AF357826

Digital Privacy and Security

Digital Privacy and Security

José Braga de Vasconcelos
Hugo Barbosa
Carla Cordeiro

Basel • Beijing • Wuhan • Barcelona • Belgrade • Novi Sad • Cluj • Manchester

Editors

José Braga de Vasconcelos
Department of Computer
Engineering and Information
Systems (DEISI)
University Lusofona
Porto
Portugal

Hugo Barbosa
Department of Computer
Engineering and Information
Systems (DEISI)
University Lusofona
Porto
Portugal

Carla Cordeiro
Department of Computer
Engineering and Information
Systems (DEISI)
University Lusofona
Porto
Portugal

Editorial Office
MDPI AG
Grosspeteranlage 5
4052 Basel, Switzerland

This is a reprint of articles from the Special Issue published online in the open access journal *Information* (ISSN 2078-2489) (available at: www.mdpi.com/journal/information/special_issues/Digital_security).

For citation purposes, cite each article independently as indicated on the article page online and as indicated below:

Lastname, A.A.; Lastname, B.B. Article Title. *Journal Name* **Year**, *Volume Number*, Page Range.

ISBN 978-3-7258-2522-6 (Hbk)
ISBN 978-3-7258-2521-9 (PDF)
doi.org/10.3390/books978-3-7258-2521-9

Contents

About the Editors

José Braga de Vasconcelos

Jose de Vasconcelos if an Associate Professor at the University Lusófona, Portugal. He obtained his PhD in Computer Science from the University of York, UK (2002). He is involved in research development in Knowledge Management and Engineering. He is Head of the Department of Computer Engineering and Information Systems at the University Lusófona, Porto. He is a Professor of Algorithms and Data Structures and Software Engineering. Also, he is a Research Integrated Member of Cognitive and People-Centric Computing (COPELABS Research Unit). Finally, he is an Academic Director at the University Lusófona of Sustainable Information Technologies for the Societies European Project that implements the Joint Masters Degree (Erasmus Mundus) in Artificial Intelligence for Sustainable Societies (AISS).

Hugo Barbosa

Hugo Barbosa graduated in Informatics Engineering: Computers and Systems (2006). He received his MSc degree in Informatics Engineering: Graphics and Multimedia Systems (2009) from the Engineering School of the Porto Polytechnic (ISEP). Currently, he works in the areas of education, games and engineering, with professional activity based on computer networks and multimedia.

Since 2010, he has been a Professor at Lusofona University, CUP for the Informatics Engineering course, and more recently he has started working at Politecnico do Porto (IPP) too. He has collaborated with the Medical Learning Methodology research in the area of interactive applications and Multimedia Systems by ID GILT/ISEP. Currently, he is a PhD student in Informatics Engineering within the Faculty of Engineering of Porto, and his research interests include Serious Games, Virtual Reality, Simulation, Player Adaptivity, Cybersecurity, and Computer Networks. He is the author of several publications in these areas. Finally, he supports journals and conferences as an Editorial Member or Reviewer, and he is also a Member of the scientific committees of these editions.

Carla Cordeiro

Carla Cordeiro holds a bachelor's and master's degree in Electrical and Computer Engineering from the Faculty of Engineering at the University of Porto (FEUP). With nearly thirty years of experience in university teaching, she is a professor at Universidade Lusófona (Porto University Center) and serves as a Guest Professor at the Instituto Superior de Engenharia do Porto (ISEP).

Her main areas of interest include Data Science, Databases, Decision Support Systems, Control Systems, Nonlinear Systems, and Mathematics, as well as innovative teaching methodologies.

Preface

Digital privacy and security have become central issues in the age of connectivity and artificial intelligence (AI). As the world increasingly adopts digital technologies, from mobile devices to healthcare systems and smart networks, including generative AI technologies, the challenges related to protecting personal data, ensuring network integrity, and resilience against cyber threats continue to grow. The intersection of public perception, human development, and digital risk significantly shapes how we address these challenges.

Public perception plays a vital role in the implementation of security policies in connected environments, as highlighted in the review "How Do Public Perceptions Affect the Security of Connected Places?". When trust in system security is low, technology adoption may decline, reducing the effectiveness of these measures. "From Cybercrime to Digital Balance" further explores how advanced digital cultures better adapt to cyber risks.

Innovations like parallel homomorphic encryption, discussed in "Secure Genomic String Search", help protect sensitive genomic data without compromising privacy. Similar advancements are applied to securing electronic medical records, ensuring patient privacy through efficient cryptographic techniques.

Mobile cybersecurity is addressed in "Explainable Machine Learning for Malware Detection on Android Applications", emphasizing the need for transparent, reliable malware detection. The security of digital ID wallets is also critical, as noted in "Assessing the Security and Privacy of Android Official ID Wallet Apps".

In healthcare, "Emerging Digital Technologies in Healthcare with a Spotlight on Cybersecurity" underscores the importance of cybersecurity, given the risks to patient data and system integrity. Additionally, "Boosting Holistic Cybersecurity Awareness with Outsourced Wide-Scope CyberSOC" highlights the value of outsourcing security operations for better threat detection.

Lastly, anonymization techniques and data recovery from social media, discussed in "Anonymization Procedures for Tabular Data" and "A Comprehensive Survey on Artifact Recovery from Social Media Platforms", are essential in the era of massive personal data generation.

This collection of works highlights the multiplicity of approaches and technological solutions being developed to tackle contemporary digital privacy and security challenges in the current AI era. From protecting personal information in healthcare systems to defending against cyber threats in critical networks, digital security is a constantly evolving field shaped by both technological advances and human interaction with these new tools.

José Braga de Vasconcelos, Hugo Barbosa, and Carla Cordeiro

Editors

 *information*

Systematic Review

How Do Public Perceptions Affect the Security of Connected Places? A Systematic Literature Review [†]

Agnieszka Dutkowska-Zuk [1], Joe Bourne [1], Chengyuan An [1], Xuan Gao [1], Oktay Cetinkaya [2], Peter Novitzky [3,4], Gideon Ogunniye [3], Rachel Cooper [1,*], David De Roure [2], Julie McCann [5], Jeremy Watson [3], Tim Watson [6] and Eleri Jones [7]

[1] Lancaster University, Lancaster LA1 4YW, UK; a.dutkowska-zuk@lancaster.ac.uk (A.D.-Z.); j.bourne@lancaster.ac.uk (J.B.); c.an1@lancaster.ac.uk (C.A.); x.gao16@lancaster.ac.uk (X.G.)

[2] University of Oxford, Oxford OX1 2JD, UK; oktay.cetinkaya@eng.ox.ac.uk (O.C.); david.deroure@oerc.ox.ac.uk (D.D.R.)

[3] University College London, London WC1E 6BT, UK; p.novitzky@ucl.ac.uk (P.N.); g.ogunniye@ucl.ac.uk (G.O.); jeremy.watson@ucl.ac.uk (J.W.)

[4] Avans University of Applied Sciences, 4817 LL Breda, The Netherlands

[5] Adaptive Emergent Systems Engineering, Imperial College London, London SW7 2BX, UK; j.mccann@imperial.ac.uk

[6] The Alan Turing Institute, London NW1 2DB, UK; tim.watson@turing.ac.uk

[7] Independent Researcher, Bangor LL57 2DG, UK; elerij@gmail.com

* Correspondence: r.cooper@lancaster.ac.uk

[†] This work is an extended version of the report commissioned by the Department for Science, Innovation and Technology (DSIT) under the title: "To what extent do public perceptions of connected places affect the security and sustainability of connected places?".

check for **updates**

Citation: Dutkowska-Zuk, A.; Bourne, J.; An, C.; Gao, X.; Cetinkaya, O.; Novitzky, P.; Ogunniye, G.; Cooper, R.; De Roure, D.; McCann, J.; et al. How Do Public Perceptions Affect the Security of Connected Places? A Systematic Literature Review. *Information* **2024**, *15*, 80. https:// doi.org/10.3390/info15020080

Academic Editors: Jose de Vasconcelos, Hugo Barbosa and Carla Cordeiro

Received: 19 November 2023
Revised: 22 December 2023
Accepted: 23 January 2024
Published: 31 January 2024

Abstract: This systematic literature review explores the scholarly debate around public perceptions and behaviors in the context of cybersecurity in connected places. It reveals that, while many articles highlight the importance of public perceptions and behaviors during a cyberattack, there is no unified consensus on how to influence them in order to minimize the attack's impact and expedite recovery. Public perceptions can affect the success and sustainability of connected places; however, exactly how and to what extent remains unknown. We argue that more research is needed on the mechanisms to assess the influence of public perceptions and associated behaviors on threats to security in connected places. Furthermore, there is a need to investigate the models and tools currently being deployed by connected place design and management to understand and influence public perceptions and behaviors. Lastly, we identify the requirements to investigate the complex relationship between the public and connected place managers, define all stakeholders clearly, and explore the patterns between specific connected place cybersecurity incidents and the methods used to transform public perceptions.

Keywords: connected places; public perception; cybersecurity; sustainability

1. Introduction

We, the authors, define connected places as a community that uses information and communication technologies with the Internet of Things (IoT) technology to "collect and analyse data to deliver new services to the built environment, and enhance the quality of living for citizens" following the National Cyber Security Centre's definition [1]. However, in addition to the promise of improved quality of living, these places also present new and potentially urgent challenges for their designers and managers: as the public interacts with data-driven technology (DDT) and the IoT within built environments, it is unknown to what extent public perceptions and behavior present security and sustainability threats.

One of the underlying technologies of connected places is the Internet of Things. Bibri defines IoT as:

"a computationally augmented everyday environment where the physical world (everyday objects) and the informational world are integrated within the ever-growing Internet infrastructure via a wide range of active and smart data-sensing devices [...]." [2] (p. 234)

IoT is mainly associated with ubiquitous computing [2], and its most popular application is the concept of smart cities [3]. Connected places can be seen as IoT applications, as long as they work as part of smart city architecture [4].

Along with the growing threat of cyberattacks on IoT and edge devices, cybersecurity has become one of the most important areas of the Internet of Things (IoT). The purpose of cybersecurity is to protect digital devices, our personal data and the services we access through them. (This research is informed by NCSC's description of cybersecurity [5]: "Cyber security's core function is to protect the devices we all use (e.g., smartphones, laptops, tablets, and computers), and the services we access-both online and at work-from theft or damage. It is also about preventing unauthorised access to the vast amounts of personal information we store on these devices, and online.") One of the challenges in IoT networks will be their security [6]. It applies to all aspects of IoT technology: hardware, network and data [7]. The user's responsibilities in the connected places' security are debatable. Hernandez-Ramos et al. [8] believe that technical solutions should not be an end user's concern in connected places. Vitunskaite et al. [9] express a similar sentiment, i.e., security should be embedded into IoT devices, and responsibility should not be placed on the people in the loop. On the other hand, Nizetic et al. found that the challenge we would face in smart cities is the operation of different sensing technologies, which "must be followed with the proper education of the population" [3] (p. 27). Connected places must withstand future attacks, be resilient and sustainable (in the way they respond and rebuild), and be accepted and adopted by citizens within them.

Therefore, in this review, we systematically investigate the concept of a *sustainable connected place* , as a connected place that continues to deliver new services to the built environment and enhance the quality of life for the public indefinitely. In this endeavor, the role of *connected place managers*, currently an under-investigated concept, which lacks a proper definition, is also the focus of our review. For the purposes of this research, we define place managers as any person with responsibility for the procurement, installation and maintenance of technologies; the handling, management, analysis and sharing of data; or, the design and enforcement of policy for the application of these technologies. It is currently unclear whether they should be responsible for the security of connected places or should be seen as users. In general, place managers are a new addition to scholarly debate and remain an overlooked area of research in the IoT field. There is a need to create tools for monitoring network operations [10] and their maintenance that could serve place managers.

While the research mentioned in this section discusses IoT environments in general, our work provides a new perspective as we specifically focus on the IoT in public spaces, where technology might not be visible at first sight to their users. Such a set-up creates a distinct synergy between public perception, cybersecurity and the sustainability of these places.

In summary, our systematic literature review (SLR) provides an overview of the current scholarly debate *"to what extent do public perceptions of connected places affect the security and sustainability of connected places?"*. The actual public perceptions of these technologies, and their acceptability, safety, and trustworthiness, are increasingly complex. Our aim is to provide a systematic state of the current knowledge, review themes in the literature, and inform future research directions concerning this emerging challenge.

2. Methods

Our SLR [11] employs the PRISMA framework [12]. The PRISMA framework guides us through the search and eligibility screening for this review. We then synthesize our findings following a qualitative thematic analysis, reporting patterns or contradictions in the literature. Our search strategy includes also the grey literature, relevant to connected places in the United Kingdom, using the same query syntax for web search.

Using the PRISMA framework, due to the emerging nature of our field of investigation, we developed a robust protocol to search, identify, and select relevant publications. The protocol was pilot-tested and calibrated prior to data collection by the authors. To achieve comprehensiveness and systematic rigor, relevant publications were retrieved using the search strategy shown in Figure 1. This strategy is discussed in detail in Section 2.1.

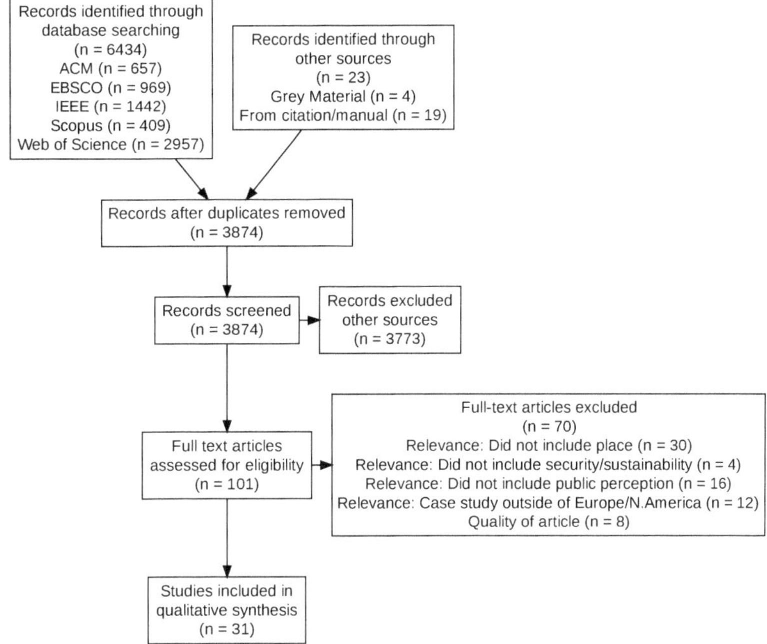

Figure 1. PRISMA Flow Diagram.

2.1. Search Strategy

After conducting initial test searches of likely databases, we refined our query syntax and eligibility criteria to create a comprehensive data set. The tests immediately revealed that it is very rare for research relevant to connected places to use the term 'connected places' and that the wide variety of types of connected places would require us to construct search terms that looked for multiple specific research problems, as opposed to one broad area. Similarly, the multifaceted and socio-technical nature of public perceptions is rarely tackled directly in the literature. Therefore, we identified the key terms that could uncover research relating to public perceptions within the scope of the policy challenge (cf. Table 1).

Table 1. Search syntax.

Constant Concept	Variable Concept
((public OR user N5 trust* OR perspective* OR attitude* OR perception* OR awareness OR accept*) AND ("cyber?security" OR cybersecurity))	Cit*; place; smart; connected; hospital; airport; station; centre OR center; port; prison; "social housing"

The databases searched were EBSCO, IEEE, ACM, Web of Science, and Scopus. These databases were selected to provide a comprehensive list of possible articles. Each database was manually searched between 9 January and 28 January 2023, with all articles found using the above query syntax added to a shared reference manager.

2.2. Eligibility Criteria

Search results were screened by at least two different researchers against the following eligibility criteria:

- *Language*: Full-text article written in English.
- *Title relevance*: Mentions user perceptions or a variable thereof; an aspect or type of connected place; and an aspect or synonym of cybersecurity and/or sustainability.
- *Abstract relevance*: Mentions user perceptions or a variable thereof; an aspect or type of connected place; and an aspect or synonym of cybersecurity and/or sustainability.
- *Geography of case studies*: Given the UK policy orientation of this review purpose, the authors agreed with DSIT's Secure Connected Place Team that only the case studies in the UK, Europe, and North America would be eligible for inclusion given their likely cultural, democratic and legal proximity; and similarity in technological readiness level.

During the screening stage by title or abstract, we excluded 3773 publications due to the nature of our broad search terms. Our aim was to find articles relevant only to specific types of connected places or referencing another article that was. The remaining articles were included in a full-text eligibility check, which evaluated the relevance and quality of an article by at least two researchers.

3. Results

This section presents the background characteristics of the process and results of our data analysis, including the details on the articles included in the literature review.

3.1. Background Characteristics

In this literature review, we screened 3874 articles before selecting 27 journal and conference articles and four pieces of grey literature that contained qualitative information on the extent to which public perceptions of connected places affect the security and sustainability of connected places.

The existing literature, both academic and grey, is predominantly technology-focused with regard to connected place security and sustainability, despite the focus on public perception of our search. The extent to which different technologies were referenced in the literature can be seen in Table 2. This table in itself contributes to our definition of connected places and supports the transferable nature of our findings, i.e., our findings may still be useful to a place that is not formally defined as a 'connected place' by the place owners or users, but which deploys and/or utilizes the technologies in this table. Four literature reviews within selected articles agree that the number of articles investigating the security impact of public perceptions is still relatively small [13–16]. Those who have investigated public perceptions tend to orient more around privacy than security [16]. The case studies included in the reviewed articles lack attention to the safety, sustainability, equity, and resilience of connected places [15].

Table 2. Technologies referenced.

Parent Category	Subcategory 1	Subcategory 2	Frequency
Application	Smart Transport		32
Application	Sensors		27
IoT devices			19
Connectivity & Data Transport	Radio Network	Wi-Fi	17
IoT Devices	Sensors	Environmental Monitoring	17
Application	E-Governance		14
IoT devices	End Point Devices	Smartphone	14
Application	Smart Lighting		13
ICT			13
IT Security			12
Application	Smart Homes		10
Application	Smart Surveillance Systems		9
IoT devices	Wearable	Wearables	9
Application	Smart Parking		8
Application	Smart Healthcare		8
Application	Smart Building		8
Big Data	Artificial Intelligence		8
Connectivity & Data Transport	Mobile Network	5G	8
IT Security	Authentication	Smart Cards	7
Data Management	Data Storage	Cloud	6
Big Data			5
IoT devices	End Point Devices	PC	5
Application	Surveillance System	CCTV	4
Application	Energy Infrastructure		4
Application	Smart Delivery Systems		4
Connectivity & Data Transport	Radio Network	Bluetooth	4
Connectivity & Data Transport	Satelite Navigation	GPS	4
Connectivity & Data Transport	Low Power Network	LoRaWAN	4
IoT devices	Smart Meters		3
IoT Platforms	Urban-Scale Iot Platforms		3
IT Security	Contactless	RFID	3
IT Security	Contactless	NFC	3
Service			3
Application	Actuators		2
Connectivity & Data Transport	ISP		2
Software	App	Waze	2
Application	Smart Building	Air Conditioning (HVAC)	1
Application	Baggage Handling Systems		1
Application	BMS		1
Application	Environmental Monitoring	Connected Forest Project	1
Application	BMS	IEQ	1
Application	Digital Twins		1
Application	Surveillance System	Smart Alarm Systems	1
Blockchain			1
Connectivity & Data Transport	Radio Network	Free Open Networks	1
Connectivity & Data Transport	Radio Network	NB-IoT	1
Connectivity & Data Transport	Low Power Network	Weightless	1
Connectivity & Data Transport	Network Layer	Zigbee	1
Connectivity & Data Transport	Low Power Network	NB-IoT	1
Connectivity & Data Transport	Network Hardware	VSAT	1
Connectivity & Data Transport	Protocol	CoAP	1
Connectivity & Data Transport	Radio Network	CWN	1
Connectivity & Data Transport	Protocol		1
Connectivity & Data Transport	Mobility Service	V2X	1
Connectivity & Data Transport	Mobility Service	VANETS	1
Connectivity & Data Transport	Protocol	DNS	1
Cyberspace	User Experience	VR	1
Cyberspace	User Experience	AR	1
Data Management	Data Management	CKAN	1
Data Management	Data Storage	USB	1
Edge Computing	Edge And Fog Computing		1
ICT	Microcontrollers		1
IoT devices	End Point Devices	Smart Batteries	1
IoT devices	End Point Devices	EUT	1
IoT devices	End Point Devices	Smart Plugs	1
IoT devices	Programmable Logic Controllers (PLCs)		1
IoT Platforms	WoTKit		1
IT Security	Authentication	PIN	1
IT Security	Authentication	MFA	1
IT Security	Encryption	PIN	1
IT Security	Authentication	readers	1
Service	Financial Service	E-Banking	1
Service	LBS provider		1
Software	App	Otonomo	1
Software	App	Corona-Warn-App	1
Software	Mobility Service	Smart Back-office Systems	1
Software	Control System Architecture	SCADA	1

3.1.1. Characteristics of Results against Query Syntax Variables

Each article was tagged against the query syntax terms. #Smart (41%) and #Cit* (33%) dominated tags that refer to place-based variables in the query syntax (Figure 2). Of the variables relating to public perspectives, #Awareness (24%), #Trust (19%), and #Perspective (17%) were the three highest in frequency (Figure 3). This represents the extent to which urban environments dominated the examples of connected places discussed within the literature.

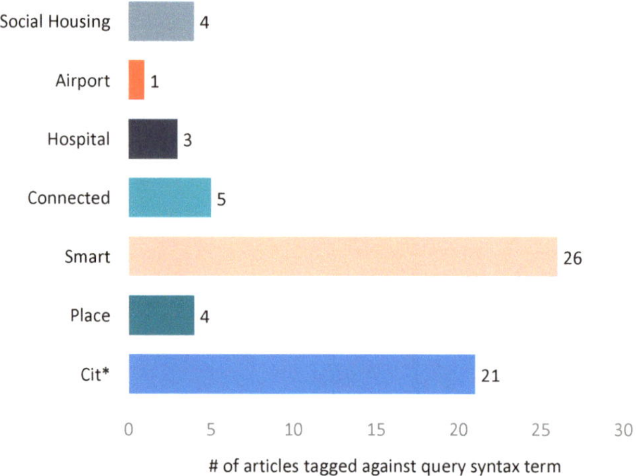

Figure 2. Connected place variable tags.

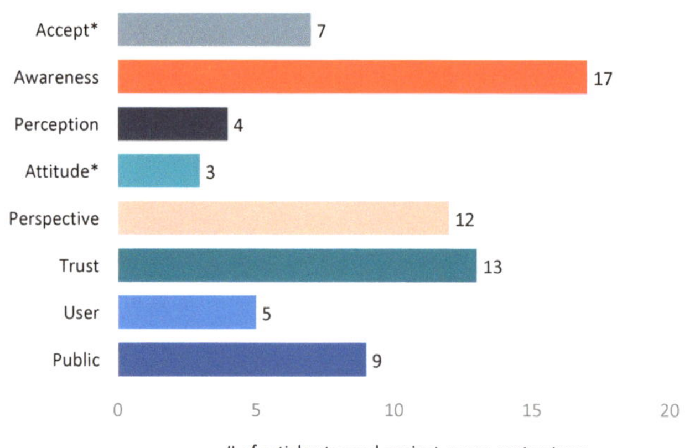

Figure 3. Public perspective variable tags.

3.1.2. Characteristics of Results by Geographic Focus

Reviewed articles that did focus on specific geography (i.e., those with a case study or survey-oriented methodology) investigated connected places in either the UK (8), wider Europe (7), or North America (1). The remaining articles had no specific geographic focus.

4. Findings

This section captures the synthesis of the literature concerning how public perceptions of connected places affect the security and sustainability of connected places. We capture both theoretical and empirical findings, to build a conceptual framework. We gather related concepts to provide a broader understanding of the research question.

4.1. Public Perceptions Influencing Public Security Behaviors

The reviewed literature suggests that the majority of the public will be oblivious to connected places [17], let alone desirable security behaviors within them [8,18]. At the same time, public perceptions and security behaviors in connected places are being influenced by different elements: the value offered by connected place technology [19]; the clarity of risks and security procedures communicated [20,21]; the ability to express concerns and participation in design and development [17,21–23]; perceptions of privacy and risk [13,23,24]; trustworthiness [8,9,16,25]; and the type and purpose of data collection [18,23].

Connected place users might be more willing to accept security and privacy risks when they perceive a space to be delivering high value, functionality, and convenience [19]. Fayoumi et al. [20] present a correlation between the explanation of security and privacy issues in an IoT system and the resulting enhanced user awareness and ability to avoid risks. However, the wide-ranging pre-existing levels of awareness amongst public users of connected places use a one-size-fits-all approach for the explanation of security and privacy issues, which is challenging. For example, many members of the public have a good understanding of network and data security processes but with low awareness of threats [26], or the information being shared by their devices in a connected place [8,18].

The degree to which the public perceives the connected place to be actively protecting them from these harms further complicates the landscape: it could lead to neglecting cybersecurity due to misleading feelings of being protected, and the controls are being taken care of elsewhere [27]. Similarly, while the public's increased awareness and risk aversion of threats is no doubt an attractive goal for connected place managers, this risk aversion may result in an unwanted consequence of residents avoiding connected places or specific technologies within them [24].

The privacy factors affecting a user's perception of security are (a) the purpose for which *data* is collected, i.e., (a.1) service or surveillance [23]; (a.2) personal or impersonal [23]; (b) the *context* that data sharing is taking place within, e.g., users are more willing to share data in the event of a friend being endangered [18]; and (c) who is collecting data, e.g., the government [13].

It is not clear from the literature to what extent security behaviors in a connected place are influenced by behaviors and experiences in cyberspace. Taher et al. [28] suggest students' privacy concerns in 'smart campus buildings' are influenced by their experiences and knowledge in other computing contexts, and that similar consent controls would be desirable. Other authors commented on the influence of the personal experience of cyberattack in cyberspace, as opposed to in a (a) *cyber–physical environment* (connected place [28]); (b) *demographic differences* (age, gender [18,29]); and (c) *pre-existing awareness* of cybersecurity vulnerabilities and controls [26]. However, none of these findings are comprehensively investigated enough to draw any applicable conclusions from.

Publications refer to privacy and security concerns that alter the likelihood of engaging with a connected place by the public. Willemsen and Cadee [30] link increased security measures with increased user-experience friction, potentially affecting the acceptability of a connected place and increasing the likelihood of a user disengaging. Van Twist et al. [13] argue that rejection of a connected place can be considered a threat to security itself. Data may become unreliable, and—in extreme instances—rejection related to mistrust can render the public themselves a threat to security [13]. This topic is further explored in Section 4.2.3.

4.2. Perspectives on Public Security Behaviors Affecting Security, and Sustainability of Connected Places

4.2.1. Reasons Public Perceptions Affect Connected Place Security and Sustainability

Hernandez-Ramos et al. [8] point to examples, e.g., the Mirai botnet attack, to demonstrate the potential for compromised IoT devices used in attacks against Information and

Communications Technology (ICT) systems and critical infrastructure (CI). They highlight that a single citizen's lack of awareness, and the resulting poor cybersecurity hygiene, could be a threat to the security of the general public and systems within a smart city [8].

A survey of 1444 residents of the US city of Denton revealed that *"approximately 55% of trust in technology by residents is related to their perception of security and privacy, which in turn influences their trust and adoption of smart-city services"* [24] (p. 618). Smart city users value safety and security, supporting increased regulation to this end. Consequently, residents are more likely to show interest in using smart city services when the applications are perceived to be innovative and privacy is assured [24].

Although intertwined, the literature suggests that privacy appears to matter slightly more to the public than (cyber)security in connected places [17]. Liesbet van Zoonen [23] argues for the importance of recognizing the public's privacy concerns to sustain support and participation. Habib et al. [24] also identify perceived cybersecurity as key to public acceptance. However, Twist et al. [13] warn that over-surveillance, often motivated by public safety, can lead to the public rejecting a connected place, hindering its sustainability. Manfreda et al. [21] list perceived privacy, innovation concept, and service quality as key factors of acceptance, with cybersecurity notably absent.

Security measures creating friction with the public need to be addressed within the context of a connected place. Willemsen and Cadee [30] present airports as public spaces, in which the trade-off between security and friction is more actively considered by place managers (i.e., the need to manage passenger comfort, processing efficiency, and security). Manfreda et al. [21] highlight the immense importance *"to analyze the trade-off between city's effectiveness and its security"* [21] (p. 277).

4.2.2. Specific Technical Vulnerabilities Affected by Public Perception

Vanolo [31] argues that personal devices are essential for the sustainability of connected places given the way an intelligent environment receives feedback from residents' smartphones. At the same time, end-user devices present the greatest security threat to connected places [9,18,19,23]. Many users' perceptions of the importance of security are very low [8,18], and often do not maintain security updates and patches. Herbert et al. [18] (p. 283) cite a 2019 study by Ali et al. [32], where more than half of 3000 global smartphone users surveyed were not aware of smartphone security and privacy. This result correlates with the findings of Ipsos Mori's *"Consumer Attitudes Towards IoT Security"* Report [33], highlighting that only 24% of Wi-Fi router owners have changed the password since purchase, and only 20% report checking the minimum support period when purchasing a smart device. Vitunskaite et al. [9] argue that the only way to control user-generated vulnerabilities of connected places is to control what is on the market.

Personal devices are often the point of access to a connected place for the public via public Wi-Fi [31]. A university-based study by Papic et al. [34] found that 43% of 110 students at Osijek University, Croatia never felt safe when using public Wi-Fi. The manner in which devices remember and automatically reconnect to Wi-Fi may present vulnerabilities to outsider attacks [25], with user behavior being key in addressing this weak link in connected place infrastructure, especially when users frequently misjudge the risky situations in the wild [29]. Willemsen and Cadee [30], writing about the arguably more security-critical environment of an airport, argue for limiting the possibility for the public to access networks in connected places, both through reducing access points and by separating public networks from internal networks.

The final technology to feature to a notable extent is smart cards. Smart cards present a good example of the assessments users make when deciding on whether or not to adopt new technology in a connected place, that of perceived usefulness, i.e., value, and perceived security [35]. Indeed, they are seen by the public, according to Bellanche-Gracia et al. [35], as guaranteeing secure transmission of sensitive data and unlocking connected places services and infrastructure. Similarly, the present smart cards serve as a good example of how connected places may *"depend more on citizens' perceptions of privacy and security risks than on the actual technological, design, or policy guarantees of privacy"* [35] (p. 474).

Notably absent from the literature are less user-orientated IoT architectures, such as sensors, low power wide area (LPWA) networks or the processing and application layers in general. These are not typically public-user-oriented and therefore not surprising in their absence. Where sensors are public user-oriented it is in a passive way with regards to user experience, i.e., the user is likely to be unaware of being 'sensed'. The literature in which sensors are featured [9,13,36] describes what happens when members of the public take far from passive actions to reject sensors in connected places, as we describe in the next section.

4.2.3. The Public as a Threat to Connected Place Security and Sustainability

Public users are positioned within the literature as influential threats [8,13] to connected place security and sustainability in various ways:

- Naive or optimistic users who may unintentionally threaten a place's security through inaction [19] or being victim to the influence of bad actors, in particular via social engineering [37];
- Allies of the place managers who are aware of threats [19] and keen to contribute to security efforts. Some articles draw a connection between trust in connected places and trust in government in general, with influence traveling in both directions [16,24,25];
- Malicious actors themselves due to the ease of causing significant damage though low-skilled cyberattacks [9,36] or rejecting surveillance through non-technical tampering, data obfuscation, or vandalism [13,36];

Isin and Ruppert [36] call for a new type of digital citizenship in which the complexities of the above can be discussed in a way that considers the multiple possible roles any member of the public may play at any time in a connected place.

4.2.4. Public Perspectives before, during, and after a Cyberattack on a Connected Place

A number of different articles focus on the public at different parts of a cybersecurity timeline: before, during, and after an attack. The vast majority focus on the role of the public as part of a socio-technical system working together, though not necessarily knowingly, to protect all parts of the system from attack [8,16,18,38]. A few articles [15,24,26,27] explore public perceptions during an attack and suggest that the importance of the public's role in the system increases significantly during this time: minimizing the impact of an attack in terms of technical damage [26] while keeping themselves safe from physical harm due to an awareness of the way an attack will affect a place's infrastructure and the mitigating actions they may have to take. Public perceptions and the ability to distinguish reliable data are very important during an attack of such, especially if this attack takes place during an existing crisis, such as natural disasters or warfare [15]. Finally, the way in which the experience of an attack affects the public perceptions of a connected place's security is disputed. Zwilling et al. [27] argue it has no effect, while Habib et al. [24] argue that it can increase rejection of connected places and present a future threat to a place's security and sustainability itself.

4.3. The Relationship between Connected Places, Their Managers and Public Perceptions, and How This Affects Security and Sustainability

4.3.1. The Various Definitions of Users, Place Managers and the Public in Connected Places Cybersecurity Research and Guidance

Related to the need for research on the multiple positions and motivations a user may manifest [25], a great deal of literature excluded from this review used the term 'user' to refer to operators and managers of connected places, referring to them as 'users' of the connected place as a tool to meet their needs, often positioning them as a customer of the designers, developers, and manufacturers of connected place technologies. This was also common across the grey materials, with government guidance using the term 'user' to refer exclusively to place managers and operators [1,38,39].

4.3.2. The Influence of Connected Place Managers and Their Relationship with the Public

The literature is divided on the influence a place manager can have on public perceptions and behaviors. Federico Cilauro [38] points towards the significance of technical factors or process factors in securing the connected place to suggest that people factors matter not. However, Vitunskaite et al. [9] point to the actions of fourth and fifth parties, i.e., those producing devices that enter the connected place, as being so critical to security that managers are powerless to influence these risks. Cilauro [38] warns against focusing on user-oriented concerns, as they may lead to over-investment in end-point security. Cilauro [38] is also critical of councils in particular, reporting that a connected place commissioner believed *"most councils do not know enough about technology or cybersecurity to procure technology"* [38] (p. 52)) and suggests this may well apply across the public sector. Others suggest that even if public perceptions do matter, place managers are helpless to influence them and should not waste their time by trying. Others, on the other hand, suggest that place managers must take a 'user-centric' approach to fully understand and overcome the security threats in connected places [25]. The gap in research on the influence of public perceptions was raised in four articles [13,15,16,21]. Liesbet van Zoonen [23] argues that connected place managers must acknowledge public concerns about privacy to maintain their support and participation.

A few articles take a very user-focused view of the privacy and security of connected places. They argue that privacy and security is a human right [16,21,40] and that it is the duty of the government to regulate connected places in a way that protects individuals' data [14]. They argue that it is the place that is the risk to the public security, not the public who is the risk to the place's security.

4.3.3. Tools, Frameworks, Models and Methods That Affect the Influence of Public Perceptions on Connected Places' Security and Sustainability

Non-technical tools proposed by the literature include a five-dimensional model for citizens' privacy in smart cities [40], privacy impact assessments [23], cybersecurity culture frameworks [26] and citizen-centric approaches of connected place design and development such as living labs, crowdsourcing and citizen participation [22,23].

Technical solutions include privacy-enhancing technologies [23] which align with the argument that public engagement is futile and the level of risk afforded to any public should be minimized to the point of irrelevance. Hernandez-Ramos et al. [8] take this further by identifying the deployment of certified devices and systems, i.e., solutions that must be created far up the connected place supply chain from the connected place manager's influence, as ways to build public trust in smart city services. However, they do not articulate how you communicate certification to the public. Louw and Van Zolms [25] make an argument for end-user information security portals or dashboards, which is a very user-centric technical solution. They suggest that these can be used to communicate training and awareness content directly to users, *"seamlessly blending in with the Wi-Fi user journey"* [25] (p. 125).

5. Discussion

In this section, we discuss the confusion and contradictions in the available literature regarding the influence of the public perspective on the security of connected places. Moreover, our analysis revealed three trade-offs, which we examine in this section. Next, we provide information regarding the limitations of our study. Lastly, based on our analysis, we provide recommendations for future research.

5.1. Confusion and Contradictions

Many of the articles reviewed point to the heightened importance of public perceptions and behavior during a cyberattack on a connected place [8,15,16,18,24,26,27,38]. However, there is no consensus on how perceptions and behavior can be influenced to minimize the impact of, and expedite recovery from, a cyberattack. This question requires further research, which can deliver up-to-date and technology-specific recommendations alongside best practices.

There is a question as to whether public Wi-Fi is a threat to the connected place, the user within a connected place, or both, given the data some users will be willing to share on insecure networks [8]. Similarly, are devices a point of security vulnerability in a connected place, or a point of data leakage, privacy threat, and over-surveillance for the member of the public within a connected place?

There is a disagreement across the literature concerning who the public is, who connected place managers are, and how aligned both groups are with the aims of a secure and sustainable connected place. There is also a contradiction across the literature concerning the aims of attempts to influence public perceptions and behaviors within connected places: are they to keep the place itself safe, i.e., its infrastructure, institutions and operations, or should they protect the public's privacy and safety? While the answer can be both, many of the reviewed articles were orientated toward one or the other motivation and did not explore the relationship between the two.

The existing literature tends to reveal the following common assumptions within connected place managers:

- Connected place security is simultaneously in the interest of both the public and place managers and these interests are not ever in conflict.
- That public users and place managers are entirely separate groups, with no individuals taking dual roles within a connected place.
- That malicious actors are 'another' separate group to public users and place managers and that users or place managers themselves always act in the interests of the other group and those within their own group.
- Place managers often focus on the technical requirements of privacy without adequate consideration of the social requirements. The technical aspects of privacy focus on the technical requirements (such as access control and data minimization) required to ensure privacy, while the social aspects focus on the privacy preferences of the public users, the relationships between public users and how such relationships impact their privacy.

Finally, it is unclear whether the most significant security and sustainability risks exist in the way end-user devices are used and maintained further up the supply chain in the standards and regulations applied to personal devices and the sensor and network technologies or within the organizational culture and practice of those delivering connected places.

5.2. Trade-Offs of Connected Places

5.2.1. Secure Places vs. Friction-Less Experiences

If connected places provide convenient solutions, members of the public may accept security and privacy risks [19]. Moreover, the lack of awareness of how to avoid privacy and security risks results in the inability to prevent them [20]. This can lead to the lack of perceived authority over users' security and privacy, or so-called learned helplessness, which further strengthens users' preference towards functionality over privacy. However, we need end users to actively take care of their security, not only for their sake but also for the sake of the system.

Users will utilize personal and public devices. Thus, connected places must develop a new side of security responsibility that would apply to both individual and collective privacy and security. However, one needs to remember the diffusion of responsibility which can take place on the level of public vs. other stakeholders, but also on the public level itself, among the end users.

Another area needing further research is the understanding of whether those who experience a data breach are more privacy and security-conscious as a result.

5.2.2. Sustainability vs. Security

As pointed out in Section 4.2.2, personal smartphones are essential for the sustainability of connected places [31], but they are the biggest security threat [9,18,19,23]. It needs to be clarified where the responsibility lies. As personal belongings, such as smartphones or smart cards, interact with connected places technology, it is still being determined who is responsible for the public's security, as well as when and how. Moreover, the perception of the public may change depending on whose responsibility it is.

5.2.3. Responsibility vs. Authority

Along with transparency, clear responsibility and agency over security and privacy, there is a need to define the public users of connected places more clearly. The gap in research on the influence of public perception has been acknowledged; however, as we pointed out at the beginning of this section, stakeholders are not precisely defined. For example, if managers of connected places are end users, it needs to be clarified.

It is also debatable whether place managers should consider their primary focus for security controls, given that public perceptions may affect the way they behave on and with their devices, or whether place managers should design and run connected places with the aim of making them resilient to user behaviors.

Furthermore, it is still being determined who has authority over data, and in what circumstances; too much on the government's side may be perceived as surveillance [13], and too little may be perceived as the public being denied their its human right to security [16,21,40]. We argue though that controlling the market [9] would not control a user's behavior with a device, particularly their likelihood to maintain antivirus or security updates and patches [25].

5.3. Limitations of This Study

Articles reviewed were often not directly addressing our research question; instead, they focus on the public discontent within a connected place [13–15], often as a rejection to perceived over-surveillance, and not necessarily relating to the impacts this has on cybersecurity, or they consider the role of an individual in a connected place caught up in cyberwarfare [15] or consider public consultation as a necessary part of designing a working and secure connected place [16].

The diverse nature of connected places also generated results that are so wide-ranging that it is difficult to develop universally applicable recommendations for every type of connected place. Articles that did identify a connection between public perceptions and public security behaviors or their adoption of connected places often applied broad observations concerning perceptions of the internet and data-driven technologies.

5.4. Recommendations for Future Research

5.4.1. Socio-Technical Approach towards Security

The four literature reviews included in our review concur with some of our own findings. We agree with their recommendations for more research into mechanisms for assessing connected place threats relating to public perception [16]. We also identified a need to address the imbalanced focus towards technical solutions for connected place security [15] and to conduct more research on how perceptions influence the security behaviors of the public [13]. They all argue for a more socio-technical approach to this challenge, another argument we concur with having evaluated our own findings.

5.4.2. User in the Loop

In addition, there is a need to explore models and tools for considering public perceptions and behaviors in connected place design and management, as well as methods through which connected place managers can influence both perceptions and behaviors, if at all. There were some participatory tools suggested by the literature [22,23,26,40]. These need further testing in different contexts, but the consensus of these arguments was that if a productive tool could be found, the public would trust, accept and sustain connected places more if individuals felt themselves to be 'in the loop'. One article [9] described an open-source platform for connected place sensor data and management in Barcelona; however, they noted that cybersecurity did not feature frequently in this discourse.

5.4.3. Transparency and Awareness Lead to Acceptance

The lack of clarity on the complex relationship between members of the public and connected place managers requires more investigation. There is a need to conduct research with the public to explore the way they position themselves within the systems keeping a connected place secure, their perceptions of their personal data and whose responsibility the protection of these data is in a connected place context. There also is a need for research that researches patterns between specific connected place cybersecurity incident causes and the methods this place deployed, previously and since, to influence public perceptions.

Lastly, our findings suggest that a lack of awareness can lead to either a lack of acceptance [30] or security [8]. Additionally, because the public may be hesitant to share personal data, it is crucial to recognize when data can and should be anonymous. An analogous example can be the wide acceptance of security and privacy restrictions at the airport. However, such a level of privacy invigilation would not be widely accepted in other public places, such as parks.

6. Conclusions

This literature review highlights the potential importance of public perceptions and behaviors concerning the security and sustainability of connected places and the need for further research to develop recommendations for minimizing the impact of attacks. The authors note that there is a lack of consensus in the literature regarding the aims of attempts to influence public perceptions and behaviors within connected places, with some focusing on protecting the infrastructure and institutions of the place, while others prioritize the privacy and safety of the public.

We reveal several assumptions within both connected place managers and researchers, including that the interests of the public and place managers are always aligned, that malicious actors are a separate group from public users and place managers and that privacy is not a subjective personal value. The authors suggest that further research is needed to explore the complex relationship between members of the public and connected place managers in the context of cybersecurity.

We acknowledge the limitations of this study, including the fact that the existing literature does often not directly address their research question and that the diverse nature of connected places makes it difficult to develop universally applicable recommendations. However, we suggest several recommendations for future research, including the need to explore models and tools for considering public perceptions and behaviors in connected place design and management, and the need to conduct research with the public to explore their perceptions of their personal data and who is responsible for protecting it in a connected place.

Author Contributions: Conceptualization, A.D.-Z., J.B., O.C., P.N. and G.O.; methodology, J.B., O.C., P.N. and G.O.; validation, R.C.; formal analysis, A.D.-Z., J.B., C.A. and X.G.; investigation, A.D.-Z., J.B., C.A. and X.G.; data curation, A.D.-Z., J.B., C.A. and X.G.; writing-original draft preparation, A.D.-Z., C.A. and X.G.; writing-review and editing, A.D.-Z., J.B., C.A., X.G., O.C., P.N., G.O., R.C., D.D.R., J.M., J.W., T.W. and E.J.; supervision, O.C., P.N. and R.C.; project administration, A.D.-Z. and J.B.; funding acquisition, J.B. All authors have read and agreed to the published version of the manuscript.

Funding: This work has been supported by the PETRAS National Centre of Excellence for IoT Systems Cybersecurity, which has been funded by the UK EPSRC under grant number EP/S035362/1.

Institutional Review Board Statement: Not applicable.

Informed Consent Statement: Not applicable.

Data Availability Statement: Not applicable.

Conflicts of Interest: The authors declare no conflicts of interest. The funding sponsors had no role in the design of the study; in the collection, analyses, or interpretation of data; in the writing of the manuscript, and in the decision to publish the results.

References

1. Connected Places Cyber Security Principles. Available online: https://www.ncsc.gov.uk/collection/connected-places-security-principles (accessed on 24 January 2023).
2. Bibri, S.E. The IoT for smart sustainable cities of the future: An analytical framework for sensor-based big data applications for environmental sustainability. *Sustain. Cities Soc.* **2018**, *38*, 230–253. [CrossRef]
3. Nižetić, S.; Šolić, P.; Gonzalez-De, D.L.D.I.; Patrono, L. Internet of Things (IoT): Opportunities, issues and challenges towards a smart and sustainable future. *J. Clean. Prod.* **2020**, *274*, 122877. [CrossRef]
4. Perković, T.; Damjanović, S.; Šolić, P.; Patrono, L.; Rodrigues, J.J. Meeting challenges in IoT: Sensing, energy efficiency, and the implementation. In Proceedings of the Fourth International Congress on Information and Communication Technology: ICICT 2019, London, UK, 6–8 September 2023; Springer: Berlin/Heidelberg, Germany, 2020; Volume 1; pp. 419–430.
5. NCSC. What Is Cyber Security? Available online: https://www.ncsc.gov.uk/section/about-ncsc/what-is-cyber-security (accessed on 9 November 2023).
6. Almusaylim, Z.A.; Alhumam, A.; Jhanjhi, N. Proposing a secure RPL based internet of things routing protocol: A review. *Ad. Hoc. Netw.* **2020**, *101*, 102096. [CrossRef]
7. Kaushik, K.; Singh, K. Security and trust in iot communications: Role and impact. In *Intelligent Communication, Control and Devices: Proceedings of ICICCD 2018*; Springer: Berlin/Heidelberg, Germany, 2019; pp. 791–798.
8. Hernandez-Ramos, J.L.; Martinez, J.A.; Savarino, V.; Angelini, M.; Napolitano, V.; Skarmeta, A.F.; Baldini, G. Security and Privacy in Internet of Things-Enabled Smart Cities: Challenges and Future Directions. *IEEE Secur. Priv.* **2021**, *19*, 12–23. [CrossRef]
9. Vitunskaite, M.; He, Y.; Brandstetter, T.; Janicke, H. Smart cities and cyber security: Are we there yet? A comparative study on the role of standards, third party risk management and security ownership. *Comput. Secur.* **2019**, *83*, 313–331. [CrossRef]
10. Kakkavas, G.; Gkatzioura, D.; Karyotis, V.; Papavassiliou, S. A review of advanced algebraic approaches enabling network tomography for future network infrastructures. *Future Internet* **2020**, *12*, 20. [CrossRef]
11. Snyder, H. Literature review as a research methodology: An overview and guidelines. *J. Bus. Res.* **2019**, *104*, 333–339. [CrossRef]
12. Page, M.J.; McKenzie, J.E.; Bossuyt, P.M.; Boutron, I.; Hoffmann, T.C.; Mulrow, C.D.; Shamseer, L.; Tetzlaff, J.M.; Akl, E.A.; Brennan, S.E.; et al. The PRISMA 2020 statement: an updated guideline for reporting systematic reviews. *Int. J. Surg.* **2021**, *88*, 105906. [CrossRef] [PubMed]
13. van Twist, A.; Ruijer, E.; Meijer, A. Smart cities & citizen discontent: A systematic review of the literature. *Gov. Inf. Q.* **2023**, *40*, 101799. [CrossRef]
14. Meijer, A.; Bolívar, M.P.R. Governing the smart city: A review of the literature on smart urban governance. *Int. Rev. Adm. Sci.* **2016**, *82*, 392–408. [CrossRef]
15. Soare, S.R. Smart Cities, Cyber Warfare and Social Disorder. In *Cyber Threats and NATO 2030: Horizon Scanning and Analysis*; CCDCOE: Tallinn, Estonia, 2020.
16. Ma, C. Smart city and cyber-security; technologies used, leading challenges and future recommendations. *Energy Rep.* **2021**, *7*, 7999–8012. [CrossRef]
17. Thomas, V.; Wang, D.; Mullagh, L.; Dunn, N. Where is Wally? In Search of Citizen Perspectives on the Smart City. *Sustainability* **2016**, *8*, 207. [CrossRef]
18. Herbert, F.; Schmidbauer-Wolf, G.M.; Reuter, C. Who Should Get My Private Data in Which Case? Evidence in the Wild. In Proceedings of the Mensch und Computer 2021, New York, NY, USA, 5–8 September 2021; MuC '21; pp. 281–293. [CrossRef]
19. Harper, S.; Mehrnezhad, M.; Mace, J.; Groß, T.; Viganò, L. User Privacy Concerns in Commercial Smart Buildings. *J. Comput. Secur.* **2022**, *30*, 465–497. [CrossRef]

20. Fayoumi, A.; Sobati-Moghadam, S.; Rajaiyan, A.; Oxley, C.; Montero, P.F.; Dahmani, A. The Cybersecurity Risks of Using Internet of Things (IoT) and Surveys of End-Users and Providers within the Domiciliary Care Sector. In Proceedings of the 2022 Sixth International Conference on Smart Cities, Internet of Things and Applications (SCIoT), Mashhad, Iran, 14–15 September 2022; pp. 1–7. [CrossRef]

21. Manfreda, A.; Ekart, N.; Mori, M.; Groznik, A. Citizens' Participation as an Important Element for Smart City Development. In Proceedings of the Re-imagining Diffusion and Adoption of Information Technology and Systems: A Continuing Conversation, Tiruchirappalli, India, 18–19 December 2020; Sharma, S.K., Dwivedi, Y.K., Metri, B., Rana, N.P., Eds.; Springer: Cham, Switzerland, 2020; IFIP Advances in Information and Communication Technology; pp. 274–284. [CrossRef]

22. Lea, R.; Blackstock, M. Smart Cities: An IoT-centric Approach. In Proceedings of the 2014 International Workshop on Web Intelligence and Smart Sensing, New York, NY, USA, 1–2 September 2014; IWWISS '14; pp. 1–2. [CrossRef]

23. van Zoonen, L. Privacy concerns in smart cities. *Gov. Inf. Q.* **2016**, *33*, 472–480. [CrossRef]

24. Habib, A.; Alsmadi, D.; Prybutok, V.R. Factors that determine residents' acceptance of smart city technologies. *Behav. Inf. Technol.* **2020**, *39*, 610–623. [CrossRef]

25. Louw, C.; Von Solms, B. Free Public Wi-Fi Security in a Smart City Context-An End User Perspective. In *Smart Cities Cybersecurity and Privacy*; Elsevier: Amsterdam, The Netherlands, 2019; p. 127. [CrossRef]

26. Georgiadou, A.; Michalitsi-Psarrou, A.; Gioulekas, F.; Stamatiadis, E.; Tzikas, A.; Gounaris, K.; Doukas, G.; Ntanos, C.; Landeiro Ribeiro, L.; Askounis, D. Hospitals' Cybersecurity Culture during the COVID-19 Crisis. *Healthcare* **2021**, *9*, 1335. [CrossRef]

27. Zwilling, M.; Klien, G.; Lesjak, D.; Wiechetek, L.; Cetin, F.; Basim, H. Cyber Security Awareness, Knowledge and Behavior: A Comparative Study. *J. Comput. Inf. Syst.* **2022**, *62*, 82–97. [CrossRef]

28. Tawer, R.; Mehrnezhad, M.; Morisset, C. "I feel spied on and I do not have any control over my data": User Privacy Perception, Preferences and Trade-offs in University Smart Buildings. *Socio-Tech. Asp. Secur.* **2022**, *2023* , 1–20.

29. Sombatruang, N.; Sasse, M.A.; Baddeley, M. Why do people use unsecure public wi-fi? An investigation of behaviour and factors driving decisions. In Proceedings of the 6th Workshop on Socio-Technical Aspects in Security and Trust, New York, NY, USA, 5 December 2016; STAST '16; pp. 61–72. [CrossRef]

30. Willemsen, B.; Cadee, M. Extending the airport boundary: Connecting physical security and cybersecurity. *J. Airpt. Manag.* **2018**, *12*, 236–247 .

31. Vanolo, A. Is there anybody out there? The place and role of citizens in tomorrow's smart cities. *Futures* **2016**, *82*, 26–36. [CrossRef]

32. Ali, M.; Rahman, M.L.; Jahan, I. Security and Privacy Awareness: A Survey for Smartphone User. *Int. J. Adv. Comput. Sci. Appl.* **2019**, *10*, 483–488. [CrossRef]

33. Ipsos MORI. Consumer Attitudes towards IoT Security. Available online: https://assets.publishing.service.gov.uk/media/607d7 e588fa8f57358f07e60/Consumer_Attitudes_Towards_IoT_Security_-_Research_Report.pdf (accessed on 31 October 2023).

34. Papic, A.; Radoja, K.; Szombathelyi, D. *Cyber Security Awareness of Croatian Students and the Personal Data Protection*; Simic, M., Ed.; University of JJ Strossmayer Osijek: Osijek, Croatia, 2022; pp. 563–574.

35. Belanche-Gracia, D.; Casaló-Ariño, L.V.; Pérez-Rueda, A. Determinants of multi-service smartcard success for smart cities development: A study based on citizens' privacy and security perceptions. *Gov. Inf. Q.* **2015**, *32*, 154–163. [CrossRef]

36. Isin, E.; Ruppert, E. *Being Digital Citizens*, 2nd ed.; Rowman & Littlefield Publishers: Lanham, MD, USA, 2020.

37. Saber, O.; Mazri, T. Smart City Security Issues: the Main Attacks and Countermeasures. *Int. Arch. Photogramm. Remote. Sens. Spat. Inf. Sci.* **2021**, *XLVI-4/W5-2021*, 465–472. [CrossRef]

38. Cilauro, F. The Connected Places Market in the UK. 2021. Available online: https://assets.publishing.service.gov.uk/media/633 d9e3ee90e0709df741cb8/The_connected_places_market_in_the_UK_2022.pdf (accesed on 20 December 2023).

39. Security-Minded Approach to Developing Smart Cities. 2022. Available online: https://www.protectuk.police.uk/advice-and-g uidance/awareness/security-minded-approach-developing-smart-cities (accesed on 20 December 2023).

40. Martinez-Balleste, A.; Perez-Martinez, P.; Solanas, A. The pursuit of citizens' privacy: A privacy-aware smart city is possible. *IEEE Commun. Mag.* **2013**, *51*, 136–141. [CrossRef]

 *information*

Article

From Cybercrime to Digital Balance: How Human Development Shapes Digital Risk Cultures

Răzvan Rughiniș [1,2], Emanuela Bran [2,3,4,*], Ana Rodica Stăiculescu [1,3,5] and Alexandru Radovici [2]

[1] Romanian Academy of Scientists, 010071 Bucharest, Romania; razvan.rughinis@upb.ro (R.R.); ana-rodica.staiculescu@fsas.unibuc.ro (A.R.S.)

[2] Faculty of Automatic Control and Computers, National University for Science and Technology Politehnica Bucharest, 060042 Bucharest, Romania; alexandru.radovici@upb.ro

[3] Doctoral School of Sociology, University of Bucharest, 010181 Bucharest, Romania

[4] Neo Networking SRL, 031786 Bucharest, Romania

[5] Faculty of Psychology, Behavioral and Legal Sciences, Andrei Saguna University of Constanta, 900196 Constanta, Romania

[*] Correspondence: emanuela.bran@s.unibuc.ro; Tel.: +40-724-021-149

Abstract: This article examines configurations of digital concerns within the European Union (EU27), a leading hub of innovation and policy development. The core objective is to uncover the social forces shaping technology acceptance and risk awareness, which are essential for fostering a resilient digital society in the EU. The study draws upon Bourdieu's concept of capital to discuss technological capital and digital habitus and Beck's risk society theory to frame the analysis of individual and national attitudes towards digital risks. Utilizing Eurobarometer data, the research operationalizes technological capital through proxy indicators of individual socioeconomic status and internet use, while country-level development indicators are used to predict aggregated national risk perception. Article contributions rely on individual- and country-level statistical analysis. Specifically, the study reveals that digital concerns are better predicted at a national level rather than individual level, being shaped by infrastructure, policy, and narrative rather than by personal technological capital. Key findings highlight a positive and a negative correlation between digital advancement with cybersecurity fears and digital literacy, respectively. HDI and DESI are relevant country-level predictors of public concerns, while CGI values are not. Using cluster analysis, we identify and interpret four digital risk cultures within the EU, each with varying foci and levels of concern, which correspond to economic, political, and cultural influences at the national level.

Keywords: cybersecurity; digital risk culture; risk society; technological capital; human development index; GCI; DESI

Citation: Rughiniș, R.; Bran, E.; Stăiculescu, A.R.; Radovici, A. From Cybercrime to Digital Balance: How Human Development Shapes Digital Risk Cultures. *Information* **2024**, *15*, 50. https://doi.org/10.3390/info15010050

Academic Editors: Jose de Vasconcelos, Hugo Barbosa and Carla Cordeiro

Received: 18 November 2023
Revised: 4 January 2024
Accepted: 12 January 2024
Published: 17 January 2024

1. Introduction

As digitalization evolves, so do the experiences and the perceptions of digital hazards [1], leading to a multifaceted interaction involving consciousness, vulnerability, and remediation. With the growing integration of societies and individuals into the digital landscape, there is a corresponding rise in their vulnerability to cyber dangers such as security breaches and misinformation campaigns. At the same time, the increased prevalence of digital platforms has led to an enhanced recognition of these potential hazards, since individuals are better informed, and societies place a larger emphasis on the dissemination of knowledge on cybersecurity and general risk communication [2]. Concurrently, the progression of digitalization introduces increasingly sophisticated instruments and tactics to address these threats. Thus, this duality gives rise to a paradox: although heightened digital exposure has the potential to magnify perceived dangers, the augmented capacities for mitigation may diminish the impression of risk or even foster a state of complacency.

The ongoing evolution of technology creates an ambivalent and dynamic interplay between digitization and the perception of risk [3], leading to continuous changes and adjustments.

The higher the digitalization level (individually and collectively), the higher the exposure to more sophisticated risks, the higher the awareness of risks, and also, conversely, the higher the means to combat risks. This leads to an ambivalent relationship between the level of digitalization and the intensity of perceived digital risks. We explore this complex relationship with regards to several dimensions of perceived digital risks and safety, namely risks pertaining to privacy and cybersecurity, digital literacy and accessibility, child well-being and mental health, and environmental sustainability.

Our research questions explore the individual and collective forces that shape digital concerns:

- How does individual-level technological capital shape perceptions of digital risks?
- How does country-level human development (measured by the Human Development Index (HDI)) and digitalization (measured by the Digital Economy and Society Index (DESI) and the Global Cybersecurity Index (GCI)) shape cultures of digital risks?
- The article investigates the individual and collective dimensions in theory and empirically. The literature review focuses on the concept of technological capital, as derived from Bourdieu's discussion of capital and habitus, and on Beck's risk society. In order to model them for statistical analysis, we propose proxy variables as indicators for each of the two concepts. The methodology describes what type of analysis was performed, and the Section 4 presents the quantitative (numerical) and qualitative (visual) outcomes. The Section 5 explains the findings comparatively within the proposed conceptual framework, followed by a conclusion which highlights the main contributions of our paper.
- At the individual level, we find, in concordance with previous studies, that digital capital, as measured through socio-demographic proxies, does not strongly shape, on aggregate, public concerns of privacy and cybersecurity. This is largely due to the ambivalent nature of the relationship between capital and risk exposure and concerns, as detailed in the Section 1. Still, at the country level, we find significant differences. Study contributions consist of identifying HDI and DESI indices as relevant predictors for country-level variability in public concerns, especially for fears regarding cybersecurity. CGI values were not relevant predictors, possibly because of a data collection lag. We also contribute to the state of the art by identifying an exploratory typology of countries that we interpret as four digital risk cultures, each with a distinctive profile of concerns and with regional specificity.

2. Literature Review

2.1. Technological Capital and Digital Habitus

Concerns about digital technologies can have individual and a collective dynamics underlined by ambivalence. At an individual level, technological capital [4] could account for observed risk perceptions. This extension of Bourdieu's concept of capital refers to the resources that individuals hold, enabling them to engage with digital technology. The digital habitus of an individual would thus comprise the set of lasting dispositions based on personal experiences and assimilated perspectives that shape perceptions, appreciations, and action regarding the digital sphere [5]. The ease with which a person uses online tools, their digital consumption habits [6], and even their susceptibility or resistance to online threats are all influenced by their digital habitus. As societies become increasingly digital, a person's digital habitus interacts with their technological capital [7], affecting how they accumulate more of it and how they deploy it in different situations.

In light of Bourdieu's conceptualization of different social fields and forms of capital, we could talk about the four dimensions of technological capital [8]. The economic dimension is related to the availability of assets such as high-performance devices, premium membership subscriptions, and high speed internet. The cultural dimension comprises skills and knowledge about the latest tech evolutions, including matters such as privacy issues or having certifications in IT-related fields. Another dimension is represented by the social technological capital [9], which comprises membership in relevant networks and groups and having connections with influencers on social media and the tech industry. Finally, there is symbolic technological capital that captures the prestige of digital expertise and presence within the digital sphere.

Technological capital can also be classified into embodied, institutionalized, and material forms of capital. These refer to skills and competences that individuals control as embodied abilities, to their acquired degrees and certifications, and to their physical and digital assets, respectively. These forms of capital can be studied indirectly through proxies such as socio-economic variables and internet use when no direct indicators are available, such as in the case of the Eurobarometer dataset that we use.

The technological capital of individuals does not exist independently of their social position. It frequently interplays with their social, cultural, and economic capital, amplifying or attenuating the positives and negatives connected with each. For example, an individual with high economic capital can easily invest part of it in material technological capital, while an individual with strong social capital and limited technological capital might struggle to maintain their network of influential connections. Consequently, the conceptual relationship between technological capital and socio-economic variables is strong, which makes it possible to use the latter as proxy indicators for the former.

Frequency of internet use is a good measurement of embodied technological capital, as it implies familiarity and comfort with digital tools and services. This form of technological capital is also indirectly revealed in the age and the gender of an individual. The younger generations have been socialized as "digital natives", growing up immersed in the digital world and exhibiting intuitive interaction skills with it. Gender is also associated with STEM skills and digital savvy, though in variable forms and intensities, as boys and men are often more encouraged than girls and women to become acquainted with technologies and to invest in them emotionally.

Education indicates primarily a form of institutionalized technological capital, being an indicator of formal training and instruction in digital skills. Embodied technological capital could also be observed indirectly through education, social class, and community size, as they shape one's encounters with the latest digital advancements. Furthermore, along with the more direct proxy estimates of material technological capital through social class and community size, gender can also act as a proxy due to the existing economic inequalities.

2.2. Risk Society and Digital Development

Beck's "Risk Society" theory highlights the transforming nature of contemporary dangers and how they alter societal perceptions and priorities of digitalization [10]. The Human Development Index (HDI), the Global Cybersecurity Index (GCI) and the Digital Economy and Society Index (DESI) can be used as proxy indicators for the risk society. HDI captures socio-economic development, which is strongly linked to digital technology advancements [11], while DESI and GCI reveal society's digital engagement and cybersecurity preparedness, respectively. Analyzing how each component relates to the risk society formulates the basis for our second research question, which explores ambivalent relationships between digitalization and digital risks, at a collective level.

The first dimension of HDI is life expectancy at birth. This strongly relates to the medical infrastructure and other life sectors such as the food industry or work environment safety, all dependent on and enhanced by digital technologies. Mean years of schooling and expected years of schooling represent the second dimension of HDI. Higher levels of education can accommodate an advanced curriculum on technologies and their multifold impact on society [12]. The third dimension, GNI per capita, indicates economic prosperity. These financial resources are at the risk of being targeted through cybercrime, but they also provide means for developing increased security infrastructures.

The Global Cybersecurity Index (GCI) captures how well a society is equipped to withstand cybersecurity issues from five different dimensions. The first one assesses the degree to which the legal system regulates data protection, critical infrastructures, and cybercrime. The next dimension focuses on national technical capabilities such as handling incidents by a Computer Incident Response Team (CIRT) and having Child Online Protection Reporting mechanisms. The third dimension watches for national cybersecurity strategies and agencies or organizations, with an additional oversight in online child protection. Another dimension measures capacity development such as conducting cyberawareness initiatives, fostering R&D programs, and cultivating national cybersecurity industries. The last dimension assesses cooperation in the form of partnerships and bilateral or multilateral agreements between agencies, firms, and countries.

Moving forward to DESI, its first dimension is represented by Connectivity. Highly connected infrastructures introduce risks related to cyberattacks and the spread of misinformation. Conversely, digital coordination helps mitigate such issues. The second dimension is Human Capital focused on digital skills [13]. This simultaneously indicates a stronger reliance on digital technologies that could represent vulnerabilities, and a higher knowledge of secure digital practices that offer protection. Use of Internet Services by citizens represents the third DESI dimension. High internet engagement may create an increased access to knowledge and a higher digital footprint along with increased digital exposure, leading to cybersecurity and privacy issues [14]. The fourth dimension is Integration of Digital Technology by businesses. A digitalized private sector is more efficient and can accommodate new business models while being at the risk of data breaches and economic espionage. Digital Public Services is the fifth dimension of DESI, and higher digitalization poses a similar threat as the previous dimension. Digitalization brings risks such as data breaches and system failures.

2.3. Previous Studies on Public Perception of Privacy and Cybersecurity Issues

To our knowledge, at the date of manuscript submission (December 2023), there were no other studies that analyzed Eurobarometer 96.1 information concerning cybersecurity concerns, though Matefi [15] discusses Europeans' perceptions of their digital rights based on the same survey.

Still, a series of authors have analyzed other Eurobarometers and dedicated surveys concerning cybersecurity and privacy concerns. For example, Lee and Wang [16] analyzed Eurobarometer 2019 data on cybersecurity fears, identifying two types of Europeans based on individual levels of online activity and cybersecurity behavior (as reported in the survey): the "at-risk class" (with higher risk) and the "cautious class" (with lower risk). At the country level, they used as predictors the Global Cybersecurity Index (GCI), GDP per capita, internet penetration, and proportion of urban population, though only internet penetration was statistically significant in discriminating between the two groups, with higher rates leading to higher proportions of the "at-risk" type. The authors also find that, at the individual level, higher digital skills are, paradoxically, associated with the at-risk class, probably due to the ambivalent relationship mediated by exposure: "Surprisingly, changes in passwords, the maintenance of security settings, and concerns about cybersecurity have all been positively associated with risky Internet users. We speculate that members of the at-risk class might engage in more online activities, and while this would make them more predisposed to being targeted online, these individuals are likely also more self-aware and recognize the potential risks of their actions" (p. 22). In a different analysis of the same Eurobarometer 2019, Lee and Kim [17] conclude that fear of cybercrime is most strongly determined by individuals' prior victimization. This finding is also supported by a systematic review of fear of cybercrime conducted by Brands and Doorn [18]. This review also identifies gender as a correlate of cybercrime concerns, with women reporting higher subjective perceptions of risks, and a positive relationship between cybercrime concerns and protective measures online, conceptualized as "constrained behavior".

Zamfirescu et al. [19] have highlighted the ambivalent relationships between online activity, experiences of cybersecurity incidents, and concerns and preventive measures taken to address them, based on Eurobarometer 87.4/2017. Although the items analyzed are different from Eurobarometer 2021 studied in this paper, and thus not directly comparable, the overall findings are consistent with our analysis. They classify European respondents into four attitudinal clusters, "avoiding", "engaging", "wary", and "aware". Similarly to our analysis, they show that socio-demographical differences as regards these types in relation to gender, age, difficulty of paying bills, and formal education are rather small. Still, countries differ markedly in the prevalence of the four types. This could possibly indicate the relevance of distinctive digital risk cultures that underlie individual attitudinal profiles. Lee and Kim [20] analyze similar data from a 2014 Eurobarometer and classify respondents into three types: uninformed users, disciplined users, and cautious users. They also conclude that country-level factors are better predictors of cybersecurity preparedness than sociodemographic factors, taking into account the GDP per capita and the Global Cybersecurity Index (GCI) values at the national level. Gomes and Dias [21] take a different approach to the Eurobarometer 2017 data, combining individual sociodemographic variables with internet use and the country-level Global Cybersecurity Index (GCI) into a multilevel factor model to predict an aggregated value of cybersecurity perceptions. They find that the GCI is a significant negative predictor for cybercrime risk perception, while individual-level predictors are significant just for self-confidence in one's abilities to use the internet and age (with negative associations) and buying goods online and male gender (with positive associations). We identify here a similar ambivalent connection, with higher digital capital indicated by GCI and self-confidence leading to lower concerns, while higher exposure indicated by online shopping and male gender leading to higher concerns.

In conclusion, previous studies regarding cybersecurity and privacy issues have highlighted the ambivalent relationship between technological capital and security concerns. Higher levels of capital enable effective action and protection, though they rely on more intense online exposure and experiences, which increase the risk surface. Starting from the review of the literature, we have chosen to add the DESI to our operationalization of the risk society, going beyond internet penetration measures studied before (which are also included in the DESI) and to examine all HDI dimensions, not just the GDP per capita, in an exploratory effort to find the best predictors that enable a modeling of cybersecurity concerns at the country level. Each dimension of the HDI, GCI, and DESI captures the ambivalent and mutual relationship between awareness level, mitigation capacity, and the outcomes of digital opportunities and threats characteristic of a risk society [22]. This ambivalent relationship between opportunities and risks was also highlighted by Bourdieu's theory of capital and its application to the digital field on an individual level. By exploring perceived digital threats through these two conceptual lenses, we will be able to trace how public opinion on digital risks is shaped.

3. Methodology

This paper is based on a secondary analysis of data collected through the Eurobarometer survey 96.1 from September to October 2021, part of which contains questions regarding digital rights and principles.

A central point of analysis throughout the paper is constituted by item QB3 "What worries you most about the increased role of digital tools and the internet in our society?", having several answer options: "Use of personal data and information by companies or public administrations", "Cyber-attacks and cybercrime such as theft or abuse of personal data, ransomware (malicious software) or phishing", "The difficulty of learning new digital skills in order to take an active part in society (e.g., working or studying online, online voting)", "The safety and well-being of children", "The difficulty some people have accessing the online world (e.g., persons with disabilities, elderly people, those living in areas with little or no internet access)", "The difficulty of disconnecting and finding a good online/offline life balance", "The environmental impact of digital products and services", "None of the above", "Other", and "Don't know". Each respondent could opt to choose or not each of these worries.

This article contains an individual-level analysis and a country-level analysis which were discussed comparatively in order to assess whether individual socio-economic status or the national properties of social structure and culture account more for the variations seen in digital worries. In the individual-level analysis, several variables were chosen as proxies for technological capital, including age, gender, age at graduation or present age if still studying, a dichotomous variable of whether somebody is currently a student or not, community size, social class, and internet use. For the country-level analysis, the HDI from 2021 and DESI from 2022 were chosen as proxies for the risk society.

The Section 4 includes the most relevant tables, while the Supplementary Material contains a more comprehensive presentation of findings. First, descriptive indicators of worries (QB3.1–QB3.7) and socio-demographic variables were obtained. Second, bivariate correlations were calculated for worries and socio-demographic variables, followed by correlations between these two categories of variables. Bivariate correlations between worries and socio-demographic variables were also performed within each of the EU27 countries. Third, two multinomial regression models were developed for predicting each of the seven worries, and their Nagelkerke Pseudo R-Square was registered. The first model (M1) includes all the previously mentioned socio-economic variables, while the second (M2) adds the country as a predictor.

The country-level analysis follows after the individual-level analysis. First, bivariate correlations were performed between each of the seven worries aggregated at country level and HDI along with DESI and GCI, both used as composite indices and separate dimensions. Second, the average mean of each worry for every country was calculated, on the basis of which an exploratory K-Means cluster analysis at the country level was carried out. Third, the four obtained clusters were interpreted according to their final cluster centers and visualized on a radar-style chart. Furthermore, the clustered countries were listed in a table and visualized on a geographical map. Cluster analysis is useful to overcome linear modelling by making possible ambivalent typologies that contain categories that vary along multiple dimensions [1,16,19,23–27].

4. Results

We proceed by first presenting descriptive statistics on the variables that represent worries captured in the Eurobarometer 96.1. For clarity, we listed them in Table 1 in descending order of the means. We observe that the order of perceived risk is issues related to cybersecurity, child safety, privacy, accessibility, life balance, digital literacy, and ecology.

Table 2 presents descriptive information for the socio-demographic variables used as proxy for individual measures of digital capital.

Next, in Table 3, we present bivariate correlations of the variables that represent worries and those that were chosen as a proxy for technological capital. In convergence with previous studies that found a low predictive value of individuals' socio-demographic position for their cybersecurity worries, such as Zamfirescu et al. [19] and Lee and Kim [20], we also find a low correlational relevance between these indicators. The analysis at an individual level displays rather low correlations, the highest values being 0.23 and 0.20. We observe that people who use the internet more have a slightly higher awareness of the dangers posed by cyber-attacks, use of personal data, and the difficulty of finding an online/offline life balance, on average, though differences highlighted by correlation coefficients are small. Furthermore, cyber-crime awareness increases with graduation age, and finding a balance is more of a concern for the younger population.

Table 1. Descriptive measures of items QB3.1–QB3.7. For all items, minimum value = 0, maximum value = 1.

Variable	Mean
Cybersecurity: QB3.2 Cyber-attacks and cybercrime such as theft or abuse of personal data, ransomware, or phishing	0.56
Child safety: QB3.4 The safety and well-being of children	0.53
Privacy: QB3.1 Use of personal data and information by companies or public administrations	0.46
Accessibility: QB3.5 The difficulty some people have accessing the online world	0.41
Life balance: QB3.6 The difficulty of disconnecting and finding a good online/offline life balance	0.34
Digital literacy: QB3.3 The difficulty of learning new digital skills in order to take an active part in society	0.26
Ecology: QB3.7 The environmental impact of digital products and services	0.23

N = 26,521; cases have been weighted for a EU27 representative sample; minimum is 0; maximum is 1; because the variables are dichotomous, we do not report the standard deviation, which is redundant with the mean.

Table 2. Descriptive measures of socio-demographic variables.

Variable	N	Minimum	Maximum	Mean	Std. Deviation
Age	26,514	15	98	49.61	18.684
Gender	26,515	0	1	0.48	0.500
Age at graduation or present age	26,154	0	93	19.60	5.476
Student dummy variable	26,154	0	1	0.09	0.289
Community	26,516	1	3	1.98	0.752
Social class	26,019	1	5	2.49	0.976
Internet use	26,521	1	7	6.21	1.742
Valid N (listwise)	25,654				

Table 3. Bivariate correlations between worries (QB3.1–QB3.7) and socio-demographic variables.

Variables	Age	Gender	Graduation Age	Student Status	Community Size	Social Class	Internet Use
Privacy	−0.10 ***	0.06 ***	**0.10 *****	0.02 **	0.02 **	0.05 ***	**0.17 *****
Cybersecurity	−0.12 ***	0.04 ***	**0.14 *****	0.06 ***	0.01	0.09 ***	**0.23 *****
Digital literacy	0.05 ***	−0.02 ***	−0.05 ***	−0.04 ***	0.00	−0.04 ***	−0.01 *
Child safety	−0.02 ***	−0.06 ***	−0.01	−0.02 ***	−0.01	−0.02 ***	0.05 ***
Accessibility	0.00	−0.03 ***	0.03 ***	−0.01	0.01	0.01	0.07 ***
Life balance	−0.20 ***	0.02 ***	**0.10 *****	**0.10 *****	0.05 ***	0.09 ***	**0.16 *****
Ecology	−0.08 ***	0.00	0.05 ***	0.05 ***	0.05 ***	0.07 ***	0.08 ***

N is between 26,019 and 26,521; statistically significant coefficients are marked with bold; $p \leq 0.05$ is marked *; $p \leq 0.01$ is marked **; $p \leq 0.001$ is marked *** Coefficients larger than 0.1 in absolute value are marked with bold.

The final step of the individual-level analysis is represented by multinomial analysis with two models, M1 and M2. Table 4 presents the obtained Pseudo R-Square Nagelkerke model values for the prediction of each digital worry. The low Nagelkerke values are not surprising, since correlations also produced rather low values. We observe that introducing the country as a predictor in the second model increases the Nagelkerke values for some of the predicted digital worries, reaching the highest value for concerns about cybersecurity. The country captures cultural and infrastructural differences, accounting for variation in cybersecurity concerns that has been explained in previous studies through macro-level indicators such as the GCI or internet penetration, as documented by Lee and Wang [16], Lee and Kim [20], and Gomez and Dias [21].

Table 4. Multinomial regression models: summary of Pseudo R-Square Nagelkerke values.

Models	Privacy	Cybersecurity	Digital Literacy	Child Safety	Accessibility	Life Balance	Ecology
Model 1: Socio-demographic variables + Internet use	0.04	0.08	0.01	0.01	0.01	0.07	0.02
Model 2: Socio-demographic variables + Internet use + Country	0.06	0.12	0.04	0.04	0.04	0.08	0.05

Socio-demographic variables: age, gender, graduation age, student status, community size, and social class.

The country-level analysis displays more intense correlation values between worries and risk society proxies, rather than individual-level technological capital proxies. Within the section of Table 5 where HDI correlations are presented, we observe that aggregated country-level cybersecurity concerns strongly correlate with the income and education components. The digital literacy concern is more characteristic of lower-income countries. Furthermore, the accessibility concern is more often found in countries with higher-quality health systems, possibly a proxy for more solidaristic societies. Regarding the DESI correlations, the human capital, tech integration, and public service components strongly correlate with perceived cybersecurity risks and negatively correlate with digital literacy concerns. Concerns with the ecological impact are negatively correlated with the education component of HDI and with the public service component of DESI, which might indicate the higher trust and optimism in societies with higher levels of development on their society's capacity to handle the environmental impact of digital technologies. Still, most GCI dimensions and its aggregated value do not correlate with digital concerns at the country level. Only its legal and organizational measures components correlate positively with public concerns for digitalization's impact on child safety, possibly indicating the influence of public debates and controversies on this topic in countries with stronger legal and organizational policies for regulating the impact of digital technologies. It is also possible that the lower correlation values for GCI are derived from its two-year lag, since the latest available values are from 2020, while DESI values are available from 2022.

Figure 1 includes a visual representation of the pattern of associations between human development (HDI) and digitalization (DESI) and digital concerns, at the country level.

Figure 2 presents scatterplots for the highest correlation values at country levels, respectively, the HDI and DESI indices with public concerns with cybersecurity. The strong correlations derive from a linear relationship that can be noticed when country values are plotted against each other.

In the next step of our analysis, we performed an exploratory K-Means cluster analysis using the mean values of each worry at a country level. Previous typological analyses at the individual level highlighted two poles of high- and low-security exposure [16], with finer classifications capturing ambivalent intermediary types [19,20]. We opted for a four-class typology, which also included intermediary types of cultures of digital risks that combine high levels of concern on some dimensions with lower levels on other dimensions. Table 6 shows the obtained final clusters which we interpreted as distinctive digital risk cultures, using their specific profile of perceived risks and concerns. We proposed a name for each risk culture, taking into account its main focus. The table header contains the proportions of each configuration within the total EU27 population and the number of member countries, along with its distinctive characteristics. Figure 3 presents the obtained values on a radar-style chart in order to better compare the four cultural profiles along the seven explored dimensions.

Table 5. Bivariate correlations between digital concerns (QB3.1–QB3.7) and HDI and DESI indices and components.

Index/Digital Concerns:	Privacy	Cybersecurity	Digital Literacy	Child Safety	Accessibility	Life Balance	Ecology
HDI 2021—Total index	**0.46** *	**0.77** **	−**0.49** **	0.32	**0.41** *	**0.44** *	−0.13
HDI Health component	**0.49** **	**0.52** **	−0.21	**0.38** *	**0.60** **	0.38	0.09
HDI Education component	0.30	**0.66** **	−**0.48** *	0.11	0.12	0.34	−**0.43** *
HDI Income component	0.30	**0.73** **	−**0.56** **	0.29	0.27	0.34	0.02
DESI 2022—Total index	0.31	**0.83** **	−**0.60** **	0.30	0.34	0.29	−0.29
DESI Human capital component	0.29	**0.84** **	−**0.59** **	0.32	0.34	0.38	−0.28
DESI Connectivity component	0.27	**0.41** *	−0.27	0.09	0.37	0.37	0.08
DESI Tech integration component	0.37	**0.77** **	−**0.42** *	0.23	**0.50** **	0.31	−0.26
DESI Public service component	0.16	**0.70** **	−**0.64** **	0.32	0.05	0.05	−**0.39** *
GCI 2020—Total index	−0.03	0.25	−0.25	0.16	0.26	0.03	−0.10
GCI Legal measures	0.11	0.36	−0.37	**0.41** *	0.27	0.11	−0.13
GCI Technical measures	−0.20	0.28	−0.30	0.06	0.07	−0.05	−0.18
GCI Organizational measures	0.25	0.28	−0.26	**0.48** *	0.04	0.06	0.01
GCI Capacity development	0.05	0.16	−0.06	0.06	0.33	0.22	0.05
GCI Cooperative measures	−0.23	−0.07	−0.04	−0.25	0.34	−0.16	−0.17

N is 27; statistically significant coefficients are marked with bold; $p \leq 0.05$ is marked *; $p \leq 0.01$ is marked **.

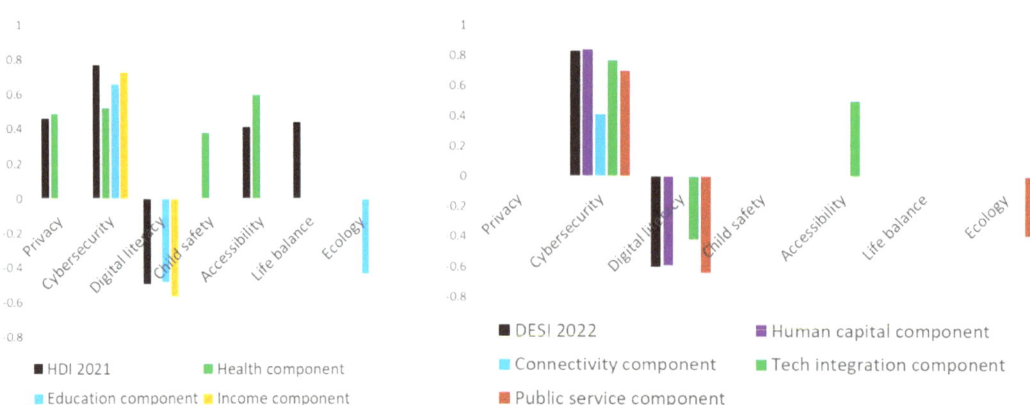

Figure 1. Visualization of correlation coefficients between digital concerns (QB3.1–QB3.7) and HDI and DESI indices and components (as presented in Table 5).

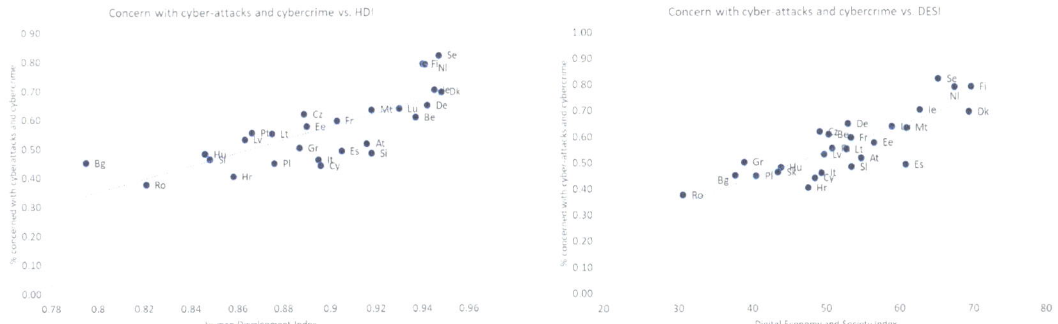

Figure 2. Scatterplot illustrating the correlations between public concerns with cyberattacks and cybercrime and HDI 2021 (Pearson correlation = 0.77) and DESI 2022 (Pearson correlation = 0.83) values, respectively, as presented in Table 5.

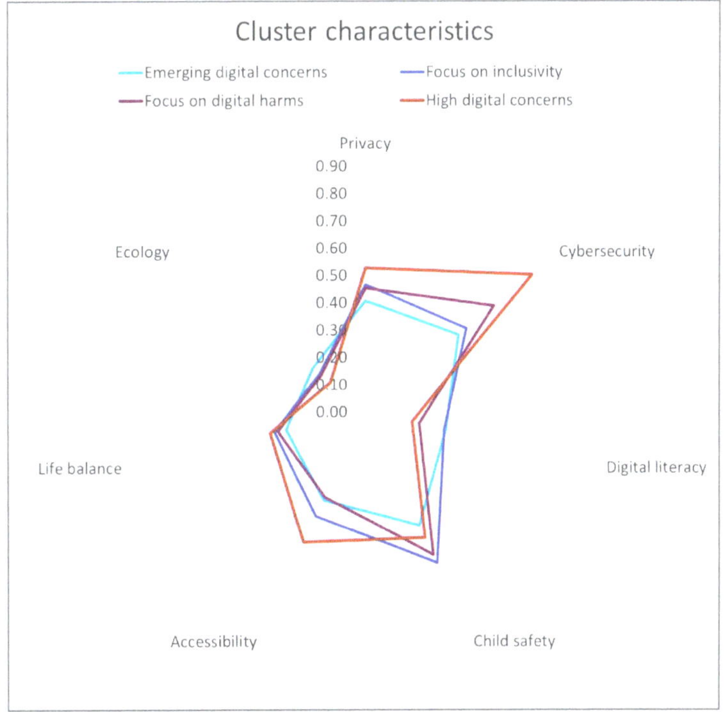

Figure 3. Radar-style chart of digital risk culture profiles.

Table 6. Cluster analysis results that highlight four digital risk culture profiles. The highest values per row are marked in bold.

Variables	Digital Risk Culture 1: Emerging Digital Concerns 32% (6 Countries)	Digital Risk Culture 2: Focus on Inclusivity 19% (7 Countries)	Digital Risk Culture 3: Focus on Harms 42% (11 Countries)	Digital Risk Culture 4: High Digital Concerns 7% (3 Countries)
Privacy	0.40	0.46	0.45	**0.52**
Cybersecurity	0.45	0.49	**0.62**	**0.80**
Digital literacy	**0.31**	**0.30**	0.21	0.18
Child safety	0.46	**0.62**	**0.58**	0.51
Accessibility	0.36	**0.43**	0.35	**0.53**
Life balance	0.30	0.35	0.34	0.37
Ecology	0.25	0.22	0.21	0.17

Header percentages represent proportions of each cluster from the EU27 population; the values represent final cluster centers; convergence was obtained on iteration 3. The largest values on each row, which define the specificity of the cluster, are marked with bold.

We notice that there are differences as well as commonalities between the four cultures of digital concerns. Cybersecurity ranks very high for all risk cultures, together with child safety and privacy, while ecological impact of digital technologies ranks lowest, with digital literacy and life balance having generally a low priority. Beyond these shared priorities, each culture has a distinctive focus. Countries with emerging digital concerns are specific in their relatively higher preoccupation with digital literacy, while countries with a focus on inclusivity prioritize child safety, accessibility, and digital literacy relatively more. Countries that focus on harm emphasize cybersecurity and child safety even more, while countries with high digital concerns are distinctive through their relative preoccupation with cybersecurity, accessibility, and privacy (see a synthesis in Table 7).

The following map shown in Figure 4 geographically delineates the identified digital risk cultures, and Table 7 contains the list of countries belonging to each configuration along with their highest concerns, listed in decreasing order of relevance within each cluster. The worries that are specific for each culture, by comparing them with the others, are marked with bold. Colors are only used to distinguish between cultural clusters, and numbering does not imply an ordinal type of variable.

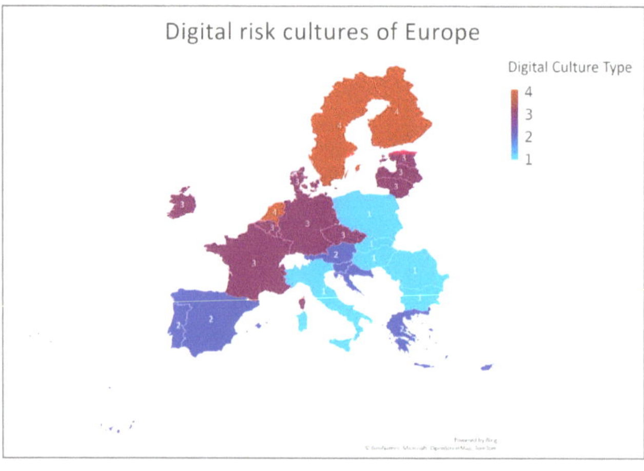

Figure 4. Geographical map of identified digital culture clusters.

Table 7. Countries belonging to each digital culture cluster.

Culture	Digital Culture 1: Emerging Digital Concerns	Digital Culture 2: Focus on Inclusivity	Digital Culture 3: Focus on Harms	Digital Culture 4: High Digital Concerns
Digital concerns	Child safety Cybersecurity Privacy Accessibility **Digital literacy** Life balance Ecology	**Child safety** Cybersecurity Privacy **Accessibility** Life balance **Digital literacy** Ecology	Cybersecurity **Child safety** Privacy Accessibility Life balance Digital literacy Ecology	Cybersecurity **Accessibility** **Privacy** Child safety Life balance Digital literacy Ecology
Countries	Bulgaria Hungary Italy Poland Romania Slovakia	Austria Croatia Cyprus Greece Portugal Slovenia Spain	Belgium Czech Republic Denmark Estonia France Germany Latvia Lithuania Luxembourg Malta Republic of Ireland	Finland Sweden The Netherlands

Worries are listed in decreasing order by level of concern within the cluster; specific worries that are higher for each cluster in comparison with the other clusters are marked in bold; countries are listed in alphabetical order.

5. Discussion

The empirical data show that concerns over digital technologies emerge at a national and regional cultural level rather than as individual attitudes related to personal socio-economic status. These cultures of digital risks could stem from the complex interplay of the forces present in a risk society as well as elements such as the system of social norms and policies, values, and structures.

The risk society theory discusses the ambivalent connection between risk perception and social development. At a European level, we observe that the analyzed digital concerns are rather frequent, presenting a mean between 56% (around one in two people fear cybercrime) and 23% (around one in four fear an environmental impact of digital tech). This finding is in line with the EU being regarded as a highly developed digital arena, though with variations between different countries and social categories, where leading tech innovations and regulatory frameworks exhibit the dynamics characteristic of modern societies between risk production and management.

There are variations in the proportion of people that are worried about different digital risks at a European or country level. High concerns over cybersecurity, privacy, and child safety and wellbeing might reflect the perceived severity of negative outcomes. Other risks related to inclusivity, life balance, and the environment might be eclipsed in comparison regarding the perceived immediacy, personal experience, and broader social narratives of technological progress.

We observe that cybersecurity concerns strongly correlate with higher HDI and DESI and with their components, especially the income component of HDI and the human capital component of DESI. This further supports Beck's theory of risk production and perception in technologically advanced societies, as these people have more at stake to lose and also a higher awareness of consequences.

Privacy concerns seem to be related to a developed health sector, probably due to the sensitivity of such data and also to the type of society reflected by this indicator. To a lesser degree, this positive correlation is also observed in the tech integration component of DESI, as highly digitalized infrastructures also represent a possible system vulnerability. Privacy concerns are lower when compared to cybersecurity, probably also because the EU is a leading policymaker in this area.

Accessibility shows a correlation pattern similar to privacy concerns but even stronger. Probably as health care standards rise, so too does the awareness towards digital inclusivity. And as integration of digital technologies becomes ubiquitous, so too does the fear of leaving behind certain individuals.

Digital literacy presents strong negative correlations with the HDI and DESI, especially with the economic component of HDI and the public service component of DESI. This might reflect the higher fear of the less digitally advanced populations of being left behind along with the trust of the digitally developed countries in the IT&C education opportunities.

Child safety, life balance, and ecology present overall lower correlation scores with country development indicators. Child safety is probably a universal concern not strongly related to development. Life balance concerns seem to arise more frequently in highly developed nations, while ecological concerns negatively correlate with educational development and digitalization of the public service. An explanation might be that the life pace in digitalized societies is sometimes disruptive to emotional health while these societies also better mitigate the ecological impact of such technologies.

The Eurobarometer data reveal four digital cultures that present distinctive profiles regarding perceived digital threats. The first digital culture we have identified extends within the geographical space of Central–Eastern Europe and Italy. The level of concerns within this culture is typically lower than the others, and the risk perception seems balanced across categories. This could be explained by these countries experiencing a transitional phase in their digital development. There is a slight emphasis on child safety and cyber-crime issues. The awareness of problems of privacy and accessibility proves the acknowledgement of challenges related to institutions and infrastructure.

The second digital culture is characteristic of Southern Europe and some Central European countries. It is characterized by a moderate overall concern profile with a focus on inclusivity. These countries place a higher emphasis on the safety and well-being of children along with a balanced online/offline life, possibly due to the cultural specifics. Furthermore, worries regarding accessibility for vulnerable populations stand out and suggest potential gaps in policy and infrastructure that need to be addressed. Medium-level concerns might suggest an awareness of the benefits of technological integration along with the acknowledgement of the pitfalls of possible disruptions.

The third digital culture occupies the space of Western Europe and includes the Baltic States and the Czech Republic. These countries also exhibit an intermediate level of digital concerns with an emphasis on possible harms of digitalization, as more advanced digital development creates awareness regarding the less anticipated risks. This deeper understanding of the complex influences of technologies is also reflected in the reduced concerns regarding digital literacy. The main characteristics of this region are a pronounced concern about cybersecurity issues followed by the safety of children online and lower concerns regarding digital skills. This is the mark of nations with advanced digital infrastructures and citizens with a consolidated digital education.

The fourth digital culture is spread across Northern Europe, where nations are some of the most digitally advanced in the world. Across these nations there is an extremely high level of concern about cyber-attacks and cybercrime. This can be explained by the advanced integration of digital services into daily life, which increases risk perception. Their second concern is accessibility, which is interesting given the actual level of development and indicates their high inclusivity standards. This region showcases Beck's idea of manufactured risks at its peak, having the highest exposure to sophisticated digital threats. While vigilant of the implications of cyberattacks, this cluster that represents the higher end of the spectrum of technological capital seems relatively comfortable with the evolution of the digital landscape related to environmental health.

Additional metrics that capture more dimensions of social development can enhance the understanding of variations in public attitudes towards cybersecurity and privacy across nations. These dimensions could be derived from a comprehensive framework that incorporates economic, cultural, political, and social elements; each of these components may influence the way the public perceives and reacts to matters pertaining to cybersecurity and privacy. As an illustration, the economic stability of a nation could be quantified using a Socio-Economic Stability Index, which incorporates indicators such as employment rates, income inequality, and economic expansion. This is a fundamental component that could shape the way the general public perceives technology and security. Societies characterized by greater economic stability may allocate greater resources towards technological infrastructure and education, resulting in heightened consciousness and comprehension of cybersecurity vulnerabilities. On the contrary, in economies characterized by lower levels of stability, the emphasis on pressing economic concerns may eclipse the significance attributed to cybersecurity, thereby resulting in a diminished level of public attention towards these matters. The perception and response of populations to cybersecurity risks could be impacted by societal attitudes toward technology, which include trust in technological advancement and openness to adopting new technologies. This could be quantified using an index of Cultural Orientation towards Technology. Cultures that demonstrate a greater propensity to embrace technological advancements are more likely to adopt cybersecurity measures in a proactive manner. The public's perception of the government's transparency and level of trust, as assessed by a Government Transparency and Trust Index, could have a bearing on their attitudes towards cybersecurity initiatives lead by the state. A metric that quantifies the degree of community engagement and social cohesion could be a Social Cohesion and Community Engagement Score. Generalized trust is important in facilitating collaborative reactions to cybersecurity risks. Strong social cohesion increases the likelihood that members of a society will collaborate to defend against cyber threats and encourage communal protective behaviors. The degree to which a nation guarantees civil liberties and personal freedoms could be assessed by a Civil Liberties and Personal Freedoms Index; this, in turn, could influence public perceptions of privacy and cybersecurity. Societies that enjoy greater freedoms frequently prioritize personal privacy to the extent that they are more vigilant and responsive to cybersecurity threats that have the potential to violate these liberties. Conversely, civil liberties that are restricted may engender a diminished level of public opposition towards intrusive cybersecurity protocols. A Globalization and International Connectivity Index, measuring the degree to which a nation is integrated into global networks for trade, travel, and communication, could capture the correlations between globalization and vulnerability to and awareness of global cybersecurity issues. Countries with extensive connectivity are more prone to confronting a wide range of cybersecurity challenges; consequently, they may possess a more sophisticated comprehension and apprehension regarding these matters. Lastly, a factor of Historical Experience with Technology and Security Incidents would consider the ways in which a nation's prior encounters with security incidents associated with technology have influenced its present-day public sentiments and policies concerning cybersecurity. Nations with a history of substantial cybersecurity threats are more likely to possess a heightened level of awareness and more comprehensive policies regarding these risks. Conversely, countries without such a background may not perceive these threats with the same severity.

6. Conclusions

The article explores the configuration of digital concerns within the EU nations, a political and cultural space leading in innovation and digital policymaking. The importance of the research stands in discussing social forces that shape technology acceptance and risk awareness, two factors that sustain building a resilient society within the advanced digital landscape of the EU. The study investigates seven digital concerns related to privacy, cybersecurity, digital literacy, child safety and wellbeing, accessibility, online/offline life balance, and environmental impact.

The Section 1 is focused on two key concepts, namely Bourdieu's capital adapted to the technological field and Beck's risk society with its ambivalent links between risk creation, mitigation, and perception. The Section 3 describes the Eurobarometer variables which are used as proxies for the technological capital within an individual-level analysis and those used as proxies for a risk society at a national aggregate level. Technological capital is operationalized through socio-economic variables and internet use that represent embodied, institutionalized, and material forms of capital. The indicators for the risk society that were explored comprise the HDI and DESI.

The Section 3 also presents the operations performed on the data including determining frequencies, computing bivariate correlations, exploring multinomial regression models, and classifying digital cultures through cluster analysis. The results revealed an accentuated variability in concerns at a national level rather than at an individual level. This implies that elements such as digital infrastructures, national policies, and broader narratives shape perceptions of the impact of technologies, rather than the digital habitus dependent on personal technological capital.

The main findings include a strong positive correlation between fear of cyberattacks and high digital development which supports Beck's theory regarding risk perception due to high exposure, deeper understanding, and irreversibility of impact. There is also a strong correlation between reduced digitalization and levels of digital literacy which further sustains the risk society theory and highlights the fear of being left behind. The cluster analysis at country level revealed four distinct digital cultures, each characterized by configurations of reduced concerns, moderate concerns with a focus on inclusivity, moderate concerns with a focus on harm, and high concerns. The specific digital risk awareness profiles align with four regions of the EU, revealing economic, political, and cultural forces that shape concerns at the national and regional levels.

One limitation of the research is with respect to the spread of the data, which is limited to the 27 countries of the EU. Even if culturally heterogeneous, the EU has a high cooperation between nations and a common strategy for technological innovation and good governance. Furthermore, studies are needed to analyze how these findings relate to the emergence of digital risk awareness within other nations around the globe. The second limitation of the study refers to the use of proxy variables for technological capital and risk society, as more direct measurements were not included in the Eurobarometer. A dedicated survey could better capture the distinctive social forces that shape public opinion on digital risks.

Supplementary Materials: R.R., E.B., A.R.S. and A.R. "From Cybercrime to Digital Balance: How Human Development Shapes Digital Risk Cultures. Supplementary Material". Available at https://bit.ly/3Gm8r3v (accessed on 16 November 2023).

Author Contributions: Conceptualization, R.R., E.B., A.R.S. and A.R.; methodology, R.R., E.B., A.R.S. and A.R.; software, E.B.; validation, R.R., E.B., A.R.S. and A.R.; formal analysis, R.R., E.B., A.R.S. and A.R.; investigation, R.R., E.B., A.R.S. and A.R.; resources, R.R.; data curation, E.B.; writing—original draft preparation, R.R., E.B., A.R.S. and A.R.; writing—review and editing, R.R., E.B., A.R.S. and A.R.; visualization, E.B.; supervision, R.R.; project administration, R.R.; funding acquisition, R.R. All authors have read and agreed to the published version of the manuscript.

Funding: This work was funded by the "Innovative Solution for Optimizing User Productivity through Multi-Modal Monitoring of Activity and Profiles—OPTIMIZE"/"Solutie Inovativa de Optimizare a Productivitatii Utilizatorilor prin Monitorizarea Multi-Modala a Activitatii si a Profilelor—OPTIMIZE" project, Contract number 366/390042/27.09.2021, MySMIS code: 121491, https://optimize.research-technology.ro/ (accessed on 16 November 2023).

Institutional Review Board Statement: Not required for secondary analysis of publicly available survey data.

Informed Consent Statement: Not required for secondary analysis of publicly available survey data.

Data Availability Statement: Publicly available datasets were analyzed in this study. (1) European Commission and European Parliament, Brussels (2022). Eurobarometer 96.1 (2021). GESIS, Cologne. ZA7846 Data file Version 1.0.0, Available at URL (accessed 1 September 2023): https://doi.org/10

.4232/1.13882. (2) UNDP (United Nations Development Programme), New York (2022). Human Development Report 2021-22: Uncertain Times, Unsettled Lives: Shaping our Future in a Transforming World, Available at URL (accessed on 1 September 2023): https://hdr.undp.org/informe-sobre-desarrollo-humano-2021-22. (3) European Commission, Brussels (2022). Digital Economy and Society Index (DESI) 2022. European Commission. Available at URL (accessed on 1 September 2023): https://digital-strategy.ec.europa.eu/en/library/digital-economy-and-society-index-desi-2022.

Conflicts of Interest: The authors declare no conflicts of interest. The funders had no role in the design of the study; in the collection, analyses, or interpretation of data; in the writing of the manuscript; or in the decision to publish the results.

References

1. Rughini, R.; Rughini, C.; Vulpe, S.N.; Rosner, D. From social netizens to data citizens: Variations of GDPR awareness in 28 European countries. *Comput. Law Secur. Rev.* **2021**, *42*, 105585. [CrossRef]
2. de las Heras-Pedrosa, C.; Sánchez-Núñez, P.; Peláez, J.I. Sentiment Analysis and Emotion Understanding during the COVID-19 Pandemic in Spain and Its Impact on Digital Ecosystems. *Int. J. Environ. Res. Public. Health* **2020**, *17*, 5542. [CrossRef] [PubMed]
3. Budeanu, A.-M.; Țurcanu, D.; Rosner, D. European Perceptions of Artificial Intelligence and Their Social Variability. In An Exploratory Study. In Proceedings of the 2023 24th International Conference on Control Systems and Computer Science (CSCS), Bucharest, Romania, 24–26 May 2023; pp. 436–443. [CrossRef]
4. Romele, A. Technological Capital: Bourdieu, Postphenomenology, and the Philosophy of Technology Beyond the Empirical Turn. *Philos. Technol.* **2021**, *34*, 483–505. [CrossRef]
5. Liébana-Cabanillas, F.; García-Maroto, I.; Muñoz-Leiva, F.; Ramos-de-Luna, I. Mobile Payment Adoption in the Age of Digital Transformation: The Case of Apple Pay. *Sustainability* **2020**, *12*, 5443. [CrossRef]
6. Talwar, S.; Talwar, M.; Kaur, P.; Dhir, A. Consumers' resistance to digital innovations: A systematic review and framework development. *Australas. Mark. J. AMJ* **2020**, *28*, 286–299. [CrossRef]
7. El-Haddadeh, R. Digital Innovation Dynamics Influence on Organisational Adoption: The Case of Cloud Computing Services. *Inf. Syst. Front.* **2020**, *22*, 985–999. [CrossRef]
8. Budeanu, A.-M.; Rosner, D. Big Data as Capital. A Case Study on the Innovation Labs Tech Accelerator. In Proceedings of the 2021 23rd International Conference on Control Systems and Computer Science (CSCS), Bucharest, Romania, 26–28 May 2021; pp. 469–475. [CrossRef]
9. Graziano, T. Social Media in Risk Perception and Disaster Management: A Geographical Perspective. In *Disaster Resilience and Human Settlements: Emerging Perspectives in the Anthropocene*; Dahiya, B., de Pascale, F., De Pietro, O., Farabollini, P., Lugeri, F.R., Mercatanti, L., Eds.; Advances in 21st Century Human Settlements; Springer Nature: Singapore, 2023; pp. 139–153. [CrossRef]
10. Sundberg, L. Towards the Digital Risk Society: A Review. *Hum. Aff.* **2023**, 1–14. [CrossRef]
11. Bolpagni, M. Cyber risk index: A socio-technical composite index for assessing risk of cyber attacks with negative outcome. *Qual. Quant.* **2022**, *56*, 1643–1659. [CrossRef]
12. Lesjak, D.; Zwilling, M.; Klein, G. Cyber crime and cyber security awareness among students: A comparative study in Israel and Slovenia. *Issues Inf. Syst.* **2019**, *20*, 80–87.
13. Vasiloiu, I.-C. Cybersecurity education in Romania—Competitive advantage in the EU market. In *Proceedings of the International Conference on Virtual Learning*, 17th ed.; The National Institute for Research & Development in Informatics—ICI Publishing House: Bucharest, Romania, 2022; pp. 297–307. [CrossRef]
14. Vimalkumar, M.; Sharma, S.K.; Singh, J.B.; Dwivedi, Y.K. 'Okay google, what about my privacy?': User's privacy perceptions and acceptance of voice based digital assistants. *Comput. Hum. Behav.* **2021**, *120*, 106763. [CrossRef]
15. Matefi, R. Digital Rights and Their Protection in the Online Environment in the Representation of EU Citizens. *Rev. Universul Jurid.* **2022**, *52*, 52–55.
16. Lee, C.S.; Wang, Y. Typology of cybercrime victimization in Europe: A multilevel latent class analysis. *Crime Delinq.* **2022**, 1–28. [CrossRef]
17. Lee, C.S.; Kim, J.H. How victims perceive fear of cybercrime: Importance of informed risk. *Crim. Justice Stud.* **2023**, *36*, 206–227. [CrossRef]
18. Brands, J.; Doorn, J.V. The measurement, intensity and determinants of fear of cybercrime: A systematic review. *Comput. Hum. Behav.* **2022**, *127*, 107082. [CrossRef]
19. Zamfirescu, R.-G.; Rughinis, C.; Hosszu, A.; Cristea, D. Cyber-security profiles of European users: A survey. In Proceedings of the 2019 22nd International Conference on Control Systems and Computer Science (CSCS), Bucharest, Romania, 28–30 May 2019; IEEE: Piscataway, NJ, USA, 2019; pp. 438–442.
20. Lee, C.S.; Kim, J.H. Latent groups of cybersecurity preparedness in Europe: Sociodemographic factors and country-level contexts. *Comput. Secur.* **2020**, *97*, 101995. [CrossRef]
21. Gomes, A.; Dias, J.G.; da Força Aérea, A. A multilevel factor analysis of the cybercrime risk perception in the European Union. In Proceedings of the Program and Book of Abstracts XXVII Meeting of the Portuguese Association for Classification and Data Analysis (CLAD), Lisboa, Portugal, 22–24 October 2020; p. 57.

22. Popkova, E.G.; Gulzat, K. Contradiction of the Digital Economy: Public Well-Being vs. Cyber Threats. In *Digital Economy: Complexity and Variety vs. Rationality*; Popkova, E.G., Sergi, B.S., Eds.; Lecture Notes in Networks and Systems; Springer International Publishing: Cham, Switzerland, 2020; pp. 112–124. [CrossRef]
23. Vulpe, S.-N.; Rughiniș, C. Social amplification of risk and "probable vaccine damage": A typology of vaccination beliefs in 28 European countries. *Vaccine* **2021**, *39*, 1508–1515. [CrossRef] [PubMed]
24. Rughiniș, C.; Vulpe, S.-N.; Flaherty, M.G.; Vasile, S. Shades of doubt: Measuring and classifying vaccination confidence in Europe. *Vaccine* **2022**, *40*, 6670–6679. [CrossRef] [PubMed]
25. Cristea, D.; Zamfirache, I.; Zamfirescu, R.-G. Vaccination against COVID-19 in Europe: A Typology Based on Cluster Analysis. *Int. J. Environ. Res. Public Health* **2022**, *19*, 8603. [CrossRef] [PubMed]
26. Zamfirescu, R.-G. Perceptions and attitudes regarding the vaccination debate in Europe: Empirical typologies and regional inequalities. *J. Comp. Res. Anthropol. Sociol.* **2021**, *12*, 47.
27. Obreja, D.M. The social side of cryptocurrency: Exploring the investors' ideological realities from Romanian Facebook groups. *New Media Soc.* **2022**, 1–18. [CrossRef]

 *information*

Article

Secure Genomic String Search with Parallel Homomorphic Encryption

Md Momin Al Aziz *, **Md Toufique Morshed Tamal** and **Noman Mohammed**

Department of Computer Science, University of Manitoba, Winnipeg , MB R3T 5V6, Canada; morshed@cs.umanitoba.ca (M.T.M.T.); noman@cs.umanitoba.ca(N.M.)
* Correspondence: azizmma@cs.umanitoba.ca

Abstract: Fully homomorphic encryption (FHE) cryptographic systems enable limitless computations over encrypted data, providing solutions to many of today's data security problems. While effective FHE platforms can address modern data security concerns in unsecure environments, the extended execution time for these platforms hinders their broader application. This project aims to enhance FHE systems through an efficient parallel framework, specifically building upon the existing torus FHE (TFHE) system chillotti2016faster. The TFHE system was chosen for its superior bootstrapping computations and precise results for countless Boolean gate evaluations, such as AND and XOR. Our first approach was to expand upon the gate operations within the current system, shifting towards algebraic circuits, and using graphics processing units (GPUs) to manage cryptographic operations in parallel. Then, we implemented this GPU-parallel FHE framework into a needed genomic data operation, specifically string search. We utilized popular string distance metrics (hamming distance, edit distance, set maximal matches) to ascertain the disparities between multiple genomic sequences in a secure context with all data and operations occurring under encryption. Our experimental data revealed that our GPU implementation vastly outperforms the former method, providing a 20-fold speedup for any 32-bit Boolean operation and a 14.5-fold increase for multiplications.This paper introduces unique enhancements to existing FHE cryptographic systems using GPUs and additional algorithms to quicken fundamental computations. Looking ahead, the presented framework can be further developed to accommodate more complex, real-world applications.

Keywords: fully homomorphic encryption; GPU parallel operations; secure computation on GPU; parallel FHE framework; secure string search using FHE

check for
updates

Citation: Aziz, M.M.A.; Tamal, M.T.M.; Mohammed, N. Secure Genomic String Search with Parallel Homomorphic Encryption. *Information* **2024**, *15*, 40. https:// doi.org/10.3390/info15010040

Academic Editors: Jose de Vasconcelos, Hugo Barbosa and Carla Cordeiro

Received: 8 November 2023
Revised: 28 December 2023
Accepted: 29 December 2023
Published: 11 January 2024

1. Introduction

In recent times, the study of fully homomorphic encryption (FHE) [1] has been a significant area of cryptographic research. FHE cryptosystems, renowned for their robust security assurances, are characterized by their ability to carry out numerous operations on encrypted data. As there is a growing demand for data-oriented applications designed to manage confidential human data, the notion of computing within the scope of encryption emerges as increasingly prevalent [2–4]. As such, FHE presents a perfect cryptographic solution to these privacy issues by facilitating arbitrary operations on encrypted data within an untrusted computational setting.

Despite the security provided by the cryptosystem, FHE's performance speed is a drawback for routine computations, leading to its limited adoption and scant real-world applications. For instance, a roughly 7-s duration is required to add two 32-bit encrypted numbers, while multiplication operations are notably slower, taking about 8 min (Table 1). To encourage the broader utilization of FHE in real-world applications, improvements to its speed are imperative—this can be achieved either through theoretical techniques to cut back on computational complexity or through simultaneous operations.

Our study suggests a parallel framework for executing FHE computations using graphics processing units (GPUs). Over the years, GPU technology has significantly contributed to various machine learning algorithms by expediting model training processes over extensive datasets. Following a similar approach, we tap into the multicore features of GPUs and propose a parallel FHE framework that uses the torus FHE (TFHE) cryptosystem [5].

Our goal is to apply the proposed FHE operations to genomic data and assess the framework's efficiency. Previously, when genomic data were processed in plain text without any protective measures, numerous safety issues surfaced [6,7]. Therefore, encrypting data during storage or computation should enhance security in case of a data breach or compromised system. Furthermore, we plan to enhance the proposed framework to include three common string search functions: hamming distance, edit distance, and set-maximal matches. These search functions hold crucial significance for applications such as ancestry search [8] and similar patients query [9,10], often involving confidential personal data. The effectiveness of these search operations is critically important, illustrated by their recent use in solving a high-profile crime case, the 'Golden State Killer' [11].

Contributions

Our study can be principally divided into two phases: (a) the development of a parallel fully homomorphic encryption (FHE) computation framework and (b) the execution of string search operations using our proposed framework. We outline our chief contributions below:

- We primarily expand Boolean gates (i.e., XOR, AND, etc.) from an existing FHE framework [12] to secure algebraic circuits comprising addition and multiplication.
- Taking full advantage of the latest enhancements in GPU architecture, we introduce parallel FHE operations. We further propose several enhancement methods, like bit coalescing, compound gates, and tree-based additions, for the execution of the secure algebraic circuits.
- We conducted a series of experiments to contrast the execution time of the sequential TFHE [12] with our proposed GPU parallel framework. Data from Table 1 demonstrate that our proposed GPU parallel method is 14.4 and 46.81 times quicker than the existing technique for standard and matrix multiplications, respectively. We also compared our performance with existing GPU-based TFHE frameworks, such as cuFHE [13], NuFHE [14], and Cingulata [15].
- Lastly, we focused on different string search operations in the genomic dataset (hamming distance, edit distance, and set-maximal matches) and executed them under encryption. Experimental outcomes reveal that the framework requires approximately 12 min to execute hamming distance and set-maximal matching on two genomic sequences with 128 genomes. In addition, for 8 genomes, the framework takes 11 min for an edit distance operation, significantly improving from the previous 5 h attempt by Cheon et al. [16].

Table 1. Comparison of the execution times (seconds) of our CPU and GPU framework for 32-bit numbers with TFHE [17], cuFHE [13], NuFHE [14], and Cingulata [15] (vector/matrix length of 32).

	Gate Op.	**Addition**		**Multiplication**	
		Regular	**Vector**	**Regular**	**Matrix (min)**
GPU-parallel	0.07	1.99	11.22	33.93	186.23
CPU-parallel	0.50	7.04	77.18	174.54	2514.34
TFHE [12]	1.40	7.04	224.31	489.93	8717.89
cuFHE [13]	-	2.03	-	132.23	-
NuFHE [14]	-	4.16	-	186	-
Cingulata [15]	-	2.16	-	50.69	-

In this work, we extend our previous work [18] on a CPU–GPU-parallel FHE framework. Notably, existing GPU-enabled TFHE libraries, cuFHE [13] and NuFHE [14], have implemented TFHE Boolean gates using GPUs, whereas our goal was to construct an optimized arithmetic circuit framework. Our design choices and algorithms reflect this improvement, and as a result, our multiplications are around 3.9 and 4.5 times faster than cuFHE and NuFHE, respectively. The code is readily available at https://github.com/UofM-DSP/CPU-GPU-TFHE (accessed on 4 January 2024).

The rest of this work is organized as follows: We discuss the required background of the work in Section 2. Section 3 discusses the underlying methods including the GPU-parallel framework and the string search operations using such parallel operations. In Section 4, we show the experimental analysis, whereas Section 5 discusses it in detail. Section 6 presents the related works, and finally, this work is concluded in Section 7.

2. Background

In this section, we describe the employed cryptographic scheme, TFHE [12], and later define the string search problem.

2.1. Torus FHE (TFHE)

In this study, we utilize torus fully homomorphic encryption (TFHE) [12], where plaintexts and ciphertexts are defined over a real torus, $\mathbb{T} = \mathbb{R}/\mathbb{Z}$, a set of real numbers called modulo 1. Ciphertexts are built through learning with errors (LWE) [19] and are expressed as torus LWE (TLWE). Here, an error term, taken from a Gaussian distribution, χ, is integrated into each ciphertext. When we consider a key size (dimension) of $m \geq 1$, a secret key present in an m-bit binary vector, and an error part of the chi distribution, an LWE sample is denoted as $(\mathbf{a}, b)$. Here, $\mathbf{a}$ signifies a vector of torus coefficients of length m (key size), with each element $\mathbf{a}_i$ derived from the uniform distribution over the real torus, and $b = \mathbf{a} \cdot \mathbf{s} + e$.

The error term (e) in the LWE sample increases and proliferates with the number of operations (for instance, addition, multiplication). Therefore, the bootstrapping technique is used to decrypt and renew the ciphertext's encryption to mitigate the noise.

TFHE views binary bits as plaintext, producing LWE samples as ciphertexts. Consequently, computations of LWE samples ($\mathbb{L}^n$) in ciphertext are equivalent to binary bit computations in plaintext. By translating binary vector representations of integer numbers into LWE sample vectors, we can represent encrypted integers. For instance, an encrypted version of an n-bit integer would be an n-LWE sample. Hence, the operations of a binary addition circuit between two n-bit numbers can parallel the equivalent operations on LWE samples of encrypted integers. In this paper, we use the terms *bit* and *LWE sample* interchangeably, and we select TFHE for the following reasons:

- Fast and Exact Bootstrapping: TFHE provides the fastest exact bootstrapping requiring around 0.1 s. Some recent encryption schemes [20,21] also propose faster bootstrapping and homomorphic computations in general. However, they do not perform exact bootstrapping and are erroneous after successive computations on the same ciphertexts.
- Ciphertext Size: Compared with the other HE schemes, TFHE offers a smaller ciphertext size as it operates on binary plaintexts (only 32 kb compared to 8mb for one 32-bit number). Nevertheless, this minimal storage advantage allows us to utilize the limited and fixed memory of GPU when we optimize the gate structures.
- Boolean Operations: TFHE also supports Boolean operations that can be extended to construct arbitrary functions. These binary bits can then be operated in parallel if their computations are independent of each other.

Current Approach: The existing application of TFHE includes foundational cryptographic functions like encryption, decryption, and all binary gate operations [12]. Notably, despite the somewhat sequential calculation of gates in the original application, the base architecture employs advanced vector extensions (AVXs) [22]. AVX, an enhancement to Intel's x86 instruction set, supports parallel vector operations. The bootstrapping process calls for substantial fast Fourier transform (FFT) operations that grow in complexity in O(n log n). The current model uses the Fastest Fourier Transform in the West (FFTW) [23], which inherently incorporates AVX.

Why TFHE? Several attempts have been made to enhance the performance and numerical operations of FHE [24–26], which are critical to our work (refer to Section 6 for details). Among the most prominent FHE schemes, torus FHE (TFHE) successfully delivers an arbitrary depth of circuits with a faster bootstrapping technique. Furthermore, it demands less storage compared with other encryption models (Table 8, available in related works for comparison). With TFHE, the plaintext message space is binary, which means that computations are entirely based on Boolean gates. Every gate operation necessitates a bootstrapping procedure in gate bootstrapping mode.

Why GPU? Most FHE schemes build upon the learning with errors (LWE) principle. In this context, plaintexts encrypted with polynomials can be portrayed using vectors. Hence, most calculations operate on vectors, making them highly parallelizable. In contrast, graphics processing units (GPUs) offer a vast number of computing cores, more so than CPUs. These cores can therefore effectively compute parallel vectors operations. Thus, these cores can be employed to parallelize FHE computations. It is crucial, however, to take into account the fixed and limited memory capacity of GPUs (8–16 GB) and their relative computing power compared with a CPU core. For in-depth comparisons, readers may refer to the Appendix A of this paper.

2.2. Sequential Framework

In this section, we present a brief overview of the sequential arithmetic circuit constructions using Boolean gates as background, which we extend later.

2.2.1. Addition

A carry-ahead 1-bit full adder circuit takes two input bits along with a carry to compute the sum and a new carry that propagates to the next bit's addition. Therefore, in a full adder, we have three inputs as a_i, b_i, and c_{i-1}, where i denotes the bit position. Here, the addition of bit a_1 and b_1 in $A, B \in \mathbb{B}^n$ requires the carry bit from a_0 and b_0. This dependency enforces the addition operation to be sequential for n-bit numbers [27]. In this work, we also used half adders for numeric increments and decrements.

2.2.2. Multiplication
Naive Approach

For two n-bit numbers, $A, B \in \mathbb{Z}$, we multiply (AND) the number A with each bit $b_i \in B$, resulting in n numbers. Then, these numbers are left shifted by i bits individually, resulting in $[n, 2n]$-bit numbers. Finally, we accumulate (reduce by addition) the n shifted numbers using addition.

Karatsuba Algorithm

We consider the divide-and-conquer Karatsuba algorithm for its improved time complexity $O(n^{\log 3})$ [28]. It relies on dividing the large input numbers and performing smaller multiplications. For n-bit inputs, the Karatsuba algorithm splits them into smaller numbers of $n/2$-bit size and replaces the multiplication with additions and subsequent multiplications (Line 12 of Algorithm 1). Later, we introduce parallel vector operations for further optimizations.

> **Algorithm 1:** Karatsuba Multiplication [28]
>
>   **Input:** $X, Y \in \mathbb{B}^n$
>   **Output:** $Z \in \mathbb{B}^{2n}$
> 2 **if** $n < n_0$ **then**
> 3 | **return** BaseMultiplication(X, Y)
> 4 **end**
> 5 $X_0 \leftarrow X \bmod 2^{n/2}$
> 6 $Y_0 \leftarrow Y \bmod 2^{n/2}$
> 7 $X_1 \leftarrow X/2^{n/2}$
> 8 $Y_1 \leftarrow Y/2^{n/2}$
> 9 $Z_0 \leftarrow$ KaratsubaMultiply(X_0, Y_0)
> 10 $Z_1 \leftarrow$ KaratsubaMultiply(X_1, Y_1)
> 11 $Z_2 \leftarrow$ KaratsubaMultiply$(X_0 + Y_0, X_1 + Y_1)$
> 12 **return** $Z_0 + (Z_2 - Z_1 - Z_0)2^n + (Z_1)2^{2n}$

2.3. CPU-Based Parallel Framework

We propose a CPU ‖ framework utilizing the multiple cores available in computers. Since the existing TFHE implementation uses AVX2, we employ that in our CPU ‖ framework.

2.3.1. Addition

Figure 1 illustrates the bitwise addition operation considered in our CPU framework. Here, any resultant bit r_i depends on its previous c_{i-1} bit. The dependency restricts incorporating any data-level parallelism in the addition circuit construction.

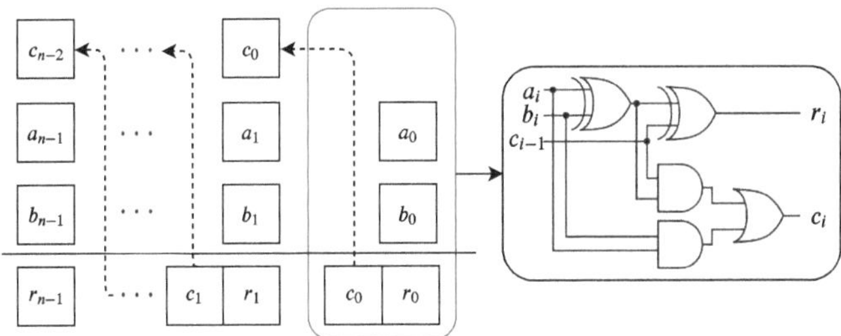

Figure 1. Bitwise addition of two n-bit numbers, A and B. a_i, b_i, c_i, and r_i are the *i*th-bit of $A, B, carry,$ and the *result*.

Here, it is possible to exploit task-level parallelism where two threads execute the XOR and AND operations (Figure 1) simultaneously. We observed that the time required to perform such fork-and-join between two threads is higher than that when executing them serially. This is partially due to the costly thread operations and eventual serial dependency of the results. Hence, we did not employ this technique for CPUs.

2.3.2. Multiplication

Among the three key operations, AND, left shift, and accumulation (addition), used in multiplications, AND and left shift can be carried out concurrently. For instance, when we have two 16-bit numbers, A and B ($\in \mathbb{B}^{16}$), and four functional threads, we distribute the AND and left shift operations among these threads.

Conversely, the accumulation operation is more demanding as it requires the execution of n additions for n-bit multiplication. This operation of accumulating values necessitates adding and storing values to the same variable, thereby rendering the operation atomic. As a result, all threads that were engaged in performing the previous AND and left shift operations must wait for the accumulation to complete. This is known as global thread synchronization [29]. However, due to its computational expensiveness, we avoid using this approach in any parallel framework.

Instead, we adopted a customized reduction operation within OpenMP [29], which exploits the globally shared memory (CPU) to store interim results. This approach predicts the addition of any results upon completion, thus avoiding the need for global thread synchronization and ultimately enhancing performance. We found that this custom reduction greatly improved performance when compared with the traditional approach of waiting for threads to complete their tasks, otherwise known as global thread synchronization.

2.4. String Search: Problem Definition

We are proposing privacy-preserving methods to measure string distances using hamming, edit distance, and set-maximal matching. We define the query string as q, whereas the target genomic sequence is denoted as y. For simplicity, we assume that all sequences have an equal number of m genes, where each gene is biallelic. Biallelic genes are represented as $\{0, 1\}$, resulting in a query to be a bit vector where $q = [q_1, q_2, \ldots, q_m]$ as $q_i \in \{0, 1\}$. On the other hand, any target sequence is defined as $y = [y_1, y_2, \ldots, y_m]$ as $y_i \in \{0, 1\}$.

In this problem, the query q and data y are encrypted with a fully homomorphic encryption (FHE) scheme [12]. Upon encryption, we denote the query as a vector of encrypted bits and is represented with $\mathbf{q}$. The encrypted data $\mathbf{y}$ is hosted in a cloud environment where a researcher is sending his/her encrypted query. Notably, the target can be a set of genomic sequences, denoted as $\mathbf{Y}$. The target is to exactly calculate or approximate a string distance score for $\mathbf{q}$ against $\mathbf{y}$ under FHE with a certain algorithm, such as hamming or edit distance. Since it is an asymmetric encryption scheme, we assume that the cloud server only has access to the public key. On the other hand, the researcher and data owner have the private key to decrypt the result and encrypt the genomic data, respectively. The targeted string distance metrics are formally defined below:

Definition 1 (*Hamming distance*). *The hamming distance* $hd(\mathbf{q}, \mathbf{y})$ *measures the difference or number of genes that are different in two sequences,* q *and* $\mathbf{y_i}$: $hd(q, \mathbf{y}) = \sum_{k \in [1,m]} (q[k] \neq \mathbf{y}[k])$.

Definition 2 (*Edit distance*). *The edit distance* $ed(\mathbf{q}, \mathbf{y})$ *between two sequences* $(\mathbf{q}, \mathbf{y})$ *is defined as the minimum cost taken over all edit sequences that transform query* $\mathbf{q}$ *into* $\mathbf{y}$. *That is,* $ed(\mathbf{x}, \mathbf{y}) = min\{C(s) | s$ *is a sequence of edit operations (insert, update, or delete) transforming* $\mathbf{q}$ *into* $\mathbf{y}\}$.

Definition 3 (*Set-maximal distance*). *A set-maximal score or distance* $sd(\mathbf{q}, \mathbf{y})$ *denotes the maximum number of consecutive matching genes between* $\mathbf{q}$ *and* $\mathbf{y}$, *which have the following conditions:*

1. *There exists some index* $k_2 > k_1$ *such that* $q[k_1, k_2] = \mathbf{y}[k_1, k_2]$ *(same substring);*
2. $q[k_1 - 1, k_2] \neq \mathbf{y_i}[k_1 - 1, j_2]$ *and* $\mathbf{q}[k_1, k_2 + 1] \neq \mathbf{y}[j_1, j_2 + 1]$; *and*
3. *For all other genes,* $k' \neq k$ *and* $k' \in [1, m]$, *if there exist* $k'_2 > k'_1$ - $\mathbf{q}[k'_1, k'_2] = \mathbf{y}[k'_1, k'_2]$ *then it must be* $k'_2 - k'_1 < k_2 - k_1$.

The set-maximal distance is defined as $sd(\mathbf{q}, \mathbf{y}) = k_2 - k_1$.

3. Methods

In this section, we outline our proposed solutions to compute the string distance metrics for the targeted algorithms. First, we propose the GPU-parallel FHE framework on top of which we build the string search operations described later.

3.1. GPU-Based Parallel Framework

In this section, we present three generalized techniques to introduce GPU parallelism (GPU ||) for any FHE computations. Then, we adopt them to implement and optimize the arithmetic operations. Notably, our CPU-parallel (CPU ||) framework is also described in Section 2.3.

3.1.1. Proposed Techniques for Parallel HE Operations

This section introduces general techniques adopted for the GPU-based parallel framework.

Parallel TFHE Construction

Figure 2 refers to the depiction of Boolean circuit computation. In this computation, every LWE sample is composed of two elements: **a** and *b*. **a** is a 32-bit integer vector determined by the secret key size (m), and its memory needs are less than those in other FHE implementations (Section 6). In this parallel TFHE construction, only the vector **a** is stored in the GPU's global memory.

Moreover, this setup uses the native CUDA-enabled FFT library (cuFFT). This library employs the parallel CUDA cores for FFT operations, with a batching technique that allows for many FFT operations to be carried out concurrently. However, the same cuFFT tool also sets a limit to the parallel number of batches. It arranges these batches in an asynchronous launch queue and processes a specific number of these batches simultaneously. This number is strictly dependent on the hardware capacity and specifications [30].

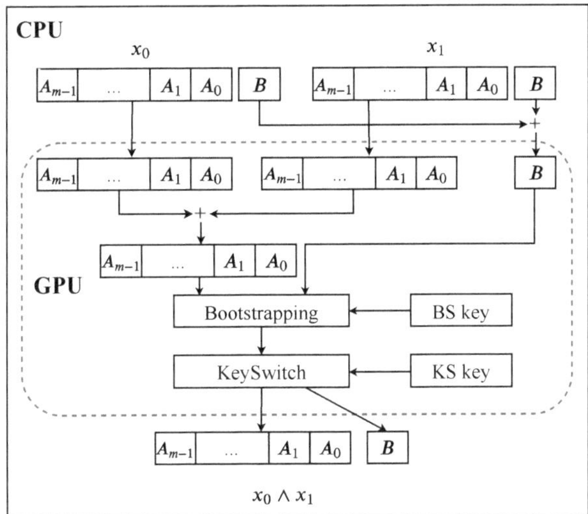

Figure 2. Arbitrary operation between two bits where BS and KS key represent bootstrapping and key switching keys, respectively.

Bit Coalescing (BC)

Bit coalescing combines n-LWE samples in a contiguous memory to represent n-encrypted bits. The encryption of an n-bit number, $X \in \mathbb{B}^n$, requires n-LWE samples (ciphertext), and each sample contains a vector of length m. Instead of treating the vectors of ciphertexts separately, we coalesce them altogether (dimension $1 \times mn$), as illustrated in Figure 3.

The main idea of such a structure is to boost parallel processes by extending the length of the vector in sequential memory. While the length of the vector is increased through vector coalescing, we incorporate additional threads to optimize parallelization and decrease execution time.

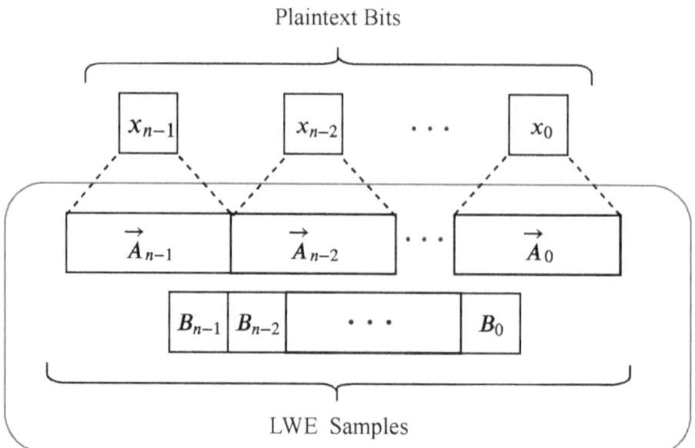

Figure 3. Coalescing n-LWE samples (ciphertexts) for n-bits where $\mathbf{A}_i$ vectors are contiguously located in GPU memory. B values for all n bits are also located togethar as the GPU memory is marked in gray.

Compound Gate

As addition is a crucial component in many arithmetic circuits, we suggest a unique gate structure known as *compound gates*. These gates provide more opportunities for parallel processes among encrypted bits. They constitute a blend of two gates and work similarly to an ordinary Boolean gate, accepting two 1-bit inputs but delivering two distinct outputs. This innovative gate structure's inspiration comes from the addition circuit. For the sum $R = A + B$, we calculate r_i and c_i using the given equations.

$$r_i = a_i \oplus b_i \oplus c_{i-1} \tag{1}$$
$$c_i = a_i \wedge b_i \mid (a_i \oplus b_i) \wedge c_{i-1} \tag{2}$$

Here, r_i, a_i, b_i, and c_i denote the ith-bit of R, A, B, and the carry, respectively. Figure 1 illustrates this computation for an n-bit addition.

While computing Equations (1) and (2), we observe that AND ($\wedge$) and XOR ($\oplus$) are computed on the same input bits. As these operations are independent, they can be combined into a single gate, which then can be computed in parallel. We name these gates as *compound gates*. Thus, $a \oplus b$ and $a \wedge b$ from Equations (1) and (2) can be computed as

$$s, c \;\; = \underbrace{a \oplus b, a \wedge b}_{CONCAT}$$

Here, the outputs of $s = a \wedge b$ and $c = a \oplus b$ are concatenated. The compound gates' construction is analogous to the task-level parallelism in CPU, where one thread performs $\wedge$, while another thread performs $\oplus$.

In GPU ||, the compound gates' operations are flexible as $\wedge$ or $\oplus$ can be replaced with any other logic gates. Furthermore, the structure is extensible up to n-bits input and $2n$-bits output.

3.1.2. Algebraic Circuits on GPU

This section presents different algebraic circuit constructions in a GPU-based parallel framework using the general techniques.

Addition: *Bitwise addition (GPU$_1$):* From the addition circuit in Section 2.3.1, we did not find any data-level parallelism. However, we noticed the presence of task-level parallelism for AND and XOR as mentioned in the compound gates' construction. Hence, we incorporated the compound gates to construct the bitwise addition circuit. We also implemented the vector addition circuits using GPU_1 to support complex circuits, such as multiplications (Section 2.2.2).

Numberwise addition (GPU$_n$): We consider another addition technique to benefit from bit coalescing. Here, we operate on all *n*-bits together. For $R = A + B$, we first store A in R ($R = A$). Then we compute $Carry = R \wedge B$, $R = R \oplus B$, and $B = Carry \ll 1$ for n times.

Here, we utilize compound gates to perform $R \wedge B$ and $R \oplus B$ in parallel. Thus, in each iteration, the input becomes two *n*-bit numbers, while in bitwise computation, the input was two single bits. On the contrary, even after using compound gates, the bitwise addition (Equations (1) and (2)) has more sequential blocks (3) than the numberwise addition (0). We analyze both in Section 4.3.

Numeric increments and decrements: We also propose half adders for numeric increments and decrements required for several operations in string search. For example, in Algorithms 3–5, we need to perform increments and decrements of an encrypted number. We use half adders and subtractors to perform the operations. In Figure 4, we show the difference of the operations. For the half adder, we perform the XOR and AND operations for all input bits for the encrypted number, while the other input is set to 1 (or 0) under encryption. The only difference for the half subtractor is that the input bit is inverted before the AND operation, which represents the carry bit.

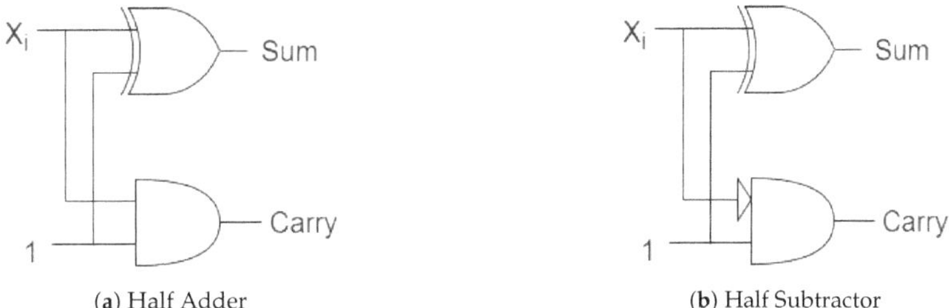

(a) Half Adder (b) Half Subtractor

Figure 4. One-bit increment and decrement using the half adder or subtractor where x_i is the input bit and the carry bit is propagated into the next bit's operation.

The sign bit for these encrypted numbers (most significant bit) also goes through the same operation as the rest of the bits. However, in this work, we cannot protect the increment against overflow as the number of bits for each encrypted number is set prior to the execution. For example, if we are incrementing a 16-bit encrypted number, and it obtains a value of $2^{15} + 1$ (1 bit reserved for the sign bit), it will not obtain a correct decrypted value. On the other hand, while decrementing by 1 for Algorithms 4 and 5, we will eventually get into negative numbers, represented by the sign bit. Therefore, we perform an OR operation in Algorithm 2 on Line 10.

Algorithm 2: Determine if input number is greater than zero

    Input: Encrypted number x with $|\mathsf{x}|$ bits, Boolean flag *hasSign* if x has sign bit
    Output: One bit representing whether x is greater than 0, *result*
2 **Procedure** greaterThanZero$(x, hasSign)$
3     $i \leftarrow 0$
4     $result \leftarrow \mathcal{E}(0)$
5   **while** $i < |\mathsf{x}| - 1$ **do**
6        $result \leftarrow result \ \bar{\text{OR}} \ \mathsf{x}[i]$
7        $i \leftarrow i + 1$
8   **end**
9   **if** *hasSign* **then**
10       $result \leftarrow result \ \bar{\text{AND}} \ (\bar{\text{NOT}} \ \mathsf{x}[|\mathsf{x}|])$
11   **end**
12   **return** *result*

Multiplication

Naive Approach: According to Section 2.2.2, multiplications have $\wedge$ and $\ll$ operations that can be executed in parallel. It will result in n-numbers where each number will have $[n, 2n]$-bits due to $\ll$. We need to accumulate these uneven-sized numbers, which cannot be distributed among the GPU threads. Furthermore, the addition presents another sequential bottleneck while adding and storing $(+ =)$ the results in the same memory location. Therefore, this serial addition will increase the execution time. In the framework, we optimize the operation by introducing a tree-based approach.

In this approach, we divide n-numbers (LWE vectors) into two $n/2$ vectors. These two $n/2$ vectors are added in parallel. We repeat the process as we divide the resultant vectors into two $n/4$ vectors and add them in parallel. The process continues until we obtain the final result. Notably, the tree-based approach requires $\log n$ steps for the accumulation. In Figure 5 for $n = 8$, all the ciphertexts underwent $\wedge$ and $\ll$ in parallel, and waited for addition. Here, L_{ij} represents the LWE samples (encrypted numbers), i is the level, and j denotes the position.

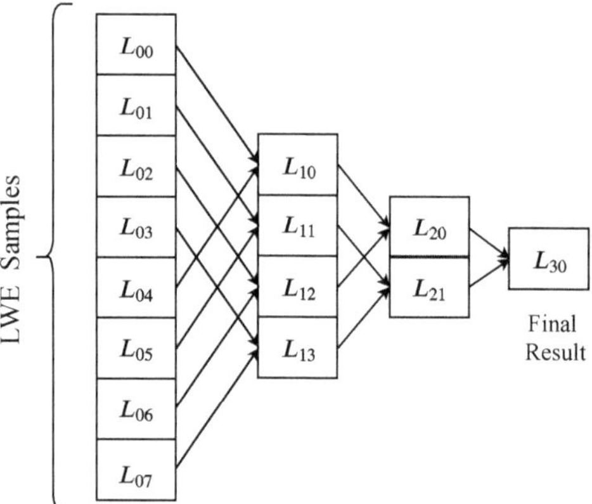

Figure 5. Accumulating $n = 8$ LWE samples (L_{ij}) in parallel using a tree-based reduction.

Karatsuba multiplication: We used the Karatsuba algorithm with some modifications in our framework to achieve further efficiency while performing multiplications. However, this algorithm requires both addition and multiplication vector operations, which tested the efficacy of these components as well. We modified the original Algorithm 1 to introduce the vector operations and rewrite the computations in Lines 9–12 as

$$\langle Temp_0, \ Temp_1 \rangle = \langle X_0, \ X_1 \rangle + \langle Y_0, \ Y_1 \rangle$$
$$\langle Z_0, \ Z_1, \ Z_2 \rangle = \langle X_0, \ X_1, \ Temp_0 \rangle \cdot \langle Y_0, \ Y_1, \ Temp_1 \rangle$$
$$\langle Temp_0, \ Temp_1 \rangle = \langle Z_2, \ Z_1 \rangle + \langle 1, \ Z_0 \rangle$$
$$Z_2 = Temp_0 + (Temp_1)'$$

In the above equations, X_0, X_1, Y_0, Y_1, Z_0, Z_1, and Z_2 are taken from the algorithm, and $\langle \ldots \rangle$ and $\cdot$ are used to denote concatenated vectors and dot product, respectively. For example, in the first equation, $Temp_0$ and $Temp_1$ store the addition of X_0, Y_0 and X_1, Y_1. It is noteworthy that in the CPU $\parallel$ framework, we utilized task-level parallelism to perform these vector operations as described in Section 2.3.

3.1.3. Bitwise Operations

In this section, the general bitwise operations required for determining the string distances are discussed. These algorithms will inherit the aforementioned algorithms and extend them accordingly based on the corresponding use cases:

Greater Than Zero

Our string distance methods on encrypted data rely on Algorithm 2 to check whether $input > 0$. Here, the algorithm takes an encrypted number as an input and checks whether it is greater than zero. This allows us to judge whether there are any set bits on the encrypted version of the number. In order to output that result, in Line 6, an encrypted bitwise OR ($\bar{O}R$) operation is performed between an encrypted bit $X[i]$ and the current *result*.

The final result also considers the sign bit as the number can be negative. Here, the sign bit is set as the most significant bit (MSB) or $X[|X|]$, which is inverted and placed on another OR operation with the *result* variable. Determining whether the input is less than 0 can also be achieved by this bit. Notably, the value of the *result* is kept encrypted throughout the computations, which is utilized in the upcoming algorithms.

Longest Consecutive Ones

Algorithm 3 is specifically designed to find the most extended series of consecutive 1 value bits in an encrypted number or bit stream. The encrypted number input, denoted as X, is left shifted in each repetition until we exhaust the bit stream, which happens after $|X|$ repetitions.

The crucial operation of this method occurs on Line 6, where X undergoes a left shift by a single unit. After this shift, an encrypted bitwise $A\bar{N}D$ operation is also performed with the preceding value of X. One check is then performed to see if the newly created X contains any 1 bit (or whether $X > 0$), and if so, a counter is incremented. This counter is linked to the *result* variable, as indicated in Algorithm 2, and increments by one each time $X > 0$.

It is crucial to underline that this algorithm is particularly applicable for set-maximal distance calculations, where encrypted haplotypes are used as the X input. This further notes that `greaterThanZero` accounts for the sign bit, which is not essential in set-maximal operations. As such, Line 10 is not considered in this specific context.

Algorithm 3: Find longest consecutive ones

   Input: Encrypted number x
   Output: *result* representing the number of the longest consecutive ones
2 **Procedure** `maxConsecutiveOnes`(X)
3     $numbits \leftarrow |\mathbf{x}|$
4     $result \leftarrow$ `greaterThanZero`$(\mathbf{x}, false)$
5   **while** $numbits > 0$ **do**
6        $\mathbf{x} \leftarrow \mathbf{x}\, A\bar{N}D\, (\mathbf{x} \ll 1)$
7        $result \leftarrow result +$ `greaterThanZero`$(\mathbf{x}, false)$
8        $numbits \leftarrow numbits - 1$
9   **end**
10   **return** *result*

Let us assume that we have an encrypted number $\mathbf{x} = \mathcal{E}(011101)$ with the sign bit $\mathcal{E}(0)$, and it contains 3 consecutive ones. Here, the result bit is set to 1 since $\mathbf{x} > 0$. In the first iteration, we perform an encrypted AND operation of $\mathbf{x}$ (011101) and $\mathbf{x} << 1$ (111010). Since the resulting $\mathbf{x}$ is greater than 0, the encrypted *result* number is incremented. In the following iteration, $\mathbf{x} = \mathcal{E}(011000)$ is multiplied (AND) with $\mathcal{E}(110000)$, which results in 010000. The result number is incremented again. However, in the subsequent iterations ($|\mathbf{x}|$ many times), the $\mathbf{x}$ values are set to 0 and result is not incremented anymore. Finally, the result from Algorithm 3 is retrieved as $\mathcal{E}(3)$.

Finding Minimum and Maximum Number

The pair of Algorithms 4 and 5 employs a method to target and identify the smallest and biggest numbers among a set of n numbers, respectively. Each encrypted number in the set, denoted as $\mathbf{x}_1, \mathbf{x}_2, \ldots, \mathbf{x}_n$, undergoes a decrement operation for every bit ($|\mathbf{x}_i|$ bit size).

The algorithms then scan to determine whether the processed number arrived at zero or if it still holds any set bit. In the process to locate the smallest number, the algorithm increments the encrypted result variable only if all numbers are beyond zero. On the contrary, to find the maximum number, the algorithm utilizes an encrypted $\bar{O}R$ operation to verify if even a single number is greater than zero.

Algorithm 4: Get minimum number among $x_1, x_2, \ldots, x_n$ encrypted positive numbers ($x_i \geq 0$)

   Input: Positive Numbers $x_1, x_2, \ldots, x_n$
   Output: Minimum encrypted number *result*
2 **Procedure** getMin$(x_1, x_2, \ldots, x_n)$
3   *numinter* $\leftarrow 2^{|x_0|}$
4   *result* $\leftarrow 0$
5   **while** *numinter* > 0 **do**
6   *gtZero* $\leftarrow \mathcal{E}(1)$
7   **foreach** $x_i \in \{x_1, \ldots, x_n\}$ **do**
8   *gtZero* $\leftarrow$ *gtZero* $\bar{\text{AND}}$ greaterThanZero(x_i)
9         $x_i \leftarrow x_i - 1$
10   **end**
11   *result* $\leftarrow$ *result* $+$ *gtZero*
12   *numinter* $\leftarrow$ *numinter* $- 1$
13   **end**
14   **return** *result*

Algorithm 5: Get maximum number among $x_1, x_2, \ldots, x_n$ encrypted positive numbers $x_i \geq 0$

   Input: Positive numbers $x_1, x_2, \ldots, x_n$
   Output: Maximum encrypted number *result*
2 **Procedure** getMax$(x_1, x_2, \ldots, x_n)$
3   *numiter* $\leftarrow 2^{|x_i|}$
4   *result* $\leftarrow \mathcal{E}(0)$
5   **while** *numiter* > 0 **do**
6   *gtZero* $\leftarrow \mathcal{E}(0)$
7   **foreach** $x_i \in \{x_1, \ldots, x_n\}$ **do**
8   *gtZero* $\leftarrow$ *gtZero* $\bar{\text{OR}}$ greaterThanZero(x_i)
9         $x_i \leftarrow x_i - 1$
10   **end**
11   *result* $\leftarrow$ *result* $+$ *gtZero*
12   *numiter* $\leftarrow$ *numiter* $- 1$
13   **end**
14   **return** *result*

In both of these algorithms, a numerical decrement process is included, represented as $x_i \leftarrow x_i - 1$. A binary half subtractor is employed for this task. However, these decrement operations may induce an underflow, considering that the input numbers xi could turn negative in any given iteration. To deal with this, we use an operation in Algorithm 2 having MSB as greaterThanZero(x_i), which emits a single bit, indicating $x_i > 0$. For identifying the smallest or largest among n numbers, this single bit (denoted as *gtZero*) is added to the result for all *numbits* instances by Algorithms 4 and 5. The final result is under encryption and utilized in edit distance approximation (Section 3.2.2) and set-maximal matches (Section 3.2.3).

Alternative Approach

As an alternative strategy, full adders can also be utilized to derive the smallest or largest numbers. For instance, deducing the maximum between x and y can be attained by calculating $x - y$. If the sign bit is unset, it implies that x is larger. Similarly, the smallest between two numbers can also be discerned by evaluating the sign bit. This method is weighed up due to the potential exponential number of iterations, considering the total bit count in Line 3 within Algorithms 5 and 4. Considering that $|x| > 16$ would necessitate numerous rounds of computations that are under encryption, for the case of $|x| \leq 16$, we resort to the previously discussed algorithms.

3.2. Secure String Search Operations

In this section, we discuss the string search operations over encrypted data utilizing the earlier algorithms.

3.2.1. Hamming Distance

Hamming distance $hd(\mathbf{q}, \mathbf{y})$ represents the bitwise difference of the input query $\mathbf{q}$ and stored sequence $\mathbf{y}$. Therefore, we perform an encrypted $X\bar{O}R$ operation between $\mathbf{q}$ and $\mathbf{y}$ where the result will have set bits (value of 1) on all occasions of mismatches. Now, we need to perform a summation of all these bits on the XOR result to obtain the hamming distance (Definition 1). Notably, we assume that the query $\mathbf{q}$ and the encrypted sequences are of the same length.

In Algorithm 6, we outline the mechanism to generate the hamming distance hd, where it contains an encrypted distance value for one target sequence $\mathbf{y}$ and query $\mathbf{q}$. This can be iterated through all sequences and performs the XOR operation between the query $\mathbf{q}$ and $\mathbf{y}_i$ sequence. Subsequently, it also adds the bits to formulate the hamming distance in Line 5. Since the *result* variable is under encryption, the addition (or increment) is oblivious as we perform the operation for every encrypted bit in *result*.

Algorithm 6: Hamming distances between a query and encrypted sequences

---

   Input: Encrypted target sequence $\mathbf{y}$ and query $\mathbf{q}$
   Output: Encrypted distances between $\mathbf{y}$ and $\mathbf{q}$, **hd**
2 **Procedure** HammingDistance($\mathbf{q}, \mathbf{y}$)
3   *result* $\leftarrow$ $\mathbf{q} \, X\bar{O}R \, \mathbf{y}$
4   **foreach** *bit* $r \in result$ **do**
5 | **hd** $\leftarrow$ **hd** $+ r$
6   **end**
7   **return hd**

3.2.2. Edit Distance Approximation

Edit distance is more complicated than hamming distance as it considers more than the bitwise difference (insertion, deletion, and subtraction). Furthermore, under plaintext, it has a $O\,(m^2)$ complexity, where m is the length of the sequence. Therefore, to reduce the complexity, we opt for the banded edit distance [10,31], where we only compute on a band of fixed size.

Algorithm 7 outlines the proposed method, where we set a fixed parameter b along with the encrypted input sequences $\mathbf{q}$ and $\mathbf{y}_i$. Apart from the initialization, we also calculate the variables *low* and *high* dictating the number of expensive operations in Line 11. Here, we calculate whether the $\mathbf{q}[i]$ and $\mathbf{y}_i[k]$ bits are the same or not using an encrypted XNOR gate. If they are not the same, then the encrypted number $d[i-1, k-1]$ needs to be incremented, which is performed with the half adder. Since we do not know the output of *same_bit*, we push that bit as carry and initialize the substitution variable. Similarly, the insertion and deletion values are set from the existing distance matrix. Finally, we calculate the minimum getMin(ins, del, sub) to predict the distance at that specific position. This is set as the new value of $d[i, k]$. Here, the three half-adder operations are run in parallel before the minimum operation.

Algorithm 7: Banded edit distance on encrypted sequence

Data: query $\mathbf{q}$, sequence $\mathbf{y}$, and band length b
Result: b-banded Edit Distance $d(\mathbf{q}, \mathbf{y})$ [31]

1   $m \leftarrow |\mathbf{q}| + 1$
2   set each element of matrix $d_{m \times m}$ to $\mathcal{E}(0)$
3   **for** $i \leftarrow 1$ **to** m **do**
4      $d[i, 0] \leftarrow \mathcal{E}(i)$;
5      $d[0, i] \leftarrow \mathcal{E}(i)$;
6   **end**
7   **for** $i \leftarrow 1$ **to** m **do**
8   **if** $i - b < 1$ **then** $low \leftarrow 1$;
9   **else** $low \leftarrow i - b$;
10   **if** $i + b > m$ **then** $high \leftarrow m$;
11   **else** $high \leftarrow i + b$;
12   **for** $k \leftarrow low$ **to** $high$ **do**
13        $same\_bit \leftarrow \mathbf{q}[i - 1]$ XNOR $\mathbf{y}[k - 1]$
14        $sub \leftarrow d[i - 1, k - 1] + same\_bit$
15        $ins \leftarrow d[i, k - 1] + 1$
16        $del \leftarrow d[i - 1, k] + 1$
17        $d[i, k] \leftarrow \texttt{getMin}(sub, ins, del)$
18   **end**
19   **end**
20   **return** $d[m, m]$;

3.2.3. Set-Maximal Distance

The set-maximal distance or match (SMM) represents the length of the longest matching substring in two sequences [32]. This allows a health-care researcher to identify genomic sequences that have more genes in common and probably are identical in their physical attributes. The distance also has applications over similar patient queries [9], secure positional Burrows–Wheeler transformation [33,34], etc.

The proposed secure set-maximal match using homomorphic encryption operation depends on Algorithm 3, $\texttt{maxConsecutiveOnes}$. Initially, we perform an encrypted XNOR between two sequences, $\mathbf{y}_i$ and query $\mathbf{q}$. Here, the XNOR operation (NOT XOR) sets a value of 1 to the positions where the sequences are matching. Now, from this XNOR result, we can perform the $\texttt{maxConsecutiveOnes}$ algorithm and obtain the highest number of set bits that are grouped together.

Suppose for a query $\mathbf{q} = 01100111$ and some input sequence $\mathbf{y}_i = 10000110$, where $\mathbf{y}_i \in \mathbf{Y}$, then $\mathbf{q}$ XNOR $\mathbf{y}_i$ will be 00011110. Now, if we perform $\texttt{maxConsecutiveOnes}(\mathbf{q}$ XNOR $\mathbf{y}_i, false)$, then the output should provide us with the encrypted result of 3. This result denotes the number of set bits on the encrypted XNOR operation, hence the set-maximal distance between $\mathbf{q}$ and $\mathbf{y}_i$.

Threshold SMM

In a threshold version of this match, we need to output only the distances beyond an input threshold t. Here, an extra operation proceeding the $\texttt{maxConsecutiveOnes}$ is required, where a simple numeric comparison with threshold t would output the result. Therefore, we can use an encrypted MUX operation [5] for this comparison. However, encrypted MUX is an expensive operation, and we can replace it with a subtraction. Therefore, we negate the $\mathcal{E}(t)$ value from the resulting $\texttt{maxConsecutiveOnes}(\mathbf{q}$ XNOR $\mathbf{y}_i, false)$. Then, we use the `greaterThanZero` algorithm on the result, which represents if the SMM distance is beyond the threshold t.

We outline the algorithm in Algorithm 8, where the threshold value is encrypted at first. The matching bits of the query and the sequence are calculated next with the XNOR operation. Subsequently, we perform the comparison operation with a maximum between *result* and $\mathcal{E}(t)$. If $\mathcal{E}(t) \geq result$, then *gt_threshold* is set as the *OR* of all bits among the **smm_distance** XNOR **enc_t** bits. Here, XNOR represents whether two vectors are the same or not and performing another logical OR among them. Lastly, we perform the AND operation with the distance. If the value of *gt_threshold* is 0, then we obtain all unset bits on the output, with set-maximal distance in the other case.

Algorithm 8: Thresholded set-maximal matching

Input: Encrypted query $\mathbf{q}$, encrypted sequence $\mathbf{y}_i \in \{\mathbf{y}_1, \ldots, \mathbf{y}_n\}$ and threshold t
Output: Encrypted SMM distance between $\mathbf{q}$ and $\mathbf{y}_i$ if it is greater than some
        value t

2   **Procedure** `SMMDistance(`$\mathbf{q}, \mathbf{y}_i, t$`)`
3   **enc_t** $\leftarrow \mathcal{E}(t)$
4   **result** $\leftarrow$ `maxConsecutiveOnes(`$\mathbf{q}$ XNOR $\mathbf{y}_i, false$`)`
5   **smm_distance** $\leftarrow$ getMax(**result**, **enc_t**)
6   *gt_threshold* $\leftarrow$ AND all bits in(**smm_distance** XNOR **enc_t**)
7   **smm_distance** $\leftarrow$!*gt_threshold* AND **smm_distance**
8   **return smm_distance**

---

4. Experimental Analysis

The experimental environment included an Intel(R) Core™ i7-2600 CPU having 16 GB system memory with an NVIDIA GeForce GTX 1080 GPU (check GPU details in Appendix A) with 8 GB memory [30]. The CPU and GPU contained 8 and 40,960 hardware threads, respectively. We used the same setup to analyze all three frameworks: sequential, CPU ||, and GPU ||.

We use two metrics for the comparison: (a) execution time and (b) speedup $= \frac{T_{seq}}{T_{par}}$. Here, T_{seq} and T_{par} are the time for computing the sequential and the parallel algorithm. In the following sections, we gradually analyze the complicated arithmetic circuits using the best results from the foregoing analysis.

4.1. GPU-Accelerated TFHE

Initially, we discuss our performance over Boolean gate operations, deemed as building blocks of any computation. Figure 6a depicts the execution time difference among the sequential, CPU ||, and GPU || frameworks for $[4, 32]$ bits. The sequential AND operation takes a minimum of 0.22 s (4 bits), while the runtime increases to 1.4 s for 32 bits.

In the GPU-parallel framework, bit coalescing facilitates the storing of LWE samples in contiguous memory and takes advantage of available vector operations. Thus, it helps to reduce the execution time from 0.22–1.4 s to 0.02–0.06 s for 4 to 32 bits. Here, for 32 bits, our techniques provide a 20× speedup. A similar improvement is foreseen in the CPU-parallel framework as we divide the number of bits by the available threads. However, the execution time increases for the CPU framework since there are only a limited number of available threads. This limited number of threads is one of the primary motivations behind the utilization of GPU.

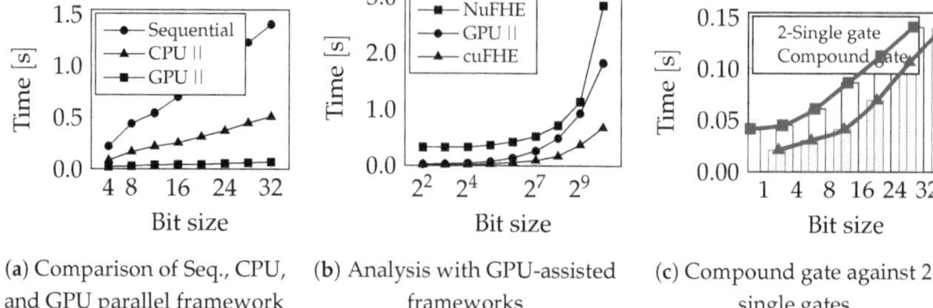

(**a**) Comparison of Seq., CPU, and GPU parallel framework

(**b**) Analysis with GPU-assisted frameworks

(**c**) Compound gate against 2 single gates

Figure 6. Performance analysis of GPU-accelerated TFHE with the sequential and CPU ∥ frameworks (**a**) and comparison with the existing GPU-assisted libraries (**b**). (**c**) presents the performance of compound gates against 2 single-gate operations, while x-axis and y-axis represent bit size and time in seconds.

Then, we further scrutinize the execution time by dividing gate operations into three major components—(a) bootstrapping, (b) key switching, and (c) miscellaneous. We select the first two as they are the most time-consuming operations and fairly generalizable to other HE schemes. Table 2 shows the difference in execution time between the sequential and the GPU parallel for $\{2, \ldots, 32\}$ bits. We show that the execution time increment is less compared with the sequential approach.

Table 2. Computation time (ms) for bootstrapping, key switching, and misc. for sequential and GPU frameworks.

Bit Size	Sequential				GPU			
n	Bootstrapping	Key Switch	Misc.	Total	Bootstrapping	Key Switch	Misc.	Total
2	68.89	17.13	27.04	113.05	19.64	2.65	0.45	22.74
4	138.02	34.18	47.97	220.17	18.86	2.69	0.08	21.63
8	275.67	68.31	96.48	440.46	27.83	2.69	0.06	30.58
16	137.25	137.25	425.22	699.72	40.70	2.91	0.44	44.06
32	274.3	274.30	852.51	1401.10	66.74	3.34	0.42	70.50

We further investigate the bootstrapping performance in the GPU-parallel framework for the Boolean gate operations. Our CUDA-enabled FFT library takes the LWE samples in batches and performs the FFT in parallel. However, due to the h/w limitations, the number of batches to be executed in parallel is limited. It can only operate on a certain number of batches at once, and next batches are kept in a queue. Hence, a sequential overhead occurs for a large number of batches that can increase the execution time.

Under the same h/w setting, we benchmark our proposed framework with the existing GPU-based libraries (cuFHE and NuFHE). Although our GPU-parallel framework outperforms NuFHE for different bit sizes (Figure 6b), the performance degrades for larger bit sizes w.r.t. cuFHE. As the cuFHE implementation focuses more on the gate level optimization, we focus on the arithmetic circuit computations. In Section 4.3, we analyze our arithmetic circuits where our framework outperforms the existing GPU libraries.

4.2. Compound Gate Analysis

According to Section 3.1.1, the compound gates are used to improve the execution time for additions or multiplications. Since the existing frameworks do not provide these optimizations, we benchmark the compound gates with the proposed single-gate computations. Figure 6c illustrates the performance of 1 compound gate over 2 single gates computed sequentially. We performed several iterations for a different number of bits

$(1, \ldots, 32)$, as shown on the x-axis while the y-axis represents the execution time. Notably, 32-bit compound gates will have two 32-bit inputs and output two 32 bits.

Here, bit coalescing improves the execution time as it takes only 0.02 s for one compound gate evaluation, compared with 0.04 s on performing 2 single gates sequentially. However, Figure 6c shows an interesting trend in the execution time between 2 single gates and 1 compound gate evaluation. The gap favoring the compound ones tends to get narrower for a higher number of bits. For example, the speedup for 1 bit happens to be $0.04/0.02 = 2$ times, whereas it reduces to 1.01 for 32 bits. The reason behind this diminishing performance is the *asynchronous launch queue* of GPUs.

As mentioned in Section 3.1.1, we use batch execution for the FFT operations. Hence, the number of parallel batches depends on the asynchronous launch queue size of the underlying GPU, which can delay the FFT operations for a large number batches. This ultimately adversely affects the speedup for large LWE sample vectors. Nevertheless, the analysis shows that the 1-bit compound gates are the most efficient, and we employ them in the following arithmetic operations.

4.3. Addition

Table 3 presents a comparative analysis of the addition operation for 16-, 24-, and 32-bit encrypted numbers. We consider our proposed frameworks: sequential, CPU ||, and GPU ||, and benchmark them with cuFHE [13], NuFHE [14], and Cingulata [15]. Furthermore, we present the performance of two variants of addition operation: $\text{GPU}_n||$ (numberwise) and $\text{GPU}_1||$ (bitwise), as discussed in Section 3.1.2.

Table 3. Execution time (s) for the n-bit addition.

Frameworks	16-Bit	24-Bit	32-Bit
Sequential	3.51	5.23	7.04
cuFHE [13]	1.00	1.51	2.03
NuFHE [14]	2.92	3.56	4.16
Cingulata [15]	1.10	1.63	2.16
Our Methods			
CPU ||	3.51	5.23	7.04
$\text{GPU}_n||$	0.94	2.55	4.44
$\text{GPU}_1||$	0.98	1.47	1.99

Table 3 demonstrates that $\text{GPU}_n||$ performs better than the sequential and CPU || circuits. GPU_n provides a $3.72\times$ speedup for 16 bits, whereas $1.58\times$ for 32 bits. However, $\text{GPU}_n||$ performs better only for 16-bit additions compared with $\text{GPU}_1||$. For 24- and 32-bit additions, $\text{GPU}_1||$ performs around $2\times$ better than $\text{GPU}_n||$. This improvement in essential as it reveals the algorithm to choose between $\text{GPU}_1||$ and $\text{GPU}_n||$.

Although both addition operations ($\text{GPU}_n||$ and $\text{GPU}_1||$) utilize compound gates, they differ in the number of input bits (n and 1 for $\text{GPU}_n||$ and $\text{GPU}_1||$, respectively). Since the compound gates perform better for smaller bits (Section 4.2), the bitwise addition performs better than the numberwise addition for 24/32-bit operations. Hence, we utilize bitwise addition for building other circuits.

NuFHE and cuFHE do not provide any arithmetic circuits in their library. Therefore, we implemented such circuits on their library and performed the same experiments. Additionally, we considered Cingulata [15] (a compiler toolchain for TFHE) and compared the execution time. Table 3 summarizes all the results, where we found that our proposed addition circuit ($\text{GPU}_1||$) outperforms the other approaches.

We further experimented on the vector additions adopting the bitwise addition and showed the analysis in Table 4. Like addition, the performance improvement on the vector addition is also noticeable. The framework scales by taking a similar execution time for smaller vector lengths $\ell \leq 8$. However, the execution time increases for longer vectors as they involve more parallel bit computations and, consequently, increase the batch size of FFT operations. The difference is clearer on 32-bit vector additions with $\ell = 32$ which takes almost twice the time of $\ell = 16$. However, for $\ell \leq 8$, the execution times are almost similar due to the parallel computations. In Section 4.2, we have discussed this issue, which relies on the FFT batch size. Notably, Figure 6c also aligns with this evidence as the larger batch size for FFT on GPUs affects the speedup. For example, $\ell = 32$ will require more FFT batches compared with $\ell = 16$, which requires more time to finish the addition operation. We did not include other frameworks in Table 4 since our GPU ‖ performed better compared with the others in Table 3.

Table 4. Execution time (s) for vector addition.

Length		16-Bit			32-Bit	
ℓ	**Seq.**	**CPU ‖**	**GPU ‖**	**Seq.**	**CPU ‖**	**GPU ‖**
4	13.98	5.07	1.27	28.05	10.02	2.56
8	27.86	9.96	1.78	56.01	19.29	3.58
16	55.66	19.65	2.82	111.3	38.77	5.70
32	111.32	38.99	5.41	224.31	77.18	11.22

4.4. Multiplication

The multiplication operation uses a sequential accumulation (reduce by addition) operation. Instead, we use a tree-based vector addition approach (discussed in Section 4.4) and gain a significant speedup. Table 5 portrays the execution times for the multiplication operations using the frameworks. Here, we employed all available threads on the machine. Like the addition circuit performance, here, GPU ‖ outperforms the sequential circuits and CPU ‖ operations by a factor of ≈ 11 and ≈ 14.5, respectively, for 32-bit multiplication.

Table 5. Multiplication execution time (s) comparison.

Frameworks	16-Bit	24-Bit	32-Bit
		Naive	
Sequential	120.64	273.82	489.94
CPU ‖	52.77	101.22	174.54
GPU ‖	11.16	22.08	33.99
cuFHE [13]	32.75	74.21	132.23
NuFHE [14]	47.72	105.48	186.00
Cingulata [15]	11.50	27.04	50.69
		Karatsuba	
CPU ‖	54.76	-	177.04
GPU ‖	7.6708	-	24.62

We further implemented the multiplication circuit on cuFHE and NuFHE. Table 5 summarizes the results comparing our proposed framework with cuFHE, NuFHE, and Cingulata. Our GPU ‖ framework is faster in execution time than the other techniques.

Notably, the performance improvement is scalable with the increasing number of bits. This is due to tree-based additions following the reduction operations and computing all Boolean gate operations by coalescing the bits altogether.

Additionally, we analyze vector multiplications available in our framework and present a comparison among the frameworks in Table 6. We found out an increase in execution time for a certain length (e.g., $\ell = 32$ on 16-bit or $\ell = 4$ on 32-bit), which is similar to the issue in vector addition (Section 4.3). Hence, the vector operations from $\ell \leq 16$ can be sequentially added to compute arbitrary vector operations. For example, we can use two $\ell = 16$ vector multiplications to compute $\ell = 32$ multiplication, resulting in around 11 min. In the vector analysis, we did not add the computations over the other frameworks since our framework surpassed their achievements for single multiplications.

Table 6. Execution time (in minutes) for vector multiplication.

Length	16-Bit			32-Bit		
ℓ	Seq.	CPU $\parallel$	GPU $\parallel$	Seq.	CPU $\parallel$	GPU $\parallel$
4	8.13	3.25	0.41	32.56	12.15	1.61
8	16.29	6.17	0.75	65.12	23.48	2.96
16	32.62	11.93	1.40	130.31	46.39	5.62
32	65.15	23.58	2.68	260.52	92.44	10.79

4.5. Karatsuba Multiplication

In Table 5, we provide execution time for 16- and 24-bit Karatsuba multiplications over encrypted numbers as well. In the CPU $\parallel$ construction of the algorithm, the execution time does not improve; rather, it increases slightly. We observed that for both 16- and 32-bit multiplications, Karatsuba outperforms the naive GPU$\parallel$ multiplication algorithm on GPU by 1.50 times. Karatsuba multiplication can also be considered a complex arithmetic operation as it comprises addition, multiplication, and vector operations. However, the CPU $\parallel$ framework did not provide such difference in performance as it took more time for the `fork-and-join` threads required by the divide-and-conquer algorithm.

4.6. String Search Operations

In Table 7, we report the execution time for the three string search operations. Here, we report the execution time in seconds, where we change the size of the genomic data. The values of $m = \{8, 16, \ldots, 256\}$ denote the number of genes for the query q and target y.

Table 7. Execution time (in seconds) for variable size query and target sequence m for different distance metrics.

Method	m					
	8	16	32	64	128	256
Hamming distance	2.89	11.84	47.95	189.81	758.73	3035.0
Set-maximal	3.76	13.3	51.24	195.72	771.08	3061.48
Set-maximal (with t)	7.15	20.67	64.43	223.14	827.76	3173.34
Edit distance	662	2577	9989	39,022	154,194	612,435

The results show that hamming distance requires the least amount of time. It is also clear from Definition 1 as it requires an XOR operation. The set-maximal matches (Definition 3) need more operations as `maxConsecutiveOnes` in Algorithm 3 employs the half adder for all bits. Furthermore, the threshold version of SMM takes more time since we need to perform the getMax operation. For example, for a target and query sequence size of $m = 128$, it takes around 14 and 13 min with and without an existing threshold. However, for a smaller size of m, we can see that the time difference is more significant as it takes 3.76 s to perform SMM, compared with 7.15 s.

Edit Distance (2) takes the highest amount of time for the same genome size m. For example, for a sequence of size $m = 32$, edit distance under FHE takes around 2 h, whereas hamming or set-maximal matches take less than a minute. Notably, in these methods, we use Algorithms 5 and 4 for $m < 32$, whereas we use the alternative (subtraction) method for larger sequences.

5. Discussion

In this section, we provide answers to the following questions about our proposed framework:

Is the proposed framework sufficient to implement any computations? This paper discusses in detail the proper implementation of Boolean gates using GPUs to enhance performance. It further explains the process of conducting basic arithmetic computations like addition, multiplication, and matrix operations using the suggested model. However, the implementation of more sophisticated algorithms like secure machine learning, as referenced in sources [35,36], is not within the scope of this paper. Future research will dive into the potential to optimize this model further for machine learning algorithms.

For the GPU ∥ framework, how do we compute on encrypted data larger than the fixed GPU memory?

Limitations like fixed GPU memory sizes and varying access speeds are common to all GPU ∥ applications. These issues also arise in deep learning when managing larger datasets. The resolution lies in segmenting the data or utilizing multiple GPUs. The model we are proposing can also apply these solutions as it is flexible enough to manage larger ciphertexts.

How can we achieve further speedup on both frameworks? In the case of the CPU ∥ model, we have tried to implement as many hardware and software level optimizations as we were able to. Nonetheless, our GPU ∥ model partially relies on the slower global GPU memory. The memory speed is crucial as different device memories have various read/write speeds. L1, or shared memory, is the fastest after the register. We used a combination of shared and global memory due to the size of the ciphertext. Going forward, we plan to use only shared memory, which is smaller but is expected to enhance the speed compared with the present method.

How would the bit security level affect the reported speedup? Currently, our model is comparable to the TFHE implementation [37], offering a security level of 110 bits, which may not be enough for certain applications. That being said, our GPU ∥ model is adaptable to any desired bit security level. However, any changes will also alter the execution times. For instance, security levels lower than 110 bits will result in faster execution and vice versa for higher bit security. Future research will incorporate and evaluate the speedup for evolving bit security levels.

Impact on computational accuracy while computing in GPUs. In the earlier GPU architecture, GPUs offered lower precision than the IEEE-754 (Available online: https://ieeexplore.ieee.org/document/8766229, accessed on 8 January 2024) floating point standard. However, the GPUs we used for testing did not have such issues as they offered double precision. Nevertheless, it is important to understand that, during FHE encryption and operations, we tend to lose precision as encrypted bits get noisier with each gate operation. Therefore, any result from FHE computation does not offer the IEEE floating point standard, to the best of our knowledge. Consequently, our framework also suffers from the same lower precision inherited by FHE limitations.

6. Related Works

6.1. Parallel Frameworks for FHE

In this section, we discuss the other HE schemes from Table 8 and categorize schemes based on their number representation:

1. Bitwise;
2. modular; and
3. approximate.

Table 8. A comparative analysis of existing homomorphic encryption schemes for different parameters on a 32-bit number.

	Year	Homomorphism	Bootstrapping	Parallelism	Bit security	Size (kb)	Add. (ms)	Mult. (ms)
RSA [38]	1978	Partial	×	×	128	0.9	×	5
Paillier [39]	1999	Partial	×	×	128	0.3	4	×
TFHE [12]	2016	Fully	Exact	AVX [22]	110	31.5	7044	489,938
HEEAN [20]	2018	Somewhat	Approximate	CPU	157	7168	11.37	1215
SEAL (BFV) [40]	2019	Somewhat	×	×	157	8806	4237	23,954
cuFHE [13]	2018	Fully	Exact	GPU	110	31.5	2032	132,231
NuFHE [14]	2018	Fully	Exact	GPU	110	31.5	4162	186,011
Cigulata [15]	2018	Fully	Exact	×	110	31.5	2160	50,690
Our Method	-	Fully	Exact	GPU	110	31.5	1991	33,930

Bitwise encryption works by encrypting the bit representation of a number. Its computation is also performed bit by bit, with each bit being handled independently of others. This characteristic is particularly beneficial for our parallel framework as the bit independence allows for parallel operation and reduces dependencies. The advantages of this process include increased speed in bootstrapping and a reduction in ciphertext size, suitable attributes considering the constraints of fixed-memory GPUs. This concept was first formalized and dubbed as GSW in 2013 [41], and has since been advanced over time [12,17,25].

Modular encryption techniques employ a fixed modulus, represented as q, that defines the size of the ciphertexts. This approach has witnessed vast improvements [42,43], particularly due to its reasonable execution time (Table 8). The quick addition and multiplication times from FV [26] and SEAL [40] demonstrate their superior speed compared with our GPU-based framework.

However, these schemes present a compromise between bootstrapping and efficiency. Often categorized as somewhat homomorphic encryption, they predefine the number of computations or the magnitude of multiplications, lacking a process for noise reduction. The resultant larger ciphertexts are consequent of large q values.

For example, we selected the ciphertext moduli of 250 and 881 bits for FV-NFLlib [26] and SEAL [40], respectively. The polynomial degrees (d) were chosen as 13 and 15 for the two frameworks as it was required to comply with the targeted bit security to populate Table 8. It is noteworthy that smaller q and d will result in a faster runtime and smaller ciphertexts, but they will limit the number of computations as well. Therefore, this modular representation requires fixing the number of homomorphic operations limiting the use cases.

Approximate number representations were recently proposed by Cheon et al. (CKKS [44]) in 2017. These schemes also provide efficient single instruction multiple data (SIMD) [45] operations similar to the modular representations as mentioned above. However, they have an inexact but efficient bootstrapping mechanism, which can be applied in less precision-demanding applications. The cryptosystem also incurs larger ciphertexts (7MB) similar to the modular approach as we tested it for $q = 1050$ and $d = 15$. Here, we did not discuss HELib [46], the first cornerstone of all HE implementations, since its cryptosystem BGV [43] is enhanced and utilized by the other modular HE schemes (such as SEAL [40]).

Our goal is to parallelize a fully homomorphic encryption (FHE) scheme. Most homomorphic encryption (HE) schemes following modular encryption are either somewhat or adopt approximate bootstrapping while requiring more memory post encryption. As a result, we opt for a bitwise bootstrappable encryption scheme: TFHE.

In terms of **hardware solutions**, few have been studied and utilized to enhance the efficiency of FHE computations. Following the formulation of FHE with ideal lattices, most efficiency enhancements have been approached from the standpoint of asymptotic runtimes. A select few approaches have dealt with the inclusion of existing multiprocessors like GPU or FPGAs [47] to achieve quicker homomorphic operations. Dai and Sunar ported another scheme, LTV [48], to GPU-based implementation [49,50]. LTV is a variant of HE that performs a limited number of operations on a given ciphertext.

Lei et al. ported FHEW-V2 [25] to GPU [51] and extended the Boolean implementation to 30-bit addition and 6-bit multiplication with a speed up to ≈2.5. Since TFHE extends FHEW and performs better than its predecessor, we consider TFHE as our baseline framework.

In 2015, a GPU-based HE scheme, CuHE [49], was proposed. However, it was not fully homomorphic as it did not have bootstrapping; hence, we did not include it in our analyses. Later in 2018, two GPU FHE libraries, cuFHE [13] and NuFHE [14], were released. Both libraries focused on optimizing the Boolean gate operations. Recently, Yang et al. [52] benchmarked cuFHE and its predecessor, TFHE, and analyzed the speedup, which we also discuss in this article (Table 8).

Our experimental analysis shows that only performing the Boolean gates in parallel is not sufficient to reduce the execution time of a higher-level circuit (i.e., multiplication). Hence, besides employing GPU for homomorphic gate operations, we focus on an arithmetic circuit. For example, we are 3.9 times faster than cuFHE in 32-bit multiplications.

Recently, Zhou et al. improved TFHE by reducing and performing the serial operations of bootstrapping in parallel [53]. However, they did use any hardware acceleration to the existing FHE operations. We consider this work as an essential future direction that can be integrated to our framework for better executing times.

Cingulata or Armadillo [15] is also a related work that proposed a compiler toolkit designed to work on homomorphically encrypted data, written in C++. Cingulata can handle a large number of parallel operations to mitigate the homomorphic encryption's performance overhead. However, in this work, we propose to perform similar optimization on GPUs, using CUDA-enabled computations.

More recently, Concrete [54], an open-source compiler using TFHE, was proposed, which simplifies the complexities of general computation under FHE. It provides several translations that allow arbitrary computations to be performed under encryption using a vanilla Python script with additional decorators. In the future, we look forward to extending our GPU-parallel features according to this framework.

6.2. Secure String Distances in Genomic Data

In one of the earlier attempts with a secure multiparty setting, Jha et al. [55] proposed a privacy-preserving genomic sequence similarity in 2008. Their paper showed three different methods to mirror the Levenshtein distance algorithm using a garbled circuit. However, for a sequence of 25 nucleotides, it took around 40 s to compute the distance metric between two strings. In 2015, Wang et al. [9] proposed an approximation of the original edit distance in a more realistic setting, where the authors utilized a reference genomic sequence to compute the edit distance. However, we analyzed its accuracy in one of our earlier works [10] and showed that the accuracy drops for longer input sequences.

In a recent attempt, Shimzu et al. [33] proposed a Burrows–Wheeler transformation for finding target queries on a genomic dataset. The authors attempted the set-maximal matches using oblivious transfer on a two-party privacy setting. However, we employ a completely different cryptographic technique as we do not require the researcher to stay active upon providing their encrypted queries. Therefore, the whole computation can be offloaded to a cloud server and harness its full computational capacity. One of the first attempts with FHE to compute edit distance was conducted by Cheon et al. [44]. Given the advances in 2017, their cryptographic scheme was impressive, though taking 16.4 s to compute a 8×8 block of string inputs. However, the underlying techniques have improved, allowing a larger string comparison using FHE techniques as we have shown in this work.

7. Conclusions

In this study, we developed algebraic circuits for fully homomorphic encryption (FHE), making them available for any complex operations. In addition, we investigated the use of CPU-level parallelism to enhance the execution speed of underlying FHE computations. A significant innovation in our work is the introduction of a GPU-level parallel framework that leverages novel optimizations such as bit coalescing, compound gate, and tree-based vector accumulation. Furthermore, we implemented this framework in genomic string operations and evaluated its effectiveness. The experimental results demonstrate that the methodology we propose is 20 times and 14.5 times quicker than the existing method for executing Boolean gates and multiplications, respectively.

Author Contributions: Conceptualization, M.M.A.A.; Methodology, M.M.A.A.; Software, M.T.M.T.; Validation, M.M.A.A. and N.M.; Writing—original draft, M.M.A.A. and M.T.M.T.; Writing—review & editing, N.M.; Supervision, N.M. All authors have read and agreed to the published version of the manuscript.

Funding: The research is supported in part by the CS UManitoba Computing Clusters and Amazon Research Grant. N.M. was supported in part by the NSERC Discovery Grants (RGPIN-04127-2022) and Falconer Emerging Researcher Rh Award.

Institutional Review Board Statement: Not applicable.

Informed Consent Statement: Not applicable.

Data Availability Statement: There are no proprietary or closed-source senstiive date used for the analysis.

Conflicts of Interest: The authors declare no conflicts of interest.

Appendix A. GPU Computational Hierarchy

A graphics processing unit (GPU) consists of a scalable array of multithreaded streaming multiprocessors (SMs). For example, our GPU for the experiments, NVIDIA GTX 1080, has 20 SMs, where SM contains 2048 individual threads. Threads are grouped into blocks, and the blocks are grouped to form grids. Threads in the blocks are split into warps (32 threads) in the same SM.

For the computational unit, the GPU includes 128 CUDA (Compute Unified Device Architecture) cores per SM. Each core execution unit has one float and one integer compute processor.

Appendix A.1. Memory Hierarchy in GPU

SMs can run in parallel with different instructions. However, all the threads of a respective SM execute the same instruction simultaneously. Therefore, GPUs are called single instruction multiple data (SIMD) machines. Besides having a large number of threads, the GPU memory system also consists of a wide variety of memories for the underlying computations. Architecturally, we divide the memory system into five categories. Figure A1 portrays the memory categories and their organization. We present a brief discussion on the memory categories:

(a)   Register;
(b)   Cache;
(c)   Shared;
(d)   Constant; and

(e)   Global.

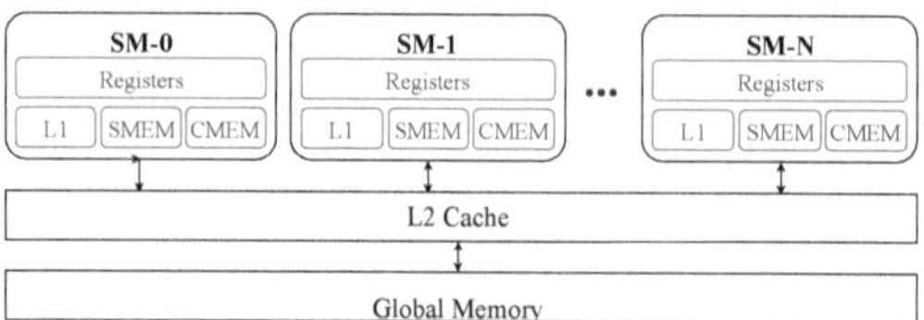

Figure A1. GPU memory hierarchy.

Register. Registers are the fastest and smallest among all memories. Registers are private to the threads.

Cache. GPUs facilitate two levels of caches, namely, L1 cache and L2 cache. In terms of latency, the L1 cache is below the registers. Each SM is equipped with a private L1 cache. On the contrary, the L2 cache has a latency that is higher than that of L1 cached and shared by all SMs.

Shared memory. Being on the SM chip, shared memory has higher bandwidth and much lower latency than the global memory. It has much lower memory space and lacks volatility.Shared memory is private to SMs as well, but public to the threads inside the SMs.

Constant memory. Constant memory resides in the device memory and is cached in the constant cache. Each SM has its own constant memory. Constant memory increases the cache hit for constant variables.

Global memory. Global memory is the largest (Table A1) among all memory categories, yet the slowest and nonpersistent. One major limitation of global memory is that it is fixed, while the main memory can be changed for the CPUs.

Table A1. A comparison between Intel(R) Core™ i7-2600 and NVIDIA GTX 1080 configurations.

	CPU	GPU
Clock speed	3.40 GHz	1734 MHz
Main memory	16 GB	8 GB
L1 cache	256 KB	48 KB
L2 cache	256 KB	2048 KB
L3 cache	8192 KB	×
Physical threads	8	40,960

Appendix A.2. Computational and Memory Hierarchy Coordination

The coordination between computation and memory hierarchy is a crucial aspect to take advantage of both faster memory and parallelism. Each thread has private local variable storage known as registers. Threads inside the same block can access the shared memory, constant memory, and L1 cache. The memories for one block are inaccessible by others inside the same SM. The number of grids can be at most the number of global memories, and the global memory is shareable from all SMs.

Bit coalescing (Section 6.1) discusses the unification of LWE samples. Hence, for a sufficiently large n-bit (LWE sample) coalescing, the memory requirement exceeds the existing shared memory. Therefore, the current GPU ‖ construction uses the global memory (the slowest). The rest of the computations use registers to store the thread-specific local variables and shared memory to share the data among the threads.

Appendix A.3. Architectural Differences with CPU

Number of cores. Modern CPUs consist of a small number of independent cores and thus confine the scopes of parallelism. GPUs, on the other hand, have an array of SMs, where each SM possesses a large number of cores. For example, in Figure A2, the CPU comprises 4 independent cores, while the GPU consists of N SMs with n CUDA cores in each SM. Thus, GPUs offer more parallel computing power for any computation.

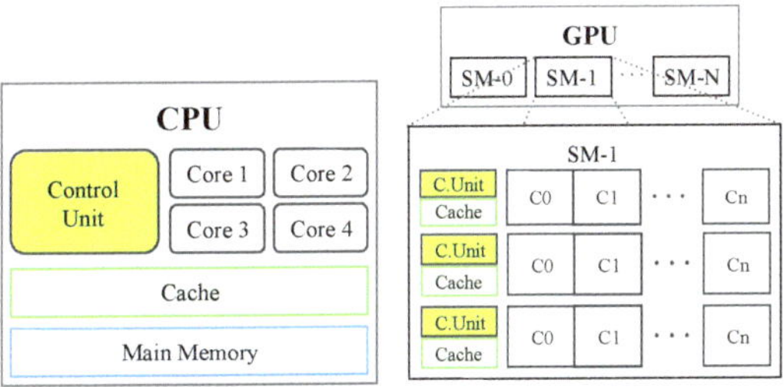

Figure A2. A schematic illustration of CPU (**a**) and GPU (**b**) architecture. Unit and C_n represent a control unit and a core in GPU, respectively. (**b**) illustrates an SM construction.

Computation complexity. Although GPUs provide more scopes of parallelism, GPU cores lack the computational power. CPU cores have higher clock cycle (3.40 GHz) than GPU (1734 MHz), as shown in Table A1. Moreover, CPU cores are capable of executing complex instruction of small data. On the contrary, a GPU core is simple and typically consists of an execution unit of integers and float numbers [56].

Memory space. Table A1 provides the storage capacity of different types of memory in the machines. Additionally, a unique aspect of CPUs is that the main memory can be modified on H/W. GPUs lack this facility as every device is shipped with fixed-size memory. This creates additional complexities like memory exhaustion while computing with a large dataset/models.

Number of threads. In modern desktop machines, the number of physical threads is equal to the number of cores. However, hyperthreading technology virtually doubles the number of threads. Thus, the CPUs can have virtual threads twice the number of cores. GPUs, on the contrary, provide thousands of cores. In GTX 1080, the total number of threads is 40,960. Therefore, the GPU is faster in data parallel algorithms.

References

1. Gentry, C. Fully homomorphic encryption using ideal lattices. In Proceedings of the STOC, Bethesda, MD, USA, 31 May 31–2 June 2009; Volume 9, pp. 169–178.
2. Pham, A.; Dacosta, I.; Endignoux, G.; Pastoriza, J.R.T.; Huguenin, K.; Hubaux, J.P. ORide: A Privacy-Preserving yet Accountable Ride-Hailing Service. In Proceedings of the 26th USENIX Security Symposium (USENIX Security 17), Vancouver, BC, Canada, 16–18 August 2017; pp. 1235–1252.
3. Kim, M.; Song, Y.; Cheon, J.H. Secure searching of biomarkers through hybrid homomorphic encryption scheme. *BMC Med. Genom.* **2017**, *10*, 42. [CrossRef] [PubMed]
4. Chen, H.; Gilad-Bachrach, R.; Han, K.; Huang, Z.; Jalali, A.; Laine, K.; Lauter, K. Logistic regression over encrypted data from fully homomorphic encryption. *BMC Med. Genom.* **2018**, *11*, 81. [CrossRef] [PubMed]
5. Morshed, T.; Alhadidi, D.; Mohammed, N. Parallel Linear Regression on Encrypted Data. In Proceedings of the In Proceedings of 16th Annual Conference on Privacy, Security and Trust (PST), Belfast, Ireland, 28–30 August 2018; pp. 1–5.
6. Naveed, M.; Ayday, E.; Clayton, E.W.; Fellay, J.; Gunter, C.A.; Hubaux, J.P.; Malin, B.A.; Wang, X. Privacy in the genomic era. *ACM Comput. Surv. (CSUR)* **2015**, *48*, 6. [CrossRef] [PubMed]
7. Aziz, M.M.A.; Sadat, M.N.; Alhadidi, D.; Wang, S.; Jiang, X.; Brown, C.L.; Mohammed, N. Privacy-preserving techniques of genomic data: A survey. *Briefings Bioinform.* **2017**, *20*, 887–895. [CrossRef]
8. 23AndMe.com. Our Health + Ancestry DNA Service—23AndMe Canada. Available online: https://www.23andme.com/en-ca/dna-health-ancestry (accessed on 20 November 2020).

9. Wang, X.S.; Huang, Y.; Zhao, Y.; Tang, H.; Wang, X.; Bu, D. Efficient genome-wide, privacy-preserving similar patient query based on private edit distance. In Proceedings of the 22Nd ACM SIGSAC Conference on Computer and Communications Security, Denver, CO, USA, 12–16 October 2015; ACM: New York, NY, USA, 2015; pp. 492–503.
10. Al Aziz, M.M.; Alhadidi, D.; Mohammed, N. Secure approximation of edit distance on genomic data. *BMC Med. Genom.* **2017**, *10*, 41. [CrossRef]
11. Guerrini, C.J.; Robinson, J.O.; Petersen, D.; McGuire, A.L. Should police have access to genetic genealogy databases? Capturing the Golden State Killer and other criminals using a controversial new forensic technique. *PLoS Biol.* **2018**, *16*, e2006906. [CrossRef]
12. Chillotti, I.; Gama, N.; Georgieva, M.; Izabachène, M. Faster fully homomorphic encryption: Bootstrapping in less than 0.1 seconds. In Proceedings of the Advances in Cryptology—ASIACRYPT 2016: 22nd International Conference on the Theory and Application of Cryptology and Information Security, Hanoi, Vietnam, 4–8 December 2016; Springer: Berlin/Heidelberg, Germany, 2016; pp. 3–33.
13. CUDA-Accelerated Fully Homomorphic Encryption Library. 2019. Available online: https://github.com/vernamlab/cuFHE (accessed on 15 December 2023).
14. NuFHE, a GPU-Powered Torus FHE Implementation. 2019. Available online: https://github.com/nucypher/nufhe (accessed on 15 December 2023).
15. Cingulata. 2019. Available online: https://github.com/CEA-LIST/Cingulata (accessed on 15 December 2023).
16. Cheon, J.H.; Kim, M.; Lauter, K. Homomorphic computation of edit distance. In Proceedings of the International Conference on Financial Cryptography and Data Security, San Juan, Puerto Rico, 26–30 January 2015; Springer: Berlin/Heidelberg, Germany, 2015; pp. 194–212.
17. Chillotti, I.; Gama, N.; Georgieva, M.; Izabachène, M. Faster packed homomorphic operations and efficient circuit bootstrapping for TFHE. In Proceedings of the International Conference on the Theory and Application of Cryptology and Information Security, Hong Kong, China, 3–7 December 2017; Springer: Berlin/Heidelberg, Germany, 2017; pp. 377–408.
18. Morshed, T.; Aziz, M.; Mohammed, N. CPU and GPU Accelerated Fully Homomorphic Encryption. In Proceedings of the 2020 IEEE International Symposium on Hardware Oriented Security and Trust (HOST), Los Alamitos, CA, USA, 7–11 December 2020; pp. 142–153. [CrossRef]
19. Regev, O. On lattices, learning with errors, random linear codes, and cryptography. *J. ACM* **2009**, *56*, 34. [CrossRef]
20. Cheon, J.H.; Han, K.; Kim, A.; Kim, M.; Song, Y. Bootstrapping for approximate homomorphic encryption. In Proceedings of the Annual International Conference on the Theory and Applications of Cryptographic Techniques, Tel Aviv, Israel, 29 April–3 May 2018; Springer: Berlin/Heidelberg, Germany, 2018; pp. 360–384.
21. Boura, C.; Gama, N.; Georgieva, M. Chimera: A Unified Framework for B/FV, TFHE and HEAAN Fully Homomorphic Encryption and Predictions for Deep Learning. *IACR Cryptol. ePrint Arch.* **2018**, *2018*, 758.
22. Lomont, C. Introduction to Intel Advanced Vector Extensions. Intel White Paper 2011, pp. 1–21. Available online: https://hpc.llnl.gov/sites/default/files/intelAVXintro.pdf (accessed on 16 December 2023).
23. Frigo, M.; Johnson, S.G. FFTW: An adaptive software architecture for the FFT. In Proceedings of the 1998 IEEE International Conference on Acoustics, Speech and Signal Processing, ICASSP'98 (Cat. No. 98CH36181), Seattle, WA, USA, 12–15 May 1998; Volume 3, pp. 1381–1384.
24. Brakerski, Z.; Gentry, C.; Halevi, S. Packed ciphertexts in LWE-based homomorphic encryption. In Proceedings of the International Workshop on Public Key Cryptography, Nara, Japan, 26 February–1 March 2013; Springer: Berlin/Heidelberg, Germany, 2013; pp. 1–13.
25. Ducas, L.; Micciancio, D. FHEW: Bootstrapping Homomorphic Encryption in Less Than a Second. Cryptology ePrint Archive, Report 2014/816,2014 . Available online: https://eprint.iacr.org/2014/816 (accessed on 20 December 2023).
26. Fan, J.; Vercauteren, F. Somewhat Practical Fully Homomorphic Encryption. *IACR Cryptol. Eprint Arch.* **2012**, *2012*, 144.
27. McGeoch, C.C. Parallel Addition. *Am. Math. Mon.* **1993**, *100*, 867–871. [CrossRef]
28. Karatsuba, A.A.; Ofman, Y.P. Multiplication of many-digital numbers by automatic computers. In *Proceedings of the Doklady Akademii Nauk*; Russian Academy of Sciences: Moskva, Russia, 1962; Volume 145, pp. 293–294.
29. Chandra, R.; Dagum, L.; Kohr, D., Menon, R.; Maydan, D.; McDonald, J. *Parallel Programming in OpenMP*; Morgan Kaufmann: Cambridge, MA, USA, 2001.
30. NVIDIA. GeForce GTX 1080 Graphics Cards from NVIDIA GeForce. Available online: https://www.nvidia.com/en-us/geforce/products/10series/geforce-gtx-1080/ (accessed on 20 December 2023).
31. Fickett, J.W. Fast optimal alignment. *Nucleic Acids Res.* **1984**, *12*, 175–179. [CrossRef]
32. Sotiraki, K.; Ghosh, E.; Chen, H. Privately computing set-maximal matches in genomic data. *BMC Med. Genom.* **2020**, *13*, 72. [CrossRef]
33. Shimizu, K.; Nuida, K.; Rätsch, G. Efficient Privacy-Preserving String Search and an Application in Genomics. *Bioinformatics* **2016**, *32*, 1652–1661. [CrossRef]
34. Durbin, R. Efficient haplotype matching and storage using the positional Burrows–Wheeler transform (PBWT). *Bioinformatics* **2014**, *30*, 1266–1272. [CrossRef]
35. Xie, P.; Bilenko, M.; Finley, T.; Gilad-Bachrach, R.; Lauter, K.; Naehrig, M. Crypto-nets: Neural networks over encrypted data. *arXiv* **2014**, arXiv:1412.6181.

36. Takabi, H.; Hesamifard, E.; Ghasemi, M. Privacy preserving multi-party machine learning with homomorphic encryption. In Proceedings of the 29th Annual Conference on Neural Information Processing Systems (NIPS), Barcelona, Spain, 5–10 December 2016.
37. Chillotti, I.; Gama, N.; Georgieva, M.; Izabachène, M. TFHE: Fast Fully Homomorphic Encryption Library. August 2016. Available online: https://tfhe.github.io/tfhe/ (accessed on 20 December 2023).
38. Rivest, R.L.; Shamir, A.; Adleman, L. A method for obtaining digital signatures and public-key cryptosystems. *Commun. ACM* **1978**, *21*, 120–126. [CrossRef]
39. Paillier, P. Public-key cryptosystems based on composite degree residuosity classes. In Proceedings of the Advances in cryptology, EUROCRYPT, Prague, Czech Republic, 2–6 May 1999; Springer: Berlin/Heidelberg, Germany, 1999; pp. 223–238.
40. Microsoft SEAL (Release 3.2). 2019. Microsoft Research, Redmond, WA. Available online: https://github.com/Microsoft/SEAL (accessed on 20 December 2023).
41. Gentry, C.; Sahai, A.; Waters, B. Homomorphic encryption from learning with errors: Conceptually-simpler, asymptotically-faster, attribute-based. In *Advances in Cryptology–CRYPTO 2013*; Springer: Berlin/Heidelberg, Germany, 2013; pp. 75–92.
42. Brakerski, Z.; Vaikuntanathan, V. Efficient fully homomorphic encryption from (standard) LWE. *SIAM J. Comput.* **2014**, *43*, 831–871. [CrossRef]
43. Brakerski, Z.; Gentry, C.; Vaikuntanathan, V. (Leveled) fully homomorphic encryption without bootstrapping. *ACM Trans. Comput. Theory* **2014**, *6*, 13. [CrossRef]
44. Cheon, J.H.; Kim, A.; Kim, M.; Song, Y. Homomorphic encryption for arithmetic of approximate numbers. In Proceedings of the International Conference on the Theory and Application of Cryptology and Information Security, Hong Kong, China, 3–7 December 2017; Springer: Berlin/Heidelberg, Germany, 2017; pp. 409–437.
45. Flynn, M.J. Some computer organizations and their effectiveness. *IEEE Trans. Comput.* **1972**, *100*, 948–960. [CrossRef]
46. Halevi, S.; Shoup, V. Algorithms in helib. In Proceedings of the Annual Cryptology Conference, Santa Barbara, CA, USA, 17–21 August 2014; Springer: Berlin/Heidelberg, Germany, 2014; pp. 554–571.
47. Doröz, Y.; Öztürk, E.; Savaş, E.; Sunar, B. Accelerating LTV based homomorphic encryption in reconfigurable hardware. In Proceedings of the International Workshop on Cryptographic Hardware and Embedded Systems, Saint-Malo, France, 13–16 September 2015; Springer: Berlin/Heidelberg, Germany, 2015; pp. 185–204.
48. López-Alt, A.; Tromer, E.; Vaikuntanathan, V. On-the-fly multiparty computation on the cloud via multikey fully homomorphic encryption. In Proceedings of the forty-fourth annual ACM symposium on Theory of computing, New York, NY, USA, 20–22 May 2012; ACM: New York, NY, USA, 2012; pp. 1219–1234.
49. Dai, W.; Sunar, B. cuHE: A homomorphic encryption accelerator library. In Proceedings of the International Conference on Cryptography and Information Security in the Balkans, Koper, Slovenia, 3–4 September 2015; Springer: Berlin/Heidelberg, Germany, 2015; pp. 169–186.
50. Dai, W.; Doröz, Y.; Sunar, B. Accelerating swhe based pirs using gpus. In Proceedings of the International Conference on Financial Cryptography and Data Security, San Juan, Puerto Rico, 26–30 January 2015; Springer: Berlin/Heidelberg, Germany, 2015; pp. 160–171.
51. Lei, X.; Guo, R.; Zhang, F.; Wang, L.; Xu, R.; Qu, G. Accelerating Homomorphic Full Adder based on FHEW Using Multicore CPU and GPUs. In Proceedings of the 2019 IEEE 21st International Conference on High Performance Computing and Communications; IEEE 17th International Conference on Smart City; IEEE 5th International Conference on Data Science and Systems (HPCC/SmartCity/DSS), Zhangjiajie, China , 10–12 August 2019.
52. Yang, H.; Yao, W.; Liu, W.; Wei, B. Efficiency Analysis of TFHE Fully Homomorphic Encryption Software Library Based on GPU. In Proceedings of the Workshops of the International Conference on Advanced Information Networking and Applications, Matsue, Japan, 27–29 March 2019; Springer: Berlin/Heidelberg, Germany, 2019; pp. 93–102.
53. Zhou, T.; Yang, X.; Liu, L.; Zhang, W.; Li, N. Faster bootstrapping with multiple addends. *IEEE Access* **2018**, *6*, 49868–49876. [CrossRef]
54. Zama. Concrete: TFHE Compiler That Converts Python Programs into FHE Equivalent, 2022. Available online: https://github.com/zama-ai/concrete (accessed on 20 December 2023).
55. Jha, S.; Kruger, L.; Shmatikov, V. Towards practical privacy for genomic computation. In Proceedings of the 2008 IEEE Symposium on Security and Privacy (sp 2008), Oakland, CA, USA, 18–21 May 2008; pp. 216–230.
56. NVidia, F. *Nvidia's Next Generation Cuda Compute Architecture*; NVidia: Santa Clara, CA, USA, 2009.

information

Article

Explainable Machine Learning for Malware Detection on Android Applications [†]

Catarina Palma [1], Artur Ferreira [1,2,*] and Mário Figueiredo [2,3]

1   ISEL, Instituto Superior de Engenharia de Lisboa, Instituto Politécnico de Lisboa, 1959-007 Lisboa, Portugal; a45241@alunos.isel.pt
2   Instituto de Telecomunicações, 1049-001 Lisboa, Portugal; mario.figueiredo@tecnico.ulisboa.pt
3   IST, Instituto Superior Técnico, Universidade de Lisboa, 1049-001 Lisboa, Portugal
*   Correspondence: artur.ferreira@isel.pt
†   This paper is an extended version of our paper published in 14th Simpósio de Informática (INForum), Porto, Portugal, 7–8 September 2023.

Abstract: The presence of malicious software (malware), for example, in Android applications (apps), has harmful or irreparable consequences to the user and/or the device. Despite the protections app stores provide to avoid malware, it keeps growing in sophistication and diffusion. In this paper, we explore the use of machine learning (ML) techniques to detect malware in Android apps. The focus is on the study of different data pre-processing, dimensionality reduction, and classification techniques, assessing the generalization ability of the learned models using public domain datasets and specifically developed apps. We find that the classifiers that achieve better performance for this task are support vector machines (SVM) and random forests (RF). We emphasize the use of feature selection (FS) techniques to reduce the data dimensionality and to identify the most relevant features in Android malware classification, leading to explainability on this task. Our approach can identify the most relevant features to classify an app as malware. Namely, we conclude that permissions play a prominent role in Android malware detection. The proposed approach reduces the data dimensionality while achieving high accuracy in identifying malware in Android apps.

Keywords: android applications; datasets; explainability; feature selection; machine learning; malware detection; numerosity balancing; security; soft computing; supervised learning

Citation: Palma, C.; Ferreira, A.; Figueiredo, M. Explainable Machine Learning for Malware Detection on Android Applications. *Information* **2024**, *15*, 25. https://doi.org/10.3390/info15010025

Academic Editors: Georgios Kambourakis, Jose de Vasconcelos, Hugo Barbosa and Carla Cordeiro

Received: 9 November 2023
Revised: 29 December 2023
Accepted: 30 December 2023
Published: 1 January 2024

1. Introduction

The worldwide use of smartphones has grown exponentially over the past decade. As of November 2023, the estimated number of smartphone users is 5.25 billion, and it continues to grow [1]. This growth has been accompanied by the popularization of Android, an open-source operating system (OS) mainly designed for touchscreen mobile devices. It is the mobile OS with the largest market share, with roughly 70% [2]. In November 2023, the app store Google Play Store had 3.718 million apps available for Android users to download [3].

The rapid wide-scale expansion of the use of smartphone devices, the increased popularity of the Android OS, and the wide variety and number of Android apps have attracted the attention of malware developers. Attackers can target a wide range of applications that deal with a significant number of user-sensitive data. They can also target the user's data on the smartphone or may use the device to carry out other attacks. Furthermore, from the attacker's perspective, the massive number of users are all targets and potential victims who can download their malware. Since the Android system has become a popular and profitable target, malicious attacks against Android mobile devices have increased. In 2021, 9.5 million malware Android packages were detected, three times more than in 2019 (3.1 million) [4]. Millions of users can download one app (possibly with malicious software) in a matter of minutes. Thus, the need to detect malicious apps is a major issue.

Some software and applications focus on security, and app stores have security and detection mechanisms to mitigate malicious apps. To some extent, these are successful, but malware keeps growing in sophistication and diffusion, sometimes easily bypassing these mechanisms. ML approaches have shown to be effective and versatile in various fields, being a milestone in the tech industry. Thus, in recent years, ML techniques have been proposed for the malware detection problem in Android applications [4–10].

Paper Contributions

This work focuses on the use of ML techniques for malware detection in Android applications, and its main contributions are the following:

- Assessing the impact of different data pre-processing techniques using four different datasets. Data pre-processing is an essential step and, to the best of our knowledge, this aspect is lacking attention in the literature on this problem.
- Enriching the literature by identifying the most decisive features for malware detection among the public-domain datasets used and identifying the ML classifiers that provide the best results.
- Expanding the literature by using real-world Android applications (developed and existing) to extend test scenarios over the ones made available by the datasets. To the best of our knowledge, no previous work has developed specific applications for malware model testing.

In this paper, we extend our previous work [11] with (non-deep) machine learning techniques, providing the following novel contributions and extensions:

- The use of real-world apps in the assessment of the ML model learned from standard datasets. We also provide a discussion on the challenges posed by the mapping from the real-world app to our learned models.
- The use of more datasets, feature selection filters, classifiers, and data pre-processing techniques, namely, different instance (numerosity) sampling techniques. The combination of these techniques on an ML pipeline is addressed and evaluated.
- A detailed and deeper discussion of the experimental results on four datasets instead of two. These four datasets have different characteristics regarding the key aspects of the data. This leads to the need to analyze the results from each dataset individually.
- For each dataset, we report the top five features that seem to be more decisive regarding malware classification, yielding some explainability on the classification. We highlight the features that most contribute to explaining the classification.

The remainder of this paper is organized as follows. Section 2 provides an overview of Android apps and related work. The proposed approach is described in Section 3. The experimental evaluation is reported in Section 4. Finally, Section 5 ends the paper with concluding remarks and directions for future work.

2. Related Work

This section briefly overviews Android malware detection, approaching ML techniques, algorithms, and datasets. It begins with a general Android app overview in Section 2.1 and malware types and security measures in Section 2.2. Then, it discusses data acquisition, namely, analysis types, and datasets in Section 2.3 and explores techniques for data pre-processing and splitting in Section 2.4. ML algorithms and their evaluation metrics are presented in Sections 2.5 and 2.6, respectively. This section ends by summarizing previous approaches to malware detection that have been proposed in the literature, in Sections 2.7 and 2.8.

2.1. Android Applications

Android is an open-source OS based on the Linux kernel, designed mainly for touchscreen mobile devices. First launched in 2008, it has many versions, with releases every few months. To understand how malware can exploit the Android OS, it is essential to know the key components of an Android app. Figure 1 depicts the elements that compose the Android package kit (APK) file of an Android app [10].

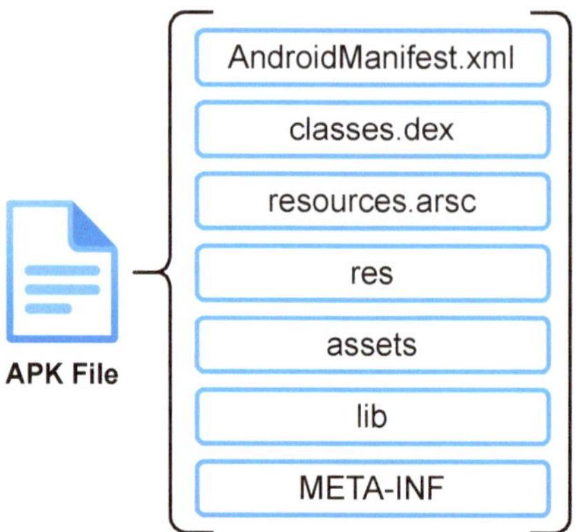

Figure 1. Components of an Android application (app).

Knowledge about the structure of an Android app allows for a better understanding of some of the critical security aspects. For instance, apps require system permissions to perform specific functionalities. Malware often exploits these accesses and permissions to perform attacks [12]. Thus, the AndroidManifest.xml file, with the permissions requested by the app, is relevant in determining if an app is malicious, as discussed in Section 2.3.

2.2. Malware on Android Applications

Malware takes different forms and approaches, such as remote access trojans, banking trojans, ransomware, adware, spyware, scareware, and premium text short message service (SMS). Malware exploits system vulnerabilities, design weaknesses, and security flaws in many Android applications that threaten end-users and/or lure the user through social engineering to install apps containing malware [13]. There are well-documented Android malware families, such as "ExpensiveWal", "HummingBad", and "Chamoi", which can be embedded or hidden in many apps available in app stores and then downloaded by millions of users.

There are several security measures to mitigate malware attacks, such as using secure internet connections, installing anti-malware apps, and the validation of the apps performed by the app stores. Android also inherits some security measures since the kernel provides application sandboxing and process isolation [12]. These security measures, to some extent, successfully mitigate malware attacks. However, sometimes they can be bypassed with a variety of techniques to hinder the identification and neutralization of malware [9].

2.3. Data Acquisition

This section provides insight into the different types of analysis used to extract features from Android apps and into some of the datasets for Android malware detection found in the literature.

2.3.1. Type of Analysis

Three types of approaches can be followed to extract features from Android apps: static, dynamic, and hybrid. Static analysis is the most popular, followed by the dynamic and hybrid approaches [10]. In static analysis, the app is analyzed in a non-runtime environment. Feature extraction is usually carried out by analyzing the code and the AndroidManifest.xml file [9]. It is generally faster and more straightforward than the other analysis types. Dynamic analysis occurs during the app's regular operation in a monitored, controlled, or sandbox environment [10] to analyze its behavior. Thus, it is computationally more demanding than static analysis [12]. Features can be extracted by analyzing network traffic, system calls, system resources, and other app behaviors [9]. Finally, hybrid analysis combines the previous two types of analysis [12]. However, as with dynamic analysis, researchers are discouraged by the time and computational resources it requires and its complexity, making it the less popular type of analysis.

2.3.2. Datasets

Several standard datasets for malware detection in Android apps are mentioned in the literature [10]. Unfortunately, frequently these are not easy to obtain. Often, the access is restricted, involving payment or authorization. In other cases, the sources may not be trustworthy.

Alkahtani and Aldhyani considered the Drebin and CICAndMal2017 datasets in their study [4], available in [14,15], respectively. The Drebin dataset, first published in 2014, contains 215 features extracted from 15,036 applications, with 9476 benign apps and 5560 malware apps from 179 different malware families. The CICAndMal2017 dataset, published in 2018, contains 183 features and 29,999 instances extracted from several sources, such as the Google Play Store. The malware samples can be organized into adware, ransomware, scareware, and SMS malware, from a total of 42 unique malware families.

The Android Malware (AM) and the Android Malware static feature (AMSF) datasets, available in [16,17], respectively, are also considered in this paper. The AM dataset was created by Martín et al. in 2016, in the context of their study [8]. It contains meta information on Android apps with 183 features and 11,476 instances. The AMSF dataset is organized into six parts, each with different features: permissions, intents, system commands, application programming interface (API) calls, API packages, and opcodes. These datasets were extracted from the same APK. In total, it contains 1062 features and 5019 samples of apps collected from the Google Play Store, APKPure, and VirusShare.

2.4. Data Pre-Processing and Splitting

This section overviews some data pre-processing and data-splitting techniques.

2.4.1. Data Pre-Processing

Data pre-processing can be generalized and aggregated into four categories [18]: cleaning, integration, reduction, and transformation. Data cleaning includes handling missing values, which can be done with different approaches, such as discarding instances with missing values or performing missing value imputation. It also addresses reformatting the data to ensure standard formats and attribute conversions, such as one-hot or label encoding. Data cleaning includes the identification of outliers and the smoothing of noisy data. Data integration consists of merging data from multiple sources into a single dataset. Data reduction techniques aim to derive a reduced representation in terms of volume, keeping the integrity of the original data. The main strategies for data reduction are dimensionality reduction, and numerosity reduction, which includes instance sampling. Dimensionality reduction can be performed by feature selection techniques, such as the relevance-redundancy feature selection(RRFS) filter approach [19]. RRFS involves discarding the weakly relevant and redundant features while keeping the relevant ones adding more value to the model. For relevance analysis, different measures can be applied, such as the unsupervised mean–median (MM) relevance measure given by

$$MM_i = |\overline{X_i} - median(X_i)|, \tag{1}$$

with $\overline{X_i}$ denoting the sample mean of feature X_i. We also consider the supervised Fisher's ratio (FR) relevance metric

$$FR_i = \frac{\left| \overline{X}_i^{(-1)} - \overline{X}_i^{(1)} \right|}{\sqrt{\text{var}(X_i)^{(-1)} + \text{var}(X_i)^{(1)}}}, \tag{2}$$

where $\overline{X}_i^{(-1)}$, $\overline{X}_i^{(1)}$, $\text{var}(X_i)^{(-1)}$, and $\text{var}(X_i)^{(1)}$ are the sample means and variances of feature X_i, for the patterns of each class. The redundancy analysis between two features, X_i and X_j, is done with the absolute cosine (AC)

$$AC_{X_i,X_j} = |cos(\theta_{X_i X_j})| = \left| \frac{\langle X_i, X_j \rangle}{||X_i|| \, ||X_j||} \right| = \frac{\sum_{k=1}^{n} X_{ik} X_{jk}}{\sqrt{\sum_{k=1}^{n} X_{ik}^2 \sum_{k=1}^{n} X_{jk}^2}}, \tag{3}$$

where $\langle , \rangle$ and $||.||$ denote the inner product and L_2 norm, respectively.

Numerosity reduction includes instance sampling, a method that balances imbalanced data. Undersampling consists of removing samples of the majority class, yielding information loss. To balance data, oversampling, which involves replicating instances of the minority class, can also be applied, yielding a higher chance of overfitting. Other techniques, such as the synthetic minority oversampling technique (SMOTE) [20], perform oversampling by creating synthetic data instead of copying existing instances.

Lastly, data transformation aims to change the data's value, structure, or format to shape it into an appropriate form. The most widely used techniques are normalization and discretization. The first involves scaling attributes to ensure they fit within a specified range. One of the most popular techniques for this task is min–max normalization. The use of discretization techniques reduces the number of continuous feature values by partitioning the feature range into intervals to replace the actual data values. The original feature values are replaced by integer indexes that represent each discretization interval, achieving a simplified representation of the data.

2.4.2. Data Splitting

Data are typically split into two or three sets: training, testing, and validation, based on random or stratified sampling. Cross-validation (CV) [21] is a resampling method that splits the data into subsets and rotates their use among them. The nested CV strategy is applied to the training, testing, and validation sets. It consists of an outer loop and an inner loop. The outer loop deals with the training and testing sets and estimates the generalization error by averaging test set scores over several dataset splits. The inner loop deals with the training and validation sets, with all subsets being obtained from the training set of the outer loop. In the inner loop, the score is approximately maximized by fitting a model to each training set and then directly maximized by selecting hyperparameters over the validation set. There are different types of CV, such as stratified K-fold CV and leave-one-out cross-validation (LOOCV). Stratified K-fold CV splits the data into K folds of approximately equal size with stratified sampling. LOOCV is the exhaustive holdout splitting approach, being a particular case of K-fold CV where K is equal to the number of instances.

2.5. Classifiers

In this section, a brief description of the classifiers used in this research is presented. Random forests(RF) [22] is an ensemble method that aggregates the output of multiple decision trees (DT) [23,24] to reach a single result. Support vector machines (SVM) [25] work by mapping data to a high-dimensional feature space to categorize data points. Even when the classes are not linearly separable, the data are transformed so that the separator can be drawn as a hyperplane that best splits the data into two classes [26]. K-nearest neighbors (KNN) [24,27] classifies a data point by a majority vote of its neighbors, with the data point being assigned to the class most common among its K nearest neighbors. Naïve Bayes (NB) classifiers follow a probabilistic approach based on Bayes' Theorem that relies on incorporating prior probability distributions to generate posterior probabilities [24,28].

As an additional technique, we also consider a classic multilayer perceptron(MLP) [29,30] as a classifier. An MLP has the advantage of learning non-linear models; the ability to train models in real-time (online learning); handling large numbers of input data; and, once trained, making quick predictions. However, it is more computationally costly than other classifiers and may be sensitive to feature scaling. We use the default implementation of MLP from the scikit-learn library, without resorting to deep learning techniques implementations.

2.6. Evaluation Metrics

This section describes the evaluation metrics used to assess the performance of the ML models. In this study, we adopt the following terminology: a true positive (TP) means to classify a malicious app as malicious correctly, a true negative (TN) is to classify a benign app as benign, a false positive (FP) is to classify a benign app as malicious, and a false negative (FN) refers to classifying a malicious app as benign. The accuracy (Acc) evaluation metric conveys the fraction of correct predictions made by the model and is given by

$$\text{Acc} = \frac{\text{TP} + \text{TN}}{\text{TP} + \text{TN} + \text{FP} + \text{FN}}. \tag{4}$$

In very unbalanced scenarios, accuracy can be misleading and other evaluation metrics are used. The positive predictive value, or precision (Prec), is given by

$$\text{Prec} = \frac{\text{TP}}{\text{TP} + \text{FP}}, \tag{5}$$

whereas the true positive rate (TPR), or sensitivity, also known as recall (Rec), is computed as

$$\text{Rec} = \frac{\text{TP}}{\text{TP} + \text{FN}}. \tag{6}$$

Finally, the F1-score, given by the harmonic mean of the precision and recall metrics

$$\text{F1} = 2\,\frac{\text{Precision} \times \text{Rec}}{\text{Precision} + \text{Rec}}, \tag{7}$$

is also considered, as well as the area under the curve—receiver operating characteristic (AUC-ROC) evaluation metric is also considered.

2.7. Overview of Machine Learning Approaches

This section focuses on the use of some common ML approaches for Android malware detection found in the literature. Section 2.8 addresses other techniques such as deep learning (DL).

Alkahtani and Aldhyani [4] applied SVM and KNN to two standard datasets: CICAndMal2017 and Drebin. SVM achieved an 80.71% accuracy with the Drebin dataset. For the CICAndMal2017 dataset, the authors claim to have achieved 100% accuracy. Regarding KNN, it achieved 81.57% on the Drebin dataset and 90% on the CICAndMal2017 dataset. Overall, SVM and KNN successfully detected malware, but SVM was more effective.

Muzaffar et al. [12] identified that many existent studies cite high accuracy rates. However, many use outdated datasets and inappropriate evaluation metrics that may be misleading. Kouliaridis and Kambourakis [9] concluded that, among the surveyed works, static analysis is the predominant approach, while publicly available datasets are often outdated. ML-based models are the most commonly used, and accuracy is the preferred evaluation metric. In studies from 2014 to 2021, RF and SVM are the most frequently employed algorithms. Wu et al. [10] provided insight into the most popular datasets used in the literature and concluded that the most used ML algorithms for Android malware detection between 2019 and 2020 were SVM, RF, and KNN.

Keyvanpour et al. [7] conducted experiments with the Drebin dataset and proposed embedding effective FS with RF. Other classifiers, such as KNN and NB, were tested, but RF outperformed other models based on several metrics. FS was shown to improve the RF classifier, with the authors reporting 99.49% accuracy and AUC of 95.6%, when using effective FS and RF with 100 trees.

Islam et al. [6] used the CCCS-CIC-AndMal2020 dataset, with 53,439 instances and 141 features. Missing data imputation was applied with the "mean" strategy, and SMOTE was used to deal with class imbalance. Min–max normalization was applied, and one-hot encoding was used for feature conversion. Recursive feature elimination (RFE) was used to perform FS, discarding 60.2% of the features. The reduced set of features lessened the complexity and improved the accuracy. The authors proposed multi-classification based on dynamic analysis, with an ensemble ML approach with weighted voting that incorporates RF, KNN, MLP, DT, SVM, and logistic regression (LR), which showed 95% accuracy.

Alomari et al. [31] proposed a multi-classification approach using the CICMalDroid2020 dataset, with 11,598 instances and 470 features. The z-score normalization, SMOTE and principal component analysis (PCA), were applied. SMOTE and z-score normalization improved the results, while PCA was not beneficial. Their approach was based on the light gradient boosting mode (LightGBM), but the performance of KNN, RF, DT, and NB was also analyzed. LightGBM presented the best accuracy and F1-score, achieving 95.49% and 95.47%, respectively.

Kouliaridis et al. [32] review the literature on Android malware detection, spanning the period from 2012 to 2020. On the Drebin, VirusShare, and AndroZoo datasets, the authors rank the importance of features with the Information Gain metric. They found that features related to permissions and intents rank higher than others. However, the single use of permission-related features alone, and the mixture of permission- and intent-related features, does not yield remarkable results in malware detection. Thus, the authors identify the need to check supplementary and more weighty features.

In another work by Kouliaridis et al. [33], the authors explore the use of the dimensionality reduction techniques PCA and t-SNE (t-distributed stochastic neighbor embedding) in malware detection. The authors propose a simple ensemble aggregated base model of similar feature types and a complex ensemble with heterogeneous base models. The experimental results on the Androzoo dataset show the adequacy of ensembles for malware detection.

The Androtomist tool for the static and dynamic analysis of applications on the Android platform is proposed by Kouliaridis et al. in [34]. This hybrid approach resorts to features stemming from static analysis along with dynamic instrumentation. The approach resorts to machine learning and signature-based detection techniques. Androtomist software is made publicly available as open source and can be installed as a web application. The authors also provide an ensemble approach with an insight on the most influencing features regarding the classification process. The approach shows promising to excellent results in terms of the accuracy, F1-score, and AUC-ROC metrics.

Potha et al. [35] find that heterogeneous ensembles can provide malware detection solutions that are better than individual models. They propose the extrinsic random-based ensemble (ERBE) method, which uses a given set of repetitions and a subset of external (malware or benign) instances. The classification features are randomly selected, and an aggregation function combines the output of all base models for each test case separately. Using solely static analysis, the ERBE method takes advantage of the availability of multiple external instances of different sizes and genres. The experimental results with the AndroZoo dataset show the effectiveness of the proposed method.

Table 1 summarizes some results reported in the existing approaches.

Table 1. Summary of some results reported in existing approaches.

Study	Dataset	Classifier	Acc (%)
Alkahtani and Aldhyani [4]	Drebin	SVM	80.71
		KNN	81.57
	CICAndMal2017	SVM	100.0
		KNN	90.00
Keyvanpour et al. [7]	Drebin	RF (with 100 DT)	99.49
Islam et al. [6]	CCCS-CIC-AndMal2020	Ensemble	95.00
AlOmari et al. [31]	CICMalDroid2020	LightGBM	95.49

2.8. Other Approaches and Surveys on the Topic

There are other approaches to detecting malware in Android apps. For example, the use of deep learning (DL) techniques has provided satisfactory results, as reported in the works by [4,10,31,36–38], in relation to detecting malware on Android apps.

An ML approach with data from the Canadian Institute for Cybersecurity is reported by Akhtar and Feng [39], showing that DT, SVM, and convolutional neural networks (CNNs) performed well, with DT being the best classifier. A hybridization of CNN and ML techniques is proposed by Hashin in [40].

The work by Djenna et al. [41] addresses the combination of behavior-based deep learning and heuristic-based approaches for malware detection, comparing them with static deep learning methods. Online learning has also been proposed by Muzaffar et al. [12]. Shaojie Yang et al. [42] proposed an Android malware detection approach based on contrastive learning. A malware detection model for malicious network traffic identification based on FS and neural networks is reported by Lu et al. [43].

Adebayo and Aziz [44] proposed an improved malware-detection model using the A-priori algorithm to learn association rules. A malware detection technique based on the semantic information of behavioral features, with a vectorized representation of the API calls sequence by a word embedding model, is proposed by Zhang et al. [45].

The DexRay technique, which converts the bytecode of the app DEX files into grayscale "vector" images and feeds them to a 1-dimensional CNN model, was proposed by [46]. Over 158k apps, DEXRAY achieves a high detection rate regarding the F1-score metric. The Hybrid malware detection framework performs a hybrid (static and dynamic) approach and was proposed by Kabakus [47].

The Androtomist tool proposed in [34] is available at https://androtomist.com (accessed on 29 December 2023) and https://github.com/billkoul/AndrotomistLite (accessed on 29 December 2023).

Malware detection is a hot topic of research with many survey and review papers. For recent surveys, please see the works by Aboaoja et al. [48], Agrawal and Trivedi [49], Almomani et al. [50], Deldar and Abadi [51], Faruki et al. [52], Gyamfi et al. [53], Kouliaridis et al. [9], Liu et al. [54], Meijin et al. [55], Muzaffar et al. [12], Naseer et al. [56], Odusami et al. [57], Razgallah et al. [58], Souri et al. [59], Qiu et al. [60], Vasani et al. [61], Wang et al. [62], and Wu et al. [10], as well as the many references therein.

3. Proposed Approach

In this section, we detail our proposed approach. In Section 3.1, we formulate our ML approach, presenting it step by step and explaining our key choices. Afterwards, in Section 3.2, the component of our approach using real-world applications is described.

3.1. Machine Learning Module

The Android malware detection task is formulated as a binary classification problem, with a benign app considered a negative sample and a malicious app as a positive one. Figure 2 depicts the first segment of the proposed approach, showing that we use binary classification datasets for which we apply different data pre-processing techniques.

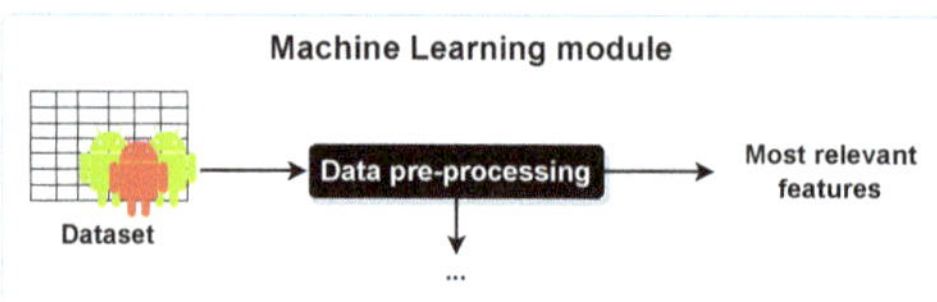

Figure 2. Partial block diagram of the proposed approach: the data pre-processing stage, which is composed of handling missing values, numerosity balancing, and feature selection. The vertical arrow points to the continuation of the ML pipeline, and the right-hand side arrow highlights that our approach identifies the most relevant features for the feature extraction module.

We start by getting data from Android apps with a dataset, such as Drebin or CICAndMal2017. Next, data pre-processing techniques, namely, techniques to handle missing values, for numerosity balancing and feature selection [63,64], are applied to properly prepare the data and to assess their impact on the model's performance. Additionally, a set of the most relevant features will be obtained with a feature selection technique. Figure 3 describes the following steps of our proposed approach, after properly preparing the data.

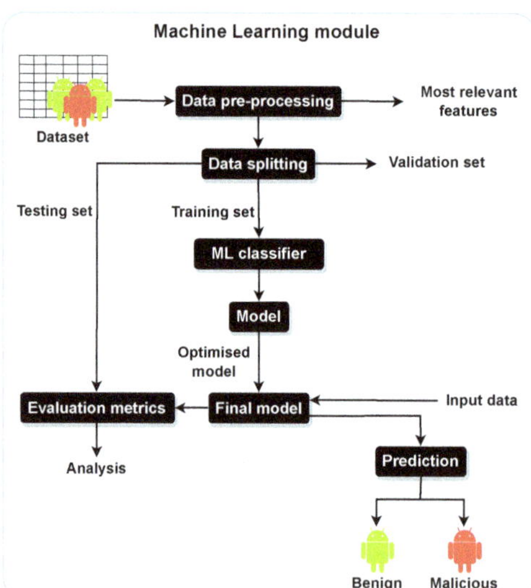

Figure 3. Partial block diagram of the proposed approach: data splitting for training and testing of the model with standard evaluation metrics. We also provide a validation set to perform hyperparameter tuning. The right-hand side arrow with input data refers to the use of data from real-world applications.

After the data pre-processing stage, three data subsets are obtained from the data splitting action: the training, testing, and validation sets. The training set is used to train/learn the model that, given input data, can make a prediction, in this case, to classify an app as benign or malicious. The testing set enables the analysis of the model through standard evaluation metrics. Based on the values reported by the evaluation metrics, the techniques used in the data pre-processing and data splitting phases can be changed or improved, thus leveraging the model's performance. The standard metrics also allow comparisons with the existing studies, as reported in Section 2.6.

Figure 4 depicts how the use of the validation set improves the model by evaluating it via the CV procedure and allowing for the tuning of the hyperparameters of the ML algorithms. This diagram also depicts the complete ML module, developed in the Python programming language, that is responsible for building, improving, and evaluating the model that will classify Android apps as benign or malicious.

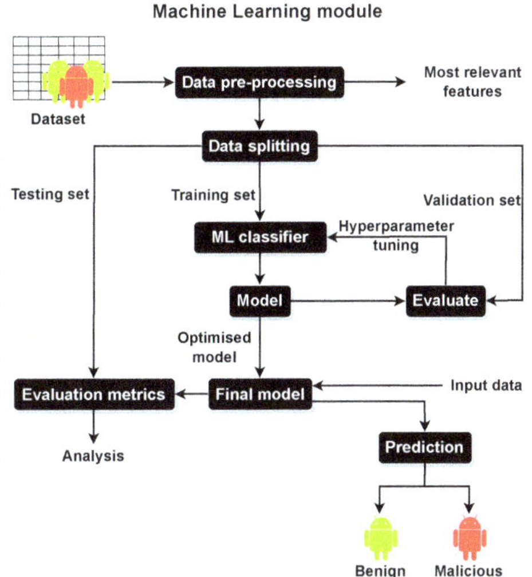

Figure 4. Full block diagram of the ML module, aggregating all the stages referenced in Figures 2 and 3 as well as the hyperparameter tunning stage.

3.2. Complete Approach—Full Block Diagram

A diagram completely representing our proposed approach is depicted in Figure 5. It incorporates the ML module from Figure 4, as well as the feature extraction module and Android applications, which are described next.

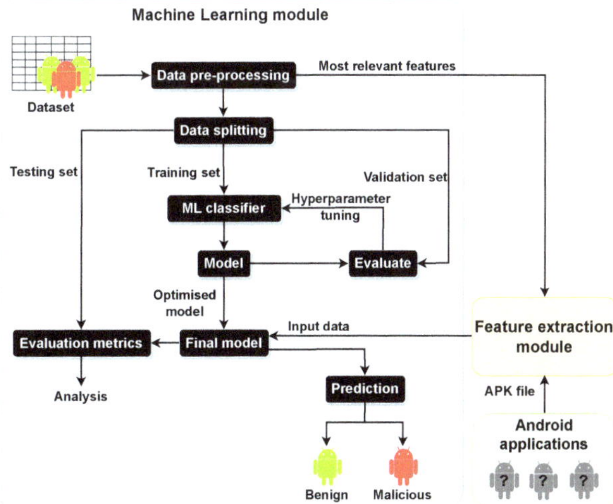

Figure 5. Full block diagram of the proposed approach with the ML module and the Android applications and feature extraction modules.

The feature extraction module follows a static analysis approach. It was developed in Python, and in Androguard, a tool and Python library to interact with Android files, which enables the extraction of the features from the Android app files. Thus, this module extracts static features from an Android app's APK file. The features sought for extraction were related to: permissions, classes, methods, intents, activities, services, receivers, providers, software, and hardware. These groups of features were preferred since they are often found in the analyzed datasets to be the most relevant features obtained via FS and are frequently mentioned in the literature in the context of static analysis.

The mapping between the extracted features and the features deemed more indicative of the presence of malware in Android apps provides the input data to the model, which can then classify/predict the Android application as benign or malicious. Here, a significant challenge emerged since the names of the features throughout the datasets are not standardized. For example, when extracting the names of the permissions required by the app, the feature `android.permission.SEND_SMS` is obtained. However, this feature in the Drebin dataset corresponds to `SEND_SMS` and in the AMSF dataset to `androidpermissionSEND_SMS`. This is an example of how the mapping between the dataset features and the features extracted from the APK file can be challenging. To improve the feature extraction module on this issue, an approach based on string similarity was adopted. With this, although the feature extraction module was not able to identify/map correctly all features, its mapping is improved.

Basic Android applications, shown on the bottom right hand side of Figure 5, were developed in the Kotlin programming language to allow for an assessment of the developed prototype of the proposed approach with real-world apps. The specifically developed apps were the following:

- 'App1', which tries to, unknowingly to the user, send an SMS message when the user clicks on the button in the app. Requests permissions regarding SMS and other features included in the top ten most relevant features in the Drebin and AMSF datasets.
- 'App2', which does not request/use any unnecessary features; thus, it is a benign app.
- 'App3', which requests permissions present among the most relevant features selected in the Drebin and AM datasets, although it does not require any of them for any functionality.

The expected labelling (ground-truth) for these apps is malicious, benign, and benign, respectively. Figure 6 depicts screen-shots of these apps.

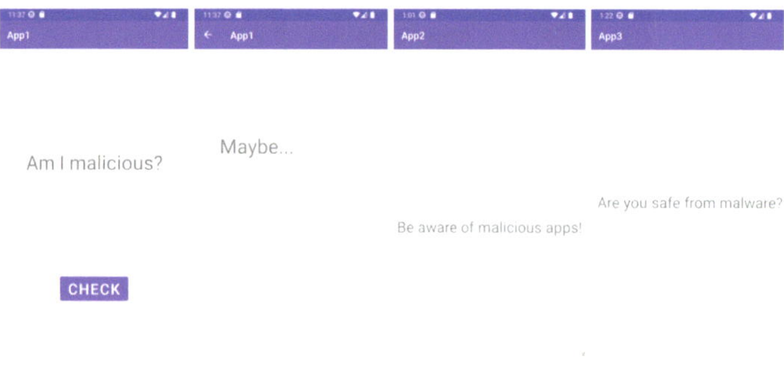

Figure 6. Developed Android applications: 'App1' (two images on the left hand-side), 'App2', and 'App3'.

4. Experimental Evaluation

We now report the experimental evaluation process, conducted using Python and the ML library 'scikit-learn'. We have considered the classifiers mentioned in Section 2.5 and the evaluation metrics described in Section 2.6.

This section is organized as follows. Section 4.1 performs dataset analysis. Baseline experimental results are presented in Section 4.2. Section 4.3 reports experimental results after applying some data pre-processing techniques. Section 4.4 presents the outcomes of applying FS. Section 4.5 displays the results obtained via CV and by performing hyperparameter tuning. Section 4.6 compares some of the obtained experimental results with those from existing studies. In Section 4.7, real-world Android applications are used to assess the prototype of the proposed approach. Finally, Section 4.8 provides an overall assessment of the experimental evaluation and a comparison with existing approaches.

4.1. Dataset Analysis

The datasets used were Drebin [14], CICAndMal2017 [15], Android Malware (AM) [16], and Android Malware static feature (AMSF) [17]. Since the proposed approach is based on static analysis, only static features are considered. Thus, dynamic features were removed if a dataset contained both types. The Drebin and AM datasets only have static features. However, the CICAndMal2017 dataset contained 110 static features and 73 dynamic features from a total of 183. The removal process was facilitated by the authors of the dataset, who properly identified the static and dynamic features. The AMSF dataset also presents static and dynamic features. Given that it was decomposed into six datasets, each one affiliated with a different group of features, only the ones containing static features were merged into the single dataset that was then used. Subsequently, the dimensionality of each used dataset is depicted in Table 2.

Table 2. Summary of the datasets considered in the experimental evaluation.

Dataset	Instances (n)	Features (d)	Available in
Drebin	15,036	215	[14]
CICAndMal2017	29,999	110	[15]
AM	11,476	182	[16]
AMSF	5019	966	[17]

The class distribution in the datasets was analyzed to evaluate if there were cases of strong imbalance. Table 3 depicts the number of instances (n) per class for each dataset.

Table 3. Class distribution for each dataset.

Dataset	Benign, n	Malicious, n	Total, n
Drebin	9476 (63.02%)	5560 (36.98%)	15,036
CICAndMal2017	9999 (33.33%)	20,000 (66.67%)	29,999
AM	8058 (70.22%)	3418 (29.78%)	11,476
AMSF	2508 (49.97%)	2511 (50.03%)	5019

Both the Drebin and CICAndMal2017 datasets present a ratio of approximately one-third between class labels. Thus, both datasets are not perfectly balanced but cannot be considered as imbalanced. The AM dataset is the most unbalanced among the chosen datasets, with the malicious class labels being less than half of the benign ones. The AMSF dataset is almost perfectly balanced. Regarding the data types of the features, Table 4 presents the number of features (d) of a categorical and non-categorical nature in each dataset. These datasets have many binary features.

Table 4. Categorical and non-categorical features (d) in each dataset.

Dataset	Categorical d	Non-Categorical d	Total d
Drebin	1	214	215
CICAndMal2017	5	105	110
AM	12	170	182
AMSF	0	966	966

Concerning the number of missing values, Table 5 exhibits the number of occurrences found in each dataset.

Table 5. Number of missing values in each dataset.

Dataset	Number of Missing Values
Drebin	0
CICAndMal2017	204
AM	19,888
AMSF	0

The Drebin and AMSF datasets have no missing values. The CICAndMal2017 dataset has 204 missing values, and the AM dataset contains 19,888 missing values. The AM dataset, among the used datasets, requires more data pre-processing tasks since it is the most unbalanced and contains the largest number of categorical features. Additionally, it possesses a high number of missing values. The Drebin and AMSF datasets require fewer data pre-processing tasks since they contain no missing values and their features are essentially numerical.

4.2. Experimental Results—Baseline

To perform the first experiments, two significant issues were addressed: categorical features and missing values, since some classifiers cannot deal with them. As a first approach, all categorical features were converted to numerical ones via label encoding. The missing values were dealt with by removing the instances that contained them unless all instances of a feature were missing; in that case, the feature was removed. On the first experiments, no validation set was obtained and no hyperparameter tuning was performed. Training and testing sets were obtained via a random stratified sampling with a 70–30 ratio for training and testing, respectively. Figures 7–9 summarize the results obtained for each dataset and classifier regarding the accuracy, F_1-score, and AUC-ROC metrics, respectively.

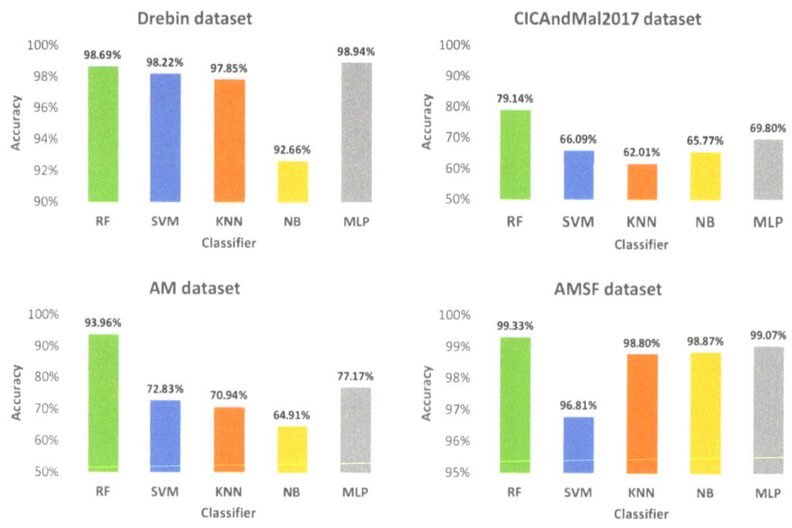

Figure 7. Accuracy (%) obtained with each classifier (RF, SVM, KNN, NB, and MLP) for each dataset. The average accuracy per classifier is 92.78%, 83.48%, 82.40%, 80.55%, and 86.24%, respectively.

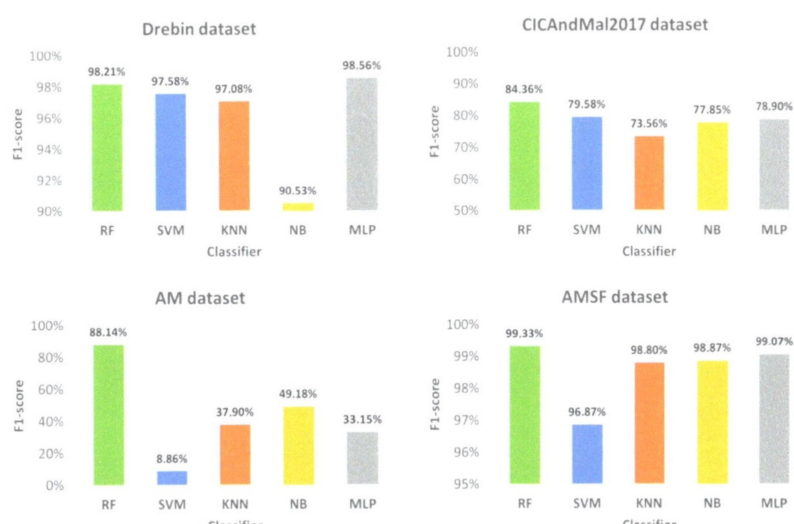

Figure 8. F1-score (%) obtained with each classifier (RF, SVM, KNN, NB, and MLP) for each dataset. The average F1-score per classifier is 92.51%, 70.72%, 76.83%, 79.10%, and 77.42%, respectively.

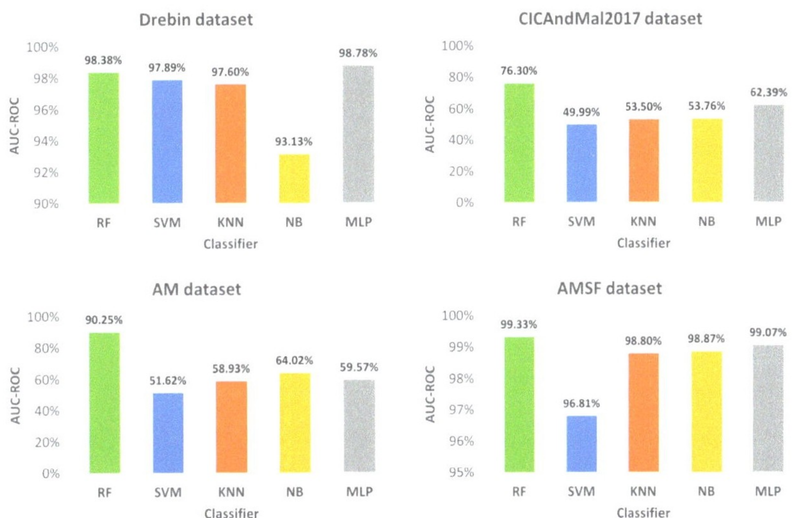

Figure 9. AUC-ROC (%) obtained with each classifier (RF, SVM, KNN, NB, and MLP) for each dataset. The average AUC-ROC per classifier is 91.06%, 74.07%, 77.20%, 77.44%, and 79.95%, respectively.

With the Drebin dataset, the best accuracy results were obtained by the MLP and RF classifiers, closely followed by SVM. Overall, all classifiers presented good results on this dataset, with the worst result being NB, with 92.66% accuracy, nevertheless a good result. The CICAndMal2017 dataset had the worst results, with the best one being 79.14% accuracy with the RF classifier and the worst 62.01% accuracy with the KNN classifier. With the AM dataset, the RF classifier obtained the best result, with the other classifiers showing less satisfactory results, with the lowest being 64.91% accuracy, with the NB classifier. For the AMSF dataset, 99.33% accuracy was obtained with the RF classifier, and the worst accuracy was 96.81% with the SVM classifier. For the F_1-score and the AUC-ROC metrics, the RF classifier attains the best results, which coincides with the findings in the literature. In the following experiments, we will address the most popular ML classifiers for this problem, which are the RF and SVM classifiers. The good results of the MLP classifier will be further explored in future work.

4.3. Experimental Results—Data Pre-Processing Stage

In this section, the results regarding different data pre-processing techniques are presented and compared with the baseline values. We address the handling of missing values, normalization, and numerosity balancing techniques.

4.3.1. Handling Missing Values

Initially, removing instances containing missing values was the method applied to deal with missing values, which yield data loss. Experiments with different methods to deal with missing values were performed to better understand their impact. We have considered the following approaches:

- Removing instances with missing values.
- Removing features with missing values.
- Missing value imputation with the mean of the explicit remaining feature values.

Since the Drebin and AMSF datasets had no missing values, only the CICAndMal2017 and AM datasets were considered in these experiments. Figure 10 depicts the accuracies obtained with different methods to deal with missing values on the AM dataset.

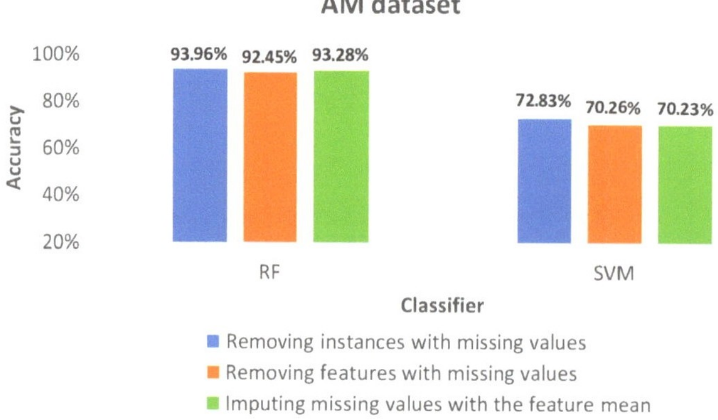

Figure 10. Accuracy (%) obtained, with the RF and SVM classifiers, for the AM dataset after applying different methods to deal with missing values.

The accuracy results obtained with the different methods to deal with missing values do not differ significantly. The same was verified with the remaining evaluation metrics. With both RF and SVM, removing instances containing missing values provided the best results in terms of accuracy. The corresponding results for the CICAndMal2017 dataset also did not vary substantially.

The results obtained by removing instances or features (containing missing values) do not differ significantly from the ones where the missing values are imputed with the estimated value based on the feature information. This is an indicator that the CICAnd-Mal2017 and AM datasets possess irrelevant data, maybe even harmful, for the training of the model. Thus, it is adequate to perform dimensionality reduction by using, for example, FS techniques. This is further explored in Section 4.4.

In the following experiments, missing value imputation with the mean strategy was the approach chosen since it does not yield data loss, being a straightforward approach that keeps the data distribution.

4.3.2. Normalization

The conversion of categorical to numerical features via label encoding can introduce large differences in the scales of features, mainly when applied to categorical features with many distinct values. Additionally, algorithms that rely on distance calculations, such as SVM, tend to be sensitive to feature scales. Normalizing features can improve the model performance and result in faster convergence since normalized features are often more interpretable by algorithms. Thus, min–max normalization was applied to accommodate values between zero and one while maintaining the original data distribution. Table 6 reports the experimental results for accuracy (Acc), F_1 score, and AUC-ROC with and without min–max normalization, for the RF and SVM classifiers for the datasets with the largest numbers of categorical features—the CICAndMal2017 and AM datasets.

Table 6. Accuracy (Acc), F_1 score and AUC-ROC with min–max normalization, using the RF and SVM classifiers on the CICAndMal2017 and AM datasets.

Classifier	Dataset	Normalization	Acc (%)	F_1 Score (%)	AUC-ROC (%)
RF	CICAndMal2017	None	79.81	84.82	77.40
		Min–max	79.62	84.72	77.06
RF	AM	None	93.28	88.02	90.28
		Min–max	93.28	88.05	90.33
SVM	CICAndMal2017	None	66.13	78.96	51.51
		Min–max	70.81	79.71	63.22
SVM	AM	None	70.23	0.00	50.00
		Min–max	90.88	82.77	85.89

Overall, the results with the RF classifier do not differ significantly, most likely because the RF algorithm does not rely on distance calculations and, thus, is generally more robust to large differences in the scales of features. The SVM classifier results greatly improve on the CICAndMal2017 and AM datasets. Namely, these results highlight how the accuracy metric can be misleading in some cases. Without min–max normalization, the SVM classifier achieved 66.13% accuracy on the CICAndMal2017 dataset. However, the AUC-ROC metric was 51.51%, suggesting a result close to a random classifier. With the min–max normalization, the AUC-ROC improved from 51.51% to 63.22%, and the accuracy improved from 66.13% to 70.81%.

These results were even more meaningful on the AM dataset, with the accuracy improving by approximately 20%, with normalization; the AUC-ROC value was previously 50% (a random classifier), and it reached 85.89% after min–max normalization. The Precision, Recall, and F_1 score metrics were 0.0%, with zero true positives. After min–max normalization, these indicators improved to 94.60%, 73.56%, and 82.77%, respectively.

4.3.3. Numerosity Balancing

To further improve the model, numerosity balancing techniques were applied to deal with data imbalance, namely, random undersampling, random oversampling, and the synthetic minority over-sampling technique (SMOTE) [20]. Table 7 reports the results, in terms of accuracy (Acc) and Recall (Rec), for the RF and SVM classifiers with the different numerosity balancing approaches for the AM dataset, the most imbalanced among all of the datasets.

Table 7. Accuracy (Acc) and Recall (Rec) values for the RF and SVM classifiers with the different numerosity balancing approaches for the AM dataset.

Classifier	Numerosity Balancing	Acc (%)	Rec (%)
RF	None	93.28	83.02
	Random undersampling	91.36	86.44
	Random oversampling	96.28	96.07
	SMOTE	94.06	91.39
SVM	None	70.81	86.00
	Random undersampling	89.18	82.44
	Random oversampling	89.47	82.75
	SMOTE	88.81	81.42

The results with the AM dataset improved significantly, with both RF and SVM classifiers, namely, with the use of random oversampling. Moreover, on the AM dataset the SVM classifier improved in terms of both accuracy and AUC-ROC, from 70.81% and 63.22%, respectively, to 89.47%. With the CICAndMal2017 dataset, the results also improved, especially with random oversampling and the RF classifier. On both Drebin and AMSF datasets, the results did not vary significantly.

Overall, random oversampling provided the best results, closely followed by SMOTE and random undersampling. The latter yields information loss, resulting in fewer training instances. SMOTE and random oversampling often provided the best results, not differing significantly between them. Random oversampling is more straightforward than SMOTE but can lead to overfitting; however, SMOTE is less prone to overfitting. Since the minority class is moderately imbalanced in the chosen datasets, random oversampling is effective. Thus, this was the chosen approach to numerosity balancing.

4.4. Experimental Results—Feature Selection

This section reports the experimental results obtained in the FS experiments, namely, with the RRFS algorithm by Ferreira and Figueiredo [19]. Different relevance measures were tested, namely, the supervised relevance measure FR and the unsupervised relevance measure MM. The redundancy measure used was the AC, with an allowed maximum similarity (M_s) between consecutive pairs of features of 0.3. Table 8 reports the accuracy (Acc) values for the SVM classifier on each dataset in the following settings: baseline (without FS), using RRFS with MM relevance, and using RRFS with the FR metric.

Table 8. Accuracy (Acc) obtained with the SVM classifier for each dataset, by not applying RRFS (original baseline) and by applying it with MM and FR relevance metrics.

Dataset	RRFS	Acc (%)
Drebin	None	98.50
	MM	94.71
	FR	96.66
CICAndMal2017	None	71.69
	MM	60.04
	FR	68.52
AM	None	89.47
	MM	86.99
	FR	84.55
AMSF	None	99.53
	MM	99.87
	FR	98.41

Overall, the results worsen slightly after applying RRFS, and the same applies to the RF classifier. However, these slight drops in accuracy in some of the results are arguably compensated for by the reduction in the number of features. The original number of features versus the number of features after applying the RRFS approach with different relevance measures for each dataset are presented in Figure 11.

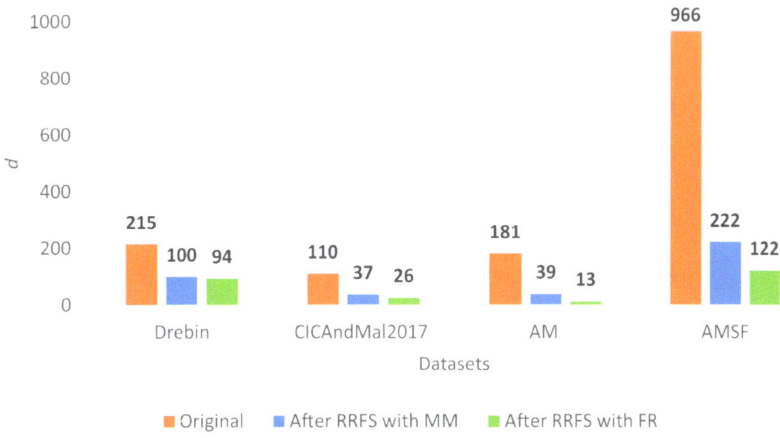

Figure 11. Number of features for each dataset, by not applying RRFS (original baseline) nnd by applying it with MM and FR relevance metrics.

Regardless of the relevance metric, the RRFS approach significantly reduced the number of features in each dataset. The supervised relevance measure FR led to a more considerable reduction in dimensionality than the unsupervised relevance measure MM. The number of reduced features combined with the evaluation metrics results indicate that the FR relevance measure presents overall better results. Thus, the use of the class label improves on the results for this task.

With the FR measure, a subset of the most relevant features is obtained. The RRFS approach continues by removing redundant features from this subset to obtain the best feature subset [19], consisting of the most relevant and non-redundant features.

The redundancy measure applied was the AC. The M_s value can define the maximum allowed similarity between pairs of features. Different values of M_s were tested (0.2, 0.3, and 0.4) to balance better the number of reduced features while maintaining good results in the evaluation metrics. The results obtained with different M_s were similar. However, a pattern could be seen where, typically, $M_s = 0.4$ would provide the best results, closely followed by $M_s = 0.3$ and then $M_s = 0.2$. The higher the M_s value, the less strict the selection is regarding redundancy between features; thus, more features are kept. Based on the results, to better accommodate both reducing features and maintaining good results, $M_s = 0.3$ seems to be the best choice.

Overall, the results with the SVM classifier seem to vary more with the use of FS than the results obtained with the RF classifier, with the latter being more robust to irrelevant features. The results with the SVM classifier suffered more influence of FS, with a tendency to get slightly worse. This could be because of the removal of too many features, which may oversimplify the model (underfitting), or the dimensionality reduction was too aggressive, leading to SVM struggling to find a reasonable decision boundary. However, the slightly worse results in terms of evaluation metrics are the cost of being able to reduce the dataset's dimensionality, with a reduction of 56% for the Drebin dataset, 76% for the CICAndMal2017 dataset, 92% for the AM dataset and 87% for the AMSF dataset.

Besides dimensionality reduction, RRFS enables the identification of the most relevant features for malware detection in Android apps, which is a key factor for the proposed approach. To better understand if the most relevant features follow a pattern or are the same among the different datasets, the five most decisive features are enumerated next.

For the Drebin dataset, RRFS (FR) selects:

1. `transact`
2. `SEND_SMS`
3. `Ljava.lang.Class.getCanonicalName`
4. `android.telephony.SmsManager`
5. `Ljava.lang.Class.getField`

For the CICAndMal2017 dataset, RRFS (FR) selects:

1. `Category`
2. `Price`
3. `Network communication : view network state (S)`
4. `Your location : access extra location provider commands (S)`
5. `System tools : set wallpaper (S)`

For the AM dataset, RRFS (FR) selects:

1. `com.android.launcher.permission.UNINSTALL_SHORTCUT`
2. `android.permission.VIBRATE`
3. `android.permission.ACCESS_FINE_LOCATION`
4. `name`
5. `android.permission.BLUETOOTH_ADMIN`
6. `android.permission.WAKE_LOCK`

For the AMSF dataset, RRFS (FR) selects:

1. `androidpermissionSEND_SMS`
2. `android.telephony.SmsManager.sendTextMessage`
3. `float-to-int`
4. `android.telephony.SmsManager`
5. `android.support.v4.widget`

The most relevant features in the Drebin and AMSF datasets are permissions and classes or methods. Permissions are the most relevant features in the AM dataset. In the CICAndMAl2017 dataset, the most relevant features are permissions and meta information. Summarizing, across the different datasets, we have that some of the most relevant features for Android malware detection are `android.permission.SEND_SMS` and `android.telephony.SmsManager`. Overall, we found that the most indicative features regarding the presence of malware in Android apps are permissions and typically SMS-related.

4.5. Experimental Results—CV and Hyperparameter Tuning

This section reports the experimental results obtained after performing the hyperparameter tuning of the RF and SVM classifiers and the use of CV. Initially, a random stratified split was applied to the datasets with a 70–30 ratio for training and testing, respectively, with no validation set considered and no hyperparameter tuning performed.

To perform the hyperparameter tuning of the RF and SVM classifiers, the function GridSearchCV [65] of the scikit-learn library was applied. This function performs an exhaustive search over specified parameter values for an estimator. The parameters of the estimator are optimized by CV. The training set is provided to the function, which splits it into training and validation sets. By default, the CV splitting strategy is stratified five-fold CV. This function also enables the specification of the hyperparameters to be optimized and their range of values.

The parameters we deemed more relevant and, thus, the parameters set during hyperparameter tuning were as follows. For the RF classifier, we considered:

- the number of trees in the range [100, 1000] with steps of 100.
- the maximum tree depth with the values 3, 5, 7, and None. The latter means the nodes are expanded until all leaves are pure or until all leaves contain less than the minimum number of samples required to split an internal node.
- the split quality measure as Gini, Entropy, or Log Loss.

For the SVM classifier, we considered:

- the regularization parameter (C) in the range [1, 20] with steps of 1.
- the kernel type to be used in the algorithm: the radial basis function (RBF) kernel, the polynomial kernel, the linear kernel, and the Sigmoid kernel.
- the kernel coefficient (gamma) for the previous kernel types (except the linear kernel).

Overall, the results improved across all evaluation metrics. However, this improvement did not surpass 2%, thus only slightly improving the performance.

To also perform CV with the training and testing sets, an outer loop for CV was added. In this case, we have a nested CV considering the CV performed in the GridSearchCV function with the training and validation sets. For the outer loop, 10-fold CV and LOOCV were applied. Here, the training time for the ML models frequently led to a "training time bottleneck" due to the limited computational resources, the number of iterations, and the number of hyperparameter combinations being tested. This was an even more significant issue with LOOCV, where the number of iterations matches the number of instances of the dataset used. As an attempt to sidestep this issue, the number of hyperparameter combinations in the GridSearchCV function was reduced by considering the values more often chosen in the optimization for each of the used datasets. However, some results still could not be obtained, namely, with LOOCV, which is much slower than 10-fold CV. Although it takes longer, its results are more stable and reliable than 10-fold CV since it uses more training samples and iterations. With 10-fold CV, some results were obtained, namely, in the form of the mean and standard deviation measures for each evaluation metric. Overall, the results were satisfying, with the mean values not differing substantially from those obtained after performing hyperparameter tuning, and the standard deviation obtained throughout the different evaluation metrics was low, indicating that the results are clustered around the mean, thus being more stable and reliable.

4.6. Comparative Analysis of Results—Discussion

In this section, some of the experimental results are compared to those from the literature, namely, the ones in Table 1. However, this comparison is not straightforward; often, the results are not directly comparable due to the use of different ML classifiers, datasets (that might not be available), and data pre-processing techniques that often are not fully described in the existing studies, with the source code also not being available for analysis. Thus, only comparisons deemed reasonable according to these aspects were made.

Since two of the datasets herein used, the Drebin and CICAndMal2017 datasets, are also used by Alkahtani and Aldhyani [4], the results obtained are briefly compared with theirs. These authors performed a random split, with 70% for training and 30% for testing. Regarding data pre-processing, only min–max normalization is mentioned. Aside from this, no other pre-processing methods or tuning of hyperparameters are mentioned. Thus, the methodology with which the results were obtained differs from ours. Since the authors did not use the RF classifier, we will compare only the SVM accuracy results. Table 9 summarizes these results.

Table 9. Comparison of the experimental results, in terms of Accuracy (%), obtained by Alkahtani and Aldhyani [4] with the SVM classifier with the ones obtained with the proposed approach using the same classifier.

Dataset	Alkahtani and Aldhyani	Proposed
Drebin	80.71	97.47
CICAndMal2017	100.00	73.22

The proposed approach presented better accuracy on the Drebin dataset, achieving 97.47% accuracy compared to the 80.71% reported by Alkahtani and Aldhyani [4]. However, regarding the CICAndMal2017 dataset, the proposed approach only achieved 73.22% compared to the accuracy of 100% claimed by the authors. This disparity in the obtained results between the two studies using the same datasets lies in the different approaches in the pre-processing applied, further emphasizing its importance since it significantly impacts the obtained results.

Regarding the most relevant features for malware detection in Android applications, Keyvanpour et al. [7] applied FS with effective and high-weight FS and reported the most relevant features on the Drebin dataset. Two features deemed more relevant to classify malware were SEND_SMS and android.telephony.SmsManager. These coincide with the most relevant features to classify malware obtained with the RRFS (with FR and $M_s = 0.3$) approach on the Drebin dataset where SEND_SMS ranked second and android.telephony.SmsManager ranked fourth, and on the AMSF dataset where they ranked first and fourth, respectively.

4.7. Experimental Results—Real-World Applications

In this section, the real-world application component of our proposed approach described in Section 3.2 and depicted in Figure 5 is assessed with real-world apps.

First, we check on the malware detection results with our three developed apps, referenced in Section 3.2 and depicted in Figure 6. The expected classifications for apps 'App1', 'App2', and 'App3', were malicious, benign, and benign, respectively. We train our ML model using each dataset and then we evaluate each app with that model. We assessed the predictions obtained with each model, and the results were as follows:

- 'App1' was classified as malicious, with the Drebin, CICAndMal2017, and AMSF datasets.
- 'App2' and 'App3' were classified as benign, with the Drebin, AM, and AMSF datasets.

To further test the developed approach, APK found online were used. As benign samples, APK of known apps were obtained from APKPure. The benign samples used were the APK files 'WhatsAppMessenger' and 'Amazon Shopping', and in both cases, they were correctly classified as benign when using the Drebin and AM datasets. Examples of malicious APK were obtained from the website [66] that presents a collection of Android malware samples. Three APK were used:

- an SMS stealer, which was classified by the ML model as benign, in most cases, thus not corresponding to the expected prediction;
- a ransomware disguised as a simple screen locker app, such that the ML model classified it as benign when learned with the Drebin and AM datasets and correctly as malicious with the CICAndMal2017 and AMSF datasets;
- an app that makes unwanted calls and has some obfuscation techniques, which the proposed approach correctly identified as malware with half of the datasets.

The proposed approach could not correctly identify malware in all cases, which was expected. The issue of feature mapping should be taken into account as it negatively influences the performance, often not identifying the features or misidentifying them. Additionally, some of the malware samples tested used obfuscation techniques, which are known to be a weakness of static analysis. Furthermore, the datasets used also greatly impact the obtained prediction.

4.8. Discussion of the Experimental Results

This section discusses and performs an overall assessment of the experimental results, with remarks on the techniques that achieved the best results across the different datasets.

The datasets that provided the best results starting at the baseline experiments were the ones requiring less data pre-processing, Drebin, and AMSF. Meanwhile, the datasets containing more missing values and categorical features, CICAndMal2017 and AM, provided worse results. AM is also the most unbalanced dataset out of the used datasets, yielding some extra learning challenges. Whether the dataset contained a large number of missing values, as was the case of the AM dataset, or none, as with Drebin and AMSF, the use of different techniques to handle missing values did not provide any noticeable result changes. Normalization was shown to greatly improve the results with the SVM classifier when there were significant differences in the scale of features, which is the case with datasets having many categorical features converted to numerical ones.

Often, the choices made in data pre-processing provided a better result for one dataset but a worse outcome for another. Thus, we found no ideal solution for all datasets. However, overall, the use of numerosity balancing techniques was shown to improve the results across all the datasets. Meanwhile, RRFS provided a significant reduction in the number of features at the cost of a slight metric decrease. Using RRFS, we were able to identify the top relevant features for classification, for each dataset. These features are mostly related to permissions and communications. The improvement of the FS stage is an aspect to improve on in future work. The extensive hyperparameter tuning stage provided very slight improvements (about 2%) on the key evaluation metrics.

5. Conclusions and Future Work

Malware in Android applications affects millions of users worldwide and is constantly evolving. Thus, its detection is a current and relevant problem. In the past few years, ML approaches have been proposed to mitigate malware in mobile applications. In this study, a prototype that resorts to ML techniques to detect malware in Android applications was developed. This task was formulated as a binary classification problem, and public domain datasets (Drebin, CICAndMal2017, AM, and AMSF) were used. Experiments were performed with RF, SVM, KNN, NB, and MLP classifiers, showing that the RF and SVM classifiers are the most suited for this problem.

Data pre-processing techniques were also explored to improve the results. Emphasis was given to FS by applying the RRFS approach to obtain the most relevant and non-redundant subset of features. Although RRFS provided slightly worse results regarding the evaluation metrics, these were arguably compensated for by the dimensionality reduction achieved in each of the used datasets. A reduction of 56% was achieved for the Drebin dataset, 76% for the CICAndMal2017 dataset, 92% for the AM dataset, and 87% for the AMSF dataset. Aside from the dimensionality reduction, RRFS selected the most relevant subset of features to identify the presence of malware. Overall, permissions have a prevalent presence among the most relevant features for Android malware detection.

A nested CV was used to evaluate the trained model better and to tune the ML algorithms hyperparameters, improving the final ML model. As for evaluation metrics, accuracy was used, but, since it can be misleading, other metrics were also applied.

The prototype of the proposed approach was assessed using real-world applications. Overall, the results were negatively impacted by the non-standardization of the dataset's feature names, which prevented accurate mapping between the extracted features and the most relevant subset of features.

The proposed approach can identify the most decisive features to classify an app as malware and greatly reduce the data dimensionality while achieving good results in identifying malware in Android applications across the various evaluation metrics.

In future work, more up-to-date datasets should be made available and used, and DL approaches and others should be further explored. Furthermore, the proposed approach could be extended to hybrid analysis and/or addressing this problem with a multiclass approach instead of a binary one. Lastly, the feature names across the datasets should have a more uniform designation and be aligned with the names of the features extracted from APK files.

Author Contributions: Conceptualization, A.F.; methodology, A.F.; software, C.P.; validation, C.P., A.F. and M.F.; writing—original draft preparation, C.P.; and writing—review and editing, C.P., A.F. and M.F. All authors have read and agreed to the published version of the manuscript.

Funding: This research was partially funded by FCT—Fundação para a Ciência e a Tecnologia, under grants number SFRH/BD/145472/2019 and UIDB/50008/2020; Instituto de Telecomunicações;

and Portuguese Recovery and Resilience Plan, through project C645008882-00000055 (NextGenAI, CenterforResponsibleAI) .

Institutional Review Board Statement: Not applicable.

Informed Consent Statement: Not applicable.

Data Availability Statement: The code and data are publicly available at https://github.com/CatarinaPalma-325/Android-Malware-Detection-with-Machine-Learning, accessed on 29 December 2023.

Conflicts of Interest: The authors declare no conflicts of interest.

References

1. How Many People Have Smartphones? | Oberlo. Available online: https://www.oberlo.com/statistics/how-many-people-have-smartphones (accessed on 29 December 2023).
2. Turner, A. Android vs. Apple Market Share: Leading Mobile OS. 2023. Available online: https://www.bankmycell.com/blog/android-vs-apple-market-share/ (accessed on 29 December 2023).
3. How Many Apps in Google Play Store? 2023. Available online: https://www.bankmycell.com/blog/number-of-google-play-store-apps/ (accessed on 29 December 2023).
4. Alkahtani, H.; Aldhyani, T.H. Artificial intelligence algorithms for malware detection in Android-operated mobile devices. *Sensors* **2022**, *22*, 2268. [CrossRef] [PubMed]
5. Pektaş, A.; Çavdar, M.; Acarman, T. Android Malware Classification by Applying Online Machine Learning. In *Computer and Information Sciences*; Czachórski, T., Gelenbe, E., Grochla, K., Lent, R., Eds.; Springer International Publishing: Cham, Switzerland, 2016; pp. 72–80.
6. Islam, R.; Sayed, M.I.; Saha, S.; Hossain, M.J.; Masud, M.A. Android malware classification using optimum feature selection and ensemble machine learning. *Internet Things Cyber-Phys. Syst.* **2023**, *3*, 100–111. [CrossRef]
7. Keyvanpour, M.R.; Barani Shirzad, M.; Heydarian, F. Android malware detection applying feature selection techniques and machine learning. *Multimed. Tools Appl.* **2023**, *82*, 9517–9531. [CrossRef]
8. Martín, A.; Calleja, A.; Menéndez, H.D.; Tapiador, J.; Camacho, D. ADROIT: Android malware detection using meta-information. In Proceedings of the 2016 IEEE Symposium Series on Computational Intelligence (SSCI), Athens, Greece, 6–9 December 2016; pp. 1–8.
9. Kouliaridis, V.; Kambourakis, G. A comprehensive survey on machine learning techniques for Android malware detection. *Information* **2021**, *12* 185. [CrossRef]
10. Wu, Q.; Zhu, X.; Liu, B. A survey of Android malware static detection technology based on machine learning. *Mob. Inform. Syst.* **2021**, *2021*, 8896013. [CrossRef]
11. Palma, C.; Ferreira, A.; Figueiredo, M. On the use of machine learning techniques to detect malware in mobile applications. In Proceedings of the 14th Simpósio de Informática (INForum), Porto, Portugal, 7–8 September 2023. Available online: https://www.inforum2023.org/Atas/paper_6478/6478-CR.pdf (accessed on 29 December 2023).
12. Muzaffar, A.; Hassen, H.R.; Lones, M.A.; Zantout, H. An in-depth review of machine learning based Android malware detection. *Comput. Secur.* **2022**, *121*, 102833. [CrossRef]
13. Alqahtani, E.J.; Zagrouba, R.; Almuhaideb, A. A Survey on Android Malware Detection Techniques Using Machine Learning Algorithms. In Proceedings of the 2019 Sixth International Conference on Software Defined Systems (SDS), Rome, Italy, 10–13 July 2019; pp. 110–117.
14. Android Malware Dataset for Machine Learning | Kaggle. Available online: https://www.kaggle.com/datasets/shashwatwork/android-malware-dataset-for-machine-learning (accessed on 29 December 2023).
15. Android Permission Dataset | Kaggle. Available online: https://www.kaggle.com/datasets/saurabhshahane/android-permission-dataset (accessed on 29 December 2023).
16. Android Malware Dataset | Kaggle. Available online: https://www.kaggle.com/datasets/saurabhshahane/android-malware-dataset (accessed on 29 December 2023).
17. Android Malware Static Feature Dataset (6 Datasets) | Kaggle. Available online: https://www.kaggle.com/datasets/laxman1216/android-static-features-datasets6-features (accessed on 29 December 2023).
18. Data Preprocessing in Machine Learning [Steps & Techniques]. Available online: https://www.v7labs.com/blog/data-preprocessing-guide (accessed on 29 December 2023).
19. Ferreira, A.; Figueiredo, M. Efficient feature selection filters for high-dimensional data. *Pattern Recognit. Lett.* **2012**, *33*, 1794–1804. [CrossRef]
20. Chawla, N.V.; Bowyer, K.W.; Hall, L.O.; Kegelmeyer, W.P. SMOTE: Synthetic minority over-sampling technique. *J. Artif. Intell. Res.* **2002**, *16*, 321–357. [CrossRef]
21. Witten, I.; Frank, E.; Hall, M.; Pal, C. *Data Mining: Practical Machine Learning Tools and Techniques*, 4th ed.; Morgan Kauffmann: Burlington, MA, USA, 2016.
22. Breiman, L. Random forests. *Mach. Learn.* **2001**, *45*, 5–32. [CrossRef]

23. Rokach, L.; Maimon, O. Top-down induction of decision trees classifiers—A survey. *IEEE Trans. Syst. Man Cybern. Part C Appl. Rev.* **2005**, *35*, 476–487. [CrossRef]
24. Alpaydin, E. *Introduction to Machine Learning*, 2nd ed.; The MIT Press: Cambridge, MA, USA, 2010.
25. Vapnik, V. *The Nature of Statistical Learning Theory*; Springer: Berlin/Heidelberg, Germany, 1999.
26. Support Vector Machines (SVM)—An Overview | By Rushikesh Pupale | Towards Data Science. Available online: https://towardsdatascience.com/https-medium-com-pupalerushikesh-svm-f4b42800e989 (accessed on 29 December 2023).
27. Aha, D.; Kibler, D.; Albert, M. Instance-based learning algorithms. *Mach. Learn.* **1991**, *6*, 37–66. [CrossRef]
28. Duda, R.; Hart, P.; Stork, D. *Pattern Classification*, 2nd ed.; John Wiley & Sons: Hoboken, NJ, USA, 2001.
29. Haykin, S. *Neural Networks: A Comprehensive Foundation*, 2nd ed.; Prentice Hall: Upper Saddle River, NJ, USA, 1999.
30. Bishop, C. *Neural Networks for Pattern Recognition*; Oxford University Press: Oxford, UK, 1995.
31. AlOmari, H.; Yaseen, Q.M.; Al-Betar, M.A. A Comparative Analysis of Machine Learning Algorithms for Android Malware Detection. *Procedia Comput. Sci.* **2023**, *220*, 763–768. [CrossRef]
32. Kouliaridis, V.; Kambourakis, G.; Peng, T. Feature Importance in Android Malware Detection. In Proceedings of the 2020 IEEE 19th International Conference on Trust, Security and Privacy in Computing and Communications (TrustCom), Guangzhou, China, 29 December 2020–1 January 2021; pp. 1449–1454. [CrossRef]
33. Kouliaridis, V.; Potha, N.; Kambourakis, G. Improving Android Malware Detection through Dimensionality Reduction Techniques. In *Machine Learning for Networking*; Renault, É., Boumerdassi, S., Mühlethaler, P., Eds.; Springer International Publishing: Cham, Switzerland, 2021; pp. 57–72.
34. Kouliaridis, V.; Kambourakis, G.; Geneiatakis, D.; Potha, N. Two Anatomists Are Better than One—Dual-Level Android Malware Detection. *Symmetry* **2020**, *12*, 1128. [CrossRef]
35. Potha, N.; Kouliaridis, V.; Kambourakis, G. An extrinsic random-based ensemble approach for android malware detection. *Connect. Sci.* **2021**, *33*, 1077–1093. [CrossRef]
36. Alqahtani, A.; Azzony, S.; Alsharafi, L.; Alaseri, M. Web-Based Malware Detection System Using Convolutional Neural Network. *Digital* **2023**, *3*, 273–285. [CrossRef]
37. Zhang, S.; Hu, C.; Wang, L.; Mihaljevic, M.J.; Xu, S.; Lan, T. A Malware Detection Approach Based on Deep Learning and Memory Forensics. *Symmetry* **2023**, *15*, 758. [CrossRef]
38. Alomari, E.S.; Nuiaa, R.R.; Alyasseri, Z.A.A.; Mohammed, H.J.; Sani, N.S.; Esa, M.I.; Musawi, B.A. Malware Detection Using Deep Learning and Correlation-Based Feature Selection. *Symmetry* **2023**, *15*, 123. [CrossRef]
39. Akhtar, M.S.; Feng, T. Malware Analysis and Detection Using Machine Learning Algorithms. *Symmetry* **2022**, *14*, 2304. [CrossRef]
40. Hashmi, S.A. Malware Detection and Classification on Different Dataset by Hybridization of CNN and Machine Learning. *Int. J. Intell. Syst. Appl. Eng.* **2023**, *12*, 650–667.
41. Djenna, A.; Bouridane, A.; Rubab, S.; Marou, I.M. Artificial Intelligence-Based Malware Detection, Analysis, and Mitigation. *Symmetry* **2023**, *15*, 677. [CrossRef]
42. Yang, S.; Wang, Y.; Xu, H.; Xu, F.; Chen, M. An Android Malware Detection and Classification Approach Based on Contrastive Lerning. *Comput. Secur.* **2022**, *123*, 102915. [CrossRef]
43. Lu, K.; Cheng, J.; Yan, A. Malware Detection Based on the Feature Selection of a Correlation Information Decision Matrix. *Mathematics* **2023**, *11*, 961. [CrossRef]
44. Adebayo, O.S.; Abdul Aziz, N. Improved malware detection model with apriori association rule and particle swarm optimization. *Secur. Commun. Netw.* **2019**, *2019*, 2850932. [CrossRef]
45. Zhang, Y.; Yang, S.; Xu, L.; Li, X.; Zhao, D. A Malware Detection Framework Based on Semantic Information of Behavioral Features. *Appl. Sci.* **2023**, *13*, 12528. [CrossRef]
46. Daoudi, N.; Samhi, J.; Kabore, A.K.; Allix, K.; Bissyandé, T.F.; Klein, J. DexRay: A Simple, yet Effective Deep Learning Approach to Android Malware Detection Based on Image Representation of Bytecode. In *Deployable Machine Learning for Security Defense*; Wang, G., Ciptadi, A., Ahmadzadeh, A., Eds.; Springer International Publishing: Cham, Switzerland, 2021; pp. 81–106.
47. Kabakuş, A.T. Hybroid: A Novel Hybrid Android Malware Detection Framework. *Erzincan Univ. J. Sci. Technol.* **2021**, *14*, 331–356. [CrossRef]
48. Aboaoja, F.A.; Zainal, A.; Ghaleb, F.A.; Al-rimy, B.A.S.; Eisa, T.A.E.; Elnour, A.A.H. Malware Detection Issues, Challenges, and Future Directions: A Survey. *Appl. Sci.* **2022**, *12*, 8482. [CrossRef]
49. Agrawal, P.; Trivedi, B. A Survey on Android Malware and their Detection Techniques. In Proceedings of the 2019 IEEE International Conference on Electrical, Computer and Communication Technologies (ICECCT), Coimbatore, India, 20–22 February 2019; pp. 1–6. [CrossRef]
50. Almomani, I.; Ahmed, M.; El-Shafai, W. Android malware analysis in a nutshell. *PLoS ONE* **2022**, *17*, e0270647. [CrossRef]
51. Deldar, F.; Abadi, M. Deep Learning for Zero-Day Malware Detection and Classification: A Survey. *ACM Comput. Surv.* **2023**, *56*, 1–37. [CrossRef]
52. Faruki, P.; Bhan, R.; Jain, V.; Bhatia, S.; El Madhoun, N.; Pamula, R. A Survey and Evaluation of Android-Based Malware Evasion Techniques and Detection Frameworks. *Information* **2023**, *14*, 374. [CrossRef]
53. Gyamfi, N.K.; Goranin, N.; Ceponis, D.; Čenys, H.A. Automated System-Level Malware Detection Using Machine Learning: A Comprehensive Review. *Appl. Sci.* **2023**, *13*, 11908. [CrossRef]

54. Liu, K.; Xu, S.; Xu, G.; Zhang, M.; Sun, D.; Liu, H. A Review of Android Malware Detection Approaches Based on Machine Learning. *IEEE Access* **2020**, *8*, 124579–124607. [CrossRef]
55. Meijin, L.; Zhiyang, F.; Junfeng, W.; Luyu, C.; Qi, Z.; Tao, Y.; Yinwei, W.; Jiaxuan, G. A Systematic Overview of Android Malware Detection. *Appl. Artif. Intell.* **2022**, *36*, 2007327. [CrossRef]
56. Naseer, M.; Rusdi, J.F.; Shanono, N.M.; Salam, S.; Muslim, Z.B.; Abu, N.A.; Abadi, I. Malware Detection: Issues and Challenges. *J. Phys. Conf. Ser.* **2021**, *1807*, 012011. [CrossRef]
57. Odusami, M.; Abayomi-Alli, O.; Misra, S.; Shobayo, O.; Damasevicius, R.; Maskeliunas, R. Android Malware Detection: A Survey. In *Applied Informatics*; Florez, H., Diaz, C., Chavarriaga, J., Eds.; Springer International Publishing: Cham, Switzerland, 2018; pp. 255–266.
58. Razgallah, A.; Khoury, R.; Hallé, S.; Khanmohammadi, K. A survey of malware detection in Android apps: Recommendations and perspectives for future research. *Comput. Sci. Rev.* **2021**, *39*, 100358. [CrossRef]
59. Souri, A.; Hosseini, R. A State-of-the-Art Survey of Malware Detection Approaches Using Data Mining Techniques. *Hum.-Centric Comput. Inf. Sci.* **2018**, *8*, 3. [CrossRef]
60. Qiu, J.; Zhang, J.; Luo, W.; Pan, L.; Nepal, S.; Xiang, Y. A Survey of Android Malware Detection with Deep Neural Models. *ACM Comput. Surv.* **2020**, *53*, 1–36. [CrossRef]
61. Vasani, V.; Bairwa, A.K.; Joshi, S.; Pljonkin, A.; Kaur, M.; Amoon, M. Comprehensive Analysis of Advanced Techniques and Vital Tools for Detecting Malware Intrusion. *Electronics* **2023**, *12*, 4299. [CrossRef]
62. Wang, D.; Chen, T.; Zhang, Z.; Zhang, N. A Survey of Android Malware Detection Based on Deep Learning. In *Machine Learning for Cyber Security*; Xu, Y., Yan, H., Teng, H., Cai, J., Li, J., Eds.; Springer International Publishing: Cham, Switzerland, 2023; pp. 228–242.
63. Guyon, I.; Gunn, S.; Nikravesh, M.; Zadeh, L. (Eds.) *Feature Extraction, Foundations and Applications*; Springer: Berlin/Heidelberg, Germany, 2006.
64. Guyon, I.; Elisseeff, A. An introduction to variable and feature selection. *J. Mach. Learn. Res. (JMLR)* **2003**, *3*, 1157–1182.
65. sklearn.model_selection.GridSearchCV—Scikit-Learn 1.3.1 Documentation. Available online: https://scikit-learn.org/stable/modules/generated/sklearn.model_selection.GridSearchCV.html (accessed on 29 December 2023).
66. Not So Boring Android Malware | Android-Malware-Samples. Available online: https://maldroid.github.io/android-malware-samples/ (accessed on 29 December 2023).

Article

Efficient and Expressive Search Scheme over Encrypted Electronic Medical Records

Xiaopei Yang [1], Yu Zhang [1,*], Yifan Wang [2] and Yin Li [3]

[1] School of Computer and Information Technology, Xinyang Normal University, Xinyang 464031, China; xiaopei94@xynu.edu.cn
[2] Department of Computer Science, Wayne State University, 42 W Warren Ave, Detroit, MI 48202, USA; yifan.wang2@wayne.edu
[3] School of Cyberspace Security, Dongguan University of Technology, Dongguan 523820, China; liyin@dgut.edu.cn
* Correspondence: zhangyu86@xynu.edu.cn

Abstract: In recent years, there has been rapid development in computer technology, leading to an increasing number of medical systems utilizing electronic medical records (EMRs) to store their clinical data. Because EMRs are very private, healthcare institutions usually encrypt these data before transferring them to cloud servers. A technique known as searchable encryption (SE) can be used by healthcare institutions to encrypt EMR data. This technique enables searching within the encrypted data without the need for decryption. However, most existing SE schemes only support keyword or range searches, which are highly inadequate for EMR data as they contain both textual and digital content. To address this issue, we have developed a novel searchable symmetric encryption scheme called SSE-RK, which is specifically designed to support both range and keyword searches, and it is easily applicable to EMR data. We accomplish this by creating a conversion technique that turns keywords and ranges into vectors. These vectors are then used to construct index tree building and search algorithms that enable simultaneous range and keyword searches. We encrypt the index tree using a secure K-Nearest Neighbor technique, which results in an effective SSE-RK approach with a search complexity that is quicker than a linear approach. Theoretical and experimental study further demonstrates that our proposed scheme surpasses previous similar schemes in terms of efficiency. Formal security analysis demonstrates that SSE-RK protects privacy for both data and queries during the search process. Consequently, it holds significant potential for a wide range of applications in EMR data. Overall, our SSE-RK scheme, which offers improved functionality and efficiency while protecting the privacy of EMR data, generally solves the shortcomings of the current SE schemes.

Keywords: searchable symmetric encryption; electronic medical record; keyword search; range search; search over encrypted data

Citation: Yang, X.; Zhang, Y.; Wang, Y.; Li, Y. Efficient and Expressive Search Scheme over Encrypted Electronic Medical Records. *Information* **2023**, *14*, 643. https://doi.org/10.3390/info14120643

Academic Editors: Jose de Vasconcelos, Hugo Barbosa and Carla Cordeiro

Received: 19 October 2023
Revised: 25 November 2023
Accepted: 29 November 2023
Published: 30 November 2023

1. Introduction

Electronic medical records use electronic devices to preserve and manage digital clinical medical records, thus replacing traditional handwritten ones. Over the past few years, with the continued development of information technology, an increasing number of medical systems are using EMRs as routine storage means. The large number of EMRs will entail large management costs for healthcare organizations. To solve this issue, EMRs can be outsourced to cloud computing service systems that have powerful storage and computing capabilities. Since medical data are highly private, medical institutions usually need to encrypt EMR data before uploading them to cloud servers to protect patient privacy. However, this protection method brings great inconvenience to the EMR retrieval operation. A simple way is to download all EMR data stored on the cloud platform to the user side and then retrieve them locally. However, this approach will cause great transmission consumption. To improve search efficiency, we can use searchable encryption

(SE) technology to encrypt these documents. This encryption technology can retrieve encrypted EMRs without decrypting them, and it can return the target documents to the querying user while protecting data security.

Motivation. SE allows data users to retrieve encrypted documents that are stored on cloud servers by utilizing an encrypted token without decrypting the documents. Thus far, most SE schemes support either multi-keywords search [1–3] or range search [4–6]. But, in a medical system, data users will perform a query containing both digital and textual fields. For an electronic medical record [7], it may contain both digital values and keywords. As shown in Figure 1, age and ID are numeric fields, while gender, disease, and department are keyword fields. Moreover, the user's query also contains both range and keywords content, e.g., age $\in$ [18, 45] AND disease $\in$ (diabetes, enteritis). If an SE scheme supporting only keyword search or range search is used to implement searching over encrypted EMR data, two EMR systems will be maintained: one that contains only text fields, and the other that contains only numeric fields. This not only increases the time and space complexities of the search process, but also reveals more intermediate information. Considering such an actual demand, it is necessary to build a SE scheme that can support range and keyword searches simultaneously.

ID	Gender	Age	Disease	Department
1	Male	60	Diabetes	Endocrine
2	Female	39	Cardiopathy	Cardiology
3	Male	70	Lung Cancer	Oncology
4	Male	23	Enteritis	Gastroenterology
5	Female	32	Conjunctivitis	Ophthalmology

Figure 1. An example of an electronic medical record.

Recently, two SE schemes [8,9] were proposed to satisfy the above practical need. In [8], Miao et al. proposed a conversion method that can transform digital points and keywords in each document to a vector representation. Using a secure K-Nearest Neighbor (KNN) algorithm to protect vector confidentiality, they presented an encryption scheme that can support range and keyword search simultaneously. Later, Wang et al. presented a SE scheme supporting spatial keyword queries. Their solution can support arbitrary geometry, as well as keyword, queries, which can be applied to realize both textual keywords and digital range queries. In their scheme, by utilizing the techniques of gray code and bloom filter, files and queries can be transformed into a series of "0-1-*" strings. For privacy preserving purposes, the obtained strings are encrypted by applying the symmetric-key hidden vector encryption (SHVE) scheme [10].

However, the above two schemes still have two issues that are causes for concern. First, only integer range query is supported in these two schemes. The reason why these two schemes cannot support decimal range searches stems from the specificity of their core methods. The scheme given in [8] uses the modulo operation to support multi-dimensional range queries. Since the modulo operation is an integer operation, this scheme can only support integer range queries. The scheme presented in [9] adopts the "gray code" encoding method to convert ranges into "0-1" bit strings. This encoding method only supports integer ranges as a legal input. However, in an electronic medical record, the range query containing decimals is very common, such as white blood cell count, blood glucose level, tumor size, etc. To overcome this shortcoming, two range encoding methods have to be given to implement range search, which can support range searches with decimals. Second, the efficiency of these two schemes could be still improved. More precisely, the scheme proposed in [8] adopts an index structure with a linear search time complexity, while the scheme in [9] will enumerate many gray codes to perform a range search. To address this issue, we take advantage of the tree-based index structure to construct an efficient SSE scheme that supports range and keyword queries simultaneously.

Contributions. In the interest of clarity, we list the major contributions of this article.

(1) We propose a keyword conversion method that can transform a collection of keywords into a vector. Furthermore, based on the characteristics of the range query, we give two ways through which to convert a range query into a vector. These vectors can be utilized to perform both range and keyword searches efficiently.

(2) We design an index tree construction algorithm to speed up the query process. The internal node of the index tree contains only one range vector, and the leaf node contains a small number of vectors for both points and keywords. Based on the index tree, through an efficient prune algorithm, the query time of the proposed scheme is sublinear to the number of documents.

(3) Through using the secure KNN scheme [11] to encrypt the index tree and query, we propose an SSE scheme that can support both range and keyword queries (SSE-RK), which can be applied in searching electronic medical records efficiently.

To show the security of the proposed scheme, we will give a detailed security analysis of SSE-RK. In addition, we conducted quantitative experiments on SSE-RK on a medical dataset. The experimental results show that the proposed scheme can effectively perform ciphertext retrieval on EMR data.

Related Work. According to the characteristics of its secret key, searchable encryption (SE) schemes are usually divided into symmetrical and asymmetrical approaches.

For searchable symmetric encryption (SSE), the data uploader and the authorized query user hold the same key. Song et al. [12] designed the first SSE scheme, which only supports single keyword queries. Goh then developed a more formal definition of security for SSE, and they utilized Bloom Filter technology to build an SSE scheme [13] that supports multi-keyword queries. Subsequently, many works [14–17] have focused on the efficiency improvement of SSE schemes. However, these schemes will return all the matched documents without sorting, which requires a great deal of computing and communication costs. To address this problem, two SSE schemes that support ranked search were proposed in [18,19]. A ranked search scheme will return the k most relevant documents based on a given similarity evaluation criterion. As a result, the solution will significantly reduce communication and storage consumption. In response to the problem that the scheme in [18,19] only supports single-keyword queries, Cao et al. proposed a ranked search scheme that supports multi-keyword queries [20]. However, the query efficiency of this scheme is linearly related to the number of documents due to its using a forward index. To improve the query efficiency, tree index-based schemes were proposed in [21,22]. The search time complexity of these schemes is sublinear to the number of documents. Recently, Liu et al. [23] presented a scheme for protecting spatial data privacy and user query privacy in location-based service providers (LBSP). The scheme uses Hilbert curves and an SSE algorithm as the basic building blocks to achieve accurate range queries. By utilizing a special inverted index structure and an oblivious memory access algorithm, an SSE scheme that supports single-keyword range queries with efficient performance was proposed in [24]. Zheng et al. [25] proposed an efficient and privacy-preserving exact set similarity search scheme under a single cloud server using symmetric key predicate encryption and B^{+}-tree indexing. By combining attribute-based encryption (ABE) with fog computing architecture, a secure and efficient fine-grained searchable data sharing and management scheme in IoT-based smart healthcare systems was introduced in [26]. This scheme can achieve secure and efficient fine-grained searchable data sharing and management. In addition, there are many works devoted to constructing SSE schemes with more expressive queries, such as semantic search [27,28] and fuzzy search [29,30], which greatly improve the flexibility of ciphertext retrieval schemes. Considering that the attributes of a document will contain both digital and keyword content, two SSE schemes [8,9] that support range and keyword queries simultaneously were proposed to meet this practical requirement. But, the efficiency and functionality of these schemes can be improved. Thus, we designed a scheme to solve these problems in this paper.

Searchable asymmetric encryption, also known as searchable public key encryption (SPE), contains a pair of secret keys in which the public key is used to encrypt the data and the private key is used for privacy queries. Boneh et al. first proposed the definition of SPE, and they created an SPE scheme that supports single keyword retrieval [31]. To support conjunctive keyword searches, Park et al. proposed a public key encryption with conjunctive keyword search (PECK) scheme [32]. To support disjunctive keyword searches, Katz et al. proposed a predicate encryption scheme [33]. To support both conjunctive and disjunctive keyword retrieval, Zhang and Lu proposed a public key encryption with a conjunctive and disjunctive keyword search (PECDK) scheme [34], which is based on the inner product encryption scheme [35]. To increase the security of SPE, an SPE that resists keyword guessing attacks [36] and an SPE with access control capability [37] have also received more attention.

Organization. The structure of this paper is as follows. The formal definition of the system and security model will be given in Section 2, and the design goals of the proposed scheme are introduced. Various conversion methods, index generation, and retrieval algorithms will be given in Section 3. Section 4 will give the concrete scheme and the security analysis of the scheme. Theoretical and experimental analysis will be given in Section 5. Section 6 concludes the paper.

2. Problem Formulation

First, we define the system model of the SSE-RK scheme. Then, the threat model faced by the SSE-RK scheme is presented. Finally, we summarize the design goals of the SSE-RK scheme. For the sake of clarity, we summarize the notation of this paper in Table 1.

Table 1. Notation descriptions in the SSE-RK scheme.

F	A set of documents $\{f_1, f_2, \ldots, f_d\}$.
d	The number of documents in F
$DIC = \{dic_1, dic_2, \ldots, dic_N\}$	The dictionary of a corpus.
$W_i = \{w_{i1}, w_{i2}, \ldots, w_{i|W_i|}\}$	The keyword set for the document f_i, where $i \in [1, d]$.
$|W_i|$	The number of keywords in W_i, and $i \in [1, N]$.
w_{ij}	The j-th keywords in W_i, and $i \in [1, N], j \in [1, |W_i|]$.
$\overrightarrow{W_i}$	The vector representation for W_i.
$p_i = \{x_{i1}, x_{i2}, \ldots, x_{im}\}$	The multi-dimension point for a document f_i, where $i \in [1, d]$.
m	The dimension of a multi-dimension point.
u	A node in the index tree.
I_u	The encrypted node u in the index.
I_T	The encrypted index tree of F.
u_p	The vector set for a multi-dimension point in a leaf node u.
$\overrightarrow{u_W}$	The vector representation for a keyword set in a leaf node u.
$\overrightarrow{u_R}$	The vector representation for a range in an internal node u.
$Q = (Q_R, Q_W)$	A query tuple.
Q_R	A query range.
Q_W	A query keyword set.
$\overrightarrow{Q_R}$	The vector representation used to search internal nodes.
Q_P	The vector set for search leaf nodes.
$\overrightarrow{Q_W}$	The vector representation for making keyword search.
T_Q	The trapdoor of the query Q.

2.1. System Model

As shown in Figure 2, similar with most SSE schemes [12–16], the system model of SSE-KR consists of three different roles: data owner (DO), data user (DU), and cloud server (CS). For SSE-RK, four main protocols are included: key generation, index building, trapdoor generation, and secure search. Specifically, the responsibility of the DO is to encrypt all documents, build secure indexes, and send them to a CS. The responsibility of the DU is to issue queries, i.e., generate secure trapdoors, and to send them to a CS. The CS is responsible for performing the secure search and returning the query results to the DU.

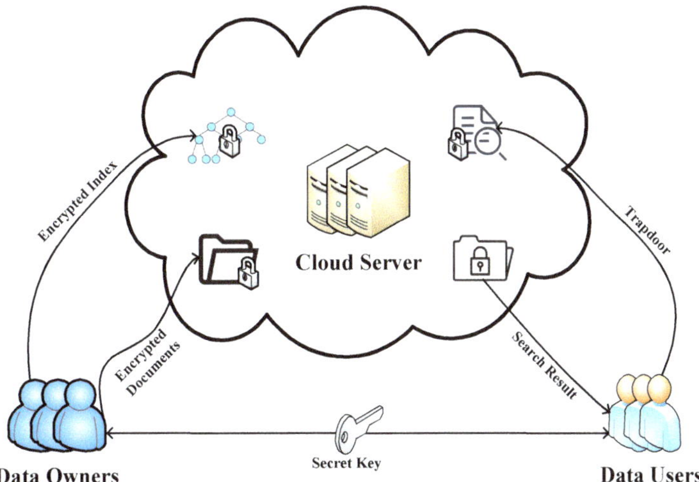

Figure 2. System model of SSE-RK.

To clarify the system model, the specific duties for each role are formally described as follows.

(1) Data owner (DO). Before outsourcing a document set $F = \{f_1, f_2, \ldots, f_d\}$ to a CS, the DO first generates the secret key, then encrypts F using traditional symmetric encryption algorithms (e.g., AES, etc.), and then constructs a secure index using the generated key. Finally, they upload the encrypted data and the secure index to a CS for storage. When a legitimate DU requests a query, the DO shares the secret key with the legitimate DU through authorization.

(2) Data user (DU). When an authorized DU wants to launch a query Q, DU generates a trapdoor using the secret key shared by DO. After this, the DU sends the trapdoor to a CS. Once the DU receives the encrypted documents back from a CS, they decrypt these documents using the secret key to recover the original plaintext.

(3) Cloud server (CS). The main function of a CS is to store files and perform retrieval. A CS stores the encrypted data and secure index uploaded by the DO. When an authorized DU uploads a trapdoor without any decryption, a CS performs a matching query on the secure index and the trapdoor, as well as returns the encrypted result of the query to the DU.

2.2. Threat Model

Through this paper, like many SE schemes [19–21], we assume that the DO and DU are credible and that the CS is "honest-but-curious". This means that the CS executes algorithms of SSE-RK honestly and correctly, but it will curiously infer and analyze obtained data to learn extra private information. According to the above assumption, the two threat models introduced in [20] were considered in the proposed scheme.

-   **Known ciphertext model.** Only contains information of ciphertexts, secure indexes, and trapdoors that can be obtained by a CS, which means that only ciphertext-only attacks can be performed in this model.
-   **Known background model.** A CS can obtain more background knowledge, e.g., term frequency (TF)-inverse document frequency (IDF), than the aforementioned model. This information is commonly acquired from documents by statistical means. The CS can conduct the statistical attack by utilizing such information.

2.3. Design Goals

Recall that our goal is to create a secure, efficient SSE scheme that supports both range and keyword searches. For the sake of clarity, we present the explicit design goals as follows.

(1) **Functionality.** The document f_i of SSE-RK contains a point set $p_i = \{x_{i1}, x_{i2}, \ldots, x_{im}\}$ and a keyword set $W_i = \{w_{i1}, w_{i2}, \ldots, w_{i|W_i|}\}$. The query Q of SSE-RK can be a hybrid of a range set $Q_R = \{[a_1, b_1], [a_2, b_2], \ldots, [a_m, b_m]\}$ and a keyword query $Q_W = \{q_1, q_2, \ldots, q_s\}$. The search result of the SSE-RK scheme can be ranked, thus meaning that SSE-RK only returns documents whose point x_{ij} is in the query range $[a_j, b_j]$ and whose keyword set W_i is strongly correlated with the query keywords Q_W as the search result, where $i \in [1, d]$ and $j \in [1, s]$.
(2) **Efficiency.** The query time of the SSE-RK is sublinear to the number of documents. Specifically, the proposed scheme has better search efficiency than other similar schemes without sacrificing much index building efficiency.
(3) **Privacy preserving.** Similar to previous schemes [19–21], the SSE-RK scheme disallows CSs to obtain extra private information. This information can be inferred from ciphertexts, secure indexes, and trapdoors. More explicitly, we list the privacy requirement of SSE-RK as follows.

    -   *Index and trapdoor privacy.* SSE-RK prevents CSs from inferring plaintext information that is hidden in indexes and trapdoors. That is to say, information including points, keywords, and their corresponding vectors cannot be disclosed to CSs.
    -   *Trapdoor unlinkability.* In real-world scenarios, CSs sometimes receive the same query request. If a CS can easily capture two trapdoors that are generated from a single query request, an adversary can launch statistical attacks, e.g., an increase in the frequency of a certain query may indicate that the user tends to retrieve popular content, thus compromising the privacy of the query request.
    -   *Keyword privacy.* CSs cannot utilize background knowledge and statistics to infer whether a trapdoor contains a particular keyword. When CSd can infer the frequency of keyword occurrences from the trapdoor, it can infer the main content of the ciphertext data.

3. Algorithms for Index Building and Searching

We first introduce some of the useful conversion methods used in the proposed scheme, which includes a keyword conversion approach and two range conversion methods. Then, based on these conversion methods, we present a method for building an index tree. This method consists of three steps: the construction of leaf nodes based on all documents; the construction of internal nodes based on all leaf nodes; and the use of a recursive algorithm that builds an index tree based on all nodes. Finally, the algorithm for searching the index tree is presented. A detailed description of these methods is proposed in the following sub-sections.

3.1. Keyword Conversion Method

In the proposed scheme, both the document and query are converted into vectors. When a query is executed, by calculating the similarity between vectors, the documents with the highest scores are returned as the search result. In our scheme, we take advantage of a keyword conversion method based on a term weighting formula called TF−IDF to implement rank search [20]. Through adopting the TF$-$IDF formula, a document and a query are converted into a TF-vector and an IDF-vector, respectively. Similar to the method introduced in [28,38], we introduce the keyword conversion method adopted in SSE-RK as follows.

(1) Creating a dictionary $DIC = \{dic_1, dic_2, \ldots, dic_N\}$ by extracting keywords in the corpus, where dic_t is a keyword and $t \in [1, N]$.

(2) Given a keyword set $W_i = \{w_{i1}, w_{i2}, \ldots, w_{i|W_i|}\}$, this approach first creates a zero vector $\overrightarrow{W_i} = \{x_{i1}, x_{i2}, \ldots, x_{iN}\}$. Then, it sets $x_{it} = TF_{w_{ij}}$ according to the Equation (1) if $w_{ij} = dic_t$, where $t \in [1, N]$, $i \in [1, d]$ and $j \in [1, |W_i|]$.

$$TF_{w_{ij}} = \frac{1 + ln(n_{w_{ij}})}{\sqrt{\sum_{w_{ij} \in W_i}(1 + ln(n_{w_{ij}}))^2}} \tag{1}$$

In Equation (1), $n_{w_{ij}}$ is the number of times w_{ij} appears in the document f_i.

(3) Given a keyword set $Q_W = \{q_1, q_2, \ldots, q_s\}$, this approach first initializes a zero vector $\overrightarrow{Q_W} = \{v_1, v_2, \ldots, v_N\}$. Then, it sets $v_t = IDF_{q_j}$ according to the Equation (2) if $q_j = dic_t$, where $t \in [1, N]$ and $j \in [1, s]$.

$$IDF_{q_j} = ln(1 + \frac{N}{n_{q_j}}) \tag{2}$$

The variable n_{q_j} in Equation (2) represents the number of documents that contains the keyword q_j.

Given $\overrightarrow{W_i}$ and $\overrightarrow{Q_W}$, we can utilize Equation (3) to calculate the similarity between f_i and Q_W.

$$Score(f_i, Q_W) = \overrightarrow{W_i} \cdot \overrightarrow{Q_W} \tag{3}$$

We can obtain a list of documents that are most relevant to the query by taking advantage of the similarity score between each document and the query.

3.2. Range Conversion Methods

For range queries, there are two frequently used operations. The first is to check whether a value x is in the range of $[a, b]$; the last is to judge whether a range $[x, y]$ intersects with a range $[a, b]$. In this subsection, to adopt the vector space model mentioned previously, we present two range conversion methods to vectorize these two operations as above.

Method M_1. Given a value x and a range $[a, b]$, we can construct Equation (4) to check whether $x \in [a, b]$.

$$\begin{aligned} f(x) &= (b - x)(x - a) \\ &= -x^2 + (b + a)x - ab \end{aligned} \tag{4}$$

Based on the root and coefficient of $f(x)$, two vectors, $\overrightarrow{x} = \{x^2, x, 1\}$ and $\overrightarrow{ab} = \{-1, a + b, -ab\}$, were created, where $\overrightarrow{x}$ and $\overrightarrow{ab}$ are for the value x and the range $[a, b]$, respectively. It is easy to verify that $x \in [a, b]$ if $\overrightarrow{x} \cdot \overrightarrow{ab} >= 0$. For simplicity, we denoted this conversion method as M_1. M_1 is used to convert the operation of whether a point belongs to a range into a vector inner product operation. When constructing the leaf nodes of an index tree, we use M_1 to convert the multi-dimensional point of a document into a set of vectors.

Method M_2. Given two ranges, $[a, b]$ and $[x, y]$, if $[a, b]$ intersects with $[x, y]$, the mid value m of $[a, b]$ must be in the range $[x - c, y + c]$, where $m = \frac{b+a}{2}$ and $c = \frac{b-a}{2}$. According to this property, Equation (5) was constructed.

$$f(x,y) = (y + c - m)(m - x + c)$$
$$= (y - a)(b - x) \tag{5}$$
$$= -ab + ax + by - xy$$

Based on Equation (5), the two vectors of $[x, y]$ and $[a, b]$ are $\overrightarrow{xy} = \{1, x, y, xy\}$ and $\overrightarrow{ab} = \{-ab, a, b, -1\}$, respectively. It can be verified that $[a, b]$ intersects with $[x, y]$ if $\overrightarrow{xy} \cdot \overrightarrow{ab} >= 0$. For simplicity, we called this conversion method M_2. M_2 was employed to convert the operation of whether two ranges intersect into a vector inner product operation. When constructing the internal nodes of an index tree, we used M_2 to convert the multi-dimensional range of an internal node into a vector.

3.3. Algorithm for Creating the Leaf Node

Since the index tree is constructed in a bottom-up manner, we built the leaf nodes first. In our scheme, each document f_i contains one multi-dimension point $p_i = \{x_{i1}, x_{i2}, \ldots, x_{im}\}$ and a keyword set W_i. The algorithm for creating leaf nodes is given in Algorithm 1. The set of leaf nodes produced by Algorithm 1 will be used as the input to the index tree building algorithm.

The formal definition of any node u on the index tree is $u = < ID, \overrightarrow{u_W}, \overrightarrow{u_R}, u_P, P_l, P_r, FID >$. ID represents the identity information of u, which is generated by a random function $GenID()$. $\overrightarrow{u_W}$ is a vector representation of the keyword set W_i associated with the leaf node, and $\overrightarrow{u_R}$ is a vector representation of the range associated with the internal node. u_P is a set of vector representations of the multi-dimensional points contained in the leaf node. P_l and P_r are pointers to the left and right child nodes, respectively. FID is the ID of the document associated with the leaf node.

The algorithm for leaf node construction is given in Algorithm 1. Specifically, for each document f_i containing the tuple (W_i, p_i), the algorithm runs $GenID()$ to assign a value to $u.ID$ and sets $u.FID$ to the identifier of f_i. Since leaf nodes have no children, both $u.P_l$ and $u.P_r$ were set to null values. Through applying the keyword conversion method introduced in Section 3.1 to W_i, we converted W_i into a keyword vector $\overrightarrow{x_i}$ and set $\overrightarrow{u_W} = \overrightarrow{x_i}$. For the point p_i of f_i, each value in p_i was transformed into a vector by adopting the method M_1. More specifically, for each $x_{ij} \in p_i$, a vector $\overrightarrow{x_{ij}} = \{x_{ij}^2, x_{ij}, 1\}$ can be created. After this, u_P is set to be $\{\overrightarrow{x_{i1}}, \overrightarrow{x_{i2}}, \ldots, \overrightarrow{x_{im}}\}$.

Algorithm 1 Creating leaf nodes.

Input: A set of tuples $\{(W_1, p_1), (W_2, p_2), \ldots, (W_d, p_d)\}$, where W_i and p_i are the keyword set and multi-dimensional point for f_i, respectively, and $i \in [1, d]$.
Output: A $LeafNodeSet$ that contains all leaf nodes.

 1: **for** each $i \in [1, d]$ **do**
 2:     initializes a leaf node u for f_i;
 3:     runs GenID() to set a unique identifier for $u.ID$, assigns the identifier of f_i to $u.FID$, and sets $u.P_l = u.P_r = NULL$.
 4:     runs the keyword conversion method to transform W_i to $\overrightarrow{x_i}$, and sets $\overrightarrow{u_W} = \overrightarrow{x_i}$;
 5:     For each $x_{ij} \in p_i$, creates a vector $\overrightarrow{x_{ij}} = \{x_{ij}^2, x_{ij}, 1\}$, and sets $u_p = \{\overrightarrow{x_{i1}}, \overrightarrow{x_{i2}}, \ldots, \overrightarrow{x_{im}}\}$.
 6:     Inserts u to $LeafNodeSet$;
 7: **end for**
 8: **return** $LeafNodeSet$

3.4. Algorithm for Building the Index Tree

The algorithm takes a set of leaf nodes as the input and builds the internal nodes of the tree in a bottom-up manner by calling the algorithm recursively, which means that an internal node is constructed by two child nodes. As such, before putting forward the tree building algorithm, we first propose a method for constructing an internal node, and we called this method M_3.

Method M_3. In our scheme, each internal node u has a set of ranges, e.g., $[x_1, y_1]$, $[x_2, y_2], \ldots, [x_m, y_m]$. Suppose that $min(\alpha, \beta)$ and $max(\alpha, \beta)$ are two simple functions, where $min(\alpha, \beta)$ and $max(\alpha, \beta)$ output the minimum and maximum values of α and β, respectively. For the two nodes u' and u'', the range of the internal node (parent node) u is constructed as follows.

(1) Let u' and u'' be two leaf nodes, where the points in u' and u'' are $p'' = \{x'_1, x'_2, \ldots, x'_m\}$ and $p'' = \{x''_1, x''_2, \ldots, x''_m\}$, respectively. For each sub-range $[x_j, y_j]$ in u, x_j and y_j are set to be $min(x'_j, x''_j)$ and $max(x'_j, x''_j)$, respectively, where $j \in [1, m]$.

(2) Let u' and u'' be two internal nodes, where the ranges in u' and u'' are $[x'_1, y'_1]$, $[x'_2, y'_2], \ldots, [x'_m, y'_m]$ and $[x''_1, y''_1]$, $[x''_2, y''_2], \ldots, [x''_m, y''_m]$, respectively. For each sub-range $[x_j, y_j]$ in u, this method sets $x_j = min(x'_j, x''_j)$ and $y_j = max(y'_j, y''_j)$, where $j \in [1, m]$.

After obtaining u's range, we need to convert the range into a range vector. Given the range $[x_1, y_1]$, $[x_2, y_2], \ldots, [x_m, y_m]$ of u, a vector $\overrightarrow{u_R} = \{1, x_1, y_1, x_1 y_1, 1, x_2, y_2, x_2 y_2, \ldots, 1, x_m, y_m, x_m y_m\}$ can be created by M_2, where $\{1, x_j, y_j, x_j y_j\}$ is the vector for the sub-range $[x_j, y_j]$.

Inspired by the index tree construction algorithm in [28,38], the approach for constructing the index tree is given in Algorithm 2. $LeafNodeSet$ contains a set of nodes. Each node in $LeafNodeSet$ does not have a parent node and is needed to be processed. The overall idea of the algorithm is to construct an internal node using every two nodes in $LeafNodeSet$ until there is only one node left in $LeafNodeSet$, which means that this unique node is the root of the tree. Specifically, suppose $LeafNodeSet[i]$ and $LeafNodeSet[i+1]$ are any two nodes in $LeafNodeSet$, then their parent node u is created as follows. First, let $u.P_l$ and $u.P_r$ point to nodes $LeafNodeSe[i]$ and $LeafNodeSet[i+1]$, respectively, and generate unique ID for u with $GenID()$; then, by taking advantage of M_3, create $\overrightarrow{u_R}$ based on the range vectors of $LeafNodeSet[i]$ and $LeafNodeSet[i+1]$; and finally, add u to $TempNodeSet$. Note that, if $|LeafNodeSet|$ is odd, the last node in $LeafNodeSet$ will be inserted to $TempNodeSet$ directly. When the parents of all nodes in $LeafNodeSet$ have been created and added to $TempNodeSet$, Algorithm 2 will be called recursively with $TempNodeSet$ as the input until the index tree is constructed.

Algorithm 2 The index tree building algorithm, declared by BuildIndexTree(LeafNodeSet)

Input: $LeafNodeSet$ including all the leaf nodes.
Output: An index tree T.

1: Sets $k = |LeafNodeSet|$;
2: **if** $k == 1$ **then**
3:    **return** $LeafNodeSet$; \\This only node is the root of the tree.
4: **end if**
5: Initializes an empty set $TempNodeSet$;
6: **for** each $i \in [1, k/2]$ **do**
7:    Constructs a parent node u for $LeafNodeSet[2 * i - 1]$ and $LeafNodeSet[2 * i]$;
8:    Utilizes $GenID()$ to generate an unique ID for $u.ID$;
9:    Sets $u.P_l = LeafNodeSet[2 * i - 1]$ and $u.P_r = LeafNodeSet[2 * i]$;
10:    Generates a vector $\overrightarrow{u_R}$ for its corresponding range according to M_3;
11:    Inserts u to $TempNodeSet$;
12: **end for**
13: **if** $k\%2 == 1$ **then**
14:    Inserts $LeafNodeSet[k]$ to $TempNodeSet$;
15: **end if**
16: $LeafNodeSet = BuildIndexTree(TempNodeSet)$; \\calls BuildIndexTree recursively.
17: **return** $LeafNodeSet$;

Example 1. *To better understand Algorithm 2, we show an example of the index tree construction in Figure 3, which consists of two steps. Suppose that $F = \{f_1, f_2, \ldots, f_8\}$, then it first transforms each document f_i into a leaf node u_i by Algorithm 2, where $i \in [1, 8]$. Concretely, for each f_i that* *contains a point p_i and a keyword set W_i, we convert p_i and W_i into u_p and $\overrightarrow{u_W}$ by utilizing M_1 and the keyword conversion method, respectively. The second step is to build the index tree based on the leaf nodes from the bottom up. More specifically, we generate the range vector $\overrightarrow{u_R}$ of each internal node u from the range vectors of its two child nodes by adopting M_3. After these two steps, the plaintext index tree is built.*

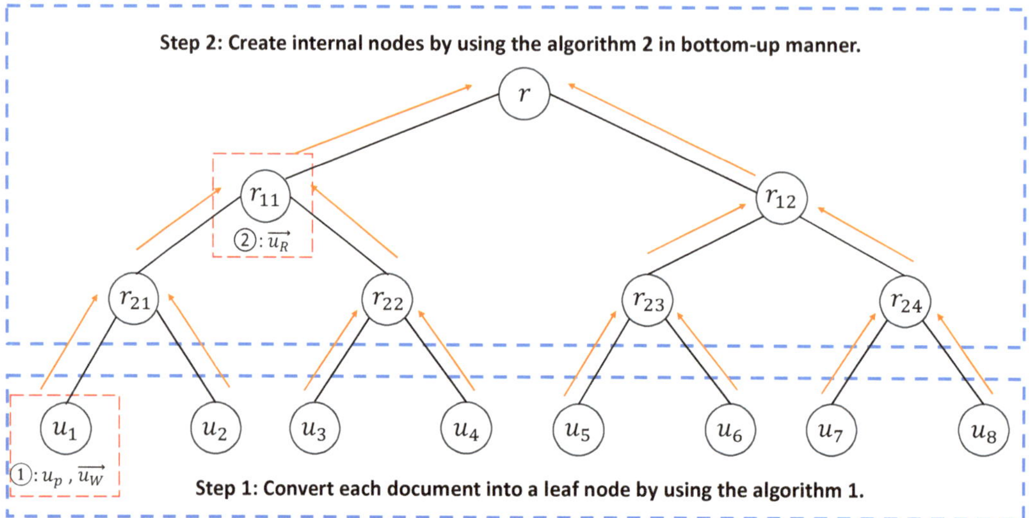

Figure 3. An example of how to build an index tree (Algorithm 2).

3.5. Algorithm for Searching the Index Tree

Before proposing the search algorithm, we first give a method for converting a query $Q = (Q_R, Q_W)$ into a query tuple that contains three elements $(\overrightarrow{Q_R}, Q_P, \overrightarrow{Q_W})$, where Q_R is a query range, Q_W is a query keyword set, $\overrightarrow{Q_R}$ is a vector used to search internal nodes, Q_P is a group of vectors used to search leaf nodes, and $\overrightarrow{Q_W}$ is a vector for conducting a keyword search. The query transformation approach, declared by *QueryTransform*, is given as follows.

(1) Given the query range Q_R, based on M_2, each sub-range $[a_j, b_j]$ is converted into $\{-a_j b_j, a_j, b_j, -1\}$, where $j \in [1, m]$. According to this conversion, a vector $\overrightarrow{Q_R} = \{-a_1 b_1, a_1, b_1, -1, -a_2 b_2, a_2, b_2, -1, \ldots, -a_m b_m, a_m, b_m, -1\}$ can be created.
(2) Based on M_1, each sub-range $[a_j, b_j]$ of Q_R is converted into $\overrightarrow{v_j} = \{-1, b_j + a_j, -a_j b_j\}$, and Q_P is set to be $\{\overrightarrow{v_1}, \overrightarrow{v_2}, \ldots, \overrightarrow{v_m}\}$.
(3) Apply the keyword conversion method to transform Q_W into $\vec{v}$, and set $\overrightarrow{Q_w} = \vec{v}$.

Inspired by the index tree search algorithm introduced in [28,38], the search algorithm used in SSE-RK is presented in Algorithm 3. In Algorithm 3, we used *RList* to store the k documents that are currently most relevant to the query and their corresponding similarity scores, as well as designate the k-score as the minimum similarity score in *RList*. Initially, *RList* is an empty list and the k-score is set to a very small number. Given a query tuple $(\overrightarrow{Q_R}, Q_p, \overrightarrow{Q_W})$ of Q, an index tree root node u, and an empty result list *RList*, the goal of the index tree search algorithm is to obtain the k documents that satisfy the range query and are most relevant to the query keywords. The search process is divided into two scenarios. (1) When an internal node is retrieved, the inner product between

$\overrightarrow{Q_R}$ and $\overrightarrow{u_R}$ is calculated. The pruning method in our scheme is verifying whether the query range $Q_R = \{[a_1, b_1], [a_2, b_2], \ldots, [a_m, b_m]\}$ in Q intersects with the range $\{[x_1, y_1], [x_2, y_2], \ldots, [x_m, y_m]\}$ in an internal node u. If the range in u intersects with the range Q_R, then it must be $\overrightarrow{u_R} \cdot \overrightarrow{Q_R} > 0$, which means that the subtree of the internal node still needs to be traversed. Thus, the algorithm continues to be called for the subtree of this node. If the inner product is less than 0, then the subtree is pruned and will not be visited further. (2) When the leaf node is retrieved, then the first step is to determine whether Q_p satisfies u_p. That is, let u_P be $\{\overrightarrow{x_1}, \overrightarrow{x_2}, \ldots, \overrightarrow{x_m}\}$, and let Q_P be $\{\overrightarrow{v_1}, \overrightarrow{v_2}, \ldots, \overrightarrow{v_m}\}$. Moreover, the search algorithm tests whether $\overrightarrow{x_j} \cdot \overrightarrow{v_j}$ equals 0 for all $j \in [1, m]$. If so, it represents that the multi-dimensional point p implied by the leaf node belongs to the query range Q_R, and that it requires further computation of the correlation score between $\overrightarrow{Q_W}$ and $\overrightarrow{u_W}$. If the score is greater than the document with the smallest relevance score in the current *RList*, the document corresponding to that leaf node is added to the *RList*, and the document with the smallest relevance score in the *RList* is removed. Otherwise, the document corresponding to this leaf node is discarded.

Algorithm 3 The index tree search algorithm, declared by SearchIndexTree($\overrightarrow{Q_R}$, Q_P, $\overrightarrow{Q_W}$, u, *RList*)

Input: A query tuple $(\overrightarrow{Q_R}, Q_P, \overrightarrow{Q_W})$ of query Q, the index tree's root node u, and an empty result list *RList*.
Output: *RList*.

1: **if** u is an internal node **then**
2:     **if** $\overrightarrow{u_R} \cdot \overrightarrow{Q_R} > 0$ **then** \\ Determine whether the query range Q_R intersects the range u_R implied by the internal node.
3:         SearchIndexTree($(\overrightarrow{Q_R}, Q_P, \overrightarrow{Q_W})$, $u.P_l$, *RList*);
4:         SearchIndexTree($(\overrightarrow{Q_R}, Q_P, \overrightarrow{Q_W})$, $u.P_r$, *RList*);
5:     **else**
6:         **return**
7:     **end if**
8: **else**
9:     **if** $\overrightarrow{x_j} \cdot \overrightarrow{v_j} = 0$ for all $j \in [1, m]$ **then** \\ Determine whether the multi-dimensional point p implied by the leaf node belongs to the query range Q_R.
10:         **if** $\overrightarrow{u_W} \cdot \overrightarrow{Q_W} > k$-score **then** \\ Calculate whether the correlation score between the document keywords and the query keywords is greater than the smallest score in the current *RList*.
11:             Removes the document with the smallest relevance score in the *RList*;
12:             Adds the tuple $< Score(u_W, Q_W), u.FID >$ to the *Rlist*;
13:             Sets the k-score to the smallest relevance score in the current *RList*;
14:         **end if**
15:     **end if**
16:     **return**
17: **end if**

Example 2. *In this example, we suppose that only the top-1 file will be returned to the data user, and Figure 4 was constructed to show the index tree search process. When using the query transformation approach, a query $Q = (Q_R, Q_W)$ is converted into a tuple $(\overrightarrow{Q_R}, Q_P, \overrightarrow{Q_W})$. According to the index tree shown in Figure 3, the search algorithm starts from the root node r and reaches the internal node r_{11} first. Since the inner product between the $\overrightarrow{u_R}$ of r_{11} and $\overrightarrow{Q_R}$ of Q was larger than 0, the search algorithm accessed its child nodes. Because the inner product between the $\overrightarrow{u_R}$ of r_{21} and $\overrightarrow{Q_R}$ of Q was smaller than 0, then the two child nodes u_1 and u_2 of r_{21} will not be reached. Since the node r_{22} matches the query Q, Algorithm 3 computes the relevant scores between u_3 and Q, as well as adds u_3 to RList directly since the number of documents in the RList had not reached the upper limit. When reaching u_4, Algorithm 3 computes the relevant score between u_4 and Q, as well as compares this score to the k-score. If the relevant score between u_4 and Q is larger than the k-score, Algorithm 3 deletes u_3 from RList and adds u_4 to RList instead; otherwise, nothing happens. When the left subtree is checked, Algorithm 3 will detect node r_{12}. Since the query Q was not related to the node r_{12}, the subtree with r_{12} as the root node would not be accessed. After this, Algorithm 3 output RList. Numbers 1–6 in Figure 4 illustrate the tree traversal process. It can be seen that subtrees* *with r_{12} or r_{21} as the tree root will not be visited. This pruning improves the query efficiency of the scheme.*

$Q = (Q_R, Q_W)$ **is converted into** $Q = (\overrightarrow{Q_R}, Q_p, \overrightarrow{Q_W})$ **by using the query conversion method.**

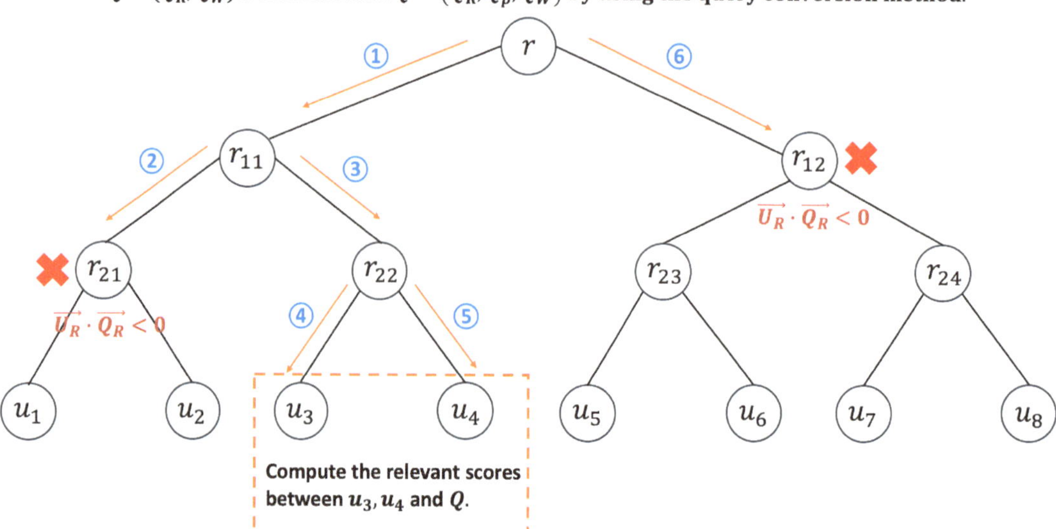

Figure 4. An example of the search process (Algorithm 3).

4. Proposed Scheme

In this section, we used the algorithms introduced in Section 3 to construct a concrete SSE-RK scheme, as well as to perform a theoretical analysis of the security of the proposed scheme.

4.1. Construction of SSE-RK

According to the system model proposed in Section 2, the SSE-RK scheme first needs to create an algorithm that can generate secret keys. Secondly, for data owners and users, SSE-RK needs to build algorithms that can generate secure searchable indexes and a trapdoor. Finally, for the cloud server, SSE-RK should construct a search algorithm to enable the secure retrieval of the encrypted index. According to the above description, the SSE-RK scheme consists of four algorithms: the secret key generation algorithm, *KeyGen*; the index building algorithm, *IndexBuild*; the trapdoor generation algorithm, *TrapdoorGen*; and the secure search algorithm, *Search*. In order to better demonstrate the relationship between the roles of the system model and the four algorithms mentioned above, we constructed Figure 5 to show the interaction process between these roles. Specifically, the DO runs the *KeyGen* algorithm to generate the secret key *sk*, and then sends *sk* to the authorized DU. The DO uses the *CreatLeafNode* algorithm (Algorithm 1) and the *BuildIndexTree* algorithm (Algorithm 2) to transform the document set into an index tree. The *IndexBuild* algorithm is then used to generate the tree into a secure index, which is then sent to a CS. Whenever the DU wants to perform a query, the DU generates a trapdoor regarding Q via the *TrapdoorGen* algorithm, which is then sent to a *CS*. Once the CS receives the trapdoor, it executes the *Search* algorithm and returns the search result, *RList*, to the DU. The detailed construction process of these four algorithms is given below.

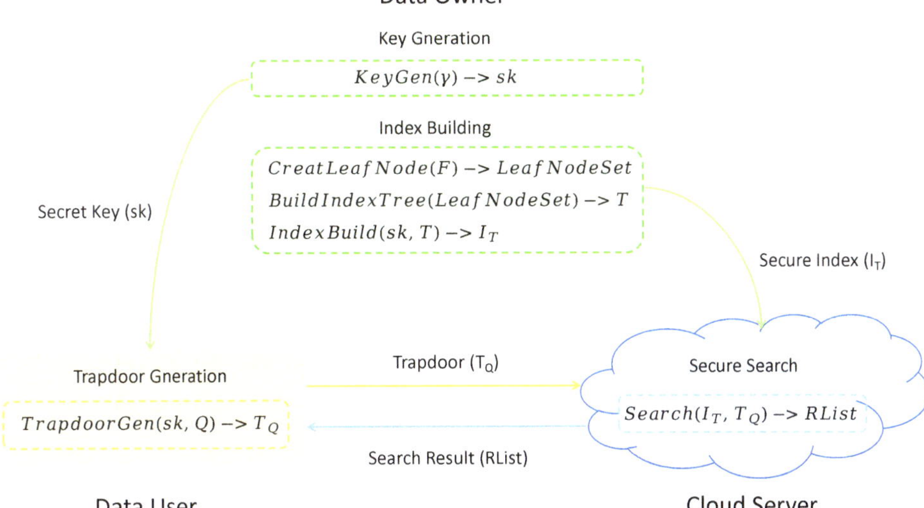

Figure 5. The process of interaction between the roles in the system model.

- **KeyGen(γ):** Given a security parameter γ as input, it first randomly generates two 3×3 invertible matrices M_{11} and M_{12}; two $4m \times 4m$ invertible matrices M_{21} and M_{22}; and two $(N+L) \times (N+L)$ invertible matrices M_{31} and M_{32}. Then, it randomly generates three vectors S_1, S_2, and S_3, where the dimensions of $S_1, S_2,$ and S_3 are 3, $4m$, and $(N+L)$, respectively. Finally, it outputs the secret key $sk = \{S_1, M_{11}, M_{12}, S_2, M_{21}, M_{22}, S_3, M_{31}, M_{32}\}$.

- **IndexBuild(sk, F):** Given the document set F, it applies Algorithm 2 to build a plaintext index tree T, and it then encrypts T. The encryption process can be classified into two situations.

  (1) For each internal node $u = < ID, NULL, \overrightarrow{u_R}, NULL, P_l, P_r, NULL >$, the algorithm generates two random vectors $\{\overrightarrow{u_R}', \overrightarrow{u_R}''\}$ of $\overrightarrow{u_R}$. More precisely, if $S_2[i] = 0$, it sets $\overrightarrow{u_R}'[i] + \overrightarrow{u_R}''[i] = \overrightarrow{u_R}[i]$; if $S_2[i] = 1$, then $\{\overrightarrow{u_R}'[i], \overrightarrow{u_R}''[i]\}$ are set to two random numbers that satisfy condition $\overrightarrow{u_R}'[i] = \overrightarrow{u_R}''[i] = \overrightarrow{u_R}[i]$, where $i \in [1, 4m]$. This procedure can be represented by the following equation.

  $$\left\{ \begin{array}{l} \overrightarrow{u_R}'[i] + \overrightarrow{u_R}''[i] = \overrightarrow{u_R}[i], \ \ if \ S_2[i] = 0; \\ \overrightarrow{u_R}'[i] = \overrightarrow{u_R}''[i] = \overrightarrow{u_R}[i], \ \ if \ S_2[i] = 1. \end{array} \right\} i \in [1, 4m].$$

  Then, it generates the encrypted internal node $I_u = < ID, NULL, \{M_{21}^T \overrightarrow{u_R}', M_{22}^T \overrightarrow{u_R}''\}, NULL, P_l, P_r, NULL >$.

  (2) For each leaf node $u = < ID, \overrightarrow{u_W}, NULL, u_P, P_l, P_r, FID >$, the encryption process contains two steps.

  - The algorithm initializes an empty set $\hat{u}_P$. For each vector $\overrightarrow{x_j}$ in u_P, the algorithm generates two random vectors $\{\overrightarrow{x_j}', \overrightarrow{x_j}''\}$ of $\overrightarrow{x_j}$, where $j \in [1, m]$. Similarly, this procedure can be represented by the following equation.

  $$\left\{ \begin{array}{l} \overrightarrow{x_j}'[i] + \overrightarrow{x_j}''[i] = \overrightarrow{x_j}[i], \ \ if \ S_1[i] = 0; \\ \overrightarrow{x_j}'[i] = \overrightarrow{x_j}''[i] = \overrightarrow{x_j}[i], \ \ if \ S_1[i] = 1. \end{array} \right\} i \in [1, 3].$$

  After this, it adds $\{M_{11}^T \overrightarrow{x_j}', M_{12}^T \overrightarrow{x_j}''\}$ into the $\hat{u}_P$.

- For the keyword vector $\overrightarrow{u_W}$ in the leaf node, the N-dimension vector $\overrightarrow{u_W}$ is stretched to a $(N + L)$-dimension vector $\overrightarrow{u_{WE}}$. For $\overrightarrow{u_{WE}}$, the value of $\overrightarrow{u_{WE}}[i]$ is set to be $\overrightarrow{u_W}[i]$ when $i \in [1, N]$, and the value of $\overrightarrow{u_{WE}}[i]$ is set as a random number ϵ_i when $i \in [N + 1, N + L]$. Then, the algorithm generates two random vectors $\{\overrightarrow{u_{WE}}', \overrightarrow{u_{WE}}''\}$ of $\overrightarrow{u_{WE}}$ according to the following equations.

$$\left\{ \begin{array}{l} \overrightarrow{u_{WE}}'[i] + \overrightarrow{u_{WE}}''[i] = \overrightarrow{u_{WE}}[i], \ \ if \ S_3[i] = 0; \\ \overrightarrow{u_{WE}}'[i] = \overrightarrow{u_{WE}}''[i] = \overrightarrow{u_{WE}}[i], \ \ if \ S_3[i] = 1. \end{array} \right\} i \in [1, N + L].$$

After these two steps, it generates the encrypted leaf node $I_u = \ < ID, \{M_{31}^T \overrightarrow{u_{WE}}', M_{32}^T \overrightarrow{u_{WE}}''\}, NULL, \hat{u}_P, P_l, P_r, FID >$.

Finally, when the encryption operation is completed for each node, the algorithm outputs the encrypted index tree I_T.

- **TrapdoorGen**(*sk*,*Q*): For a query $Q = (Q_R, Q_W)$, this algorithm applies the query conversion method introduced in Section 3.5 to generates a query tuple $(\overrightarrow{Q_R}, Q_P, \overrightarrow{Q_W})$. After this, it will encrypt the query tuple. The encryption process can be classified into three situations.

(1) For $\overrightarrow{Q_R}$, it generates two random vectors $\{\overrightarrow{Q_R}', \overrightarrow{Q_R}''\}$. This division process is similar to the index building algorithm and can still be represented by the following equation.

$$\left\{ \begin{array}{l} \overrightarrow{Q_R}'[i] + \overrightarrow{Q_R}''[i] = \overrightarrow{Q_R}[i], \ \ if \ S_2[i] = 0; \\ \overrightarrow{Q_R}'[i] = \overrightarrow{Q_R}''[i] = \overrightarrow{Q_R}[i], \ \ if \ S_2[i] = 1. \end{array} \right\} i \in [1, 4m].$$

After this, it replaces $\overrightarrow{Q_R}$ with $\{M_{21}^{-1}\overrightarrow{Q_R}', M_{22}^{-1}\overrightarrow{Q_R}''\}$.

(2) The algorithm initializes an empty set $\hat{Q}_P$. For each vector $\overrightarrow{v_j}$ in Q_P, the algorithm generates two random vectors $\{\overrightarrow{v_j}', \overrightarrow{v_j}''\}$ of $\overrightarrow{v_j}$ according to the following equations, where $j \in [1, m]$.

$$\left\{ \begin{array}{l} \overrightarrow{v_j}'[i] + \overrightarrow{v_j}''[i] = \overrightarrow{v_j}[i], \ \ if \ S_1[i] = 0; \\ \overrightarrow{v_j}'[i] = \overrightarrow{v_j}''[i] = \overrightarrow{v_j}[i], \ \ if \ S_1[i] = 1. \end{array} \right\} i \in [1, 3].$$

After this, it adds each $\{M_{11}^{-1}\overrightarrow{v_j}', M_{12}^{-1}\overrightarrow{v_j}''\}$ into $\hat{Q}_P$.

(3) The N-dimension vector $\overrightarrow{Q_W}$ is expanded to a $(N + L)$-dimension vector $\overrightarrow{Q_{WE}}$. For each $i \in [1, N]$, it sets $\overrightarrow{Q_{WE}}[i] = \overrightarrow{Q_W}[i]$. For each $i \in [N + 1, N + L]$, it chooses a random number 0 or 1, and it sets $\overrightarrow{Q_{WE}}[i]$ to be equal to 0 or 1. Then, it adopts the following equations to create two random vectors $\{\overrightarrow{Q_{WE}}', \overrightarrow{Q_{WE}}''\}$.

$$\left\{ \begin{array}{l} \overrightarrow{Q_{WE}}'[i] + \overrightarrow{Q_{WE}}''[i] = \overrightarrow{Q_{WE}}[i], \ \ if \ S_3[i] = 0; \\ \overrightarrow{Q_{WE}}'[i] = \overrightarrow{Q_{WE}}''[i] = \overrightarrow{Q_{WE}}[i], \ \ if \ S_3[i] = 1. \end{array} \right\} i \in [1, N + L].$$

After this, it replaces $\overrightarrow{Q_W}$ with $\{M_{31}^{-1}\overrightarrow{Q_{WE}}', M_{32}^{-1}\overrightarrow{Q_{WE}}''\}$.

Finally, this algorithm outputs the trapdoor $T_Q = \{\{M_{21}^{-1}\overrightarrow{Q_R}', M_{22}^{-1}\overrightarrow{Q_R}''\}, \hat{Q}_P, \{M_{31}^{-1}\overrightarrow{Q_{WE}}', M_{32}^{-1}\overrightarrow{Q_{WE}}''\}\}$ for Q.

- **Search** (I_T, T_Q): Given an encrypted index tree I_T and a trapdoor T_Q, this algorithm executes the search operation in a pre-order traversal manner. When an internal node

$I_u = <ID, NULL, \{M_{21}^T \overrightarrow{u_R}', M_{22}^T \overrightarrow{u_R}''\}, NULL, P_l, P_r, NULL>$ is accessed, it computes the following:

$$(M_{21}^T \overrightarrow{u_R}' \cdot M_{21}^{-1} \overrightarrow{Q_R}') + (M_{22}^T \overrightarrow{u_R}'' \cdot M_{22}^{-1} \overrightarrow{Q_R}'') = \overrightarrow{u_R}' \cdot \overrightarrow{Q_R}' + \overrightarrow{u_R}'' \cdot \overrightarrow{Q_R}''$$
$$= \overrightarrow{u_R} \cdot \overrightarrow{Q_R} \tag{6}$$

When reaching a leaf node $I_u = <ID, \{M_{31}^T \overrightarrow{u_{WE}}', M_{32}^T \overrightarrow{u_{WE}}''\}, NULL, \hat{u}_P, P_l, P_r, FID>$, the computation process has two steps.

(1) For each $\overrightarrow{x_j}', \overrightarrow{x_j}''$ in $\hat{u}_P$ and each $\overrightarrow{v_j}', \overrightarrow{v_j}''$ in $\hat{Q}_P$, where $j \in [1, m]$, it computes the following:

$$(M_{11}^T \overrightarrow{x_j}' \cdot M_{11}^{-1} \overrightarrow{v_j}') + (M_{12}^T \overrightarrow{x_j}'' \cdot M_{12}^{-1} \overrightarrow{v_j}'') = \overrightarrow{x_j}' \cdot \overrightarrow{v_j}' + \overrightarrow{x_j}'' \cdot \overrightarrow{v_j}''$$
$$= \overrightarrow{x_j} \cdot \overrightarrow{v_j} \tag{7}$$

(2) To evaluate the relevance score, it computes the following:

$$(M_{31}^T \overrightarrow{u_{WE}}' \cdot M_{31}^{-1} \overrightarrow{Q_{WE}}') + (M_{32}^T \overrightarrow{u_{WE}}'' \cdot M_{32}^{-1} \overrightarrow{Q_{WE}}'') = \overrightarrow{u_{WE}}' \cdot \overrightarrow{Q_{WE}}' + \overrightarrow{u_{WE}}'' \cdot \overrightarrow{Q_{WE}}''$$
$$= \overrightarrow{u_{WE}} \cdot \overrightarrow{Q_{WE}} \tag{8}$$

According to the above Equations (6)–(8), the computation result between the encrypted node I_u and the trapdoor T_Q is identical to that between the plaintext u and the query Q. Thus, this algorithm can take advantage of Algorithm 3 to execute a ranked search.

4.2. Security Analysis

As described in Section 2.3, the proposed scheme needs to satisfy three security requirements such as "Index and trapdoor privacy", "Trapdoor Unlinkability", and "Keyword privacy". In the following, we will analyze the security of the proposed solution in detail based on these three requirements.

Index and trapdoor privacy. For a privacy-preserving scheme, the objective is to preserve as much sensitive information about the adversary as possible while successfully obtaining the correct result. Based on the method in [39], we give the following definition before conducting the security proof.

History: According to Table 1, $F = \{f_1, f_2, \ldots, f_d\}$ is the set of documents, where f_i represents the i-th document, I_T is the index tree constructed from F using the index building algorithm, and $Q_S = \{Q_1, Q_2, \ldots Q_t\}$ is the set of queries that have been executed. The history associated with Q_S is defined as $H_{Q_S} = \{F, I_T, Q_S\}$.

View: View represents what can be seen by adversaries in the scheme. Specifically, we use the AES scheme to encrypt F. The ciphertext of F is denoted as $C*$. Furthermore, we use the secure KNN scheme to encrypt the index tree and queries. The encrypted index tree and trapdoors are denoted as I_T* and T_D*, respectively. The adversary's view is defined as $\{C*, I_T*, T_D*\}$.

Trace: Traces of history are additional information that adversaries can obtain during the execution of a scheme. It is mainly the access pattern and search pattern leaked by the user when the user makes queries on the encrypted index I_T* when using the trapdoor collection T_D*. The access pattern is the query results that correspond to each query, while the search pattern is a matrix where, if the element in row i and column j of the matrix is 1, then it means that the query condition q_i is the same as the query condition q_j.

Based on the definitions of the terms above, we give the following lemma and provide detailed steps of the proof of the lemma.

Lemma 1. *Given the two histories with the same trace, the proposed scheme is said to be secure if the adversaries of the probability polynomial time cannot distinguish their views.*

Proof. For a particular trace, if a polynomial-time simulator S exists, it can generate a simulated index $I_{T_S}*$, a series of simulated trapdoors $T_{D_S}*$, and a simulated encrypted document set C_S*, i.e., a simulated $view_S = \{C_S*, I_{T_S}*, T_{D_S}*\}$. We say that the proposed scheme is secure if the adversary cannot distinguish the simulated $view_S$ from the real view with a non-negligible probability. Below, we give the concrete simulation procedure for the proof.

- S generates a simulated encrypted document set C_S*. Firstly, S generates $f_i^S \in \{0,1\}^{\{|f_i|\}}$, where $1 \le i \le d$ and $\{0,1\}^{\{|f_i|\}}$ are represented as a binary string of length $|f_i|$. Then, S encrypts f_i^S to create f_i^S* such that $|f_i^S*| = |f_i*|$, where $|f_i^S*|$ and $|f_i*|$ are the ciphertexts of f_i^S and f_i, respectively. Finally, S outputs $C_S* = \{f_i^S*|1 \le i \le d\}$. Since the AES scheme is secure, it is guaranteed that C_S* and $C*$ cannot be distinguished by an adversary.

- S generates the simulated trapdoor set $T_{D_S}*$. S generates t query conditions, i.e., $Q' = \{Q_1', Q_2', ..., Q_t'\}$. For each Q_j', the *TrapdoorGen* algorithm can be utilized to produce it as a trapdoor, where $1 \le j \le t$. Since the essence of the *TrapdoorGen* algorithm is to encrypt Q_j' using the secure KNN scheme, it ensures that $T_{D_S}*$ and T_D* cannot be distinguished by an adversary.

- S generates the simulated index tree $I_{T_S}*$. For each simulated document f_i^S, S generates the simulated multi-dimensional point p_i^S and the keyword set W_i^S based on the query set Q'. For each query $Q_j' = (Q_R^j, Q_W^j)$ in which $1 \le j \le t$, the p_i^S generated by S needs to satisfy $p_i \in Q_R^j$ and $p_i^S \in Q_R^j$ and $Score(W_i, Q_W^j) = Score(W_i^S, Q_W^j)$. Here, p_i and W_i are the multi-dimensional point and keyword set of the real document f_i, respectively, where $1 \le i \le d$. S will generate a simulated index tree I_{T_S} for all the the simulated points and keyword sets using the index tree building algorithm, and it will encrypt the I_{T_S} using the *IndexBuild* algorithm to create an encrypted index tree $I_{T_S}*$. Since the secure KNN scheme we use is secure under a known ciphertext model, the SSE-RK scheme can guarantee the indistinguishability of $I_{T_S}*$ from I_T*.

By utilizing the $T_{D_S}*$ to query $I_{T_S}*$, it can be verified that the simulated $view_S$ will produce the same trace as the real view. Since the AES and secure KNN schemes are provably secure, this means that, based on the same trace, there is no probabilistic polynomial time adversary that can distinguish between the simulated $view_S$ and the real view. Therefore, we argue that the proposed scheme is secure. $\square$

Trapdoor unlinkability. The proposed scheme will first expand the keyword vector $\overrightarrow{Q_W}$ into a vector $\overrightarrow{Q_{WE}}$ that contains "noise" in the process of generating trapdoors. Here, "noisy" refers to the random integer that is added in the third step of the *TrapdoorGen* algorithm when expanding $\overrightarrow{Q_W}$ into $\overrightarrow{Q_{WE}}$. Since the added "noise" is random, even the same $\overrightarrow{Q_W}$ will be expanded into a different $\overrightarrow{Q_{WE}}$. In addition, the $\overrightarrow{Q_{WE}}$ is randomly partitioned in the process of encrypting $\overrightarrow{Q_{WE}}$ via the secure KNN scheme. Based on the above two operations, the SSE-RK scheme can encrypt the same Q into different trapdoors, thus achieving the unlinkability of the trapdoors.

Keyword privacy. Since the attacker can obtain the statistical information of the dataset under the known background model, it can make use of the word frequency information to analyze the query keywords in the trapdoor. To avoid such an attack, the proposed scheme expands the keyword vector $\overrightarrow{u_W}$ for each node when building the index tree. Specifically, vector $\overrightarrow{u_W}$ is extended with L dimensions, where each dimension is set to a random "noise" ϵ_i. In this way, the similarity score of any query is obfuscated by the value of $\sum \epsilon_i$. As L increases, the probability of obtaining the same similarity score for the same query will be further reduced due to the interference of $\sum \epsilon_i$. Although the addition of "noise" increases privacy, it leads to a decrease in search precision. To balance privacy and precision, as analyzed in [21], we can make a trade-off by adjusting L and ϵ_i.

5. Performance Evaluation

In order to better demonstrate the performance of the proposed scheme, we will perform a theoretical analysis of the proposed scheme based on the experimental results. The experimental data are obtained from 50,000 documents, which were randomly selected from a real medical dataset named "OHSUMED" [39]. The experimental *PC* contained an Intel(R) Core(TM) i7@2.90GHz CPU and 16 GB RAM. To better illustrate the merit of the proposed scheme, we performed simulation experiments on two schemes related to the proposed scheme, and we then compared them with our scheme. The performance comparison mainly focused on three aspects: index building, trapdoor generation, and ciphertext retrieval. For convenience, we denote the two schemes [8,9] to be compared by Miao18 and Wang19, and we listed some of the parameters that may affect the efficiency of these schemes in Table 2. In addition, we constructed Table 3 to show the efficiency comparison between these schemes. In the next sub-section, we will verify the theoretical analysis through experimental data and validate the effectiveness of the proposed scheme.

Table 2. Notations for the comparison analysis.

N	The number of keywords in the dictionary.
d	The number of documents in the corpus.
m	The dimension of the point in the document.
L	The average length of a query range.
M	The dimension of bloom filter used in Wang19.
θ	The average number of documents that match the query.

Table 3. Comparative analysis of the scheme efficiency.

Schemes	Index Building	Trapdoor Generation	Search
Miao18	$2d(N+3m)^2$	$(N+3m)^2$	$d(N+3m)$
Wang19	dLM^2	LM^2	$L(M+m)$
SSE-RK	dm^2+dN^2	$(N+3m)^2+(4m)^2$	$\theta(N+7m)$

5.1. Efficiency of Index Building

According to Figure 6, the time cost of the index building in Miao18 is squarely related to N and linearly associated with d. This is because the vector length of each document of Miao18 is $N+3m$. Thus, its index encryption process needs to perform $d(N+3m)^2$ product operations. For Wang19, since each leaf node contains m points and a BF vector of length M, the d leaf nodes in its index tree need to perform the $d(m+M)$ encryption operations of SHVE. In addition, since the internal node contains m ranges $[a_i, b_i]$ and a BF vector, the internal node needs to perform the $dL(m+M)$ encryption operations of SHVE, where L is the average length of $[a_i, b_i]$ and $i \in [1, m]$. Because the range of the internal node needs to include the points associated with all its leaf nodes, L will increase as d increases. Based on the above analysis, it can be inferred that the time consumption of index building in Wang19 is proportional to d^2. This conclusion is corroborated by the experimental results shown in Figure 6a. In addition, since Wang19 uses BF to index its keyword domain, the index-building time of Wang19 is independent of N. For the proposed scheme, since each leaf node of the index tree corresponds to a vector of length $N+3m$, the encryption of the leaf nodes needs to perform $d(N+3m)^2$ product operations. Moreover, the internal node corresponds to a vector of length $4m$, so the internal node needs to perform $d*m^2$ product operations. Since m is much smaller than d and N, we reckon that the time cost of index building in the SSE-RK scheme is squarely related to N and linearly associated with d. The experimental results in Figure 6 are consistent with the theoretical analysis.

To sum up, as shown in Figure 6, the time cost of index building in Wang19 is much longer than that of Miao18 and the proposed scheme because its encryption process requires enumerating all points in the range associated with the internal node, and the SHVE encryption operation it uses is more time-consuming than the product operation. In addition, the time cost of index building in the SSE-RK scheme is slightly more than that of Miao18 because the proposed scheme needs to encrypt d internal nodes.

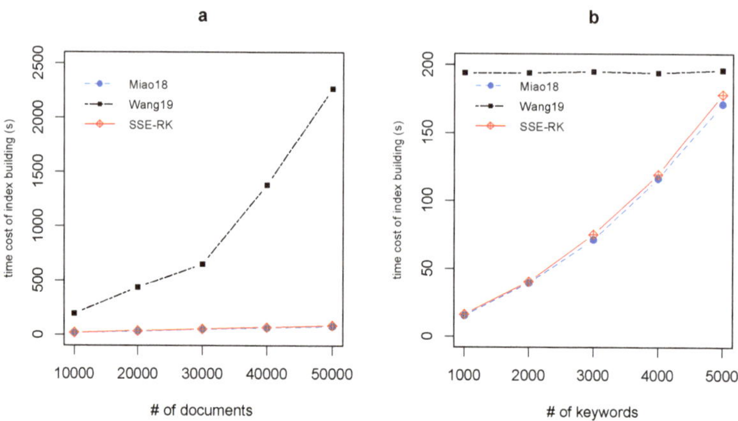

Figure 6. Impact of d (**a**) and N (**b**) on the time consumption of index building. N = (1000; 2000; 3000; 4000; 5000) and d = (10,000; 20,000; 30,000; 40,000; 50,000).

5.2. Efficiency of Trapdoor Generation

For Miao18, the vector length of its trapdoor is $N + 3m$; as such, its trapdoor generation process needs to execute $(N + 3m)^2$ product operations. For Wang19, assuming that its query range length is L, its trapdoor generation needs to execute the $L(m + M)$ key generation operations of SHVE since its query contains $L(m + M)$ vectors. The trapdoor of the proposed scheme contains two vectors. One's length is $N + 3m$ and the other's length is $4m$. Thus, its trapdoor generation process needs to execute $(N + 3m)^2 + (4m)^2$ product operations.

According to Figure 7a, it can be seen that all schemes are independent of d. Furthermore, the proposed scheme requires slightly more trapdoor generation time compared to Miao18. And the time cost of trapdoor generation in Wang19 is more than that of the other two schemes. This result could be explained by the fact that the time consumption of the key generation algorithm of SHVE used in Wang19 is more than that of the product operation in Miao18 and our scheme. In addition, according to Figure 7b, it can be seen that both Miao18 and the proposed scheme are squared with N, while Wang19 is independent of N. As N keeps increasing, the time cost of trapdoor generation in Miao18 and the SSE-RK scheme will be higher than that of Wang19.

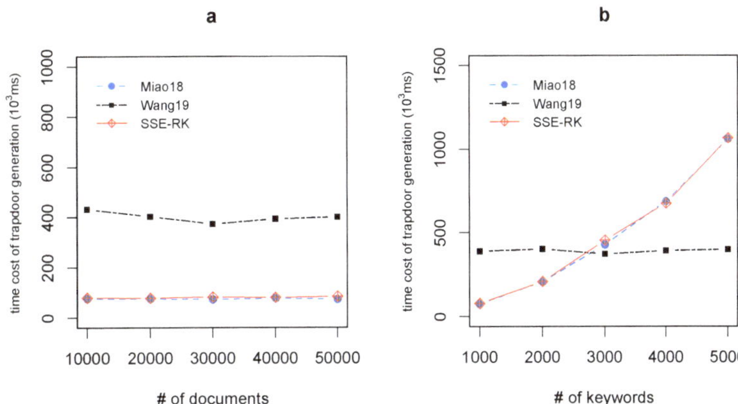

Figure 7. Impact of d (**a**) and N (**b**) on the time cost of trapdoor generation. N = (1000; 2000; 3000; 4000; 5000) and d = (10,000; 20,000; 30,000; 40,000; 50,000)

5.3. Efficiency of Search

For Miao18, since the vector length of each document is $N + 3m$, the test algorithm requires performing $d(N + 3m)$ product operations. Considering that the index structure of Wang19 is a tree, assuming that θ represents the average number of documents that satisfy the query, its test algorithm needs to visit at least θ internal, as well as θ leaf, nodes. The test algorithm requires performing the $L(m + N)$ and $m + M$ decryption operations of SHVE for each internal node and leaf node, respectively. Thus, the total test time complexity is $\theta L(m + N)$. For the proposed scheme, like Wang19, it is necessary to visit at least θ internal, as well as θ leaf, nodes. For each internal node and leaf node, $4m$ and $3m + N$ product operations need to be performed, respectively. Thus, at least $\theta(7m + N)$ product operations need to be performed in total.

The results in Figure 8 corroborate the above analysis. As shown in Figure 8a, the proposed scheme has a sub-linear relationship with d as d increases. Compared with Miao18, the test time of the proposed scheme is lower since the proposed scheme utilizes the tree structure to reduce the access of a large number of irrelevant documents, thus making θ much smaller than d. Although both Wang19 and our scheme utilize the tree structure to improve the query efficiency, the search efficiency of the SSE-RK scheme is preferable to that of Wang19 since the decryption operation of SHVE is more time-consuming than the product operation. According to Figure 8b, the query time of Wang19 is independent of N, while that of Miao18 and our scheme grows slightly as N increases. Since the decryption operation of SHVE used by Wang19 is more time-consuming than the product operation, its query efficiency is still the lowest.

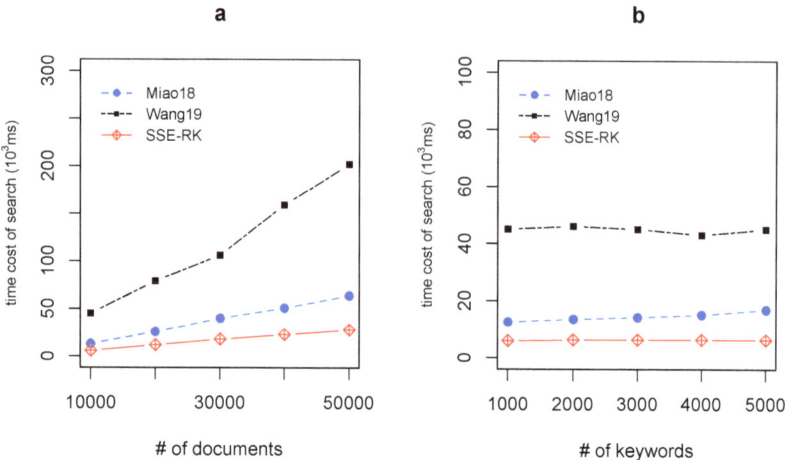

Figure 8. Impact of d (**a**) and N (**b**) on the time cost of search. N = (1000; 2000; 3000; 4000; 5000) and d = (10,000; 20,000; 30,000; 40,000; 50,000)

5.4. Discussion

As shown in the experimental results, when d = 10,000 and $N = 1000$, the time cost of search in SSE-RK is 5.9 s while that in Miao18 is 12.7 s. However, the index building time of SSE-RK is nearly 2 s longer than that of Miao18. Since search operations are more frequent than index building operations, we can argue that SSE-RK is more practical than Miao18. Compared with Wang19, the proposed scheme has a significant improvement in index construction and query efficiency. Although the time cost of trapdoor generation in Wang19 is less than that of the proposed scheme when N gradually increases, we reckon that the SSE-RK scheme is still practical since the trapdoor generation operation is a relatively small part of the overall user query process. The experimental analysis shows that Wang19 is less efficient. An objective reason for this is that Wang19 is designed to realize queries for arbitrary geometric ranges. In contrast, the proposed scheme and Miao18 are specifically designed to support range and keyword searches. In conclusion, based on the experimental results, we can find that the proposed scheme improves the query efficiency without sacrificing too much index building time. Considering the need for frequent queries on EMR data, we believe the proposed solution is more suitable for medical information systems.

Most of the existing SSE schemes only support keyword search. Compared to these schemes, the proposed scheme can support more complex query conditions. In order to quantify the cost of enhanced query functionality, we chose a highly efficient SSE scheme that only supports keyword search for an experimental comparison. We denote this scheme Zhang22 [38], and we show the experimental results in Figure 9. The experimental data show that the proposed scheme has an advantage in terms of index building time. This is because the internal nodes of the index tree of SSE-RK are constructed using range data, while that of Zhang22 are created using keyword vectors. Thus, the time complexity of the index tree building of SSE-RK is $dN^2 + dm^2$, while that of Zhang22 is $2dN^2$. The trapdoor generation time for the proposed scheme is a little higher than the one for Zhang22. This is because the trapdoor for SSE-RK will include range information in addition to keyword information. The search time for the proposed scheme is somewhat higher than the search time for Zhang22. This is because the query process of SSE-RK not only involves the similarity calculation of the keyword vectors, but also the determination of whether the ranges overlap. Zhang22, on the contrary, only needs to perform the similarity calculation of the keyword vectors. Therefore, the search time complexity of the proposed scheme is $7m + N$, while that of Zhang22 is N. The experiment results illustrate that the proposed scheme does incur a certain query cost when implementing more complex query conditions. Therefore, meaningful future work could be to improve the search efficiency of the scheme.

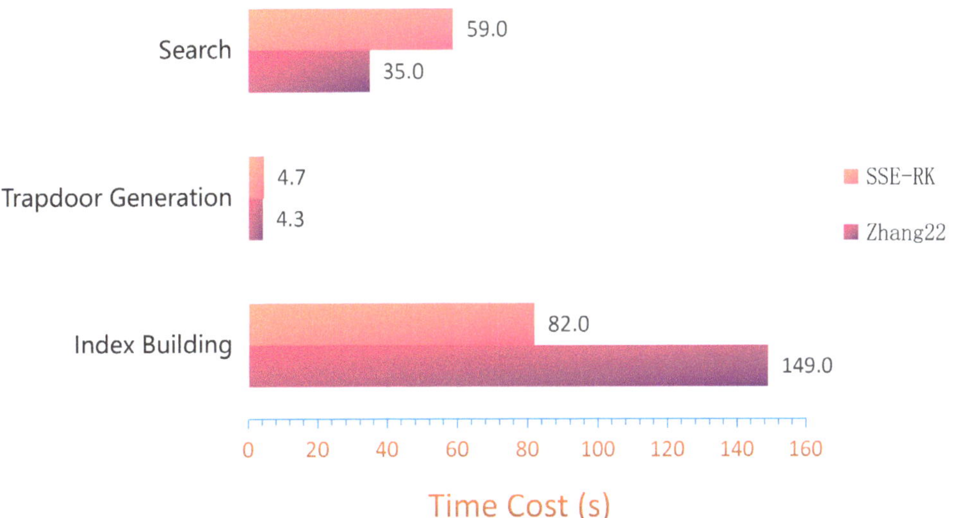

Figure 9. Comparison with the SSE scheme that supports only keyword search.

In addition, since the SSE-RK scheme can support both range and keyword search, it can also be utilized in applications such as location-based services [40] and protein prediction systems [41], etc. It is not difficult to find that the data in these applications will generally contain both numeric and textual types.

6. Conclusions

In this paper, we constructed a searchable encryption scheme that supports both range and keyword queries, and this scheme can perform a secure and fast search over encrypted EMR data. The construction of the SSE-RK scheme is divided into three main parts. Firstly, a keyword conversion method and two range conversion methods were proposed. These methods can transform keyword sets, range sets, and multi-dimensional points into vectors. Secondly, we designed an index tree-building algorithm. This algorithm makes use of the converted vectors to build all of the documents into a binary balanced tree in a bottom-up manner. Finally, the security of the SSE-RK scheme is ensured by encrypting each node in the index tree with a secure KNN algorithm. Furthermore, it is experimentally demonstrated that the query efficiency of the proposed scheme is sub-linearly related to the number of EMRs, and that it has better practicality than previous similar schemes.

In medical information systems, in addition to the range and keyword queries, user queries usually include more query conditions, such as in fuzzy queries, semantic queries, and Boolean queries. Therefore, our future work is to build a searchable encryption scheme that supports complex query conditions to enable a more accurate search over EMR data.

Author Contributions: Conceptualization, X.Y., Y.Z., and Y.L.; Data curation, Y.Z. and Y.L.; Formal analysis, X.Y., Y.Z., and Y.L.; Funding acquisition, Y.Z. and Y.L.; Methodology, X.Y. and Y.Z.; Software, Y.Z. and Y.W.; Validation, X.Y., Y.Z., and Y.L.; Writing—original draft, X.Y. and Y.Z.; Writing— review & editing, Y.Z., Y.L., and Y.W. All authors have read and agreed to the published version of the manuscript.

Funding: This work was supported by the National Natural Science Foundation of China (grant nos. 61972090 and 31872704), the Natural Science Foundation of Henan (grant no. 202300410339), and the Nanhu Scholars Program for Young Scholars of XYNU.

Data Availability Statement: The data used to support the findings of this study are available from the website, URL: https://trec.nist.gov/data/t9_filtering.html (accessed on 29 September 2023).

Conflicts of Interest: The authors declare no conflict of interest.

References

1.	Li, H.; Yang, Y.; Luan, T.H.; Liang, X.; Zhou, L.; Shen, X.S. Enabling fine-grained multi-keyword search supporting classified sub-dictionaries over encrypted cloud data. *IEEE Trans. Dependable Secur. Comput.* **2015**, *13*, 312–325. [CrossRef]
2.	Sun, W.; Liu, X.; Lou, W.; Hou, Y.T.; Li, H. Catch you if you lie to me: Efficient verifiable conjunctive keyword search over large dynamic encrypted cloud data. In Proceedings of the 2015 IEEE Conference on Computer Communications (INFOCOM), Hong Kong, China, 26 April–1 May 2015; pp. 2110–2118.
3.	Miao, Y.; Weng, J.; Liu, X.; Choo, Ki.R.; Liu, Z.; Li, H. Enabling verifiable multiple keywords search over encrypted cloud data. *Inf. Sci.* **2018**, *465*, 21–37. [CrossRef]
4.	Zhu, H.; Lu, R.; Huang, C.; Chen, L.; Li, H. An efficient privacy-preserving location-based services query scheme in outsourced cloud. *IEEE Trans. Veh. Technol.* **2015**, *65*, 7729–7739. [CrossRef]
5.	Wang, B.; Li, M.; Wang, H. Geometric range search on encrypted spatial data. *IEEE Trans. Inf. Forensics Secur.* **2015**, *11*, 704–719. [CrossRef]
6.	Xu, G.; Li, H.; Dai, Y.; Yang, K.; Lin, X. Enabling efficient and geometric range query with access control over encrypted spatial data. *IEEE Trans. Inf. Forensics Secur.* **2018**, *14*, 870–885. [CrossRef]
7.	Tang, Q. Public key encryption schemes supporting equality test with authorisation of different granularity. *Int. J. Appl. Cryptogr.* **2012**, *2*, 304–321. [CrossRef]
8.	Miao, Y.; Liu, X.; Deng, R.H.; Wu, H.; Li, H.; Li, J.; Wu, D. Hybrid keyword-field search with efficient key management for industrial internet of things. *IEEE Trans. Ind. Inform.* **2018**, *15*, 3206–3217. [CrossRef]
9.	Wang, X.; Ma, J.; Liu, X.; Deng, R.H.; Miao, Y.; Zhu, D.; Ma, Z. Search me in the dark: Privacy-preserving boolean range query over encrypted spatial data. In Proceedings of the IEEE INFOCOM 2020—IEEE Conference on Computer Communications, Toronto, ON, Canada, 6–9 July 2020; pp. 2253–2262.
10.	Lai, S.; Patranabis, S.; Sakzad, A.; Liu, J.K.; Mukhopadhyay, D.; Steinfeld, R.; Sun, S.; Liu, D.; Zuo, C. Result pattern hiding searchable encryption for conjunctive queries. In Proceedings of the 2018 ACM SIGSAC Conference on Computer and Communications Security, Toronto, ON, Canada, 15–19 October 2018; pp. 745–762.
11.	Wong, W.K.; Cheung, D.W.; Kao, B.; Mamoulis, N. Secure kNN computation on encrypted databases. In Proceedings of the 2009 ACM SIGMOD International Conference on Management of Data, Providence, RI, USA, 29 June–2 July 2009; pp. 139–152.
12.	Song, D.; Wagner, D.; Perrig, A. Practical techniques for searching on encrypted data. In Proceedings of the IEEE Symposium on Research in Security and Privacy, Berkeley, CA, USA, 14–17 May 2000; pp. 44–55.
13.	Goh, E.J. Secure indexes. *IACR Cryptol. Eprint Arch.* **2003**, *2003*, 216.
14.	Byun, J.W.; Lee, D.H.; Lim, J. Efficient conjunctive keyword search on encrypted data storage system. In Proceedings of the European Public Key Infrastructure Workshop, Turin, Italy, 19–20 June 2006; Springer: Berlin/Heidelberg, Germany, 2006; pp. 184–196.
15.	Ballard, L.; Kamara, S.; Monrose, F. Achieving efficient conjunctive keyword searches over encrypted data. In Proceedings of the International Conference on Information and Communications Security, Beijing, China, 10–13 December 2005; Springer: Berlin/Heidelberg, Germany, 2005; pp. 414–426.
16.	Zhu, Y.; Ma, D.; Wang, S. Secure data retrieval of outsourced data with complex query support. In Proceedings of the 2012 32nd International Conference on Distributed Computing Systems Workshops, Macau, China, 18–21 June 2012; pp. 481–490.
17.	Curtmola, R.; Garay, J.; Kamara, S.; Ostrovsky, R. Searchable symmetric encryption: Improved definitions and efficient constructions. *J. Comput. Secur.* **2011**, *19*, 895–934. [CrossRef]
18.	Zerr, S.; Olmedilla, D.; Nejdl, W.; Siberski, W. Zerber+R: Top-k retrieval from a confidential index. In Proceedings of the 12th International Conference on Extending Database Technology: Advances in Database Technology, Saint Petersburg, Russia, 24–26 March 2009; pp. 439–449.
19.	Wang, C.; Cao, N.; Ren, K.; Lou, W. Enabling Secure and Efficient Ranked Keyword Search over Outsourced Cloud Data. *IEEE Trans. Parallel Distrib. Syst.* **2012**, *23*, 1467–1479. [CrossRef]
20.	Cao, N.; Wang, C.; Li, M.; Ren, K.; Lou, W. Privacy-preserving multi-keyword ranked search over encrypted cloud data. *IEEE Trans. Parallel Distrib. Syst.* **2013**, *25*, 222–233. [CrossRef]
21.	Xia, Z.; Wang, X.; Sun, X.; Wang, Q. A Secure and Dynamic Multi-Keyword Ranked Search Scheme over Encrypted Cloud Data. *IEEE Trans. Parallel Distrib. Syst.* **2016**, *27*, 340–352. [CrossRef]
22.	Guo, C.; Zhuang, R.; Chang, C.; Yuan, Q. Dynamic multi-keyword ranked search based on bloom filter over encrypted cloud data. *IEEE Access* **2019**, *7*, 35826–35837. [CrossRef]

23. Liu, Z.; Wu, L.; Meng, W.; Wang, H.; Wang, W. Accurate range query with privacy preservation for outsourced location-based service in IOT. *IEEE Internet Things J.* **2021**, *8*, 14322–14337. [CrossRef]
24. Molla, E.; Rizomiliotis, P.; Gritzalis, S. Efficient searchable symmetric encryption supporting range queries. *Int. J. Inf. Secur.* **2023**, *22*, 785–798. [CrossRef]
25. Zheng, Y.; Lu, R.; Guan, Y.; Shao, J.; Zhu, H. Achieving efficient and privacy-preserving exact set similarity search over encrypted data. *IEEE Trans. Dependable Secur. Comput.* **2020**, *19*, 1090–1103. [CrossRef]
26. Gupta, B.B.; Lytras, M.D. Fog-enabled secure and efficient fine-grained searchable data sharing and management scheme for IoT-based healthcare systems. *IEEE Trans. Eng. Manag.* **2022**. [CrossRef]
27. Fu, Z.; Ren, K.; Shu, J.; Sun, X.; Huang, F. Enabling personalized search over encrypted outsourced data with efficiency improvement. *IEEE Trans. Parallel Distrib. Syst.* **2015**, *27*, 2546–2559. [CrossRef]
28. Zhang, Y.; Li, Y.; Wang, Y. Efficient Searchable Symmetric Encryption Supporting Dynamic Multikeyword Ranked Search. *Secur. Commun. Netw.* **2020**, *2020*, 7298518. [CrossRef]
29. Fu, Z.; Wu, X.; Guan, C.; Sun, X.; Ren, K. Toward Efficient Multi-Keyword Fuzzy Search over Encrypted Outsourced Data with Accuracy Improvement. *IEEE Trans. Inf. Forensics Secur.* **2017**, *11*, 2706–2716. [CrossRef]
30. Kuzu, M.; Islam, M.S.; Kantarcioglu, M. Efficient similarity search over encrypted data. In Proceedings of the 2012 IEEE 28th International Conference on Data Engineering, Arlington, VA, USA, 1–5 April 2012; pp. 1156–1167.
31. Boneh, D.; Crescenzo, G.D.; Ostrovsky, R.; Persiano, G. Public key encryption with keyword search. In Proceedings of the International Conference on the Theory and Applications of Cryptographic Techniques, Interlaken, Switzerland, 2–6 May 2004; Springer: Berlin/Heidelberg, Germany, 2004; pp. 506–522.
32. Park, D.J.; Kim, K.; Lee, P.J. Public key encryption with conjunctive field keyword search. In Proceedings of the International Workshop on Information Security Applications, Jeju, Republic of Korea, 23–25 August 2004; Springer: Berlin/Heidelberg, Germany, 2004; pp. 73–86.
33. Katz, J.; Sahai, A.; Waters, B. Predicate encryption supporting disjunctions, polynomial equations, and inner products. In Proceedings of the Annual International Conference on the Theory and Applications of Cryptographic Techniques, Istanbul, Turkey, 13–17 April 2008; Springer: Berlin/Heidelberg, Germany, 2008; pp. 146–162.
34. Zhang, Y.; Li, Y.; Wang, Y. Secure and Efficient Searchable Public Key Encryption for Resource Constrained Environment Based on Pairings under Prime Order Group. *Secur. Commun. Netw.* **2019**, *2019*, 5280806. [CrossRef]
35. Kim, I.; Hwang, S.O.; Park, J.H.; Park, C. An Efficient Predicate Encryption with Constant Pairing Computations and Minimum Costs. *IEEE Trans. Comput.* **2016**, *65*, 2947–2958. [CrossRef]
36. Zhang, R.; Wang, J.; Song, Z.; Wang, X. An enhanced searchable encryption scheme for secure data outsourcing. *Sci. China Inf. Sci.* **2020**, *63*, 132102. [CrossRef]
37. Miao, Y.; Liu, X.; Choo, K.K.R.; Deng, R.H.; Li, J.; Li, H.; Ma, J. Privacy-preserving attribute-based keyword search in shared multi-owner setting. *IEEE Trans. Dependable Secur. Comput.* **2019**, *18*, 1080–1094. [CrossRef]
38. He, W.; Zhang, Y.; Li, Y. Fast, Searchable, Symmetric Encryption Scheme Supporting Ranked Search. *Symmetry* **2022**, *14*, 1029. [CrossRef]
39. Hersh, W.; Buckley, C.; Leone, T.J.; Hickam, D. OHSUMED:An interactive retrieval evaluation and new large test collection for research. In Proceedings of the 17th Annual International ACM SIGIR Conference on Research and Development in Information Retrieval, Dublin, Ireland, 3–6 July 1994; pp. 192–201.
40. Shin, K.G.; Ju, X.; Chen, Z.; Hu, X. Privacy protection for users of location-based services. *IEEE Wirel. Commun.* **2012**, *19*, 30–39. [CrossRef]
41. Zhang, J.; Liang, X.; Zhou, F.; Li, B.; Li, Y. TYLER, a fast method that accurately predicts cyclin-dependent proteins by using computation-based motifs and sequence-derived features. *Math. Biosci. Eng.* **2021**, *18*, 6410–6429.

 *information*

Review

A Systematic Literature Review on Human Ear Biometrics: Approaches, Algorithms, and Trend in the Last Decade

Oyediran George Oyebiyi [1], Adebayo Abayomi-Alli [1,*], Oluwasefunmi 'Tale Arogundade [1], Atika Qazi [2], Agbotiname Lucky Imoize [3,4,*] and Joseph Bamidele Awotunde [5]

[1] Department of Computer Science, Federal University of Agriculture, Abeokuta 110124, Nigeria
[2] Centre for Lifelong Learning, Universiti Brunei Darussalam, Jalan Tungku Link, Gadong BE1410, Brunei
[3] Department of Electrical and Electronics Engineering, Faculty of Engineering, University of Lagos, Akoka, Lagos 100213, Nigeria
[4] Department of Electrical Engineering and Information Technology, Institute of Digital Communication, Ruhr University, 44801 Bochum, Germany
[5] Department of Computer Science, Faculty of Information and Communication Sciences, University of Ilorin, Ilorin 240003, Nigeria
* Correspondence: abayomiallia@funaab.edu.ng (A.A.-A.); aimoize@unilag.edu.ng (A.L.I.)

Abstract: Biometric technology is fast gaining pace as a veritable developmental tool. So far, biometric procedures have been predominantly used to ensure identity and ear recognition techniques continue to provide very robust research prospects. This paper proposes to identify and review present techniques for ear biometrics using certain parameters: machine learning methods, and procedures and provide directions for future research. Ten databases were accessed, including ACM, Wiley, IEEE, Springer, Emerald, Elsevier, Sage, MIT, Taylor & Francis, and Science Direct, and 1121 publications were retrieved. In order to obtain relevant materials, some articles were excused using certain criteria such as abstract eligibility, duplicity, and uncertainty (indeterminate method). As a result, 73 papers were selected for in-depth assessment and significance. A quantitative analysis was carried out on the identified works using search strategies: source, technique, datasets, status, and architecture. A Quantitative Analysis (QA) of feature extraction methods was carried out on the selected studies with a geometric approach indicating the highest value at 36%, followed by the local method at 27%. Several architectures, such as Convolutional Neural Network, restricted Boltzmann machine, auto-encoder, deep belief network, and other unspecified architectures, showed 38%, 28%, 21%, 5%, and 4%, respectively. Essentially, this survey also provides the various status of existing methods used in classifying related studies. A taxonomy of the current methodologies of ear recognition system was presented along with a publicly available occlussion and pose sensitive black ear image dataset of 970 images. The study concludes with the need for researchers to consider improvements in the speed and security of available feature extraction algorithms.

Keywords: biometric technology; ear recognition systems; feature extraction; classification methods; convolutional neural network; restricted Boltzmann machine

Citation: Oyebiyi, O.G.; Abayomi-Alli, A.; Arogundade, O.'T.; Qazi, A.; Imoize, A.L.; Awotunde, J.B. A Systematic Literature Review on Human Ear Biometrics: Approaches, Algorithms, and Trend in the Last Decade. *Information* **2023**, *14*, 192. https://doi.org/10.3390/info14030192

Academic Editors: Jose de Vasconcelos, Hugo Barbosa, Carla Cordeiro and Alessandra Lumini

Received: 19 December 2022
Revised: 13 March 2023
Accepted: 15 March 2023
Published: 17 March 2023

1. Introduction

Globally, over 1.5 billion people are without proper identification proof [1]. Establishing a person's identity, together with connected privileges, is an increasing source of concern for governments all over the world, as it constitutes a major requirement for the attainment of Sustainable Development Goals (SDG).

A formal means of personal identity verification is a primary requirement in modern societies. The inability to establish one's identity can significantly hamper access to basic rights, government, and other essential services. The task of effectively identifying an individual involves the use of biometrics technology. Biometric recognition involves using specialized devices to capture the image of an individual's feature and computer software to extract, encrypt, store, and match these features [2]. It typically involves the use of unique features such as the face, ear signature, gait, voice, fingerprint, etc., for automatic computerized identification systems.

A biometric system is principally a pattern recognition system that obtains biometric data from an individual, mines a feature set from the data acquired, and compares this feature set against the stored template in the database [3].

Computer-based biometric systems have become available primarily due to increasing technological sophistication and computing capabilities. The face is a prominent example of an innate human biometric used for identification [4]. It is a major feature for identification due to its uniqueness [5]. However, an upward surge in the global population coupled with cultural diversities makes effective identification more profound, particularly as traditional identification such as passwords, locks and pin codes are gradually becoming vulnerable to theft, sabotage, or loss hence the need for more reliable traits like the ear [6]. The recent global pandemic caused by the novel corona virus (COVID-19) has led to the compulsory use of face masks in public [7]. Consequently, this new dressing standard poses a serious challenge to facial recognition in public [8]. Further still, the challenge is further emphasized in the performance of recognition systems, particularly in surveillance scenarios, because the masks have occluded a large portion of the face [9] and have made the attention to ear recognition research even more important. Although strategies for ear recognition systems (ERS) were long conceived, actual implementation did not occur until much later [10]. Ear images are a promising feature that has been lately advanced as a biometric resource [11]. For instance, the human ears have an immediately foreseeable background, and scholarly work on the symmetric features of the human ear has continued to generate new interest [12]. For instance, structural features of the human ear abound, thereby making it readily suitable for robust processing and applications. Not only does the ear represent an unchanged biometric trait over time, but it also possesses characteristics applicable to every individual, such as distinctiveness, collectability, universality, and permanence [13].

The advantages of the external ear as a biometric feature include:

1. Fewer inconsistencies in ear structure due to advancement in age compared with a face.
2. Reliable ear outline throughout an individual life cycle.
3. The distinctiveness of the external ear shape is not affected by moods, emotions, other expressions, etc.
4. Restricted surface ear surface area leads to faster processing compared with a face.
5. It is easier to capture the human ear even at a distance.
6. The procedure is non-invasive. Beards, spectacles, and makeup cannot alter the appearance of the ear.

In summary, this study aims to conduct a Systematic Literature Review (SLR) on human ear biometric and recognition systems. The emphasis is on the contributions of deep learning to improving and enhancing ear recognition system performance vis-a-vis traditional machine learning methods. Subsequent sections of this paper are organized as follows: Section 2 highlights the sequence, search methods, and other strategies used in this study. Results obtained are presented in Section 3, with a follow-up discussion in Section 4. Lastly, Section 5 highlights the research outcomes and challenges and presents a current taxonomy of the ear recognition system.

2. Research Method

Research studies on human ear biometrics abound. These studies, mostly digital, were scientifically analyzed using quantitative methods to highlight significant trends and developments in ear recognition systems. The search procedure used in [1] was adopted and used for this study to provide answers to the following research questions:

RQ1: What is state of the art in ear recognition research?

RQ2: What has deep learning contributed to ear recognition in the last decade?

RQ3: Is there sufficient publicly available data for ear recognition research?
The research questions though intertwined motivates conducting this SLR.

2.1. Search Attributes

The methods of human ear recognition can be roughly divided into traditional and methods based on deep learning, [14] with studies particularly more inclined towards the latter.

Biometrics has, over time, evolved to include deep learning of artificial neural networks (ANN), [15]. Deep Convolutional Neural Networks are mathematical models that simulate the functional attributes of human biological neural networks [16]. They represent multiple data layers with multiple abstraction stages through learning to generate precise models autonomously [17]. Research into ear recognition using neural networks with varying performances has been in existence for a while. Several variants of ANN, such as the convolutional neural network (CNN) are applicable in advancing various biometric modalities. Studies suggest that approaches applying CNN epitomize state-of-the-art performance in object detection, segmentation, and image classification, particularly in unconstrained settings [18].

One of the initial efforts at the neural network for ear recognition was described by [19], which employed local binary patterns and CNN with a recognition accuracy of 93.3%. Recent advances in CNN for developing verification and identification systems have considerably pushed the development of image classification and object detection [20]. It combines a large set of parameters than traditional neural networks, thereby generating improved performance [16].

2.2. Search Queries

In other to obtain a robust and comprehensive collection of related articles that have significantly contributed to ERS, the following search criteria were used:

1. Boolean operators of "OR or "AND" to retrieve data.
2. Keywords generated from the research question as search parameters.
3. Restriction to some publication types and publishers.
4. Identifiers from related work.

Search results displayed outcomes with keywords and Boolean combinations such as (human ear) AND (deep convolutionary network (OR) biometrics), (Identification (OR) recognition (OR) deep-learning (OR) feature extraction). A logical procedure of review of the contributions of neural networks to ERS was conducted through a numerical assessment to identify innovative patterns, methods, and techniques in the ear recognition domain. Table 1 indicates the number of articles downloaded from respective indexed databases.

Table 1. Articles downloaded from indexed database.

S/n	Digital Library	No. Articles	Percentage (%)
1	Taylor & Francis	89	7.9
2	Science Direct	157	14
3	IEEE	255	22.7
4	Emerald	48	4.2
5	ACM	73	6.5
6	Sage	55	4.9
7	Springer	201	17.9
8	Elsevier	137	12.2
9	Wiley	45	4.0
10	MIT	61	5.4
	Total	1121	100

Search Stage 1 (Information Extraction): an in-depth search of seven electronic databases showed an initial total article count of 1121 and was further subjected to a careful selection process.

Search Stage 2 (Screening): after the removal of 784 duplicate and 245 irrelevant articles/works of literature, a residual quantity of 92 was obtained for onward analysis.

Search Stage 3 (Eligibility Determination): in obtaining appropriate articles relevant to the study, 92 articles were shortlisted. Subsequently, 18 articles were dropped for lack of clear-cut methodology.

Search Stage 4 (Inclusion): in-line with the research aim, the Authors conducted a quality check for the residual articles and concluded on 74 for further systematic review.

The summary of the search procedure from stage 1 (information extraction), stage 2 (screening), stage 3 (eligibility determination) to stage 4 (inclusion) are represented in the Preferred Reporting Items for Systematic Reviews and Meta-Analyses (PRISMA) flowchart in Figure 1. Preliminary results from search criteria were obtained from Google Scholar, Scopus, Springer, Science Direct, ACM, Emerald, and IEEE explore databases using a search criterion of publications not later than ten (10) years.

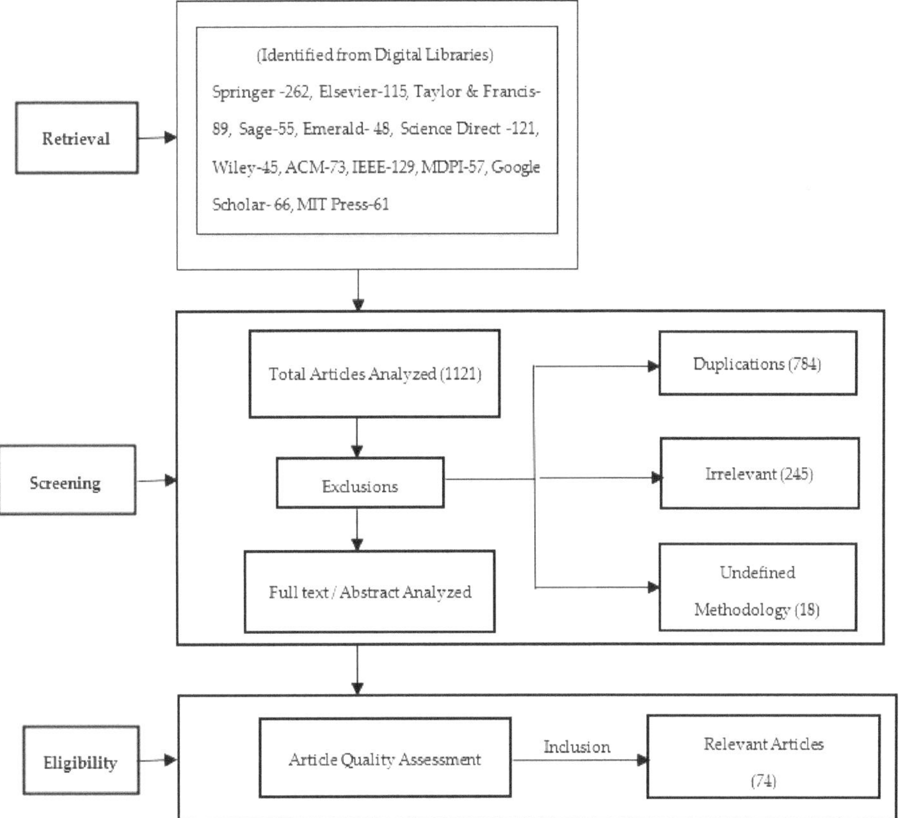

Figure 1. PRISMA flow chart for the search procedure.

2.3. Search Strategy

After a preliminary assessment of requirements suitable for answering the research questions, a predominance of varied knowledge repositories ranging from journal articles, online blogs, and bulletins to book chapters were returned. Five (5) main sources which include journals, conferences, workshops, book chapters and original thesis were selected for the review. A total of 74 articles were carefully selected based on relevance with 52 journal articles, 9 conference proceedings, 5 workshop reports, 5 theses and 3 book chapters.

2.4. Article Source (AS)

Ten (10) electronic databases, including Taylor & Francis, Springer, Elsevier, Emerald, Wiley, Science Direct, IEEE, ACM, Sage, and MIT, provided data for extraction using keywords and related terms in the study. The sources include workshops, conference proceedings, journal publications, original thesis, and book chapters.

2.5. Ear Databases

This section presents a review of databases used in ear detection and recognition. Ear databases are crucial in developing and evaluating ERS and algorithms. Existing databases are in different sizes with varied factors of influence ranging from illumination to the angle of the pose. A summary of existing databases used in ear recognition research studies is presented in Table 2. A number of these databases are either publicly available or can be acquired under license.

Table 2. Existing ear recognition research databases.

S/n	Catalogue	Year	Total Images	Sides	Volunteers	Description	Available
1	VGGFace-Ear	2022	234651	both	660	Iner and intra subject variations in pose, age, illumination and ethnicity.	Free
2	UERC	2019	11000	Both	3690	Three image datasets to train and test images under varied parameters	Free
3	EarVN1.0	2018	28412	N/A	164	Images captured under varied pose, illumination, and occlusion conditions	Free
4	USTB-HELLOEAR (A)	2017	336572	Both	104	Pose variations	Free
5	USTB-HELLOEAR (B)	2017	275909	Both	466	Left and right images captured in uncontrolled conditions	Free
6	WebEars	2017	1000	N/A	N/A	Images captured under varied conditions	Free
7	HelloEars	2017	610000	Both	1570	Images captured in a controlled environment	Free
8	AWE	2016	1000	Both	100	Images captured in the wild in an uncontrolled environment	Free
9	UND	2014	NA	Both	N/A	Different image collections with varied images captured in 3D.	Free
10	XM2VTS	2014	4 Footages	Both	295	32 khz 16-bit audio/video files	Not Free
11	UMIST	2014	564	Both	20	Head rotation from the left-hand side to the frontal view	Free
12	UBEAR	2011	4497	Both	127	Images captured in an uncontrolled environment with different poses and occlusion	Free
13	WPUT	2010	2071	Both	501	Varied illumination	Free
14	YSU	2009	2590		259	Angle images between 0 and 90	Free
15	IIT Delhi	2007	493	Right	125	3 Images taken indoor	Free
16	WVU	2006	460	Both	402	2 min audio-visual from both sides	Free
17	USTB (4)	2005	8500	Both	500	15-degree differences using 17 cameras	Free

Table 2. *Cont.*

S/n	Catalogue	Year	Total Images	Sides	Volunteers	Description	Available
18	USTB (3)	2004	1738	Right	79	Dual images at 5-degree variation till 60.	Free
19	USTB (2)	2003	308	Right	77	Varying degrees of illumination at +30 and −30 degrees	Free
20	USTB (1)	2002	180	Right	60	Different illumination conditions at a trivial angle	Free
21	UND (E)	2002	942	Both	302	Both 2D and 3D pictures	Free
22	UND (F)	2003	464	Side	114	Side profile appearance	Free
23	UND (G)	2005	738	Side	235	2D and 3D pictures	Free
24	UND (J2)	2005	1800	Both	415	2D and 3D pictures	Free
25	IITD	2007	663	Right	121	Greyscale images with slight angle variations.	Free
26	PERPINAN	1995	102	Left	17	Images with minor pose variations captured in a controlled environment	Free
27	AMI	NA	700	Both	100	Fixed Illumination	Free
28	NCKU	N/A	330	Both	90	37 images for each respondent	Free

2.6. Methods of Classification

The techniques of ear recognition can be grouped into four broad categories: hybrid, geometric, holistic, and local methods [10].

2.6.1. Geometric Approach

Research on geometric tendencies of the human ear dates to early 1890, when a French researcher, Alphonse Bertillon, suggested the potential of the human ear in identifying subjects [21]. Additional improvements using geometric features promoted the development of a Voronoi illustration with adjacency graphs [22].

The geometric method involves the extraction and analysis of geometric features of the human ear. These ranges from canny edge detection and contours to statistical features [23]. Ear image edges are computed after noise reduction using a Gaussian filter in canny edge detection. Edges are then connected to generate a pattern [24]. The contours of the ear start and end points are also useful information sources applicable in generating ear features and recognizable patterns [25]. Other feature-based statistical methods present ear images using parameters such as ear height, width, and angles between ear portions [26]. The work [27] presents a detailed taxonomy of ear features used for recognition by both machines and humans, such as texture, structure, and details. Typical texture-related features include ear type, skin colour; ear size, and shape, all extractable using linear discriminant analysis and principal component analysis algorithms. Ear features also use more prominent methods like local binary pattern [28], SIFT [29], and Gabor filters [30], on ear structures such as lobes, contours, and folds of the ear to represent the distinctiveness of the ear.

However, distortion invariant methods in ear geometry make only the required details available, thereby making this approach over-dependent on edge detectors such that only geometric ear information is considered with little emphasis on texture information.

2.6.2. Holistic Approach

In the holistic method, the overall stance of the ear is used to calculate input representations. It provides reasonable performance, particularly for suitably processed images. Hence, the approach requires normalization procedures before the extraction of desired features to ensure quality performance.

In this study, several studies on holistic techniques were reviewed. Ref. [31] conducted preliminary research on Force Field Transformation (FFT) for automatic ear recognition and returned a recognition rate of 99% on about 252 images in the XM2VTS database. Ref. [32] furthered the application of FFT with the underlying principle of Newton's law of gravitation to consider symmetric image pixels.

Experiments on the USTB IV database by [33] registered a comparatively low recognition rate of 72.2%. Gabor filters are also capable of identifying detailed texture data. When fused, its recognition accuracy varies between 92.06% and 95.93% [32]. Dimensionality reduction techniques such as PCA [31,34], ICA [35] and matrix factorization [36], feed higher-dimension vectors into lower dimensions while retaining their distinct features. Selected wavelet coefficients were used by [37] in repeated steps to represent features of ear images from the IITK database with a stated recognition accuracy of 96% [38] in their experiment on the UND and FEUD databases identified the suitability of sparse representations in changing degrees of illumination and pose.

In [39], numerical methods were used in composing six varied feature vectors that serve as feedback for a back propagation neural network for classifying moment invariant feature sets.

2.6.3. Local Approach

The local method depends on local areas of certain locations in an image to the extent of encoding texture details such that the region of interest does not automatically match structurally significant parts. Studies such as [40] present SIFT as a robust algorithm suitable for feature extraction under changing conditions. For instance, SIFT can accommodate variants in the pose for about 20 degrees [32]. Generally, assigning landmarks to ear images before training ensures proper filtering and matching operations in the local technique. Though SIFT landmarks have been very high such that obtaining an exact assignment is experimentally impossible, [41] attained a recognition rate of 91.5% with the XM2VTS database with possibilities for further improvements to 96%. Subsequent studies by [42] decomposed ear images into distinct colour segments with a reduced error margin that identifies and calculate unique identifiers for each key point detected. Unlike other approaches, local descriptors have varying degrees of complexity and are often combined with hybrid techniques to provide further reliable results in ear recognition [43].

2.6.4. Hybrid Approach

The hybrid technique involves the use of multiple parameters to improve the performance of recognition systems [5]. Edge models are initially generated from training images before adjustments into actual edges, as shown in [44]. Similarly, a fusion of Tchebichef moment descriptors and the triangle ratio method was experimentally determined in [45], while [46] achieved a recognition accurate of 99.2% in the USTB II database.

The study of [47] famously combined PCA and wavelets, while [39] opted for a fusion of Haar wavelet and LBP. The sparse representation algorithm by [48] was used on gray-level positioning features before initial dimension reduction procedures with LDA by [49]. In wavelet transforms, coefficient thresholds are required to obtain feature vectors that are particularly useful in the recognition and identification systems [50].

2.7. Ear Recognition Stages

In ear recognition systems, ear images are captured using a specific device. The images are then subjected to a preliminary stage of determining potential regions of interest using algorithms before being processed by a classifier, where details are enhanced before further procedures [51]. Essentially, the stages required in ear recognition are highlighted below:

2.7.1. Pre-Processing

This is the first step in ensuring the usability of acquired images. It involves the removal of unwanted background information (noise) before further processing. The techniques used are divided into intensity and filter methods.

Intensity Method: Analysing coloured images for edge and feature detection can be very complex [23]. Hence, a 3-conduit (RGB) image is often reduced to a single pathway (grayscale) to minimize complexity [52]. A method of spreading image intensity across a histogram, known as histogram equalization, is also sometimes applicable.

Filter method: In the filter method, noise reduction and feature enhancements are achieved using fuzzy technology [24]. Mean or median and Gaussian and Gabor filters are prominent examples of achieving a similar purpose.

2.7.2. Feature Extraction

The task of reducing the dimensions of an image for proper identification is known as feature extraction [53]. The features of an image must be precisely and correctly extracted using certain constituents of ear images, such as texture, colour, and shape. Subsequently, research parameters have been established to further determine the performance of recognition systems [9].

2.7.3. Classification

The classification or authentication stage is the final stage in the recognition process, where the feature set of the probe image is compared with a database image using various authentication techniques [23]. Many studies have been conducted on the stages involved in recognition of ear patterns. A summary of the common methods used by researchers for developing efficient and effective ERS is presented in Table 3.

Table 3. Summary of common methods in different stages of human ear recognition.

Pre-Processing	Feature Extraction	Decision-Making and Classification
Filter Method Log Gabor Filter [54] Gaussian filter [55] Middle filter [55,56] Fuzzy filter [24] Intensity Method Histogram equalization [53,57] RBG—grayscale [25,55]	Geometric Method Numerical technique [58] Ear contour [25] Detection of the edge [59] Appearance Based Method Descriptors of features [60] Reduction of Dimension [61] Force field Transformations [62] Wavelet Method [63]	Neural networks [64] Normalized cross-correlation [53] SVM classifier [64,65], K-Nearest Neighbours [28] Minimum Distance Classifier [50]

2.8. Deep Learning Approaches in Ear Recognition

In this study, a relationship between the most crucial stage (feature extraction) and classification techniques in relation to the volume of Authors is established.

Although deep-based schemes are often data-hungry, requiring significant processing time, several light, computationally fast variants have recently evolved [66,67].

In deep learning, more prominent feature extraction techniques include Gabor Mean [54], ANN Classifier, Haar wavelet ([50], Linear Discriminant Analysis (LDA) [68,69], Back Propagation Neural Network [70], FFT [23], Principal Component Analysis (PCA), [71], Edge-based method [12] and Voronoi diagrams [20].

Over time, the field of ear recognition has naturally developed along traditional machine learning methods, with few of its methods showing resilience to unconstrained conditions, including lightning and pose variations [69], hence inhibiting the overall performance of traditional systems.

Traditional ear detection and feature extraction methods typically rely on physiological attributes of the ear for normalization, feature extraction and classification [69,72]. For instance, in [73], training of various geometrical attributes of the ear was conducted with neural classifiers before the appearance of the inner and outer ear was suggested by [74]. Similarly, a combination of ear shape, average, centroid, and distance between pixels has been used to extract features using contour algorithms [75] geometrically. The work [58] extracted features using exterior ear edge and other local geometric features. Though these procedures appear straightforward, the performance level is often significantly low due to other salient processes involved [23].

Techniques involving subspace learning such as PCA, LDA and ICA, sometimes referred to as "Eigenears" have been experimentally determined suitably in local ear contour feature extraction [23]. More recently, The work [61] used a combination of multi-discriminative attributes and dimension reduction techniques to locally extract features of the ear. Such fusion techniques are referred to as hybrid and are usually more computationally expensive but with higher recognition performance over individual local, holistic, and geometric methods [76].

Nevertheless, traditional learning methods in ear recognition are severely hampered by more complex realities [72]. Even more interesting is the recent research focus which involves obtaining ear images in unrestrained conditions, generally referred to as in the wild. Traditional approaches to human ear recognition often rely on the preliminary processing of images, complex feature extraction, and determination of suitable classifiers [70]. These challenges have opened a new landscape as the research focus has gradually shifted to the automation of biometric identification [77].

3. Results Analysis

This section presents a discussion of search strategy outcomes to provide answers to research questions. Subsequently, different subsections are structured to highlight interpretations of the findings.

3.1. Search Strategy 1: Source

RQ1: What is state of the art in ear recognition research?

In the initial phase, a categorized search was used to identify similar articles on ERS and Neural Networks using paper titles and related keywords before developing a concluding search technique. The search for similar works was conducted for articles between 2010 and 2020 from the following sources: Springer, Elsevier, ACM, IEEE, Sage, Wiley, MIT Press, Taylor & Francis, Emerald and Science Direct. Figure 1 shows the number of relevant articles from selected sources, thus addressing RQ1.

3.2. Relevance of Publication

The 74 selected publications show that IEEE had the highest number with 15 relevant articles, followed by Springer having 12 relevant articles, Elsevier published 11, while Science Direct published 9 relevant articles. Taylor & Francis, Emerald, ACM, and Sage had 8, 8, 7 and 3 articles, respectively, while Wiley and MIT had one relevant publication each.

Ear recognition technique remains an active area of research that continues to generate diverse interest. The total number of relevant publications and the corresponding levels of citation from 2011 to 2020 is 2, 3, 5, 5, 4, 8, 7, 12, 10, and 13, respectively. Thus, confirming the steady rise in neural network techniques with the year 2020 having the highest number of relevant articles within the decade.

Although diverse methods of pre-processing, feature extraction and classification exist in the recognition process, there is an upward surge in the use of neural network methods for classification in ear recognition systems. Reasons for this might be inferred from the increasing demand for more fool proof biometric identification systems requiring large datasets and the ability of neural networks to train very large data sets autonomously.

3.3. Search Strategy 3: (Method)

Ear recognition techniques vary. Overtime, several Authors, have experimentally determined the performance of ERS using single or combined approaches on a wide array of datasets. Table 4 presents a summary of identified works containing metrics used in ear recognition.

Table 4. Summary of Performance metrics used in Traditional and Deep learning techniques in selected articles.

Traditional Learning Technique			
True Acceptance Rate [6,78–83]	Template capacity [5,84–86]	False Acceptance Rate [4,6,21,23,83,87–91]	Equal Error Rate [92–94]
Matching Speed [3,95]	Recognition Accuracy [14,15,24,28,68,85,96–105]	Recall [106–108]	Precision [40,95,102,109–111]
Deep Learning Techniques			
True Acceptance Rate [110–114]	Template capacity [115]	False Acceptance Rate [110–114].	Equal Error Rate [72,114]
Matching Speed [61,115–117]	Recognition Accuracy [70,118–121]	Recall [57,77,122–125]	Precision [126,127]

Previous studies have highlighted the numerous methods applied in the process of ear recognition, including local, holistic, geometric, and hybrid. The study on 74 existing related literature carefully selected from several works of literature [7–180] revealed that 65%, 20%, 12% and 8% of the studies employed local, hybrid, holistic, and geometric methods, respectively. Although several works of literature on ear biometrics abound, a concise summary of some existing ear recognition approaches from the list is presented in Table 5. A summary of the Pros and Cons of different sub-areas in Ear Recognition Stages is given in Table 6 in Section 4.

Table 5. Comparative summary of ear recognition approaches.

Reference.	Year	Method	Type	Dataset	Performance (%)
[7]	2010	PCA and NN	Holistic	UBEAR	96
[18]	2022	Deep Learning	CNN	VGGFace	NA
[23]	2019	NA	NA	NA	NA
[27]	2016	Geometric features	Geometric features	CP	88
[31]	2003	Force field transform	Holistic	Own	NA
[31]	2003	PCA	Holistic	UND(E)	71.6
[35]	2005	Matrix factorization	Holistic	USTB II	91
[38]	2008	Sparse representation	Holistic	UND	96.9
[39]	2010	Moment invariant method	Holistic	Own	91.8
[40]	2010	SIFT	Local	XM2VTS	96
[41]	2007	Combination of pre-filtered points and SIFT	Local	XM2VTS	91.5
[47]	2007	PCA and wavelet transformation	Hybrid	USTB II, CP	90.5
[47]	2007	Inpainting techniques, neural networks	CNN, Traditional learning	UERC	75
[48]	2013	SIFT	Local	CP	78.8
[49]	2014	Hybrid-based on SURF LDA AND NN	Hybrid	Own	97

Table 5. *Cont.*

Reference.	Year	Method	Type	Dataset	Performance (%)
[41]	2007	Combination of pre-filtered points and SIFT	Local	XM2VTS	91.5
[47]	2007	PCA and wavelet transformation	Hybrid	USTB II, CP	90.5
[47]	2007	Inpainting techniques, neural networks	CNN, Traditional learning	UERC	75
[48]	2013	SIFT	Local	CP	78.8
[49]	2014	Hybrid-based on SURF LDA AND NN	Hybrid	Own	97
[49]	2014	Neural networks	Deep CNN	UERC	99.7
[72]	2019	Neural Networks	CNN	AMI	75.6
[73]	1999	Orthogonal log-Gabor filter pairs	Local	IITD II	95.9
[75]	2005	Ear framework geometry	Geometric	Own	86.2
[81]	2013	Not Applicable (NA)	NA	NA	NA
[85]	2019	NA	NA	NA	NA
[87]	2019	Neural networks	CNN	-	-
[92]	2020	Deep learning	CNN	NA	97
[98]	2014	Edge image dimension	Geometric	USTB II	85
[107]	2016	CNN	Local	Avila Police School & Bisite Video	80.5 & 79.2
[107]	2013	Deep neural network	CNN	Avila Police School	84
[108]	2017	Traditional Machine Learning	YOLO, Multilayer perceptron	Own	82
[117]	2018	Maximum and minimum height lines	Geometric	USTDB&IIT Delhi	98.3 & 99.6
[119]	2018	Deep Learning	CNN	Open image dataset	85
[123]	2023	Neural networks	CNN	AMI, UND, Video Dataset, UBEAR	98
[128]	2010	PCA	Holistic	Own	40
[129]	2002	ICA	Holistic	Own	94.1
[130]	2014	Log-Gabor wavelets	Local	UND	90
[131]	2007	Multi-Matcher	Hybrid	UND(E)	80
[132]	2007	Log-Gabor filters	Local	XM2VTS	85.7
[133]	2008	LBP and Haar Wavelet transformation	Hybrid	USTB III	92.4
[134]	2008	Improved locally linear embedding	Holistic	USTB III	90
[135]	2008	Null Kernel discriminant analysis	Holistic	USTB I	97.7
[136]	2008	Gabor filters	Local	UND(E)	84
[137]	2009	Block portioning and Gabor transformation	Local	USTB II	100

Table 5. *Cont.*

Reference.	Year	Method	Type	Dataset	Performance (%)
[138]	2009	2D quadrature filter	Local	IITD I	96.5
[140]	2013	Sparse representation classification	Holistic	USTB III	90
[141]	2019	Multi-level fusion	Hybrid	USTB II	99.2
[142]	2014	Enhanced SURF with NN	Local	IITK 1	2.8
[143]	2014	Non-linear curvelet features	Local	IITD II	96.2
[144]	2014	BSIF	Local	IITD II	97.3
[145]	2014	LPQ	Local	Several	93.1
[146]	2014	LPQ, BSIF, LBP, HOG with LDA	Hybrid	UND-J2, AMI, IITK	98.7
[147]	2014	Weighted wavelet transforms and DCT	Hybrid	Own	98.1
[148]	2015	Haar wavelet and LBP	Hybrid	IITD	94.5
[149]	2016	BSIF	Local	IITD I, IITD II	96.7 & 97.3
[150]	2015	Multi-bags-of-features histogram	Local	IITD I	6.3
[151]	2015	Gabor filters	Local	IITD II	92.4
[153]	2017	Modular neural network	Hybrid	USTB	99
[154]	2018	Biased normalized cut and morphological operations	Deep Neural Network	Own	95
[155]	2018	Traditional machine learning	Local	NA	NA
[156]	2020	Deep learning	CNN	Own	95
[157]	2020	Traditional Machine Learning	Sparse Representation	USTB III	NA
[158]	2022	Traditional Machine Learning	Hybrid	IITDelhi	NA
[159]	2022	Deep Learning	SIFT and ANN	IITDelhi	NA
[180]	2022	Global and local ear prints	Hybrid	FEARID	91.3

In this study, the authors of selected articles were divided into five groups. These categories represent the level of the ERS implementation in the article in terms of if the study was based on:

1. an **assessment** of existing algorithms on a given dataset (A);
2. a **proposed** or yet-to-be-evaluated techniques (S);
3. a **designed** templates using existing procedures (D);
4. **planning and assessment** with studies based on established procedures (PA);
5. newly **proposed** and **executed** techniques (PE).

The results showed A, S, D, PA and PE returned 26, 19, 8, 9, 13 articles respectively. The details of the articles in each category is in Table 7 (see Section 4).

Results show that 25.33% of the methods used in the selected articles were suggested (proposed) and not implemented. This might not be unconnected with the availability of limited ear databases collected in unrestrained situations for experimental studies.

RQ2: What are the contributions of deep learning to ear recognition in the last decade?

At present, acceptance of deep learning techniques is increasing as it combines the traditional steps in the recognition process into single connecting models [72]. Deep learning algorithms have overcome many of the challenges associated with machine learning algorithms, particularly those associated with feature extraction techniques, while also having the ability for biometric image transformations. Consequently, attempts at ear detection using neural networks though initially limited are rapidly gaining pace. Early attempts by [160] focused on multi-class projection extreme learning machine methods to augment performance. In [10], a concise and detailed review of advances in ear detection using machine learning was presented. Geometric morphometric and Neural Networks were suggested in [57] to compare non-automated instances. Ref. [87] developed a neural network model to authenticate responses originating from the human ear with a 7.56% and 13.3% increase in identification and verification tasks, respectively.

However, variants of the neural network such as Convolutional Neural Networks (CNN) have shown remarkable performance against conventional systems [161]. The CNN design originates from [162], it is majorly a multi-layer network with capabilities to handle several invariants [169]. Subsequent experimental studies have gradually adapted its use to the recognition of specific human biometric traits. It eliminates cumbersome pre-processing procedures associated with traditional methods [163,164] and its robustness against texture and shape makes it dominant over traditional approaches [20,24].

Experimental studies by [72] compared the performance of some traditional ear recognition approaches to a variant of CNN with results above 22% of the initial descriptors. Nonetheless, ear recognition using deep neural networks is still significantly hampered by limited ear recognition databases and few experimental images leading to data augmentation [18].

RQ3: Is there sufficient publicly available data for ear recognition research?

A summary of findings from Table 2 indicates a predominance of free publicly available ear databases. This research identifies 27 publicly available datasets. Findings studies suggest the existence of publicly available ear databases since 1995, however, ear databases have grown to further accommodate different poses, angles, occlusion, and modes of collection.

Ear biometrics represents an active field of research. Nevertheless, ear image databases are very rare and usually strongly limited [165]. Further still, an absence of a unified large-scale publicly available ear database still represents a major challenge in the overall objective evaluation of ear recognition systems.

For instance, as of 2017, the reported performance of ear-recognition techniques has surpassed the rank-1 recognition rate of 90% on most available datasets [10]. This fact suggests that though technology has reached a level of maturity that easily handles images captured in laboratory-like settings, presently available ear databases are inadequate. Consequently, more challenging datasets are needed to identify open problems and provide room for further advancements.

3.4. Comparison with Related Surveys

ERS is not so popular compared to other biometric systems like fingerprints, faces, Veins, iris etc, [113]. Data augmentation of images in neural networks is often a challenging factor. Hence [166] suggested a learning method using limited datasets to train the network in ear image recognition. Similarly, Ref. [69] proposed a means of ear identification using transfer learning. Ref. [10] also recommended a mean method to improve the performance of datasets and suggested various architectures and controlled learning on previously trained datasets to develop a widely accessible CNN-based ear recognition method. In order to improve upon factors that affect image acquisition techniques such as contrast, position, and light intensity, a framework for ear localization using a histogram of oriented gradient (HOG) and support vector machine (SVM) was developed by [116] before subsequent CNN classification. A discriminant method was suggested by [61] to extract ear features in a pecking order, while [21] introduced dual images using SVM to tackle the challenge of limited images per subject. In exploring hand-crafted options, Ref. [167] combined CNN and handcrafted features to augment deep learning techniques, thus suggesting that deep learning can be complemented with other techniques.

This survey extended the review from [23], whose focus was mainly on the three core phases of ear biometric research: pre-processing, feature extraction and authentication. Consequently, a comprehensive overview of the contributions of prior research efforts is further amplified with particular emphasis on methods used for feature extraction and classification process. Despite previous reviews, this study focuses on qualitative and quantitative analysis of prevailing techniques through diverse search strategies as done in [11]. To the best of our knowledge, this study is the first to provide an in-depth novel synopsis and grouping of research approaches in ear biometric using different categories: existing approaches and methods.

Table 7 in Section 4 shows shows the predominantly used ear databases amongst several researchers from the list of reviewed articles.

A careful review of selected publications revealed some factors highlighted below as major determinants of the challenge raised in R3.

1. Poor feature selection: the application of feature selection is very diverse as it aims to reduce factors that can affect the performance of classifiers. Many images are acquired with several inherent background noises. Invariably, poor feature selection results in poor classification.

2. Hardware Dependence: A common drawback identified from selected works of literature is the resource-intensive tendencies of neural networks and other associated costs. They often require large volumes of data for training, placing heavy computational demand on processors.

3. Gaps between industry, implementation, research, and deployment: studies from reviewed articles revealed a missing link between the industries, researchers, and other stakeholders such that the majority of the related experimental studies were performed for purely academic purposes, hence limiting the potential to fine-tune existing technologies to suit user requirements.

Consequently, a need for merging research with actual deployment at user-ends is crucial in assessing the strengths and weaknesses of recognition systems and in providing relevant state-of-the-art systems capable of mitigating emerging vulnerabilities.

3.5. State of the Art in Ear Biometrics over the Last Decade

In the past few years, ear biometrics have been very prominent in achieving state of the art status applicable within the fields of human verification and identification [173]. Although poor quality images have often been a demerit, improved methods have since been developed to tackle it. Research from various authors, Refs. [181,182] have consistently explored novel approaches targeted at optimal performance of ear biometric systems. Typically, concentration on ear biometrics have been largely focused on the approaches of ear detection. This is seen from the study in [183–189]. The fundamental goal of researchers for years has been and continues to be developing ear recognition model that can overcome all detection challenges [183], but ear detection remains an image segmentation problem. In [184], deep CNN and contextual information was applied for ear detection in the 2D side of the face image. A single stage architecture was used to perform detection and classification with scale invariance. A context-provider in Context-aware Ear Detection Network (ContexedNet) developed in [190], extracts probability maps from the input image corresponding to facial element locations, and a model specifically designed to segment ears that incorporates the probability maps into a context-aware segmentation-based ear recognition algorithm. Extensive tests were conducted on the AWE and UBEAR datasets to evaluate ContexedNet, and the results were very encouraging when compared to other state-of-the-art methods. In [185], a deep learning object detector called Faster R-CNN was developed based on CNN, PCA and genetic algorithm (GA) for feature extraction, dimensionality reduction and selection, respectively. The work [186] went further to propose a deep network for segmenting and normalising ear print patterns, the model was trained using the IITD dataset.

Furthermore, the authors in [113] proposed a method for ear detection based on Faster Region-based Convolutional Neural Networks (Faster R-CNNs). On the UBEAR and UND dataset, the model was demonstrated to assure highly competitive outcomes by building on advancements in the general object detection area. El-Naggar et al. later presented a theoretically related method in [191], which once more showed the effectiveness of the Faster R-CNN architecture for ear identification. A geometric deep learning-based method for ear recognition was reported [76]. The suggested model uses Gaussian mixture models to define convolutional filters and permits the use of CNNs on graphs (GMMs). Based on this idea, the authors develop a framework for competitive detection that is both highly rotation-resistant (i.e., rotation equivariant) and has other advantageous features. Using a multi-path model topology and detection grouping, the authors [123] proposed a CNN-based method for ear detection that locates ear regions in the images. This method's core idea is to search for ears at various scales, like contextual modules seen in contemporary object identification frameworks like [192,193], to enhance detection the authors in [190] employed general object detection models with contextual modules for the job of ear detection, exploring a related approach.

The work in [187], studied ear landmarks detection while utilising the image contract, Laplace filter and Gaussian blurring techniques. Sobel Edge detector and modified adaptive search window was applied for highlighting ear edges and detecting region while [188] automatically identified the primary anatomical contour features in depth map pictures to detect the auricular elements of the ear. Ear Mask Extraction (EME) network, normalization algorithm and a novel Siamese-based CNN (CG-ERNet) was used to segment, align, and extract deep ear features, respectively in [189]. Curvature Gabor filters were used by CG-ERNet to take advantage of domain-specific information while triplet loss, triplet selection, and adaptive margin were adopted for better loss convergence.

Recent technological advancements in the field of artificial intelligence and particularly convolutional neural networks have inspired improved computer visions leading to improved detection, recognition, regression, and classification issues in ear biometrics. Some of these innovations are highlighted in [189] to include object detection methods such as F-RCNN, Mask-RCNN, SSD, VGG. Though these methods often have several non-linear layers, a myriad of parameters may be used in further training the ear recognition databases.

The work [194] employed a deep unsupervised active learning (DUAL) model to learn new features on the ear images while testing without any feedback or correction. Using conditional Deep Convolutional Generative Adversarial Networks (DCGAN) and Convolutional Neural Network (CNN) models, a framework that includes a generative model for colouring dark and grayscale images as well as a classification model was proposed in this [195]. When tested on the limited AMI and the unconstrained AWE ear datasets, the model displayed encouraging results. A quick CNN-like network (TR-ICANet) was suggested for ear print recognition in [67]. While PCA was used to geometrically normalize scale and posture, CNN was employed to detect the ear landmarks and convolutional filters were learned through an unsupervised learning method utilizing Independent Component Analysis (ICA).

Selecting and weighting characteristics has an impact on most ear identification techniques; this is a difficult problem in ERS and other pattern recognition applications [196]. The authors presented a deep CNN feature learning Mahalanobis distance metric technique. Discriminant correlation analysis was used to reduce dimensionality, Mahalanobis distance was learned based on LogDet divergence metric, and K-nearest neighbour was implemented for ear detection, various deep features are retrieved by adopting VGG and ResNet pre-trained models. In [197], unrestricted ear recognition was examined using a transformer neural network dubbed Vision transformer (ViT) and data-efficient image transformers (DeiTs). The recognition accuracy of the ViT-Ear and DeiT-Ear models was at par with previous CNN-based techniques and other deep learning algorithms. Without data augmentation procedures, ViT and DeiTs models was shown to outperform ResNets. The authors in [198], utilized Deep Residual Networks (ResNet) to create ear recognition models that acts as feature extractors in feeding an SVM classifier. ResNet was trained and improved utilizing a training corpus of various ear datasets. To improve the performance of the entire system, ensembles of networks with different depths were deployed.

A six layer deep convolutional neural network design was proposed in [199] to supplement the other biometric systems in a pandemic scenario. When deployed in conjunction with an appropriate surveillance system, the method was found to be very effective at identifying people in huge crowds in uncontrolled environments. The Particle Swarm Optimization (PSO)-based ERS was presented in [200] and evaluated with 50 photos and 150 images using the AMI EAR database. The recognition accuracy was 98% and 96.6%, respectively, which is superior to other benchmark approaches like PCA and Scale Invariant Feature Transform (SIFT).

Despite the advances in deep learning, ear recognition approaches have since grown to include bi and multi-modal methods. For instance, the works [201,202] underscores the accuracy of multimodal biometric systems in uncontrolled scenarios by integrating ear and face profile. Each biometrics' texture characteristics were extracted using a histogram-based local descriptor, local directional patterns, binarized statistical picture features, and local phase quantization. At the feature and score levels, the local descriptors from both modalities were combined to create the KNN classifier for human identification [201]. In [202], a high-dimensional feature vector was utilized to independently represent the ear and face modalities in the frequency and spatial domains utilizing local phase quantization (LPQ) and local directional patterns (LDP). To create more non-linear and discriminative characteristics for the kNN classifier's use in identifying persons, the feature set was merged with kernel discriminative common vector (KDCV). Experimental results on two benchmark datasets demonstrated that the suggested strategy outperforms individual modalities and other cutting-edge techniques in terms of performance.

3.6. Threats to Validity

Considering the related threats to the review procedures and possibly inaccurate data extraction, the highlighted papers in this review were selected based on the earlier described process. The details in Figure 1 reflects some of the answers raised in the research questions. There are numerous articles that no doubt may extend beyond the search parameters used; hence the possibility of exclusion of one or more vital but related articles remains likely. Consequently, a reference check was carried out at the initial stage to prevent any omission of such articles. The final article selection was based on parameters such as precision of the information, quality assessment and clear methodology. Also, the articles were further evaluated by comparing results published by various Authors to avoid overestimation.

4. Discussions, Limitations, and Taxonomy

This study underscores the contributions of deep learning to ear recognition systems while also highlighting a summary of contemporary techniques discussed in other studies. Security is paramount and accurate recognition of target elements from pre-processing to classification is critical in ensuring the integrity of any biometric system. The contributions of deep learning are multifaceted and far-reaching. Studies reviewed affirm the enormous work done in ERS using minimum distance and support vector machines.

However, newer methods capable of autonomously training large sets of data remain under explored. Based on the articles selected, the advantages and disadvantages of the various sub-units in ear recognition stages are indicated in Table 6. A small number of novel classification approaches exist for ERS. The work [168] highlighted a few bio-inspired algorithms, such as cuckoo search, particle swarm optimization, etc. Although some of the listed algorithms have widespread application domains, their significance is primarily for unraveling the optimization challenge in the location search. Consequently, in-depth knowledge of deep learning in pre-processing and feature extraction stages of ear recognition systems is required in subsequent research.

Table 6. Summary of the Pros and Cons of different sub-areas in Ear Recognition Stages.

Stage	Sub-Area	Pros	Cons
Pre-processing	Filter method	No need for object segmentation	Aligned ears are at a disadvantage
		Graceful degradation is a major boost	Some details may be lost
		Suitable for non-aligned images	Limited bandwidth is a drawback
	Intensity method	Reduced computational difficulty	Distorted uniform images are concealed
		Spin and reflection invariant	Poor performance against scaling
		Limited false matches	Copy and paste regions of an image cannot be detected
Feature Extraction	Geometric method	Suitable for obtaining a non-varying feature	Increased computation requirements
		Methods are easy to implement	Results can sometimes be inaccurate
		Image orientations are detected	Susceptible to noise
	Appearance Method	Very robust, particularly in 2-dimensional space	Performance decreases with size
		Any image characteristics is extracted as a feature	Average accuracy is less compared with other methods
		Minimized false matches	Cannot handle certain compressions
		It can be used with a few selected features	Illumination is a significant factor
		Recognition accuracy is high	Good-quality images are required
Classification	Neural Networks	Non-linear problems are easily resolved	Inability to model a few numbers of training datasets
	Support Vector	Increased performance with gap in classes	Large datasets are unsuitable in SVM
		Improved memory utilization	Noise is not effectively controlled
		Improved memory utilization	Limited explanation for classification

4.1. Limitations

In line with the study research questions, a thorough review of research articles on the contributions of deep learning to ERS was conducted, with 74 publications eventually identified as sufficient to achieve the research objectives. However, most of the papers listed were published between 2015 to 2022. Therefore, we cannot categorically state that all available studies in this research domain have been exhausted, considering the rate and volume of published research articles. Also, non-English articles were not considered during the article search.

4.2. Specific Contributions

Presently, the need to develop a black ear-pose invariant ear recognition database is motivated by the following:

1. This study identifies a need to evaluate the performance of ear recognition systems with ear images of different races before they are deployed in real-world scenarios. However, existing ear recognition databases contain mostly Caucasian ear images, while other minority ethnic groups such as blacks, Asians, and Arabs are ignored [169].

2. The black race form 18.2% of the total world population, however, previous research endeavors toward black ear recognition have not been established, and there is no publicly available dataset dedicated to black ear recognition in the works of literature reviewed.
3. This study observed that ear recognition images are often partially or fully occluded by hair, dress, headphone, hat/cap, scarf, rings, and other obstacles [170]. Such occlusions and viewpoints may cause a significant decline in the performance of the ear recognition algorithm (ERA) during identification or verification tasks [171]. Therefore, reliable ear recognition should be equipped with automated detection of occlusion to avoid misclassification due to occluded samples [51].

Therefore, the ear image samples were collected from 152 African (black-skinned) individuals from a public university in Nigeria. The dataset contains left and right ear images of the volunteers in varying pose angles of $0°$, $30°$, and $60°$, respectively, with the ear images containing head scarfs, earrings, ear plugs, etc., thus, making the dataset pose and occlusion invariant. The corpus is published and publicly available to researchers at [203] with a total of 907 black ear images. Figure 2 shows the pose angles of the left and right ear images as captured for each volunteer.

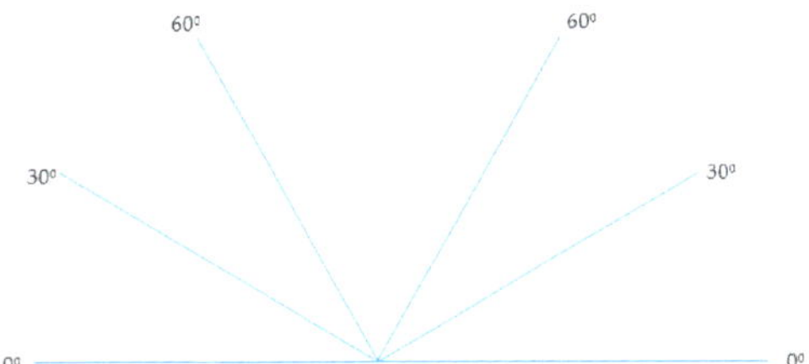

Figure 2. Pose of angles of the left and right ear images.

Also, this study classified current state-of-the-art techniques to reflect the contributions of the highlighted works under three core categories: approaches, performance parameters, and trait selection [204]. Figure 3 provides an explicit description of this taxonomy. The complete classification results of the articles is presented in Table 7.

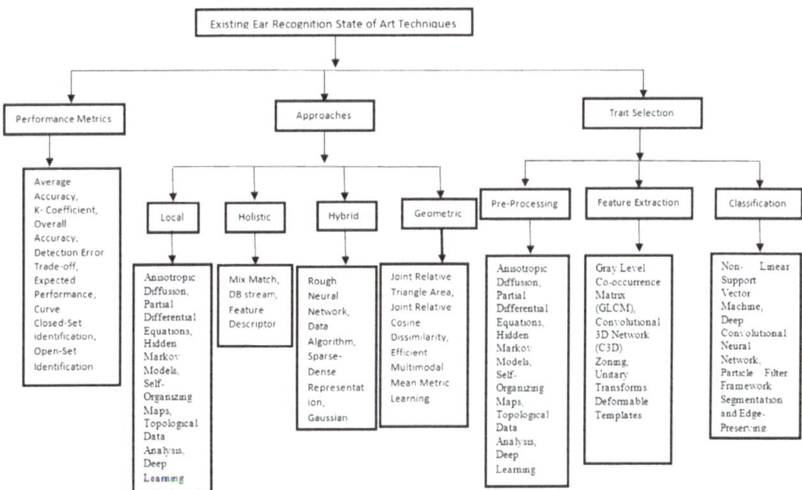

Figure 3. A Taxonomy showing ear recognition state of the art methodology.

Table 7. Article classification result.

Year	Authors	Dataset	Approaches				Methods		Architecture			Status				
			Holistic	Local	Geometric	Hybrid	TL	DL	CNN	Others	Unspecified	Assessment (A)	Proposed (S)	Designed (D)	Planned & Assessed (P&A)	Proposed & Executed (P&E)
2016	[3]							x	x							x
2017	[5]							x		x						
2019	[6]	x						x	x			x				
2010	[7]						x				x					
2017b	[10]	x				x	x				x					
2019	[12]	x					x							x		
2016	[16]	x						x	x							x
2018	[17]	x						x	x							x
2022	[18]	x						x	x							
2018	[20]	x						x	x					x		
2017	[24]	x						x	x							
2012	[25]	x				x	x					x	x			
2012	[28]	x					x			x			x			
2016	[29]	x						x	x							
2018	[34]	x						x	x					x		
2010	[39]	x						x				x		x		
2010	[40]	x		x			x							x		
2018	[43]				x			x				x	x			
2013	[46]	x		x			x			x			x			
2013	[48]	x			x		x					x			x	
2014	[49]	x		x			x					x	x			
2015	[50]	x		x			x					x	x			
2021	[51]	x						x								
2016	[52]			x			x					x	x			
2016	[53]	x						x	x							
2011	[55]	x		x			x					x		x		
2015	[56]	x			x		x					x	x			
2016	[57]	x			x			x	x							x
2014	[58]								x					x		
2018	[59]	x						x	x							x
2018	[60]	x						x	x					x		
2016	[61]	x			x		x						x			
2016	[64]	x		x			x									

Table 7. *Cont.*

Year	Authors	Dataset	Approaches				Methods		Architecture		Status					
			Holistic	Local	Geometric	Hybrid	TL	DL	CNN	Others	Unspecified	Assessment (A)	Proposed (S)	Designed (D)	Planned & Assessed (P&A)	Proposed & Executed (P&E)
2015	[65]	x		x			x				x	x				
2022	[66]	x						x	x							x
2018	[69]	x						x		x					x	
2019	[72]	x						x	x							x
2019	[76]	x						x	x					x		
2020	[77]	x														x
2018	[78]	x						x			x	x				
2014	[79]	x				x	x				x					
2011	[80]	x												x		
2013	[81]	x		x			x									x
2020	[83]						x		x			x				
2019	[87]	x				x	x				x	x				
2020	[88]	x					x			x					x	
2010	[91]	x		x			x			x		x				
2020	[92]	x						x	x						x	
2017	[93]							x	x							
2018	[94]	x						x	x				x			
2016	[95]	x		x			x						x			
2014	[98]	x		x			x		x							
2018	[99]	x		x			x				x					
2014	[100]						x				x				x	
2019	[101]	x						x	x				x			
2018	[102]	x			x		x				x					
2017	[104]						x				x					
2013	[106]	x		x			x							x		
2016	[107]	x						x					x			
2020	[108]	x					x				x					
2017	[109]	x			x		x				x					
2017	[110]	x						x	x				x			
2020	[111]						x			x						
2020	[112]							x	x						x	
2017	[113]	x						x					x			
2019	[116]	x						x	x				x			

Table 7. *Cont.*

Year	Authors	Dataset	Approaches				Methods		Architecture			Status				
			Holistic	Local	Geometric	Hybrid	TL	DL	CNN	Others	Unspecified	Assessment (A)	Proposed (S)	Designed (D)	Planned & Assessed (P&A)	Proposed & Executed (P&E)
2018	[119]	x						x	x							
2020	[121]	x						x	x			x				
2019	[123]	x						x	x							x
2014	[124]	x		x			x			x		x				
2016	[126]	x						x	x							x
2010	[127]	x		x			x				x	x				
2013	[140]	x					x		x							
2013	[141]	x		x			x			x			x			
2014	[142]	x		x			x			x			x			
2014	[143]	x						x		x		x				
2015	[150]	x				x	x						x			
2020	[156]	x						x	x					x		
2020	[157]	x						x	x			x				
2019	[166]	x						x	x			x				
2018	[167]	x						x	x					x		
2010	[179]	x		x			x				x	x				
2020	[183]	x						x	x				x			
2021	[184]	x														
2021	[185]	x						x	x				x			
2021	[186]	x						x						x		
2021	[187]	x					x						x			
2021	[188]						x						x			
2021	[189]	x						x		x						x
2021	[190]	x				x	x						x			
2021	[194]							x		x						x
2021	[195]	x						x	x				x			
2021	[196]	x						x	x							x
2021	[198]	x						x		x						x
2021	[199]	x						x	x				x			
2022	[202]	x		x			x						x			

5. Conclusions and Future Direction

Although a high volume of research is geared toward improving the recognition accuracy of biometric systems, none of these techniques has shown 100% accuracy. In this study, an SLR showing the current contributions of deep learning to ear recognition in different stages is presented. Before the screening, a total number of 1121 articles was returned during a preliminary search followed by a thorough analysis of existing contributions of deep learning, research questions, and the various methods used in the recognition process. In the end, 74 articles were deemed relevant to the study and were selected for further analysis.

In terms of the number of publications per year, results indicate that significant contributions were made to ear recognition in 2018, as it had 18 relevant articles, closely followed by 2016 with 16 articles. Results based on contributions from Deep learning obtained from Table 7 showed CNN, other architectures and non- unspecified architectures had 51.95%, 18.18%, and 29.87%, contributions, respectively. Similarly, local, geometric and hybrid feature extraction approaches had 60.61%, 18.18% and 21.21%, respectively. For studies that employed existing or developed image databases, the analysis revealed that 85.42% (82) articles used one database or another in their studies, while 14 did not use any database.

Contrastingly, results from analyzing the status of articles showed gap between proposed methods (S) and proposed & executed works (P&E) which accounted for 25.33% and 17.33%, respectively. Articles that assessed existing algorithms (A), designed a templates (D) or planned and assessed using established procedures (PA) had 34.67%, 10.67%, and 12.0%, respectively.

Traditional machine learning methods was used in 45 (48.91%) of the articles while 47 (51.09%) employed deep learning methods. This is due to increase in the ER datasets sizes.

Further still, an examination of selected performance metrics of recognition accuracy, template capacity, true acceptance rate, false acceptance rate, false rejection rate, equal error rate, precision, recall, and matching speed used by the Authors of selected articles was systematically determined. Interestingly, most studies on ear recognition system are assessment of existing algorithms on a given dataset followed by newly proposed or yet to be evaluated techniques.

In real-life applications, speed is of great essence. Future works should investigate various enhancement techniques to improve the speed of feature extraction algorithms in ERS. Although ear biometric technology is renowned for its long history of use, particularly in developed countries, it is still enjoying rapid growth and potential with increasingly dynamic but secure classification procedures. Establishing an efficient and foolproof ear biometric recognition system is not only a growing concern but also an opportunity to explore the inherent gaps in feature extraction and classification procedures targeted at accurate authentication or identification tasks.

Author Contributions: The manuscript was written through the contributions of all authors. O.G.O., was responsible for the conceptualization of the topic; article gathering and sorting were carried out by O.G.O., A.A.-A., O.'T.A. and A.Q.; manuscript writing and original drafting and formal analysis were carried out by O.G.O., A.A.-A., O.'T.A., A.Q., A.L.I. and J.B.A.; writing of reviews and editing were carried out by A.A.-A., O.'T.A., A.Q., A.L.I., J.B.A. and A.A.-A. led the overall research activity. All authors have read and agreed to the published version of the manuscript.

Funding: The work of Agbotiname Lucky Imoize is supported by the Nigerian Petroleum Technology Development Fund (PTDF) and the German Academic Exchange Service (DAAD) through the Nigerian-German Postgraduate Program under grant 57473408.

Data Availability Statement: The black ear recognition dataset is publicly available. Other data that supports the findings in this paper are available from the corresponding author upon reasonable request.

Conflicts of Interest: The authors declare no conflict of interest.

References

1. World Bank Group. *Identification for Development Strategic Framework*; Working Paper; World Bank Group: Washington, DC, USA, 2016.
2. Atick, J. The Identity Ecosystem of Rwanda. A Case Study of a Performant ID System in an African Development Context. *ID4Africa Rep.* **2016**, 1–38. Available online: https://citizenshiprightsafrica.org/the-identity-ecosystem-of-rwanda-a-case-study-of-a-performant-id-system-in-an-african-development-context/ (accessed on 17 December 2022).
3. Saranya, M.; Cyril, G.L.I.; Santhosh, R.R. An approach towards ear feature extraction for human identification. In Proceedings of the International Conference on Electrical, Electronics and Optimization Techniques (ICEEOT 2016), Chennai, India, 3–5 March 2016; pp. 4824–4828. [CrossRef]
4. Unar, J.; Seng, W.C.; Abbasi, A. A review of biometric technology along with trends and prospects. *Pattern Recognit.* **2014**, *47*, 2673–2688. [CrossRef]
5. Emersic, Z.; Stepec, D.; Struc, V.; Peer, P. Training Convolutional Neural Networks with Limited Training Data for Ear Recognition in the Wild. In Proceedings of the International Conference on Automatic Face Gesture Recognition, Washington, DC, USA, 30 May–3 June 2017; pp. 987–994. [CrossRef]
6. Wang, Z.; Yang, J.; Zhu, Y. Review of Ear Biometrics. *Arch. Comput. Methods Eng.* **2019**, *28*, 149–180. [CrossRef]
7. Alaraj, M.; Hou, J.; Fukami, T. A neural network based human identification framework using ear images. In Proceedings of the International Technical Conference of IEEE Region 10, Fukuoka, Japan, 21–24 November 2010; pp. 1595–1600.
8. Song, L.; Gong, D.; Li, Z.; Liu, C.; Liu, W. Occlusion Robust Face Recognition Based on Mask Learning with Pairwise Differential Siamese Network. In Proceedings of the IEEE/CVF International Conference on Computer Vision, Seoul, Korea, 27 October–2 November 2019; pp. 773–782. [CrossRef]
9. Li, P.; Prieto, L.; Mery, D.; Flynn, P.J. On Low-Resolution Face Recognition in the Wild: Comparisons and New Techniques. *IEEE Trans. Inf. Forensics Secur.* **2019**, *14*, 2000–2012. [CrossRef]
10. Emersic, Z.; Struc, V.; Peer, P. Ear recognition: More than a survey. *Neurocomputing* **2017**, *255*, 26–39. [CrossRef]
11. Abayomi-Alli, O.; Misra, S.; Abayomi-Alli, A.; Odusami, M. A review of soft techniques for SMS spam classification: Methods, approaches and applications. *Eng. Appl. Artif. Intell.* **2019**, *86*, 197–212. [CrossRef]
12. Youbi, Z.; Boubchir, L.; Boukrouche, A. Human ear recognition based on local multi-scale LBP features with city-block distance. *Multi. Tools Appl.* **2019**, *78*, 14425–14441. [CrossRef]
13. Madhusudhan, M.V.; Basavaraju, R.; Hegde, C. Secured Human Authentication Using Finger-Vein Patterns. In *Data Management, Analytics, and Innovation. Advances in Intelligent Systems and Computing*; Balas, V., Sharma, N., Chakrabarti, A., Eds.; Springer: Singapore, 2019; pp. 311–320. [CrossRef]
14. Lei, Y.; Qian, J.; Pan, D.; Xu, T. Research on Small Sample Dynamic Human Ear Recognition Based on Deep Learning. *Sensors* **2022**, *22*, 1718. [CrossRef]
15. Chen, Y.; Chen, W.; Wei, C.; Wang, Y. Occlusion aware face in painting via generative adversarial networks. In Proceedings of the Image Processing (ICIP), International Conference on IEEE, Beijing, China, 17–20 September 2017; pp. 1202–1206.
16. Tian, L.; Mu, Z. Ear recognition based on deep convolutional network. In Proceedings of the 9th International Congress on Image and Signal Processing, Biomedical Engineering, and Informatics (CISP-BMEI 2016), Datong, China, 15–17 October 2016; pp. 437–441. [CrossRef]
17. Labati, R.D.; Muñoz, E.; Piuri, V.; Sassi, R.; Scotti, F. Deep-ECG: Convolutional Neural Networks for ECG biometric recognition. *Pattern Recognit. Lett.* **2019**, *126*, 78–85. [CrossRef]
18. Ramos-Cooper, S.; Gomez-Nieto, E.; Camara-Chavez, G. VGGFace-Ear: An Extended Dataset for Unconstrained Ear Recognition. *Sensors* **2022**, *22*, 1752. [CrossRef]
19. Guo, Y.; Xu, Z. Ear Recognition Using a New Local Matching Approach. In Proceedings of the 15th IEEE International Conference on Image Processing (ICIP), San Diego, CA, USA, 12–15 October 2008; pp. 289–293.
20. Raghavendra, R.; Raja, K.B.; Venkatesh, S.; Busch, C. Improved ear verification after surgery—An approach based on collaborative representation of locally competitive features. *Pattern Recognit.* **2018**, *83*, 416–429. [CrossRef]
21. Bertillon, A. *La Photographie Judiciaire, Avec un Appendice Classificationetl Identification Anthropométriques*; Technical Report; Gauthier-Villars: Paris, France, 1890.
22. Burge, M.; Burger, W. Ear biometrics in computer vision. In Proceedings of the 15th International Conference on Pattern Recognition. ICPR-2000, Barcelona, Spain, 3–7 September 2000; pp. 822–826.
23. Alva, M.; Srinivasaraghavan, A.; Sonawane, K. A Review on Techniques for Ear Biometrics. In Proceedings of the IEEE International Conference on Electrical, Computer and Communication Technologies (ICECCT), Coimbatore, India, 20–22 February 2019; pp. 1–6. [CrossRef]
24. Chowdhury, M.; Islam, R.; Gao, J. Robust ear biometric recognition using neural network. In Proceedings of the 12th IEEE Conference on Industrial Electronics and Applications (ICIEA), Siem Reap, Cambodia, 18–20 June 2017; pp. 1855–1859.
25. Kumar, R.; Dhenakaran, S. Pixel based feature extraction for ear biometrics. In Proceedings of the IEEE International Conference on Machine Vision and Image Processing (MVIP), Coimbatore, India, 14–15 December 2012; pp. 40–43.
26. Rahman, M.; Islam, R.; Bhuiyan, I.; Ahmed, B.; Islam, A. Person identification using ear biometrics. *Int. J. Comput. Internet Manag.* **2007**, *15*, 1–8.

27. El-Naggar, S.; Abaza, A.; Bourlai, T. On a taxonomy of ear features. In Proceedings of the IEEE Symposium on Technologies for Homeland Security; HST2016, Waltham, MA, USA, 10–11 May 2016; pp. 1–6. [CrossRef]
28. Damer, N.; Führer, B. Ear Recognition Using Multi-Scale Histogram of Oriented Gradients. In Proceedings of the Eighth International Conference on Intelligent Information Hiding and Multimedia Signal Processing, Piraeus-Athens, Greece, 18–20 July 2012; pp. 21–24.
29. Tiwari, S.; Singh, A.; Singh, S. Comparison of Adult and Infant Ear Images for Biometric Recognition. In Proceedings of the Fourth International Conference on Parallel Distribution Grid Computing, Waknaghat, India, 22–24 December 2016; pp. 4–9.
30. Tariq, A.; Anjum, M.; Akram, M. Personal identification using computerized human ear recognition system. In Proceedings of the 2011 International Conference on Computer Science and Network Technology, Harbin, China, 24–26 December 2011; pp. 50–54.
31. Chang, K.; Bowyer, K.; Sarkar, S.; Victor, B. Comparison and combination of ear and face images in appearance-based biometrics. *IEEE Trans. Pattern Anal. Mach. Intell.* **2003**, *25*, 1160–1165. [CrossRef]
32. Pflug, A.; Busch, C. Ear biometrics: A survey of detection, feature extraction and recognition methods. *IET Biom.* **2012**, *1*, 114–129. [CrossRef]
33. Dong, J.; Mu, Z. Multi-pose ear recognition based on force field transformation. In Proceedings of the 2nd International Symposium on Intelligence in Information Technology Applications, Shanghai, China, 20–22 December 2008; pp. 771–775.
34. Xiao, X.; Zhou, Y. Two-Dimensional Quaternion PCA and Sparse PCA. *IEEE Trans. Neural Networks Learn. Syst.* **2018**, *30*, 2028–2042. [CrossRef] [PubMed]
35. Zhang, J.; Mu, C.; Qu, W.; Liu, M.; Zhang, Y. A novel approach for ear recognition based on ICA and RBF network. In Proceedings of the International Conference on Machine Learning and Cybernetics, Guangzhou, China, 18–21 August 2005; pp. 4511–4515.
36. Yuan, L.; Mu, C.; Zhang, Y.; Liu, K. Ear recognition using improved non-negative matrix factorization. In Proceedings of the International Conference on Pattern Recognition, Hong Kong, China, 20–24 August 2006; pp. 501–504.
37. Sana, A.; Gupta, P.; Purkai, R. Ear Biometrics: A New Approach. In *Advances in Pattern Recognition*; Pal, P., Ed.; World Scientific Publishing: Singapore, 2007; pp. 46–50.
38. Naseem, I.; Togneri, R.; Bennamoun, M. *Sparse Representation for Ear Biometrics*; Bebis, G., Boyle, R., Parvin, B., Koracin, D., Remagnino, P., Porikli, F., Eds.; Advances in Visual Computing: San Diego, CA, USA, 2008; pp. 336–345.
39. Wang, X.-Q.; Xia, H.-Y.; Wang, Z.-L. The Research of Ear Identification Based On Improved Algorithm of Moment Invariant. In Proceedings of the 2010 Third International Conference on Information and Computing, Wuxi, China, 4–6 June 2010; Volume 1, pp. 58–60. [CrossRef]
40. Bustard, J.D.; Nixon, M.S. Toward Unconstrained Ear Recognition From Two-Dimensional Images. *IEEE Trans. Syst. Man Cybern. Part A Syst. Humans* **2010**, *40*, 486–494. [CrossRef]
41. Arbab-Zavar, B.; Nixon, S.; Hurley, J. On model-based analysis of ear biometrics. In Proceedings of the Conference on Biometrics: Theory, Applications and Systems, Crystal City, VA, USA, 27–29 September 2007; pp. 1–5.
42. Kisku, R.; Mehrotra, H.; Gupta, P.; Sing, K. SIFT-Based ear recognition by fusion of detected key-points from color similarity slice regions. In Proceedings of the IEEE International Conference on Advances in Computational Tools for Engineering Applications (ACTEA), Beirut, Lebanon, 15–17 July 2009; pp. 380–385.
43. Emersic, Z.; Playa, O.; Struc, V.; Peer, P. Towards accessories-aware ear recognition. In Proceedings of the 2018 IEEE International Work Conference on Bioinspired Intelligence (IWOBI), San Carlos, Costa Rica, 18–20 July 2018; pp. 1–8.
44. Jeges, E.; Mate, L. Model-Based Human Ear Localization and Feature Extraction. *Int. J. Intell. Comput. Med. Sci. Image Pro.* **2007**, *1*, 101–112.
45. Liu, H.; Yan, J. Multi-view Ear Shape Feature Extraction and Reconstruction. In Proceedings of the Third International IEEE Conference on Signal-Image Technologies and Internet-Based System (SITIS), Shanghai, China, 16–18 December 2007; pp. 652–658.
46. Lakshmanan, L. Efficient person authentication based on multi-level fusion of ear scores. *IET Biom.* **2013**, *2*, 97–106. [CrossRef]
47. Nosrati, M.S.; Faez, K.; Faradji, F. Using 2D wavelet and principal component analysis for personal identification based On 2D ear structure. In Proceedings of the International Conference on Intelligent and Advanced Systems, Kuala Lumpur, Malaysia, 25–28 November 2007; pp. 616–620. [CrossRef]
48. Kumar, A.; Chan, T.-S. Robust ear identification using sparse representation of local texture descriptors. *Pattern Recognit.* **2013**, *46*, 73–85. [CrossRef]
49. Galdamez, P.; Arrieta, A.G.; Ramon, M. Ear recognition using a hybrid approach based on neural networks. In Proceedings of the International Conference on Information Fusion, Salamanca, Spain, 7–10 July 2014; pp. 1–6.
50. Mahajan, A.S.B.; Karande, K.J. PCA and DWT based multimodal biometric recognition system. In Proceedings of the International Conference on Pervasive Computing (ICPC), Pune, India, 8–10 January 2015; pp. 1–4. [CrossRef]
51. Quoc, H.N.; Hoang, V.T. Real-Time Human Ear Detection Based on the Joint of Yolo and RetinaFace. *Complexity* **2021**, *2021*, 7918165. [CrossRef]
52. Panchakshari, P.; Tale, S. Performance analysis of fusion methods for EAR biometrics. In Proceedings of the 2016 IEEE International Conference on Recent Trends in Electronics, Information & Communication Technology (RTEICT), Bangalore, India, 20–21 May 2016; pp. 1191–1194. [CrossRef]
53. Ghoualmi, L.; Draa, A.; Chikhi, S. An ear biometric system based on artificial bees and the scale invariant feature transform. *Expert Syst. Appl.* **2016**, *57*, 49–61. [CrossRef]

54. Mishra, S.; Kulkarni, S.; Marakarkandy, B. A neoteric approach for ear biometrics using multilinear PCA. In Proceedings of the International Conference and Workshop on Electronics and Telecommunication Engineering (ICWET 2016), Mumbai, India, 26–27 February 2016. [CrossRef]
55. Kumar, A.; Hanmandlu, M.; Kuldeep, M.; Gupta, H.M. Automatic ear detection for online biometric applications. In Proceedings of the 2011 3rd International Conference on Computer Vision, Pattern Recognition, Image Processing and Graphics, Hubli, India, 15–17 December 2011.
56. Anwar, A.S.; Ghany, K.K.A.; Elmahdy, H. Human Ear Recognition Using Geometrical Features Extraction. *Procedia Comput. Sci.* **2015**, *65*, 529–537. [CrossRef]
57. Cintas, C.; Quinto-Sánchez, M.; Acuña, V.; Paschetta, C.; de Azevedo, S.; de Cerqueira, C.C.S.; Ramallo, V.; Gallo, C.; Poletti, G.; Bortolini, M.C.; et al. Automatic ear detection and feature extraction using Geometric Morphometrics and convolutional neural networks. *IET Biom.* **2017**, *6*, 211–223. [CrossRef]
58. Rahman, M.; Sadi, R.; Islam, R. Human ear recognition using geometric features. In Proceedings of the International Conference on Electrical Information and Communication Technology (EICT), Khulna, Bangladesh, 5–8 March 2014; pp. 1–4.
59. Canny Edge Detection. Fourier.eng.hmc.edu. 2018. Available online: http://fourier.eng.hmc.edu/e161/lectures/canny/node1.html (accessed on 18 December 2022).
60. Omara, I.; Li, X.; Xiao, G.; Adil, K.; Zuo, W. Discriminative Local Feature Fusion for Ear Recognition Problem. In Proceedings of the 2018 8th International Conference on Bioscience, Biochemistry and Bioinformatics (ICBBB), Tokyo, Japan, 18–20 January 2018; pp. 139–145. [CrossRef]
61. Omara, I.; Li, F.; Zhang, H.; Zuo, W. A novel geometric feature extraction method for ear recognition. *Expert Syst. Appl.* **2016**, *65*, 127–135. [CrossRef]
62. Hurley, D.; Nixon, M.; Carter, J. Force Field Energy Functionals for Ear Biometrics. *Comput. Vis. Image Underst.* **2005**, *98*, 491–512. [CrossRef]
63. Polin, Z.; Kabir, E.; Sadi, S. 2D human-ear recognition using geometric features. In Proceedings of the 7th International Conference on Electrical and Computer Engineering, Dhaka, Bangladesh, 20–22 December 2012; pp. 9–12.
64. Benzaoui, A.; Adjabi, I.; Boukrouche, A. Person identification based on ear morphology. In Proceedings of the International Conference on Advanced Aspects of Software Engineering (ICAASE), Constantine, Algeria, 29–30 October 2016; pp. 1–5.
65. Benzaoui, A.; Hezil, I.; Boukrouche, A. Identity recognition based on the external shape of the human ear. In Proceedings of the 2015 International Conference on Applied Research in Computer Science and Engineering (ICAR), Beirut, Lebanon, 8–9 October 2015; pp. 1–5.
66. Sharkas, M. Ear recognition with ensemble classifiers: A deep learning approach. *Multi. Tools Appl.* **2022**, *81*, 43919–43945. [CrossRef]
67. Korichi, A.; Slatnia, S.; Aiadi, O. TR-ICANet: A Fast Unsupervised Deep-Learning-Based Scheme for Unconstrained Ear Recognition. *Arab. J. Sci. Eng.* **2022**, *47*, 9887–9898. [CrossRef]
68. Pflug, A.; Busch, C.; Ross, A. 2D ear classification based on unsupervised clustering. In Proceedings of the International Joint Conference on Biometrics, Clearwater, FL, USA, 29 September–2 October 2014; pp. 1–8.
69. Dodge, S.; Mounsef, J.; Karam, L. Unconstrained ear recognition using deep neural networks. *IET Biom.* **2018**, *7*, 207–214. [CrossRef]
70. Ying, T.; Shining, W.; Wanxiang, L. Human ear recognition based on deep convolutional neural network. In Proceedings of the 30th Chinese Control and Decision Conference (2018 CCDC), Shenyang, China, 9–11 June 2018; pp. 1830–1835. [CrossRef]
71. Zarachoff, M.M.; Sheikh-Akbari, A.; Monekosso, D. Multi-band PCA based ear recognition technique. *Multi. Tools Appl.* **2022**, *82*, 2077–2099. [CrossRef]
72. Alshazly, H.; Linse, C.; Barth, E.; Martinetz, T. Handcrafted versus CNN Features for Ear Recognition. *Symmetry* **2019**, *11*, 1493. [CrossRef]
73. Moreno, B.; Sanchez, A.; Velez, J. On the use of outer ear images for personal identification in security applications. In Proceedings of the IEEE 33rd Annual International, Carnahan Conference on Security Technology, Madrid, Spain, 5–7 October 1999; pp. 469–476. [CrossRef]
74. Mu, Z.; Yuan, L.; Xu, Z.; Xi, D.; Qi, S. *Shape and Structural Feature Based Ear Recognition*; Springer: Berlin/Heidelberg, Germany, 2004; pp. 663–670. [CrossRef]
75. Choras, M. Ear biometrics based on geometrical feature extraction. *Electron. Lett. Comput. Vis. Image Anal.* **2005**, *5*, 84–95. [CrossRef]
76. Tomczyk, A.; Szczepaniak, P.S. Ear Detection Using Convolutional Neural Network on Graphs with Filter Rotation. *Sensors* **2019**, *19*, 5510. [CrossRef] [PubMed]
77. Abdellatef, E.; Omran, E.M.; Soliman, R.F.; Ismail, N.A.; Elrahman, S.E.S.E.A.; Ismail, K.N.; Rihan, M.; El-Samie, F.E.A.; Eisa, A.A. Fusion of deep-learned and hand-crafted features for cancelable recognition systems. *Soft Comput.* **2020**, *24*, 15189–15208. [CrossRef]
78. Traore, I.; Alshahrani, M.; Obaidat, M.S. State of the art and perspectives on traditional and emerging biometrics: A survey. *Secur. Priv.* **2018**, *1*, e44. [CrossRef]
79. Prakash, S.; Gupta, P. Human recognition using 3D ear images. *Neurocomputing* **2014**, *140*, 317–325. [CrossRef]

80. Raposo, R.; Hoyle, E.; Peixinho, A.; Proenca, H. UBEAR: A dataset of ear images captured on-the-move in uncontrolled conditions. In Proceedings of the 2011 IEEE Workshop on Computational Intelligence in Biometrics and Identity Management (CIBIM), Paris, France, 11–15 April 2011; pp. 84–90. [CrossRef]

81. Abaza, A.; Bourlai, T. On ear-based human identification in the mid-wave infrared spectrum. *Image Vis. Comput.* **2013**, *31*, 640–648. [CrossRef]

82. Pandiar, A.; Ntalianis, K. *Palanisamy, Intelligent Computing, Information and Control Systems, Advances in Intelligent Systems and Computing 1039*; Springer: Berlin/Heidelberg, Germany, 2019; pp. 176–185.

83. Nait-Ali, A. (Ed.) *Hidden Biometrics*; Springer: Berlin/Heidelberg, Germany, 2020. [CrossRef]

84. Srinivas, N.; Flynn, P.J.; Bruegge, R.W.V. Human Identification Using Automatic and Semi-Automatically Detected Facial Marks. *J. Forensic Sci.* **2015**, *61*, S117–S130. [CrossRef]

85. Almisreb, A.; Jamil, N. *Advanced Technologies in Robotics and Intelligent Systems*; Proceedings of ITR 2019; Springer: Berlin/Heidelberg, Germany, 2012; pp. 199–203. [CrossRef]

86. Almisreb, A.; Jamil, N. Automated Ear Segmentation in Various Illumination Conditions. In Proceedings of the IEEE 8th International Colloquium on Signal Processing and Its Applications, Malacca, Malaysia, 23–25 March 2012; pp. 199–203.

87. Kang, J.S.; Lawryshyn, Y.; Hatzinakos, D. Neural Network Architecture and Transient Evoked Otoacoustic Emission (TEOAE) Biometrics for Identification and Verification. *IEEE Trans. Inf. Forensics Secur.* **2019**, *15*, 2291–2301. [CrossRef]

88. Rane, M.E.; Bhadade, U.S. Multimodal score level fusion for recognition using face and palmprint. *Int. J. Electr. Eng. Educ.* **2020**. [CrossRef]

89. Saini, R.; Rana, N. Comparison of Various Biometrics Methods. *Int. J. Adv. Sci. Technol.* **2014**, *2*, 24–30.

90. Patil, S. Biometric Recognition Using Unimodal and Multimodal Features. *Int. J. Innov. Res. Comput. Commun. Eng.* **2014**, *2*, 6824–6829.

91. Khan, B.; Khan, M.; Alghathbar, K. Biometrics and identity management for homeland security applications in Saudi Arabia. *Afr. J. Bus. Manag.* **2010**, *4*, 3296–3306.

92. Zhang, J.; Ma, Q.; Cui, X.; Guo, H.; Wang, K.; Zhu, D. High-throughput corn ear screening method based on two-pathway convolutional neural network. *Comput. Electron. Agric.* **2020**, *179*, 105525. [CrossRef]

93. Bansal, J.; Das, K.N.; Nagar, A.; Deep, K.; Ojha, A. Soft Computing for Problem Solving. In *Advances in Intelligent Systems and Computing*; Springer: Singapore, 2017; pp. 1–9. [CrossRef]

94. Earnest, E.; Hansley, E.; Segundo, P.; Sarkar, S. Employing fusion of learned and handcrafted Feature for unconstrained ear recognition. *IET Biom.* **2018**, *7*, 215–223.

95. Chen, L.; Mu, Z. Partial Data Ear Recognition From One Sample per Person. *IEEE Trans. Hum. Mach. Syst.* **2016**, *46*, 799–809. [CrossRef]

96. Wang, X.; Yuan, W. Gabor wavelets and General Discriminant analysis for ear recognition. In Proceedings of the 8th World Congress on Intelligent Control and Automation, Jinan, China, 7–9 July 2010; pp. 6305–6308. [CrossRef]

97. Fahmi, P.A.; Kodirov, E.; Choi, D.J.; Lee, G.S.; Azli, A.M.F.; Sayeed, S. Implicit Authentication based on Ear Shape Biometrics using Smartphone Camera during a call. In Proceedings of the IEEE International Conference on Systems, Man and Cybernetics, Seoul, Korea, 14–17 October 2012; pp. 2272–2276.

98. Ariffin, S.M.Z.S.Z.; Jamil, N. Cross-band ear recognition in low or variant illumination environments. In Proceedings of the International Symposium on Biometrics and Security Technologies (ISBAST), Kuala Lumpur, Malaysia, 26–27 August 2014; pp. 90–94. [CrossRef]

99. Al Rahhal, M.M.; Mekhalfi, M.L.; Guermoui, M.; Othman, E.; Lei, B.; Mahmood, A. A Dense Phase Descriptor for Human Ear Recognition. *IEEE Access* **2018**, *6*, 11883–11887. [CrossRef]

100. Oravec, M. Feature extraction and classification by machine learning methods for biometric recognition of face and iris. In Proceedings of the ELMAR-2014, Zadar, Croatia, 10–12 September 2014; pp. 1–4. [CrossRef]

101. Wu, Y.; Chen, Z.; Sun, D.; Zhao, L.; Zhou, C.; Yue, W. Human Ear Recognition Using HOG with PCA Dimension Reduction and LBP. In Proceedings of the 2019 IEEE 9th International Conference on Electronics Information and Emergency Communication (ICEIEC), Beijing, China, 12–14 July 2019; pp. 72–75. [CrossRef]

102. Sable, A.H.; Talbar, S.N. An Adaptive Entropy Based Scale Invariant Face Recognition Face Altered by Plastic Surgery. *Pattern Recognit. Image Anal.* **2018**, *28*, 813–829. [CrossRef]

103. Mali, K.; Bhattacharya, S. Comparative Study of Different Biometric Features. *Int. J. Adv. Res. Comput. Commun. Eng.* **2013**, *2*, 30–35.

104. Kandgaonkar, T.V.; Mente, R.S.; Shinde, A.R.; Raut, S.D. Ear Biometrics: A Survey on Ear Image Databases and Techniques for Ear Detection and Recognition. *IBMRD's J. Manag. Res.* **2015**, *4*, 88–103. [CrossRef]

105. Sikarwar, R.; Yadav, P. An Approach to Face Detection and Feature Extraction using Canny Method. *Int. J. Comput. Appl.* **2017**, *163*, 1–5. [CrossRef]

106. Maity, S. 3D Ear Biometrics and Surveillance Video Based Biometrics. Ph.D. Thesis, University of Miami, Miami, FL, USA, 2017; p. 1789, Open Access Dissertations. Available online: https://scholarlyrepository.miami.edu/oa_dissertations/1789 (accessed on 5 December 2022).

107. Mamta; Hanmandlu, M. Robust ear based authentication using Local Principal Independent Components. *Expert Syst. Appl.* **2013**, *40*, 6478–6490. [CrossRef]

108. Galdámez, P.L.; Raveane, W.; Arrieta, A.G. A brief review of the ear recognition process using deep neural networks. *J. Appl. Log.* **2017**, *24*, 62–70. [CrossRef]
109. Li, L.; Zhong, B.; Hutmacher, C.; Liang, Y.; Horrey, W.J.; Xu, X. Detection of driver manual distraction via image-based hand and ear recognition. *Accid. Anal. Prev.* **2020**, *137*, 105432. [CrossRef] [PubMed]
110. Nguyen, K.; Fookes, C.; Sridharan, S.; Tistarelli, M.; Nixon, M. Super-resolution for biometrics: A comprehensive survey. *Pattern Recognit.* **2018**, *78*, 23–42. [CrossRef]
111. HaCohen-Kerner, Y.; Hagege, R. Language and Gender Classification of Speech Files Using Supervised Machine Learning Methods. *Cybern. Syst.* **2017**, *48*, 510–535. [CrossRef]
112. Kaur, P.; Krishan, K.; Sharma, S.K.; Kanchan, T. Facial-recognition algorithms: A literature review. *Med. Sci. Law* **2020**, *60*, 131–139. [CrossRef] [PubMed]
113. Pedrycz, W.; Chen, S. Deep Learning: Algorithms and Applications. In *Studies in Computational Intelligence*; Springer: Berlin/Heidelberg, Germany, 2020; pp. 157–170. [CrossRef]
114. Zhang, Y.; Mu, Z. Ear Detection under Uncontrolled Conditions with Multiple Scale Faster Region-Based Convolutional Neural Networks. *Symmetry* **2017**, *9*, 53. [CrossRef]
115. Eyiokur, F.I.; Yaman, D.; Ekenel, H.K. Domain adaptation for ear recognition using deep convolutional neural networks. *IET Biom.* **2018**, *7*, 199–206. [CrossRef]
116. Kandaswamy, C.; Monteiro, J.C.; Silva, L.M.; Cardoso, J.S. Multi-source deep transfer learning for cross-sensor biometrics. *Neural Comput. Appl.* **2016**, *28*, 2461–2475. [CrossRef]
117. Sinha, H.; Manekar, R.; Sinha, Y.; Ajmera, P.K. Convolutional Neural Network-Based Human Identification Using Outer Ear Images. In *Soft Computing for Problem Solving*; Springer: Berlin/Heidelberg, Germany, 2018; pp. 707–719. [CrossRef]
118. Xu, X.; Liu, Y.; Cao, S.; Lu, L. An Efficient and Lightweight Method for Human Ear Recognition Based on MobileNet. *Wirel. Commun. Mob. Comput.* **2022**, *2022*, 9069007. [CrossRef]
119. Hidayati, N.; Maulidah, M.; Saputra, E.P. Ear Identification Using Convolution Neural Network. Available online: www.iocscience.org/ejournal/index.php/mantik/article/download/2263/1800 (accessed on 18 December 2022).
120. Madec, S.; Jin, X.; Lu, H.; De Solan, B.; Liu, S.; Duyme, F.; Heritier, E.; Baret, F. Ear density estimation from high resolution RGB imagery using deep learning technique. *Agric. For. Meteorol.* **2018**, *264*, 225–234. [CrossRef]
121. Mikolajczyk, M.; Growchoski, M. Data augmentation for improving deep learning in image classification. In Proceedings of the 2018 International Interdisciplinary PhD Workshop (IIPhDW), Świnoujście, Poland, 9–12 May 2018; pp. 215–224.
122. Jiang, R.; Tsun, L.; Crookes, D.; Meng, W.; Rosenberger, C. *Deep Biometrics, Unsupervised and Semi-Supervised Learning*; Springer: Berlin/Heidelberg, Germany, 2020; pp. 238–322. [CrossRef]
123. Pereira, T.M.; Conceição, R.C.; Sencadas, V.; Sebastião, R. Biometric Recognition: A Systematic Review on Electrocardiogram Data Acquisition Methods. *Sensors* **2023**, *23*, 1507. [CrossRef]
124. Raveane, W.; Galdámez, P.L.; Arrieta, M.A.G. Ear Detection and Localization with Convolutional Neural Networks in Natural Images and Videos. *Processes* **2019**, *7*, 457. [CrossRef]
125. Martinez, A.; Moritz, N.; Meyer, B. *Should Deep Neural Nets Have Ears? The Role of Auditory Features in Deep Learning Approaches*; Interspeech: Incheon, Korea, 2014; pp. 1–5.
126. Jamil, N.; Almisreb, A.; Ariffin, S.; Din, N.; Hamzah, R. Can Convolution Neural Network (CNN) Triumph in Ear Recognition of Uniform Illumination Variant? *Indones. J. Electr. Eng. Comput. Sci.* **2018**, *11*, 558–566.
127. de Campos, L.M.L.; de Oliveira, R.C.L.; Roisenberg, M. Optimization of neural networks through grammatical evolution and a genetic algorithm. *Expert Syst. Appl.* **2016**, *56*, 368–384. [CrossRef]
128. El-Bakry, H.; Mastorakis, N. Ear Recognition by using Neural networks. *J. Math. Methods Appl. Comput.* **2010**, 770–804. Available online: https://www.researchgate.net/profile/Hazem-El-Bakry/publication/228387551_Ear_recognition_by_using_neural_networks/links/553fa82c0cf2320416eb244b/Ear-recognition-by-using-neural-networks.pdf (accessed on 18 December 2022).
129. Victor, B.; Bowyer, K.; Sarkar, S. An evaluation of face and ear biometrics. In Proceedings of the International Conference on Pattern Recognition, Quebec City, QC, Canada, 11–15 August 2002; Volume 1, pp. 429–432.
130. Jacob, L.; Raju, G. Ear recognition using texture features-a novel approach. In *Advances in Signal Processing and Intelligent Recognition Systems*; Springer International Publishing: New York, NY, USA, 2014; pp. 1–12.
131. Kumar, A.; Zhang, D. Ear authentication using Log-Gabor wavelets. In Proceedings of the Symposium on Defense and Security, International Society for Optics and Photonics, Orlando, FL, USA, 9–13 April 2007; pp. 1–5.
132. Lumini, A.; Nanni, L. An improved BioHashing for human authentication. *Pattern Recognit.* **2007**, *40*, 1057–1065. [CrossRef]
133. Arbab-Zavar, B.; Nixon, M. Robust Log-Gabor Filter for Ear Biometrics. In Proceedings of the International Conference on Pattern Recognition (ICPR 2008), Tampa, FL, USA, 8–11 December 2008; pp. 1–4.
134. Wang, Y.; Mu, Z.-C.; Zeng, H. Block-based and multi-resolution methods for ear recognition using wavelet transform and uniform local binary patterns. In Proceedings of the Pattern Recognition, 2008, ICPR 2008, 19th International Conference, Tampa, FL, USA, 8–11 December; 2008; pp. 1–4. [CrossRef]
135. Xie, Z.; Mu, Z. Ear recognition using LLE and IDLLE algorithm. In Proceedings of the 19th International Conference on Pattern Recognition, Tampa, FL, USA, 8–11 December 2008; pp. 1–4. [CrossRef]
136. Zhang, Z.; Liu, H. Multi-view ear recognition based on B-Spline pose manifold construction. In Proceedings of the 7th World Congress on Intelligent Control and Automation, Chongqing, China, 25–27 June 2008; pp. 2416–2421. [CrossRef]

137. Nanni, L.; Lumini, A. Fusion of color spaces for ear authentication. *Pattern Recognit.* **2009**, *42*, 1906–1913. [CrossRef]
138. Xiaoyun, W.; Weiqi, Y. Human ear recognition based on block segmentation. In Proceedings of the Cyber—Enabled Distributed Computing and Knowledge Discovery, Zhangjiajie, China, 10–11 October 2009; pp. 262–266.
139. Chan, S.; Kumar, A. Reliable ear identification using 2-D quadrature filters. *Pattern Recognit. Lett.* **2012**, *33*, 1870–1881. [CrossRef]
140. Ganapathi, I.I.; Prakash, S.; Dave, I.R.; Bakshi, S. Unconstrained ear detection using ensemble-based convolutional neural network model. *Concurr. Comput. Pract. Exp.* **2019**, *32*, e5197. [CrossRef]
141. Baoqing, Z.; Zhichun, M.; Chen, J.; Jiyuan, D. A robust algorithm for ear recognition under partial occlusion. In Proceedings of the Chinese Control Conference, Xi'an, China, 26–28 July 2013; pp. 3800–3804.
142. Kacar, U.; Kirci, M. ScoreNet: Deep Cascade Score Level Fusion for Unconstrained Ear Recognition. Available online: https://ietresearch.onlinelibrary.wiley.com/doi/pdfdirect/10.1049/iet-bmt.2018.5065 (accessed on 18 December 2022).
143. Wang, Y.; Cheng, K.; Zhao, S.; Xu, E. Human Ear Image Recognition Method Using PCA and Fisherface Complementary Double Feature Extraction. Available online: https://ojs.istp-press.com/jait/article/download/146/159 (accessed on 18 December 2022).
144. Basit, A.; Shoaib, M. A human ear recognition method using nonlinear curvelet feature subspace. *Int. J. Comput. Math.* **2014**, *91*, 616–624. [CrossRef]
145. Benzaoui, A.; Hadid, A.; Boukrouche, A. Ear biometric recognition using local texture descriptors. *J. Electron. Imaging* **2014**, *23*, 053008. [CrossRef]
146. Khorsandi, R.; Abdel-Mottaleb, M. Gender classification using 2-D ear images and sparse representation. In Proceedings of the 2013 IEEE Workshop on Applications of Computer Vision (WACV), Clearwater Beach, FL, USA, 15–17 January 2013; pp. 461–466. [CrossRef]
147. Pflug, A.; Paul, N.; Busch, N. A comparative study on texture and surface descriptors for ear biometrics. In Proceedings of the International Carnahan Conference on Security Technology, Rome, Italy, 13–16 October 2014; pp. 1–6.
148. Ying, T.; Debin, Z.; Baihuan, Z. Ear recognition based on weighted wavelet transform and DCT. In Proceedings of the Chinese Conference on Control and Decision, Changsha, China, 31 May–2 June 2014; pp. 4410–4414.
149. Chattopadhyay, P.K.; Bhatia, S. Morphological examination of ear: A study of an Indian population. *Leg. Med.* **2009**, *11*, S190–S193. [CrossRef] [PubMed]
150. Krishan, K.; Kanchan, T.; Thakur, S. A study of morphological variations of the human ear for its applications in personal identification. *Egypt. J. Forensic Sci.* **2019**, *9*, 1–11. [CrossRef]
151. Houcine, B.; Hakim, D.; Amir, B.; Hani, B.A.; Bourouba, H. Ear recognition based on Multi-bags-of-features histogram. In Proceedings of the International Conference on Control, Engineering Information Technology, Tlemcen, Algeria, 25–27 May 2015; pp. 1–6. [CrossRef]
152. Meraoumia, A.; Chitroub, S.; Bouridane, A. An automated ear identification system using Gabor filter responses. In Proceedings of the International Conference on New Circuits and Systems, Grenoble, France, 7–10 June 2015; pp. 1–4.
153. Morales, A.; Diaz, M.; Llinas-Sanchez, G.; Ferrer, M. Ear print recognition based on an ensemble of global and local features. In Proceedings of the International Carnahan Conference on Security Technology, Taipei, Taiwan, 21–24 September 2015; pp. 253–258.
154. Sánchez, D.; Melin, P.; Castillo, O. Optimization of modular granular neural networks using a firefly algorithm for human recognition. *Eng. Appl. Artif. Intell.* **2017**, *64*, 172–186. [CrossRef]
155. Almisreb, A.; Jamil, N.; Din, M. Utilizing AlexNet Deep Transfer Learning for Ear Recognition. In Proceedings of the 4th International Conference on Information Retrieval and Knowledge Management (CAMP), Kota Kinabalu, Malaysia, 26–28 March 2018; pp. 1–5.
156. Wiseman, K.B.; McCreery, R.W.; Walker, E.A. Hearing Thresholds, Speech Recognition, and Audibility as Indicators for Modifying Intervention in Children With Hearing Aids. *Ear Hear.* **2023**. [CrossRef]
157. Khan, M.A.; Kwon, S.; Choo, J.; Hong, S.J.; Kang, S.H.; Park, I.-H.; Kim, S.K. Automatic detection of tympanic membrane and middle ear infection from oto-endoscopic images via convolutional neural networks. *Neural Netw.* **2020**, *126*, 384–394. [CrossRef] [PubMed]
158. Ma, Y.; Huang, Z.; Wang, X.; Huang, K. An Overview of Multimodal Biometrics Using the Face and Ear. *Math. Probl. Eng.* **2020**, *2020*, 6802905. [CrossRef]
159. Hazra, A.; Choudhury, S.; Bhattacharyya, N.; Chaki, N. *An Intelligent Scheme for Human Ear Recognition Based on Shape and Amplitude Features. Advanced Computing Systems for Security: 13. Lecture Notes in Networks and Systems, 241*; Chaki, R., Chaki, N., Cortesi, A., Saeed, K., Eds.; Advanced Springer: Berlin/Heidelberg, Germany, 2022. [CrossRef]
160. Jeyabharathi, J.; Devi, S.; Krishnan, B.; Samuel, R.; Anees, M.I.; Jegadeesan, R. Human Ear Identification System Using Shape and structural feature based on SIFT and ANN Classifier. In Proceedings of the International Conference on Communication, Computing and Internet of Things (IC3IoT), Chennai, India, 10–11 March 2022; pp. 1–6. [CrossRef]
161. Xu, X.; Lu, L.; Zhang, X.; Lu, H.; Deng, W. Multispectral palmprint recognition using multiclass projection extreme learning machine and digital shearlet transform. *Neural Comput. Appl.* **2016**, *27*, 143–153. [CrossRef]
162. Borodo, S.; Shamsuddin, S.; Hasan, S. Big Data Platforms and Techniques. *Indones. J. Electr. Eng. Comput. Sci.* **2016**, *1*, 191–200. [CrossRef]
163. Hubel, D.H.; Wiesel, T.N. Receptive fields of single neurones in the cat's striate cortex. *J. Physiol.* **1959**, *148*, 574–591. [CrossRef] [PubMed]
164. Booysens, A.; Viriri, S. Ear biometrics using deep learning: A survey. *Appl. Comput. Intell. Soft Comput.* **2022**, *2022*. [CrossRef]

165. Zhao, H.M.; Yao, R.; Xu, L.; Yuan, Y.; Li, G.Y.; Deng, W. Study on a Novel Fault Damage Degree Identification Method Using High-Order Differential Mathematical Morphology Gradient Spectrum Entropy. *Entropy* **2018**, *20*, 682. [CrossRef] [PubMed]
166. Gonzalez, E.; Alvarez, L.; Mazorra, L. Normalization and feature extraction on ear images. In Proceedings of the IEEE International Carnahan Conference on Security, Newton, MA, USA, 15–18 October 2012; pp. 97–104. [CrossRef]
167. Zhang, J.; Yu, W.; Yang, X.; Deng, F. Few-shot learning for ear recognition. In Proceedings of the 2019 International Conference on Image, Video and Signal Processing, New York, NY, USA, 25–28 February 2019; pp. 50–54. [CrossRef]
168. Zou, Q.; Wang, C.; Yang, S.; Chen, B. A compact periocular recognition system based on deep learning framework AttenMidNet with the attention mechanism. *Multimed. Tools Appl.* **2022**. [CrossRef]
169. Shafi'I, M.; Latiff, M.; Chiroma, H.; Osho, O.; Abdul-Salaam, G.; Abubakar, A.; Herawan, T. A Review on Mobile SMS Spam Filtering Techniques. *IEEE Access* **2017**, *5*, 15650–15666. [CrossRef]
170. Perkowitz, S. The Bias in the Machine: Facial Recognition Technology and Racial Disparities. *MIT Case Stud. Soc. Ethic Responsib. Comput.* **2021**. [CrossRef]
171. Kamboj, A.; Rani, R.; Nigam, A. A comprehensive survey and deep learning-based approach for human recognition using ear biometric. *Vis. Comput.* **2021**, *38*, 2383–2416. [CrossRef]
172. Othman, R.; Alizadeh, F.; Sutherland, A. A novel approach for occluded ear recognition based on shape context. In Proceedings of the 2018 International Conference on Advanced Science and Engineering (ICOASE), Duhok, Iraq, 9–11 October 2018; pp. 93–98.
173. Zangeneh, E.; Rahmati, M.; Mohsenzadeh, Y. Low resolution face recognition using a two-branch deep convolutional neural network architecture. *Expert Syst. Appl.* **2020**, *139*, 112854. [CrossRef]
174. Toprak, I.; Toygar, Ö. Detection of spoofing attacks for ear biometrics through image quality assessment and deep learning. *Expert Syst. Appl.* **2021**, *172*, 114600. [CrossRef]
175. Rahim, M.; Rehman, A.; Kurniawan, F.; Saba, T. Biometrics for Human Classification Based on Region Features Mining. *Biomed. Res.* **2017**, *28*, 4660–4664.
176. Hurley, D.; Nixon, M.; Carter, J. Automatic ear recognition by force field transformations. In Proceedings of the IEE Colloquium on Visual Biometrics, Ref. No. 2000/018, London, UK, 2 March 2000; pp. 1–5.
177. Abaza, A.; Ross, A.; Herbert, C.; Harrison, M.; Nixon, M. A survey on ear biometrics. *ACM Comput. Surv.* **2013**, *45*, 1–35. [CrossRef]
178. Chowdhury, D.P.; Bakshi, S.; Sa, P.K.; Majhi, B. Wavelet energy feature based source camera identification for ear biometric images. *Pattern Recognit. Lett.* **2018**, *130*, 139–147. [CrossRef]
179. Miccini, R.; Spagnol, S. HRTF Individualization using Deep Learning. In Proceedings of the 2020 IEEE Conference on Virtual Reality and 3D User Interfaces Abstracts and Workshops (VRW), Atlanta, GA, USA, 22–26 March 2020; pp. 390–395.
180. Bargal, S.A.; Welles, A.; Chan, C.R.; Howes, S.; Sclaroff, S.; Ragan, E.; Johnson, C.; Gill, C. Image-based Ear Biometric Smartphone App for Patient Identification in Field Settings. In Proceedings of the 10th International Conference on Computer Vision Theory and Applications, Berlin, Germany, 11–14 March 2010; pp. 171–179. [CrossRef]
181. Agarwal, R. Local and Global Features Based on Ear Recognition System. In *International Conference on Artificial Intelligence and Sustainable Engineering*; Sanyal, G., Travieso-González, C.M., Awasthi, S., Pinto, C.M., Purushothama, B.R., Eds.; Lecture Notes in Electrical Engineering; Springer: Singapore, 2022; p. 837. [CrossRef]
182. Chowdhury, D.P.; Bakshi, S.; Pero, C.; Olague, G.; Sa, P.K. Privacy Preserving Ear Recognition System Using Transfer Learning in Industry 4.0. In *IEEE Transactions on Industrial Informatics*; IEEE: New York, NY, USA, 2022; pp. 1–10. [CrossRef]
183. Minaee, S.; Abdolrashidi, A.; Su, H.; Bennamoun, M.; Zhang, D. Biometrics recognition using deep learning: A survey. *Artif. Intell. Rev.* **2023**, 1–49. [CrossRef]
184. Kamboj, A.; Rani, R.; Nigam, A.; Jha, R.R. CED-Net: Context-aware ear detection network for unconstrained images. *Pattern Anal. Appl.* **2020**, *24*, 779–800. [CrossRef]
185. Ganapathi, I.I.; Ali, S.S.; Prakash, S.; Vu, N.S.; Werghi, N. A Survey of 3D Ear Recognition Techniques. *ACM Comput. Surv.* **2023**, *55*, 1–36. [CrossRef]
186. Alkababji, A.M.; Mohammed, O.H. Real time ear recognition using deep learning. *TELKOMNIKA Telecommun. Comput. Electron. Control* **2021**, *19*, 523–530. [CrossRef]
187. Hamdany, A.H.S.; Ebrahem, A.T.; Alkababji, A.M. Earprint recognition using deep learning technique. *TELKOMNIKA Telecommun. Comput. Electron. Control.* **2021**, *19*, 432–437. [CrossRef]
188. Hadi, R.A.; George, L.E.; Ahmed, Z.J. Automatic human ear detection approach using modified adaptive search window technique. *TELKOMNIKA Telecommun. Comput. Electron. Control* **2021**, *19*, 507–514. [CrossRef]
189. Mussi, E.; Servi, M.; Facchini, F.; Furferi, R.; Governi, L.; Volpe, Y. A novel ear elements segmentation algorithm on depth map images. *Comput. Biol. Med.* **2021**, *129*, 104157. [CrossRef]
190. Kamboj, A.; Rani, R.; Nigam, A. CG-ERNet: A lightweight Curvature Gabor filtering based ear recognition network for data scarce scenario. *Multi. Tools Appl.* **2021**, *80*, 26571–26613. [CrossRef]
191. Emersic, Z.; Susanj, D.; Meden, B.; Peer, P.; Struc, V. ContexedNet: Context–Aware Ear Detection in Unconstrained Settings. *IEEE Access* **2021**, *9*, 145175–145190. [CrossRef]
192. El-Naggar, S.; Abaza, A.; Bourlai, T. Ear Detection in the Wild Using Faster R-CNN Deep Learning. In Proceedings of the 2018 IEEE/ACM International Conference on Advances in Social Networks Analysis and Mining (ASONAM), Barcelona, Spain, 28–31 August 2018; pp. 1124–1130. [CrossRef]

193. Tang, X.; Du, D.K.; He, Z.; Liu, J. *PyramidBox: A Context-Assisted Single Shot Face Detector*; Springer: Berlin/Heidelberg, Germany, 2018; pp. 812–828. [CrossRef]

194. Najibi, M.; Samangouei, P.; Chellappa, R.; Davis, L.S. SSH: Single Stage Headless Face Detector. In Proceedings of the 2017 IEEE International Conference on Computer Vision (ICCV), Venice, Italy, 22–29 October 2017; pp. 4875–4884. [CrossRef]

195. Khaldi, Y.; Benzaoui, A.; Ouahabi, A.; Jacques, S.; Taleb-Ahmed, A. Ear Recognition Based on Deep Unsupervised Active Learning. *IEEE Sens. J.* **2021**, *21*, 20704–20713. [CrossRef]

196. Khaldi, Y.; Benzaoui, A. A new framework for grayscale ear images recognition using generative adversarial networks under unconstrained conditions. *Evol. Syst.* **2021**, *12*, 923–934. [CrossRef]

197. Omara, I.; Hagag, A.; Ma, G.; El-Samie, F.E.A.; Song, E. A novel approach for ear recognition: Learning Mahalanobis distance features from deep CNNs. *Mach. Vis. Appl.* **2021**, *32*, 38. [CrossRef]

198. Alejo, M.B. Unconstrained Ear Recognition Using Transformers. *Jordanian J. Comput. Inf. Technol.* **2021**, *7*, 326–336. [CrossRef]

199. Alshazly, H.; Linse, C.; Barth, E.; Idris, S.A.; Martinetz, T. Towards Explainable Ear Recognition Systems Using Deep Residual Networks. *IEEE Access* **2021**, *9*, 122254–122273. [CrossRef]

200. Priyadharshini, R.A.; Arivazhagan, S.; Arun, M. A deep learning approach for person identification using ear biometrics. *Appl. Intell.* **2020**, *51*, 2161–2172. [CrossRef] [PubMed]

201. Lavanya, B.; Inbarani, H.H.; Azar, A.T.; Fouad, K.M.; Koubaa, A.; Kamal, N.A.; Lala, I.R. Particle Swarm Optimization Ear Identification System. In *Soft Computing Applications. SOFA 2018. Advances in Intelligent Systems and Computing*; Balas, V., Jain, L., Balas, M., Shahbazova, S., Eds.; Springer: Berlin/Heidelberg, Germany, 2020; pp. 372–384. [CrossRef]

202. Sarangi, P.P.; Panda, M.; Mishra, S.; Mishra, B.S.P. Multimodal biometric recognition using human ear and profile face: An improved approach. In *Cognitive Data Science in Sustainable Computing, Machine Learning for Biometrics*; Sarangi, P.P., Ed.; Elsevier: Amsterdam, The Netherlands; pp. 47–63. [CrossRef]

203. Sarangi, P.P.; Nayak, D.R.; Panda, M.; Majhi, B. A feature-level fusion based improved multimodal biometric recognition system using ear and profile face. *J. Ambient. Intell. Humaniz. Comput.* **2022**, *13*, 1867–1898. [CrossRef]

204. Abayomi-Alli, A.; Bioku, E.; Folorunso, O.; Dawodu, G.A.; Awotunde, J.B. An Occlusion and Pose Sensitive Image Dataset for Black Ear Recognition. Available online: https://zenodo.org/record/7715970#.ZBPQjPZBxPZ (accessed on 18 December 2022).

 *information*

Review

Emerging Digital Technologies in Healthcare with a Spotlight on Cybersecurity: A Narrative Review

Ahmed Arafa [1,2,*] , **Haytham A. Sheerah** [3] **and Shada Alsalamah** [4,5]

1   Department of Preventive Cardiology, National Cerebral and Cardiovascular Center, Suita 564-8565, Japan
2   Department of Public Health and Community Medicine, Faculty of Medicine, Beni-Suef University, Beni-Suef 62521, Egypt
3   International Collaborations, Ministry of Health, Riyadh 11176, Saudi Arabia; hasheerah@moh.gov.sa
4   Information Systems Department, College of Computer and Information Sciences, King Saud University, Riyadh 11362, Saudi Arabia; saalsalamah@ksu.edu.sa
5   Digital Health and Innovation Department, World Health Organization, CH-1211 Geneva, Switzerland
*   Correspondence: ahmed011172@med.bsu.edu.eg; Tel.: +81-6-6170-1070 (ext. 60239); Fax: +81-6-6170-1824

Abstract: Emerging digital technologies, such as telemedicine, artificial intelligence, the Internet of Medical Things, blockchain, and visual and augmented reality, have revolutionized the delivery of and access to healthcare services. Such technologies allow for real-time health monitoring, disease diagnosis, chronic disease management, outbreak surveillance, and rehabilitation. They help personalize treatment plans, identify trends, contribute to drug development, and enhance public health management. While emerging digital technologies have numerous benefits, they may also introduce new risks and vulnerabilities that can compromise the confidentiality, integrity, and availability of sensitive healthcare information. This review article discussed, in brief, the key emerging digital technologies in the health sector and the unique threats introduced by these technologies. We also highlighted the risks relevant to digital health cybersecurity, such as data breaches, medical device vulnerabilities, phishing, insider and third-party risks, and ransomware attacks. We suggest that the cybersecurity framework should include developing a comprehensive cybersecurity strategy, conducting regular risk assessments, implementing strong access control, encrypting data, educating staff, implementing secure network segmentation, backing up data regularly, monitoring and detecting anomalies, establishing an incident response plan, sharing threat intelligence, and auditing third-party vendors.

Keywords: artificial intelligence; blockchain; cybersecurity; digital health; emerging digital technologies; healthcare; telehealth

Citation: Arafa, A.; Sheerah, H.A.; Alsalamah, S. Emerging Digital Technologies in Healthcare with a Spotlight on Cybersecurity: A Narrative Review. *Information* **2023**, *14*, 640. https://doi.org/10.3390/info14120640

Academic Editors: Jose de Vasconcelos, Hugo Barbosa and Carla Cordeiro

Received: 19 October 2023
Revised: 8 November 2023
Accepted: 28 November 2023
Published: 29 November 2023

1. Introduction

The healthcare industry has witnessed a profound transformation fueled by rapid advancements in digital technologies. Over the past few decades, emerging digital technologies have surfaced as powerful catalysts for innovation in healthcare. Telemedicine, wearable devices, electronic health records, the Internet of Things (IoT) in healthcare, artificial intelligence (AI), and blockchain technology are just a few examples of the technologies that have rapidly transformed the sector. Telemedicine has made healthcare more accessible by enabling remote consultations, wearable devices have allowed for continuous patient monitoring, electronic health records have streamlined record-keeping and data sharing, and AI has offered remarkable insights for diagnosis and treatment. The utilization of these technologies has improved healthcare efficiency and effectiveness, but it has also introduced new challenges [1–3].

The integration of digital technologies in healthcare has opened up Pandora's box of vulnerabilities. Interconnected devices, often with inadequate security measures, can be a point of entry for cyberattacks. Patient data, a prime target for hackers, are at risk of theft or unauthorized access. The rapid pace of innovation sometimes means that security considerations are an afterthought, leaving systems and devices unprepared to face evolving threats. Moreover, the human element, including healthcare staff and patients, can also inadvertently introduce vulnerabilities through actions such as sharing passwords, falling victim to phishing attacks or failing to update software and systems regularly. As such, the vulnerabilities related to emerging digital technologies in healthcare demand a vigilant and proactive response [4–6].

Specifically, cybersecurity threats in healthcare have been on the rise, posing significant risks to patient safety and data integrity. Malware attacks, ransomware incidents, and data breaches have the potential to disrupt healthcare services, compromise patient records, and jeopardize the trust between healthcare providers and their patients. The consequences of these threats extend beyond financial losses, with the potential for harm to patient health and wellbeing. Moreover, healthcare institutions also face legal and reputational repercussions, making cybersecurity a paramount concern. Understanding these threats and their potential impacts is crucial in the ongoing effort to safeguard the healthcare industry from malicious actions [5–7].

In response to the growing threats, healthcare organizations have been actively developing and implementing cybersecurity best practices. The approach includes ensuring robust security measures across digital healthcare systems, securing endpoints and networks, encrypting sensitive data, and training personnel to recognize and mitigate cyber risks. Furthermore, regulatory frameworks and standards mandate certain cybersecurity measures to protect patient data. Collaboration among healthcare stakeholders, governments, and the cybersecurity industry has also been instrumental in developing effective strategies to bolster the security of emerging digital technologies in healthcare [5–7].

In this context, the World Health Organization's (WHO) Global Strategy on Digital Health 2020–2025 highlighted the need for harnessing the power of digital technologies alongside strengthening data protection and privacy measures in digital health systems. These strategic objectives underscore the importance of establishing robust legal and regulatory frameworks to safeguard the privacy, confidentiality, and integrity of personal health data [8].

In an era where technology has the potential to revolutionize healthcare, it is crucial to strike a balance between harnessing the power of these digital advancements and ensuring that they do not become vectors of harm. In doing so, we can pave the way for a future where emerging digital technologies in healthcare can be harnessed to their full potential, delivering optimal patient care while safeguarding patient data and well-being from the ever-present cybersecurity threats.

Unlike previous review articles that discussed certain technical areas related to emerging digital technologies, this review article will navigate through interconnected facets of emerging digital technologies in healthcare and cybersecurity, aiming to provide a comprehensive understanding of the current landscape, especially for healthcare workers. By exploring the benefits, vulnerabilities, threats, and best practices in healthcare cybersecurity, readers will gain insights into the intricate dance between innovation and security within the healthcare sector.

2. Methods

The primary objective of this narrative review is to provide a comprehensive and insightful overview of emerging digital technologies in healthcare, with a particular focus on cybersecurity considerations. We aim to synthesize the existing literature to understand the current landscape of digital technologies in healthcare and the challenges and opportunities related to cybersecurity within this context (Table 1).

Table 1. A summary of items discussed in this narrative review.

Emerging Digital Technologies in Healthcare	Vulnerabilities Related to Emerging Digital Technologies in Healthcare	Cybersecurity Threats in Healthcare	Cybersecurity Best Practices in the Health Sector
• Mobile health applications (mHealth apps), wearable Internet of Things (WIoT), and personalized health (pHealth)	• Cybersecurity	• Data breaches	• Develop a comprehensive cybersecurity strategy
• Big data analytics	• Interoperability	• Medical device vulnerabilities	• Conduct regular risk assessments
• Cloud computing	• Regulatory compliance	• Phishing	• Implement strong access controls
• Internet of Medical Things (IoMT)	• Ethical considerations	• Insider risks	• Encrypt data
• Virtual reality (VR) and augmented reality (AR)	• Provider and patient education	• Third-party risks	• Educate and train staff
• Telemedicine and telehealth	• Infrastructure	• Ransomware attacks	• Implement secure network segmentation
• Artificial intelligence (AI) and machine learning (ML)			• Regularly back up data
• Distributed Ledger Technology (DLT) and blockchain			• Monitor and detect anomalies
			• Establish an incident response plan
			• Collaborate and share threat intelligence
			• Regularly audit and assess third-party vendors

We accessed a variety of academic databases, including, but not limited to, PubMed and Scopus. We employed a combination of keywords and phrases, including "digital technologies in healthcare", "eHealth", "mHealth", "telemedicine", "cybersecurity", "healthcare data security", "emerging technologies in healthcare", and related terms. These keywords were used in various combinations to maximize the relevance of the search results. Non-peer-reviewed studies and studies published in languages other than English were not sought.

The results and insights extracted from the selected literature were synthesized in a narrative format. This narrative review does not include a meta-analysis but instead provides a qualitative analysis of the themes, trends, and issues related to the adoption of digital technologies in healthcare and the challenges posed by cybersecurity. Due to the multi-faceted nature of our topic, the need to cover several aspects related to emerging digital technologies in healthcare and threats related to their application, and the large number of articles investigating specific areas, we could not systematically obtain all related articles, and we focused on narrative and systematic reviews instead. We believe that a narrative review may allow healthcare workers to obtain a more comprehensive view of emerging digital technologies in healthcare and cybersecurity. Nevertheless, it is important to acknowledge that this narrative review may be subject to certain limitations. The inclusion criteria may introduce selection bias, and the rapidly evolving nature of the field might mean that some emerging developments may not be adequately covered.

3. Emerging Digital Technologies in Healthcare

There are several emerging digital technologies that are making an impact on healthcare. These technologies use digital platforms, connectivity, and data to transform various aspects of healthcare delivery, patient engagement, and research. Regardless of the technology, they all mainly aim to connect health workers and patients to enable a seamless flow of medical information between healthcare settings for informed decision-making purposes [8] (Table 2).

Table 2. A summary of the main features of emerging digital technologies in healthcare.

Features	Summary
Types and uses of mobile health applications (mHealth apps)	Health tracking, medication, telemedicine and telehealth, fitness, mental health, health record, and health education
Features of wearable Internet of Things (WIoT)	Wireless mobility, intelligence and interactivity, sustainability, simple operation, and portability
Types of big data streams	Clinical data from electronic medical records, biometric data from medical devices, financial data from relevant financial records, patient data from questionnaires and surveys, and social media data from social network
Implications of cloud computing	Relying on software, providing security and interoperability, performing clinical tasks, supporting patient-centeredness, facilitating collaboration, and increasing service mobility and flexibility
Steps of the Internet of Medical Things (IoMT)	Collecting and analyzing data, informing healthcare providers, patients, or other medical devices, and sending real-time recommendations
Uses of virtual reality (VR) and augmented reality (AR)	Medical training, surgical planning, remote consultations, and patient education
Challenges to virtual reality (VR) and augmented reality (AR)	High cost, difficulty in integrating VR and AR with existing healthcare infrastructure, and ethical and legal considerations
Types of telemedicine	Remote patient monitoring, store-and-forward telemedicine, real-time telemedicine, and physician-to-physician consultation
Uses of artificial intelligence (AI) and machine learning (ML)	Analyzing medical data, developing personalized treatment plans, remotely tracking patient vital signs, symptoms, and adherence to treatment plans, and automating routine administrative tasks, such as appointment scheduling, documentation, and data entry
Applications of blockchain technology	Health data exchange, medical supply chain management, clinical trials and research, health insurance and claims processing, and personal health records

3.1. Mobile Health Applications (mHealth Apps), Wearable Internet of Things (WIoT), and Personalized Health (pHealth)

mHealth apps are applications designed for mobile devices, such as smartphones and tablets, that aim to support healthcare delivery and promote wellness. They vary widely in terms of content, accessibility, interactivity, connectivity, and security [9]. They offer a wide range of functionalities and can be categorized into the following several types, based on their uses: (1) health tracking apps, which focus on monitoring and tracking health-related data, such as physical activity, sleep patterns, nutrition, and vital signs; (2) medication apps, which send reminders for medication doses, track adherence, provide information about drug interactions, and enable users to maintain a medication schedule; (3) telemedicine and telehealth apps, which enable patients to connect with healthcare providers through video calls, text messaging, or voice calls, allowing for remote diagnosis, monitoring, and treatment; (4) fitness apps, which offer workout tracking, personalized training plans, and step counting; (5) mental health apps, which provide resources for mental health support, stress management, and mindfulness practices; (6) health record apps, which enable users to store, access, and manage their personal health information and keep track of their medical history, test results, vaccinations, and appointments; and (7) health education apps, which provide health-related education, information, and resources [9–12].

WIoT interconnects wearable sensors to enable the monitoring of human factors and other data, which is useful in enhancing individuals' everyday quality of life. The main features of WIoT are as follows: (1) wireless mobility, (2) intelligence and interactivity, (3) sustainability, (4) simple operation, and (5) portability [10]. They can be categorized, per their applications, into four areas: (1) health monitoring, (2) disease diagnosis, (3) chronic disease management, and (4) rehabilitation [10].

pHealth refers to the use of digital health technologies, data analytics, and personalized medicine approaches to tailor healthcare and preventive interventions to patients' characteristics, needs, and preferences. The concept of pHealth aims to move away from the traditional "one-size-fits-all" approach to healthcare and move toward more personalized and patient-centered care. pHealth uses various technologies, such as WIoT, mHealth apps, genetic testing, and remote monitoring tools, to collect and analyze vast amounts of data about an individual's health status, behaviors, and lifestyle factors. By combining these data with advanced analytics, healthcare providers can gain deeper insights into a person's health profile and make more informed and targeted health decisions [13].

However, several challenges face the wide application of mHealth apps and WIoT, such as the lack of industry standards, obstacles in reaching user-friendly solutions, cybersecurity concerns, and technical problems [9–12].

3.2. Big Data Analytics

Big data streams include various types of data: (1) clinical data from electronic medical records, hospital information systems, image centers, laboratories, and pharmacies; (2) biometric data from medical devices that monitor vital signs, body composition, etc.; (3) financial data, constituting records of relevant financial operations; (4) scientific research data; (5) patient data, including treatment preferences, satisfaction levels, self-administered information about their lifestyle and sociodemographic factors; and (6) social media data [14]. Big data analytics involves processing and analyzing a huge amount of data. This processing may vary in terms of data volume, speed of generation, heterogeneity, inconsistency, quality, and value [14]. Big data analytics has become increasingly used to improve clinical decision-making, identify trends, contribute to drug development, and enhance public health management [14–17]. However, big data analytics faces several challenges related to storage, processing, finding and fixing troubles, and security issues [16,17].

3.3. Cloud Computing

Cloud computing offers scalable and cost-effective storage and processing capabilities for healthcare organizations. It enables secure access to medical records, facilitates data sharing and collaboration, and supports telemedicine and remote monitoring [18–21]. The implications of cloud computing in healthcare can be summarized in the following points: (1) relying on software, especially software as a service (SaaS), platform as a service (PaaS), and infrastructure as a service (IaaS); (2) providing security and interoperability; (3) performing clinical tasks; (4) supporting patient-centeredness; (5) facilitating collaboration; and (6) increasing service mobility and flexibility [19]. However, the lack of regulations, system outages, lack of control, and security issues remain potential challenges [19–21] (Figure 1).

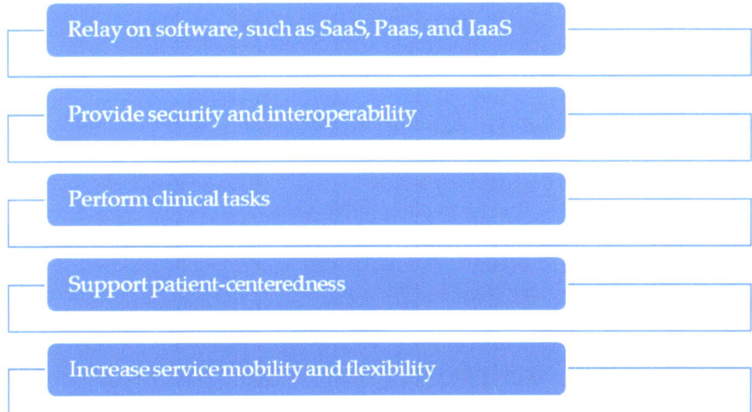

Figure 1. Characteristics of cloud computing as an emerging digital technology in healthcare.

3.4. Internet of Medical Things (IoMT)

The IoMT refers to the interconnected network of medical devices, sensors, and wearable technologies, such as smartwatches, fitness trackers, and glucose monitors. These devices collect and transmit instantaneous health data, allowing for remote patient monitoring, early disease detection, and personalized care [22–24]. The IoMT framework-based digital healthcare includes several stages. First, the patient's data are collected using smart wearable or implanted devices that are connected by a body or wireless sensor network, then analyzed, and finally, predictions are drawn. Healthcare providers, patients, or other medical devices can be automatically approached to be informed of the current medical condition or future potential health outcome. Finally, the IoMT provides real-time recommendations about what should be conducted to manage the current medical condition and prevent future complications [22]. Nevertheless, the IoMT faces challenges related to data privacy, a potential lack of accuracy, especially when massive data are processed, and the high cost of installing and maintaining the devices [22–24].

3.5. Virtual Reality (VR) and Augmented Reality (AR)

VR and AR technologies create interactive experiences for medical training, surgical planning, and patient education. While VR can simulate realistic medical scenarios for training healthcare professionals, AR overlays digital information in the real world, aiding in surgical navigation and medical imaging [25–28]. In medical training, VR and AR technologies provide interactive environments for medical students, allowing them to simulate surgeries, practice complex procedures, and learn anatomy in a realistic and risk-free manner. These technologies enable hands-on experiences and improve learning outcomes. Surgeons can use VR and AR to visualize patient-specific anatomical structures and plan complex surgeries. VR can be used in rehabilitation to create engaging and motivating environments for patients. It can be used to simulate real-life scenarios and exercises, helping patients to regain motor skills, improve balance, and manage pain. AR can provide feedback and guidance during physical therapy sessions. Furthermore, VR and AR can facilitate remote consultations by providing virtual meeting spaces where healthcare providers can interact with patients and review medical data. It allows for better collaboration, faster diagnoses, and reduced travel burdens for patients [25–28]. The main challenge of VR and AR is the high cost of high-quality headsets, sensors, and computing systems. Moreover, integrating VR and AR systems with existing healthcare infrastructure, electronic health records, and medical imaging systems can be complex. Furthermore, the use of VR and AR in healthcare raises ethical and legal considerations related to patient privacy, data security, and informed consent [25–28].

3.6. Telemedicine and Telehealth

Telemedicine refers to the remote delivery of healthcare services, including medical consultations, diagnoses, and treatment, using telecommunications technology. The main types of telemedicine are remote patient monitoring, store-and-forward telemedicine, real-time interactive telemedicine, and physician-to-physician consultation [29–32]. It poses several advantages, such as providing convenient access to healthcare, especially for those in remote areas, eliminating travel expenses and time off work for patients, and reducing hospital admissions. However, many barriers should be considered, such as technological difficulties, particularly in rural and low-income areas, privacy and security concerns, limited physical examination, reimbursement and regulatory problems, and diagnostic limitations [29–32].

Telehealth is a broader term that encompasses a wider range of healthcare services and activities beyond merely clinical care. It includes the use of digital communication technologies to provide healthcare-related information, education, and administrative services. It can involve remote patient monitoring, health education through online platforms, electronic health record systems, mobile health apps, and administrative tasks such as scheduling appointments and processing medical bills [29–32] (Figure 2).

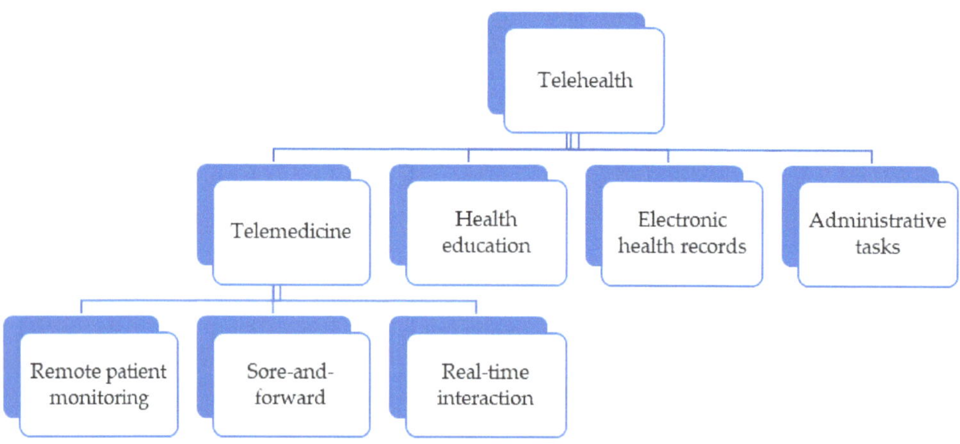

Figure 2. Telehealth as an emerging digital technology in healthcare.

3.7. Artificial Intelligence (AI) and Machine Learning (ML)

AI refers to the ability of machines to mimic human behavior by learning from data using self-learning technologies (such as data mining, pattern recognition, and natural language processing) to understand the way the human brain works. ML is a subset of AI that can also improve with experience. With such techniques, AI and ML have the potential to revolutionize healthcare. They can analyze vast amounts of medical data, including medical images, lab results, and patient records, to aid in the diagnosis of diseases. By analyzing individual patient data, AI and ML can develop personalized treatment plans based on factors, such as medical history, genetics, and lifestyle. AI-powered monitoring devices can remotely track patient vital signs, symptoms, and adherence to treatment plans. ML algorithms can detect trends and anomalies, alerting healthcare providers to potential issues. Furthermore, AI can automate routine administrative tasks, such as appointment scheduling, documentation, and data entry, allowing healthcare professionals to focus more on patient care [33–36]. However, data privacy concerns, a lack of quality data, inadequate interpretations, the lack of a skilled workforce, and regulatory and legal shortages are the main barriers to the wide application of AI and ML in medical facilities [37,38].

3.8. Distributed Ledger Technology (DLT) and Blockchain

DLT is a decentralized and distributed digital system that records transactions and data across multiple computers or nodes. In a distributed ledger, each participant has a copy of the data, and changes made to the ledger are synchronized across all copies. This approach ensures the transparency, security, and immutability of data, since alterations require consensus among the network participants. Blockchain is a specific type of DLT that uses cryptographic techniques to secure and validate transactions. It is a chain of blocks, where each block contains a list of transactions and a reference to the previous block, forming an unbroken and tamper-evident chain. The key features of blockchain include decentralization, immutability, and transparency. Blockchain technology has several potential applications, such as (1) health data exchange: blockchain can facilitate and secure interoperable exchange of patient health records among healthcare providers while maintaining data privacy and consent; (2) medical supply chain management: blockchain can track the movement of pharmaceuticals, medical devices, and supplies, ensuring authenticity, quality control, and reducing the risk of counterfeit products; (3) clinical trials and research: blockchain can enhance transparency and data integrity in clinical trials, helping to prevent data manipulation and improving the research process; (4) health insurance and claims processing: blockchain can streamline insurance processes, reduce fraud, and improve the accuracy and speed of claims processing; and (5) personal health records: blockchain can enable patients to have more control over their health data, allowing them to share specific information with healthcare providers and researchers while maintaining ownership and privacy (Figure 3). Implementing blockchain in healthcare requires addressing challenges such as regulatory compliance, data standardization, scalability, and ensuring that private patient data remains secure [39–43].

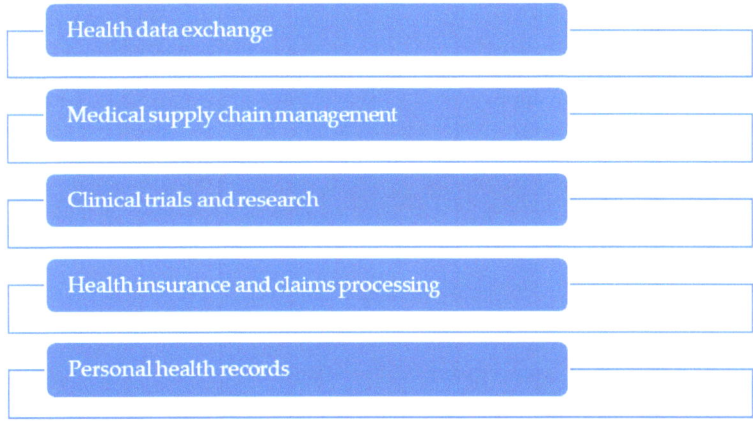

Figure 3. Applications of blockchain as an emerging digital technology in healthcare.

4. Vulnerabilities Related to Emerging Digital Technologies in Healthcare

While emerging digital technologies have numerous benefits, they also introduce new threats and vulnerabilities that can compromise the confidentiality, integrity, and availability of sensitive healthcare information.

4.1. Cybersecurity

The increased use of digital technologies in healthcare generates and collects vast amounts of sensitive patient data. Ensuring robust data security and privacy measures is crucial to protect against data breaches, unauthorized access, and the potential misuse of personal health information. Medical facilities should implement strong encryption, access controls, and data anonymization techniques to safeguard patient data [44–51]; this topic is described below with more details.

4.2. Interoperability

Interoperability refers to the ability of different digital systems and technologies to exchange and use data seamlessly. Interoperability challenges could be due to the following. (1) A lack of standardization: The absence of widely adopted standards for data formats, interfaces, and communication makes it difficult for systems to exchange and interpret data accurately. (2) Fragmented systems and technical heterogeneity: Healthcare organizations often use multiple digital systems, such as electronic health records, imaging systems, laboratory systems, and telemedicine platforms. Bridging the gaps between these systems to enable data exchange is a significant challenge. (3) Data security: Healthcare data are highly sensitive and subject to strict privacy regulations. Ensuring secure and private data exchange between digital systems while complying with security regulations adds complexity to achieving interoperability. (4) Inadequate infrastructure: Several medical facilities may use outdated technologies with limited data exchange capabilities. Integrating newer digital technologies with older systems is challenging. Addressing these challenges requires collaborative efforts among stakeholders, including healthcare organizations, technology vendors, standardization bodies, and regulatory agencies [52–54].

4.3. Regulatory Compliance

Healthcare is an industry with numerous legal and regulatory requirements. Compliance with these regulations becomes more complex with the adoption of digital technologies, especially in multiple jurisdictional settings. Medical facilities should navigate the regulatory landscape and ensure that their digital systems adhere to the necessary privacy and security standards [55–57]. Several regulatory bodies pertain to digital health technologies. In the US, for example, the Health Insurance Portability and Accountability Act (HIPAA) has established standards for the protection of patient health information, while the Food and Drug Administration (FDA) regulates medical devices, including certain digital health technologies, such as software applications, wearables, and telehealth devices [56]. In the European Union, the General Data Protection Regulation (GDPR) has applied rules for the protection of personal data, while the Medical Device Regulation (MDR) regulates medical devices, including those related to digital health [55]. Nevertheless, these regulations struggle to keep pace with the rapid advancements in digital healthcare. Furthermore, several digital technologies fall into gray regulatory areas, such as guidelines and frameworks. In addition, regulatory bodies face challenges in monitoring evolving digital technologies, detecting non-compliance, and enforcing regulations effectively [56].

4.4. Ethical Considerations

The use of emerging digital technologies in healthcare raises ethical questions related to data ownership, consent, transparency, and bias. The main ethical considerations can be summarized in the following points: (1) data privacy and security: digital technologies generate vast amounts of sensitive patient data, raising concerns about privacy breaches and data security; (2) informed consent issues: patients should be adequately informed about the potential risks, benefits, and possible uses of their data, enabling them to make informed decisions about their participation in digital health initiatives; (3) algorithm bias: AI and machine learning algorithms can inadvertently introduce bias, leading to unequal treatment and disparities in healthcare outcomes; (4) patient autonomy: patients should have the ability to make choices about the use, sharing, and retention of their health information; (5) access and equity: technological literacy, socioeconomic disparities, and geographical location can create barriers to access; (6) transparency: AI and machine learning algorithms can be complex and difficult to understand, making it challenging to explain their decisions or actions; and (7) accountability: establishing clear lines of accountability and defining liability frameworks becomes essential to protect both patients and healthcare providers [58–60].

4.5. Provider and Patient Education

The successful adoption and utilization of emerging digital technologies require adequate education and training for healthcare providers and patients. Healthcare providers should be proficient in using these technologies effectively, while patients need to be educated about the benefits, risks, and privacy considerations related to the use of digital tools [61–63].

4.6. Infrastructure

The infrastructure required to support emerging digital technologies may be lacking in certain regions or medical facilities. The main components of the infrastructure needed for installing digital technologies in medical facilities are the following: (1) a reliable and high-speed network to provide seamless connectivity and data transmission, (2) hardware and devices, (3) an electronic health recording system, and (4) technical support and maintenance [64,65].

5. Cybersecurity Threats in Healthcare

Insufficient cybersecurity regulations and procedures in medical facilities pose significant threats to patient safety, data integrity, and healthcare management. The healthcare sector has become an attractive target for cybercriminals due to the high value of medical records.

5.1. Data Breaches

Breached data can include medical records, personal identifiers, financial data, and insurance details. The stolen data can be sold to advertising agencies or used for identity theft or financial fraud, leading to significant harm to individuals and reputational damage to medical facilities [66,67].

5.2. Medical Device Vulnerabilities

The increasing use of interconnected medical devices, such as infusion pumps, pacemakers, and imaging systems, introduces vulnerabilities. These devices may have outdated software or weak security controls, making them susceptible to cyberattacks [68,69].

5.3. Phishing

Phishing attacks target healthcare employees through deceptive emails, phone calls, or text messages. These attacks could trick individuals into revealing sensitive information or granting unauthorized access, leading to data breaches [70–72].

5.4. Insider Risks

Insiders, including employees, contractors, or partners, pose a significant cybersecurity risk. Insider threats can involve intentional actions, such as stealing or leaking data, or unintentional actions, such as inadvertently exposing sensitive information [73–76].

5.5. Third-Party Risks

Medical facilities often collaborate with third-party vendors, suppliers, and partners, increasing the attack surface. Weak security practices in these third-party systems can be exploited by cybercriminals to obtain unauthorized access to healthcare networks [75,76].

5.6. Ransomware Attacks

Ransomware has emerged as a major threat to medical facilities. These attacks involve malicious software that encrypts data, rendering it inaccessible until a ransom is paid. Ransomware can lead to significant disruptions in healthcare services, compromise patient care, and result in financial losses [77,78].

6. Cybersecurity Best Practices in the Health Sector: A Framework for Healthcare Settings

6.1. Develop a Comprehensive Cybersecurity Strategy

Medical facilities should establish a robust cybersecurity strategy that outlines clear objectives, policies, and procedures for protecting patient data and critical infrastructure. This strategy should encompass prevention, detection, response, and recovery mechanisms to address potential cyber threats effectively [45,46,79,80].

6.2. Conduct Regular Risk Assessments

Regular risk assessments help identify vulnerabilities and potential entry points for cyberattacks. By assessing the security posture of systems, networks, and devices, healthcare organizations can proactively identify and mitigate potential risks and weaknesses [79,80].

6.3. Implement Strong Access Controls

Strong access controls are essential to prevent unauthorized access to sensitive patient data. Implementing multi-factor authentication, strong passwords, and role-based access control ensures that only authorized individuals can access critical information [80].

6.4. Encrypt Data

Encryption is a fundamental measure for protecting patient data. It ensures that even if data were to be intercepted or stolen, they remain unreadable and unusable. Encryption should be applied to data at rest, in transit, and during backup processes [81,82].

6.5. Educate and Train Staff

Human error remains a significant factor in cybersecurity incidents. Medical facilities should conduct regular training and awareness programs to educate employees about cybersecurity risks, best practices, and the importance of following security protocols [83]. This education can take various forms, including lectures, seminars, and even games [84–86].

6.6. Implement Secure Network Segmentation

The segmentation of networks and systems within healthcare environments helps contain potential breaches and limit the lateral movement of attackers. By separating different areas of the network and implementing strict access controls between them, medical facilities can reduce the impact of a successful cyberattack [87].

6.7. Regularly Back up Data

Backing up data is crucial to ensure continuity and recovery from potential ransomware attacks or data loss incidents. Backups should be encrypted, stored securely, and tested regularly to verify their integrity and the ability to restore data effectively [88,89].

6.8. Monitor and Detect Anomalies

Implementing robust monitoring and detection systems can help identify and respond to cybersecurity incidents promptly. Intrusion detection and prevention systems, security information and event management tools, and immediate log analysis can aid in detecting and mitigating threats promptly [80].

6.9. Establish an Incident Response Plan

Medical facilities should have a well-defined incident response plan in place. This plan outlines the steps to be taken in the event of a cybersecurity incident, including communication protocols, containment measures, forensic investigation procedures, and recovery strategies [80].

6.10. Collaborate and Share Threat Intelligence

Medical facilities should actively participate in information sharing and collaborate with industry peers, government agencies, and cybersecurity organizations to stay updated on emerging threats, vulnerabilities, and best practices. Sharing threat intelligence enhances the collective ability to defend against cyber threats [90].

6.11. Regularly Audit and Assess Third-Party Vendors

Medical facilities often work with third-party vendors who have access to patient data or provide critical services. It is essential to assess the security practices of these vendors and ensure they meet stringent cybersecurity standards.

7. Conclusions

Emerging digital technologies are transforming the landscape of healthcare, ushering in an era of innovation and efficiency. These technologies, including mHealth apps, wearables, big data analytics, cloud computing, blockchain, IoMT, VR, AR, telemedicine, AI, and ML, are instrumental in revolutionizing healthcare services. mHealth apps and wearables empower individuals to monitor their health in real time, fostering proactive healthcare management. Big data analytics enable healthcare professionals to extract valuable insights from vast datasets, personalizing treatment plans and identifying disease trends for public health benefit. Cloud computing facilitates seamless data sharing and storage, enhancing collaboration and accessibility. Blockchain technology ensures the integrity and security of medical records, assuaging concerns about data privacy and accuracy. IoMT devices connect healthcare systems, enhancing patient care coordination and remote monitoring. VR and AR technologies have applications in medical training and patient engagement, while telemedicine and telehealth platforms bridge geographical gaps, providing access to medical expertise and services. AI and ML algorithms aid in diagnosis and treatment, revolutionizing healthcare delivery. However, these transformative technologies also confront several challenges, such as cybersecurity threats, interoperability issues, regulatory complexities, ethical dilemmas, and the need for comprehensive provider and patient education. Infrastructure limitations further impede their widespread adoption. To mitigate cybersecurity risks, a robust framework is essential. This framework includes developing a comprehensive cybersecurity strategy, conducting regular risk assessments, enforcing strict access controls, data encryption, staff education, secure network segmentation, routine data backups, anomaly detection, incident response planning, threat intelligence sharing, and third-party vendor audits. By addressing these challenges, healthcare can harness the full potential of these digital innovations to improve patient care and public health outcomes.

Author Contributions: Conceptualization, A.A. and S.A.; methodology, A.A.; software, A.A.; validation, A.A., H.A.S. and S.A.; formal analysis, A.A.; investigation, A.A.; resources, A.A., H.A.S. and S.A.; data curation, A.A.; writing—original draft preparation, A.A.; writing—review and editing, A.A., H.A.S. and S.A.; visualization, A.A., H.A.S. and S.A.; supervision, A.A.; project administration, A.A.; funding acquisition, S.A. All authors have read and agreed to the published version of the manuscript.

Funding: This research received no external funding.

Data Availability Statement: No new data was created.

Conflicts of Interest: The authors declare no conflict of interest.

References

1. Stern, A.D.; Brönneke, J.; Debatin, J.F.; Hagen, J.; Matthies, H.; Patel, S.; Clay, I.; Eskofier, B.; Herr, A.; Hoeller, K.; et al. Advancing digital health applications: Priorities for innovation in real-world evidence generation. *Lancet Digit. Health* **2022**, *4*, e200–e206. [CrossRef] [PubMed]
2. Ronquillo, Y.; Meyers, A.; Korvek, S.J. *Digital Health*; StatPearls Publishing: Treasure Island, FL, USA, 2023.
3. Stoumpos, A.I.; Kitsios, F.; Talias, M.A. Digital transformation in healthcare: Technology acceptance and its applications. *Int. J. Environ. Res. Public Health* **2023**, *20*, 3407. [CrossRef] [PubMed]
4. Neves, A.L.; Burgers, J. Digital technologies in primary care: Implications for patient care and future research. *Eur. J. Gen. Pract.* **2022**, *28*, 203–208. [CrossRef] [PubMed]
5. Giansanti, D. Ten years of telehealth and digital healthcare: Where are we? *Healthcare* **2023**, *11*, 875. [CrossRef] [PubMed]

6.   Mesko, B. Health IT and digital health: The future of health technology is diverse. *J. Clin. Transl. Res.* **2018**, *3* (Suppl. S3), 431–434. [CrossRef] [PubMed]

7.   Ibrahim, M.S.; Yusoff, H.M.; Abu Bakar, Y.I.; Aung, M.M.T.; Abas, M.I.; Ramli, R.A. Digital health for quality healthcare: A systematic mapping of review studies. *Digit. Health* **2022**, *8*, 20552076221085810. [CrossRef] [PubMed]

8.   Mariano, B. Towards a global strategy on digital health. *Bull. World Health Organ.* **2020**, *98*, 231. [CrossRef] [PubMed]

9.   Nouri, R.; RNiakan Kalhori, S.; Ghazisaeedi, M.; Marchand, G.; Yasini, M. Criteria for assessing the quality of mHealth apps: A systematic review. *J. Am. Med. Inform. Assoc.* **2018**, *25*, 1089–1098. [CrossRef]

10.   Lu, L.; Zhang, J.; Xie, Y.; Gao, F.; Xu, S.; Wu, X.; Ye, Z. Wearable health devices in health care: Narrative systematic review. *JMIR Mhealth Uhealth* **2020**, *8*, e18907. [CrossRef]

11.   Smuck, M.; Odonkor, C.A.; Wilt, J.K.; Schmidt, N.; Swiernik, M.A. The emerging clinical role of wearables: Factors for successful implementation in healthcare. *NPJ Digit. Med.* **2021**, *4*, 45. [CrossRef]

12.   Canali, S.; Schiaffonati, V.; Aliverti, A. Challenges and recommendations for wearable devices in digital health: Data quality, interoperability, health equity, fairness. *PLoS Digit Health* **2022**, *1*, e0000104. [CrossRef] [PubMed]

13.   Alsalamah, H.A.; Nasser, S.; Alsalamah, S.; Almohana, A.I.; Alanazi, A.; Alrrshaid, F. Wholesome Coin: A pHealth solution to reduce high obesity rates in Gulf Cooperation Council countries using cryptocurrency. *Front. Blockchain* **2021**, *4*, 654539. [CrossRef]

14.   Batko, K.; Ślęzak, A. The use of big data analytics in healthcare. *J. Big Data* **2022**, *9*, 3. [CrossRef] [PubMed]

15.   Piovani, D.; Bonovas, S. Real world-big data analytics in healthcare. *Int. J. Environ. Res. Public Health* **2022**, *19*, 11677. [CrossRef] [PubMed]

16.   Cozzoli, N.; Salvatore, F.P.; Faccilongo, N.; Milone, M. How can big data analytics be used for healthcare organization management? Literary framework and future research from a systematic review. *BMC Health Serv. Res.* **2022**, *22*, 809. [CrossRef] [PubMed]

17.   Nascimento, I.J.B.D.; Marcolino, M.S.; Abdulazeem, H.M.; Weerasekara, I.; Azzopardi-Muscat, N.; Gonçalves, M.A.; Novillo-Ortiz, D. Impact of big data analytics on people's health: Overview of systematic reviews and recommendations for future studies. *J. Med. Internet Res.* **2021**, *23*, e27275. [CrossRef] [PubMed]

18.   Mehrtak, M.; SeyedAlinaghi, S.; MohsseniPour, M.; Noori, T.; Karimi, A.; Shamsabadi, A.; Heydari, M.; Barzegary, A.; Mirzapour, P.; Soleymanzadeh, M.; et al. Security challenges and solutions using healthcare cloud computing. *J. Med. Life* **2021**, *14*, 448–461. [CrossRef]

19.   Gao, F.; Thiebes, S.; Sunyaev, A. Rethinking the meaning of cloud computing for health care: A taxonomic perspective and future research directions. *J. Med. Internet Res.* **2018**, *20*, e10041. [CrossRef]

20.   Gu, D.; Yang, X.; Deng, S.; Liang, C.; Wang, X.; Wu, J.; Guo, J. Tracking knowledge evolution in cloud health care research: Knowledge map and common word analysis. *J. Med. Internet Res.* **2020**, *22*, e15142. [CrossRef]

21.   Cresswell, K.; Domínguez Hernández, A.; Williams, R.; Sheikh, A. Key challenges and opportunities for cloud technology in health care: Semistructured interview study. *JMIR Hum. Factors* **2022**, *9*, e31246. [CrossRef]

22.   Srivastava, J.; Routray, S.; Ahmad, S.; Waris, M.M. Internet of Medical Things (IoMT)-based smart healthcare system: Trends and progress. *Comput. Intell. Neurosci.* **2022**, *2022*, 7218113. [CrossRef]

23.   Dwivedi, R.; Mehrotra, D.; Chandra, S. Potential of Internet of Medical Things (IoMT) applications in building a smart healthcare system: A systematic review. *J. Oral. Biol. Craniofac. Res.* **2022**, *12*, 302–318. [CrossRef]

24.   Sadhu, P.K.; Yanambaka, V.P.; Abdelgawad, A.; Yelamarthi, K. Prospect of Internet of Medical Things: A review on security requirements and solutions. *Sensors* **2022**, *22*, 5517. [CrossRef]

25.   Bhugaonkar, K.; Bhugaonkar, R.; Masne, N. The trend of metaverse and augmented & virtual reality extending to the healthcare system. *Cureus* **2022**, *14*, e29071.

26.   Yeung, A.W.K.; Tosevska, A.; Klager, E.; Eibensteiner, F.; Laxar, D.; Stoyanov, J.; Glisic, M.; Zeiner, S.; Kulnik, S.T.; Crutzen, R.; et al. Virtual and augmented reality applications in medicine: Analysis of the scientific literature. *J. Med. Internet Res.* **2021**, *23*, e25499. [CrossRef]

27.   Kassutto, S.M.; Baston, C.; Clancy, C. Virtual, augmented, and alternate reality in medical education: Socially distanced but fully immersed. *ATS Sch.* **2021**, *2*, 651–664. [CrossRef]

28.   Syed Abdul, S.; Upadhyay, U.; Salcedo, D.; Lin, C.W. Virtual reality enhancing medical education and practice: Brief communication. *Digit. Health* **2022**, *8*, 20552076221143948. [CrossRef]

29.   Gajarawala, S.N.; Pelkowski, J.N. Telehealth benefits and barriers. *J. Nurse Pract.* **2021**, *17*, 218–221. [CrossRef]

30.   Kichloo, A.; Albosta, M.; Dettloff, K.; Wani, F.; El-Amir, Z.; Singh, J.; Aljadah, M.; Chakinala, R.C.; Kanugula, A.K.; Solanki, S.; et al. Telemedicine, the current COVID-19 pandemic and the future: A narrative review and perspectives moving forward in the USA. *Fam. Med. Community Health* **2020**, *8*, e000530. [CrossRef]

31.   Al-Hazmi, A.M.; Sheerah, H.A.; Arafa, A. Perspectives on telemedicine during the era of COVID-19; what can Saudi Arabia do? *Int. J. Environ. Res. Public Health* **2021**, *18*, 10617. [CrossRef]

32.   Ibrahim, A.E.; Magdy, M.; Khalaf, E.M.; Mostafa, A.; Arafa, A. Teledermatology in the time of COVID-19. *Int. J. Clin. Pract.* **2021**, *75*, e15000. [CrossRef]

33.   Bajwa, J.; Munir, U.; Nori, A.; Williams, B. Artificial intelligence in healthcare: Transforming the practice of medicine. *Future Heal. J.* **2021**, *8*, e188–e194. [CrossRef]

34. Briganti, G.; Le Moine, O. Artificial intelligence in medicine: Today and tomorrow. *Front. Med.* **2020**, *7*, 27. [CrossRef]
35. Habehh, H.; Gohel, S. Machine learning in healthcare. *Curr. Genom.* **2021**, *22*, 291–300. [CrossRef]
36. Althenayan, A.S.; AlSalamah, S.A.; Aly, S.; Nouh, T.; Mirza, A.A. Detection and classification of COVID-19 by radiological imaging modalities using deep learning techniques: A literature review. *Appl. Sci.* **2022**, *12*, 10535. [CrossRef]
37. Pujari, S.; Reis, A.; Zhao, Y.; Alsalamah, S.; Serhan, F.; Reeder, J.C.; Labrique, A.B. Artificial intelligence for global health: Cautious optimism with safeguards. *Bull. World Health Organ.* **2023**, *101*, 364. [CrossRef]
38. Oala, L.; Murchison, A.G.; Balachandran, P.; Choudhary, S.; Fehr, J.; Leite, A.W.; Goldschmidt, P.G.; Johner, C.; Schörverth, E.D.M.; Nakasi, R.; et al. Machine learning for health: Algorithm auditing & quality control. *J. Med. Syst.* **2021**, *45*, 105.
39. Alsalamah, H.A.; Alsuwailem, G.; Bin Rajeh, F.; Alharbi, S.; AlQahtani, S.; AlArifi, R.; AlShargi, S.; Alsalamah, S.A.; Alsalamah, S. eHomeCaregiving: A diabetes patient-centered blockchain ecosystem for COVID-19 caregiving. *Front. Blockchain* **2021**, *4*, 477012. [CrossRef]
40. Alsalamah, S.; Alsalamah, H.A.; Nouh, T.; Alsalamah, S.A. Healthyblockchain for global patients. *Comput. Mater. Contin.* **2021**, *68*, 2431–2449. [CrossRef]
41. Kurdi, H.; Alsalamah, S.; Alatawi, A.; Alfaraj, S.; Altoaimy, L.; Ahmed, S.H. HealthyBroker: A trustworthy blockchain-based multi-cloud broker for patient-centered ehealth services. *Electronics* **2019**, *8*, 602. [CrossRef]
42. Saeed, H.; Malik, H.; Bashir, U.; Ahmad, A.; Riaz, S.; Ilyas, M.; Bukhari, W.A.; Khan, M.I.A. Blockchain technology in healthcare: A systematic review. *PLoS ONE* **2022**, *17*, e0266462. [CrossRef]
43. Elangovan, D.; Long, C.S.; Bakrin, F.S.; Tan, C.S.; Goh, K.W.; Yeoh, S.F.; Loy, M.J.; Hussain, Z.; Lee, K.S.; Idris, A.C.; et al. The use of blockchain technology in the health care sector: Systematic review. *JMIR Med. Inform.* **2022**, *10*, e17278. [CrossRef]
44. Jalali, M.S.; Kaiser, J.P. Cybersecurity in hospitals: A systematic, organizational perspective. *J. Med. Internet Res.* **2018**, *20*, e10059. [CrossRef]
45. He, Y.; Aliyu, A.; Evans, M.; Luo, C. Health care cybersecurity challenges and solutions under the climate of COVID-19: Scoping review. *J. Med. Internet Res.* **2021**, *23*, e21747. [CrossRef]
46. Argaw, S.T.; Troncoso-Pastoriza, J.R.; Lacey, D.; Florin, M.-V.; Calcavecchia, F.; Anderson, D.; Burleson, W.; Vogel, J.-M.; O'leary, C.; Eshaya-Chauvin, B.; et al. Cybersecurity of hospitals: Discussing the challenges and working towards mitigating the risks. *BMC Med. Inform. Decis. Mak.* **2020**, *20*, 146. [CrossRef]
47. Kruse, C.S.; Frederick, B.; Jacobson, T.; Monticone, D.K. Cybersecurity in healthcare: A systematic review of modern threats and trends. *Technol. Health Care* **2017**, *25*, 1–10. [CrossRef]
48. Coventry, L.; Branley, D. Cybersecurity in healthcare: A narrative review of trends, threats and ways forward. *Maturitas* **2018**, *113*, 48–52. [CrossRef]
49. Giansanti, D. Cybersecurity and the digital-health: The challenge of this millennium. *Healthcare* **2021**, *9*, 62. [CrossRef] [PubMed]
50. Jalali, M.S.; Razak, S.; Gordon, W.; Perakslis, E.; Madnick, S. Health care and cybersecurity: Bibliometric analysis of the literature. *J. Med. Internet Res.* **2019**, *21*, e12644. [CrossRef] [PubMed]
51. Niki, O.; Saira, G.; Arvind, S.; Mike, D. Cyber-attacks are a permanent and substantial threat to health systems: Education must reflect that. *Digit. Health* **2022**, *8*, 20552076221104665. [CrossRef] [PubMed]
52. Lehne, M.; Sass, J.; Essenwanger, A.; Schepers, J.; Thun, S. Why digital medicine depends on interoperability. *NPJ Digit. Med.* **2019**, *2*, 79. [CrossRef] [PubMed]
53. Martin, L.T.; Nelson, C.; Yeung, D.; Acosta, J.D.; Qureshi, N.; Blagg, T.; Chandra, A. The issues of interoperability and data connectedness for public health. *Big Data* **2022**, *10*, S19–S24. [CrossRef]
54. Torab-Miandoab, A.; Samad-Soltani, T.; Jodati, A.; Rezaei-Hachesu, P. Interoperability of heterogeneous health information systems: A systematic literature review. *BMC Med. Inform. Decis. Mak.* **2023**, *23*, 18. [CrossRef] [PubMed]
55. Hussein, R.; Wurhofer, D.; Strumegger, E.M.; Stainer-Hochgatterer, A.; Kulnik, S.T.; Crutzen, R.; Niebauer, J. General Data Protection Regulation (GDPR) toolkit for digital health. *Stud. Health Technol. Inform.* **2022**, *290*, 222–226. [PubMed]
56. Torous, J.; Stern, A.D.; Bourgeois, F.T. Regulatory considerations to keep pace with innovation in digital health products. *NPJ Digit. Med.* **2022**, *5*, 121. [CrossRef]
57. Rodriguez-Villa, E.; Torous, J. Regulating digital health technologies with transparency: The case for dynamic and multi-stakeholder evaluation. *BMC Med.* **2019**, *17*, 226. [CrossRef]
58. Brall, C.; Schröder-Bäck, P.; Maeckelberghe, E. Ethical aspects of digital health from a justice point of view. *Eur. J. Public Health* **2019**, *29* (Suppl. S3), 18–22. [CrossRef]
59. Zarif, A. The ethical challenges facing the widespread adoption of digital healthcare technology. *Health Technol.* **2022**, *12*, 175–179. [CrossRef]
60. Maeckelberghe, E.; Zdunek, K.; Marceglia, S.; Farsides, B.; Rigby, M. The ethical challenges of personalized digital health. *Front. Med.* **2023**, *10*, 1123863. [CrossRef]
61. Jarva, E.; Oikarinen, A.; Andersson, J.; Tuomikoski, A.M.; Kääriäinen, M.; Meriläinen, M.; Mikkonen, K. Healthcare professionals' perceptions of digital health competence: A qualitative descriptive study. *Nurs. Open* **2022**, *9*, 1379–1393. [CrossRef]
62. Wubante, S.M.; Tegegne, M.D. Health professionals knowledge of telemedicine and its associated factors working at private hospitals in resource-limited settings. *Front. Digit. Health* **2022**, *4*, 976566. [CrossRef] [PubMed]
63. Ghaddaripouri, K.; Mousavi Baigi, S.F.; Abbaszadeh, A.; Mazaheri Habibi, M.R. Attitude, awareness, and knowledge of telemedicine among medical students: A systematic review of cross-sectional studies. *Health Sci. Rep.* **2023**, *6*, e1156. [CrossRef]

64. Duggal, M.; El Ayadi, A.; Duggal, B.; Reynolds, N.; Bascaran, C. Editorial: Challenges in implementing digital health in public health settings in low and middle income countries. *Front. Public Health* **2023**, *10*, 1090303. [CrossRef] [PubMed]

65. Hadjiat, Y. Healthcare inequity and digital health-a bridge for the divide, or further erosion of the chasm? *PLoS Digit. Health* **2023**, *2*, e0000268. [CrossRef]

66. Seh, A.H.; Zarour, M.; Alenezi, M.; Sarkar, A.K.; Agrawal, A.; Kumar, R.; Ahmad Khan, R. Healthcare data breaches: Insights and implications. *Healthcare* **2020**, *8*, 133. [CrossRef]

67. Koczkodaj, W.W.; Masiak, J.; Mazurek, M.; Strzałka, D.; Zabrodskii, P.F. Massive health record breaches evidenced by the Office for Civil Rights data. *Iran. J. Public Health* **2019**, *48*, 278–288. [CrossRef]

68. Williams, P.A.; Woodward, A.J. Cybersecurity vulnerabilities in medical devices: A complex environment and multifaceted problem. *Med. Devices* **2015**, *8*, 305–316. [CrossRef]

69. Ransford, B.; Kramer, D.B.; Kune, D.F.; de Medeiros, J.A.; Yan, C.; Xu, W.; Crawford, T.; Fu, K. Cybersecurity and medical devices: A practical guide for cardiac electrophysiologists. *Pacing. Clin. Electrophysiol.* **2017**, *40*, 913–917. [CrossRef]

70. Priestman, W.; Anstis, T.; Sebire, I.G.; Sridharan, S.; Sebire, N.J. Phishing in healthcare organisations: Threats, mitigation and approaches. *BMJ Health Care Inform.* **2019**, *26*, e100031. [CrossRef]

71. Abdelhamid, M. The role of health concerns in phishing susceptibility: Survey design study. *J. Med. Internet Res.* **2020**, *22*, e18394. [CrossRef] [PubMed]

72. Gordon, W.J.; Wright, A.; Aiyagari, R.; Corbo, L.; Glynn, R.J.; Kadakia, J.; Kufahl, J.; Mazzone, C.; Noga, J.; Parkulo, M.; et al. Assessment of employee susceptibility to phishing attacks at US health care institutions. *JAMA Netw. Open* **2019**, *2*, e190393. [CrossRef] [PubMed]

73. Chapman, P. Are your IT staff ready for the pandemic-driven insider threat? *Netw. Secur.* **2020**, *2020*, 8–11. [CrossRef]

74. Khan, N.; JHoughton, R.; Sharples, S. Understanding factors that influence unintentional insider threat: A framework to counteract unintentional risks. *Cogn. Technol. Work* **2022**, *24*, 393–421. [CrossRef]

75. Yeo, L.H.; Banfield, J. Human factors in electronic health records cybersecurity breach: An exploratory analysis. *Perspect Health Inf. Manag.* **2022**, *19*, 1i. [PubMed]

76. Nifakos, S.; Chandramouli, K.; Nikolaou, C.K.; Papachristou, P.; Koch, S.; Panaousis, E.; Bonacina, S. Influence of human factors on cyber security within healthcare organisations: A systematic review. *Sensors* **2021**, *21*, 5119. [CrossRef] [PubMed]

77. Neprash, H.T.; McGlave, C.C.; Cross, D.A.; Virnig, B.A.; Puskarich, M.A.; Huling, J.D.; Rozenshtein, A.Z.; Nikpay, S.S. Trends in ransomware attacks on US hospitals, clinics, and other health care delivery organizations, 2016–2021. *JAMA Health Forum.* **2022**, *3*, e224873. [CrossRef] [PubMed]

78. Dameff, C.; Tully, J.; Chan, T.C.; Castillo, E.M.; Savage, S.; Maysent, P.; Hemmen, T.M.; Clay, B.J.; Longhurst, C.A. Ransomware Attack associated with disruptions at adjacent emergency departments in the US. *JAMA Netw. Open* **2023**, *6*, e2312270. [CrossRef] [PubMed]

79. Argaw, S.T.; Bempong, N.E.; Eshaya-Chauvin, B.; Flahault, A. The state of research on cyberattacks against hospitals and available best practice recommendations: A scoping review. *BMC Med. Inform. Decis. Mak.* **2019**, *19*, 10. [CrossRef]

80. Borky, J.M.; Bradley, T.H. Protecting information with cybersecurity. *Eff. Model-Based Syst. Eng.* **2018**, 345–404. [CrossRef]

81. Almalawi, A.; Khan, A.I.; Alsolami, F.; Abushark, Y.B.; Alfakeeh, A.S. Managing security of healthcare data for a modern healthcare system. *Sensors* **2023**, *23*, 3612. [CrossRef]

82. Sarosh, P.; Parah, S.A.; Bhat, G.M. An efficient image encryption scheme for healthcare applications. *Multimed. Tools Appl.* **2022**, *81*, 7253–7270. [CrossRef]

83. Hijji, M.; Alam, G. Cybersecurity Awareness and Training (CAT) framework for remote working employees. *Sensors* **2022**, *22*, 8663. [CrossRef]

84. Arain, M.A.; Tarraf, R.; Ahmad, A. Assessing staff awareness and effectiveness of educational training on IT security and privacy in a large healthcare organization. *J. Multidiscip Health* **2019**, *12*, 73–81. [CrossRef] [PubMed]

85. Kamerer, J.L.; McDermott, D.S. Cyber hygiene concepts for nursing education. *Nurse Educ. Today* **2023**, *130*, 105940. [CrossRef] [PubMed]

86. Rubia, F.; Affan, Y.; Lin, L.; Jianmin, W. How persuasive is a phishing email? A phishing game for phishing awareness. *J. Comp. Secur.* **2019**, *27*, 581–612.

87. Johansson, D.; Jönsson, P.; Ivarsson, B.; Christiansson, M. Information technology and medical technology personnel's perception regarding segmentation of medical devices: A focus group study. *Healthcare* **2020**, *8*, 23. [CrossRef] [PubMed]

88. Zarour, M.; Alenezi, M.; Ansari, M.T.J.; Pandey, A.K.; Ahmad, M.; Agrawal, A.; Kumar, R.; Khan, R.A. Ensuring data integrity of healthcare information in the era of digital health. *Health Technol. Lett.* **2021**, *8*, 66–77. [CrossRef] [PubMed]

89. Seo, H.J.; Kim, H.H.; Kim, J.H. A SWOT analysis of the various backup scenarios used in electronic medical record systems. *Health Inform. Res.* **2011**, *17*, 162–171. [CrossRef]

90. Mallinder, J.; Drabwell, P. Cyber security: A critical examination of information sharing versus data sensitivity issues for organisations at risk of cyber attack. *J. Bus. Contin. Emer. Plan* **2014**, *7*, 103–111.

information

Review

A Comprehensive Survey on Artifact Recovery from Social Media Platforms: Approaches and Future Research Directions

Khushi Gupta, Damilola Oladimeji, Cihan Varol *, Amar Rasheed and Narasimha Shahshidhar

Department of Computer Science, Sam Houston State University, Huntsville, TX 77340, USA;
kxg095@shsu.edu (K.G.); dko011@shsu.edu (D.O.); axr249@shsu.edu (A.R.); nks001@shsu.edu (N.S.)
* Correspondence: cxv007@shsu.edu

Abstract: Social media applications have been ubiquitous in modern society, and their usage has grown exponentially over the years. With the widespread adoption of these platforms, social media has evolved into a significant origin of digital evidence in the domain of digital forensics. The increasing utilization of social media has caused an increase in the number of studies focusing on artifact (digital remnants of data) recovery from these platforms. As a result, we aim to present a comprehensive survey of the existing literature from the past 15 years on artifact recovery from social media applications in digital forensics. We analyze various approaches and techniques employed for artifact recovery, structuring our review on well-defined analysis focus categories, which are memory, disk, and network. By scrutinizing the available literature, we determine the trends and commonalities in existing research and further identify gaps in existing literature and areas of opportunity for future research in this field. The survey is expected to provide a valuable resource for academicians, digital forensics professionals, and researchers by enhancing their comprehension of the current state of the art in artifact recovery from social media applications. Additionally, it highlights the need for continued research to keep up with social media's constantly evolving nature and its consequent impact on digital forensics.

Keywords: artifact analysis; digital forensics; disk forensics; memory forensics; network forensics; social media forensics

check for
updates

Citation: Gupta, K.; Oladimeji, D.; Varol, C.; Rasheed, A.; Shahshidhar, N. A Comprehensive Survey on Artifact Recovery from Social Media Platforms: Approaches and Future Research Directions. *Information* **2023**, *14*, 629. https://doi.org/ 10.3390/info14120629

Academic Editors: Jose de Vasconcelos, Hugo Barbosa and Carla Cordeiro

Received: 10 October 2023
Revised: 16 November 2023
Accepted: 16 November 2023
Published: 24 November 2023

1. Introduction

The term "Social Media" refers to a variety of interactive online platforms, chat rooms, and internet forums. They all have their own unique features and purposes that encourage seamless user connectivity, interactive information exchange, and data transfer via internet-mediated communications. Social media is becoming a vital aspect of modern civilization as a result of the broad adoption of new technology and the internet's pervasiveness in the lives of billions of people globally [1]. Some of the most popular social media applications include WhatsApp, Facebook, and Instagram. The COVID-19 outbreak and the resulting lockdowns further allowed deeper penetration of social media applications into users' daily lives. This made the growth of social media applications like TikTok even more prominent. Statistics for January 2023 state that 59% of the world's population uses social media for an average of 2 h and 31 min per day [2].

As a result of the extensive communication and widespread user engagement facilitated by social media applications, they have emerged as a new avenue for criminal activities known as social media-mediated crimes. These crimes are becoming advanced in nature, owing to the vast information exchange that takes place between millions of devices across the globe [3–6]. Social media applications give cybercriminals a platform to manipulate personal data and use it to perpetrate crimes [7]. Some of the crimes committed through social media platforms include spam (unwanted messages embedded with harmful links that lure users into giving personal information) [8], online identity theft (involves taking someone's identity without their consent with the motive of committing fraud or financial theft) [9], cyberbullying (harassing, humiliating, or threatening another through the internet) [10], sexual exploitation (using someone's sexuality for personal or financial gain, often through coercion or manipulation), and many other crimes.

Digital forensics is the process of identifying, acquiring, processing, analyzing, and reporting on data stored electronically [11]. The combination of social media and digital forensics has given rise to a new field called Social Media Forensics (SMF) [12]. SMF is the process of collecting, analyzing, and preserving digital evidence from social media platforms. Over the last ten years, it has been acknowledged as a distinct branch of digital forensics. In legal cases concerning cyber crime where the perpetrator, victim, or witnesses may have used social media platforms, social media artifacts are essential as evidence [7,13]. Social media artifacts in the context of digital forensic investigations refer to the digital traces, remnants, or pieces of data left behind by using social media platforms. Common social media artifacts include chats, posts, geolocation, timestamps, deleted chats, and much more.

These artifacts can be valuable sources of evidence in various types of investigations. Trials involving the use of evidence from social media evidence are continuously increasing. In 2016, only in the United States, 14,000 decisions were observed, out of which 9500 heavily relied on evidence from social media [13], which is twice as high as the number in 2015. Due to the exclusion of cases in which social media content was used but no decision was made, it should be noted that these numbers are significantly lower than the actual number of investigations. They do, however, emphasize the undeniable significance of social media data.

One positive aspect of social media crimes is that criminals often leave digital footprints of their deeds, which is where social media forensics comes into play. Among various types of cybercrimes taking place, cybercrimes executed via social media platforms, also called online social network (OSN) crimes, have recently accelerated in number. Thus, there is a critical need for forensic analysis of digital platforms operating social media applications, as these platforms can be used for criminal activity, terrorism, and other unlawful actions. When properly explored for its potential, social media content can prove to be an outstanding source of digital evidence for digital forensics investigators. The information available about potential victims and suspects on social media is endless. It offers a dynamic dataset of user-generated information, such as posts, friend lists, images, geographical information, videos, demographics, and more.

In this article, we review the current state of research in social media forensics. It provides an overview of the current technical practices for the extraction and analysis of social media evidence. The primary objective is to identify the gaps in current practices and explicitly outline the future research objective for social media forensics. The rest of the paper is arranged as follows. Section 2 of this article will provide a brief overview and history of the domain of social media forensics, highlighting the importance of social media as evidence in legal proceedings. Section 3 highlights the parameters the study is structured upon. The methodology of the paper is explained in Section 4. Sections 5–7 will review research work on various analysis aspects such as memory, network, and disk, respectively. Section 8 examines emerging trends discerned throughout this review. Section 9 outlines some of the challenges faced in this domain and future research focus areas to address them. Finally, Section 10 presents our concluding remarks.

2. Background

The inception of using social media evidence was first reported in 2009 in the trial of the United States v. Drew in California. In this case, the convicted woman had allegedly created a fake MySpace (a social media application) profile, leading to the suicide of a young girl. However, the formal recognition of the potential role of social media evidence in litigation was brought to light by John G. Browning [14]. His research highlighted the increasing use of social media and scenarios where the utilization of evidence from social media becomes an inherent aspect of legal proceedings. In 2011, Zainudin et al. [15] contributed to this growing field by presenting a comprehensive social media forensics investigation model, bolstering utilizing online social networking (OSN) data as evidence. Additionally, in 2014, Keyvanpour et al. [16] referred to social media forensics as digital forensics 2.0 and suggested that this sub-domain is the future of digital forensics.

SMF is a growing domain, having only existed for over ten years. A study conducted by Damshenas et al. in 2014 presented a review of emerging trends in digital forensics but refrained from listing social media forensics as one of the domains due to the scarcity of publications addressing this subject [17]. Additionally, [18] reviewed the situation of evidence acquisition, admissibility, and legal jurisdiction in the domain of social media forensics. Therefore, a review of the domain of social media forensics is needed to assess the current state of the field, which will help us examine the challenges faced and how we can address them [18]. The objective of this survey paper is to address the following research questions:

- What are the current state-of-the-art artifact recovery techniques used in digital forensics from social media applications?
- What are the trends in research related to artifact recovery in social media applications?
- What are the current gaps in the literature that need to be focused on?
- What are the future research directions for artifact recovery from social media applications in digital forensics, and how can these techniques be improved to serve the needs of digital forensics practitioners better?

3. Preliminary Information

In this section, we conduct a comprehensive analysis of different methodologies used by various studies in SMF. We examined these studies based on several research parameters to provide an in-depth analysis of the correlation of the applied methodologies to SMF artifact recovery, as shown in Figure 1. They are essential aspects that define and shape this research. These parameters include the research objective, the framework used to conduct the investigation, the analysis focus, the experimental setup, and the tools employed by the authors. They explain what the study is about, and how it was conducted. The parameters are further discussed in depth in the subsequent subsections.

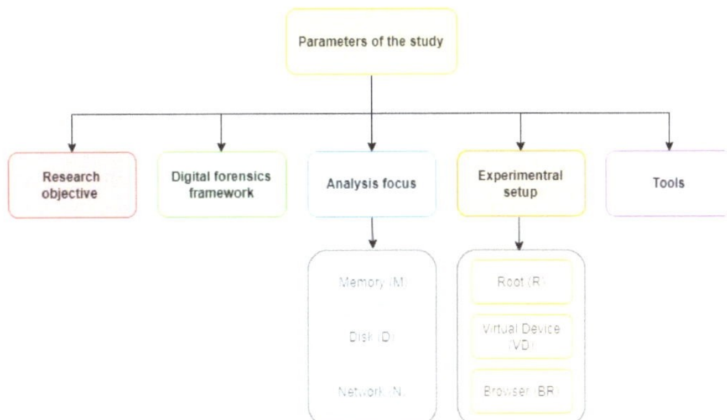

Figure 1. Study parameters.

3.1. Research Objectives

Numerous research initiatives within the field of social media forensics pursue various research objectives, from the recovery of digital evidence to the development of tools and the analysis of underlying databases and code. Below are the most common research objectives addressed, as shown in Table 1:

- **Artifact analysis**: Investigating digital traces and artifacts left behind by social media platforms upon conducting user activity.
- **Recovering deleted chats**: Recovering deleted chats on social media platforms to reconstruct digital interactions.
- **Decrypting messages/traffic**: Research on methodologies for decrypting encrypted messages and network traffic within social media applications.
- **Comparison of tools**: Evaluating different forensic tools on social media investigations, identifying their strengths and weaknesses.
- **Artifact correlation**: Establishing connections among different types of digital artifacts collected during the examination.
- **Tool creation**: Creating software for social media forensics.
- **Creating a forensic taxonomy**: Developing comprehensive taxonomies and categorizations to classify various types of digital evidence and artifacts encountered in social media investigations.
- **Database structure and analysis**: Analyzing the underlying structure of social media databases to gain insights into data storage and retrieval mechanisms.
- **Source code analysis**: Analyzing the source code of social media applications to uncover vulnerabilities, backdoors, or hidden features that may have forensic significance.

Table 1. Research objectives.

Research Objective	References
Artifact Analysis	[7,19–125]
Recovering deleted chats	[126–128]
Decrypting databases/traffic	[40,72,83,129–136]
Comparison of tools	[47,51,56,109,112,127,128,137–141]
Artifact correlation	[67,77,134,142,143]
Tool creation	[33,93,144–149]
Creating a forensic taxonomy	[49,150,151]
Database structure and analysis	[36,52,131]
Source code analysis	[23,32,142]

3.2. Common Digital Forensics Frameworks

Various digital forensic frameworks are employed to ensure methodical and structured investigations. These frameworks serve as invaluable resources for digital forensic practitioners, offering guidelines, protocols, and methodologies to ensure that investigations are carried out systematically in accordance with recognized industry standards. These frameworks are explained below:

- **National Institute of Standards and Technology (NIST)**: NIST offers a comprehensive framework that provides guidelines and standards for digital forensic investigations. It consists of four phases, namely collection, examination, analysis, and presentation [152], as shown in Figure 2.
- **Association of Chief Police Officers (ACPO)**: The ACPO framework is widely adopted in law enforcement agencies in the United Kingdom. It outlines procedures and best practices for handling digital evidence in criminal investigations [92].
- **McKemmish Framework**: Developed by Margaret McKemmish, this framework focuses on the digital preservation aspect of forensic investigations. It emphasizes the need to maintain the integrity and authenticity of digital evidence over time [153].
- **Digital Forensic Research Workshop (DFRWS)**: DFRWS is a community-driven organization that has contributed significantly to developing digital forensic standards and methodologies. Its framework consists of six stages, namely identification, preservation, collection, examination, analysis, and presentation [154].

- **National Institute of Justice (NIJ)**: The NIJ framework caters to the specific needs of the criminal justice community in the United States. It addresses forensic procedures, evidence handling, and the integration of digital evidence into the criminal justice system [155].
- **iPhone Forensic Framework (iFF)**: Existing commercial solutions and approaches in the field of iPhone forensics tend to be costly and complex, often demanding supplementary hardware for the investigative process. Consequently, Husain et al. [156] introduced a simple framework for iPhone forensic examination, comprising three main stages: data retrieval, data examination, and data presentation. This framework proved to be effective in extracting evidence from an iPhone.
- **International Digital Forensics Investigation Framework 2 (IDFIF 2)**: IDFIF 2 is an updated version of the IDFIF framework intended to enhance the global standardization of digital forensic practices. It focuses on promoting international cooperation and consistency in digital investigations [157].

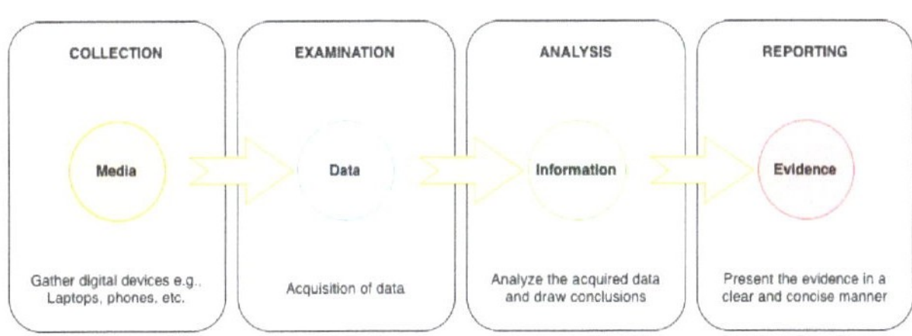

Figure 2. The NIST framework.

Among the most prevalent frameworks utilized by researchers are NIST [7,26,47,51, 52,68,84,95,97,98,102,103,109,117,124,127,138–140], ACPO [35,50,87], McKemmish [41,61], DFRWS [110,112,118], NIJ [56], iFF [21,156], IDFIF2 [90]. Out of all these frameworks, the NIST framework, as shown in Figure 2, is the most commonly utilized across the studies examined for this review. Its comprehensiveness, covering all aspects of digital forensics from evidence collection to reporting, makes it adaptable to diverse investigative scenarios. Additionally, NIST's commitment to regular updates ensures its relevance in an ever-evolving field. These factors collectively make the NIST forensic framework a preferred choice in the digital forensics community.

3.3. Analysis Focus

Social media artifacts can be found in various locations within a computing device. Researchers and digital forensics experts typically focus on three primary aspects when examining social media applications: the disk, memory, and network. Hence, we structure our review of existing literature to reflect these analysis aspects.

- *Disk*: The disk is essentially the storage of a device, primarily the hard drive and solid-state drives in computers and NAND flash chips in phones. The data in the disk provide numerous artifacts from social media applications, such as user-identifiable information, timestamps, media (photos and videos), chats, and much more.
- *Memory*: Memory refers to the volatile storage areas of a device, such as the Random Access Memory (RAM). Almost all applications use volatile memory to store data temporarily, such as the current state, open applications, active processes, etc. This provides access to real-time information, such as passwords, user activities, and more, making it valuable for investigations.
- *Network*: Analyzing network data involves monitoring and capturing network traffic exchanged. It allows investigators to track and analyze data in transit, potentially uncovering valuable evidence related to social media activities. This aspect is crucial as it involves real-time communication.

Figure 3 shows the frequency of the existing literature in each category of analysis focus surveyed in the paper. Additionally, the graph also depicts the frequency of each operating system under these categories. The figure depicts that the most tackled focus area of social media forensic investigations is the disk. The disk is commonly prioritized because social media applications store a substantial amount of user data on the disk, encompassing profiles, messages, posts, and multimedia content, even after users delete or modify their data. Moreover, unlike data in memory or network traffic, which are typically transient and may be overwritten or disappear once the device is turned off or the session ends, data on the disk are relatively stable. Additionally, comprehensive forensic tools and techniques are well-established for disk analysis, allowing for thorough analysis.

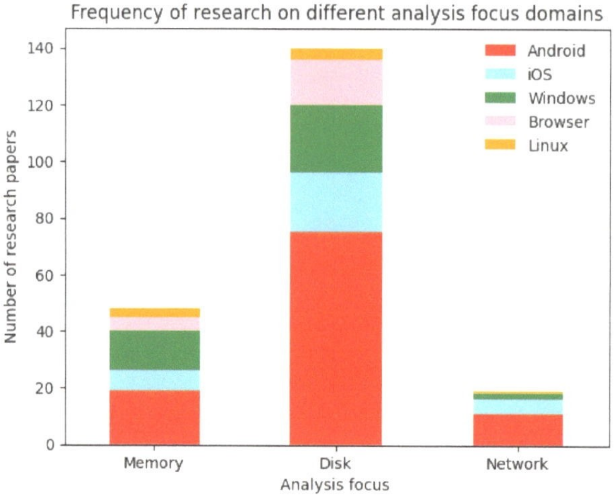

Figure 3. Frequency of surveyed literature based on the analysis focus.

3.4. Experimental Setup

The outcomes of various research experiments can vary significantly depending on the specific experimental setup chosen by the researcher. The common setup parameters employed by researchers in the field of social media forensics include:

- ***Rooting or Jailbreaking***: One of the critical decisions researchers make is whether to root (for Android) or jailbreak (for iOS) the mobile device under investigation. Rooting or jailbreaking grants the researcher elevated privileges and access to parts of the device that are typically restricted. This decision can significantly impact the types of data that can be accessed and the methods employed for data extraction.
- ***Virtual device environment***: Some experiments are conducted in a controlled environment using virtual devices or emulators. These virtual environments mimic the behavior of real devices and can be useful for testing and research without affecting physical devices.
- ***Web browser***: Another approach involves conducting experiments through a web browser interface. This method can be advantageous for studying web-based applications and online social media user activities and the subsequent traces of evidence the browser leaves.

Figure 4 depicts the tools that are used for different experimental setups used by researchers. These tools enable the researchers to create the foundation for conducting their experiments. This figure is divided into three common experimental setups utilized: (a) conducting digital forensic analysis of browser data, (b) creating virtualized environments of a device (mobile device or desktop), and (c) rooting a mobile device. Under each category, we list the common tools utilized for each experimental setup.

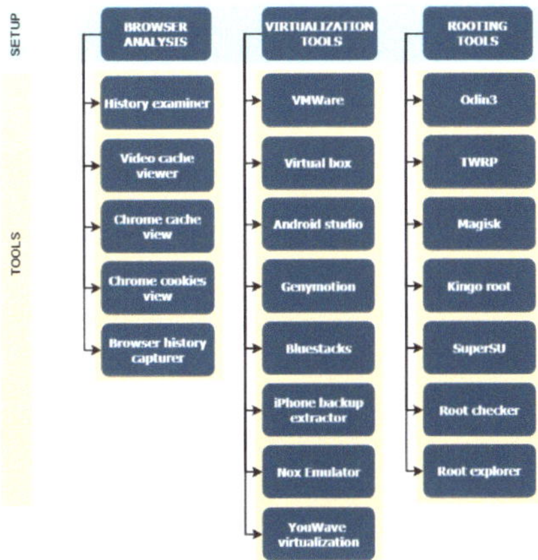

Figure 4. Common experimental setup tools.

3.5. Digital Forensics Tools

Social media forensics relies on a diverse array of specialized tools to analyze digital evidence effectively. These tools encompass a wide spectrum of functions for various digital devices. Each tool serves a unique role in the examination process, enabling researchers to dissect digital devices to reveal critical social media artifacts.

Figure 5 is organized by categorizing digital forensic tools based on the purpose of their utilization within the analysis focus areas (memory, network, and disk). The tools are further subdivided based on their specific usage within each focus area. For memory analysis, the tools are grouped into acquisition and analysis tools. In the case of network analysis, they are categorized as analysis and proxy tools, while for disk analysis, tools are further categorized into acquisition, analysis, and decryption tools.

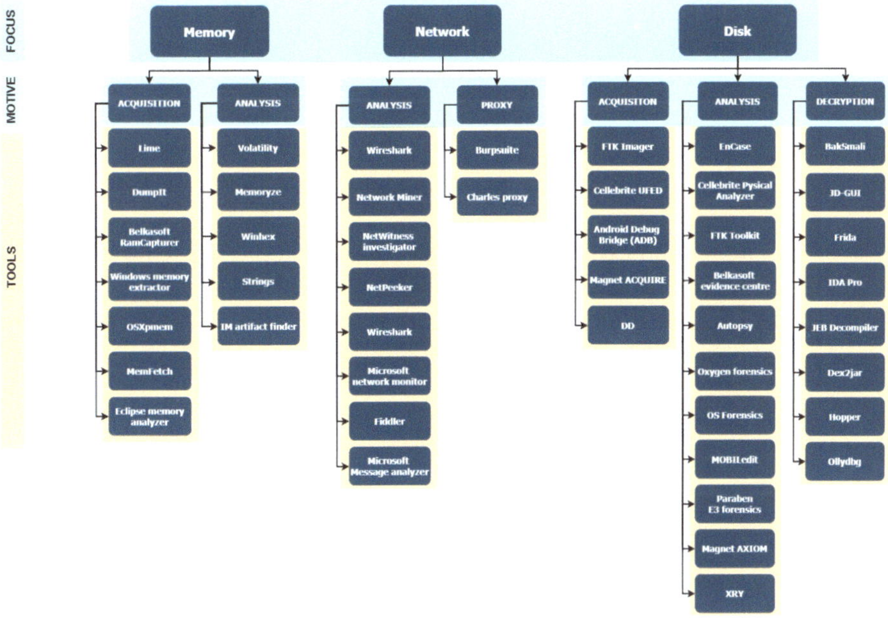

Figure 5. Common digital forensic tools.

4. Methodology

This paper presents a thorough review of approximately 170 research articles spanning the last 15 years, aiming to identify the literature on artifact recovery from social media platforms. The approach used in this study is illustrated in Figure 6, where "n" represents the number of articles. A search was conducted using electronic databases such as the Institute of Electrical and Electronics Engineers (IEEE) Xplore Digital Library, ACM Digital Library, Science Direct, and Springer Nature.

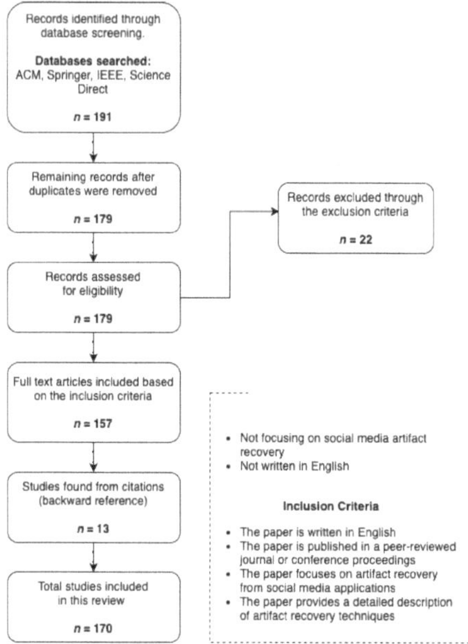

Figure 6. Methodology.

The search keywords included "artifact recovery", "social media applications", "digital forensics", "forensic investigation", and "social media forensics". The criteria for including papers were as follows: (1) the paper is written in English, (2) the paper is published in a peer-reviewed journal or conference proceedings, (3) the paper focuses on artifact recovery from social media applications in digital forensics, and (4) the paper provides a detailed description of the artifact recovery techniques and methods used. Subsequently, the chosen papers were evaluated based on the following criteria: (1) the type of social media application studied, (2) the techniques and methods used for artifact recovery, and (3) the contribution of the research in digital forensics.

Organization of the Research

In the following sections, we analyze existing the literature tackling artifact recovery on various social media applications, particularly following the structure outlined in Section 3.3. Hence, we have organized them to discuss the literature focusing on memory analysis in Section 4, while Section 5 discusses existing works that relate to network analysis, and finally, we thoroughly examine papers that perform disk analysis in Section 6.

Additionally, throughout the paper, we grouped the recovered artifacts into five distinct categories, as shown in Figure 7. Dividing the artifacts into separate categories helped organize evidence and findings from various studies. It also helped us analyze and discuss related findings together. These categories are detailed below:

- ***User information***: This category contains artifacts that reveal critical data points on a user's personal information.
- ***User activities***: This group of artifacts reveals information about user activities on social media platforms.
- ***Metadata***: Metadata consists of crucial information like timestamps and geolocation, providing valuable context to other artifacts retrieved.
- ***Password***: This category refers to the user account password being recovered.
- ***Encryption key***: Encryption key artifacts are commonly recovered from studies focusing on database decryption of social media applications. They are used to decrypt the database.

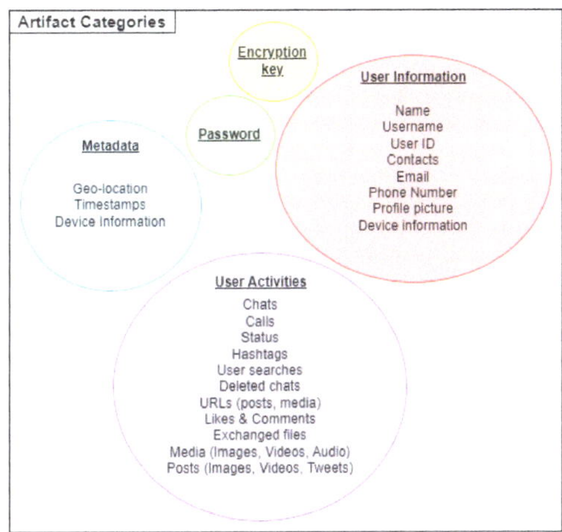

Figure 7. Artifact categories.

In each analysis focus category, we present a comprehensive overview of the reviewed literature through tables. These tables outline details such as social media applications studied, browser information (pertinent to web applications), utilization of a virtual device (VD), rooted status of the mobile device (R), tools utilized for acquisition and analysis, and the collected artifacts. To indicate the use of a virtual device or the rooted status of the device, we use "Y" for affirmative instances and "N" for negative instances. Furthermore, the indication of a specific browser and the recovered artifact categories is represented by a checkmark ("✓"), signifying usage, while a cross (×), denotes that the specified browser was not used, and the corresponding artifact category was not recovered. Additionally, we use "N/A" for certain information not provided in the original research reviewed.

The categories reviewed in this paper play a pivotal role in illuminating the methodologies employed in the studies under review. By meticulously outlining the parameters above, the review paper furnishes readers with a comprehensive understanding of the research methodologies. This detailed inclusion facilitates meaningful comparisons between diverse studies, enabling researchers to discern patterns, trends, and variations in methodologies. Such comparative analysis contributes to the synthesis of existing knowledge and aids in the identification of best practices within the realm of digital forensics. Furthermore, the incorporation of these categories serves as a diagnostic tool, allowing for the identification of gaps in the current body of research.

5. Memory Analysis Focus

Memory forensics is a branch of digital forensics that focuses on the analysis and extraction of digital evidence from a computer's volatile memory, also known as RAM. Volatile memory stores data temporarily while a computer is powered on and actively running [158]. Some of the data stored by the RAM include:

- program data (data related to currently running applications);
- process data (data related to currently running processes such as open files and data for execution);
- user data (data generated or modified by the users);
- network data (network connections);
- graphics data (video and graphics data including contents of the screen and graphics used in applications);
- user sessions (Information about user sessions, including user login credentials, active user profiles, and session-related data);
- browser data (data related to open tabs, history, cookies, and cached web content).

With a treasure trove of user and system information stored by the RAM, memory forensics is indispensable for investigating social media applications. Owing to its ability to capture a wide range of data, different researchers analyze the volatile memory of digital devices for various research purposes. The majority of the research is carried out to uncover what kinds of evidentiary artifacts related to social media applications can be found from the memory [57,59,60,76,78,159], whereas other researchers look for specific kinds of artifacts such as deleted chats [126] or encryption keys [83]. Additional research goals behind examining volatile memory for social media evidence are also to decrypt databases [129] and for the creation of tools for analysis of memory artifacts from social media applications [145,149].

5.1. Memory Acquisition

The memory forensics process typically involves two main phases: memory acquisition and memory analysis. Some of the most common tools used for memory acquisition in the literature include DumpIt [60,83,150] and LiMe (Linux Memory Extractor) [25,81,82,134], while other acquisition tools include FTK Imager [84], Android Debug Bridge [34,38,82], and Belkasoft Ram capturer [84]. From the review of the existing literature, it is seen that DumpIt is the most common choice for memory acquisition in Windows machines. It is a command-line memory tool that specializes in acquiring the contents of physical RAM primarily from Windows systems. The acquired memory (memory dump) is then output in a raw format, which can then be further analyzed using memory analysis tools. However, one of the tool's limitations is that it leaves a digital footprint on the memory [83], which can taint the memory dump acquired.

While DumpIt is the most prominent tool used for memory acquisition on Windows platforms, LiMe is the most prominent memory acquisition tool for Linux kernels and Linux-based devices such as Android. It is an open-source tool that can perform full memory captures. LiMe supports two memory acquisition methods, one via the transfer control protocol (TCP) network and the other via local storage, such as SD cards [81]. It is noteworthy that LiMe requires that the device be rooted to perform the acquisition [134]. This is because LiMe needs access to the kernel's memory space, which contains critical system information and data from running processes. Additionally, LiMe functions by loading a kernel module into the running kernel to create a memory snapshot. The access levels to perform all these functions are protected for security reasons. Thus, root access needs to be granted to capture memory using LiMe.

While some researchers prefer conducting experiments on physical devices, others use virtualization. Virtualization allows Windows systems to be configured on VMWare and Android Virtual Devices (AVDs) configured using platforms such as Android Mobile Device Emulator. When researchers use virtual devices, the process of acquiring a memory dump becomes streamlined. In the case of Windows systems, researchers can capture the memory by creating a snapshot, such as a .vmem file, while using VMWare, as performed by Chang et al. [59]. In the context of AVDs, researchers can bypass the need for device rooting since it can be preconfigured to grant root access to users within the virtual environment, as performed by Anglano et al. [134].

5.2. Memory Analysis

After acquiring a memory dump, memory analysis is the next phase. It is the process of examining the contents of the volatile memory to extract valuable information and evidence for investigative purposes. The most common tool for memory analysis is Volatility [33,81,83,85,126,134]. Volatility is a versatile open-source memory forensics tool. It provides a wide range of plugins to analyze memory dumps from various operating systems, such as Windows, Linux, and MacOS. Volatility can be used to extract information about running processes, network connections, registry keys, and much more. However, one of the major drawbacks of Volatility is the limited support for Linux and Mac operating systems. Analysis of these operating systems may require the researcher to create specific profiles for the particular operating system version in use.

Other than Volatility, many research methodologies prefer using hex editors to analyze memory dumps [25,37,59,60,81,83–85,145]. Hex editors are widely used for memory analysis for several important reasons. They provide a low-level representation of data, allowing investigators the opportunity to inspect the contents of the memory byte by byte. This level of granularity is required to identify data patterns needed to extract evidence. Another important reason for using hex editors is the ability to search for specific strings or patterns within the memory dump, which is one of the most employed methods used by researchers to look for evidence in the memory [59,77,78,81,83,84].

In the same line, the tool "Strings" is another popular tool for extracting a sequence of characters. A string of text is usually passed to search throughout the memory dump. The lines of the dump containing the matching text strings are then extracted. This is a traditional method used to analyze volatile memory [160]. Strings is commonly employed for this task as it supports large raw files, hexadecimal, ASCII, Unicode, and regular expressions. Other memory analysis tools used to conduct memory analysis in the literature include FTK toolkit [25,78,80] and EnCase [37,59].

In an effort to conduct a thorough examination of the remnants left by the LINE application on a Windows 10 system, Chang et al. [59] carry out investigations with different configurations of the environment. One of the configurations included conducting anti-forensic activities, such as deleting the application using CCleaner. This approach yielded a noteworthy discovery, revealing trace evidence of LINE activity, encompassing chats, usernames, and user files persisting in the system's RAM. Despite the relatively limited number of artifacts, the recoverability of artifacts remains intact.

While most of the memory analysis conducted on platforms is aimed at recovering evidence from social media applications locally downloaded on the device, some researchers have tackled memory forensics to recover evidence from browsers running social media web applications [25,58,94,97–101,148]. As seen in Table 2, the most targeted browser researchers use is Google Chrome because it is one of the most widely used web browsers globally, with a significant market share [161]. Its popularity makes it a prime target for forensic researchers because it represents a large portion of users' online activities. One of the most common research objectives related to browsers was to compare the artifacts uncovered from using social media web applications across different browsers [97–99]. The findings from these research experiments reveal that using different browsers can yield a discrepancy in recovered artifacts. This is due to variations in their architecture, data storage mechanisms, and how they manage user information. Hence, it is important to consider the browser's characteristics in any forensic investigation.

Table 2. Memory analysis on browser.

Ref	Application	Browser				VD		Tools		Artifacts			
		Google Chrome	Firefox	Internet Explorer	Microsoft Edge		Acquisition	Analysis		User Information	User activities	Metadata	Password
[25]	Facebook, Twitter, Google+, Telegram	×	✓	×	×	N	Lime	FTK Toolkit, HxD		✓	✓	✓	✓
[58]	Twitter	✓	×	✓	×	Y	N/A	Winhex, Memoryze, FTK Imager		✓	✓	×	✓
[94]	LinkedIn	✓	✓	×	✓	N	Mandiant	FTK Imager		✓	✓	×	✓
[98]	Instagram	✓	×	✓	×	Y	N/A	Winhex		✓	✓	×	×
[99]	Instagram	✓	✓	✓	×	Y	N/A	WinHex		✓	✓	×	×
[100]	TikTok	✓	×	×	×	N	DumpIt	HxD		×	✓	×	×
[101]	Google Meet	✓	✓	×	✓	Y	Volatility	Strings, FTK Imager		✓	✓	×	×
[148]	Facebook, Skype, Twitter, Hangouts, WhatsApp, Telegram	✓	✓	×	✓	Y	N/A	Strings, grep		✓	✓	✓	×

5.3. Artifact Recovery from Memory

Most of the existing literature in the domain of memory analysis for social media evidence exists for the purpose of determining and exploring what artifacts can be uncovered upon analysis. We have illustrated the existing literature in Table 3. Upon surveying the literature, it is seen that many artifacts can be gathered from analyzing the memory. Some of these artifacts include chats [36,38,57,77,83–85,126,150], contacts [33,60,76, 77,149], media (URLs to photos, videos, images) [33,60,84,150], deleted chats [59], passwords [60,76,145,149,159], user profile information [83], geolocation data [84,150], and timestamps [59,77,126,150].

The chat feature is one of the most popular features in social media applications. It has become a central component of social media applications, contributing to user engagement. Chat features provide a convenient way to engage with other users in real time with options for multimedia sharing. Recovering chat artifacts is paramount in social media forensics due to the wealth of crucial evidence they contain. These chat records provide evidence of online interactions, offering invaluable insights into user behavior, relationships, intents, and activities on social media platforms. By examining chat artifacts, investigators can uncover evidence of cybercrimes, harassment, fraud, impersonation, and much more. Furthermore, these artifacts aid in verifying user identities and establishing a contextual understanding of events.

Passwords and encryption keys are crucial pieces of evidence that can be recovered from the forensic analysis of RAM (Random Access Memory). This is due to how computer systems handle sensitive data during their operation. When a user logs into a system or an application, their password or encryption key is temporarily loaded into RAM to facilitate authentication or data decryption. Even after the user logs out or the application is closed, fragments or residues of this sensitive information may persist in RAM for a certain duration. Modern operating systems and applications also use caching mechanisms to enhance performance, temporarily storing credentials in RAM. Moreover, when data are being actively used or processed, encryption keys must be loaded into RAM to decrypt those data on the fly, making them potentially accessible through RAM analysis.

Passwords hold the key to unlocking valuable evidence. They not only grant access to a user's social media profiles but also provide insights into their online activities, connections, and potentially illicit actions. In cases involving cybercrimes, cyberbullying, or online harassment, gaining access to a suspect's social media accounts can reveal critical evidence, including private messages, deleted content, and interactions with victims. This information is indispensable for investigations, as it can help establish motives, uncover hidden activities, and facilitate the identification of culprits.

Table 3. Existing literature on artifact recovery from memory.

Platform	Ref	Application	R	VD	Tools		Artifacts				
					Acquisition	Analysis	User Information	User activities	Metadata	Password	Encryption key
Windows	[57]	Digsby	N	N	N/A	Encase	✓	✓	✓	×	×
	[60]	LinkedIn	N	N	DumpIt	WinHex	✓	✓	×	✓	×
	[76]	Skype	N	Y	N/A	RSA keyfinder, AES Keyfinder, Volatility, Hex editor	×	×	×	✓	✓
	[77]	Facebook	N	N	Helix	FTK Toolkit, HxD	✓	✓	✓	×	×
	[83]	Google Hangouts	N	N	DumpIt	Volatility, WinHex	✓	✓	×	×	✓
	[84]	Line	N	N	Ramcapturer, FTK Imager	WinHex	×	✓	✓	×	×
	[126]	IMO	N	N	Custom python script	Volatility, Windbg	✓	✓	✓	×	×
	[145]	Digsby	N	N	N/A	WinHex	✓	×	×	✓	×
	[149]	Telegram	N	Y	Windows memory extractor	IM artifact finder	×	✓	✓	✓	×
	[150]	Skype, WhatsApp, Viber, Facebook	N	N	DumpIt	Strings	✓	✓	✓	×	×
Android	[33]	WhatsApp	Y	Y	Memfetch	Volatility	×	✓	✓	×	×
	[34]	Skype	Y	Y	ADB, DDMS	Eclipse memory analyzer, grep	×	✓	×	×	×
	[35]	Wickr	Y	N	Android tool memory dump	Strings	✓	×	×	×	×
	[36]	Wickr, Telegram	N	N	Memory dump app	String, grep	✓	×	×	×	×
	[37]	Line	Y	Y	N/A	Winhex, EnCase	✓	✓	×	×	×
	[38]	KIK	N	Y	ADB	Grep, JHAT	×	✓	×	×	×
	[78]	Viber	N	N	Android SDK	FTK Toolkit	✓	×	×	×	×
	[80]	Skype, MSN	N	N	Android SDK	FTK Toolkit	✓	×	×	×	×
	[81]	WeChat	N	N	Lime	WinHex, Volatility	×	✓	×	×	×
	[82]	Facebook, Viber, WhatsApp	Y	N	Lime, ADB	Custom script	✓	✓	✓	×	×
	[130]	Private text messaging, Wickr	Y	N	N/A	N/A	×	×	×	✓	×
	[134]	ChatSecure	Y	Y	Lime	Volatility	×	×	×	×	✓
Linux	[25]	Facebook, twitter, google+, telegram, openwapp, LINE	N	N	Lime	FTK Toolkit, HxD	✓	✓	×	✓	×
	[85]	Discord, Slack	N	Y	N/A	Volatility, WxHexeditor	✓	✓	×	×	×
iOS	[150]	Skype, WhatsApp, Viber, Facebook	N	N	DumpIt	Strings	✓	✓	✓	×	×

6. Network Analysis Focus

The continually surging popularity of online services compels security experts and law enforcement agencies to seek innovative approaches for investigating cybercrimes and obtaining court-admissible evidence. There are a few researchers who have conducted forensic analysis on the disk in an effort to investigate encrypted databases of secured social media applications [125,132], but such approaches fall short when it comes to investigating end-to-end encrypted data. In such a case, network forensics comes in handy. Network forensics is a specialized branch of digital forensics that focuses on the collection, analysis, and interpretation of network traffic and data to uncover evidence related to cybercrimes and security incidents. It involves systematically examining network logs, packet captures, configuration files, and other network-related data sources to reconstruct events and recover network traffic artifacts [162,163]. Network traffic analysis is of paramount importance in the field of SMF. The existing literature solidifies this by showing that network traffic is a rich source of evidence for social media user interactions (posts, messages, and calls), as shown in Table 4. These data are crucial for reconstructing events, establishing timelines, and identifying involved parties in forensic investigations by revealing insights into user behavior, connections, and engagement patterns.

Table 4. Existing literature on network forensics investigation for social media applications.

Purpose	Ref	Application	System	R	Wireshark	Others	Artifacts
Traffic characterization	[43]	IMO	Android, iOS	Y	✓	N/A	Chats, Calls, Ports, IP add.
	[70]	Skype	Windows	N	✓	Netpeeker	Logins, Calls, Codec, Port
	[74]	Whatsapp	Android	N	✓	N/A	Chats
	[75]	Signal	Android	N	✓	N/A	Chats, Media, Calls, IP add.
Traffic decryption	[71]	Whatsapp	Android	N	✓	Pidgin	Calls, Phone no., Codec
Artifacts	[39]	Line	Android	Y	N	Logcat, Shark for root	Protocol, IP add.
	[40]	Telegram, Line, Kakaotalk	Android	Y	✓	Logcat	Timestamp, Protocol, IP add.
	[41]	Facebook, Twitter, Google+, Linkedin	Android, iOS	N	✓	N/A	IP add., Domain name, Timestamp, Protocol, Certificate
	[42]	Whatsapp, Viber, Instagram, Snapchat, Facebook	Android, iOS	N	✓	Network miner, Netwitness Investigator	Chats, Media, Location, Password, Server links
	[45]	Skype	Windows	Y	N	Microsoft message analyzer, Snooper	Calls, protocol, Codec, Phone no.
	[72]	Facebook, Twitter, Telegram	Firefox OS	N	✓	Network miner, Microsoft network monitor	IP add., Port, Certificate, Timestamps
	[73]	Telegram, Viber, Snapchat, Discord, etc.	iOS	N	✓	Charles proxy, Burp suite, Network miner	Chats, Location, Contacts, Password

Social media applications facilitate the transfer of substantial data volumes across communication networks, encompassing various formats, with network packets being the most prevalent. Network packets hold useful user online activity data. When effectively captured, stored, and processed, they can yield valuable assets in forensic investigations and provide admissible evidence [164]. The de facto format for capturing network packets is libpcap. The Pcap Next-Generation Capture File Format (pcapng) has succeeded the traditional pcap format. The information extracted from these network packets can be used as evidence either directly or indirectly. For example, some information contained in the packets, including the sender and receiver IP addresses, port numbers, etc., along with the transferred data, can be used directly as evidence. In contrast, indirect information derived from multiple packets can also be used as evidence. This includes streams of packets sent from a particular host to another one in a certain pattern, which might indicate a specific user activity.

Many social media applications offer end-to-end encryption. These applications have attracted significant attention from users, driven by escalating concerns regarding their privacy. Notable social media applications, including Signal, WhatsApp, Facebook Messenger, and WeChat, have incorporated robust end-to-end encryption techniques during data transmission to safeguard user data's security and privacy. Signal, for instance, asserts the use of the highly secure Signal Protocol for communication. However, it is important to acknowledge that malicious actors also capitalize on the protective attributes of end-to-end encryption in these apps. Consequently, the presence of these security features presents an attractive medium for digital crime and fraudulent activities. Various researchers conduct network forensics for several reasons. Some of the most prominent reasons for conducting network forensics on social media applications include (1) traffic characterization [43,70,74,75], (2) traffic decryption [71], and lastly, (3) recovering artifacts [39–42,45,72,73], as shown in Table 4.

6.1. Common Research Aims for Network Forensics

Traffic characterization aims to identify user activities through the network traffic. The classification of user activities is performed by finding certain fixed patterns in network traffic. As most of the social media applications are secure and traffic flows are HTTPS-encapsulated, gaining access to the actual contents of information being exchanged between an app client and the servers is difficult. However, identification of a particular app and its user's activities is made possible by establishing behavior analysis of the traffic. This is performed by finding out a number of fixed patterns that are considered useful to identify the application over the network and to classify user activities.

The decryption of network traffic involves transforming encrypted data into their original, human-readable form. When data are transmitted over a network, they are often encrypted to protect their confidentiality and security. Decryption, therefore, serves as the means to unveil the content of these encrypted communications, making it comprehensible for analysis and investigation. To extract artifacts from network traffic, researchers establish a controlled network environment. Within this controlled setting, they simulate a sequence of user interactions within the application under examination. Subsequently, they capture the network traffic that results from these actions, meticulously dissecting and reconstructing evidentiary traces of potentially suspect data. This process allows for a comprehensive examination of digital footprints and potential forensic evidence within the network traffic, shedding light on user activities.

Many researchers have also incorporated the idea of using firewalls into the network forensic investigation [43,70,75,165]. Deploying a firewall within the investigation network enhances the ability to effectively monitor app behavior. Firewall rules are employed to verify the app's default behavior, enabling the imposition of restrictions and the identification of any hidden or alternative app behaviors. Additionally, this approach facilitates the observation of client–server connectivity design patterns, ports, and server ranges.

Using a firewall helps in understanding connectivity patterns by regulating traffic through different rule sets. A firewall can be used to restrict client traffic and compel the exposure of the client to alternate connectivity methods. Azab et al. [43,70] configured firewall rule sets to block out TCP ports that the application would regularly communicate on to understand the changes in network connectivity patterns. Moreover, firewalls can also be used to filter out traffic not concerning the experiment so that the researchers can focus on traffic corresponding to the experiment, as performed in [70,75]. Another use case of employing a firewall includes blocking server IP addresses, as performed in [75], which would result in reduced functionality of the application.

6.2. Common Network Forensics Tools

The heart of network packet analysis relies on packet capturing and analysis. One of the most utilized packet capture and analysis softwares used by researchers in the field is Wireshark [41–43,70,71,74]. In 1998, Gerald Combs introduced Ethereal, a packet analyzer that was later rebranded as Wireshark in 2006 [166]. Wireshark is a versatile open-source network protocol analyzer that can capture and analyze a vast array of protocols and traffic types. It can analyze protocols from simple HTTP/HTTPS protocols to complex protocols such as TCP, DNS, UDP, ICMP, etc. It has an exceedingly user-friendly graphical user interface (GUI) tailored for packet analysis [167]. This GUI features a packet browser capable of simultaneously displaying a list of packets, along with detailed information and packet bytes of the currently selected packet.

Other than Wireshark, Network Miner and Charles proxy are other common network packet analysis tools. NetworkMiner is a network analysis tool designed for passive network packet capturing and forensic analysis. Its primary function is to extract valuable information and artifacts from captured network traffic. NetworkMiner can dissect and analyze network packets to reveal insights such as IP addresses, domain names, usernames, file transfers, etc. It aids in reconstructing network conversations, allowing forensic analysts to piece together the chronology of network events. Additionally, The Charles Web Debugging Proxy, developed by Karl von Randow in 2002, is a versatile web debugging proxy tool that primarily serves the function of monitoring and intercepting network traffic between a user's device and the internet. Its core purpose is to provide detailed insights into the HTTP and HTTPS traffic generated by web browsers or mobile applications. Charles Proxy allows users to inspect, analyze, and manipulate this traffic in real time.

6.3. Network Forensics Artifacts

Artifacts from network analysis primarily stem from monitoring and examining network traffic. These artifacts encompass data packets, communication logs, metadata detailing network interactions, and information related to IP addresses, ports, and protocols. IP addresses are fundamental to network forensic analysis. They help identify the source and destination of network traffic. However, we cannot solely depend on IP addresses for our investigation due to their dynamic nature. IP addresses often cannot be directly linked to a person [168] or a specific geolocation [169]. Some other prominent artifacts that can be gathered during a network forensic analysis include port numbers [43,72], protocols [39–41,45], domain names [41], certificates [72] used, and timestamps [39,41,72].

Port numbers help differentiate services and applications on a network, while protocols specify the rules and format of the network communication. They determine how data are structured, transmitted, and interpreted and help investigators understand the nature of network traffic. Certificates, specifically SSL/TLS certificates, are critical for securing web communications by encrypting data transmitted over HTTPS connections. They include details about the website's identity, encryption algorithms, and validity. Another common artifact retrieved is timestamps. They provide chronological information about network events.

Most of the authors of the existing literature focus on the artifacts from user activities related to chats [74] and calls [45,70,71]. This is because the most common user activities performed on social media applications are communication, such as chatting and calling. In light of this aim, Cents et al. [74] identified sent and received WhatsApp chat messages between a phone and the WhatsApp servers by detecting patterns in wiretap data. Wiretap data are utilized since it is difficult to trace any signs of network traffic monitoring by the suspect. Furthermore, Karpisek et al. [71] focused on decrypting WhatsApp network traffic to uncover information related to a call, while Azab et al. and Nicoletti et al. [45,70] examined the Skype application to characterize network traffic and retrieve artifacts related to calls, respectively. Some of the most prominent artifacts recovered from the above are audio codecs [45,70,71], call establishment and termination [70,71], call duration [71], and phone numbers [45,71].

7. Disk Analysis Focus

While conducting analysis on digital systems, it is paramount to analyze the storage media contained in these systems. This is because they are major sources of evidence, often holding a wealth of information that can provide critical insights into user activities. These storage media, including hard drives, solid-state drives, NAND chips (Android storage), and many more, serve as repositories of both active and historical data, making them central to the investigative process in digital forensics.

Disk analysis can be applied across a spectrum of platforms encompassing various operating systems, including Windows, Android, and iOS. Social media applications are often downloaded and installed on devices operating with these diverse systems. Each social media application possesses its own database, serving as the repository for user data, as shown in Figure 8. Researchers engage in digital forensic analysis of the disk to scrutinize these databases, conducting detailed investigations to recover artifacts and shed light on user activities within the social media sphere.

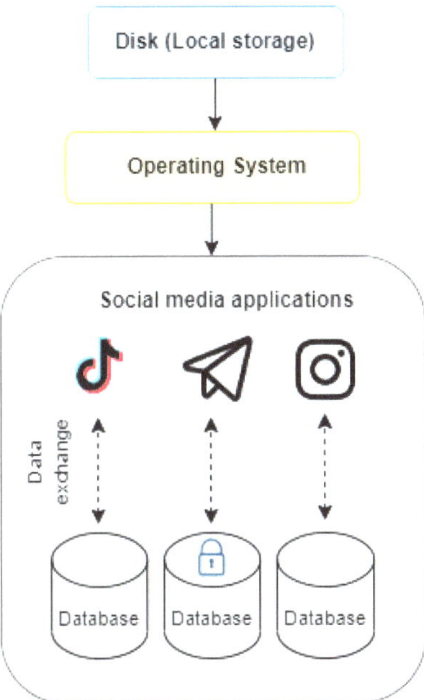

Figure 8. Key parameters in the digital forensic analysis of the disk: operating system and individual social media databases (sometimes encrypted).

7.1. Experimental Setup

The process of conducting disk analysis begins with the researcher preparing the platform they intend to use for experimentation. This platform can be either a physical computer or a virtual machine, depending on the nature of the investigation. On the other hand, in the case of mobile devices, researchers may also choose to root (for Android) or jailbreak (for iOS) the phones to gain administrative privileges and access to restricted areas of the device.

7.1.1. Virtualized Environments

To conduct digital forensics experiments, researchers either use physical devices or virtualized environments. Virtual environments rely on software that can simulate a physical device. In the rapidly changing landscape of technology, leveraging virtual machines for digital forensic analysis is increasingly advantageous. As technology evolves, new operating systems, file formats, and software environments emerge. Virtual machines adapt readily to these changes by enabling the creation of specialized, up-to-date analysis environments. This adaptability ensures that forensic analysts can keep pace with the latest technologies and forensic tools, ensuring their investigations remain effective and relevant in an ever-evolving digital world.

Virtualized devices, indeed, make it simple and cost-effective to run experiments on a variety of different virtual devices (featuring different hardware and software combinations). Furthermore, they allow a third party to use virtualized devices identical to those we used in our experiments, as well as to control their operational conditions so that the same conditions holding at the moment of our experiments can be replicated on them. In this way, repeatability is ensured.

Many researchers prefer to use virtual machines for several key reasons [30,46,50,53, 58,59,106,107,135,136,142,143]. Virtual machines provide a controlled and isolated environment for conducting forensic analysis. They also allow for creating a snapshot or clone to restore the original system or previous versions of the system, as performed by [30].

Additionally, they allow researchers to create replicas of the digital environment for use in different experiments [107]. Moreover, virtual machines can also be set up to accommodate various configurations for different experiments, as performed by [59].

VMWare Workstation is the most widely used tool for emulating desktop computers [59,61], whereas the most common virtualization tool researchers utilize to emulate an Android device is Genymotion [53,107,135]. Other utilized platforms include Android Studio [50], Android mobile device emulator [134,142], YouWave Virtualization [143], and Nox emulator.

Virtualization makes it easier to extract the data on the phone because virtualization tools implement internal storage as memory files, which can be acquired and analyzed. This makes the process greatly simplified, as it reduces the need for acquisition tools. For example, YouWave Virtualization implements the internal storage of the phone as a VirtualBox storage file [143] that can be parsed by a suitable tool for analysis. Additionally, virtualization platforms can be configured to grant root access to the virtualized devices [142], which removes the need for researchers to perform the tedious task of rooting the phone, hence making the experiment much simpler to conduct. Moreover, researchers also conduct virtualization in their experiment to look for any discrepancies in the results revealed from a physical device and a virtualized device, as performed in [135,143].

7.1.2. Rooting (Android)

Many researchers root their Android devices as part of the experimental setup before performing the experiments [39,40,105,106,111,127,128,140]. Rooting plays an important role in the forensic analysis of an Android device because it provides investigators with the elevated privileges necessary for accessing and retrieving data at the system level. Given that a significant portion of crucial files resides within the system partition of Android devices [120], rooting becomes a requisite step in obtaining vital evidence from the device. This step potentially allows for more data retrieval than if the device was unrooted [33]. Rooting not only allows access to protected directories containing user data (i.e., the/data/data directory), but it also allows users to back up some or all of the files located within these directories, making it easier for a logical acquisition to be conducted through backup applications. The most common tool used to root Android devices is Odin [7,66,123,124]. Other common rooting tools include Root explorer [37], TWRP (Team Win Recovery Project) [120,128], Root checker [122,140], Magisk [128,136], and Kingo root [115].

7.1.3. Jailbreaking (iPhones)

Just like rooting grants administrative access to Android devices, jailbreaking elevates iPhone privileges and removes software restrictions. Jailbreaking not only provides administrative privileges but also eliminates device software limitations. Ovens et al. [22,43] focused on analyzing the KIK messenger app to locate and examine artifacts created or altered by the application. To accomplish this, they conducted their investigation on an iPhone that had been jailbroken. By jailbreaking the device, they achieved the following objectives: (1) observed files modified or generated by the app during its operation, (2) bypassed the file system's access restrictions, and (3) installed and executed third-party applications essential for their analysis. In their research, the taig jailbreak tool facilitated access to the iOS file system, while Cydia, a software manager, allowed for the installation of necessary third-party tools not supported by Apple.

7.2. Disk Forensic Analysis Tools

In the realm of digital forensics investigations, researchers employ a diverse array of tools to extract and scrutinize social media evidence. These tools serve different purposes; some are dedicated to acquiring data from devices, while others are exclusively designed for data analysis. Nevertheless, many of these tools exhibit the versatility to execute both acquisition and analysis tasks seamlessly. Moreover, it is worth noting that certain tools are tailored for specific operating systems, limiting their applicability to particular platforms.

Furthermore, within the spectrum of digital forensics tools, a distinction exists between those that are freely available or open-source and those that are proprietary, as shown in Table 5. This table is structured to provide a comprehensive overview by categorizing data according to the specific operating systems, the experiment's objectives, the retrieved artifacts, and the tools employed for both data acquisition and analysis. Furthermore, this table highlights the accessibility of these tools by subcategorizing them into two distinct groups, i.e., free and proprietary.

Table 5. Existing literature on disk forensics investigation for social media applications.

OS	Purpose	Artifacts	Tools	
			Acquisition	Analysis
Windows	Artifact Recovery	User Activities [129–131]	**Free** FTK Imager	**Free** HxD, WinHex
		User Information and User Activities [26,32,60,66,69,137]	**Backup** My Backup	**Proprietary** Oxygen forensics, UFED PA
		User Information, User Activities, and Metadata [27–29,59,93,147]	**Proprietary** Magnet AXIOM process, UFED Touch	**Registry** Regshot, Reg decoder, Registry editor
	Database Decryption	[129–131]	Ollydbg, JEB compiler, IDA Pro, Hopper	HxD
iOS/Mac	Artifact Recovery	User Activities [64] User Information and User Activities [21,23,24,43,65–67,69]	**Free** iTunes	**Free** DB Browser for SQLite, pslist editor, HxD
		User Information, User Activities, and Metadata [19,20,22,41,68,170]	**Proprietary** Cellebrite UFED, UFED Touch	**Proprietary** Magnet AXIOM examine, UFED PA
	Database Decryption	[35,37,39,127]	Ollydbg, JEB compiler, IDA Pro, Hopper	HxD
Android (rooted)	Artifact Recovery	User Activities [35,37,39,127] User Information, and User Activities [24,34,68,102,103,106,107,116–118,125,138,142]	**Free** ADB, My Backup Pro, Titanium backup, Helium backup	**Free** HxD, WinHex, DB Browser for SQLite
		User Information, User Activities, and Metadata [27,43,66,88,104,105,108–110,112,114,115,119,120,128,139,140,170]	**Proprietary** Magnet Axiom Process, Magnet Acquire, MOBILedit forensic, UFED Touch, UFED 4PC, XRY	**Proprietary** Oxygen forensics, Magnet Axiom examine, UFED PA
	Database Decryption	[39,134–136]	Ollydbg, JEB compiler, IDA Pro, Dex2jar	HxD
Android (non-rooted)	Artifact Recovery	User Activities [42,52,55,64] User Information and User Activities [41,48,53,65,67,144]	**Proprietary** Cellebrite UFED, Oxygen forensics, MOBILedit forensics, Magnet AXIOM process, Wondershare Dr.Fone, XRY	**Free** DB Browser for SQLite, SQLite Viewer, Autopsy, AccessData FTK, HxD
		User Information, User Activities, and Metadata [36,47,49–51,54,56,143]		**Proprietary** Magnet AXIOM examine, Belkasoft evidence centre, UFED PA

1. *Free tools:* Our analysis reveals that the choice of free data acquisition tools is contingent upon the operating system under examination. For Windows, FTK Imager emerges as the predominant option, while iOS investigations frequently employ iTunes, and Android device data acquisition commonly relies on ADB (Android Debug Bridge) [134] and backup utilities. Conversely, analysis tools exhibit a higher degree of consistency in their utilization across various operating systems. Hex editors and DB Browser for SQLite rank as the most widely used analysis tools, with a notable exception being plist editors, which are specifically tailored for examining

.plist files—these are key/value persistent storage files—found on iOS and macOS operating systems.

2. *Proprietary tools:* Proprietary tools represent closed-source software applications that are developed and exclusively owned by specific organizations. Typically, these tools necessitate the acquisition of licenses for authorized usage. Moreover, the outcomes produced by these tools are generally accepted in a court of law, making it difficult to dispute their findings. Notable players in the field of digital forensics software include Cellebrite, Magnet Forensics, Belkasoft, and Oxygen Forensics, among others. These companies often categorize their software offerings based on distinct functionalities. For instance, Cellebrite distinguishes between the Cellebrite UFED (Universal Forensic Extraction Device), tailored for data extraction, and the Cellebrite PA (Physical Analyzer), designed for in-depth analysis. Similarly, Magnet Forensics offers the Magnet AXIOM Process for data acquisition and the Magnet AXIOM Examine for comprehensive analysis [67,127,134]. Other proprietary tools renowned for their data extraction capabilities encompass XRY, MOBILedit Forensics, Wondershare Dr.Fone, and Belkasoft Evidence Centre.

The selection of tools varies depending on the research objectives. While the aforementioned tools are primarily employed for artifact recovery, a distinct set of software tools comes into play when the focus shifts to database decryption. This specialized category encompasses tools such as OllyDbg, JEB Compiler, IDA Pro, Hopper, and Dex2jar. OllyDbg is a debugger and reverse engineering tool. IDA Pro (Interactive Disassembler Professional) and Hopper are disassembly and reverse engineering tools. Lastly, Dex2jar is a set of tools and utilities used for Android application analysis and reverse engineering.

7.3. Disk Forensic Acquisition

Once the experimental setup is completed, researchers conduct their experiments by emulating user interactions on the social media application to elicit the application to generate and store data on the device's memory. The next step is to acquire an image (copy) of the device to preserve original evidence and recover relevant artifacts. To extract data from the device, researchers use one of the three acquisition methods: logical acquisition [19, 21,42,64,65,67,69,170,171], full file system [46,64], or physical acquisition [32].

1. *Logical acquisition:* Logical acquisition involves extracting data at a higher level of abstraction, which mainly includes specific files and data from the device. However, it does not capture deleted files or data stored in unallocated disk space. Logical acquisitions are commonly conducted using ADB and backup applications [36,39,40, 52,170,172]. These tools help researchers extract application-specific files, directories, and user data. Android Debug Bridge (ADB) is a command-line tool used for managing Android devices. ADB facilitates communication between a computer and an Android device over a USB connection or a network connection (Wi-Fi or Ethernet). Additionally, there are many backup applications that allow users to backup data—including application data—mainly to the device's internal memory, to an external SD card, or to some designated cloud storage. These data can then be analyzed using forensic tools.

2. *Full File system acquisition:* Full file system extraction is an acquisition in which all the data and metadata related to a device's file system are collected and preserved as part of an investigation. This method captures the complete hierarchical structure of files, directories, and associated file attributes, such as timestamps, permissions, and file sizes. On the other hand, physical acquisition involves the creation of a bit-for-bit copy or clone of the entire device, which yields more information than a logical extraction would [32].

3. *Physical acquisition:* A physical acquisition is a common type of acquisition conducted by researchers [64,111]. It typically provides more evidence than full file system acquisition [69] because it captures not only the file system structures but also the entire contents of the storage device at a lower level, including unallocated space, deleted

files, and fragmented data. Tools such as Cellebrite UFED are most prominently used for full file system and physical extractions [64].

7.4. Disk Forensic Analysis

Once the data are acquired, researchers then analyze the data to recover artifacts. The two main kinds of analysis procedures used by researchers are manual analysis [22,39,40, 69,143] and automated analysis.

1. *Manual analysis*: Manual analysis pertains to the investigator's non-automated (manual) efforts in searching for populated artifacts. Manual and automated digital forensics analyses differ in how they handle digital evidence. Manual analysis relies on human expertise, where forensic investigators actively examine evidence, search for relevant artifacts, and make informed judgments based on their experience. While this approach is flexible and customizable, it is time-consuming and requires specialized knowledge and skills. To conduct manual analysis, most researchers use DB Browser for SQLite to analyze the database files [111,115,118,128] and hex editors such as HxD or WinHex [27,28,59,60,111,147].

2. *Automated analysis*: Automated analysis relies on specialized software tools and scripts to process and analyze digital evidence without direct human intervention. Automated analysis is usually conducted by specialized tools such as Oxygen forensics, Cellebrite UFED Physical analyzer, and others [32,55,65]. Many research articles have employed proprietary tools for automatically analyzing social media data. The most commonly used tools for analysis are MOBILedit, Belkasoft Evidence Center, Oxygen Forensics, Cellebrite Physical Analyzer, Magnet AXIOM, and Internet Evidence Finder [56,109,112,123,128].

3. *Source code analysis*: While data analysis of social media applications is the most common way to retrieve artifacts in SMF investigations, Gregorio et al. [23,32] proposed a methodology that will supplement the analysis of artifacts with steps such as studying open knowledge sources (books, related blogs, technical papers) and the source code of the application. It is seen that this methodology yields a broad amount of information. Consequently, it becomes important to delve into open knowledge and dissect the source code to comprehend the data extracted from application artifacts. The collective implementation of these three steps streamlines analysis and traceability and also mitigates reliance on forensic tools. Although this analysis methodology yielded more artifacts than the artifact analysis step yielded alone, there are some limitations to this methodology. In some cases, it is not possible to apply some of the steps due to a lack of information in the open knowledge sources, information from non-trusted sources, or a lack of public source code.

Windows-Specific Forensic Analysis

Here, we review the analysis of data and artifacts unique to the Windows operating environment. These review areas focus on the registry (a centralized database that stores configuration settings and options for both the operating system and installed applications) and Windows phone (a smartphone that runs on the Windows operating system). While Windows phones have been discontinued, it is noteworthy that certain researchers have undertaken digital forensic analyses of social media applications on the platform.

1. *Windows registry*: Analyzing the registry during a forensic investigation in Windows systems is crucial. The registry encapsulates a wealth of information that includes system configurations, user activities, and program execution records. Registry information can be extracted and examined from a forensic image, i.e., a disk copy of the original evidence. To that end, authors of [28,60] also analyze the registry during their forensic investigation. Some of the major tools used for registry analysis are Registry Editor and Regshot. Some of the artifacts revealed from registry analysis include information on the application, such as the model ID and install time [28,60]. Other prominent artifacts include contact photos retrieved from LinkedIn [60].

2. *Windows Phone*: Besides Windows systems, researchers have also explored conducting forensic analysis on Windows Phones. While conducting a forensic analysis of WhatsApp data on a Windows phone, Shortall et al. [65] acquired data using the DD command. This was because, at the time of writing, no tool could be used to acquire data from a Windows Phone. A few years later, while analyzing Telegram on the same platform, Gregorio et al. [32] opted for a physical acquisition using Cellebrite UFED Touch. Both experiments involved analysis using the tools Cellebrite UFED Physical Analyzer and Oxygen forensics, but unfortunately, almost no artifacts were recovered. In the case of WhatsApp, the authors recovered media and an encrypted database, but for Telegram, no artifacts were recovered.

7.5. Aims of Disk Forensic Analysis

As earlier stated in Section 3.1, there are a range of research objectives fulfilled by conducting the analysis of the disk, such as artifact recovery, decryption of databases, reconstruction of chats, and creation of tools, among many more. Therefore, in this section, we elucidate the diverse objectives that motivate researchers to engage in disk forensic analysis.

7.5.1. Organization of Data

Social media applications store vast amounts of user-generated data. Thus, it is key to understand the folder structure to identify where these data are stored within the device, thereby making it easier to locate and retrieve relevant evidence. Azhar et al. [36] and Tri et al. [52] conduct digital forensics analysis on social media applications to understand the organization of data in social media applications.

Azhar et al. [36] analyzed the data structures of Wickr and Telegram. The authors selected these two applications due to their ephemeral messaging features. Various forensic analysis techniques were employed to retrieve artifacts from these applications. This is because Wickr and Telegram employ several security measures, and the nature of recovered artifacts differs based on the type of acquisition. The analysis phase consisted of analyzing the application file (.apk) and the data directories of the application. In Wickr, the authors extracted the "classes.dex" file from the application. The .dex file revealed all the class definitions used by Wickr, giving further insights into the operation of the application, such as the encryption mechanism used [35]. At the same time, the analysis of the data directory revealed the workings of the ephemeral function of Wickr, bringing light to the fact that Wickr stores its received messages in encrypted ".wic" files [35,36]. Additionally, the analysis of Telegram revealed the storage mechanisms of its normal and secret chats.

In the same vein, Tri et al. [52] conducted a forensic analysis to determine the structure of folders in the IMO application. A logical acquisition was conducted, which was manually analyzed, revealing the folder structure of IMO. The results revealed that the IMO data directory consists of six folders, out of which two have subfolders. These subfolders consisted of images and videos populated by user activities, which can be further analyzed to recover artifacts.

7.5.2. Artifact Analysis

A common purpose for conducting social media forensic investigations on the disk is to recover artifacts. Digital forensics artifacts are pieces of information that are left behind on digital devices as a result of user activities. Social media platforms generate a wide range of artifacts, such as chats, private messages, posts, comments, calls, and many more. These artifacts are essential components of digital forensic investigations and provide valuable evidence that can be used to reconstruct events, analyze user behavior, and establish a timeline of digital activities. Many researchers aim to retrieve artifacts when conducting digital forensic analysis of social media applications [26–32,60,65,66,69,137,147].

There is a plethora of artifacts that can be extracted from social media analysis by performing a digital forensics investigation on the disk. Additionally, due to the functionality of different social media applications, the extracted artifacts in an investigation can differ. Thus, Azfar et al. [121] created a forensic taxonomy of thirty popular social media applications, classifying the extracted artifacts into four categories, namely User and contact information, Exchanged messages, Timestamps, and User location, as well as other artifacts.

7.5.3. Analysis of Privacy Features

Social media applications increasingly incorporate features like private chats and chat delete/unsend options to address privacy concerns. However, these features can also be misused for secretive or malicious purposes. For this reason, many researchers focus on analyzing artifacts related to private chats, unsent messages, and deleted chats [35,39,55, 111,127,128,173].

Satrya et al. [39] conducted an extensive analysis of both regular and private chat conversations within popular messaging applications such as Telegram, KakaoTalk, and Line on Android. In the case of Telegram, the researchers discovered that the contents of both regular and secret chats could be easily accessed and read using the SQLite Browser tool. For Line, the results revealed a complete absence of encryption for Line's regular chat artifacts. However, Line's hidden chat feature demonstrated a slightly different behavior. Although it also lacked encryption, it possessed a self-destruct mechanism that necessitated the timely acquisition of the chat data before they are irretrievably lost. In the context of KakaoTalk, the authors could only retrieve the last message within a chat activity.

Unsending chats is another privacy feature offered by social media applications. Hermawan et al. [55] analyzed an Android phone with the objective of identifying any retrievable artifacts associated with user actions involving the "unsending" of messages. The analysis was conducted on Skype, Viber, Snapchat, Facebook, Telegram, Line, Instagram, and Whatsapp using proprietary tools such as MOBILedit and UFED PA. The results reveal that artifacts of "unsend" messages can be found on all platforms except Line and Snapchat.

Many researchers have also researched the recoverable artifacts from deleted and disappearing chats. Vasilaras et al. studied the recovery of deleted chats on Telegram, Salamh et al. [127] examined the forensic artifacts of WhatsApp's "delete for everyone" feature, while Kumar et al. [111] analyzed the retrievable artifacts from Instagram's vanish feature (messages which would disappear). In all three research experiments, the recovery of artifacts was made possible by the presence of the Write Ahead Log (WAL). The WAL file serves as a form of journal, maintaining a comprehensive record of all transactions that have been executed but not yet applied to the primary database. Utilizing the WAL as a journaling mode ensures the integrity of the primary database by committing changes to a separate file until a checkpoint is reached. Examination of the WAL file yields insights into the most recent state of the database. For instance, data recently deleted and absent from the primary database may still be retrievable from the database's WAL file.

7.5.4. Reconstruction of Artifacts

Social media artifacts often contain critical evidence related to cybercrime and other malicious activities. However, simply collecting digital data is not enough. Understanding the context is vital. Decoding and interpreting the artifacts can help with the comprehension of the artifacts, providing insights into the chronology of the events that took place. Furthermore, the reconstruction of artifacts can prove to be invaluable in creating timelines, identifying patterns of behavior, and understanding the sequence of events. To this end, a few researchers have focused on reconstructing social media artifacts [40,134,143].

Anglano et al. [143] discussed the process of decoding and interpreting all the artifacts and data produced by WhatsApp Messenger on Android devices. They further illustrate how these artifacts can be correlated to deduce diverse forms of information that would remain incomprehensible if each were examined in isolation. Notably, the authors provide a detailed exploration of the structure of the contacts and chat databases, enabling the interpretation of stored data. These artifacts were subsequently correlated, revealing valuable insights, including the identification of added, blocked, and deleted contacts, alongside the reconstruction of chat histories and their contents. This insightful analysis was rendered possible through the utilization of WhatsApp's log files, which record user activities and allow the authors to correlate information seamlessly between the log files and the databases.

In subsequent studies conducted by Anglano et al. [134] and Satrya et al. [40], the authors pursued a common objective, each focusing on distinct messaging applications—ChatSecure (an application that allows a user to communicate via multiple existing instant messaging accounts on a unified platform) and Telegram Messenger, respectively. Within their investigations, both research papers detailed the structural aspects of various application database tables, including components such as contacts, accounts, and messages. Consequently, these studies provide comprehensive guidance on how to analyze and correlate the data stored within the databases of ChatSecure and Telegram Messenger. This analytical approach yields insights into identifying IM accounts utilized by both the user and their friends in ChatSecure, as well as the reconstruction of messages, contacts, and file exchange chronologies specific to each application.

7.5.5. Decryption of Databases

Storing user information in databases on the disk raises significant privacy concerns, notably regarding the potential exposure of users' confidential data, including chats, photos, and personally identifiable information [174]. Typically, social media applications store user data within databases located on the device where the application is installed. One of the more common databases seen in this review is LevelDB, which is an open-source on-disk key-value store developed by Google. LevelDb is used by Microsoft Teams [31], Discord [29,30], Riot.im [30], and others. These database files contain extensive information about the user and their activities. To safeguard these data, social media applications commonly employ encryption measures, ensuring that only the application itself can access the stored information. Numerous researchers have investigated the decryption of these internal databases within social media applications [129,131,132].

Decryption procedures often entail deciphering the backup files associated with applications. These backup files are typically encrypted to protect user data. To retrieve artifacts, researchers utilize specialized techniques to decrypt these files. Once decrypted, investigators can analyze the artifacts, such as messages, images, and other user-generated content, shedding light on user activities.

Krishnapriya et al. [119] analyzed the Signal application data using an encrypted backup file to locate artifacts on an Android device. The authors manually acquired the backup file (.backup file) using ADB, which was then decrypted using a command line tool called Signal backup decryptor with a 30-digit passphrase. The database file in the backup was then analyzed for artifacts corresponding to user activity, such as user profiles, contacts, and messages.

Using a similar methodology of decrypting backup databases, Gudi et al. [133] decrypt WhatsApp backup databases (msgstore.db) on an Android device. The authors used a tool called "WhatsApp Key/DB Extractor" to extract the SQLite encrypted database in a decrypted format. The output is then processed by WhatsApp extract tool to output the database information in a human-readable format.

Additionally, Choi et al. [131] studied the backup process of KakaoTalk by reverse engineering the application to analyze the encryption process. They revealed that the key to the backup file could be generated using the user's password and a unique nine-digit number, which is assigned in the order of user registration on the app. If a weak password is used, the nine-digit number can easily be brute forced, leading to the encryption key [132]. Additionally, in a future study, Choi et al. [132] revealed that KakaoTalk and NateOn no longer required the user password to generate the encryption key. Instead, it required device-specific information such as the unique identifier, the model name, and the serial number. In the same line, Kim et al. [129] decrypted Telegram chat databases. It uses an

SQLite extension module called SQLCipher. The authors identified its parameters, which derived the encryption key.

Further analysis of research articles tackling the decryption of application databases revealed that the preferences.xml (and its variants) file could be a useful piece in the puzzle of decryption application databases [134–136]. Additionally, it is seen that many applications make use of SQLCipher to encrypt application databases [130,134,135].

Son et al. [136] research the decryption process of signal databases on a rooted Android device. Signal uses the Android Keystore to protect the encryption key. Thus, the authors developed an application to extract the key from the Android Keystore, as it cannot be extracted directly. To decrypt the Signal application's encrypted database ("signal.db"), you need to acquire a value called "pref_database_encrypted_secret" from the "org.thoughtcrime.securesms_preferences.xml" file. This value is a JSON string with the 'data' (cipher text and authentication tag), 'iv' (initialization vector) as a key, and its corresponding values, both of which are required for the decryption key. As a result, the database, multimedia, and log files could be decrypted.

Furthermore, Anglano et al. [134] focused on the methodology of decrypting Chat-Secure databases. ChatSecure employs SQLCipher for database encryption, with the encryption key being internally generated by the application, maintaining user confidentiality. This key remains securely stored within the device's volatile memory to facilitate decryption by ChatSecure as needed. However, to enhance security and prevent unauthorized access, ChatSecure utilizes the CacheWord library. This library encrypts the key using a user-defined secret passphrase and stores it within an XML file named "info.guardianproject.cacheword.prefs.xml", found in the "shared_prefs" directory. This layered security approach ensures that adversaries cannot decipher the databases using the saved secret key alone.

In a related context, Wu et al. [135] delved into the decryption procedures applied to WeChat's database. WeChat utilizes SQLCipher to encrypt chat message databases. Key data, such as chat records and configurations generated during WeChat's operation, are stored within three specific subdirectories, namely "databases", "shared_prefs", and "MicroMsg". The "databases" and "shared_prefs" directories house user authentication information and configuration files, while the "MicroMsg" directory stores crucial user activity data. When WeChat is initiated, it assigns a unique "uin" (User Identification Number) identifier to each user. Through analysis of the decompiled WeChat App code, the authors discerned that the decryption key is derived from the International Mobile Equipment Identity (IMEI) of the smartphone and the "uin" of the current WeChat user. Extraction of IMEI and "uin" data can be achieved from configuration files like "CompatibilityInfo.cfg" and "system_config_prefs.xml".

7.5.6. Creating Tools

Another application of conducting digital forensics analysis on social media applications is to create a tool. After thoroughly investigating the recovered artifacts and the structure of Discord's cache on various operating systems such as Windows, Linux, and Mac, Motylinkski et al. [147] developed a tool called DiscFor, which automatically retrieves all data stored on local Discord files, sparing the need for manual inspection of cache or JSON files. It can function both as a standalone Python script and as an executable file compatible with multiple systems.

Along the same lines, Anglano et al. [144] designed a software called "AnForA" that automates the activities carried out to forensically analyze Android applications. It begins by installing the target application onto a virtualized Android device. Subsequently, a series of experiments are conducted in which specific actions replicating the user interactions with the app are automatically executed within the application. The system then actively observes and monitors the device's file systems, allowing for the identification and correlation of data generated or altered during each action with the corresponding user interaction.

7.5.7. Browser Analysis

Performing forensic analysis on disk storage also enables the examination of social media web applications. Numerous researchers have engaged in forensic analysis of browser data stored on disks to recover valuable social media artifacts. The most common web browser chosen for such experiments is Google Chrome [86,90,96,175], likely attributed to its widespread usage, rendering it a primary focus for forensic investigations.

As depicted in Table 6, throughout the existing literature, the prevailing tool for acquiring web browser data has been FTK Imager, with an exception where iTunes is utilized to gather data from the Safari web browser [87]. As for the analysis phase, prominent tools encompass hex editors and DB Browser for SQLite, which are instrumental in delving into the database files of web browsers. In addition to these mainstream tools, specialized software such as ChromeCacheView, VideoCacheView, and Browser History capture tools have been developed with the specific purpose of analyzing web browser data. These tools are tailored to dissect various aspects of web browser data, including cache contents and browsing history.

Table 6. Disk analysis on browser.

Ref	Application	Browser					VD	Tools		Artifacts			
		Google Chrome	Firefox	Internet Explorer	Microsoft Edge	Microsoft Edge		Acquisition	Analysis	User Information	User activities	Metadata	Password
[86]	AIM, Meebo, E-buddy, Google Talk	×	×	✓	×	×	N	FTK Imager	FTK Toolkit	✓	✓	✓	×
[87]	AIM, Yahoo, Google Talk	×	×	×	×	✓	N	iTunes	DB Browser for SQLite, MobileSyncBrowser	✓	×	✓	✓
[88]	Facebook	✓	✓	✓	×	×	N	Encase	Encase	✓	✓	✓	×
[89]	Facebook	×	×	✓	×	×	Y	N/A	Internet Evidence Finder	×	✓	✓	×
[90]	WhatsApp	✓	×	×	×	×	N	FTK Imager	DB Browser for SQLite	✓	×	✓	×
[91]	Facebook	✓	✓	✓	×	×	N	N/A	FTK Toolkit	✓	✓	×	×
[93]	WhatsApp	✓	×	×	×	×	N	N/A	BrowSwEx	×	✓	✓	×
[94]	LinkedIn	✓	✓	×	✓	×	N	FTK Imager	FTK Imager	✓	✓	×	×
[95]	TikTok	✓	×	×	×	×	N	FTK Imager	FTK Imager, VideoCacheView, Browser History Capture	✓	✓	×	×
[96]	Discord	✓	×	×	×	×	N	N/A	DB Browser for SQLite, ChromeCacheView, HxD	✓	✓	✓	×
[98]	Instagram	✓	×	✓	×	×	Y	N/A	DB Browser for SQLite, WinHex	✓	✓	✓	×
[99]	Instagram	✓	✓	✓	×	×	Y	N/A	DB Browser for SQLite, WinHex	✓	✓	×	×
[100]	TikTok	✓	×	×	×	×	N	N/A	DB Browser for SQLite, History examiner, HxD, VideoCacheViewer	✓	✓	×	×
[101]	Google Meet	✓	✓	×	✓	×	Y	FTK Imager	ChromeCacheView, ChromeCookiesView, DB Browser for SQLite, Autopsy	✓	✓	✓	×
[176]	Youtube, Facebook	✓	×	×	×	×	N	N/A	ChromeCacheView, X-ways	×	✓	×	×

8. Trends in Social Media Forensics

Social media platforms can capture and store massive amounts of user-generated content, making them valuable evidence sources in both civil and criminal cases. The reliability and timeliness of this evidence can play a significant role in determining the end result of a case.

The literature review findings reveal that Facebook [56,89,91], Whatsapp [33,65,143], and Skype [45,76,137] are the most commonly studied social media applications. These applications have been extensively studied due to their widespread use and popularity. This is also evident in the tools that are exclusively designed to analyze data from these specific applications, such as SkypeAlyzer [137] and Whatsapp Viewer [133], among others. Other popular social media applications, such as Instagram [53,110,111], Twitter [97,140,146], Signal [75,117,118], and Telegram [23,142,149], have also been extensively studied. It is worth noting that in some applications, such as Snapchat, very little evidence is recovered due to the ephemeral nature of the communication and the deletion of the artifacts [55,67].

Most research on social media applications has focused on the Android platform in mobile phones [54,55,124], as shown in Figure 3. This is because Android is the market dominator in the global smartphone market [121]. This makes it the prime target for malicious actors to conduct their activities, thus making it the most prominent environment for digital forensic scrutiny. Additionally, Android's open-source nature grants forensic experts deep insight into its underlying code, facilitating the development of specialized tools and techniques for analysis. The diverse hardware ecosystem on which Android operates presents both challenges and opportunities, demanding adaptability in forensic approaches to accommodate various device configurations. The platform's rich app ecosystem, user customization options, cloud integration, and evolving security features all contribute to its significance in digital forensics. Furthermore, legal considerations often place Android devices at the center of criminal cases, necessitating the continuous development of expertise in Android device analysis. However, with the increasing popularity of iOS devices, more attention is being given to the iOS platform [42,68,73]. It is also interesting to note that in mobile platforms such as Blackberry, no traces of evidence could be recovered, making it a very secure platform [7,66]. Although Blackberry platforms are the most secure, their usage has diminished over the years.

Regarding desktop computers and laptops, Windows is the most extensively studied platform [28,132,150], leaving a gap in the research on the Mac OS and Linux operating systems. The Windows operating system has earned its status as one of the most researched platforms in digital forensics investigations for several compelling reasons. Firstly, Windows has long been the dominant operating system for personal computers, meaning a substantial portion of digital data and potential evidence are hosted on Windows devices. Its ubiquity makes it a prime focus for forensic experts, as it is frequently involved in a wide spectrum of criminal activities. Additionally, Windows' complex and extensive architecture presents a rich landscape for forensic analysis, with various artifacts, logs, and registry entries offering valuable insights into user activities and system behavior. Furthermore, the wide range of Windows versions and configurations encountered in the field challenges investigators to continually adapt their techniques and tools, enhancing the need for ongoing research.

Examining social media applications on desktops or laptops additionally provides the opportunity to explore the web-based components of these platforms, offering a comprehensive view of users' online interactions and behaviors, both within the desktop application and across web interfaces. However, only a few studies have examined social media applications on web browsers [97,148,176], indicating a significant potential for further research in this area.

The analyses of memory, disk, and network are the three main focus areas encompassing the research analyzed in this survey. Among these, disk storage is the most frequently studied focus area [54], while network analysis has been the least studied [41]. Disk analysis is frequently studied in digital forensic investigations of social media applications due to the central role of local storage in storing user-generated data, making it a primary source of valuable evidence. Additionally, a wealth of specialized forensic tools exists to efficiently extract and examine data from storage devices, which have evolved to cater to the complex storage structures used by modern social media applications. On the other hand, network analysis is less commonly studied due to challenges such as the use of encrypted communication, the volume of data, and their ephemeral nature. Network analysis is often secondary to disk analysis in typical investigations, where local storage holds the primary cache of user data.

Different analysis focus areas require specialized forensic tools for acquisition and analysis. For example, for memory analysis, the widely used tools for collection were Lime, FTK Imager, and DumpIt [82,97,150]. Volatility was widely adopted for analyzing memory [85]. The most commonly used tools to analyze network traffic were Wireshark and Network Miner [72].

Lastly, it was observed that although most research focused on recovering artifacts from social media applications, their purposes varied. While most articles concentrated on artifact recovery from common use cases of an application, such as online shop fraud [84], defamation crimes [95], pornography [56], cyberbullying [110], and web phishing [117], some papers specifically focused on artifacts related to particular application features, such as the "unsend message" feature [55], or a specific storage medium such as Indexed DB [93]. Furthermore, some articles also focused on creating a forensic taxonomy [49], decryption of databases [129,132], comparing tools [140], comparing different versions of applications [135], comparing platforms [66], artifacts recovered in different web browsers [97], detecting patterns in network traffic [74], creating tools [144,148], and reconstructing the sequence of chat messages [134].

Our findings in this review provide a comprehensive understanding of the various approaches and techniques used for artifact recovery. We also highlighted the need for continued research to improve the efficiency and accuracy of artifact recovery from social media applications in digital forensics.

9. Challenges and Future Research Focus in SMF

The increasing use of social media platforms has made artifact recovery a critical area of research in digital forensics. Our survey offers a comprehensive and systematic review of the current literature on artifact recovery from social media applications in digital forensics. The outcomes of this review were utilized to pinpoint crucial areas for further research in artifact recovery from social media applications that stem from the challenges identified.

1. *Social media data in the cloud*: The field of social media forensics is developing quickly, and one aspect that has not been given much attention is the investigation of evidence stored in the cloud. With the increasing number of people using social media apps that keep their data in the cloud, it is now vital to concentrate on analyzing cloud data. However, cloud storage presents a significant difficulty for digital forensic investigators, as traditional forensic methods may not be enough to access and analyze cloud data [128]. Therefore, it is crucial to conduct research into the digital forensics of social media app cloud data to create more effective ways of recovering and analyzing artifacts. This research will enhance the efficiency of digital forensic investigations and help tackle the emerging challenges related to cloud-based digital evidence.

2. *Lack of standard methodology for conducting social media forensics analysis*: It is crucial to create a comprehensive framework for social media forensics to guide future research [177]. While there are existing frameworks like NIST, NIJ, and ACPO that researchers use for digital forensic extraction and analysis, they are not tailored to the unique challenges presented by social media applications. Therefore, a new framework that specifically addresses the collection and analysis of data from social media platforms is necessary. This framework should offer a thorough approach to artifact recovery and tackle the unique challenges that arise from social media platforms.

3. *Lack of specialized tools for social media forensics*: There is a need for further research on integrating social media data into traditional forensic tools. Most current digital forensics tools are not equipped to handle social media data effectively. Therefore, it is necessary to explore methods of integrating social media data into traditional forensics tools to enhance analysis and artifact recovery.

4. *Vast amounts of social media data*: One particular area that could be addressed is the analysis of deleted and hidden data. Social media platforms allow users to delete or conceal their data, and it is essential to explore the potential for artifact recovery from such data. In addition, social media platform APIs can be used as a source of data for artifacts. These APIs offer a way to access the data stored on social media platforms, and their potential for artifact recovery in digital forensics has yet to be fully explored. Future research can focus on investigating these APIs and their potential for artifact recovery.

5. *Heterogeneous and disparate sources of data*: They pose significant challenges for investigators and analysts. On social media applications, digital evidence is created in a variety of forms, including text, photographs, videos, and location-based information. Hence, the huge volume and disparity of data across many platforms makes it a difficult undertaking to efficiently acquire, analyze, and document this information. Investigators must deal with data consistency, dependability, and authenticity difficulties. Furthermore, individuals' differing privacy settings and data access rights hamper the recovery and investigation of digital evidence. As a result, dealing with the challenges of processing diverse and divergent data sources in social media forensics necessitates not just strong technological skills, but also a thorough awareness of legal and ethical aspects of the digital investigative process.

6. *Adaptation of Machine Learning and Deep Learning models in SMF*: The use of machine learning models is highly promising for automating the process of artifact extraction from social media platforms. Specifically, deep learning models can be trained to identify relevant patterns and features within social media data, which can greatly enhance the efficiency and accuracy of artifact recovery. However, using these models may require technical expertise that some digital forensic professionals may not possess.

The examination of the current literature on artifact recovery from social media platforms in digital forensics emphasizes the importance of continued research. The future research directions outlined in this study can provide useful guidance for professionals and researchers working in digital forensics. Moreover, since social media applications are continuously evolving and introducing new features, research must be conducted to keep up with the rapidly changing landscape of social media forensics.

10. Conclusions

In this survey, we examined over 170 existing works in the literature tackling digital forensic analysis on several social media applications. We carry out an extensive examination delving into a wide range of analysis foci, research objectives, tools, and techniques relating to the field of social media forensics. We have structured this survey to emphasize that there are several research objectives behind conducting investigations on social media applications, such as artifact recovery, decryption of databases, and tool creation, to name a few. We also highlighted the most common digital forensic frameworks employed by most of the research reviewed. Subsequently, the reviewed papers were categorized into specific groups that outline the core research areas of the SMF investigation, particularly focusing on network, memory, and disk analysis. Furthermore, we delve into the platforms on which this research was conducted and the specialized tools subsequently employed for data acquisition and analysis. As a result, we developed a taxonomy for grouping the artifacts recovered during the investigation's analysis.

Our examination of existing research has illuminated prevalent trends in the field, simultaneously exposing gaps for future exploration. While data extraction from application databases on mobile devices has been extensively studied, a notable void exists in research addressing the retrieval and analysis of data from cloud storage—a prominent mode of data storage nowadays. Furthermore, our review underscores a lack of standardized methodologies or frameworks in the realm of digital forensics investigations of social media applications, where a conspicuous gap persists. Notably, the absence of a standardized methodology poses a significant challenge to the coherence of findings in this domain.

Lastly, despite the widespread manual techniques employed in analyzing social media data, there is a promising opportunity for future studies to leverage machine learning and deep learning models for the automation of large-scale social media data analysis. This potential shift towards automation could streamline and enhance the efficiency of digital forensics investigations in the ever-evolving domain of social media forensics.

Author Contributions: Conceptualization, K.G. and C.V.; methodology, K.G., and D.O.; validation, D.O.; formal analysis, K.G., D.O. and C.V.; investigation, K.G.; resources, C.V.; data curation, K.G. and D.O.; writing—original draft preparation, K.G. and D.O.; writing—review and editing, C.V., A.R. and N.S.; visualization, D.O.; supervision, C.V., A.R. and N.S.; project administration, C.V.; funding acquisition, C.V. All authors have read and agreed to the published version of the manuscript.

Funding: This research received no external funding.

Data Availability Statement: No new data were created or analyzed in this study. Data sharing is not applicable to this article.

Conflicts of Interest: The authors declare no conflict of interest.

References

1. Ma, B.; Tao, Z.; Ma, R.; Wang, C.; Li, J.; Li, X. A High-Performance Robust Reversible Data Hiding Algorithm Based on Polar Harmonic Fourier Moments. *IEEE Trans. Circuits Syst. Video Technol.* 2023, *early access*. [CrossRef]
2. Chaffey, D. Global Social Media Statistics Research Summary 2022 [June 2022]. 2023. Available online: https://www.smartinsights.com/social-media-marketing/social-media-strategy/new-global-social-media-research/ (accessed on 12 May 2023).
3. Alqatawna, J.; Madain, A.; Al-Zoubi, A.; Al-Sayyed, R. Online social networks security: Threats, attacks, and future directions. In *Social Media Shaping e-Publishing and Academia*; Springer: Berlin/Heidelberg, Germany, 2017; pp. 121–132.
4. Rathore, S.; Sharma, P.K.; Loia, V.; Jeong, Y.S.; Park, J.H. Social network security: Issues, challenges, threats, and solutions. *Inf. Sci.* **2017**, *421*, 43–69. [CrossRef]
5. Fire, M.; Goldschmidt, R.; Elovici, Y. Online social networks: Threats and solutions. *IEEE Commun. Surv. Tutor.* **2014**, *16*, 2019–2036. [CrossRef]
6. Patel, P.; Kannoorpatti, K.; Shanmugam, B.; Azam, S.; Yeo, K.C. A theoretical review of social media usage by cyber-criminals. In Proceedings of the 2017 International Conference on Computer Communication and Informatics (ICCCI), Coimbatore, India, 5–7 January 2017; pp. 1–6.
7. Al Mutawa, N.; Baggili, I.; Marrington, A. Forensic analysis of social networking applications on mobile devices. *Digit. Investig.* **2012**, *9*, S24–S33. [CrossRef]
8. Luo, W.; Liu, J.; Liu, J.; Fan, C. An analysis of security in social networks. In Proceedings of the 2009 Eighth IEEE International Conference on Dependable, Autonomic and Secure Computing, Chengdu, China, 12–14 December 2009; pp. 648–651.
9. Norden, S. How the Internet Has Changed the Face of Crime. 2013. Available online: https://scholarscommons.fgcu.edu/esploro/outputs/doctoral/How-the-Internet-has-Changed-the/99383341581306570 (accessed on 12 May 2023).
10. Dredge, R.; Gleeson, J.; De la Piedad Garcia, X. Cyberbullying in social networking sites: An adolescent victim's perspective. *Comput. Hum. Behav.* **2014**, *36*, 13–20. [CrossRef]
11. Garfinkel, S.L. Digital forensics research: The next 10 years. *Digit. Investig.* **2010**, *7*, S64–S73. [CrossRef]
12. Basumatary, B.; Kalita, H.K. Social media forensics—A holistic review. In Proceedings of the 2022 9th International Conference on Computing for Sustainable Global Development (INDIACom), New Delhi, India, 23–25 March 2022; pp. 590–597.
13. Reddy, S.T.; Mothe, R.; Sunil, G.; Harshavardhan, A.; Korra, S.N. Collecting the evidences and forensic analysis on social networks: Disputes and trends in research. *Stud. Rosenthal. J. Study Res.* **2019**, *XII*, 183–192.
14. Browning, J.G. Digging for the digital dirt: Discovery and use of evidence from social media sites. *SMU Sci. Tech. Law Rev.* **2010**, *14*, 465.
15. Zainudin, N.M.; Merabti, M.; Llewellyn-Jones, D. Online social networks as supporting evidence: A digital forensic investigation model and its application design. In Proceedings of the 2011 International Conference on Research and Innovation in Information Systems, Kuala Lumpur, Malaysia, 23–24 November 2011; pp. 1–6.
16. Keyvanpour, M.; Moradi, M.; Hasanzadeh, F. Digital forensics 2.0: A review on social networks forensics. In *Computational Intelligence in Digital Forensics: Forensic Investigation and Applications*; Springer: Cham, Switzerland, 2014; pp. 17–46.
17. Damshenas, M.; Dehghantanha, A.; Mahmoud, R. A survey on digital forensics trends. *Int. J. Cyber-Secur. Digit. Forensics* **2014**, *3*, 209–235.
18. Arshad, H.; Jantan, A.; Omolara, E. Evidence collection and forensics on social networks: Research challenges and directions. *Digit. Investig.* **2019**, *28*, 126–138. [CrossRef]
19. Tso, Y.C.; Wang, S.J.; Huang, C.T.; Wang, W.J. iPhone social networking for evidence investigations using iTunes forensics. In Proceedings of the 6th International Conference on Ubiquitous Information Management and Communication, Kuala Lumpur, Malaysia, 20–22 February 2012; pp. 1–7.

20. Gao, F.; Zhang, Y. Analysis of WeChat on iPhone. In Proceedings of the 2nd International Symposium on Computer, Communication, Control and Automation, Shijiazhuang, China, 22–24 February 2013; Atlantis Press: Amsterdam, The Netherlands, 2013; pp. 278–281.

21. Al Mushcab, R.; Gladyshev, P. Forensic analysis of instagram and path on an iPhone 5s mobile device. In Proceedings of the 2015 IEEE Symposium on Computers and Communication (ISCC), Larnaca, Cyprus, 6–9 July 2015; pp. 146–151.

22. Ovens, K.M.; Morison, G. Forensic analysis of kik messenger on ios devices. *Digit. Investig.* **2016**, *17*, 40–52. [CrossRef]

23. Gregorio, J.; Alarcos, B.; Gardel, A. Forensic analysis of Telegram messenger desktop on macOS. *Int. J. Res. Eng. Sci.* **2018**, *6*, 39–48.

24. Iqbal, A.; Marrington, A.; Baggili, I. Forensic artifacts of the ChatON Instant Messaging application. In Proceedings of the 2013 8th International Workshop on Systematic Approaches to Digital Forensics Engineering (SADFE), Hong Kong, China, 21–22 November 2013; pp. 1–6.

25. Yusoff, M.N.; Dehghantanha, A.; Mahmod, R. Forensic investigation of social media and instant messaging services in Firefox OS: Facebook, Twitter, Google+, Telegram, OpenWapp, and Line as case studies. In *Contemporary Digital Forensic Investigations of Cloud and Mobile Applications*; Elsevier: Amsterdam, The Netherlands, 2017; pp. 41–62.

26. Majeed, A.; Zia, H.; Imran, R.; Saleem, S. Forensic analysis of three social media apps in windows 10. In Proceedings of the 2015 12th International Conference on High-Capacity Optical Networks and Enabling/Emerging Technologies (HONET), Islamabad, Pakistan, 21–23 December 2015; pp. 1–5.

27. Lee, C.; Chung, M. Digital forensic analysis on Window8 style UI instant messenger applications. In *Computer Science and Its Applications*; Springer: Berlin/Heidelberg, Germany, 2015; pp. 1037–1042.

28. Majeed, A.; Saleem, S. Forensic analysis of social media apps in windows 10. *NUST J. Eng. Sci.* **2017**, *10*, 37–45.

29. Moffitt, K.; Karabiyik, U.; Hutchinson, S.; Yoon, Y.H. Discord forensics: The logs keep growing. In Proceedings of the 2021 IEEE 11th Annual Computing and Communication Workshop and Conference (CCWC), Las Vegas, NV, USA, 27–30 January 2021; pp. 0993–0999.

30. Schipper, G.C.; Seelt, R.; Le-Khac, N.A. Forensic analysis of Matrix protocol and Riot. im application. *Forensic Sci. Int. Digit. Investig.* **2021**, *36*, 301118. [CrossRef]

31. Paligu, F.; Varol, C. Microsoft Teams desktop application forensic investigations utilizing IndexedDB storage. *J. Forensic Sci.* **2022**, *67*, 1513–1533. [CrossRef]

32. Gregorio, J.; Gardel, A.; Alarcos, B. Forensic analysis of telegram messenger for windows phone. *Digit. Investig.* **2017**, *22*, 88–106. [CrossRef]

33. Thakur, N.S. Forensic Analysis of WhatsApp on Android Smartphones. 2013. Available online: https://scholarworks.uno.edu/td/1706/ (accessed on 12 May 2023).

34. Al-Saleh, M.I.; Forihat, Y.A. Skype forensics in android devices. *Int. J. Comput. Appl.* **2013**, *78*, 38–44. [CrossRef]

35. Barton, T.; Azhar, M. Forensic analysis of the recovery of Wickr's ephemeral data on Android platforms. In Proceedings of the First International Conference on Cyber-Technologies and Cyber-Systems, IARIA, Venice, Italy, 9–13 October 2016; pp. 35–40.

36. Azhar, M.; Barton, T.E.A. Forensic analysis of secure ephemeral messaging applications on android platforms. In *Proceedings of the International Conference on Global Security, Safety, and Sustainability*; Springer: Berlin/Heidelberg, Germany, 2017; pp. 27–41.

37. Chang, M.S.; Chang, C.Y. Forensic analysis of LINE messenger on android. *J. Comput.* **2018**, *29*, 11–20.

38. Al-Rawashdeh, A.M.; Al-Sharif, Z.A.; Al-Saleh, M.I.; Shatnawi, A.S. A post-mortem forensic approach for the kik messenger on android. In Proceedings of the 2020 11th International Conference on Information and Communication Systems (ICICS), Irbid, Jordan, 7–9 April 2020; pp. 079–084.

39. Satrya, G.B.; Daely, P.T.; Shin, S.Y. Android forensics analysis: Private chat on social messenger. In Proceedings of the 2016 Eighth International Conference on Ubiquitous and Future Networks (ICUFN), Vienna, Austria, 5–8 July 2016; pp. 430–435.

40. Satrya, G.B.; Nugroho, M.A. Digital forensics study of internet messenger: Line artifact analysis in Android OS. In Proceedings of the 2016 International Conference on Control, Electronics, Renewable Energy and Communications (ICCEREC), Bandung, Indonesia, 13–15 September 2016; pp. 23–29.

41. Norouzizadeh Dezfouli, F.; Dehghantanha, A.; Eterovic-Soric, B.; Choo, K.K.R. Investigating Social Networking applications on smartphones detecting Facebook, Twitter, LinkedIn and Google+ artefacts on Android and iOS platforms. *Aust. J. Forensic Sci.* **2016**, *48*, 469–488. [CrossRef]

42. Walnycky, D.; Baggili, I.; Marrington, A.; Moore, J.; Breitinger, F. Network and device forensic analysis of android social-messaging applications. *Digit. Investig.* **2015**, *14*, S77–S84. [CrossRef]

43. Sudozai, M.; Saleem, S.; Buchanan, W.J.; Habib, N.; Zia, H. Forensics study of IMO call and chat app. *Digit. Investig.* **2018**, *25*, 5–23. [CrossRef]

44. Zhang, H.; Chen, L.; Liu, Q. Digital forensic analysis of instant messaging applications on android smartphones. In Proceedings of the 2018 International Conference on Computing, Networking and Communications (ICNC), Maui, HI, USA, 5–8 March 2018; pp. 647–651.

45. Nicoletti, M.; Bernaschi, M. Forensic analysis of Microsoft Skype for Business. *Digit. Investig.* **2019**, *29*, 159–179. [CrossRef]

46. Mahajan, A.; Dahiya, M.; Sanghvi, H.P. Forensic analysis of instant messenger applications on android devices. *arXiv* **2013**, arXiv:1304.4915.

47. Riadi, I. Forensic investigation technique on android's blackberry messenger using nist framework. *Int. J. Cyber-Secur. Digit. Forensics* **2017**, *6*, 198–206. [CrossRef]
48. Alyahya, T.; Kausar, F. Snapchat analysis to discover digital forensic artifacts on android smartphone. *Procedia Comput. Sci.* **2017**, *109*, 1035–1040. [CrossRef]
49. Azfar, A.; Choo, K.K.R.; Liu, L. Forensic taxonomy of android social apps. *J. Forensic Sci.* **2017**, *62*, 435–456. [CrossRef] [PubMed]
50. Ashawa, M.; Ogwuche, I. Forensic data extraction and analysis of left artifacts on emulated android phones: A case study of instant messaging applications. *Seizure* **2017**, *19*, 16. [CrossRef]
51. Riadi, I.; Yudhana, A.; Putra, M.C.F. Forensic Tool Comparison on Instagram Digital Evidence Based on Android with The NIST Method. *Sci. J. Inform.* **2018**, *5*, 235–247. [CrossRef]
52. Tri, M.K.; Riadi, I.; Prayudi, Y. Forensics acquisition and analysis method of imo messenger. *Int. J. Comput. Appl.* **2018**, *179*, 9–14.
53. Alisabeth, C.; Pramadi, Y.R. Forensic analysis of instagram on android. In *Proceedings of the IOP Conference Series: Materials Science and Engineering*; IOP Publishing: Bristol, UK, 2020; Volume 1007, p. 012116.
54. Akinbi, A.; Ojie, E. Forensic analysis of open-source XMPP/Jabber multi-client instant messaging apps on Android smartphones. *SN Appl. Sci.* **2021**, *3*, 1–14. [CrossRef]
55. Hermawan, T.; Suryanto, Y.; Alief, F.; Roselina, L. Android forensic tools analysis for unsend chat on social media. In Proceedings of the 2020 3rd International Seminar on Research of Information Technology and Intelligent Systems (ISRITI), Yogyakarta, Indonesia, 10–11 December 2020; pp. 233–238.
56. Ardiningtias, S.R. A Comparative Analysis of Digital Forensic Investigation Tools on Facebook Messenger Applications. *J. Cyber Secur. Mobil.* **2022**, *11*, 655–672.
57. Yasin, M.; Kausar, F.; Aleisa, E.; Kim, J. Correlating messages from multiple IM networks to identify digital forensic artifacts. *Electron. Commer. Res.* **2014**, *14*, 369–387. [CrossRef]
58. Chang, M.; Chang, C.Y. Twitter social network forensics on Windows 10. *Int. J. Innov. Sci. Eng. Technol.* **2016**, *3*, 55–60.
59. Chang, M.S.; Chang, C.Y. Line messenger forensics on windows 10. *J. Comput.* **2019**, *30*, 114–125.
60. Bashir, S.; Abbas, H.; Shafqat, N.; Iqbal, W.; Saleem, K. Forensic Analysis of LinkedIn's Desktop Application on Windows 10 OS. In *Proceedings of the 16th International Conference on Information Technology-New Generations (ITNG 2019)*; Springer: Berlin/Heidelberg, Germany, 2019; pp. 57–62.
61. Yang, T.Y.; Dehghantanha, A.; Choo, K.K.R.; Muda, Z. Windows instant messaging app forensics: Facebook and Skype as case studies. *PLoS ONE* **2016**, *11*, e0150300. [CrossRef]
62. Mahr, A.; Cichon, M.; Mateo, S.; Grajeda, C.; Baggili, I. Zooming into the pandemic! A forensic analysis of the Zoom Application. *Forensic Sci. Int. Digit. Investig.* **2021**, *36*, 301107. [CrossRef]
63. Khalid, Z.; Iqbal, F.; Kamoun, F.; Hussain, M.; Khan, L.A. Forensic Analysis of the Cisco WebEx Application. In Proceedings of the 2021 5th Cyber Security in Networking Conference (CSNet), Abu Dhabi, United Arab Emirates, 12–14 October 2021; pp. 90–97.
64. Le-Khac, N.A.; Sgaras, C.; Kechadi, T. Forensic acquisition and analysis of Tango VoIP. In Proceedings of the International Conference on Challenges in IT, Engineering and Technology (ICCIET 2014), Phuket, Thailand, 17–18 July 2014.
65. Shortall, A.; Azhar, M.H.B. Forensic acquisitions of WhatsApp data on popular mobile platforms. In Proceedings of the 2015 Sixth International Conference on Emerging Security Technologies (EST), Braunschweig, Germany, 3–5 September 2015; pp. 13–17.
66. Awan, F.A. Forensic examination of social networking applications on smartphones. In Proceedings of the 2015 Conference on Information Assurance and Cyber Security (CIACS), Rawalpindi, Pakistan, 18 December 2015; pp. 36–43.
67. Aji, M.P.; Riadi, I.; Lutfhi, A. The digital forensic analysis of snapchat application using XML records. *J. Theor. Appl. Inf. Technol.* **2017**, *95*.
68. Keim, Y.; Hutchinson, S.; Shrivastava, A.; Karabiyik, U. Forensic Analysis of TikTok Alternatives on Android and iOS Devices: Byte, Dubsmash, and Triller. *Electronics* **2022**, *11*, 2972. [CrossRef]
69. Bowling, H.; Seigfried-Spellar, K.; Karabiyik, U.; Rogers, M. We are meeting on Microsoft Teams: Forensic analysis in Windows, Android, and iOS operating systems. *J. Forensic Sci.* **2023**, *68*, 434–460. [CrossRef]
70. Azab, A.; Watters, P.; Layton, R. Characterising network traffic for skype forensics. In Proceedings of the 2012 Third Cybercrime and Trustworthy Computing Workshop, Ballarat, Australia, 29–30 October 2012; pp. 19–27.
71. Karpisek, F.; Baggili, I.; Breitinger, F. WhatsApp network forensics: Decrypting and understanding the WhatsApp call signaling messages. *Digit. Investig.* **2015**, *15*, 110–118. [CrossRef]
72. Yusoff, M.N.; Dehghantanha, A.; Mahmod, R. Network Traffic Forensics on Firefox Mobile OS: Facebook, Twitter, and Telegram as Case Studies. In *Contemporary Digital Forensic Investigations of Cloud and Mobile Applications*; Elsevier: Amsterdam, The Netherlands, 2017; pp. 63–78.
73. Bhatt, A.J.; Gupta, C.; Mittal, S. Network forensics analysis of iOS social networking and messaging Apps. In Proceedings of the 2018 Eleventh International Conference on Contemporary Computing (IC3), Noida, India, 2–4 August 2018; pp. 1–6.
74. Cents, R.; Le-Khac, N.A. Towards a New Approach to Identify WhatsApp Messages. In Proceedings of the 2020 IEEE 19th International Conference on Trust, Security and Privacy in Computing and Communications (TrustCom), Guangzhou, China, 29 December–1 January 2020; pp. 1895–1902.
75. Afzal, A.; Hussain, M.; Saleem, S.; Shahzad, M.K.; Ho, A.T.; Jung, K.H. Encrypted Network Traffic Analysis of Secure Instant Messaging Application: A Case Study of Signal Messenger App. *Appl. Sci.* **2021**, *11*, 7789. [CrossRef]

76. Simon, M.; Slay, J. Recovery of skype application activity data from physical memory. In Proceedings of the 2010 International Conference on Availability, Reliability and Security, Krakow, Poland, 15–18 February 2010; pp. 283–288.

77. Chu, H.C.; Deng, D.J.; Park, J.H. Live data mining concerning social networking forensics based on a facebook session through aggregation of social data. *IEEE J. Sel. Areas Commun.* **2011**, *29*, 1368–1376. [CrossRef]

78. Chu, H.C.; Yang, S.W.; Wang, S.J.; Park, J.H. The partial digital evidence disclosure in respect to the instant messaging embedded in viber application regarding an android smart phone. In *Information Technology Convergence, Secure and Trust Computing, and Data Management*; Springer: Berlin/Heidelberg, Germany, 2012; pp. 171–178.

79. Sgaras, C.; Kechadi, M.; Le-Khac, N.A. Forensics acquisition and analysis of instant messaging and VoIP applications. In *Computational Forensics*; Springer: Berlin/Heidelberg, Germany, 2012; pp. 188–199.

80. Chu, H.C.; Lo, C.H.; Chao, H.C. The disclosure of an Android smartphone's digital footprint respecting the Instant Messaging utilizing Skype and MSN. *Electron. Commer. Res.* **2013**, *13*, 399–410. [CrossRef]

81. Zhou, F.; Yang, Y.; Ding, Z.; Sun, G. Dump and analysis of android volatile memory on wechat. In Proceedings of the 2015 IEEE International Conference on Communications (ICC), London, UK, 8–12 June 2015; pp. 7151–7156.

82. Nisioti, A.; Mylonas, A.; Katos, V.; Yoo, P.D.; Chryssanthou, A. You can run but you cannot hide from memory: Extracting IM evidence of Android apps. In Proceedings of the 2017 IEEE Symposium on Computers and Communications (ISCC), Heraklion, Crete, Greece, 3–6 July 2017; pp. 457–464.

83. Kazim, A.; Almaeeni, F.; Al Ali, S.; Iqbal, F.; Al-Hussaeni, K. Memory forensics: Recovering chat messages and encryption master key. In Proceedings of the 2019 10th International Conference on Information and Communication Systems (ICICS), Irbid, Jordan, 11–13 June 2019; pp. 58–64.

84. Riadi, I.; Sunardi, S.; Rauli, M.E. Live forensics analysis of line app on proprietary operating system. *Kinetik Game Technol. Inf. Syst. Comput. Netw. Comput. Electron. Control* **2019**, *4*, 305–314. [CrossRef]

85. Davis, M.; McInnes, B.; Ahmed, I. Forensic investigation of instant messaging services on linux OS: Discord and Slack as case studies. *Forensic Sci. Int. Digit. Investig.* **2022**, *42*, 301401. [CrossRef]

86. Kiley, M.; Dankner, S.; Rogers, M. Forensic analysis of volatile instant messaging. In *Proceedings of the IFIP International Conference on Digital Forensics*; Springer: Berlin/Heidelberg, Germany, 2008; pp. 129–138.

87. Husain, M.I.; Sridhar, R. iForensics: Forensic analysis of instant messaging on smart phones. In *Proceedings of the International Conference on Digital Forensics and Cyber Crime*; Springer: Berlin/Heidelberg, Germany, 2009; pp. 9–18.

88. Al Mutawa, N.; Al Awadhi, I.; Baggili, I.; Marrington, A. Forensic artifacts of Facebook's instant messaging service. In Proceedings of the 2011 International Conference for Internet Technology and Secured Transactions, Abu Dhabi, United Arab Emirates, 11–14 December 2011; pp. 771–776.

89. Baca, M.; Cosic, J.; Cosic, Z. Forensic analysis of social networks (case study). In Proceedings of the ITI 2013 35th International Conference on Information Technology Interfaces, Dubrovnik, Croatia, 24–27 June 2013; pp. 219–223.

90. Actoriano, B.; Riadi, I. Forensic Investigation on WhatsApp Web Using Framework Integrated Digital Forensic Investigation Framework Version 2. *Int. J. Cyber-Secur. Digit. Forensics (IJCSDF)* **2018**, *7*, 410–419.

91. Cloyd, T.; Osborn, T.; Ellingboe, B.; Glisson, W.B.; Choo, K.K.R. Browser analysis of residual facebook data. In Proceedings of the 2018 17th IEEE International Conference on Trust, Security and Privacy in Computing and Communications/12th IEEE International Conference on Big Data Science and Engineering (TrustCom/BigDataSE), New York, NY, USA, 1–3 August 2018; pp. 1440–1445.

92. Horsman, G. ACPO principles for digital evidence: Time for an update? *Forensic Sci. Int. Rep.* **2020**, *2*, 100076. [CrossRef]

93. Paligu, F.; Varol, C. Browser forensic investigations of whatsapp web utilizing indexeddb persistent storage. *Future Internet* **2020**, *12*, 184. [CrossRef]

94. Chang, M.S.; Yen, C.P. LinkedIn Social Media Forensics on Windows 10. *Int. J. Netw. Secur.* **2020**, *22*, 321–330.

95. Pandela, T.; Riadi, I. Browser forensics on web-based tiktok applications. *Int. J. Comput. Appl.* **2020**, *175*, 47–52. [CrossRef]

96. Gupta, K.; Varol, C.; Zhou, B. Digital forensic analysis of discord on google chrome. *Forensic Sci. Int. Digit. Investig.* **2023**, *44*, 301479. [CrossRef]

97. Cusack, B.; Alshaifi, S. Mining Social Networking Sites for Digital Evidence. In Proceedings of the 13th Australian Digital Forensics Conference, Perth, WA, Australia, 30 November–2 December 2015; pp. 15–21.

98. Chang, M.S. Evidence gathering of instagram on windows 10. *Int. J. Innov. Sci. Eng. Technol.* **2016**, *3*.

99. Chang, M.S.; Yen, C.P. Forensic Analysis of Social Networks Based on Instagram. *Int. J. Netw. Secur.* **2019**, *21*, 850–860.

100. Al-Duwairi, B.; Shatnawi, A.S.; Jaradat, H.; Al-Musa, A.; Al-Awadat, H. On the Digital Forensics of Social Networking Web-based Applications. In Proceedings of the 2022 10th International Symposium on Digital Forensics and Security (ISDFS), Istanbul, Turkey, 6–7 June 2022; pp. 1–6.

101. Iqbal, F.; Khalid, Z.; Marrington, A.; Shah, B.; Hung, P.C. Forensic investigation of Google Meet for memory and browser artifacts. *Forensic Sci. Int. Digit. Investig.* **2022**, *43*, 301448. [CrossRef]

102. Idowu, S.; Dominic, E.D.; Okolie, S.; Goga, N. Security vulnerabilities of skype application artifacts: A digital forensic approach. *Int. J. Appl. Inf. Syst* **2019**, *12*, 5–10.

103. Iqbal, A.; Alobaidli, H.; Almarzooqi, A.; Jones, A. LINE IM app forensic analysis. In Proceedings of the 12th International Conference on High-Capacity Optical Networks and Enabling/Emerging Technologies (HONET-ICT 2015), Islamabad, Pakistan, 21–23 December 2015.

104. Kara, İ. Digital forensic analysis of discord mobile application on android based smartphones. *Acta Infol.* **2022**, *6*, 189–198. [CrossRef]
105. Khoa, N.H.; Duy, P.T.; Do Hoang, H.; Pham, V.H. Forensic analysis of tiktok application to seek digital artifacts on android smartphone. In Proceedings of the 2020 RIVF International Conference on Computing and Communication Technologies (RIVF), Ho Chi Minh City, Vietnam, 14–15 October 2020; pp. 1–5.
106. Domingues, P.; Nogueira, R.; Francisco, J.C.; Frade, M. Post-mortem digital forensic artifacts of TikTok Android App. In Proceedings of the 15th International Conference on Availability, Reliability and Security (ARES), Virtual, 25–28 August 2020; pp. 1–42.
107. Agrawal, A.K.; Sharma, A.; Khatri, P. Digital forensic analysis of Facebook app in virtual environment. In Proceedings of the 2019 6th International Conference on Computing for Sustainable Global Development (INDIACom), New Delhi, India, 13–15 March 2019; pp. 660–664.
108. Ntonja, M.; Ashawa, M. Examining artifacts generated by setting Facebook Messenger as a default SMS application on Android: Implication for personal data privacy. *Secur. Priv.* **2020**, *3*, e128. [CrossRef]
109. Yudhana, A.; Riadi, I.; Anshori, I. Identification of Digital Evidence Facebook Messenger on Mobile Phone With National Institute of Standards Technology (Nist) Method. *J. Ilm. Kursor* **2018**, *9*. [CrossRef]
110. Pambayun, S.; Riadi, I. Investigation on instagram android-based using digital forensics research workshop framework. *Int. J. Comput. Appl.* **2020**, *175*, 15–21. [CrossRef]
111. Kumar, S.T.; Karabiyik, U. Instagram Forensic Analysis Revisited: Does anything really vanish? In Proceedings of the 2021 International Symposium on Networks, Computers and Communications (ISNCC), Dubai, United Arab Emirates, 31 October–2 November 2021; pp. 1–6.
112. Ichsan, A.N.; Riadi, I. Mobile Forensic on Android-Based IMO Messenger Services Using Digital Forensic Research Workshop (DFRWS) Method. *Int. J. Comput. Appl.* **2021**, *174*, 34–40. [CrossRef]
113. Mehrotra, T.; Mehtre, B. Forensic analysis of Wickr application on android devices. In Proceedings of the 2013 IEEE International Conference on Computational Intelligence and Computing Research, Madurai, India, 26–28 December 2013; pp. 1–6.
114. AlZahrani, A.; Wani, M.A.; Bhat, W.A. Forensic analysis of Twitch video streaming activities on Android. *J. Forensic Sci.* **2021**, *66*, 1721–1741. [CrossRef]
115. Akbal, E.; Baloglu, I.; Tuncer, T.; Dogan, S. Forensic analysis of BiP Messenger on android smartphones. *Aust. J. Forensic Sci.* **2020**, *52*, 590–609. [CrossRef]
116. Manna, F.; Agrawal, A.K. Forensic Analysis of Blue Talk (Random Chat). In *Artificial Intelligence and Communication Technologies*; Soft Computing Research Society: New Delhi, India, 2023; pp. 83–89.
117. Irawan, T.; Riadi, I. Mobile Forensic Signal Instant Messenger Services in Case of Web Phishing using National Institute of Standards and Technology Method. *Int. J. Comput. Appl.* **2022**, *184*, 30–40. [CrossRef]
118. Prayogo, A.G.; Riadi, I. Digital Forensic Signal Instant Messages Services in Case of Cyberbullying using Digital Forensic Research Workshop Method. *Int. J. Comput. Appl.* **2022**, *184*, 21–29. [CrossRef]
119. Krishnapriya, S.; Priyanka, V.; Kumar, S.S. Forensic Extraction and Analysis of Signal Application in Android Phones. In Proceedings of the 2021 International Conference on Forensics, Analytics, Big Data, Security (FABS), Bengaluru, India, 21–22 December 2021; Volume 1, pp. 1–6.
120. Agrawal, V.; Tapaswi, S. Forensic analysis of Google Allo messenger on Android platform. *Inf. Comput. Secur.* **2019**, *27*, 62–80. [CrossRef]
121. Azfar, A.; Choo, K.K.R.; Liu, L. An android social app forensics adversary model. In Proceedings of the 2016 49th Hawaii International Conference on System Sciences (HICSS), Koloa, HI, USA, 5–8 January 2016; pp. 5597–5606.
122. Lone, A.H.; Badroo, F.A.; Chudhary, K.R.; Khalique, A. Implementation of forensic analysis procedures for whatsapp and viber android applications. *Int. J. Comput. Appl.* **2015**, *128*, 26–33.
123. Dargahi, T.; Dehghantanha, A.; Conti, M. Forensics analysis of Android mobile VoIP apps. In *Contemporary Digital Forensic Investigations of Cloud and Mobile Applications*; Elsevier: Amsterdam, The Netherlands, 2017; pp. 7–20.
124. Onovakpuri, P.E. Forensics Analysis of Skype, Viber and WhatsApp Messenger on Android Platform. *Int. J. Cyber-Secur. Digit. Forensics* **2018**, *7*, 119–132. [CrossRef]
125. Rathi, K.; Karabiyik, U.; Aderibigbe, T.; Chi, H. Forensic analysis of encrypted instant messaging applications on Android. In Proceedings of the 2018 6th International Symposium on Digital Forensic and Security (ISDFS), Antalya, Turkey, 22–25 March 2018; pp. 1–6.
126. Ababneh, A.; Awwad, M.A.; Al-Saleh, M.I. IMO forensics in android and windows systems. In Proceedings of the 2017 8th International Conference on Information, Intelligence, Systems & Applications (IISA), Larnaca, Cyprus, 27–30 August 2017; pp. 1–6.
127. Salamh, F.E.; Karabiyik, U.; Rogers, M.K. Asynchronous forensic investigative approach to recover deleted data from instant messaging applications. In Proceedings of the 2020 International Symposium on Networks, Computers and Communications (ISNCC), Montreal, QC, Canada, 20–22 October 2020; pp. 1–6.
128. Vasilaras, A.; Dosis, D.; Kotsis, M.; Rizomiliotis, P. Retrieving deleted records from Telegram. *Forensic Sci. Int. Digit. Investig.* **2022**, *43*, 301447. [CrossRef]

129. Kim, G.; Park, M.; Lee, S.; Park, Y.; Lee, I.; Kim, J. A study on the decryption methods of telegram X and BBM-Enterprise databases in mobile and PC. *Forensic Sci. Int. Digit. Investig.* **2020**, *35*, 300998. [CrossRef]
130. Kim, G.; Kim, S.; Park, M.; Park, Y.; Lee, I.; Kim, J. Forensic analysis of instant messaging apps: Decrypting Wickr and private text messaging data. *Forensic Sci. Int. Digit. Investig.* **2021**, *37*, 301138. [CrossRef]
131. Choi, J.; Park, J.; Kim, H. Forensic analysis of the backup database file in KakaoTalk messenger. In Proceedings of the 2017 IEEE International Conference on Big Data and Smart Computing (BigComp), Jeju Island, Republic of Korea, 13–16 February 2017; pp. 156–161.
132. Choi, J.; Yu, J.; Hyun, S.; Kim, H. Digital forensic analysis of encrypted database files in instant messaging applications on Windows operating systems: Case study with KakaoTalk, NateOn and QQ messenger. *Digit. Investig.* **2019**, *28*, S50–S59. [CrossRef]
133. Gudipaty, L.; Jhala, K. Whatsapp forensics: Decryption of encrypted whatsapp databases on non rooted android devices. *J. Inf. Technol. Softw. Eng.* **2015**, *5*, 2.
134. Anglano, C.; Canonico, M.; Guazzone, M. Forensic analysis of the ChatSecure instant messaging application on android smartphones. *Digit. Investig.* **2016**, *19*, 44–59. [CrossRef]
135. Wu, S.; Zhang, Y.; Wang, X.; Xiong, X.; Du, L. Forensic analysis of WeChat on Android smartphones. *Digit. Investig.* **2017**, *21*, 3–10. [CrossRef]
136. Son, J.; Kim, Y.W.; Oh, D.B.; Kim, K. Forensic analysis of instant messengers: Decrypt Signal, Wickr, and Threema. *Forensic Sci. Int. Digit. Investig.* **2022**, *40*, 301347. [CrossRef]
137. Meißner, T.; Kröger, K.; Creutzburg, R. Client-side Skype forensics: An overview. *Multimed. Content Mob. Devices* **2013**, *8667*, 272–283.
138. Umar, R.; Riadi, I.; Zamroni, G.M. A comparative study of forensic tools for WhatsApp analysis using NIST measurements. *Int. J. Adv. Comput. Sci. Appl.* **2017**, *8*, 69–75. [CrossRef]
139. Riadi, I.; Sunardi, S.; Fauzan, A. Examination of digital evidence on android-based line messenger. *Int. J. Cyber-Secur. Digit. Forensics (IJCSDF)* **2018**, *7*, 337–343. [CrossRef]
140. Raji, M.; Wimmer, H.; Haddad, R.J. Analyzing data from an android smartphone while comparing between two forensic tools. In Proceedings of the SoutheastCon 2018, St. Petersburg, FL. USA, 19–22 April 2018; pp. 1–6.
141. Muflih, G.Z.; Sunardi, S.; Riadi, I.; Yudhana, A.; Azmi, H.I. Comparison of Forensic Tools on Social Media Services Using the Digital Forensic Research Workshop Method (DFRWS). *JIKO (Jurnal Inform. Dan Komputer)* **2023**, *6*. [CrossRef]
142. Anglano, C.; Canonico, M.; Guazzone, M. Forensic analysis of telegram messenger on android smartphones. *Digit. Investig.* **2017**, *23*, 31–49. [CrossRef]
143. Anglano, C. Forensic analysis of WhatsApp Messenger on Android smartphones. *Digit. Investig.* **2014**, *11*, 201–213. [CrossRef]
144. Anglano, C.; Canonico, M.; Guazzone, M. The android forensics automator (anfora): A tool for the automated forensic analysis of android applications. *Comput. Secur.* **2020**, *88*, 101650. [CrossRef]
145. Yasin, M.; Abulaish, M. DigLA—A Digsby log analysis tool to identify forensic artifacts. *Digit. Investig.* **2013**, *9*, 222–234. [CrossRef]
146. Casser, T.; Ketel, M. Developing a forensics tool for social media. In Proceedings of the 2014 ACM Southeast Regional Conference, Kennesaw, GA, USA, 28–29 March 2014; pp. 1–4.
147. Motyliński, M.; MacDermott, Á.; Iqbal, F.; Hussain, M.; Aleem, S. Digital forensic acquisition and analysis of discord applications. In Proceedings of the 2020 International Conference on Communications, Computing, Cybersecurity, and Informatics (CCCI), Sharjah, United Arab Emirates, 3–5 November 2020; pp. 1–7.
148. Barradas, D.; Brito, T.; Duarte, D.; Santos, N.; Rodrigues, L. Forensic analysis of communication records of messaging applications from physical memory. *Comput. Secur.* **2019**, *86*, 484–497. [CrossRef]
149. Fernández-Álvarez, P.; Rodríguez, R.J. Extraction and analysis of retrievable memory artifacts from Windows Telegram Desktop application. *Forensic Sci. Int. Digit. Investig.* **2022**, *40*, 301342. [CrossRef]
150. Thantilage, R.D.; Le Khac, N.A. Framework for the retrieval of social media and instant messaging evidence from volatile memory. In Proceedings of the 2019 18th IEEE International Conference on Trust, Security and Privacy in Computing and Communications/13th IEEE International Conference on Big Data Science and Engineering (TrustCom/BigDataSE), Rotorua, New Zealand, 5–8 August 2019; pp. 476–482.
151. Yan, S.; Choo, K.K.R.; Le-Khac, N.A. Signal instant messenger forensics. In *A Practical Hands-On Approach to Database Forensics*; Springer: Berlin/Heidelberg, Germany, 2022; pp. 27–92.
152. Kent, K.; Chevalier, S.; Grance, T.; Dang, H. Sp 800-86. Guide to Integrating Forensic Techniques into Incident Response. 2006. Available online: https://csrc.nist.gov/pubs/sp/800/86/final (accessed on 12 May 2023).
153. McKemmish, R. *What Is Forensic Computing?*; Australian Institute of Criminology Canberra: Canberra, Australia, 1999.
154. Baryamureeba, V.; Tushabe, F. The enhanced digital investigation process model. In Proceedings of the Digital Forensic Research Conference, Baltimore, MD, USA, 11–13 August 2004.
155. Garvey, T.; LaBerge, J.W.G. Forensic Intelligence Models: Assessment of Current Practices in the United and Internationally. Available online: https://nij.ojp.gov/library/publications/forensic-intelligence-models-assessment-current-practices-united-states-and (accessed on 12 May 2023).

156. Husain, M.I.; Baggili, I.; Sridhar, R. A simple cost-effective framework for iPhone forensic analysis. In Proceedings of the Digital Forensics and Cyber Crime: Second International ICST Conference, ICDF2C 2010, Abu Dhabi, United Arab Emirates, 4–6 October 2010; Springer: Berlin/Heidelberg, Germany, 2011; pp. 27–37.

157. Ruuhwan, R.; Riadi, I.; Prayudi, Y. Evaluation of integrated digital forensics investigation framework for the investigation of smartphones using soft system methodology. *Int. J. Electr. Comput. Eng.* **2017**, *7*, 2806–2817. [CrossRef]

158. Inoue, H.; Adelstein, F.; Joyce, R.A. Visualization in testing a volatile memory forensic tool. *Digit. Investig.* **2011**, *8*, S42–S51. [CrossRef]

159. Ghafarian, A.; Fredy, J. Investigating Instagram Privacy Through Memory Forensics. In *Proceedings of the Science and Information Conference*; Springer: Berlin/Heidelberg, Germany, 2023; pp. 1263–1273.

160. Garcia, G.L. Forensic physical memory analysis: An overview of tools and techniques. In Proceedings of the TKK T-110.5290 Seminar on Network Security, TKK, Helsinki, Finland, 11–12 October 2007; Volume 207, pp. 305–320.

161. Oberlo. Most Popular Web Browsers in 2022. Oberlo. 2022. Available online: https://www.oberlo.com/statistics/browser-market-share (accessed on 11 September 2022).

162. Sikos, L.F. Packet analysis for network forensics: A comprehensive survey. *Forensic Sci. Int. Digit. Investig.* **2020**, *32*, 200892. [CrossRef]

163. Montasari, R.; Hill, R.; Carpenter, V.; Montaseri, F. Digital forensic investigation of social media, acquisition and analysis of digital evidence. *Int. J. Strateg. Eng. (IJoSE)* **2019**, *2*, 52–60. [CrossRef]

164. Nikkel, B.J. Generalizing sources of live network evidence. *Digit. Investig.* **2005**, *2*, 193–200. [CrossRef]

165. Umrani, A.; Javed, Y.; Iftikhar, M. Network forensic analysis of Twitter application on Android OS. In Proceedings of the 2022 International Conference on Frontiers of Information Technology (FIT), Islamabad, Pakistan, Islamabad, Pakistan, 12–13 December 2022; pp. 249–254.

166. Beale, J.; Orebaugh, A.; Ramirez, G. *Wireshark & Ethereal Network Protocol Analyzer Toolkit*; Elsevier: Amsterdam, The Netherlands, 2006.

167. Sanders, C. *Practical Packet Analysis: Using Wireshark to Solve Real-World Network Problems*; No Starch Press: San Francisco, CA, USA, 2017.

168. Clarke, N.; Li, F.; Furnell, S. A novel privacy preserving user identification approach for network traffic. *Comput. Secur.* **2017**, *70*, 335–350. [CrossRef]

169. Afanasyev, M.; Kohno, T.; Ma, J.; Murphy, N.; Savage, S.; Snoeren, A.C.; Voelker, G.M. Privacy-preserving network forensics. *Commun. ACM* **2011**, *54*, 78–87. [CrossRef]

170. Al Mushcab, R.; Gladyshev, P. The significance of different backup applications in retrieving social networking forensic artifacts from Android-based mobile devices. In Proceedings of the 2015 Second International Conference on Information Security and Cyber Forensics (InfoSec), Cape Town, South Africa, 15–17 November 2015; pp. 66–71.

171. Hweidi, R.F.A.; Jazzar, M.; Eleyan, A.; Bejaoui, T. Forensics Investigation on Social Media Apps and Web Apps Messaging in Android Smartphone. In Proceedings of the 2023 International Conference on Smart Applications, Communications and Networking (SmartNets), Instanbul, Turkey, 25–27 July 2023; pp. 1–7.

172. Makate, A.; Muduva, M.; Chaudhary, N.K.; Chiwariro, R. Setting the Tone for Sound Forensic Investigations on Android-Based Social Media Platforms. *Int. J. Res. Appl. Sci. Eng. Technol.* **2023**, *11*. [CrossRef]

173. Khweiled, R.; Jazzar, M.; Eleyan, A.; Bejaoui, T. Using SQLite Structure Analysis To Retrieve Unsent Messages On WhatsApp Messaging Application. In Proceedings of the 2022 International Conference on Smart Applications, Communications and Networking (SmartNets), Palapye, Botswana, 29 November–1 December 2022; pp. 01–06.

174. Kobsa, A.; Patil, S.; Meyer, B. Privacy in instant messaging: An impression management model. *Behav. Inf. Technol.* **2012**, *31*, 355–370. [CrossRef]

175. Mistry, N.; Vora, S. Cloud and Social Media Forensics. In *Modern Forensic Tools and Devices: Trends in Criminal Investigation*; John Wiley & Sons: Hoboken, NJ, USA, 2023; pp. 41–63.

176. Horsman, G. Reconstructing streamed video content: A case study on YouTube and Facebook Live stream content in the Chrome web browser cache. *Digit. Investig.* **2018**, *26*, S30–S37. [CrossRef]

177. Al-Mousa, M.R.; Al-Zaqebah, Q.; Al-Ghanim, M.; Samara, G.; Al-Matarneh, S.; Asassfeh, M. Examining Digital Forensic Evidence for Android Applications. In Proceedings of the 2022 International Arab Conference on Information Technology (ACIT), Abu Dhabi, United Arab Emirates, 22–24 November 2022; pp. 1–8.

information

Article

Securing the Network: A Red and Blue Cybersecurity Competition Case Study

Cristian Chindrus [†] and Constantin-Florin Caruntu [*,†]

Department of Automatic Control and Applied Informatics, "Gheorghe Asachi" Technical University of Iasi, 700050 Iasi, Romania; cristian.chindrus@student.tuiasi.ro
* Correspondence: caruntuc@ac.tuiasi.ro
[†] These authors contributed equally to this work.

Abstract: In today's dynamic and evolving digital landscape, safeguarding network infrastructure against cyber threats has become a paramount concern for organizations worldwide. This paper presents a novel and practical approach to enhancing cybersecurity readiness. The competition, designed as a simulated cyber battleground, involves a Red Team emulating attackers and a Blue Team defending against their orchestrated assaults. Over two days, multiple teams engage in strategic maneuvers to breach and fortify digital defenses. The core objective of this study is to assess the efficacy of the Red and Blue cybersecurity competition in fostering real-world incident response capabilities and honing the skills of cybersecurity practitioners. This paper delves into the competition's structural framework, including the intricate network architecture and the roles of the participating teams. This study gauges the competition's impact on enhancing teamwork and incident response strategies by analyzing participant performance data and outcomes. The findings underscore the significance of immersive training experiences in cultivating proactive cybersecurity mindsets. Participants not only showcase heightened proficiency in countering cyber threats but also develop a profound understanding of attacker methodologies. Furthermore, the competition fosters an environment of continuous learning and knowledge exchange, propelling participants toward heightened cyber resilience.

Keywords: cybersecurity; Red and Blue Team; collaborative training; cybersecuritycompetitions; incident response; attack scenarios

Citation: Chindrus, C.; Caruntu, C.-F. Securing the Network: A Red and Blue Cybersecurity Competition Case Study. *Information* **2023**, *14*, 587. https://doi.org/10.3390/info14110587

Academic Editors: Jose de Vasconcelos, Hugo Barbosa and Carla Cordeiro

Received: 29 September 2023
Revised: 24 October 2023
Accepted: 25 October 2023
Published: 26 October 2023

1. Introduction

In the contemporary digital era, characterized by an increasing reliance on interconnected technology, the safeguarding of network infrastructure against a rapidly evolving spectrum of cyber threats has emerged as a critical imperative. Cybersecurity, once a niche concern, has now become a central pillar in the operations of organizations across industries [1]. The growing sophistication of malicious actors, coupled with the increasing frequency and impact of cyber incidents, has underscored the urgency for organizations to fortify their cyber defenses and equip their workforce with advanced incident response capabilities.

As organizations face these challenges, innovative approaches to cybersecurity training have gained prominence. Traditional methods, though essential, often fall short in providing the real-world, dynamic scenarios necessary to prepare cybersecurity professionals for the intricacies of modern cyber threats. In response, cybersecurity competitions have emerged as a dynamic and immersive training methodology, offering a simulated battleground where defenders and attackers engage in strategic encounters [2].

Cybersecurity encompasses strategies and measures to safeguard digital systems and information from unauthorized access and cyber threats. This field has grown significantly in response to the rising challenges. Key tactics include firewalls, encryption, strong passwords, and threat detection. The authors of [3] outline the top five current cybersecurity challenges and emphasize the importance of awareness in protecting digital environments from electronic threats. Artificial intelligence (AI) empowers cybersecurity by automating tasks, enhancing threat detection, and bolstering defenses. A systematic review of AI applications in cybersecurity can be found in [4]. It categorizes these AI use cases using a National Institute of Standards and Technology (NIST) cybersecurity framework, providing a comprehensive view of AI's potential to enhance security across various domains. Cybersecurity social networking is an evolving interdisciplinary field that tackles security issues within the realm of social networks. The research in [5] defines risk as the combination of consequences and the likelihood of occurrence, highlighting risk assessment as a critical task in the broader context of IT security. This approach encompasses physical, hardware, software, network, and human resources, integrating multiple protection levels and strategies.

This paper explores the field of cybersecurity competitions, focusing on the intriguing domain of Red and Blue Cybersecurity Competitions. Such competitions simulate adversarial scenarios, pitting Red teams, and emulating attackers, against Blue teams, tasked with defending critical digital assets. This study proposes a thorough examination of the competition's conception, design, execution, and the resulting outcomes. Through a combination of qualitative and quantitative analyses, this research endeavors to provide a holistic understanding of the competition's effectiveness in enhancing participants' defensive and offensive cybersecurity skills. Moreover, this study aspires to contribute to the broader field of cybersecurity education by extrapolating insights and lessons from the competition's structure and outcomes, potentially informing the development of more robust and impactful training paradigms in the realm of cyber defense and offense.

The authors in [6] present a comprehensive framework for competence development and assessment in hybrid cybersecurity exercises. With the rise of security threats, especially in cyber defense exercises (CDX), the framework targets the effective evaluation of diverse participant skills. It optimizes CDX to include all teams, even non-technical trainees, enhancing resource utilization and cybersecurity awareness. Covering formative assessment, team composition, objectives, and exercise flow, the framework enriches cybersecurity training methodologies. Developed through empirical research, it offers insights into diverse trainee-focused hybrid exercises. Yamin et al. [7] explore cybersecurity training by studying cyber ranges and security testbeds, emphasizing their essential role in counteracting cyber threats and crimes. It investigates two training forms: one enhancing security professionals' threat defense skills, and the other raising cybersecurity awareness among non-security professionals and the public. This study examines how specialized infrastructures like cyber ranges enable hands-on learning and scenario execution.

In [8], the authors present a holistic method for combined Red and Blue Team assessments, vital for evaluating network/system security and detecting vulnerabilities. These assessments encompass diverse operational, managerial, and technical tasks, emphasizing key principles. The paper introduces a dedicated Red and Blue Team methodology as a guide for effective security audits and penetration testing. This methodology enhances assessment robustness and cybersecurity readiness. Andreolini et al. [9] describe a novel framework for evaluating trainee performance in modern cybersecurity exercises. It includes a distributed monitoring architecture to capture trainee activity data, a directed graph-based algorithm for modeling actions, and novel scoring algorithms based on graph operations. These algorithms comprehensively assess trainee attributes like speed and precision, enabling precise progress measurement and error identification—overcoming limitations in common cyber ranges.

The primary objective of this study is to assess the efficacy of Red and Blue Cybersecurity Competitions in cultivating robust incident response capabilities and enhancing the overall cybersecurity readiness of participants. By delving into the competition's intricacies, examining participant performance data, and evaluating the impact on technical expertise and strategic thinking, this paper seeks to provide valuable insights into the potential of this innovative training paradigm.

In preceding studies, the core system [10] and system architecture [11] have been presented in individual cases. The outcomes elucidated in those analyses relate to the inaugural instance of the competition. However, in the current paper, we wish to outline the following:

- A comprehensive overview of all elements within each subsystem, providing a holistic view of the competition.
- A comparative analysis based on two editions of the competition.
- In comparison with [12], the findings highlight the continuous improvement in participants' skills and capabilities when addressing real-world incidents and challenges.
- This assessment underscores the competition's effectiveness as a practical learning platform that closely mirrors real-world scenarios and not just a presentation of cybersecurity impact as in [13].

In the following sections, we will delve into the methodology, structure, and outcomes of the Red and Blue Cybersecurity Competition. By exploring the nuances of this immersive training approach, we aim to shed light on its transformative potential in equipping cybersecurity professionals to navigate the complex and ever-evolving landscape of cyber threats.

2. Importance of Competition in Cybersecurity Training

With the evolution of cybersecurity, the concept of competition has garnered substantial recognition as an essential driver for fostering effective training methodologies. This section embarks on a comprehensive exploration of the profound significance that competition holds within the domain of cybersecurity training. By delving into its multifaceted dimensions and discerning the extensive benefits it imparts, we gain insights into how competition propels training strategies to new heights of efficacy.

Competition, when exploited within the context of cybersecurity training, assumes a multifaceted role that extends beyond its conventional connotations. At its core, competition offers an immersive and dynamic environment where individuals and teams engage in strategic maneuvers and tactical confrontations [14]. This interactive setting not only mirrors real-world scenarios but also serves as an incubator for the cultivation of essential skills and attributes.

A primary dimension of competition in cybersecurity training lies in its ability to instill a heightened sense of urgency and resourcefulness. Participants are compelled to navigate intricate challenges and adversaries, often under stringent time constraints. This pressured environment stimulates quick thinking, decision-making agility, and the ability to adapt swiftly to unforeseen circumstances—all indispensable qualities in the cybersecurity landscape, where rapid responses to emerging threats are paramount.

Moreover, competition acts for the refinement of communication, collaboration, and teamwork—attributes that are pivotal in effective cybersecurity operations. As participants engage in tactical endeavors, the interplay of diverse skill sets and perspectives fosters a dynamic exchange of ideas and strategies. This collaborative ethos mirrors the real-world synergy required among cybersecurity professionals to combat multifaceted threats [15].

Beyond its experiential advantages, competition also significantly contributes to the psychological and emotional aspects of cybersecurity training. The inherent drive to excel and outperform peers fuels a culture of continuous improvement and self-motivation. Participants cultivate a resilient mindset, where the pursuit of excellence becomes a cornerstone of their professional ethos.

2.1. The Role of Competition in Cybersecurity

Competition, a formidable force in the realm of cybersecurity training, has the power to inject dynamism and intensity into the learning process. Within this context, competition constructs an immersive arena where participants are not merely passive learners but active contenders. This environment propels individuals to harness their accumulated knowledge, technical skills, and strategic insight to overcome their opponents, effectively simulating the real-world combat between defenders and threat actors.

At its core, the essence of competition lies in its capacity to stimulate multifaceted cognitive responses. Participants are galvanized by the inherent challenge to prove their worth, fostering a state of heightened engagement and awareness. The spirit of competition serves as a forge that sparks critical thinking, innovative problem-solving, and the cultivation of an agile mindset—qualities inherently demanded by the intricate and ever-evolving cybersecurity landscape [16].

Furthermore, competition introduces an element of urgency that mirrors the time-sensitive nature of cybersecurity incidents. In this pressured environment, participants are compelled to make swift, yet calculated decisions. This experiential facet not only augments the participants' technical proficiency but also nurtures their capacity to analyze complex scenarios under time constraints—an indispensable attribute in the face of emergent cyber threats.

In essence, competition transcends the boundaries of a conventional learning paradigm, encapsulating the true spirit of cybersecurity. By creating an environment that mirrors the high-stakes struggle between defenders and adversaries, competition not only imparts technical skills but also forges a resilient and adaptable mindset. As we delve further into this paper, we unravel the various dimensions through which competition intertwines with cybersecurity training, underscoring its role as a transformative force in preparing cybersecurity professionals for the complex challenges that lie ahead.

2.2. Advantages of Competition in Cybersecurity Training

The integration of competition into the cybersecurity training presents a number of advantages that significantly augment the efficacy of the learning experience. Foremost, this approach transcends theoretical comprehension, immersing participants into authentic scenarios that mirror the intricacies of real-world cyber challenges. The act of decision-making takes on tangible consequences, compelling individuals to navigate the intricate maze of cybersecurity with a practical perspective [17]. The pressure inherent in competitive environments acts as a furnace, shaping the development of resilience and composed responses—attributes indispensable for skillful incident management.

Beyond its immersive qualities, competition lays the foundation for a culture of perpetual enhancement. The competitive ethos serves as a powerful motivator, propelling participants to remain attuned to the ever-evolving threat landscape and on top of innovative defensive stratagems. Incentivized by the drive to secure victory, participants are inherently inclined toward dynamic learning, wherein knowledge is not static but constantly refined in response to emerging challenges.

Furthermore, the collaborative fabric intrinsic to competitive frameworks encourages a rich exchange of insights. The pooling of diverse expertise becomes a hallmark of competition, as participants collaboratively decipher complex dilemmas. This knowledge-sharing paradigm not only accelerates problem-solving but also cultivates a collective intelligence that thrives on mutual support and the synergy of minds.

2.3. Examples of Competitions

These exercises emulate real-world attack scenarios, pitting offensive "Red Teams" against defensive "Blue Teams". The Red Teams employ sophisticated tactics to infiltrate systems, while the Blue Teams adeptly counteract these assaults. Such competitions underscore the importance of effective teamwork, strategic thinking, and rapid decision-making in cybersecurity defense. Examples of competitions are Locked Shields and DEFCON, which are described in what follows.

The "Locked Shields" exercise stands as a seminal Red Team (RT) versus Blue Team (BT) cybersecurity exercise, uniting member nations and partners of the Cooperative Cyber Defence Center of Excellence (CCDCOE) [18]. This training paradigm converges the collective expertise of diverse entities to navigate the intricate labyrinth of modern cyber warfare.

Within the exercise's conceptual framework, the stage is set on a fictional island nation, Berylia, located in the northern reaches of the Atlantic Ocean. Berylia grapples with a burgeoning security crisis, emblematic of contemporary cyberattacks, as orchestrated attacks target both military and civilian IT systems. This wave of cyber attacks is creating a cascading domino effect, disrupting the very fabric of Berylian governance, military operations, communication networks, water treatment facilities, and the electricity grid. Unraveling in the wake of this turmoil is a palpable surge of public unrest and protests, underscoring the tangible ramifications of cyber chaos [19].

In an innovative stride, the exercise's domain encompasses the emulation of a central bank's reserve management and financial messaging systems, marking an unprecedented inclusion. Furthermore, the integration of a 5G standalone mobile communication platform underscores a visionary facet of critical infrastructure. This strategic maneuver serves a dual purpose—it imparts cyber defenders with firsthand experience in grappling with nascent technological shifts while presenting an opportune testing ground for safeguarding forthcoming advancements.

Capture the flag (CTF) competitions constitute a cornerstone of the cybersecurity training paradigm, designed to scrutinize participants' technical prowess through a series of intellectually demanding phases [20]. Regrettably, despite a predominantly tech-savvy audience, these CTF events often fail to captivate, akin to observing diligent students tackling complex homework assignments. The unhurried cadence of these competitions, spanning entire days or even multiple days, further adds to the challenge of sustaining audience engagement [21].

In emblematic instances like DEFCON, the unfolding of competition progress is relayed to the audience in a rudimentary spreadsheet format, succinctly encapsulating each team's journey in safeguarding their networks or probing vulnerabilities [22]. Yet, beneath this seemingly mundane surface, the CTF competition conceals moments of technical ingenuity, punctuated by consequential tactical choices and intricate adversarial maneuvers. These turning points have the power to decide the winner, unraveling the intricate web of how, why, and where success was forged.

3. Red and Blue Team Training

In the rapidly evolving landscape of contemporary cybersecurity, the concept of Red and Blue Team Training has emerged as a strategic imperative in bolstering digital defenses. This section presents a comprehensive investigation into the world of Red and Blue Team Training, delving deeply into its foundational elements, operational distinctions, methodologies, and the substantial benefits it confers in elevating organizational cybersecurity readiness [23].

Red and Blue Team Training represents a dynamic paradigm in cybersecurity education and preparation. Rooted in a simulation-based approach, it mirrors real-world cyber conflict scenarios by pitting offensive "Red Teams" against defensive "Blue Teams". The Red Teams, akin to adversarial entities, orchestrate sophisticated attacks to exploit vulnerabilities, while the Blue Teams ardently safeguard digital assets by detecting, countering, and neutralizing the incursions.

This immersive training methodology transcends theoretical instruction, offering a hands-on platform where participants engage in a high-stakes, adversarial competition. Beyond technical acumen, it nurtures strategic thinking, adaptive problem-solving, and real-time decision-making in the face of dynamic threats.

In the evolving landscape of modern cybersecurity, the paradigm of Red and Blue Team Training stands as a formidable entity, and strengthens the fortifications of digital defenses. This section undertakes an extensive exploration into the far-reaching influence of Red and Blue Team Training, unraveling the complexity of its operational dynamics and showing the key factors that underpin its effectiveness [24].

At its core, Red and Blue Team Training embodies a holistic approach to cybersecurity preparedness. The Red Team, embodying the role of the aggressor, employs an arsenal of tactics mirroring real-world threat actors to infiltrate an organization's digital ecosystem. Counterbalancing this, the Blue Team emerges as the guardian, orchestrating a vigilant defense to counter and neutralize the simulated attacks launched by their adversarial counterpart [23].

Within the complex field of cybersecurity education, the adoption of Red and Blue Team Training stands as a potent avenue for nurturing skilled defenders and adept adversaries. However, this section pivots toward the multifaceted challenges that frequently impact the trajectory of effective training. It further delves into pioneering strategies devised to transcend these impediments, while concurrently scrutinizing methodologies geared toward a comprehensive evaluation of the genuine efficacy of Red and Blue Team Training initiatives [1].

Moreover, Red and Blue Team Training promotes collaboration and synergy among cybersecurity practitioners. The interplay between Red and Blue Teams cultivates a holistic understanding of attack vectors, enabling defenders to proactively fortify their defenses.

3.1. Definition of Red and Blue Teams

In the intricate struggle of cybersecurity, Red and Blue Teams emerge as the embodiment of adversaries and defenders [24]. The Red Team embodies the attacker's persona, utilizing an array of offensive tactics to breach an organization's digital fortifications. In stark contrast, the Blue Team embodies the role of guardians, orchestrating countermeasures to repel and mitigate the simulated assaults orchestrated by the Red Team [25]. This dynamic exchange sets the stage for a controlled arena fostering skill refinement, incident response augmentation, and the revelation of security weak points.

The Red Team's role as aggressors entails the execution of multifaceted attack vectors, mirroring the techniques used by actual threat actors. Their endeavors span from exploiting software vulnerabilities to social engineering, painting a vivid picture of the diverse threat landscape. In parallel, the Blue Team's tenacity is demonstrated through proactive threat detection, rapid incident containment, and the fortification of digital perimeters [26].

The synergy between these teams materializes in the form of invaluable learning opportunities. The adversarial context enables cybersecurity professionals to fine-tune their defensive strategies while evolving to predict and thwart emergent attack patterns. The combination of Red and Blue Teams, underpinned by robust training methodologies, culminates in a virtuous cycle of skill growth and organizational resilience.

In the realm of cybersecurity, a dilemma occurs, defining the distinct tactical trajectories of Red and Blue Teams. These two entities, while unified in the pursuit of bolstering digital security, adopt roles as starkly opposed as they are complementary [13]. The Red Team assumes the mantle of the adversary, venturing into the digital domain with the aim of probing, exploiting, and laying bare vulnerabilities that may otherwise remain concealed. In stark contrast, the Blue Team ascends as the vigilant guardian, entrusted with the pivotal responsibility of identifying, mitigating, and orchestrating countermeasures against the simulated threats propagated by the Red Team [26].

3.2. How Red and Blue Team Training Works

At the forefront of contemporary cybersecurity, the paradigm of Red and Blue Team Training unfolds as a carefully constructed arena, emulating the tumultuous landscapes of actual cyber attack scenarios. In this dynamic enactment, the Red Team, analogous to a framework of virtual attackers, mobilizes an array of intricate hacking techniques. Their objective resonates with that of genuine threat actors—to infiltrate and compromise an organization's digital infrastructure [27].

In a synchronous battle of defense and offense, the Blue Team stands resolute, assuming the mantle of sentinels charged with the safeguarding of the organization's digital domain. Their endeavor encompasses not only the detection of the Red Team's intricate maneuvers but also the analytical prowess to discern the motives and methodologies that underpin these attacks. Through swift and strategic action, the Blue Team endeavors to thwart the Red Team's advances, neutralizing their impact and fortifying the organization's cyber defenses.

This realm of simulation serves as an priceless pool, forging the skills and resilience of cybersecurity practitioners. The immersive experience granted by Red and Blue Team Training offers a veritable playground for participants to hone their capacities in responding adeptly to the ever-evolving spectrum of cyber threats. By navigating this virtual battlefield, participants cultivate a refined skill set, augmented by practical insights and strategic dexterity [13]. Thus, the synergy between simulated scenarios and real-world challenges engenders a robust cadre of cybersecurity professionals adept in countering the countless permutations of digital intrusion.

3.3. How Red and Blue Team Training Improves Cybersecurity Posture

In dissecting the mechanics of Red and Blue Team Training, emphasis is placed on the pivotal role of experiential learning. Participants are immersed in realistic scenarios, transcending theoretical realms to navigate authentic decision-making processes with real-world implications. This hands-on engagement cultivates resilience and composure, attributes paramount to effective incident response.

In the relentless search of cybersecurity excellence, Red and Blue Team Training emerges as a pivotal pillar. Central to this methodology is a simulated real-world scenario, wherein participants immerse themselves in the intricate dance of adversaries. The Red Team, assuming the role of aggressors, employs sophisticated tactics to breach systems, while the Blue Team, the trusted defenders, adeptly counters these incursions. This dynamic synergy fosters a comprehensive skill set encompassing proactive threat detection, rapid incident response, and strategic vulnerability mitigation [28].

The impact of Red and Blue Team Training resonates across the multidimensional landscape of cybersecurity readiness. By submerging participants in authentic adversarial contexts, the training nurtures an acute grasp of attack vectors, vulnerabilities, and defensive strategies. This experiential mode of learning empowers participants to discern nuanced signs of compromise, facilitating swift and precise countermeasures.

Moreover, Red and Blue Team Training forges enduring resilience and adaptability in cybersecurity practitioners. The competitive and ever-evolving exercises refine the participants' ability to navigate fluid threats, giving them the agility to counter complicated attacks. The collaborative spirit of this training fosters teamwork and efficient communication across diverse skill sets, underscoring the paramount importance of a united defensive front. As this exploration unfolds, subsequent sections delve deeper, unraveling the strategic intricacies of Red and Blue Team Training's orchestration in enhancing cybersecurity prowess.

3.4. Best Practices for Implementing Red and Blue Team Training

The implementation of Red and Blue Team Training necessitates a deliberate and strategic approach to amplify its transformative influence. To ensure its efficacy, a set of best practices takes center stage [8]:

- **Targeted Skill Development:** Tailoring training objectives to the unique needs and proficiency levels of participants emerges as a cornerstone. This customization not only optimizes skill augmentation but also harmonizes training outcomes with organizational cybersecurity aspirations.
- **Realistic Scenario Design:** The crafting of scenarios mirroring real-world challenges assumes paramount importance. This entails encompassing a spectrum of attack vectors, system configurations, and industry-relevant scenarios. Such fidelity to realism lays the foundation for cultivating practical and nuanced problem-solving skills.
- **Continuous Learning Cycle:** Embracing a cyclical training model that champions iterative learning constitutes an essential element. Post-exercise assessments and

structured debriefings serve as conduits for perpetuating knowledge retention and gradual enhancement over time.

- **Interdisciplinary Collaboration:** The promotion of cross-functional collaboration between Red and Blue Teams emerges as a cornerstone. This interplay mirrors the symbiosis requisite for effective cybersecurity defense. By embracing diverse perspectives, participants are fortified with a holistic outlook, nurturing multifaceted cybersecurity strategies.
- **Feedback and Evaluation:** The regular assessment of participant performance accompanied by robust feedback mechanisms assumes pivotal importance. This iterative feedback loop not only informs the fine-tuning of training methodologies but also underpins the continuous evolution of training outcomes.

3.5. Common Challenges Faced during Red and Blue Team Training

While Red and Blue Team Training offers transformative benefits in cybersecurity education as detailed in the previous section, it is imperative to acknowledge and address the potential hurdles that can hinder its optimal execution. This section undertakes a comprehensive analysis of these challenges, encompassing a spectrum of technical intricacies to logistical considerations, each warranting meticulous contemplation [29]:

1. *Resource Limitations:* The successful implementation of Red and Blue Team Training hinges on the availability of essential resources, including time, personnel, and appropriate technology. Acquiring and configuring requisite tools, establishing suitable training environments, and securing proficient trainers can present substantial obstacles.
2. *Realism and Relevance:* A cornerstone of effective training lies in crafting scenarios that authentically emulate contemporary cyber threats. Achieving the delicate equilibrium between realistic simulations and predefined training objectives is paramount to ensure that the acquired skills translate into practical proficiency.
3. *Team Dynamics and Communication:* The collaborative dynamic between Red and Blue Teams hinges upon uninterrupted communication and synchronized strategic maneuvers. Overcoming potential barriers in communication, fostering a harmonious team environment, and aligning tactical approaches require dedicated efforts.
4. *Skill Diversity:* Participants engaged in Red and Blue Team Training invariably possess diverse levels of technical insight and domain expertise. Tailoring training protocols to accommodate this spectrum of skill sets while upholding meaningful engagement and skill enhancement poses a multifaceted challenge.

3.6. Strategies for Overcoming These Challenges

In response to the multifaceted challenges inherent in Red and Blue Team Training, a strategic toolkit of innovative approaches emerges as an imperative. These solutions are designed to transcend obstacles, fostering an environment that leads to optimal training outcomes and cybersecurity readiness [30]:

1. *Adoption of Simulation Technology:* Embracing cutting-edge simulation technologies serves as a potent remedy for resource constraints. These platforms offer a cost-effective and scalable avenue to replicate intricate cyber scenarios, mitigating challenges posed by limited resources and facilitating immersive experiential learning.
2. *Customized Scenario Development:* Tailoring training scenarios to mirror an organization's unique cybersecurity landscape elevates training relevance and participant engagement. By mirroring real-world vulnerabilities and incidents, participants hone skills that directly translate into bolstered defense mechanisms.
3. *Communication Enhancement Workshops:* Integrating specialized communication workshops into training regimens can enhance interpersonal skills, facilitating seamless information exchange and collaboration between Red and Blue Teams. Effective communication is pivotal to coordinated defense maneuvers.
4. *Adoption of Progressive Learning Pathways:* Implementing a tiered training framework accommodates participants with divergent skill levels. This modular approach en-

sures inclusivity, allowing novices and experts alike to engage at their proficiency level, fostering a culture of continuous learning and skill enhancement.

In the journey to optimize the effectiveness of Red and Blue Team Training, proactively addressing challenges and devising adaptable strategies assume a pivotal role. By confronting these challenges head-on and delineating effective strategies and assessment methodologies, this paper takes significant strides in advancing our understanding of the intricate dynamics that encompass cybersecurity training. Moreover, it underscores the compelling need for a perpetually evolving paradigm in response to the ever-changing landscape of cybersecurity, ensuring the training remains at the forefront of educational excellence.

4. Red and Blue Competition for Cybersecurity Training—Case Study

Through the paradigm of a Red Team and Blue Team cybersecurity simulation, the Red Team assumes the role of an ethical hacker, strategically endeavoring to exploit vulnerabilities that have been identified by the Blue Team. This simulation embodies the concept of penetration testing, a process that involves replicating the techniques and methodologies employed by real-world attackers. This pragmatic approach signifies a departure from relying solely on theoretical capabilities and security equipment, instead anchoring the company's defense mechanisms in their actual performance when confronted with genuine threats.

The essence of red teaming lies in its capacity to provide an authentic assessment of an organization's cybersecurity incident response capabilities. By simulating genuine attack scenarios, red teaming serves as a test for an organization's preparedness to counter sophisticated cyber threats. In direct contrast, the Blue Team undertakes the role of network defenders within this simulation. Their pivotal role involves identifying and rectifying vulnerabilities, effectively learning which aspects within the organizational framework require attention and improvement. Furthermore, their engagement enhances their ability to swiftly respond to and mitigate potential breaches.

While prevention is widely acknowledged as a cornerstone of cybersecurity, this simulation underscores the equal significance of detection and remediation. These three facets together fortify an organization's overall defense capability. By fusing the proactive measures of the Blue Team with the probing initiatives of the Red Team, this simulation cultivates a holistic approach to cybersecurity that not only safeguards against potential attacks but also bolsters the organization's capacity to effectively counteract them.

4.1. The Architecture of Red and Blue Competition

The network architecture designed for such a scenario initially appears simplistic, as illustrated in the diagram below (Figure 1). It necessitates the deployment of a router, a core system, and a series of subnets, corresponding in number to the participating teams. These subnets are intended to house vulnerable systems that demand protection through the identification and resolution of security issues. Moreover, these virtual machines (VMs) are employed to launch attacks on opposing teams, aimed at flag identification. In our specific instance, there exist six VMs, each endowed with distinct vulnerabilities.

A notable challenge posed by this architecture pertains to the multitude of rules imperative for the configuration of the router. The initial set of regulations seeks to proscribe direct entry to the VMs owned by rival teams. Access to these systems is exclusively sanctioned within the boundaries of the originating team's designated subnet. With the competition segmented into three distinct phases, each phase presenting two available VMs, new sets of rules are needed. These subsequent regulations function to constrain and obstruct access to the VMs during each competition phase.

In every stage of the competition, a grace period is afforded, granting teams the opportunity to familiarize themselves with their assigned systems. However, during this interval, access to the adversarial teams' VMs is prohibited. Subsequently, another set of three rules is implemented, governing the interaction between any two teams for each given time period.

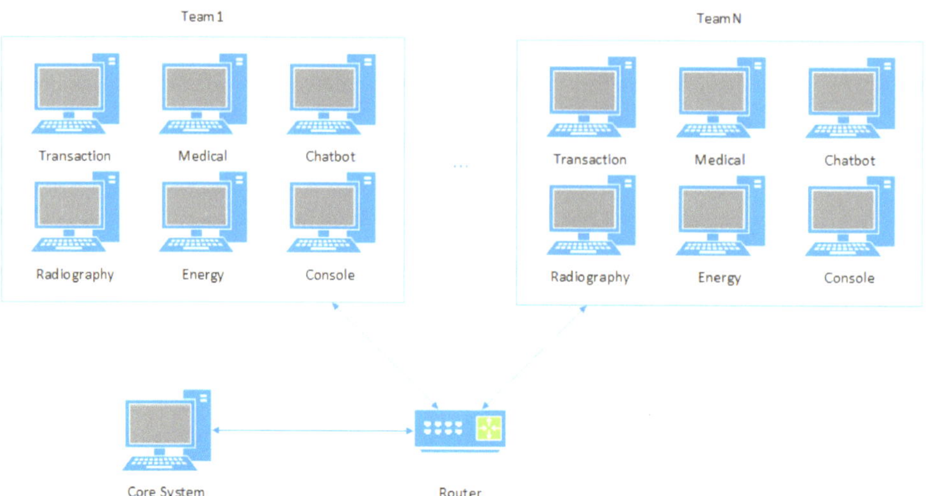

Figure 1. Network's architecture.

A selection of six VMs was chosen to cover a wide range of vulnerabilities and facilitate broad participation in this competition. It was determined that effectively addressing the tasks required between two and four participants for each of the two VMs. Additionally, the infrastructure of the cyber range dictated that there should be between 20 and 25 participating teams, introducing a new constraint regarding the number of vulnerable VMs. To resolve as many vulnerabilities identified by the Blue Team as possible and enable the Red Team to automate attacks, it was decided to progressively unlock challenges over the course of the competition's three phases.

An additional stipulation imposed for the fair conduct of the competition mandates that teams exclusively access the VM corresponding to their assigned mission. For example, a team associated with VM1 can only exploit vulnerabilities intrinsic to VM1, which is linked to the opposing team's objectives. This requirement translates into the establishment of six rules, corresponding to the number of missions, for every connection between two teams.

Virtual machines are configured and deployed through the utilization of Ansible scripts, which offer the flexibility to delineate essential hardware prerequisites and other pertinent parameters. It is advised that VMs adhere to the recommended hardware specifications encompassing two central processing units (CPUs), four gigabytes of random access memory (RAM), and a 40-gigabyte hard disk capacity. Conversely, the core system necessitates a more robust hardware configuration, mandating a minimum of 16 CPUs, 64 gigabytes of RAM, and a hard disk capacity of 100 gigabytes. Notably, the implementation of this framework does not entail the need for specialized hardware equipment. The only requisites involve the employment of servers that align with the stipulated hardware prerequisites, ensuring an optimal and seamless execution of the system.

To further challenge the detection capabilities of both the opposing teams and the core system, a mechanism is implemented whereby all traffic visible within a team's designated subnet emanates from a singular IP address. This IP address corresponds to the default gateway aligned with each network segment. The obscuring of IPs across subnets is realized through the execution of network address translation (NAT) for each source IP.

The culmination of these regulations entails an intricate web of rules, necessitating multiplication to accommodate the number of participating teams. This multiplication concludes in a substantial volume of rules, an extensive collection that mandates real-time management during the competition's runtime.

4.2. Vulnerabilities Description

The cybersecurity competition features a collection of six distinct virtual machines, each engineered to incorporate a diverse range of vulnerabilities. These vulnerabilities have been intentionally incorporated to rigorously evaluate the incident response proficiency of the participating individuals. Throughout the competition's progression, a strategic approach was adopted, revealing sets of two virtual machines during each sequential phase. This methodical revealing of VMs ensured a controlled and incremental escalation of challenge complexity, allowing participants to gradually adapt to evolving scenarios. The distribution of vulnerabilities across these virtual machines enabled the evaluation of participants' adeptness in identifying and mitigating a spectrum of cyber threats. This systematic structure facilitated a comprehensive assessment of the contestants' capabilities, contributing to an enhanced understanding of their preparedness in the dynamic realm of cybersecurity.

4.2.1. First Phase

In the first phase, participants were provided with a set of VMs characterized by a low level of complexity. This strategic approach aimed at facilitating the accommodation of participants to the unique competition format. By providing VMs with relatively manageable challenges, participants were given the opportunity to familiarize themselves with the new competition framework.

The initial virtual machine, referred to as "Transaction", functions to replicate transactional processes within multiple blockchain wallets. This simulation deliberately incorporates a series of vulnerabilities inspired by the intricacies of cryptocurrency wallet operations. Notably, this virtual machine presents a spectrum of at least five distinct methods for exploitation, encompassing a susceptible API and a collection of misconfigurations inherent in the application's developmental phase.

Subsequently, the second virtual machine, denominated as "Medical", emulates the online platform of a medical clinic. Termed "Medical", this virtual environment introduces an array of vulnerabilities, encompassing local file inclusion (LFI), remote code execution (RCE), SQL injection, and JSON web token (JWT) attacks. Additionally, the presence of diverse authentication token issues adds complexity to this virtual realm, effectively challenging participants' capacities for effective incident response.

This comprehensive scenario serves as a rigorous testing ground, probing participants' adeptness in identifying and mitigating intricate cybersecurity threats. The virtual machines, Transaction and Medical, mirror real-world situations, thereby furnishing participants with an opportunity to hone their technical skills, tactical decision-making, and their ability to navigate multifaceted security vulnerabilities. Such experiential learning not only enhances participants' cybersecurity readiness but also reinforces their understanding of the evolving threat landscape.

4.2.2. Second Phase

In the context of the second phase, the augmentation of the scenario involved the preparation of two additional virtual machines to further challenge participants' cybersecurity prowess.

The first of these virtual machines, called "Chatbot", emulates a functional chat service, as suggested by its nomenclature. The VM was meticulously designed with a curated set of predefined questions, accompanied by a series of code development intricacies deliberately introduced into its framework. Within this construct, three pivotal vulnerabilities were strategically embedded: SQL Injection, Command Injection, and Directory Traversal. The successful exploitation of these vulnerabilities demanded the acquisition of unauthorized access to a specific user account, thereby facilitating the retrieval of decryption keys and consequently granting access to concealed information of utmost importance.

Concurrently, the second supplementary virtual machine, emblematic of an X-ray clinic's web page, emerged as a complex challenge. This virtual environment catered to functions such as appointment scheduling and provision of analysis data. Within its construct, two distinct web vulnerabilities, namely XML External Entity (XXE) and Local File Inclusion, were meticulously incorporated. The LFI vulnerability enabled the manipulation of appointment-related files without undergoing stringent validation, consequently allowing unauthorized access to the database directly through the browser. Furthermore, an inadvertent active FTP server and a designated port-operating server were discovered within this virtual machine, unintentionally expanding its attack surface. This port served as a conduit through which physicians could access their schedules, thus inadvertently introducing an additional layer of vulnerability.

This augmentation in the scenario not only fostered an intensified testing ground for participants but also served as a comprehensive exercise in identifying, exploiting, and mitigating multifaceted vulnerabilities. This experiential learning platform, characterized by intricately engineered virtual machines, served to enhance participants' tactical skills, strategic decision-making, and overall preparedness in the realm of cybersecurity.

4.2.3. Third Phase

In the final phase of the competition, the landscape evolved to encompass a distinct industrial focus, where two virtual machines were introduced to emulate intricate scenarios reflective of the industrial sector's cybersecurity challenges.

The first of these VMs, aptly named "Energy", entailed the simulation of a Supervisory Control and Data Acquisition (SCADA) communication protocol governing interactions among multiple power stations. Each individual VM in this configuration held four distinct pieces of information pertaining to the respective power station. Crucially, one specific piece of data, concerning nuclear fuel—a critical and sensitive component—was intended to remain strictly inaccessible. However, vulnerabilities stemming from the developmental intricacies of the specialized protocol introduced misconfigurations, thereby potentially exposing confidential nuclear fuel data. Notably, a maintenance window further heightened the vulnerability, temporarily rendering the entire plant susceptible to potential breaches.

The second VM in this phase encompassed an administration console emblematic of an industrial power plant. It resembled a Linux terminal in terms of its interface, albeit tailored to execute functions pertinent to the industrial realm. Unfortunately, the control software manufacturer's oversights became evident within this construct. Notable vulnerabilities included the inadvertent exposure of credential encryption mechanisms and inadequately conducted checks on certain instructions. These oversights inadvertently furnished potential attackers with exploitable entry points, enabling them to manipulate the encryption process and execute commands beyond the confines of standard user privileges.

This phase of the competition thus presented participants with intricate industrial-based scenarios, spotlighting the critical importance of safeguarding sensitive industrial systems against potential threats. By navigating these intricate challenges, participants honed their ability to discern vulnerabilities, execute precise incident responses, and fortify the digital defense mechanisms that underpin industrial operations.

4.3. Core System Structure for Red and Blue Competition

The Red and Blue mission incorporates an infrastructure comprising a core system and a series of network segments, the count of which corresponds to the number of participating teams. This intricate setup is responsible for scrutinizing the services hosted on each team's virtual machines, validating submitted flags, and allocating points accordingly. Each distinct segment is exclusively designated for a particular team and encompasses a cluster of VMs equipped with diverse vulnerable services, totaling six such segments. The interconnection of these segments is facilitated by a router, which enforces a set of rules governing inter-team permissions. These rules include restrictions such as permitting solely direct access to a team's own network and implementing network address translation to obscure the actual IPs of both the adversary teams and the core system.

Central to the proposed scenario is the core system, functioning as the orchestrator of this training exercise (Figure 2). This system is structured around three discrete yet interdependent components: GenerateThings (GT), ServicesMonitor (SM), and ValidateFlags (VF). All these modules are governed by a configuration file dictating start and end dates, as the exercise may span multiple days. Notably, the core system possesses the capacity to discern days, team identities, mission designations, team IPs, and the epoch's duration—the period when flags undergo modification, among other parameters.

This intricate setup forms the backbone of the training exercise, enabling participants to engage in real-world simulations of cyber scenarios, fostering hands-on experience, and enhancing their incident response, threat detection, and defensive capabilities.

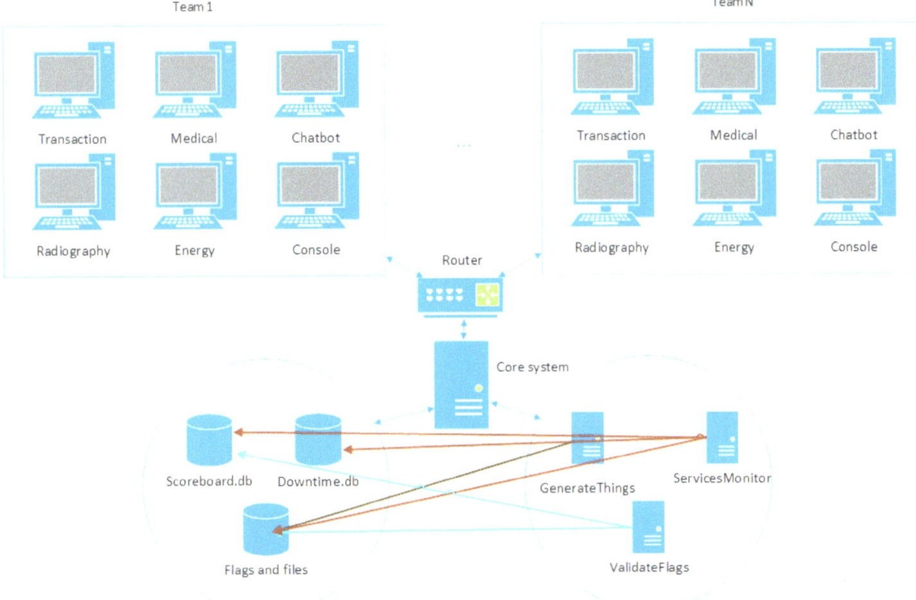

Figure 2. Core system architecture.

4.3.1. Module I—GenerateThings

The core module, known as GenerateThings, serves as the central hub responsible for producing an array of crucial data components, including flags, usernames, login credentials, and decryption keys. These elements are meticulously tailored to each distinct mission and team, rendering them unique in nature. GT's operations are meticulously synchronized with the temporal rhythm of epochs, delineated by predetermined time intervals. The generated data are systematically organized within local storage, arranged through a designated folder system characterized by explicit nomenclature. All information created by this module will be unique for each team, both in the initial generation and in epoch regeneration.

The main steps executed by the GT module are as follows (Figure 3):

- **getConfig():** Extracting information regarding the scenario's operation mode (e.g., number of missions, epoch duration, defensive time intervals, IP addresses of missions) from the configuration file config.txt;
- **generate():** Creating files/information specific to each mission;
- **sendData():** Transmitting files/information to each virtual machine;
- **saveHistory():** The generated information is saved in the storage area of the core system.

Moreover, GT undertakes the task of facilitating the operational efficiency of the ValidateFlags component. In pursuit of this objective, flags are duplicated into a separate file, securely preserved within a predefined directory path. The architecture of these folders is deliberately engineered to offer intuitive and user-friendly access to the diverse information generated within each epoch. This meticulous structuring serves to expedite debugging processes, particularly in scenarios demanding unanticipated interventions.

Concurrently, GT assumes a key function in updating mission-specific flags and associated information, all orchestrated according to the temporal cadence established by the epoch's duration. These updates are methodically propagated through a standardized user profile omnipresent across all virtual machines. This user profile equally serves as the conduit for Secure Shell (SSH) connections, instrumental in transferring files to designated mission locations. Subsequently, these files are endowed with the requisite privileges, facilitating seamless integration into the VMs' operational ecosystem.

A key intrinsic facet of the GT pertains to its rigorous validation of flag submissions. In instances where submissions fail to meet the required criteria, GT initiates an automated retry protocol. Transmission attempts are recurrently reinitiated at one-minute intervals, persisting for a maximum of three endeavors. This robust error management mechanism ensures that critical data are transmitted securely, enhancing the reliability and effectiveness of the overall system.

4.3.2. Module II—ServicesMonitor

The ServicesMonitor module assumes a role in overseeing the vigilant surveillance of services specific to each mission. It executes a comprehensive array of availability assessments, encompassing four distinct categories: FailWrite (FW), FailConnect (FC), FailRead (FR), and FailFunctional (FF). FW signifies the incapacity to establish an SSH connection with the designated machine, a difficult situation attributed to potential SSH service anomalies, connection permissions, or even the virtual machine's shutdown status. FC, on the other hand, designates the inability to establish a connection between the monitoring system and the designated application port.

Should the ServicesMonitor encounter an inability to legitimately acquire mission-specific data, denoted as the "flag", the issue is categorized as FR. The culmination of its evaluation entails an intricate and comprehensive examination of the service's functionalities. This assessment, denoting FF, encompasses diverse evaluations such as application registration, login procedures, or the accessibility of specific web pages. A failed outcome in any of these assessments results in the classification of FF.

The steps executed by the Validate Flags module are as follows (Figure 3):

- **getConfig():** Extracting information regarding the scenario's operation mode (e.g., number of missions, epoch duration, defensive time intervals, IP addresses of missions) from the configuration file config.txt;
- **FChecks():** Verification of service availability for each service. These checks include: FW, FC, FR, FF;
- **checkAlive():** Verification in case a service changes its status (from active to inactive or vice versa) and recording this change in a temporary list;
- **deployThreads():** Instantiation of a number of threads equal to the number of teams and loading them with the initial set of checks;
- **threads():**
  1. **updateDowntime():** Continuous calculation of the availability score and its update in the corresponding database (downtime.db);
  2. **resetTmpScore():** Resetting the temporary score (closely related to step three) in case a service changes its status;
- **setServiceStatus():** Changing the status of services that have changed in the databases responsible for displaying information on the scoreboard (scoreboard.db);
- **logging():** Saving the information provided by service checks in corresponding files in the storage area.

The data found by the ServicesMonitor are methodically archived within a dedicated database, supplemented by the duration of service unavailability. This temporal metric holds substantial importance as a contributory factor to team scoring, albeit in a detrimental manner. Concomitantly, these instances of service downtime are logged in a separate database, carefully tailored for individual teams and their corresponding missions. This systematic segregation is imperative to authenticate the precision of the ultimate availability calculation. This calculation, computed exponentially across the total exercise duration, is subsequently rendered as a percentage, encapsulating the comprehensive assessment of service viability.

4.3.3. Module III—ValidateFlags

The final constituent module within the core system framework is the ValidateFlags module. Its primary function encompasses the validation of flags submitted by each participating team. This pivotal module assumes the responsibility of cross-referencing the transmitted flag with the corresponding entry within the internal database, located in the previously indicated destination. Furthermore, the VF module is tasked with conducting a dual assessment: first, it scrutinizes whether the information dispatched to the module deviates from the validating team's generated value; second, it evaluates the currency of the information in consideration of potential epoch transitions.

The steps executed by the VF module are as follows (Figure 3):

- **getConfig()**: Extracting information regarding the scenario's operation mode (e.g., number of missions, epoch duration, defensive time intervals, IP addresses of missions) from the configuration file config.txt;
- **submitFlag()**: Event triggered when the module receives a flag validation request from a team;
- **saveHistory()**: Saving the request made by the team in the storage area of the core system;
- **changeOff&Def()**: Updating the offensive and defensive status for both the attacking and defending teams;
- **checks()**: A series of verifications to validate a flag. These checks include:
  1. **tooManyPairs()**: The maximum number of flags that can be submitted for validation to the core system cannot exceed the total number of teams minus one;
  2. **expired()**: Flags fall into the "expired" category if they are submitted in an epoch different from the one in which they were generated;
  3. **alreadySubmitted()**: Flags are categorized as "alreadySubmitted" if a team attempts to validate the same valid flag for the second time;
  4. **ownToken()**: Flags fall into this category if the token submitted belongs to the same team attempting validation; in such cases, the core system does not award points for validating one's own flags;
  5. **invalid()**: Flags that do not fit into any of the above categories undergo a one-to-one comparison with the valid flag stored. If the comparison results in a negative match, the flag falls into the "invalid" category, and no points are awarded. The same negative result is generated if the submitted flag does not adhere to the expected format;
  6. **valid()**: In contrast to the previous comparison, if the comparison result is positive for both flags, the submitted flag is considered valid, and the team is awarded the corresponding points.
- **getPoints()**: Calculating the score to be awarded to the team that successfully submits a valid flag based on the positions of the two teams in the rankings (the attacking team and the defending team);
- **insertFlag()**: Inserting the valid flag into the storage area as a valid request made by the team;
- **updateUptime()**: Updating the availability score for each team individually and the overall availability score (uptime) on the scoreboard.

For each accurately entered flag, a participant receives a quantified allocation of points. This point attribution hinges on a logical algorithm: if the attacking team surpasses the attacked team in the ranking, the scoring player secures points equivalent to the ranking differential. Conversely, if the attacked team holds a superior position, the scoring participant obtains a singular point.

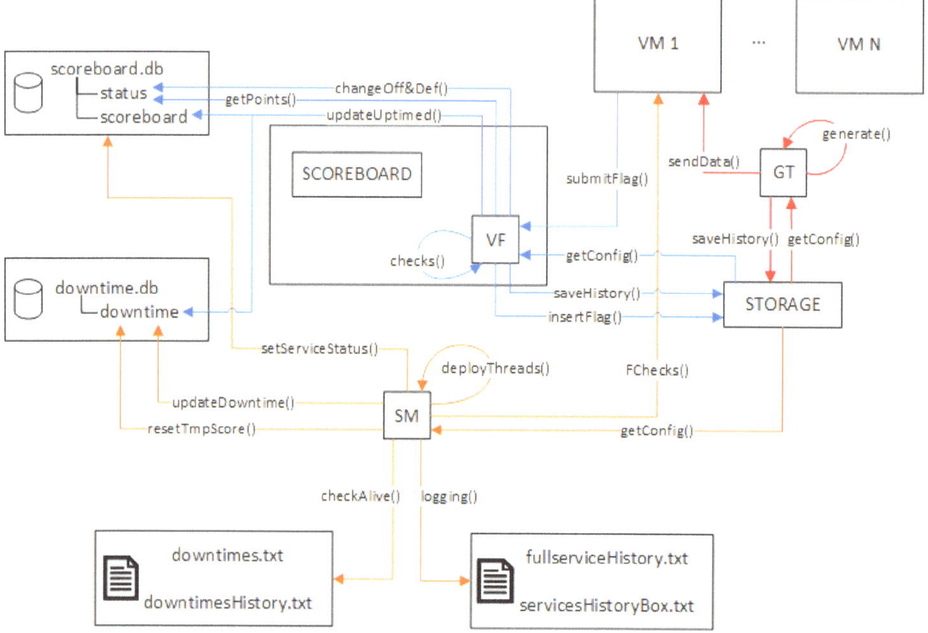

Figure 3. Core system implementation.

Beyond its fundamental flag validation role, the VF module is endowed with supplementary utility. It can be effectively leveraged to establish an intuitive graphical interface, tailored for real-time score monitoring and service availability oversight. Additionally, the module's capabilities extend to the monitoring of historical performance, extending its purview to encompass the tracking of the latest six epochs. This multifunctional attribute amplifies the versatility and comprehensive utility of the ValidateFlags module within the context of the overarching cybersecurity competition infrastructure.

Each of the aforementioned modules has incorporated a feature known as *Panic_mode*. This function serves a crucial role in managing unforeseen contingencies that may arise, such as the sudden shutdown or reboot of any of the modules during the course of the exercise. The *Panic_mode* function operates by assessing the status of the module at the instance of a shutdown, closely reviewing the tasks that had been successfully executed up to that juncture. Subsequently, it resumes operation from the precise point at which the *Panic_mode* function was invoked.

This *Panic_mode* mechanism serves as a strategic safeguard, ensuring the robustness and resilience of the system architecture in the face of unexpected disruptions. By effectively preserving the progress made prior to the shutdown event, the *Panic_mode* function contributes to the continuity and stability of the exercise, minimizing potential downtime and optimizing the overall training experience.

5. Illustrative Results

The Red and Blue competition entailed the collaboration of teams composed of six persons, resulting in a mixed and diverse community of expertise. Taking place over two days, the competition encompassed a three-phase sequence, each revealing novel challenges that progressively evolved in complexity, as described in Section 4.2. Exceeding initial projections, the competition's outcomes were remarkable, primarily attributed to the enthusiastic reception of participants toward the novel approach integrated into the competition.

The ValidateFlags module can also be leveraged to develop a graphical user interface for real-time monitoring of scores and service availability, as illustrated in Figure 4. This interface enables users to track the status of the most recent six epochs. In Figure 4, areas highlighted in red indicate the epoch during which a flag was successfully obtained from the opposing team. The rightmost box signifies the most recent epoch, while the box preceding it represents the state two epochs ago. Conversely, blue markings indicate the last two epochs in which a flag was captured by the respective team. This graphical representation offers an at-a-glance view of flag acquisition trends and team performance over time.

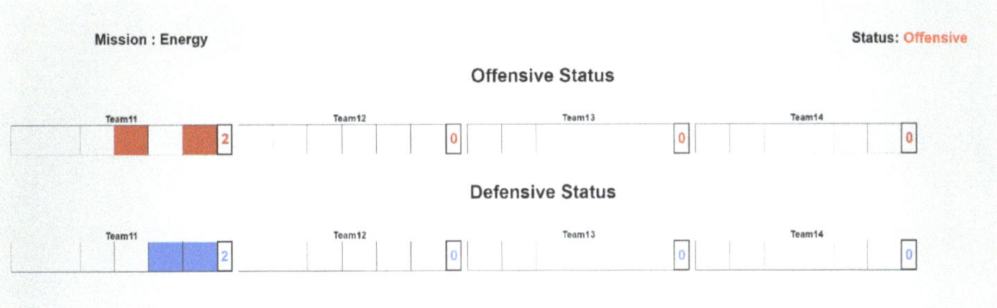

Figure 4. Last six epochs status.

A team's final score, as presented in the ranking provided in Figure 5, is determined by the following formula:

$$score = (score_{offensive} + score_{defensive}) \cdot uptime, \tag{1}$$

Here, the offensive score represents the points a team earns by successfully capturing flags, while the defensive score corresponds to the total number of flags that remain unobtained by opposing teams in a given epoch.

To calculate the total availability points $total_{AP}$, which represent the maximum achievable availability for a team throughout the exercise, the following equation is used:

$$total_{AP} = 3600 \cdot n_{missions} \cdot n_{hours/day} \cdot n_{days}, \tag{2}$$

where

- $n_{missions}$ is the total number of missions;
- $n_{hours/day}$ is the number of hours played each day;
- n_{days} is the total number of days allocated for the exercise.

Each mission has its own downtime ($downtime_{mission}$), and the summation of downtime for all missions results in

$$sum_{downtime} = \sum_{i=0}^{n_{missions}} downtime_{mission}[i]. \tag{3}$$

Using Equations (2) and (3), one can determine the overall period of availability, expressed as a percentage:

$$uptime = \frac{total_{AP} - sum_{downtime}}{total_{AP}} \cdot 100. \tag{4}$$

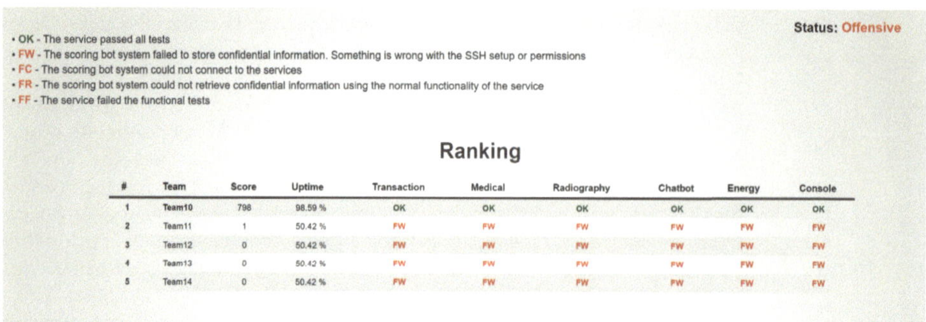

Figure 5. Ranking status.

The results of the comparison between the two completed Red and Blue cybersecurity competitions reveal interesting trends and improvements in various aspects of the participants' performance.

In the inaugural competition, involving a total of 20 participating teams, a discernible average skill enhancement of approximately 75% was noted through a self-assessment metric. This notable improvement underscores the competition's efficacy in fostering a steep learning curve among participants. Moreover, a progressive decrease in the average incident response time was observed as the competition advanced, illustrating heightened agility and seamless coordination among the participating teams.

In the subsequent iteration of the competition, which encompassed 25 participating teams, the trends displayed an even more encouraging trajectory. The average enhancement in skills experienced a notable uptick, reaching 85%. This elevation underscores the sustained efficacy of the competition in cultivating and advancing participants' proficiencies in the cybersecurity domain.

An analysis of participants' self-assessment regarding skill enhancement, presented in Table 1, conducted before and after the competition, unveiled substantial advancements. Initially, in the pre-competition survey, a mere 40% of the participants self-identified as possessing advanced skills. However, following their engagement in the competition, this metric notably surged to an impressive 85%. These findings imply that the practical experience acquired throughout the competition played a pivotal role in bolstering participants' assurance and proficiency in the realm of cybersecurity practices.

Table 1. Self-assessment of skill enhancement.

Skill Level	Before Competition (%)	After Competition (%)
Novice	25	5
Intermediate	35	10
Advanced	40	85

Table 2 illustrates an analysis of vulnerability exploitation rates across both iterations of the competition highlights the evolving proficiency of the participants. In the initial competition, only 30% of the vulnerabilities identified were effectively exploited by the teams. Remarkably, this rate surged to 65% in the subsequent competition, indicating a heightened grasp of attack vectors and techniques among the participants. This observed trend points toward a significant enhancement in the participants' ability to strategically exploit identified vulnerabilities.

Table 2. Vulnerability exploitation rates.

Competition	Identified Vulnerabilities	Exploited Vulnerabilities (%)
First	50	30
Second	60	65

The influence of team collaboration on competition performance is clearly visible from the collected data (Table 3). In the inaugural competition, teams that enthusiastically embraced cross-functional collaboration between Red and Blue Teams exhibited an average performance superiority of 45% over their counterparts. Notably, this pattern persisted in the subsequent competition, reiterating the crucial role of collaborative strategies in fostering adept cybersecurity defense. The consistent positive correlation between collaboration and enhanced performance underscores the importance of teamwork and knowledge exchange in the context of cybersecurity competitions.

Table 3. Impact of team collaboration on performance.

Collaboration Level	Performance Improvement (%)
Low	0
Moderate	25
High	45

Table 4 presents an interesting pattern surfaced when analyzing the detection-to-exploitation ratios in both conducted competitions. During the inaugural competition, the ratio stood at approximately 3:1, elucidating that teams exhibited a higher proficiency in identifying vulnerabilities compared to exploiting them. However, this dynamic evolved in the subsequent competition, as the ratio shifted to 1:1, signifying that teams had refined their offensive skills. This transition highlighted their achievement of a smooth balance between the capacities of vulnerability detection and exploitation, underscoring the evolution of participants' offensive strategies and technical skills.

Table 4. Detection vs. exploitation ratios.

Competition	Detection: Exploitation Ratio
First	3:1
Second	1:1

Analysis of post-competition surveys revealed a notable increase in the confidence of the participants, shown in Table 5. Initially, in the first competition, only 50% of the participants expressed a strong assurance in their capacity to effectively manage real-world cyber threats. However, following the culmination of the second competition, this figure experienced a remarkable escalation to 85%. This substantial increase underscores the profound impact of hands-on engagement within the competition, accentuating how practical exposure contributes to boosting participants' confidence in their ability to address complex cybersecurity challenges.

Table 5. Post-competition confidence.

Confidence Level	After First Competition (%)	After Second Competition (%)
Low	30	10
Moderate	20	5
High	50	85

The performance of the core system is graphically depicted in Figure 6, where measurements were recorded at hourly intervals to approximate the system's ability to handle requests per second. Notably, due to the distinctive nature of this Red and Blue competition compared to the traditional Red vs. Blue approach, a discernible trend emerges. On the first day of the competition, the system's request handling capacity was comparatively lower. However, as participants grew accustomed to this innovative approach, their responsiveness increased significantly on the second day, peaking at a remarkable 49,834 requests per second.

Furthermore, Figure 6 also highlights that, toward the end of the exercise, a substantial volume of requests continued to be processed. This sustained interest from participating teams underscores the appeal and effectiveness of the proposed competition strategy. It is notable that the core system's architecture has been meticulously designed to leverage multi-threading, a critical factor contributing to the optimization of processing time. This graph primarily represents the requests directed to the ValidateFlags module for flag validation. Simultaneously, ServicesMonitor and GenerateThings services operated in parallel, placing an additional workload on the core system.

In the second edition of the competition, there is a notable increase in the overall volume of requests, surpassing the figures recorded in the first edition. A new peak of 57,429 requests per second is observed, indicating the growing popularity and participation in this unique cybersecurity competition model.

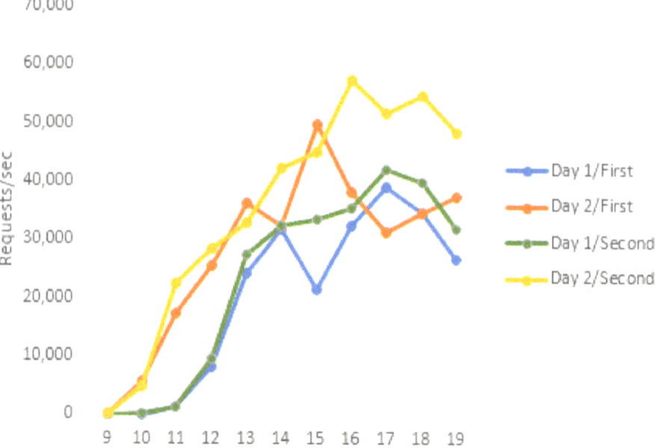

Figure 6. Core system performance.

To enhance the clarity of the results depicted in Figure 6, we performed additional calculations using the total daily counts from Table 6. These measurements represent the number of requests recorded at specific hours. As a result, it is possible for certain values to be lower than the previous measurements, depending on the timing of the data recording. This variability arises from the specific moments at which these data points were logged. It is evident that, in the second edition, there is an increase in the number of requests for each day.

Table 6. Total requests/day.

Edition	Day	Number of Requests
One	1	219,664
One	2	308,836
Two	1	253,822
Two	2	389,166

Taken together, the outcomes of these two competitions distinctly underscore a consistent and positive progression in participants' proficiencies, collaborative dynamics, and adeptness in incident response. This outcome robustly underscores the efficacy of the

Red and Blue cybersecurity competition framework as a model for cultivating a vibrant and interactive learning environment. The documented trends affirm that this model actively stimulates skill refinement and teamwork while improving participants' abilities to skillfully manage cyber incidents.

6. Discussion

An analysis of the compiled statistical data, following the execution of two iterations of the competition, revealed a consistent trend—all participants demonstrated visible enhancements in their knowledge and competence regarding incident response throughout the duration of the competition. This observation underscores the efficacy of the Red and Blue Teams competition in fostering learning and the cultivation of skillsets among the participants.

The participants' enthusiasm for the novel competition format considerably contributed to the favorable outcomes. This open embrace facilitated active engagement with the presented challenges, thereby enabling the augmentation of their comprehension of cybersecurity concepts and the refinement of their incident response proficiencies. By offering a dynamic and invigorating setting, the competition structure facilitated hands-on skill acquisition and the application of theoretical insights to authentic real-world scenarios.

We have presented in detail the structure of the main components that make such a competition possible, namely core system and system architecture. The tables presented in the previous section show how this new competition improves the competences of the participants. Figure 6 also illustrates the performance that the core system can achieve, demonstrating that the created infrastructure can be easily scaled.

For the first competition, the impact of collaboration on performance enhancement was particularly remarkable. Teams that actively engaged in higher levels of collaborative efforts showcased a more pronounced improvement in their performance metrics. This emphasizes the pivotal role of teamwork and the exchange of knowledge within the framework of such competitive scenarios.

The ratio of vulnerability detection to exploitation exhibited a favorable trend. Teams demonstrated the capacity to identify vulnerabilities at a rate surpassing the adversaries' ability to exploit them promptly, highlighting the successful implementation of robust defensive strategies.

Notably, participants' post-competition confidence level experienced a substantial elevation, measuring at an impressive 60%. This outcome signifies a significant boost in participants' self-assurance in their acquired skills as a direct consequence of their involvement in the competition.

In the second iteration of the competition, the incident response time exhibited further refinement, indicating a heightened state of readiness and improved decision-making capabilities among the teams. The continued significance of collaboration was evident, as teams showcased varying degrees of progress directly correlated with their collaborative endeavors.

Consistency was observed in the detection-to-exploitation ratio across the competitions. This consistency highlights participants' adeptness in responding promptly to identified vulnerabilities, thereby minimizing potential risks.

Remarkably, post-competition confidence levels registered a substantial increase, reaching an impressive 75%. This elevation reinforces the competition's positive influence on the participants' self-assurance in their cybersecurity aptitude.

Through the intense challenges and strategic gameplay of the competition, participants not only enhance their technical skills but also cultivate qualities crucial in cybersecurity professionals: critical thinking, adaptability, and teamwork. The simulation of actual attack scenarios provides a controlled environment to learn and evolve, enabling participants to grasp the intricacies of cyber threats and mitigation strategies.

Moreover, the competitive atmosphere fosters an eagerness to stay updated with the latest threat trends, thereby reinforcing a culture of continuous improvement. As participants navigate through simulated breaches and fortify defenses, they emerge with a deeper understanding of the asymmetrical nature of cybersecurity and the need for holistic approaches.

The Red and Blue cybersecurity competition encapsulates the essence of collaboration and rivalry, uniting diverse skill sets toward a common goal of fortifying digital landscapes. This immersive experience equips participants with practical insights and hones their ability to orchestrate a proactive defense. Ultimately, the competition not only trains the next generation of cybersecurity experts but also underscores the critical importance of constant vigilance, collaboration, and innovation in securing networks against the relentless tide of cyber threats.

7. Conclusions

In conclusion, the conducted Red and Blue Cybersecurity Competitions have provided invaluable insights into the effectiveness of this novel approach in enhancing participants' skills, promoting collaboration, and refining incident response capabilities. The two competitions showcased consistent improvements across various parameters, such as skill enhancement, incident response time, collaboration impact, vulnerability exploitation rates, and post-competition confidence levels. These outcomes collectively underline the potency of the Red and Blue competition model in fostering a dynamic learning environment that bridges theoretical knowledge with practical experience. The competitions' positive impact on participants' confidence, coupled with the evident growth in their abilities, emphasizes the significance of experiential learning in cybersecurity education. As the digital landscape continues to evolve, this competition model offers a promising avenue for training and preparing cybersecurity professionals to effectively tackle the evolving challenges of the cyber realm.

We have demonstrated that there are numerous benefits associated with the integration of the two teams. We presented an architecture upon which such a competition can be built. VMs with intentionally created vulnerabilities were introduced, alongside the Core System containing all its functionalities. Following the successful completion of two editions of this competition, we discussed how participants' skills have improved and emphasized the value it brings to the training of incident response teams. This approach underscores the significance of such combined training exercises in strengthening cybersecurity readiness.

Author Contributions: Conceptualization, C.C. and C.-F.C.; methodology, C.C. and C.-F.C.; software, C.C.; validation, C.C. and C.-F.C.; formal analysis, C.C. and C.-F.C.; investigation, C.C.; resources, C.C.; data curation, C.C.; writing—original draft preparation, C.C.; writing—review and editing, C.C. and C.-F.C.; visualization, C.C.; supervision, C.-F.C.; project administration, C.-F.C.; funding acquisition, C.-F.C. All authors have read and agreed to the published version of the manuscript.

Funding: Part of this research was supported by the project "Collaborative environment for developing OpenStack-based cloud architectures with applications in RTI" SMIS 124998 from The European Regional Development Fund through the Competitiveness Operational Program 2014–2020, priority axis 1: Research, technological development and innovation (RTI)—the POC/398/1/1 program.

Institutional Review Board Statement: Not applicable.

Informed Consent Statement: Not applicable.

Data Availability Statement: Not applicable.

Acknowledgments: Not applicable.

Conflicts of Interest: The authors declare no conflicts of interest. The funders had no role in the design of the study; in the collection, analyses, or interpretation of data; in the writing of the manuscript; or in the decision to publish the results.

Abbreviations

The following abbreviations are used in this manuscript:

AI	Artificial Intelligence
API	Application Programming Interface
BT	Blue Team
CCDCOE	Cyber Defence Center of Excellence
CDX	Cyber Defense Exercises
CPUs	Central Processing Units
CTF	Capture the Flag
FC	FailConnect
FF	FailFunctional
FR	FailRead
FTP	File Transfer Protocol
FW	FailWrite
GT	GenerateThings
IP	Internet Protocol
JWT	JSON Web Token
LFI	Local File Inclusion
NAT	Network Address Translation
NIST	National Institute of Standards and Technology
RAM	Random Access Memory
RCE	Remote Code Execution
RT	Red Team
SCADA	Supervisory Control and Data Acquisition
SM	ServicesMonitor
SSH	Secure Shell
VF	ValidateFlags
VMs	Virtual machines
XXE	XML External Entity

References

1. Karjalainen, M.; Kokkonen, T. Comprehensive cyber arena; the next generation cyber range. In Proceedings of the IEEE European Symposium on Security and Privacy Workshops, Genoa, Italy, 6–10 June 2022 ; pp. 11–16.
2. Attiah, A.; Chatterjee, M.; Zou, C.C. A game theoretic approach to model cyber attack and defense strategies. In Proceedings of the International Conference on Communications, Kansas City, MO, USA, 20–24 May 2018; pp. 1–7.
3. Mijwil, M.; Unogwu, O.J.; Filali, Y.; Bala, I.; Al-Shahwani, H. Exploring the Top Five Evolving Threats in Cybersecurity: An In-Depth Overview. *Mesopotamian J. Cybersecur.* **2023**, *2023*, 57–63. [CrossRef]
4. Kaur, R.; Gabrijelčič, D.; Klobučar, T. Artificial intelligence for cybersecurity: Literature review and future research directions. *Inf. Fusion* **2023**, *97*, 101804. [CrossRef]
5. Aktayeva, A.; Makatov, Y.; Tulegenovna, A.K.; Dautov, A.; Niyazova, R.; Zhamankarin, M.; Khan, S. Cybersecurity Risk Assessments within Critical Infrastructure Social Networks. *Data* **2023**, *8*, 156
6. Brilingaitė, A.; Bukauskas, L.; Juozapavičius, A. A framework for competence development and assessment in hybrid cybersecurity exercises. *Comput. Secur.* **2020**, *88*, 101607. [CrossRef]
7. Yamin, M.M.; Katt, B.; Gkioulos, V. Cyber ranges and security testbeds: Scenarios, functions, tools and architecture. *Comput. Secur.* **2020**, *88*, 101636. [CrossRef]
8. Veerasamy, N. High-Level Methodology for Carrying out Combined Red and Blue Teams. In Proceedings of the 2nd International Conference on Computer and Electrical Engineering, Dubai, United Arab Emirates, 28–30 December 2009; pp. 416–420.
9. Andreolini, M.; Colacino, V.G.; Colajanni, M.; Marchetti, M. A framework for the evaluation of trainee performance in cyber range exercises. *Mob. Netw. Appl.* **2020**, *25*, 236–247. [CrossRef]
10. Chindrus, C.; Caruntu, C.F. Development and Testing of a Core System for Red and Blue Scenario in Cyber Security Incidents. In Proceedings of the 15th International Conference on Security of Information and Networks, Sousse, Tunisia, 11–13 November 2022; pp. 1–7.
11. Chindrus, C.; Caruntu, C.F. Challenges and Solutions in Designing a Network Architecture for Red and Blue Cybersecurity Competitions. In Proceedings of the 27th International Conference on System Theory, Control and Computing, Timisoara, Romania, 11–13 October 2023.
12. Newhouse, W.; Keith, S.; Scribner, B.; Witte, G. National initiative for cybersecurity education (NICE) cybersecurity workforce framework. *Nist Spec. Publ.* **2017**, *800*, 181.

13. DeCusatis, C.; Bavaro, J.; Cannistraci, T.; Griffin, B.; Jenkins, J.; Ronan, M. Red-blue team exercises for cybersecurity training during a pandemic. In Proceedings of the IEEE 11th Annual Computing and Communication Workshop and Conference, Las Vegas, NV, USA, 27–30 January 2021; pp. 1055–1060.

14. Bock, K.; Hughey, G.; Levin, D. King of the hill: A novel cybersecurity competition for teaching penetration testing. In Proceedings of the USENIX Workshop on Advances in Security Education, Baltimore, MD, USA, 8 June 2018.

15. Cheung, R.S.; Cohen, J.P.; Lo, H.Z.; Elia, F.; Carrillo-Marquez, V. Effectiveness of cybersecurity competitions. In Proceedings of the International Conference on Security and Management, The Steering Committee of The World Congress in Computer Science, Las Vegas, NV, USA, 2012 ; p. 1.

16. Katsantonis, M.; Fouliras, P.; Mavridis, I. Conceptual analysis of cyber security education based on live competitions. In Proceedings of the IEEE Global Engineering Education Conference, Athens, Greece, 25–28 April 2017; pp. 771–779.

17. Katsantonis, M.N.; Mavridis, I.; Gritzalis, D. Design and evaluation of cofelet-based approaches for cyber security learning and training. *Comput. Secur.* **2021**, *105*, 102263. [CrossRef]

18. Smeets, M. The Role of Military Cyber Exercises: A Case Study of Locked Shields. In Proceedings of the 2022 14th International Conference on Cyber Conflict: Keep Moving! (CyCon), Tallinn, Estonia, 31 May–3 June 2022; Volume 700, pp. 9–25.

19. Känzig, N.; Meier, R.; Gambazzi, L.; Lenders, V.; Vanbever, L. Machine Learning-based Detection of C&C Channels with a Focus on the Locked Shields Cyber Defense Exercise. In Proceedings of the 2019 11th International Conference on Cyber Conflict (CyCon), Tallinn, Estonia, 28–31 May 2019; Volume 900, pp. 1–19.

20. Svabensky, V.; Celeda, P.; Vykopal, J.; Brisakova, S. Cybersecurity knowledge and skills taught in capture the flag challenges. *Comput. Secur.* **2021**, *102*, 102154. [CrossRef]

21. Karagiannis, S.; Ntantogian, C.; Magkos, E.; Ribeiro, L.L.; Campos, L. PocketCTF: A Fully Featured Approach for Hosting Portable Attack and Defense Cybersecurity Exercises. *Information* **2021**, *12*, 318. [CrossRef]

22. Senanayake, R.; Porras, P.; Kaehler, J. Revolutionizing the Visual Design of Capture the Flag (CTF) Competitions. In *HCI for Cybersecurity, Privacy and Trust, Proceedings of the First International Conference, HCI-CPT 2019, Held as Part of the 21st HCI International Conference, HCII 2019, Orlando, FL, USA, 26–31 July 2019*; Springer: Cham, Switzerland, 2019; pp. 339–352.

23. Haney, J.M.; Paul, C.L. Toward integrated tactical operations for Red/Blue cyber defense teams. In Proceedings of the Workshop on Security Information Workers at Symposium on Usable Privacy and Security, Baltimore, MD, USA, 12–14 August 2018.

24. Alothman, B.; Alhajraf, A.; Alajmi, R.; Farraj, R.A.; Alshareef, N.; Khan, M. Developing a Cyber Incident Exercises Model to Educate Security Teams. *Electronics* **2022**, *11*, 1575. [CrossRef]

25. Kovacevic, I.; Gros, S. Red Teams-Pentesters, APTs, or Neither. In Proceedings of the MIPRO, Opatija, Croatia, 21–25 May 2012; pp. 1242–1249.

26. Kokkonen, T.; Puuska, S. Blue team communication and reporting for enhancing situational awareness from white team perspective in cyber security exercises. In *Internet of Things, Smart Spaces, and Next Generation Networks and Systems*; Springer: Cham, Switzerland, 2018; pp. 277–288.

27. Thomas, L.J.; Balders, M.; Countney, Z.; Zhong, C.; Yao, J.; Xu, C. Cybersecurity Education: From beginners to advanced players in cybersecurity competitions. In Proceedings of the International Conference on Intelligence and Security Informatics, Shenzhen, China, 1–3 July 2019; pp. 149–151.

28. Shen, C.C.; Chiou, Y.M.; Mouza, C.; Rutherford, T. Work-in-Progress-Design and Evaluation of Mixed Reality Programs for Cybersecurity Education. In Proceedings of the 7th International Conference of the Immersive Learning Research Network, Eureka, CA, USA, 17 May–10 June 2021; pp. 1–3.

29. Seker, E.; Ozbenli, H.H. The concept of cyber defence exercises (cdx): Planning, execution, evaluation. In Proceedings of the International Conference on Cyber Security and Protection of Digital Services, Glasgow, UK, 11–12 June 2018; pp. 1–9.

30. Khan, M.A.; Merabet, A.; Alkaabi, S.; Sayed, H.E. Game-based learning platform to enhance cybersecurity education. *Educ. Inf. Technol.* **2022**, *27*, 5153–5177. [CrossRef]

Review

Anonymization Procedures for Tabular Data: An Explanatory Technical and Legal Synthesis

Robert Aufschläger [1,*], Jakob Folz [1], Elena März [2], Johann Guggumos [2], Michael Heigl [1], Benedikt Buchner [2] and Martin Schramm [1]

[1] Technology Campus Vilshofen, Deggendorf Institute of Technology, 94474 Vilshofen an der Donau, Germany; jakob.folz@th-deg.de (J.F.); michael.heigl@th-deg.de (M.H.); martin.schramm@th-deg.de (M.S.)

[2] Faculty of Law, University of Augsburg, 86159 Augsburg, Germany; elena.maerz@jura.uni-augsburg.de (E.M.); johann.guggumos@jura.uni-augsburg.de (J.G.); benedikt.buchner@jura.uni-augsburg.de (B.B.)

* Correspondence: robert.aufschlaeger@th-deg.de

Abstract: In the European Union, Data Controllers and Data Processors, who work with personal data, have to comply with the General Data Protection Regulation and other applicable laws. This affects the storing and processing of personal data. But some data processing in data mining or statistical analyses does not require any personal reference to the data. Thus, personal context can be removed. For these use cases, to comply with applicable laws, any existing personal information has to be removed by applying the so-called anonymization. However, anonymization should maintain data utility. Therefore, the concept of anonymization is a double-edged sword with an intrinsic trade-off: privacy enforcement vs. utility preservation. The former might not be entirely guaranteed when anonymized data are published as Open Data. In theory and practice, there exist diverse approaches to conduct and score anonymization. This explanatory synthesis discusses the technical perspectives on the anonymization of tabular data with a special emphasis on the European Union's legal base. The studied methods for conducting anonymization, and scoring the anonymization procedure and the resulting anonymity are explained in unifying terminology. The examined methods and scores cover both categorical and numerical data. The examined scores involve data utility, information preservation, and privacy models. In practice-relevant examples, methods and scores are experimentally tested on records from the UCI Machine Learning Repository's "Census Income (Adult)" dataset.

Keywords: emerging technologies and applications; multimedia content management; privacy and trust

Citation: Aufschläger, R.; Folz, J.; März, E.; Guggumos, J.; Heigl, M.; Buchner, B.; Schramm, M. Anonymization Procedures for Tabular Data: An Explanatory Technical and Legal Synthesis. *Information* **2023**, *14*, 487. https://doi.org/10.3390/info14090487

Academic Editors: Jose de Vasconcelos, Hugo Barbosa and Carla Cordeiro

Received: 2 August 2023
Revised: 22 August 2023
Accepted: 29 August 2023
Published: 1 September 2023

1. Introduction

Working with personalized data is a highly risky task. Not only in sensitive sectors like health and finance, personal data has to be protected. Personal data can occur in vast varieties. Nevertheless, in practice, personal data are often stored in structured tabular datasets, and this work focuses on tabular datasets as objects of study.

Violating the regulations in force, such as the General Data Protection Regulation (GDPR) by the European Union (EU), can lead to severe penalties. More importantly, from an ethical perspective, data leakage can cause irreversible and irreparable damage.

However, removing personal information, i.e., called anonymizing, is a challenging task that comes with a trade-off. On the one hand, after anonymizing, no personal references should be possible. This can only be achieved by manipulating or even deleting data. On the other hand, the data utility should be maintained. Hereby, we refer to "data utility" as any measure to rate how useful data are for given tasks.

Furthermore, anonymization is highly task-dependent, and due to the lack of specialized Open Data, Data Controllers and Data Processors cannot rely on given experiences.

In the following, this article looks at the anonymization of tabular data from the legal perspective of the GDPR. We describe practice-relevant anonymization terms, methods, and scores for tabular data in a technical manner while enforcing common terminology and explaining the legal setting for anonymizing tabular data.

This explanatory synthesis aims to distill and organize the wealth of information from a multitude of versatile sources in the context of anonymizing tabular data. We aim to bring the information into a clear and structured format to grasp the key concepts, trends, and current ambiguities. Our approach seeks to ensure both comparability and broad applicability, focusing on achieving general validity in practical use cases.

The main contributions of this review paper can be summarized as follows:

1. Terminology and taxonomy establishment of anonymization methods for tabular data:
   This review introduces a unifying terminology for anonymization methods specific to tabular data. Furthermore, the paper presents a novel taxonomy that categorizes these methods, providing a structured framework that enhances clarity and organization within tabular data anonymization.

2. Comprehensive summary of information loss, utility loss, and privacy metrics in the context of anonymizing tabular data:
   By conducting an extensive exploration, this paper offers a comprehensive overview of methods used to quantitatively assess the impact of anonymization on information and utility in tabular data. By providing an overview of the so-called privacy models, along with precise definitions aligned with the established terminology, the paper reviews and explains the trade-offs between privacy protection and data utility, with special attention to the Curse of Dimensionality. This contribution facilitates a deeper understanding of the complex interplay between anonymization and the quality of tabular data.

3. Integration of anonymization of tabular data with legal considerations and risk assessments:
   Last but not least, this review bridges the gap between technical practices and legal considerations by analyzing how state-of-the-art anonymization methods align with case law and legislation. By elucidating the connection between anonymization techniques and the legal context, the paper provides valuable insights into the regulatory landscape surrounding tabular data anonymization. This integration of technical insights with legal implications is essential for researchers, practitioners, and policymakers alike, contributing to a more holistic approach to data anonymization. The paper conducts a risk assessment for privacy metrics and discusses present issues regarding implementing anonymization procedures for tabular data. Further, it examines possible gaps in the interplay of legislation and research from both technical and legal perspectives. Based on the limited sources of literature and case law, conclusions on the evaluation of the procedures were summarized and were partially drawn using deduction.

In summary, these three main contributions collectively provide interdisciplinary insights for assessing data quality impact and promote a well-informed integration of technical and legal aspects in the domain of tabular data anonymization.

2. Background

This article does not consider the anonymization of graph data or unstructured data, where high dimensionality adds additional constraints [1]. We solely focus on tabular data that can be extracted from relational databases. Due to their reliability and widespread tools, relational databases are used in a wide range of applications across various industries. Thus, anonymizing tabular data in relational databases is a practice-relevant task. In this matter, protecting privacy is the main goal. Further, it facilitates the development of new applications with the possible publishing of Open Data.

We only consider data that have string or atomic data types, e.g., Boolean, integer, character, and float, as attribute data types. From a conceptual point of view, we only distinguish between categorical and numerical attributes, which can be reduced to the data types of string and float in implementations. Characters and integers might be typecast, respectively. We define records as single entries in the database. Individuals might be related to more than one record. This happens when records are created by user events, such as purchase records. Though we relate to relational databases and their taxonomy, to emphasize the anonymization task, instead of using the term "primary key", we use the term Direct Identifier. Instead of talking about a "super key", we say Quasi-Identifier (QI). A QI refers to a set of attributes where the attributes are not identifiers by themselves, but together as a whole might enable the unique identification of records in a database. The QI denotes the characteristics on which linking can be enforced [2]. The QI contains the attributes that are likely to appear in other known datasets, and in the context of privacy models, there is the assumption that a data holder can identify attributes in their private data that may also appear in external information and thus can accurately identify the QI [3]. Further, by considering the same attribute values of a QI, the dataset of records is split into disjunct subsets that form equivalence classes. In the following, we call these equivalence classes groups. If a group consists of $k \in \mathbb{N}$ entries, we call the group a k-group. Besides Direct Identifiers and (potentially more than one) QIs, there are the so-called Sensitive Attributes (SAs), which, importantly, should not be assignable to individuals after applying anonymization. In Section 4, we give the mathematical setting for the data to study. In contrast to pseudonymization, where re-identification is possible but is not within the scope of this article, anonymization does not allow Direct Identifiers at all. For this reason, in anonymization, removing Direct Identifiers is always the first step to take (e.g., in [4]). For the sake of simplicity, we assume that this step is already performed and define the data model on top of it. For the sake of consistency and comparability, throughout the article, we use the Adult dataset from the UCI Machine Learning Repository [5] ("Census income" dataset) for visualizing examples.

3. Related Work

Related work can be categorized into several categories depending on the data format, the perspective (technical or legal), and the use case. The first listed works take a technical perspective and deal with different data types and use cases in anonymization.

The survey [6] by Abdul Majeed et al. gives a comprehensive overview of anonymization techniques used in privacy-preserving data publishing (PPDP) and divides them into the anonymization of graphs and tabular data. Although anonymization techniques for tabular data are presented, the focus of the survey is on graph data in the context of social media. The survey concludes that privacy guidelines must be considered not only at the anonymization level, but in all stages, such as collection, preprocessing, anonymization, sharing, and analysis.

In the literature, most often, the approaches to anonymization are context-sensitive.

Another example is [7], where the authors discuss anonymizing Public Participation Geographic Information System (PPGIS) data by first identifying privacy concerns, referring to the European GDPR as the legal guideline. The authors claim to have reached a satisfactory level of anonymization after applying generalization to non-spatial attributes and perturbations to primary personal spatial data.

Also in [8], by Olatunji et al., anonymization methods for relational and graph data are the focus but with an emphasis on the medical field. Further, in addition to the various anonymization methods, an overview of various attack methods and tools used in the field of anonymization is given. The evaluation is focused on two main objectives, which are performed on the Medical Information Mart for Intensive Care (MIMIC-III) dataset anonymized with the ARX data anonymization tool [9]. In the anonymization procedure, the differences in the accuracy of the predictions between anonymized data and de-anonymized data are shown. In this use case, generalization has less impact on accuracy than suppression, and it is not necessary to anonymize all attributes but only specific ones.

Again—considering anonymization procedures—in [10], Jakob et al. present a data anonymization pipeline for publishing an anonymized dataset based on COVID-19 records. The goal is to provide anonymized data to the public promptly after publication, while protecting the dataset consisting of 16 attributes against various attacks. The pipeline itself is tailored to one dataset. All Direct Identifiers were removed, and the remaining variables were evaluated using [11] to determine whether they had to be classified as QIs or not.

In [12], the authors examine privacy threats in data analytics and briefly list privacy preservation techniques. Additionally, they propose a new privacy preservation technique using a data lake for unstructured data.

In the literature review in [13], the authors list 13 tools and their anonymization techniques. They identify Open Source anonymization tools for tabular data and give a short summary for each tool. Also, they give an overview of which privacy model is supported by which tool. However, they focus on a literature review and do not give in-depth evaluations of the tools. Last but not least, they derive recommendations for tools to use for anonymizing phenotype datasets with different properties and in different contexts in the area of biology. Besides anonymization methods, some of the literature focuses on the scoring of anonymity and privacy.

In the survey [14], the authors list system user privacy metrics. They list over 80 privacy metrics and categorize into different privacy aspects. Further, they highlight the individuality of single scenarios and present a method for how to choose privacy metrics based on questions that help to choose privacy metrics for a given scenario. Whereas the authors unify and simplify the metric notation when possible, they do not focus on the use case of tabular data and do not describe anonymization methods for tabular data (in a unifying manner). Further, they do not consider the legal perspective.

The following works take a legal perspective but do not fill the gap between legal and technical requirements. The legal understanding is not congruent with technology development, and there are different definitions of identifiable and non-identifiable data in different countries.

In [15], the authors discuss different levels of anonymization of tabular health data in the jurisdictions of the US, EU, and Switzerland. They call for legislation that respects technological advances and provides clearer legal certainty. They propose a move towards fine-grained legal definition and classification of re-identification steps. In the technical analysis, the paper considers only two anonymization methods, removal of Direct Identifiers and perturbation, and gives a schematic overview of classification for levels of data anonymization. The data are classified into identifying data, pseudonymized data, pseudo-anonymized data, aggregated data, (irreversibly) anonymized data, and anonymous data.

In [1], the authors consider the even more opaque regulations regarding anonymizing unstructured data, such as text documents or images. They examine the identifiability test in Recital 26 to understand which conditions must be met for the anonymization of unstructured data. Further, they examine both approaches that will be discussed in Sections 6.3 and 6.4.

From a conceptual perspective, in [16], the authors call for a paradigm shift from anonymization towards transparency, accountability, and intervenability, because full anonymization, in many cases, is non-feasible to implement, and solely relying on anonymization often leads to undesired results.

In summary, it can be seen that there is an increasing demand for practical anonymization solutions due to the rising number of privacy data breaches and the increasing number of data. With the establishment of new processing paradigms, the relevance of user data anonymization will continue to increase. However, current approaches need significant improvement, and there is a need to develop new practical approaches that enable the balancing act between privacy and utility.

4. Technical Perspective

The following model omits the existence of Direct Identifiers and just deals with one QI and several SAs. Furthermore, to make the setting comprehensible, we use the terms table, database, and dataset interchangeably. Let $D = \{R_1, R_2, \ldots, R_n\}$ be a database modeled as a multiset with $n \in \mathbb{N}$ not necessarily distinct records, where $R_i \in A_1 \times A_2 \times \cdots \times A_r \times A_{r+1} \times \ldots \times A_{r+t}$, $i = 1, \ldots, n$, are database entries composed of attribute values; $r \in \mathbb{N}$ is the number of attributes that are part of the QI; $t \in \mathbb{N}_0$ is the number of non QI attributes; A_j, $j = 1, \ldots, r + t$, is the set of possible attribute values of the attribute indexed by j; and the first r attributes represent the QI. In the following, let $|\cdot|$ denote the cardinality of a set, and more specifically, let $|D|$ denote the number of distinct records in database D. As several records can potentially be assigned to one individual, n records correspond to $m \leq n$ individuals with QI attributes $\{U_1, U_2, \ldots, U_m\}$, where $U_i \in A_1 \times A_2 \times \ldots \times A_r$, $i = 1, \ldots, m$. We assume that given data are preprocessed and individuals can only be assigned to one individual, i.e., $|D| = m = n$. Further, let $SA \subseteq \{A_1, \ldots, A_{r+t}\}$ denote the SAs as a subset of all attributes. For the sake of simplicity, in the article, without loss of generality, we restrict the numerical attributes to $A_i \subset \mathbb{R}$ and the categorical attributes to $A_i \subset \mathbb{N}$, $i = 1, \ldots, r + t$. Let R_i, $i \in \{1, \ldots, n\}$ denote the i-th entry and $R_i(j)$, $j \in \{1, \ldots, r + t\}$ denote the value of the j-th attribute of the i-th entry in the database. Figure 1 visualizes the data structure to be studied.

	attr. 1	**…**	**attr. r**	**attr. r + 1**	**…**	**attr. r + t**
R_i	$R_i(1)$	…	$R_i(r)$	$R_i(r + 1)$	…	$R_i(r + t)$

Figure 1. The considered data model. The first r attributes form a QI. All attributes indexed from 1 to $r + t$ are potentially SAs. The considered data model does not contain Direct Identifiers.

Before scoring certain levels of anonymity for a dataset with personal data, we give an overview of common anonymization methods. We aim to cover relevant methods for tabular data in as detailed a manner as necessary. We are aware that not all methods are described in detail and that research is being carried out on newer approaches. However, in this article, we focus on the most important methods that are state-of-the-art and/or common practice. Some anonymization methods use the information given by the QI. In that case, it is important to note that there might be more than one QI (super key) in a database, and often, several choices of QI have to be considered to score anonymization. For the sake of simplicity and because the following definitions do not limit the use of multiple QIs, where needed, we use a fixed set of attributes as a single QI. In the following, we categorize anonymization methods in seven categories (Sections 4.1–4.7), where not all are necessarily based on QIs. The considered methods are given in the taxonomy in Figure 2. This taxonomy represents a hierarchical structure that classifies anonymization methods into different levels of categories and subcategories, reflecting their relationships.

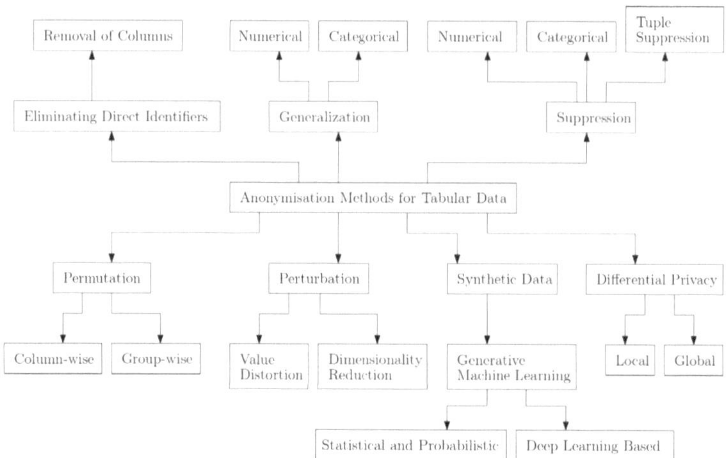

Figure 2. Taxonomy of anonymization methods for tabular data.

4.1. Eliminating Direct Identifiers

Direct Identifiers are attributes that allow for the immediate re-identification of data entries. Therefore, due to the GDPR definition of anonymization, removing the Direct Identifier is compulsory and usually the first step in any anonymization of personal tabular data. Direct Identifiers, often referred to as IDs, do not usually contain valuable information and can simply be removed. A more detailed description can be found in the Health Insurance Portability and Accountability Act (HIPAA) Privacy Rule [17] by the United States Department of Health and Human Services, which specifies a Safe Harbor method that requires certain Direct Identifiers of individuals to be removed. The 18 Direct Identifiers that are required to be removed according to the Safe Harbor method can be found in Table 1. To the best of our knowledge, there is no EU counterpart to the HIPAA.

Table 1. Direct Identifiers in the HIPAA Safe Harbor method.

No.	Direct Identifier	No.	Direct Identifier
1	Names	10	Social security numbers
2	All geographic subdivisions smaller than a state	11	IP addresses
3	All elements of dates (except year) directly related to an individual	12	Medical record numbers
4	Telephone numbers	13	Biometric identifiers, including finger and voice prints
5	Vehicle identifiers and serial numbers	14	Health plan beneficiary numbers
6	Fax numbers	15	Full-face photographs and any comparable images
7	Device identifiers and serial numbers	16	Account numbers
8	Email addresses	17	Any other unique identifier
9	URLs	18	Certificate/license numbers

4.2. Generalization

In generalization, the level of detail is coarsened. As a result, given the attributes of individuals, re-identification in the dataset should be impossible. Further, generalization limits the possibility of finding correlations between different attribute columns and datasets. This also makes it difficult to combine and assign records to an individual. There are several types of generalizations, such as subtree generalization, full-domain generalization, unrestricted subtree generalization, cell generalization, and multi-dimensional generalization [6]. generalization for categorical attributes can be defined as follows (c.f. [18]): Let $\overline{A}_j \subseteq \mathcal{P}(A_j)$ be a set of subsets of A_j.

A mapping

$$g : A_1 \times \ldots \times A_r \to \overline{A}_1 \times \ldots \times \overline{A}_r \tag{1}$$

is called a record generalization if and only if for any record's QI $(b_1, \ldots, b_r) \in A_1 \times \ldots \times A_r$ and $(B_1, \ldots, B_r) := g(b_1, \ldots, b_r) \in \overline{A}_1 \times \ldots \times \overline{A}_r$, it holds that $b_j \in B_j$, $j = 1, \ldots, r$.

Let

$$g_i : A_1 \times \ldots \times A_r \to \overline{A}_1 \times \ldots \times \overline{A}_r, \ i = 1, \ldots, n \tag{2}$$

be record generalizations. With $\overline{R}_i := g_i(R_i)$, $i = 1, \ldots n$, we call $g(D) := \{\overline{R}_1, \ldots, \overline{R}_n\}$ a generalization of database D.

The trivial generalization of an attribute is defined as

$$g : A \to \overline{A}, \ b \mapsto \{b\}. \tag{3}$$

Often, generalization is achieved by generalizing attribute values by replacing parts of the value with a special character, for example, "$*$".

Generalization is sometimes also named recoding and can be categorized according to the strategies used [19]. There is a classification in global or local recoding. Global recoding refers to the process of mapping a chosen value to the same generalized value or value set across all records in the dataset. In contrast, local recoding allows the same value to be mapped to different generalized values in each anonymized group. For the sake of simplicity, we use the word generalization instead of recoding. Generalization offers flexibility in data anonymization, but it also requires more careful consideration to ensure that the privacy of individuals is still protected. Further, there is the classification into single- and multi-dimensional generalizations. Here, single-dimensional generalization involves mapping each attribute individually.

$$g : A_1 \times \ldots \times A_r \to \overline{A}_1 \times \ldots \times \overline{A}_r, \tag{4}$$

In contrast, multi-dimensional generalization involves mapping the Cartesian Product of multiple attributes.

$$g : A_1 \times \ldots \times A_r \to \overline{B}_1 \times \ldots \times \overline{B}_s, \ s < r, \tag{5}$$

where B_i, $i = 1, \ldots, s$, is a set in $\{A_1, \ldots, A_r\}$ or is a Cartesian Product of sets $A_{k_1} \times \ldots \times A_{k_l}$, $1 < l \leq r$. When dealing with numerical attributes, generalization can be implemented using discretization, where attribute values are discretized into same-length intervals. The approach is also referred to as value-class membership [20]. Let $L \in \mathbb{N}$ be the interval size. Then, discretization can be defined as

$$g : \mathbb{R} \to \{[a, b) \mid a, b \in \mathbb{R}, \ a < b\}, \ \lambda \mapsto I, \tag{6}$$

where g maps the real number λ to half-open real interval

$$I = [lower, \ upper) := \left[\left\lfloor \frac{\lambda}{L} \right\rfloor L, \ \left\lfloor \frac{\lambda}{L} \right\rfloor L + L \right), \tag{7}$$

where I has length L and $\lfloor \cdot \rfloor$ represents the floor function, which rounds down to the nearest integer. If one wants to discretize to tenths or even smaller decimal places, one can multiply L and the attribute values in the corresponding column with $10, 100, \ldots$ before applying discretization and with the multiplicative inverse of $10, 100, \ldots$ after applying discretization. In practice, due to the often vast possibilities of generalizing tabular data, a generalization strategy has to be found. Note that data consisting of categorical and numerical attributes can incorporate different generalizations for different attributes and different database entries (Equations (2)–(6)).

An example for applying generalization and discretization to the Adult dataset is given in Figure 3.

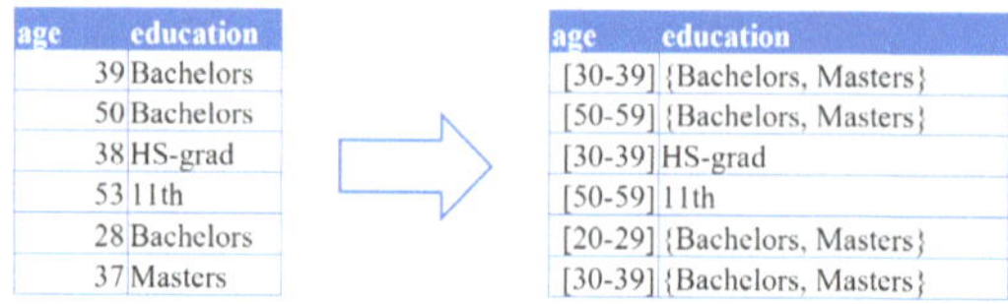

Figure 3. Example. Visualizing both generalization and discretization by projecting the first six records of Adult on the columns `age` and `education`. In the categorical attribute column `education`, the attribute values "Bachelors" and "Masters" are summarized to a set with both values. In the numerical attribute column `age`, the values for `age` are discretized in intervals of size 10.

4.3. Suppression

Suppression (or Data Masking) can be defined as a special type of generalization [18]. To be specific, suppression using generalization resp. total generalization can be achieved by applying $g(b_1, \ldots, b_r) = (\overline{b_1}, \ldots, \overline{b_r})$, $\overline{b_j} \in \{b_j, *\}$ for every database record $(b_1, \ldots, b_r) \in A_1 \times \ldots \times A_r$, where $* := A_j$ or $* := \varnothing$, when suppressing categorical attribute values. To suppress numerical attribute values, we can define $* := f(A_j)$ with $f : \mathbb{R} \to \mathbb{R}$, where f is a statistical function such as mean, sum, variance, standard deviation, median, mode, min, and max. An example of suppression is given in Figure 4.

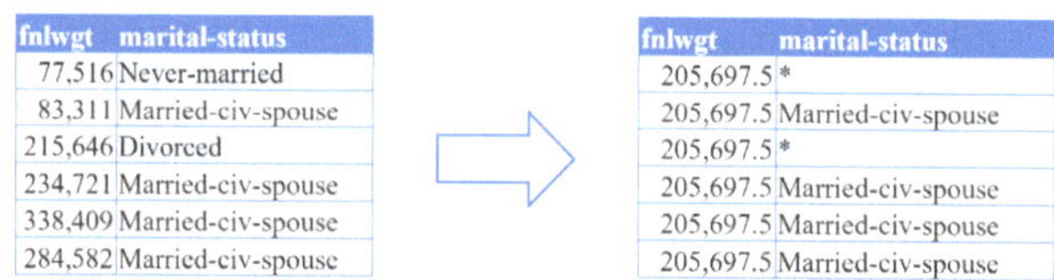

Figure 4. Example. Visualizing suppression of the numerical attribute column `fnlwgt` (final weight: number of units in the target population that the responding record represents) by replacing every column value with the mean value of all column values. Visualizing suppression of the categorical attribute column `marital-status` by replacing the values with *, which denotes all possible values or the empty set.

Another concept of suppression is tuple suppression, which can be used to deal with outliers. Thereby, given a positive $k \in \mathbb{N}$ for the desired k-anonymity, the database entries in groups with less than k-entries are deleted [21].

4.4. Permutation

With permutation, the order of an individual QI's attribute values within a column is swapped. Mathematically, a permutation is defined as a bijective function that maps a finite set to itself. Let

$$\sigma : \{1, 2, \ldots, n\}^n \to \{1, 2, \ldots, n\}^n,$$
$$(i_1, i_2, \ldots, i_n) \mapsto (\sigma(i_1), \sigma(i_2), \ldots, \sigma(i_n)) \tag{8}$$

be a permutation of record indices.

Considering only column j of the records of a database, we define a column permutation as

$$\pi : A_j^n \to A_j^n, \ (R_i(j))_{i=1,\ldots,n} \mapsto \left(R_{\sigma(i)}(j) \right)_{i=1,\ldots,n}. \tag{9}$$

This reassigns information among columns, potentially breaking important relationships among attributes. This can result in a subsequent deterioration of analyses where the relationships are relevant. An example of column permutation is given in Figure 5.

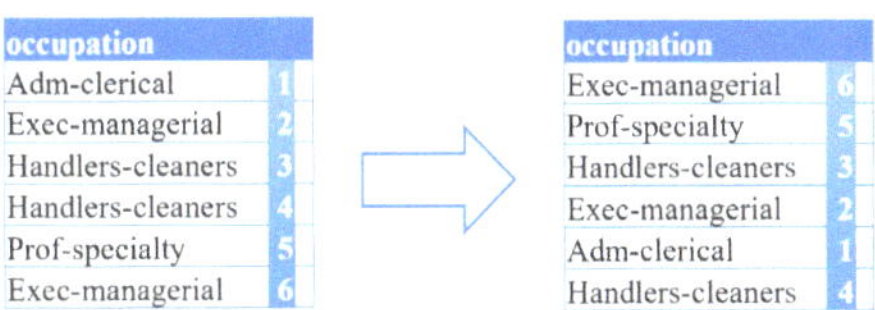

Figure 5. Example. Visualizing permutation of the column `occupation` in the cutout of the first six rows in the Adult dataset. The attached indices point out the change in order by applying permutation. No attribute values are deleted, but the ordering inside the column is very likely destroyed.

4.5. Perturbation

In perturbation, additive or multiplicative noise is applied to the original data. However, without a careful choice of noise, there is the possibility that utility is hampered. On the contrary, especially in the case of outliers, applying noise might not be enough to ensure privacy after anonymization achieved using perturbation. Perturbation is mainly applied to SAs. In [20], the perturbation approaches provide modified values for SAs. The authors consider two methods for modifying SAs without using information about QIs. Besides value-class membership or discretization, which is here explained in generalization (Section 4.2), the authors use value distortion as a method for privacy preservation in data mining. Hereby, for every attribute value $R_i(j)$, $i = 1, \ldots, n$, in an attribute column j, the value $R_i(j)$ is replaced with the value $R_i(j) + \rho$, where $\rho \in \mathbb{R}$ is additive noise drawn from a random variable with continuous uniform distribution $r \sim U(-a, a)$, $a > 0$, or with normal distribution $r \sim \mathcal{N}(\mu, \sigma)$ with mean $\mu = 0$ and standard deviation $\sigma > 0$.

Probability distribution-based methods might also be referred to as perturbation. However, because these methods replace the original data as a whole, we list these approaches in Synthetic Data (Section 4.7). The same applies to dimensionality reduction-based anonymization methods, which we also list in Synthetic Data.

Section 4.6 studies a more sophisticated field of perturbations, namely, Differential Privacy (DP), which is the state of the art in privacy-preserving ML.

4.6. Differential Privacy

Differential Privacy, introduced by Cynthia Dwork in [22], is a mathematical technique that allows for the meaningful analysis of data while preserving the privacy of individuals in a dataset. The idea is to add random noise to data in such a way that—as it is the goal in anonymization—no inferences can be made about personal and sensitive data. DP is implemented in different variants depending on the use case, where anonymization is only a sub-task in a vast variety of use cases. Generally, there is a division into local [23] and global DP [24]. The local DP model does not require any assumptions about the server, whereas the global DP model is a central privacy model that assumes the existence of a trusted server. As a result, the processing frameworks for global and local DP differ significantly. However, the definition of local DP can be embedded into the definition of global DP as a special case where the number of database records equals one.

Common techniques to implement local DP are the Laplace and Exponential mechanisms [24], and Randomized Response [25].

In the context of global DP, there are novel output-specific variants of DP for ML training processes, where ML models are applied to sensitive data and model weights are manipulated in order to preclude successful membership or attribute inference attacks. For example, in Differentially Private Stochastic Gradient Descent (DP-SGD) [26], instead of adding noise to the data themselves, gradients (i.e., the multi-variable derivative of the loss function with respect to the weight parameters) are manipulated to obtain privacy-preserving Neural Network models. Adapting the training process is also referred to as private training. Whereas private training only adjusts the training process and leads to private predictions, private prediction itself is a DP technique to prevent privacy violations by limiting the amount of information about the training data that can be obtained from a series of model predictions. Whereas private training operates on model parameters, private prediction perturbs model outputs [27]. The privacy models' *k*-anonymity, *l*-diversity, and *t*-closeness rely on deterministic mechanisms and can be calculated given the database and a QI. On the contrary, global DP does not depend only on the QI but also on the whole database and a randomized mechanism M in connection with a data-driven algorithm, such as database queries, statistical analysis, or ML algorithms. The most basic definition of the so-called (ϵ, δ)-DP includes the definition of a randomized algorithm, probability simplex, and the distance between two databases based on the ℓ_1-norm of the difference of histograms. This definition of DP requires that for every pair of "neighbouring" databases X, Y (given as histograms), it is extremely unlikely that, ex post facto, the observed value $M(X)$ resp. $M(Y)$ is much more or much less likely to be generated when the input database is X than when the input database is Y [24]. Two databases are called neighbors if the resulting histograms $x, y \in \{0,1\}^{|\mathcal{X}|}$ only differ in at most one record, where in our setting, $x_i, y_i \in \{0,1\}$, $i = 1, \ldots, |\mathcal{X}|$ is the number of non-duplicate records with the same type in X resp. Y, where $\mathcal{X} \supseteq D$ is the record "universe". More in detail, the (ϵ, δ)-DP for a randomized algorithm M with domain $\{0,1\}^{|\mathcal{X}|}$ is defined by the inequality below, where $\epsilon > 0$, $\delta \geq 0$ are privacy constraints.

For all $S \subseteq range(M)$ (subset of the possible outputs of M) and $x, y \in \{0,1\}^{|\mathcal{X}|}$, such that $\|x - y\|_1 \leq 1$, we have

$$Pr[M(X) \in S] \leq e^\epsilon Pr[M(Y) \in S] + \delta. \tag{10}$$

The smaller the value of the so-called privacy budget ϵ, the stronger the privacy guarantee. Additionally, parameter δ is a small constant term that is usually set to a very small value to ensure that the formula holds with high probability. In summary, DP guarantees that the output of a randomized algorithm does not reveal much about any individual in the dataset, even if an adversary has access to all other records in the database. There are promising approaches, such as in [28], where the authors propose a general and scalable approach for differentially private synthetic data generation that also works for tabular data.

4.7. Synthetic Data

Whereas the above approaches directly manipulate dataset entries, with synthetic approaches, new data are generated based on extracted and representative information from the original data. For the sake of simplicity, the following synthetic approaches to generate data are only described for numerical data. However, by using a reasonable coding method (such as one-hot encoding), categorical data might be converted into numerical data, and vice versa.

In [29], to improve anonymization using generalization for *k*-anonymity, the so-called condensation method was introduced. The approach is related to probability distribution-based perturbation methods. Thereby, the resulting numerical attribute values closely match the statistical characteristics of the original attribute values, including inter-attribute correlations (second order) and mean values (first order). Condensation does not require hierarchical domain generalizations and fits both static data (static condensation) and dynamic data streams (dynamic condensation). In summary, this approach condenses records into groups of predefined size, where each group maintains a certain level of statistical information (mean, covariance). The authors test the accuracy of a simple *K*-Nearest Neighbor classifier on different labeled datasets and show that condensation allows for high levels of privacy without noticeably compromising classification accuracy. Further, the authors find that by using static condensation for anonymization, in many cases, even better classification accuracy can be achieved. This is because the implied removal of anomalies cancels out the negative impact of adding noise. In summary, condensation produces synthetic data by creating a new perturbed dataset with similar dataset characteristics. The mentioned paper states the corresponding algorithm to calculate statically condensed group statistics: first-order and second-order sum per attribute and total number of records. Afterwards, given the calculated group statistics, by building the covariance matrix of attributes for every group, the eigenvectors and eigenvalues of the covariance matrix can be calculated using eigendecomposition. To construct new data, the authors assume that the data within each group is independently and uniformly distributed along each eigenvector with a variance equal to the corresponding eigenvalue.

Another approach to improving privacy preservation when creating synthetic data is to bind Principal Component Analysis (PCA) or Linear Discriminant Analysis (LDA) with DP [30]. In the paper, considering the PCA-based approach, a perturbed covariance matrix (real and symmetric) is decomposed into eigenvalues and eigenvectors, and Laplace noise is applied on the resulting eigenvectors to generate noisy data. The introduced differential PCA-based privacy-preserving data publishing mechanism satisfies ϵ-Differential Privacy and yields better utility in comparison to the Laplace and Exponential mechanisms, even when having the same privacy budget.

In [31], the authors propose a sparsified Singular Value Decomposition (SVD) for data distortion to protect privacy. Given the dataset—often a sparse—matrix $D \in \mathbb{R}^{n \times m}$, the SVD of D is $D =: U\Sigma V^T$, where U is an $n \times n$ orthonormal matrix; $\Sigma := diag[\sigma_1, \sigma_2, \ldots, \sigma_s]$, $\sigma_i \geq 0$, $1 \leq i \leq s$ with $s := \min\{m, n\}$ is an $n \times m$ diagonal matrix whose non-negative diagonal entries are in descending order; and V^T is an $m \times m$ orthonormal matrix. Due to the property of descending variation in $\sigma_1, \ldots, \sigma_s$, data can be compressed to lower dimensionality while preserving utility. This is achieved by using only the first $1 \leq d \leq s$ columns of U, the $d \times d$ upper left submatrix of Σ, and the first d rows from V^T: U_d, Σ_d, V_d^T. The matrix $D^d := U_d \Sigma_d V_d^T$ to represent D can be interpreted as a reduced dataset of D that can be used for mining on the original dataset, D. In contrast to SVD, in sparsified SVD, entries in U_d and V_d^T that are below a threshold are set to zero to obtain a sparsified data matrix $\overline{D}^d$. By thresholding values in U_d and V_d^T to zero and by dropping less important features in D, data are distorted, which makes it harder to estimate values and records in D. However, the most important features are kept. Therefore, the approach aims to maintain the utility of the original dataset, D.

Overall, from a technical perspective, when considering eigenvector-based approaches to generate synthetic data, a numerically stable algorithm including suitable matrix preprocessing for the eigenvalue problem at hand has to be selected. Last but not least, eigenvector-based approaches can also help mitigate the Curse of Dimensionality in data anonymization [32]. The Curse of Dimensionality and its relation to anonymization methods are explained in more detail in Section 5.5.

More recent generative ML models that are often based on deep learning can effectively create synthetic and anonymous data. Generative models aim to approximate a real-world joint probability distribution, such that the original dataset only represents samples pulled from the learned distribution. One common use case of generative models is to fix class imbalances or to apply domain transfer. However, generative approaches can also be used to generate anonymous data. Importantly, considering privacy preservation, the generated data should not allow for (membership/attribute) inferences about specific training data. When it comes to tabular data, in [33], the authors create synthetic tabular data by adapting a Generative Adversarial Network (GAN) that incorporates a Long Short-Term Memory (LSTM) Neural Network in the generator and a Fully Connected Neural Network in the discriminator. Other examples for synthetic tabular data based on GANs can be found in the papers [34,35]. However, just considering a generative ML model by itself does not imply the privacy preservation of training data. Therefore, generative ML might be combined with DP as a potential way out [36]. This again also applies to tabular data; c.f. [37].

5. Utility vs. Privacy

In anonymization, there is always the trade-off of removing information vs. keeping utility. In the literature, two main concepts are used to model the change in utility when applying anonymizing: information loss (Section 5.1) and utility loss (Section 5.2).

To give an overview, we categorize and list the studied anonymization scores in Section 5 in Table 2.

Table 2. Overview of information losses, utility losses/measurements, and privacy models when applying anonymization methods to tabular data

Measurement	Method
Information loss	Conditional entropy [18] Monotone entropy [18] Non-uniform entropy [18] Information loss on a per-attribute basis [38] Relative condensation loss [39] Euclidean distance [40]
Utility loss	Average group size [41] Normalized average equivalence class size metric [42] Discernibility metric [21,42,43] Proportion of suppressed records ML utility Earth Mover Distance [44] z-Test statistics [7]
Privacy models	k-Anonymity [3] Mondrian multi-dimensional k-anonymity [42] l-Diversity [45] t-Closeness [46] Privacy probability of non-re-identification [47]

In the following subsections, we explain the measurements and methods in greater detail. Further, we give insights into the occurring phenomena of the so-called Curse of Dimensionality in the context of anonymizing tabular data.

5.1. Information Loss

Conditional entropy assesses the amount of information that is lost with anonymization in terms of generalization and suppression of categorical attributes. In [18], the authors study the problem of achieving k-anonymity using generalization and suppression with minimal loss of information. As a solution to the problem, they prove that the stated problem is NP-hard and present an algorithm with an approximation guarantee of $O(\ln\ k)$-anonymity. The calculation of information loss based on entropy builds on probability distributions for each of the attributes. Let X_j denote the categorical value of attribute A_j, $j = 1, \ldots r$, in a randomly selected record from a dataset D consisting of only categorical data. Then, for $a \in A_j$, $j \in \{1, 2, \ldots, r\}$,

$$Pr[X_j = a] := \frac{|\{1 \leq i \leq n : R_i(j) = a\}|}{n}. \tag{11}$$

Let $B_j \subseteq A_j$. Then, the conditional entropy of X_j given B_j is defined as follows:

$$H(X_j|B_j) := \\ -\sum_{b_j \in B_j} Pr[X_j = b_j|X_j \in B_j] \log_2 (Pr[X_j = b_j|X_j \in B_j]). \tag{12}$$

Loosely speaking, conditional entropy measures the average amount of uncertainty in X_j given the knowledge that X_j takes values from B_j.

Given $g(D) = \{\overline{R_1}, \overline{R_2}, \ldots, \overline{R_n}\}$, a generalization of D, the entropy measure of the loss of information caused by generalizing D into $g(D)$ is defined as

$$\Pi_e(D, g(D)) := \sum_{i=1}^{n} \sum_{j=1}^{r} H(X_j | \overline{R}_i(j)). \tag{13}$$

If $\overline{R}_i$, $i \in \{1, \ldots, n\}$, is no generalization at all, i.e., $|\overline{R}_i(j)| = 1$, we have $H(X_j | \overline{R}_i(j)) = 0$, and there is no uncertainty. On the other hand, if $\overline{R}_i(j) = A_j$, there is maximal uncertainty. An example of entropy information loss is given in Figure 6.

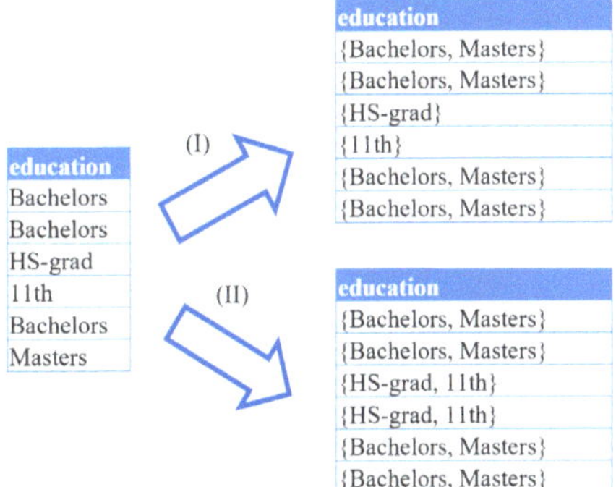

Figure 6. Example. Entropy information loss when generalizing the column `education` of the cutout of the first six rows in the Adult dataset. In generalization (I), we obtain $\Pi_e(D, g(D)) \approx 3.25$, which means lower information loss than in generalization (II), where $\Pi_e(D, g(D)) \approx 5.25$.

In [18], the authors also use other variants of entropy measures, namely, the so-called monotone entropy measure and non-uniform entropy measure, with different characteristics. However, the authors claim that the entropy measure is a more appropriate measure when it comes to privacy.

Given a dataset $D = \{R_i \mid i = 1, \ldots, n\}$ consisting of only numerical attributes and a discretization $g(D) = \{\overline{R}_i(j) \mid i = 1, \ldots, n, \, j = 1, \ldots, r\}$ of D, the information loss on a per-attribute basis can be calculated with the following formula [38]:

$$\Pi(D, g(D)) := \frac{1}{n \cdot r} \sum_{i=1}^{n} \sum_{j=1}^{r} \frac{upper_{ij} - lower_{ij}}{\max_j - \min_j}, \tag{14}$$

where $upper_{ij}$ and $lower_{ij}$ are the upper and lower bounds of generalized attribute value interval $\overline{R}_i(j)$, and $\min_j := \min_{i=1,\ldots,n}\{R_{ij}\}$ and $\max_j := \max_{i=1,\ldots,n}\{R_{ij}\}$, i.e., the minimum and maximum attribute values before generalization.

Based on condensation (Section 4.7) for k-anonymity, in [39], the so-called relative condensation loss is defined to score information loss in anonymization. Given anonymized tabular data $\overline{D}$, the relative condensation loss is group-wise-defined and represents a minimum level of information loss. For $g \in groups$, where $groups$ are the groups of anonymized data $\overline{D}$,

$$\mathcal{L}(g) := \frac{\max_{\overline{R}_i, \overline{R}_k \in g, \, i \neq k} \|\overline{R}_i - \overline{R}_k\|_2}{\max_{\overline{R}_i, \overline{R}_k \in \overline{D}, \, i \neq k} \|\overline{R}_i - \overline{R}_k\|_2} \in (0, 1], \tag{15}$$

where $\|\cdot\|_2$ denotes the 2-norm and anonymized entries $\overline{R}_i$, $i = 1, \ldots, n \in \mathbb{R}^d$, are quantified as real vectors of dimension $d \in \mathbb{N}$, $d \geq r$. Different values of $\mathcal{L}(g)$ for the different $g \in groups$ can be aggregated ($avg, \max, \ldots$) to a total information loss $\mathcal{L}(\overline{D})$.

Last but not least, in [40], the authors use the average Euclidean distance to measure information loss:

$$IL(D, g(D)) := \frac{1}{n} \sum_{i=1}^{n} dist\left(R_i, \overline{R}_i\right), \tag{16}$$

where *dist* defines the Euclidean distance between data records. Note that in the case of non-real-valued attributes in the dataset, the records have to be vectorized before applying *dist*. An example of numerical information loss is given in Figure 7.

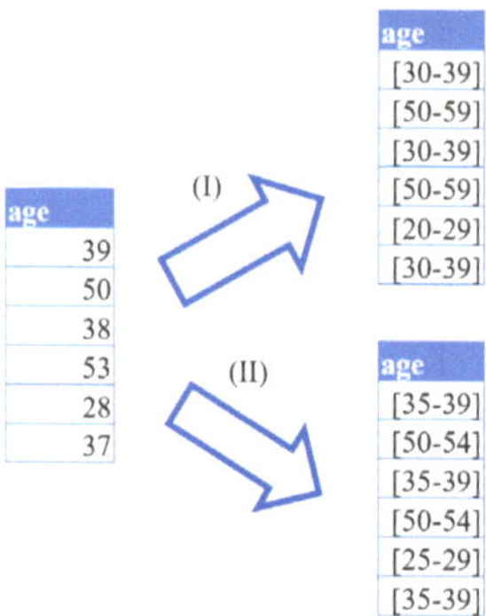

Figure 7. Example. Numerical information loss when generalizing the column age of the cutout of the first six rows in the Adult dataset. In generalization (I), we obtain $\Pi(D, g(D)) \approx 0.36$ and $IL(D, g(D)) \approx 3.33$, which means higher information loss than in generalization (II), where $\Pi(D, g(D)) = 0.16$ and $IL(D, g(D)) \approx 1.17$. In this example, to apply *ID*, intervals are vectorized by calculating the mean of the minimum and maximum values.

If there is a mixture of categorical and numerical attributes in D, the summands of the combined sum have to be weighted accordingly. Relative condensation loss can be used for both categorical and numerical data by defining feature embeddings for categorical data.

5.2. Utility Loss

As mentioned above, the entropy measure can only be used for processing categorical attributes. However, they lack the capability to deal with numerical data. By designing a utility loss that can deal with both categorical and numerical attribute values, we can overcome this downside. In [44], the authors quantify utility by calculating the distance between the relative frequency distributions of each data attribute in the original data and the sanitized data. The distance is based on the Earth Mover Distance (EMD). Further, z-test statistics can be utilized to examine whether significant differences exist between variables in the original and the anonymized data [7]. Another method to score the utility of anonymization that can be used for evaluations is the average size of groups [41],

$$group_{AVG}(D) := \frac{|D|}{|groups|}, \tag{17}$$

or the normalized average equivalence class size metric [42], defined by the formula

$$C_{AVG}(D) := \frac{|D|}{|groups| \cdot k}, \tag{18}$$

or the so-called, commonly used discernibility metric, which scores the number of database entries that are indistinguishable from each other [21,42,43] and penalizes large group sizes,

$$C_{DM}(D) := \sum_{group \in groups} |group|^2. \tag{19}$$

The listed group-size-based metrics $group_{AVG}$, C_{AVG}, and C_{DM} should be minimized to maintain utility while aiming for k-anonymity with k greater than or equal to a predefined positive integer.

Taking into account record suppression (Section 4.3), the proportion of suppressed records in the total number of records before anonymization can also be used to measure the loss of utility. However, applying record suppression to obtain k-anonymity extends group sizes and thus group-size-based metrics.

In contrast to the above approaches, when the context is known in advance, there is the possibility to measure the data utility by scoring the output of ML algorithms that use anonymized data for training. For example, in [38], anonymized labeled data are scored by calculating the F-measure after applying K-Nearest Neighbor to classify molecules that are given as numerical attributes. Considering the Adult dataset, in [48], the authors apply different ML algorithms (K-Nearest Neighbor, Random Forest, Adaptive Boosting, Gradient Tree Boosting) to anonymized data. However, they just apply record suppression for anonymization. In the following, we call this type of score ML utility.

5.3. Privacy Models

There are common models to determine if records in a dataset can be re-identified. Yet, the models have weaknesses that can potentially be exploited by attackers. In the following, we solely focus on the definitions and give examples. In Section 6.7, we list the models' weaknesses and embed the definitions in a legal context.

5.3.1. k-Anonymity

The so-called k-anonymity, first introduced in [3], $k \in \mathbb{N}^+$, $k \leq n$, is a dataset property for anonymization that considers a QI. If the attributes of the QI for each record in the dataset are identical to at least $k - 1$ other records in the dataset, the dataset is called k-anonymous. When having k-anonymity, groups consist of at least k-records. Technically, k-anonymity is defined by

$$k := \min_{group \in groups} |group|.$$

To give an example, Figure 8 shows a database R, where the four attributes `education`, `education-num`, `capital-loss`, `native-country` build a QI and the attribute `age` is an SA. In Figure 8, generalization and discretization are applied, affecting the attributes `education`, `education-num`, `native-country` in such a way that at least two records in the table always have the same QI, leading to k-anonymity with $k = 2$. To be precise, the data are split into two groups: $\{R_1, R_2, R_5, R_6\}$ and $\{R_3, R_4\}$.

The privacy metric of k-anonymity might be combined with different metrics. For example, the authors in [42] introduce the so-called Mondrian multi-dimensional k-anonymity as a multi-dimensional generalization model for k-anonymity. The paper proposes a greedy metric approximation algorithm that offers flexibility and incorporates general-purpose metrics such as the discernibility metric or the normalized average equivalence class size metric (Section 5.2).

age	workclass	fnlwgt	education	education-num	marital-status	occupation	relationship	race	sex	capital-gain	capital-loss	hours-per-week	native-country	income
39	State-gov	77,516	Bachelors	13	Never-married	Adm-clerical	Not-in-family	White	Male	2,174	0	40	United-States	<=50K
50	Self-emp-not-inc	83,311	Bachelors	13	Married-civ-spouse	Exec-managerial	Husband	White	Male	0	0	13	United-States	<=50K
38	Private	215,646	HS-grad	9	Divorced	Handlers-cleaners	Not-in-family	White	Male	0	0	40	United-States	<=50K
53	Private	234,721	11th	7	Married-civ-spouse	Handlers-cleaners	Husband	Black	Male	0	0	40	United-States	<=50K
28	Private	338,409	Bachelors	13	Married-civ-spouse	Prof-specialty	Wife	Black	Female	0	0	40	Cuba	<=50K
37	Private	284,582	Masters	14	Married-civ-spouse	Exec-managerial	Wife	White	Female	0	0	40	United-States	<=50K

age	workclass	fnlwgt	education	education-num	marital-status	occupation	relationship	race	sex	capital-gain	capital-loss	hours-per-week	native-country	income
39	State-gov	77,516	('Bachelors', 'Masters')	(10.0, 14.0)	Never-married	Adm-clerical	Not-in-family	White	Male	2,174	0	40	(United-States, Cuba)	<=50K
50	Self-emp-not-inc	83,311	('Bachelors', 'Masters')	(10.0, 14.0)	Married-civ-spouse	Exec-managerial	Husband	White	Male	0	0	13	(United-States, Cuba)	<=50K
38	Private	215,646	('HS-grad', '11th')	(5.0, 9.0)	Divorced	Handlers-cleaners	Not-in-family	White	Male	0	0	40	(United-States, Cuba)	<=50K
53	Private	234,721	('HS-grad', '11th')	(5.0, 9.0)	Married-civ-spouse	Handlers-cleaners	Husband	Black	Male	0	0	40	(United-States, Cuba)	<=50K
28	Private	338,409	('Bachelors', 'Masters')	(10.0, 14.0)	Married-civ-spouse	Prof-specialty	Wife	Black	Female	0	0	40	(United-States, Cuba)	<=50K
37	Private	284,582	('Bachelors', 'Masters')	(10.0, 14.0)	Married-civ-spouse	Exec-managerial	Wife	White	Female	0	0	40	(United-States, Cuba)	<=50K

Figure 8. Example. The first six rows of the Adult dataset, where the blue-background attributes `education`, `education-num`, `capital-loss`, `native-country` define a QI (just artificially chosen as the QI for demonstration purposes!). Column sorting can be applied to fit the data scheme (Figure 1). The transformed six-row database fulfills k-anonymity with $k = 2$, whereas before discretization in the column `education-num` and generalizations in the columns `education` and `native-country`, the groups had a minimum group size of one. The background colors (orange and yellow) visualize group correspondence, where the attributes in the chosen QI are identical for every record in the group.

5.3.2. *l*-Diversity

l-Diversity, introduced in [45], a second common model for anonymization, considers SAs and gives additional privacy protection to k-anonymity. Again, it considers groups of records with the same QI. When having distinct l-diversity, $l \in \mathbb{N}^+$, $l \leq n$, each group has at least l different attribute values for every SA. Therefore, it is not possible to assign a single attribute value to all records of a group, and group membership does not imply assigning a unique SA to a person. Utilizing l-diversity for scoring anonymity can be challenging, as it depends on the variety of values an SA can have. Technically, l-diversity is defined as

$$l := \min_{group \in groups} |\{R(j) \mid R \in group\}|, \tag{20}$$

where $j \in \{1, \ldots, r + t\}$ denotes the column index of the SA. Given the example at the bottom of Figure 8 and the SA age in every group, all values of age are diverse, and each group consists of two records. Therefore, we have l-diversity with $l = 2$. For the SA `workclass`, there would be l-diversity with $l = 1$.

5.3.3. *t*-Closeness

t-Closeness [46] again takes into account SA values. Whereas l-diversity considers the variety of SA values in single groups, t-closeness checks the granularity of SA values in a single group in comparison to the overall value distribution in the dataset. A group is said to have t-closeness if the EMD between the relative frequency distribution of an SA in this group and the relative frequency distribution of the attribute in the whole dataset is no more than a threshold $t > 0$. A dataset is said to have t-closeness if all equivalence classes have t-closeness. Originally, the authors considered the EMD for this purpose (for comparison, see Section 5.2). The distance is calculated differently for integer, numerical, and categorical attributes. Given a dataset D with an SA at index $s \in \{1, \ldots, r + t\}$, the t-closeness of the dataset is defined as

$$t(D) := \max_{group \in groups} EMD(P, Q_{group}), \tag{21}$$

where the following apply:

- D is the dataset;
- P is the relative frequency distribution of all attribute values in the column of the SA in dataset D;

- Q_{group} is the relative frequency distribution of all attribute values in the column of the SA within *group* that is an equivalence class of dataset D and is obtained by a given QI;
- $EMD(P, Q)$ is the EMD between two relative frequency distributions and depends on the attributes' value type.

Given two ordered relative frequency distributions P and Q of integer values, the ordered EMD is defined as follows:

$$EMD(P, Q) := \frac{1}{o - 1} \sum_{i=0}^{o-1} \left| \sum_{j=0}^{i} (P - Q)_j \right|, \tag{22}$$

where the following apply:

- o is the number of distinct integer attribute values in the SA column;
- P and Q are two relative frequency distributions as histograms (integers are ordered in ascending order).

Given two ordered relative frequency distributions P and Q of categorical values, the equal EMD is defined as follows:

$$EMD(P, Q) := \frac{1}{2} \sum_{i=0}^{o-1} |(P - Q)_i|, \tag{23}$$

where the following apply:

- o is the number of distinct categorical attribute values in the SA column;
- P and Q are two relative frequency distributions as histograms (integers are ordered in ascending order).

Given the example at the bottom of Figure 8 and the sensitive integer attribute age, there would be t-closeness with $t = 0.2$, due to

$$EMD(P_1, Q) = 0.1$$

and

$$EMD(P_2, Q) = 0.2,$$

where P_1 is the orange group with four records and P_2 is the yellow group with two records.

5.4. Re-Identification Risk Quantification

Besides information loss, utility scoring, and privacy models, there is a fourth important method to score anonymization, namely, quantifying the probability of re-identification risk. Privacy models can only be calculated given the anonymized tabular dataset, and information loss and utility scores evaluate the application of anonymization regarding utility preservation. Re-identification risk can be calculated given an anonymized dataset plus an individual's attribute value(s) as background knowledge. The re-identification risk method particularly takes into account the very realistic danger of the so-called inference attacks. For example, in [47], the authors define a score that incorporates the uniqueness, uniformity, and correlation of attribute values. They quantify the re-identification risk by calculating a joint probability of the non-uniqueness and non-uniformity of records. From a technical perspective, the re-identification risk is modeled as a Markov process. We adapt the definition of the probability (PR) of re-identifying a record R to our setting assuming a unit record dataset D, i.e., not having event data. Further, we restrict the definition to attributes that are part of the QI, i.e., to the first r attributes in the dataset. We define the probability (PR) of re-identifying a record R given its attribute values at indices $J \subseteq \{1, \ldots, r\}$ as follows:

$$PR(R(J)) := 1.0 - PP(R(J)) \cdot n), \tag{24}$$

where n is the total number of records in the dataset and $PP(R(J))$ is the privacy probability of non-re-identifying record R in dataset D with a subset of attribute values of record R at attribute indices J, i.e., $R(J)$. PP is calculated by utilizing the Markov Model risk score. Without loss of generality, we re-index the ordered set of attribute values $\{R(1), \ldots, R(r)\}$, define the ordered set $\{R(2), \ldots, R(m)\} := \{R(1), \ldots, R(r)\} \setminus R(J)$, and let $R(1) := R(J)$. Then, the privacy probability of non-re-identifying record R in dataset D with a subset of attribute values of record R at attribute indices J is defined as

$$
\begin{aligned}
PP(R(J)) := P(R(J)) \cdot (1 - P(R|R(J))) \\
\cdot \prod_{1 \le j \le m-1} P(R(j+1)|R(j))(1 - P(R|R(j+1))),
\end{aligned}
\tag{25}
$$

where the following apply:

- $P(R(J)) := Pr[X_j = R(j), j \in J]$;
- $P(R|R(J)) := Pr[X_i = R(i), i \notin J | X_j = R(j), j \in J]$;
- $P(R(j+1)|R(j)) := Pr[X_{j+1} = R(j+1)|X_j = R(j)]$;
- $P(R|R(j+1)) := Pr[X_i = R(i), i \notin J | X_{j+1} = R(j+1)]$.

Calculating the average PR for all records in the dataset yields

$$
PR(D, J) := \frac{1}{n} \sum_{i=1}^{n} PR(R_i(J)).
\tag{26}
$$

Considering the dataset given in Figure 9 as an example, given the attribute value "Bachelors" for education in dataset record R_1, the privacy probability of re-identifying the record is $PR(R_1(\{1\})) = 0.9$. The calculation of the start probability, i.e., attribute uniqueness, $P(R_1(\{1\}) \approx 0.386$, is equivalent to the re-identification-risk score, RIR, which is efficiently calculated with CSIRO's R4 tool [49]. Given the attribute value "HS-grad" for education in dataset record R_3, the privacy probability of re-identifying this record is the highest, as $PR(R_3(\{1\})) = 1.0$, and the RIR score is $P(R_3(\{1\}) = 1.0$. Whereas the RIR score does not depend on the order of attributes, PR depends on the attribute indices and also takes into account inter-attribute relations. Besides the average privacy probability of re-identifying records, the paper [47] describes the minimum, maximum, median, and marketer re-identification risk based on the calculated PR values of all dataset records to score the re-identification risk of a dataset.

	education	sex	hours-per-week
R_1	Bachelors	M	40
R_2	Bachelors	M	13
R_3	HS-grad	M	40
R_4	11th	M	40
R_5	Bachelors	F	40
R_6	Masters	F	40

Figure 9. Example. Projecting the first six rows of the Adult set on the attributes `education`, `sex`, `hours-per-week`. The PR score assumes that attribute values are known and subsequently calculates the risk of re-identifying a single record (in the case of unit record data). Having knowledge about different values of the attribute `education` (yellow resp. orange) leads to different privacy probabilities of re-identifying a record (record R_1 resp. R_3).

5.5. Curse of Dimensionality

The phenomena of the Curse of Dimensionality, first mentioned in [50] in the context of linear equations, refer to the increase in computational complexity and requirements for data analysis as the number of variables (dimensions/attributes) grows. This increase makes it more and more difficult to find optimal solutions for high-dimensional problems. Considering anonymization, most privacy models on multivariate tabular data lead to poor utility if enforced on datasets with many attributes [32]. Aggarwal has already shown in [39] that large-sized QIs lead to difficult anonymization, having previously presented condensation [29] (described in Section 4.7) as a synthetic approach to anonymization to achieve k-anonymity. Besides showing the openness inference attacks in terms of probability when having high-dimensional data, in an experimental analysis, it is visualized that anonymizing high-dimensional data, even for only 2-anonymity, leads to unacceptable information loss. However, high-dimensional data potentially have inter-attribute correlations that—despite the theoretic Curse of Dimensionality—can be used to better anonymize them in terms of utility preservation. Therefore, to overcome the Curse of Dimensionality in anonymization, in the so-called Vertical Fragmentation, the data are first partitioned into disjoint sets of correlating attributes and subsequently anonymized and assembled after the anonymization step [38]. This approach is method-agnostic, as it can be used with all anonymization methods described in Section 4. Given the attributes $A_1, \ldots, A_{r+t}$, a vertical fragmentation $\mathcal{F}$ of the attributes is a partitioning of the attributes in fragments $\mathcal{F} = \{F_1, \ldots, F_f\}$ s.t. $\forall i \in \{1, \ldots, f\} : F_i \subseteq \{A_1, \ldots, A_{r+t}\}, F_i \cap F_j = \varnothing, i \neq j$ and $\bigcup_{i=1,\ldots,f} F_i = \{A_1, \ldots, A_f\}$, where $i, j \in \{1, \ldots, r+t\}$. Considering the single fragments, groups can be formed, and k-anonymity, calculated. However, there are a vast number of possibilities for vertical fragmentation depending on the number of attributes. Therefore, systematic vertical fragmentation that takes into account inter-attribute correlations and post-utility after anonymization has to be chosen. The approach in [38] focuses on classification problems and attempts to maximize the amount of non-redundant information contained in single fragments while also striving for high utility of fragments to conduct the classification task. The authors propose the so-called Fragmentation Minimum Redundancy Maximum Relevance (FMRMR) metric to head into beneficial fragmentation. In the following, let F^j, $j = 1, \ldots, |F|$, denote indexed attributes of fragment F and A^C be the class attribute in the database. The "supervised" FMRMR metric is calculated with the formula

$$FMRMR(\mathcal{F}) := \sum_{F \in \mathcal{F}} (V_F - W_F), \tag{27}$$

where

$$V_F := \frac{1}{|F|} \sum_{j=1}^{|F|} I\left(A^c, F^j\right) \tag{28}$$

is the total mutual information between the attributes and class attribute A^C in fragment F of fragmentation $\mathcal{F}$ and

$$W_F := \frac{1}{|F|^2} \sum_{k=1}^{|F|} \sum_{j=1}^{|F|} I\left(F^k, F^j\right), \tag{29}$$

is the total pairwise mutual information between the attributes in fragment F of fragmentation $\mathcal{F}$. The formula [51]

$$I(A_k, A_j) := \sum_{a_k \in R(k)} \sum_{a_j \in R(j)} Pr\left[X_k = a_k,\ X_j = a_j\right]$$
$$\log_2 \left(\frac{Pr\left[X_k = a_k,\ X_j = a_j\right]}{Pr\left[X_k = a_k\right] Pr\left[X_j = a_j\right]} \right) \tag{30}$$

defines the mutual information between attributes A_k and A_j, where X_k, X_j are discrete random variables as defined in Section 5.1 and the joint probability distribution is defined as

$$Pr[X_k = a,\ X_j = b] :=$$
$$\frac{|\{1 \leq i \leq n : R_i(k) = a,\ R_i(j) = b\}|}{n}, \tag{31}$$

where $a \in R(k)$, $b \in R(j)$ are values of the corresponding column. Note that if X_k and X_j are independent random variables, we have $I(A_k, A_j) = 0$, and the columns are non-redundant.

With Equation (27), the fragment utility for the classification task at hand is maximized (Equation (28)) while minimizing the mutual information and redundancy of attributes inside the fragment (Equation (29)). Above, we described the procedure in the context of a supervised application. However, vertical fragmentation can also be used in the context of an unsupervised application by adding one or more common attributes to the single fragments to enforce correspondence between fragments. Therefore, when having an unsupervised task at hand, an "unsupervised" FMRMR metric might be defined by adapting Equation (27):

$$uFMRMR(\mathcal{F}_{ext}) := - \sum_{Fe \in \mathcal{F}_{ext}} W_{Fe}, \tag{32}$$

where $\mathcal{F}_{ext} := \{Fe_1, \ldots, Fe_f\}$ is obtained from fragmentation $\mathcal{F} = \{F_1, \ldots, F_f\}$ by adding one or more common attribute(s) $A \subset \{A_1, \ldots, A_{r+t}\}$ to each fragment: $\forall i = 1, \ldots, f :$ $Fe_i := F_i \cup A$.

To sum up, the vertical fragmentation approach aims to alleviate the negative effects of the Curse of Dimensionality. By choosing suitable discrete or continuous probability distributions depending on the given data, after possibly necessary preprocessing like discretizing values, the approach can be used in principle for both categorical and numerical data. Figure 10 visualizes the mutual information of all attribute pairs of the Adult dataset in a symmetric matrix.

The Curse of Dimensionality also occurs in DP. For example, in [52], the authors state that Randomized Response suffers from the Curse of Dimensionality. There is a trade-off between applying Randomized Response to single attributes and applying Randomized Response to a set of attributes simultaneously. Depending on the number of records, the latter might lead to poor utility of the estimated distribution of the original data, and applying Randomized Response to single attributes implies a poor estimated joint distribution of the original data. The authors propose an algorithm to cluster attributes with high mutual dependencies and apply Randomized Response to single clusters jointly. Their measure of dependency between two attributes A_k, A_j is based on the absolute value of the Pearson Correlation and Cramér's V Statistic $V(A_k, A_j)$. In Randomized Response, $|Corr(A_k, A_j)|$ can be calculated given discretized numerical attributes A_k, A_j, and Cramér's V Statistic $V(A_k, A_j)$ can be calculated given categorical attributes A_k, A_j that have no ordering. In their experimental results, they empirically evaluate the phenomenon on the multivariate Adult dataset.

The Pearson Correlation of attributes A_j, A_k is defined as

$$|Corr(A_k, A_j)| := \left| \frac{\sum_{i=1}^{n} \left(A_j^{(i)} - \bar{A}_j \right) \left(A_k^{(i)} - \bar{A}_k \right)}{\sqrt{\sum_{i=1}^{n} \left(A_j^{(i)} - \bar{A}_j \right)^2 \sum_{i=1}^{n} \left(A_k^{(i)} - \bar{A}_k \right)^2}} \right|, \tag{33}$$

where $\bar{A}_j$ resp. $\bar{A}_k$ denote the mean value of attributes A_j resp. A_k.

Let r^j be the number of categories of attribute A_j and r^k be the number of categories of attribute A_k. In the scope of the following formula, let $\{1, \ldots, r^j\}$ be the set of categories of attribute A_j and $\{1, \ldots, r^k\}$ be the set of categories of attribute A_k.

Then, Cramér's V Statistic of attributes A_j, A_k is defined as

$$V_{jk} = \sqrt{\frac{\chi_{jk}^2 / n}{\min(r^j - 1, r^k - 1)}}, \tag{34}$$

where

$$\chi^2 := \sum_{p=1}^{r^j} \sum_{q=1}^{r^k} \frac{(n \cdot Pr[X_j = p, X_k = q] - n \cdot Pr[X_j = p] \cdot Pr[X_k = q])^2}{n \cdot Pr[X_j = p] \cdot Pr[X_k = q]} \tag{35}$$

is the chi-squared independence statistic.

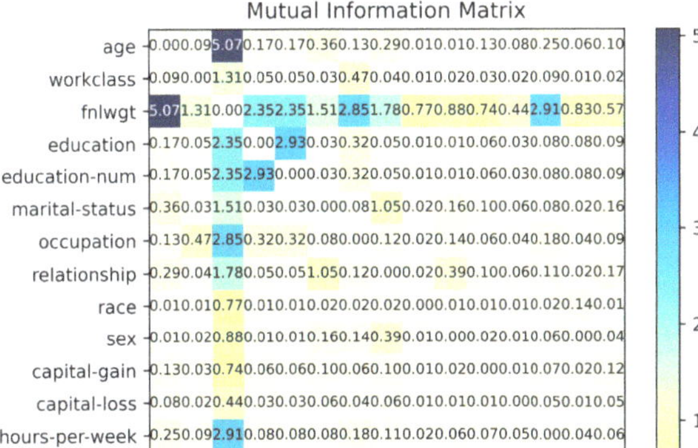

Figure 10. Example. Considering the Adult dataset as an example, this dataset can be used for the supervised training of a machine learning algorithm to classify persons having income $\leq$ USD 50 K. The categorical attributes `education` and `education-num` contain highly mutual information ($I(A_{education}, A_{education-num}) \approx 2.93$) and might be part of different fragments, whereas the categorical attributes `race` and `sex` do not contain highly mutual information ($I(A_{race}, A_{sex}) \approx 0.01$) and can be part of the same fragment in vertical fragmentation. The calculated mutual information values are based on the training dataset (without the test data) of the Adult dataset. The matrix is symmetric because the function in (30) is symmetric. The values are rounded to two decimal places.

Figure 11 shows an example where the absolute value of the Pearson Correlation and Cramér's V Statistic are calculated for numerical resp. categorical attributes in the Adult dataset.

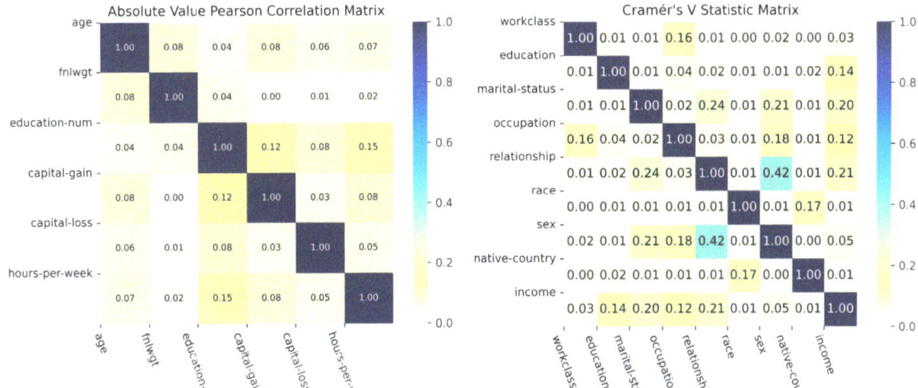

Figure 11. Example. Absolute values of Pearson Correlation coefficients and Cramér's V Statistic coefficients in the Adult dataset. Both matrices are symmetric. The values are rounded to two decimal places.

6. Legal Perspective

Sections 4 and 5 have presented technical procedures, and the consequences of the anonymization of tabular datasets have been worked out. To comply with the legal requirement for anonymization in the EU, especially concerning the GDPR, the legal basis and prerequisites must be elaborated. Based on this, conclusions about the legally secure and robust anonymization of tabular data can be drawn. In general, the legal literature on anonymization is not restricted to structured data.

However, the literature discussed in this review can be straightforwardly related to tabular data but not to unstructured data.

Firstly, we look at the legal aspects of data anonymization in general. The legal framework and requirements for handling anonymized data are analyzed. Subsequently, the problem of anonymizing tabular data is addressed, and existing legislation, analyzed. Particular attention is paid to the GDPR, which must be interpreted as the legal basis for this problem. Furthermore, different approaches to anonymizing data are considered. Especially, the absolute and relative theories of anonymization are discussed, and the different legal interpretations are highlighted. Lastly, an evaluation of the privacy models is carried out with an individual evaluation of the k-anonymity, l-diversity, and t-closeness privacy models, which serve as common approaches to anonymizing tabular data. Relevant factors such as the effectiveness and security of anonymization techniques are considered.

6.1. Synopsis of the Problem

When publishing data, the GDPR sets the framework and requirements for lawful publication. The aim of this law is to protect the individual's right to informational self-determination, i.e., the individual's own influence on the dissemination and collection of personal data is to be preserved [53].

The European GDPR refers in its scope exclusively to personal data. This means that all data that cannot be traced back to an identifiable person fall outside the scope of protection and are generally available as Open Data. Despite the considerable importance of the distinction between personal reference and anonymity, the GDPR does not regulate this but merely presupposes the concept of anonymity as a counterpart to personal data.

According to Art. 4 (1) GDPR "personal data means any information relating to an identified or identifiable natural person ('data subject'); an identifiable natural person is one who can be identified, directly or indirectly, in particular by reference to an identifier such as a name, an identification number, location data, an online identifier, or to one or more factors specific to the physical, physiological, genetic, mental, economic, cultural, or social identity of that natural person". In this context, the Article 29 Data Protection Working Party stated, in Opinion 4/2007 WP 136, that identification is normally achieved using particular pieces of information, which are called "identifiers" [54]. They are distinguished in "directly" and "indirectly" identifiers.

Thereby—in the context of tabular data—in our terminology, "directly" identifier refers to a Direct Identifier and "indirectly" identifier refers to an attribute that is part of a QI. A person may be directly identified by name, whereas they may be identified indirectly by a telephone number, car registration, or by a combination of significant criteria, which allows them to be recognized by narrowing down the group to which they belong (age, occupation, place of residence) [54].

Particularly with regard to Indirect Identifiers, the issue arises when a reference to a person still exists. Some characteristics are so unique that someone can be identified with no effort ("present Prime Minister of Spain"), but a combination of several different details may also be specific enough to narrow it down to one person, especially if someone has access to additional information [54]. According to this, sufficient anonymization only exists if this personal reference is removed and is not traceable [55].

Hereby, it should be pointed out that in [54], "[...] it is not necessary for the information to be considered as personal data that it is contained in a structured database or file".

However, the given examples mostly refer to structured data, as they are given in tabular datasets.

Further, as Recital 26 to the GDPR states, "the principles of data protection should therefore not apply to anonymous information, namely, information, which does not relate to an identified or identifiable natural person or to personal data rendered anonymous in such a manner that the data subject is not or no longer identifiable".

Anonymization occurs when personal data are changed in such a way that the person behind them can no longer be identified by personal and factual circumstances [56]. This also applies to the remaining or otherwise related datasets in their entirety [57]. The complexity of anonymity, therefore, lies in the definition, which is difficult to delimit and determine, of which datasets have which attributes that are sufficiently related to a person. This can only be performed with an intensive examination of the type and scope of the existing data and the data to be anonymized [57].

To obtain meaningful Open Data, a careful and difficult balance between sufficient information and effective anonymization to protect data subjects is necessary. Basically, anonymization must be distinguished from pseudonymization, which is essentially characterized by the fact that the data and persons can be identified again by using a code or key [55]. So far, pseudonymization has been considered insufficient and treated as personal data [56]. However, the European General Court (EGC) recently ruled that under certain circumstances, pseudonymous data may not fall under the scope of the GDPR if the data recipient lacks means for re-identification. The critical factor is whether the recipient has access to the decryption key or can obtain it. If not, the data are not considered personal data and thus do not fall under the GDPR [58].

6.2. Recital 26

Recital 26 to the GDPR further demands "to ascertain whether means are reasonably likely to be used to identify the natural person, account should be taken of all objective factors, such as the costs of and the amount of time required for identification, taking into consideration the available technology at the time of the processing and technological developments".

In determining the relevant knowledge and means, Recital 26, therefore, requires a risk analysis to evaluate the likelihood of the risk of re-identification. In this analysis, an objective standard must be used, and in principle, a purely abstract standard of measurement must be applied, not the subjective interests and motivation for the use of such data. Under certain circumstances, however, these must also be included in the assessment criteria [53].

The risk of re-identification must, therefore, be assessed on a case-by-case basis. However, the interpretation of these requirements and the extent to which the available knowledge and means of third parties are to be taken into account are controversial. In this context, the spectrum of opinions is divided with regard to the requirements for the feasibility of establishing a connection to a person. It is questionable whether it depends on the respective Data Controller (relative personal reference) or whether anybody can establish the personal reference (absolute personal reference) [53].

6.3. Absolute Personal Reference/Zero-Risk Approach

The absolute approach shows two main considerations. On the one hand, it is about the group of people who must be considered potential de-anonymizers. The other is the re-identification risk that still exists due to the means available to this group of people. According to the absolute personal reference approach, a person becomes identifiable if anybody at all can re-establish the personal reference. All means available to this third party must be deliberated over. Hence, this approach can only be met if all anonymization is fully and completely irreversible and the capability of de-anonymization is eliminated [59]. In this regard, it is sometimes demanded that the original and thus still personal data records are deleted after anonymization has been implemented [60]. This refers to Tuple

Suppression, which is explained in Section 4.3. According to this approach, they are still personal data when a Data Controller does not delete the original data and hands over the anonymized dataset [61]. Accordingly, all possibilities for reversing the anonymization process must be taken into contemplation. This also includes illegal means of obtaining special knowledge as well as potential infringements of professional confidentiality [62].

To a greater extent, nevertheless, such a scale should not be required and is simply not feasible, according to the state of the art [63]. This also reflects both the telos of the law and the wording of Recital 26. Recital 26 states that "all the means reasonably likely to be used" should be deliberated. Hence, the GDPR does not consider all and every possibility of de-anonymization. It more likely supports a risk-based approach to it, which must be evaluated on the basis of the circumstances of the individual case.

Furthermore, following this absolute approach would mean that most data must still be considered personal, making true anonymization practically impossible. The main issue lies in the fact that there can never be complete certainty that no one else possesses additional knowledge or data that could potentially lead to re-identification [64].

6.4. Relative Personal Reference/Risk-Based Approach

The relative approach also exhibits two considerations that run parallel to those of the absolute approach. First, the circle of persons who need to be focused on is tighter. Secondly, the relative approach acknowledges a certain risk of de-identification [62,64]. Moreover, when dealing with Open Data, the choice between the relative and absolute approaches becomes largely inconsequential. The very nature of Open Data dictates that they should be accessible to a broad and diverse audience, opening the data to virtually anybody interested in utilizing them. As a result, the practical reality of Open Data means that considerations must extend to any potential data recipient, since they all have access to the shared data. Therefore, it is necessary to consider anybody as a potential de-anonymizer. The absolute and relative approaches thus lead to the same result. However, a key distinction between the relative approach and the absolute one emerges concerning the treatment of re-identification risk. While the absolute approach aspires to eliminate any possibility of re-identification, the relative approach recognizes that a certain level of re-identification risk may persist. The decisive factor is then the assessment of the risk and the inclusion of risk factors.

6.5. Tightened Relative Personal Reference of the EU's Court of Justice

The EU's Court of Justice (ECJ) developed a conciliatory, relative approach to establishing the reference to persons in the context of a preliminary ruling in 2016. In this respect, the ECJ dealt with the question of the extent to which the knowledge and means of third parties should be included in accordance with Recital 26, so we are referring to anonymized data. The decisive issue was whether dynamic IP addresses constitute personal data. The crucial question was which conditions must be met for a Data Controller to "reasonably" have access to the data held by a third party [64]. As General Advocate Sanchez pointed out, Recital 26 does not refer to any means that may be used by anybody but constrains these means to "likely reasonably to use".

Therefore, a risk-based approach is more in line with the wording. Third parties are persons to whom any person may reasonably turn to obtain additional data or knowledge for the purpose of identification. After all, the General Advocate set forth that "otherwise [...] it would be virtually impossible to discriminate between the various means, since it would always be possible to imagine the hypothetical contingency of a third party who, no matter how inaccessible to the [data controller], could—now or in the future—have additional relevant data to assist in the identification of a [person]" [64].

This restriction of the absolute theory and tightening of the relative theory have been endorsed by the ECJ. In this respect, the absolute theory is limited to the extent that additional knowledge, which can only be gained using illegal methods or is practically impossible on account of the fact that it requires a disproportionate effort in terms of time, cost, and manpower [64]. Thus, the risk of identification appears to be negligible [64].

The relative approach, on the other hand, is tightened to the effect that they are still to be considered personal data if there are legal means that can be used to obtain additional knowledge from a third party that can enable the identification of a person [64]. However, the extent to which such legal means are available and whether it is reasonable to expect them to be used remains an open question. This concretization work is, therefore, incumbent on the national courts [64].

6.6. Evaluation Standards for the Risk Assessment of the Techniques

The Art. 29 Data Protection Working Party sets out various criteria for assessing the risk of individuals being identifiable or determinable when personal data are anonymized. The individual risk groups are merely a framework for evaluating the risk of identification. These principles should always be applied to the individual case and require a thorough evaluation. According to the idea of the data protection authority, Data Controllers should submit a final risk evaluation to the relevant authority. This is recommended as a general concept that a Data Controller drafts for his existing and expected datasets.

The first aspect of risks is singling out individuals from datasets [61]. The initial point is anonymized data records that have been generalized, for example. The aim of a legally secure anonymization process is to form these groups on such a scale that an individual assignment of attributes to a single person is no longer possible [65]. This is to be achieved by ensuring that the combined group has several identical attributes. The danger of singling out, therefore, exists within small group formations as well as with extreme attributes, since these are easier to assign. If persons in group formations still have unique characteristics of attributes, this favors classification. In order to prevent singling out, an appropriately large number of similar attributes must be chosen based on the evaluation of the individual case and the dataset. In this evaluation process, special attention should be paid to preserving the information content [61]. Consequently, if the k-groups are becoming too large, the information value can be reduced or falsified. Therefore, the information content of the dataset should always be taken into account, as this can result in data being rendered unrecognizable or falsified. In this way, the Data Controller can maintain the information content of other attributes and still guarantee anonymity.

The second risk factor relates to the linkability of data [61]. In relation to an anonymous dataset, this must be considered in combination with two individually anonymous datasets. If a Data Controller publishes several anonymized datasets, these must also preserve anonymity in their entirety. If individual persons can be determined from the combination of these two datasets, because individual attributes can now be linked together, the data are still to be considered personal [66]. In this respect, this approach has substantial uncertainty. It is questionable, and not yet clarified, which data are to be considered for this purpose. Certainly, the entirety of the publication is to be taken into account, but it is debatable whether data already published by third parties are also to be included [67]. Or, what probably leads to the widest extension, whether third parties have data at their disposal with which a linkage leads to the identifiability of individuals. Again, the jurisprudence of the ECJ can be used, that is, only additional knowledge that can be obtained by legal means is taken into consideration.

The last criterion set by the Art. 29 Data Protection Working Party is the so-called inference [61]. This is the most difficult requirement to circumvent. Basically, it means that conclusions can be drawn from datasets for the entirety of persons. In view of the challenges of anonymization, it rather demands that no conclusions that could be used to infer an individual person can be drawn from the published dataset. Here, too, there is a lack of concreteness in differentiation from singling out. However, reference attributes are probably more limited to the individual dataset from which assumptions could be drawn.

In the further outlook, each anonymization concept and method is, therefore, examined with regard to these three risk factors [61]. Other aspects may also be included as risks in the evaluation, so the standard for these three aspects from the perspective of the "motivated intruder" must always be set. This "motivated intruder test" is intended to test the anonymization carried out for its stability and, as above, is based on the individual case. The motivation of the intruder is inevitably measured according to the value and information content of the dataset.

6.7. Legal Evaluation

This subsection conducts a legal evaluation by embedding technical terms such as privacy models in a legal context.

6.7.1. Identifiers, Quasi-Identifiers, and Sensitive Attributes

In the process of anonymization using the individual models, the QIs are to be determined and evaluated. For example, these might include dates of specific events (death, birth, discharge from a hospital, etc.), postal codes, sex, ethnicity, etc. [68]. One can orient oneself towards an assessment system that evaluates and assesses the attributes. This should essentially identify all SAs, also in the sense of the GDPR. For this purpose, all variables are listed and evaluated within the framework of three case groups. The assessment ranges from low (1) to medium (2) to high (3). The first category for the individual variables is "replication", in which the information is assessed according to how consistently it appears in connection with a person. A low score is given to measured blood pressure, while a high score is given to a person's date of birth. The second group is concerned with the "availability" of the information. The decisive factor, here, is how available this information or variable is for third parties to re-identify. As already shown above, the ECJ's standard also affects this assessment as to how far-reaching additional knowledge is to be taken into account. Therefore, the laboratory values of a person are difficult to obtain, whereas, as in the example of the "Breyer" case, the person behind an IP address can certainly be obtained by legal means if there is a legitimate interest. This should also be considered for public registers, such as the land registry. The last category concerns "distinguishability", according to which it is possible to assess how people can be distinguished from each other by means of individual values. For example, a ZIP code with a complete reproduction is to be classified as higher than one with a shortened reproduction [11].

6.7.2. k-Anonymity

The privacy model k-anonymity, which is defined in Section 5.3.1, ensures that given a QI, each record is indistinguishable from at least $k - 1$ other records, making it more difficult for attackers to identify individuals by their attributes [3]. The degree of privacy protection depends on the quality and quantity of attributes in the dataset and the choice of k. The larger k, the larger its group, and the more securely an individual is protected from re-identification.

Singling out within a k-group is made more difficult by the fact that all individuals have the same QI and are indistinguishable based on them, such that individuals can hide behind the k-group.

However, Data Processors must also consider the risk of attribute disclosure, where an attacker can infer sensitive information about an individual even if they cannot directly re-identify them. This may still be possible with linkability and inference. Linkability of records may still be possible, because the probability of $1/k$ with small k is sufficient to make correlations about affected individuals among records in a k-group.

Another deficit of the k-anonymity model is that attacks are not closed with inference techniques [65]. If all k-individuals belong to the same group and it is known to which group an individual belongs, it is very easy to determine the value of a property. Attackers are able to extract information from the dataset and make inferences about the affected individuals, whether it is included in the dataset or not.

Therefore, whether this model alone ensures compliance with the anonymization requirement of the GDPR is largely negated. To achieve robust anonymization, additional models such as *l*-diversity or *t*-closeness can be used.

Nevertheless, the model is used in anonymization applications because it provides the basic structure for anonymization when values are not to be corrupted, as it is the case with perturbation. The LEOSS cohort study [10] uses an anonymization pipeline built on k equal to 11 by applying the ARX tool [9]. Thus, they follow the recommendation of the Art. 29 Data Protection Working Party (WP216) [61], which evaluates a k-value less than or equal to 10 as insufficient. The k-value depends, among other things, on the number of aggregated attributes [57] used in a QI. In the NAPKON study, the qualitative analysis of the attributes included in the dataset was controlled for the risk of linkage or selection by reducing the uniqueness of the combinations of the variables age, sex, quarter, and year of diagnosis and cohort [69].

6.7.3. *l*-Diversity

The privacy model *l*-diversity, which is defined in Section 5.3.2, was introduced as an extension of k-anonymity to compensate one of its major shortcomings: the failure to account for the distribution of SAs within each group of k-indistinguishable individuals [45]. This deficiency can lead to the disclosure of SAs resulting from the merging to k-groups. The advancement aims to ensure that deterministic attacks using inference techniques are no longer possible by guaranteeing that the individual attributes in each equivalence class have at least l different values, so that attackers are always guaranteed significant uncertainty about a particular affected individual [61].

Thus, the evaluation in [68] shows two different shortcomings of *l*-diversity, when the l values for each SA are not well represented. A similarity attack can be performed when the SAs fulfill the criterion of *l*-diversity but are semantically similar. Despite meeting the requirement of *l*-diversity, it is possible to learn that someone has cancer when every attribute value is a specific form of cancer. An attack on skewness can be made when the overall distribution is skewed. Then, *l*-diversity cannot prevent attribute disclosure. This is the case when the distribution of attribute values in a dataset consists predominantly of one of two possible values and a k-group has the other value except for one entry. This allows assumptions to be derived about this group that an attacker can use.

Despite possible protection from inference techniques, linkability may still be possible even with diversification because this risk still remains on k-anonymity settings. Only the risk of singling out can be prevented when implementing *l*-Diversity as an extension of k-anonymity. *l*-diversity processes just the SAs that were initially unaffected. Unlike k-anonymity, there is no recommendation from WP216 for a threshold of l.

This privacy model is suitable for protecting data from attacks using inference techniques when the values are well distributed and represented. However, it should be noted that this technique cannot prevent information leakage if the attribute values within a group are inconsistently distributed, have low bandwidth, or are semantically similar. Eventually, the concept of *l*-diversity provides room for attacks using inference techniques [61].

6.7.4. *t*-Closeness

The privacy model *t*-closeness, which is defined in Section 5.3.3, deals with a new measure of security and complements *l*-diversity [46]. It takes into account the unavoidable gain in knowledge of an attacker when considering all SA values in the entire dataset. *t*-Closeness represents a measure of minimal knowledge gain that results from considering a generalized k-group compared with the entire dataset. This also means that any group of individuals, indistinguishable on the basis of the QI, behind which a person is anonymized, can hardly be distinguished from any other group with respect to their SA values by the *t*-closeness-defined measure. Thus, a person's data are better protected in their anonymizing group than was the case with *l*-diversity, since this group hardly reveals more information than the entire distribution.

In the specific case where the attribute values within a group are non-uniformly distributed, have a narrow range of values, or are semantically similar, an approach known as *t*-closeness is applied. This represents a further improvement in anonymization using generalization and consists of a procedure in which the data are partitioned into groups in such a way that the original distribution of the attribute values in the original dataset is reproduced as far as possible [61]. However, WP216 has not given any recommendation for the *t*-value, so it depends on case-by-case consideration. One approach would be to incrementally increase the *t*-value if re-identification by an attacker with the current value is still possible.

With *t*-closeness, a dataset processed with *k*-anonymity is improved regarding the risk of inference and was implemented in the LEOSS cohort study [10], with *t* equal to 0.5.

Nevertheless, data anonymized using *k*-anonymity and *t*-closeness are still vulnerable to inference techniques and have to reviewed case by case. Whereas in *k*-anonymity and *l*-diversity, large values mean better privacy, in *t*-closeness, small values mean better privacy.

6.7.5. Differential Privacy

DP, which is defined in Section 4.6, applied as a randomized process, manipulates data in such a way that the direct link between data and the data subject can be removed [61]. There are several mechanisms that satisfy the defined anonymity criterion and are applicable to different types of data. The method ensures the protection of individual data by modifying the results by adding random noise. This can limit a potential attacker's ability to draw conclusions about the attribute value of a single data point, even if they know all the attribute values of the other data points. By adding random noise, the influence of a single data point on the statistical result is hidden [70]. With regard to the risk criteria, it can be seen that singling out can be prevented under certain circumstances. Linking and inference can still be possible with multiple applications and are thus dependent on the so-called privacy budget, which refers to parameter ϵ in Section 4.6.

6.7.6. Synthetic Data

As explained in Section 4.7, synthetic approaches can be used as a workaround to anonymize tabular data. Artificially generated synthetic data retain the statistical characteristics of the original data. This process can involve utilizing a machine learning model that comprehends the structure and statistical distribution of the original data to create synthetic data. Preserving the statistical properties of the original data is vital, as it enables data analysts to derive significant insights from the synthetic data, treating them as if they were drawn directly from the original dataset. To introduce a diverse range of data, the generation process may incorporate a certain level of unrelated randomness into synthetic data [71].

Synthetic data can help to ensure that an individual's records are not singled out or linked. However, if an adversary knows of the presence of a person in the original dataset, even if that person cannot be individualized, sensitive inferences such as attribute disclosure may still be possible, as shown in [72]. Moreover, machine learning models can be exposed to privacy attacks by the so-called Membership Inference Attacks or Model Inversion Attacks [73].

6.7.7. Risk Assessment Overview

Based on the findings in Sections 6.7.2–6.7.6, Table 3 gives an overview of risk assessments of the discussed privacy models and privacy-enhancing technologies for anonymizing tabular data. We only rate with respect to the attack scenarios that are described by the Art. 29 Data Protection Working Party: singling out, linkability, and inference.

Table 3. Risk assessment for anonymization methods of tabular data. (1): Risk depends on chosen k. (2): It does not take into account similarity attacks. (3): Based on k-anonymity. (4): Risk depends on value distribution of Sensitive Attributes. (5): Risk depends on privacy budget. (6): Might be combined with DP. +: The method can be considered a strategy to defend against the attack scenario. −: The method cannot solely be considered a defense strategy against the attack scenario.

	Singling Out	Linkability	Inference
k-Anonymity	+	− (1)	− (2)
l-Diversity	+ (3)	− (1,3)	+ (2,4)
t-Closeness	+ (3)	− (1,3)	+ (2,4)
DP	+	+ (5)	+ (5)
Synthetic data	+	+	− (6)

7. Discussion

In our exploration of anonymization methods and scores for tabular data, some unclarities and issues are present.

Foremost is the uncertainty surrounding the choice of QIs and thresholds for privacy models. A fundamental challenge is the inability to make a priori assumptions about the knowledge an adversary possesses regarding records in tabular data. Often, there is a vast array of potential QIs that could be exploited, which goes hand in hand with the lack of context understanding.

This issue is further complicated by the fact that the privacy models adopted only cover specific scenarios, leaving room for specific attack scenarios to succeed.

Further, to maximize privacy protection, we may compromise the data utility. A potential solution might be found in combining different anonymization methods, each addressing specific weaknesses. For instance, use-case-specific DP can be applied to provide an additional layer of security. However, implementation details and the actual compatibility of methods are yet to be thoroughly studied. As an example, the interaction between t-closeness and group formation has shown that the elimination of group records to achieve certain t-closeness, k-anonymity, and l-diversity can unintentionally lead to higher t. This can potentially compromise the achieved anonymization.

Moreover, the structure and composition of the dataset themselves poses a challenge. Often, SAs are the target variables, thereby making their concealment problematic. Privacy models, such as l-diversity, depend on the number of attribute values for the SA, meaning that the effectiveness of the method varies based on the characteristics of the dataset. When it comes to anonymizing high-dimensional tabular data, as described in Section 5.5, one also has to deal with the Curse of Dimensionality.

Anonymizing the Adult dataset into k-anonymity with $k > 10$ still yields comparable utility for different ML models, but this is data- and task-dependent and DP might additionally be applied in model inference [48].

As Wagner et al. [14] have recommended, a selection of multiple metrics to cover multiple aspects of privacy should be pursued. This approach allows for more robust privacy protection, minimizing the chances of oversights and weaknesses.

The implementation of these privacy protection measures presents its own set of challenges. To begin with, different types of data, such as categorical and numerical, necessitate different approaches. Some attributes might even possess dual characteristics, complicating the anonymization procedure. Different possible definitions and ways of implementing these methods add to the complexity. Privacy models must also be adapted to data types, with a clear understanding of the differences between integers and floating-point numbers, or categorical versus numerical data types. Additionally, applying these methods often involves a trial-and-error process. Multi-stage anonymization is a potential strategy that might yield better results, though the complexity and difficulty of execution cannot be underestimated. For example, achieving certain k-anonymity using generalization and suppression with minimal loss of information [18] is an NP-hard problem. This implies that execution time could be exponential in the worst-case scenarios—a factor that needs to be tested and considered in the implementation phase.

Last but not least, the context of data—whether they are fixed or streaming—poses another challenge. Privacy protection measures for streaming or online data may require a different approach, considering the time and space complexity involved.

Future research should focus on addressing these issues, providing a more comprehensive and effective solution to data anonymization of tabular data.

8. Conclusions

In conclusion, this article has examined the technical and legal considerations of data anonymization and explored different approaches to solving this problem.

From the legal perspective, based on our analysis and legal evaluation, the following conclusions can be drawn. The risk-based approach, in alignment with the ECJ case law in the "Breyer" case, highlights the importance of considering legally obtainable additional knowledge when assessing the acceptable re-identification risk. This approach enhances the understanding of data anonymity by taking into account relevant information that can potentially lead to re-identification. Due to the missing legal requirements for robust anonymization, a recommendation for k-anonymity with k greater than 10 was made by the Article 29 Data Protection Working Party in WP216 [61]. Prior to implementing k-anonymity, it is crucial to identify the QIs using the evaluation table and the provided evaluation system. Furthermore, the opinion suggests the use of t-closeness. Similarly, there are no legal requirements at this point to ensure legally compliant anonymization. Only in [10], a t-value set at 0.5 was considered to be a high level of privacy protection. However, since the risk-based approach is based on individual-case assessment, it must be considered that these values should not be considered universally applicable. The ongoing uncertainty makes anonymization still a challenging endeavor. In addition, it is important to note that for anonymized data, future consideration of the EU Data Governance Act, particularly in relation to data rooms and the security of such data, becomes crucial. The Data Governance Act aims to establish a framework for secure and responsible data sharing that ensures data protection and governance in data rooms.

Future research and advancements in the field should continue to explore the legal and technical aspects of data anonymization, taking into account evolving legislation, court rulings, and emerging best practices. By staying abreast of these developments and adhering to appropriate standards, a data-driven environment that respects privacy, safeguards personal information, and promotes responsible data sharing practices can be fostered.

Anonymization procedures can support the creation of Open Data. Similar to Open Source, Open Data represent an economically and socially relevant concept. For example, it is part of the digital strategy resp. the Open Data strategy of the current resp. the previous federal government in Germany. However, a challenge may be that under the current European regulations, in the near future, all data might be classified as personal data as a result of moving forward into a data-driven world. In [74], this is named the Law of Everything. The reason for this is the widely defined rules on data protection and the definition of the terms "information" and "personal data" by the GDPR. This is accelerated by the rapid advances in technology, which enable ever greater interpretability of data as well as the increased collection of information in real time. The Law of Everything is an approach with a worthy goal but not one that can be implemented sustainably with current procedures.

Author Contributions: Conceptualization, R.A.; Methodology, R.A., J.F., J.G. and E.M.; Software, R.A.; Validation, R.A., J.F. and M.H.; Formal analysis, R.A.; Investigation, R.A. and J.F.; Resources, R.A., J.F., J.G. and E.M.; Data curation, R.A.; Writing—original draft preparation, R.A., J.G. and E.M.; Writing—review and editing, R.A., J.F., M.H., B.B. and M.S.; Visualization, R.A. and J.F.; Supervision, M.H., B.B. and M.S.; Project administration, M.H., B.B. and M.S.; Funding acquisition, M.H. and M.S. All authors have read and agreed to the published version of the manuscript.

Funding: The research project EAsyAnon ("Verbundprojekt: Empfehlungs- und Auditsystem zur Anonymisierung", funding indicator: 16KISA128K) is funded by the European Union under the umbrella of the funding guideline "Forschungsnetzwerk Anonymisierung für eine sichere Datennutzung" from the German Federal Ministry of Education and Research (BMBF).

Institutional Review Board Statement: Not applicable.

Informed Consent Statement: Not applicable.

Data Availability Statement: The dataset Adult used in this study for experiments is openly available to download from the UCI Machine Learning Repository. Data can be found at https://archive.ics.uci.edu/dataset/2/adult (accessed on 15 May 2023).

Conflicts of Interest: The authors declare no conflict of interest.

Abbreviations

The following abbreviations are used in this manuscript:

DP	Differential Privacy
DP-SGD	Differentially Private Stochastic Gradient Descent
ECJ	European Court of Justice
EGC	European General Court
EU	European Union
FMRMR	Fragmentation Minimum Redundancy Maximum Relevance
GAN	Generative Adversarial Network
GDPR	General Data Protection Regulation
HIPAA	Health Insurance Portability and Accountability Act
LDA	Linear Discriminant Analysis
LSTM	Long Short-Term Memory
MIMIC-III	Medical Information Mart for Intensive Care
PCA	Principal Component Analysis
PPDP	Privacy-preserving data publishing
PPGIS	Public Participation Geographic Information System
QI	Quasi-Identifier
SA	Sensitive Attribute
SVD	Singular Value Decomposition

References

1. Weitzenboeck, E.M.; Lison, P.; Cyndecka, M.; Langford, M. The GDPR and unstructured data: Is anonymization possible? *Int. Data Priv. Law* **2022**, *12*, 184–206. [CrossRef]
2. Samarati, P.; Sweeney, L. Protecting privacy when disclosing information: K-anonymity and its enforcement through generalization and suppression. In Proceedings of the IEEE Symposium on Security and Privacy, Oakland, CA, USA, 3–6 May 1998; pp. 1–19.
3. Sweeney, L. K-Anonymity: A Model for Protecting Privacy. *Int. J. Uncertain. Fuzziness-Knowl.-Based Syst.* **2002**, *10*, 557–570. [CrossRef]
4. Ford, E.; Tyler, R.; Johnston, N.; Spencer-Hughes, V.; Evans, G.; Elsom, J.; Madzvamuse, A.; Clay, J.; Gilchrist, K.; Rees-Roberts, M. Challenges Encountered and Lessons Learned when Using a Novel Anonymised Linked Dataset of Health and Social Care Records for Public Health Intelligence: The Sussex Integrated Dataset. *Information* **2023**, *14*, 106. [CrossRef]
5. Becker, B.; Kohavi, R. Adult. UCI Machine Learning Repository. 1996. Available online: https://archive-beta.ics.uci.edu/dataset/2/adult (accessed on 15 May 2023).
6. Majeed, A.; Lee, S. Anonymization Techniques for Privacy Preserving Data Publishing: A Comprehensive Survey. *IEEE Access* **2021**, *9*, 8512–8545. [CrossRef]
7. Hasanzadeh, K.; Kajosaari, A.; Häggman, D.; Kyttä, M. A context sensitive approach to anonymizing public participation GIS data: From development to the assessment of anonymization effects on data quality. *Comput. Environ. Urban Syst.* **2020**, *83*, 101513. .: 10.1016/j.compenvurbsys.2020.101513. [CrossRef]
8. Olatunji, I.E.; Rauch, J.; Katzensteiner, M.; Khosla, M. A review of anonymization for healthcare data. In *Big Data*; Mary Ann Liebert, Inc.: New Rochelle, NY, USA, 2022.
9. Prasser, F.; Kohlmayer, F. Putting statistical disclosure control into practice: The ARX data anonymization tool. In *Medical Data Privacy Handbook*; Springer: Cham, Switzerland, 2015; pp. 111–148.

10. Jakob, C.E.M.; Kohlmayer, F.; Meurers, T.; Vehreschild, J.J.; Prasser, F. Design and evaluation of a data anonymization pipeline to promote Open Science on COVID-19. *Sci. Data* **2020**, *7*, 435. [CrossRef]

11. Malin, B.; Loukides, G.; Benitez, K.; Clayton, E.W. Identifiability in biobanks: Models, measures, and mitigation strategies. *Hum. Genet.* **2011**, *130*, 383–392. [CrossRef]

12. Ram Mohan Rao, P.; Murali Krishna, S.; Siva Kumar, A. Privacy preservation techniques in big data analytics: A survey. *J. Big Data* **2018**, *5*, 33. [CrossRef]

13. Haber, A.C.; Sax, U.; Prasser, F.; the NFDI4Health Consortium. Open tools for quantitative anonymization of tabular phenotype data: literature review. *Briefings Bioinform.* **2022**, *23*, bbac440. [CrossRef]

14. Wagner, I.; Eckhoff, D. Technical Privacy Metrics. *ACM Comput. Surv.* **2018**, *51*, 1–38. [CrossRef]

15. Vokinger, K.; Stekhoven, D.; Krauthammer, M. Lost in Anonymization—A Data Anonymization Reference Classification Merging Legal and Technical Considerations. *J. Law Med. Ethics* **2020**, *48*, 228–231. [CrossRef] [PubMed]

16. Zibuschka, J.; Kurowski, S.; Roßnagel, H.; Schunck, C.H.; Zimmermann, C. Anonymization Is Dead—Long Live Privacy. In Proceedings of the Open Identity Summit 2019, Garmisch-Partenkirchen, Germany, 28–29 March 2019; Roßnagel, H., Wagner, S., Hühnlein, D., Eds.; Gesellschaft für Informatik: Bonn, Germany, 2019; pp. 71–82.

17. Rights (OCR), Office for Civil. Methods for De-Identification of PHI. HHS.gov. 2012. Available online: https://www.hhs.gov/hipaa/for-professionals/privacy/special-topics/de-identification/index.html (accessed on 21 July 2023).

18. Gionis, A.; Tassa, T. k-Anonymization with Minimal Loss of Information. *IEEE Trans. Knowl. Data Eng.* **2009**, *21*, 206–219. [CrossRef]

19. Terrovitis, M.; Mamoulis, N.; Kalnis, P. Local and global recoding methods for anonymizing set-valued data. *VLDB J.* **2011**, *20*, 83–106. [CrossRef]

20. Agrawal, R.; Srikant, R. Privacy-Preserving Data Mining. In Proceedings of the SIGMOD '00: Proceedings of the 2000 ACM SIGMOD International Conference on Management of Data, Dallas, TX, USA, 16–18 May 2000; Association for Computing Machinery: New York, NY, USA, 2000; pp. 439–450. [CrossRef]

21. Bayardo, R.; Agrawal, R. Data privacy through optimal k-anonymization. In Proceedings of the 21st International Conference on Data Engineering (ICDE'05), Tokyo, Japan, 5–8 April 2005; pp. 217–228. [CrossRef]

22. Dwork, C. Differential Privacy. In *Automata, Languages and Programming, Proceedings of the 33rd International Colloquium on Automata, Languages and Programming, Part II (ICALP 2006), Venice, Italy, 10–14 July 2006*; Springer: Berlin/Heidelberg, Germany, 2006, Volume 4052, pp. 1–12.

23. Wang, T.; Zhang, X.; Feng, J.; Yang, X. A Comprehensive Survey on Local Differential Privacy toward Data Statistics and Analysis. *Sensors* **2020**, *20*, 7030. [CrossRef]

24. Dwork, C.; Roth, A. The algorithmic foundations of differential privacy. *Found. Trends Theor. Comput. Sci.* **2014**, *9*, 211–407. [CrossRef]

25. Wang, Y.; Wu, X.; Hu, D. Using Randomized Response for Differential Privacy Preserving Data Collection. In Proceedings of the EDBT/ICDT Workshops, Bordeaux, France, 15 March 2016.

26. Abadi, M.; Chu, A.; Goodfellow, I.; McMahan, H.B.; Mironov, I.; Talwar, K.; Zhang, L. Deep Learning with Differential Privacy. In Proceedings of the 2016 ACM SIGSAC Conference on Computer and Communications Security, Vienna, Austria, 24–28 October 2016; pp. 308–318. [CrossRef]

27. van der Maaten, L.; Hannun, A.Y. The Trade-Offs of Private Prediction. *arXiv* **2020**, arXiv:2007.05089.

28. McKenna, R.; Miklau, G.; Sheldon, D. Winning the NIST Contest: A scalable and general approach to differentially private synthetic data. *arXiv* **2021**, arXiv:2108.04978.

29. Aggarwal, C.C.; Yu, P.S. A condensation approach to privacy preserving data mining. In *Advances in Database Technology-EDBT 2004, Proceedings of the International Conference on Extending Database Technology, Crete, Greece, 14–18 March 2004*; Springer: Berlin/Heidelberg, Germany, 2004, pp. 183–199.

30. Jiang, X.; Ji, Z.; Wang, S.; Mohammed, N.; Cheng, S.; Ohno-Machado, L. Differential-Private Data Publishing Through Component Analysis. *Trans. Data Priv.* **2013**, *6*, 19–34.

31. Xu, S.; Zhang, J.; Han, D.; Wang, J. Singular value decomposition based data distortion strategy for privacy protection. *Knowl. Inf. Syst.* **2006**, *10*, 383–397. [CrossRef]

32. Soria-Comas, J.; Domingo-Ferrer, J. Mitigating the Curse of Dimensionality in Data Anonymization. In Proceedings of the Modeling Decisions for Artificial Intelligence: 16th International Conference, MDAI 2019, Milan, Italy, 4–6 September 2019; Springer: Berlin/Heidelberg, Germany, 2019; pp. 346–355.

33. Xu, L.; Veeramachaneni, K. Synthesizing Tabular Data using Generative Adversarial Networks. *arXiv* **2018**, arXiv:1811.11264.

34. Park, N.; Mohammadi, M.; Gorde, K.; Jajodia, S.; Park, H.; Kim, Y. Data Synthesis based on Generative Adversarial Networks. *arXiv* **2018**, arXiv:1806.03384.

35. Xu, L.; Skoularidou, M.; Cuesta-Infante, A.; Veeramachaneni, K. Modeling Tabular data using Conditional GAN. *arXiv* **2019**, arXiv:1907.00503.

36. Xie, L.; Lin, K.; Wang, S.; Wang, F.; Zhou, J. Differentially Private Generative Adversarial Network. *arXiv* **2018**, arXiv:1802.06739.

37. Kunar, A.; Birke, R.; Zhao, Z.; Chen, L. DTGAN: Differential Private Training for Tabular GANs. *arXiv* **2021**, arXiv:2107.02521.

38. Zakerzadeh, H.; Aggrawal, C.C.; Barker, K. Towards Breaking the Curse of Dimensionality for High-Dimensional Privacy. In Proceedings of the 2014 SIAM International Conference on Data Mining, Philadelphia, PA, USA, 24–26 April 2014.

39. Aggarwal, C.C. On K-Anonymity and the Curse of Dimensionality. In Proceedings of the VLDB '05: 31st International Conference on Very Large Data Bases, Trondheim, Norway, 30 August–2 September 2005; pp. 901–909.
40. Salas, J.; Torra, V. A General Algorithm for k-anonymity on Dynamic Databases. In Proceedings of the DPM/CBT@ESORICS, Barcelona, Spain, 6–7 September 2018.
41. Xu, J.; Wang, W.; Pei, J.; Wang, X.; Shi, B.; Fu, A. Utility-based anonymization for privacy preservation with less information loss. *SIGKDD Explor.* **2006**, *8*, 21–30. [CrossRef]
42. LeFevre, K.; DeWitt, D.; Ramakrishnan, R. Mondrian Multidimensional K-Anonymity. In Proceedings of the 22nd International Conference on Data Engineering (ICDE'06), Atlanta, GA, USA, 3–8 April 2006; p. 25. [CrossRef]
43. Elabd, E.; Abd elkader, H.; Mubarak, A.A. L—Diversity-Based Semantic Anonymaztion for Data Publishing. *Int. J. Inf. Technol. Comput. Sci.* **2015**, *7*, 1–7. [CrossRef]
44. Wang, X.; Chou, J.K.; Chen, W.; Guan, H.; Chen, W.; Lao, T.; Ma, K.L. A Utility-Aware Visual Approach for Anonymizing Multi-Attribute Tabular Data. *IEEE Trans. Vis. Comput. Graph.* **2018**, *24*, 351–360. [CrossRef]
45. Machanavajjhala, A.; Gehrke, J.; Kifer, D.; Venkitasubramaniam, M. L-diversity: Privacy beyond k-anonymity. In Proceedings of the 22nd International Conference on Data Engineering (ICDE'06), Atlanta, GA, USA, 3–8 April 2006; p. 24. [CrossRef]
46. Li, N.; Li, T.; Venkatasubramanian, S. t-Closeness: Privacy Beyond k-Anonymity and l-Diversity. In Proceedings of the 2007 IEEE 23rd International Conference on Data Engineering, Istanbul, Turkey, 15 April 2006–20 April 2007; pp. 106–115. [CrossRef]
47. Vatsalan, D.; Rakotoarivelo, T.; Bhaskar, R.; Tyler, P.; Ladjal, D. Privacy risk quantification in education data using Markov model. *Br. J. Educ. Technol.* **2022**, *53*, 804–821. [CrossRef]
48. Díaz, J.S.P.; García, Á.L. Comparison of machine learning models applied on anonymized data with different techniques. *arXiv* **2023**, arXiv:2305.07415.
49. CSIRO. Metrics and Frameworks for Privacy Risk Assessments, CSIRO: Canberra, Australia, Adopted on 12 July 2021. 2021. Available online: https://www.csiro.au/en/research/technology-space/cyber/Metrics-and-frameworks-for-privacy-risk-assessments (accessed on 4 June 2023).
50. Bellman, R. *Dynamic Programming*, 1st ed.; Princeton University Press: Princeton, NJ, USA, 1957.
51. Ding, C.; Peng, H. Minimum redundancy feature selection from microarray gene expression data. In Proceedings of the 2003 IEEE Bioinformatics Conference. CSB2003, Stanford, CA, USA, 11–14 August 2003; pp. 523–528. [CrossRef]
52. Domingo-Ferrer, J.; Soria-Comas, J. Multi-Dimensional Randomized Response. *arXiv* **2020**, arXiv:2010.10881.
53. Kühling, J.; Buchner, B. (Eds.) *Datenschutz-Grundverordnung BDSG: Kommentar*, 3rd ed.; C.H.Beck: Bayern, Germany, 2020.
54. Article 29 Data Protection Working Party. Opinion 4/2007 on the Concept of Personal Data, WP136, Adopted on 20 June 2007. 2007. Available online: https://ec.europa.eu/justice/article-29/documentation/opinion-recommendation/files/2007/wp136_en.pdf (accessed on 5 May 2023).
55. Auer-Reinsdorff, A.; Conrad, I. (Eds.) Früher unter dem Titel: Beck'sches Mandats-Handbuch IT-Recht. In *Handbuch IT-und Datenschutzrecht*, 2nd ed.; C.H.Beck: Bayern, Germany, 2016.
56. Paal, B.P.; Pauly, D.A.; Ernst, S. *Datenschutz-Grundverordnung, Bundesdatenschutzgesetz*; C.H.Beck: Bayern, Germany, 2021.
57. Specht, L.; Mantz, R. Handbuch europäisches und deutsches Datenschutzrecht. In *Bereichsspezifischer Datenschutz in Privatwirtschaft und öffentlichem Sektor*; C.H.Beck: München, Germany, 2019.
58. *Case T-557/20*; Single Resolution Board v European Data Protection Supervisor. ECLI:EU:T:2023:219. Official Journal of the European Union: Brussel, Belgium, 2023. Available online: https://eur-lex.europa.eu/legal-content/EN/TXT/PDF/?uri=CELEX:62020TA0557 (accessed on 1 July 2023).
59. Groos, D.; van Veen, E.B. Anonymised data and the rule of law. *Eur. Data Prot. L. Rev.* **2020**, *6*, 498. [CrossRef]
60. Finck, M.; Pallas, F. They who must not be identified—distinguishing personal from non-personal data under the GDPR. *Int. Data Priv. Law* **2020**, *10*, 11–36. [CrossRef]
61. Article 29 Data Protection Working Party. *Opinion 5/2014 on Anonymisation Techniques*; WP216, Adopted on 10 April 2014; Directorate-General for Justice and Consumers: Brussel, Belgium, 2014. Available online: https://ec.europa.eu/justice/article-29/documentation/opinion-recommendation/files/2014/wp216_en.pdf (accessed on 1 July 2023).
62. Bergt, M. Die Bestimmbarkeit als Grundproblem des Datenschutzrechts—Überblick über den Theorienstreit und Lösungsvorschlag. *Z. Datenschutz* **2015**, *365*, 345–396.
63. Burkert, C.; Federrath, H.; Marx, M.; Schwarz, M. Positionspapier zur Anonymisierung unter der DSGVO unter Besonderer Berücksichtigung der TK-Branche. Konsultationsverfahren des BfDI. 10 February 2020. Available online: https://www.bfdi.bund.de/SharedDocs/Downloads/DE/Konsultationsverfahren/1_Anonymisierung/Positionspapier-Anonymisierung.html (accessed on 11 May 2023).
64. *Case C-582/14*; Patrick Breyer v Bundesrepublik Deutschland. ECLI:EU:C:2016:779. Court of Justice of the European Union: Brussel, Belgium, 2016. Available online: https://eur-lex.europa.eu/legal-content/EN/TXT/PDF/?uri=CELEX:62014CJ0582 (accessed on 1 July 2023).
65. Schwartmann, R.; Jaspers, A.; Lepperhoff, N.; Weiß, S.; Meier, M. Practice Guide to Anonymising Personal Data; Foundation for Data Protection, Leipzig 2022. Available online: https://stiftungdatenschutz.org/fileadmin/Redaktion/Dokumente/Anonymisierung_personenbezogener_Daten/SDS_Practice_Guide_to_Anonymising-Web-EN.pdf (accessed on 10 June 2023).
66. Bischoff, C. Pseudonymisierung und Anonymisierung von personenbezogenen Forschungsdaten im Rahmen klinischer Prüfungen von Arzneimitteln (Teil I)-Gesetzliche Anforderungen. *Pharma Recht* **2020**, *6*, 309–388.

67. Simitis, S.; Hornung, G.; Spiecker gen. Döhmann, I. *Datenschutzrecht: DSGVO mit BDSG*; Nomos: Baden-Baden, Germany, 2019; Volume 1.
68. Csányi, G.M.; Nagy, D.; Vági, R.; Vadász, J.P.; Orosz, T. Challenges and Open Problems of Legal Document Anonymization. *Symmetry* **2021**, *13*, 1490. [CrossRef]
69. Koll, C.E.; Hopff, S.M.; Meurers, T.; Lee, C.H.; Kohls, M.; Stellbrink, C.; Thibeault, C.; Reinke, L.; Steinbrecher, S.; Schreiber, S.; et al. Statistical biases due to anonymization evaluated in an open clinical dataset from COVID-19 patients. *Sci. Data* **2022**, *9*, 776. [CrossRef]
70. Dewes, A. Verfahren zur Anonymisierung und Pseudonymisierung von Daten. In *Datenwirtschaft und Datentechnologie: Wie aus Daten Wert Entsteht*; Springer: Berlin/Heidelberg, Germany, 2022; pp. 183–201. [CrossRef]
71. Giomi, M.; Boenisch, F.; Wehmeyer, C.; Tasnádi, B. A Unified Framework for Quantifying Privacy Risk in Synthetic Data. *arXiv* **2022**, arXiv:2211.10459.
72. López, C.A.F. On the legal nature of synthetic data. In Proceedings of the NeurIPS 2022 Workshop on Synthetic Data for Empowering ML Research, New Orleans, LA, USA, 2 December 2022.
73. Veale, M.; Binns, R.; Edwards, L. Algorithms that Remember: Model Inversion Attacks and Data Protection Law. *Philos. Trans. R. Soc. Math. Phys. Eng. Sci.* **2018**, *376*, 20180083. [CrossRef]
74. Purtova, N. The law of everything. Broad concept of personal data and future of EU data protection law. *Law Innov. Technol.* **2018**, *10*, 40–81. [CrossRef]

Article

Assessing the Security and Privacy of Android Official ID Wallet Apps

Vasileios Kouliaridis [1,*,†] , Georgios Karopoulos [1,†] and Georgios Kambourakis [2,†]

1   European Commission, Joint Research Centre (JRC), 21027 Ispra, Italy; georgios.karopoulos@ec.europa.eu
2   Department of Information and Communication Systems Engineering, University of the Aegean, 83200 Karlovasi, Greece; gkamb@aegean.gr
*   Correspondence: vasileios.kouliaridis@ec.europa.eu
†   These authors contributed equally to this work.

Abstract: With the increasing use of smartphones for a wide variety of online services, states and countries are issuing official applications to store government-issued documents that can be used for identification (e.g., electronic identity cards), health (e.g., vaccination certificates), and transport (e.g., driver's licenses). However, the privacy and security risks associated with the storage of sensitive personal information on such apps are a major concern. This work presents a thorough analysis of official Android wallet apps, focusing mainly on apps used to store identification documents and/or driver's licenses. Specifically, we examine the security and privacy level of such apps using three analysis tools and discuss the key findings and the risks involved. We additionally explore Android app security best practices and various security measures that can be employed to mitigate these risks, such as updating deprecated components and libraries. Altogether, our findings demonstrate that, while there are various security measures available, there is still a need for more comprehensive solutions to address the privacy and security risks associated with the use of Android wallet apps.

Keywords: Android privacy; Android security; wallet apps

Citation: Kouliaridis, V.; Karopoulos, G.; Kambourakis, G. Assessing the Security and Privacy of Android Official ID Wallet Apps. *Information* **2023**, *14*, 457. https://doi.org/10.3390/info14080457

Academic Editors: Jose de Vasconcelos, Hugo Barbosa and Carla Cordeiro

Received: 24 July 2023
Revised: 10 August 2023
Accepted: 11 August 2023
Published: 13 August 2023

1. Introduction

The increasing reliance on mobile devices for accessing online services has led to the development of various wallet applications (apps), which allow citizens to upload and store government issued documents, such as vaccination certificates, identity documents (IDs), and driver's licenses (DLs). The electronic IDs and DLs stored in a wallet app contain the same information as their physical counterparts, i.e., personal information such as name, date of birth, and photo, as well as a unique identifier, document issue, and expiration date. Depending on the state or country of issue, these electronic copies may be used for various purposes, including accessing government services, opening bank accounts, conducting online transactions, identification in public services, and police inspections. The European Commission has proposed a European Digital Identity using a digital wallet [1]; more recently, the launch of EU-wide digital driving licenses [2] was also announced. In addition, the US Transportation Security Administration (TSA) currently accepts some mobile IDs and DLs in a number of US airports [3]. With regard to the end user, it is foreseen that, globally, one in two people will use a mobile wallet by 2025 [4], increasing the number of mobile wallets in use from 2.8 billion at the end of 2020 to 4.8 billion by the end of 2025.

While holding all identification documents in one place may seem convenient, it also raises serious concerns regarding the privacy and security offered by these apps to users and their sensitive personal information, as shown in relevant research [5–10]. The potential risks associated with the storage of ID copies on Android apps are numerous. For instance, the mobile device can be lost or stolen, or the app can be compromised by malware or other more direct attacks. In such cases, the ID copy can be accessed by unauthorized parties, who can use the information for nefarious purposes, such as identity theft or financial fraud.

Furthermore, even if the app itself is not compromised, it may still collect and transmit personal data to third-party servers without the user's knowledge or consent, posing a significant threat to privacy. In Jan 2021, a person was sentenced to five years in prison after using a state-authorized digital driver's license mobile app to defraud three credit unions and four banks [11]. According to a recent report [12] from McAfee, 15 million Americans had their identity stolen in 2021. Based on data gathered by Finanso.se [13], one in five Europeans have experienced identity theft fraud between 2020 and 2022. In 39% of these cases, the attackers used the victim's phone to steal their identity [13].

To address these key concerns, app providers must follow security and privacy best practices during the app's lifecycle, aiming to prevent theft of sensitive personal information. Regarding the Android ecosystem, there exist several noteworthy standards and best practices for developing secure software, including the Android developer website [14], the Open Worldwide Application Security Project (OWASP) mobile top 10 project [15], and the Japan Smartphone Security Association (JSSEC) Android application secure design/secure coding guidebook [16]. Additionally, there are several works in the literature that focus on the security of the Android OS, such as [17,18]. However, compliance to these practices is often limited by the complexity of the underlying technology, the developer's level of technical expertise, and the lack of standardized security protocols and policies. Moreover, the development of such apps may be outsourced to third parties who perform these functions on behalf of the solution provider. In such a case, trust is indirect, and sometimes cannot be fully assessed.

The present work focuses on mobile wallets that support IDs and DLs, offering the first, to our knowledge, exhaustive review and examination of this topic based on three app security analysis tools. Precisely, the contributions of this study are as follows:

- We present an overview of the existing official mobile apps supporting IDs and DLs, as well as the privacy and security risks associated with storing digital ID and DL documents. The term "official" means apps that are either offered by governmental agencies (state-sponsored) or by a mobile operating system (OS), say, Android or iOS.
- We collect and analyze existing Android apps for ID and DL storage using three *.apk* analysis tools, present the discovered vulnerabilities of each app, and discuss key findings.
- We offer recommendations for app developers and relevant stakeholders to enhance the privacy and security of ID and DL storage in Android apps.

The rest of this paper is structured as follows. The next section surveys official ID/DL wallet apps. Section 4 presents the vulnerability analysis results. Section 5 details the key findings of the previous section and provides recommendations to improve the security status of the analyzed apps. The last section concludes the paper.

2. Related Work

The domain of ID/DL wallet apps is rather new and, to the best of our knowledge, there is no previous work tackling the issue of ID/DL wallet app security and privacy. There is, however, a large volume of work of a similar nature evaluating generic Android app security and privacy.

Filiol and Irola [19] analyzed numerous mobile apps in the banking domain. The authors showed that almost all apps were prone to known vulnerabilities, endangering users' private data, sometimes severely. The authors also discussed the certification process for apps available on a secure market. Kaur et al. [20] presented a security assessment of the Android e-wallet apps provided by Canada's leading banks. According to their analysis, all apps were found to be vulnerable against trivial attack vectors.

In the health domain, Papageorgiou et al. [7] provided a security and privacy analysis of popular freeware mobile health apps. The authors employed both static and dynamic analysis, as well as custom testing of each application. Their analysis demonstrated that the majority of apps neither follow well-known practices and guidelines nor comply with data protection regulations. Kouliaridis et al. [8] focused on contact tracing apps used for decelerating the spread of infectious diseases. They analyzed all official Android contact tracing apps deployed by European countries by means of dynamic instrumentation. Their findings revealed that these apps may put users' security and privacy at risk due to an assortment of weaknesses, vulnerabilities, and misconfigurations. Karopoulos et al. [9] examined existing initiatives for COVID-19 digital certificates undertaken by organizations and countries worldwide. As part of their study, they analyzed official Android apps for COVID-19 digital certificates to reveal possible security and privacy issues affecting the end user. Their results demonstrated that, overall, the schemes developed by European countries provide a higher level of privacy protection compared to those from Asia and America.

In the automotive domain, Mandal et al. [21] analyzed Android infotainment apps against a list of possible exposure scenarios. Their results showed that almost 80% of these apps were potentially vulnerable. Chatzoglou et al. [10] provided a security assessment of all the official car management apps offered by major car manufacturers operating in Europe. The apps were assessed for vulnerabilities and possible weak security practices. Their analysis reported numerous issues, ranging from privacy-invasive permissions and API calls, to potentially exploitable common weakness enumeration (CWE) and common vulnerabilities and exposures (CVE)—identified weaknesses and vulnerabilities.

Regarding the use of cryptography, Egele et al. [22] developed an automatic analysis technique to find Android apps on Google Play that use cryptographic APIs. The authors reported that 88% of these apps misused cryptographic APIs, making at least one mistake that resulted in decreasing the maximum achievable security level. To this end, they provided recommendations to improve the cryptographic security of such apps. Chatzikonstantinou et al. [23] evaluated the use of cryptography in 49 Android apps whose operation is related to data encryption. Their results revealed that the majority of these apps, i.e., around 88%, presented at least one type of cryptographic weakness. The authors provided guidelines and best practices for developers, to aid in the development of more secure apps.

More recently, Chatzoglou et al. [24] performed a fully fledged analysis of more than 40 mainstream internet of things (IoT) official Android apps belonging to six popular categories of home/office and wearable devices. They pinpointed that most of the examined apps were susceptible to an assortment of security and privacy issues, including transmission of cleartext traffic, outdated software components, no protection against reverse engineering, and others. They concluded that the attack surface for an IoT device is significantly augmented because of the security weaknesses in the accompanying app.

Although more and more manufactures are relying on trusted execution environments (TEEs) to shield their devices, Ref. [25] provides an extensive analysis and categorization of existing vulnerabilities in TEEs and shows the design flaws that lead to them. The authors in [26], released new state of the art mobile app datasets along with an in-depth analysis of their static characteristics to aid the detection of Android malware with the use of both shallow and deep learning techniques.

The objective of the above summary of analyses of Android apps is to highlight the main issues related to the security and privacy of different types of apps. Overall, previous work in the field underlines that even officially certified Android apps, also under the scrutiny of the official Google Play app store, present numerous issues that can potentially endanger users' security and privacy. In the rest of this paper, we perform similar analyses to investigate whether this holds true for recently launched ID/DL apps as well, given that this is still an unexplored field.

3. ID/DL Wallet Apps Worldwide

As already pointed out in Section 1, ID/DL wallet apps can be classified in two main categories: either state-sponsored or offered by a mobile operating system (OS). The former category of wallet apps are developed under the auspices of the government of a specific country or state. Apart from state-sponsored apps, the main mobile OS platforms, that is, Android and iOS that together account for more than 99% of the respective market share [27,28], have announced support for mobile IDs and/or mobile DLs. The fact that both of these platforms are active in the domain of mobile ID/DL is a key factor towards the wide adoption of such solutions.

Looking at the current support by mobile platforms, in December 2022, Google announced support for storing state IDs and DLs from selected US states in Google Wallet as a beta feature [29]. On the iOS side, Apple announced in 2021 that some US states had signed up to make available state IDs and DLs in Apple Wallet [30]. According to the US Transportation Security Administration (TSA) [3], various airports around the US currently accept mobile IDs and DLs stored in Apple Wallet issued by the Arizona, Colorado, and Maryland states.

It should be noted here that mobile-OS-supported IDs and DLs could possibly entail similar security risks as ID wallet apps. More specifically, in some use cases, the service might require unlocking the smartphone to access the ID/DL and handing out the unlocked device to the interested, authorized party, i.e., police or other public or private service agent. On the other hand, if the electronic ID and DL are available without the need to unlock the phone, the personal information contained in them will be visible to anyone who picks up the device. A balanced use case scenario between security and usability would provide access to the electronic ID/DL using biometric authentication, without unlocking the smartphone.

In this work, we only consider official, state-sponsored ID/DL wallet apps for the Android OS. To our knowledge, the 18 official ID/DL wallet apps available as of the time of writing of this paper are those listed in Table 1.

Table 1. Outline of the examined apps (ID: identity document, DL: driver's license).

Country/State	App Name	ID	DL	Downloads	Android Version	App Providers
North America						
Louisiana, USA	LA wallet [31]	Yes	Yes	500 K	5.0+	State of Louisiana
Colorado, USA	myColorado [32]	Yes	No	100 K	8.1+	State of Colorado—Governor's Office of IT
Florida, USA	FL Smart ID: Thales [33]	No	Yes	10 K	6.0+	Florida Department of Highway Safety and Motor Vehicles
Georgia, USA	DDS 2 GO [34]	No	Yes	500 K	5.1+	Georgia Department of Driver Services
Oklahoma, USA	Oklahoma Mobile ID [35]	Yes	No	100 K	6.0+	Idemia R&D
Delaware, USA	Delaware Mobile ID [36]	Yes	No	10 K	6.0+	Idemia R&D
Utah, USA	GET Mobile ID [37]	Yes	Yes	10 K	8.0+	GET Group NA
USA	Airside Digital Identity [38]	Yes	Yes	10 K	8.0+	American Airlines/Airside Mobile Inc.
Canada	eID-Me Digital ID [39]	Yes	No	10 K	8.0+	Bluink Ltd.

Table 1. *Cont.*

Country/State	App Name	ID	DL	Downloads	Android Version	App Providers
Europe						
Austria	eAusweise [40]	No	Yes	100 K	8.0+	Bundesministerium für Finanzen
Denmark	Kørekort [41]	No	Yes	500 K	8.0+	Digitaliseringsstyrelsen
Germany	Verimi ID wallet [42]	Yes	Yes	100 K	7.0+	Verimi
Greece	Gov.gr Wallet [43]	Yes	Yes	500 K	8.0+	Hellenic Republic
Netherlands	KopieID [44]	Yes	No	1 M	7.0+	Rijksoverheid
Portugal	id.gov.pt [45]	Yes	Yes	500 K	4.2+	AMA, IP
Spain	mi DGT [46]	No	Yes	5 M	5.1+	DGT oficial
Asia						
Telangana, India	RTA m-wallet [47]	No	Yes	5 K	5.0+	Transport Department Govt. of Telangana
Oceania						
Australia	Service NSW [48]	No	Yes	1 M	6.0+	Service NSW

4. Vulnerability Analysis

The aim of this section is to present key results regarding the vulnerability analysis of the wallet apps given in Table 1. Specifically, the 18 ID/DL wallet apps were collected from Google Play with a freeze date of 1 June 2023. Each of them was statically analyzed using three tools, namely, Ostorlab [49], Mobile Security Framework (MobSF) [50], and Androtomist [51]. The detailed results of the security assessment performed with the aforementioned tools can be found in [52].

Ostorlab is a cloud-based security platform that caters for dynamic and static analysis of mobile apps. It allows users to scan an app for vulnerabilities, such as insecure injection, outdated dependencies, hardcoded secrets, weak cryptography, cleartext communication, configuration issues, and improper use of permissions. The tool also provides a detailed report of the findings, including the severity of each vulnerability, i.e., *low*, *medium*, or *high*. Moreover, it provides recommendations for remediation. According to the tool's web page, more than 10K companies and security professionals rely on it for Android app penetration testing. The overall risk rating of the app is calculated by aggregating the individual ratings of each vulnerability. More specifically, Ostorlab uses the following techniques to find vulnerabilities:

- Configuration checks for insecure settings. These settings include Android native parameters, e.g., in the AndroidManifest.xml.
- Third-party dependency analysis to find all application dependencies of all supported frameworks, as well as statically compiled dependencies, and identify a large set of libraries. The tool then tries to match these libraries against its known vulnerabilities database.
- Hardcoded secrets scanning, i.e., API keys, passwords, tokens, encryption keys, and initialization vectors (IVs).
- Taint analysis to identify vulnerabilities, such as SQL injection, command injection, or the use of hardcoded keys.

In contrast to MobSF, Ostorlab reports the use of outdated dependencies. Additionally, Ostorlab also checks supply chain vulnerabilities, such as dependency confusion, namely, attacks directed against third-party dependencies in an app. Recall that third-party dependencies refer to libraries, frameworks, and other software built by external parties and are embedded into the app.

MobSF is one of the all-in-one tools recommended by the OWASP Mobile Security Testing Guide [53]. MobSF is a popular open-source mobile app security testing framework that allows users to perform static and dynamic analysis of Android apps. The static analysis includes source code, binary, tracker analysis, and configuration analysis, while the dynamic analysis is based on runtime behavior analysis, code injection, and traffic interception. The tool can be used to identify vulnerabilities, such as sensitive data disclosure, insecure cryptography, and insecure communications. It also provides detailed reports on the findings, including a list of vulnerabilities, their respective CWE, and a score using the common vulnerability scoring system (CVSS), i.e., 0–3.9 = low, 4–6.9 = medium, and 7–10 = high. To compute an overall score for the app, first, a severity level, high, warning, or good, is assigned to each vulnerability by MobSF. The final score of the app is calculated by first assigning a perfect score of 100 and then for each vulnerability applying the following:

- severity high—subtracting 15 from the score;
- severity warning—subtracting 10 from the score;
- severity good—adding 5 to the score.

Apart from the above-mentioned well-known tools, the authors used an self-developed tool that, however, has already been used in relevant research. The reason for using this tool in conjunction with the other two is that it gave us more fine-grained control over the analysis process. Androtomist is an automated and configurable tool, which combines static and dynamic analysis to evaluate Android app behavior. In the context of this paper, it has been used to statically analyze each app and extract components from the manifest file, such as activities, services, and broadcast receivers. Activities are used when one app invokes a component of another app instead of calling the whole app. For example, a social media app can call the email composer component of an email app. However, an activity constitutes a potential entry point for malicious entities if not properly secured, increasing the attack surface of the app. A service, on the other hand, is an app component that runs in the background without providing a user interface, such as a service handling network tasks, playing music, or performing file I/O operations. Furthermore, a service can remain active even when the user switches to another application. Broadcast receivers are used to send and receive messages between apps, such as notifications or alarms. If an app's broadcast receiver is not secured properly, it may allow other apps to intercept and read the messages. This can lead to sensitive information being leaked, such as passwords or personal data. Finally, Androtomist employs static taint analysis, which aids in finding complex vulnerabilities spanning long code paths.

By using three separate tools, this work aims to provide a comprehensive understanding of the security and privacy level of the examined Android apps. Our results rely on static analysis only and focus on code vulnerabilities; Table 2 summarizes the analysis results per tool. Specifically, the table presents Ostorlab's risk raking, MobSF's security score, and the number of exported activities, services, and receivers reported by the Androtomist tool.

Table 2. Vulnerability analysis results: high risk and low risk security scores have been emphasized with bold font.

App Name	Ostorlab Risk Rating	MobSF Security Score (%)	Exported Activities-Services-Receivers
LA wallet	**High**	Medium (45)	1-4-1
myColorado	**High**	Medium (53)	1-0-1
FL Smart ID: Thales	**High**	Medium (57)	1-1-1
DDS 2 GO	Medium	**Low (38)**	2-1-1
Oklahoma Mobile ID	**High**	Medium (60)	3-0-3

Table 2. *Cont.*

App Name	Ostorlab Risk Rating	MobSF Security Score (%)	Exported Activities-Services-Receivers
Delaware Mobile ID	High	Medium (55)	3-0-2
GET Mobile ID	High	High (69)	3-3-1
Airside Digital Identity	Low	Medium (62)	2-2-2
eID-Me Digital ID	High	Medium (56)	1-1-1
eAusweise	Low	Medium (60)	6-0-1
Kørekort	Low	Medium (60)	0-1-1
Verimi ID wallet	Medium	Medium (64)	1-2-2
Gov.gr Wallet	High	Medium (56)	2-2-2
KopieID	Low	Medium (62)	1-0-0
id.gov.pt	High	Medium (51)	1-0-1
mi DGT	High	Medium (51)	7-1-2
RTA m-wallet	High	Medium (44)	0-1-1
Service NSW	High	Medium (44)	2-2-5

5. Discussion

This section wraps up our key findings from the vulnerability analysis of Section 4, for each of the three tools, namely, Ostorlab, MobSF, and Androtomist. Recall that the analytical results per tool can be found in [52].

5.1. Ostorlab

In order to provide a global overview, we summarize the top vulnerabilities identified by Ostorlab and MobSF in Figure 1; in the rest of this subsection, we analyze our findings with Ostorlab. Our analysis showed 47 cases of use of outdated vulnerable components in 14 apps, which can be exploited by malicious parties; most of these cases have a high risk rating. Third-party libraries should be updated to the latest version during the development phase and application updates should be issued to patch vulnerable components. Regarding cryptography use, all but one of the apps were found not to follow best practices by using hardcoded keys, storing secret information in the app, using non-random or insecure random values, supporting deprecated cipher suites, or performing incorrect certificate validation. Note that insufficient cryptography is placed in the fifth position of the latest OWASP top 10 mobile risks list [15]. In addition, three apps, i.e., "DDS 2 GO", "Service NSW", and "mi DGT" have set the *usesCleartextTraffic* attribute to "true", which indicates that the apps intend to exchange or allow cleartext network traffic. In the OWASP top 10 mobile risks list, insecure communication is placed in the third position. Obviously, given that such apps are used for storing ID/DL documents, cleartext network traffic could allow data theft over the network simply by means of packet sniffing. In total, 12, or approximately 67%, of the apps have a high risk rating according to Ostorlab.

Notably, all apps have been flagged with the "task highjacking" warning [54]. Task hijacking can be used to perform phishing attacks. This is a noteworthy issue, as an attacker could potentially capture and read triggered intents. For example, CVE-2020-0096, also known as "Standhogg 2.0", can potentially exploit this issue in unpatched Android OS v8, 8.1, and 9. According to Android's guidelines for "task affinities" [55], setting the "android:launchMode" attribute in the <activity> tag to "singleInstance" forbids other activities to be part of its task. Furthermore, setting the "android:taskAffinity" attribute to an empty string in the <activity> tag forces the activities to use a randomly generated task affinity. Last but not least, by using explicit intents, developers can specify which application will satisfy the intent. In addition, approximately 61% of the apps were flagged with the "intent spoofing" warning [56]. This vulnerability can be exploited by sending an intent towards an app's exported component, i.e., activity, receiver, or service, to obtain unauthorized access. Each exported component should check the caller's identity prior to executing any tasks. Ostrolab also suggests requiring *signature* or *signatureorsystem* level permissions to limit a component's exposure to a set of trusted applications [56]. Finally, there were many warnings flagging potential risks; in most cases, these warnings are false positives or do not pose a significant risk. Nevertheless, developers should examine these cases as well to identify potential security or privacy issues.

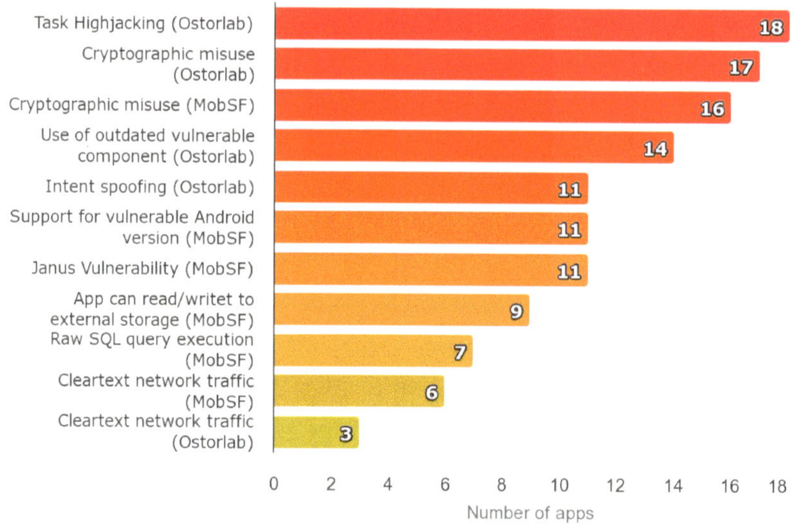

Figure 1. Top vulnerabilities as reported by Ostorlab and MobSF.

5.2. MobSF

As already mentioned in Section 4, in contrast to Ostorlab, MobSF provides a security score, where a higher score indicates a more secure app. Overall, out of the 18 apps, only "GET Mobile ID" received a low security risk score ($>71\%$), 16 apps were granted a medium score (41%–70%), and "DDS 2 GO" received a high risk score ($<40\%$); an overview of the results is presented in Figure 2.

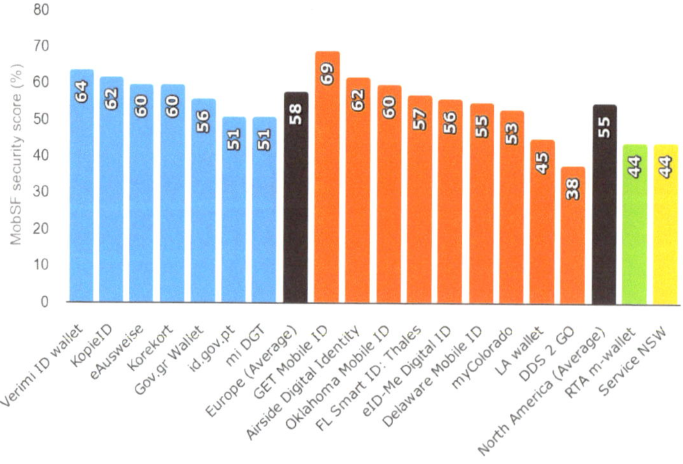

Figure 2. MobFS security score results, a higher score indicates a more secure app (blue: Europe, orange: North America, green: Asia, yellow: Oceania).

As noted earlier, a summary of the top vulnerabilities identified by both Ostorlab and MobSF is provided in Figure 1; in the rest of this subsection we analyze our findings with MobSF. According to MobSF, more than half (11) of the apps appear to be vulnerable to the so called "Janus vulnerability", documented in CVE-2017-13156 [57]. This vulnerability allows attackers to modify apps without affecting their signatures, i.e., adding extra bytes to the android package kit (APK) and DEX (Dalvik virtual machine executable) files. However, it only affects Android devices before v8.1, when signed with the v1 signature scheme. A similarly high proportion of apps, approximately 56% (10 out of 18), can be installed on a vulnerable Android version. Furthermore, all but two apps present at least one cryptographic misuse or warning; the exceptions are "mi DGT" and "Oklahoma Mobile ID". In addition, one-third of the apps use SQLite and execute raw SQL queries, which could lead to SQL injection attacks. Another important finding was that six of the apps allowed cleartext traffic in general or to/from specific network domains or IP addresses. As already stated above, in the OWASP top 10 mobile risks list, this warning is placed in the third position. Finally, 14 out of the 18 apps received the "insertion of sensitive information into log file" warning (CWE-532 [58]). While logging information is helpful during the development stage of an app, it must be stripped away before the app becomes publicly available. Precisely, an attacker could analyze the logs to extract private information stored on them. Finally, 50% of the apps received the "insecure data storage" warning (CWE-276) as they can read/write to external storage. This can be dangerous as any app can read data written to external storage. This warning is placed in the second position in the OWASP top 10 mobile risks list.

MobSF also logs third-party trackers that may be utilized by each app. We focus on six common tracker categories.

- Crash reporters: These trackers notify developers upon a crash event, informing them about the respective error.
- Analytics trackers: Collect usage information, e.g., time users spent on the app and top features used.
- Profiling trackers: Attempt to profile users with the purpose of optimizing personalized advertising.
- Identification trackers: Gather information with the purpose of ultimately matching a digital (user) identity with the real person.
- Ads: These trackers focus on serving personalized advertisements to the users.
- Location trackers: By using location services, these trackers obtain the geographical location of the user to improve location-based personalized advertisements.

As shown in Figure 3, app analysis revealed that all but three apps use trackers. The exceptions are "eAusweise", "Verimi ID wallet", and "GET Mobile ID". On the other hand, 13 apps use the *Firebase* Google analytics service as a method to measure users' engagement with them. Furthermore, seven apps exploit Google crashLytics to track code issues and app crashes. Additionally, "Delaware Mobile ID" and "Oklahoma Mobile ID" use AppsFlyer, which tracks all app-related events that are generated by clients, to improve personalized advertisements, as well as Localytics, which is a marketing tool used to engage users via targeted push and in-app messages (ads). Last but not least, "KopieID" uses Countly, which tracks and analyzes user behavior.

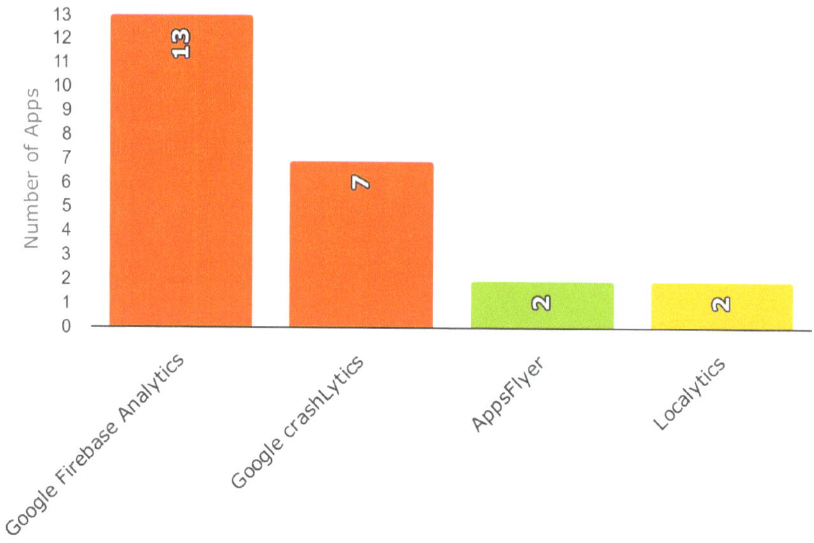

Figure 3. Top trackers used.

5.3. Androtomist

Finally, Androtomist was used to decompile each app, extract their manifest file, and log their exported components. In addition, taint analysis was also performed to extract possible data leaks. According to our results, none of the analyzed apps has exported content providers. On the other hand, two-thirds of the apps have at least one exported service (exceptions are "myColorado", "Oklahoma Mobile ID", "Delaware Mobile ID", "eAusweise", "KopieID", and "ip.gov.pt"). Furthermore, 16 apps have at least one exported activity (exceptions are "RTA m-wallet" and "Kørekort") and all apps except "KopieID" have at least one exported receiver.

When comparing the exported components of each, it is noted that "mi DGT" and "eAusweise" have seven and six exported activities, respectively, while the rest of the apps have three or less exported activities. Moreover, "LA wallet" has the most (four) exported services, while "Service NSW" has the most (five) exported receivers.

To prevent data leaks through broadcast receivers, app developers should implement appropriate security measures, such as setting proper permissions, restricting access to sensitive data, and using encrypted communication channels. Android end users should also be cautious when granting permissions to apps and limit access to sensitive data whenever possible. Android apps can set exported components, i.e., components that can be used by other applications, but often do not properly restrict which applications can launch the component or access the data they contain [59]. Additionally, we employed taint analysis on all apps and our results did not reveal any leaks.

5.4. Key Takeaways

As shown in Table 2, Europe has a lower percentage of high risk apps and a higher average security score than North America, as measured with Ostorlab. Specifically, three out of seven apps have a high risk rating in Europe, compared to seven out of nine apps in North America. Similarly, based on MobSF's results, Europe performs better with a security score of 58% compared to 55% of North American apps, as shown in Table 2 and Figure 2. Equally important is the number of CWEs reported by MobSF, i.e., 4 CWEs per application on average in Europe vs. 5.2 CWEs per app on average in North America.

With reference to Figure 1, which depicts the top vulnerabilities from both MobFS and Ostorlab, it is apparent that the tools are complementary to each other, reporting some common as well as unique findings. Furthermore, MobFS scores the security of apps, while Ostorlab measures the opposite, i.e., their security risk. As such, the use of both tools played an important role in identifying a variety of warnings and vulnerabilities.

It is also important here to comment on the overall results presented in Table 2. As it has already been briefly discussed previously, the three analysis tools assess different aspects of each app. Ostorlab has three extra analysis sections, including taint analysis, which makes it report more information. Moreover, Ostorlab reports risk ratings, meaning that even if an app has a single high risk vulnerability, then it is considered a high risk app. MobSF reports security scores by adding or subtracting points from a base score of 100%. This means that, on the one hand, identified vulnerabilities decrease but, on the other, good practices increase the score. For this reason, it is quite rare for an app to receive a low security score, unless it is a malware. Regarding Androtomist, the exported components used in the context of this work are only a small part of the analysis, whereas the other tools perform a much deeper analysis. Summing up, to achieve an overall idea of the security posture of an app, one should consider the results of all the three tools in a combinatorial manner in order to obtain an approximation of the total level of risk.

6. Conclusions

This paper conducted a comprehensive analysis concentrating on security and privacy aspects of the so far available ID/DL wallet apps. In other words, we attempt to answer the key question: Are these apps free of vulnerabilities which are known to the community, say, already documented in a CVE ID? To this end, three different software tools were used to analyze such apps and identify vulnerabilities. Our findings revealed significant (even critical but straightforward) security flaws that considerably increase the attack surface and could severely undermine the overall end user's security and privacy. Additionally, suggestions for app developers that enhance the security of these apps were discussed. It can be said that the overall picture is not so encouraging, suggesting that app creators and other stakeholders should devote more attention to security and privacy, not treating them as an afterthought. Actually, this tendency in tossing security aside, typically in favor of functionality, is corroborated by the related work as detailed in Section 2. Notably, the Android platform is currently working on its own ID wallet service [29], which could serve as an alternative solution for governments considering ID wallet app development. Future research should include a security evaluation of this component. Furthermore, cybersecurity policies such as those introduced by the European Commission [60] can provide guidance to member states in developing more secure and resilient solutions.

Author Contributions: Conceptualization, V.K. and G.K. (Georgios Karopoulos); data curation, V.K.; formal analysis, V.K., G.K. (Georgios Karopoulos), and G.K. (Georgios Kambourakis); investigation, V.K. and G.K. (Georgios Karopoulos); methodology, V.K., G.K. (Georgios Karopoulos), and G.K. (Georgios Kambourakis); resources, V.K. and G.K. (Georgios Kambourakis); software, V.K.; supervision, G.K. (Georgios Kambourakis); validation, G.K. (Georgios Karopoulos) and G.K. (Georgios Kambourakis); visualization, V.K., G.K. (Georgios Karopoulos) and G.K. (Georgios Kambourakis); writing—original draft, V.K. and G.K. (Georgios Karopoulos); writing—review and editing, V.K., G.K. (Georgios Karopoulos) and G.K. (Georgios Kambourakis). All authors have read and agreed to the published version of the manuscript

Funding: This research received no external funding.

Institutional Review Board Statement: Not applicable.

Informed Consent Statement: Not applicable.

Data Availability Statement: Results from our analysis can be found at https://github.com/billkoul/AndroidIDWalletApps (accessed on 4 July 2023).

Conflicts of Interest: The authors declare no conflict of interest.

Abbreviations

The following abbreviations are used in this manuscript:

APK	Android application package
CVE	Common vulnerabilities and exposures
CWE	Common weakness enumeration
DL	Driver's license
ID	Identity document
IoT	Internet of things
IV	Initialization vectors
JSSEC	Japan smartphone security association
OWASP	Open worldwide application security project
SQL	Structured query language

References

1. European Commission. European Digital Identity. Available online: https://commission.europa.eu/strategy-and-policy/priorities-2019-2024/europe-fit-digital-age/european-digital-identity_en (accessed on 4 July 2023).
2. European Commission. Road Safety: Commission Proposes Updated Requirements for Driving Licences and Better Cross-Border Enforcement of Road Traffic Rules. Available online: https://ec.europa.eu/commission/presscorner/detail/en/ip_23_1145 (accessed on 4 July 2023).
3. Transportation Security Administration . When Will the Phased Digital ID Rollout Start? Which Airports/States Will Be First in Line for This New Technology? Available online: https://www.tsa.gov/travel/frequently-asked-questions/when-will-phased-digital-id-rollout-start-which-airportsstates (accessed on 4 July 2023).
4. GLOBE NEWSWIRE. Study: More than Half of the World's Population Will Use Mobile Wallets by 2025. Available online: https://www.globenewswire.com/en/news-release/2021/07/08/2259605/0/en/Study-More-than-half-of-the-world-s-population-will-use-mobile-wallets-by-2025.html (accessed on 4 July 2023).
5. Damopoulos, D.; Kambourakis, G.; Anagnostopoulos, M.; Gritzalis, S.; Park, J.H. User privacy and modern mobile services: are they on the same path? *Pers. Ubiquitous Comput.* **2013**, *17*, 1437–1448. [CrossRef]
6. Papamartzivanos, D.; Damopoulos, D.; Kambourakis, G. A cloud-based architecture to crowdsource mobile app privacy leaks. In Proceedings of the 18th Panhellenic Conference on Informatics, PCI '14, Athens, Greece, 2–4 October 2014; ACM: New York, NY, USA, 2014, pp. 59:1–59:6. [CrossRef]
7. Papageorgiou, A.; Strigkos, M.; Politou, E.; Alepis, E.; Solanas, A.; Patsakis, C. Security and Privacy Analysis of Mobile Health Applications: The Alarming State of Practice. *IEEE Access* **2018**, *6*, 9390–9403. [CrossRef]
8. Kouliaridis, V.; Kambourakis, G.; Chatzoglou, E.; Geneiatakis, D.; Wang, H. Dissecting contact tracing apps in the Android platform. *PLoS ONE* **2021**, *16*, 1–28. [CrossRef]
9. Karopoulos, G.; Hernandez-Ramos, J.L.; Kouliaridis, V.; Kambourakis, G. A Survey on Digital Certificates Approaches for the COVID-19 Pandemic. *IEEE Access* **2021**, *9*, 138003–138025. [CrossRef]
10. Chatzoglou, E.; Kambourakis, G.; Kouliaridis, V. A Multi-Tier Security Analysis of Official Car Management Apps for Android. *Future Internet* **2021**, *13*, 58. [CrossRef]
11. Louisiana Man Uses Digital Driver's License to Defraud Credit Unions & Banks. Available online: https://www.cutimes.com/2023/03/16/louisiana-man-uses-digital-drivers-license-to-defraud-credit-unions-banks/?slreturn=20230708061731 (accessed on 4 July 2023).
12. A Guide to Identity Theft Statistics for 2023. Available online: https://www.mcafee.com/learn/a-guide-to-identity-theft-statistics/ (accessed on 4 July 2023).
13. One in Five Europeans Have Experienced Identity Theft Fraud in the Last Two Years. Available online: https://finanso.se/one-in-five-europeans-have-experienced-identity-theft-fraud-in-the-last-two-years/ (accessed on 4 July 2023).
14. Android. App Security Best Practices. Available online: https://developer.android.com/topic/security/best-practices (accessed on 4 July 2023).
15. OWASP Mobile Top 10. Available online: https://owasp.org/www-project-mobile-top-10/ (accessed on 4 July 2023).
16. jssec. Android Application Secure Design/Secure Coding Guidebook. Available online: https://www.jssec.org/dl/android_securecoding_en_20220117/index.html (accessed on 2022 4 July 2023).

17. Garg, S.; Baliyan, N. Comparative Analysis of Android and IOS from Security Viewpoint. *Comput. Sci. Rev.* **2021**, *40*, 100372. [CrossRef]
18. Sarkar, A.; Goyal, A.; Hicks, D.; Sarkar, D.; Hazra, S. Android Application Development: A Brief Overview of Android Platforms and Evolution of Security Systems. In Proceedings of the 2019 Third International Conference on I-SMAC (IoT in Social, Mobile, Analytics and Cloud) (I-SMAC), Palladam, India, 12–14 December 2019; pp. 73–79. [CrossRef]
19. Filiol, E.; Irolla, P. Security of Mobile Banking... and of Other Mobile Apps. In Proceedings of the Black Hat Asia, Singapore, 24–27 March 2015; pp. 1–22.
20. Kaur, R.; Li, Y.; Iqbal, J.; Gonzalez, H.; Stakhanova, N. A Security Assessment of HCE-NFC Enabled E-Wallet Banking Android Apps. In Proceedings of the 2018 IEEE 42nd Annual Computer Software and Applications Conference (COMPSAC), Tokyo, Japan, 23–27 July 2018; Volume 02, pp. 492–497. [CrossRef]
21. Mandal, A.K.; Cortesi, A.; Ferrara, P.; Panarotto, F.; Spoto, F. Vulnerability analysis of android auto infotainment apps. In Proceedings of the 15th ACM International Conference on Computing Frontiers, Ischia, Italy, 8–10 May 2018; pp. 183–190.
22. Egele, M.; Brumley, D.; Fratantonio, Y.; Kruegel, C. An Empirical Study of Cryptographic Misuse in Android Applications. In Proceedings of the 2013 ACM SIGSAC Conference on Computer & Communications Security, Berlin, Germany, 4–8 November 2013; Association for Computing Machinery: New York, NY, USA, 2013; p. 73–84. [CrossRef]
23. Chatzikonstantinou, A.; Ntantogian, C.; Karopoulos, G.; Xenakis, C. Evaluation of Cryptography Usage in Android Applications. *EAI Endorsed Trans. Secur. Saf.* **2016**, *3*, e4. [CrossRef]
24. Chatzoglou, E.; Kambourakis, G.; Smiliotopoulos, C. Let the Cat out of the Bag: Popular Android IoT Apps under Security Scrutiny. *Sensors* **2022**, *22*, 513. [CrossRef] [PubMed]
25. Muñoz, A.; Ríos, R.; Román, R.; López, J. A survey on the (in)security of trusted execution environments. *Comput. Secur.* **2023**, *129*, 103180. [CrossRef]
26. Gómez, A.; Muñoz, A. Deep Learning-Based Attack Detection and Classification in Android Devices. *Electronics* **2023**, *12*, 3253. [CrossRef]
27. Statista. Mobile Operating Systems' Market Share Worldwide from 1st Quarter 2009 to 4th Quarter 2022. Available online: https://www.statista.com/statistics/272698/global-market-share-held-by-mobile-operating-systems-since-2009/ (accessed on 4 July 2023).
28. Statcounter. Mobile Operating System Market Share Worldwide. Available online: https://gs.statcounter.com/os-market-share/mobile/worldwide (accessed on 4 July 2023).
29. Google Inc.. What's New in Google System Updates. Available online: https://support.google.com/product-documentation/answer/11412553 (accessed on 2022 4 July 2023).
30. Apple Inc.. Apple Announces First States Signed Up to Adopt Driver's Licenses and State IDs in Apple Wallet. Available online: https://www.apple.com/newsroom/2021/09/apple-announces-first-states-to-adopt-drivers-licenses-and-state-ids-in-wallet/ (accessed on 4 July 2023).
31. Lawallet App. Available online: https://play.google.com/store/apps/details?id=gov.la.omv.lawallet (accessed on 4 July 2023).
32. MyColorado App. Available online: https://play.google.com/store/apps/details?id=com.soc.mycolorado (accessed on 4 July 2023).
33. FL Smart ID App. Available online: https://play.google.com/store/apps/details?id=com.thalesgroup.dis.idv.fl.holder.prd (accessed on 4 July 2023).
34. dds2go App. Available online: https://play.google.com/store/apps/details?id=gov.ga.dds.gadds (accessed on 4 July 2023).
35. Oklahoma Mobile ID App. Available online: https://play.google.com/store/apps/details?id=com.idemia.mobileid.us.ok (accessed on 4 July 2023).
36. Delaware Mobile ID App. Available online: https://play.google.com/store/apps/details?id=com.idemia.mobileid.us.de (accessed on 4 July 2023).
37. GET Mobile ID. Available online: https://play.google.com/store/apps/details?id=com.getgroupna.mdl.app.utah (accessed on 4 July 2023).
38. Airside Digital Identity. Available online: https://play.google.com/store/apps/details?id=com.airsidemobile.digitalid.android.prod (accessed on 4 July 2023).
39. eID-Me Digital ID App. Available online: https://play.google.com/store/apps/details?id=ca.bluink.eid_me_and (accessed on 4 July 2023).
40. eAusweise App. Available online: https://play.google.com/store/apps/details?id=at.gv.oe.awp.eausweise (accessed on 4 July 2023).
41. Kørekort app. Available online: https://play.google.com/store/apps/details?id=dk.digst.mdl (accessed on 4 July 2023).
42. Verimi ID Wallet App. Available online: https://play.google.com/store/apps/details?id=com.verimi (accessed on 4 July 2023).
43. gov.gr App. Available online: https://play.google.com/store/apps/details?id=gr.gov.wallet (accessed on 4 July 2023).
44. Kopie ID App. Available online: https://play.google.com/store/apps/details?id=com.milvum.kopieid (accessed on 4 July 2023).
45. id.gov.pt App. Available online: https://play.google.com/store/apps/details?id=id.gov.pt (accessed on 4 July 2023).
46. mi DGT App. Available online: https://play.google.com/store/apps/details?id=com.dgt.midgt&hl=en (accessed on 4 July 2023).

47. RTA m-Wallet App. Available online: https://play.google.com/store/apps/details?id=tsgovt.com.mywalet (accessed on 4 July 2023).
48. Service NSW App. Available online: https://play.google.com/store/apps/details?id=au.gov.nsw.service (accessed on 4 July 2023).
49. Ostorlab. Mobile Application Security Testing. Available online: https://www.ostorlab.co/product/mobile (accessed on 4 July 2023).
50. Abraham, A.; Schlecht, D.; Dobrushin, M.; Nadal, V. Mobile security framework (MobSF). Available online: https://github.com/MobSF/Mobile-Security-Framework-MobSF (accessed on 4 July 2023).
51. Kouliaridis, V.; Kambourakis, G.; Geneiatakis, D.; Potha, N. Two Anatomists Are Better than One-Dual-Level Android Malware Detection. *Symmetry* **2020**, *12*, 1128. [CrossRef]
52. Android Official ID Wallet Apps–Analysis Results. Available online: https://github.com/billkoul/AndroidIDWalletApps (accessed on 4 July 2023).
53. OWASP Mobile App Security. Available online: https://owasp.org/www-project-mobile-app-security/ (accessed on 4 July 2023).
54. Task Hijacking. Available online: https://docs.ostorlab.co/kb/APK_TASK_HIJACKING/ (accessed on 4 July 2023).
55. Handle Affinities. Available online: https://developer.android.com/guide/components/activities/tasks-and-back-stack#Affinities (accessed on 4 July 2023).
56. Intent Spoofing. Available online: https://docs.ostorlab.co/kb/INTENT_SPOOFING/ (accessed on 4 July 2023).
57. CVE-2017-13156. Available online: https://nvd.nist.gov/vuln/detail/CVE-2017-13156 (accessed on 4 July 2023).
58. CWE-532: Insertion of Sensitive Information into Log File. Available online: https://cwe.mitre.org/data/definitions/532.html (accessed on 4 July 2023).
59. CWE-926: Improper Export of Android Application Components. Available online: https://cwe.mitre.org/data/definitions/926.html (accessed on 4 July 2023).
60. European Commission. Cybersecurity Policies. Available online: https://digital-strategy.ec.europa.eu/en/policies/cybersecurity-policies (accessed on 4 July 2023).

 *information*

Article

Blockchain Data Availability Scheme with Strong Data Privacy Protection

Xinyu Liu [1], Shan Ji [2,*], Xiaowan Wang [3], Liang Liu [2] and Yongjun Ren [1]

[1] Engineering Research Center of Digital Forensics, Ministry of Education, School of Computer Science, Nanjing University of Information Science and Technology, Nanjing 210044, China

[2] College of Computer Science and Technology, Nanjing University of Aeronautics and Astronautics, Nanjing 210016, China

[3] College of Digital Arts, Xi'an University of Posts & Telecommunications, Xi'an 710061, China

* Correspondence: shanji@nuaa.edu.cn; Tel.: +86-189-3659-1811

Abstract: Blockchain, with its characteristics of non-tamperability and decentralization, has had a profound impact on various fields of society and has set off a boom in the research and application of blockchain technology. However, blockchain technology faces the problem of data availability attacks during its application, which greatly limits the scope and domain of blockchain applications. One of the most advantageous researches to address this problem is the scalable data availability solution that integrates coding theory design into the Merkle tree promise. Based on this scheme, this paper combines a zero-knowledge accumulator with higher efficiency and security with local repair coding, and proposes a data availability scheme with strong dataset privacy protection. The scheme first encodes the data block information on the blockchain to ensure tamper-proof data, and then uses a zero-knowledge accumulator to store the encoded data block information. Its main purpose is to use zero-knowledge property to protect the accumulation set information stored in the accumulator from being leaked and to ensure that no other information about the accumulation set is revealed during the data transmission. It fundamentally reduces the possibility of attackers generating fraudulent information by imitating block data and further resists data availability attacks.

Keywords: blockchain; privacy protection; data availability; zero knowledge accumulator

Citation: Liu, X.; Ji, S.; Wang, X.; Liu, L.; Ren, Y. Blockchain Data Availability Scheme with Strong Data Privacy Protection. *Information* **2023**, *14*, 88. https://doi.org/10.3390/info14020088

Academic Editors: Jose de Vasconcelos, Hugo Barbosa and Carla Cordeiro

Received: 18 November 2022
Revised: 30 January 2023
Accepted: 1 February 2023
Published: 2 February 2023

1. Introduction

Public blockchains, such as Bitcoin [1] and Ether [2], have proven themselves to be secure in practice. One of them, Bitcoin, has gone through more than a decade of secure and real-time operations, but at the cost of deteriorating performance [3]. To address this problem, various consensus layers and off-chain extension methods have been introduced: For example, ACeD, which is a scalable data availability solution that adds coding theory to the Merkle tree commitment to ensure efficiency and tamper resistance [4]; a new fraud prevention and data availability system that reduces the trade-off between on-chain capacity and security by enabling light clients to receive and verify proofs of fraud for invalid blocks from full nodes; and rollup information scattering with provable retrievability, a scheme that uses linear erasure codes and homomorphic vector commitments to design a storage and communication efficient protocol. These schemes address the scalable data availability problem of blockchain from different perspectives through different implementations. This paper aims to improve the blockchain data availability scheme based on the above scheme, and proposes a blockchain data availability scheme with strong dataset privacy protection (DPP-DA).

This paper proposes an intermediate "data availability verification" mechanism between the side blockchain (i.e., smaller blockchains) and the trusted blockchain (i.e., larger blockchains). The side blockchain transmits data to the verification layer, which then transmits verifiable membership witnesses to the trusted blockchain and ensures that the data is available in the side blockchain. N verification nodes work together to verify whether the proposed blocks are searchable (that is, data is available) before submitting it to the trusted blockchain. The key problem is how to share data securely and efficiently among nodes to verify the availability of data.

The solution of this paper is to use local repair codes [5–7] so that different nodes receive different encoding blocks. To ensure the integrity and correctness of the encoded blocks, we use zero-knowledge accumulators [8,9] to provide membership proofs for any block, but malicious block producers can hide malicious data, so the probability of reconstructing a block is very small and negligible. Nodes can detect such attacks by broadcasting what they receive and decoding data forwarded by others to confirm that the data is correct.

In order to find a scalable solution to the problem of data availability verification, the method based on local repair code must prevent error encoding attacks while minimizing the cost of storage and communication. The local repair code has low communication complexity and high data repair ability. When the storage node is a hostile node, the storage and download overhead is also low.

While solving the problem of data availability of blockchain, the threat of data privacy in a blockchain system will become a more important research issue. If there is no data privacy protection, the data will be easily leaked, and attackers will be more likely to attack the blockchain by imitating the leaked data, fraudulently cheating the blockchain in the process of data transmission, thus increasing the probability of data availability attacks. Therefore, it is also important to ensure the data privacy protection performance of the blockchain.

The existing various privacy protection mechanisms [10–12] and implementation technologies protect blockchain privacy from different aspects. Therefore, in a blockchain system that actually considers privacy protection, multiple technologies are usually integrated to achieve a more comprehensive privacy protection effect [13,14]. For the privacy of user information, the current protection mechanisms still have a lot of room for development, but the existing implementation technologies can not completely solve the threat to privacy protection. There are deficiencies in security, performance, scalability, and so on. Overall, with the continuous development of applications and demands, blockchain technology will gradually tend to improve in terms of privacy protection. Among them, zero-knowledge proof technology [15,16] is effective in solving the data privacy protection of blockchain.

In this paper, based on the zero-knowledge proof technique, we introduce and design a zero-knowledge accumulator based on bilinear mapping [17] to propose a powerful privacy-preserving enhancement scheme for datasets, which also provides hidden guarantees: accumulation values and witnesses do not leak dynamic sets that evolve through element insertion/deletion. At the same time, in addition to the results that can be queried, they do not disclose any information about the set, protecting not only the initially accumulated set, but also all accumulative updates. It also allows membership and non-membership proofs, it can compute membership witnesses, and it supports efficient updating of accumulative values due to insertions and deletions in sets. Membership and non-membership queries for a set can be responded to without revealing any other information about the set. This scheme not only enhances the security assurance of datasets, but also maintains the same efficient performance.

2. Related Work

Blockchain scaling: For a given node network, achieving the highest throughput and lowest latency blockchain that can be operated by consensus has always been a major focus area [18]. The off-chain payment network indirectly increases the transaction throughput of the system by processing large amounts of transaction data offline while using the blockchain to handle exceptions in the off-chain payment process [19]. The consensus mechanism of Bitcoin PoW [20,21] ensures the consistency of the state of the blockchain in the open network (weak consistency), but it does not consider the efficiency of the blockchain. So, Eyal et al. [22] proposed the Bitcon-NG scheme, which aims to increase the number of transaction confirmations in each round of consensus, so as to improve the transaction throughput of the system. The transaction throughput of the system can also be improved by designing a reliable sharding mechanism in an open blockchain network, based on the sharding technique [23,24] borrowed from the traditional distributed database domain. In this paper, starting from another form of blockchain extension, we design and implement an intermediate verification layer that can carry out scalable security interaction between the side blockchain and trusted blockchain.

Data availability: When blockchain nodes cannot access all data, they are vulnerable to data availability attacks [25]. One solution is to use the light node to provide warnings to the full node to notify the malicious block proponents of misbehavior and encode the blockchain data to improve the efficiency of fraud prevention. It was first used in 2D Reed-Solomon codes [26,27] and was then generalized by cryptographic hash accumulators encoding Merkle trees to generate block promises. In this paper, we propose a local repair encoding for validation operations: this encoding, combined with a zero-knowledge accumulator, allows efficient and secure validation of data between verification nodes.

Improving the scalability of the blockchain leads to a vulnerablilty to data availability attacks. That is, the amount of data increases with the improvement of the scalability of the blockchain, so it is very important for nodes to determine whether malicious transactions are hidden in the block when a new block is generated. Therefore, the aim of the scalable data availability scheme is to improve the scalability of the blockchain and at the same time solve the data availability attacks caused by malicious nodes.

Data privacy protection: With the wide application of blockchain technology, blockchain is facing more and more security threats and challenges [28,29]. Blockchain does not rely on central nodes, and transaction records, such as addresses and transaction amounts of participating users, are often made public on the blockchain, making it easy for nodes to verify, store transaction contents, and reach consensus. However, this open and transparent nature of the blockchain will likely lead to user privacy leaks [30,31]. The varying security performance and ability of each blockchain node to combat information leakage increases the risk of data privacy leakage [32]. The flaws of various programs in the blockchain will also expose the blockchain system to huge security risks. In this paper, we design a powerful data privacy protection scheme using zero-knowledge accumulators, which allow the membership and non-membership of sets to be answered without revealing any other information about the set at query time and allow membership and non-membership proofs, can compute membership witness, and support the efficient updating of accumulation values due to insertions and deletions in sets. Accumulators with zero-knowledge can be thought of as "honest submitter" relaxations of zero-knowledge sets.

3. System and Security Models

The system consists of four parts: trusted blockchain (proof of storage block), client (node providing data in side blockchain), zero knowledge accumulator, and intermediate verification layer to ensure data availability. The system structure is shown in Figure 1.

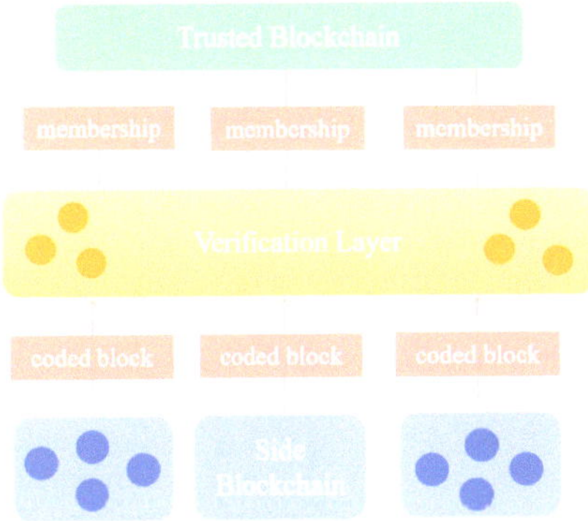

Figure 1. System structure.

3.1. Network Models and Assumptions

This part contains two types of nodes: verification nodes and client nodes. The specific flow of the intermediate verification layer is shown in Figure 2.

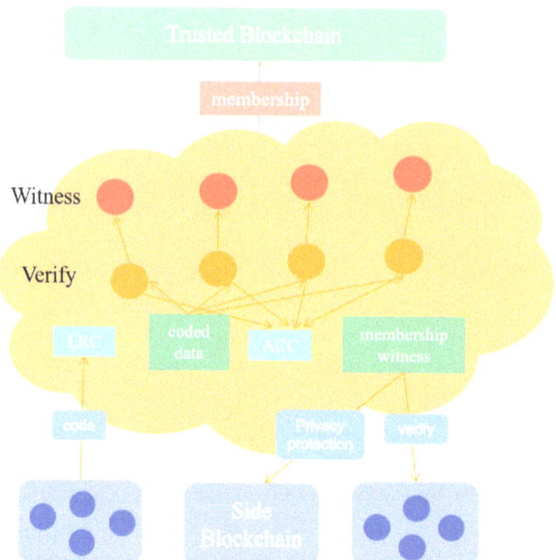

Figure 2. Intermediate verification layer.

Verification nodes are the main participants in the verification layer. They receive block submitted requests from the client of the side blockchain, including the block header and a set of data blocks. After ensuring that the data is complete and correct, they determine whether the block is available by verification and submit the result to the trusted blockchain.

Zero knowledge accumulator stores the block information on the blockchain to provide privacy for the client, and then the client receives the block and requests the verification layer to submit the block. They update the information periodically based on the membership witness from the trusted blockchain and inquire the verification node about the block witnessed by the non-membership witness as needed.

A key assumption of the verification model is that trusted blockchains have a persistent data sequence and service activeness. In addition, we assume that honest nodes are in the majority in the verification layer. The verification node is connected to all clients. The network is synchronized and the communication is certified and reliable.

3.2. Data Privacy Protection Model

Block data of the blockchain is stored using a zero-knowledge accumulator, where the accumulation values and proofs are not disclosed for dynamic sets inserted and deleted through elements. During data transfer in trusted blockchains and side blockchains, privacy protection is provided for any dynamic changes in data generated by the set in the accumulator, i.e., set membership and non-membership queries can be answered without revealing any other information about the set.

Data storage: Each block is connected to a zero-knowledge accumulator, which compressively stores the encoded block data and forms a large accumulation set in the accumulator.

Dynamic operations: Dynamically and efficiently query, add, delete and other operations to cumulative sets. Accumulated values do not leak for dynamic sets that change through element insertion/deletion.

Set membership and non-membership proofs: Membership and non-membership proofs are generated for sets of data stored in accumulators, and set membership and non-membership proofs can query these proofs without disclosing any other information about these datasets.

3.3. Verification Model

Reducing the storage burden and ensuring data availability through the intermediate verification layer is of vital importance. The verification layer network consists of several zero-knowledge accumulators and blocks to form N verification nodes, which can transmit data with the client and provide data availability services. There are opponents that can damage several authentication nodes. Any node that is not damaged is called an honest node.

In the verification layer, data blocks are the basic data units. The following steps are required to submit and retrieve block b for data availability verification.

1. Generation blocks: When a client wants to commit block b to a trusted blockchain, it runs the accumulation set (b, D) of accumulators connected to the block to generate membership witnesses for block b and a set of D blocks $D_1, \ldots, D_m$ generates membership witnesses Wit_D.
2. Dispersion blocks: The client runs the decentralized protocol disperse $(B, (D_1, \ldots, D_m), N)$, and specifies that different data blocks are sent to N different verification nodes.
3. Verification termination: Verification nodes query membership witnesses to finalize and accept their witnesses to write certain blocks in the trusted blockchain.
4. Retrieve data: The client retrieves a set of blocks of any witnesses Wit_D that has been verified by the verification layer by initiating a request (retrieve, Wit_D).
5. Decoded data: Any client can run primitive decoding $\left(W_D, \{ Wit_{D_i} \}_{i \in S} \right)$ to decode the blocks in the retrieved block $\{ Wit_{D_i} \}_{i \in S}$. The decoder also returns the proof of the membership associated with the witness for decoding block b.

We describe the security of the verification model, that is, the data availability scheme, and define the data availability verification, as follows.

In the data availability verification of the trusted block chain, the client submits the block and the trusted block chain receives the witness with the following properties:

1. Termination: When an honest client requests block b decentralized, block b will eventually be approved and the witness will be transferred to the trusted blockchain.
2. Availability: Dispersion is acceptable if a client wants to retrieve Wit_D and the verification layer is able to provide it with block b or empty block $\varnothing$ and prove that the client is related to Wit_D.
3. Correctness: If two honest clients running (Retrieve, Wit_D) at the same time receive b_1 and b_2, then $b_1 = b_2$. If the client initiating the dispersion is honest, it needs to satisfy the original dispersion block $b_1 = b$.

4. Technical Description

In this section, bilinear mappings, zero knowledge accumulators, and local repair codes are described and constructed, respectively. These techniques are described in more detail in Refs. [5,8,33], respectively. Readers can refer to these studies for further information.

4.1. Bilinear Mapping

The basic bilinear accumulator is a paired bilinear mapping based on the n-strong Diffie–Hellman assumption [33]. Pairing: $e\colon G_1 \times G_2 \to G_T$, where G_1, G_2 and G_T are cyclic groups of prime order p. We require pairing e to satisfy the following attributes.

Bilinearity: $e\left(u^a, v^b \right) = e(u, v)^{ab}$, where $u \in G_1, v \in G_2, a, b \in Z_p$.

Non-degeneracy: There is at least element $g_1 \in G_1, g_2 \in G_2$ that satisfies $e(g_1, g_2) \neq 1$.

Calculability: For any $u \in G_1, v \in G_2$, there is a polynomial time algorithm related to a given security parameter λ, which can efficiently calculate $e(u, v)$.

We call $(p, G_1, G_2, G_T, e, g_1, g_2)$ a bilinear paired tuple as the output of a probabilistic polynomial time algorithm running on input 1^λ. When choosing cyclic groups G_1 and G_2, we usually consider the security of accumulators, that is $G_1 \neq G_2$, we choose asymmetric cyclic groups.

Suppose g_1, g_2 is the generator of G_1, G_2, then $e(g_1, g_2)$ is the generator of $G_T, k \in Z_p^*$. The accumulated value for the dataset $D = \{d_1, \ldots, d_n\}$ is $A(D) = g_1 \Pi_{d \in D}(d + k)$.

For any subset D_0 of the set D, its membership witness $W(D_0)$ is the accumulative value of removing D_0 from the set $D : W(D_0) = g_1 \Pi_{d \in D \setminus D_0}(d + k)$.

Verify that the membership witness $W(D_0)$ is correct or not, we can judge whether $e\big(W(D_0), g_2 \Pi_{d_0 \in D_0}(d_0 + k)\big) = e(A(D), g_2)$ is true or not.

4.2. Zero-Knowledge Accumulator

The zero-knowledge accumulator is a dynamic universal accumulator based on bilinear mapping. It has all the properties of dynamic universal accumulator and achieves perfect zero-knowledge property. It supports membership witness and non-membership witness, and it supports insertion and deletion of sets for efficient updating of accumulative values. The following is a definition of dynamic universal accumulator and zero-knowledgeability.

There are five probabilistic polynomial-time algorithms in the dynamic universal accumulator (GenKey, Setup, Witness, Verify, Update). It represents the set D with accumulative values, which contains elements from the domain D. It supports queries of the form "$d \in D$?". Where $d \in D$ and the update of the current collection (e.g., using the "insert d" or "delete d" operations). The algorithm for the dynamic universal accumulator runs between the owner, the server, and the client, as described below. A tuple of algorithms constitutes the accumulator.

Five PPT algorithms comprise the dynamic universal accumulator, DUA = (GenKey, Setup, Witness, Verify, Update) defined as follows:

$$(sk, vk) \leftarrow \text{GenKey}\left(1^\lambda\right)$$

The key generation algorithm takes security parameters λ as input, and then outputs the public verification key vk and the secret key sk saved by the owner, which are responded by the client during the verification query.

$$(acc, ek, aux) \leftarrow \text{Setup}(sk, D)$$

The owner runs this setup algorithm. It takes as input the source set D and generates an accumulative value Acc that is published to both the server and client, along with the evaluation key ek and the auxiliary information aux that is only sent to the server for proof construction.

$$(b, w) \leftarrow \text{Witness}(acc, D, d, ek, aux)$$

The server runs the witness algorithm. It inputs the evaluation keyword ek, the accumulative value acc, the set D, and the query element d. It outputs an indication of whether the boolean value b is in the set and the witness w of the answer.

$$(\text{accept}/\text{reject}) \leftarrow \text{Verify}(acc, d, b, w, vk)$$

The client runs the verification algorithm. It inputs accumulative value acc, public key vk, queried element d, boolean value b, witness w, and outputs accept/reject.

$$(acc', ek', aux') \leftarrow \text{Update}(acc, D, d, sk, aux, upd)$$

This update algorithm inputs the current set with its accumulative values and auxiliary information and inserts element d into D, if $upd = 1$ or removes element d from D, if $upd = 0$. The algorithm outputs $\perp$ if $upd = 1$ and $d \in D$, (similarly, if $upd = 0$ and $d \notin D$), indicating that the update is invalid. Otherwise, it outputs (acc', ek', aux'), where acc' is the new accumulative value corresponding to the set $D \cup \{d\}$ or $D \setminus \{d\}, ek'$ is the modified evaluation keyword, and aux' is the auxiliary information of the set (both are sent to the server only).

As a result of changing accumulative values, we need the WitUpdate function in order to update the existing witnesses efficiently.

$$(upd, w') \leftarrow \text{WitUpdate}'(acc, acc', d, w, y, ek', aux, aux', upd)$$

The WitUpdate algorithm will run after the update is called. It takes as input the old and new accumulative values and auxiliary information based on the binary value upd, the evaluation keyword ek' that updates the output, and the elements inserted or removed from the set d. It also uses different elements y and their existing witnesses w (which can be membership or non-membership witnesses). A new witness w' about y of the new set d' is output. This output must match what can be calculated by running Witness (acc', d', y, ek', aux').

Zero-knowledgeness: Let X be a binary function. For a query, $X(query, d, D)) = 1$ when and only when $d \in D$ or update $D(\text{update}, d, c, D)) = 1$ when $(c = 1 \wedge d \notin D)$ or $(c = 0 \wedge d \in D)$. Let RealAdv (1^λ) Ideadv, and Sim(1^λ) be the game between the challenger, the adversary Adv, and the simulator $Sim = (Sim_1, Sim_2)$, defined as follows:

RealAdv (1^λ):

Setup: The challenger runs $(sk, vk) \leftarrow \text{GenKey}(1^\lambda)$ and sends the vk to Adv. The latter selects the set D_0 with $|D_0| \in \text{Poly}(\lambda)$ and sends it to the challenger, which in turn runs setup (sk, D_0) to obtain (acc_0, ek_0, aux_0). Then, it sends acc_0 to Adv and sets $(D, acc, ek, aux) \leftarrow (D_0, acc_0, ek_0, aux_0)$.

Query: For $i = 1, \ldots, l$, where $l \in \text{poly}(\lambda)$, Adv outputs (op, x_i, c_i), where $op \in$ query, update $\}$ and $c_i \in \{0, 1\}$:

If op = query: Challenger runs $(b, w_i) \leftarrow$ witness (acc, D, d_i, ek, aux) and returns output to Adv.

If op = update: Challenger runs Update$(acc, D, d_i, sk, aux,)$. Update the set if the output is not $\bot$, and accordingly get d_i, set$(D, acc, ek, aux) \leftarrow (d_i, acc_i, ek_i, aux_i)$ and forward acc to Adv. Otherwise, output $\bot$.

Response: The opponent outputs a bit x.

IdealAdv (1^λ) :

Setup: The simulator Sim_1, with input1 1^λ, outputs a vk and forwards it to Adv. The adversary chooses a set D_0 with $|D_0| \in \text{poly}(\lambda)$. Sim_1 responds with acc_0 and maintains the state $state_S$. Finally, let $(D, acc) \leftarrow (D_0, acc_0)$.

Query: For $i = 1, \ldots, l$, Adv outputs (op, x_i, c_i), where $op \in \{$query, update$\}$ and $c_i \in \{0, 1\}$:

If op = query: The simulator runs $(b, w_i) \leftarrow Sim_2(acc, x_i, state_S, D(\text{query}, d_i, D))$ and returns the output to Adv.

If op = update: The simulator runs $Sim_2(acc, state_S, X(\text{update}, d_i, c_i, D))$. If the output of D (update, d_i, c_i, D) is 1, such that $D \leftarrow D_i \cup d_i$ in $c_1 = 1$ and $D \leftarrow D_i \backslash d_i$ in $c_1 = 0$ and according to a valid update, X is always the placeholder variable for the latest set version, but the simulator never observes the variable. The simulator responds to adv with acc_0.

4.3. Local Repair Code

Let F_q be a finite field consisting of q elements. Denote the set $\{1, 2, \ldots, n\}$ by $[n]$. In layman's terms, a given codeword is a grouping code with local restorability r if each coordinate of a given codeword can be recovered by accessing a maximum of r other coordinates of the codeword, it is a block code with local repairable r.

Let $C \subseteq F_q^n$ be a q-element grouping code of length n. For each $\alpha \in F_q$ and $i \in [n]$, define $C(i, \alpha) := \{c = (c_1, \ldots, c_n) \in : c_i = \alpha\}$. For a subset $I \subseteq [n] \backslash \{i\}$, we denote by $C_I(i, \alpha)$ the projection of $C(i, \alpha)$ onto I. A code E is said to be a locally restorative code with local restorability r if for each $i \in [n]$, there exists a subset $I_i \subseteq \backslash \{i\}$ satisfying $|I_i| \leq r$ such that for any $\alpha \neq \beta$, the codes $E_{I_i}(i, \alpha)$ and $E_{I_i}(i, \beta)$ are disjoint.

5. Performance Guarantee

5.1. Data Privacy Protection Security Analysis

To ensure the security of blockchain data privacy protection, the security of the zero-knowledge accumulator needs to be analyzed. The two main aspects include completeness and reliability.

One of the properties of the cryptographic accumulator is completeness, that is, the witness of the output of any call sequence through the scheme algorithm, because the state of the set at the time of witness generation is correctly verified with an almost negligible probability.

Completeness. Let the elements in D assimilate the set which is constructed after calling the update algorithm (starting from the set D_0) and for ek_i, Aux_i as well. The dynamic universal accumulator is complete if for all sets D_0, where $|D_0|$ and $l \geq 0$ are polynomials in λ and for all $d_i \in D$, for $0 = 1, \ldots, l$, there is a negligible function $v(\lambda)$, then the dynamic universal accumulator is said to be complete such that:

$$\Pr \left[\begin{array}{c} (sk, vk) \leftarrow \text{GenKey}(1^\lambda); (e_0, acc_0, aux_0) \leftarrow \text{Setup}(sk, D_0) \\ \{(acc_{i+1}, ek_{i+1}, aux_{i+1}) \leftarrow \text{Update}(acc_i, D_i, d_i, sk, aux, upd_i)\}_{0 \leq i \leq l} \\ (b, w) \leftarrow \text{Witness}(acc_l, D_l, d, e_l, aux_l) : \text{Verify}(acc, d, b, w, vk) = \text{accept} \end{array} \right] \geq 1 - v(\lambda) \quad (1)$$

where the probability of the algorithm exceeds its randomness.

The second property is reliability. It reflects the fact that the adversarial server cannot provide proof of acceptance if the request is incorrect.

Reliability: that is to say, Adv has the right to access all algorithms in the scheme and is required to generate a statement and the witness of the statement in the competition, but Adv cannot win.

For all PPT adversaries Adv and all 1-polynomials in λ running on input 1^λ, the randomness of the coins that take over the algorithm and Adv has a negligible probability of winning the following game:

Setup: Challenger runs $(sk, vk) \leftarrow \text{GenKey}(1^\lambda)$ and sends vk to Adv, who responds with set D_0. The challenger runs $(ek_0, acc_0) \leftarrow \text{set}(sk, D_0)$ and sends the output to the adversary.

Updates: The challenger starts the list L and inserts the tuple (acc_0, d_0). After this, for $i = 0$, the opponent releases update x_i and receives the updated output $(acc_i, D_i, d_i, sk, aux_i, upd_i)$ from the challenger. After each call to update, if the output is not $\perp$, the challenger appends the returned (acc_{i+1}, D_{i+1}) to L. or else, it appends (acc_i, D_i).

Challenge: A triple (d^*, b^*, w^*) is output by the adversary along with an index j. Let $L[j]$ be (acc_j, D_i). The adversary will win the game if the following occurs:

$$\text{Verify}(acc_j, d^*, b^*, w^*, vk) = \text{accept} \wedge \left((d^* \in D_j \wedge b^* = 0) \vee (d^* \notin D_j \wedge b^* = 1) \right) \quad (2)$$

The discussion on the conditions for winning the game should take place on this point. In particular, Adv output set D^* and the accumulative value $acc*$ and may be used to calculate the latter to cater to the randomization of the accumulator.

5.2. Security Analysis of Data Availability Scheme

In order to demonstrate that the data availability scheme is secure if the trusted blockchain is durable and secure, we prove the following properties.

Verification termination: In data availability verification, dispersion is accepted only if a membership witness is submitted to the trusted blockchain. If honest client requests are scattered, but there is no membership witness in the trusted blockchain, then either no membership witness is submitted, or no new transactions are accepted. By querying the membership witness Wit_D, even if all the damaged nodes cannot provide any information, the data can still be considered available by membership proof and the membership witness will be presented, so the trusted blockchain is not active, which contradicts our assumption.

Availability: If decentralization is accepted, there is a membership witness in the trusted blockchain, and the verification node has proved the block. Because the trusted blockchain is persistent, the membership witness can be obtained as long as the client retrieves the block, and at least M/N nodes will respond through the stored zero-knowledge accumulator connected to the block. On receiving a group block from a partial node of the side blockchain, for applying a local repair code with local repairability r and a feasible dispersion algorithm $(b, (D_1, \ldots, D_m), N)$ of the data availability verification layer, if dispersion is accepted, the verification is able to provide block b or empty block $\varnothing$ and prove its relation to Wit_D whenever an honest client requests retrieval.

6. Performance Analysis

6.1. Storage and Communication

We deployed our solution implementation on Linux cloud hardware with a 6-core CPU, 32 GB RAM, 128 GB SSD, and 40 Gpbs network interface (for data verification layer and side blockchain nodes). The central goals of the system are dataset privacy protection and data availability. Based on Table 1, we define four key performance metrics for the system, let N be the number of nodes, M be the number of blocks, and b be the size of each block. The coded repair rate of the local repair code measures the fault tolerance of the model. Consider the simplest scaling solution, which is to spread the data across the network without duplication. The "storage overhead" refers to the ratio of the total storage cost to the actual storage information. Considering that the blocks in each node are connected to a zero-knowledge accumulator to compress the stored data, the storage overhead is $O(N)$, which indicates that the storage cost increases linearly with the network size. The system implements $O(1)$ storage in case of client honesty and $O(Logb)$ storage in case of client corruption. When applying 1D-RS codes [34], the worst-case scenario is that the adversary sends a block verification node with incorrect encoding and needs to download $O(B)$ data for fraud prevention. The data availability verification system in this paper achieves a near-optimal overhead, requiring only $O(Logb)$ proofs to be downloaded. For a given block, the communication efficiency of the data availability verification system in this paper is $O(B)$.

Table 1. System performance indicators.

Fault Tolerance	Scalability	Storage Overhead	Communication Efficiency
$O(b)$	$O(N)$	$O(Logb)$	$O(B)$

6.2. Bandwidth Consumption during Local Repair Code Encoding

We can calculate the amount of bandwidth consumed by the nodes during the encoding process. The bandwidth consumption of the node is determined by evaluating the bandwidth consumption of the d encoding fragments stored by each node. The bandwidth consumption of the node during encoding varies for $k = 10, 20, 30, 40, 50, 60$, and $d = 4, 5, 6$, where k denotes the total number of encoded fragments. Figure 3 shows the change in bandwidth consumption when the encoding fragments are stored during encoding. When d is fixed, the larger k is fixed, and the less bandwidth is consumed for storing the encoded fragment during encoding, and when k is fixed, the larger d is, and the greater bandwidth is consumed for storing the encoded fragment during encoding. Therefore, the size of bandwidth occupied by nodes for data transmission is related to the amount of encoded data allocated to nodes for storage. When the block size is relatively large, the bandwidth occupation and the amount of stored data can be measured to choose a better solution, but with the current block size of the mainstream blockchain, the bandwidth occupied by data transmission between nodes within a group is small.

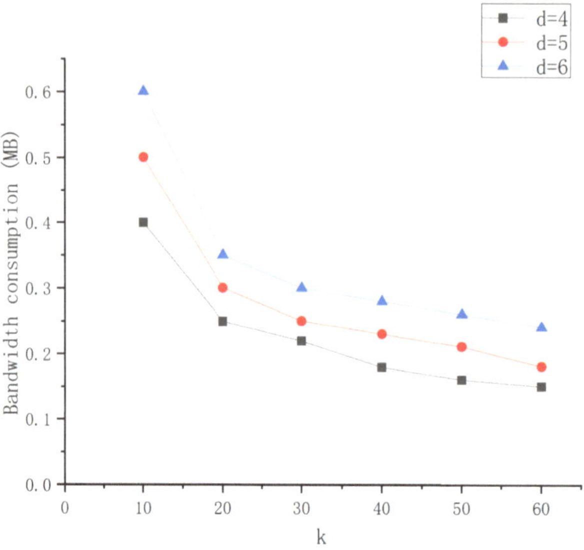

Figure 3. Bandwidth consumption during encoding.

In the experiments, the repair rate of erroneous nodes was calculated and the total encoded data volume of the nodes was evaluated at the number of erroneous nodes $p = 1, 2, 3$, respectively. $n = 20, 40, 60, 80, 100, 120$ is the repair rate of the erroneous nodes. Figure 4 shows the variation of the repair rate of the error nodes. We can know that when p is fixed, the larger n is, and the slower the repair rate of the error nodes in each slice, and when n is fixed, the smaller p is, and the faster the repair rate of the error nodes.

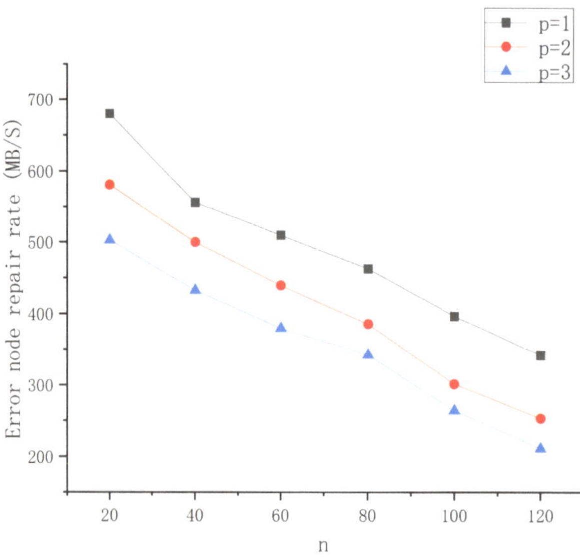

Figure 4. Error node repair rate.

6.3. Comparison of Schemes

We compare the data availability scheme with strong dataset privacy protection (DPP-DA) in this paper with the ACeD data availability scheme, the 1D-RS scheme [35,36], using regenerable codes, and the AVID [37] scheme. The differences between the three in terms of latency, throughput, and fault tolerance are analyzed, respectively. The results are shown in Table 2. In terms of latency, the local repair codes used in this paper are more efficient compared to Merkle tree coding and regenerable codes. It is more effective in reducing the blockchain time delay. In terms of throughput, DPP-DA has a higher improvement compared with the other two schemes, because compressed storage by accumulator can improve the throughput of blockchain. In terms of fault tolerance, the fault tolerance of blockchain is influenced by the coding repair rate, where the coding repair ability of local repair codes is higher than other codes, so the data availability scheme based on local repair codes is more fault tolerant.

Table 2. Performance comparison.

Metrics	ACeD	1D-RS	AVID	DPP-DA
Latency	around 80 s	around 100 s	around 90 s	around 75 s
Throughput	around 1300 tps	around 1000 tps	around 1200 tps	more than 1500 tps
Fault tolerance	affected by code repair rate	affected by code repair rate	affected by code repair rate	affected by code repair rate

7. Conclusions

By investigating previous data availability scheme, this paper puts forward a new blockchain-based data availability scheme. The original coded Merkle tree is replaced by a zero-knowledge accumulator with local repair coding with higher efficiency and security, and then the zero-knowledge performance of the zero-knowledge accumulator is used to achieve strong data privacy protection performance considering the privacy security of the data. Finally, a blockchain data availability scheme with strong privacy protection for datasets is proposed. The scheme first ensures tamper-proof data by encoding the data block information on the blockchain, and then stores the encoded data block information on the blockchain using a zero-knowledge accumulator to protect the accumulation set information stored in the accumulator from being compromised. It fundamentally reduces the possibility of attackers generating fraudulent information by imitating the information of data blocks on the blockchain.

Author Contributions: X.L. and Y.R. were responsible for conceptual analysis, methodological analysis, and writing the original draft. X.W. and L.L. were responsible for thesis revision and review. S.J. was responsible for review, supervision, and project administration. All authors have read and agreed to the published version of the manuscript.

Funding: This work was supported by the National Key R&D Program of China (Grant No. 2021YFB27-00500), and it was also supported by the National Natural Science Foundation of China (Grant No. 62072249, 62076125). This work was also supported by the National Key R&D Program of Guangdong Province (Grant No. 2020B0101090002), and the Natural Science Foundation of Jiangsu Province (Grant No. BK20200418, BE2020106).

Data Availability Statement: The datasets generated and analyzed during the current study are not publicly available due to restricted data sources but are available from the corresponding author on reasonable request.

Conflicts of Interest: The authors declare no conflict of interest.

References

1. Nakamoto, S. Bitcoin: A Peer-to-Peer Electronic Cash System. *Decentralized Bus. Rev.* **2008**, *21260*, 21260.
2. Chen, H.; Pendleton, M.; Njilla, L.; Xu, S.H. A survey on Ethereum systems security. Vulnerabilities, attacks, and defenses. *ACM Comput. Surv.* **2021**, *53*, 1–43. [CrossRef]

3.   Ren, Y.J.; Zhu, F.; Wang, J.; Sharma, P.; Ghosh, U. Novel vote scheme for decision-making feedback based on blockchain in internet of vehicles. *IEEE Trans. Intell. Transp.* **2021**, *21*, 1639–1648. [CrossRef]
4.   Sheng, P.Y.; Xue, B.W.; Kannan, S.; Viswanath, P. ACeD: Scalable data availability oracle. In Proceedings of the International Conference on Financial Cryptography and Data Security, Virtual Event, 1–5 March 2021; Springer: Berlin/Heidelberg, Germany, 2021; pp. 299–318.
5.   Papailiopoulos, D.S.; Dimakis, A.G. Locally repairable codes. *IEEE Trans. Inf. Theory* **2014**, *60*, 5843–5855. [CrossRef]
6.   Huang, P.; Yaakobi, E.; Uchikawa, H.; Siegel, P.H. Binary linear locally repairable codes. *IEEE Trans. Inf. Theory* **2016**, *62*, 6268–6283. [CrossRef]
7.   Luo, Y.; Xing, C.; Yuan, C. Optimal locally repairable codes of distance 3 and 4 via cyclic codes. *IEEE Trans. Inf. Theory* **2019**, *65*, 1048–1053. [CrossRef]
8.   Esha, G.; Olga, O.; Dimitrios, P.; Roberto, T.; Nikos, T. Zero-knowledge accumulators and set operations. *Cryptol. Eprint Arch.* **2016**, *10032*, 1–46.
9.   Campanelli, M.; Mathias, H. Curve trees: Practical and transparent zero-knowledge accumulators. *Cryptol. Eprint Arch.* **2022**, *756*, 1–18.
10.   Li, T.; Qian, Q.; Ren, Y.J.; Ren, Y.Z.; Xia, J.Y. Privacy-preserving recommendation based on kernel method in cloud computing. *Comput. Mater. Contin.* **2021**, *66*, 779–791. [CrossRef]
11.   Feng, Q.; He, D.B.; Zeadally, S.; KhurramKhan, M.; Kumar, N. A survey on privacy protection in blockchain system. *J. Netw. Comput. Appl.* **2019**, *126*, 45–58. [CrossRef]
12.   Mohammed, B.; Abdulghani, A.A.; Mohd, A.B.I.; Ali, S.S.; Muhammad, K.K. Comprehensive Survey on Big Data Privacy Protection. *IEEE Access* **2022**, *8*, 20067–20079.
13.   Liang, W.; Yang, Y.; Yang, C.; Hu, Y.H.; Xie, S.Y.; Li, K.C.; Cao, J.N. PDPChain: A consortium blockchain-based privacy protection scheme for personal data. *IEEE Trans. Reliab.* **2022**, 1–13.
14.   Ren, Y.J.; Huang, D.; Wang, W.H.; Yu, X.F. BSMD: A blockchain-based secure storage mechanism for big spatio-temporal data. *Future Gener. Comput. Syst.* **2023**, *138*, 328–338. [CrossRef]
15.   Benarroch, D.; Campanelli, M.; Fiore, D.; Kobi, G.; Dimitris, K. Zero-knowledge proofs for set membership: Efficient, succinct, modular. In Proceedings of the International Conference on Financial Cryptography and Data Security, Virtual Event, 1–5 March 2021; Springer: Berlin/Heidelberg, Germany, 2021; pp. 393–414.
16.   Sun, X.Q.; Yu, F.R.; Zhang, P.; Sun, Z.W.; Xie, W.X.; Peng, X. A survey on zero-knowledge proof in blockchain. *IEEE Netw.* **2021**, *35*, 198–205. [CrossRef]
17.   Ren, Y.J.; Qi, J.; Liu, Y.P.; Wang, J.; Kim, G. Integrity verification mechanism of sensor data based on bilinear map accumulator. *ACM Trans. Internet Technol.* **2021**, *21*, 1–20. [CrossRef]
18.   Zhou, Q.H.; Huang, H.W.; Zheng, Z.B.; Bian, J. Solutions to scalability of blockchain: A survey. *IEEE Access* **2020**, *8*, 16440–16455. [CrossRef]
19.   Novo, O. Scalable access management in IoT using blockchain: A performance evaluation. *IEEE Internet Things J.* **2019**, *6*, 4694–4701. [CrossRef]
20.   Panda, S.S.; Mohanta, B.K.; Satapathy, U.; Jena, D.; Gountia, D.; Patra, T.K. Study of blockchain based decentralized consensus algorithms. In Proceedings of the TENCON 2019—2019 IEEE Region 10 Conference (TENCON), Kochi, India, 17–20 October 2019; pp. 908–913.
21.   Ren, Y.J.; Zhu, F.J.; Kumar, S.P.; Wang, T.; Wang, J. Data query mechanism based on hash computing power of blockchain in internet of things. *Sensors* **2020**, *20*, 207. [CrossRef]
22.   Eyal, I.; Gencer, A.E.; Renesse, R.V. Bitcoin-NG: A scalable blockchain protocol. In Proceedings of the 13th USENIX Symposium on Networked Systems Design and Implementation (NSDI'16), Santa Clara, CA, USA, 16–18 March 2016; pp. 45–59.
23.   Yun, J.; Goh, Y.; Chung, J.M. DQN-based optimization framework for secure sharded blockchain systems. *IEEE Internet Things J.* **2021**, *8*, 708–722. [CrossRef]
24.   Mizrahi, A.; Rottenstreich, O. Blockchain state sharding with space-aware representations. *IEEE Trans. Netw. Serv. Manag.* **2021**, *18*, 1571–1583. [CrossRef]
25.   Yu, M.C.; Saeid, S.; Li, S.Z.; Salman, A.; Sreeram, K.; Pramod, V. Coded merkle tree: Solving data availability attacks in blockchains. In Proceedings of the International Conference on Financial Cryptography and Data Security, Kota Kinabalu, Malaysia, 10–14 February 2020; Springer: Cham, Switzerland, 2020; Volume 12059, pp. 114–134.
26.   Martńnez-Peñas, U.; Kschischang, F.R. Reliable and secure multishot network coding using linearized reed-solomon codes. *IEEE Trans. Inf. Theory* **2019**, *65*, 4785–4803. [CrossRef]
27.   Papamanthou, C.; Roberto, T.; Nikos, T. Authenticated hash tables based on cryptographic accumulators. *Algorithmica* **2016**, *74*, 664–712. [CrossRef]
28.   Ren, Y.J.; Leng, Y.; Cheng, Y.P.; Wang, J. Secure data storage based on blockchain and coding in edge computing. *Math. Biosci. Eng.* **2019**, *16*, 1874–1892. [CrossRef] [PubMed]
29.   Tavani, H.T.; Moor, J.H. Privacy protection, control of information, and privacy-enhancing technologies. *ACM Sigcas Comput. Soc.* **2001**, *31*, 6–11. [CrossRef]
30.   Gong, J.; Mei, Y.R.; Xiang, F.; Hong, H.S.; Sun, Y.B.; Sun, Z.X. A data privacy protection scheme for Internet of things based on blockchain. *Trans. Emerg. Telecommun. Technol.* **2021**, *32*, e4010. [CrossRef]

31. Ren, Y.J.; Leng, Y.; Qi, J.; Pradip, K.S.; Wang, J. Multiple cloud storage mechanism based on blockchain in smart homes. *Future Gener. Comput. Syst.* **2021**, *115*, 304–313. [CrossRef]
32. Boneh, D.; Bunz, B.; Fisch, B. Batching techniques for accumulators with applications to IOPs and stateless blockchains. In Proceedings of the Annual International Cryptology Conference, Santa Barbara, CA, USA, 18–22 August 2019; Springer: Cham, Switzerland, 2019; pp. 561–586.
33. Thakur, S. Batching non-membership proofs with bilinear accumulators. *IACR Cryptol. ePrint Arch.* **2019**, 1–22. Available online: https://eprint.iacr.org/2019/1147 (accessed on 8 November 2022).
34. Halbawi, W.; Liu, Z.; Hassibi, B. Balanced Reed-Solomon codes. In Proceedings of the 2016 IEEE International Symposium on Information Theory (ISIT), Barcelona, Spain, 10–15 July 2016; pp. 935–939.
35. Sarkar, M.N.I.; Meegahapola, L.G.; Datta, M. Reactive power management in renewable rich power grids: A review of grid-codes, renewable generators, support devices, control strategies and optimization algorithms. *IEEE Access* **2018**, *6*, 41458–41489. [CrossRef]
36. Chen, H.C.H.; Lee, P.P.C. Enabling data integrity protection in regenerating-coding-based cloud storage: Theory and implementation. *IEEE Trans. Parallel Distrib. Syst.* **2014**, *25*, 407–416. [CrossRef]
37. Cachin, C.; Tessaro, S. Asynchronous verifiable information dispersal. *IEEE Symp. Reliab. Distrib. Syst.* **2014**, *25*, 191–201.

Article

Analysis of the Impact of Age, Education and Gender on Individuals' Perception of Label Efficacy for Online Content

Matthew Spradling [1,*] and Jeremy Straub [2,*]

1. College of Innovation and Technology, University of Michigan-Flint, Flint, MI 48502, USA
2. Department of Computer Science, North Dakota State University, Fargo, ND 58105, USA
* Correspondence: mjspra@umich.edu (M.S.); jeremy.straub@ndsu.edu (J.S.); Tel.: +1-(810)-766-6735 (M.S.); +1-(701)-231-8196 (J.S.)

Abstract: Online content is consumed by most Americans and is a primary source of their news information. It impacts millions' perception of the world around them. Problematically, individuals who seek to deceive or manipulate the public can use targeted online content to do so and this content is readily consumed and believed by many. The use of labeling as a way to alert consumers of potential deceptive content has been proposed. This paper looks at factors which impact its perceived trustworthiness and, thus, potential use by Americans and analyzes these factors based on age, education level and gender. This analysis shows that, while labeling and all label types enjoy broad support, the level of support and uncertainty about labeling varies by age and education level with different labels outperforming for given age and education levels. Gender, alternately, was not shown to have a tremendous impact on respondents' perspectives regarding labeling; however, females where shown to support labeling more, on average, but also report more uncertainty.

Keywords: deceptive online content; age; education; gender; fake news; content labeling; efficacy

Citation: Spradling, M.; Straub, J. Analysis of the Impact of Age, Education and Gender on Individuals' Perception of Label Efficacy for Online Content. *Information* **2022**, *13*, 516. https://doi.org/10.3390/info13110516

Academic Editors: Jose de Vasconcelos, Hugo Barbosa and Carla Cordeiro

Received: 13 September 2022
Accepted: 25 October 2022
Published: 28 October 2022

Publisher's Note: MDPI stays neutral with regard to jurisdictional claims in published maps and institutional affiliations.

1. Introduction

The internet has been a powerful force to connect the world. It has provided a voice for those without access to traditional forms of mass communications and a means for dissidents to organize against governments that they consider to be oppressive. It provides everyone connected to it the potential to communicate with the masses. However, the same mechanisms that provide these benefits also can create problems, when used for nefarious means.

A growing number of incidents show the power of online content to manipulate the public—for political and other purposes—with misinformation and disinformation. Deceptive online content has been blamed for interference with the 2016 U.S. presidential election [1], the Brexit vote [2] and elections in other countries around the world [3]. It has driven physical violence, such as an armed standoff in a pizza parlor [4], and has been used by multiple foreign influence campaigns [5].

The threat here is significant. Keys [6] has termed the current era as being one of "post-truth" while Lee [7] has described fake news as a "sinister force" that is a threat to democracy. Tong et al. [8] contend that a "weaponization of fake news" has occurred. With 55% of Americans indicating that they get at least some of their news from social media [9] and 75% indicating that they have believed fake headlines [10,11], the scope of the problem is pronounced.

Labeling has been proposed as a possible solution to this issue. Fuhr et al. [12] proposed a nutrition-style label which Lespagnol et al. [13], Vincentius et al. [14], and others have proposed additions to. Prior work has analyzed the need for online content labeling [15] and the perception of labeling data by university community members [16]. A broader study, using a United States population representative sample, has also been analyzed to assess

American's perspectives with regard to online labeling [17]. U.S. population representative data has also been analyzed to assess consumers' perception of labeling efficacy, based on their income level, party affiliation and level of internet usage [18] and to assess how factors impact content trustworthiness differently, based on age, education and gender [19].

This paper builds on this prior work by looking at how age, education and gender impact the perception of online content labeling efficacy. It continues, in Section 2, with a discussion of prior work that informs the work presented herein. Section 3 presents data regarding the study instrument used to collect the data analyzed herein and respondents' demographics. Sections 4–6 present analysis for three types of labels (informational, warning and supplemental information) and Section 7 analyzes broader trends across the data presented for specific labels. The paper concludes and discusses potential areas of future work, in Section 8.

2. Background

This section provides a review of prior work in three areas which serve as a foundation for the work presented herein. First, a discussion of online deceptive content and the problems it poses is presented. Then, product labeling is discussed, in Section 2.2. Finally, labeling's potential use for combatting deceptive online content is reviewed, in Section 2.3.

2.1. Online Deceptive Content and Its Impact

At one point, the term 'fake news' was used to refer to content that publishers and readers knew was comedically false [20]. While the content might have been presented in a similar format to news content, it was not designed to fool people (though it sometimes did [21]). More recently, the term has been used to refer to deliberately deceptive content which is designed to be manipulative [22].

For many, the term fake news became well known during the 2016 U.S. presidential election. Grinberg et al. [23] estimated that 6% of news content was fake during this time period and Lazer et al. [24] estimated that Americans had, on average, consumed between one and three fake articles. Bovet and Makse [25] determined that, during the election, a quarter of tweets were "fake or extremely biased news" Fake news was also prevalent in the Brexit movement [2,5] and in least 20 other countries [3].

The impact of fake news spans across society. College students, for example, indicated that they expected social media news to be inaccurate [26]; however, despite this, individuals in the 18 to 29 year-old age group use social media more frequently than others and indicate trusting it more [26,27]. Fake news can confuse members of the public of all ages [28], has started an armed standoff [29] and has even been used to circulate inaccurate and potentially dangerous health information [30].

2.2. Product Labeling

Warning and information labels are used on numerous products. Information labels, such as the nutrition facts labels placed on food items (shown in Figure 1a) and energy labels (shown in Figure 1b) placed on electronic devices, seek to provide consumers with information in a standardized format to allow them to make decisions and comparisons between products. Warning labels are also placed on products, such as alcohol and tobacco, to promote healthy consumption decisions. However, the goal of warning labels is typically to limit consumption of the product, either in general or by a potentially vulnerable subgroup.

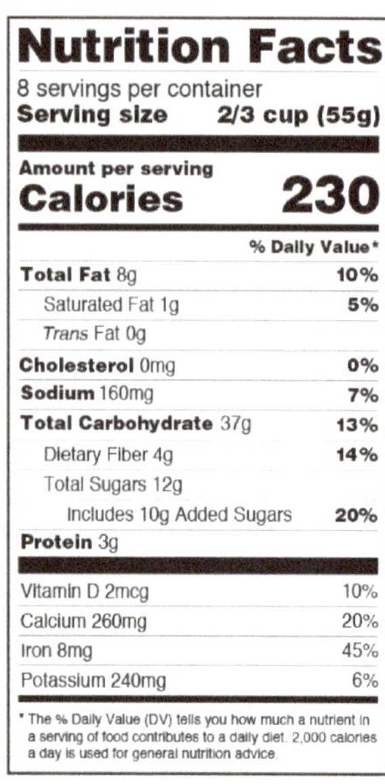

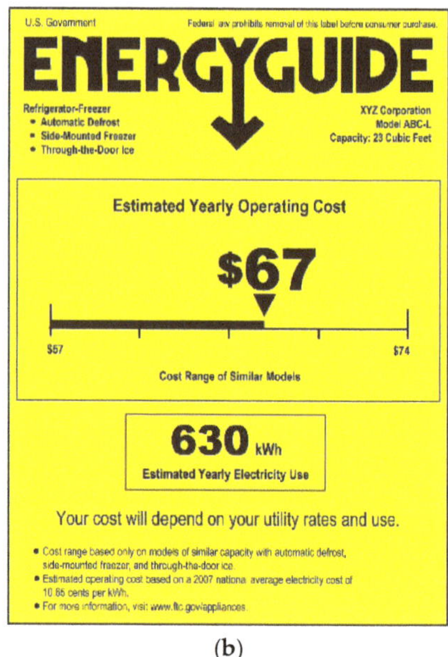

(**a**)(**b**)

Figure 1. (**a**) Nutrition Facts label format (modified from [31]), left, and (**b**) energy guide label format [32], right.

Tobacco warning labels have been shown to be effective at communicating how dangerous the product is and preventing youth from starting smoking [33]. The current cigarette packaging labels in the United States date back to 1984 [34] and carry a text-based surgeon general's warning [35]. Labels containing images have been shown to have more impact than text warnings. The FDA proposed "graphic" labels [36] (an example of which is shown in Figure 2); however, these labels were not implemented due to objections from tobacco companies [37], which were upheld by the courts [37,38] which found that the packaging requirements violated the First Amendment of the United States Constitution [39].

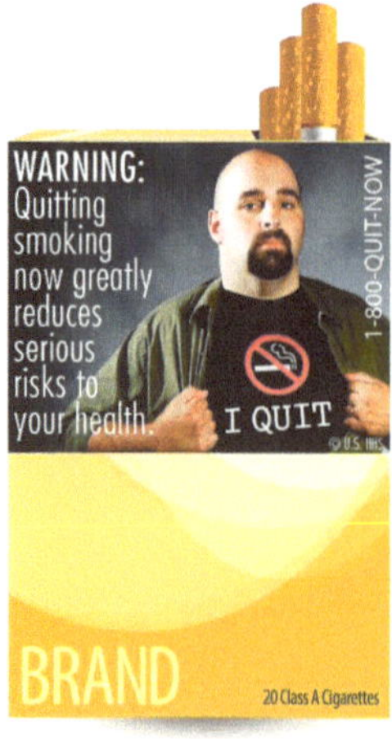

Figure 2. Example of the FDA's proposed cigarette labels in 2011 [40].

The FDA proposed new labels, in 2019 [39] (examples of which are shown in Figure 3), which were planned to launch in June of 2021. These labels build upon the graphical approach shown in Figure 1. Their required use has been delayed several times [41]. Similar efforts have been undertaken by other countries. New Zealand's Smoke-free Environments Regulations of 1999, for example, require tobacco products to include a graphic health warning [42]. While the law was challenged by the tobacco industry, it was ultimately adopted and had significant support from the public [42].

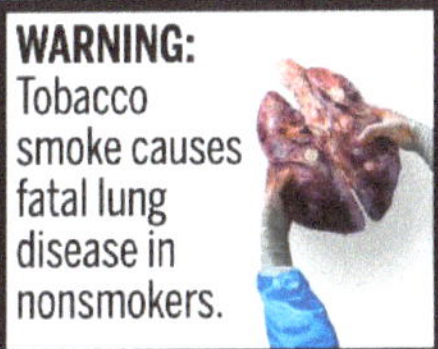

Figure 3. Examples of the cigarette labels proposed in 2019 [43].

Labeling has also been implemented, in the United States, for movies, television and music. MPAA rating labels are placed on movies and V-Chip ratings [44–46] are assigned to television programs. Some music, with explicit lyrics, carries a warning label to that effect [47]. Many movies also carry an anti-piracy warning from the U.S. Federal Bureau of Investigation which warns consumers about the risks of piracy to attempt to deter it [48]. All of these content labeling systems involved government coordination and collaboration with industry, to varying degrees.

2.3. Online Content Labeling

Labeling may be similarly valuable for online content to aid in information consumption decision-making. Lazer et al. [24] suggested that consumers could be aided by both preventing their exposure to deceptive content and helping them evaluate it.

Deceptive content hosting websites, though, may be uninterested in self-regulation and resistant to industry and government labeling. These sites may prefer that consumers consume their misinformation due to ideological [49] or advertising revenue generation [50] goals. Government mandated online content labeling, in the United States, may face considerable legal challenges. The decision preventing the FDA from requiring graphic health cigarette warnings was due to free speech concerns [39] of a potentially less protected nature (product sales [51]) than online content.

U.S. law is not the only consideration, of course, as online deceptive content is inherently an international challenge. In the United States, government required content labeling may face constitutional challenges as an infringement upon publishers' free speech rights [52]. Numerous other countries have their own regulations that must also be considered. The People's Republic of China, for example, has a law, the Information Network and Internet Security, Protection and Management Regulations of 1997, which proscribes "making falsehoods or distorting the truth, spreading rumors, destroying the order of society" which may dictate the removal of misinformation. If information is censored by the government content labeling may be unneeded as the content will no longer be available for others' viewing [53].

Ethiopia, Cote d'Ivoire and Malawi also have laws that proscribe publishing false information [54]. Bangladesh created a law "to control the spread of online misinformation" [55] and Indonesian laws threaten jail sentences, of up to a decade, for "spreading false information or news that intentionally causes public disorder" [56]. Alternately, the European Union has created a framework for "digital platforms' self-regulation" [56]. Other countries' laws vary. Yadav et al. [57] identified and analyzed over 100 national laws which have different requirements and scopes.

While online content labeling can draw from several sources, it presents numerous challenges. A key challenge is how to determine what label to assign to a given article.

Deceptive content must first be identified before it can be labeled with a warning. Numerous techniques are possible (see [58,59]). Approaches can be manual, automatic or combine both. Articles' style, authors and distributors, and even network analysis can be used to identify deceptive content [60]. Wang demonstrated an automated approach, using machine learning with manually annotations. Automated technique examples include machine learning techniques with and without manual annotations [61], natural language processing [62], deep [63], mixed graph [64] and graph-attention [65] neural networks and neural stacking [66]. Techniques which analyze social networks [67], signal detection [68], and emotion cognizance [69] have also been proposed. Shao et al. suggested [70] that a multi-modal ensemble approach may provide the benefits of both single mode and multi-modal analysis and outperform other approaches. Rapti et al. [71], have also proposed a model for considering fake news using a "disinformation blueprint" which may allow deceptive content to be identified more holistically.

Approaches to identifying deceptive content using influence analysis [72,73] have been proposed, such as Budak, Agrawal and Abbadi's [74] "competing cascades dissipating in a network" method, and the use of a heuristic based on degree centrality [74]. Suchia et al. [75] proposed an approach to detect rumors that piggyback alongside legitimate news stories but add incorrect information. Fairbanks et al. [76], noting the prevalence of politically charged deceptive content, created a technique that classifies text as containing "liberal words", "conservative words", and "fake news words". The fake news words category, though, was shown to be unreliable.

Taxonomies for labeling have been proposed by Tandoc, Lim and Ling [10] (who developed a system including "satire", "parody", "fabrication", "manipulation", "propaganda", and "advertising") and Bakir and McStay [77]. Online content publishers have also created their own systems. Twitter introduced Birdwatch, which is based on manual evaluation of Twitter posts by other users [78]. Wikipedia has published a list of news sources that includes reliability information (https://en.wikipedia.org/wiki/Wikipedia: Reliable_sources/Perennial_sources) (accessed on 26 October 2022).

3. Survey and Respondents

A survey was conducted with a goal of understanding Americans' news content consumption decision making perceptions. The survey instrument and the data collection process are discussed in Section 3.1 and the labels whose efficacy was evaluated are discussed in Section 3.2. Respondent demographics are discussed in Section 3.3. Finally, Section 3.4 discusses the analysis methodology used herein.

3.1. Survey Instrument and Data Collection

The survey utilized in [16] was modified for use for this study. It was edited to reduce the target response time to 15 min and to combine the three surveys, which were administered independently for [16]. Questions which were redundant between the surveys were removed and the revised survey was reviewed by the authors and Qualtrics staff. As part of Qualtrics standard procedure, a limited pilot was used to validate the instrument. As no issues were detected during the pilot study, the pilot responses were included in the dataset, based on Qualtrics' standard practices.

For each proposed label type, respondents were presented with the label and description of how it would appear when browsing social media. For each label, participants were asked the same five questions regarding the its helpfulness: whether or not they found it annoying, whether they would use it, whether they believed other people would use it, and whether they believed it would be helpful in judging the trustworthiness of news articles. These question categories and the text of the questions from the survey instrument are presented in Table 1.

Table 1. Survey instrument questions for each label instrument. Respondents were presented with each proposed label instrument and were asked the following questions.

Question Category	Text from Survey Instrument
Helpfulness	Would you find this label helpful?
Annoyingness	Would you find this label annoying?
Usefulness	Would you review this label when viewing news articles on social media?
Others' usefulness	Would others review this label when viewing news articles on social media?
Trustworthiness judging	Would it be useful for judging the trustworthiness of news articles?

By asking "would you find this label helpful", the survey identified the general positive or negative attitude of the participant towards using the label, without asking specifically where this sentiment comments from. The remaining questions help to establish the source of this perception. For example, a participant may find the label to be useful for judging trustworthiness yet find it annoying and unlikely to be utilized in practice. This could suggest a problem with the design of the label rather than the type of information being presented in it. Some label styles present a larger amount of information than others, providing more details at the cost of being larger. Responses regarding "usefulness for judging trustworthiness" can be compared to perceptions of "annoyingness" to observe trade-off between brevity and verbosity. All of this information helps to inform the design of future labeling mechanisms.

The specific topic presented in the labels, "Trouble at High Speed West Middle School", was chosen to be an apolitical topic which would not influence respondents' attitude toward the label. While sounding news-like, it avoids addressing a real-world issue and uses a fictitious school name. The headline is meant to avoid distracting from the label design itself and thus biasing responses. Were the headline to focus on a particular news item (for example, about the 2020 US presidential election), respondents' responses may be confounded by being based on both their opinions regarding the topic and the label design. A key area for future work will involve testing the efficacy of labels in a real-world setting with real instances of legitimate news and misinformation. This study seeks to characterize attitudes towards the label instruments themselves without such confounding concerns.

The data analyzed herein was collected by Qualtrics International Inc. using a quota-based stratified sampling technique using the survey instrument modified from [16]. The recruiting plan was targeted to obtain population proportionate participation, based on gender, age, income level and political affiliation.

The survey was administered in October of 2021 and approximately 550 responses were collected. Of these, 500 are part of the population representative sample. As respondents were offered a completion-based incentive, most responses are complete. In this paper, all responses which answer the relevant demographic and response questions are included in the analysis.

3.2. News Article Labels

The informational labels in the study, which are discussed in Section 4, utilize the labeling categories (title, author, authority, etc.) originally proposed by Fuhr et al. [12], as discussed in [16]. Informational labels 1 and 2 each provide the label categories and their values without any further explanation. These can be seen as 'pure' informational labels, where the user must interpret the information, as no interpretation is provided by the label.

Informational labels 1 and 3 also include the article's original headline, image, and introductory text. This preserves more of the original article's elements which are intended to be attractive to the user and draw them into clicking the link and viewing the article. This is similar to how nutrition facts are added to the side of a container while still including the product's branding information and imagery. Informational label 3 provides additional supporting information for each label category, helping the user to interpret it.

Unlike informational labels 1 and 3, informational label 2 appears as a pop-up, covering some of the original article's elements. Relevant information, such as the title is retained;

but the article's image and summary text are not visible. Like the cigarette labeling design, shown in Figure 2, this style of label blocks potentially attractive advertising elements for the article, such as the image. The goal of this is to allow the user to make a decision without being emotionally persuaded by factors other than the information about the article.

Warning labels 1, 2, and 3 alert the user that "The information in this article is advertised as fact. However, the information has not been verified by any trustworthy sources". This goes further than the informational labels, warning the user to be on guard, should they decide to view the article. In each case, the user can still allowed to proceed by clicking the forward button.

Warning label 1 appears as a pop-up, preventing the user from seeing the article's elements (similar to how the cigarette warnings in Figure 2 block half of the front of the carton). Warning label 2 appears beneath the normal headline elements of the article, making it less intrusive. Warning label 3 is presented as an intermediary webpage which is displayed after clicking on an article but before viewing its contents. This is similar to the intermediary page generated by some web browsers when clicking an unsafe link (e.g., one which may lead to computer viruses).

Finally, a supplemental informational label is presented. This style of label provides specific supporting fact-checked information which is directly related to the claims of the article. Rather than making any statement as to the veracity of the article's claims, it simply makes it easier for the user to compare those claims to facts from trusted sources. This style of label is similar to those used by Twitter and YouTube during the 2020 US presidential election, where tweets or videos making claims about the election results would sometimes be augmented with links to supplementary information from well-known news sources [15].

3.3. Respondent Demographics

Due to the population representativeness goal, respondents are well distributed across demographic groups. Approximately 51% were female and 49% were male. Only a small number of respondents indicated a non-binary gender (less than 1%). Because of the small sample size, non-binary gender's impact could not be analyzed further.

Respondents from ten age groups (starting at 18 years of age) were included in the study. The breakdown of respondents amongst these age groups is presented in Table 2.

Table 2. Respondents' age distribution [17].

18–24	25–29	30–34	35–39	40–44	45–49	50–54	55–59	60–64	65 and Older
10.57%	10.93%	11.29%	10.04%	8.96%	6.63%	6.09%	12.54%	12.19%	10.75%
59	61	63	56	50	37	34	70	68	60

Respondents from seven educational levels participated in this study. The distribution of respondents between education levels is presented in Table 3. High school graduates, who have not completed a college degree, comprised just under 50% of the study population. Nearly a quarter of respondents held a bachelor's degree. Associate's and master's degree holders each comprised just over 10% of respondents. High school graduates without collegiate education and doctoral degree holders also comprised small parts (less than 5% each) of the survey population.

Table 3. Respondents' education distribution [17].

Some High School (No Degree)	High School Degree	Some College (No Degree)	Associate's Degree	Bachelor's Degree	Master's Degree	Doctoral Degree
4.68%	25.72%	23.20%	11.51%	22.12%	10.25%	2.52%
26	143	129	64	123	57	14

3.4. Analysis Methodology

The Qualtrics online system and Microsoft Excel software were used to perform data analysis. Each question was analyzed in terms of three demographic characteristics (age, education and gender) to ascertain the extent to which each demographic characteristic impacted respondents' perceptions of each label. This data is presented and analyzed in Sections 4–6. Section 7 considers trends present across the multiple demographic groups and questions.

4. Informational Label Related Data and Analysis

This section presents and analyzes data regarding informational labels. These labels present details in a manner similar to food nutrition fact labels and are designed to allow viewers to consider the relevant information and then to decide whether they want to consume the content or not. For each label, five types of data were collected and are analyzed in terms of three metrics. Respondents were asked about each label's helpfulness, annoyingness, whether they would use the label, whether others would use the label and whether the label would help in assessing article trustworthiness. Respondents could answer yes, no or unsure. The data from these questions is analyzed, in this section, in terms of respondents' age, education level and gender.

The helpfulness of informational label 1 (shown in Figure 4), when it appears underneath a news article automatically, is considered in Figures 5–7. Respondents answered the question "would you find this label helpful?".

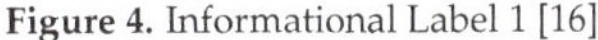

M

Trouble at High Speed West Middle School

High Speed West Middle School in deadlock due to boys refusing to say the word "hello", opting only to refer to people as "Gamers."
1 week ago

Title: Trouble at High Speed West Middle School
Author: Michael Scott
Fact: 73%
Opinion: 27%
Emotion: 35

Authority: 2/10
Viral: True
Topicality: 3/10
Reading level: 12th grade
Technicality: 2/10

Figure 4. Informational Label 1 [16].

In terms of age, there is a decline in perceived helpfulness as age increases. There are slight spikes in yes responses at the 40–44, 55–59, and 65 and older age groups. The number of uncertain responses shows no discernible pattern. Age groups other than 35–39, 45–49, and 60–64 show at least 50% answering yes even when uncertainty is factored in. When uncertainty is not considered, only the 60–64 age group maintains less than 50% yes responses.

By education level, there is a larger decline as education level increases from the some high school up to the bachelor's degree education levels. There is a spike at the master's degree level, which is maintained at the doctoral degree level, when uncertainty is not factored in. When uncertainty is introduced, doctoral degree holders' support is less pronounced than master's degree holders, due to a higher level of uncertainty amongst doctoral degree holders. Education groups, other than associate's and bachelor's degree holders, have at least 50% answering yes, even when uncertainty is factored in. Both of these groups show at least 50% answering "yes" when uncertainty is not considered.

By gender, there are more yes answers among females than male respondents and nearly equal levels of uncertainty. Both groups have at least 50% of respondents answering yes, even when uncertainty is factored in.

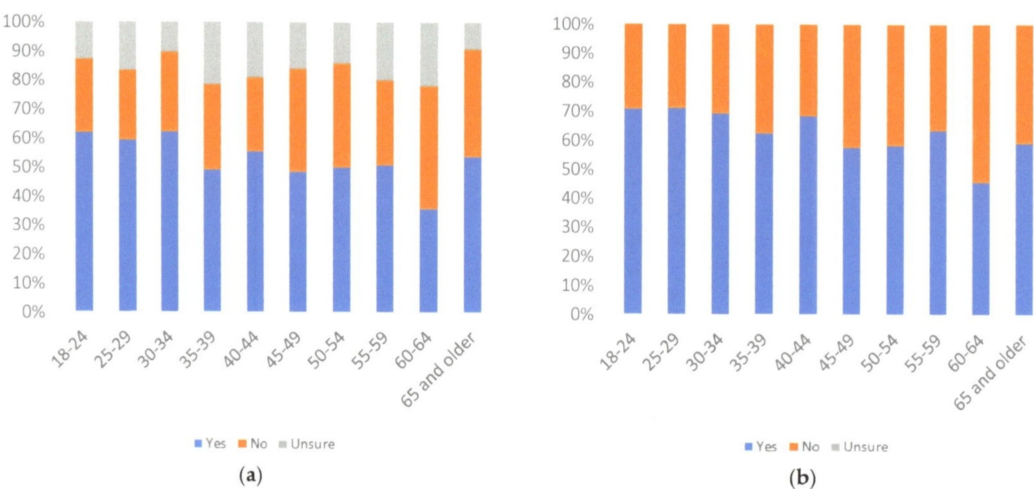

Figure 5. Label helpfulness, by age group: (**a**) with uncertain respondents (left) and (**b**) without uncertain respondents (right).

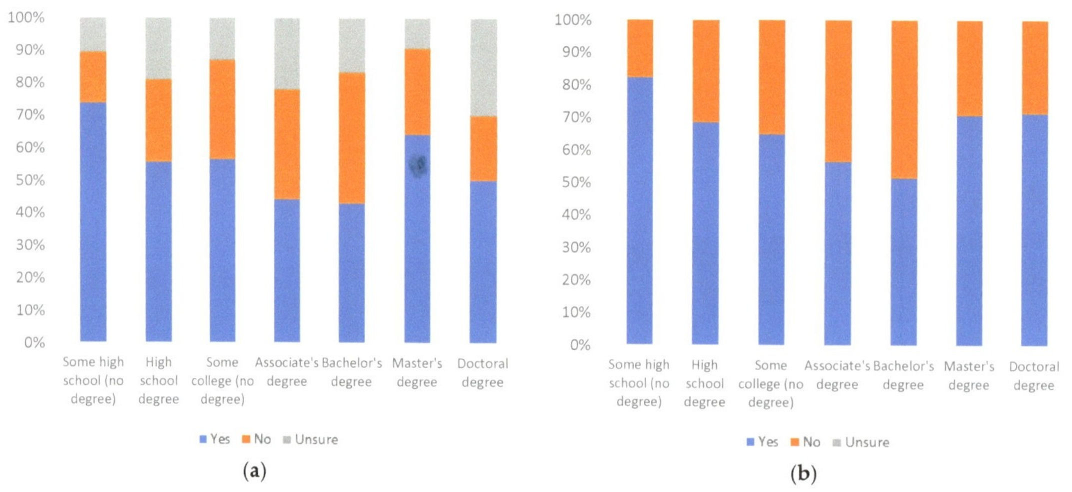

Figure 6. Label helpfulness, by education level: (**a**) with uncertain respondents (left) and (**b**) without uncertain respondents (right).

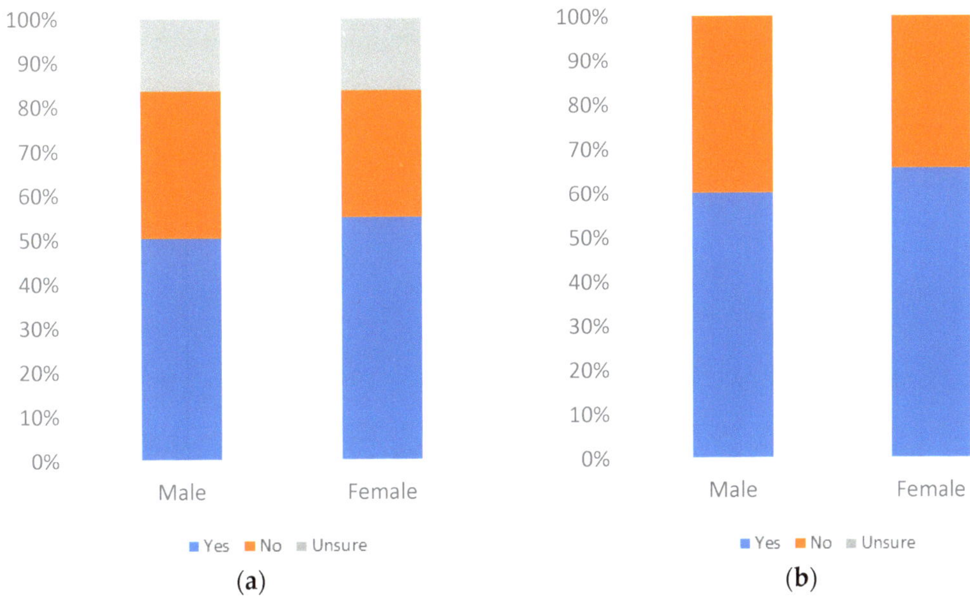

Figure 7. Label helpfulness, by gender: (**a**) with uncertain respondents (left) and (**b**) without uncertain respondents (right).

Figures 8–10 consider annoyingness of informational label 1, with respondents answering the question "would you find this label annoying?".

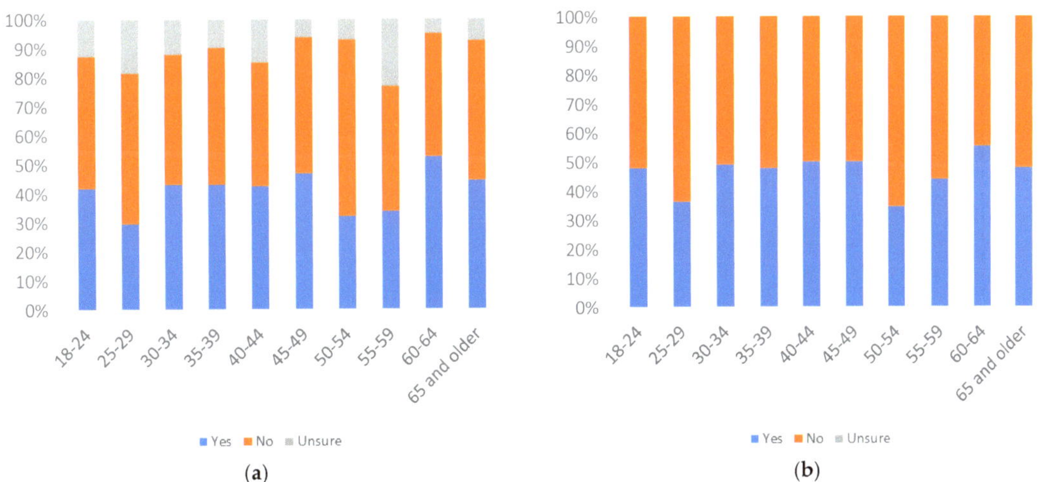

Figure 8. Label annoyingness, by age group: (**a**) with uncertain respondents (left) and (**b**) without uncertain respondents (right).

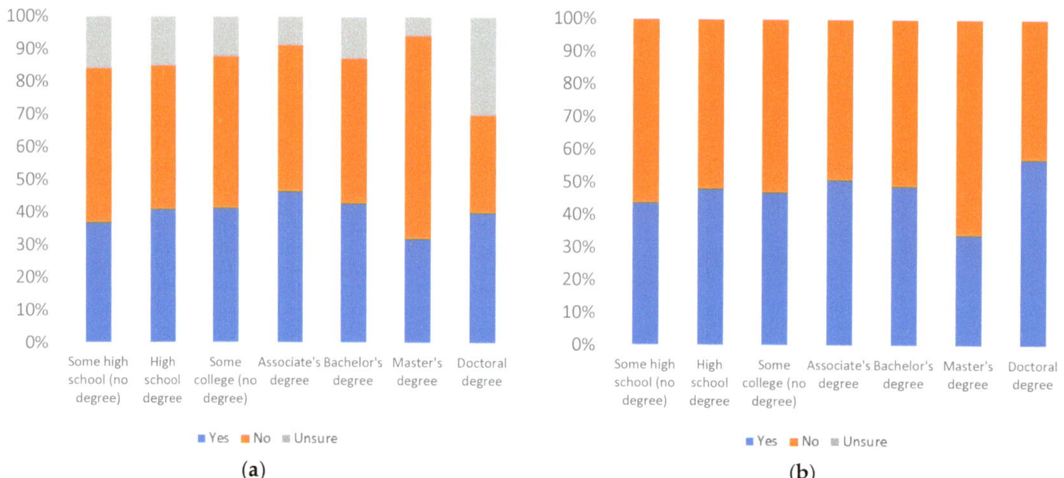

Figure 9. Label annoyingness, by education level: (**a**) with uncertain respondents (left) and (**b**) without uncertain respondents (right).

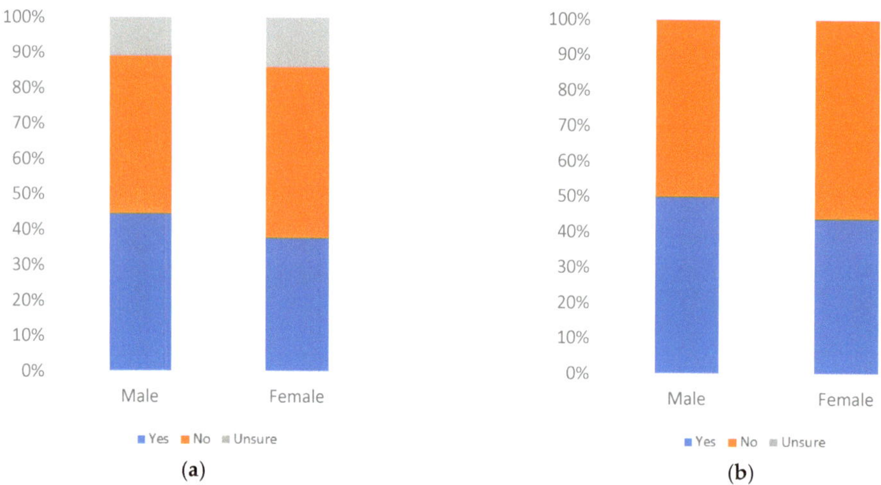

Figure 10. Label annoyingness, by gender: (**a**) with uncertain respondents (left) and (**b**) without uncertain respondents (right).

In terms of age, there is no clear pattern of decline or increase in perceived annoyingness as age increases. There are drops in yes responses at the 25–29, 50–54, and 55–59 age groups and an increase at the 60–64 age group. The number of uncertain responses also shows no discernable pattern. All age groups have less than 50% answering yes, when uncertainty is factored in. Only the 60–64 age group has greater than 50% yes responses, when uncertainty is not considered. This indicates a low level of annoyingness overall, amongst most age groups.

By education level, there is an increase in perceived annoyingness up to the associate's degree level, then a decline up to the master's degree level. Finally, there is a spike at the doctoral degree level. The spike at the doctoral degree level is less pronounced, once uncertainty is factored in, as doctoral degree holders show the largest level of uncertainty. All education groups have less than 50% of respondents answering yes, with uncertainty factored in. Only doctoral degree holders have at least 50% yes responses, when uncertainty is not considered. This indicates a low level of annoyingness overall, amongst most education groups.

By gender, there are more yes responses among males than females and more uncertainty among female respondents. Both groups have less than 50% of respondents answering yes, even when uncertainty is not considered. This indicates a low level of annoyingness overall, amongst both gender groups.

Figures 11–13 consider likelihood that respondents will personally use informational label 1, with respondents answering the question "would you review this label when viewing news articles on social media?".

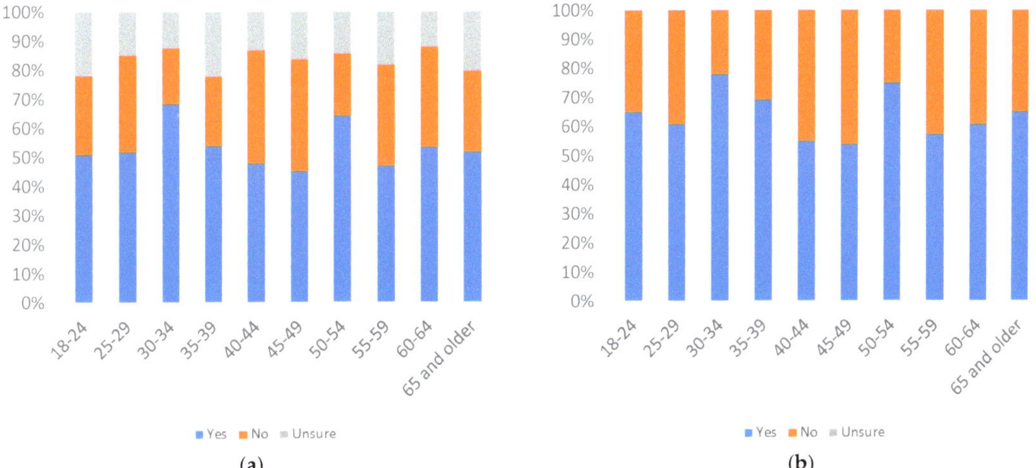

Figure 11. Label use, by age group: (**a**) with uncertain respondents (left) and (**b**) without uncertain respondents (right).

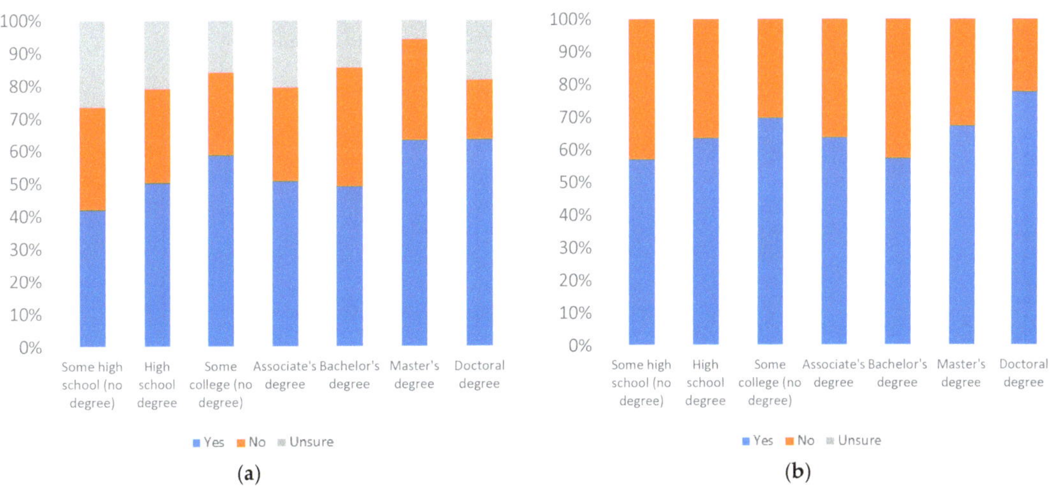

Figure 12. Label use, by education level: (**a**) with uncertain respondents (left) and (**b**) without uncertain respondents (right).

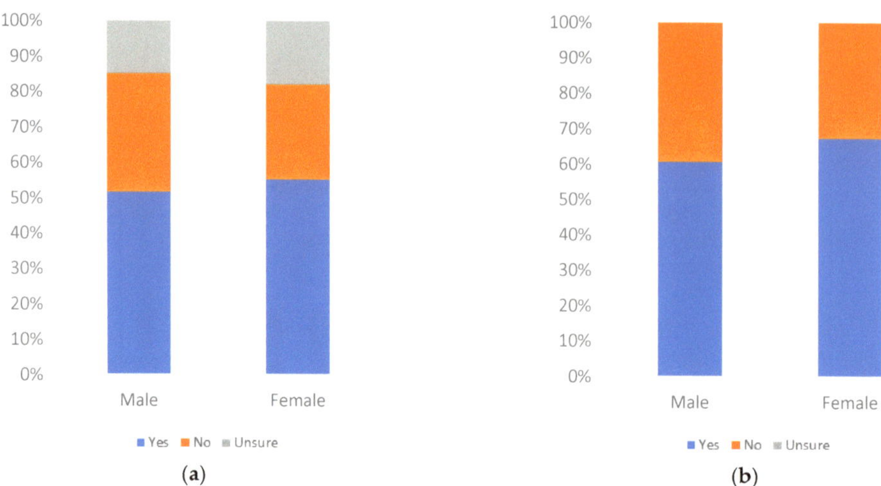

Figure 13. Label use, by gender: (**a**) with uncertain respondents (left) and (**b**) without uncertain respondents (right).

In terms of age, there is no clear pattern of decline or increase in perceived personal usage as age increases. There are spikes in yes responses at the 30–34, 35–39, and 50–54 age groups. The number of uncertain responses also shows no discernible pattern. All age groups, other than 40–44, 45–49 and 55–59, have at least 50% of respondents answering yes, even when uncertainty is factored in. All groups have at least 50% yes responses when uncertainty is not considered.

By education level, there is an overall increase in yes responses, as education level increases. The lowest percentage of yes responses is at the some high school education level, and while the percentage of yes responses declines from the some college to bachelor's degree levels, it increases again up to its peak at the doctoral degree level. Only three of the seven education groups (some college, master's degree, and doctoral degree) have at least 50% yes responses, when uncertainty is factored in. All groups have at least a 50% level of yes responses, when uncertainty is not considered.

By gender, there are more yes responses among females than males and slightly higher uncertainty among females. Both groups have greater than 50% answering yes, even with uncertainty.

Figures 14–16 consider respondents' perception of the likelihood of others to use informational label 1, with respondents answering the question "would others review this label when viewing news articles on social media?".

In terms of age, there is no clear pattern of decline or increase in perceived use by others as age increases. There is a notable drop in yes responses for the 45–49 age group. The number of uncertain responses also shows no discernible pattern, but there is a high level of uncertainty amongst all groups. All age groups other than the 25–29 and 30–34 groups have less than 50% answering yes, when factoring in uncertainty. When uncertainty is not considered, only the 45–49 age group answers yes less than 50% of the time.

By education level, there is an increase in uncertainty level as education level increases. The number of yes responses declined from the some college to the Bachelor's degree levels, but then it increases up to the doctoral degree level. While only two education groups, the some high school and some college groups, have at least 50% yes responses, when uncertainty is factored in, all groups show at least 50% yes responses when uncertainty is not considered.

By gender, there are slightly more yes responses among female respondents and a nearly identical level of uncertainty between males and females. Both groups have less than 50% yes responses, with uncertainty factored in and greater than 50% yes responses, when uncertainty is not considered.

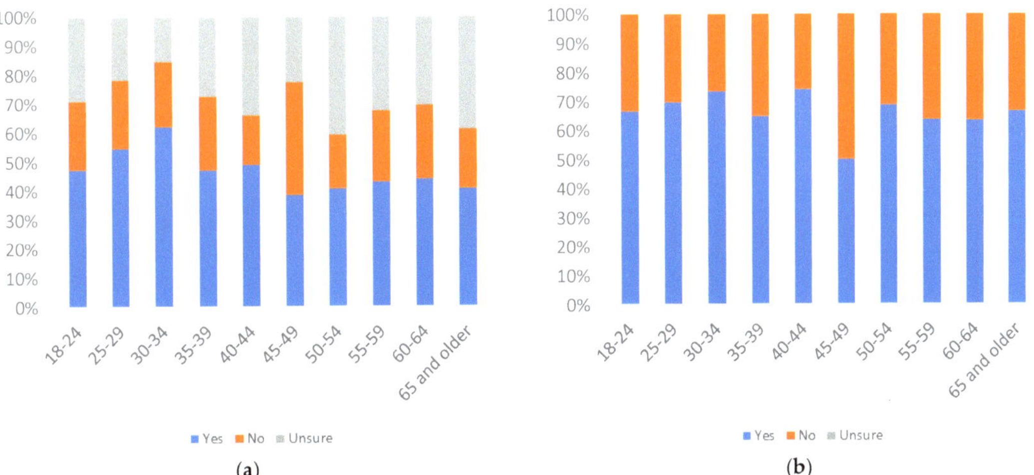

(a)

(b)

Figure 14. Label others' use, by age group: (**a**) with uncertain respondents (left) and (**b**) without uncertain respondents (right).

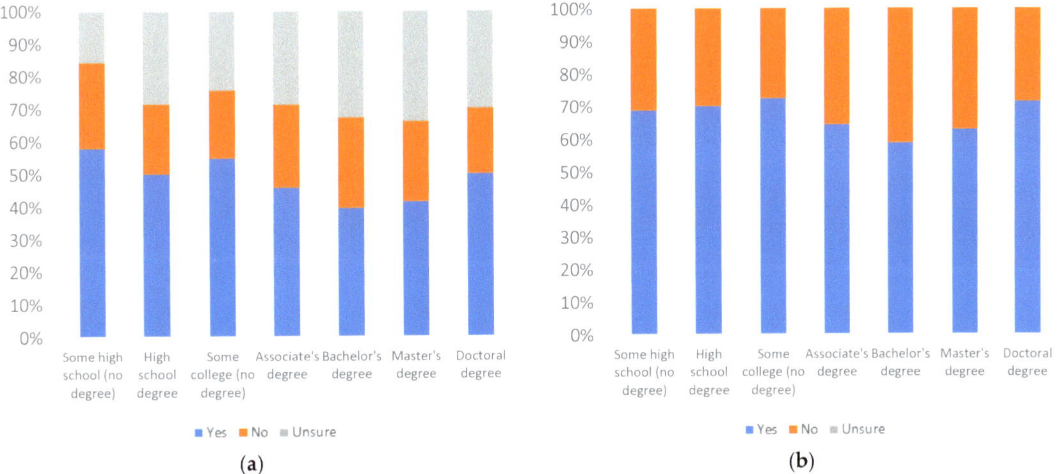

(a)

(b)

Figure 15. Label others' use, by education level: (**a**) with uncertain respondents (left) and (**b**) without uncertain respondents (right).

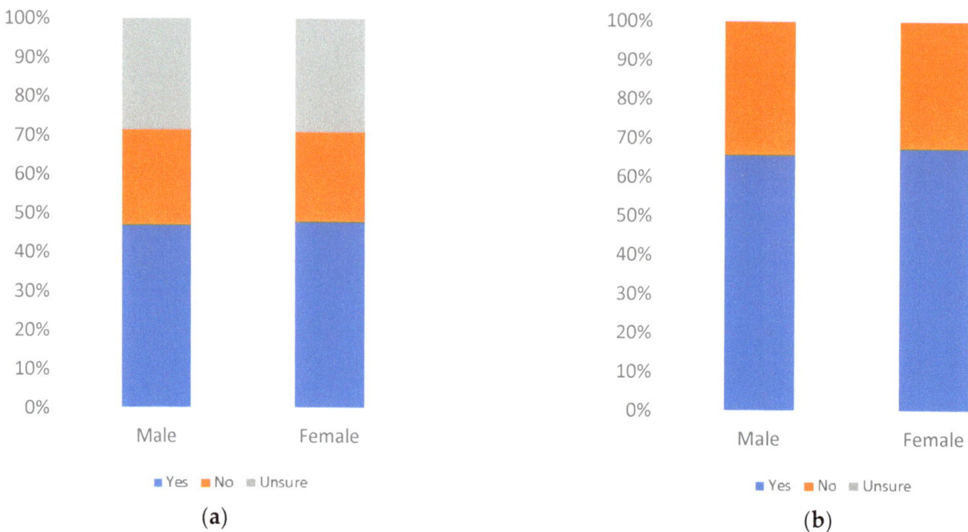

Figure 16. Label others' use, by gender: (**a**) with uncertain respondents (left) and (**b**) without uncertain respondents (right).

Figures 17–19 consider the value of informational label 1 in gauging trustworthiness, with respondents answering the question "would it be useful for judging the trustworthiness of news articles?".

In terms of age, there is a decline in yes responses from the 25–29 age group, up to the 60–64 age group. Against this trend, there is a downward spike at the 18–24 age group and an upward spike at the 65 and older age group. The uncertainty level shows no discernible pattern. The only four age groups to have at least 50% yes responses, when uncertainty is factored in, are the 18–24, 25–29, 30–34, and 65 and older groups. All age groups have at least 50% yes responses, when uncertainty is not considered.

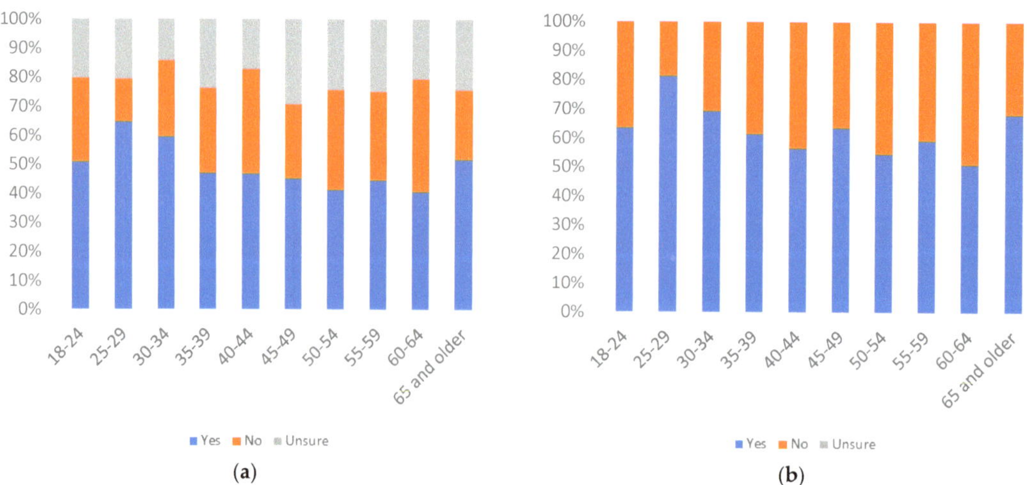

Figure 17. Label trustworthiness judging use, by age group: (**a**) with uncertain respondents (left) and (**b**) without uncertain respondents (right).

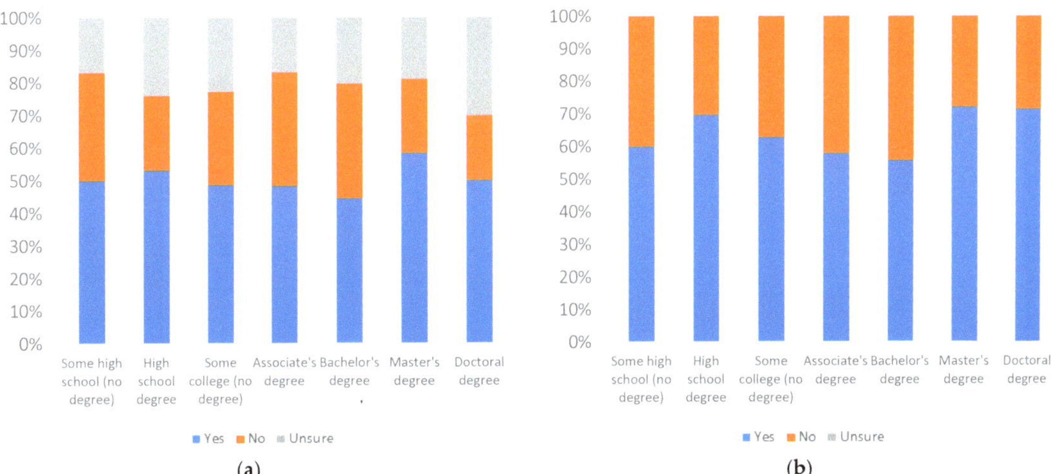

Figure 18. Label trustworthiness judging use, by education level: (**a**) with uncertain respondents (left) and (**b**) without uncertain respondents (right).

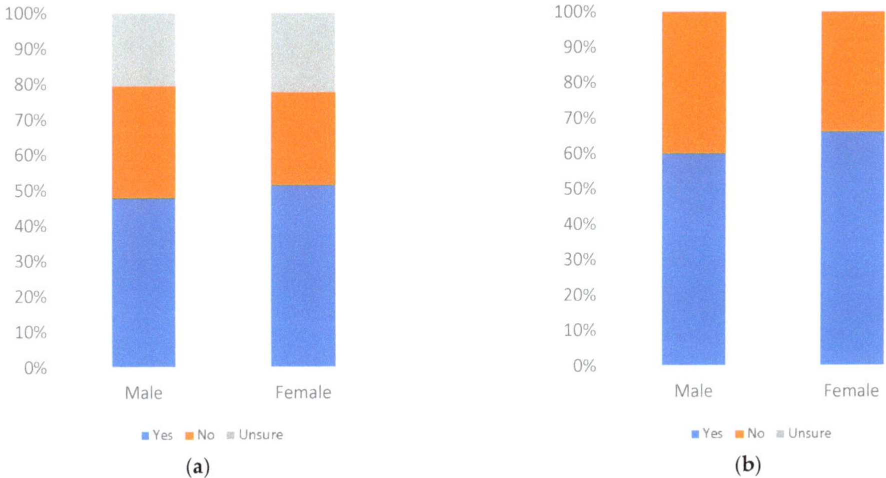

Figure 19. Label trustworthiness judging use, by gender: (**a**) with uncertain respondents (left) and (**b**) without uncertain respondents (right).

By education level, there is a decline in yes responses from the high school degree to the bachelor's degree levels followed by a spike at the master's degree and doctoral degree levels. Much of the increase in yes responses at the doctoral degree level is not present when uncertainty is factored in. While only three groups (high school, master's degree, and doctoral degree) have at least 50% yes responses, when uncertainty is factored in, all groups have at least 50% yes responses, when uncertainty is not considered.

By gender, females have an increase in the number of yes responses and are the only group to have at least 50% yes responses, even when uncertainty is considered. Both groups have at least 50% yes responses, when uncertainty is not factored in.

The helpfulness of informational label 2 (shown in Figure 20), when it pops up in front of a news article automatically, is considered in Figures 21–23. Respondents answered the question "would you find this label helpful?".

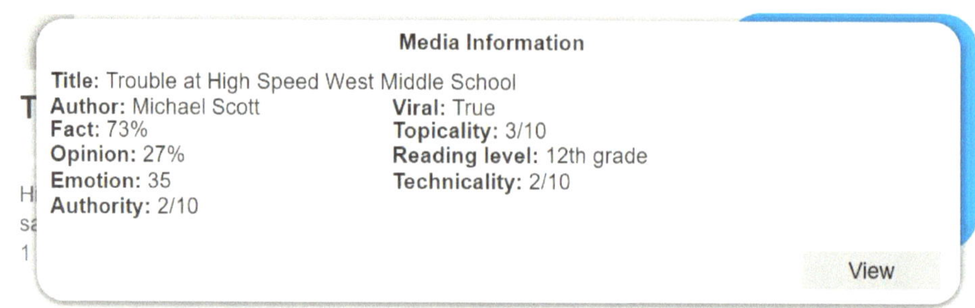

Figure 20. Informational label 2 [16].

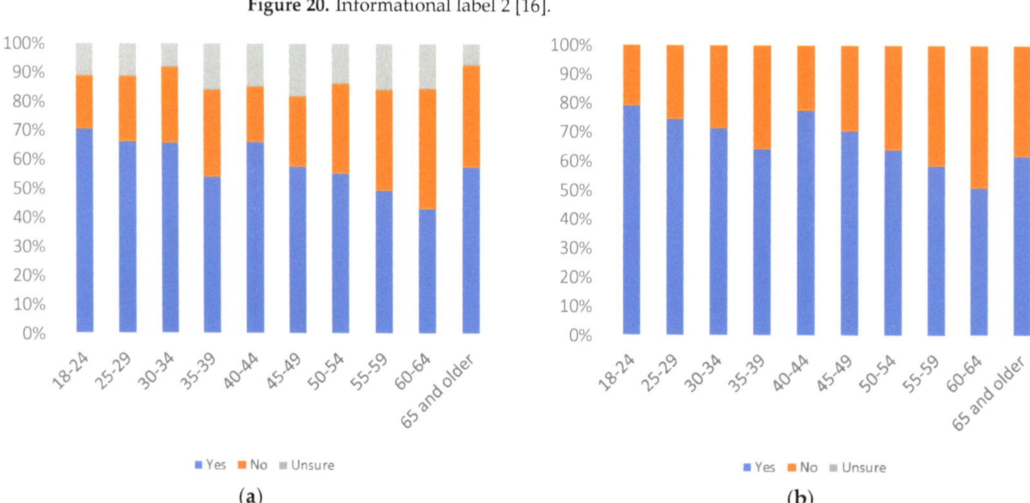

Figure 21. Label helpfulness, by age group: (**a**) with uncertain respondents (left) and (**b**) without uncertain respondents (right).

In terms of age, there are two waves of decline in yes responses, as age decreases. The first is from the 18–24 age group to the 35–39 age group. This is followed by a spike, and then another decline from the 40–44 to 60–64 age groups, followed by another spike. These waves remain consistent, even with uncertainty considered. While the 55–59 and 60–64 age groups have less than 50% yes responses, when uncertainty is considered, even these two groups have at least 50% yes responses when uncertainty is not factored in.

By education level, there is a gradual decline in yes responses as education level increases. There is a slight increase at the master's degree level, and a very high level of uncertainty in the some high school group. The doctoral degree holders group reports less than 50% yes responses, when uncertainty is considered. When uncertainty is removed, all groups have at least 50% yes responses.

By gender, females have more yes responses, as well as a higher uncertainty level. Both gender groups have at least 50% yes responses, even when uncertainty is factored in.

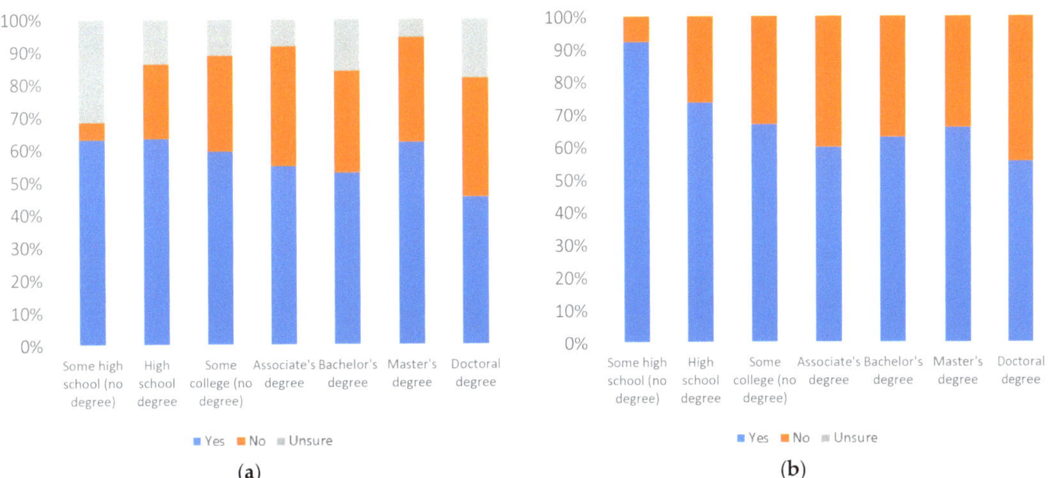

Figure 22. Label helpfulness, by education level: (**a**) with uncertain respondents (left) and (**b**) without uncertain respondents (right).

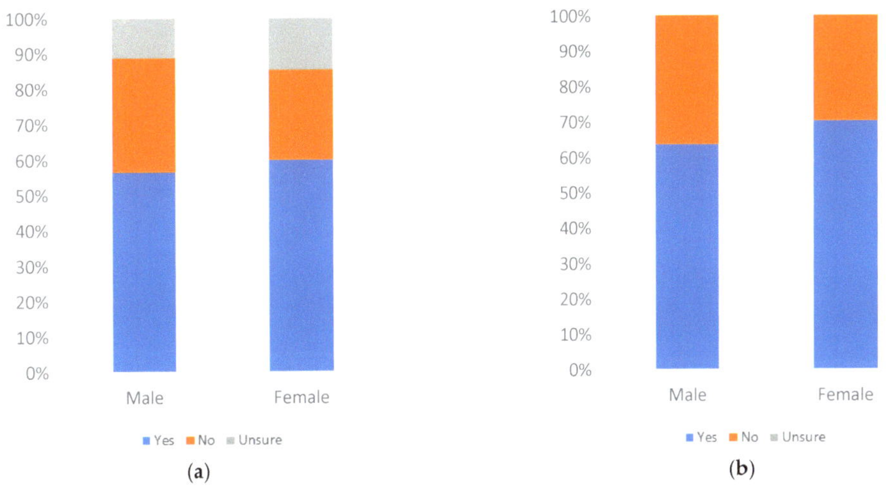

Figure 23. Label helpfulness, by gender: (**a**) with uncertain respondents (left) and (**b**) without uncertain respondents (right).

Figures 24–26 consider annoyingness of informational label 2, with respondents answering the question "would you find this label annoying?".

In terms of age, there are three peaks of yes responses. There is an increase from ages 18–24 to 35–39, followed by a decline to the 45–49 age group. Then, oscillating increases and decreases are present, up to the 65 and older age group. The uncertainty responses show no discernible pattern. Only the 30–34, 35–39 and 60–64 age groups have at least 50% yes responses, when uncertainty is considered. Without uncertainty factored in, the 50–54 age group additionally has at least 50% yes responses. This indicates a low level of annoyingness, amongst most age groups.

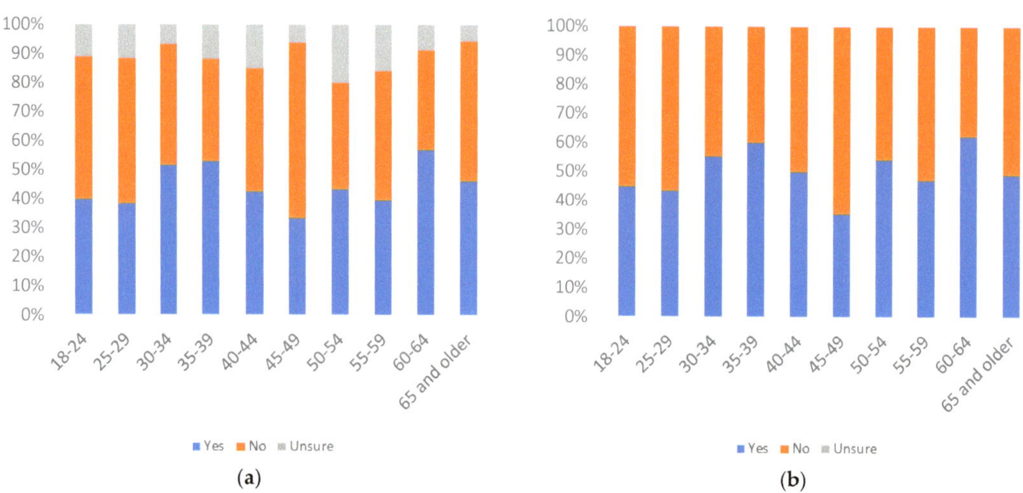

Figure 24. Label annoyingness, by age group: (**a**) with uncertain respondents (left) and (**b**) without uncertain respondents (right).

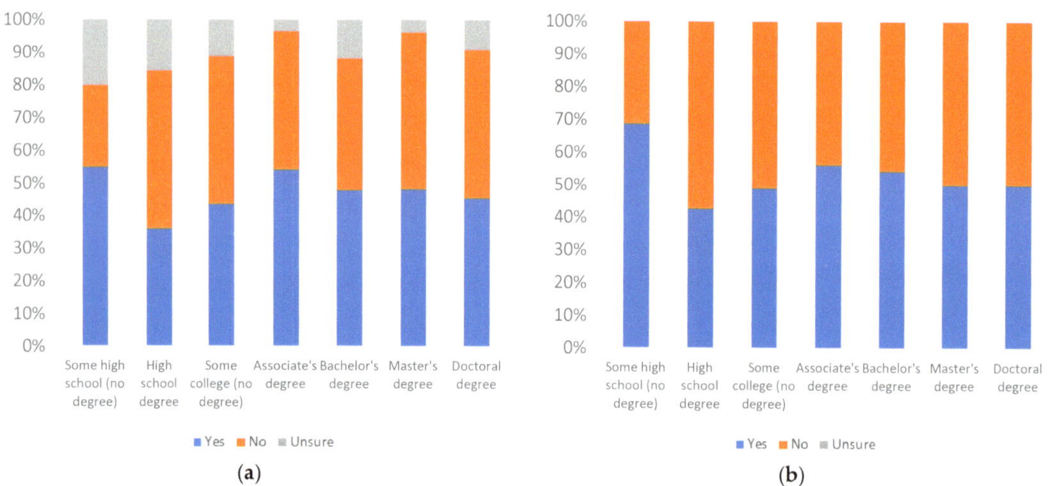

Figure 25. Label annoyingness, by education level: (**a**) with uncertain respondents (left) and (**b**) without uncertain respondents (right).

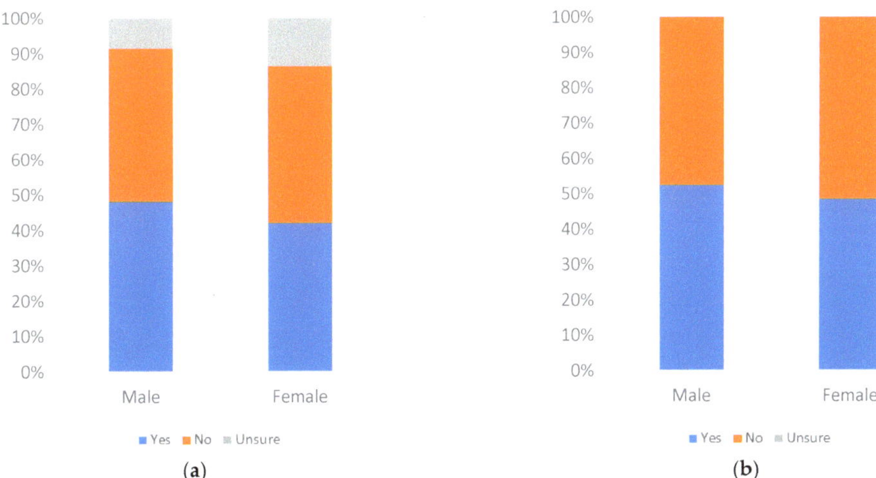

Figure 26. Label annoyingness, by gender: (**a**) with uncertain respondents (left) and (**b**) without uncertain respondents (right).

When considering education level, there is a spike in perceived annoyingness at the some high school education level. Amongst other education levels, the number of yes responses peaks at the associate's degree level. Uncertainty levels, similarly, have a valley at the associate's degree level, with fewer than 5% of associate's degree respondents reporting uncertainty. When uncertainty is factored in, only the some high school and associate's degree education levels have at least 50% yes responses. Bachelor's degree holders also report 50% yes responses, when uncertainty is not considered. This indicates a low level of annoyingness amongst most education groups.

By gender, females have less yes responses, as well as a greater uncertainty level. Both gender groups report less than 50% yes responses, when uncertainty is considered, though male respondents report greater than 50% yes responses, when uncertainty is not factored in. This indicates that males find the label more annoying than females.

Figures 27–29 consider respondents likelihood to personally use informational label 2, with respondents answering the question "would you review this label when viewing news articles on social media?".

In terms of age, there are two peaks of yes responses. There is an increase from the 18–24 to 30–34 age groups, followed by a decline to the 35–39 age group. Then, there is an increase, at the 40–44 age group, followed by a general decline. The decline at higher age groups, becomes an increase, when uncertainty is factored in. The 65 and older age group's level of uncertainty accounts for this shift. All age groups, other than 18–24, answered at least 50% yes, even when uncertainty is factored in. The 18–24 age group remains below 50%, even without uncertainty considered.

By education level, the number of yes responses remains relatively consistent, when uncertainty is not considered. Uncertainty decreases as education level increases, up to the master's degree level, then it increases sharply at the doctoral degree level. All groups other than the some high school and doctoral degree levels have at least 50% yes responses, when uncertainty is factored in. Without uncertainty, all groups have at least 50% yes responses.

By gender, the levels of support are almost equal, except for a higher level of uncertainty being reported among female respondents. Both groups have at least a 50% level of yes responses, even with uncertainty factored in.

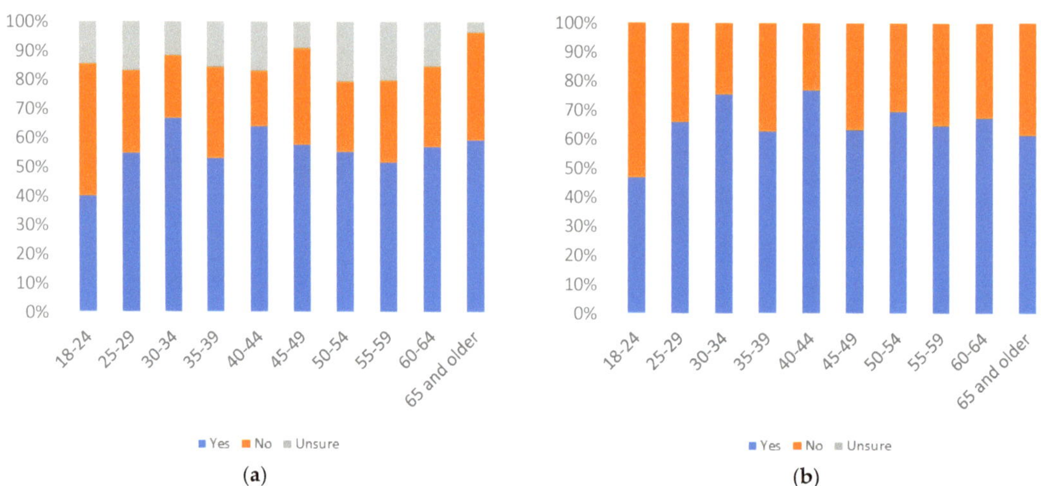

Figure 27. Label use, by age group: (**a**) with uncertain respondents (left) and (**b**) without uncertain respondents (right).

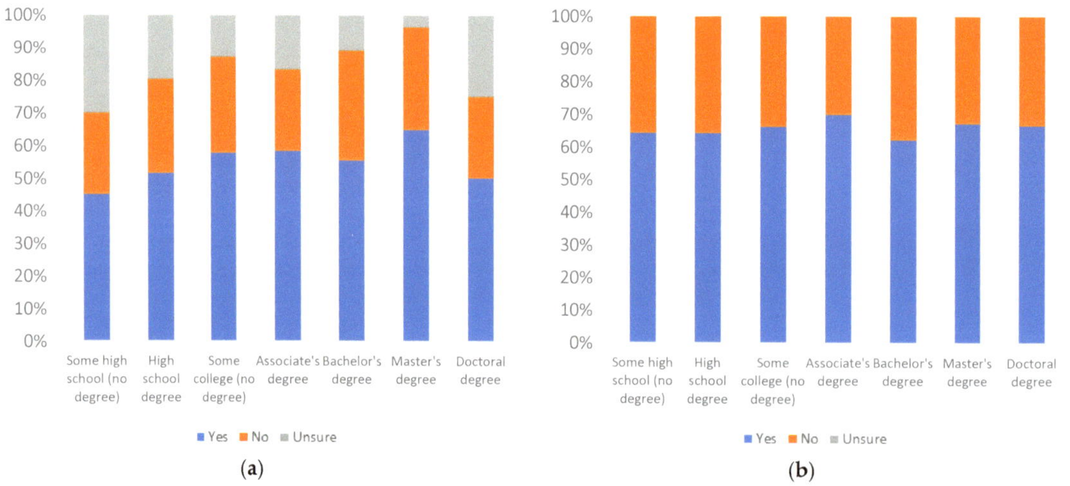

Figure 28. Label use, by education level: (**a**) with uncertain respondents (left) and (**b**) without uncertain respondents (right).

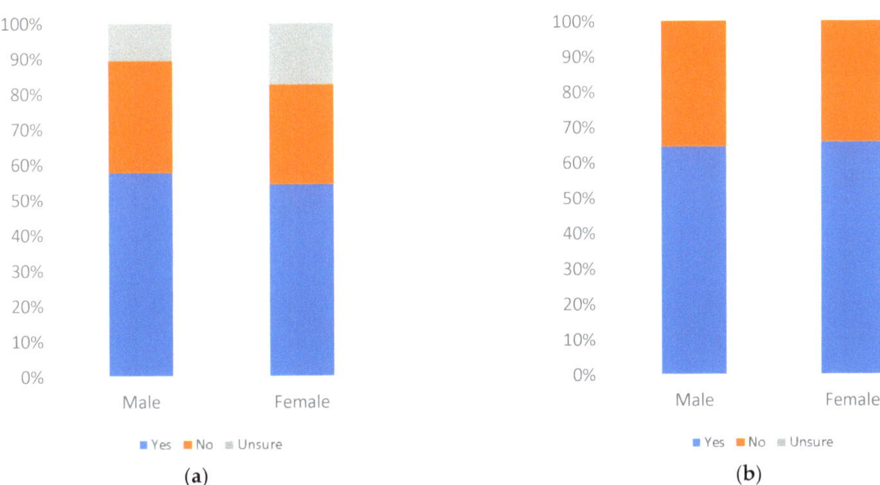

Figure 29. Label use, by gender: (**a**) with uncertain respondents (left) and (**b**) without uncertain respondents (right).

Figures 30–32 consider respondents' perception of likelihood of others to use informational label 2, with respondents answering the question "would others review this label when viewing news articles on social media?".

There is no clear pattern of increasing or decreasing support as age increases. There are spikes in the number of yes responses at the 30–34, 40–44, and 50–54 age groups, which are apparent even with uncertainty factored in. Overall, the level of uncertainty is relatively high. While only three age groups (30–34, 40–44, and 50–54) have at least 50% yes responses, when uncertainty is factored in, all groups have at least 50% yes responses, when uncertainty is not considered.

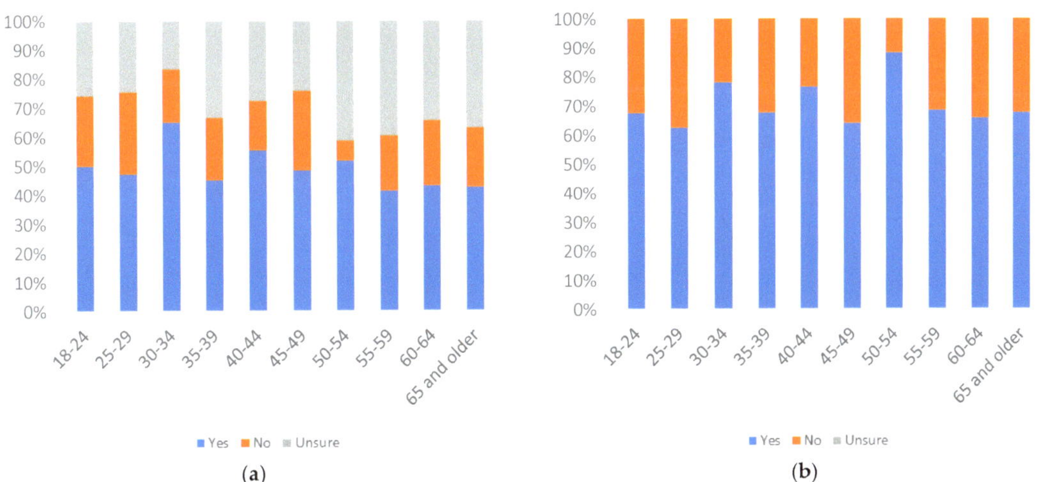

Figure 30. Label others' use, by age group: (**a**) with uncertain respondents (left) and (**b**) without uncertain respondents (right).

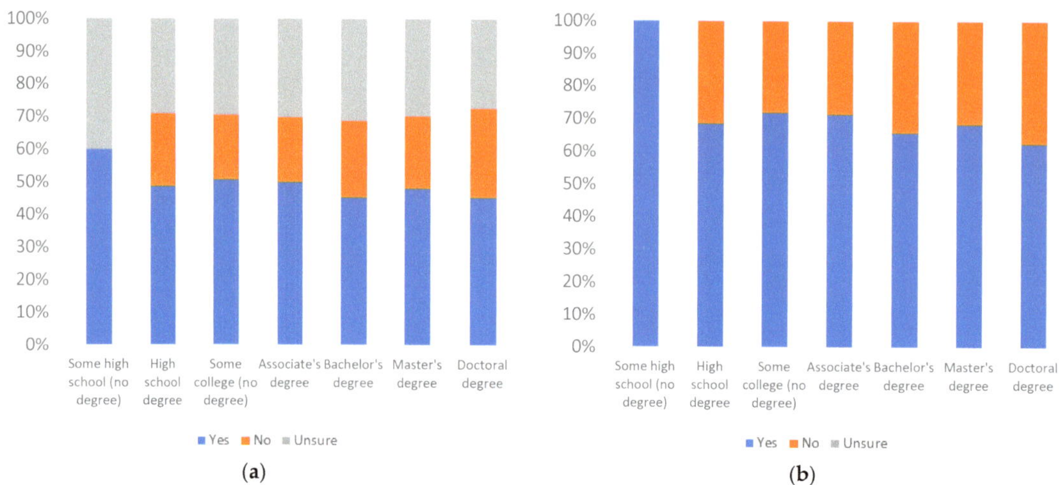

Figure 31. Label others' use, by education level: (**a**) with uncertain respondents (left) and (**b**) without uncertain respondents (right).

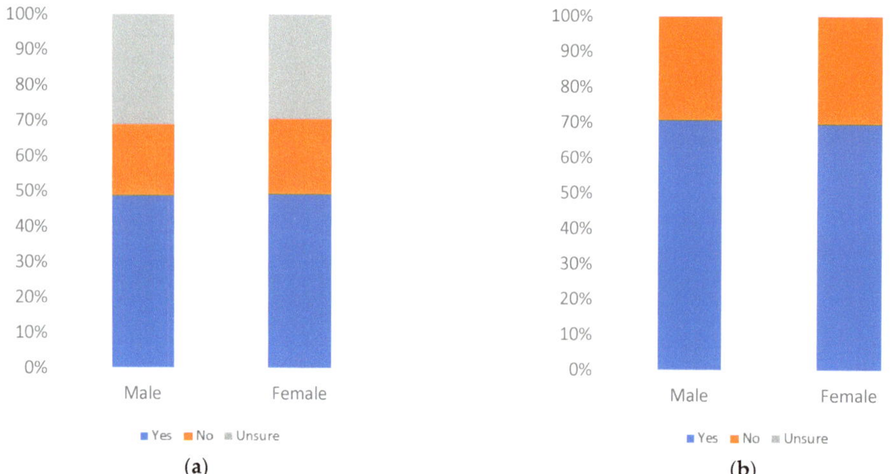

Figure 32. Label others' use, by gender: (**a**) with uncertain respondents (left) and (**b**) without uncertain respondents (right).

By education level, responses are relatively consistent, except for a surprising level (100%) of support in the some high school group, when uncertainty is not considered. It should be noted, however, that the some high school group reports approximately 40% uncertainty, so the apparent level of enthusiasm is not as strong, given the higher level of uncertainty surrounding this question. While only the some high school group has at least 50% yes responses, with uncertainty factored in, all education level groups have at least 50% yes responses, without considering uncertainty.

By gender, the levels of support are almost equal, even with uncertainty considered. While both genders have less than 50% yes responses, when uncertainty is considered, both groups have greater than 50% yes responses, when uncertainty is removed.

Figures 33–35 consider the value of informational label 2 for gauging trustworthiness, with respondents answering the question "would it be useful for judging the trustworthiness of news articles?".

In terms of age, there are three peaks in yes responses: one is at the 25–29 and 30–34 age groups. A second is at the 45–49 age group. A final peak is at the 65 and older age group. There is a spike in uncertainty for the 35–39 age group and an increase in uncertainty from the 40–44 to 60–64 age groups. The uncertainty level for this question is relatively high. When uncertainty is factored in, only the 18–24, 35–39, 55–59 and 60–64 age groups have less than 50% yes responses. Without uncertainty, all age groups report at least 50% yes responses.

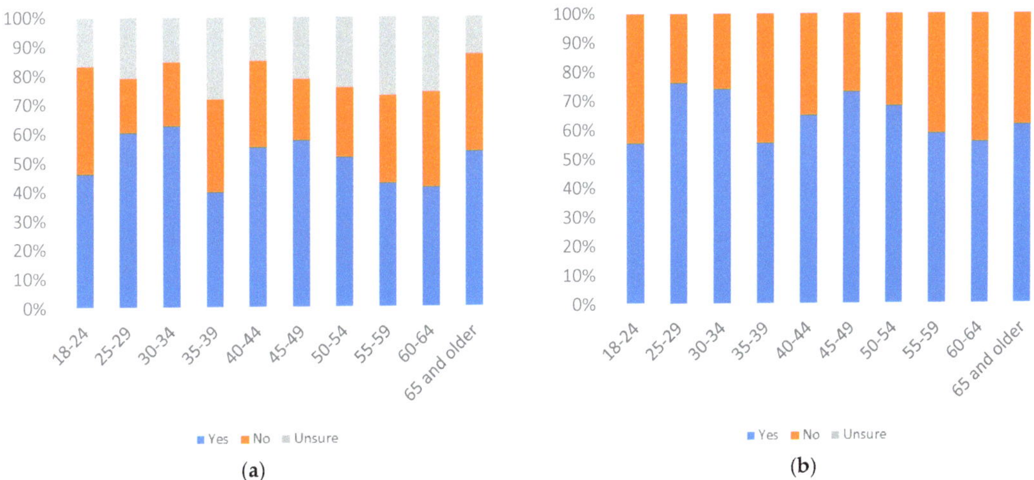

Figure 33. Label trustworthiness judging use, by age group: (**a**) with uncertain respondents (left) and (**b**) without uncertain respondents (right).

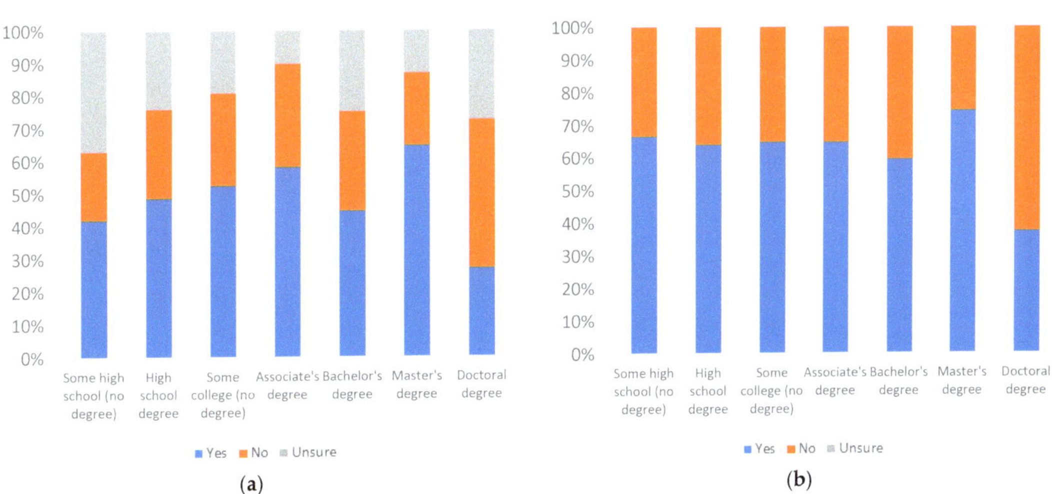

Figure 34. Label trustworthiness judging use, by education level: (**a**) with uncertain respondents (left) and (**b**) without uncertain respondents (right).

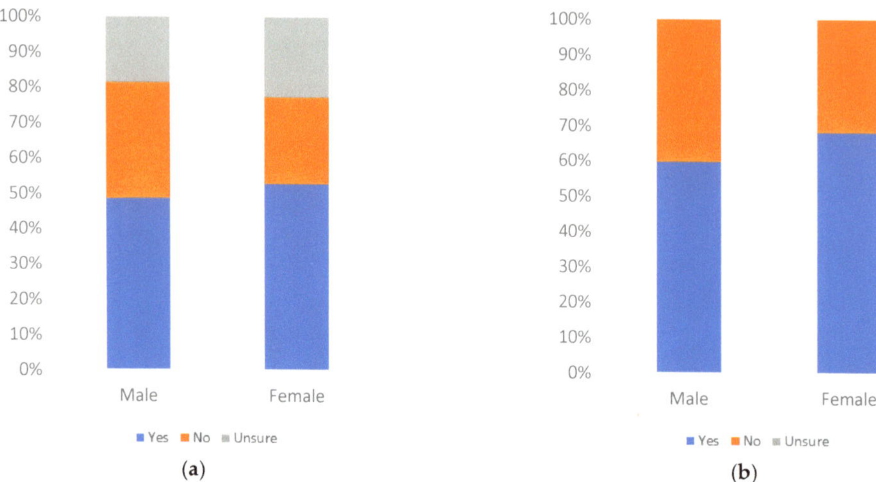

Figure 35. Label trustworthiness judging use, by gender: (**a**) with uncertain respondents (left) and (**b**) without uncertain respondents (right).

By education level, yes responses are consistent, except for a spike at the master's degree level, followed by a drop at the doctoral degree level. Uncertainty exhibits two valleys, with one low point at the associate's degree level and a second at the master's degree level. Only the some college, associate's degree, and master's degree education levels report at least 50% yes responses, when uncertainty is considered. Without uncertainty, all but the doctoral degree group report at least 50% yes responses.

By gender, female respondents have a higher number of yes responses than makes but also a higher level of uncertainty. With uncertainty factored in, only the female respondents have at least 50% yes responses. Without uncertainty, both groups reach this threshold.

The helpfulness of informational label 3 (shown in Figure 36), when it appears underneath a news article automatically, is considered in Figures 37–39. Respondents answered the question "would you find this label helpful?".

In terms of age, there are two plateaus in yes responses, with a drop at the 35–39 age group. These plateaus remain consistent even when uncertainty is included. All age groups report at least 50% yes responses even when uncertainty is considered.

By education level, there is a spike in support by the some high school group, when uncertainty is not considered. When uncertainty is factored in, this spike is not present, due to a high level of uncertainty at the some high school education group; however, a new spike appears at the master's degree group, due to their relatively low uncertainty. Even when uncertainty is included, all education groups report at least 50% yes responses.

By gender, female respondents report a significantly higher level of yes responses, while uncertainty is similar for both groups. Both groups have at least 50% yes responses, even when including uncertainty.

M

Trouble at High Speed West Middle School

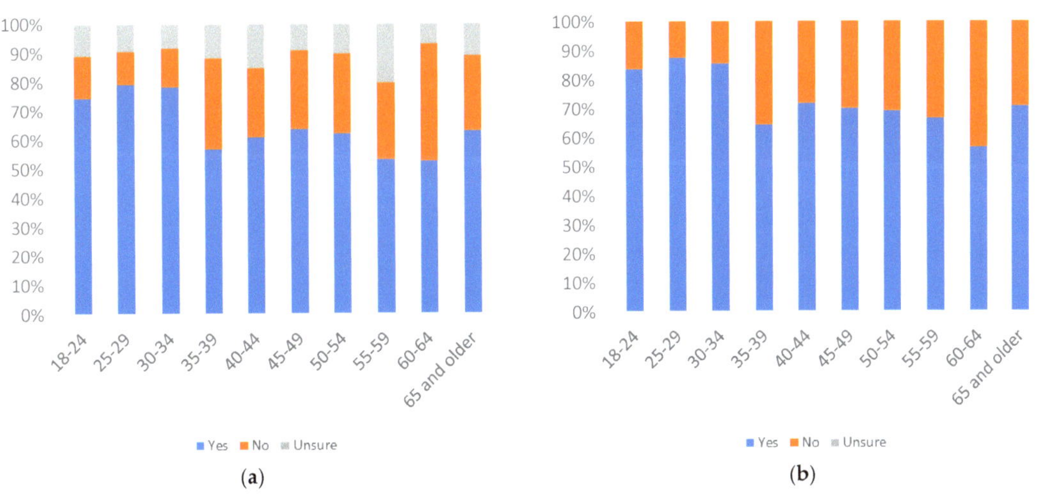

High Speed West Middle School in deadlock due to boys refusing to
say the word "hello", opting only to refer to people as "Gamers."
1 week ago

Title: Trouble at High Speed West Middle School
Author: Michael Scott
Fact: 73%
This is the percentage of words written as what the author
believes is fact. Taken as an average over the total number of
prepositions. Often credible sources have a percentage hovering
around 60%

Opinion: 27%
This is the percentage of words written as what the author
expresses as opinion. Taken as an average over the total number
of prepositions. Often credible sources that aren't opinion pieces
have 10-20%

Emotion: 12%
The usage of words are charged with positive or negative
connotations. This is calculated over the average number of
words. Often credible sources have less than 7%

Authority: 2/10
Calculated out of 10. based upon the importance of the source
how often the source produces accurate content. and if the source
is widely trusted by the public. Often credible sources have at least
level 3.

Viral: True
Whether or not the article is moving rapidly and widely
over the internet from one source to another. Viral
media may not yet be verified as accurate

Topicality: 3/10
This is a score of how relevant the article is to the current
content being produced by other media sources. Articles
with topicality greater than 7 cover subjects which are
currently widely discussed in media

Reading level: 12th grade
The level of education required to understand the the
grammatical correctness. vocabulary. and syntax of the text
Often credible sources have atleast a 9th grade reading
level

Technicality: 2/10
The amount of domain knowledge required to be able to
understand what the information in the media is conveying
The score is how hard it would be for someone outside the
field to comprehend. Often credible sources have around
level 3

Figure 36. Informational label 3 [16].

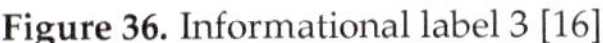

(a)   (b)

Figure 37. Label helpfulness, by age group: (**a**) with uncertain respondents (left) and (**b**) without
uncertain respondents (right).

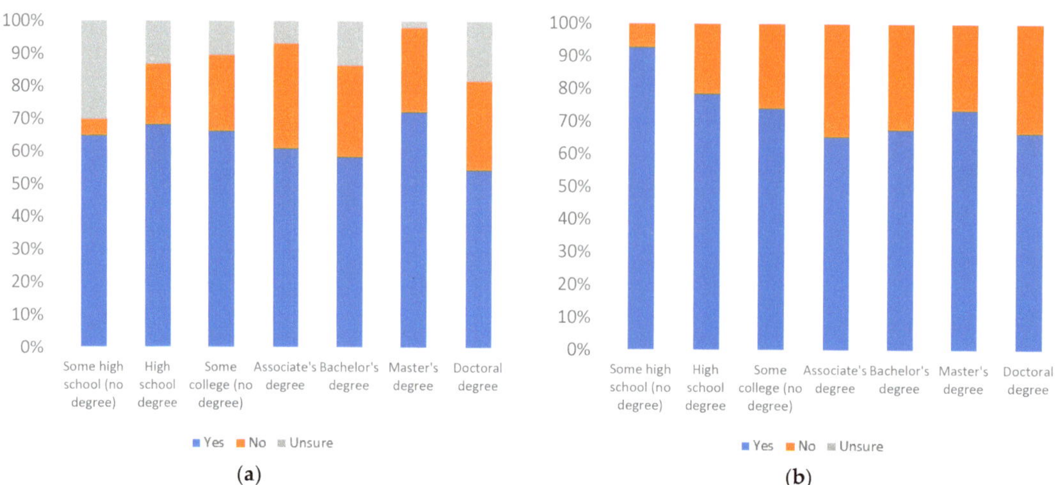

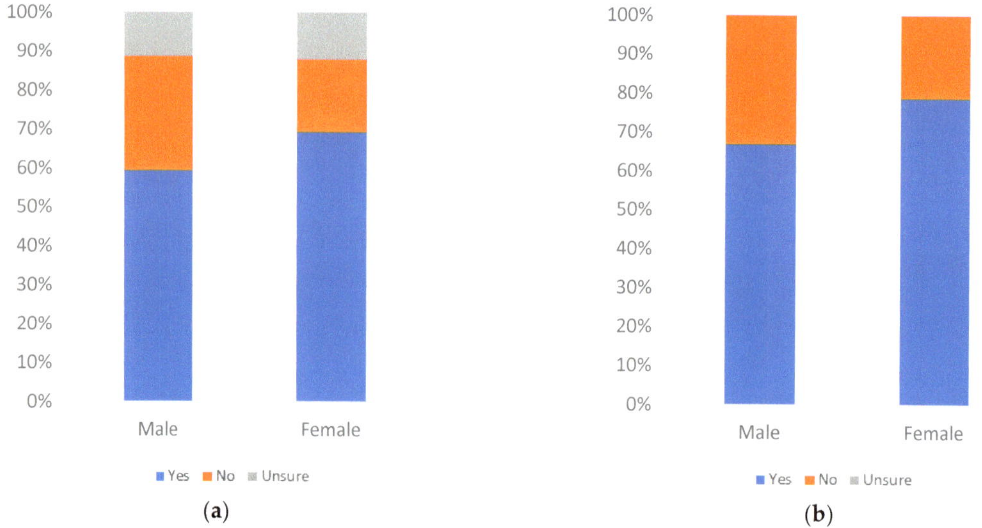

Figure 38. Label helpfulness, by education level: (**a**) with uncertain respondents (left) and (**b**) without uncertain respondents (right).

Figure 39. Label helpfulness, by gender: (**a**) with uncertain respondents (left) and (**b**) without uncertain respondents (right).

Figures 40–42 consider annoyingness of informational label 3, with respondents answering the question "would you find this label annoying?".

In terms of age, there is a decline in yes responses from the 18–24 to 30–34 age groups. This is followed by an increase from the 30–34 to 50–54 age groups. Support oscillates over the 55–59, 60–64 and 65 and older age groups. Only four age groups (45–49, 50–54, 60–64, and 65 and older) have at least 50% yes responses, when uncertainty is factored in. When uncertainty is not considered, the 35–39, 40–44, and 55–59 age groups also reach this threshold. This indicates that there is a moderate feeling of annoyance towards the label, across the 35–39 and older age groups.

By education level, there is no clear pattern of increase or decrease as education level increases. The highest level of uncertainty is seen amongst those with some high school education, while the master's degree education level group reports no uncertainty. When uncertainty is factored in, only the associate's degree education level group has at least 50% yes responses. Without uncertainty, the high school degree, bachelor's degree, and doctoral degree groups also report at least 50% yes responses. This shows no clear pattern of increasing or decreasing levels of annoyance, with changing education levels.

By gender, males report a slightly higher level of annoyance, while females report a higher level of uncertainty. Neither group reports at least a 50% yes response level, when uncertainty is considered; however, male respondents meet this threshold when uncertainty is removed.

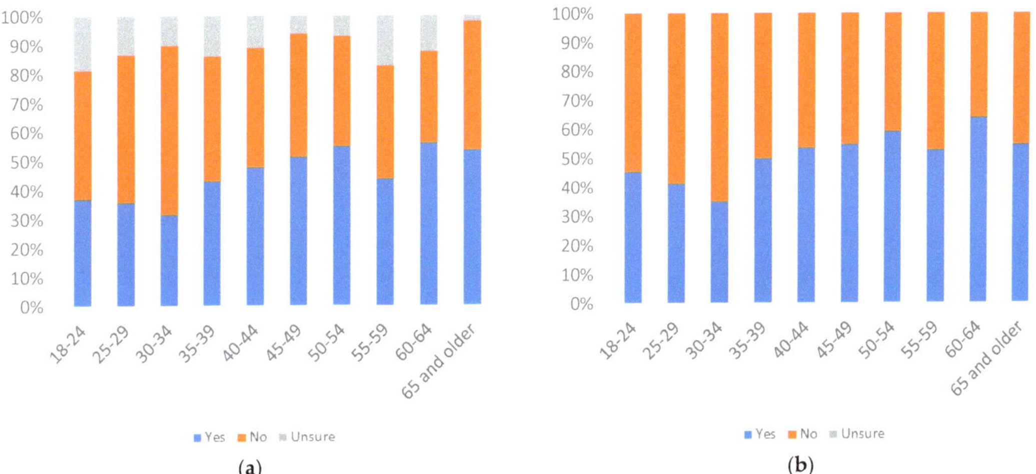

Figure 40. Label annoyingness, by age group: (**a**) with uncertain respondents (left) and (**b**) without uncertain respondents (right).

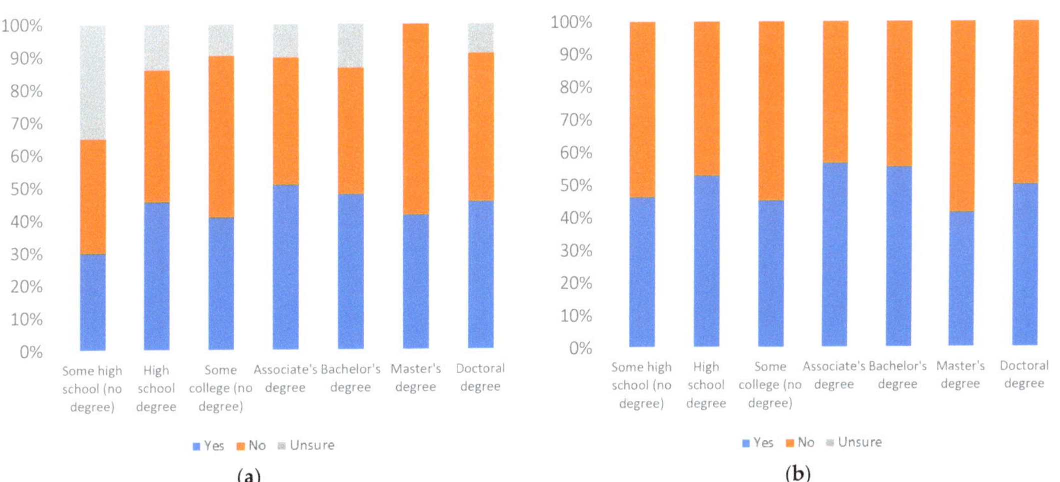

Figure 41. Label annoyingness, by education level: (**a**) with uncertain respondents (left) and (**b**) without uncertain respondents (right).

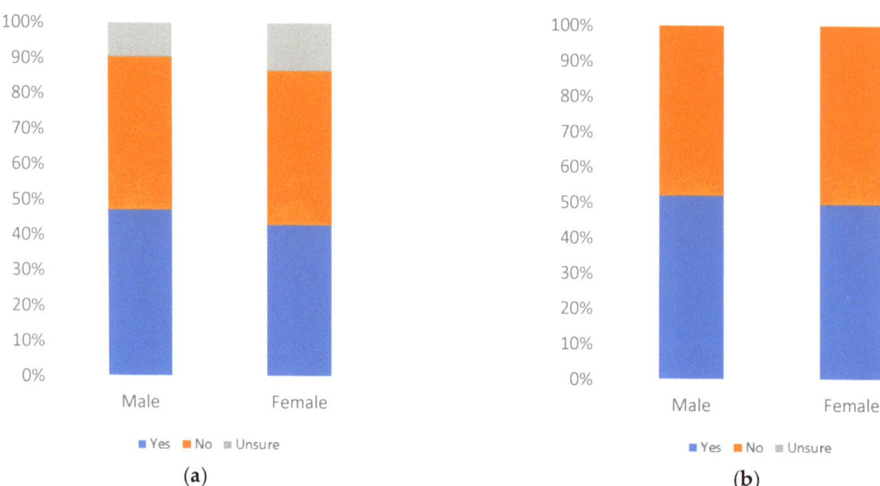

Figure 42. Label annoyingness, by gender: (**a**) with uncertain respondents (left) and (**b**) without uncertain respondents (right).

Figures 43–45 consider the likelihood of respondents personally using informational label 3, with respondents answering the question "would you review this label when viewing news articles on social media?".

In terms of age, there is no clear pattern of increase or decrease, as age increases. The most noticeable drops in yes responses occurs with the 18–24, 35–39, and 45–49 age groups. Amongst these, while the 18–24 and 35–39 groups report a high level of uncertainty, the 45–49 age group reports almost no uncertainty. All but the 18–24 and 35–39 age groups report at least 50% yes responses when uncertainty is considered. With uncertainty removed, every age group meets the 50% yes threshold.

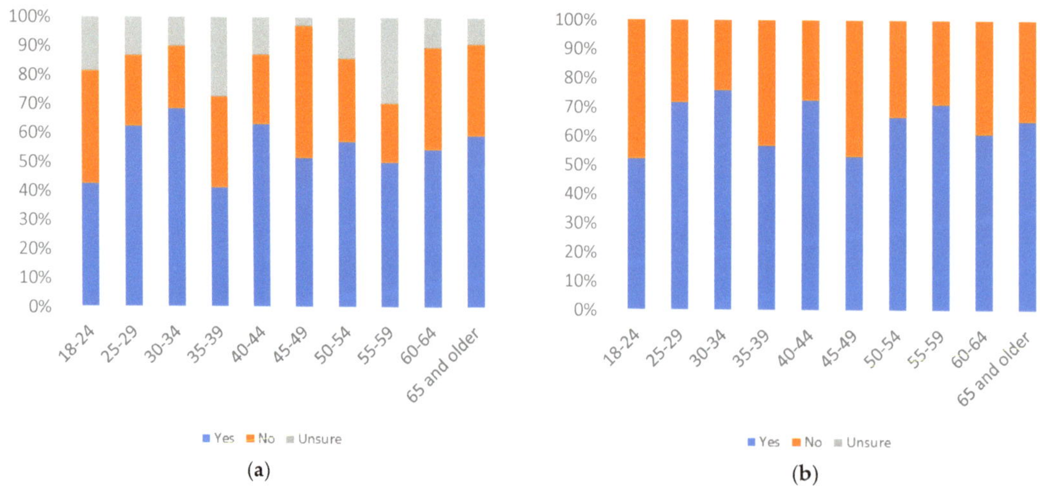

Figure 43. Label use, by age group: (**a**) with uncertain respondents (left) and (**b**) without uncertain respondents (right).

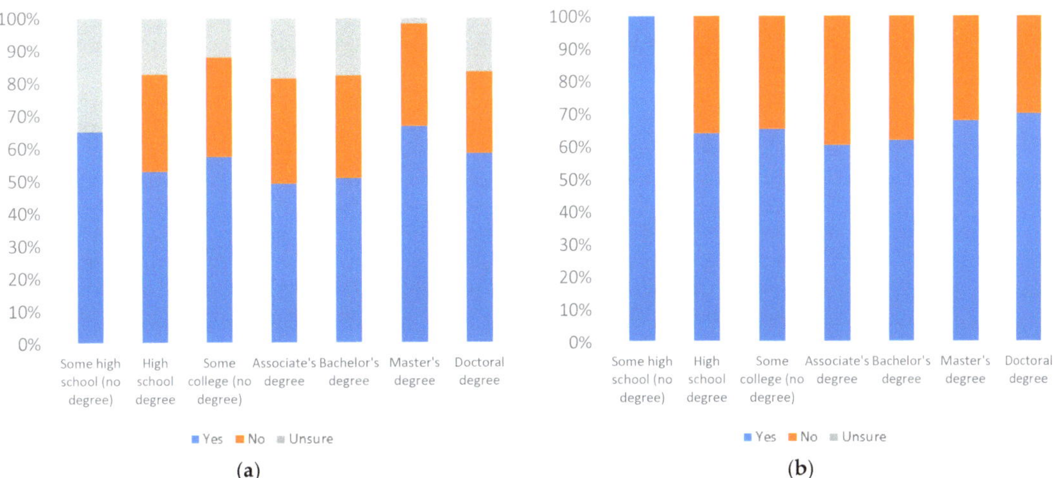

Figure 44. Label use, by education level: (**a**) with uncertain respondents (left) and (**b**) without uncertain respondents (right).

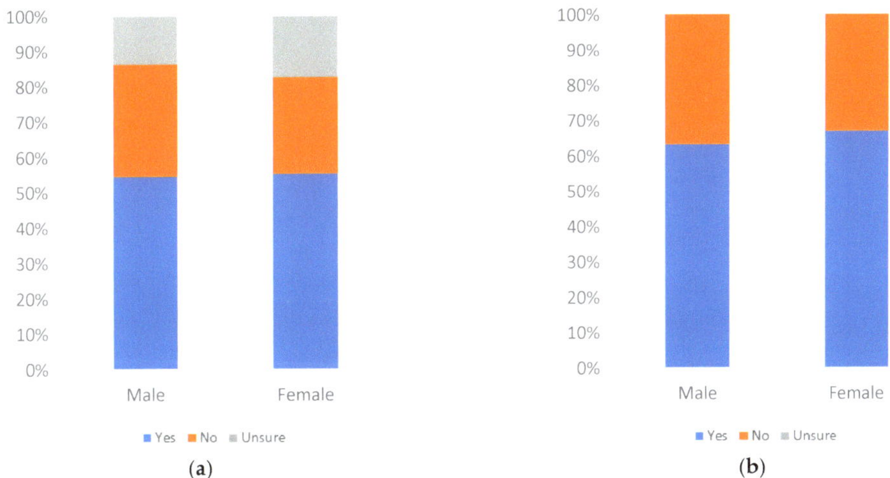

Figure 45. Label use, by gender: (**a**) with uncertain respondents (left) and (**b**) without uncertain respondents (right).

By education level, responses are relatively consistent, when uncertainty is not considered except for another surprising 100% yes response from the some high school education level group. Again, the uncertainty level of this education group tends to place it closer to the other groups, while the master's degree education group spikes, due to a low level of uncertainty. Recalling Figure 31, which considered the likelihood of others to use informational label 2, an almost identical dynamic of responses was found amongst age groups. However, in this case in Figure 44, the question is regarding personal use, rather than the usage of others. When uncertainty is considered, only the associate's degree education level group has fewer than 50% yes responses. With uncertainty eliminated, even this group reaches above the 50% yes response level threshold.

By gender, females report more yes responses than males, as well as a higher level of uncertainty. Both groups report at least 50% yes responses, even when uncertainty is included.

Figures 46–48 consider respondents' perception of the likelihood of others to use informational label 3, with respondents answering the question "would others review this label when viewing news articles on social media?".

In terms of age, when uncertainty is not factored in, there is a gradual decline in yes responses from the 25–29 to 65 and over age groups, with the exception of a spike at the 40–44 age group and a slight recovery at 50–54 age group. The lowest point for yes responses, though, is at the 18–24 age group. When uncertainty is included, the percentage of yes responses shows the same pattern of decline, but with no spike at the 40–44 age group, a steep drop at the 35–39 age group, and some recovery at the 65 and older age group. The uncertainty level for this question is relatively high. When uncertainty is considered, only four age groups (25–29, 30–34, 40–44, and 45–49) report at least a 50% level of yes responses. When uncertainty is removed, all but the 18–24 age group reach the 50% yes threshold.

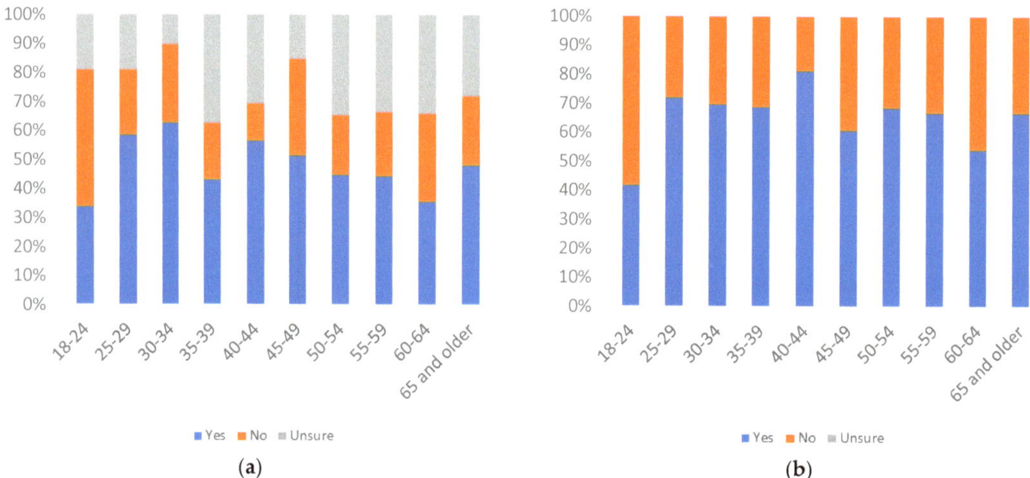

Figure 46. Label others' use, by age group: (**a**) with uncertain respondents (left) and (**b**) without uncertain respondents (right).

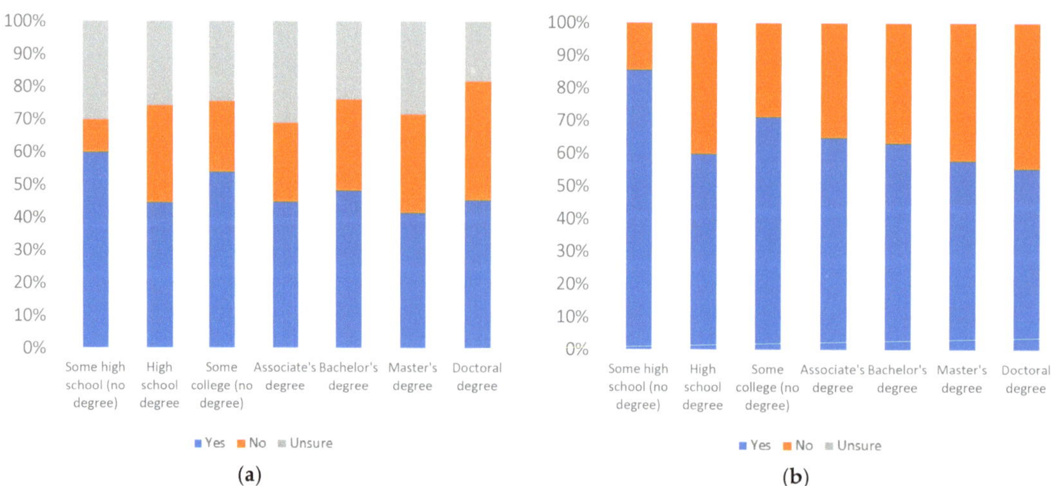

Figure 47. Label others' use, by education level: (**a**) with uncertain respondents (left) and (**b**) without uncertain respondents (right).

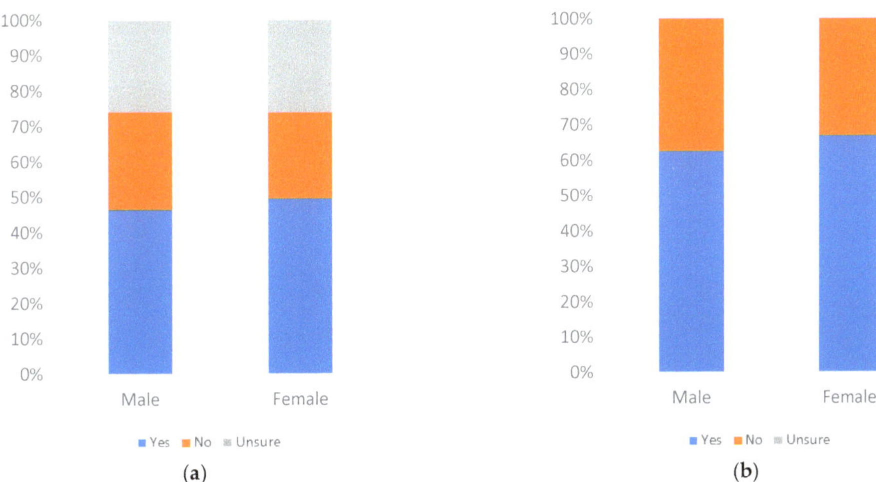

Figure 48. Label others' use, by gender: (**a**) with uncertain respondents (left) and (**b**) without uncertain respondents (right).

By education level, there is a consistent decline in yes responses, as education level increases. As one exception, there is a sharper drop at the high school degree age group. Uncertainty levels are mostly consistent across education groups. While only the some high school and some college (no degree) groups report at least 50% "yes" responses, when uncertainty is factored in. All groups reach this threshold, when uncertainty is removed.

By gender, female respondents report yes more frequently than males, while the two groups share approximately the same level of uncertainty. Neither group exceeds 50% yes responses, when uncertainty is included; however, both groups reach this threshold when uncertainty is removed.

Figures 49–51 consider the value of informational label 3 for gauging articles' trustworthiness, with respondents answering the question "would it be useful for judging the trustworthiness of news articles?".

In terms of age, there is no clear pattern of yes responses increasing or decreasing as age increases. There are noticeable drops in yes responses at the 18–24, 35–39 and 50–54 age groups and a spike in uncertainty for the 35–39 age group. Only the 30–34 and 50–54 age groups report fewer than 50% yes responses, when uncertainty is included. Without uncertainty factored in, all age groups report at least 50% yes responses.

By education level, there is a consistent decline in yes responses, as education level increases, except for a slight recovery at the master's degree level. Uncertainty levels are highest for the some high school group and lowest for the associate's degree and master's degree groups. However, they are otherwise relatively consistent. All groups, other than the doctoral degree holders, report at least 50% yes responses, even when uncertainty is considered. With uncertainty removed, even the doctoral degree holders reach the 50% yes threshold.

By gender, there are significantly greater yes responses among female respondents, as well as slightly higher uncertainty, among females. Both groups report at least 50% yes responses, even when uncertainty is considered.

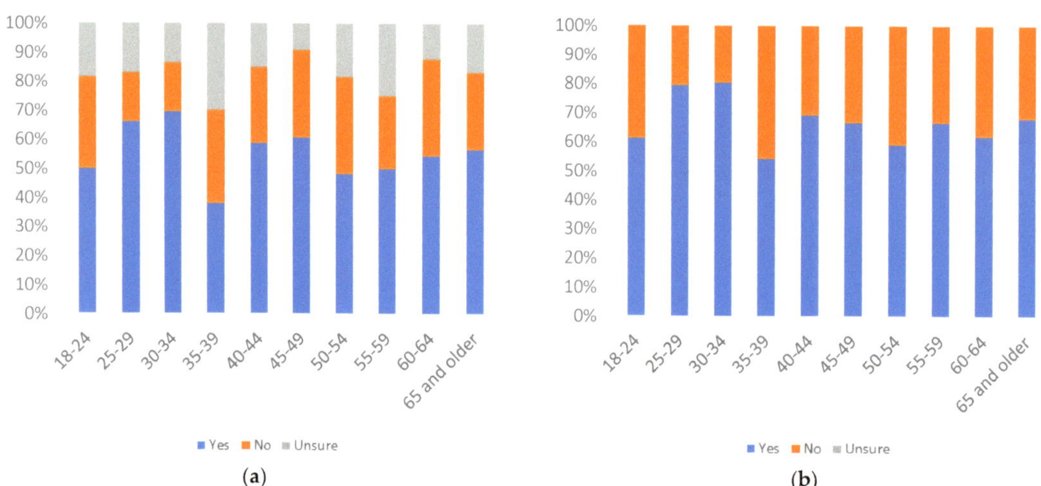

Figure 49. Label trustworthiness judging use, by age group: (**a**) with uncertain respondents (left) and (**b**) without uncertain respondents (right).

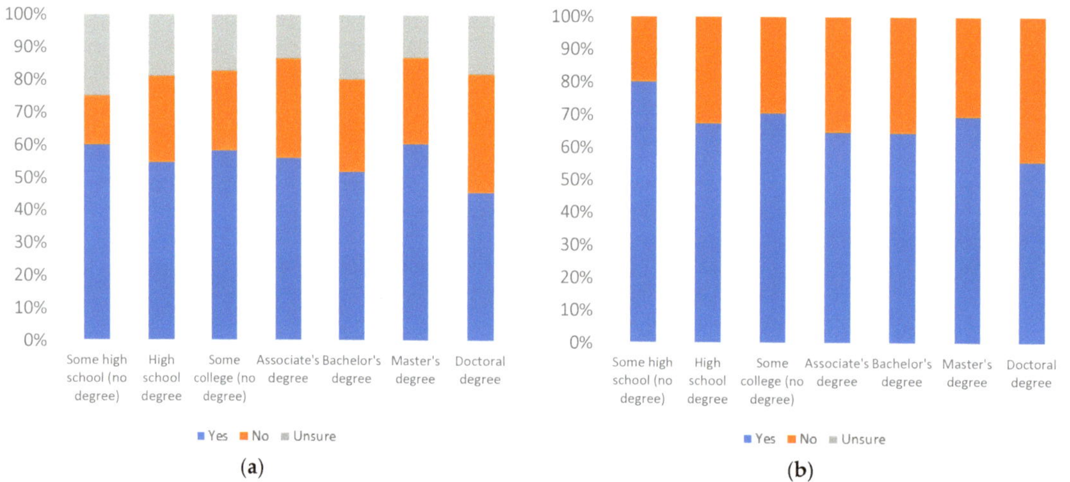

Figure 50. Label trustworthiness judging use, by education level: (**a**) with uncertain respondents (left) and (**b**) without uncertain respondents (right).

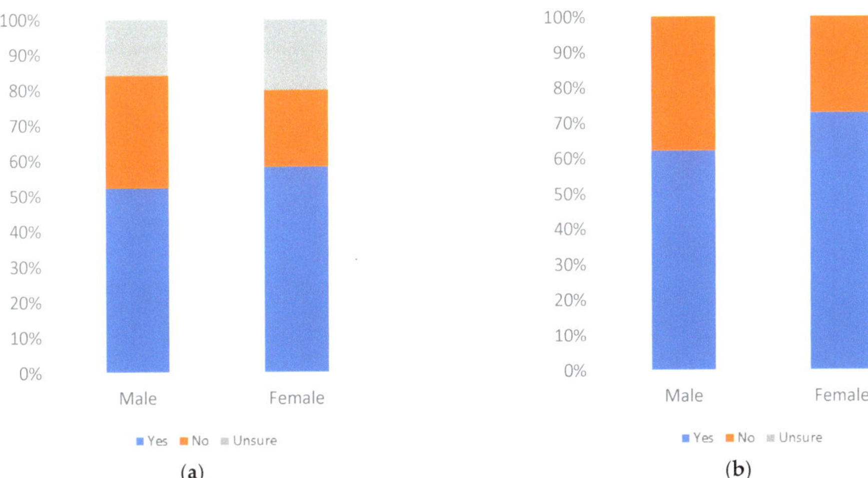

Figure 51. Label trustworthiness judging use, by gender: (**a**) with uncertain respondents (left) and (**b**) without uncertain respondents (right).

5. Warning Label Related Data and Analysis

In addition to the informational labels, which present salient details in a neutral manner, labels which provide a specific caution or warning statement to viewers were also considered. Respondents' perspectives regarding these labels are discussed in this section. Again, respondents were asked about the helpfulness, annoyingness, whether they would use the label, whether they thought others would use the label and whether they thought that the label would aid in assessing article trustworthiness. The data from these questions was analyzed in terms of respondents' age, education level and gender.

The helpfulness of warning label 1 (Figure 52), when it appears on top of an article that is deemed unsafe, is considered in Figures 53–55. Respondents were asked to answer the question "would you find this label helpful?".

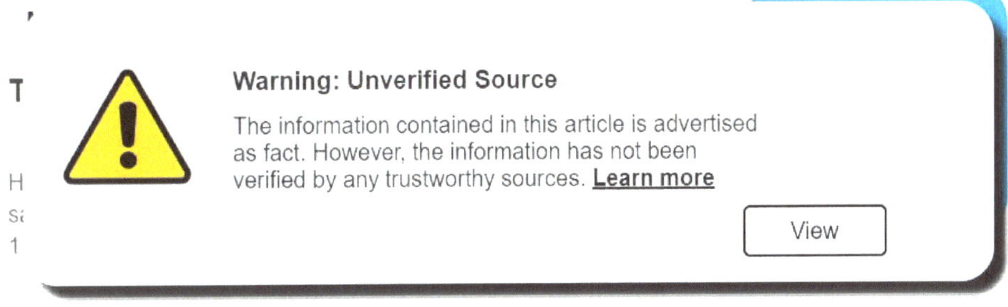

Figure 52. Warning label 1 [16].

In terms of age, there is a sudden drop in yes responses at the 35–39 age group, followed by a steady increase. Otherwise, responses are generally consistent when uncertainty is not considered. Even when uncertainty is not considered, all age groups report at least 50% yes responses.

By education level, there is a slow decline in yes responses as education level increases. Uncertainty is most pronounced at the lowest and highest education levels. However, even with uncertainty factored in, all age groups report at least 50% yes responses.

Information **2022**, *13*, 516

By gender, female respondents have both the highest yes response rate and the highest uncertainty level. Both gender groups have at least 50% yes responses, even when uncertainty is included.

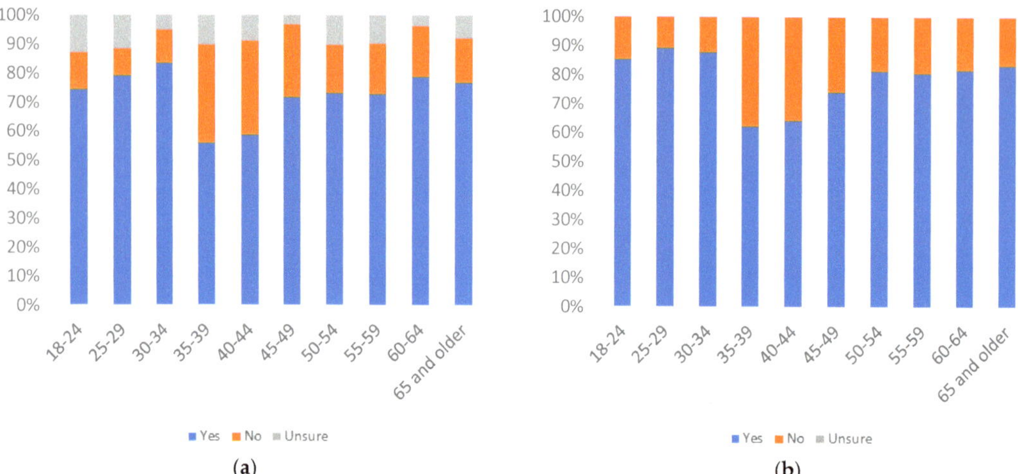

Figure 53. Label helpfulness, by age group: (**a**) with uncertain respondents (left) and (**b**) without uncertain respondents (right).

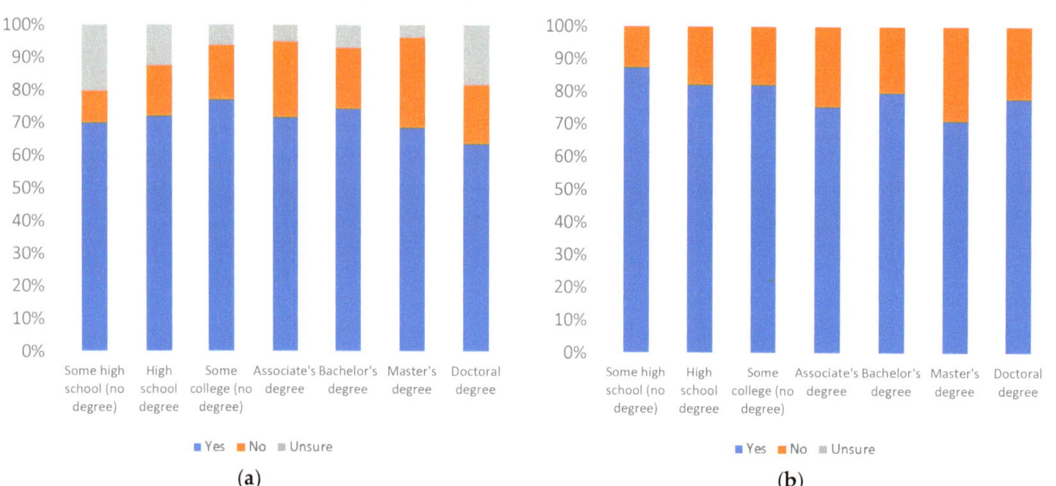

Figure 54. Label helpfulness, by education level: (**a**) with uncertain respondents (left) and (**b**) without uncertain respondents (right).

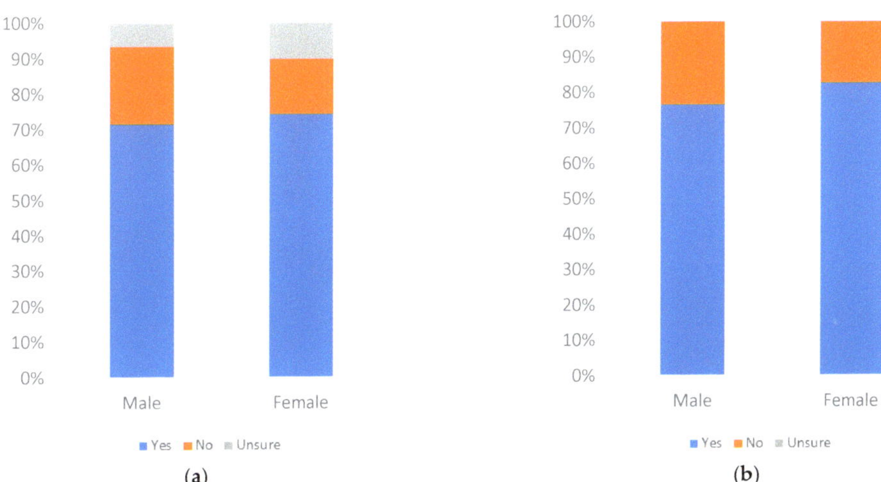

(a)   (b)

Figure 55. Label helpfulness, by gender: (**a**) with uncertain respondents (left) and (**b**) without uncertain respondents (right).

Figures 56–58 consider respondents' perceptions of the annoyingness of warning label 1, with respondents answering the question "would you find this label annoying?".

In terms of age, there is a peak in yes responses at the 40–44 age group, with yes responses rising steadily from the 18–24 to 40–44 age groups and then dropping again to the 55–59 age group. There is then a second, smaller peak from the 55–59 age group to the 65 and older age group. Whether uncertainty is included or not, the only age group to exceed 50% yes responses is the 40–44 age group. This indicates an overall low level of annoyance across most age groups.

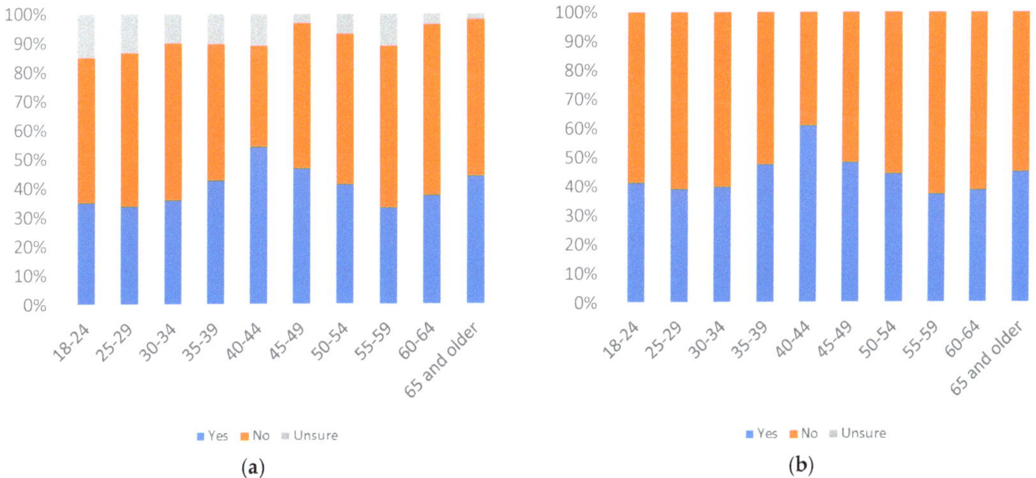

(a)   (b)

Figure 56. Label annoyingness, by age group: (**a**) with uncertain respondents (left) and (**b**) without uncertain respondents (right).

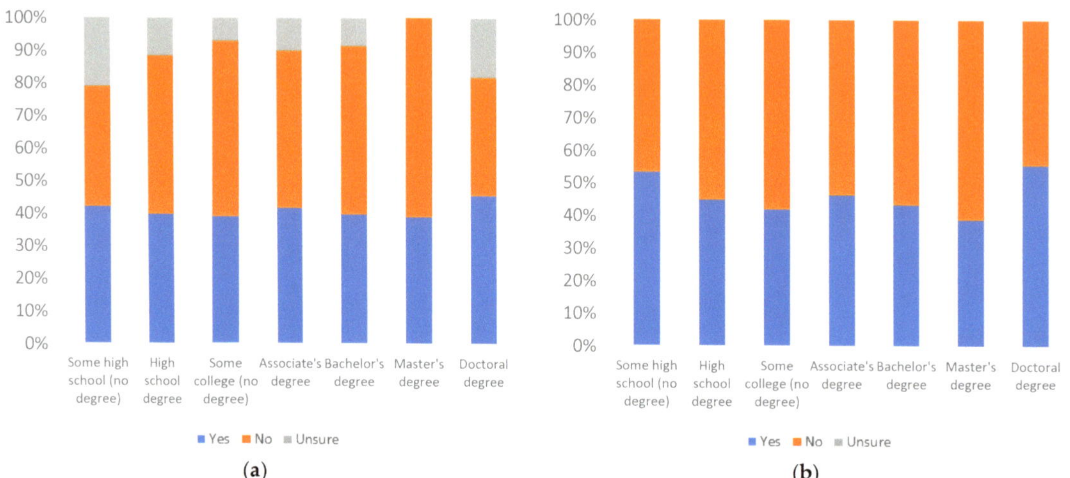

Figure 57. Label annoyingness, by education level: (**a**) with uncertain respondents (left) and (**b**) without uncertain respondents (right).

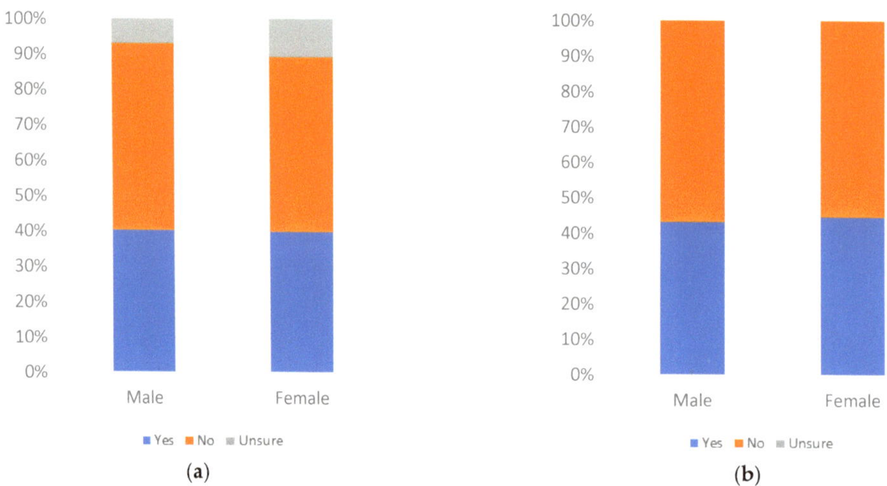

Figure 58. Label annoyingness, by gender: (**a**) with uncertain respondents (left) and (**b**) without uncertain respondents (right).

By education level, yes responses spike slightly for the some high school (no degree) and doctoral degree groups, when uncertainty is not considered, and otherwise remains relatively consistent. Results are consistent, even for these groups, when uncertainty is considered, as there are spikes in uncertainty for both groups. The percentage of respondents answering yes exceeds 50% only for these two groups, and only when uncertainty is not considered.

By gender, male and female yes response levels are nearly equal, with a slightly higher yes response and uncertainty level for females. Both groups remain under 50% yes responses, even without uncertainty included.

Figures 59–61 consider respondents' likelihood of personally using warning label 1, with respondents answering the question "would you review this label when viewing news articles on social media?".

In terms of age, there are peaks at the 25–29, 50–54, and 60–64 age groups. The steepest decline in yes responses occurs between the 30–34 and 35–39 age groups. This drop is even more pronounced, when uncertainty is also included. Only the 40–44 age group has below 50% yes responses, and then only when uncertainty is included.

By education level, there is a small peak at the associate's degree education level. Due to a higher-than-average level of uncertainty, the some high school (no degree) group drops under 50% yes, when uncertainty is included. Without uncertainty considered, all groups report above 50% yes responses.

By gender, there is an increase in the number of yes responses among female respondents in addition to a higher level of uncertainty. Both groups report greater than 50% yes responses, even when uncertainty is included.

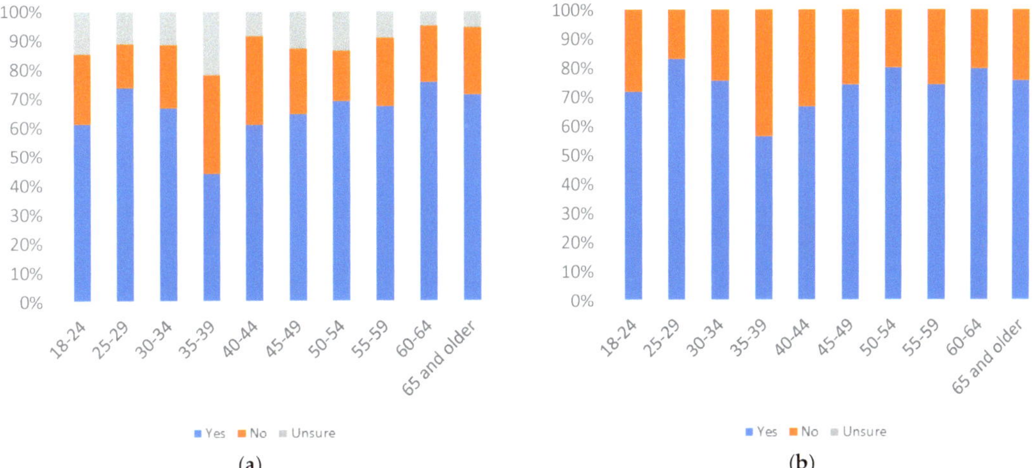

Figure 59. Label use, by age group: (**a**) with uncertain respondents (left) and (**b**) without uncertain respondents (right).

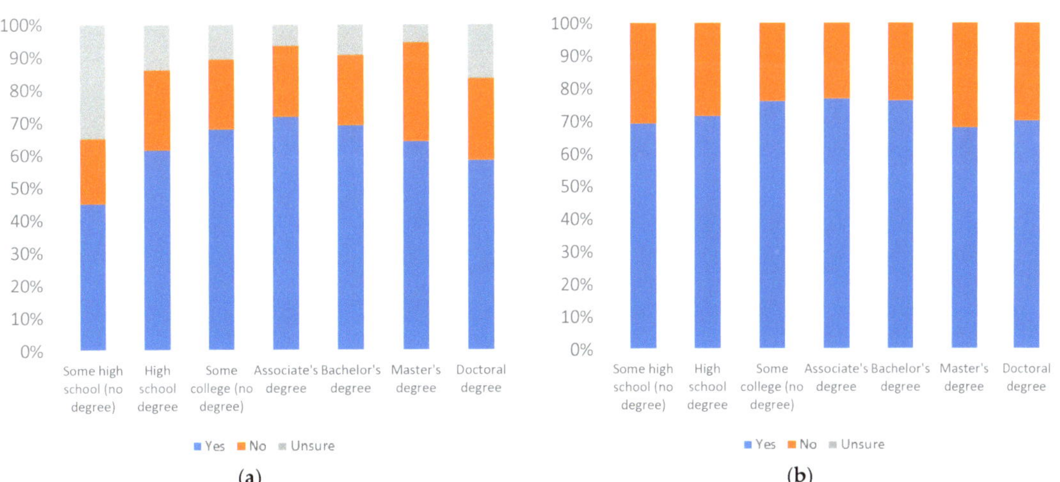

Figure 60. Label use, by education level: (**a**) with uncertain respondents (left) and (**b**) without uncertain respondents (right).

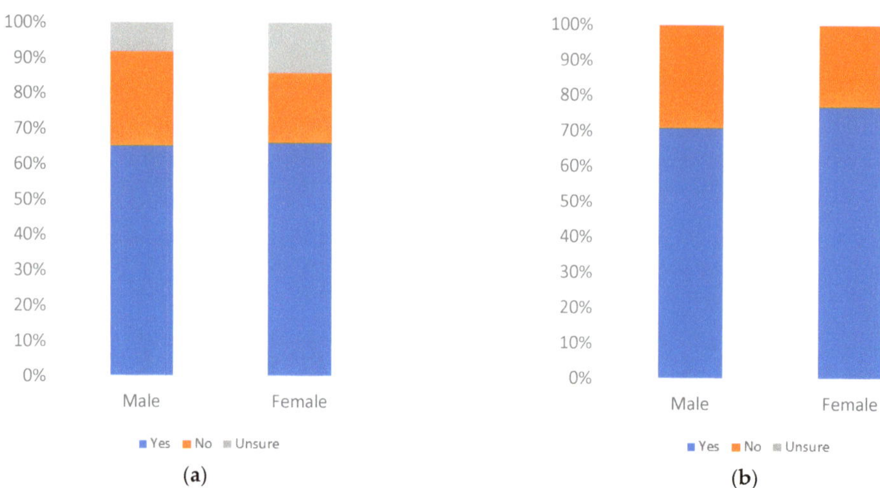

Figure 61. Label use, by gender: (**a**) with uncertain respondents (left) and (**b**) without uncertain respondents (right).

Figures 62–64 consider respondents' perspective as to the likelihood of others to use warning label 1, with respondents answering the question "would others review this label when viewing news articles on social media?".

In terms of age, results appear somewhat consistent, when uncertainty is not considered. There is a plateau from the 45–49 to 65 and older age groups. There is a slow decline from the 25–29 to 40–44 age groups, and a drop at the 18–24 age group. Uncertainty levels are generally high. Once uncertainty is introduced, the results change significantly, with three waves of increase at 18–24 to 30–34, 35–39 to 45–49, and 50–54 to 65 and older. Each of these waves bottoms out either just above or just below 50% yes responses, with only two (35–39 and 50–54) dropping below 50%, with uncertainty included. Without uncertainty, all age groups exceed 50% yes responses.

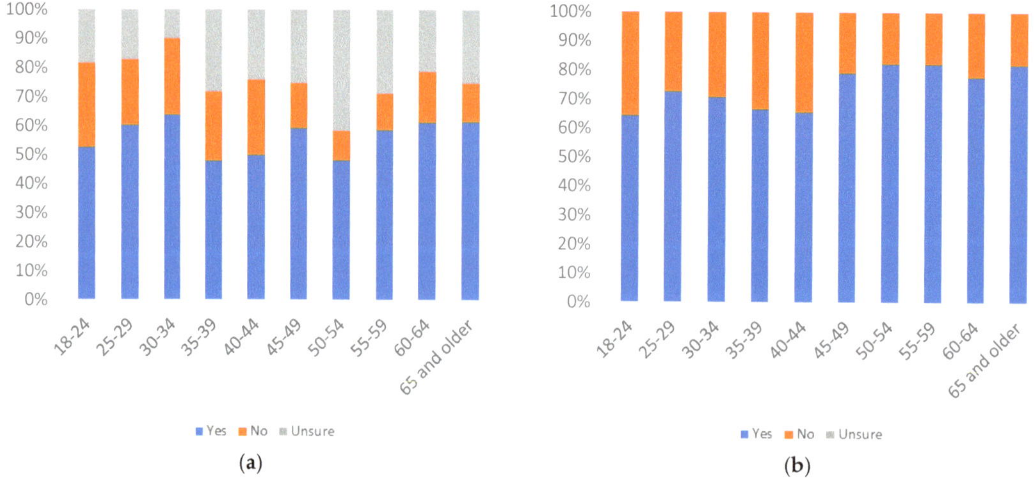

Figure 62. Label others' use, by age group: (**a**) with uncertain respondents (left) and (**b**) without uncertain respondents (right).

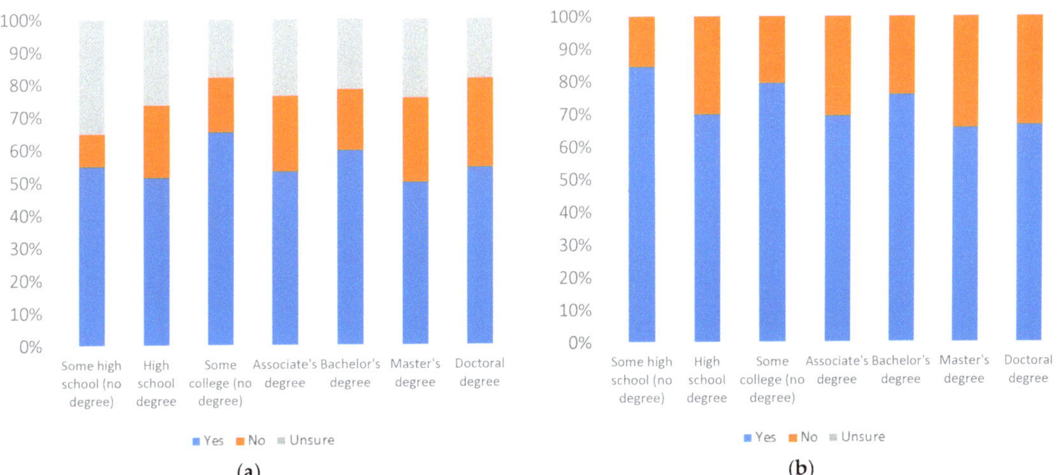

Figure 63. Label others' use, by education level: (**a**) with uncertain respondents (left) and (**b**) without uncertain respondents (right).

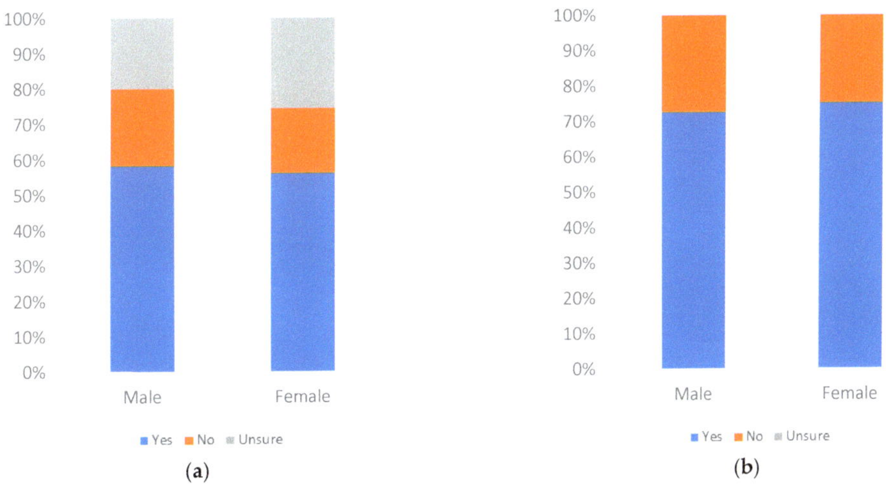

Figure 64. Label others' use, by gender: (**a**) with uncertain respondents (left) and (**b**) without uncertain respondents (right).

By education level, there is a decline in the level of yes responses, as education level increases, when uncertainty is not considered. With the consideration of uncertainty, results are instead relatively consistent. The exceptions, in both cases, are spikes at the some college (no degree) and bachelor's degree education level groups. All education groups meet or exceed 50% yes responses, even when uncertainty is considered.

By gender, females report a higher level of uncertainty and slightly lower level of yes responses; though female yes responses are a higher proportion when uncertainty is not considered. Both groups exceed 50% yes responses, even when uncertainty is included.

Figures 65–67 consider the value of warning label 1 for gauging article trustworthiness, with respondents answering the question "would it be useful for judging the trustworthiness of news articles?".

In terms of age, there are three waves of increasing yes responses, when uncertainty is considered, at the 18–24 to 30–34, 35–39 to 45–49, and 40–54 to 65 and older age groups. Similar waves exist, when uncertainty is removed, though there is a spike at the 25–29 age group which is due to a higher level of uncertainty for that group. Only the 35–39 age group has under 50% yes responses, and then only when uncertainty is included.

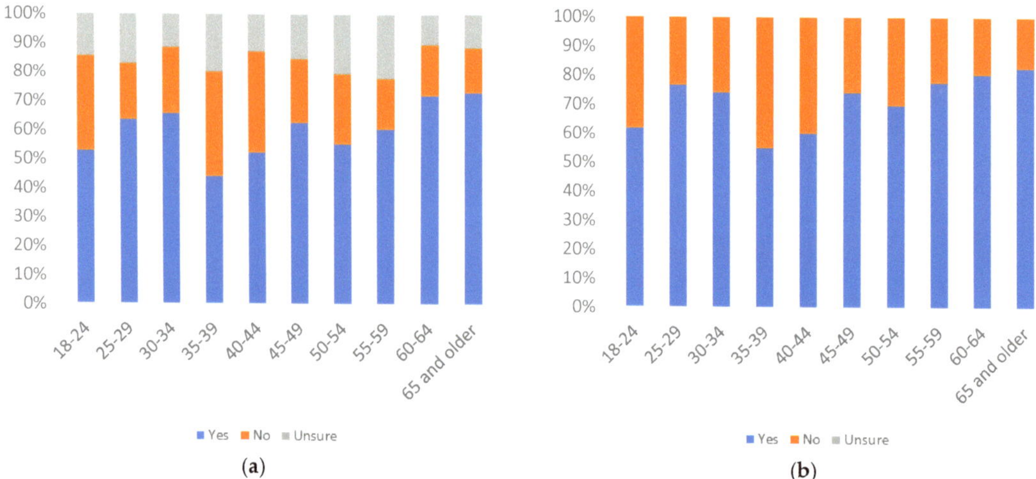

Figure 65. Label trustworthiness judging use, by age group: (**a**) with uncertain respondents (left) and (**b**) without uncertain respondents (right).

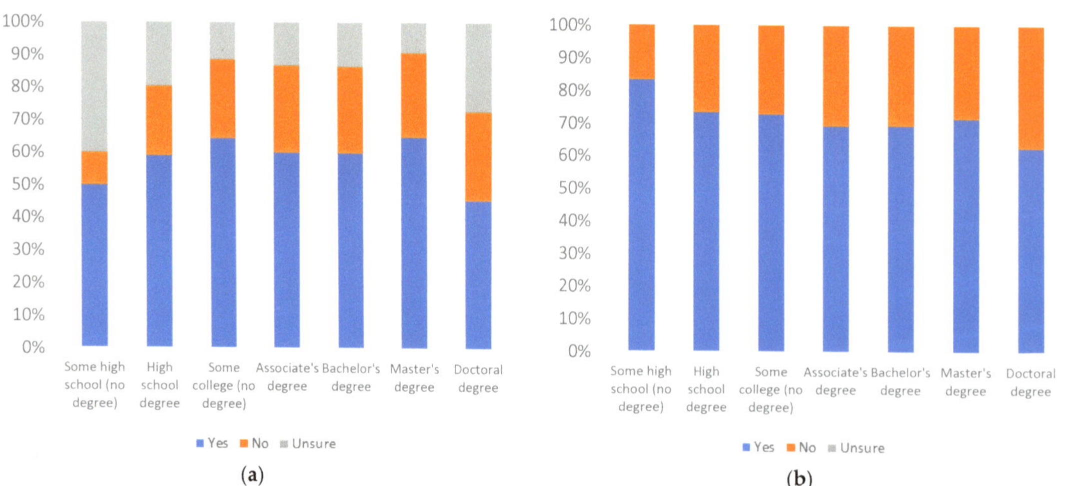

Figure 66. Label trustworthiness judging use, by education level: (**a**) with uncertain respondents (left) and (**b**) without uncertain respondents (right).

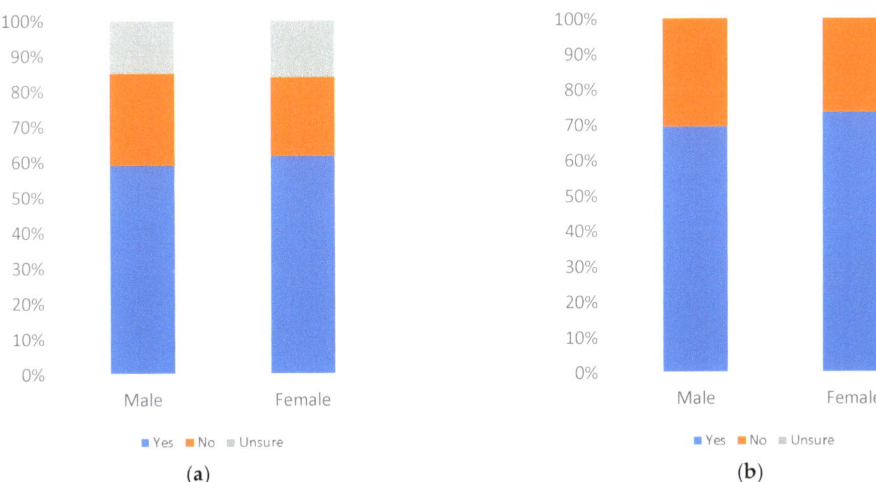

Figure 67. Label trustworthiness judging use, by gender: (**a**) with uncertain respondents (left) and (**b**) without uncertain respondents (right).

By education level, the some high school (no degree) group and doctoral degree group show higher than average uncertainty levels. As a result, while there appears to be a gradual decrease in yes responses, when uncertainty is not included, this becomes a gradual increase (not including doctoral degree holders), when uncertainty is introduced. Only doctoral degree holders have less than 50% yes responses, and then only when uncertainty is included.

By gender, females have a higher percentage of yes responses, while both groups have approximately the same level of uncertainty. Both groups report higher than 50% yes responses, even when uncertainty is included.

The helpfulness of warning label 2 (shown in Figure 68), when it appears underneath a news article that is deemed unsafe, is considered in Figures 69–71. Respondents answer the question "would you find this label helpful?".

M

Trouble at High Speed West Middle School

Figure 68. Warning label 2 [16].

In terms of age, results are relatively consistent, except for drops in yes response levels at the 35–39, 45–49, 60–64 and 65 and older age groups. These drops appear even when uncertainty is considered, though only the 45–49 age group drops below 50% yes response levels. When uncertainty is not included, all age groups exceed 50% yes responses.

By education level, there is a gradual decline in yes responses, as education level increases and a graduate decrease in uncertainty from the some high school (no degree) level up to the associate's degree holders education level. All education levels report a greater than 50% yes response rate, even when uncertainty is included.

By gender, female respondents report higher both a higher number of yes responses and a higher level of uncertainty. Both groups have a greater than 50% yes response rate, even when uncertainty is considered.

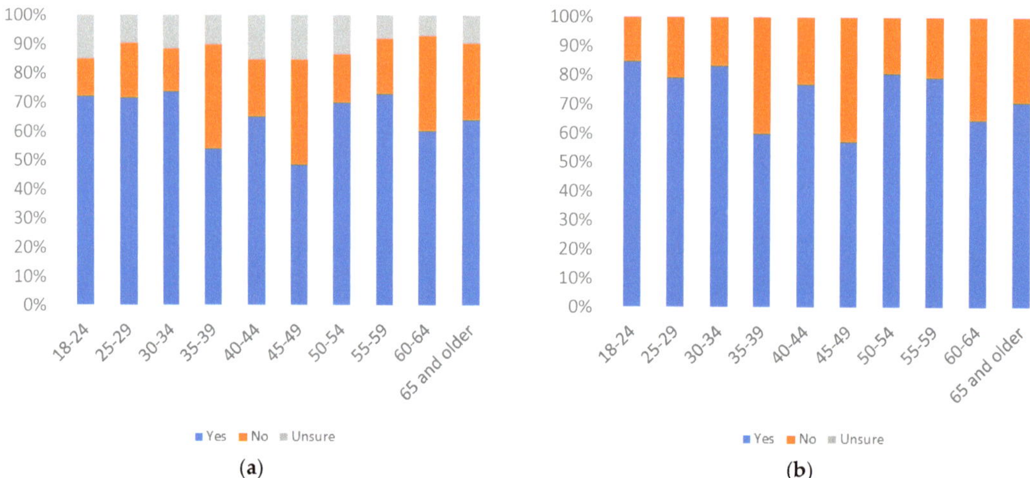

Figure 69. Label helpfulness, by age group: (**a**) with uncertain respondents (left) and (**b**) without uncertain respondents (right).

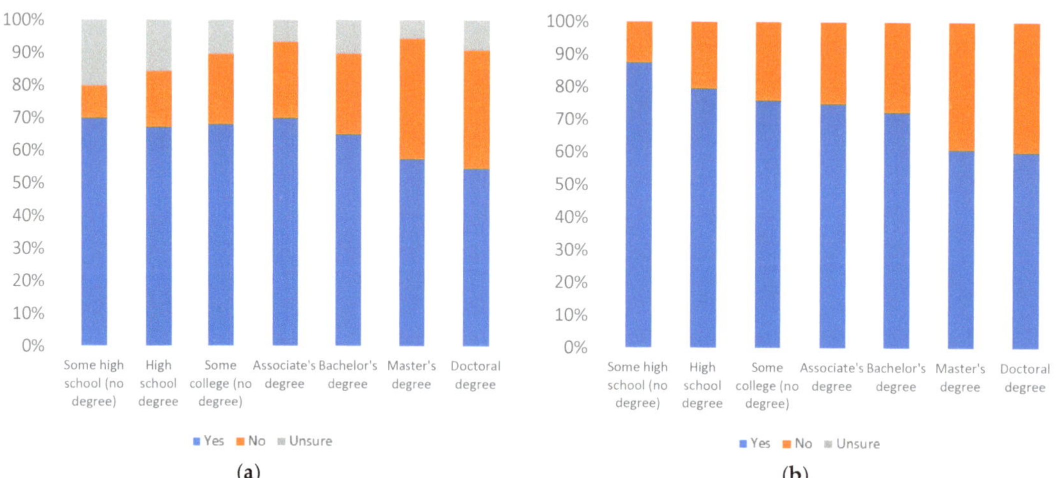

Figure 70. Label helpfulness, by education level: (**a**) with uncertain respondents (left) and (**b**) without uncertain respondents (right).

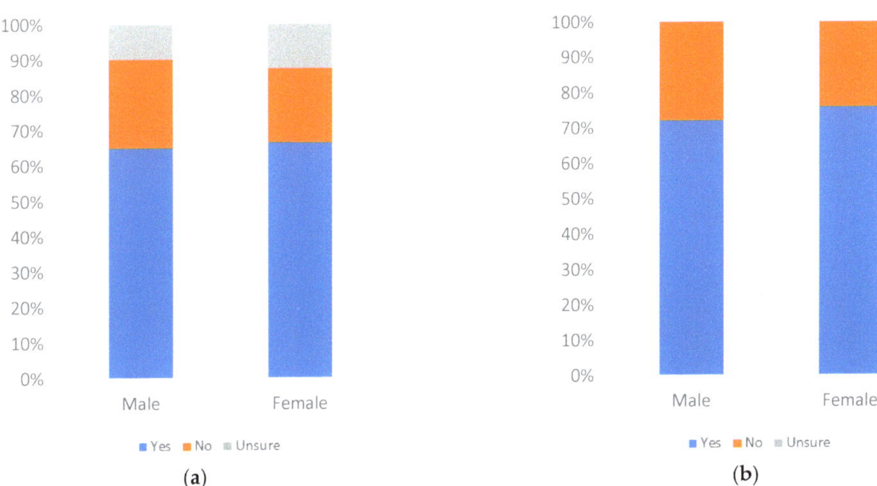

Figure 71. Label helpfulness, by gender: (**a**) with uncertain respondents (left) and (**b**) without uncertain respondents (right).

Figures 72–74 consider the annoyingness of warning label 2, with respondents answering the question "would you find this label annoying?".

In terms of age, there is no apparent general pattern of increase or decrease as age increases. There is a decline from the 18–24 to 35–39 age groups, when uncertainty is not included; however, this decline is less notable, when uncertainty is introduced. There is a spike at the 40–44 age group, a drop at the 50–54 age group, and another spike at the 60–64 age group. All groups report less than 50% yes responses, even when uncertainty is not included, meaning that annoyance is relatively low, across all age groups.

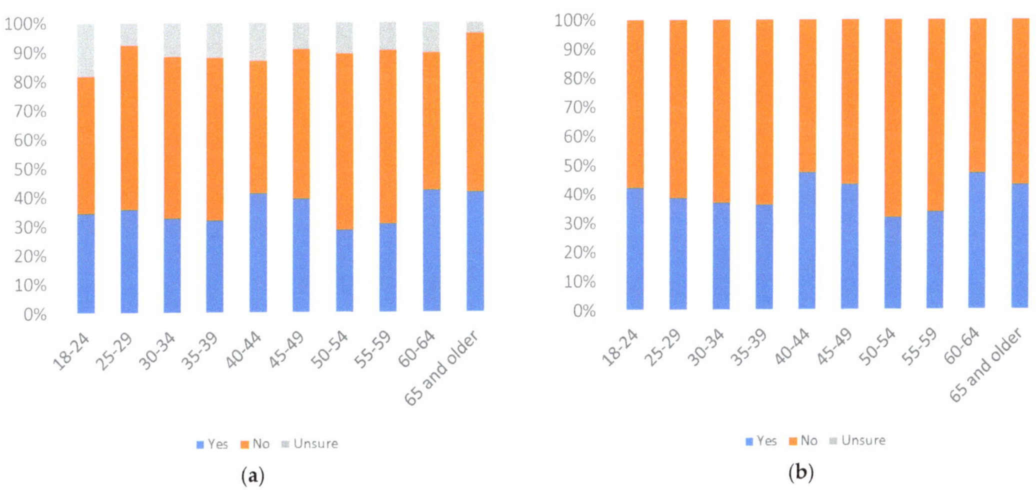

Figure 72. Label annoyingness, by age group: (**a**) with uncertain respondents (left) and (**b**) without uncertain respondents (right).

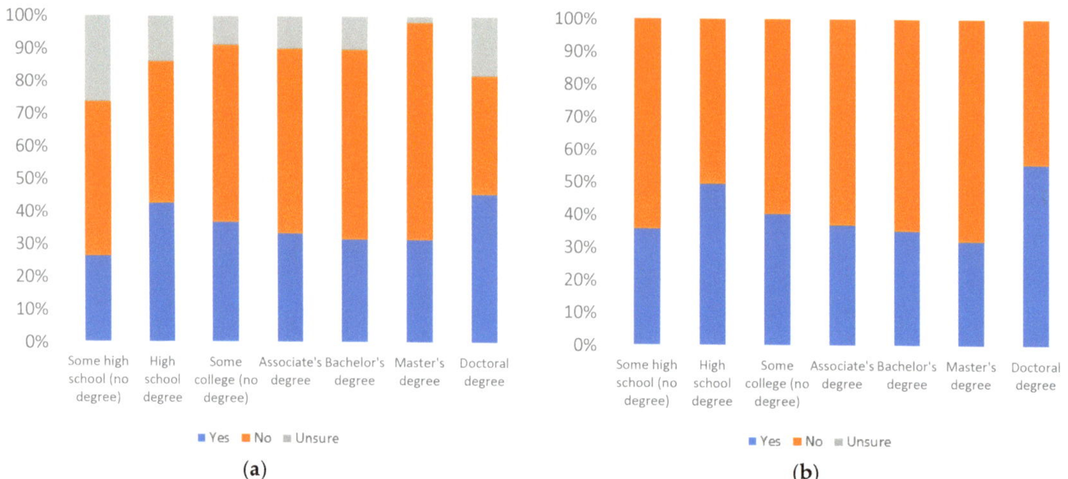

Figure 73. Label annoyingness, by education level: (**a**) with uncertain respondents (left) and (**b**) without uncertain respondents (right).

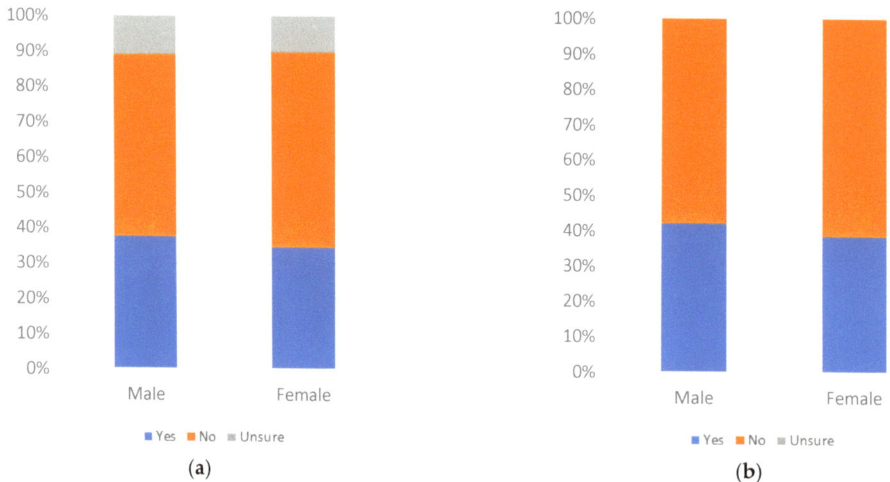

Figure 74. Label annoyingness, by gender: (**a**) with uncertain respondents (left) and (**b**) without uncertain respondents (right).

By education level, there is a decline in yes responses from the high school degree educational level up to master's degree holders, with a drop at the some high school (no degree) level and a spike for doctoral degree holders. Uncertainty is highest for the some high school (no degree) and doctoral degree groups as well. While yes responses remain below 50% for all education groups, when uncertainty is included, doctoral degree holders exceed 50% yes responses, when uncertainty is removed. This indicates a low level of annoyance, across most education levels.

By gender, male respondents report a higher percentage of yes responses and a higher uncertainty level than females. Neither group exceeds 50% yes responses, even when uncertainty is not included, meaning that annoyance is relatively low regardless of gender.

Figures 75–77 consider likelihood of respondents' to personally use warning label 2, with respondents answering the question "would you review this label when viewing news articles on social media?".

In terms of age, there is no apparent general pattern of increase or decrease as age increases. There are sharp drops at the 18–24, 35–39 and 45–49 age groups, even when uncertainty is included; however, no age group drops below 50% yes responses, even considering uncertainty.

By education level, the some high school (no degree) and doctoral degree levels have the highest uncertainty. When uncertainty is not considered, there is a large spike in yes responses for the some high school (no degree) group. Otherwise, the results are relatively consistent across education levels. Yes responses remain at or above 50% for all education levels, even when uncertainty is considered.

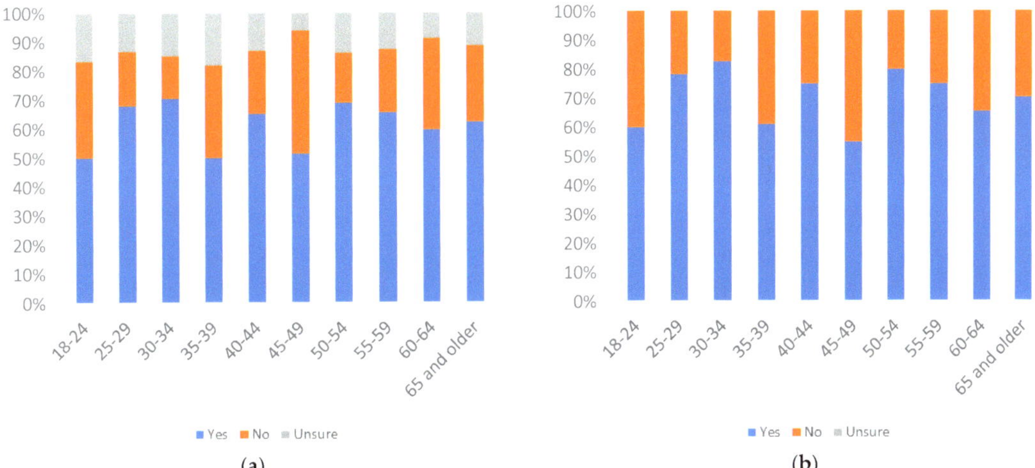

(a)

(b)

Figure 75. Label use, by age group: (**a**) with uncertain respondents (left) and (**b**) without uncertain respondents (right).

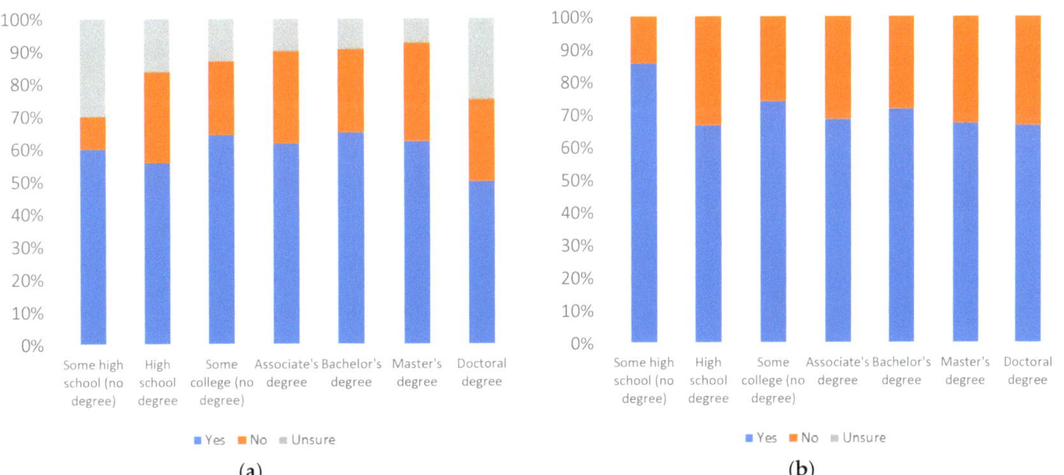

(a)

(b)

Figure 76. Label use, by education level: (**a**) with uncertain respondents (left) and (**b**) without uncertain respondents (right).

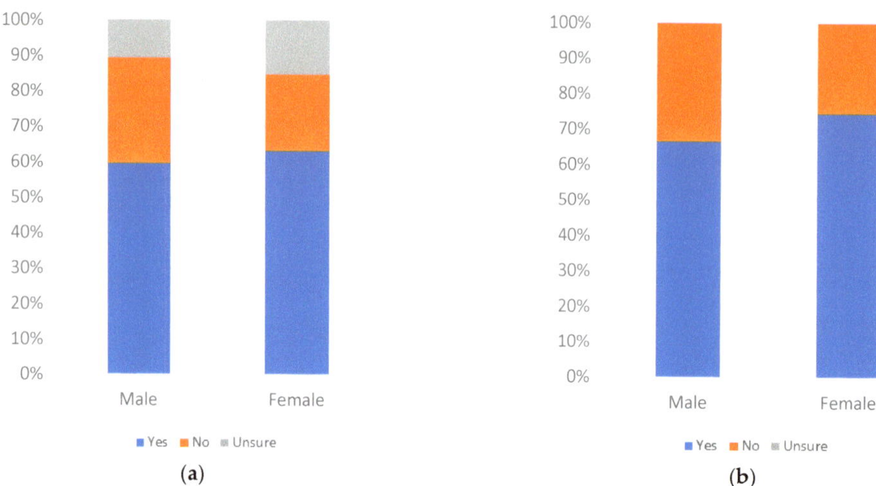

Figure 77. Label use, by gender: (**a**) with uncertain respondents (left) and (**b**) without uncertain respondents (right).

By gender, females report a higher percentage of yes responses and a higher uncertainty level than males. Both groups have over 50% yes responses, even when uncertainty is included.

Figures 78–80 consider respondents' perception of the likelihood of others to use warning label 2, with respondents answering the question "would others review this label when viewing news articles on social media?".

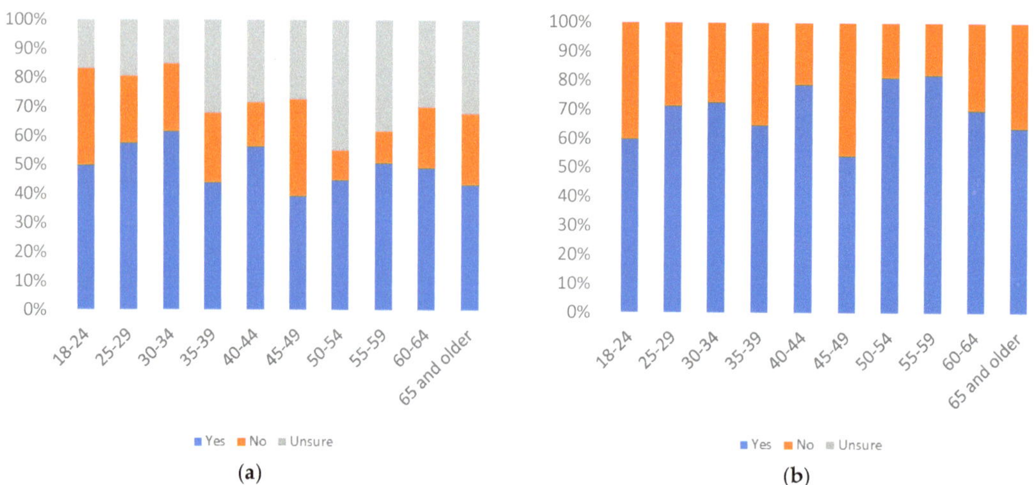

Figure 78. Label others' use, by age group: (**a**) with uncertain respondents (left) and (**b**) without uncertain respondents (right).

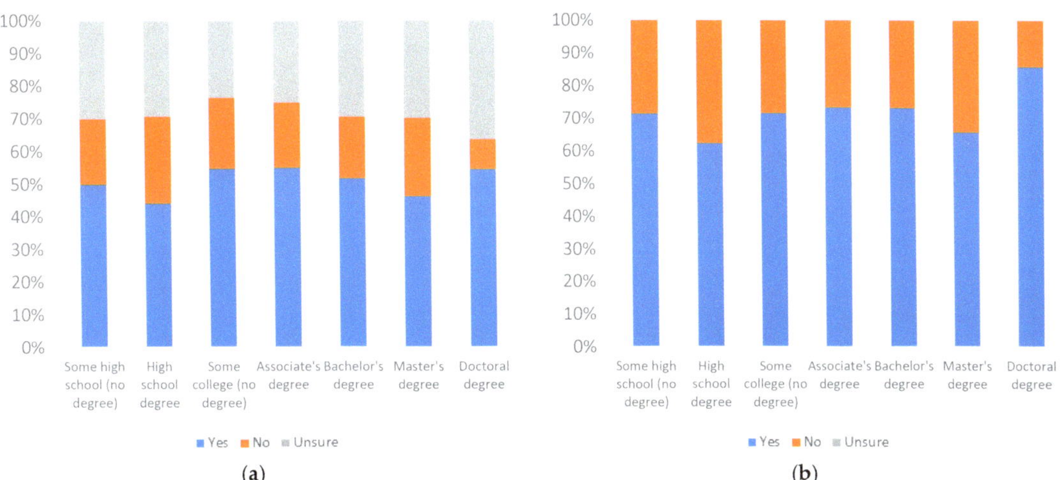

Figure 79. Label others' use, by education level: (**a**) with uncertain respondents (left) and (**b**) without uncertain respondents (right).

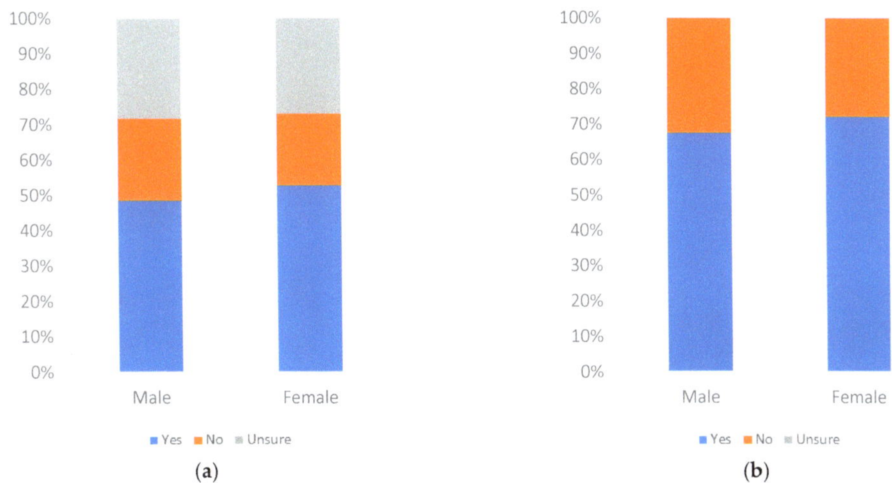

Figure 80. Label others' use, by gender: (**a**) with uncertain respondents (left) and (**b**) without uncertain respondents (right).

In terms of age, there are three peaks in yes responses at the 30–34, 40–44, and 55–59 age groups. These are apparent whether uncertainty is considered or not. The peaks are more gradual, though, when uncertainty is included. There are high levels of uncertainty for the 50–54 and 55–59 age groups, which smooth the curve from the 45–49 to the 65 and older age groups. Uncertainty is relatively high across all age groups. With uncertainty considered, the 35–39, 45–49, 50–54, 60–64 and 65 and older age groups all have below 50% yes responses. When uncertainty is not included, all age groups exceed 50% yes responses, indicating the magnitude of uncertainty present.

By education level, yes responses are relatively consistent, when uncertainty is considered. This is due to an exceptionally high level of uncertainty amongst doctoral degree holders. When uncertainty is omitted, yes responses for doctoral degree holders appear to spike. All education levels other than high school degree and master's degree have at least a 50% yes response rate, even when uncertainty is included. When uncertainty is omitted, all education levels exceed 50% yes responses.

By gender, female respondents report a higher percentage of yes responses, while male respondents report a higher level of uncertainty. Consequently, male respondents fall below 50% yes responses, when uncertainty is included. Both groups exceed 50% yes responses, when uncertainty is ignored.

Figures 81–83 consider the value of warning label 2 for gauging article trustworthiness, with respondents answering the question "would it be useful for judging the trustworthiness of news articles?".

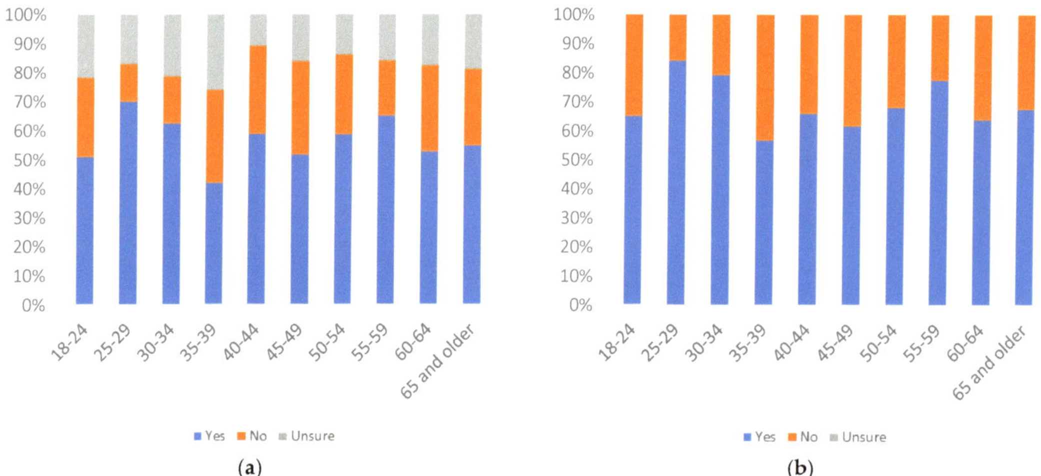

(a) (b)

Figure 81. Label trustworthiness judging use, by age group: (**a**) with uncertain respondents (left) and (**b**) without uncertain respondents (right).

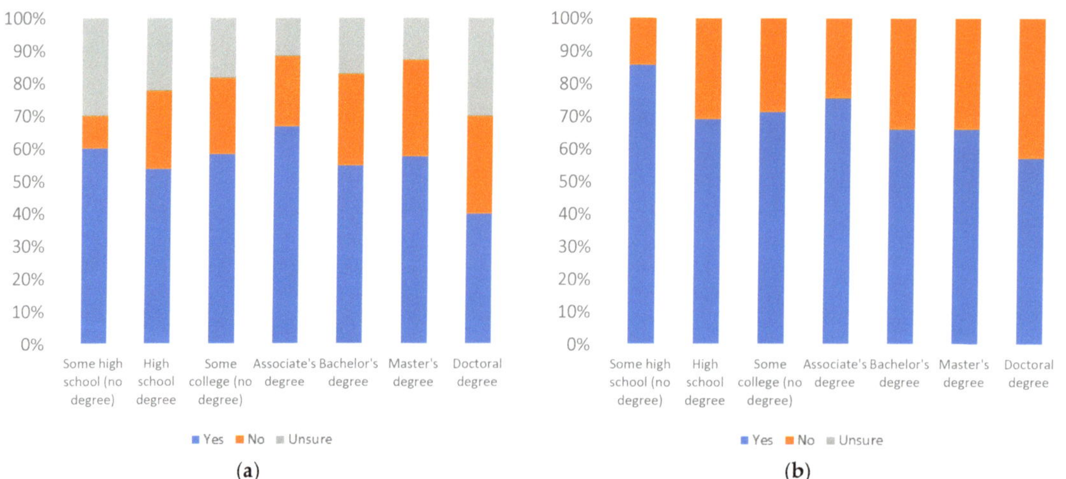

(a) (b)

Figure 82. Label trustworthiness judging use, by education level: (**a**) with uncertain respondents (left) and (**b**) without uncertain respondents (right).

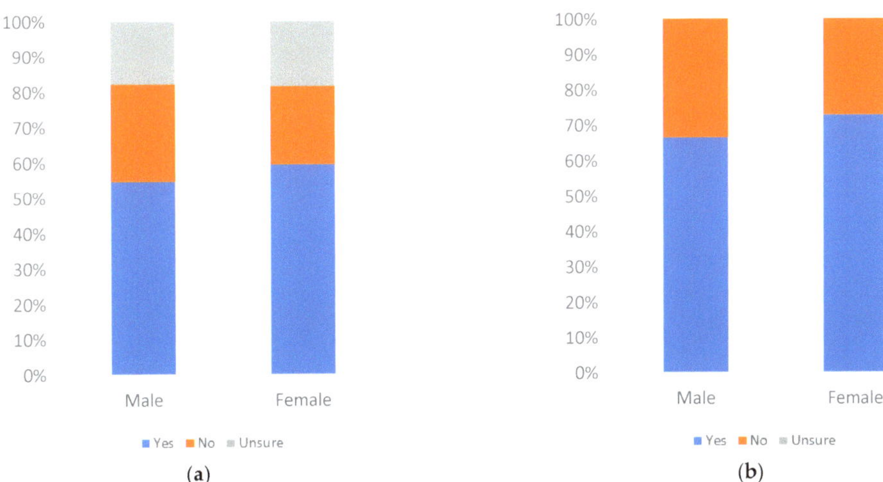

Figure 83. Label trustworthiness judging use, by gender: (**a**) with uncertain respondents (left) and (**b**) without uncertain respondents (right).

In terms of age, there is no apparent pattern of increase or decrease as age increases. The percentage of yes responses drops for the 35–39 age group, while it spikes at the 25–29, 30–34, and 55–59 age groups. Only the 35–39 age group has below 50% yes responses, and this is only when uncertainty is included. Without uncertainty's inclusion, all age groups exceed 50% yes responses.

By education level, there is a general decline in uncertainty from the some high school (no degree) level to the master's degree level, followed by a sharp increase at the doctoral degree level which matches the peak seen at the some high school (no degree) level. Like prior results in this study, it may be inferred that, for most label styles, doctoral degree holders reach a point in their education where they are more likely to question their own beliefs, and that otherwise certainty tends to increase as education level increases. There is a spike in yes responses for the some high school (no degree) group, when uncertainty is not included. Only doctoral degree holders have below 50% yes responses, and then only when uncertainty is included.

By gender, females report a higher percentage of yes responses, while uncertainty levels are similar for both groups. Both groups exceed 50% yes responses, even when uncertainty is included.

The helpfulness of warning label 3 (shown in Figure 84), when it appears after clicking a link to an article but before the article's contents are displayed, is considered in Figures 85–87. Respondents answer the question would you find this label helpful?

In terms of age, there are three waves of decline: from 18–24 to 25–29, from 30–34 to 45–49, and from 50–54 to 65 and older. There is a slight recovery at the 65 and older group, when uncertainty is considered, due to a very low level of uncertainty for that age group. Only the 45–49 age group has below 50% yes responses, and then only when uncertainty is included.

By education level, yes response levels are relatively consistent, when uncertainty is included, other than a drop for doctoral degree holders. Due to a very high level of uncertainty, the some high school (no degree) education level has an apparent spike in the proportion of yes responses, when uncertainty is not considered. Only doctoral degree holders drop below 50% yes responses, and then only when uncertainty is included.

By gender, female respondents are far more likely to report yes despite similar uncertainty levels for both genders. Both genders report above 50% yes responses, even with uncertainty included.

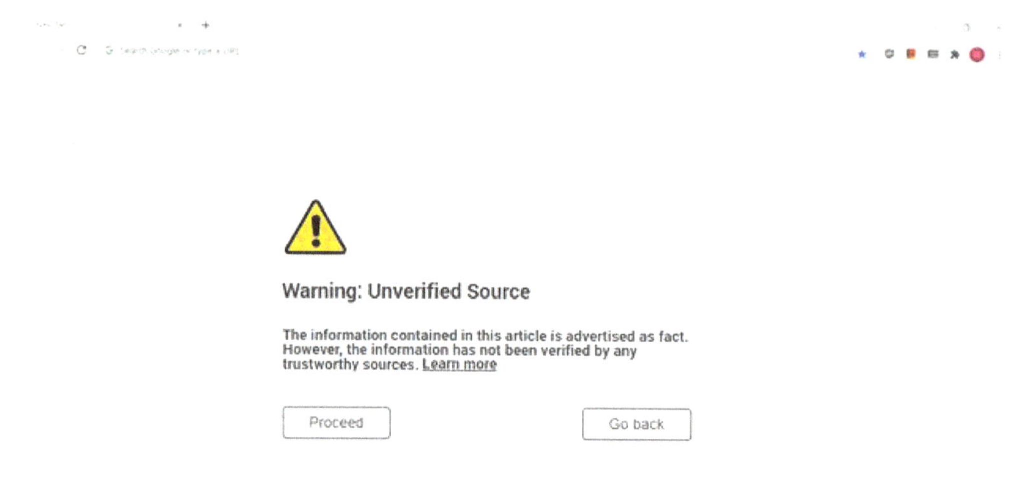

Figure 84. Warning label 3 [16].

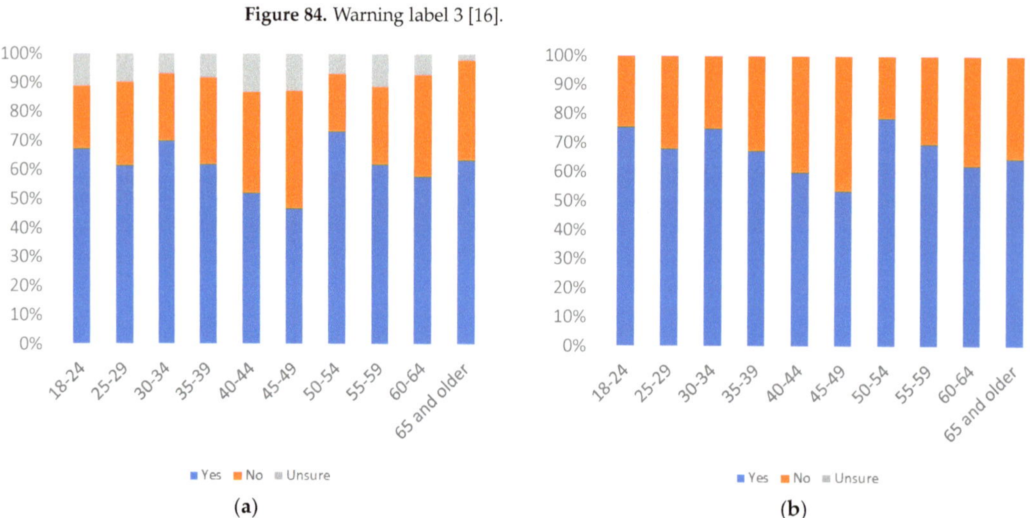

(**a**) (**b**)

Figure 85. Label helpfulness, by age group: (**a**) with uncertain respondents (left) and (**b**) without uncertain respondents (right).

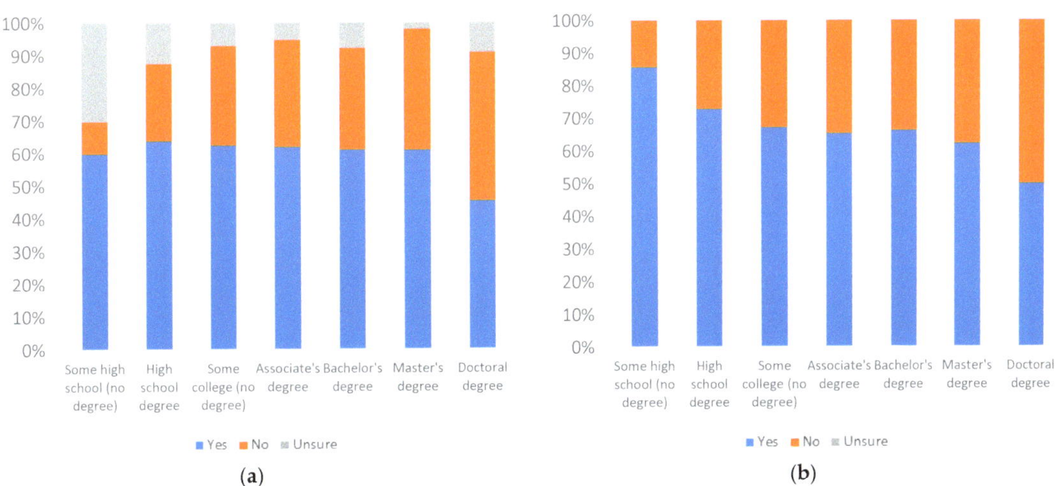

Figure 86. Label helpfulness, by education level: (**a**) with uncertain respondents (left) and (**b**) without uncertain respondents (right).

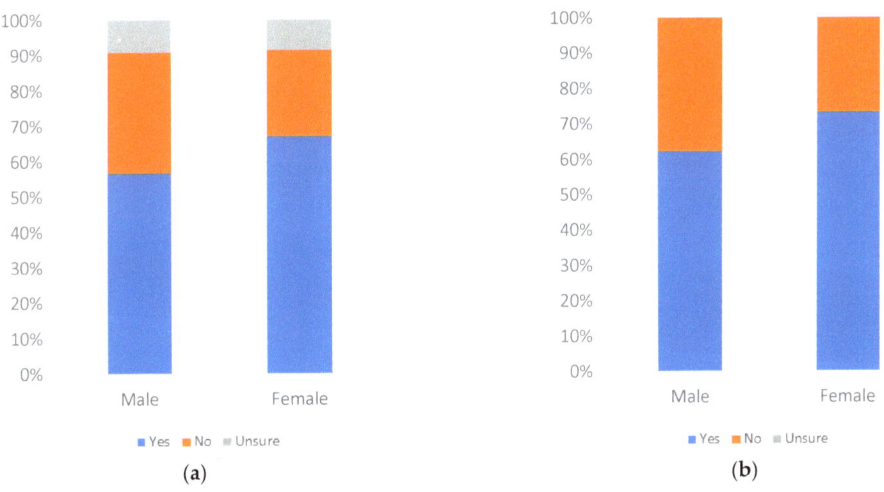

Figure 87. Label helpfulness, by gender: (**a**) with uncertain respondents (left) and (**b**) without uncertain respondents (right).

Figures 88–90 consider annoyingness of warning label 3, with respondents answering the question "would you find this label annoying?".

In terms of age, there is a clear curve peaking at the 40–44 age group, whether uncertainty is included or not. Only the 40–44 and 45–49 age groups exceed 50% yes responses, when uncertainty is included. When uncertainty is not included, only these two groups and the 35–39 age group exceed a 50% yes response level. As such, for most age groups the level of annoyance is relatively low.

By education level, there are two peaks at the some college (no degree) and master's degree levels, whether uncertainty is included or otherwise. Uncertainty peaks at the some high school (no degree) group. All groups have below a 50% yes response level, when uncertainty is included. When uncertainty is not included, only the some college (no degree) group exceeds a 50% proportion of yes responses. This shows that the annoyance level is relatively low, across education levels.

By gender, female and male responses are nearly identical, both in terms of the proportion of yes responses and the level of uncertainty. Both have under 50% yes responses, whether uncertainty is considered or not.

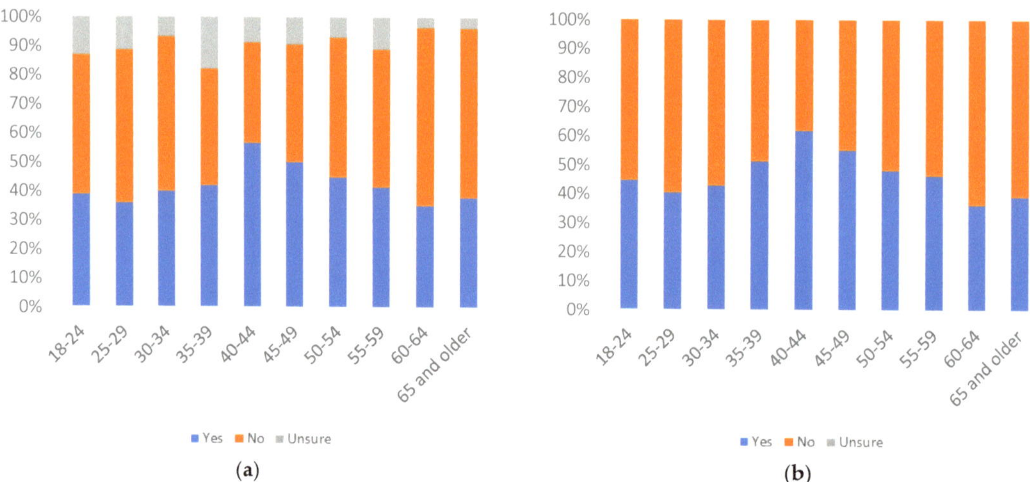

Figure 88. Label annoyingness, by age group: (**a**) with uncertain respondents (left) and (**b**) without uncertain respondents (right).

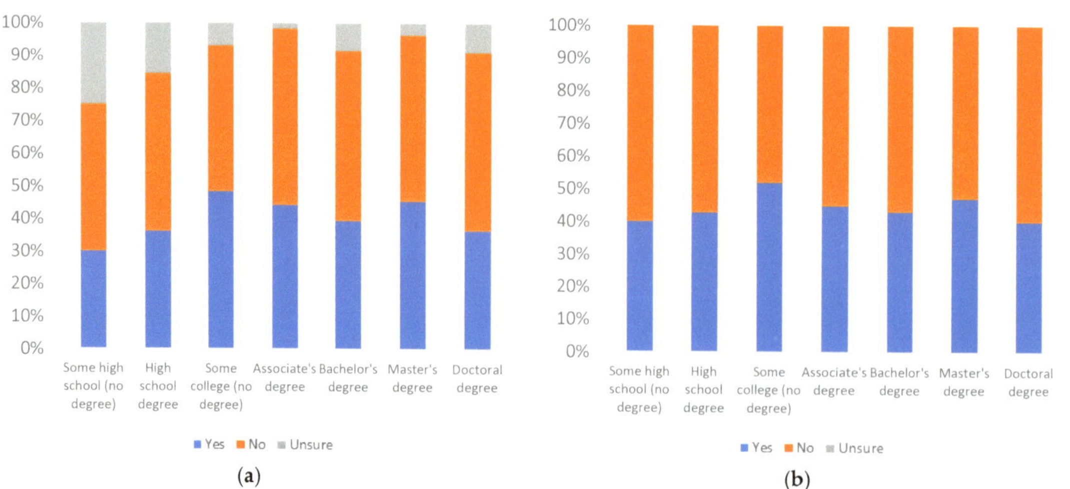

Figure 89. Label annoyingness, by education level: (**a**) with uncertain respondents (left) and (**b**) without uncertain respondents (right).

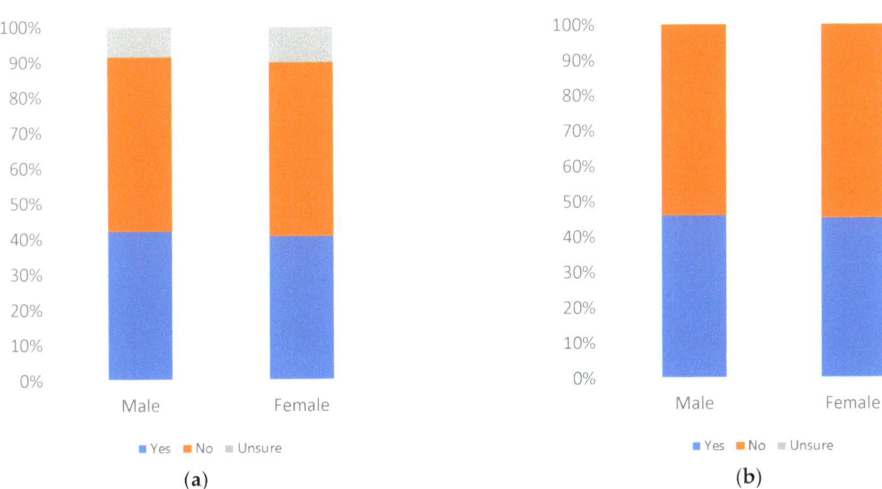

Figure 90. Label annoyingness, by gender: (**a**) with uncertain respondents (left) and (**b**) without uncertain respondents (right).

Figures 91–93 consider likelihood of respondents to personally use warning label 3, with respondents answering the question "would you review this label when viewing news articles on social media?".

In terms of age, there is no clear pattern of increase or decrease in yes responses, as age increases. Uncertainty tends to increase from the 30–34 to 50–54 age groups. It then declines up to the 65 and older age group. There are spikes in yes responses for the 30–34, 40–44, and 50–54 age groups, with a gradual decline from the 50–54 to 65 and older age groups. Only the 35–39 and 45–49 age groups have below 50% yes responses, when uncertainty is included. When uncertainty is not included, the proportion of yes responses remains over 50% for all age groups.

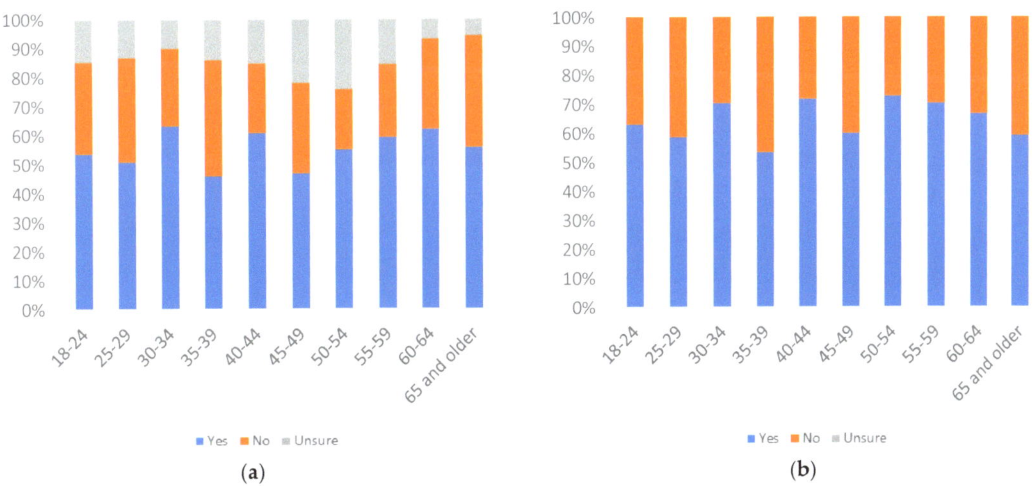

Figure 91. Label use, by age group: (**a**) with uncertain respondents (left) and (**b**) without uncertain respondents (right).

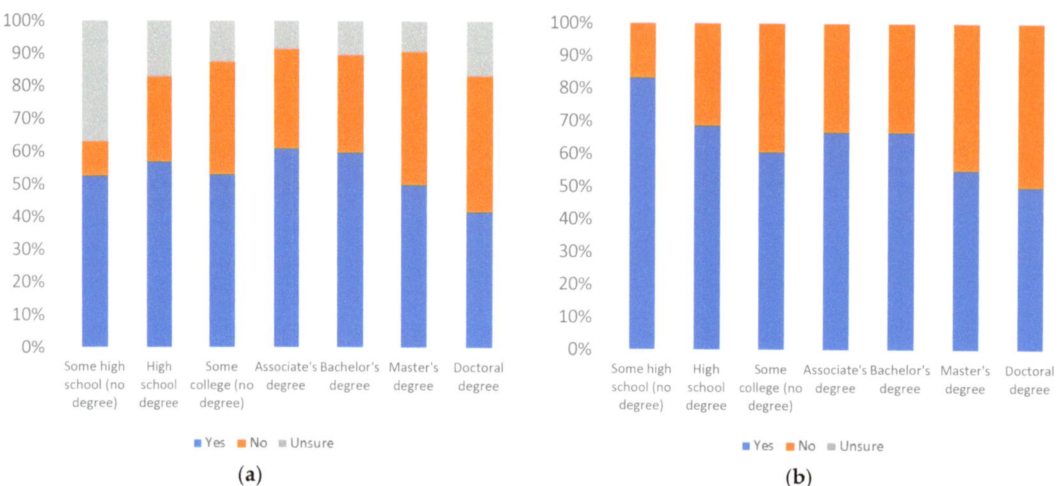

Figure 92. Label use, by education level: (**a**) with uncertain respondents (left) and (**b**) without uncertain respondents (right).

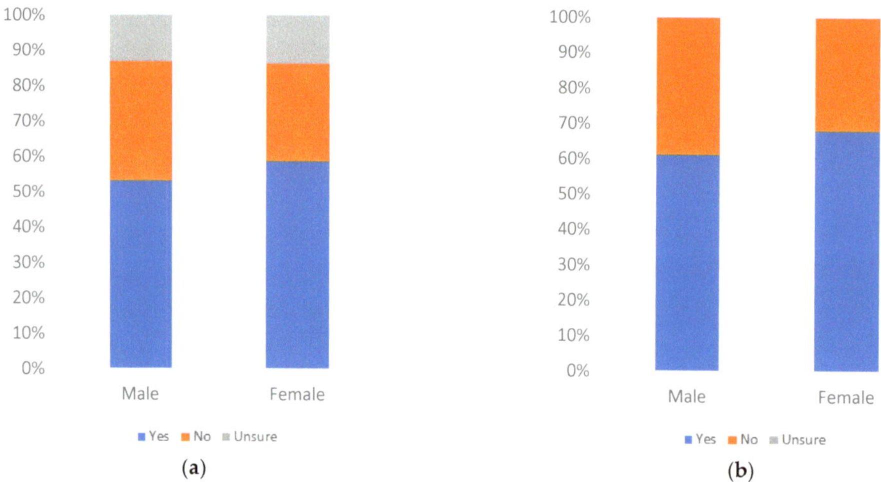

Figure 93. Label use, by gender: (**a**) with uncertain respondents (left) and (**b**) without uncertain respondents (right).

By education level, there results are relatively consistent, when uncertainty is included except for a decline from the bachelor's degree to doctoral degree education levels. There is a spike in the proportion of yes responses for the some high school (no degree) group, when this group's high level of uncertainty is included. Only the doctoral degree holders have below 50% yes responses, and then only when uncertainty is included.

By gender, there are more yes responses among females, while uncertainty remains similar for both groups. Both groups have above 50% yes responses, even when uncertainty is included.

Figures 94–96 consider respondents' perception of the likelihood of others to use warning label 3, with respondents answering the question "would others review this label when viewing news articles on social media?".

In terms of age, there is no clear pattern of consistent increase or decrease in yes responses, as age increases. Uncertainty tends to decrease as age increases, with sharp spikes in uncertainty at the 35–39 and 50–54 age groups. Despite the similarly in uncertainty levels, the 35–39 age group shows a sharp drop in the proportion of yes responses, relative to most age groups, while the 50–54 age group shows a sharp increase. Another sharp drop in yes responses is seen at the 18–24 age group. Uncertainty levels are relatively high across all age groups. When uncertainty is included, only a subset of age groups (25–29, 30–34, 40–44, 50–54, and 60–64) have at least 50% yes responses. When uncertainty is removed, only the 18–25 age group has a proportion of yes responses below 50%.

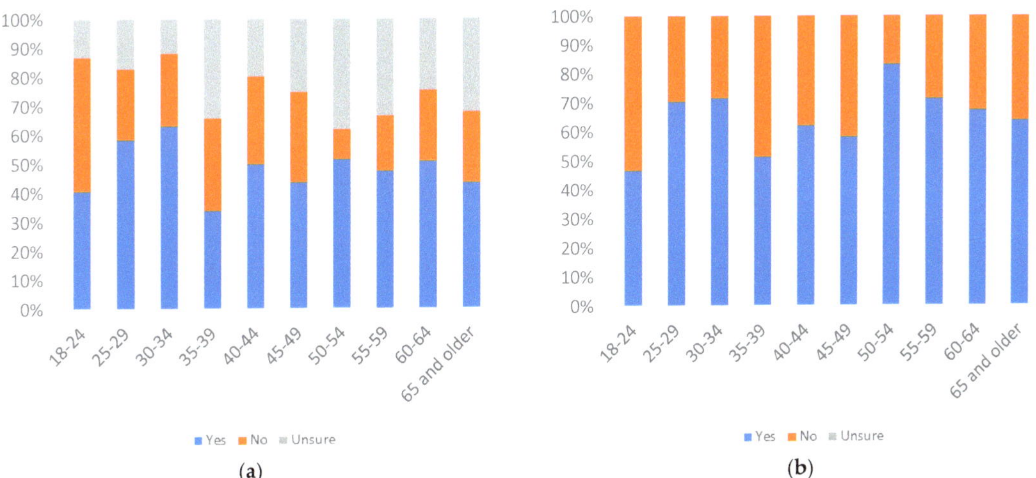

Figure 94. Label others' use, by age group: (**a**) with uncertain respondents (left) and (**b**) without uncertain respondents (right).

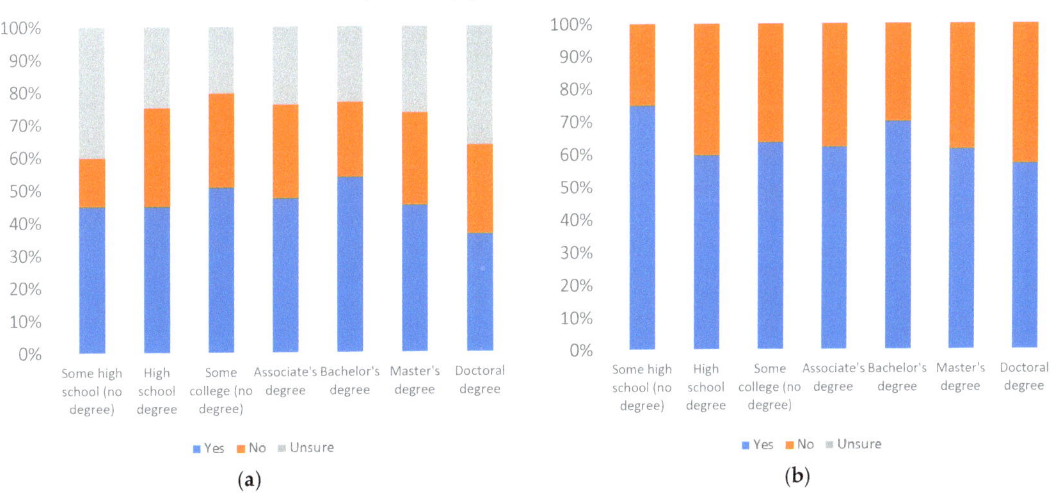

Figure 95. Label others' use, by education level: (**a**) with uncertain respondents (left) and (**b**) without uncertain respondents (right).

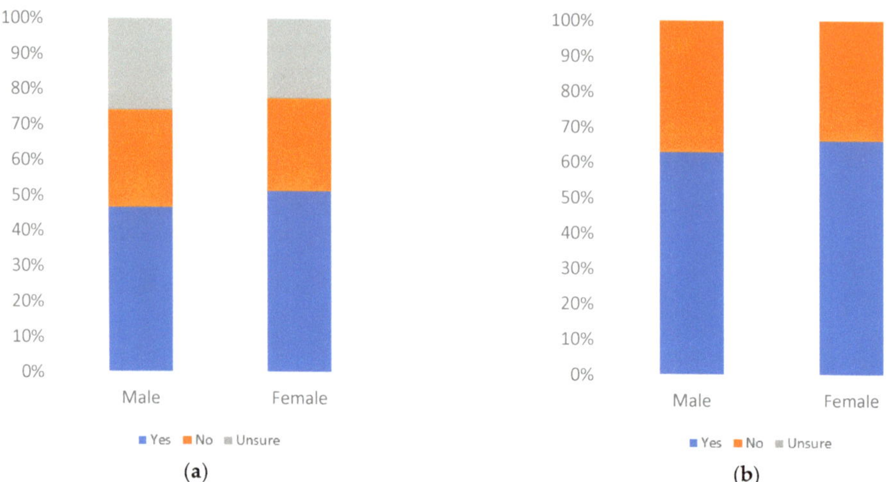

Figure 96. Label others' use, by gender: (**a**) with uncertain respondents (left) and (**b**) without uncertain respondents (right).

By education level, there is a slight peak in support at the bachelor's degree level, when uncertainty is included. Uncertainty is at its highest for the some high school (no degree) and doctoral degree groups. The some high school (no degree) group has an apparent spike in the proportion of yes responses, when uncertainty is omitted. With uncertainty included, only the some college (no degree) and bachelor's degree education groups have at least 50% yes responses. When uncertainty is removed, all groups exceed a 50% proportion of yes responses.

By gender, there are more yes responses among females and slightly greater uncertainty among males. Males report less than 50% yes responses, when uncertainty is included. Both groups exceed a 50% proportion of yes responses, when uncertainty is removed.

Figures 97–99 consider the value of warning label 3 for gauging articles' trustworthiness, with respondents answering the question "would it be useful for judging the trustworthiness of news articles?".

In terms of age, there are three peaks in yes responses: at the 25–29, 40–44, and 50–54 age groups. The 35–39 age group has a particularly pronounced drop in yes responses, in addition to a higher-than-average level of uncertainty. Only the 35–39 and 45–49 age groups have below 50% yes responses, when uncertainty is included. Only the 35–39 age group has a proportion of yes responses below 50%, when uncertainty is not considered.

By education level, results are relatively consistent, with a drop in yes responses for doctoral degree holders. The some high school (no degree) group has a higher proportion of yes responses, when uncertainty is not considered. The some high school (no degree) and doctoral degree groups have the highest uncertainty levels. With uncertainty considered, only these two groups have below 50% yes responses. Without uncertainty, the proportion of yes responses is at or above 50% for all education levels.

By gender, females have a higher percentage of "yes" responses, while uncertainty levels are similar for both groups. Both groups have a percentage of yes responses at or above 50%, even when uncertainty is included.

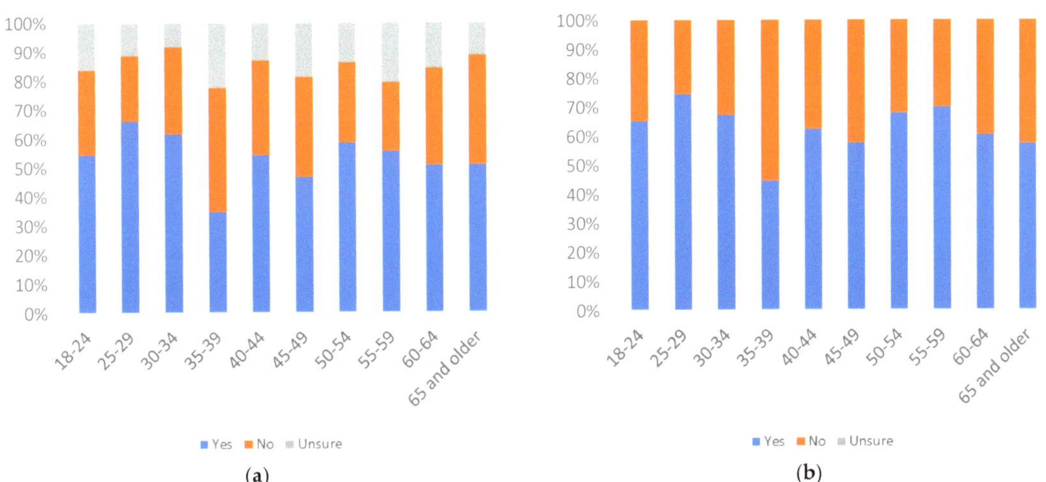

Figure 97. Label trustworthiness judging use, by age group: (**a**) with uncertain respondents (left) and (**b**) without uncertain respondents (right).

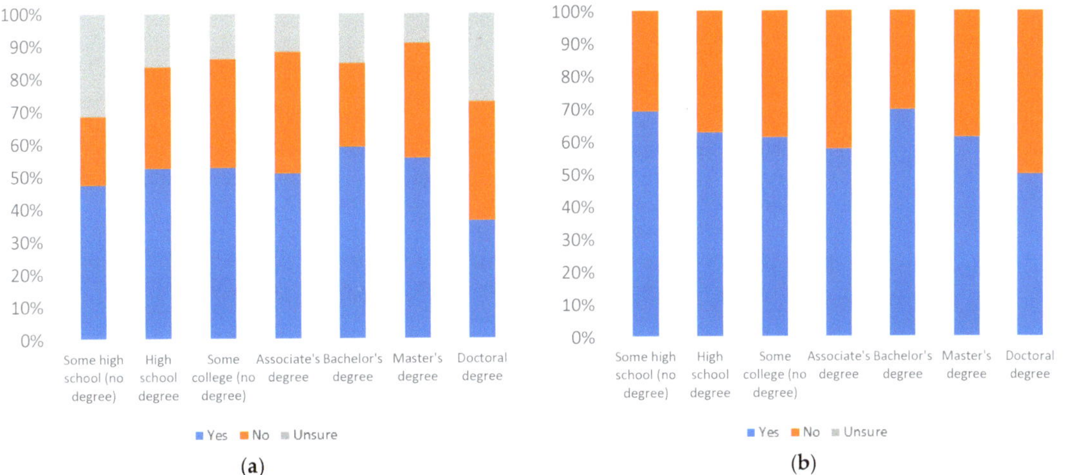

Figure 98. Label trustworthiness judging use, by education level: (**a**) with uncertain respondents (left) and (**b**) without uncertain respondents (right).

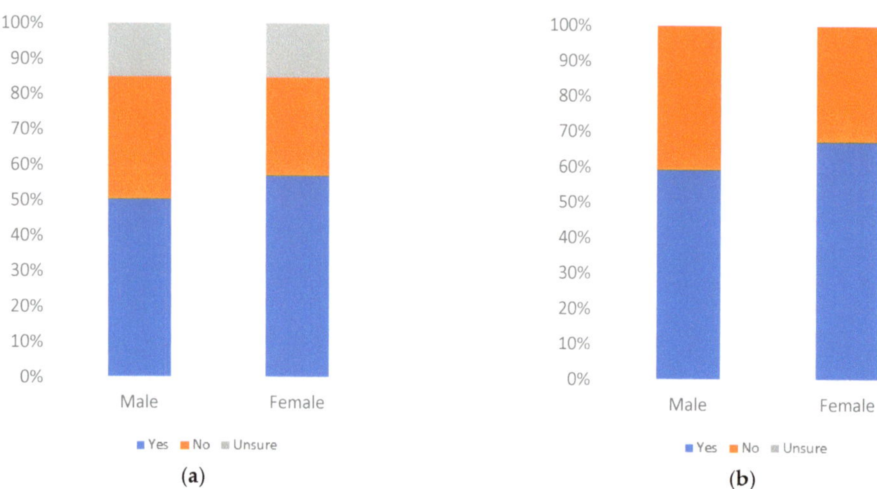

Figure 99. Label trustworthiness judging use, by gender: (**a**) with uncertain respondents (left) and (**b**) without uncertain respondents (right).

6. Supplemental Information Label Related Data and Analysis

Finally, a third type of labels—supplemental information labels—are considered. These labels provide additional details about the content of a page and a link to a location where more details can be obtained from a trusted news source. Again, respondents were asked about the helpfulness, annoyingness, whether they would use the label, whether they thought others would use the label and whether they thought the label would be helpful for assessing articles' trustworthiness. Respondents' answers to these questions were analyzed in terms of their age, education level and gender in this section.

The helpfulness of the supplemental information label (shown in Figure 100), when it is appended to any article, regardless of its accuracy, is considered in Figures 101–103. Respondents answered the question "would you find this label helpful?".

M

Trouble at High Speed West Middle School

High Speed West Middle School in deadlock due to boys refusing to say the word "hello", opting only to refer to people as "Gamers."
1 week ago

This article makes claims regarding High Speed West Middle School's bylaws. High Speed West Middle School's website has the complete school bylaws publicly available.

LEARN MORE

Figure 100. Supplemental information label [16].

In terms of age, there are two clear curves, with the larger curve peaking at the 30–34 age group and the smaller curve peaking at the 50–54 and 55–59 age groups. Uncertainty levels show no clear pattern, as age increases. It reaches its the highest level at the

40–44 age group and is at the 50–54 age group. The 40–44 and 45–49 age groups have under 50% yes responses, when uncertainty is included. All groups exceed a 50% proportion of yes responses, when uncertainty is not included.

By education level, yes responses remain relatively consistent with a slight spike at the associate's degree level and a decline at the doctoral degree level. Uncertainty spikes for the some high school (no degree) education level, though all groups have at least a 50% level of yes responses, even when uncertainty is included.

By gender, there is a significantly higher level of yes responses for female responses, as well as a slightly higher level of uncertainty. Both groups have over 50% yes responses, even when considering uncertainty.

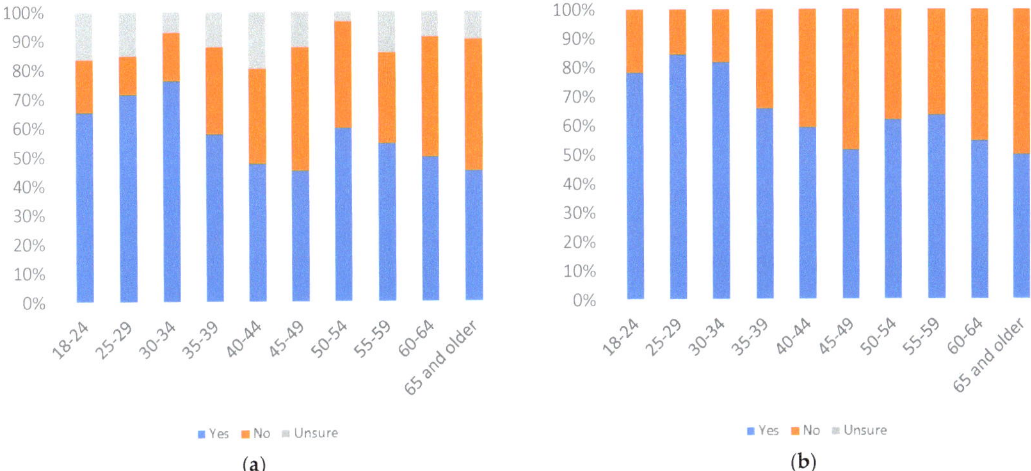

Figure 101. Label helpfulness, by age group: (**a**) with uncertain respondents (left) and (**b**) without uncertain respondents (right).

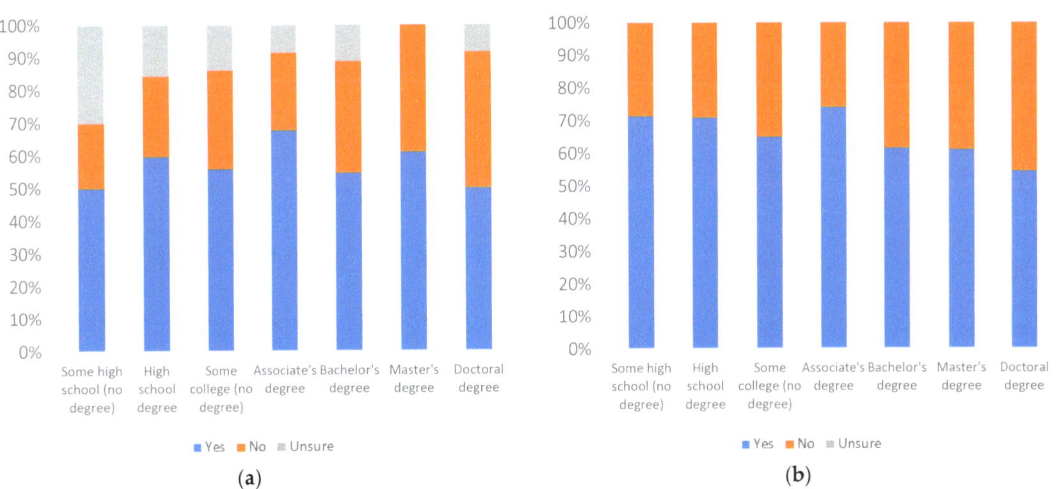

Figure 102. Label helpfulness, by education level: (**a**) with uncertain respondents (left) and (**b**) without uncertain respondents (right).

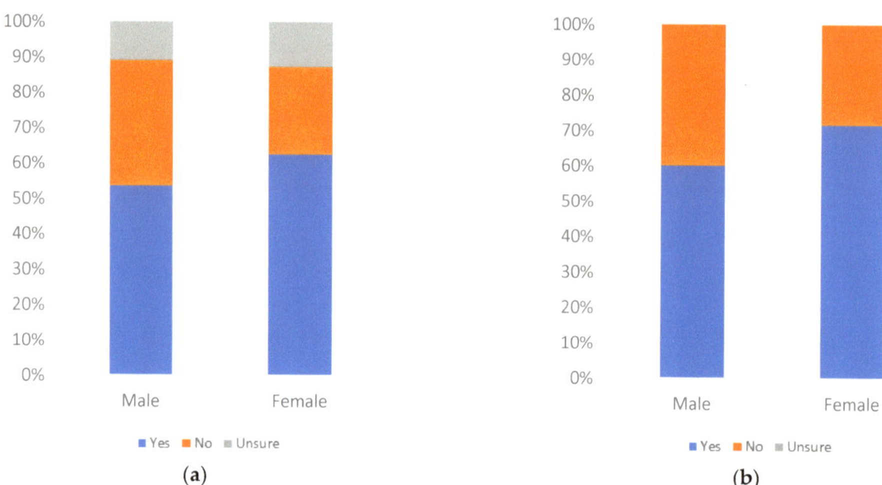

Figure 103. Label helpfulness, by gender: (**a**) with uncertain respondents (left) and (**b**) without uncertain respondents (right).

Figures 104–106 consider the annoyingness of the supplemental information label, with respondents answering the question "would you find this label annoying?".

In terms of age, there is a peak at the 40–44 age group followed by a decline and consistency, at higher age groups. Uncertainty is particularly low for the 30–34 and 50–54 age groups, while uncertainty is highest for the 18–24 and 55–59 age groups. Only the 40–44 age group exceeds 50% yes responses, with uncertainty included. The proportion of yes responses also reaches 50% for the 55–59 age group, when uncertainty is excluded. This demonstrates that the level of annoyance is low across most age groups.

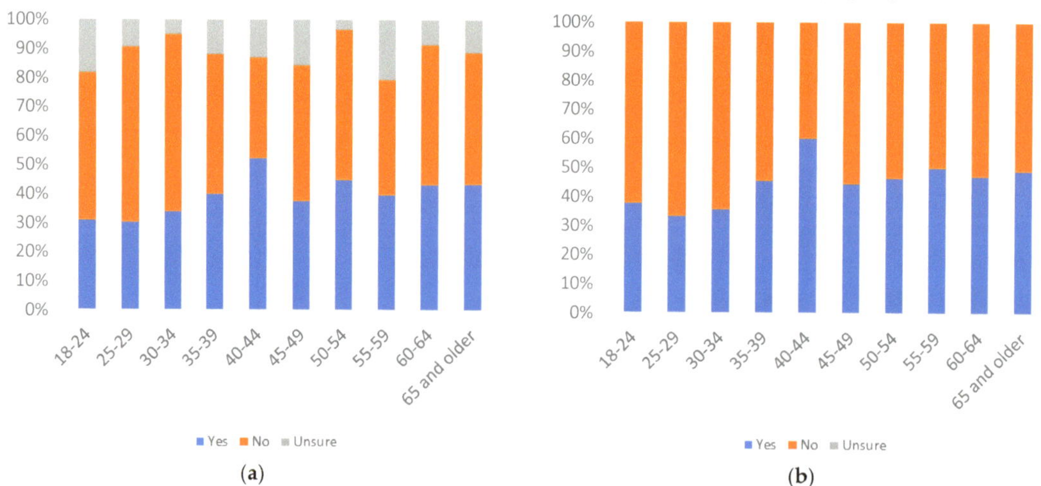

Figure 104. Label annoyingness, by age group: (**a**) with uncertain respondents (left) and (**b**) without uncertain respondents (right).

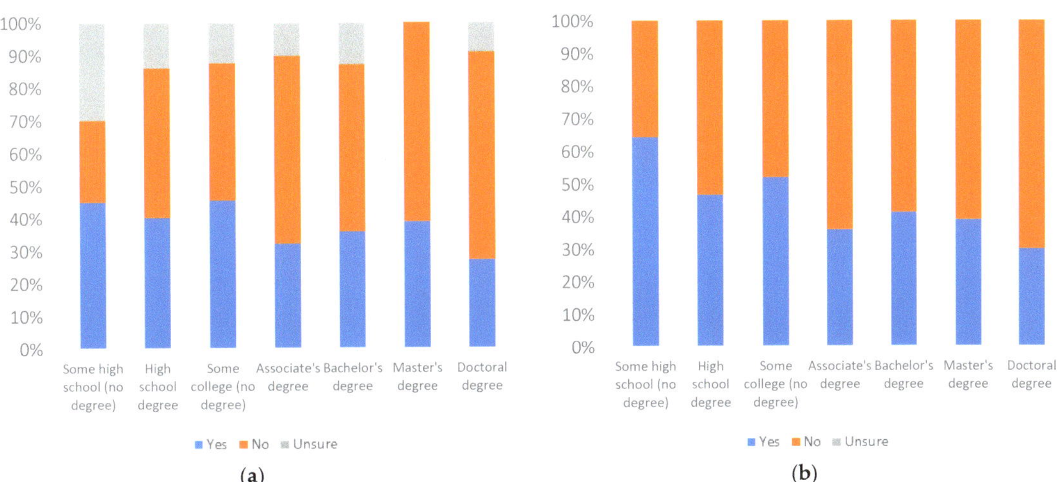

Figure 105. Label annoyingness, by education level: (**a**) with uncertain respondents (left) and (**b**) without uncertain respondents (right).

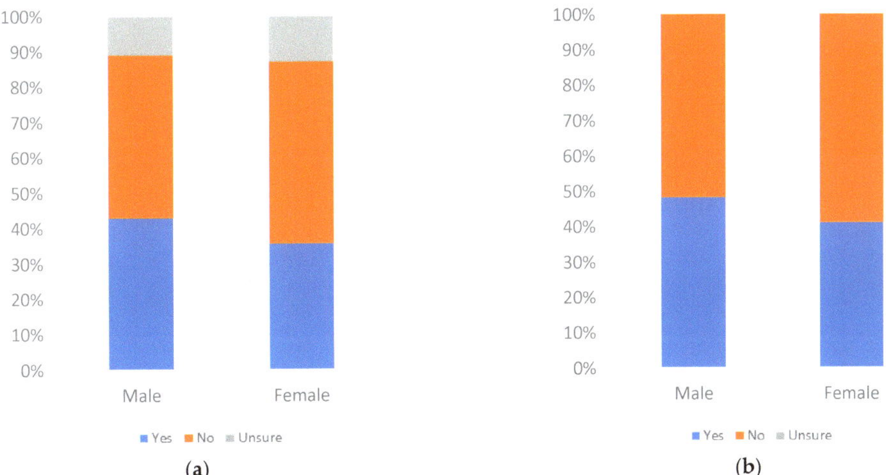

Figure 106. Label annoyingness, by gender: (**a**) with uncertain respondents (left) and (**b**) without uncertain respondents (right).

By education level, there is a gradual decline in yes responses, as education level increases. There is a spike at the some college (no degree) group. As with most prior questions, the some high school (no degree) group shows the highest level of uncertainty. Interestingly, the master's degree group reports 0% uncertainty. No group reaches the threshold of 50% yes responses, when uncertainty is considered. When uncertainty is removed, only the some high school (no degree) and some college (no degree) groups exceed a 50% proportion of yes responses. This indicates a low level of annoyance across most education levels.

By gender, males have a higher percentage of yes responses, while females have a slightly higher level of uncertainty. Neither group exceeds 50% yes responses, even when uncertainty is not included.

Figures 107–109 consider respondents' likelihood to personally use the supplemental information label, with respondents answering the question "would you review this label when viewing news articles on social media?".

In terms of age, there is a clear curve with yes responses peaking at the 30–34 age group. This group also has the lowest level of uncertainty. When uncertainty is considered, four groups fail to reach the 50% threshold for yes responses: 18–24, 45–49, 55–59, and 65 and older. Without uncertainty, only the 65 and older age group falls below a 50% proportion of yes responses.

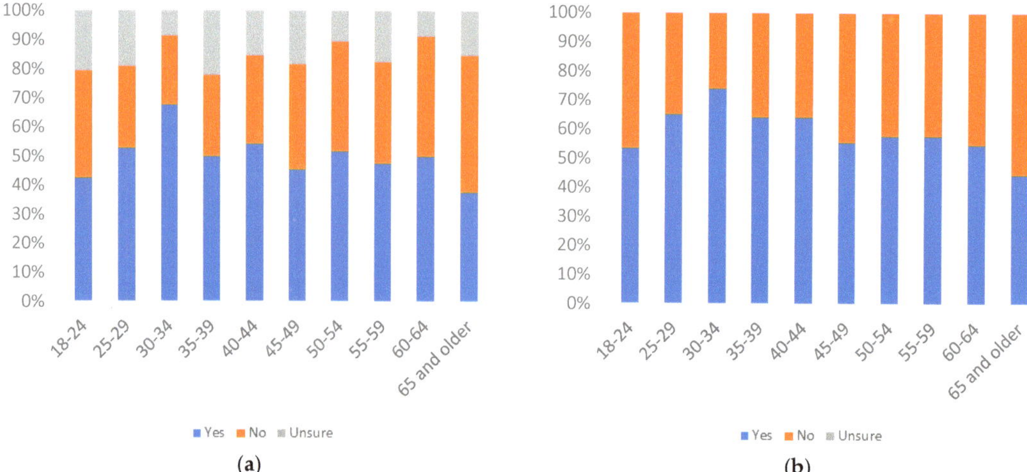

Figure 107. Label use, by age group: (**a**) with uncertain respondents (left) and (**b**) without uncertain respondents (right).

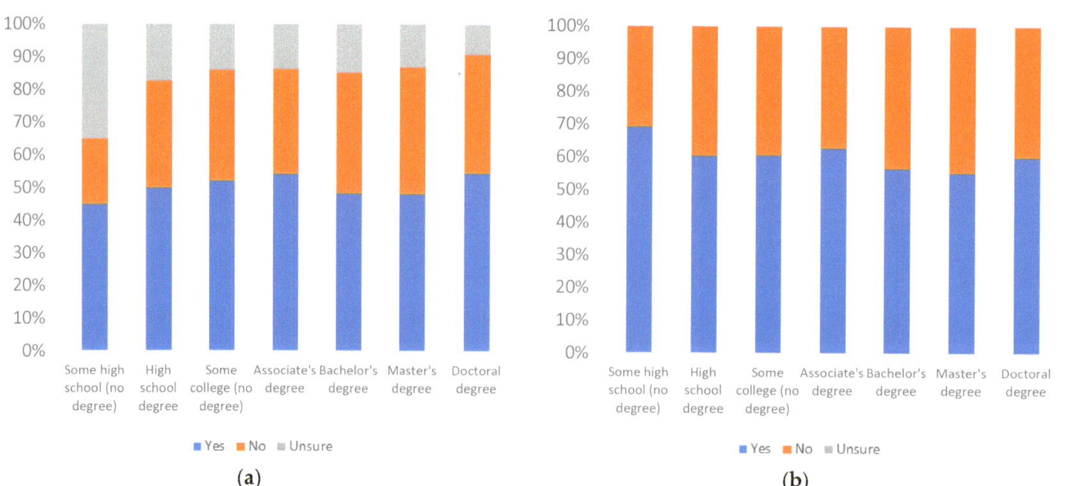

Figure 108. Label use, by education level: (**a**) with uncertain respondents (left) and (**b**) without uncertain respondents (right).

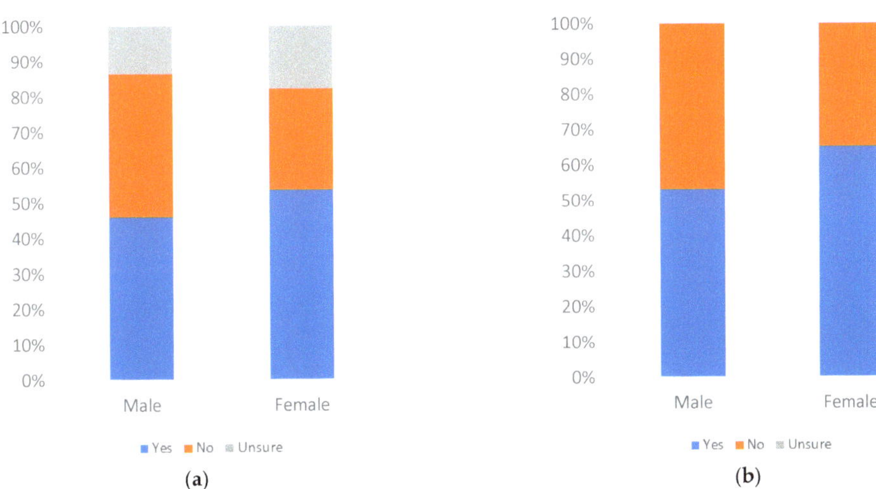

Figure 109. Label use, by gender: (**a**) with uncertain respondents (left) and (**b**) without uncertain respondents (right).

Responses are relatively flat across education levels, though uncertainty is again highest for the some high school (no degree) group. Three groups (some high school (no degree), bachelor's degree, and master's degree) have below a 50% yes response level, when uncertainty is included. When uncertainty is excluded, all educational levels exceed a 50% proportion of yes responses.

By gender, females respond yes more frequently than males, in addition to reporting a higher level of uncertainty. The male respondents have below 50% yes responses, when uncertainty is included. Both groups exceed a 50% proportion of yes responses, when uncertainty is not considered.

Figures 110–112 consider respondents' perception of the likelihood of others to use the supplemental information label, with respondents answering the question "would others review this label when viewing news articles on social media?".

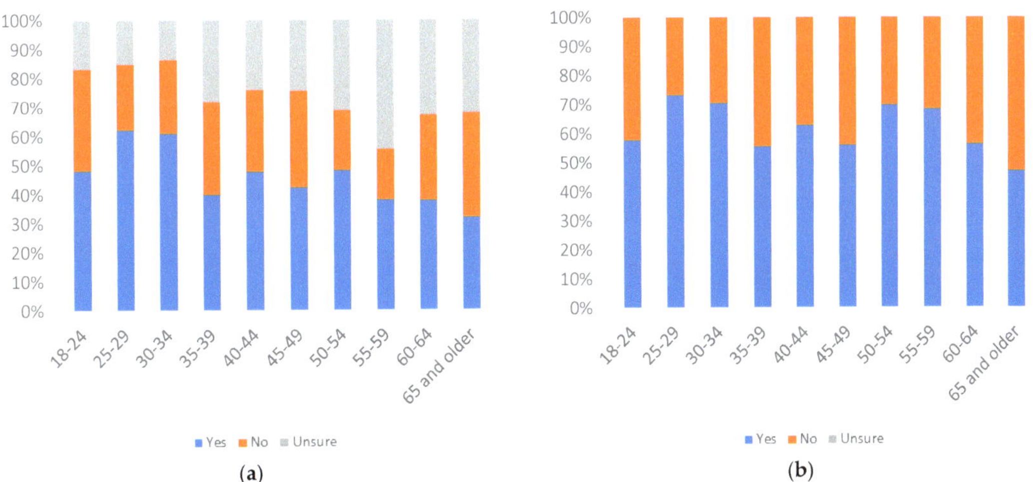

Figure 110. Label others' use, by age group: (**a**) with uncertain respondents (left) and (**b**) without uncertain respondents (right).

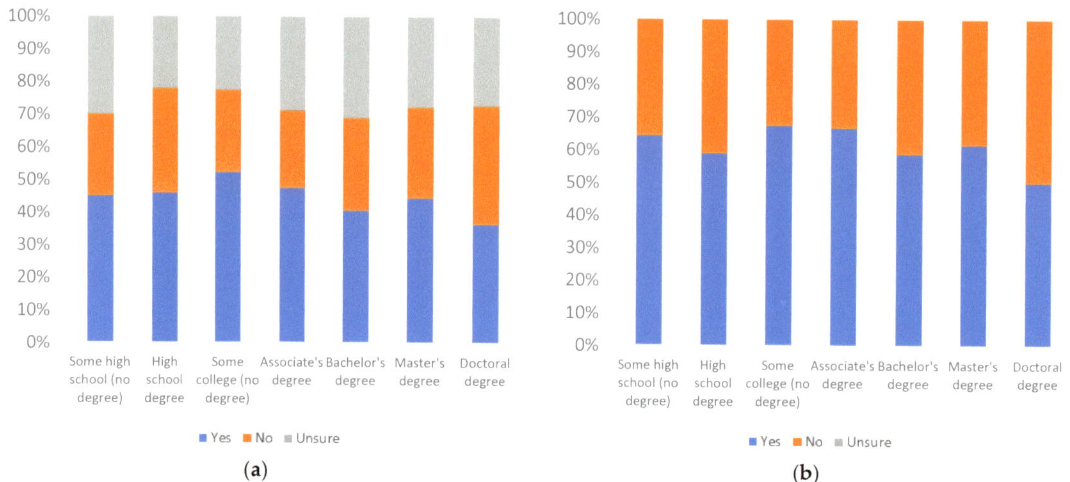

Figure 111. Label others' use, by education level: (**a**) with uncertain respondents (left) and (**b**) without uncertain respondents (right).

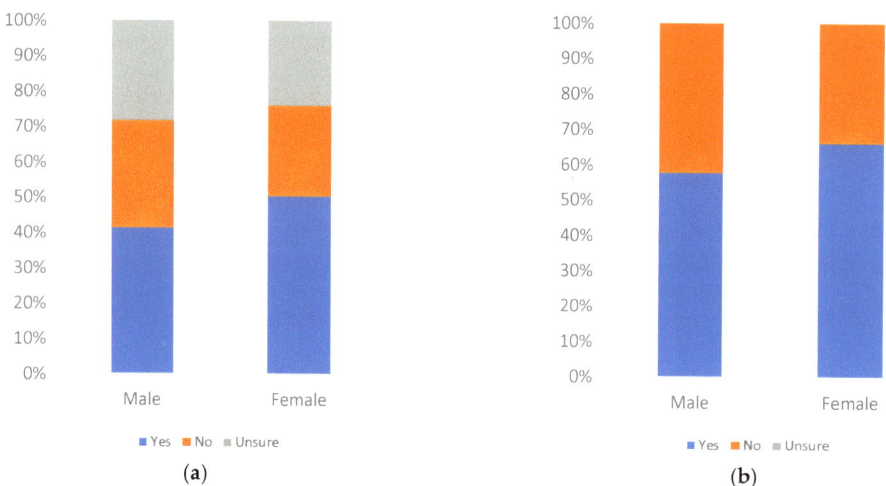

Figure 112. Label others' use, by gender: (**a**) with uncertain respondents (left) and (**b**) without uncertain respondents (right).

In terms of age, there are spikes at three age groups, when uncertainty is included: the 25–29 and 30–34 age groups (jointly forming one peak), the 40–44 age group, and the 50–54 age group. These same peaks exist when uncertainty is removed, though the 55–59 age group also shows a peak in this case, due to it's higher-than-average uncertainty. In general, uncertainty across all groups is relatively high for this question. Consequently, while only two groups (25–29 and 30–34) exceed 50% yes responses when considering uncertainty, all groups—other than the 65 and older age group—exceed a 50% proportion of yes responses, when uncertainty is excluded.

Responses are relatively consistent across education levels, with the lowest point at the doctoral degree level. Unlike most other questions, where the some high school (no degree) and doctoral degree education levels are frequently the high points for uncertainty, on this question uncertainty is relatively consistent (but pronounced) across all education levels.

Only the some college (no degree) group exceeds 50% yes responses, when uncertainty is included. All groups have at least a 50% proportion of yes responses, when uncertainty is removed.

By gender, females more frequently respond with yes than males, while males report a higher level of uncertainty. Males have below 50% yes responses when uncertainty is included. Both gender groups exceed a 50% proportion of yes responses, when uncertainty is eliminated.

Figures 113–115 consider the value of the supplemental information label for gauging article trustworthiness, with respondents answering the question "would it be useful for judging the trustworthiness of news articles?".

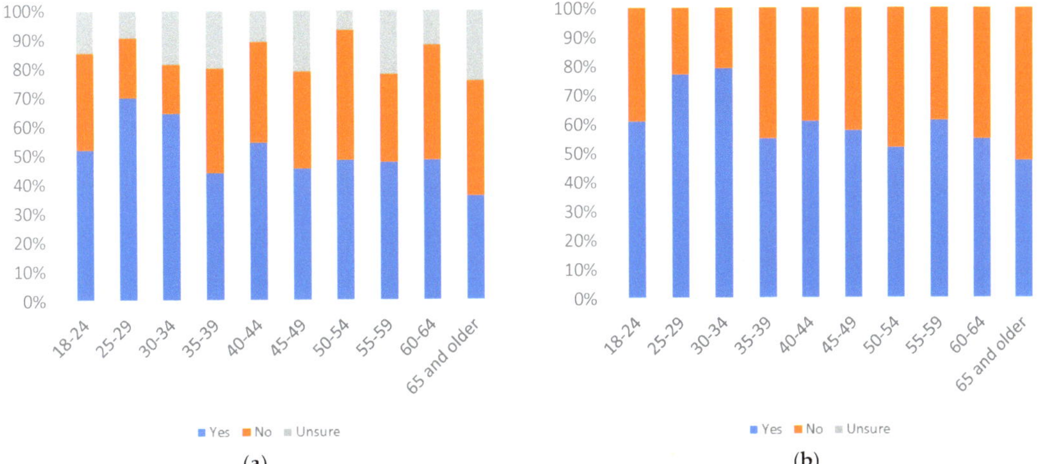

Figure 113. Label trustworthiness judging use, by age group: (**a**) with uncertain respondents (left) and (**b**) without uncertain respondents (right).

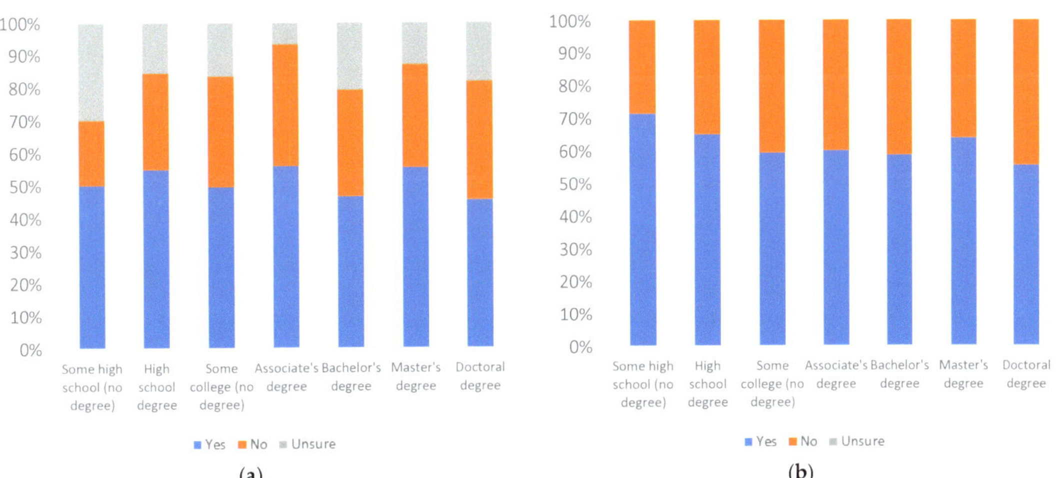

Figure 114. Label trustworthiness judging use, by education level: (**a**) with uncertain respondents (left) and (**b**) without uncertain respondents (right).

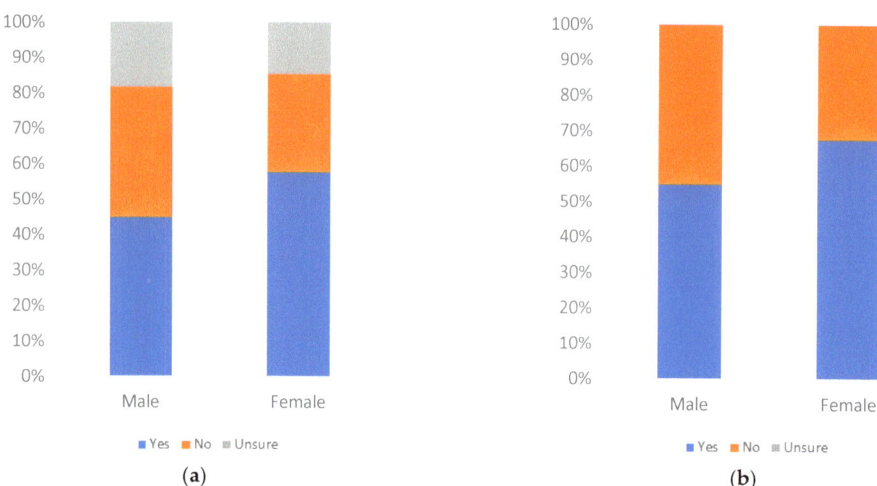

Figure 115. Label trustworthiness judging use, by gender: (**a**) with uncertain respondents (left) and (**b**) without uncertain respondents (right).

In terms of age, the level of yes responses is relatively consistent, except for a spike at the 25–29 and 30–34 age groups. Uncertainty is at its lowest level at the 50–54 age group but seems to vary unpredictably as age increases. Less than half of age groups report at least 50% yes responses, when uncertainty is included. These groups tend to be younger, including the 18–24, 25–29, 30–34 and 40–44 age groups. When uncertainty is eliminated, all age groups other than 65 and older exceed a 50% proportion of "yes" responses.

Responses are relatively consistent across education levels when uncertainty is included. The proportion of yes responses trends downward, as education level increases, when uncertainty is ignored. The highest uncertainty level is exhibited by the some high school (no degree) education level, once again, while associate's degree holders express the lowest level of uncertainty, in this case. Only two education levels (bachelor's degree and doctoral degree) have below 50% yes responses, when uncertainty is included. All groups exceed a 50% proportion of yes responses, when uncertainty is not considered.

By gender, females respond far more frequently with yes than do males, while males reported a higher level of uncertainty. Males have less than 50% yes responses, when uncertainty is included. Both groups exceed a 50% proportion of yes responses, when uncertainty is excluded.

7. Broader Analysis and Analysis of Implications

This section discusses trends across the different label types, demographics and questions. Notably, respondents were overall very positive about the use of labels. In most cases, the majority of respondents indicated answers supportive of the use of labels, such finding them helpful, not annoying, indicating that they and others would use them and saying that they would be useful for evaluating articles' trustworthiness.

Of course, some labels were better received than others. In the informational labels, for example, the third informational label was the best received by the youngest age groups, with approximately 70% of those between 18 and 34 finding the first informational label helpful (not considering those indicating uncertainty), versus an average of approximately 75% for the second informational label and 85% for the third. Notably, different trends existed between these labels as well, for these groups. The first had relative similarity between the three age groups (18–24, 25–29 and 30–34), while the second exhibited a downward trend with age and the third had an increase between the first two age groups, followed by a decline between the second and third labels. Most labels exhibited a drop in support at the 35–39 demographic; however, this was notably less pronounced for warning label 3, which has only a small difference between the 30–34 and 35–39 age groups and continues falling from the 35–39 vale at the 40–49 age levels. The supplemental information label shows a drop at 35–39; however, it continues dropping at 40–44, while—in many other cases, such as warning label 2—the support rebounds in the next age level up.

Table 4 provides an overview of the trends present, by demographic, for all of the label types and questions. Notably, there is not a consistent theme of declining or increasing by age or education level. In some cases, no clear trend is present. In others, conflicting trends are seen for a given metric at different age or education levels. Differences in trend type are also present across the different labels and questions.

Overall, the age-correlated responses show the most variability between responses. The education level data (which, of course, does have an implicit but imperfect correlation with age), shows a more moderate level of fluctuations. The gender-correlated data, on the other hand, shows that there is a limited amount of difference between genders, for most questions, with several label-question combinations having results between males and females which differ between them.

Uncertainty is also measured and, in many cases, decreases—at least partially across the range—with additional age or education. Males and females exhibit different levels of uncertainty across various label and question combinations; however, there is not a consistent pattern to which gender is more or less uncertain that perfectly correlates with specific labels or question types. In general, though, females indicate greater levels of uncertainty (having greater uncertainty reported in 25 out of 35 label question combinations). Females also indicate stronger support for labeling (indicated by greater yes responses for all questions, except annoyingness, and no for annoyingness), responding with support in 28 out 35 label-question combinations.

For all labeling categories, the annoyingness level is either the same for both males and females or higher for males than females. Conversely, the reverse is observed with regard to helpfulness, across all label styles.

There are also gender differences by label style. More males than females indicated that they would use informational label 2, while females indicated this more with respect to all of the other label styles. Females also indicated being more confident than males that others would use each labeling style (including informational label 2). Finally, except for informational label 1, more females than males indicated that each label style would be useful in judging the trustworthiness of a news article.

While some gender-difference is shown in specific label preference, the trend is broader than being related to any single label. This demonstrates that the higher level of support shown by females is likely unrelated to specific elements of the design of particular labels.

The lack of a clear pattern of responses or the presence of conflicting patterns is present for many of the demographic-analyzed individual label question responses. Of the 105 demographic-question-label combinations, just under a third (33) have no clear pattern or evidence of conflicting trends. Slightly more (36) of the combinations have no clear pattern or conflicting trends related to uncertainty. In approximately two-thirds (22) of these, there is a lack of a clear pattern (or conflicting trends) in both the demographic responses and the uncertainty.

Considering the four categories that are associated with label support (all except annoyingness), 24 demographic-question-label combinations have a decreasing association of support with increased age or education level. Four of the annoyingness demographic-question-label combinations show an increase with age/education, a similar indication of support-declining with increasing age or education. Alternately, only six combinations (outside of the annoyingness question, which has three support-increasing decrease response combinations) show a trend of increasing with greater age or education. Only one demographic-question-label combination (informational label 2's self-use) has only minimal change amongst levels.

Table 4. Overview of trends in responses and respondents' demographics.

		Helpfulness	Annoyingness	Use	Others' Use	Trustworthiness
Informational 1	Age	Decreases	No clear pattern	No clear pattern	No clear pattern	Partial decrease
	(UNCT)	No clear pattern	No clear pattern	No clear pattern	No clear pattern	No clear pattern
	Education	Partial decrease	No clear pattern	Two partial increases	No clear pattern	Partial decrease
	(UNCT)	No clear pattern	Partial slight decrease	Partial decrease	Decrease	No clear pattern
	Gender	Female slightly higher	Male slightly higher	Female slightly higher	Same	Male slightly higher
	(UNCT)	Same	Female slightly higher	Female slightly higher	Same	Female slightly higher
Informational 2	Age	Two partial decreases	No clear pattern	Partial increase	No clear pattern	No clear pattern
	(UNCT)	Partial increase	No clear pattern	No clear pattern	No clear pattern	No clear pattern
	Education	Decreases	Partial increase	Minimal change	No clear pattern	No clear pattern
	(UNCT)	No clear pattern	Partial decrease	Partial decrease	No clear pattern	Partial decrease
	Gender	Female higher	Male higher	Male slightly higher	Same	Female slightly higher
	(UNCT)	Female higher	Male higher	Female higher	Male slightly higher	Female higher
Informational 3	Age	No clear pattern	Partial increase	Two partial increases	No clear pattern	No clear pattern
	(UNCT)	No clear pattern	Partial decrease	No clear pattern	Two partial decreases	No clear pattern
	Education	Partial decrease	Partial increase	No clear pattern	Partial decrease	Decrease
	(UNCT)	Partial decrease	Partial decrease	No clear pattern	Partial decrease	Partial decrease
	Gender	Female higher	Male higher	Female slightly higher	Female higher	Female higher
	(UNCT)	Female slightly higher	Female higher	Female slightly higher	Same	Female higher

Table 4. *Cont.*

		Helpfulness	Annoyingness	Use	Others' Use	Trustworthiness
Warning 1	Age	Partial increase	Conflicting trends	Conflicting trends	No clear pattern	Partial increase
	(UNCT)	No clear pattern	No clear pattern	No clear pattern	Two partial decreases	Conflicting Trends
	Education	Decreases	Two partial decreases	Partial slight increase	Decrease	Decrease
	(UNCT)	Partial decrease	No clear pattern	Partial decrease	Partial decrease	Partial decrease
	Gender	Female higher	Same	Female higher	Female slightly higher	Female higher
	(UNCT)	Female higher	Female slightly higher	Female higher	Female higher	Female higher
Warning 2	Age	No clear pattern	No clear pattern	No clear pattern	No clear pattern	No clear pattern
	(UNCT)	No clear pattern	No clear pattern	Conflicting trends	No clear pattern	Conflicting Trends
	Education	Decreases	Partial decrease	No clear pattern	No clear pattern	Conflicting Trends
	(UNCT)	Partial decrease	Partial decrease	Partial decrease	No clear pattern	Partial decrease
	Gender	Female higher	Male higher	Female higher	Female higher	Female higher
	(UNCT)	Female higher	Male higher	Female higher	Female slightly higher	Female slightly higher
Warning 3	Age	Two partial decreases	Conflicting trends	Partial decrease	Partial decrease	No clear pattern
	(UNCT)	No clear pattern	No clear pattern	Conflicting trends	No clear pattern	No clear pattern
	Education	Decreases	Conflicting trends	Partial decrease	No clear pattern	Two partial decreases
	(UNCT)	Partial decrease	Partial decrease	Two partial decreases	Partial decrease	Partial decrease
	Gender	Female higher	Same	Female higher	Female higher	Female higher
	(UNCT)	Male slightly higher	Female slightly higher	Female slightly higher	Male higher	Female slightly higher

Table 4. *Cont.*

		Helpfulness	Annoyingness	Use	Others' Use	Trustworthiness
Supplemental Information	Age	Two partial decreases	Two partial increases	Conflicting trends	No clear pattern	Conflicting Trends
	(UNCT)	Conflicting trends	Conflicting trends	No clear pattern	Two partial decreases	No clear pattern
	Education	Partial decrease	Decrease	No clear pattern	Partial decrease	Partial decrease
	(UNCT)	Partial decrease	Partial decrease	Partial decrease	No clear pattern	Partial decrease
	Gender	Female higher	Male higher	Female higher	Female higher	Female higher
	(UNCT)	Female slightly higher	Female slightly higher	Female higher	Male higher	Male higher

This data suggests that the age and education demographics of an online content labeling system user are very important, when choosing the type of label to use, to maximize the efficacy of the system. However, the limited number of overarching trends, which run the entire spectrum of the age or education range, mean that system designers and administrators will need to make nuanced decisions based on specific users' demographics. The data presented herein, when multiple label types' absolute values are compared for particular demographic values, can inform these decisions. Of course, these initial heuristic decisions should also be refined based on the behavior of a given user, learned over time, as any given user's behaviors may not align perfectly with others in the particular demographic group being assessed.

8. Conclusions and Future Work

This paper has analyzed data from a national study of American's attitudes towards online content labels, in terms of age, education level and gender. It has shown that females are more supportive of labels, generally, than males; however, they also indicate greater confusion regarding their efficacy. Additionally, while females show more support, the difference in support levels between the two genders is—for many labels and considerations—relatively limited. The impact of gender on label efficacy appears to be broader than an association with specific label styles and elements, as females evidence stronger support than males across label styles and survey questions, with a very limited number of exceptions.

In terms of education level and age, it has been shown that the perceived efficacy of labels and support for them generally decreases with age; however, a majority of respondents at all ages and education levels indicated support for the labels (when excluding responses indicating uncertainty). Label annoyingness, was shown to have a positive correlation, for four labels. This perhaps indicates that some respondents found the information to be unneeded for their age and experience. A few labels were shown to have a positive correlation between age/education and support.

As youth have been identified as a key demographic that may benefit from online content labeling, it is beneficial that this study shows that the labels may be particularly useful for this demographic. Furthermore, the study has identified certain labels that may be particularly beneficial for younger users, such as informational label 3. Other age and education levels, though, may be better served with other labels.

It is clear that age and education level have a significant impact on label efficacy; however, the impact is more nuanced than an overarching trend. In some cases, conflicting trends are shown at different points along the age or education level spectrum, which may indicate gaining more (or less) benefit, up until a point, and then having that benefit decline. There may also be generational and lifestyle factors that are responsible for some of the discontinuous changes within the data. There is also a possibility of unknown confounding variables being present. In any case, the data presented and analyzed herein can inform label-selection decision making, based on the demographics of the individual being targeted to use the label.

Building upon this work, needed future work includes conducting observations of respondent's decision making when using a simulated system to ascertain whether individuals predicted behaviors and their actual ones align, with regard to the topic of this study. A variety of activities are also needed in the broader context of online content labeling. These include the development of new and enhanced technologies to detect intentionally deceptive content, new labels designs to assess the efficacy of and policy analysis to consider how content labeling can be most effectively implemented in real-world environments.

Author Contributions: Conceptualization, J.S. and M.S.; methodology, J.S. and M.S.; resources, J.S.; writing—original draft preparation, J.S. and M.S.; writing—review and editing, J.S. and M.S.; project administration, J.S.; funding acquisition, J.S. All authors have read and agreed to the published version of the manuscript.

Funding: Partial support for this work was provided by the NDSU Challey Institute for Global Innovation and Growth. Funding for the article publication charge was provided by the Hayek Fund for Scholars at the Institute for Human Studies at George Mason University.

Institutional Review Board Statement: The study was conducted according to the guidelines of the Declaration of Helsinki, and approved by the Institutional Review Board of North Dakota State University (protocol IRB0003884, approved 23 September 2021).

Informed Consent Statement: Informed consent was obtained from all subjects involved in the study.

Data Availability Statement: A data release, via a data journal publication, is planned once initial analysis of all data is complete.

Acknowledgments: Thanks are given to Jade Kanemitsu from Qualtrics International Inc. for the management of the data collection process. Thanks are also given to Ryan Suttle, Scott Hogan and Rachel Aumaugher who developed many of the questions that were used in this study during their earlier work (which was presented in [16]). Thanks are given to Bob Fedor who generated an earlier set of figures using this data (which were not used in this paper).

Conflicts of Interest: The authors declare no conflict of interest. The funders had no role in the design of the study; in the collection, analyses, or interpretation of data; in the writing of the manuscript, or in the decision to publish the results.

References

1. Allcott, H.; Gentzkow, M. Social Media and Fake News in the 2016 Election. *J. Econ. Perspect.* **2017**, *31*, 211–236. [CrossRef]
2. Bastos, M.T.; Mercea, D. The Brexit Botnet and User-Generated Hyperpartisan News. *Soc. Sci. Comput. Rev.* **2017**, *37*, 38–54. [CrossRef]
3. Cunha, E.; Magno, G.; Caetano, J.; Teixeira, D.; Almeida, V. Fake News as We Feel It: Perception and Conceptualization of the Term "Fake News" in the Media. *Lect. Notes Comput. Sci. Incl. Subser. Lect. Notes Artif. Intell. Lect. Notes Bioinform.* **2018**, *11185*, 151–166. [CrossRef]
4. Aisch, G.; Huang, J.; Kang, C. Dissecting the #PizzaGate Conspiracy Theories-The New York Times. *New York Times*, 2016, Volume 10, p. 2. Available online: https://www.nytimes.com/interactive/2016/12/10/business/media/pizzagate.html (accessed on 1 September 2022).
5. McGaughey, E. Could Brexit be Void? *King's Law J.* **2018**, *29*, 331–343. [CrossRef]
6. Keyes, R. *The Post-Truth Era: Dishonesty and Deception in Contemporary Life*; St. Martin's Press: New York, NY, USA, 2004.
7. Lee, T. The global rise of "fake news" and the threat to democratic elections in the USA. *Public Adm. Policy* **2019**, *22*, 15–24. [CrossRef]
8. Tong, C.; Gill, H.; Li, J.; Valenzuela, S.; Rojas, H. "Fake News Is Anything They Say!"—Conceptualization and Weaponization of Fake News among the American Public. *Mass Commun. Soc.* **2020**, *23*, 755–778. [CrossRef]
9. More Americans Are Getting Their News From Social Media. Available online: https://www.forbes.com/sites/petersuciu/2019/10/11/more-americans-are-getting-their-news-from-social-media/#589ec4d43e17 (accessed on 1 February 2020).
10. Tandoc, E.C.; Lim, W.; Ling, R. Defining "Fake News" A typology of scholarly definitions. *Digit. J.* **2018**, *6*, 137–153. [CrossRef]
11. Silverman, C.; Singer-Vine, J. Most Americans Who See Fake News Believe It, New Survey Says. *BuzzFeed News*, 2016. Available online: https://www.buzzfeednews.com/article/craigsilverman/fake-news-survey (accessed on 1 September 2022).
12. Fuhr, N.; Giachanou, A.; Grefenstette, G.; Gurevych, I.; Hanselowski, A.; Jarvelin, K.; Jones, R.; Liu, Y.; Mothe, J.; Nejdl, W.; et al. An Information Nutritional Label for Online Documents. *ACM SIGIR Forum* **2018**, *51*, 46–66. [CrossRef]
13. Lespagnol, C.; Mothe, J.; Ullah, M.Z. Information Nutritional Label and Word Embedding to Estimate Information Check-Worthiness. In Proceedings of the 42nd International ACM SIGIR Conference on Research and Development in Information Retrieval, ACM, Paris, France, 21–25 July 2019; pp. 941–944.
14. Vincentius, K.; Aggarwal, P.; Sahan, A.; Högden, B.; Madan, N.; Bangaru, A.; Schwenger, C.; Muradov, F.; Aker, A. Information Nutrition Labels: A Plugin for Online News Evaluation. In *First Workshop on Fact Extraction and VERification*; Association for Computational Linguistics: Brussels, Belgium, 2018; pp. 28–33.
15. Spradling, M.; Straub, J.; Strong, J. Protection from 'Fake News': The Need for Descriptive Factual Labeling for Online Content. *Future Internet* **2021**, *13*, 142. [CrossRef]
16. Suttle, R.; Hogan, S.; Aumaugher, R.; Spradling, M.; Merrigan, Z.; Straub, J. University Community Members' Perceptions of Labels for Online Media. *Future Internet* **2021**, *13*, 281. [CrossRef]
17. Straub, J.; Spradling, M. Americans' Perspectives on Online Media Warning Labels. *Behav. Sci.* **2022**, *12*, 59. [CrossRef] [PubMed]

18. Straub, J.; Spradling, M.; Fedor, B. Assessment of Consumer Perception of Online Content Label Efficacy by Income Level, Party Affiliation and Online Use Levels. *Information* **2022**, *13*, 252. [CrossRef]
19. Straub, J.; Spradling, M.; Fedor, B. Assessment of Factors Impacting the Perception of Online Content Trustworthiness by Age, Education and Gender. *Societies* **2022**, *12*, 61. [CrossRef]
20. Ott, B. Some Good News about the News: 5 Reasons Why 'Fake' News is Better than Fox 'News'-Flow. Flow A Crit. *Forum Telev. Media Cult.* **2005**, *2*, 316–317.
21. Kim, S. All the Times People Were Fooled by the Onion. Available online: https://abcnews.go.com/International/times-people-fooled-onion/story?id=31444478 (accessed on 4 February 2022).
22. Saez-Trumper, D. Fake Tweet Buster: A Webtool to Identify Users Promoting Fake News on Twitter. In Proceedings of the 25th ACM Conference on Hypertext and Social Media, ACM, Santiago, Chile, 1–4 September 2014.
23. Grinberg, N.; Joseph, K.; Friedland, L.; Swire-Thompson, B.; Lazer, D. Fake news on Twitter during the 2016 U.S. presidential election. *Science* **2019**, *363*, 374–378. [CrossRef] [PubMed]
24. Lazer, D.M.J.; Baum, M.A.; Benkler, Y.; Berinsky, A.J.; Greenhill, K.M.; Menczer, F.; Metzger, M.J.; Nyhan, B.; Pennycook, G.; Rothschild, D.; et al. The science of fake news. *Science* **2018**, *3*, 1094–1096. [CrossRef]
25. Bovet, A.; Makse, H.A. Influence of fake news in Twitter during the 2016 US presidential election. *Nat. Commun.* **2019**, *10*, 1657. [CrossRef]
26. Shearer, E.; Matsa, K.E. News Use across Social Media Platforms 2018. Available online: https://www.pewresearch.org/journalism/2018/09/10/news-use-across-social-media-platforms-2018/ (accessed on 21 September 2021).
27. Fatilua, J. Who trusts social media? *Comput. Human Behav.* **2018**, *81*, 303–315. [CrossRef]
28. Balmas, M. When Fake News Becomes Real: Combined Exposure to Multiple News Sources and Political Attitudes of Inefficacy, Alienation, and Cynicism. *Commun. Res.* **2014**, *41*, 430–454. [CrossRef]
29. Kang, C.; Goldman, A. *Washington Pizzeria Attack, Fake News Brought Real Guns*; New York Times: New York, NY, USA, 2016.
30. Haithcox-Dennis, M. Reject, Correct, Redirect: Using Web Annotation to Combat Fake Health Information—A Commentary. *Am. J. Health Educ.* **2018**, *49*, 206–209. [CrossRef]
31. U.S. Food and Drug Administration Changes to the Nutrition Facts Label. Available online: https://www.fda.gov/food/food-labeling-nutrition/changes-nutrition-facts-label (accessed on 14 December 2020).
32. U.S. Department of Energy Estimating Appliance and Home Electronic Energy Use. Available online: https://www.energy.gov/energysaver/estimating-appliance-and-home-electronic-energy-use (accessed on 10 January 2022).
33. Hammond, D. Health warning messages on tobacco products: A review. *Tob. Control.* **2011**, *20*, 327–337. [CrossRef] [PubMed]
34. Lomeli, N.; Funke, D. *Fact Check: Cigarette Warning Labels in US Haven't Changed Since 1984*; USA Today: Tysons Corner, VA, USA, 2022.
35. Hiilamo, H.; Crosbie, E.; Glantz, S.A. The evolution of health warning labels on cigarette packs: The role of precedents, and tobacco industry strategies to block diffusion. *Tob. Control* **2014**, *23*, e2. [CrossRef] [PubMed]
36. Hensley, S. Be Warned: FDA Unveils Graphic Cigarette Labels. *NPR Website*, 2011. Available online: https://www.npr.org/sections/health-shots/2011/06/21/137316580/be-warned-fda-unveils-graphic-cigarette-labels (accessed on 1 February 2020).
37. CBS News Judge Blocks FDA Requirement for Graphic Tobacco Warning Labels. Available online: https://www.cbsnews.com/news/judge-blocks-fda-requirement-for-graphic-tobacco-warning-labels/ (accessed on 1 March 2022).
38. Ingram, D.; Yukhananov, A.U.S. Court Strikes down Graphic Warnings on Cigarettes. Available online: https://www.reuters.com/article/us-usa-cigarettes-labels/u-s-court-strikes-down-graphic-warnings-on-cigarettes-idUSBRE87N0NL20120824 (accessed on 1 March 2022).
39. U.S. Food & Drug Administration FDA Proposes New Required Health Warnings with Color Images for Cigarette Packages and Advertisements to Promote Greater Public Understanding of Negative Health Consequences of Smoking. Available online: https://www.fda.gov/news-events/press-announcements/fda-proposes-new-required-health-warnings-color-images-cigarette-packages-and-advertisements-promote (accessed on 1 March 2022).
40. FDA Label Imaegs. Available online: https://web.archive.org/web/20120302084657/http://www.fda.gov/downloads/TobaccoProducts/Labeling/CigaretteWarningLabels/UCM259974.zip (accessed on 1 March 2022).
41. Craver, R. Tobacco Manufacturers Gain Three More Months before Graphic-Warning Labels Required on Cigarette Packs | Local | Journalnow.com. Available online: https://journalnow.com/business/local/tobacco-manufacturers-gain-three-more-months-before-graphic-warning-labels-required-on-cigarette-packs/article_fd8915b6-8f43-11ec-aad6-2f790b9bdb5a.html (accessed on 1 March 2022).
42. Hoek, J.; Wilson, N.; Allen, M.; Edwards, R.; Thomson, G.; Li, J. Lessons from New Zealand's introduction of pictorial health warnings on tobacco packaging. *Bull. World Health Organ* **2010**, *88*, 861–866. [CrossRef] [PubMed]
43. U.S. Food & Drug Administration Cigarette Labeling and Health Warning Requirements | FDA. Available online: https://www.fda.gov/tobacco-products/labeling-and-warning-statements-tobacco-products/cigarette-labeling-and-health-warning-requirements (accessed on 1 March 2022).
44. Motion Picture Association Inc.; National Association of Theatre Owners Inc. CLASSIFICATION AND RATING RULES; Sherman Oaks, California, 2020. Available online: https://www.filmratings.com/Content/Downloads/rating_rules.pdf (accessed on 27 October 2022).
45. WELCOME TO FilmRatings.com. Available online: https://www.filmratings.com/ (accessed on 1 February 2020).
46. The V-Chip: Options to Restrict What Your Children Watch on TV | Federal Communications Commission. Available online: https://www.fcc.gov/consumers/guides/v-chip-putting-restrictions-what-your-children-watch (accessed on 1 February 2020).
47. Harrington, R. Record Industry Unveils Lyrics Warning Label. Available online: https://www.washingtonpost.com/archive/lifestyle/1990/05/10/record-industry-unveils-lyrics-warning-label/6fc30515-ac8a-4e5d-9abd-a06a34cb54f2/ (accessed on 28 February 2022).

48. U.S. Federal Bureau of Investigation FBI Anti-Piracy Warning Seal. Available online: https://www.fbi.gov/investigate/white-collar-crime/piracy-ip-theft/fbi-anti-piracy-warning-seal (accessed on 1 March 2022).
49. Baptista, J.P.; Gradim, A. Understanding Fake News Consumption: A Review. *Soc. Sci.* **2020**, *9*, 185. [CrossRef]
50. Braun, J.A.; Eklund, J.L. Fake News, Real Money: Ad Tech Platforms, Profit-Driven Hoaxes, and the Business of Journalism. *Digit. J.* **2019**, *7*, 1–21. [CrossRef]
51. Rostron, A. Pragmatism, Paternalism, and the Constitutional Protection of Commercial Speech. *Vt. Law Rev.* **2012**, *37*, 527–589.
52. United States Constitution, First Amendment.
53. U.S. Embassy Beijing New PRC Internet Regulation. Available online: https://irp.fas.org/world/china/netreg.htm (accessed on 28 February 2022).
54. Diagne, A.; Finlay, A.; Gaye, S.; Gichunge, W.; Pretorius, C.; Schiffrin, A.; Cunliffe-Jones, P.; Onumah, C. *Misinformation Policy in Sub-Saharan Africa*; University of Westminster Press: London, UK, 2021; p. 224. [CrossRef]
55. Haque, M.M.; Yousuf, M.; Alam, A.S.; Saha, P.; Ahmed, S.I.; Hassan, N. Combating Misinformation in Bangladesh. *Proc. ACM Hum. Comput. Interact* **2020**, *4*, 130. [CrossRef]
56. Carson, A.; Fallon, L. *Fighting Fake News: A Study of Online Misinformation Regulation in the Asia Pacific*; La Trobe University: Melbourne, Australia, 2021. [CrossRef]
57. Yadav, K.; Erdoğdu, U.; Siwakoti, S.; Shapiro, J.N.; Wanless, A. Countries have more than 100 laws on the books to combat misinformation. How well do they work? *Bull. At. Sci.* **2021**, *77*, 124–128. [CrossRef]
58. Kumar, P.J.S.; Devi, P.R.; Sai, N.R.; Kumar, S.S.; Benarji, T. Battling Fake News: A Survey on Mitigation Techniques and Identification. In Proceedings of the 2021 5th International Conference on Trends in Electronics and Informatics (ICOEI), Tirunelveli, India, 3–5 June 2021; pp. 829–835. [CrossRef]
59. Sharma, K.; Qian, F.; Jiang, H.; Ruchansky, N.; Zhang, M.; Liu, Y. Combating fake news: A survey on identification and mitigation techniques. *ACM Trans. Intell. Syst. Technol.* **2019**, *10*, 1–42. [CrossRef]
60. Zhou, X.; Zafarani, R. A Survey of Fake News: Fundamental Theories, Detection Methods, and Opportunities. *ACM Comput. Surv.* **2020**, *53*, 1–40. [CrossRef]
61. Wang, W.Y. "Liar, Liar Pants on Fire": A New Benchmark Dataset for Fake News Detection. *arXiv* **2017**, arXiv:1705.00648,.
62. De Oliveira, N.R.; Pisa, P.S.; Lopez, M.A.; de Medeiros, D.S.V.; Mattos, D.M.F. Identifying Fake News on Social Networks Based on Natural Language Processing: Trends and Challenges. *Information* **2021**, *12*, 38. [CrossRef]
63. Deepak, S.; Chitturi, B. Deep neural approach to Fake-News identification. *Procedia Comput. Sci.* **2020**, *167*, 2236–2243. [CrossRef]
64. Guo, Z.; Yu, K.; Jolfaei, A.; Li, G.; Ding, F.; Beheshti, A. Mixed Graph Neural Network-Based Fake News Detection for Sustainable Vehicular Social Networks. *IEEE Trans. Intell. Transp. Syst.* **2022**, 1–13. [CrossRef]
65. Yuan, H.; Zheng, J.; Ye, Q.; Qian, Y.; Zhang, Y. Improving fake news detection with domain-adversarial and graph-attention neural network. *Decis. Support Syst.* **2021**, *151*, 113633. [CrossRef]
66. Koloski, B.; Stepišnik-Perdih, T.; Pollak, S.; Škrlj, B. Identification of COVID-19 Related Fake News via Neural Stacking. *Commun. Comput. Inf. Sci.* **2021**, *1402*, 177–188. [CrossRef]
67. Hebroune, O.; Benhiba, L. *User-Enriched Embedding for Fake News Detection on Social Media*; Springer: Cham, Switzerland, 2022; pp. 581–599. [CrossRef]
68. Batailler, C.; Brannon, S.M.; Teas, P.E.; Gawronski, B. A Signal Detection Approach to Understanding the Identification of Fake News. *Perspect. Psychol. Sci.* **2022**, *17*, 78–98. [CrossRef]
69. Anoop, K.; Deepak, P.; Lajish, L.V. Emotion cognizance improves health fake news identification. In Proceedings of the 24th International Database Engineering & Applications Symposium (IDEAS 2020), Incheon, Korea, 12–18 August 2020.
70. Shao, Y.; Sun, J.; Zhang, T.; Jiang, Y.; Ma, J.; Li, J. Fake News Detection Based on Multi-Modal Classifier Ensemble. In Proceedings of the 1st International Workshop on Multimedia AI against Disinformation, Newark, NJ, USA, 27–30 June 2022. [CrossRef]
71. Rapti, M.; Tsakalidis, G.; Petridou, S.; Vergidis, K. Fake News Incidents through the Lens of the DCAM Disinformation Blueprint. *Information* **2022**, *13*, 306. [CrossRef]
72. Chen, W.; Wang, Y.; Yang, S. Efficient influence maximization in social networks. In Proceedings of the 2010 IEEE International Conference on Data Mining, Miami, FL, USA, 6–9 December 2009. [CrossRef]
73. Chen, W.; Yuan, Y.; Zhang, L. Scalable influence maximization in social networks under the linear threshold model. In Proceedings of the 2010 IEEE International Conference on Data Mining, Sydney, Australia, 13–17 December 2010. [CrossRef]
74. Budak, C.; Agrawal, D.; Abbadi, A. El Limiting the spread of misinformation in social networks. In Proceedings of the 20th International Conference on World Wide Web, Hyderabad, India, 28 March–1 April 2011; pp. 665–674. [CrossRef]
75. Jain, S.; Sharma, V.; Kaushal, R. Towards automated real-time detection of misinformation on Twitter. In Proceedings of the 2016 International Conference on Advances in Computing, Communications and Informatics (ICACCI), Jaipur, India, 21–24 September 2016; pp. 2015–2020. [CrossRef]
76. Fairbanks, J.; Fitch, N.; Knauf, N.; Briscoe, E. Credibility Assessment in the News: Do we need to read? In Proceedings of the MIS2 Workshop held in conjuction with 11th Int'l Conference on Web Search and Data Mining, ACM, Del Ray, CA, USA, 5–9 February 2018.
77. Bakir, V.; McStay, A. Fake News and The Economy of Emotions. *Digit. J.* **2018**, *6*, 154–175. [CrossRef]
78. Pröllochs, N. Community-Based Fact-Checking on Twitter's Birdwatch Platform. *arXiv* **2021**, arXiv:2104.07175.

Article

SMS-I: Intelligent Security for Cyber–Physical Systems

Eva Maia *, Norberto Sousa, Nuno Oliveira, Sinan Wannous, Orlando Sousa and Isabel Praça

GECAD—Research Group on Intelligent Engineering and Computing for Advanced Innovation and Development, School of Engineering of the Polytechnic of Porto (ISEP), 4249-015 Porto, Portugal
* Correspondence: egm@isep.ipp.pt

Abstract: Critical infrastructures are an attractive target for attackers, mainly due to the catastrophic impact of these attacks on society. In addition, the cyber–physical nature of these infrastructures makes them more vulnerable to cyber–physical threats and makes the detection, investigation, and remediation of security attacks more difficult. Therefore, improving cyber–physical correlations, forensics investigations, and Incident response tasks is of paramount importance. This work describes the SMS-I tool that allows the improvement of these security aspects in critical infrastructures. Data from heterogeneous systems, over different time frames, are received and correlated. Both physical and logical security are unified and additional security details are analysed to find attack evidence. Different Artificial Intelligence (AI) methodologies are used to process and analyse the multi-dimensional data exploring the temporal correlation between cyber and physical Alerts and going beyond traditional techniques to detect unusual Events, and then find evidence of attacks. SMS-I's Intelligent Dashboard supports decision makers in a deep analysis of how the breaches and the assets were explored and compromised. It assists and facilitates the security analysts using graphical dashboards and Alert classification suggestions. Therefore, they can more easily identify anomalous situations that can be related to possible Incident occurrences. Users can also explore information, with different levels of detail, including logical information and technical specifications. SMS-I also integrates with a scalable and open Security Incident Response Platform (TheHive) that enables the sharing of information about security Incidents and helps different organizations better understand threats and proactively defend their systems and networks.

Keywords: cyber–physical systems; digital forensics; cyber–physical systems forensics; machine learning; rule mining; security incident response

Citation: Maia, E.; Sousa, N.; Oliveira, N.; Wannous, S.; Sousa, O; Praça, I. SMS-I: Intelligent Security for Cyber–Physical Systems. *Information* **2022**, *13*, 403. https://doi.org/10.3390/info13090403

Academic Editors: Jose de Vasconcelos, Hugo Barbosa and Carla Cordeiro

Received: 12 July 2022
Accepted: 22 August 2022
Published: 25 August 2022

Publisher's Note: MDPI stays neutral with regard to jurisdictional claims in published maps and institutional affiliations.

1. Introduction

Cyber–physical systems (CPS) combine the physical and cyber worlds, which allows an improvement of the entire operating environment by adding different promising capabilities to these environments [1]. Therefore, CPS are being used in several domains, including manufacturing processes, healthcare, transportation, and commercial and residential smart buildings [2]. For example, recently, several studies have been done to explore the full potential of CPS in the context of Industry 4.0 [3,4]. This can happen because CPS use and integrate different technologies, from software systems, networks, and sensors to hardware devices such as microcontrollers and actuators. However, this combination enabling interactions between cyber and physical components, not only brings new and more complex paths of attack but also increases the attack impact, since an event caused by a cyber component can have a huge impact on physical ones or vice-versa [5]. The connections between the physical systems and the critical software components are especially vulnerable, since with a cyber attack in these connections the attacker can manipulate, disrupt or power off the physical system [6]. Thus, beyond damage to cyber and physical components, a cyber–physical attack can also have major consequences that may include human deaths and injuries, infrastructure damages, loss of resources, and machine breakdowns or malfunctions. Furthermore, these damages can have an even greater impact on critical infrastructure such as hospitals and airports. Stuxnet worm [7], the US power grid attack [8], German steel-mill Incident [9], the Ukrainian power grid Incident [10], and the recent Florida Water Treatment Plant [11] and Colonial Pipeline [12] attacks, are some examples of security attacks on CPS that have caused huge impacts on the normal operation of the systems.

After an attack, it is crucial to understand how it was performed, who did it and why it happened. This will help to understand which assets were compromised but also will allow the creation of defense mechanisms for future attacks [13]. For that, security analysts need to analyse and investigate several sources of information. In CPS, this investigation process becomes much wider and complex, due to the amount of components that need to be analysed. Not only software and hardware components need to be considered but also all interactions across all CPS. Several investigations have been done to develop tools to secure CPS as well as techniques and frameworks to evaluate CPS security; however, CPS forensic investigation area is still in its early stage. Mohamed et al. [14] reviewed examples of current research efforts in the field and the types of tools and methods proposed for CPS forensics. The authors also discussed some issues and challenges in the domain that need to be addressed. One of the issues pointed out was the need for data analytics tools to find correlations between digital and physical evidence. Furthermore, Fausto et al. [15] pointed out that finding complex attack patterns through the combination of physical and cyber Events is a very challenging task. Moreover, they stated that the correlation strategies of heterogeneous Events for security reasons, and the techniques and algorithms to exploit this correlation are still open issues.

Additionally, for a successful correlation of the security Events, it is essential to keep track of the currently handled Events. For that, cybersecurity teams typically use ticketing systems that allow the follow up of the event for analysis, after the reporting, and until closure. However, due to the complexity of modern attacks, increasingly multi-step, the Events handled can be part of a larger attack that spans different parts of systems. Thus, the information crucial to detecting such attacks is often distributed in time and space, which makes detection difficult. Hence, an important feature of these systems is the collaboration among the security professionals, such as Security Operations Center (SOC) and Computer Emergency Response Team (CERT) security analysts, with diverse knowledge, skills and experience, to improve the quality of their investigation. Moreover, collaboration is important not only between the security professionals of the same institution, but also between companies, sectors, and even countries to improve the exchange of information to prevent, mitigate and recover from cyber-attacks. Collaboration between these actors is crucial to restricting the spread of new attacks, particularly zero-day attacks. Sharing new vulnerabilities, attacks, breaches or any other type of information allows a proactive detection of these newly identified threats [16]. This way, the company, sector or even country under attack will benefit from the analysis and correlation actions previously defined by others to resolve the same or similar issues. Governments with their national cybernetic emergencies response team (CERT) or CSIRT are boosting this collaboration to provide support in information security Incidents to the government or corporate entities for the management of cybersecurity and cyberdefense. In addition, European regulatory directives [17] and technical recommendations [18] are promoting actions to ensure a high common level of network and information security across the Union, by developing technologies and procedures for sharing security information to combat modern attacks and mitigate their effects in a timely manner. [19] The aim is to work in a collaborative framework between the CERTs and CSIRTs of the governments that allow the share of information at the taxonomy level about vulnerabilities and reports to be interconnected, providing a large scale security situation awareness which is in turn critical to the overall security posture of an entire nation [20].

In this work, we describe the SMS-I tool, which deals with the analysis of data from heterogeneous systems over different time frames, correlates them to find evidence of the causes of an attack, and supports the definition of remediation measures in a collaborative way. SMS-I was firstly designed in the scope of the SATIE project, which aimed to build a security Toolkit [21] in order to protect critical air transport infrastructure against combined cyber–physical threats by improving the cyber–physical correlations, forensics investigations and dynamic impact assessment at airports. However, SMS-I can work with data from any security CPS since it analyses additional security details, providing contextual and semantic data to identify causes for security events and threats. Furthermore, Machine Learning (ML) methodologies have been applied for outlier detection, exploring the temporal correlation between cyber and physical Alerts, going beyond traditional one-class algorithms, and considering ensemble methods to detect unusual events, taking into account its sequential nature, which may help to find evidence of attacks. An intelligent dashboard is also part of the SMS-I in order to support decision makers in a deep analysis of how the breaches and the assets were explored and compromised. SMS-I also integrates with a scalable and open Security Incident Response Platform (TheHive) that enables the sharing of information about security Incidents. This can make the difference to the organizations security, since this collaborative sharing of information can help different organizations better understand threats and proactively defend their systems and networks.

SMS-I can be easily extended with new modules that can increase its capabilities. Therefore, this work presents a more complete version of the SMS-I tool. A first draft was presented at [22], and a more complete version of this draft was presented at [23]. This work shows in more detail the capabilities presented in the previous works, but also introduces a new capability: the Incident response. Therefore, the main contributions of this paper are:

- detail the SMS-I tool capabilities. The different components of this investigation tool are fully described in this work, presenting its different features;
- present all the different experiments done regarding the SMS-I Machine Learning Engine. Some of these results are already presented in the previous papers; however, in this work, we detail all the work carried out and the results obtained;
- introduce the Incident response capability of SMS-I tool. This is a new SMS-I capability that promotes the sharing of information between organizations. The integration of this feature with TheHive is also detailed in this work;
- show SMS-I Intelligent dashboard in detail, highlighting the added value for the security analysts of each view;
- demonstrate the convenience and usefulness of the SMS-I tool in the decision-making process of security analysts, using a very simple and realistic example.

The remainder of this paper is organized as follows: in Section 2, we introduce the SMS-I architecture, and we briefly describe each component. The Machine Learning Engine is the heart of the SMS-I tool. Hence, Section 3 presents this SMS-I component with more detail. Section 4 describes the SMS-I intelligent dashboard, another important element of the SMS-I tool. The SMS-I Incident Response capability is detailed in Section 5. In the scope of SATIE project, the SMS-I tool was validated and demonstrated in three different airports. Section 6 briefly describes an example that shows the ability of SMS-I to support the security experts work. Finally, the conclusions are presented in Section 7.

2. SMS-I Tool Overview

SMS-I is a forensics investigation system that was initially designed to be part of the SATIE security Toolkit. However, as already mentioned, it can be part of any security system. To explain the integration of SMS-I in a security environment, we will use the SATIE example. Note that the referred SATIE systems can be easily replaced by any other similar security systems.

In the SATIE security environment, cyber and physical sensors are scattered across the whole airport's infrastructure, collecting vast amounts of Events related to the airport system's activity. These Events are sent to the Correlation Engine (CEngine), a pattern matching mechanism that contains expert written rules which are periodically reviewed and updated under a strict protocol, to possibly identify abnormal behaviour. When a set of Events trigger a specific rule, an Alert is originated and sent to the Incident Management

Portal (IMP). In the IMP, after investigating the Alert occurrence, the security operator classifies Alerts as either Incidents or not, triggering a security response. SMS-I tool inspects these Incident and Alert occurrences to provide a deeper analysis of an attack. For that, the system periodically fetches data from the CEngine and the IMP using HTTP(S) requests to obtain Alerts and Incidents generated by the SATIE Toolkit. These data are parsed into predefined formats and stored in specific indexes of the SMS-I Database. This is a crucial part of the SMS-I tool since it allows the system to keep track of the new data that is generated within the SATIE Environment. Then, the SMS-I ML Engine gets this new data and executes the ML models capable of determining, for each Alert, the probability of it being an Incident based on its own features, features of related Events and the features of other Alerts of a regarded time window (Incident Prediction). The employed models are expected to grow smarter over time with system usage. SMS-I ML engine also analyses these data to understand if the system already has remediation measures for the Incident that have occurred and, if not, supports the security analyst in its definition (Incident Response). Additionally, using the Association Rule Mining (ARM) Engine, the SMS-I ML Engine provides an API endpoint for executing rule mining algorithms on the SMS-I Database data according to a set of parameters specified in the request header (Association Rules). It retrieves the list of association rules to identify potential relationships between Alerts for a given timeframe.

The SMS-I Intelligent Dashboard provides a Graphical User Interface of all of these data that handle the interaction with the security analyst. It encapsulates Kibana dashboards and allows the operator to make use of several functionalities such as consulting Alert lists, performing filtering, mining new association rules, managing association rule base, and consulting Alert details. SMS-I also integrates with the TheHive Incident management tool that allows the collaborative investigation of Incidents. TheHIVE platform is a popular and recommended tool for the management of Incident cases [20]. It is tightly integrated with MISP (Malware Information Sharing Platform), which allows the exchange of information on information security Incidents, both internally and between other security teams. TheHive platform can be complemented with the Cortex engine to analyze the Incidents using advanced intelligence. An overview of the SMS-I architecture can be seen in Figure 1.

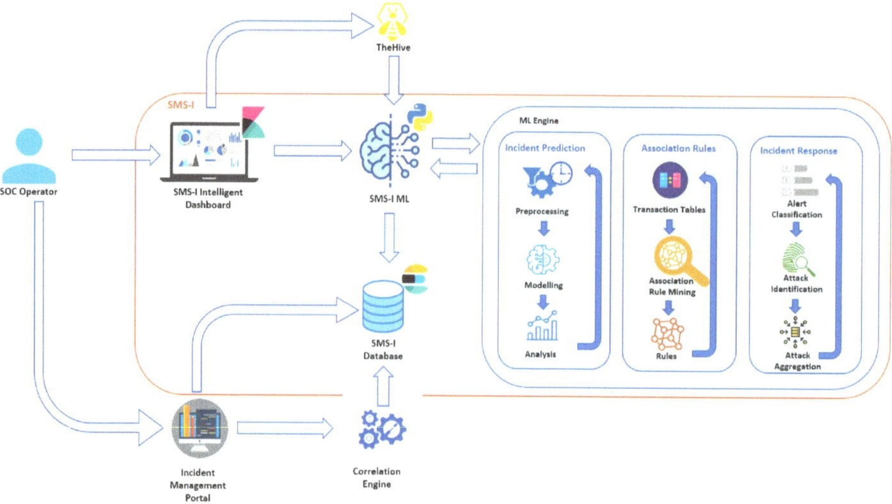

Figure 1. SMS-I architecture overview.

2.1. SMS-I Integration

In this section, SMS-I functionality and integration features are described. The SATIE system's security framework from the SMS-I perspective will be used to provide a better understanding of both SMS-I functionalities and its integration with other SATIE Tools such as the CEngine and the IMP. Note that this should be seen just as an example, and the referred tools can be easily replaced by other security tools, as already mentioned.

As a first step, it is crucial to formally define the fundamental business concepts—Events, Alerts, and Incidents—since they are constantly mentioned throughout the document:

- **Events** are discrete change of state or status of an Asset or group of Assets. They can have multiple heterogeneous sources and are categorized as either cyber or physical, depending on the system that originated them. They contain low-level information about the system's activity, such as network traffic or baggage handling system data. Specific Events may trigger Alerts.
- **Alerts** are notifications that a specific attack has been directed at an organization's information systems. They are triggered when abnormal activity is detected. They are usually related to several Events that have triggered security rules.
- An **Incident** results from the classification of Alerts by the SOC operator. They represent real identified threats to the system. Additionally, it has some sort of impact within the organization, which is described by its severity and completion level.

Unified Modeling Language (UML) and a combination of C4 Model [24] with 4+1 Architectural View Model [25] are used as a formalism to graphically represent software architecture from different views with different degrees of granularity. For example, the following diagram, Figure 2, provides a logic view of the SATIE security ecosystem without the SMS-I tool.

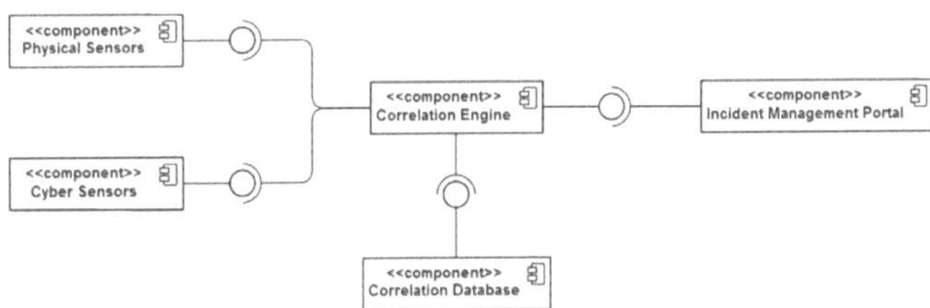

Figure 2. SATIE security ecosystem without SMS-I tool.

Different cyber and physical sensors present in the airport's infrastructure send a large amount of Events related to the airport system's activity. CEngine receives all these Events and stores them in the Correlation Database. When a set of Events triggers a specific rule of CEngine, an Alert is sent to the IMP to be analysed by a security expert and classified as an Incident or not, triggering a security response if needed.

SMS-I, as a forensics investigation system, will use an intelligent layer to help the security expert to inspect Incident and Alert occurrences. For that, the system periodically fetches data from the CEngine and the IMP, using HTTP(S) requests to obtain new Events, Alerts and Incidents generated by the SATIE Toolkit. These data are processed and stored in the Investigation Database of SMS-I, so it can be used by a web application to display several useful visualizations and by an ML Engine. The internal architecture of the SMS-I tool is described in greater detail in the next section. The following diagram, Figure 3, places SMS-I in the context of the SATIE solution as example of integration.

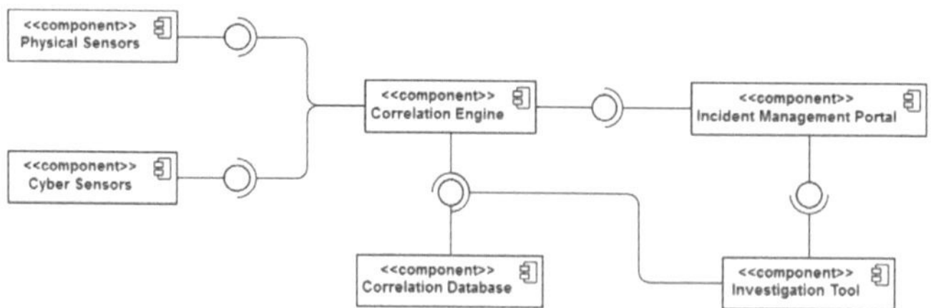

Figure 3. SATIE security ecosystem with SMS-I.

2.2. SMS-I Internal Architecture

SMS-I is a complex system with many different software requirements such as periodic data synchronization, Incident prediction and response computing with ML Engine, association rule mining, dashboard visualization and a series of other functionalities involving different lists and filters. To assure separation of concerns, modularity, and maintainability the system's architecture was designed with the Single Responsibility Principle (SRP) [26] in mind and inspired by a microservices-oriented architecture. Therefore, SMS-I is composed of multiple components with specific well-defined responsibilities. The internal architecture of the forensics investigation system is described in Figure 4.

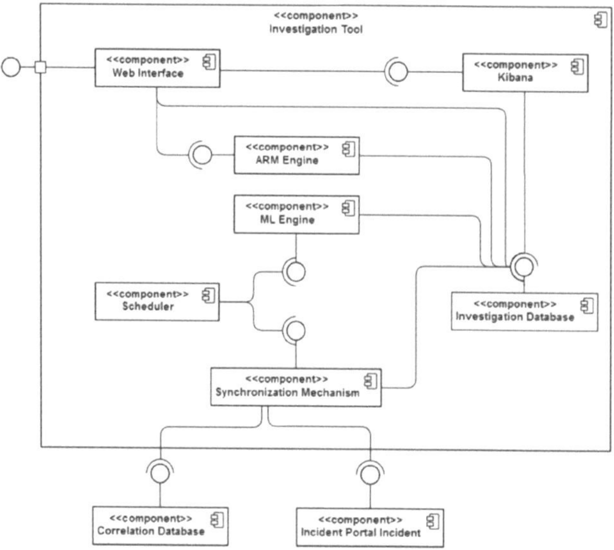

Figure 4. SMS-I architecture.

Each component of the SMS-I architecture can be described as follows:

- **Synchronization Mechanism:** It is the component responsible for acquiring new Events, Alerts and Incidents from the Correlation Engine and the Incident Management Portal, parsing them into predefined formats and storing them into specific indexes of the Investigation Database. The synchronization mechanism is one of the most critical processes of the SMS-I since it allows the system to keep track of the new data generated within the SATIE Environment. Additionally, as new Alerts are added to the database, they are also processed by the ML Engine. The synchronization process is represented in Figure 5.
- **ML Engine:** The ML Engine is responsible for executing the ML models capable of determining, for each Alert, the probability of it being an Incident based on its own

features, features of related Events and the features of other Alerts of a regarded time window. The employed models are expected to grow smarter over time with system usage. The ML engine also analyses the data received from an Incident response point of view, taking into account a collaborative approach and providing confidence scores over other related cases.

- **Scheduler:** The Scheduler performs the orchestration of both Synchronization Mechanism and ML Engine by triggering their execution by a configurable time constraint (e.g., every five minutes, every hour, every day).
- **ARM Engine:** The Association Rule Mining (ARM) Engine provides an API endpoint for executing rule mining algorithms on the Investigation Database data according to a set of parameters specified in the request header. It retrieves the list of generated rules.
- **Investigation Database:** It corresponds to an Elastic Search database that stores all system data—Events, Alerts, Incidents, ML probabilities and association rules.
- **Kibana:** It is part of the ELK Stack and can be described as an interface to the Investigation Database. It provides several methods to build interesting visualizations that are combined to produce intuitive and informative dashboards for inspecting the system's behaviour over time.
- **Web Application:** It provides a Graphical User Interface (GUI) that handles the interaction with the SOC operator. It encapsulates the Kibana dashboards and allows the operator to make use of several functionalities such as consulting Alert lists, performing filtration, mining new association rules, managing association rule base and consulting Alert details.

An Authentication module also grants authentication to the Web Application by matching user credentials with those stored in a shared LDAP server between all SATIE Tools. Lightweight directory access protocol (LDAP) is a protocol for accessing and maintaining data through directory servers often used for authentication and storing information about users, groups, and applications. This implementation allows every user to access every SATIE Tool with the same credentials.

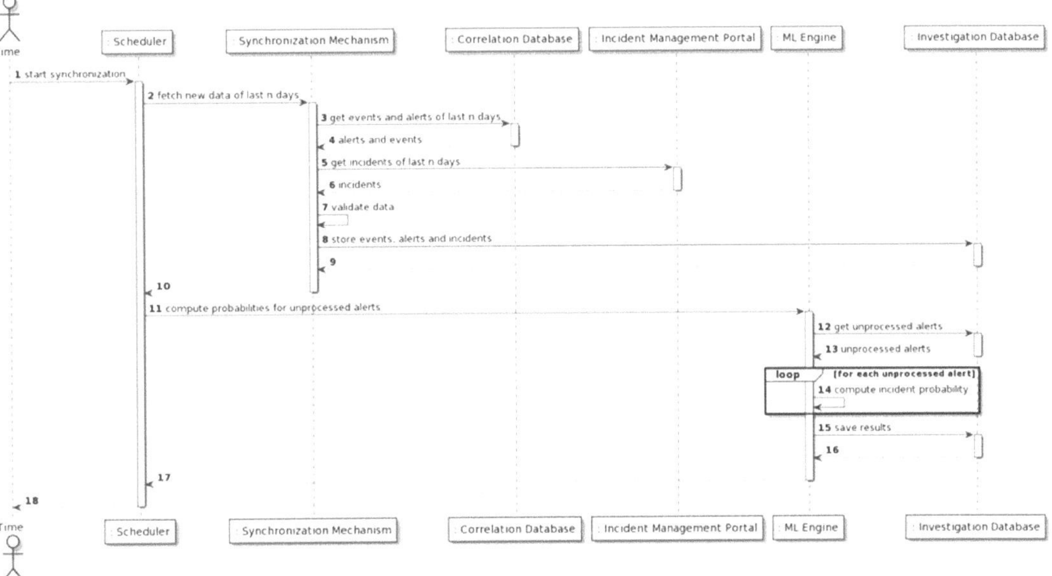

Figure 5. SMS-I Synchronization process.

3. SMS-I Machine Learning Engine

The ML methods present in the SMS-I can be categorized into three groups: Incident probability prediction, association rule mining and Incident response. For the first, supervised algorithms were trained on the sequential data of cyber and physical Alerts to predict the probability of a given Alert being an Incident based on previous occurrences. The second group of methods uses the same data to derive new correlation rules between Alerts that can be analysed to understand the complex pattern inherent to such data. The third group analyses the data to understand if the needed mitigation measures are already in place for the Incident reported. All these groups will be described in the following sections.

3.1. Incident Probabilities

There are many approaches for building ML models that can efficiently detect anomalies in time series data. To properly investigate and explore state of the art methods for such task, a study on public datasets was first performed. One of the difficulties of this study was to find an appropriate testbed for testing the employed methods performance. Currently, in the literature, there is not a huge amount of cyber–physical datasets being one of the most relevant the Secure Water Treatment (SWaT) dataset [27]. However, the physical data are too context-specific and there is no sufficient guarantees that a method able to safeguard a water treatment facility is going to exhibit the same kind of performance in the airport security domain, since they regard different physical sensors. The solution to this problem was to consider only the data from the network under study, which are more general and share many similarities between several domains, providing a better estimate of the model's performance. For example, the same kind of attacks, such as brute force and denial of service can be performed on many different networks to disrupt one or several services. Therefore, we decided to consider network intrusion detection datasets. And despite the lack of good and reliable datasets has been appointed in the literature as one of the main obstacles in intrusion detection research [28], some datasets were recently introduced to solve this issue, namely NSW-NB15 [29], CICIDS2017 [30] and CIDDS-001 [28]. From all the ones previously mentioned, CIDDS-001 was the one selected to be used for several reasons, such as the number of records, the recording period duration and the considered attack types. A comparison between the datasets mentioned above can be found in Table 1.

Table 1. Dataset comparison.

Dataset	Year	Format	Count	Duration	Kind
NSW-NB15	2015	packet, other	2 M	31 h	Emulated
CICIDS2017	2017	uni. flow	3.1 M	5 Days	Emulated
CIDDS-001	2017	uni. flow	33 M	28 Days	Emulated and Real

Anomaly detection for the CIDDS-001 dataset, considering the AttackType label, was addressed using two different approaches: single-flow and multi-flow. The first regards individual flows as separate records and attempts to find differences between normal and attack related ones. The latter considers a given window of flows, performing an analysis on the entire data sequence to detect anomalies. For each approach three ML algorithms were experimented and compared: Random Forest (RF), Multi-player Perception (MLP) and Long-Short Term Memory (LSTM). In the next sections, we briefly describe this work. For more detail please see [31].

3.1.1. Incident Probabilities Testbed

The CIDDS-001 network traffic data are represented in unidirectional netflow format which, is a universal standard. The data were recorded for approximately four weeks from two different environments, an emulated small business environment, OpenStack, and External Server, which captured real traffic from the internet. The OpenStack environment includes several clients and servers, such as e-mail and web server. In this testbed, four different types of attacks were performed: ping scans, port scans, brute forces and denial of service. The considered traffic data regards several features such as source and destination ports, source and destination IPs, communication protocol, number of transmitted bytes, number of transmitted packets, flow duration and TCP flags. Additionally, the data has three different labels, Class, AttackType and AttackDescription. For this investigation, the AttackType label was used since it provides a categorization of the different attacks that were performed. The considered algorithms were trained with this label so that they could recognise and distinguish the different attacks present in the testbed.

Random Forest (RF) is a supervised learning algorithm that uses an ensemble of decision trees, useful for classification or regression problems. Each decision tree that composes the "forest" reaches a prediction and the results of all of them is selected by majority voting or the average of outputs. By having multiple uncorrelated models for each of the trees, the possible individual errors of each one were diluted, relying on the "wisdom of the crowd" [32]. Another helpful model for classification and regression is a feed-forward neural network, Multilayer Perceptron (MLP). An MLP is a network of several layers of nodes, or neurons, each one with an activation function that maps the weighted inputs to the output of each node. Although feed forward means the data moves in only one direction, this model does benefit from back propagation during training, where the error between the prediction and the real value is fed back through the network to adjust the weights of each connection [33]. Due to the nature of the dataset used, a Long Short-Term Memory model were also employed. This neural network, unlike normal feed forward networks such as the previous example, has feedback connections. This allows it to process sequences of data such as network or Intrusion Detection System (IDS) [34].

3.1.2. TestBed Results

For evaluating and comparing the algorithms performance the dataset was split into three sets, training, validation and testing. The models were trained using the labelled data of the train set and their predictions were computed for the validation and testing set. By comparing these predictions with the real values several indicators of the methods performance can be calculated such as:

$$\text{Accuracy} = \frac{\text{Number of correct predictions}}{\text{Total number of predictions}}, \quad \text{Precision} = \frac{\text{Correct positives}}{\text{Total number of positives}},$$

$$\text{Recall} = \frac{\text{Correct positives}}{\text{Total number of positive samples}}, \quad \text{F1-score} = \frac{2 \times \text{Precision} \times \text{Recall}}{\text{Precision} + \text{Recall}},$$

$$\text{FPR} = \frac{\text{number of false positives}}{\text{total number of negatives}}.$$

Accuracy is biased towards the majority class, normal traffic, since it is obtained by dividing the number of correct predictions by the total number of observations. Hence, F1-score provides a better evaluation of an algorithm's performance since it is the harmonic mean of precision and recall. For the single-flow approach the obtained results are presented in Table 2.

Table 2. Results for the single-flow approach.

Model	Accuracy	Precision	Recall	F1-Score	FPR
LSTM	99.91	98.37	71.40	74.23	00.05
RF	99.90	79.43	95.68	85.04	00.02
MLP	99.92	78.68	73.75	75.79	00.06

Analysing the results, it can be said that the best performing model was the RF with a F1-score of 85.04, it also exhibits lower recall in comparison to its value of precision. On the other hand, the LSTM has better precision with lower recall presenting an F1-score of 74.23. The MLP is quite balanced in terms of both metrics which resulted in an F1-score of 75.79, higher than the one of the LSTM. The RF also presents the lowest occurrence of false alarms, a FPR of 00.02 being arguably the best model for the single flow viewpoint.

For the multi-flow approach, the results are quite different. With the increase of the flow window size the results of the LSTM keep improving while the ones of RF and MLP decrease. Nevertheless, the RF for a window of 10 flows presents an F1-score of 89.82, close to the best value found, 91.66, for the LSTM with a window size of 70. The methods performance over the increase of window size is represented in Figure 6.

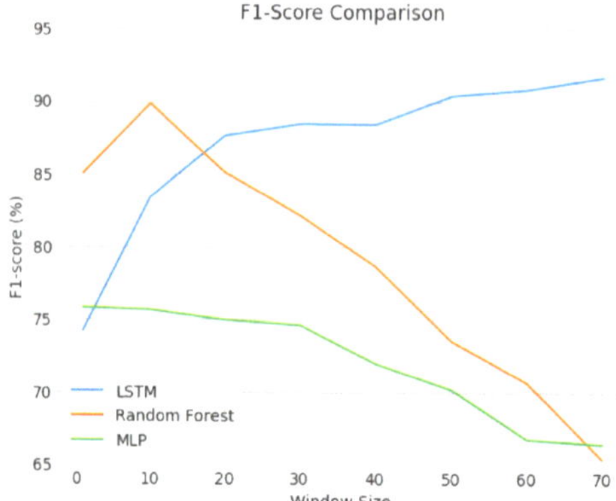

Figure 6. Performance over window size.

The best performing models are LSTM-70 and RF-10, and they share the same value of FPR (Table 3). However, the LSTM presents a higher precision and lower recall in comparison with the RF. Since the values of these metrics are more balanced for the LSTM 94.03 precision and 89.71 recall, it results in the highest F1-score, 91.66. The complete results are presented in Table 3.

Table 3. Results for the multi-flow approach.

Model	Accuracy	Precision	Recall	F1-Score	FPR
LSTM-70	99.94	94.03	89.71	91.66	00.04
RF-10	99.95	96.83	85.65	89.82	00.04

These results lead to believe that the multi-flow approach outperforms the single-flow-based one and that the LSTM is a robust algorithm for understanding complex patterns in sequential data, in particularly, network traffic data. Furthermore, the algorithms performance seems to keep improving as the window size grows larger. Optimizing the value of the window can be a crucial point for obtaining the best possible intrusion detection classifier for the CIDDS-001 context.

3.1.3. SATIE Toolkit Preliminary Results

The normal usage of the SATIE Toolkit and the scenario simulation runs produced, on a regular basis, several Alerts and Incidents. These data, although not being the best to serve as testbed for ML models, were used to obtain some preliminary results for the Incident probability algorithm. These experiments were essential to understand which approaches are better for the SATIE data and how well can the algorithms distinguish between malicious Alerts, which were tagged as Incidents, and false positive Alerts. The considered dataset was built with data extracted from the Investigation Database, which was in turn obtained by the Synchronization Mechanism continuous execution. All the Alerts related to Incidents, 368, were labelled as malicious while the remaining ones, 9215, were marked as normal. The dataset is not large in terms of data volume and has a high-class imbalance since more than 96% of records are benign. These characteristics made the application of deep learning approaches such as MLP and LSTM unviable. Additionally, there were multiple challenges regarding data quality such as Alerts related to Incidents that were not manually labelled in the IMP, Alerts with a lot of empty fields that were only generated to test SATIE Tools and many repeated entries due to simulations that are executed daily. To mitigate these problems, every feature with over 60% missing values were discarded as well as all the Alerts related to the repeated daily executions. Furthermore, an oversampling method, Synthetic Minority Oversampling Technique (SMOTE) was used to produce synthetic examples of Incidents to minimize the class imbalance.

The data, after being pre-processed, was split into two sets: 70% for training and 30% for the test. Then, a RF model was used as a classifier (RF-1), obtaining an accuracy of 98.08%. However, the value of F1-score, 60.94%, indicated that the model was performing poorly on the minority class, failing to classify most of the Incidents. In an attempt to improve the obtained results, three time-based features were engineered for a given window of time (30 min): the number of Alerts, the number of distinct sensors and the most common sensor. With these new features, the accuracy and F1-score of this new classifier (RF-2) improved significantly, 98.54% and 76.60% respectively. The preliminary results lead us to believe that an approach which combines both individual Alert features and time-based engineered features can work quite well on the SATIE data. On the other hand, the dataset extracted from the Correlation Engine, despite its limitations, was a good starting point to fine tune the SMS-I ML algorithms. This was improved using the different scenario simulation executions that were executed on the platform, learning new patterns that was used to identify Incidents more accurately in the demonstration phase.

3.2. Association Rule Mining

Apriori is a very popular algorithm for data mining focusing on association rules, developed by Agrawal and Srikan in 1994 [35]. It identifies the items or patterns in a transactional dataset and then relates frequent occurrences to those patterns, generating association rules to describe them [36]. These rules are comprised of statements that describe the relationships between seemingly unrelated items inside a transaction.

Let $X = \{i_1, 1_2, \ldots, i_m\}$ be the set of all items concerned in a dataset, and $T = \{t_1, t_2, \ldots, t_m\}$ be a set of transactions, where each transaction is a set of items. The association rule, noted as $X \Rightarrow Y$ indicates a certain relation between two itemsets X and Y. An association rule $X \Rightarrow Y$ is supported if the percentage of transactions that contain both itemset X and Y in T exceeds a certain threshold, called support threshold, i.e., $\mathtt{Support}(X \Rightarrow Y) = \frac{\text{Number of transactions containing } X \text{ and } Y}{\text{Total number of transactions}}$. Furthermore, the confidence for the association rule $X \Rightarrow Y$ is defined by the percentage of transactions that contain itemset Y among transactions containing itemset X, i.e., $\mathtt{Confidence}(X \Rightarrow Y) = \frac{\text{Number of transactions containing } X \text{ and } Y}{\text{Number of transactions containing } X}$. The support represents the usefulness of the discovered rule and the confidence represents certainty of the rule. Lift is a simple correlation measuring whether X and Y are independent or dependent and correlated Events. It is calculated by $\mathtt{Lift}(X \Rightarrow Y) = \frac{\text{Number of transactions containing } X \text{ and } Y / \text{Number of transactions containing } X}{\text{Percentage of transactions containing } Y}$. If a rule has a lift of one, X and Y are independent and no rule will be generated containing either event. If a rule has a lift greater than one, X and Y are dependent and correlated positively.

To build the association rule mining for the SMS-I tool, using the apriori algorithm, the sequences of Alerts in a mineable database were grouped by using a certain criterion to form transactions. That criterion is a time window, and the focus will be the name of the sensor that originated the Alert. In order to compile the transactional dataset, for each Alert, the selected window was subtracted to its "detect_date" field. From the obtained time range, all Alerts that fell inside that interval were joined and a list with their sensor's name was created, performing this operation on all entries, and obtaining the set of transactions. Using this set of transactions several rules are generated to allow the user to understand the correlation of the different sensor Alerts in an attack.

3.3. Incident Response

After positive identification of an Alert as a security threat, measures need to be taken to limit the impact of the attack. These mitigation measures are usually described in procedures that detail, step-by-step, how to proceed when dealing with a given type of attack. These procedures are then compiled into playbooks [37] that can be extended to perform other important tasks in the mitigation or remediation process, tailored to the organization that is using them. A "phishing email" playbook, for example, might not only include the normal steps of deleting emails from affected inboxes and running scans on the machines of victims to make sure nothing was compromised, but also send out personalized memos raising awareness about this type of attack.

Compiling a list of playbooks for different types of attacks allows automation of much of their steps, considerably streamlining a SOCs workflow [37]. Additionally, multiple Alerts originating from the same type of attack, or even the same attack, can be aggregated in cases where playbooks can be applied to all the Alerts in a case at the same time.

In order to further automate cybersecurity, and focusing on Incident Response in a SOC workflow, a new module of SMS-I tool (Incident Response) was designed to be capable of slotting into current SOC tools, as a way of enriching incoming Alerts. This module is leveraged as a decision support system, employing multiple models to perform identification and classification of Alerts, adding their results as another point of consideration for security expert analysis. The additional information helps analysts not only decide if a given Alert is in fact an attack, but also by identifying which case contains playbooks to treat similar Alerts.

SMS-I Incident Response module aims to tackle two problems of the SOC pipeline: classification of incoming Alerts for security threats (Alert Classification); and grouping of similar Alerts in cases for bulk processing (Alert Aggregation). Although different in their nature, both of these are classification problems where a set of data points are categorized into classes. In this context, the data points will be Alerts and the classes their possible label.

In the Alert Classification problem, only two possible classes exist for an Alert, either attack or normal. In contrast, in the Attack Aggregation problem, the possible classes are the existing cases in the system. Furthermore, the nature of the data for Attack Aggregation binary classification problem guarantees that all the future incoming entries will only ever be of two possible types.On the other hand, classifying each Alert into groups will fail when a never before seen Alert, i.e., from a new type of attack, arrives in the queue. In this case, the multiclass classification model, trained with known classes will incorrectly identify the new Alert as one of the existing classes. For this reason, a middle step needs to exist between both classification problems—Attack Identification. After being classified as an attack by the first model, the system needs to decide if this Alert is similar to other Alerts already in the database or if it is a new one. As such, an anomaly detection model will be trained with Alerts already in the system to create a baseline of known Alerts, filtering any outliers and skipping the final step. The third model is trained on groups of Alerts that compose a case, selecting the relevant case for every incoming entry. The sequence of these three steps can be seen in Figure 7.

Each of the three different phases of the SMS-I Incident Response module, requires ML models tuned to the unique specifications of their given problem. These models will undergo a selection stage where data originating from the final system is used to train and compare the results among them.

3.3.1. Alert Classification

The first step in this Incident Response pipeline will analyse an Alert in order to classify it as an attack, or not attack. If the Alert receives the "not attack" classification, then the Alert is the result of a false positive and can be safely disregarded. On the other hand, if the Alert is considered an attack, it will continue to the next step of this pipeline. This binary classification problem is extensively studied in this domain, with multiple models continually being researched in the literature [38–40]. Three models were selected for this first step:

- **Random Forest**, as already mentioned, is a tree based model, employing a set of decision trees and taking in account the output of each one. A decision tree aggregates datapoints by iteratively splitting the features of a given dataset into consecutive binary nodes, ending each branch on its outcome, or label. Although very good with low complexity data, higher sized trees can lead to overfitting. Random Forest models mitigate this issue by using an ensemble of unrelated decision trees and consolidating their results, achieving significant results in the literature for both classification and regression problems.
- **Support-Vector Machines (SVM)** [41] is a probabilistic model that maps training data to points in space, and finds the hyperplane with the maximum margin that separates the two classes. Newer data points are mapped in space in the same way and classified according to which side of the hyperplane they have landed. This model is a very robust classifier with the caveat that it is limited to binary-class classification.
- Similarly to Random Forest, **XgBoost** [42] is an ensemble of decision trees, but using a gradient boosting algorithm. Instead of concurrently training a group of decision tree models and averaging their output, models are trained consecutively using the residuals from each iteration to train the next one.

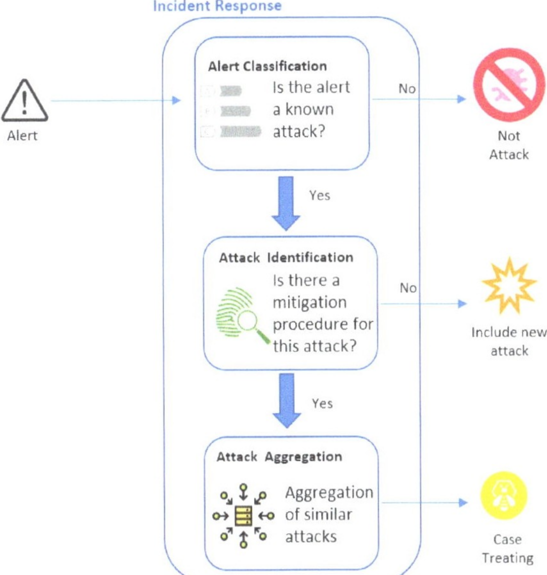

Figure 7. SMS-I Incident Response module Architecture.

3.3.2. Attack Identification

In order to classify an incoming Alert as "unknown", an anomaly detection based approach was selected. Although this approach is not uncommon for the cybersecurity domain, it is normally applied to the detection of attacks, whereas here, it is used to identify Alerts different from everything in the system.

After classification in the first step, an Alert classified as attack is analysed for known information. The objective is to aggregate this new Alert with other Alerts in the system. If the incoming Alert is known, it will be assigned to a case containing playbooks on how to deal with this type of attack. If it is unknown, the Alert is marked as such, to be analysed and procedures prepared on how to deal with this type of attack. For this novel use case, two models were picked from the literature, as the most suitable:

- **Isolation Forest** [43] is a tree based model that uses distance between data points to detect outliers, hinging on the principle that outliers are distinct from normal data. During the construction of the binary tree, data are grouped into branches according to their similarity, with more similar entries needing longer branches to differentiate them. As such, data closer to the root of the tree can be considered an anomaly since it was easily distinguishable from the rest.
- **One-Class Support-Vector Machines** [44] is a similar implementation to SVM but instead of using an hyperplane to separate two classes, it uses an hypersphere around normal data and classifies new data based on its distance to the sphere.

3.3.3. Attack Aggregation

Finally, in the third step, Alerts previously marked as both "attack" and "known" in previous steps are matched to the Alerts in the system, searching for a suitable case to be assigned to, allowing automatic application of remediation or mitigation techniques contained in the related playbook.

The multiple possible results for this step, cases, makes this a multiclass classification problem, a subset of normal classification. As such, some models from the first step were also selected:

- **Random Forest** due to its robust results and straightforward implementation, behaving no differently in binary and multiclass classification problems.
- Although models such as **Support-Vector Machines** in its most simple type only supports binary classification, implementations exist where the problem is compartmentalized into multiple binary classification problems followed by the same principle: discovering the hyperplane that linearly separates classes [45,46].
- **K-Nearest Neighbors (KNN)** [47] uses distance between datapoints to identify clusters of similar data. Despite its good results it is not very scalable due to being computationally demanding.

3.4. Preliminary Results

Despite our first evaluation of which models should be used for each phase of the SMS-I Incident Response module, we need to test them in a dataset to select the one that should be deployed. For that, we used the testbed dataset already described in Section 3.1.1. In Table 4, we present the results for each phase. Note that we only consider the models described in the previous section, because they have already been chosen as the best approaches to be tested.

Table 4. Incident Response Experiment Results.

Steps	Models	Accuracy	F1-Score	Macro F1-Score
Alert Classification	RF	97.1	69.2	96.8
	SVM	97.3	63.1	96.5
	XgBoost	97.3	70.4	96.9
Attack Identification	IF	80.9	82.8	80.8
	One Class SVM	67.6	73.7	65.6
Attack Aggregation	RF	80.2	58.5	77.8
	SVM	80.2	59.2	78.3
	KNN	88.3	54.9	85.4

F1-score was selected as the metric of choice given its good balance between Precision and Recall while paying attention to class imbalance existent in the data. This imbalance can also be observed in the difference between macro and weighted metrics, since macro metrics take into account the number of each class' members during result calculations. As such, for the first and third steps, the macro F1-score was used to evaluate the impact differently sized classes have in the final results. For the second phase F1-score was also used, only this time focusing on the score for the outlier class, i.e., the Alerts considered unknown to the system. For the first and second step of the SMS-I Incident Management module, tree based models achieved the best performance in the experiments, with XgBoost and Isolation Forest respectively selected for the mentioned steps. For the third step's experiments, although a mostly inconclusive affair due to the closeness of results, SVM did manage to edge out ahead.

4. SMS-I Intelligent Dashboard

SMS-I allows the analysis of data from heterogeneous systems over different time frames. To provide this information regarding the system's Events, Alerts, and Incidents in a useful way, it implements a visualization tool—the SMS-I Intelligent Dashboard. Furthermore, it assists and facilitates the security analyst's work using graphical dashboards and Alert classification suggestions, which derive from the SMS-I ML Engine previously presented. Consequently, users can more easily identify anomalous situations that can be related to possible Incident occurrences. They can also explore information, with varying levels of detail, including logical information and technical specifications. An overview of the different information provided can be seen in Figure 8.

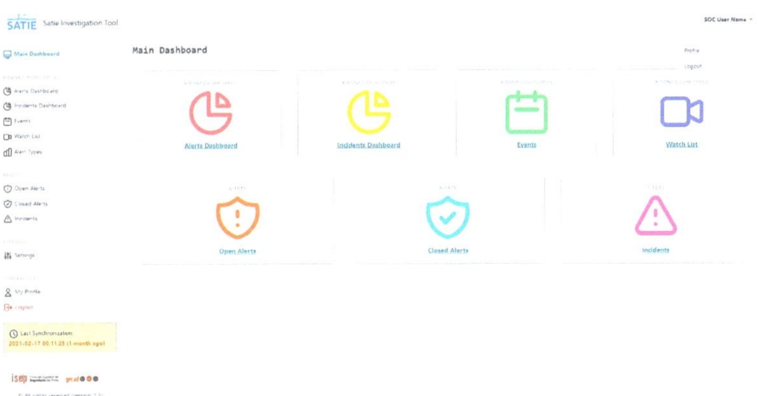

Figure 8. SMS-I Intelligent Dashboard overview.

Two different detailed dashboards were accessible: Alerts and Incidents Dashboards. Both were developed using Elasticsearch and Kibana technologies. Elasticsearch is responsible for the analysis, normalization, enrichment and storage of Alert and Incident data, as well as data provided by ML algorithms. Then, these data are accessed by Kibana to create these two dashboards, which allow the user to search and visualize airport security related data.

The Alerts Dashboard includes all data related to airport security Alerts generated by the different cyber and physical Threat Detection Systems available in the SATIE Toolkit. One of the main goals of this dashboard is to monitor the quantity, nature, and severity of Alerts, considering their Incident prediction probability, which is calculated by the SMS-I ML Engine. More than 70% of security analysts feel overwhelmed with the number of Alerts and Incidents they need to investigate for a day [48]. In addition, more than 50% of organizations receive over 10,000 Alerts daily, which can lead to Alert fatigue and neglect. Therefore, to maintain SOC efficiency and reduce the impact of the investigation on the responsible personnel, it is essential to control the quantity of received Alerts and Incidents. Therefore, a set of graphics and metrics were added to this dashboard (see Figure 9) to monitor the number of Alerts received to help avoid a sudden overload of Alerts by monitoring the total number of cyber and physical Alerts. In addition, an Alert gauge was added to ensure that an overwhelming quantity of Alerts is not reached.

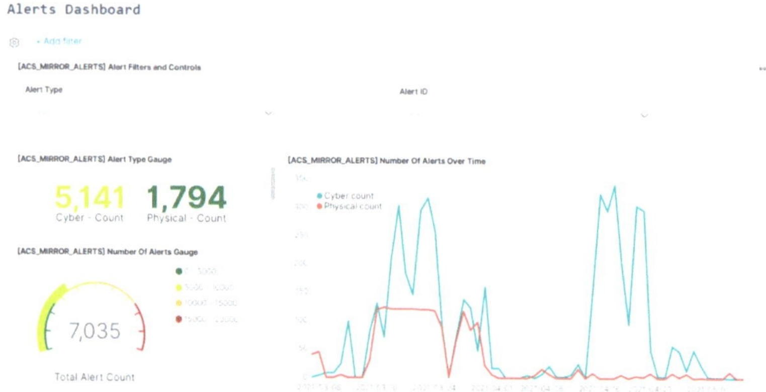

Figure 9. SMS-I Intelligent Dashboard: Alert quantity monitoring visualizations.

The severity of Alerts is another important parameter that needs to be monitored by security analysts, since Alert's severity defines if the Alert should be ignored or if there is a need to conduct a more thorough investigation. For the SATIE project, four severity levels were defined: high, medium, low, and info. Besides controlling the number of Alerts for each severity level, to avoid the overburdening of security analysts, using the Alerts dashboard is also possible to monitor the date of occurrence of Alerts (see Figure 10). This is useful to perform pattern and trend identification and to study previous Incidents and preceding Alerts.

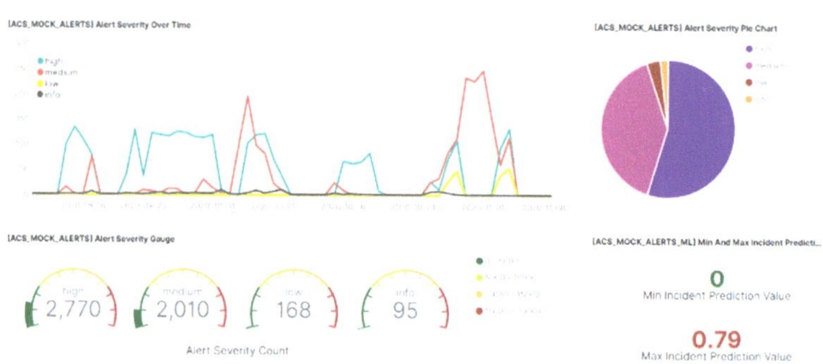

Figure 10. Alerts Dashboard—Alert severity monitoring visualizations.

The results provided by the ML engine regarding the Incident prediction probability, in other words, the probability of an Alert representing an Incident, can also be visualized in the Alerts dashboard (Figure 11). A set of graphics and metrics display, from 0% to 100%, the number of Alerts that possess a certain probability of being an Incident, as well as the average Incident prediction probability. In the example shown, most Alerts have an

Incident prediction probability lower than 35%, which leads to a low average probability value. This means that overall, there probably is not an occurrence of an Incident.

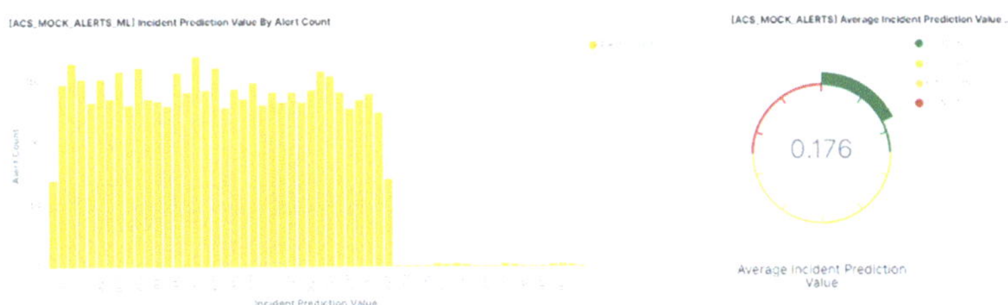

Figure 11. Alerts Dashboard—Incident prediction probability visualizations.

The most common source and target IPs and ports are also displayed to the user in the Alerts Dashboard (Figure 12). This information can be very valuable for the security analyst, as it helps to discover information about the attacks, namely where they come from and what the targets are.

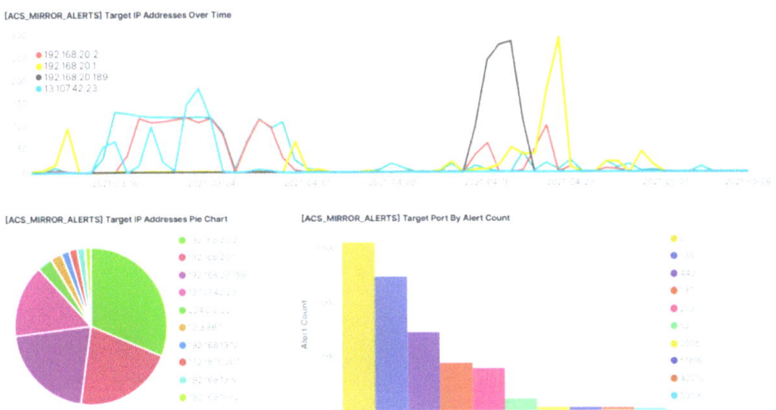

Figure 12. Alerts Dashboard—Target IP and Ports visualizations. Note that IPs have been obfuscated for security reasons.

The Incidents Dashboard aggregates all detected Incidents related to airport security. This dashboard follows the structure of the Alerts Dashboard by monitoring the quantity, nature, and severity of Incidents (Figure 13). Thus, similar to what happens with the Alerts Dashboard, it has similar visualizations available to the user, displaying information regarding Incident quantity monitoring and Incident severity monitoring.

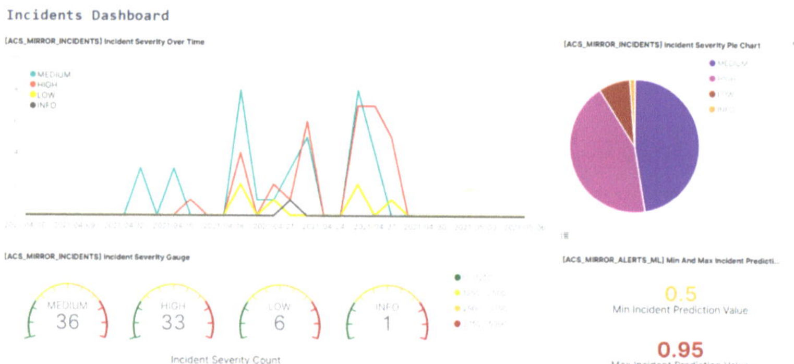

Figure 13. Incidents Dashboard—Incidents severity monitoring visualizations.

SMS-I Intelligent Dashboard also makes available a set of different visualizations. Events timeline is one of them. It provides ability to security analysts to preview a timeline of Events within the system. Events are displayed in the form of an ordered timeline, with summarized info of each event (Figure 14). Filters can be applied to customize the timeline, such as: maximum Alerts number, minimum Incident probability, and time range.

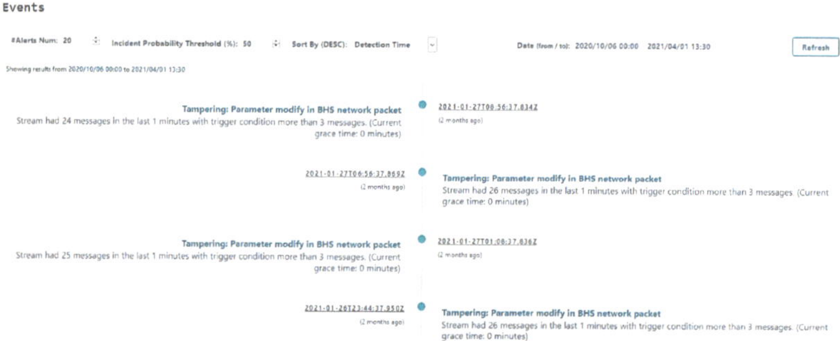

Figure 14. SMS-I Intelligent Dashboard: Events timeline.

A Watch List section is also available and allows users to preview a list of the latest Alerts within the system (Figure 15). Alerts in this list are being displayed in the form of aligned cards, with summarized info of each Alert within the corresponding card. The list can be sorted by detection time or Incident probability, and filtered by maximum Alerts number, minimum Incident probability, and time range.

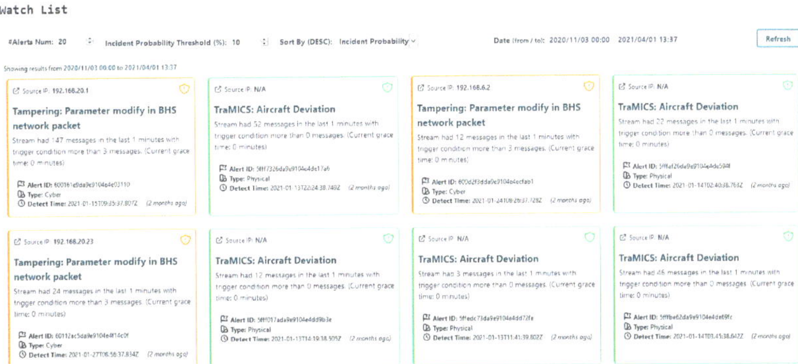

Figure 15. Watch List with example Alerts.

Each card within the list has highlights of the Alert details (Figure 16). Users can click on any card to display the full details of the corresponding Alert (Figure 17). Furthermore, cards are displayed using indexed colours that reflect the severity level of each Alert (red for High, orange for Medium, and Green for low).

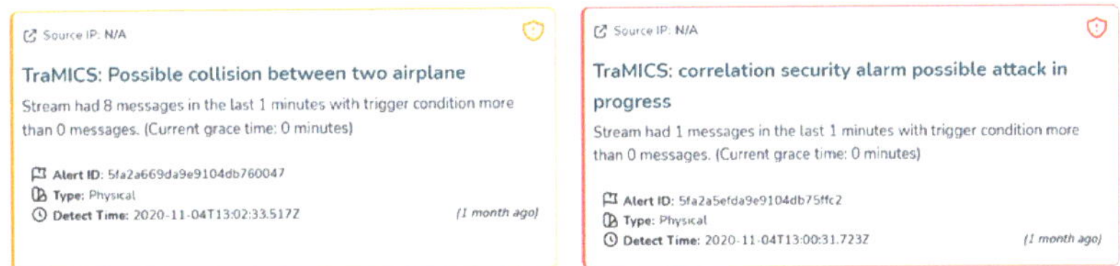

Figure 16. Watch List Alert Cards example (see [49] for more information on TraMICS).

When the user clicks on a specific Alert Card, the corresponding Alert details will be displayed. Details include the Alert title and description, information identifying the Alert, the source and target details, and the probability of this Alert being an Incident.

If the card is a specific Incident Card, the corresponding Incident details as well as the related Alerts will be displayed (Figure 18).

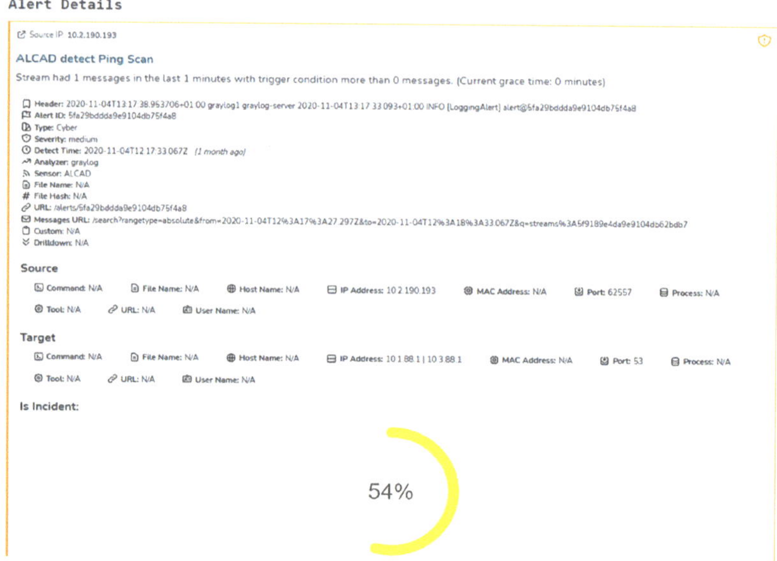

Figure 17. Alert Details example.

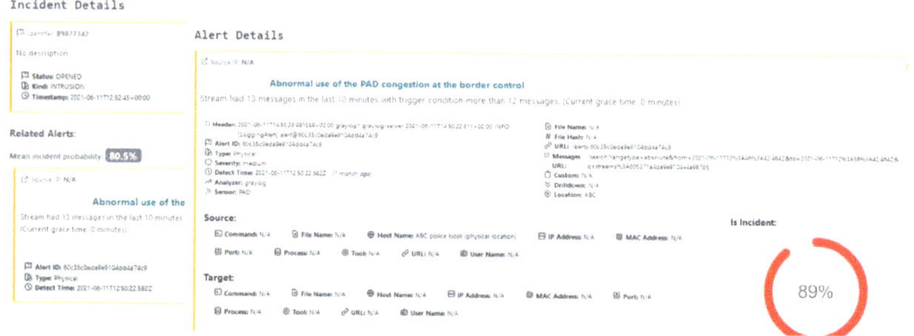

Figure 18. SMS-I Intelligent Dashboard: Incident and Alert details example.

It is also possible to display the distribution of Alerts as per their types (physical/cyber), and due to multiple levels of aggregation (no aggregation, by minutes, by hours, by days, …), using the Alert Types section of SMS-I Dashboard (Figure 19). Alerts can be also filtered by their type, Incident probability, and detection time.

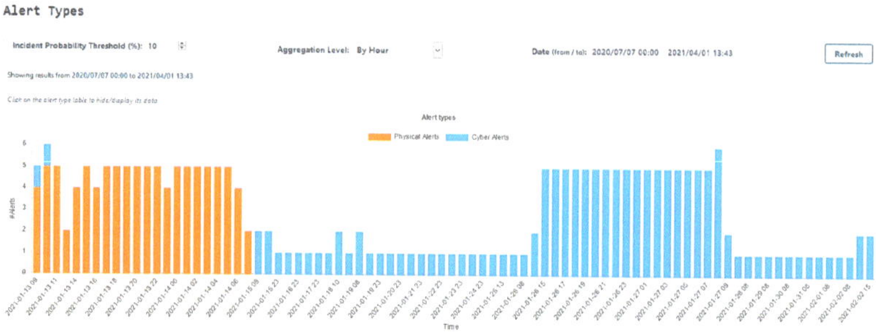

Figure 19. Alert Types visualization.

Another important part of SMS-I Intelligent Dashboard is the Association Rules functionality (Figure 20) which allows security analysts to automatically generate rules that can help them understand, using historical data, the correlation of the different sensor Alerts in an attack. The security analyst can customize the parameters, namely the time window, the support and confidence, to generate different rules.

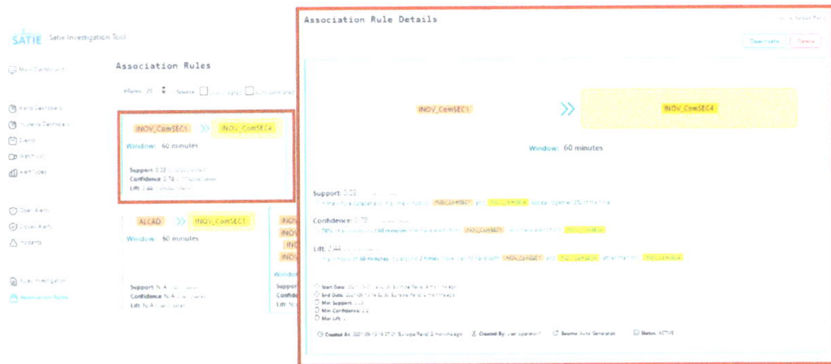

Figure 20. SMS-I Intelligent Dashboard: Association rules visualization.

5. SMS-I Incident Response Integration

TheHive is an Incident management tool focused on Incident analysis used by security analysts to manage Incidents and give them an adequate treatment. This tool is often used by the organizations due to its open-source implementation, and collaboration focused functionalities. TheHive is designed to support multi-enterprise SOCs in a collaborative Incident management and orchestration environment. This allows security analysts and experts to share information between partners and work on cases collaboratively. Furthermore, TheHive contains connections to security threat databases, namely MISP, receiving up-to-date intelligence on any new security threats.

SMS-I allows a direct integration with the TheHive tool. Due to TheHive's highly collaboration focused functionalities, this integration can be described as in Figure 21, with the novel SMS-I Incident Response module capturing incoming Alerts from multiple sources and, after ML analysis, augmenting their information with intelligent classification.

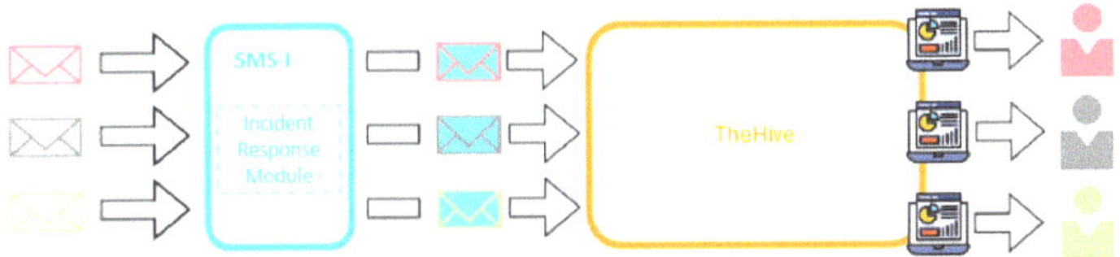

Figure 21. SMS-I Incident Response module information flow.

The improved Alerts are then submitted to TheHive's new Alert queue, waiting for manual verification (Figure 22). When security analysts log in to TheHive to perform this verification, they can use the ML analysis contained in each Alert to help decide on how to proceed with each one. This information is very useful, since the security analyst does not need to try to understand if there already exist similar attacks in the database, for example. This information is already provided by SMS-I in the additional fields of the Alert (Figure 23).

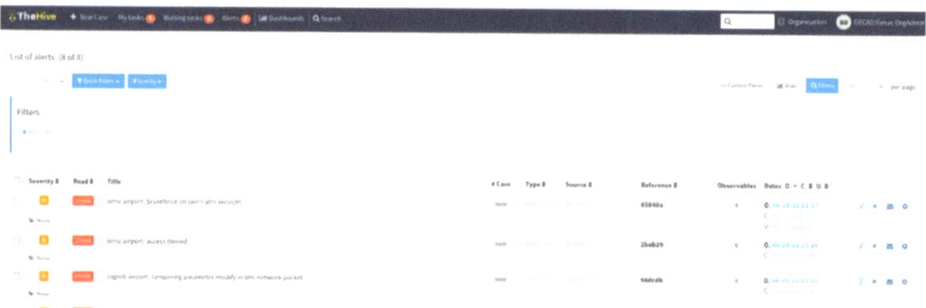

Figure 22. TheHive Alert Queue.

TheHive utilizes its own concept of observables [50], stateful properties of an Alert that are likely to indicate an intrusion, allowing investigations to be run on individual or groups of observables to verify their compromise level (Figure 23). Therefore, source IP, file hash, or sender email domain are fields contained in an Alert received by SMS-I that can be considered observables. In the scope of TheHive, this is information that may indicate an attack. Since SMS-I already provides this information, the security analyst does not need to manually add it.

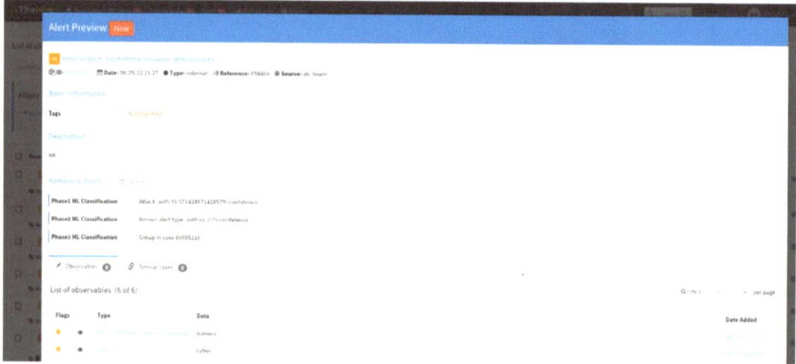

Figure 23. TheHive Alert Example.

6. SMS-I Demonstration

SMS-I tool was validated and demonstrated in the scope of the SATIE project, using a simulation platform and in the pilot sites [51–53]. The different security analysts were first introduced to the platform. First, we explained the purpose of the SMS-I tool as a whole, and then we showed how they can get useful insights from the information in the SMS-I Intelligent Dashboard. Then, the security analysts used the SMS-I tool through the SMS-I Intelligent Dashboard. During the simulations and then in the demonstrations several data and opinions were gathered and used to fine tune the tool and refine the SMS-I ML engine. All the experiments also highlighted the need to have tools such as SMS-I, that intelligently correlate the different cyber and physical security Alerts and assist the security analysts to detect highly sophisticated attacks of this time and the future. IBM stated that it took an average of 287 days to identify and contain a data breach in 2020 [54]. This detection time demonstrates how difficult is for companies to detect and mitigate cyber attacks [55]. This is even more difficult in CPS, where attacks usually involve multistage and multiple components. Moreover, the analytic tasks conducted by security analysts rely heavily on a cognitive decision-making process that can differ between analysts, depending on their technical knowledge or level of experience [56]. This is why it is so important to have intelligent tools, as SMS-I, to support security analyst decisions.

To demonstrate the efficiency of the different tools in the SATIE toolkit several realistic scenarios incorporating a considerable number of potential cyber and physical attacks were defined. In one of these threat scenarios, an attacker seeks to perform cyber attacks on the Airport Operation Control Center (AOCC) system to manipulate the information displayed in the Flight Information Display System (FIDS), thus giving origin to passenger movements which result in an irregular and disorderly movement of people in the terminal, and odd plane movements on the platform to create confusion on the apron. The attacker's first actions can be used to demonstrate the effectiveness of the SMS-I tool and the help it can give to security analysts in their decision-making process. The scenario starts with an attacker who sends a spear-phishing email to a computer with administrator privileges. An employee opens the email on that computer and clicks on the link which allows the malware to be downloaded and executed. This malware allows the attacker to take remote control of the computer. Then, the attacker performs a network scan to determine the network address and port of the Airport Operation Database server—his main target. From a security analyst's perspective, it is important to correlate both Events and understand that they are steps of the same multi-step attack. However, due to the difficulty of analyzing these different Events, which can be, for example, observed and classified by different analysts, they are sometimes classified as isolated Events instead of being correlated and aggregated. This was what happened in the demonstration of this scenario. The security operator reported the corresponding Alerts as two different Incidents, as can be seen in Figure 24.

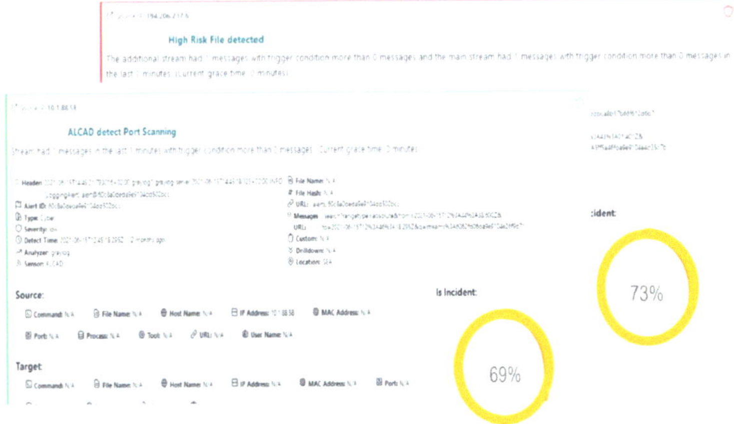

Figure 24. SMS-I Intelligent Dashboard: Malware Detection by Malware Analyser and Network Scan detection by ALCAD system (part of SATIE Toolkit) [57].

Moreover, the port scanning Alert was classified as a low severity Incident, which should not be the case since it is already the second step of the multi-step attack.

Using the SMS-I Intelligent Dashboard, after the reporting of the Incident by the security operator, the security expert can observe that. Despite this being an Incident that was reported as a low severity Incident, it is related to an Alert that has a 69% probability of being an Incident (Figure 24), thus it should be reported with higher severity. Similarly, the SMS-I Incident Response module classifies the port scan Alert as an attack with 66% confidence (Figure 25), while not discovering similar Alerts in the system. This means a playbook should be created with steps mitigating this type of attack so that future attacks of the same type can more easily be treated.

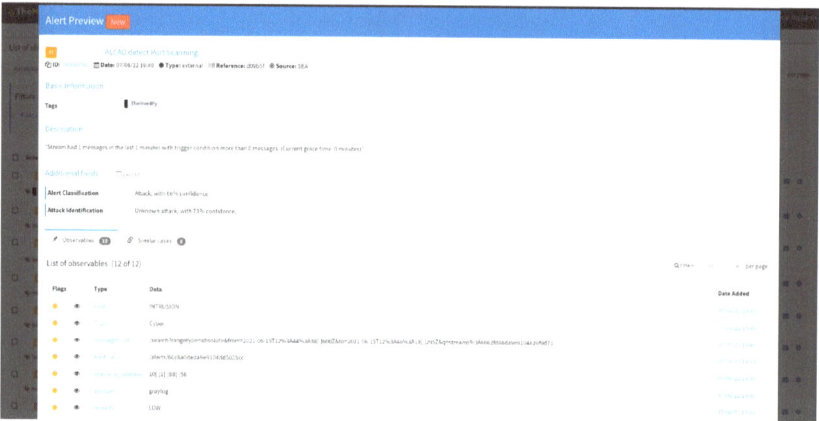

Figure 25. SMS-I Incident Response results for Network Scan example (TheHive view).

Furthermore, using association rules, the security analyst can understand that the malware and the network scan Alerts are correlated and should be reported as being part of the same Incident (Figure 26). This information can also be added to the playbook to have more information about this type of attacks.

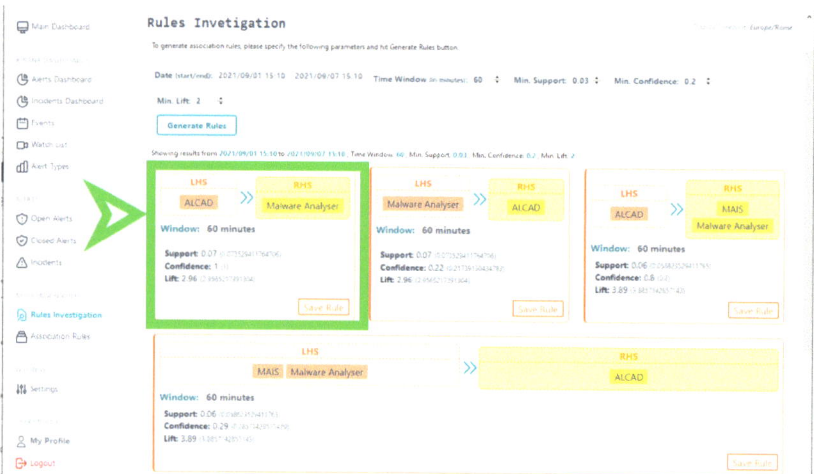

Figure 26. Association Rules generated by SMS-I tool. The rule marked is the one generated by the example described.

Therefore, with this demonstration, we showed not only the ability of the SMS-I to support the security experts work, but it also allowed us, using a very simple "real" example, to illustrate the need for intelligent tools that can assist security analysts in their decision-making process. Using the SMS-I tool, the security analyst can understand the weaknesses of the first security analysis and have intelligent suggestions on how to combat and even resolve them. Different suggestions are provided to the analyst to define mitigation measures to avoid future attacks. Furthermore, SMS-I also simplifies the sharing of information, through TheHive platform, to support the security awareness of other partners.

7. Conclusions

This work describes the SMS-I tool that allows the improvement of the forensics investigation in cyber–physical systems. It is a complex system composed by multiple components with specific functions, namely periodic data synchronization, Incident prediction and response, association rule mining, dashboard visualization, and a several other functionalities involving different lists and filters.

Several AI approaches were used to process and analyse the multi-dimensional data exploring the temporal correlation between cyber and physical Alerts. Supervised algorithms were trained on the sequential data of cyber and physical Alerts to predict the probability of a given Alert to be an Incident based on previous occurrences. The results obtained suggest that the multi-flow approach outperforms the single-flow-based one and that the LSTM is a robust algorithm to understand complex patterns in sequential data, in particularly, network traffic data. Forest-based models achieved the best performance in all tasks considering Incident response analysis. In addition, several association rules can be created by applying different ML techniques that allows the user to understand the correlation of the different data in an attack.

All the information can be visualized in the SMS-I Intelligent Dashboard. Several graphical dashboards, with different levels of detail can be used to easily identify anomalous situations that can be related to possible Incident occurrences. Furthermore, the information provided by the ML algorithms, namely the Incident probability can be analysed on SMS-I intelligent dashboard. Moreover, for an additional insight about the association rules, a management of the association rules by the security analysts can also be done.

The integration between SMS-I tool and TheHive, an Incident management tool, was presented. This integration supports the collaboration among the security professionals, not only inside the same institution but also between companies. Furthermore, SMS-I provides an extra intelligent layer that adds useful information to the security occurrences, which is automatically displayed in the Incident management tool facilitating information sharing and improving the quality of the investigation.

SMS-I tool was tested in different European airports in the scope of SATIE project. A very simple and authentic example, presented in this work, demonstrated the convenience and usefulness of the SMS-I tool in the decision-making process of security analysts. As future work, we plan to test SMS-I in other cyber–physical systems to improve the results across the board. On the system's side, a greatest improvement could be an automatic retraining of the models, using labeled data from the SOC.

Author Contributions: Conceptualization, E.M., N.S., N.O., S.W., O.S. and I.P.; methodology, E.M., N.S., N.O., S.W., O.S. and I.P.; software, N.S., N.O. and S.W.; validation, E.M., N.S., N.O., S.W., O.S. and I.P.; formal analysis, E.M., N.S., N.O., S.W., O.S. and I.P.; investigation, E.M., N.S., N.O., S.W., O.S. and I.P.; writing—original draft preparation, E.M., N.S., N.O. and S.W.; writing—review and editing, E.M., O.S. and I.P.; visualization, N.S., N.O. and S.W.; supervision, E.M., O.S. and I.P.; project administration, E.M. and I.P.; funding acquisition, I.P. All authors have read and agreed to the published version of the manuscript.

Funding: This research was funded by the Horizon 2020 Framework Programme under grant agreement No 832969. This output reflects the views only of the author(s), and the European Union cannot be held responsible for any use which may be made of the information contained therein. For more information on the project see: http://satie-h2020.eu/.

Institutional Review Board Statement: Not applicable.

Informed Consent Statement: Not applicable.

Conflicts of Interest: The authors declare no conflict of interest.

References

1. Lee, E.A. Cyber Physical Systems: Design Challenges. In Proceedings of the 2008 11th IEEE International Symposium on Object and Component-Oriented Real-Time Distributed Computing (ISORC), Orlando, FL, USA, 5–7 May 2008; pp. 363–369. [CrossRef]
2. Gunes, V.; Peter, S.; Givargis, T.; Vahid, F. A Survey on Concepts, Applications, and Challenges in Cyber–physical Systems. *KSII Trans. Internet Inf. Syst.* **2014**, *8*, 4242–4268.
3. Oks, S.J.; Jalowski, M.; Lechner, M.; Mirschberger, S.; Merklein, M.; Vogel-Heuser, B.; Möslein, K.M. Cyber–physical systems in the context of Industry 4.0: A review, categorization and outlook. *Inf. Syst. Front.* 2022; *early access.*
4. Lozano, C.V.; Vijayan, K.K. Literature review on Cyber Physical Systems Design. *Procedia Manuf.* **2020**, *45*, 295–300. [CrossRef]
5. Loukas, G. Cyber–Physical Attacks: A Growing Invisible Threat. Butterworth-Heinemann Is an Imprint of Elsevier. 2015. Available online: https://www.elsevier.com/books/cyber-physical-attacks/loukas/978-0-12-801290-1 (accessed on 4 July 2022).
6. Kim, S.; Park, K.J. A Survey on Machine-Learning Based Security Design for Cyber–physical Systems. *Appl. Sci.* **2021**, *11*, 5458. [CrossRef]
7. Karnouskos, S. Stuxnet worm impact on industrial cyber–physical system security. In Proceedings of the 37th Annual Conference of the IEEE Industrial Electronics Society, Melbourne, VIC, Australia, 7–10 November 2011; pp. 4490–4494.
8. Plumer, C. It's Way too Easy to Cause a Massive Blackout in the US. 2014. Available online: https://www.vox.com/2014/4/14/5604992/us-power-grid-vulnerability (accessed on 4 July 2022).
9. Colatin, S.D.T. Steel Mill in Germany. 2014. Available online: https://cyberlaw.ccdcoe.org/wiki/Steel_mill_in_Germany_(2014) (accessed on 4 July 2022).
10. Lee, R.M.; Assante, M.J.; Conway, T. Analysis of the Cyber Attack on the Ukrainian Power Grid. *E-ISAC* **2016**. Available online: https://nsarchive.gwu.edu/sites/default/files/documents/3891751/SANS-and-Electricity-Information-Sharing-and.pdf (accessed on 4 July 2022).
11. Kardon, S. Florida Water Treatment Plant Hit With Cyber Attack. 2021. Available online: https://www.industrialdefender.com/florida-water-treatment-plant-cyber-attack/ (accessed on 4 July 2022).
12. Sanger, D.E.; Krauss, C.; Perlroth, N. Cyberattack Forces a Shutdown of a Top U.S. Pipeline. 2021. Available online: https://www.nytimes.com/2021/05/08/us/politics/cyberattack-colonial-pipeline.html (accessed on 4 July 2022).
13. Jin, A.S.; Hogewood, L.; Fries, S.; Lambert, J.H.; Fiondella, L.; Strelzoff, A.; Boone, J.; Fleckner, K.; Linkov, I. Resilience of Cyber–physical Systems: Role of AI, Digital Twins, and Edge Computing. *IEEE Eng. Manag. Rev.* **2022**, *50*, 195–203. [CrossRef]
14. Mohamed, N.; Al-Jaroodi, J.; Jawhar, I. Cyber–Physical Systems Forensics: Today and Tomorrow. *J. Sens. Actuator Netw.* **2020**, *9*, 37. [CrossRef]
15. Fausto, A.; Gaggero, G.B.; Patrone, F.; Girdinio, P.; Marchese, M. Toward the Integration of Cyber and Physical Security Monitoring Systems for Critical Infrastructures. *Sensors* **2021**, *21*, 6970. [CrossRef] [PubMed]
16. Rajivan, P.; Cooke, N. Impact of team collaboration on cybersecurity situational awareness. In *Lecture Notes in Computer Science (Including Subseries Lecture Notes in Artificial Intelligence and Lecture Notes in Bioinformatics)*; Springer: Berlin/Heidelberg, Germany, 2017; Volume 10030, pp. 203–226. [CrossRef]
17. Parliament, E. The NIS2 Directive: A High Common Level of Cybersecurity in the EU. 2022. Available online: https://www.europarl.europa.eu/thinktank/en/document/EPRS_BRI(2021)689333 (accessed on 4 July 2022).
18. European Union Agency for Network; Information Security. The NIS2 DiDetect, SHARE, Protect. Solutions for Improving Threat Data Exchange among CERTs. 2013. Available online: https://www.eurohttps://www.enisa.europa.eu/publications/detect-share-protect-solutions-for-improving-threat-data-exchange-among-certs/at_download/fullReport (accessed on 4 July 2022).
19. Settanni, G.; Skopik, F.; Shovgenya, Y.; Fiedler, R.; Carolan, M.; Conroy, D.; Boettinger, K.; Gall, M.; Brost, G.; Ponchel, C.; et al. A collaborative cyber incident management system for European interconnected critical infrastructures. *J. Inf. Secur. Appl.* **2017**, *34*, 166–182. [CrossRef]
20. Bernal, A.E.; Monterrubio, S.M.M.; Fuente, J.P.; Crespo, R.G.; and, E.V. Methodology for Computer Security Incident Response Teams into IoT Strategy. *KSII Trans. Internet Inf. Syst.* **2021**, *15*, 1909–1928. [CrossRef]
21. Köpke, C. Impact Propagation in Airport Systems. In Proceedings of the 2nd International Workshop on Cyber–physical Security for Critical Infrastructures Protection (CPS4CIP 2021), Darmstadt, Germany, 4–8 October 2021; Springer International Publishing: Cham, Switzerland, 2021; pp. 191–206.
22. Macedo, I.; Wanous, S.; Oliveira, N.; Sousa, O.; Praça, I. A Tool to Support the Investigation and Visualization of Cyber and/or Physical Incidents. In Proceedings of the WorldCIST 9th World Conference on Information Systems and Technologies, Azores, Portugal, 30 March–2 April 2021; Rocha, Á., Ed.; Springer International Publishing: Cham, Switzerland, 2021; pp. 130–140.
23. Maia, E.; Sousa, N.; Oliveira, N.; Wannous, S.; Praça, I. SMS-I: An Intelligent Correlation tool for Cyber–physical Systems. In Proceedings of the 2022 5th International Conference DPSC2022, Porto, Portugal, 19–20 January 2022.
24. Brown, S. The C4 Model for Visualising Software Architecture. 2022. Available online: https://c4model.com/ (accessed on 4 July 2022).
25. Poole, C.; Huisman, J. Using extreme programming in a maintenance environment. *IEEE Softw.* **2001**, *18*, 42–50. [CrossRef]
26. Martin, R.C. *Agile Software Development: Principles, Patterns and Practices*; Prentice Hall PTR: Englewood Cliffs, NJ, USA, 2003.
27. Taormina, R.; Galelli, S.; Tippenhauer, N.; Salomons, E.; Ostfeld, A.; Eliades, D.; Aghashahi, M.; Sundararajan, R.; Pourahmadi, M.; Banks, M.; et al. Battle of the Attack Detection Algorithms: Disclosing cyber attacks on water distribution networks. *J. Water Resour. Plan. Manag.* **2018**, *144*. [CrossRef]

28. Ring, M.; Wunderlich, S.; Grüdl, D.; Landes, D.; Hotho, A. Flow-Based Benchmark Data Sets for Intrusion Detection. In Proceedings of the 16th European Conference on Cyber Warfare and Security (ECCWS), Dublin, Ireland, 29–30 June 2017; pp. 361–369.

29. Moustafa, N.; Slay, J. UNSW-NB15: A comprehensive data set for network intrusion detection systems (UNSW-NB15 network data set). In Proceedings of the 2015 Annual Military Communications and Information Systems (MilCIS), Canberra, Australia, 10–12 November 2015; pp. 1–6. [CrossRef]

30. Sharafaldin., I.; Habibi Lashkari., A.; Ghorbani., A.A. Toward Generating a New Intrusion Detection Dataset and Intrusion Traffic Characterization. In Proceedings of the 4th International Conference on Information Systems Security and Privacy (ICISSP), Funchal, Madeira, 22–24 January 2018; SciTePress: Setúbal, Portugal, 2018; pp. 108–116.

31. Oliveira, N.; Praça, I.; Maia, E.; Sousa, O. Intelligent Cyber Attack Detection and Classification for Network-Based Intrusion Detection Systems. *Appl. Sci.* **2021**, *11*, 1674. [CrossRef]

32. Zhang, C.; Ma, Y. *Ensemble Machine Learning: Methods and Applications*; Springer: Berlin/Heidelberg, Germany, 2012.

33. Gardner, M.W.; Dorling, S. Artificial neural networks (the multilayer perceptron)—A review of applications in the atmospheric sciences. *Atmos. Environ.* **1998**, *32*, 2627–2636. [CrossRef]

34. Gwon, H.; Lee, C.; Keum, R.; Choi, H. Network intrusion detection based on LSTM and feature embedding. *arXiv* **2019**, arXiv:1911.11552.

35. Agrawal, R.; Srikant, R. Fast Algorithms for Mining Association Rules in Large Databases. In Proceedings of the 20th International Conference on Very Large Data Bases, Santiago de Chile, Chile, 12–15 September 1994; VLDB '94; Morgan Kaufmann Publishers Inc.: San Francisco, CA, USA, 1994; pp. 487–499.

36. Han, J.; Kamber, M.; Pei, J. *Data Mining Concepts and Techniques*; 3rd ed.; Morgan Kaufmann Publishers: Waltham, MA, USA, 2012.

37. Applebaum, A.; Johnson, S.; Limiero, M.; Smith, M. Playbook oriented cyber response. In Proceedings of the 2018 National Cyber Summit (NCS), Huntsville, AL, USA, 5–7 June 2018; pp. 8–15.

38. Martínez Torres, J.; Iglesias Comesa na, C.; García-Nieto, P.J. Machine learning techniques applied to cybersecurity. *Int. J. Mach. Learn. Cybern.* **2019**, *10*, 2823–2836. [CrossRef]

39. Alqahtani, H.; Sarker, I.H.; Kalim, A.; Hossain, M.; Md, S.; Ikhlaq, S.; Hossain, S. Cyber intrusion detection using machine learning classification techniques. In *International Conference on Computing Science, Communication and Security*; Springer: Berlin/Heidelberg, Germany, 2020; pp. 121–131.

40. Sarker, I.H.; Abushark, Y.B.; Alsolami, F.; Khan, A.I. Intrudtree: A machine learning based cyber security intrusion detection model. *Symmetry* **2020**, *12*, 754. [CrossRef]

41. Mammone, A.; Turchi, M.; Cristianini, N. Support vector machines. In *Wiley Interdisciplinary Reviews: Computational Statistics*; Wiley: Hoboken, NJ, USA, 2009; pp. 283–289.

42. Chen, T.; He, T.; Benesty, M.; Khotilovich, V.; Tang, Y.; Cho, H.; Chen, K. Xgboost: Extreme Gradient Boosting; R Package Version 0.4-2. 2015. Available online: https://cran.r-project.org/web/packages/xgboost/vignettes/xgboost.pdf (accessed on 4 July 2022).

43. Liu, F.T.; Ting, K.M.; Zhou, Z.H. Isolation forest. In Proceedings of the 2008 Eighth IEEE International Conference on Data Mining, Pisa, Italy, 15–19 December 2008; pp. 413–422.

44. Schölkopf, B.; Williamson, R.C.; Smola, A.; Shawe-Taylor, J.; Platt, J. Support vector method for novelty detection. *Adv. Neural Inf. Process. Syst.* **1999**, *12*, 582–588.

45. Wang, Z.; Xue, X. Multi-class support vector machine. In *Support Vector Machines Applications*; Springer: Berlin/Heidelberg, Germany, 2014; pp. 23–48.

46. Franc, V.; Hlaváč, V. Multi-class support vector machine. In Proceedings of the 2002 International Conference on Pattern Recognition, Quebec City, QC, Canada, 11–15 August 2002; Volume 2, pp. 236–239.

47. Guo, G.; Wang, H.; Bell, D.; Bi, Y.; Greer, K. KNN model-based approach in classification. In *OTM Confederated International Conferences on the Move to Meaningful Internet Systems*; Springer: Berlin/Heidelberg, Germany, 2003; pp. 986–996.

48. Casey, T. Survey: 27 Percent of IT Professionals Receive More Than 1 Million Security Alerts Daily. 2018. Available online: https://www.imperva.com/blog/27-percent-of-it-professionals-receive-more-than-1-million-security-alerts-daily/ (accessed on 4 July 2022).

49. Schaper, M.; Gluchshenko, O.; Muth, K.; Tyburzy, L.; Rusko, M.; Trnka, M. The Traffic Management Intrusion and Compliance System as Security Situation Assessment System at an Air Traffic Controller's Working Position. In Proceedings of the 31st European Safety and Reliability Conference ESREL, Angers, France, 19–23 September 2021; pp. 2825–2831.

50. Barnum, S.; Martin, R.; Worrell, B.; Kirillov, I. *The Cybox Language Specification*; The MITRE Corporation: McLean, VA, USA, 2012.

51. SATIE_Consortium. D6.3 Test and Validation Results on the Simulation Platform. Technical Report. 2021. Available online: https://satie-h2020.eu/wp-content/uploads/2022/01/SATIE_D6.3_Test-and-validation-results-on-the-simulation-platform_PU_v1.0_compressed.pdf (accessed on 4 July 2022).

52. SATIE_Consortium. D6.5 Report about Demonstration and Results in Athens Airport. Technical Report. 2021. Available online: https://satie-h2020.eu/wp-content/uploads/2022/01/SATIE_D6.5_Report-about-demonstration-and-results-in-Athens-airport_PU_v1.0_compressed.pdf (accessed on 4 July 2022).

53. SATIE_Consortium. D6.6 Report about Demonstration and Results in Milan Airport. Technical Report. 2021. Available online: https://satie-h2020.eu/wp-content/uploads/2022/01/SATIE_D6.6_Report-about-demonstration-and-results-in-Milan-airport_PU_v1.0_compressed-1.pdf (accessed on 4 July 2022).
54. IBM Security. *Cost of a Data Breach Report 2021*; IBM Security: Tulsa, OK, USA, 2021.
55. Vielberth, M.; Böhm, F.; Fichtinger, I.; Pernul, G. Security Operations Center: A Systematic Study and Open Challenges. *IEEE Access* **2020**, *8*, 227756–227779. [CrossRef]
56. Daniel, C.; Gill, T.; Hevner, A.; Mullarkey, M. A Deep Neural Network Approach to Tracing Paths in Cybersecurity Investigations. In Proceedings of the 2020 International Conference on Data Mining Workshops (ICDMW), Sorrento, Italy, 17–20 November 2020; pp. 472–479.
57. Reuschling, F.; Carstengerdes, N.; Stelkens-Kobsch, T.H.; Burke, K.; Oudin, T.; Schaper, M.; Apolinário, F.; Praca, I.; Perlepes, L. *Toolkit to Enhance Cyber-Physical Security of Critical Infrastructures in Air Transport*; Now Publishers: Norwell, MA, USA, 2021.

 *information*

Article

Boosting Holistic Cybersecurity Awareness with Outsourced Wide-Scope CyberSOC: A Generalization from a Spanish Public Organization Study

Manuel Domínguez-Dorado [1,*], Francisco J. Rodríguez-Pérez [2], Javier Carmona-Murillo [2], David Cortés-Polo [2] and Jesús Calle-Cancho [3]

[1] Department of Domains, Information Systems and Digital Toolkit, Public Business Entity Red.es., 28020 Madrid, Spain
[2] Department of Computing and Telematics Systems Engineering, University of Extremadura, 10003 Cáceres, Spain
[3] Extremadura Research Center for Advanced Technologies (CETA-CIEMAT), 10200 Trujillo, Spain
* Correspondence: manuel.dominguez@red.es; Tel.: +34-747-756-532

Abstract: Public sector organizations are facing an escalating challenge with the increasing volume and complexity of cyberattacks, which disrupt essential public services and jeopardize citizen data and privacy. Effective cybersecurity management has become an urgent necessity. To combat these threats comprehensively, the active involvement of all functional areas is crucial, necessitating a heightened holistic cybersecurity awareness among tactical and operational teams responsible for implementing security measures. Public entities face various challenges in maintaining this awareness, including difficulties in building a skilled cybersecurity workforce, coordinating mixed internal and external teams, and adapting to the outsourcing trend, which includes cybersecurity operations centers (CyberSOCs). Our research began with an extensive literature analysis to expand our insights derived from previous works, followed by a Spanish case study in collaboration with a digitization-focused public organization. The study revealed common features shared by public organizations globally. Collaborating with this public entity, we developed strategies tailored to its characteristics and transferrable to other public organizations. As a result, we propose the "Wide-Scope CyberSOC" as an innovative outsourced solution to enhance holistic awareness among the cross-functional cybersecurity team and facilitate comprehensive cybersecurity adoption within public organizations. We have also documented essential requirements for public entities when contracting Wide-Scope CyberSOC services to ensure alignment with their specific needs, accompanied by a management framework for seamless operation.

Keywords: cyberSOC outsourcing; holistic cybersecurity; public sector cyber-resilience; tactical-operational cybersecurity management; wide-scope cyberSOC

 check for
updates

Citation: Domínguez-Dorado, M.;
Rodríguez-Pérez, F.J.; Carmona-
Murillo, J.; Cortés-Polo, D.;
Calle-Cancho, J. Boosting Holistic
Cybersecurity Awareness with
Outsourced Wide-Scope CyberSOC:
A Generalization from a Spanish
Public Organization Study.
Information **2023**, *14*, 586. https://
doi.org/10.3390/info14110586

Academic Editors: Jose de
Vasconcelos, Hugo Barbosa
and Carla Cordeiro

Received: 12 September 2023
Revised: 17 October 2023
Accepted: 23 October 2023
Published: 25 October 2023

1. Introduction

A multitude of definitions exist for the concept of cybersecurity. One of the wider definitions can be located in the work of Domínguez-Dorado et al. [1], which is closely intertwined with the notion of cyberspace. Cyberspace, defined as a network comprising interconnected information systems facilitated by communication networks, serves as the arena where individuals and entities interact and carry out their activities. This environment possesses distinct attributes, including high dynamism, common ground where each organization exercises control over a portion, a substantial reliance on third parties, and a necessity to prioritize not only information, but also the continuity of business processes and assets. Furthermore, it demands a focus on cyber resilience, among other considerations. Within this context, cybersecurity emerges as the discipline entrusted with the responsibility of managing and mitigating the threats, risks, and circumstances originating from this intricate cyberspace. A cyberattack, one of the most common of the mentioned cyber threats, encompasses any deliberate endeavor aimed at illicitly acquiring, disclosing, modifying, incapacitating, or annihilating data, applications, or other assets by means of unauthorized access to a network, computer system, or digital device. Furthermore, it is worth noting that attackers need not always gain access to any element within the organization's infrastructure. A mere misinformation campaign can suffice to tarnish the organization's reputation and trustworthiness. It is widely recognized that in the 21st Century, cybersecurity must be approached holistically. However, many organizations still struggle to effectively implement this approach due to a lack of alignment with traditional information security standards and practices. While an information security approach permits handling the cybersecurity aspects in many cases, it might be insufficient, alone, to address some of the risks and threats that emerge from cyberspace and for that reason, it is sometimes recommended to the adopt a more suitable cybersecurity approach as explained in von Solms and van Niekerk [2], and Reid and van Niekerk [3]. Therefore, achieving true holism and effective cybersecurity in practice remains a challenge for many organizations.

In various instances, the obstacles in achieving holistic cybersecurity deployment stem from issues tied to the cross-functional cybersecurity workforce and their capacity to establish a holistic approach to address the ever-evolving cyber threats landscape. This will be further elucidated in the forthcoming sections. For instance, one of the reasons that public sector organizations often outsource their cybersecurity needs, such as managed cybersecurity services or CyberSOC services, is the difficulty in recruiting and retaining civil servants with the necessary cybersecurity skills as stated in works as Furnell [4], De Zan [5], Reeder and Alan [6], or DeCrosta [7]. This is a problem faced by organizations across the public and private sectors, but it is particularly acute in the public sector for which we recommend the studies of Shava and Hofisi [8], Ngwenyama et al. [9], or Nizich [10], where the high demand and high salaries for cybersecurity professionals in the private sector can make it difficult to attract and retain talent. Additionally, when it comes to externalized CyberSOC contracts, these contracts must be renewed on a periodic basis, which can make it difficult to retain talent even when outsourcing these services. As a result, public sector organizations may struggle to maintain a consistent and effective approach to cybersecurity.

Relying heavily on outsourced services for their operational needs is also an impediment to focusing on a holistic framework, Reh Lee et al. [11]. Public sector entities often have a large number of highly skilled managers at various levels, but the hands-on work is frequently carried out by personnel from outsourced services providers. As a result, tactical-operational teams in these organizations are often composed of a mix of in-house staff and personnel from external service providers. These outsourced services are typically focused on specific areas, such as communications, software development, legal advising, human resources, or facilities management, and are typically only available to the specific area that contracted them. This fragmented approach creates obstacles to achieving holistic cybersecurity. Nevertheless, when a decision has been made to outsource a CyberSOC, this situation can be tapped as the foundation for building a truly holistic approach to cybersecurity, particularly in public sector organizations. To achieve this goal, the CyberSOC should be able to propose cybersecurity actions that can be implemented across the organization to achieve the necessary level of holism. This requires a cross-functional vision, as the nature of cybersecurity is inherently holistic. At the same time, the tactical-operational teams responsible for implementing these cybersecurity measures must be skilled in their respective areas of expertise to effectively design and implement cybersecurity safeguards in the "last mile". Unfortunately, it is often the case that neither the CyberSOC is adequately equipped to prescribe cybersecurity actions across all domains, nor are tactical-operational teams trained to apply their expertise to cybersecurity holistically, Onwibiko and Ouazzane [12].

Taking the aforementioned considerations into account, in this work, we address the enhancement of the organization's cybersecurity workforce capabilities to implement and maintain holistic cybersecurity. Our study commences with the necessity of implementing a model for managing holistic cybersecurity from the lower levels of a Spanish public organization. To attain this objective, we initiated a thorough examination of the existing literature, aiming to identify aspects highlighted in a prior work [1] and potential requisites for its practical application within the context of public sector. Subsequently, we conducted an in-depth analysis of the participating entity, which agreed to serve as a case study that could be generalized aid similar organizations. In this sense, the participating public entity contributed not only by providing information for analysis at the beginning of the study, but also actively participated in defining the solution presented in this paper. They shared their firsthand expertise and played a crucial role in identifying and addressing early implementation issues, adding substantial value to the research effort. The purpose of this analysis was to confirm the presence of insights we had identified as common during our examination of the existing literature, within the studied public organization. If these insights are indeed present, the same strategies devised for our specific use case should prove advantageous for public sector entities on a broader scale.

As a result of our investigation in cooperation with the participating entity, and in order to couple with the features of public sector organizations, we suggest introducing a new category of outsourced CyberSOC, which we refer to as the Wide-Scope CyberSOC. This innovative CyberSOC not only needs to incorporate a holistic cybersecurity approach into its daily operations, but also must possess the capability to convey this perspective and knowledge to every member of the cross-functional, diverse cybersecurity team, thereby empowering them to actively engage in this collaborative approach. As part of our study, we identify the key elements and requirements that a public organization should demand from the provider offering such a Wide-Scope CyberSOC service. This ensures that it facilitates the improvement of worker capabilities in the context of holistic cybersecurity.

As part of this endeavor, we draw upon existing frameworks and prior knowledge, such as the CyberTOMP framework and previous research on outsourcing and workforce training, among others. By amalgamating these resources with additional components, we streamline the process of implementing comprehensive cybersecurity measures within public organizations.

The remainder of this document is organized as follows: In Section 2, a review of research relevant for our proposal are carried out. Section 3 provides a detailed description of the methodology and steps employed in our study, including a literature review as an expanded and detailed version of the introduction. Section 4 presents the key findings obtained throughout the research and Section 5 summarizes the most significant conclusions of our study and presents the future lines of work that arise from it.

2. Analysis of the State of the Art

Starting at this juncture, we initiated an analysis of the existing literature. Our aim was to select relevant works that could facilitate an expansion of our knowledge, particularly regarding insights derived from one of our prior studies [1]. Additionally, we sought to identify any unique requirements or specific needs that might surface when applying the aforementioned work to a public sector organization. At this stage, our primary objective was to pinpoint common features, requirements, or needs that were shared by public organizations on a global scale. Table 1 provides a comprehensive overview of the collection of works we analyzed. However, a detailed contextualization of these works is provided in the subsequent paragraphs.

In recent decades, there has been a growing consensus regarding the meaning of cybersecurity and how it differs from previous approaches such as technology security and information security, represented by the works of Schatz et al. [2,13]. Cybersecurity emerges from the concept of cyberspace, which is a network of interconnected information services that allows people and organizations to conduct their activities and businesses beyond the physical boundaries of traditional organizations. As a result, much of the ecosystem in which organizations operate falls outside of their control, and the dependence of business activities on this "uncontrolled" part has increased over time. This new environment gives rise to new threats, risks, and countermeasures that must be properly addressed; Ghelani addresses this problem in [14].

Table 1. Studies examined to ascertain whether the identified characteristics could be extrapolated to the entire Public Sector.

Topic	Analyzed Source
Holistic cybersecurity foundations and cybersecurity context in public sector	[2,3,13,15–34]
Tactical-operational cybersecurity workforce management	[1,35–47]
Cybersecurity talent development and retention	[4–10,48–66]
Outsourcing in public sector	[11,67–88]
Outsourcing CyberSOC services	[89–95]

Slowly but surely, organizations are beginning to adopt practical approaches to cybersecurity management. However, these efforts are often limited to the strategic level and rely on information security standards rather than specific cybersecurity frameworks, as analyzed by Sulistyowati et al. in [15]. There has been relatively little progress in applying cybersecurity management to lower levels, which are crucial for achieving effective cybersecurity.

The situation in the public sector is even more challenging. Private companies are often early adopters of new technologies and approaches, while public sector organizations are typically slower to adopt these innovations due to a variety of constraints such as regulatory frameworks, contracting timeframes, hiring restrictions, career development opportunities, and excessive bureaucracy; Srinivas et al. goes deep in this topic in [16]. As a result, public sector entities may struggle to adapt nimbly to changes in the cybersecurity landscape. In many cases, they resort to outsourcing services in order to alleviate these challenges.

2.1. The Importance of a Holistic Approach to Cybersecurity

Cybersecurity differs from previous approaches in several ways, with the main differences stemming from the emergence of a new environment: the cyberspace. As a critical component in every digitized organization, cyberspace poses unique challenges since organizations cannot have complete control over it but have near complete dependency. As mentioned in the introduction *"a mere misinformation campaign can suffice to tarnish the organization's reputation and trustworthiness"*. The threats and risks that emerge from this environment require unity of action and a broader holistic approach as studied in Ahmed et al. [17], and while some research has been conducted in this area as described by Atoum et al. in [18], much more work remains to achieve an acceptable level of holism, something that is covered by Kranemburg and Le Gars [19], and to cover those specific threats emanating from cyberspace for which an information security approach does not fit well. Recent studies also suggest the need to extend this holism not only within the organization itself, but also to its network of collaborators, civil organizations, government entities, and citizens, in order to provide the necessary unity of action to effectively respond to threats and risks, as investigated in [20] by Del-Real and Díaz-Fernández.

In order to effectively respond to risks and threats emanating from cyberspace, a holistic approach to cybersecurity must involve all functional areas of the organization. This requires a cross-functional approach that considers the unique perspectives and challenges of each area in order to develop comprehensive and effective cybersecurity strategies and, of course, it requires that the involved cross-functional cybersecurity workforce poses a high level of awareness regarding their potential contribution to the overall cybersecurity. Moreover, holism should not be a merely theoretical concept but had better instead to focus on practical implementation. While there have been some advances in achieving this holism in practice, most of these efforts have focused on the strategic level, with less attention given to bringing holism down to the tactical and operational levels of the organization. It is at these lower levels that the necessary safeguards for effective cybersecurity are implemented, though, and thus, it is essential to address the obstacles that prevent organizations from achieving true holism in their tactical-operational approach to cybersecurity.

2.2. Tactical-Operational Cybersecurity Workforce Management

There are several works that address cybersecurity management from different points of view: Rothrock et al. examine it from the board of director's perspective in [45]; the municipalities' points of view are reviewed by Preis and Susskind in [41]; the work by Limba et al. in [46] is centered in critical infrastructures; Yigit et al. focus on the assessment of cybersecurity capabilities in [37]; Rajan et al. focused on cross-functional collaboration in [38]; etc. All of these are very useful studies that have made possible several advances in cybersecurity. However, none of them are comprehensive models that can be used within an organization to handle cybersecurity at tactical and operational levels with a managerial approach. From our perspective, holism can only be achieved by designing and applying managerial techniques not only to lower levels, but also from lower levels, from those who must cooperate in the short and medium term to execute and design cybersecurity safeguards in the last mile, as considered by Axon et al. in [39].

While there are a few existing works that address holism at different levels, including the tactical and operational levels, there is still a need for further research and development in this area in order to effectively manage cybersecurity at these levels.

In [40], a work by Antunes et al., a good analysis is carried out after a practical implementation of an information security and a cybersecurity program in small and medium-size enterprises (SMEs) in Portugal. It takes into account the required controls and their degree of implementation, and profiles SMEs to apply proportional security measures. However, it does not provide details on the coordination mechanism for the multidisciplinary cybersecurity workforce and is based on the ISO 27001 standard for information security rather than cybersecurity. The authors themselves recognize this as a limitation. This analysis focuses on characterizing the participating SMEs in order to align the various safeguards with their specific needs.

The work developed by Domínguez-Dorado et al. in [1] proposed a more comprehensive set of procedural elements that explicitly enable cybersecurity management at the tactical and operational levels is defined as CyberTOMP framework. It is based on the most important cybersecurity frameworks and initiatives, and its authors have created a unified list of potential cybersecurity actions. These actions, also called "expected outcomes", are clustered into three implementation groups that can be applied to business assets with different cybersecurity needs, making it easier to select the appropriate cybersecurity controls, a selection of controls mechanism that is also covered by Breier and Hudec in [47].

While this framework is designed specifically for managing cybersecurity at the tactical and operational levels, it also allows for alignment with strategic cybersecurity goals through the use of the business impact analysis, that, according to Quinn et al. in [36], is a good tool to inform risk prioritization, and the cybersecurity master plan as hooks, which allows unifying cybersecurity and business continuity in a single framework, something described in [43] by Phillips and Tanner. This approach allows organizations to maintain a focus on their overall cybersecurity objectives while also addressing the specific challenges and needs at the tactical and operational levels and this allows the framework to be independent of the strategic standard chosen by the organization, while still providing complementary support. The study of Domínguez-Dorado et al. in [1] follows a practical approach and provides step-by-step processes, procedures, and guidance for identifying cybersecurity actions through a collaborative process that engages all functional areas of the organization. It is additionally supported by tools that facilitate the attainment of agreements on the necessary set of cybersecurity actions [35]. This approach allows for the development of holistic cybersecurity actions that are agreed upon and assigned to the functional areas involved in cybersecurity. The focus of this framework on business assets, which are understood as manageable and understandable units of cybersecurity, is a growing trend in the field as can be extracted from the works of Clark et al. [42] and Kure and Islam [44].

Nonetheless, although this framework provides a useful approach for managing cybersecurity at the tactical and operational levels, there is room to improve. For instance, it can be enhanced to identify the skills and training required by different functional areas of the organization in order to effectively carry out their cybersecurity tasks. Without the necessary skills and training, it is difficult for organizations to fully implement this framework and achieve the desired results.

Summarizing, to ensure the effectiveness of tactical and operational cybersecurity management, it is essential to develop mechanisms that can provide the necessary capabilities and expertise at these levels. This can be achieved through training programs, hiring qualified personnel, and implementing systems and processes that support the effective management of cybersecurity at the tactical and operational levels, or it can be achieved by acquiring this knowledge from specialized third parties. By taking these steps, organizations can better prepare themselves to effectively manage cybersecurity risks and threats and ensure that their overall cybersecurity efforts are successful.

2.3. Cybersecurity Talent Development and Retention

The development and retention of cybersecurity talent is a pressing issue in today's world. The rapid expansion of the cyberspace and the growing dependence of organizations on it have led to a shortage of cybersecurity professionals. The pandemic of COVID-19 has exacerbated this situation, as organizations have had to provide remote access and services to their employees, making them more vulnerable to cyber-attacks. This has motivated an increased demand for cybersecurity specialists, as organizations strive to protect themselves against these threats.

The shortage of cybersecurity talent has an indirect effect on organizations: in high-demand conditions, organizations are less able to retain cybersecurity-skilled personnel because many companies are competing for the same talent.

Training the existing workforce is an option, but it comes with the risk of losing skilled personnel due to the high demand for cybersecurity professionals. Despite this, providing training to the existing workforce can be beneficial in the short term, as it allows organizations to develop the skills of their employees and improve their ability to manage cybersecurity risks and threats. However, it is important for organizations to carefully consider their training strategies, as they need to ensure that they can retain their trained personnel in the long term. It is likely that more educated, motivated, and well-paid public employees will be easier for organizations to retain, as identified by Dahlstöm et al. [64].

There is an increasing number of research works that address this situation from different perspectives; for instance, in [4], the authors present evidence of the cybersecurity workforce shortage and the different forms of qualification that are available to meet the needs. The work presented in [5] show that this shortage is due in part to the high demand for cybersecurity specialists, as well as the limited availability of relevant training programs and qualifications. In response to this problem, some public organizations have turned to national skills competitions to create interest in cybersecurity and attract qualified personnel. In a work by Ahmad et al. [62], the authors propose to use incident management as a way to improve organizational learning in cybersecurity topics. This approach focuses on using real-life incidents to provide practical experience and training for cybersecurity personnel, with the aim of increasing their knowledge and expertise. The research carried out in [56] by Ahmad et al. highlights the need for interdisciplinary cybersecurity education and proposes a curriculum roadmap that integrates cybersecurity across technical and non-technical curricula. This approach seeks to address the current shortage of cybersecurity talent by providing a more comprehensive education on the subject. The research presented in [6] proposes three promising approaches to identify, recruit, and develop cybersecurity talent from both technical and non-technical personnel. These approaches aim to address the shortage of skilled cybersecurity professionals and improve organizations' ability to retain their talent. In [57], Chowdhury and Gkioulos identify cybersecurity training offerings for critical infrastructure protection and the key performance indicators that allow evaluating their effectiveness. In research by Noche [58], a comprehensive review of empirical studies aimed at developing the cybersecurity workforce is presented. Gamification is proposed as a method to improve the cybersecurity training of individuals responsible for protecting critical infrastructure in [54] by Ashley et al. In [60], a study by Kävrestad and Nohlberg, a review of evaluation strategies for cybersecurity training is presented with the aim of minimizing the impact of human factors on cyberattacks. In an investigation by Hulatt and Stavrou [59], the authors present the need for a multidisciplinary cybersecurity workforce that includes professionals from various backgrounds beyond traditional ones such as computing and Information Technology (IT). The authors of [55], Justice et al., analyze the future needs of the cybersecurity workforce. In [61], Maurer et al. identify the specific cybersecurity and professional skills required by those responsible for cybersecurity. These skills are necessary to ensure the effectiveness of tactical and operational cybersecurity management. Finally, in [7], the study analyses the quantitative and qualitative factors that contribute to the current shortage of cybersecurity professionals.

Overall, the shortage of cybersecurity talent is a growing concern for organizations, as it reduces their ability to effectively manage cybersecurity risks and protect against potential threats. This shortage is particularly acute at the tactical and operational levels, where hands-on skills are essential. Intense competition for skilled personnel has made it difficult for organizations to attract and retain the talent they need, leading to further declines in their ability to manage cybersecurity effectively. In order to address this issue, organizations must develop effective strategies to attract and retain cybersecurity talent, particularly at the tactical and operational levels. This will require a comprehensive approach that includes training programs, hiring qualified personnel, and implementing systems and processes that support effective cybersecurity management.

2.4. Outsourcing in Public Sector

There are various forms of potential collaboration in public service delivery, as Kekez et al. analyze in [85], with outsourcing being one of the most common. The decision to outsource is often driven by a desire to reduce costs, as investigated by Santos and Fontana in [71] and improve efficiency. By transferring certain business processes or functions to an external provider, a company can benefit from their expertise and specialized capabilities. Additionally, outsourcing can provide access to a global talent pool, allowing companies to tap into a wider range of skills and knowledge. In addition to cost savings and access to specialized skills, outsourcing can also help a business to focus on its core competencies and drive growth. As such, this is a strategy that is often considered by public organizations looking to streamline their operations and improve their public services.

Although there are some differences between public and private outsourcing, which is explored in [87] by Burnes and Anastasiadis, the motivations for outsourcing are similar across both public and private sectors, with cost control and reduction, focus on core capabilities, and access to supplier expertise and technologies being among the key drivers as supported by works carried out by Marco-Simó and Pastor-Collado [74] or Bogoviz et al. [77], but also to face exceptional situations like the pandemic of COVID-19 as analyzed in [75] by van der Wal. Public organizations are generally well-equipped with individuals who have the necessary skills and expertise to manage tasks and processes effectively. However, they frequently face challenges when it comes to staffing the most technical and operational tasks, which require specialized knowledge and expertise. As a result, these organizations may struggle to effectively perform these tasks, leading to reduced efficiency and performance.

In order to overcome these challenges, many public organizations turn their strategic plans to outsourcing through public-private contracts, as examined in Pavelko et al. [70]. These contracts provide a legal framework for defining the roles and responsibilities of each party, as well as the terms of the relationship between the public and private sectors. They also help to ensure that the activities and services provided under the contract are organized and carried out in a manner that is consistent with the parties' respective rights and obligations, something studied in the research of Bloomfield et al. [78]. The accurate definition of service requirements within these contracts is a key factor for Proscovia in [79] to successful outsourcing, which will later depend on managing the outsourcing relationship well after the decision is made, which is evaluated in [69] by Heikkilä and Cordon. The lack of service requirements definitions when outsourcing in public sector led to a falling quality of the provided public services.

Outsourcing is a controversial topic. There are many interesting works that discuss the pros and cons of outsourcing in the public sector under different circumstances such as those carried out by Tayauova, Lobao et al., Aswini, Sánchez, Rizwan and Bhatti, Johansson and Siverbo, and Andersson et al. in [76,81–83,86,88] or [80], respectively, among others. Although this debate is outside the scope of our study, we mention them here to highlight the significance of the outsourcing approach for public sector entities.

While outsourcing can have a slight negative effect on the performance and perception of in-house employees [11], it is often necessary in order to ensure that tactical-operational teams have the necessary skills and expertise. But as a result of outsourcing, tactical-operational teams in the public sector are often composed of a mix of public sector employees and outsourced or insourced personnel.

It is also important to note that by outsourcing any service, the outsourcing organization is expanding its supply chain, which can lead to additional risks, including in the realm of cybersecurity. Some of these topics are covered in Nasrulddin et al. [72] and Repetto et al. [73].

2.5. Outsourcing CyberSOC Services

A CyberSOC, is a specialized unit that is focused on monitoring, detecting, and responding to cyber threats in real time. Among the main duties of a CyberSOC the following are included, as determined in Saraiva and Mateus-Coelho [90]:

- Continuous monitoring of an organization's networks and systems for signs of potential cyber threats;
- Detection of cyber threats through the use of advanced technology and analysis of security data;
- Response to detected threats, including implementing countermeasures to prevent or mitigate the impact of the threat;
- Communication with relevant stakeholders, such as the organization's leadership and other security teams, about detected threats and response efforts;
- Ongoing analysis of security data to identify patterns and trends that can help improve the organization's overall security posture.

In addition to these core duties, a CyberSOC may also be responsible for providing training and education to the organization's staff on cybersecurity best practices, as well as collaborating with other security teams and external partners to share information and coordinate efforts to defend against cyber threats. Overall, the role of a CyberSOC is essential in helping organizations protect themselves from the constantly evolving threat landscape of the digital world, as analyzed in [91] by Shutock and Dietrich, and assess their readiness level, something evaluated in [92] by Georgiadou et al.

From our perspective, this set of capabilities and responsibilities, especially the non-core ones, can be tapped by the organization to turn the CyberSOC into the cornerstone over which develop real holistic cybersecurity. Although in public administration, where outsourcing is something very common, this possibility cannot be extrapolated directly, due to the existence of cross-functional tactical and operational teams composed by employees and outsourced workforce.

From a cybersecurity perspective, the presence of mixed multidisciplinary in-house/outsourced tactical and operational teams, which experience high levels of turnover every few years, is not necessarily a problem, but it does present a challenging situation that must be managed carefully in order to ensure effective holistic cybersecurity across the organization.

The above could be even more challenging if the CyberSOC service itself is outsourced, which is also a common practice in public sector and involves roles with high cybersecurity skills, as questioned in Nugraha [94]. Although outsourcing also has advantages, as mentioned in previous paragraphs, the cons are relevant in this case, according to Ti Dun et al. [93], and several efforts have to be made to enhance the communication between the public entity's manager and the provider of CyberSOC services, which is analyzed in [95] by Kokulu et al. In view of the above, we are of the opinion that one potential disadvantage of outsourcing a CyberSOC is the loss of control over the security of the organization's systems and data. When a CyberSOC is managed by an external provider, the organization loses the ability to directly oversee and manage the security measures in place to protect its systems and data. This can make it difficult to ensure that the necessary security protocols are being followed and can increase the risk of security breaches or other incidents. Another disadvantage is the potential for reduced flexibility and responsiveness. When a CyberSOC is outsourced, the organization is reliant on the external provider for the timely detection and response to security threats. If the provider is unable to respond quickly or effectively, this can leave the organization vulnerable to security breaches or other incidents. Lastly, assigning an outsourced CyberSOC to prescribe cybersecurity tasks for all of the organization's functional areas that are also partially outsourced can lead to conflicts and a lack of coordination between service providers. This can potentially be challenging to resolve and can impact the organization's cybersecurity strategy.

As previously mentioned, there are several situations in which public sector organizations may need to outsource their CyberSOC services. In order for these outsourced CyberSOCs to be able to provide cybersecurity recommendations for all of the organization's functional areas and support their implementation, the outsourcing public entity must put in some effort upfront to identify the necessary capabilities of the CyberSOC and include them as requirements in the related technical specifications. However, these public organizations are often outsourcing their CyberSOC services due to a lack of knowledge and skills, making it difficult for them to identify the necessary requirements. It is necessary to simplify this process in order to ensure that the requirements for the service provider of an outsourced CyberSOC align with the needs of the public organization to develop effective, comprehensive cybersecurity.

2.6. Insights after Reviewing the State of the Art

After conducting a thorough review to identify the unique circumstances and issues that prevent the achievement of effective, comprehensive cybersecurity in public sector organizations, we found that:

- The role of tactical-operational cross-functional teams in cybersecurity management is crucial, as they are responsible for implementing the actual cybersecurity countermeasures within the organization and provide the corresponding holism. There is a dearth of research studies that examine this specific niche from a managerial standpoint, thereby creating a void that hampers the implementation of a comprehensive cybersecurity management approach. It is imperative that such an approach be undertaken at these levels to prevent the formation of isolated units, both within the public and private sectors;
- Currently, there is a shortage of cybersecurity professionals that is expected to continue in the short and medium term. This shortage is particularly acute in public sector organizations, which often have personnel capable of managing at all levels but lack technical staff with hands-on expertise. Therefore, it is imperative to undertake certain actions aimed at raising awareness among the cross-functional cybersecurity workforce regarding the implications of their specific areas of expertise in the broader realm of cybersecurity. This will enable them to become personnel who possess the necessary expertise and managerial acumen to effectively confront the prevailing cyber threats;
- Public sector entities heavily rely on the practice of outsourcing. One of the reasons for that is to gain access to technical staff with hands-on expertise, trying to avoid the mentioned workforce shortage. As a result, their cross-functional tactical-operational teams are often composed of a mix of employees and outsourced workers, which are frequently replaced as their outsourcing contracts come to an end. It is common for public organizations to also outsource CyberSOC services. Although outsourcing appears to be a necessary step in many instances, it is crucial that it is executed in a manner that ensures the service provider aligns with the cybersecurity requirements

of the business. Specifically, it must be capable of facilitating the implementation of a comprehensive tactical-operational cybersecurity management approach.

3. Method

The present research is driven by the real need of a public sector entity, at its own initiative, to undertake an ambitious program to implement a tactical-operational management model for cybersecurity, providing the required holism to tackle current cyber threats. The mentioned organization is a Spanish public organization, which is involved in promoting technology in all spheres of society. It employs approximately 300 individuals and comprises five departments along with sixteen primary functional areas. Exploiting this need and in mutual agreement with the involved organization, we conducted a research project aimed at providing a series of valuable contributions not only to that organization, but also to other public entities with similar needs.

We undertook the research employing a business analysis methodology, evaluating the capacities of the public entity to effectively implement a comprehensive tactical-operational cybersecurity management approach, which holds the potential to foster a substantial transformation in the cybersecurity culture. Our study was divided into four phases grouped in two stages:

- Stage 1. Pre-study of public sector requirements and context
  - o Phase 1. In this phase, after a systematic analysis of the existing literature was carried out, the corresponding insights were analyzed and organized to detect whether the features, requirements, and impediments to deploy a truly holistic cybersecurity management model are shared by different public sector organizations worldwide; this phase corresponds to the work described in Section 2.
  - o Phase 2. During this phase, a series of meetings were conducted with the participating organization to discuss the prerequisites for implementing a comprehensive cybersecurity management model. These discussions aimed to enable the organization to assess challenges and barriers that could impede the adoption of such a model. Additionally, the organization shared anonymously, and whenever possible, information about other public entities it is related to, which allowed gathering relevant insight both directly and indirectly. This phase focused on determining the organization's capability to fulfill the model's requirements and identify potential obstacles. Continuing with our work, the information retrieved in the mentioned meetings was channelized using the Strengths, Weaknesses, Opportunities, and Threats (SWOT) analysis technique described by Benzaghta et al. in [96] to analyze deeply and systematically de current circumstances of the participating public entity. We also determine at this point whether the resulting insights coincide with the common features identified for public organizations in a wider context.
  - o Phase 3. At this stage, we identified a specific set of actionable strategies that we understood as universally applicable to all public sector entities due the fact that they share common root characteristics as determined in Phase 1 and Phase 2. These strategies were aimed at the successful implementation of a comprehensive tactical-operational cybersecurity management model. This model takes into consideration the distinctive attributes of the public organizations identified in the previous phase and we use the Threats, Opportunities, Weaknesses, and Strengths (TOWS) matrix technique, described in Pasaribu et al. [97], to analyze the external opportunities and threats and compare them to the organization's strengths and weaknesses, resulting in a set of actionable strategies. The combined use of SWOT–TOWS analysis is common to analyze and interpret systems, especially to develop strategies; the work of Hattangadi in [98] analyzes them together.
- Stage 2. Model development.
  - o Phase 4. Finally, we carried out our proposal to develop the identified strategies, that would allow public entities to seamlessly adopt a holistic management model

of cybersecurity, taking into account and incorporating the previously identified peculiarities and facing the existing specific challenges of public entities. Throughout the duration of this phase, the research team benefited from the active engagement of the participating public entity. Their involvement enriched the solutions devised by providing insights from the perspective of the recipient institution.

3.1. Stage 1: Pre-Study of Public Sector Requirements and Context

During this stage, encompassing all tasks within phases 1, 2, and 3, we conducted a comprehensive preliminary study to systematically analyze the context surrounding public sector entities. This analysis extended to the international perspective through a state-of-the-art review and to our specific Spanish case study. The overarching objective at this stage was to acquire an in-depth understanding of the requirements and characteristics unique to public sector organizations, enabling them to effectively address the challenges faced by the cross-functional cybersecurity workforce in implementing holistic cybersecurity. Armed with this knowledge, we aimed to identify the most advantageous strategies for any model seeking to address these challenges and seamlessly integrate with public sector entities. We leveraged these identified strategies in the subsequent development of our proposal.

In phase 2, several meetings were held with the participating organization, aimed at discussing the requirements that need to be met to implement a holistic cybersecurity management model. The main purpose of these meetings was to analyze its specific context, gathering relevant information about its strengths and weaknesses, as well as the existing opportunities and threats in relation to the implementation of a holistic cybersecurity model. Moreover, throughout the entire process, the participating organization provided anonymous information concerning other similar public entities with which it had relationships, pertaining to the same aspects being analyzed in its case. As a result, the study incorporates direct information provided by the organization itself, as well as secondary information concerning third parties, provided by the organization but in an indirect way, thus necessitating a more in-depth subsequent analysis. Based on these, and with the gathered information, a SWOT analysis was conducted, which succinctly represented the characteristics of the organization and its starting conditions to address the process of deploying a holistic model that enables the enhancement of its cybersecurity (Table 2).

Table 2. SWOT analysis based on the information provided by the participating entity regarding its own strengths, weaknesses, opportunities, and threats, as well as those of third-party public entities.

	Strengths	Weakness
Internal	<ul><li>Their personnel are highly skilled as managers;</li><li>Have much experience in outsourcing processes and can contract the required skilled service providers if needed;</li><li>Can provide long term stable employment;</li><li>They are not necessarily under the pressure of a profit goal but driven by the vocation of public utility.</li></ul>	<ul><li>Have difficulty to retain and develop the career of cybersecurity personnel;</li><li>Lack of personnel skilled in hands-on tasks;</li><li>Their teams are often composed by in-house and outsourced personnel;</li><li>They are silo-based organizations where cross-domain collaboration is difficult.</li></ul>
	Opportunities	Threats
External	<ul><li>There is an increasing interest that public organizations enhance their cybersecurity capabilities;</li><li>Can partner with private sector organizations to leverage their expertise and technology to improve cybersecurity;</li><li>Those public organizations able to offer cyber-resilient services will be more valued;</li><li>More funding is available for public organization to modernize in terms of cybersecurity.</li></ul>	<ul><li>Private sector can attract potential employees more effectively;</li><li>Regulations hinder to contract the same service providers continuously;</li><li>The number of cyber criminals seeking to target public sector organizations is increasing;</li><li>Cyber threats are constantly evolving, and the public sector may struggle to keep up with the latest threats and technologies. This can lead to a reactive approach to cybersecurity rather than a proactive one.</li></ul>
	Positive	Negative

From this phase, we obtained a comprehensive understanding of the organization's potential to implement the intended model. The positive aspects can be summarized as a high capacity for management and expertise in outsourcing, coupled with a growing interest and allocation of budget towards enhancing cybersecurity in the public sector. The negative aspects primarily revolve around the public entity's challenges in developing and retaining technical cybersecurity talent, as well as difficulties in adapting to highly dynamic changes or implementing a collaborative internal working system.

In conclusion of this stage, we have come to the realization that the common characteristics we found in the analysis of the state of the art are also present in the participating entity and the rest of entities we analyzed indirectly. Extensive literature exists that describes similar circumstances in public organizations worldwide. Henceforth, we possessed sufficient confidence to perceive this situation as a widespread phenomenon within public sector organizations aspiring to implement a comprehensive tactical-operational cybersecurity management approach. At this point in our study, we had gathered sufficient evidence to suggest that the participating organization exhibited similar characteristics to other public entities worldwide in terms of their potential to implement a holistic cybersecurity management model. This encouraged us to believe that the solution we were developing for the participating entity could also be beneficial to other organizations with similar profiles.

Finally, in the third phase, we employed the prior analysis as an input to a TOWS matrix with the objective of translating the insights from Phase 1 and Phase 2 into actionable strategies. The resulting strategies were:

- Strengths and Opportunities (SO) strategies, commonly referred to as the "Maxi-Maxi Strategy", encompass the utilization of strengths to optimize opportunities. In a TOWS analysis, this type of strategy is considered highly proactive and has a higher likelihood of yielding success. In our case, the public organization could leverage its expertise, skills, and capabilities in public procurement and outsourcing to effectively utilize the available funding. By establishing public-private contracts, the organization can transform itself into a resilient entity in the field of cybersecurity and provide better and more secure public services;
- Strengths and Threats (ST) strategies, commonly referred to as the "Maxi-Mini Strategy", involve leveraging strengths to mitigate threats. In our study, by leveraging the growing allocation of funds for cybersecurity enhancements and the heightened focus on modernizing and fortifying public entities and services, the public organization can seize the opportunity to engage public sector companies. This strategic move aims to facilitate the organization's adaptation to the dynamic, challenging, and rapidly evolving contexts of cybersecurity and cyber threats;
- Weakness and Opportunities (WO) strategies, commonly referred to as the "Mini-Maxi Strategy", encompass the approach of minimizing weaknesses by capitalizing on available opportunities. In our work, the growing allocation of funds for cybersecurity enhancements, coupled with the heightened emphasis on modernizing and fortifying public entities and services, presents an opportunity for the public organization to utilize outsourced personnel, augment the cybersecurity skills and career progression of its existing employees, and establish methodological foundations to foster true holism;
- Weaknesses and Threats (WT) strategies, also recognized as the "Mini-Mini Strategy", are employed to minimize weaknesses and evade threats. Within a TOWS analysis, this type of strategy is considered highly reactive/defensive and may not be as reliable in generating success. Due to this rationale, this strategy is not deemed conducive to steering the advancement of our proposal.

In summary, our objective in this research was to find a mechanism that would facilitate the development of the described strategies, namely, the SO, ST, and WO strategies. Essentially, this mechanism should be based on the outsourcing of services, leveraging existing resources and the interest in cybersecurity within the context of public sector entities. Its purpose would be to enhance the cybersecurity skills of various functional areas within the organization, improve its talent retention capabilities, implement a holistic model, and establish a cybersecurity management context that seamlessly orchestrates all these elements.

3.2. Stage 2: Model Development

The second stage of our research began with the inputs from stage 1, namely, the strategies required for a model aiming to address the challenges of deploying holistic cybersecurity by the cross-functional cybersecurity workforce in public sector organizations. In this specific context, the strategies previously defined were adjusted to accommodate the unique characteristics of public entities, ensuring that the resulting model would be well-suited to their needs.

Throughout Phase 4, we formulated our proposal to execute the strategies delineated in the preceding stage. Following thorough deliberations, we made the strategic choice to harness the outsourcing capabilities of public sector entities and establish a novel type of outsourced CyberSOC. This strategic decision was aimed at bolstering the cybersecurity proficiency of the cross-functional workforce while aligning with the specific contextual considerations, strengths, and weaknesses unique to public sector organizations. The outcome of this phase, as detailed in the following sections, are the results of our research: a novel concept called the "Wide-Scope CyberSOC" along with the essential documentation and procedural elements for its easy and efficient implementation within public sector organizations.

As mentioned, our proposal involves the utilization of an outsourced CyberSOC service, equipped with specialized capabilities that serve as the foundation for fostering a holistic approach to cybersecurity management within the organization. We designated this novel CyberSOC type as "Wide-Scope CyberSOC".

In order to materialize this Wide-Scope CyberSOC, we deemed it imperative to consider several pivotal aspects, as depicted in Figure 1:

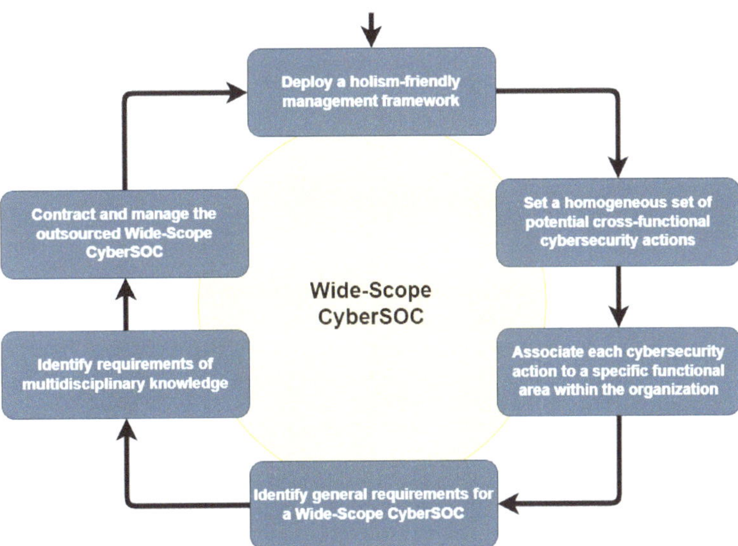

Figure 1. Key aspects to be taken into consideration to seamlessly integrate a Wide-Scope CyberSOC into the organization, enabling a holistic management of cybersecurity.

- The establishment of a cybersecurity management framework that can deliver the necessary holism at lower organizational levels is imperative. Contracting a Wide-Scope CyberSOC to assist the organization in overcoming silos and adopting a holistic approach would be futile if the procedural foundations to support such an extended CyberSOC have not been put in place. Consequently, based on the reasons outlined in Section 2.2, we opted for the CyberTOMP framework.

- Since the Wide-Scope CyberSOC is intended to provide guidance and assistance in designing and implementing multidisciplinary cybersecurity measures, it is essential to pre-identify the potential set of such cybersecurity actions. This enables us to contractually demand support for each of these actions. As our proposal is based on CyberTOMP, this set of actions is already identified within this framework. The Unified List of Expected Outcomes (ULEO) of CyberTOMP (Table 3) precisely represents a compilation of potential cybersecurity actions. There, every unified expected outcome is represented together with its corresponding function and category from the cybersecurity framework of National Institute of Standards and Technology (NIST). Each expected outcome in the ULEO has its own identifier. Expected outcomes from [99] are identified with the prefix "9D", those from [100] are identified with the prefix "CSC", and the remainder are identified using the original terminology from [101]. Furthermore, the associated Implementation Groups (IGs), to which the unified expected outcome should be applied, are determined. This enables the development of a proportionate cybersecurity approach, as lower IGs define the unified expected outcomes applicable to assets of lower criticality, while higher IGs pertain to assets with greater criticality. Additionally, leveraging this list for our proposal allows us to utilize the associated set of metrics concerning its implementation and the cybersecurity status of each asset to which they are applied.

Table 3. A fragment of the ULEO, as defined in the CyberTOMP framework, included for informational purposes.

NIST Function	NIST Category	Unified Expected Outcome	IG1	IG2	IG3
Protect	PR.PT	9D-4		√	√
Protect	PR.PT	CSC-4.12			√
.	.	.	.	.	.
.	.	.	.	.	.
.	.	.	.	.	.
Protect	PR.PT	PR.PT-5	√	√	√

- It is also crucial to identify which functional area should be responsible for each of these cybersecurity actions, ensuring that the contribution of each functional area to overall cybersecurity enables genuine holistic cybersecurity. Furthermore, this allows the Wide-Scope CyberSOC to focus its efforts on supporting each area in developing specific cybersecurity actions from the perspective of its specialized field. During our research efforts, we conducted a detailed analysis of the various functional areas involved in cybersecurity, as defined in CyberTOMP (Table 4). We also examined the specific scope of each cybersecurity action and established the association between functional areas and corresponding actions in all cases, as described in [99,100,102]. The comprehensive results of our investigation can be found in Appendix A.

Table 4. Functional areas of the organization involved in holistic cybersecurity, as defined in the reference framework used in our proposal.

Area ID	Area's Main Cybersecurity Responsibilities
FA1	In charge of the security of Internet of Things (IoT) devices.
FA2	Implementation of active defense measures, vulnerabilities management, threat hunting, Security Information and Event Management (SIEM) operation, activities within a CyberSOC, and incident response.
FA3	Human resources preparation regarding cybersecurity threats through continuous training and its reinforcement, as well as the design and execution of practical cybersecurity exercises

Table 4. *Cont.*

Area ID	Area's Main Cybersecurity Responsibilities
FA4	Analysis of internal and external threats, exchange of threat intelligence with third parties, and preparation and incorporation of Indicators of Compromise (IoCs).
FA5	Surveillance of the applicable regulation and its incorporation into cybersecurity. Key Performance Indicators (KPI) monitoring, establishment of strategies, policies, standards, processes, procedures, and corporate instructions.
FA6	Risk treatment, business continuity management, crisis management, establishing the organization's position regarding cyber risks, insurance contracting, risk registration, auditing, definition of groups of risk management, and definition of those responsible and owners of the processes and assets.
FA7	Cybersecurity risk analysis, vulnerability scanning, supply chain risk identification and analysis, asset inventory, risk monitoring, penetration testing of infrastructure, people, or information systems.
FA8	Leading the secure software development cycle, continuous integration and deployment, user experience security, software quality, API security, identification of information flows in information systems, management of the free software used and the static or dynamic analysis of the code.
FA9	Management, development, implementation, and verification of compliance with the standards and regulations defined at the corporate level for cybersecurity: CIS controls [100], CIS Community Defense Model [103], MITRE matrix [104,105], NIST framework [101] for the improvement of cybersecurity of critical infrastructures or the family of standards ISO27000, CyberTOMP.
FA10	Management, definition, implementation, operation, prevention, etc., in relation to cryptography, key and certificate management, encryption standards, security engineering, access controls with or without multiple authentication factors, single sign-on, privileged access management, identity management, identity federation, cloud security, container security, endpoint security, data protection and prevention of data leakage, network design to prevent distributed denial of service attacks, development and secure configuration of systems, patch and update management and the establishment of secure reference configurations.
FA11	Promote study, education and training, attendance at conferences and participation in related professional groups, training, or certification.
FA12	Internal and external corporate communication, social networks management, marketing and the establishment and maintenance of institutional relationship with interested third parties with whom the organization maintains some type of contact.

- Given that the Wide-Scope CyberSOC is going to be outsourced to third parties, it is highly advisable to establish a set of general requirements that clearly distinguish what is being contracted as a Wide-Scope CyberSOC and not merely a technologically focused CyberSOC. This is important because many service providers tend to offer traditional, technology-focused CyberSOC services by default. In the context of a public entity that has outsourced some of its workforce and has an external CyberSOC, we define a Wide-Scope CyberSOC as a CyberSOC with the following general requirements:
  - o Must poses the necessary skills and capabilities to understand, design, prescribe, advise, and monitor cybersecurity actions that can be executed by every functional area within an organization that can contribute to the organization's strategic common effort, with a particular focus on those functional areas that fall outside of the realm of computing or information technologies;
  - o Must be capable of positioning itself within the context of each organization's functional areas, and from this vantage point, be able to understand the implications (including what, how, where, when, and who) of these areas of expertise with regards to cybersecurity. In fact, a Wide-Scope CyberSOC must be an expert in all fields of knowledge that are relevant to cybersecurity. Not only in the most technological ones;
  - o Must be aware that those functional areas that do not typically participate in cybersecurity may not be conscious of the fact that they can significantly contribute to improving the overall state of cybersecurity from within their own areas of expertise. As such, a Wide-Scope CyberSOC must also act as a mentor to enhance

the awareness of these functional areas and develop their cybersecurity skills from the perspective of their areas of expertise;

o   Must be able to understand the organizational context and address circumstances where the functional areas with which it engages in cybersecurity may be partially outsourced and frequently renewed. Its mode of operation must be adapted to this situation in a seamless manner.

Drawing upon the characteristics of public entities that we have identified, and supported by the body of research we have examined and presented in Table 1, we have proposed the preceding paragraphs as general requirements for public entities when engaging a service provider for CyberSOC outsourcing.

This approach allows us to leverage the existing presence of an outsourced, technology-focused CyberSOC to offer a more comprehensive perspective on cybersecurity. Simultaneously, it enhances the awareness of the cybersecurity workforce regarding its potential contributions to the overall cybersecurity posture of the organization. While there may be alternative approaches, we believe that ours takes into account factors already prevalent in public organizations, which we have directly and indirectly analyzed in previous phases. These factors include the widespread adoption of outsourcing, the existence of mixed operational teams comprising both in-house and outsourced personnel, the challenges associated with acquiring cybersecurity talent, and the imperative need to augment cybersecurity skills to address the shortage in the cybersecurity workforce, among others. In our conception of a Wide-Scope CyberSOC, it must be proficient enough to serve as the cybersecurity reference unit within the organization and train cross-functional personnel applying a learning-by-doing approach, as explained in [106] by Deng et al., and also providing mentorship and coaching as needed, following the guidelines of [107–110] by Hamburg, Burrel, Ndueso et al., and Corradini, respectively. It is also necessary that the outsourced Wide-Scope CyberSOC has the ability of enhancing the cybersecurity awareness of workers, as in [65,66]. It should serve as a facilitating element that enables the continuous enhancement of cybersecurity capabilities and knowledge within each functional area involved in corporate cybersecurity, rather than solely designing and implementing these measures firsthand.

While it is not mandatory, it is advisable for the Wide-Scope CyberSOC to be viewed as a collective asset of the entire cross-functional cybersecurity workforce. Given that this new CyberSOC will be more deeply involved in the daily cybersecurity activities of various functional areas, we recommend positioning it within the organization in a way that minimizes the potential for any functional area to perceive conflicts of interest or biases, something identified by Monzelo and Nunes [111] or Badhwar [112], as shown in Figure 2.

- As a preliminary step before contracting the Wide-Scope CyberSOC service, it is also essential to turn the desired multidisciplinary capabilities, skills, and knowledge into explicit requirements for the service that any potential service provider must meet. These requirements will enable them to effectively mentor and provide the necessary support to the various functional areas contributing to cybersecurity. As part of our study, we have conducted this analysis and defined the necessary prerequisites, which can be directly incorporated into the technical specifications of the Wide-Scope CyberSOC. The specific knowledge requirements can be found in Appendix A;
- Finally, after addressing all the relevant points explained in this section, the public entity will be able to outsource the Wide-Scope CyberSOC service using its expertise in public procurement. Once the service is contracted, it should be managed using the existing procedures in the selected model, CyberTOMP. Figure 3 illustrates the specific activities of the tactical-operational cybersecurity management process defined in CyberTOMP, where the Wide-Scope CyberSOC should play a key role by contributing its expertise and acting as a cohesive element among the various functional areas of the organization. Furthermore, aside from the aforementioned aspect, which pertains exclusively to the set of steps/tasks delineated in the CyberTOMP proposal, the Wide-Scope CyberSOC must also undertake the activities typically associated with a

traditional CyberSOC. These activities may encompass actions within the realms of identify, protect, detect, respond, and recover approaches, as is customary.

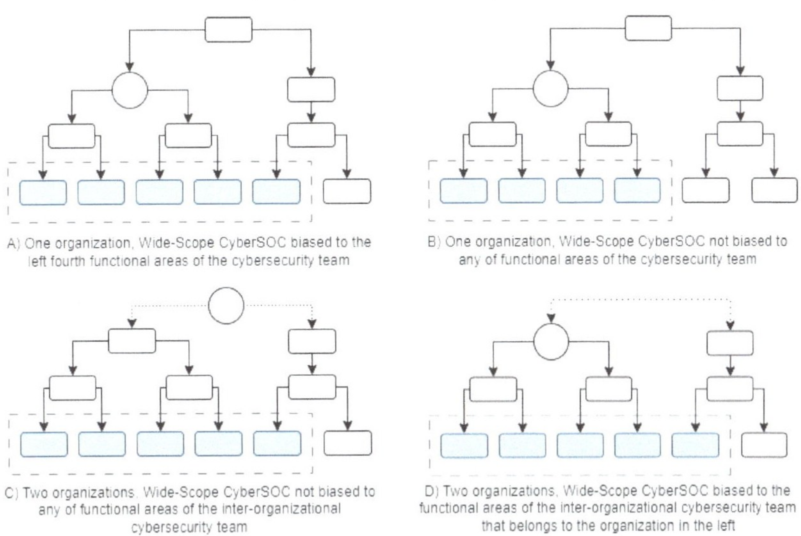

Figure 2. Here are four examples of organizational structures. In (**B**,**C**), the Wide-Scope CyberSOC (represented by a circle) is less likely to be perceived as biased, as every functional area involved in cybersecurity (shown in gray) that makes up the multidisciplinary cybersecurity team (enclosed by a dashed rectangle) has direct access to it, even if they belong to different organizations. Conversely, this is not the case in scenarios (**A**,**D**).

Figure 3. Tasks defined within the CyberTOMP framework in which the Wide-Scope CyberSOC can assume a significant role.

3.3. Assessing the Wide-Scope CyberSOC Effect on the Deployment of Holistic Cybersecurity

The core objective of our proposal is to ease the implementation of holistic cybersecurity by enhancing the capabilities of the cross-functional cybersecurity workforce, which includes individuals from both the public and private sectors. Our aim is to empower them to better comprehend and apply their roles, leveraging their specific expertise to contribute effectively to the overall organizational cybersecurity strategy.

To achieve this goal, we advocate for the adoption of the innovative Wide-Scope CyberSOC. It is crucial to underscore that our ultimate objective is to fortify the cybersecurity situational awareness of the personnel involved. To this end, we believe that evaluating and measuring the situational awareness of the cybersecurity cross-functional team over time, post-implementation of the Wide-Scope CyberSOC within the organization, serves as a robust means of validating the effectiveness of the Wide-Scope CyberSOC in simplifying the deployment of holistic cybersecurity.

To facilitate this measurement, we propose the utilization of structured questionnaires tailored to assess personnel's situational awareness skills across four key areas, in line with the requirements we recommend imposing on the Wide-Scope CyberSOC:

1. Grasping the holistic nature of cybersecurity and the extensive spectrum of potential, applicable cybersecurity actions;
2. Recognizing the responsibilities associated with each functional area and appreciating the critical importance of collective engagement in achieving the highest cybersecurity standards;
3. Understanding the imperative need for proportional cybersecurity measures, aligned with the criticality of assets;
4. Acknowledging that various approaches can be employed to attain the same objectives, thus enabling the distribution of cybersecurity efforts and resources throughout the organization to foster collaborative equilibrium.

Given that situational awareness training is inherently an ongoing process, it may take a substantial amount of time before conclusive results are obtained. Nevertheless, successive measurements should exhibit an upward trend in these skills among the cross-functional cybersecurity workforce.

4. Results and Discussion

The current research project addresses a genuine need of a Public Sector entity engaged in defining and implementing a holistic cybersecurity management model: the necessity to attain a comprehensive level of cybersecurity awareness among their personnel. With the collaboration of this organization, we undertook this work with the intention of ensuring that the outcomes, tools, and elements developed could also be applicable to other public sector entities. Our motivation lies not only in a sense of public service but also in the potential for collaboration and further evolution of the proposal.

To ensure this, we conducted our work adhering to the standard formal or semi-formal methods as described: We conducted an analysis of a relevant set of research works found in the current literature. Our goal was to identify requirements stemming from one of our previous studies and the need emerging from its applicability to a public sector entity. Subsequently, through interviews and work sessions, we assessed the entity's situation and specific characteristics regarding the adoption of a holistic model for cybersecurity management. Concurrently, we indirectly gathered information on similar characteristics in other public organizations from the same organization. We employed SWOT analysis technique, to systematically organize and categorize these attributes, to confirm these characteristics were similar to the common ones, we analyzed scrutinizing the international literature. This was crucial to develop a proposal applicable to all public organizations, not just the study participant. The outcome confirmed shared characteristics, and for that reason, we assumed they share a common scenario and could benefit from our proposal. Using a TOWS analysis technique, we identified successful strategies, guiding a coherent approach in our proposal's design. To implement the identified strategies, and taking into account the features of public sector organizations, we designed an extended-capabilities CyberSOC that facilitates the adoption of the holistic model tactically and operationally by increasing the holistic cybersecurity awareness level of the cybersecurity workforce.

To the best of our knowledge, and after extensive periods of research, we have not encountered a study that addresses the development of holistic cybersecurity capabilities at the lower levels of the organization while also considering the specificities of public sector entities and their operational methods. Our proposal specifically targets this gap within public organizations.

As a contribution resulting from this study, we coined the new concept, "Wide-Scope CyberSOC", which defines such a CyberSOC with extended capabilities. This CyberSOC can be easily outsourced, thanks to our identification of a well-structured, common, and multidisciplinary set of cybersecurity actions that has been also associated with each organization's functional area involved in cybersecurity. We then transformed this set into directly applicable requirements when drafting technical specifications for the procurement of such services. As a result of this process, the outsourced Wide-Scope CyberSOC is managed and evaluated consistently, seamlessly integrated into a specific framework for the holistic, tactical-operational management of cybersecurity. These contributions can be found, summarized, and organized, in Appendix A.

The Wide-Scope CyberSOC will be capable of actively participating in and facilitating the tactical-operational cybersecurity team in various activities. These activities include identifying cybersecurity requirements, breaking down business assets, identifying functional areas involved in their cybersecurity, analyzing the cyber threat landscape, and adapting the organization accordingly. Additionally, the CyberSOC will be instrumental in designing and implementing cross-functional cybersecurity measures. This empowered CyberSOC will serve as a cornerstone, expediting the adoption of a multidisciplinary approach to cybersecurity management within the public organization.

As part of our study, in cooperation with the participating public entity, we have designed its first Wide-Scope CyberSOC. It underwent a public tender process, with various security service providers submitting their offers. The organization has since implemented and is currently managing its first Wide-Scope CyberSOC based on the guidelines outlined in this study. In the meanwhile, we are assessing the effect of introducing the Wide-Scope CyberSOC in this public sector organization following the method described in Section 3.3. Initial measurements show promise, but further data collection and maturation are required before presenting the results to the general public, which will take a considerable amount of time.

We devoted a substantial amount of effort to carefully plan our research approach, ensuring that the results would not only be beneficial for the participating public organization, but also applicable to other public sector organizations internationally. While we are confident that it aligns well with the Spanish case study, we conducted and took the necessary precautions to facilitate its applicability to a broader range of public organizations, and we acknowledge that no research is immune to the possibility of unintentional biases or errors. We have identified two potential areas where these unlikely events could occur:

- The generalization process in our research was built upon the presence of common features and circumstances identified in the global literature pertaining to public sector organizations, along with the parallel existence of these same insights within the public organization participating in our study. This alignment allowed us to establish a connection that led us to recognize that the insights from our case study are applicable to other public organizations worldwide. To ensure the reliability of our approach, we deliberately selected a comprehensive array of research works for the analysis of current literature concerning public sector organizations. This approach was taken specifically to reduce the risk of selecting only a few sources that might not accurately represent these public organizations. Nonetheless, despite our efforts, there is a slight possibility that our selection of research works may have been influenced by unconscious bias;

- On the other hand, we have introduced a method to evaluate the effectiveness of our proposal, which we are currently applying to the participating organization in our study. The initial results appear promising, but they require extended assessment over time to thoroughly ascertain the model's benefits. Furthermore, since this is a generalization based on a single case study, the only application thus far has been the one conducted as part of our research. Additional applications will offer valuable data to refine our proposal if necessary.

While we have not identified any of the situations mentioned, and despite our vigilance and awareness, we acknowledge that these could be two points where additional checks could be beneficial to strengthen our work. Therefore, we encourage third parties to independently analyze the generalization process we conducted and implement the model in other public organizations to verify the results or propose enhancements that contribute to the body of knowledge related to holistic cybersecurity management in public sector organizations.

5. Conclusions and Future Work

As highlighted in the introduction, organizations across various sectors, both public and private, are becoming increasingly reliant on cyberspace, a realm beyond complete control, rendering them susceptible to dynamic cyber threats. This vulnerability exposes organizations to potential risks, including business disruptions and sensitive data breaches. For public entities, such risks translate into an inability to deliver essential public services and a failure to safeguard citizens' data and privacy. To address this challenge effectively, an enhanced cybersecurity awareness among the cybersecurity workforce is essential. We have identified common characteristics among public sector organizations, enabling us to propose a comprehensive solution that equips them to navigate cyberspace securely. Our proposal introduces a novel outsourced CyberSOC, the Wide-Scope CyberSOC, designed to facilitate the development of holistic cybersecurity skills within the workforce and stream-line holistic cybersecurity management in public sector organizations. This work offers a valuable framework applicable to any public entity, particularly those heavily engaged in digital citizen services, where the exposure to the expanding cyber threats landscape is significant. Additionally, we have outlined the comprehensive set of requirements that public organizations should request from Wide-Scope CyberSOC service providers to en-sure the fulfillment of necessary functionalities. As part of future work, we are exploring the development of specific tools to simplify the operations of Wide-Scope CyberSOCs and enhance the holistic cybersecurity awareness of cross-functional cybersecurity teams.

Author Contributions: Conceptualization, M.D.-D., F.J.R.-P., J.C.-M., D.C.-P. and J.C.-C.; methodology, M.D.-D., F.J.R.-P., J.C.-M., D.C.-P. and J.C.-C.; software, M.D.-D., F.J.R.-P., J.C.-M., D.C.-P. and J.C.-C.; validation, M.D.-D., F.J.R.-P., J.C.-M., D.C.-P. and J.C.-C.; formal analysis, M.D.-D., F.J.R.-P., J.C.-M., D.C.-P. and J.C.-C.; investigation, M.D.-D., F.J.R.-P., J.C.-M., D.C.-P. and J.C.-C.; resources, M.D.-D., F.J.R.-P., J.C.-M., D.C.-P. and J.C.-C.; data curation, M.D.-D., F.J.R.-P., J.C.-M., D.C.-P. and J.C.-C.; writing—original draft preparation, M.D.-D., F.J.R.-P., J.C.-M., D.C.-P. and J.C.-C.; writing—review and editing, M.D.-D., F.J.R.-P., J.C.-M., D.C.-P. and J.C.-C.; visualization, M.D.-D., F.J.R.-P., J.C.-M., D.C.-P. and J.C.-C.; super-vision, M.D.-D., F.J.R.-P., J.C.-M., D.C.-P. and J.C.-C.; project administration, M.D.-D., F.J.R.-P., J.C.-M., D.C.-P. and J.C.-C.; funding acquisition, M.D.-D., F.J.R.-P., J.C.-M., D.C.-P. and J.C.-C. All authors have read and agreed to the published version of the manuscript.

Funding: This research was funded in part by TED2021-131699B-I00/ MCIN/ AEI/ 10.13039/501100011033/ European Union NextGenerationEU/PRTR.

Data Availability Statement: No new data were created or analyzed in this study. Data sharing is not applicable to this article.

Conflicts of Interest: The authors declare no conflict of interest. The funders had no role in the design of the study; in the collection, analyses, or interpretation of data; in the writing of the manuscript; or in the decision to publish the results.

Appendix A

Table A1. Knowledge Requirements to Contract Wide-Scope CyberSOC Services.

NIST Function	NIST Category	Unified Expected Outcome	IG1	IG2	IG3	Main Area ID	Knowledge Requirement: "The Wide-Scope CyberSOC must be Skilled to Help Cross-Functional Teams in…"
Identify	ID.AM	CSC-1.1	√	√	√	FA7	Establishing and maintaining a detailed enterprise asset inventory with the potential to store or process data.
Identify	ID.AM	CSC-12.4		√	√	FA10	Establishing and maintaining architecture diagrams.
Identify	ID.AM	CSC-14.1	√	√	√	FA3	Establishing and maintaining a security awareness program.
Identify	ID.AM	CSC-2.2	√	√	√	FA8	Ensuring that only authorized, supported software is used.
Identify	ID.AM	CSC-3.1	√	√	√	FA5	Establishing and maintaining a process for data management
Identify	ID.AM	CSC-3.2	√	√	√	FA10	Establishing and maintaining a data inventory.
Identify	ID.AM	CSC-3.6	√	√	√	FA10	Identifying data on end-user devices that has encryption requirements.
Identify	ID.AM	CSC-3.7		√	√	FA9	Establishing and maintaining a data classification scheme
Identify	ID.AM	ID.AM-1	√	√	√	FA7	Establishing and maintaining detailed inventory of physical devices and systems.
Identify	ID.AM	ID.AM-2	√	√	√	FA8	Inventorying all software platforms and applications within the organization.
Identify	ID.AM	ID.AM-3		√	√	FA8	Mapping organizational communication and data flows.
Identify	ID.BE	9D-1		√	√	FA7	Analyzing the business environment to determine potential ways of deterring attacks.
Identify	ID.BE	ID.BE-1			√	FA6	Identifying and communicating the organization's role in the supply chain.
Identify	ID.BE	ID.BE-2			√	FA6	Identifying and communicating the organization's place in critical infrastructure and its industry sector.
Identify	ID.BE	ID.BE-3			√	FA5	Establishing and communicating priorities for organizational mission, objectives, and activities.
Identify	ID.BE	ID.BE-4			√	FA5	Establishing dependencies and critical functions for delivery of critical services.
Identify	ID.BE	ID.BE-5			√	FA5	Establishing resilience requirements to support delivery of critical services for all operating states.
Identify	ID.GV	CSC-17.4		√	√	FA5	Establishing, maintaining an incident response process.
Identify	ID.GV	ID.GV-1	√	√	√	FA5	Establishing and communicating organizational cybersecurity policy.
Identify	ID.GV	ID.GV-2		√	√	FA9	Coordinating and aligning cybersecurity roles and responsibilities with internal roles and external partners.
Identify	ID.GV	ID.GV-3			√	FA5	Understanding and managing legal and regulatory requirements regarding cybersecurity.

Table A1. *Cont.*

NIST Function	NIST Category	Unified Expected Outcome	IG1	IG2	IG3	Main Area ID	Knowledge Requirement: "The Wide-Scope CyberSOC must be Skilled to Help Cross-Functional Teams in…"
Identify	ID.GV	ID.GV-4			√	FA5	Ensuring governance and risk management processes address cybersecurity risks.
Identify	ID.RA	9D-1		√	√	FA7	Ensuring that the organization understands the risk of vulnerabilities and the necessity of deterring their exploitation.
Identify	ID.RA	CSC-18.2		√	√	FA7	Conducting periodic external penetration tests in order to enhance understanding of cyber risks.
Identify	ID.RA	CSC-18.5			√	FA7	Conducting periodic internal penetration tests in order to enhance understanding of cyber risks.
Identify	ID.RA	CSC-3.7		√	√	FA9	Assessing the current validity of the data classification scheme in relation to existing risks.
Identify	ID.RA	ID.RA-1	√	√	√	FA7	Identifying and documenting assets vulnerabilities.
Identify	ID.RA	ID.RA-2			√	FA4	Ensuring cyber threat intelligence is received from information sharing forums and sources.
Identify	ID.RA	ID.RA-3			√	FA4	Identifying and document threats, both internal and external.
Identify	ID.RA	ID.RA-4			√	FA6	Identifying potential business impacts and likelihoods.
Identify	ID.RA	ID.RA-6			√	FA6	Identifying and prioritizing risk responses.
Identify	ID.RM	9D-8		√	√	FA2	Comprehending the potential risks that necessitate redirecting attackers to alternative targets.
Identify	ID.RM	ID.RM-1			√	FA6	Ensuring risk management processes are established, managed, and agreed to by organizational stakeholders.
Identify	ID.RM	ID.RM-2			√	FA6	Determining and clearly expressing organizational risk tolerance.
Identify	ID.RM	ID.RM-3			√	FA6	Informing the organization's risk tolerance by its role in critical infrastructure and sector specific risk analysis.
Identify	ID.SC	ID.SC-1		√	√	FA5	Identifying, establishing, assessing, and managing cyber supply chain risk management processes.
Identify	ID.SC	ID.SC-2	√	√	√	FA5	Identifying, prioritizing, and assessing third party partners of information systems, components, and services, using a cybersecurity supply chain risk assessment process.
Identify	ID.SC	ID.SC-3		√	√	FA9	Ensuring contracts with suppliers and third-party are designed to meet the goals of an organization's cybersecurity program and cybersecurity supply chain management plan.
Identify	ID.SC	ID.SC-4			√	FA6	Auditing, testing, and evaluating suppliers and third-party partners to confirm they are meeting their contractual obligations.
Identify	ID.SC	ID.SC-5	√	√	√	FA9	Conducting response and recovery planning and testing with suppliers and third-party providers.
Protect	PR.AC	CSC-12.5		√	√	FA10	Centralizing network authentication, authorization, and auditing.

Table A1. *Cont.*

NIST Function	NIST Category	Unified Expected Outcome	IG1	IG2	IG3	Main Area ID	Knowledge Requirement: "The Wide-Scope CyberSOC must be Skilled to Help Cross-Functional Teams in…"
Protect	PR.AC	CSC-12.6		√	√	FA10	Employing secure network management and communication protocols.
Protect	PR.AC	CSC-13.4		√	√	FA10	Conducting traffic filtering between network segments
Protect	PR.AC	CSC-4.7	√	√	√	FA10	Managing default accounts on enterprise assets and software.
Protect	PR.AC	CSC-5.2	√	√	√	FA10	Using unique passwords for all enterprise assets.
Protect	PR.AC	CSC-5.6		√	√	FA10	Centralizing account management.
Protect	PR.AC	CSC-6.8			√	FA10	Deploying and maintaining Role-Based Access Control (RBAC)
Protect	PR.AC	PR.AC-1	√	√	√	FA10	Ensuring identities and credentials are issued, managed, verified, revoked, and audited for authorized devices, users, and processes.
Protect	PR.AC	PR.AC-2			√	FA7	Ensuring physical access to assets is managed and protected.
Protect	PR.AC	PR.AC-3	√	√	√	FA10	Ensuring remote access is managed.
Protect	PR.AC	PR.AC-4	√	√	√	FA10	Ensuring access permissions and authorizations are managed, incorporating the principles of least privilege and separation of duties.
Protect	PR.AC	PR.AC-5	√	√	√	FA10	Ensuring network integrity is protected.
Protect	PR.AC	PR.AC-6			√	FA10	Ensuring identities are proofed and bound to credentials and asserted in interactions.
Protect	PR.AC	PR.AC-7	√	√	√	FA10	Ensuring users, devices, and other assets are authenticated commensurate with the risk of the transaction.
Protect	PR.AT	CSC-14.9		√	√	FA3	Conducting role-specific security awareness and skills training.
Protect	PR.AT	CSC-15.4		√	√	FA5	Ensuring service provider contracts include security requirements.
Protect	PR.AT	PR.AT-1	√	√	√	FA3	Ensuring all users are informed and trained.
Protect	PR.AT	PR.AT-2		√	√	FA3	Ensuring privileged users understand their roles and responsibilities.
Protect	PR.DS	9D-6			√	FA8	Dispersing protective measures throughout the payload to safeguard the data.
Protect	PR.DS	CSC-3.4	√	√	√	FA10	Enforcing data retention in accordance with the risk strategy.
Protect	PR.DS	PR.DS-1		√	√	FA10	Ensuring data-at-rest is protected.
Protect	PR.DS	PR.DS-2		√	√	FA10	Ensuring data-in-transit is protected.
Protect	PR.DS	PR.DS-3	√	√	√	FA10	Ensuring assets are formally managed throughout removal, transfers, and disposition.
Protect	PR.DS	PR.DS-4			√	FA10	Adjusting capacity to ensure availability is maintained.
Protect	PR.DS	PR.DS-5			√	FA10	Ensuring protections against data leaks are implemented.
Protect	PR.DS	PR.DS-6		√	√	FA10	Ensuring integrity checking mechanisms are used to verify software, firmware, and information integrity.

Table A1. *Cont.*

NIST Function	NIST Category	Unified Expected Outcome	IG1	IG2	IG3	Main Area ID	Knowledge Requirement: "The Wide-Scope CyberSOC must be Skilled to Help Cross-Functional Teams in…"
Protect	PR.DS	PR.DS-7		√	√	FA10	Ensuring the development and testing environment(s) are separate from the production environment.
Protect	PR.DS	PR.DS-8			√	FA10	Ensuring integrity checking mechanisms are used to verify hardware integrity.
Protect	PR.IP	9D-3		√	√	FA2	Enhancing the difficulty of accessing the protected information beyond the attacker's skills.
Protect	PR.IP	9D-5		√	√	FA2	Investigating the threat in depth in order to prevent access to protected information using a multi-layered approach.
Protect	PR.IP	9D-8		√	√	FA2	Implementing measures to divert attackers in order to protect the information.
Protect	PR.IP	9D-9	√	√	√	FA2	Implementing measures in depth that become increasingly challenging and less visible as they approach the asset.
Protect	PR.IP	CSC-11.1	√	√	√	FA10	Establishing and maintaining a process for data recovery.
Protect	PR.IP	CSC-16.1		√	√	FA8	Establishing and maintaining a secure application development process.
Protect	PR.IP	CSC-16.14			√	FA4	Undertaking comprehensive threat modelling.
Protect	PR.IP	CSC-18.4			√	FA7	Validating the security measures deployed to protect information following each penetration test.
Protect	PR.IP	CSC-2.5		√	√	FA5	Creating an allow list of authorized software in order to protect information.
Protect	PR.IP	CSC-2.6		√	√	FA5	Creating an allow list of authorized libraries in order to protect information.
Protect	PR.IP	CSC-2.7			√	FA5	Creating an allow list of authorized scripts in order to protect information.
Protect	PR.IP	CSC-4.3	√	√	√	FA10	Configuring automatic session locking on enterprise assets to protect the information.
Protect	PR.IP	PR.IP-1	√	√	√	FA5	Ensuring a baseline configuration of information technology/industrial control systems is created and maintained incorporating security principles.
Protect	PR.IP	PR.IP-10		√	√	FA5	Ensuring response and recovery plans are tested.
Protect	PR.IP	PR.IP-11	√	√	√	FA11	Incorporating cybersecurity into human resources practices for information handling.
Protect	PR.IP	PR.IP-12		√	√	FA7	Developing and implementing a vulnerability management plan.
Protect	PR.IP	PR.IP-2		√	√	FA10	Implementing a system development life cycle to manage systems.
Protect	PR.IP	PR.IP-3			√	FA5	Designing a configuration change control process.
Protect	PR.IP	PR.IP-4	√	√	√	FA10	Ensuring backups of information are conducted, maintained, and tested.
Protect	PR.IP	PR.IP-5			√	FA5	Ensuring policy and regulations regarding the physical operating environment for organizational assets are met.

Table A1. *Cont.*

NIST Function	NIST Category	Unified Expected Outcome	IG1	IG2	IG3	Main Area ID	Knowledge Requirement: "The Wide-Scope CyberSOC must be Skilled to Help Cross-Functional Teams in…"
Protect	PR.IP	PR.IP-6	√	√	√	FA10	Ensuring data is destroyed according to policy.
Protect	PR.IP	PR.IP-7		√	√	FA5	Ensuring protection processes are improved.
Protect	PR.IP	PR.IP-8			√	FA2	Ensuring effectiveness of protection technologies is shared.
Protect	PR.IP	PR.IP-9	√	√	√	FA5	Ensuring response plans and recovery plans are in place and managed.
Protect	PR.MA	9D-5		√	√	FA2	Conducting maintenance activities on all layers of the asset.
Protect	PR.MA	9D-9		√	√	FA2	Carrying out maintenance tasks to ensure depth of defense.
Protect	PR.MA	CSC-12.1	√	√	√	FA10	Carrying out maintenance to ensure the network infrastructure is up to date.
Protect	PR.MA	CSC-12.3		√	√	FA10	Managing the network infrastructure with a security-oriented approach.
Protect	PR.MA	CSC-13.5		√	√	FA10	Carrying out maintenance actions to ensure assets remotely connecting to enterprise resources comply with the organization's requirements.
Protect	PR.MA	CSC-16.13			√	FA2	Performing root cause analysis on security vulnerabilities.
Protect	PR.MA	CSC-18.3		√	√	FA10	Remediating penetration test findings.
Protect	PR.MA	CSC-4.2	√	√	√	FA5	Carrying out tasks to securely configure the network infrastructure in accordance with established processes.
Protect	PR.MA	CSC-4.6	√	√	√	FA10	Carrying out security maintenance tasks on enterprise assets and software.
Protect	PR.MA	CSC-4.8		√	√	FA10	Uninstalling or disabling unnecessary services on enterprise assets and software.
Protect	PR.MA	CSC-4.9		√	√	FA10	Configuring trusted DNS servers on enterprise assets.
Protect	PR.MA	CSC-7.3	√	√	√	FA10	Performing automated operating system patch management.
Protect	PR.MA	CSC-8.1	√	√	√	FA5	Establishing and maintaining an audit log management process.
Protect	PR.MA	CSC-8.10		√	√	FA10	Retaining audit logs.
Protect	PR.MA	CSC-8.3	√	√	√	FA10	Ensuring adequate audit log storage.
Protect	PR.MA	CSC-8.9		√	√	FA10	Centralizing audit log collection and retention.
Protect	PR.MA	PR.MA-1			√	FA10	Ensuring maintenance and repair of organizational assets are performed and logged, with approved and controlled tools.
Protect	PR.PT	9D-4		√	√	FA2	Implementing differentiated protections to address each threat specifically.
Protect	PR.PT	9D-7			√	FA2	Employing decoys to distract attackers.
Protect	PR.PT	CSC-4.12			√	FA10	Separating enterprise workspaces on mobile end-user devices
Protect	PR.PT	CSC-4.4	√	√	√	FA10	Implementing and managing a firewall on servers

Table A1. *Cont.*

NIST Function	NIST Category	Unified Expected Outcome	IG1	IG2	IG3	Main Area ID	Knowledge Requirement: "The Wide-Scope CyberSOC must be Skilled to Help Cross-Functional Teams in…"
Protect	PR.PT	CSC-4.5	√	√	√	FA10	Implementing and managing a firewall on end-user devices
Protect	PR.PT	CSC-9.5		√	√	FA10	Implementing DMARC.
Protect	PR.PT	PR.PT-1	√	√	√	FA10	Ensuring audit/log records are determined, documented, implemented, and reviewed in accordance with policy.
Protect	PR.PT	PR.PT-2	√	√	√	FA10	Ensuring removable media is protected and its use restricted according to policy.
Protect	PR.PT	PR.PT-3			√	FA10	Ensuring the principle of least functionality is incorporated by configuring systems to provide only essential capabilities.
Protect	PR.PT	PR.PT-4			√	FA10	Ensuring communications and control networks are protected.
Protect	PR.PT	PR.PT-5	√	√	√	FA10	Ensuring mechanisms are implemented to achieve resilience requirements in normal and adverse situations.
Detect	DA.AE	CSC-8.12			√	FA10	Collecting service provider logs to detect anomalies.
Detect	DA.AE	DE.AE-1		√	√	FA10	Establishing and maintaining a baseline of operations and expected data flows for users and systems.
Detect	DA.AE	DE.AE-2		√	√	FA2	Analyzing detected events to understand attack targets and methods.
Detect	DA.AE	DE.AE-3	√	√	√	FA2	Collecting and correlating event data correlated from multiple sources and sensors.
Detect	DA.AE	DE.AE-4			√	FA2	Determining impact of events.
Detect	DA.AE	DE.AE-5			√	FA2	Establishing incident alert thresholds.
Detect	DE.CM	CSC-13.1		√	√	FA2	Centralizing security event alerting
Detect	DE.CM	CSC-13.5		√	√	FA10	Monitoring access control for assets remotely connecting to enterprise resources.
Detect	DE.CM	CSC-3.14			√	FA10	Logging access to sensitive data.
Detect	DE.CM	DE.CM-1		√	√	FA2	Ensuring the network is monitored to detect potential cybersecurity events.
Detect	DE.CM	DE.CM-2			√	FA1	Ensuring the physical environment is monitored to detect potential cybersecurity events.
Detect	DE.CM	DE.CM-3			√	FA10	Ensuring personnel activity is monitored to detect potential cybersecurity events.
Detect	DE.CM	DE.CM-4	√	√	√	FA2	Detecting malicious code.
Detect	DE.CM	DE.CM-5			√	FA2	Detecting unauthorized mobile code.
Detect	DE.CM	DE.CM-6			√	FA2	Monitoring external service provider activity to detect potential cybersecurity events.
Detect	DE.CM	DE.CM-7	√	√	√	FA2	Monitoring for unauthorized personnel, connections, devices, and software.
Detect	DE.CM	DE.CM-8		√	√	FA7	Conducting periodic vulnerability scans
Detect	DE.DP	CSC-17.1	√	√	√	FA5	Designating personnel, including key and backup, to manage incident handling.

Table A1. *Cont.*

NIST Function	NIST Category	Unified Expected Outcome	IG1	IG2	IG3	Main Area ID	Knowledge Requirement: "The Wide-Scope CyberSOC must be Skilled to Help Cross-Functional Teams in…"
Detect	DE.DP	CSC-17.4		√	√	FA5	Testing the incident response process to ensure it includes awareness of anomalous events.
Detect	DE.DP	CSC-17.5		√	√	FA5	Assigning key cross-functional roles and responsibilities in relation to incident response.
Detect	DE.DP	DE.DP-2			√	FA2	Ensuring detection activities comply with all applicable requirements.
Detect	DE.DP	DE.DP-3			√	FA10	Testing detection processes.
Detect	DE.DP	DE.DP-5			√	FA5	Continuously improving detection processes.
Respond	RS.AN	CSC-17.9			√	FA5	Establishing and maintaining security incident thresholds to ensure effective response.
Respond	RS.AN	RS.AN-1		√	√	FA2	Ensuring notifications from detection systems are investigated.
Respond	RS.AN	RS.AN-2			√	FA2	Ensuring the impact of the incident is understood.
Respond	RS.AN	RS.AN-3			√	FA2	Ensuring forensics are performed.
Respond	RS.AN	RS.AN-5		√	√	FA5	Ensuring processes are established to receive, analyze, and respond to vulnerabilities disclosed to the organization from internal and external sources.
Respond	RS.CO	CSC-17.4	√	√	√	FA5	Communicating the incident response process.
Respond	RS.CO	CSC-17.5		√	√	FA5	Communicating key cross-functional roles and responsibilities in relation to incident response.
Respond	RS.CO	RS.CO-5			√	FA4	Ensuring voluntary information sharing occurs with external stakeholders to achieve broader cybersecurity situational awareness.
Respond	RS.IM	RS.IM-1		√	√	FA5	Ensuring response plans incorporate lessons learned.
Respond	RS.IM	RS.IM-2		√	√	FA5	Response strategies are updated.
Respond	RS.MI	CSC-1.2	√	√	√	FA10	Ensuring that a process is in place to address unauthorized assets.
Respond	RS.MI	CSC-4.10		√	√	FA10	Enforcing remote wipe capability on portable end-user devices
Respond	RS.MI	CSC-7.7		√	√	FA10	Remediating detected vulnerabilities and weakness.
Respond	RS.MI	RS.MI-1			√	FA2	Containing incidents.
Respond	RS.MI	RS.MI-2			√	FA2	Mitigating incidents.
Respond	RS.MI	RS.MI-3			√	FA2	Mitigating newly identified vulnerabilities or documenting them as accepted risks.
Respond	RS.RP	CSC-17.6		√	√	FA5	Defining mechanisms for communicating during incident response.
Respond	RS.RP	RS.RP-1			√	FA2	Ensuring a response plan is executed during or after an incident.
Recover	RC.CO	RC.CO-1			√	FA12	Managing public relations.
Recover	RC.CO	RC.CO-2			√	FA12	Repairing the reputation after an incident.
Recover	RC.CO	RC.CO-3			√	FA12	Communicating recovery activities to internal and external stakeholders as well as executive and management teams.

Table A1. *Cont.*

NIST Function	NIST Category	Unified Expected Outcome	IG1	IG2	IG3	Main Area ID	Knowledge Requirement: "The Wide-Scope CyberSOC must be Skilled to Help Cross-Functional Teams in…"
Recover	RC.IM	RC.IM-1			√	FA5	Ensuring recovery plans incorporate lessons learned.
Recover	RC.IM	RC.IM-2			√	FA5	Ensuring recovery strategies are updated.
Recover	RC.RP	RC.RP-1			√	FA2	Ensuring a recovery plan is executed during or after a cybersecurity incident.

References

1. Domínguez-Dorado, M.; Carmona-Murillo, J.; Cortés-Polo, D.; Rodríguez-Pérez, F.J. CyberTOMP: A Novel Systematic Framework to Manage Asset-Focused Cybersecurity From Tactical and Operational Levels. *IEEE Access* **2022**, *10*, 122454–122485. [CrossRef]
2. von Solms, R.; van Niekerk, J. From information security to cyber security. *Comput. Secur.* **2013**, *38*, 97–102. [CrossRef]
3. Reid, R.; van Niekerk, J. From information security to cyber security cultures. In Proceedings of the Information Security for South Africa, Johannesburg, South Africa, 13–14 August 2014.
4. Furnell, S. The cybersecurity workforce and skills. *Comput. Secur.* **2012**, *100*, 102080. [CrossRef]
5. De Zan, T. Mitigating the Cyber Security Skills Shortage: The Influence of National Skills Competitions on Cyber Security Interest. Ph.D. Thesis, Department of Education and Centre for Doctoral Training in Cyber Security, Linacre College, University of Oxford, Oxford, UK, 2021.
6. Reeder, F.; Alan, P. *What Works in Finding Elite Cybersecurity Talent: Promising Practices for Chief Information Officers*; CIO.org: Newport, UK, 2021.
7. DeCrosta, J. Bridging the Gap: An Exploration of the Quantitative and Qualitative Factors Influencing the Cybersecurity Workforce Shortage. Ph.D. Thesis, Utica College, Utica, NY, USA, 2021.
8. Shava, E.; Hofisi, C. Challenges and Opportunities for Public Administration in the Fourth Industrial Revolution. *Afr. J. Public Aff.* **2017**, *9*, 203–215.
9. Ngwenyama, O.; Henriksen, H.Z.; Hardt, D. Public management challenges in the digital risk society: A Critical Analysis of the Public Debate on Implementation of the Danish NemID. *Eur. J. Inf. Syst.* **2023**, *32*, 108–126. [CrossRef]
10. Nizich, M. Preparing the Cybersecurity Workforce of Tomorrow. In *The Cybersecurity Workforce of Tomorrow (The Future of Work)*; Emerald Group Publishing Limited: Bingley, UK, 2023; pp. 117–146.
11. Lee, G.R.; Lee, S.; Malatesta, D.; Fernández, S. Outsourcing and Organizational Performance: The Employee Perspective. *Am. Rev. Public Adm.* **2019**, *49*, 973–986. [CrossRef]
12. Onwubiko, C.; Ouazzane, K. Challenges towards Building an effective Cyber Security Operations Centre. *Int. J. Cyber Situational Aware.* **2019**, *4*, 11–39. [CrossRef]
13. Schatz, D.; Bashroush, R.; Wall, J. Towards a More Representative Defifinition of Cyber Security. *J. Digit. Forensics Secur. Law* **2017**, *12*, 53–74.
14. Ghelani, D. Cyber Security, Cyber Threats, Implications and Future. *Am. J. Sci. Eng. Technol.* **2022**, *3*, 12–19.
15. Sulistyowati, D.; Handayani, F.; Suryanto, Y. Comparative Analysis and Design of Cybersecurity Maturity Assessment Methodology Using NIST CSF, COBIT, ISO/IEC 27002 and PCI DSS. *Int. J. Inform. Vis.* **2020**, *4*, 225–230. [CrossRef]
16. Srinivas, J.; Das, A.K.; Kumar, N. Government regulations in cyber security: Framework, standards and recommendations. *Future Gener. Comput. Syst.* **2019**, *92*, 178–188. [CrossRef]
17. Soomro, Z.A.; Shah, M.H.; Ahmed, J. Information security management needs more holistic approach: A literature review. *Int. J. Inf. Manag.* **2016**, *36*, 215–225. [CrossRef]
18. Atoum, I.; Otoom, A.; Ali, A.A. A holistic cyber security implementation framework. *Inf. Manag. Comput. Secur.* **2014**, *22*, 251–264. [CrossRef]
19. van Kranenburg, R.; Le Gars, G. The Cybersecurity Aspects of New Entities Need a Cybernetic, Holistic Perspective. *Int. J. Cyber Forensic Adv. Threat Investig.* **2021**, *1*, 2. [CrossRef]
20. Del-Real, C.; Díaz-Fernández, A.M. Understanding the plural landscape of cybersecurity governance in Spain: A matter of capital exchange. *Int. Cybersecur. Law Rev.* **2022**, *3*, 313–343. [CrossRef]
21. Oruj, Z. Cyber security: Contemporary cyber threats and national strategies. *Distance Educ. Ukr. Innov. Norm.-Leg. Pedagog. Asp.* **2023**, *1*, 100–116.
22. Sharikov, P. Contemporary Cybersecurity Challenges. In *The Implications of Emerging Technologies in the Euro-Atlantic Space*; Palgrave Macmillan: Cham, Switzerland; Basel, Switzerland, 2023; pp. 143–157.
23. Cavelty, M.D.; Smeets, M. Regulatory cybersecurity governance in the making: The formation of ENISA and its struggle for epistemic authority. *J. Eur. Public Policy* **2023**, *30*, 1330–1352. [CrossRef]
24. Kosseff, J. Upgrading Cybersecurity Law. *Houst. Law Rev. Forthcom.* **2023**, 1–33. [CrossRef]

25. Creemers, R. The Chinese Conception of Cybersecurity: A Conceptual, Institutional and Regulatory Genealogy. *J. Contemp. China* **2023**, 1–16. [CrossRef]
26. Mijwil, M.M.; Filali, Y.; Aljanabi, M.; Bounabi, M.; Al-Shahwani, H. The Purpose of Cybersecurity Governance in the Digital Transformation of Public Services and Protecting the Digital Environment. *Mesopotamian J. Cybersecur.* **2023**, *2023*, 1–6.
27. Abazi, B. Establishing the National Cybersecurity (Resilience) Ecosystem. *IFAC-PapersOnLine* **2022**, *55*, 42–47. [CrossRef]
28. ENISA. *ENISA Threat Landscape 2022*; European Union Agency for Cybersecurity: Heaclión, Greece, 2022.
29. Hinkley, S. *Technology in the Public Sector and the Future of Government Work*; UC Berkeley Labor Center: Berkeley, CA, USA, 2022.
30. Norris, D.F.; Mateczun, L.K.; Forno, R.F. What the Literature Says About Local Government Cybersecurity. In *Cybersecurity and Local Government*; Wiley Data and Cybersecurity: Hoboken, NJ, USA, 2022; pp. 47–66.
31. CCN-CERT. *Ciberamenazas y Tendencias: Eidición 2022*; Centro Criptológico Nacional: Madrid, Spain, 2022.
32. Farrand, B.; Carrapico, H. Digital sovereignty and taking back control: From regulatory capitalism to regulatory mercantilism in EU cybersecurity. *Eur. Sefcurity* **2022**, *31*, 435–453. [CrossRef]
33. Al Mehairi, A.; Zgheib, R.; Abdellatif, T.M.; Conchon, E. Cyber Security Strategies While Safeguarding Information Systems in Public/Private Sectors. In *Electronic Governance with Emerging Technologies, Proceedings of the EGETC 2022, Tampico, Mexico, 12–14 September 2022*; Communications in Computer and Information Science; Springer: Cham, Switzerland, 2022; pp. 49–63.
34. Blondin, D.; Boin, A. Cooperation in the Face of Transboundary Crisis: A Framework for Analysis. *Perspect. Public Manag. Gov.* **2020**, *3*, 197–209. [CrossRef]
35. Domínguez-Dorado, M.; Cortés-Polo, D.; Carmona-Murillo, J.; Rodríguez-Pérez, F.J.; Galeano-Brajones, J. Fast, Lightweight, and Efficient Cybersecurity Optimization for Tactical–Operational Management. *Appl. Sci.* **2023**, *13*, 6327. [CrossRef]
36. Quinn, S.; Ivy, N.; Barrett, M.; Feldman, L.; Topper, D.; Witte, G.; Gardner, R.K. *Using Business Impact Analysis to Inform Risk Prioritization and Response*; NIST Interagency Report NIST IR 8286D; NIST: Gaithersburg, MD, USA, 2022.
37. Ozkan, B.Y.; van Lingen, S.; Spruit, M. The Cybersecurity Focus Area Maturity (CYSFAM) Model. *J. Cybersecur. Priv.* **2021**, *1*, 119–139. [CrossRef]
38. Rajan, R.; Rana, N.P.; Parameswar, N.; Dhir, S.; Sushil; Dwivedi, Y.K.K. Developing a modified total interpretive structural model (M-TISM) for organizational strategic cybersecurity management. *Technol. Forecast. Soc. Change* **2021**, *170*, 120872. [CrossRef]
39. Axon, L.; Erola, A.; van Rensburg, A.J.; Nurse, J.R.C.; Goldsmith, M.; Creese, S. Practitioners' Views on Cybersecurity Control Adoption and Effectiveness. In Proceedings of the ARES 2021: The 16th International Conference on Availability, Reliability and Security, Vienna, Austria, 17–20 August 2021; ACM ICPS. ACM: New York, NY, USA, 2021; pp. 1–10.
40. Antunes, M.; Maximiano, M.; Gomes, R.; Pinto, D. Information Security and Cybersecurity Management: A Case Study with SMEs in Portugal. *J. Cybersecur. Priv.* **2021**, *1*, 219–238. [CrossRef]
41. Preis, B.; Susskind, L. Municipal Cybersecurity: More Work Needs to be Done. *Urban Aff. Rev.* **2020**, *58*, 614–629. [CrossRef]
42. Clark, M.; Espinosa, J.; Delone, W. Defending Organizational Assets: A Preliminary Framework for Cybersecurity Success and Knowledge Alignment. In Proceedings of the 53rd Hawaii International Conference on System Sciences, Maui, HI, USA, 7–10 January 2020; pp. 4283–4292.
43. Phillips, R.; Tanner, B. Breaking down silos between business continuity and cyber security. *J. Bus. Contin. Emerg. Plan.* **2019**, *12*, 224–232.
44. Kure, H.I.; Islam, S. Assets focus risk management framework for critical infrastructure cybersecurity risk management. *IET Cyber-Phys. Syst. Theory Appl.* **2019**, *4*, 332–340. [CrossRef]
45. Rothrock, R.A.; Kaplan, J.; Van Der Oord, F. The Board's Role in Managing Cybersecurity Risks. *MIT Sloan Manag. Rev.* **2018**, *59*, 12–15.
46. Limba, T.; Plėta, T.; Agafonov, K.; Damkus, M. Cyber security management model for critical infrastructure. *Entrep. Sustain. Issues* **2017**, *4*, 559–573. [CrossRef]
47. Breier, J.; Hudec, L. On Selecting Critical Security Controls. In Proceedings of the 2013 International Conference on Availability, Reliability and Security, Regensburg, Germany, 2–6 September 2013; IEEE: New York, NY, USA, 2013; pp. 1–7.
48. Almoughem, K.A.B.M. The Future of Cybersecurity Workforce Development. *Acad. J. Res. Sci. Publ.* **2023**, *4*, 37–48. [CrossRef]
49. Shah, A.; Ganesan, R.; Jajodia, S.; Cam, H.; Hutchinson, S. A Novel Team Formation Framework based on Performance in a Cybersecurity Operations Center. *IEEE Trans. Serv. Comput. Early Access* **2023**, *16*, 2359–2371. [CrossRef]
50. Adetoye, B.; Fong, R.C.-W. Building a Resilient Cybersecurity Workforce: A Multidisciplinary Solution to the Problem of High Turnover of Cybersecurity Analysts. In *Cybersecurity in the Age of Smart Societies*; Springer: Cham, Switzerland, 2023; pp. 61–87.
51. Balon, T.; Baggili, I. Cybercompetitions: A survey of competitions, tools, and systems to support cybersecurity education. *Educ. Inf. Technol.* **2023**, *28*, 11759–11791. [CrossRef]
52. Nadua, F.-D.-L.; Escandor, L.; Bangayan, M.; Vigonte, F.; Abante, M.V. Identifying Incentives to Address Attrition in the Government Cybersecurity Workforce. 2023; pp. 1–21. Available online: https://ssrn.com/abstract=4382110 (accessed on 16 October 2023).
53. Fisk, N.; Kelly, N.M.; Liebrock, L. Cybersecurity Communities of Practice: Strategies for Creating Gateways to Participation. *Comput. Secur.* **2023**, *132*, 103188. [CrossRef]
54. Ashley, T.D.; Kwon, R.; Gourisetti, S.N.G.; Katsis, C.; Bonebrake, C.A.; Boyd, P.A. Gamification of Cybersecurity for Workforce Development in Critical Infrastructure. *IEEE Access* **2022**, *10*, 112487–112501. [CrossRef]

55. Justice, C.; Sample, C.; Loo, S.M.; Ball, A.; Hampton, C. Future Needs of the Cybersecurity Workforce. In Proceedings of the 17th International Conference on Cyber Warfare and Security, Albany, NY, USA, 17–18 March 2022; Academic Conferences International Limited: South Oxfordshire, UK, 2022; Volume 17, pp. 81–91.

56. Ahmad, N.; Laplante, P.A.; DeFranco, J.F.; Kassab, M. A Cybersecurity Educated Community. *IEEE Trans. Emerg. Top. Comput.* **2022**, *10*, 1456–1463. [CrossRef]

57. Chowdhury, N.; Gkioulos, V. Cyber security training for critical infrastructure protection: A literature review. *Comput. Sci. Rev.* **2021**, *40*, 100361. [CrossRef]

58. Noche, E.B. A Literature Review of Empirical Studies on Cyber Security Workforce Development. *Asian J. Multidiscip. Stud.* **2021**, *4*, 65–73.

59. Hulatt, D.; Stavrou, E. The Development of a Multidisciplinary CybersecurityWorkforce: An Investigation. In *Human Aspects of Information Security and Assurance, Proceedings of the 15th IFIP WG 11.12 International Symposium, HAISA 2021*; Virtual, 7–9 July 2021, Springer: Cham, Switzerland, 2021; pp. 138–147.

60. Kävrestad, J.; Nohlberg, M. Evaluation Strategies for Cybersecurity Training Methods: A Literature Review. In *Human Aspects of Information Security and Assurance, Proceedings of the 15th IFIP WG 11.12 International Symposium, HAISA 2021*; Virtual, 7–9 July 2021, Springer: Cham, Switzerland, 2021; pp. 102–112.

61. Maurer, C.; Summer, M.; Mazzola, D.; Pearlson, K.; Jacks, T. The Cybersecurity Skills Survey: Response to the 2020 SIM IT Trends Study. In Proceedings of the SIGMIS-CPR'21: 2021 on Computers and People Research Conference, Virtual, 30 June 2021; ACM: Hamburg, Germany, 2021; pp. 35–37.

62. Ahmad, K.C.A.; Desouza, S.B.; Manyard, H.N.; Baskerville, R.L. How integration of cyber security management and incident response enables organizational learning. *J. Assoc. Inf. Sci. Technol.* **2020**, *71*, 939–953. [CrossRef]

63. McNulty, M.; Kettani, H. On Cybersecurity Education for Non-technical Learners. In Proceedings of the 2020 3rd International Conference on Information and Computer Technologies (ICICT), San Jose, CA, USA, 9–12 March 2020; IEEE: New York, NY, USA, 2020; pp. 413–416.

64. Dahlström, C.; Nistotskaya, M.; Tyrberg, M. Outsourcing, bureaucratic personnel quality and citizen satisfaction with public services. *Public Adm.* **2018**, *96*, 218–233. [CrossRef]

65. Affan, Y.; Lin, L.; Rubia, F.; Wang, J. Improving software security awareness using a serious game. *IET Softw. Spec. Issue Gamification Persuas. Games Softw.* **2019**, *13*, 159–169.

66. Rubia, F.; Affan, Y.; Lin, L.; Wang, J. Strategies for counteracting social engineering attacks. *Comput. Fraud. Secur.* **2022**, *2022*, 15–19. [CrossRef]

67. Aragão, J.P.S.; Fontana, M.E. Guidelines for public sector managers on assessing the impact of outsourcing on business continuity strategies: A Brazilian case. *J. Glob. Oper. Strateg. Sourc.* **2023**, *16*, 118–141. [CrossRef]

68. Gowun, P.; Brunjes, B.M. Engaging Citizens in Government Contracting: A Theoretical Approach for the Role of Social Service Nonprofits. *Perspect. Public Manag. Gov.* **2022**, *5*, 317–329.

69. Heikkilä, J.; Cordon, C. Outsourcing: A core or non-core strategic management decision? *Brief. Entrep. Financ.* **2022**, *11*, 183–193. [CrossRef]

70. Pavelko, O.; Lazaryshyna, I.; Dukhnovska, L.; Sharova, S.; Oliinyk, T.; Donenko, I. Construction Development and Its Impact on the Construction Enterprises Financial Results. *Stud. Appl. Econ.* **2021**, *39*, 1–11. [CrossRef]

71. Aragão, J.P.S.; Fontana, M.E. Outsourcing Strategies in Public Services under Budgetary Constraints: Analysing Perceptions of Public Managers. *Public Organ. Rev.* **2021**, *22*, 61–77. [CrossRef]

72. Latif, M.N.A.; Aziz, N.A.A.; Hussin, N.S.N.; Aziz, Z.A. Cyber security in supply chain management: A systematic review. *LogForum* **2021**, *17*, 49–57. [CrossRef]

73. Repetto, M.; Carrega, A.; Rapuzzi, R. An architecture to manage security operations for digital service chains. *Future Gener. Comput. Syst.* **2021**, *115*, 251–266. [CrossRef]

74. Marco-Simó, J.M.; Pastor-Collado, J.A. IT Outsourcing in the Public Sector: A Descriptive Framework from a Literature Review. *J. Glob. Inf. Technol. Manag.* **2020**, *23*, 25–52. [CrossRef]

75. van der Wal, Z. Being a Public Manager in Times of Crisis: The Art of Managing Stakeholders, Political Masters, and Collaborative Networks. *Public Adm. Rev.* **2020**, *80*, 759–764. [CrossRef] [PubMed]

76. Rizwan, H.; Bhatti, S.N. Impacts of Outsourcing on Quality: A Case Study of an Electronics Sector. *Bahria Univ. J. Manag. Technol.* **2020**, *2*, 16–23.

77. Bogoviz, A.V.; Berezhnoi, A.V.; Mezhov, I.S.S.; Titova, O.V.; Kryukova, O.G. Decision Making in Modern Business Systems by the Principles of Outsourcing. In *Specifics of Decision Making in Modern Business Systems*; Emerald Publishing Limited: Leeds, UK, 2019; pp. 141–148.

78. Bloomfield, K.; Williams, T.; Bovis, C.; Merali, Y. Systemic risk in major public contracts. *Int. J. Forecast.* **2019**, *35*, 667–676. [CrossRef]

79. Proscovia, S. The impact of new public management through outsourcing on the management of government information: The case of Sweden. *Rec. Manag. J.* **2019**, *29*, 134–151.

80. Andersson, F.; Jordahl, H.; Josephson, J. Outsourcing Public Services: Contractibility, Cost, and Quality. *CESifo Econ. Stud.* **2019**, *65*, 349–372. [CrossRef]

81. Soliño, A.S. Sustainability of Public Services: Is Outsourcing the Answer? *Sustainability* **2019**, *11*, 7231. [CrossRef]

82. Lobao, L.; Gray, M.; Cox, K.; Kitson, M. The shrinking state? Understanding the assault on the public sector. *Camb. J. Reg. Econ. Soc.* **2018**, *11*, 389–408. [CrossRef]
83. Aswini, K. Advantages and Disadvantages of Outsourcing. *Shanlax Int. J. Commer.* **2018**, *6*, 7–9.
84. Pupion, P.-C. Research on Public Strategic Management requiring a new theoretical framework. *Gest. Manag. Public* **2018**, *6*, 6–13.
85. Kekez, A.; Howlett, M.; Ramesh, M. Varieties of collaboration in public service delivery. *Policy Des. Pract.* **2018**, *1*, 243–252. [CrossRef]
86. Johansson, T.; Siverbo, S. The relationship between supplier control and competition in public sector outsourcing. *Financ. Account. Manag. Gov. Public Serv. Charities* **2018**, *34*, 268–287. [CrossRef]
87. Burnes, B.; Anastasiadis, A. Outsourcing: A public-private sector comparison. *Supply Chain Manag. Int. J.* **2016**, *8*, 355–366. [CrossRef]
88. Tayauova, G. Advantages and disadvantages of outsourcing: Analysis of outsourcing practices of Kazakhstan banks. *Procedia-Soc. Behav. Sci.* **2012**, *41*, 188–195. [CrossRef]
89. Schmid, A.U.; Knudsen, S.; Niehoff, T.; Schwietz, K. Planning Distributed Security Operations Centers in Multi-Cloud Landscapes A Systematic Approach, Generalized from A Case Study. *Res. Sq.* **2023**, 1–18. [CrossRef]
90. Saraiva, M.; Mateus-Coelho, N. CyberSoc Framework a Systematic Review of the State-of-Art. *Procedia Comput. Sci.* **2022**, *204*, 961–972. [CrossRef]
91. Shutock, M.; Dietrich, G. Security Operations Centers: A Holistic View on Problems and Solutions. In Proceedings of the 55th Hawaii International Conference on System Sciences, Virtual, 4–7 January 2022.
92. Georgiadou, A.; Mouzakitis, S.; Bounas, K.; Askounis, D. A Cyber-Security Culture Framework for Assessing Organization Readiness. *J. Comput. Inf. Syst.* **2022**, *62*, 452–462. [CrossRef]
93. Dun, Y.T.; Razak, M.F.A.; Zolkiplib, M.F.; Bee, T.F.; Firdaus, A. Grasp on next generation security operation centre (NGSOC): Comparative study. *Int. J. Nonlinear Anal. Appl.* **2022**, *12*, 869–895.
94. Nugraha, I. A Review on the Role of Modern SOC in Cybersecurity Operations. *Int. J. Curr. Sci. Res. Rev.* **2021**, *4*, 408–414. [CrossRef]
95. Kokulu, F.B.; Soneji, A.; Bao, T.; Shoshitaishvili, Y.; Zhao, Z.; Doupé, A.; Ahn, G. Matched and Mismatched SOCs: A Qualitative Study on Security Operations Center Issues. In Proceedings of the CCS '19: 2019 ACM SIGSAC Conference on Computer and Communications Security, London, UK, 11–15 November 2019; ACM: New York, NY, USA, 2019; pp. 1955–1970.
96. Benzaghta, M.A.; Elwalda, A.; Mousa, M.M.; Erkan, I.; Rahman, M. SWOT analysis applications: An integrative literature review. *J. Glob. Bus. Insights* **2021**, *6*, 55–73. [CrossRef]
97. Pasaribu, R.D.; Shalsabila, D.; Djatmiko, T. Revamping business strategy using Business Model Canvas (BMC), SWOT analysis, and TOWS matrix. *Herit. Sustain. Dev.* **2023**, *5*, 1–18. [CrossRef]
98. Hattangadi, V. SWOT & TOWS are Effective Tools for Strategic Formulation. *Eur. Econ. Lett.* **2023**, *13*, 977–981.
99. Wilson, K.S.; Kiy, M.A. Some Fundamental Cybersecurity Concepts. *IEEE Access* **2014**, *2*, 116–124. [CrossRef]
100. CIS. *CIS Critical Controls (R)*; Center for Internet Security: New York, NY, USA, 2021.
101. NIST. *Framework for Improving Critical Infrastructure Cybersecurity v1.1*; National Institute of Standards and Technology: Gaithersburg, MD, USA, 2018.
102. NIST. *Security and Privacy Controls for Information Systems and Organizations*; SP 800-53 Rev. 5; NIST: Gaithersburg, MD, USA, 2020.
103. Center for Internet Security. *CIS Community Defense Model v2.0*; Center for Internet Security: New York, NY, USA, 2021.
104. Strom, B.E.; Applebaum, A.; Miller, D.P.; Nickels, K.C.; Pennington, A.G.; Thomas, C.B. *MITRE ATT and CK(C): Design and Philosophy*; Defense Technical Information Center: Fort Belvoir, VA, USA, 2018.
105. Kwon, R.; Ashley, T.; Castleberry, J.; Mckenzie, P.; Gourisetti, S.N.G. Cyber Threat Dictionary Using MITRE ATT&CK Matrix and NIST Cybersecurity Framework Mapping. In Proceedings of the 2020 Resilience Week (RWS), Salt Lake City, UT, USA, 19–23 October 2020; IEEE: New York, NY, USA, 2020; pp. 106–112.
106. Deng, S.; Guan, X.; Xu, J. The coopetition effect of learning-by-doing in outsourcing. *Int. J. Prod. Res.* **2021**, *59*, 516–541. [CrossRef]
107. Hamburg, I. Interdisciplinary Training and Mentoring for Cyber Security in Companies. In *Handbook of Research on Cyber Crime and Information Privacy*; IGI Global: Hershey, PA, USA, 2021; pp. 356–371.
108. Burrel, D.N. Assessing the value of executive leadership coaches for cybersecurity project managers. *Int. J. Hum. Cap. Inf. Technol. Prof.* **2019**, *10*, 20–32. [CrossRef]
109. John, S.N.; Noma-Osaghae, E.; Oajide, F.; Okokpujie, K. *Cybersecurity Education: The Skills Gap, Hurdle! In Innovations in Cybersecurity Education*; Springer: Cham, Switzerland, 2020; pp. 361–376.
110. Corradini, I. Training Methods. In *Building a Cybersecurity Culture in Organizations*; Studies in Systems, Decision and Control; Springer: Cham, Switzerland, 2020; Volume 284, pp. 115–133.
111. Monzelo, P.; Nunes, S. The Role of the Chief Information Security Officer (CISO) in Organizations. In *CAPSI 2019 Proceedings*; CAPSI: Toronto, ON, Canada, 2019; pp. 1–14.
112. Badhwar, R. *See Something, Do Something! In The CISO's Transformation*; Springer: Cham, Switzerland, 2021; pp. 45–53.

information

Article

Assessment of Consumer Perception of Online Content Label Efficacy by Income Level, Party Affiliation and Online Use Levels

Jeremy Straub [1,*], Matthew Spradling [2] and Bob Fedor [1]

[1] Department of Computer Science, North Dakota State University, Fargo, ND 58105, USA; robert.fedor@ndsu.edu

[2] Department of Mathematics and Applied Sciences, University of Michigan Flint, Flint, MI 48502, USA; mjspra@umich.edu

* Correspondence: jeremy.straub@ndsu.edu; Tel.: +1-701-231-8196

Abstract: Deceptive online content represents a potentially severe threat to society. This content has shown to have the capability to manipulate individuals' beliefs, voting and activities. It is a demonstrably effective way for foreign adversaries to create domestic strife in open societies. It is also, by virtue of the magnitude of content, very difficult to combat. Solutions ranging from censorship to inaction have been proposed. One solution that has been suggested is labeling content to indicate its accuracy or characteristics. This would provide an indication or even warning regarding content that may be deceptive in nature, helping content consumers make informed decisions. If successful, this approach would avoid limitations on content creators' freedom of speech while also mitigating the problems caused by deceptive content. To determine whether this approach could be effective, this paper presents the results of a national survey aimed at understanding how content labeling impacts online content consumption decision making. To ascertain the impact of potential labeling techniques on different portions of the population, it analyzes labels' efficacy in terms of income level, political party affiliation and online usage time. This, thus, facilitates determining whether the labeling may be effective and also aids in understating whether its effectiveness may vary by demographic group.

Keywords: online content labeling; fake news; trust; income level; party affiliation; online time

Citation: Straub, J.; Spradling, M.; Fedor, B. Assessment of Consumer Perception of Online Content Label Efficacy by Income Level, Party Affiliation and Online Use Levels. *Information* **2022**, *13*, 252. https://doi.org/10.3390/info13050252

Academic Editors: Jose de Vasconcelos, Hugo Barbosa and Carla Cordeiro

Received: 15 March 2022
Accepted: 9 May 2022
Published: 13 May 2022

Publisher's Note: MDPI stays neutral with regard to jurisdictional claims in published maps and institutional affiliations.

1. Introduction

Deceptive online content in the form of misinformation, mal-information, and disinformation, which is commonly referred to as "fake news", is a growing problem [1]. Each form of fake news shares a commonality of including inaccurate, incomplete, or misleading information posing as accurate news. Misinformation includes falsehoods that were not necessarily created with the intention to misinform. Disinformation, by contrast, is false information created to intentionally deceive. Mal-information, similarly, is created with the intention of deception, but it uses selective facts while omitting important details in order to form the deception. Fake news is sometimes targeted at specific demographic groups to enhance and target its effect. Tong et al. [2] contend that some current uses actually represent a "weaponization of fake news".

Fake news has been blamed for election interference in multiple countries worldwide [1] and was identified as a driving force in the United Kingdom's departure from the European Union [3]. Allegations of its use as part of foreign influence campaigns [4] abound. The problem is so pronounced that Lee [5] labeled it a "sinister force" that threatens democracy itself.

Due to the magnitude and impact of the problem, a variety of potential solutions have been proposed. These have included restricting internet access [6], content filtering [7], and detecting and removing content [8]. Problematically, little consensus on which standards should be used for these exists. It is also likely that these techniques would run afoul of many democracies' speech freedom protections. Another possible solution, content labeling [9], has been proposed. Unlike the earlier solutions, labeling does not prevent (or remove) speech. Instead, it provides additional information as context and, in some cases, warns information consumers about particularly problematic content.

While content labeling does not have the speech restriction issues of other techniques, it also does not prevent access to the content. Thus, its effectiveness as a solution to the issues of fake news' spread and impact depend on the impact of labeling on consumers' consumption decisions and post-consumption activities.

This paper aimed to determine what the impact of different label types will be on these behaviors. It presents and analyzes the results of a national survey in the United States on consumers' preferences and their beliefs regarding the effectiveness of different labeling approaches. From these results, this paper drew conclusions regarding the effectiveness of content labeling. The impact and effectiveness were analyzed based on respondents' income levels, political party affiliations and online usage time to ascertain whether labels' impact would be fairly consistent across the population or whether its effectiveness would differ by group. This data will inform the development and prospective deployment of a content labeling system. In addition to suggesting whether it will be effective overall, it also facilitates determining whether targeted training and other roll-out activities would be needed to encourage system adoption and use and to improve its effectiveness among various demographic groups.

This paper continues with a review of prior work in Section 2. Section 3 presents an overview of the survey administration process and demographic details about the respondents. Sections 4–6 present and analyze data on several different types of labeling. Then, Section 7 assesses the implications of the data presented in the previous three sections. Finally, Section 8 presents the key conclusions of the paper and discusses needed areas of future work.

2. Background

This section presents prior work in several areas that provide a foundation upon which the current work draws. First, prior work related to fake news and deceptive online content is presented. Next, content labeling in other areas is discussed. Finally, prior work on online content labeling is reviewed.

2.1. Fake News and Deceptive Content Online

Early "fake news" referred to satirical content that viewers and readers knew was false and comedic [10]. This content, while having similarities to news in formatting, was not designed to fool people (though it occasionally did [11]). In the mid-2010s, though, the use of the term changed and deliberately deceptive—often political—content, designed to manipulate readers grew in prevalence on the Internet [12]. By 2016, deceptive content fake news had become a notable part of the online news content. In the United States, approximately 6% of all news content was fake during the presidential election [13], and it is estimated that each American had, on average, consumed one to three fake articles [14]. In the United Kingdom, fake content was helping to drive the Brexit movement [3,4]. On Twitter, Bovet and Makse [15] calculated that 25% of tweets during this period were "fake or extremely biased news". Cunha et al. [1] showed that this extended well beyond the United States and the United Kingdom to at least 20 other countries.

Beyond the effects on elections, the societal impacts are pronounced. The impact of fake news content on youth is one area of concern. College students surveyed indicated that they expected news on social media to be inaccurate [16]; however, 18–29 year olds generally use social media more frequently than other age groups and trust those sources more than average [16,17].

Fake news causes actual harm. It has been identified as confusing the public [18] and was even involved in starting an armed standoff [19]. It has also been blamed for circulating damaging health-related information [20]. In response to these issues, a variety of techniques have been developed for mitigating its efficacy and spread. This has led to the development of a number of attempted detection methods with various degrees of success [21]. Tandoc, Lim and Ling [22] even went so far as to develop a classification scheme for fake news content.

While both automated and manual labeling can be performed, a key challenge is how to present the results of this labeling to the prospective reader to maximize its notability and safety impact. Several types of labeling have been proposed [23] as a technique to mitigate deceptive content while not infringing upon content creators' speech rights.

2.2. Content Labeling for Other Applications

Product warning labels, such as those displayed on alcohol and tobacco products, are designed to promote public health. The goal of a warning label in this space is to limit consumption of the product, either by the entire target market or by a vulnerable subgroup. Tobacco product warning labels have a low cost of implementation, but they have been shown to be highly effective at communicating the dangers of tobacco and discouraging young people from taking up the habit [24]. While tobacco companies have shown willingness to implement warning labels of a sort, they have fought strongly against implementation of the most effective forms of warning labels. Current cigarette packaging regulations in the United States date back to 1984 [25] and carry only a text-based Surgeon General's warning [26], using one of four required statements [27].

Graphic health warning labels (containing images such as lungs afflicted with cancer) have been shown to have a great deal more impact than simple text warnings; however, their adoption has been slow. Initially, the FDA proposed "graphic" labels [28], such as those shown in Figure 1, which the tobacco industry contended [29] forced "cigarette makers to display government anti-smoking advocacy more prominently than their own branding". The requirement to use this packaging was not upheld by the courts [29,30], as it was found to violate the First Amendment [31].

Figure 1. The FDA's proposed cigarette labels from 2011 [32].

In 2019, the FDA proposed new labels which were "based on–and within the limits of–both science and the law" [31]. These labels, shown in Figure 2, were planned to launch in June of 2021; however, they have been delayed at least seven times and are currently planned to be required as of 9 April 2023 [33].

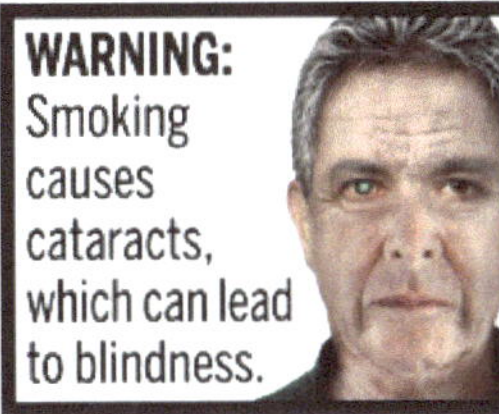

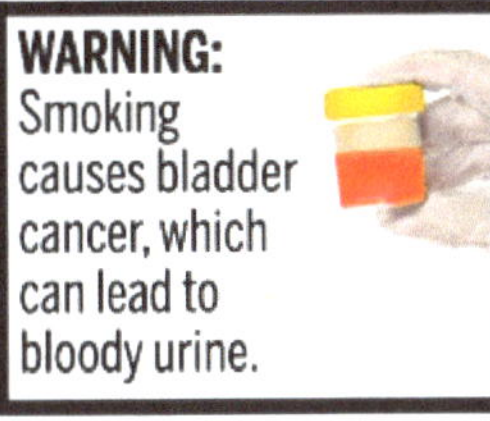

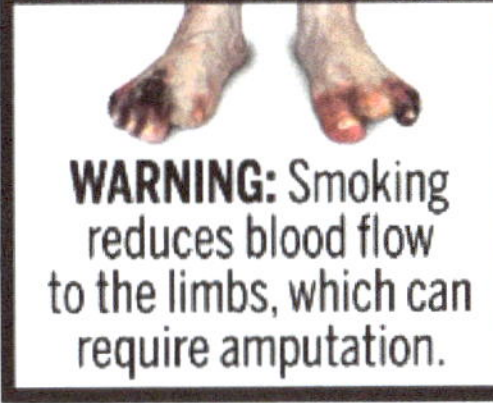

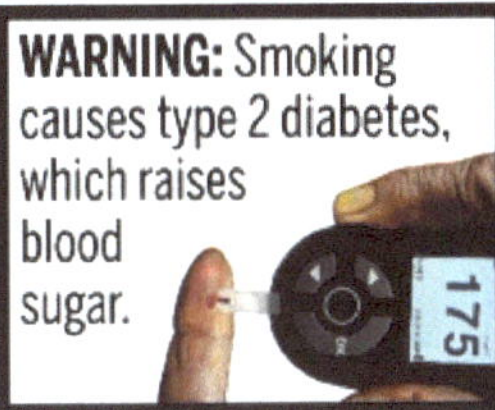

Figure 2. Cigarette labels proposed in 2019 [34].

Websites that present intentional news-style misinformation may be uninterested in self-regulation and, similar to cigarette manufacturers, may be resistant to industry and government labeling requirements that deter users from visiting their sites, reading the misinformation and producing ideological goals [35] or generating advertising revenue [36]. In the case of tobacco, efforts to implement graphic health warning labels have been successful in some nations through government regulation. In New Zealand, the Smoke-Free Environments Regulations of 1999 required that tobacco products include graphic health warnings. This legislation faced legal challenges by the tobacco industry, just as similar legislation has in the United States, but ultimately it was adopted and enjoyed strong public support [37].

Online content labeling may be more legally problematic than cigarette labeling, if required by a government. As previously noted, a federal court prevented the FDA from requiring its 2011 graphic health cigarette warnings due to the presence of free speech concerns [31]. Notably, the cigarette manufacturers were not trying to engage in pure speech but instead speech related to selling their product (which has been held, in some cases, to be less protected [38]). Even with this lower standard of projection than online content would likely enjoy, the labeling requirement was proscribed.

In the United States, thus, labeling may be most effectively implemented by industry self-regulation or collaborative industry–government cooperation. A variety of examples of effective content regulation, developed by or in conjunction with relevant industries, exist. The MPAA movie and V-Chip television ratings [39–41] and explicit lyric warning labels [42] for music are several such examples. In the case of anti-piracy warnings, the US Federal Bureau of Investigation created a voluntary program that allows content creators to warn consumers about the legal risks of piracy activities [43]. Arguably, in this case, the interests of the content producers were well aligned with the agency's, which is not the case in many other areas where labeling is used.

Deceptive online content is inherently an international challenge. The regulations that may impact the implementation of labeling vary considerably. The freedom of speech guaranteed by the United States Constitution serves as an argument against government required content labeling, which could be taken to infringe upon the speech rights of the publisher [44]. Other countries, though, have regulations with different focuses. The People's Republic of China's Computer Information Network and Internet Security, Protection and Management Regulations of 1997, for example, prohibits internet users from "making falsehoods or distorting the truth, spreading rumors, destroying the order of society". Under these regulations, content labeling may be unnecessary as misinformation should be removed entirely rather than simply to be labeled as such [45].

Other countries have similar laws. Ethiopian law, for example, prohibits certain types of "false accusations", Cote d'Ivoire prohibits "'false information' that could harm the reputation of institutions" and Malawi's laws proscribe the "publication of false statements that may 'cause fear and alarm to the public or do disturb the public peace'" [46]. Bangladesh, while having constitutional protections for free expression, created a law "to control the spread of online misinformation" that has, according to Haque et al. [47], been used to jail journalists and close publications. Indonesia has laws that can jail those convicted of "spreading false information or news that intentionally causes public disorder" for up to a decade [48]. The European Union, on the other hand, has taken actions to "facilitate digital platforms' self-regulation to tackle misinformation and disinformation", which have been met with, at least, partial success [48]. Other countries' laws vary. Yadav et al.'s work [49] demonstrates the diversity of regulation. They identified and analyzed over 100 national laws with conflicting purposes, varying scopes and which met with different levels of success.

2.3. Online Misinformation Detection and Content Labeling

Online content labeling can draw from labeling for television, movies and video games as well as from product labeling. However, it presents several challenges. First, a source for the label's content must be identified. Second, the design of the label itself must be acceptable to content consumers so that they are willing to use it.

Fake news labeling begins with its identification and classification. Identification drives label display, while classification is key to the information that is provided on the label. A variety of forms of identification are possible (see [50,51] for an extended discussion). Manually curated, automatically generated or hybrid manual/automated approaches can be utilized. Zhou and Zafarani [21] describe identification approaches based on style, network analysis and distributing users. Wang [52] demonstrated an automated approach using machine learning with manual annotations. A variety of other automated techniques exist including those that use graph-attention neural networks [53], natural language processing [54], neural stacking [55] and deep neural networks [56]. The social sciences have also contributed through the consideration of emotion cognizance [57] and the use of signal detection approaches [58].

Multiple industry-implemented examples also exist. Twitter's Birdwatch service utilizes manual curation of Twitter posts by users [59]. Wikipedia, similarly, maintains a manually curated list of news sources that is annotated with details regarding their reliability (https://en.wikipedia.org/wiki/Wikipedia:Reliable_sources/Perennial_sources).

Several taxonomies for deceptive online content have been proposed. Tandoc, Lim and Ling [22] developed a classification system that included the categories "satire", "parody", "fabrication", "manipulation", "propaganda" and "advertising". Bakir and McStay [60] had one more category in their system which had the groupings of:

- "False connection (where headlines, visuals or captions do not support the content)";
- "False context (genuine content shared with false contextual information)";

- "Manipulated content (genuine imagery/information manipulated to deceive)";
- "Misleading content (misleading use of information to frame an issue or individual)";
- "Imposter content (genuine sources are impersonated)";
- "Fabricated content (100 per cent false, designed to deceive and harm)";
- "Satire/parody (with potential to fool but no intention to cause harm)".

Perhaps the most important information to label, for consumer protection, is deliberate mal-information and disinformation. One approach to this is through influence analysis. Identifying influential nodes in social networks has been well studied. While the optimization problem is NP-hard, identification can be approximated such as by using Monte Carlo simulation [61,62]. Early work on the spread of misinformation in social media built upon this notion of influential nodes, modeling the problem in terms of what Budak, Agrawal and Abbadi [63] refer to as "competing cascades dissipating in a network". The multi-campaign independent cascade model (MCICM) considers the diffusion of two competing information campaigns, such as the case where one campaign represents the truth, and the second campaign represents misinformation. The core problem, eventual influence limitation (EIL), is to minimize the number of nodes that will adopt the message of the misinformation campaign given a limited budget for the counterinfluence campaign. While the EIL problem is NP-hard to optimize, the authors found initial success with a degree centrality heuristic [63].

More recently, real-time detection of misinformation, disinformation and mal-information spreading on Twitter has been accomplished with some success. Suchia et al. [64] proposed an early algorithm that identifies actively propagated "rumors", defined by the authors as information "many people believe to be true" but that diverges from the facts available on "verified news channels". As an example, if a trending headline observes the fact that the CEO of Corporation X is stepping down and an unverified claim that Corporation X will declare bankruptcy is trending along with it, the supposed bankruptcy story would be the "rumor". The notion is that a rumor is detected as piggybacking alongside one or more legitimate news stories, adding misinformation, mal-information or disinformation to the real narrative.

Trends in the spread of misinformation related to the COVID-19 pandemic [65] have been a particular focus of investigation. One study [66], conducted using data available through the Twitter Streaming API from January to March 2020, reviewed 2,792,513 tweets; 18,168,161 retweets; 456,878 quoted retweets on the subject in over 30 languages with 55.2% in English. Approximately 40.5% of the original tweets contained links to external sources, and these sources were investigated by the researchers. This research showed that only 0.6% of tweets were sharing one of five common myths about the spread, treatment and origins of COVID-19. However, the study also found that just as few, only 0.51%, linked to "reputable health sources", such as the Centers for Disease Control or the World Health Organization, preferring instead to link to popular news media (13%) or other less reliable sources.

The identification of misinformation, mal-information and disinformation is only a portion of the challenge, though. Once potentially harmful content is identified, the next question becomes what to do about it.

The United States' 2016 and 2020 presidential elections were instructive in this regard. Trends regarding the spread of misinformation surrounding the election on Twitter and other social media sites were analyzed [13,67]. Perhaps in response to this, numerous social media platforms, such as Facebook, Twitter, Instagram and YouTube, began labeling social media posts and videos in the run-up to the 2020 United States Presidential Election to combat the spread of misinformation surrounding the candidates, rules about in-person and mail-in voting and the election results themselves [68,69]. A public dataset of over one billion "tweets" (Twitter posts) was released, initially from 1 December 2020 through 22 January 2021 but later expanded to include earlier and later tweets [70]. A separate study [71] of tweets from 1 November 2020 through 8 January 2021 from the Twitter account of former United States President Donald Trump was conducted, covering the days before the 2020 election up until the date that Donald Trump's account was suspended by Twitter. During this period, Twitter flagged numerous tweets from the former President as containing misinformation, disinformation or mal-information related to the 2020 election. These flags appeared as a content label viewable to Twitter users. In some cases, called "hard intervention" by the authors, the original tweet was unable to be liked or replied to and was concealed behind the label, requiring the user to click a button to view the content after reviewing the warning regarding the misinformation. Other "soft interventions" provided a warning as to the content being misleading but did not prevent the tweet from being interacted with or covered behind the "view" button.

This study [71] found that while hard interventions were successful in preventing the spread of individual tweets, tweets having a soft intervention spread over social media further and longer than tweets that were not flagged at all. This does not necessarily indicate that a soft flag caused the tweet to spread more frequently. Given that the content of a "soft flagged" tweet may have been more interesting to users than a typical "unflagged" tweet, the "soft flagged" tweets may have naturally spread more than those that did not receive a flag, simply due to the quality of the content. Indeed, those tweets that received a soft flag may have spread even further without soft intervention than with it. To know whether a label design has a causal effect on a social media post's propagation, a more controlled study would need to compare the circulation of identical posts, some of which are "soft labeled" and some of which are not, in separate study groups. The study did show that this style of soft intervention used by Twitter was not sufficient to fully deter the spread of Donald Trump's tweets regarding the 2020 election results. Better methods with clear analysis of the causal effects on propagation are still needed to address the issue.

While identification and classification are a key step, the primary focus of this work was on labeling and built upon the labels proposed by Fuhr et al. [23]. This work proposes several media labeling categories including factuality vs. opinion statements; readability and reading level; the current level of virality of the topic's spread online; the usage of emotionally charged words and phrases; the level of public controversy surrounding the topic; the authority and credibility of the source; the degree of field-specific technical knowledge required to interpret the paper; how topical is the document. It also discusses numerous detection methods already available for generating information regarding each category, though future work may improve further upon these methods for specific application to informational labeling techniques.

An addition to this model was proposed by Lespagnol et al. [72] to include "information check-worthiness", while Vincentius et al. [73] also suggested an expansion to include source, article popularity and political bias categories.

Political bias has been a source of significant concern [74], particularly given the use of the term "fake news" as a way of attacking political adversaries' content. Fairbanks et al. [75] created a technique that perhaps offers a partial solution by classifying text as "liberal words", "conservative words" and "fake news words"; however, the fake news category was unreliable.

In prior work, the benefits and approaches to labeling have been discussed [9]. This included presenting a comparison of online media labeling technology to product labeling such as the "nutrition facts" labeling utilized in the United States, the ESRB rating system for video games and FDA warning labels for cigarette packaging. Based on this, it considered multiple paths for developing online media labeling techniques and their potential consequences.

Additionally, the perspectives of university community members [76] and all Americans [77] with regard to content labeling were assessed. University community members' label preferences were also analyzed [76].

The study of the perceptions of university members on online media labeling compared two demographically diverse university communities within the United States. It included questions relating to participants' views regarding multiple label categories (including those proposed by Fuhr et al. [23]). These categories included the article's title, publisher, publication date, author, sponsors, author's political affiliations, the sponsor's political affiliations, the publisher's political affiliations, writing quality, topic virality, topic controversy level, the reading level and the use of field-specific technical statements. It also gauged respondents' perspectives on and receptiveness to several labeling styles that were previously [9] developed.

This label preference analysis [76] utilized questions similar to the ones for which data were analyzed herein. Each respondent was asked how much they used a particular category of information, how much they believed other people used that category and how much they believe the category ought to be ideally used. This work showed that respondents tended to prefer informational labels over blocking labels, and that they would prefer to have information that they can then use to make decisions from rather than to be told simply whether a media source is trustworthy. This suggests that a "nutrition facts"-style informational label may be preferred by these communities.

3. Survey Administration and Respondent Characteristics

This section describes the methods used for this study. Specifically, it provides details regarding the survey that was used to collect the data that are analyzed in Sections 4–6. First, the survey instrument is discussed. Then, the process of survey administration is reviewed. Finally, the demographic characteristics of the respondents are presented.

3.1. Survey Instrument

A survey instrument was created that was based on the one utilized in [76]. The survey was edited for brevity with a target completion time of 15 min (or less). The new survey combined the questions from the three separate surveys utilized in [76]. Much of the editing involved the removal of questions. Some were removed due to the fact of being redundant among the three surveys (e.g., the demographic questions); others were removed for brevity. Limited editing for consistency and clarity of the newly combined survey was also performed. The final survey was reviewed by the authors and the Qualtrics survey staff before it was put to use. The survey administration plan started with a short-term pilot study, which served to validate the revised instrument before the full-scale survey. No issues were detected during this pilot phase; therefore, these responses were utilized as part of the dataset and applied to the applicable quotas based on Qualtrics' survey administration procedures.

3.2. Survey Administration

A quota-based stratified sampling technique was utilized to collect the data presented and analyzed herein. Data were collected by Qualtrics International Inc., through the use of the survey instrument that was described previously and based on the instrument used in [76].

Qualtrics recruited respondents based on providing a population proportionate representation in terms of the key demographics of income level, age, gender and political affiliation. The survey was administered in October of 2021 and approximately 550 responses were collected. Of these, 500 were part of the population's representative sample; however, all responses that included an answer to the applicable demographic and response question being analyzed were considered herein. Respondents were given an incentive based on complete survey submission. Thus, the vast majority of responses were complete.

3.3. Respondent Demographic Details

Respondent demographics are presented in this section. Due to the quota-based stratified technique used (which was described in the previous section), the respondents were well distributed across the key demographics. In terms of gender, approximately 49% of respondents were male and 51% were female. A small number of respondents (less than 1%) indicated a non-binary gender; however, due to the limited number of responses and small sample size, the perspectives of non-binary respondents could not be analyzed.

In terms of the age demographic, approximately 11% of respondents were in the 18–24, 25–29 and 30–34 age groups (each). Approximately 10% of respondents were aged 35–39, and 9% of respondents were aged 40–44. The 45–49 age range composed 7% of respondents, and 6% of respondents were aged 50–54. The 55–59 age group included 14% of respondents, and 12% of respondents were aged 60–64. Finally, 11% of respondents were in the 65 and older age group.

Respondents also had various levels of educational attainment. High school graduates (without college attendance) constituted 26% of respondents. An additional 23% had completed some college but not a degree. Associate degree graduates (without higher degrees) constituted 12% of respondents, and bachelor's degree graduates (without higher degrees) constituted 22% of respondents. Approximately 13% of respondents held graduate degrees with 10% holding master's degrees and 3% holding doctorates. Finally, 5% of respondents reported that they had not completed high school.

4. Informational Labels

This section considers the impact of informational labels on Americans' news content consumption behaviors. It presents and discusses the results from several survey questions relevant to informational labels. Respondents were presented with multiple potential labels and asked five questions about each regarding whether they would find it helpful or annoying, whether they and others would use the label and whether they found it useful for judging content's trustworthiness.

4.1. Informational Label with Article Summary

The first of these labels is presented in Figure 3. This informational label presents the title of the article, a brief text overview and an image from the article. It then presents ten pieces of information about the article that could be used by prospective readers to assess it and to determine whether they will choose to read it or not. Figures A1–A15, in Appendix A, present respondents' views about the utility of this type of a label. Error bars are included on these and all data figures to depict the standard error level for each type of response.

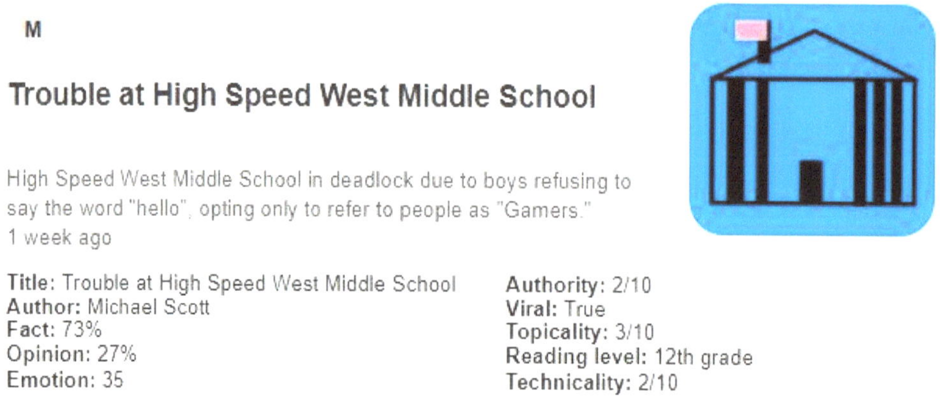

Figure 3. Informational label with article summary [76].

Respondents were first asked whether they would find this label helpful. Responses to this question, analyzed by income level, political party affiliation and internet usage levels, are presented in Figures A1–A3, respectively. Each figure shows the responses including (left) and excluding (right) "unsure" responses.

Figure A1 shows that most respondents, who had an opinion, found the labels to be helpful. The level of uncertainty fluctuated notably by income level, with the greatest numbers of individuals reporting being unsure at the lowest, highest and USD 75,000–99,999 income levels. When considering only "yes" and "no" responses, a trend of a slight decline in perceived helpfulness with increasing income level is shown in Figure A1 (right). Overall, though, there was not a tremendous difference between perceived helpfulness across different income levels. It is notable that there was an increase in perceived helpfulness between the USD 50,000 and USD 75,000 income levels. This trend was also present in the data for some other questions related to other labels.

Figure A2 considers respondents' perceptions of helpfulness by political party affiliation. Democrats were more certain about their responses than Republicans and independents/other party members and also found the label to be more helpful. Notably, the difference between Democrats and Republicans was smaller than the difference between Democrats and independents/other party members for both uncertainty and helpfulness. Similar with the age data, there was no tremendous variation in usefulness perception across the different political affiliations.

Next, perceived helpfulness was analyzed in terms of internet usage level. Notably, the level of uncertainty did not correlate with either greater or lower levels of internet usage (as the greatest uncertainty levels are reported in the highest and lowest usage level categories). There was a slight trend with respondents indicating greater helpfulness of the label with higher levels of internet usage.

Respondents were also asked about the annoyingness of the label. Figures 5, A4 and A6 present the data related to annoyingness.

Figure A4 presents the levels of annoyingness of the label reported by income levels. Notably, several levels (comparing Figures A1 and A4) had reduced uncertainty reported as compared to helpfulness. Additionally, while most respondents did not find the labels annoying (i.e., a no answer), this was only slightly above half. There was also a trend of declining level of annoyance from the USD 25,000–49,999 to the USD 100,000–124,999 income levels, though the USD 125,000 income level had the highest level of annoyance reported, overall, and the USD 24,999 and less group had more individuals reporting the label being annoying then the next group up.

Next, annoyingness was analyzed in terms of political party affiliation. While the levels of uncertainty reported mirrored those reported for the helpfulness question for this label, the three affiliation groups had minimal differences between the number of respondents reporting the label as being annoying.

The responses for annoyingness by internet usage level also mirrored those for helpfulness. This was the case both for the level of uncertainty reported and for the number of individuals indicating that the labels were annoying (and not annoying).

Respondents were next asked whether they would be willing to review the label presented in Figure 3. Data related to respondents' willingness are presented in Figures A7–A9. In Figure A7, there was a slight trend in reduced uncertainty with higher income levels and a similar trend in being less willing to review, which also correlated with higher income levels. In both cases, the USD 75,000 and USD 125,000 and higher income levels bucked the trend, reporting greater uncertainty than the next lower income level and more willingness to review.

Willingness to review was next assessed by political affiliation. Notably, Republicans showed a significantly lower level of willingness to review than Democrats and less than that of independent/other party members. This is notable, as more Republican respondents had indicated the label to be helpful and fewer had indicated it being annoying compared to independents/other party members. Thus, it appeared that Republicans' wiliness to use the labeling was notably influenced by factors other than the label itself. Despite the differences between helpfulness, annoyingness and willingness to use levels, the uncertainty levels by affiliation mirrored the helpfulness and annoyingness ones.

The data related to willingness to use by internet use level are also interestingly different from the helpfulness and annoyingness data. While a similar pattern of uncertainty response was still present (albeit less pronounced and fluctuating), increased willingness to use the label had a very strong correlation with increased internet usage levels.

Respondents were next asked about others' willingness to review. These data are shown in Figure A10. While higher levels of uncertainty were reported by those with higher income levels, no clear trend in the perception of others' willingness to use the label was present. Over half of all groups indicated believing that others would use the labels, and two groups had over 70% who reported being willing. It is notable that, in this data, there was a sharp decline at the USD 50,000 income level followed by an increase at the USD 75,000 income level.

Figure A11 presents data regarding the willingness of others to use the label based on political affiliation. The same patterns in individuals' own willingness to use the label were present in the willingness of others to use data, albeit they were somewhat less pronounced. Again, Democrats had the highest belief in the willingness of others to use and the lowest uncertainty. Independents/other party affiliates had the highest uncertainty and Republications reported the lowest willingness of others to use the label. This may be indicative of individuals associating with those that share their political views but being moderated by the fact that they also associate with those that do not share their political views.

The data for willingness of others to use the label correlated with internet usage level are presented in Figure A12. There was no consistent pattern in this area. This is likely indicative of individuals associating with others with all levels of internet usage (as opposed to principally associating with those with similar internet usage levels as themselves). This is notably different from the political party affiliation responses discussed immediately above (shown in Figure A11) as well as the trend of increasing willingness to review by internet usage (shown in Figure A9).

The final question regarding the first label indicates its level of usefulness in judging trustworthiness. These data are presented in Figures A13–A15. Figure A13 shows the relationship between perceived trustworthiness judgement usefulness and income level. It shows that uncertainty decreased with income level (with the highest income level not following this trend), and perceived usefulness decreased with income level (with the highest income group, again, not following this trend). There was, again, an increase in perceived usefulness between the USD 50,000 and USD 75,000 income levels.

Trustworthiness judgement usefulness was next assessed by political affiliation. As with the willingness to use data, Democrats reported the lowest uncertainty and highest perceived judgement usefulness. Independents/other party members reported the highest uncertainty and Republicans indicated the lowest level of perceived utility for assessing trustworthiness. Notably, over half of all three political parties indicated that they believed this label would be useful for assessing trustworthiness.

Perceived trustworthiness assessment utility was also analyzed by internet usage level. Mirroring the data presented in Figure A9, there was a general trend of decreased uncertainty and increased perception of usefulness associated with higher internet usage levels. Notably, the highest usage group was lower, in both categories, than the usage level below it; however, it still reported lower uncertainty and higher perceived utility than the lowest internet usage level.

4.2. Informational Label without Article Summary

A second label was assessed, which is shown in Figure 4. This label presents the article's characteristic data that the first label (Figure 3) provided. However, it lacks the article overview and article image. Figures A16–A30, in Appendix A, present the relevant respondent perception data regarding this label design.

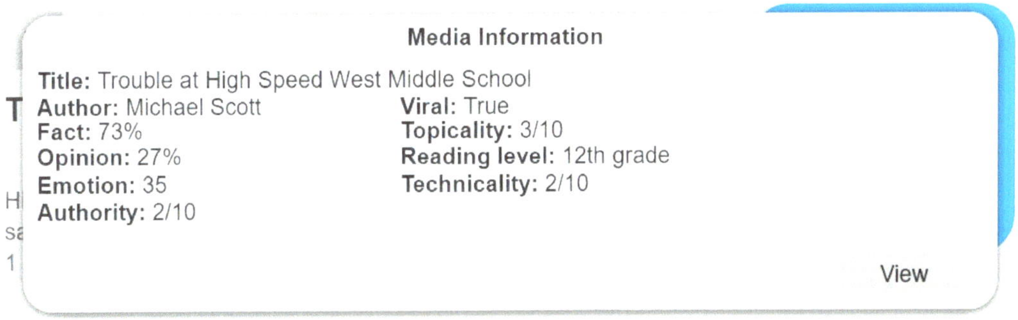

Media Information

Title: Trouble at High Speed West Middle School

Author: Michael Scott   **Viral:** True

Fact: 73%   **Topicality:** 3/10

Opinion: 27%   **Reading level:** 12th grade

Emotion: 35   **Technicality:** 2/10

Authority: 2/10

View

Figure 4. Informational label without article summary [76].

Figures A16–A19 present data regarding the perceived helpfulness of the second informational label. Figure A16 characterizes the impact of income level on respondents' perception of the helpfulness of the label. There was a partial trend of reduced uncertainty with increased income level at the lowest three income levels; however, no clear trend was present after this. The perception of helpfulness showed two downward trends. One existed at the three lowest income levels. It reset at USD 75,000 in annual income, and a second downward trend started at this point. There was a similar increase at the USD 75,000 annual income level for information label 1 (Figure A1), though that increase was less pronounced than what was seen for information label 2.

Figure A17 shows the impact of political affiliation on respondents' helpfulness perceptions. As is common with many responses, Democrats had the lowest level of uncertainty and believed the label to be helpful the most often. Republicans had the second lowest uncertainty level and the second highest helpfulness perception for label 2.

Figure A18 shows the impact of internet usage on respondents' perception of the second informational label's helpfulness. Two slight trends were present. A slight reduction in respondents' levels of uncertainty and an increase in respondents' helpfulness perceptions were present with increased online usage time.

Next, Figures A19–A21 present data regarding the perceived annoyingness of the second label. Figure A19 shows a correlation between increased income levels and decreased uncertainty regarding annoyingness. There was also a slight trend of increased annoyingness being reported by individuals with higher income levels.

Figure A20 shows the perception of annoyingness by political affiliation. The pattern shown in several previous questions of Democrats having the lowest uncertainty and greatest favorability toward the label was also present here. However, it was much less pronounced than with several of the other question responses. Democrats and Republicans were nearly tied in terms of finding the label annoying, while notably more independents/other party members found the label annoying than either Democrats or Republicans.

Figure A21 shows the annoyingness perception of label 2 by internet usage level. There was no notable pattern of association between respondents' level of internet usage and annoyingness perception, either in terms of the level of uncertainty reported or in terms of finding the label annoying or not.

Figures A22–A24 characterize respondents' indication of their own willingness to use informational label 2. Figure A22 characterizes respondents' willingness to use the label in terms of income level. A general trend of reduced uncertainty with increased income level was present. In addition, a trend of reduced willingness with higher income level was present up to the USD 75,000 point. As with the question regarding helpfulness, there was a similar increase in willingness to review from the USD 50,000 to the USD 75,000 income levels for both labels, though it was, again, more pronounced for the second label.

Figure A23 presents respondents' willingness to use the second informational label in terms of party affiliation. While Democrats indicated the highest willingness to use the label (followed by independents/other party members, with just slightly more willingness than Republicans), it is notable that Republicans had the lowest uncertainty for this label. The difference between the uncertainty levels was limited, albeit.

Figure A24 presents respondents' willingness to use the label in terms of online usage levels. There was a slight trend of increasing willingness to use the label with increased online usage. There was also a trend of reducing uncertainty with increased online usage, which was present at all but the highest usage level.

Figures A25–A27 present respondents' perceptions of others' willingness to review the label. Figure A25 presents this in terms of income level. There was no clear trend present in terms of a correlation between income level and willingness to review or uncertainty about this question. There was a notable increase between the USD 50,000 and USD 75,000 income levels, after a decline leading up to the USD 50,000 income level.

Figure A26 considers respondents' perceptions of others' willingness to use the second label by political party. As in many other cases, Democrats had the highest willingness to use the label (followed by independents/other party members) and the lowest uncertainty (followed by Republicans).

Figure A27 considers respondents' perceptions of others' willingness to review the label in terms of internet usage level. A trend of declining uncertainty with increasing usage level was shown (however, the highest usage level bucked this trend). There was no notable level of difference between willingness to use responses and usage level, though.

Finally, for this label, respondents were asked whether they would find the label useful for judging article trustworthiness. These data are presented in Figures A28–A30. Figure A28 presents respondents' perceptions of the utility of label 2 for judging trustworthiness by income level. While a trend existed regarding reduced uncertainty with increasing income level (which the highest income level, again, bucked), no clear trend was present in the actual willingness responses by income level. Again, there was an increase in perceived usefulness between the USD 50,000 and USD 75,000 income levels.

Figure A29 considers willingness to use the second label by political affiliation. Again, Democrats perceived the label the most positively, with the highest willingness to use percentage and lowest uncertainty. Republicans had the second lowest uncertainty and second highest willingness to use, followed (with limited difference) by independents/other party affiliates. This was, of course, somewhat different from the trend shown in previous political party-related data.

Figure A30 presents data regarding the judging usefulness of label 2 in terms of internet usage levels. This data show a trend of decreasing uncertainty and increasing perceived usefulness with increasing internet usage level; however, the level of difference between the usage level groups was limited.

4.3. Informational Label including Article Summary and Component Descriptions

Respondent perceptions were also solicited regarding a third type of informational label. This label presents all of the information from labels 1 and 2 (including the description and graphic from Figure 3). It also includes a brief description of what each piece of article metric data means to aid in the interpretation of the data. This third label is presented in Figure 5. Data related to this label are presented in Figures A31–A35, in Appendix A.

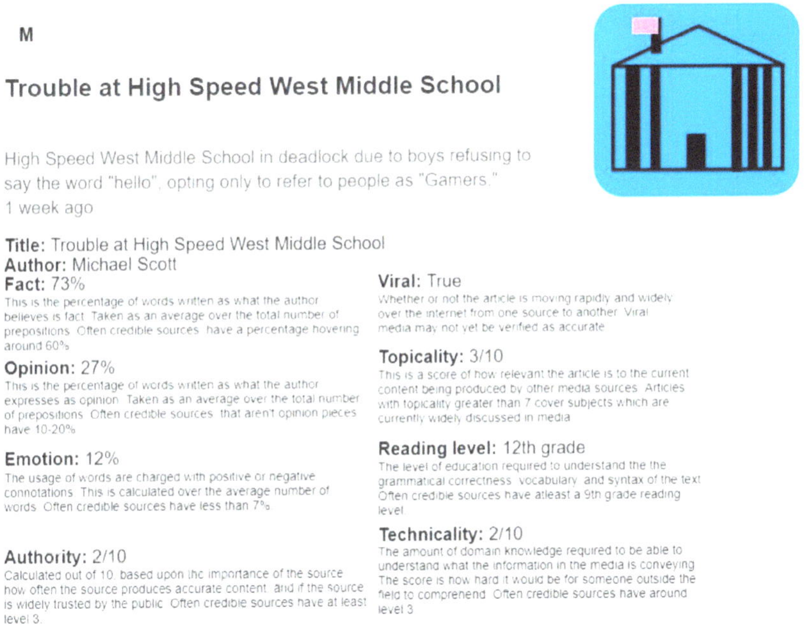

Figure 5. Informational label with article summary and component score descriptions [76].

Data regarding the helpfulness of the third informational label is presented in Figures A31–A33. Figure A31 shows the number of respondents indicating perceived helpfulness of the label by income level. While there was no overarching trend in these data, the uncertainty and perceived helpfulness decreased with increased income across the three lowest levels of the data. The perceived helpfulness then increased for the next two levels, though a similar trend with uncertainty was not present. The highest income level did not participate in either of these trends. As with the previous two labels, there was an increase in perceived helpfulness between the USD 50,000 and USD 75,000 income levels, though it was less pronounced than for the second label (Figure A16). In this instance, the trend differed, as there was a continued increase in perceived helpfulness for the third label at the USD 100,000 income level; however, it showed a similar pattern between the USD 50,000–75,000 income levels as was present in previous label styles.

Figure A32 shows the perceived helpfulness of the third label by political affiliation. As was true in many cases, Democrats reported the lowest uncertainty and highest perceived helpfulness. This was followed by the Republicans (for both uncertainty and helpfulness) and then independents/other party members.

Data presenting the helpfulness of label 3 by internet usage level are shown in Figure A33. These data show no clear trend related to uncertainty; however, a trend of increased perception of usefulness with higher internet usage was present at the lower three levels of internet usage. This trend was bucked by the highest internet usage level.

Figures A34–A36 characterize the perceptions of the annoyingness of label 3. Figure A34 presents the perceptions of annoyingness in terms of income level. There was a general trend of declining uncertainty with increasing income level, with some deviations. There was also a trend of increasing perceived annoyingness up to the USD 50,000–74,999 income group followed by declining perceived annoyingness. The highest income level bucked this trend, with annoyingness reported at a similar level to the USD 50,000–74,999 group. Once again, between the USD 50,000 and USD 75,000 income levels, a trend was present. In the case of annoyingness, this trend presented itself as a decrease, rather than the increases generally found for helpfulness and usefulness.

Figure A35 characterizes the annoyingness of the label by political affiliation. Once again, Democrats perceived the label the most positively, having the lowest uncertainty and lowest annoyance reported. Republicans and independent/other party members had similar higher uncertainty and annoyingness levels.

Figure A36 shows perception of annoyingness of the third informational label in terms of internet usage level. While there was a very slight trend regarding reduced uncertainty with increased internet usage, no trend was present in the internet-usage-associated annoyingness data itself.

Figures A37–A39 present data regarding respondents' willingness to use informational label 3. Figure A37 shows the willingness level correlated with income level. There were no notable trends present in either the uncertainty level or income level associated with the willingness level data itself. It is notable, though, that respondents' willingness to review, once again, increased from the USD 50,000 to the USD 75,000 income levels.

Figure A38 presents the willingness to review data correlated with party affiliation. As was the case with some frequency, Democrats had the lowest uncertainty and highest positive perception of the label. Republicans had slightly less uncertainty than independents/other party members and indicated willingness to use with slightly less frequency.

Figure A39 presents the willingness to use data related to label 3 correlated with internet usage levels. A trend of declining uncertainty was present across the lowest three levels, and a trend of increased willingness to use was present (with slight a deviation at the 3–5 h level) across all four levels.

Figures A40–A42 present data regarding respondents' perceptions of others' willingness to review the third informational label. Figure A40 presents this data by income level. As shown in Figure A40, there are no notable trends in the correlation between income level and others' willingness to review the third informational label. Perceived willingness of others to review increases when between the USD 50,000 and USD 75,000 income levels, as was observed for the first (Figure A7) and second (Figure A25) labels.

Figure A41 shows respondents' perceptions of others' willingness to review in terms of political affiliation. Notably, as has been common, Democrats have the lowest uncertainty and highest willingness to use the label. This is followed by Republicans and then independents/other party members.

Figure A42 presents respondents' perceptions of others' willingness to review the third informational label by internet usage level. There are slight trends of reducing uncertainty and increasing willingness to review the label (with a deviation at the 3–5 h level) with greater internet usage time.

Focus now turns to the utility of the third informational label for assessing the trustworthiness of an article. Figures A43–A45 present data related to this. Figure A45, in particular, presents data regarding the association between income level and perceived usefulness for trustworthiness assessment. There is a slight trend of decreasing uncertainty and increasing perception of trustworthiness assessment utility with increased income level, for this label. Notably, the highest income bracket does not participate in either of these trends. Once again, there is a decrease in perceived usefulness from the USD 25,000 to USD 50,000 income levels followed by an increase at the USD 75,000 income level.

Figure A44 presents data regarding trustworthiness determination utility associated with party affiliation. As was frequently the case, Democrats had the lowest uncertainty level and highest trustworthiness determination utility level. For uncertainty, Republicans had only slightly more uncertainty than Democrats did for this label. The difference was more pronounced for the difference in perceived trustworthiness determination, though the Republicans also found there to be more utility from this label than independents/other party members.

Finally, Figure A45 presents the trustworthiness judging utility data correlated with internet usage levels. There was a clear trend in this data of reducing uncertainty with increasing internet usage levels. There was also a trend of slightly increasing trustworthiness judging utility with increasing internet usage levels.

5. Warning Labels

Focus now turns to warning labels. This section presents and discusses the results from several survey questions relevant to warning labels (paralleling the discussion of information labels in Section 4). Respondents were presented with three warning labels to review and then indicated their perspectives.

5.1. Warning Label including Description

Figure 6 presents the first warning label. This label pops up in front of the content, has a warning icon and explains the rationale for the warning.

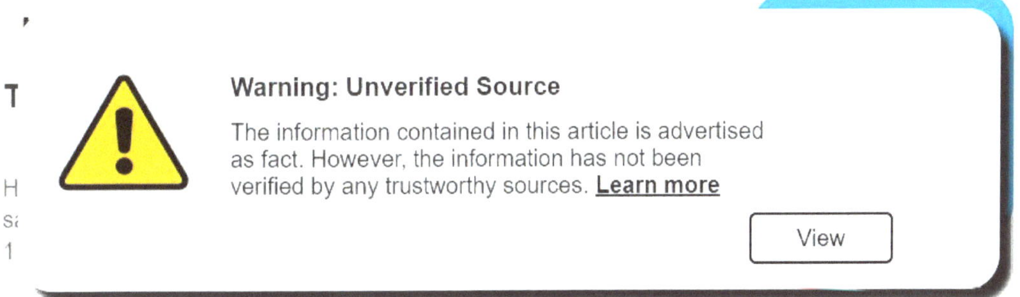

Figure 6. Warning label with description [76].

Figures 7–9 present data related to respondents' perception of the helpfulness of warning label 1 (Figure 6). Figure 7 presents perceptions of helpfulness in terms of income level. Notably, there was comparatively small (to the informational labels) uncertainty, which had a slight trend of reduction with increasing income level. There was also a high level of individuals reporting helpfulness (above 70% for all income levels), with a slight trend of reduction in helpfulness perception with increasing income level.

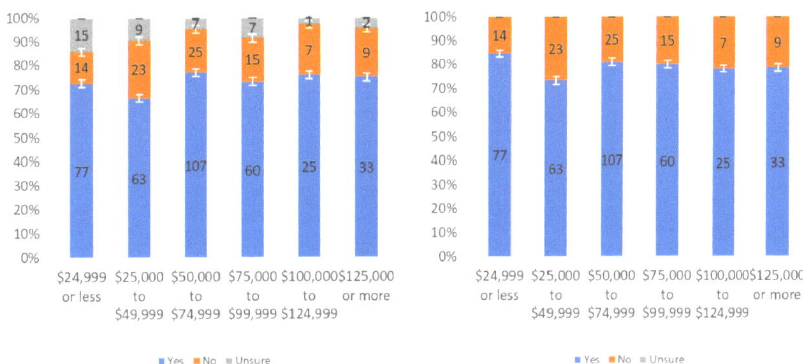

Figure 7. Responses regarding label helpfulness by income level including (**left**) and excluding (**right**) unsure responses.

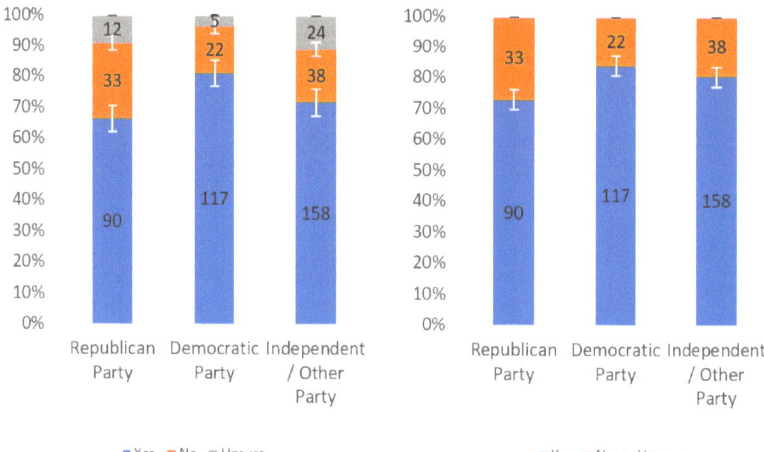

Figure 8. Responses regarding label helpfulness by political affiliation including (**left**) and excluding (**right**) unsure responses.

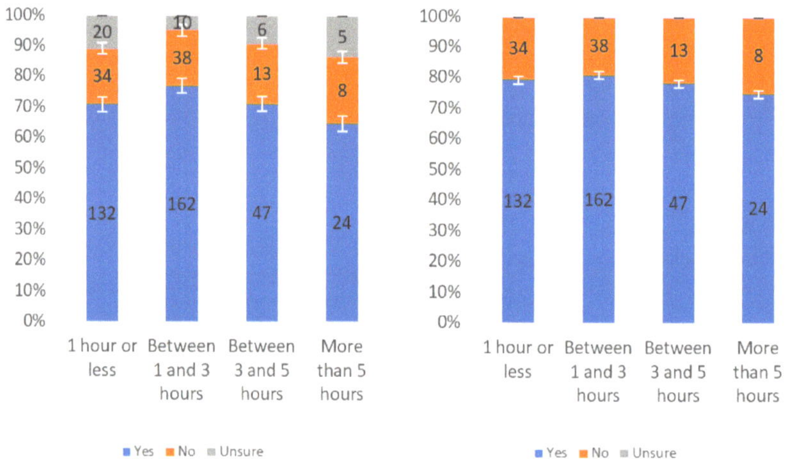

Figure 9. Responses regarding label helpfulness by internet usage level including (**left**) and excluding (**right**) unsure responses.

Figure 8 presents the helpfulness perceptions by respondents' political affiliations. As with the informational labels, Democrats had the best perceptions of the label with the lowest uncertainty and highest levels of finding it helpful. Republicans had the second lowest uncertainty, while independents/other party members had the second highest level of perception of helpfulness.

Figure 9 considers helpfulness of the first warning label by internet usage level. There was a slight downward trend at the three highest levels of usage for perception of helpfulness. This was coupled with a growing level of reported uncertainty.

Respondents were asked about the annoyingness of the first warning label, and these results are presented in Figures 10–12. Figure 10 presents the annoyingness perception based on respondents' income levels. While there was a trend toward a slight decrease in uncertainty with increased income levels, no trend existed in the annoyingness perceptions themselves.

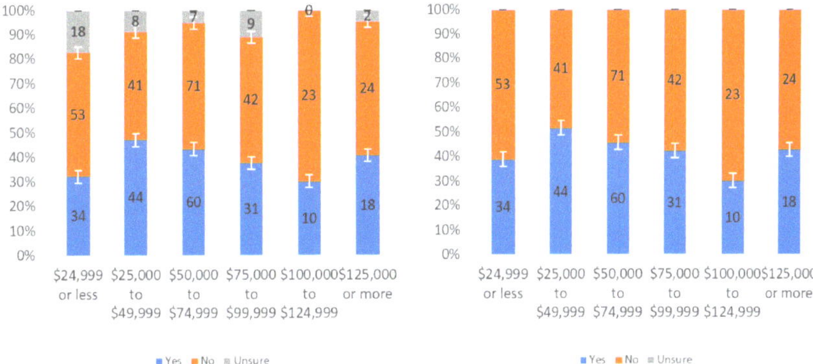

Figure 10. Responses regarding label annoyingness by income level including (**left**) and excluding (**right**) unsure responses.

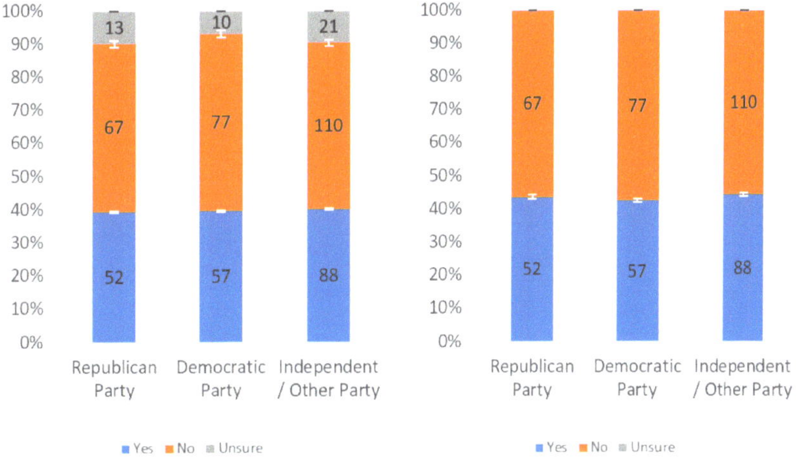

Figure 11. Responses regarding label annoyingness by political affiliation including (**left**) and excluding (**right**) unsure responses.

Figure 11 presents the annoyingness perceptions in terms of respondents' political affiliations. Notably there was very little deviation between the political affiliations' responses. The three groups had nearly identical annoyingness perception levels, and the difference among the uncertainty levels was not practically significant.

There were also no notable trends present in the annoyingness data presented in terms of internet usage level in Figure 12. There was minor and practically insignificant variation present.

Focus now turns to respondents' responses regarding their willingness to use the first warning label. Data related to this are presented in Figures 13–15. Figure 15 shows willingness to use in terms of respondents' income levels. There was a trend present regarding reduced uncertainty, generally, with increased income levels. There was also a slight reduction in willingness to use with increasing income levels; however, the reduction was not practically significant.

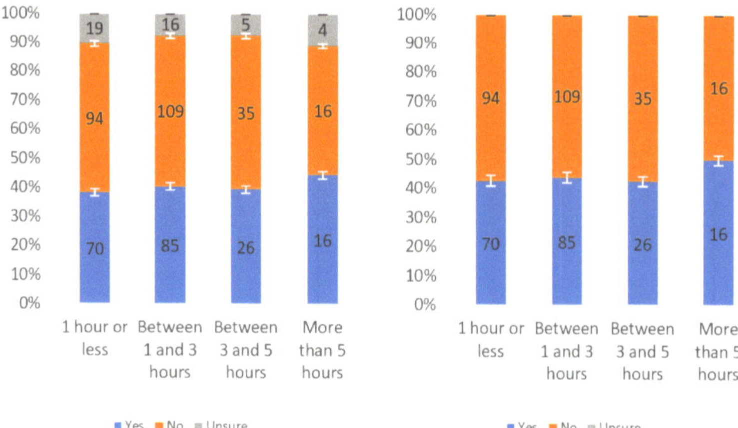

Figure 12. Responses regarding label annoyingness by internet usage level including (**left**) and excluding (**right**) unsure responses.

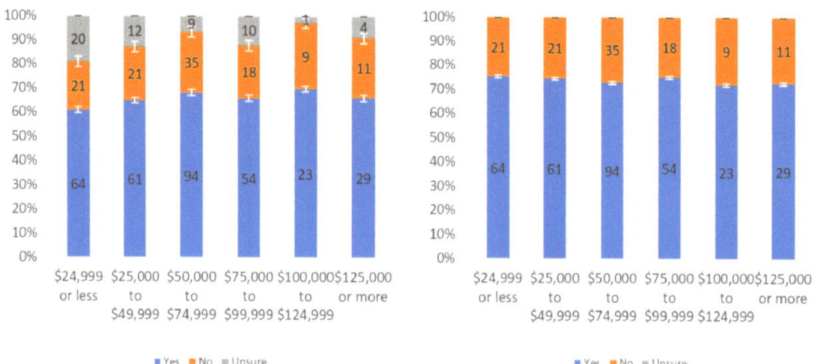

Figure 13. Responses regarding respondents' willingness to review by income level including (**left**) and excluding (**right**) unsure responses.

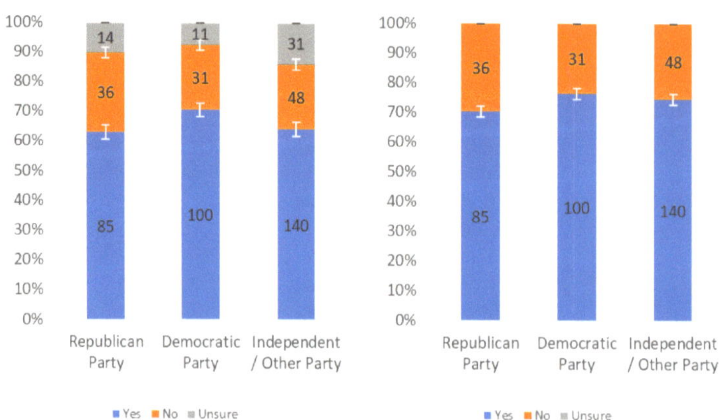

Figure 14. Responses regarding respondents' willingness to review by party affiliation including (**left**) and excluding (**right**) unsure responses.

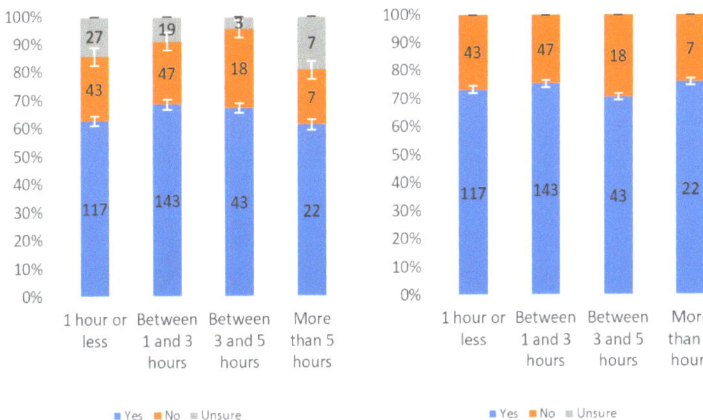

Figure 15. Responses regarding respondents' willingness to review by internet usage level including (**left**) and excluding (**right**) unsure responses.

The willingness to use data is now considered in terms of respondents' political affiliations. Again, the variations among the different groups were relatively small. The Democrats had the most favorable views of the label with the lowest uncertainty and highest levels of willing to use responses. Republicans had the second lowest uncertainty level, while independents/other party members had the second highest level willingness to use. Notably, the willingness to use (among those not indicating uncertainty) was at approximately 70% or above for all three political affiliation groups.

Figure 15 presents the willingness to use data in terms of online usage time. There was neither a clear trend in the willingness to use levels nor differences among the groups that were practically significant. There was a trend of reducing uncertainty levels with increased online usage among the three lowest levels; however, the highest online usage level also had the highest uncertainty, bucking this trend.

Figures 16–18 characterize respondents' perceptions of others willingness to use the first warning label. Figure 16 presents the willingness to use data in terms of income levels. No clear trend existed with regard to willingness to use the label and income level. A trend of reduced uncertainty with increased income level was present at the three highest levels. It is notable that for the first warning label, this was the only question where a notable increase was observed between the USD 50,000 and USD 75,000 income levels.

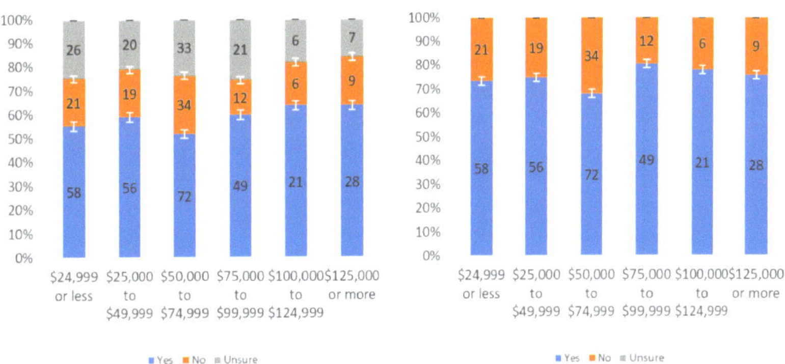

Figure 16. Responses regarding others' willingness to review by income level including (**left**) and excluding (**right**) unsure responses.

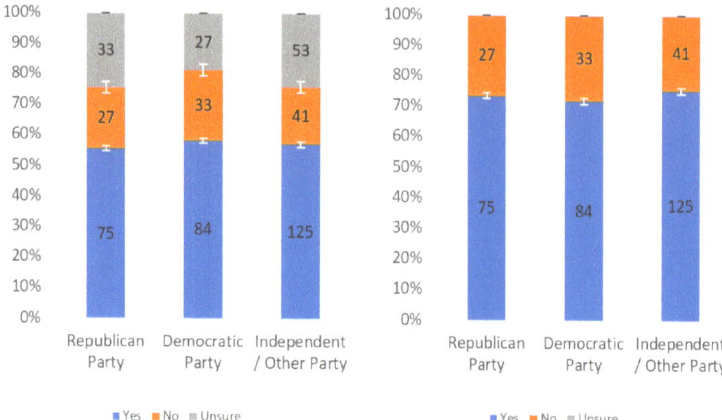

Figure 17. Responses regarding others' willingness to review by party affiliation including (**left**) and excluding (**right**) unsure responses.

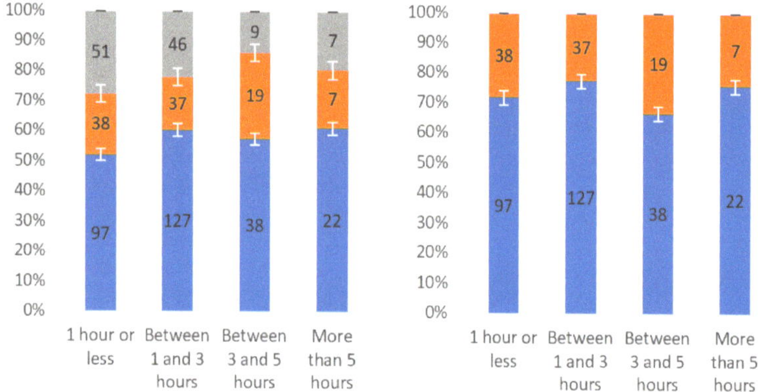

Figure 18. Responses regarding others' willingness to review by internet usage level including (**left**) and excluding (**right**) unsure responses.

Figure 17 presents respondents' perception of others' willingness to use the first warning label in terms of political affiliation. Notably, while Democrats had the lowest uncertainty, they also had the lowest willingness level, with independents/other party members and Republicans reporting higher levels of belief in others being willing to use the label.

Finally, Figure 18 presents respondents' perception of others' willingness to use the first warning label in terms of respondents' online usage levels. There was reduced uncertainty with increased online usage at all but the top level of usage. No trend, however, was present in the willingness data correlated with online usage levels.

Figures 19–21 present data regarding the utility of the label for judging the trustworthiness of the article. Figure 21 presents this in terms of income level. In this figure, there is a clear trend of reducing uncertainty with increased income levels in this data. However, no trends were obvious in the judging utility responses themselves.

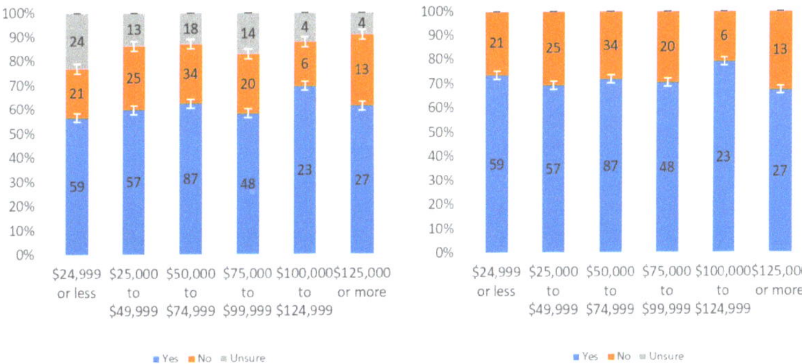

Figure 19. Responses regarding usefulness in judging trustworthiness by income level including (**left**) and excluding (**right**) unsure responses.

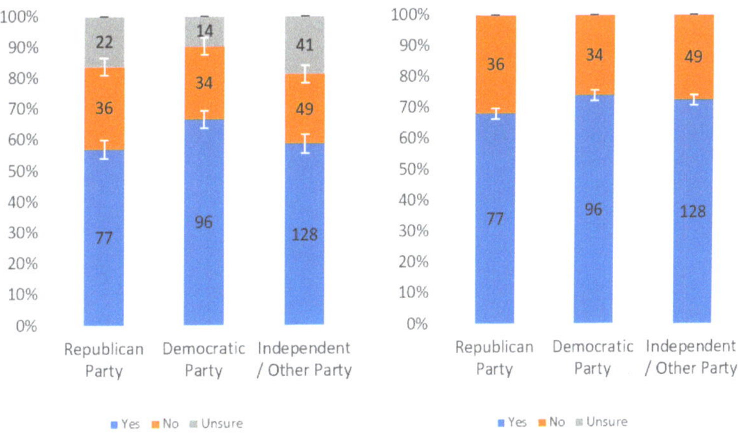

Figure 20. Responses regarding usefulness in judging trustworthiness by party affiliation including (**left**) and excluding (**right**) unsure responses.

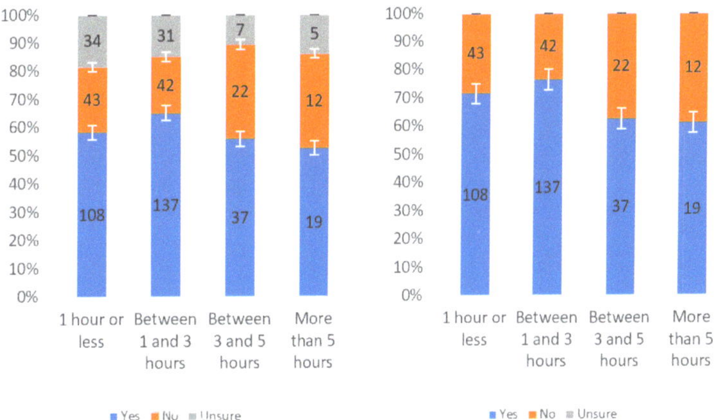

Figure 21. Responses regarding usefulness in judging trustworthiness by internet usage level including (**left**) and excluding (**right**) unsure responses.

Figure 20 presents the trustworthiness judging utility data perceptions in terms of respondents' political affiliation. While there were larger differences in uncertainty level, the difference between the levels of judging utility perceptions, themselves, were limited. As in many cases, Democrat respondents indicated the lowest uncertainty and highest perceived judging utility. The difference in perceived utility levels were quite low, though, and not practically significant.

Figure 21 presents the judging utility data in terms of respondents' online usage levels. There was a general trend of decreasing uncertainty with increased online usage. There was also a general trend of decreased perceptions of judging effectiveness with increased online usage levels.

5.2. Warning Label including Summary

A second type of warning label is presented in Figure 22. This label has a less prominent warning icon and explanation of why the warning is being displayed. It also provides a brief summary of the article and a picture from the article. Data related to this second article are presented in Figures 23–38.

M

Trouble at High Speed West Middle School

High Speed West Middle School in deadlock due to boys refusing to say the word "hello", opting only to refer to people as "Gamers."
1 week ago

Warning: Unverified Source

The information contained in this article is advertised as fact. However, the information has not been verified by any trustworthy sources. Learn more

Figure 22. Warning label with article summary [76].

Figures 23–25 present data regarding the perceived helpfulness of the second warning label. Figure 23 presents the helpfulness data in terms of respondents' income level. While there was a reduction in uncertainty with growing income level, in all but the highest income level group, there was no notable trend shown in terms of an association between helpfulness perception and income level.

Figure 24 depicts respondents' perceptions regarding the helpfulness of the second warning label in terms of political affiliation. As in many cases, Democrat respondents had the lowest uncertainty level and highest perception of helpfulness. Republicans had both the second lowest uncertainty and second highest perceived helpfulness responses for this label. Figure 25 presents respondents' perceptions of label helpfulness in terms of their internet usage levels. There were no clear trends present for either the uncertainty levels or the helpfulness perception levels. The differences in helpfulness perception levels were also not practically significant.

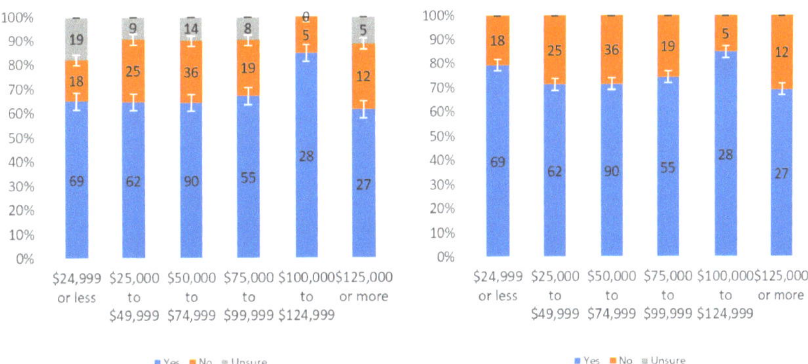

Figure 23. Responses regarding label helpfulness by income level including (**left**) and excluding (**right**) unsure responses.

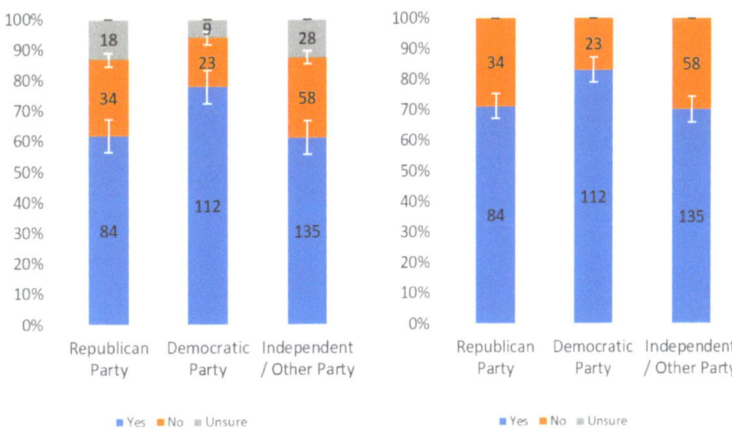

Figure 24. Responses regarding label helpfulness by party affiliation including (**left**) and excluding (**right**) unsure responses.

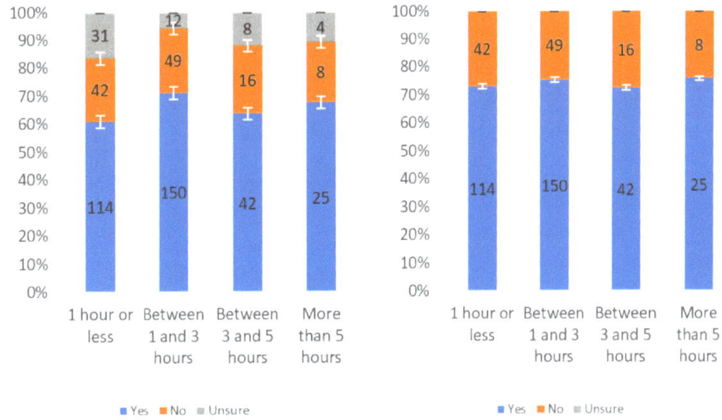

Figure 25. Responses regarding label helpfulness by internet usage level including (**left**) and excluding (**right**) unsure responses.

The focus now turns to respondents' perception of the second warning label's annoyingness. These data are presented in Figures 26–28. Figure 26 presents this data in terms of respondents' income levels. While Figure 26 shows a noticeable trend of reducing uncertainty with income level (excluding the highest income level group), there was no notable correlation between annoyingness perception and income level.

Figure 27 presents the correlation between annoyingness perception of the second warning level and political affiliation. As usual, the Democratic respondents had the highest perceptions of the label, and they had the lowest uncertainty and the lowest annoyingness levels. Republicans had the second lowest uncertainty and annoyingness levels.

Figure 28 presents the annoyingness level data in terms of online usage time. There was a noticeable reduction in uncertainty with increasing online usage amongst the three lowest usage levels; however, no notable trend was present among the annoyingness level data itself.

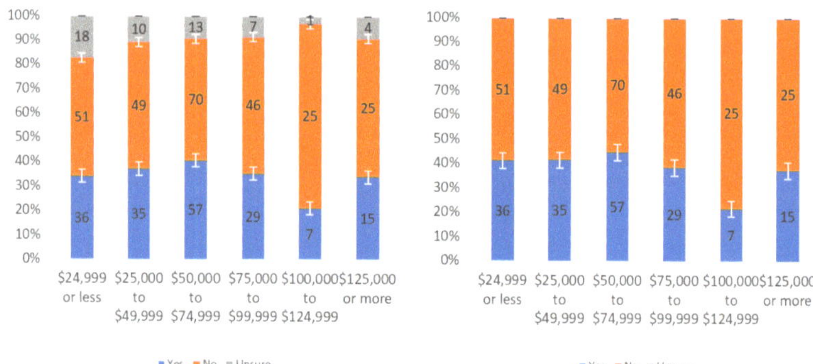

Figure 26. Responses regarding label annoyingness by income level including (**left**) and excluding (**right**) unsure responses.

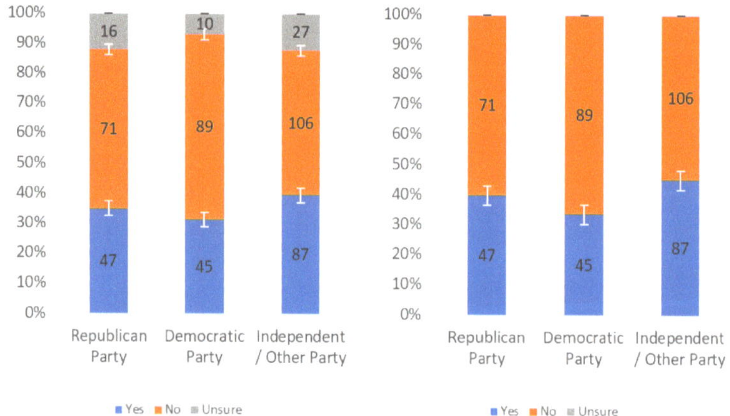

Figure 27. Responses regarding label annoyingness by political affiliation including (**left**) and excluding (**right**) unsure responses.

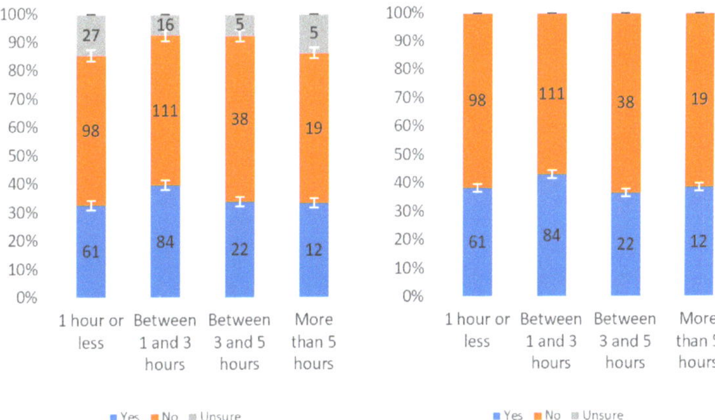

Figure 28. Responses regarding label annoyingness by internet usage level including (**left**) and excluding (**right**) unsure responses.

Next, respondents' willingness to use the second warning label is considered. These data are presented in Figures 29–31. Figure 29 presents this in terms of respondents' income levels. No clear trend was present in this data for either the uncertainty or willingness in terms of income level, though there was, once again, a decrease from the USD 25,000 to USD 50,000 income levels followed by an increase at the USD 75,000 income level.

Figure 30 presents the willingness data in terms of political affiliation. As typical, Democrats had less uncertainty and the highest willingness to use the label. Independents/other party members had the second lowest uncertainty, while Republicans had the second highest willingness to use. While there were noticeable differences in uncertainty levels, the differences in willingness to use levels were less pronounced.

Figure 31 presents the data regarding willingness to use for the second warning label in terms of respondents' online usage levels. The figure shows (with deviation at the highest usage level) a downward trend in uncertainty and a positive trend in willingness to use the label with increasing levels of internet usage.

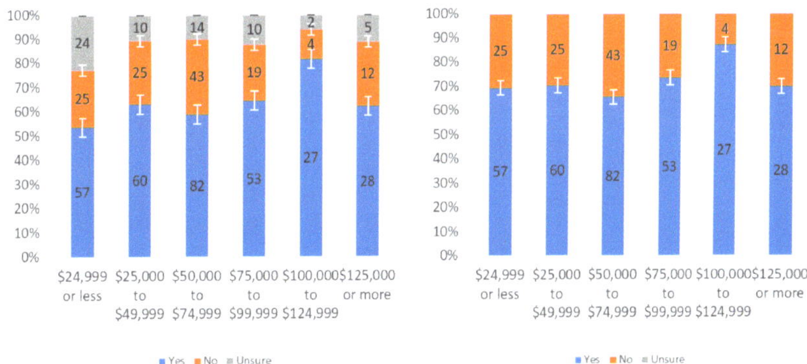

Figure 29. Responses regarding respondents' willingness to review by income level including (**left**) and excluding (**right**) unsure responses.

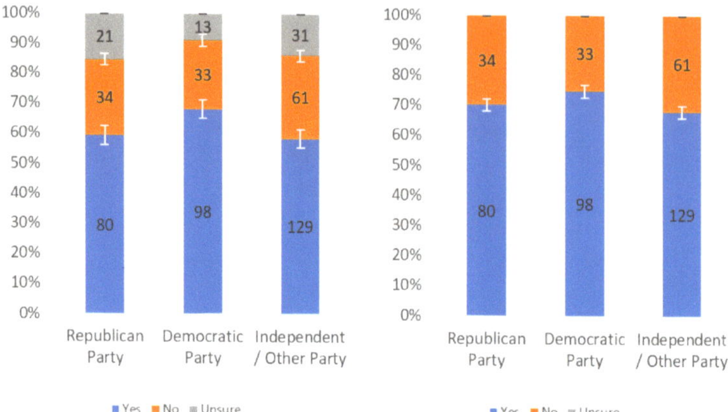

Figure 30. Responses regarding respondents' willingness to review by party affiliation including (**left**) and excluding (**right**) unsure responses.

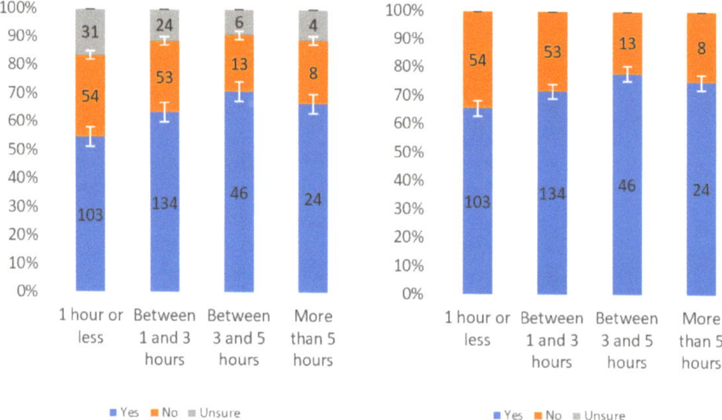

Figure 31. Responses regarding respondents' willingness to review by internet usage level including (**left**) and excluding (**right**) unsure responses.

Figures 32–34 present data related to respondents' perception of others' willingness to use the second warning label. Figure 32 presents this data in terms of respondents' income levels. There was no notable trend present in terms of either uncertainty or willingness correlated with income levels with one exception: the previously observed trend at the USD 50,000 and USD 75,000 income levels was again present. There was a sharp decline at the USD 50,000 income level followed by a sharp increase at the USD 75,000 income level.

Figure 33 shows data regarding respondents' perceptions of others' willingness to use the second warning label in terms of political affiliation. As typical, Democrats reported the lowest uncertainty and highest wiliness to use. Republications had the second lowest uncertainty and independents/other party members had the second highest willingness to use levels. Notably, the difference among the three groups' willingness to use levels was quite small.

Figure 34 presents respondents' perceptions of others' willingness to use the second warning label in terms of online usage level. There were trends of decreasing uncertainty and increasing willingness to use the label with increasing online usage levels among the lowest three usage levels. Notably, the differences between the willingness levels were quite small and much smaller than the difference between the uncertainty levels.

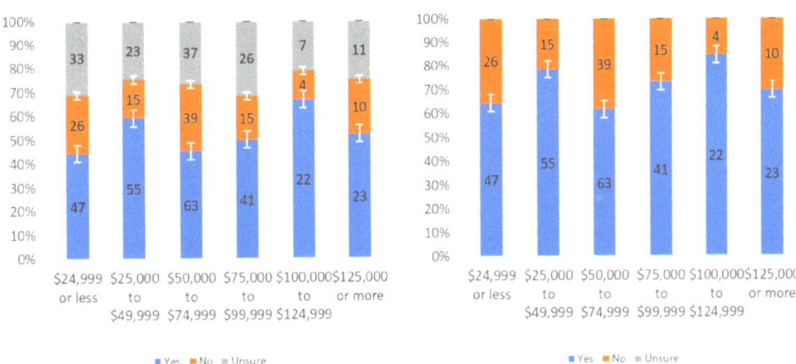

Figure 32. Responses regarding others' willingness to review by income level including (**left**) and excluding (**right**) unsure responses.

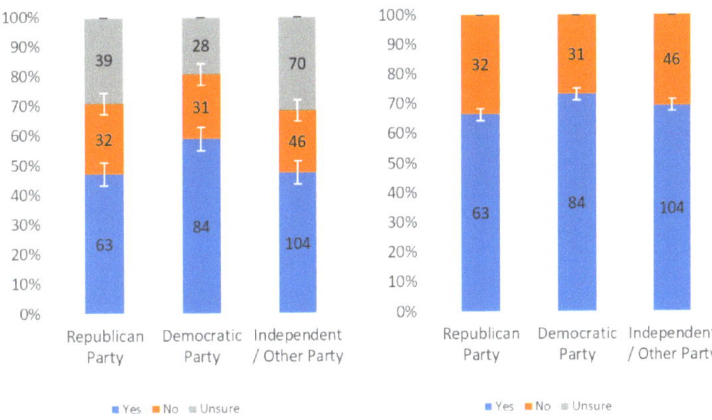

Figure 33. Responses regarding others' willingness to review by party affiliation including (**left**) and excluding (**right**) unsure responses.

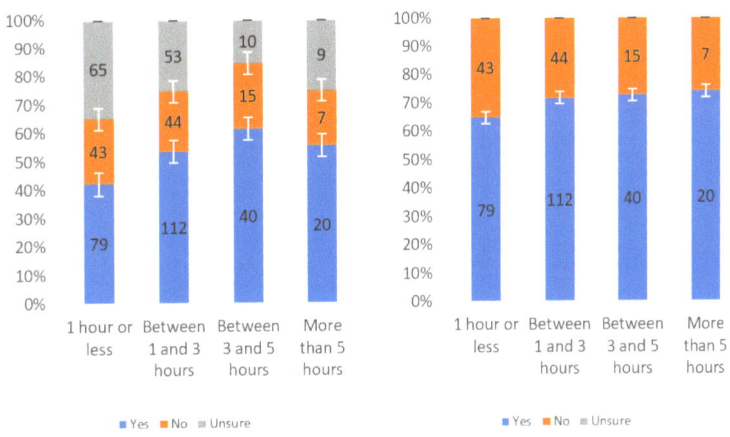

Figure 34. Responses regarding others' willingness to review by internet usage level including (**left**) and excluding (**right**) unsure responses.

Figures 35–37 present data regarding respondents' perception of the use of the second warning label for judging the trustworthiness of online content. Figure 35 presents this data in terms of income level. There was a noticeable trend amongst all but the highest income level of declining uncertainty and increased perception of utility for judging trustworthiness. Once more, perceived usefulness declined from the USD 25,000 to USD 50,000 income levels and then increased again at the USD 75,000 income level.

Figure 36 presents respondents' perceptions of utility for assessing article trustworthiness in terms of political affiliation. As typical, Democrat respondents reported the lowest uncertainty and highest trustworthiness determination utility. Republicans reported the second lowest uncertainty level and second highest utility levels.

Finally, Figure 37 presents respondents' perceptions of the usefulness of the second warning label for judging trustworthiness in terms of internet usage level. While there was a trend present of declining uncertainty with increased usage level, there was no noticeable trend in the utility perception levels themselves.

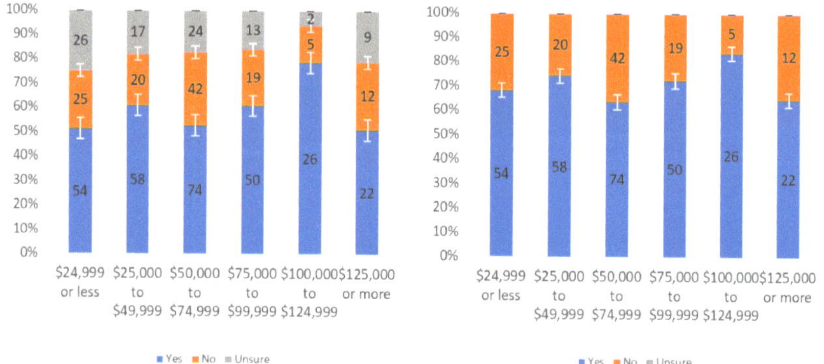

Figure 35. Responses regarding usefulness in judging trustworthiness by income level including (**left**) and excluding (**right**) unsure responses.

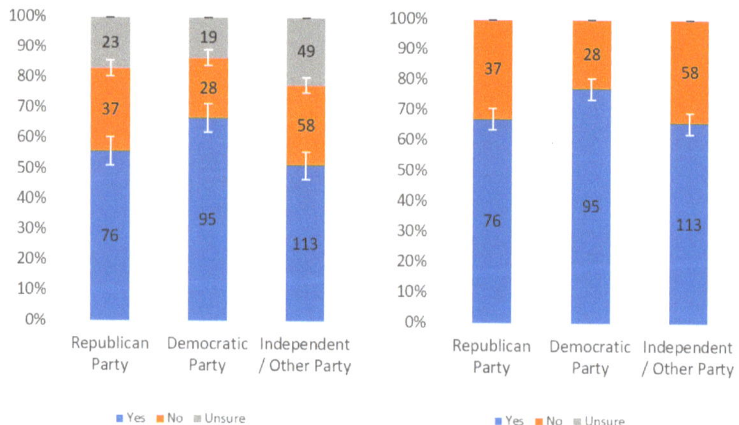

Figure 36. Responses regarding usefulness in judging trustworthiness by party affiliation including (**left**) and excluding (**right**) unsure responses.

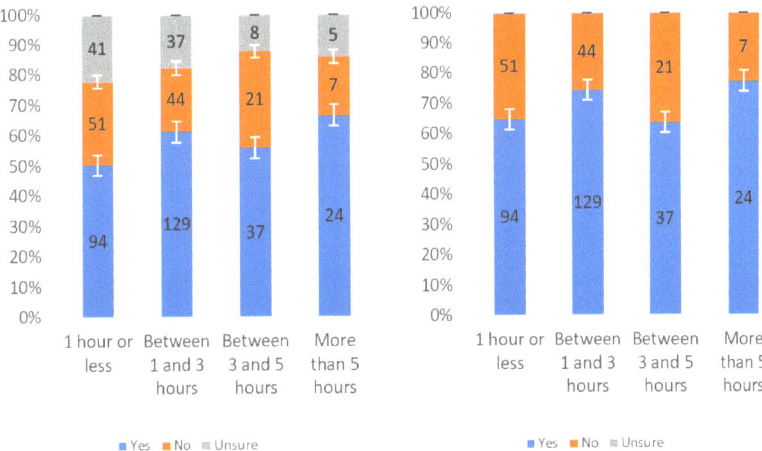

Figure 37. Responses regarding usefulness in judging trustworthiness by internet usage level including (**left**) and excluding (**right**) unsure responses.

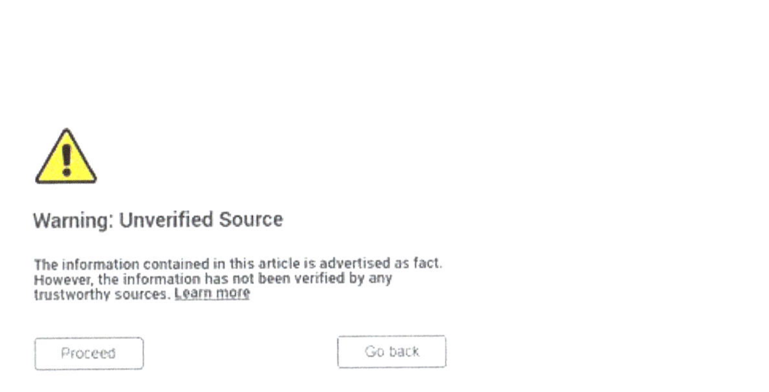

Figure 38. Blocking warning label [76].

5.3. Blocking Warning Label

Focus now turns to the third type of warning label, a blocking warning label. This label is presented on a separate page that loads before the content page loads and must be clicked through to view the content. It has a prominent warning icon and explanation of why a warning is being issued for the content. This third warning label is presented in Figure 38. Data related to respondents' perceptions of it are presented in Figures 39–53.

Figures 39–41 present data regarding the helpfulness of the blocking label. Figure 39 presents this data in terms of income level. Not notable trend was present in the uncertainty or helpfulness data. A blocky variation of the trend, which peaked at the USD 25,000 and USD 75,000 income levels, was observed again in these data.

Figure 40 presents helpfulness data for the blocking label in terms of political affiliation. As typical, Democrats had lower levels of uncertainty and higher levels of helpfulness. Republicans had the second lowest uncertainty and second highest perceptions of helpfulness.

Figure 41 presents the helpfulness data in terms of respondents' internet usage levels. There was a downward trend present between higher usage levels and greater uncertainty. The level of usefulness also exhibited a slight trend upwards with increased internet usage. The latter is in contrast to other labels which had trends that were almost the opposite.

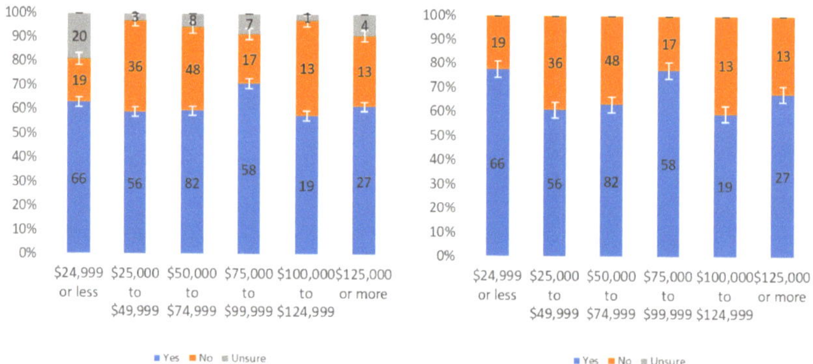

Figure 39. Responses regarding label helpfulness by income level including (**left**) and excluding (**right**) unsure responses.

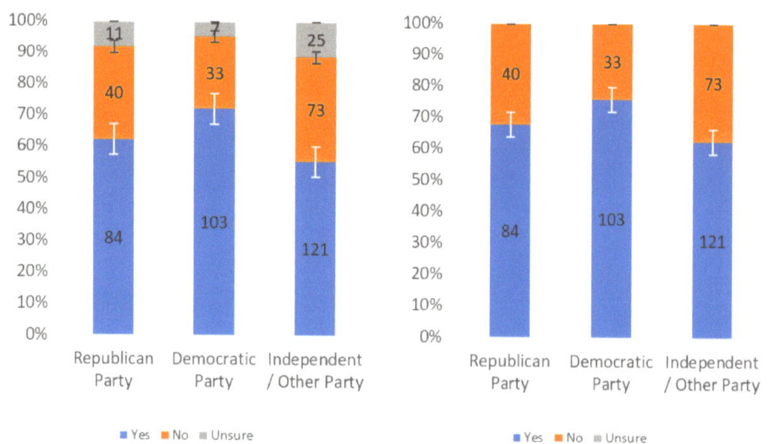

Figure 40. Responses regarding label helpfulness by party affiliation including (**left**) and excluding (**right**) unsure responses.

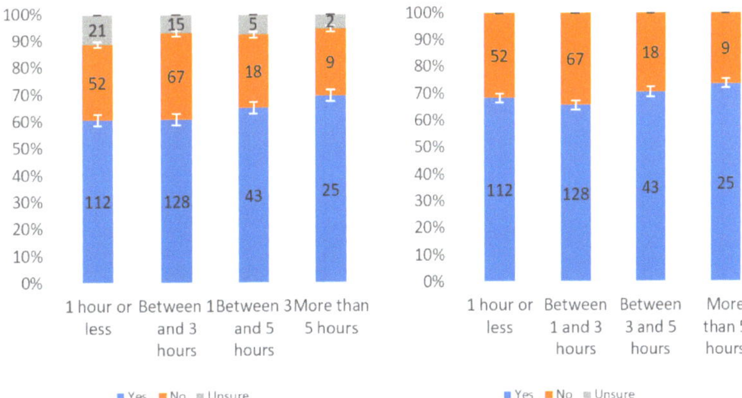

Figure 41. Responses regarding label helpfulness by internet usage level including (**left**) and excluding (**right**) unsure responses.

Figures 42–44 present data regarding the annoyingness of the blocking label. Figure 42 presents these data in terms of respondents' income levels. There was no clear trend in either the uncertainty level or annoyingness perception across all levels, though smaller trends existed in each. Most notably, there was a trend between the USD 25,000 and USD 99,999 income levels of decreased annoyingness perception associated with increasing income levels.

Figure 43 presents data regarding annoyingness in terms of political affiliation. While the recurring trend of Democrats having the lowest uncertainty was present, there was only a slight difference in the levels of annoyingness reported by political affiliation. Republicans also reported the lowest level of annoyingness. This differs from the typical situation of Democrats reacting more favorably towards most labels.

Figure 44 presents the annoyingness data for the blocking label in terms of online usage time. These data had a slight trough in annoyingness at the 1–3 h level (which was also the trough for uncertainty levels). The differences in annoyingness among the different internet usage levels were limited.

Now, focus turns to respondents' willingness to use the blocking label. There was a noticeable trend, shown in Figure 45, of declining uncertainty with increased income throughout the income levels. No clear trend was present in the willingness data itself. There was, again, a small increase from the USD 50,000 to USD 75,000 income levels.

Figure 46 presents the willingness to use data by political affiliation. This data mirrors that for other labels. Again, Democrats had the most favorable view of the label and the lowest uncertainty. Nearly 70% of Democrats indicated willingness to use as opposed to just under 65% of Republicans. Approximately 60% of independents/other party members indicated willingness, placing them at the lowest level of willingness. Republicans also had the second lowest uncertainly levels, behind Democrats.

Figure 47 presents the willingness to use levels in terms of online usage level. A trend of decline with increased usage was present in the lowest three of the four uncertainty levels. The willingness to use the blocking label had a negative correlation with increased online usage at these same three levels.

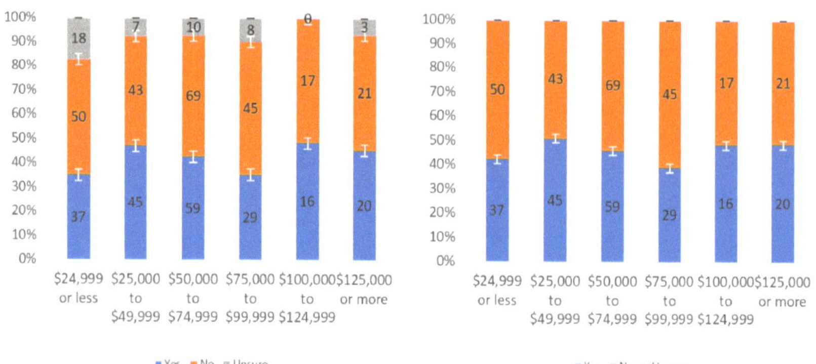

Figure 42. Responses regarding label annoyingness by income level including (**left**) and excluding (**right**) unsure responses.

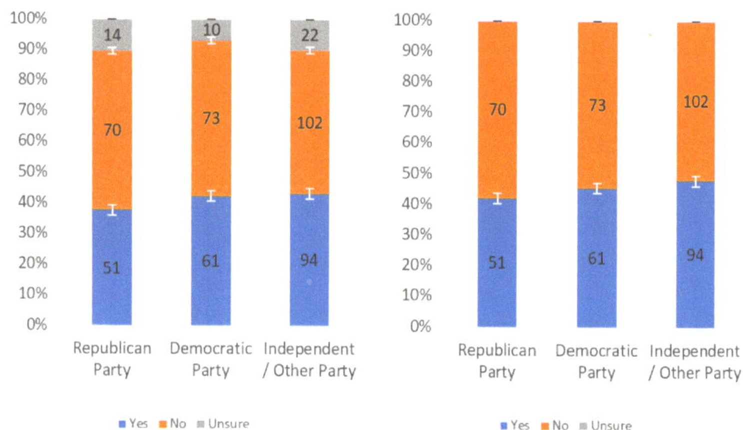

Figure 43. Responses regarding label annoyingness by party affiliation including (**left**) and excluding (**right**) unsure responses.

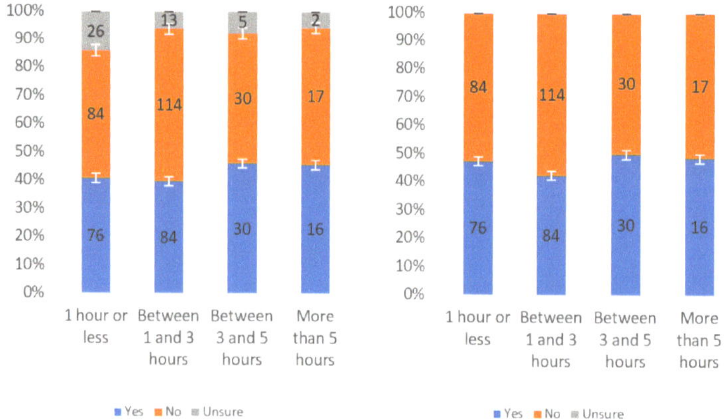

Figure 44. Responses regarding label annoyingness by internet usage level including (**left**) and excluding (**right**) unsure responses.

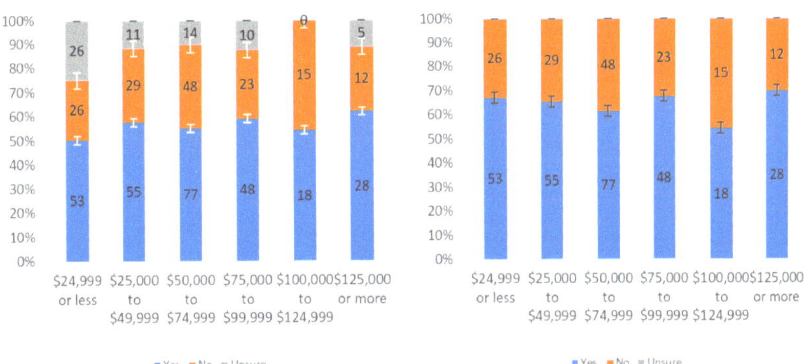

Figure 45. Responses regarding respondents' willingness to review by income level including (**left**) and excluding (**right**) unsure responses.

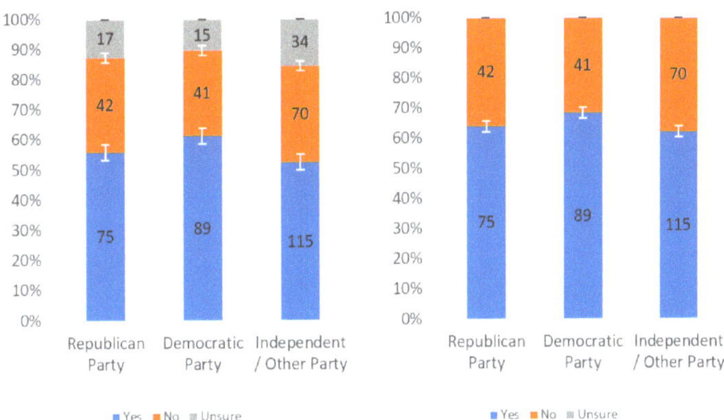

Figure 46. Responses regarding respondents' willingness to review by party affiliation including (**left**) and excluding (**right**) unsure responses.

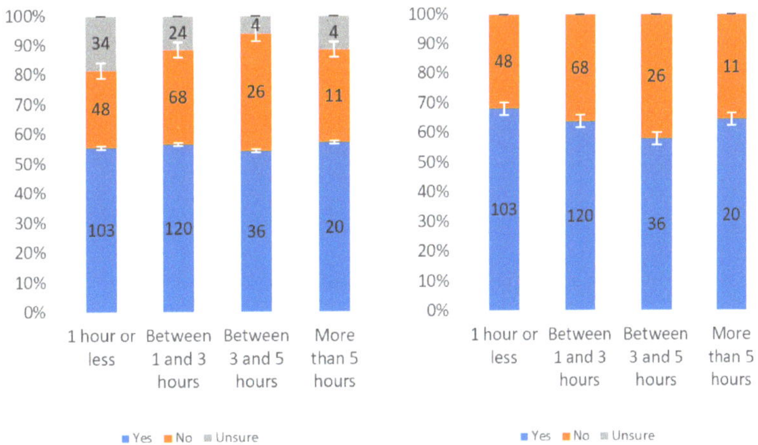

Figure 47. Responses regarding respondents' willingness to review by internet usage level including (**left**) and excluding (**right**) unsure responses.

Figures 48–50 present data regarding respondents' perceptions of others' willingness to use the label. Figure 48 presents this by income levels. The data show a trend of decreasing uncertainty with increasing income level and a less noticeable trend of decreasing perception of others' willingness to use the label with income level. There was a small decline from the USD 24,999 or less to USD 50,000 income levels followed by a sharp increase at the USD 75,000 income level, with a more pronounced decline following this.

Figure 49 presents respondents' perceptions of others' willingness to use the labels in terms of political affiliation. Democrats and independents indicated others to be more likely to use the label, for this particular label. Democrats had the lowest uncertainty, followed by Republicans. Independent/other party members indicated uncertainty more than Democrats and Republicans; however, Republicans indicated the lowest level of thinking others would use the label.

Figure 50 presents the willingness to use data in terms of online usage time. A very slight decline with increased usage levels was present in the willingness data. Decreasing uncertainty with increased income levels was shown for the three lowest income brackets.

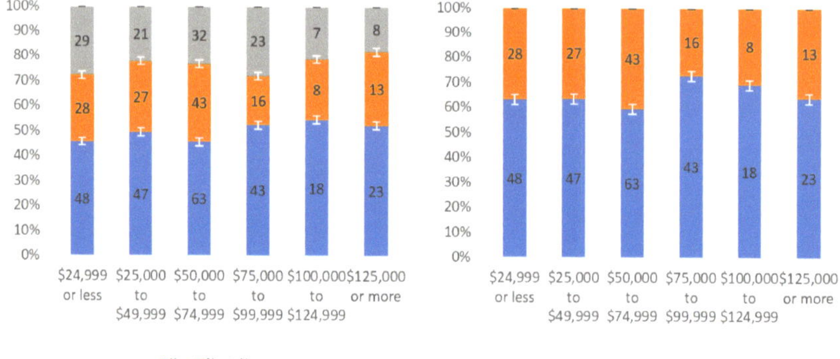

Figure 48. Responses regarding others' willingness to review by income level including (**left**) and excluding (**right**) unsure responses.

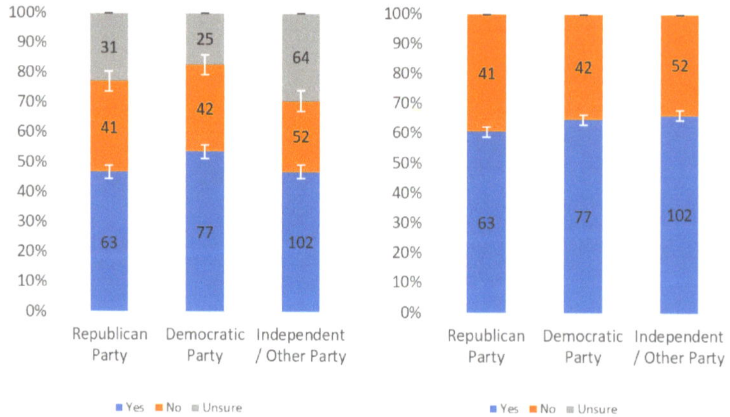

Figure 49. Responses regarding others' willingness to review by political affiliation including (**left**) and excluding (**right**) unsure responses.

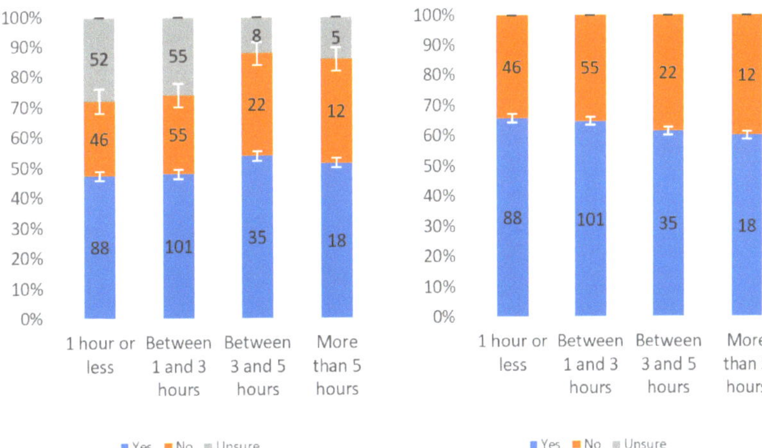

Figure 50. Responses regarding others' willingness to review by internet usage level including (**left**) and excluding (**right**) unsure responses.

Focus now turns to the blocking label's utility for judging trustworthiness. Figures 51–53 present data related to this. Figure 51 presents data related to income levels. While there was no clear trend regarding uncertainty, there was a slight positive correlation, with deviations at the USD 50,000 and USD 100,000 levels between increased income levels and perception of utility for judging trustworthiness.

In Figure 52, which presents trustworthiness judging utility by political affiliation, the recurring pattern of Democrats having the lowest (though only marginally, in this case) uncertainty levels and highest utility levels was again present. In this instance, Republicans had the second least uncertainty (just slightly less than the Democrats), while the independents/other party members and Republicans had similar utility levels.

Finally, Figure 53 presents the trustworthiness judging utility data in terms of internet usage level. No notable correlation between greater internet usage and utility was shown. Uncertainty had a clear trend of declining with increased internet usage levels.

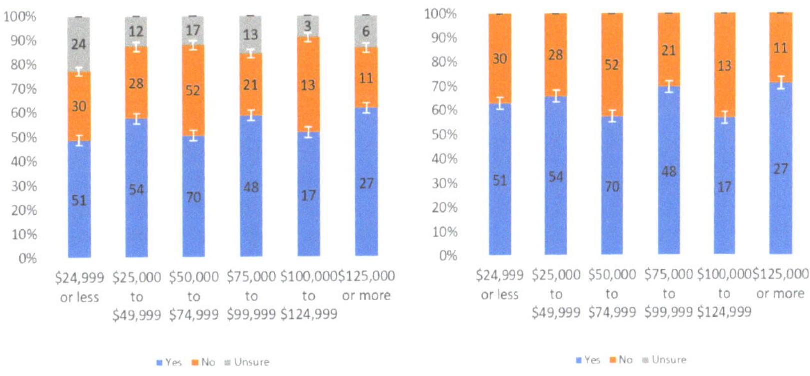

Figure 51. Responses regarding usefulness in judging trustworthiness by income level including (**left**) and excluding (**right**) unsure responses.

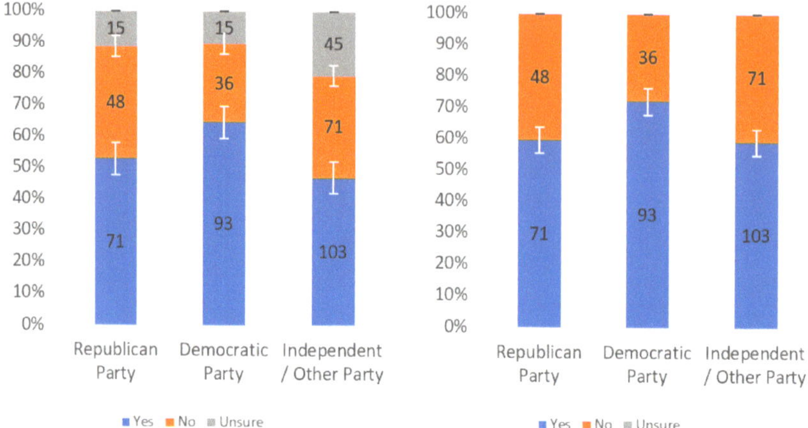

Figure 52. Responses regarding usefulness in judging trustworthiness by party affiliation including (**left**) and excluding (**right**) unsure responses.

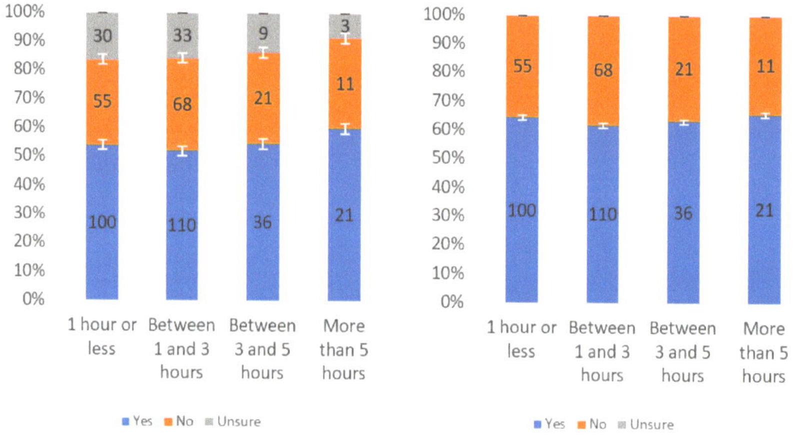

Figure 53. Responses regarding usefulness in judging trustworthiness by internet usage level including (**left**) and excluding (**right**) unsure responses.

6. Supplemental Information Labels

Finally, a third type of label—one that provides supplemental information—is assessed. As in Sections 4 and 5 for informational and warning labels, respectively, this section presents and discusses the results from several survey questions relevant to supplemental information labels. Figure 54 presents the example of this type of figure that was presented to respondents in the survey. As the figure shows, this label provides the title of the article, a brief summary of the article and a picture from the article. It then has a "learn more" box that provides a link to factual details relevant to claims made in the article.

M

Trouble at High Speed West Middle School

High Speed West Middle School in deadlock due to boys refusing to
say the word "hello", opting only to refer to people as "Gamers."
1 week ago

This article makes claims regarding High Speed West Middle School's bylaws.
High Speed West Middle School's website has the complete school bylaws
publicly available.

Figure 54. "Learn more" additional information label [76].

Figures 55–57 present data regarding respondents' perceptions of the helpfulness of
this label. Figure 55 presents data in terms of income levels. While there was no notable
trend related to the uncertainty level, the label had a negative correlation between increased
income levels and perception of helpfulness at the lowest income levels, followed by
increasing perception of helpfulness at higher ones.

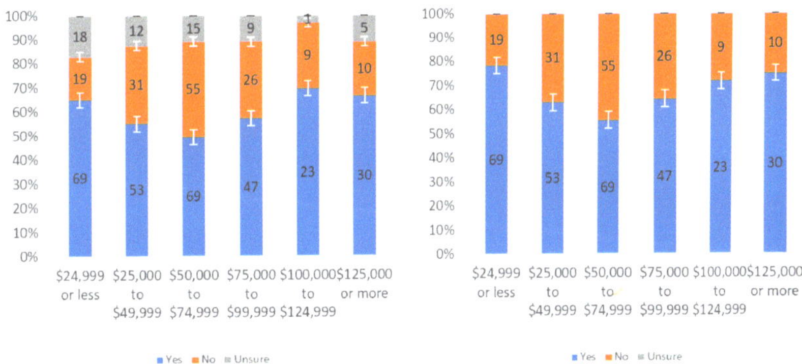

Figure 55. Responses regarding label helpfulness by income level including (**left**) and excluding
(**right**) unsure responses.

Figure 56 shows the helpfulness data in association with political affiliation. As usual,
Democrat respondents found the label to be the most helpful. They also had the lowest
level of uncertainty. Republican respondents had slightly more uncertainty and slightly less
perceptions of helpfulness. Independents/other party members had higher uncertainty
and lower helpfulness perceptions.

The helpfulness data are also presented in terms of correlation with online usage levels.
While there was a limited decline in uncertainty shown in the lower three levels of internet
usage, a positive trend was present in the actual helpfulness data associated with these
internet usage levels.

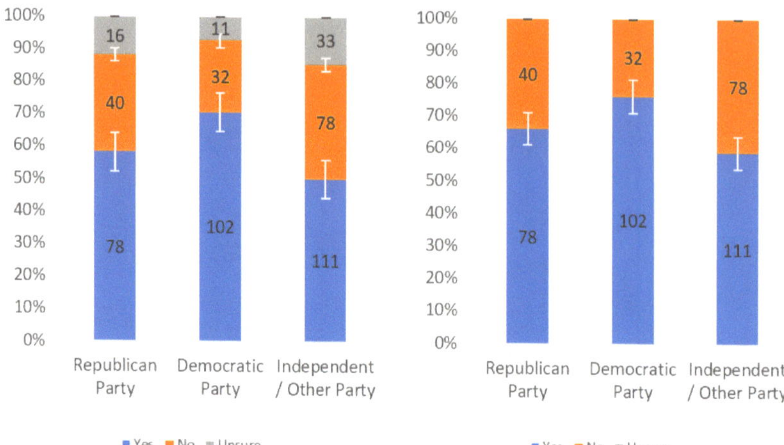

Figure 56. Responses regarding label helpfulness by party affiliation including (**left**) and excluding (**right**) unsure responses.

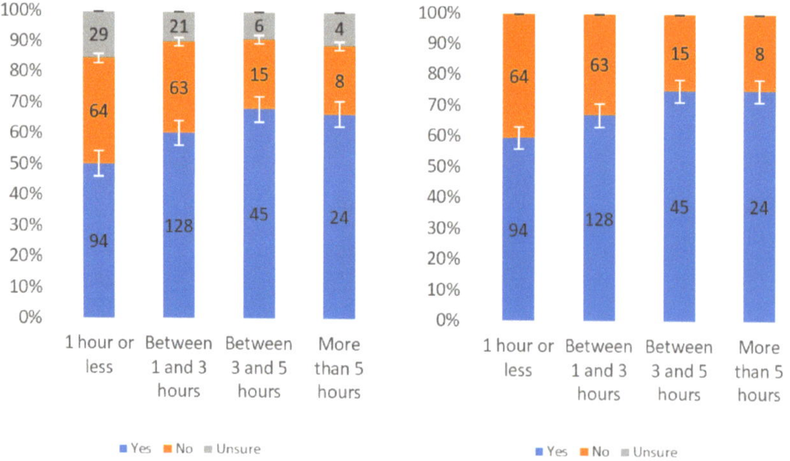

Figure 57. Responses regarding label helpfulness by internet usage level including (**left**) and excluding (**right**) unsure responses.

Next, the annoyingness of the label is assessed. Figures 58–60 present data related to the annoyingness of the supplemental information label. Figure 58 presents data in association with income level. There was a general minor positive association in the uncertainty data, and there was a limited negative correlation between increased income level and perception of annoyingness, excluding the lowest income bracket.

The annoyingness data are presented associated with political affiliation in Figure 59. As typical, Democrats had the lowest uncertainly level. Democrats also found the label the least annoying, followed—with only a slight difference between each—by Republicans and independents.

The annoyingness data are presented in Figure 60 in terms of online usage levels. In this data, the uncertainty values decreased with increased internet usage levels. The annoyingness level values also declined with increased levels of internet usage, except for a very slight increase between the highest two levels.

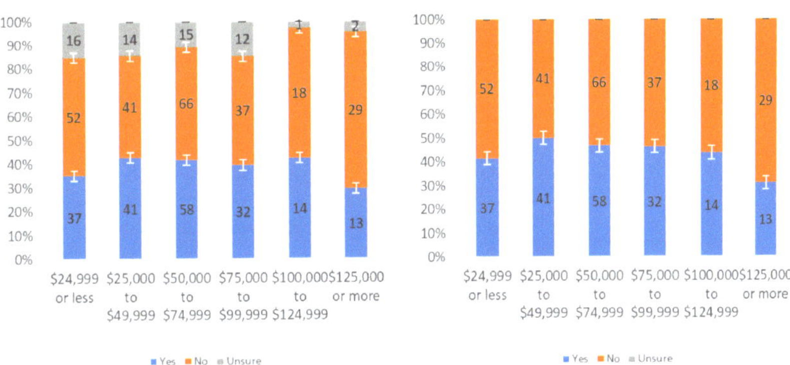

Figure 58. Responses regarding label annoyingness by income level including (**left**) and excluding (**right**) unsure responses.

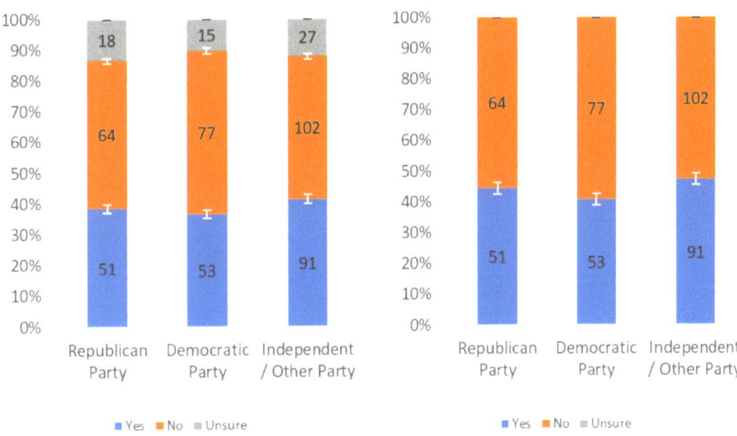

Figure 59. Responses regarding label annoyingness by party affiliation including (**left**) and excluding (**right**) unsure responses.

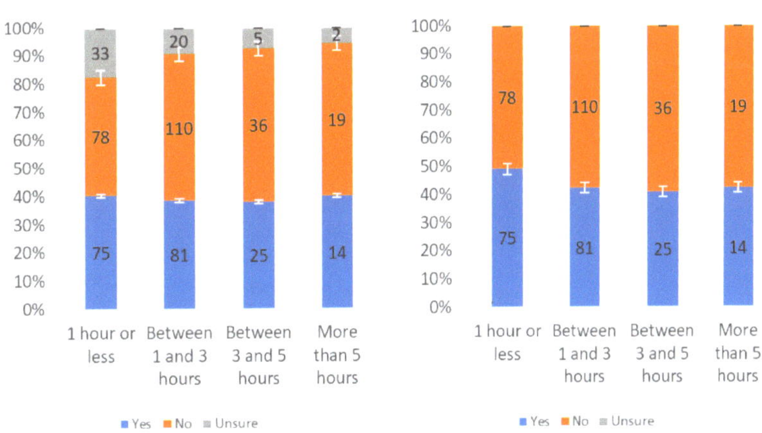

Figure 60. Responses regarding label annoyingness by internet usage level including (**left**) and excluding (**right**) unsure responses.

Focus now turns to respondents' willingness to use the supplemental information label. Figures 61–63 present data related to this. Figure 61 presents data in terms of income level. There was no notable correlation trend between income level and willingness to use. The level of uncertainty declined relatively steadily with increased income level at the lowest three levels; however, no trend was present at higher levels.

Next, in Figure 62, willingness to use data for the supplemental information label is presented in terms of association with political affiliation. As typical, Democrat respondents indicated the lowest uncertainty and also the highest level of usage willingness. Republicans had the second lowest uncertainty and the second highest level of willingness to use.

Figure 63 characterizes respondents' willingness to use the label correlated with internet usage levels. There was a general trend of positive correlation between increased levels of online usage and increased levels of willingness to use the supplemental information label. There was also a small correlation between decreased levels of uncertainty and increased internet usage levels.

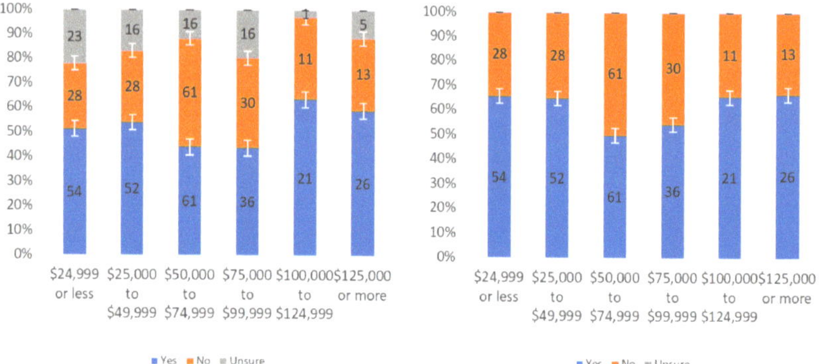

Figure 61. Responses regarding respondents' willingness to review by income level including (**left**) and excluding (**right**) unsure responses.

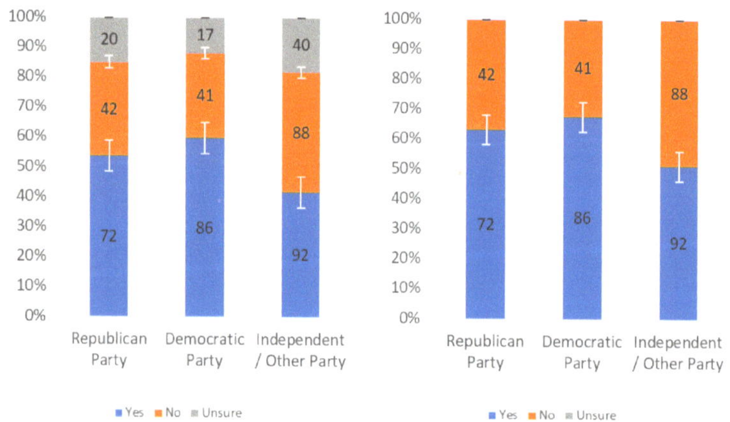

Figure 62. Responses regarding respondents' willingness to review by party affiliation including (**left**) and excluding (**right**) unsure responses.

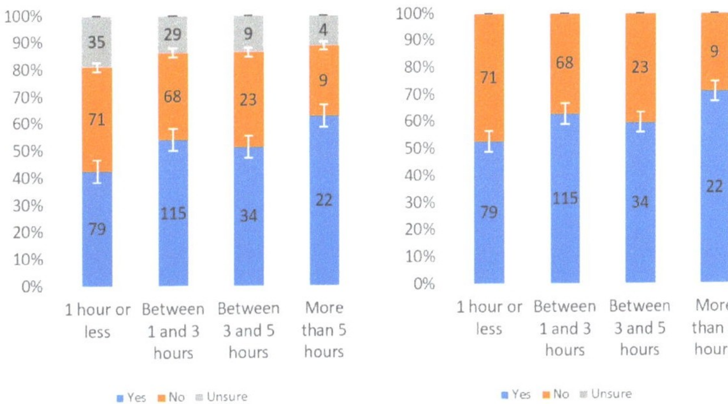

Figure 63. Responses regarding respondents' willingness to review by internet usage level including (**left**) and excluding (**right**) unsure responses.

Now, focus turns to respondents' perceptions of others' willingness to use the supplemental information label. Data related to this is presented in Figures 64–66. Figure 64 presents this in terms of income level. The data show no clear trend between uncertainty and increased income levels. There was also no clear overarching trend visible in the others' willingness level data.

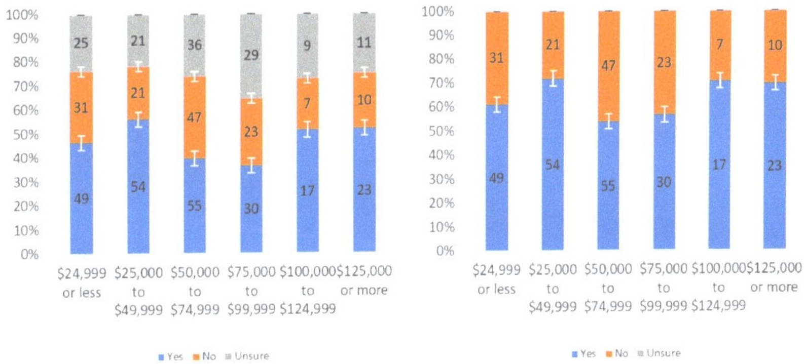

Figure 64. Responses regarding others' willingness to review by income level including (**left**) and excluding (**right**) unsure responses.

Figure 65 shows the others' willingness data correlated with political affiliation. As is typical, Democrats had the lowest level of uncertainty and the highest level of perceived willingness of others to use the labels. Republicans had the second lowest uncertainty levels and the second highest others' willingness levels.

Figure 66 presents the others' willingness to use data in terms of internet usage level. A clear trend of increased perception of others' willingness correlated with increased internet usage was present. The lowest three levels of internet usage also had a trend of decreased uncertainty with increased internet usage.

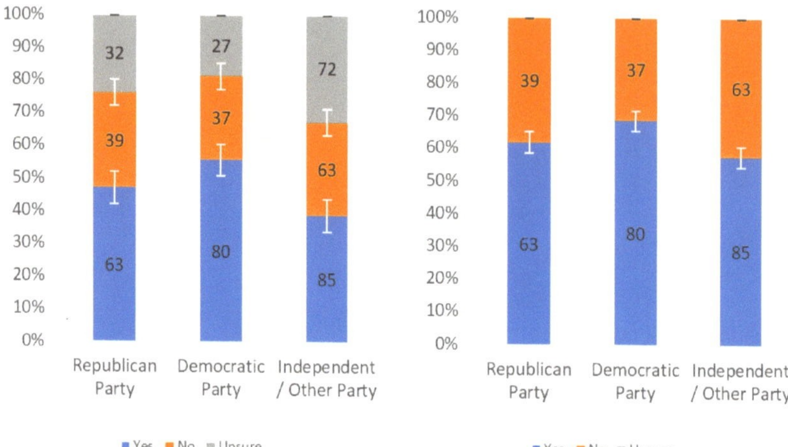

Figure 65. Responses regarding others' willingness to review by party affiliation including (**left**) and excluding (**right**) unsure responses.

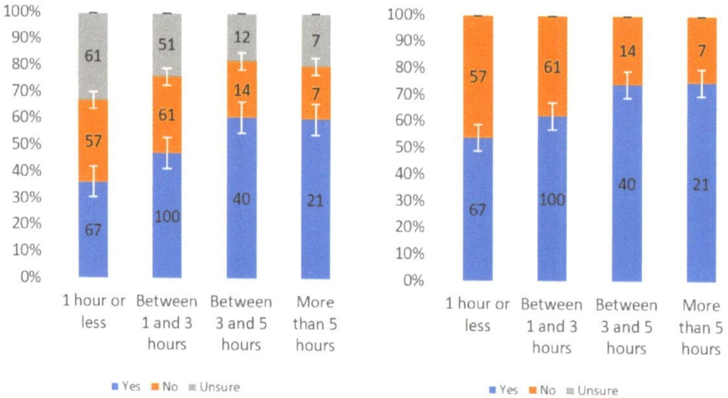

Figure 66. Responses regarding others' willingness to review by internet usage level including (**left**) and excluding (**right**) unsure responses.

Finally, the label's efficacy for judging trustworthiness is assessed. Figures 67–69 present data related to this. Figure 67 presents this data associated with income level. No clear trends were present in either the uncertainty level or usefulness data.

The trustworthiness judging efficacy data are presented in terms of political affiliation in Figure 68. As typical, Democrats reported lower uncertainty and higher levels of perceived trustworthiness judging efficacy. Republicans had the second highest uncertainty and the second highest level of trustworthiness judging efficacy belief. Independents reported the greatest uncertainty and lowest usefulness among the three groups.

Finally, the trustworthiness judging efficacy of the supplemental information label is considered relative to online usage levels. For both the uncertainty and usefulness values, a trend was present. The first trend was decreasing uncertainty with increased usage, and the second trend was an increasing perceived utility for judging trustworthiness that was positively associated with increased internet usage.

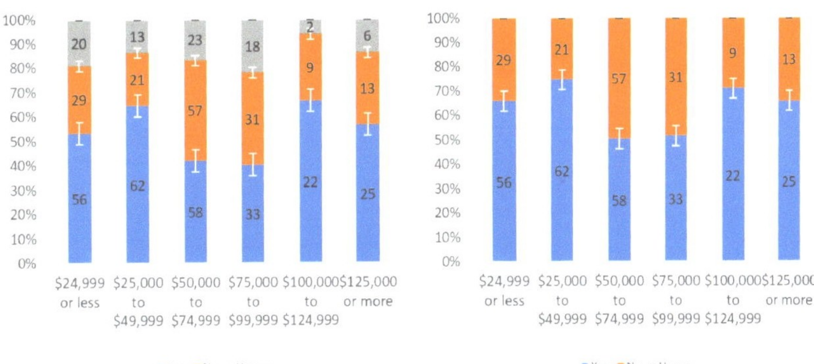

Figure 67. Responses regarding usefulness in judging trustworthiness by income level including (**left**) and excluding (**right**) unsure responses.

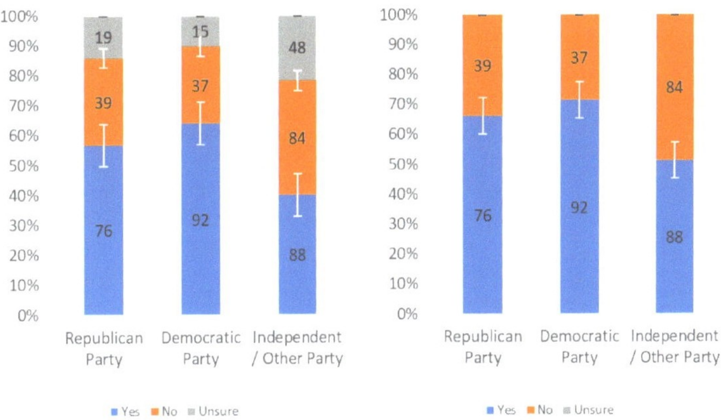

Figure 68. Responses regarding usefulness in judging trustworthiness by party affiliation including (**left**) and excluding (**right**) unsure responses.

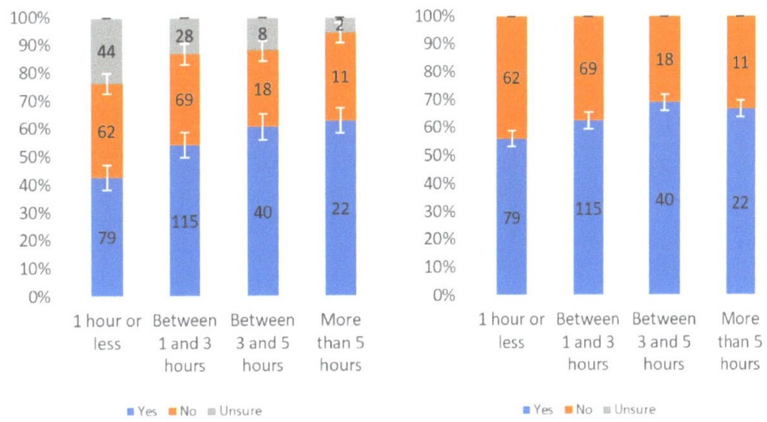

Figure 69. Responses regarding usefulness in judging trustworthiness by internet usage level including (**left**) and excluding (**right**) unsure responses.

7. Analysis and Implications

This section presents comparative analysis of the data presented in the previous sections. First, the trends present in the data, which were previously discussed, are briefly summarized and key patterns are identified. Then, the level of willingness of respondents and respondents' perceived willingness of others to use each label is compared between labels and by income level, political affiliation and online usage levels. Finally, respondents' willingness to use each label is compared to their perceived willingness of others for each label and based on income level, political affiliation and online usage levels.

Table 1 presents the trends present throughout the data for the seven labels in terms of income level. Several overarching trends are present. First, in general, metrics regarding the perception of the labels decreased with increased income. There were two limited exceptions to this. The first was annoyingness, which showed a slight positive association with income level in one instance, no notable trend in two instances, conflicting trends in one instance and a partial negative association in two instances. The second was trustworthiness, which had a marginal positive association in one instance and a partial positive association in another instance (it also had one negative, one partial negative and two no notable associations). Generally, though, the labels were seen less positively with increased income levels (and as more annoying, in at least one case). The number of respondents indicating uncertainty also had a strong negative correlation with increased income. Thus, respondents can be taken to be less supportive of the labels and more certain of this belief with increased income levels. An exception to this rule was seen at the USD 75,000 income level, which, for some labels, showed an increase in support for positive question categories (i.e., helpfulness, self-willingness, others'-willingness and usefulness) relative to the USD 50,000 income level. Similarly, there was a decrease, in some cases, in "annoyance" when shifting from the USD 50,000 to the USD 75,000 income level.

The three labels that showed an at least somewhat positive trend in perceived trust with increasing income were the labels with the most information. Informational label 3 has the extended description of each metric presented and warning label 2 presents the article summary along with the rationale for the warning. The supplemental information label provides a link to a relevant source. This may be indicative of those with higher income levels seeking more information for their decision making. It may be that a label with more information on it (or perhaps linked to from it) than any of the ones analyzed herein would perform the best for higher income groups. This is a potential topic for future work to analyze.

Table 2 compares the trends in the perception of labels based on respondents' political affiliations. Most notable from reviewing these data was that in almost all cases, Democratic Party-affiliated respondents found the labels the most helpful and useful for judging trustworthiness, and they believed that they and others were most likely to use them. In most cases, Democrats found the labels the least annoying or there was a tie for finding them the least annoying. Because of this, the most notable data elements were those where this pattern did not hold. In terms of the metric, there were only two instances of this: independents/other party affiliates indicated others' willingness to use warning labels 1 and 3 at a higher level than Democrats. Similarly, on the uncertainty side, there was a single exception: Republicans had higher certainty for self-willingness for informational label 2. However, even with these two deviations, the pattern of higher support for labels by Democrats is very clear and pronounced.

Table 3, similar to Tables 1 and 2, compares the trends in the perception of labels based on respondents' online usage levels. This data were far more varied than the data in the previous table and were, in some cases, somewhat contradictory in potential meaning. Looking at the metric data, informational label 1 had positive correlations (of various levels) to all metrics except others' willingness to use the label. Notably, the only strong positive correlation was for self-willingness, which increased with online usage levels. However, the slight and partial positives for helpfulness and judging trustworthiness (which aligned with the positive for self-willingness) were at odds with the partial positive for annoyingness. However, these differences are marginal.

Table 1. Trends for label types for income level data.

	Metric	**Uncertainty**
Informational Label 1		
Helpfulness	Two negatives	Partial negative
Annoyingness	Partial negative	Fluctuates
Self-Willingness	Slightly negative	Slightly negative
Others' Willingness	Partial negative	Partial positive
Judging Trustworthiness	Negative	Partial negative
Informational Label 2		
Helpfulness	Two negatives	Not notable
Annoyingness	Slightly positive	Negative
Self-Willingness	Partial negative	Partial negative
Others' Willingness	Not notable	Not notable
Judging Trustworthiness	Partial negative	Not notable
Informational Label 3		
Helpfulness	Conflicting trends	Partial negative
Annoyingness	Conflicting trends	Negative
Self-Willingness	Not notable	Not notable
Others' Willingness	Not notable	Not notable
Judging Trustworthiness	Partial positive	Partial slight negative
Warning Label 1		
Helpfulness	Slightly negative	Slightly negative
Annoyingness	Not notable	Slightly negative
Self-Willingness	Slightly negative	Negative
Others' Willingness	Partial negative	Partial negative
Judging Trustworthiness	Not notable	Negative
Warning Label 2		
Helpfulness	Not notable	Partial negative
Annoyingness	Not notable	Partial negative
Self-Willingness	Not notable	Not notable
Others' Willingness	Not notable	Not notable
Judging Trustworthiness	Marginally Positive	Negative
Warning Label 3 (Blocking)		
Helpfulness	Not notable	Not notable
Annoyingness	Partial negative	Partial negative
Self-Willingness	Partial slight negative	Negative
Others' Willingness	Partial negative	Slightly negative
Judging Trustworthiness	Not notable	Not notable
Supplemental Info. Label		
Helpfulness	Conflicting trends	Partial slight negative
Annoyingness	Partial negative	Partial negative
Self-Willingness	Partial positive	Partial negative
Others' Willingness	Not notable	Partial negative
Judging Trustworthiness	Not notable	Not notable

Table 2. Trends for label types for political affiliation data.

	Metric	Uncertainty
Informational Label 1		
Helpfulness	Democrats most helpful	Democrats most sure
Annoyingness	Effective tie	Democrats slightly surer
Self-Willingness	Democrats most willing	Democrats most sure
Others' Willingness	Democrats most willing	Democrats most sure
Judging Trustworthiness	Democrats most useful	Democrats most sure
Informational Label 2		
Helpfulness	Democrats most helpful	Democrats most sure
Annoyingness	Democrats slightly less annoying	Democrats slightly surer
Self-Willingness	Democrats most willing	Republicans slightly surer
Others' Willingness	Democrats most willing	Democrats most sure
Judging Trustworthiness	Democrats most useful	Democrats most sure
Informational Label 3		
Helpfulness	Democrats most helpful	Democrats slightly surer
Annoyingness	Democrats less annoying	Democrats most sure
Self-Willingness	Democrats most willing	Democrats most sure
Others' Willingness	Democrats most willing	Democrats most sure
Judging Trustworthiness	Democrats most useful	Democrats slightly surer
Warning Label 1		
Helpfulness	Democrats most helpful	Democrats slightly surer
Annoyingness	Effective tie	Democrats very slightly surer
Self-Willingness	Democrats slightly more willing	Democrats slightly surer
Others' Willingness	Independents slightly more willing	Democrats slightly surer
Judging Trustworthiness	Democrats slightly more useful	Democrats most sure
Warning Label 2		
Helpfulness	Democrats most helpful	Democrats most sure
Annoyingness	Democrats less annoying	Democrats most sure
Self-Willingness	Democrats slightly more willing	Democrats most sure
Others' Willingness	Democrats slightly more willing	Democrats most sure
Judging Trustworthiness	Democrats most useful	Democrats slightly surer
Warning Label 3 (Blocking)		
Helpfulness	Democrats most helpful	Democrats very slightly surer
Annoyingness	Effective tie	Democrats very slightly surer
Self-Willingness	Democrats slightly more willing	Democrats slightly surer
Others' Willingness	Independents most willing	Democrats most sure
Judging Trustworthiness	Democrats most useful	Democrats very slightly surer
Supplemental Information Label		
Helpfulness	Democrats most helpful	Democrats surer
Annoyingness	Democrats slightly less annoying	Democrats slightly surer
Self-Willingness	Democrats most willing	Democrats most sure
Others' Willingness	Democrats most willing	Democrats most sure
Judging Trustworthiness	Democrats most useful	Democrats most sure

Table 3. Trends for label types for online usage level data.

	Metric	Uncertainty
Informational Label 1		
Helpfulness	Slightly positive	Not notable
Annoyingness	Partial positive	Partial negative
Self-Willingness	Positive	Not notable
Others' Willingness	Not notable	Partial negative
Judging Trustworthiness	Partial positive	Partial negative
Informational Label 2		
Helpfulness	Slightly positive	Not notable
Annoyingness	Not notable	Not notable
Self-Willingness	Slightly positive	Partial negative
Others' Willingness	Not notable	Partial negative
Judging Trustworthiness	Slightly negative	Slightly positive
Informational Label 3		
Helpfulness	Partial positive	Not notable
Annoyingness	Slightly negative	Not notable
Self-Willingness	Partial negative	Positive
Others' Willingness	Slightly negative	Positive
Judging Trustworthiness	Slightly positive	Negative
Warning Label 1		
Helpfulness	Partial negative	Partial positive
Annoyingness	Not notable	Not notable
Self-Willingness	Not notable	Partial negative
Others' Willingness	Not notable	Slightly negative
Judging Trustworthiness	Negative	Slightly negative
Warning Label 2		
Helpfulness	Not notable	Not notable
Annoyingness	Not notable	Partial negative
Self-Willingness	Partial negative	Partial positive
Others' Willingness	Partial negative	Partial positive
Judging Trustworthiness	Not notable	Negative
Warning Label 3 (Blocking)		
Helpfulness	Partial slight positive	Slightly negative
Annoyingness	Not notable	Negative
Self-Willingness	Partial negative	Partial negative
Others' Willingness	Slightly negative	Negative
Judging Trustworthiness	Not notable	Slightly negative
Supplemental Info. Label		
Helpfulness	Partial positive	Partial negative
Annoyingness	Partial slight negative	Negative
Self-Willingness	Positive	Slightly negative
Others' Willingness	Positive	Partial negative
Judging Trustworthiness	Partial positive	Negative

Informational label 2 is similarly confusing with slight positive correlations between online usage time and helpfulness and self-willingness and a slight negative correlation with judging trustworthiness. Informational label three has similarly conflicting trends with the helpfulness, annoyingness and judging trustworthiness trends suggesting one pattern while both willingness metrics suggest a conflicting one. Again, though, these differences are somewhat marginal due to the slight and partial nature of these trends.

Warning labels 1 and 2 had more consistent trends. In cases where trends were present, label support had a negative correlation with increased online usage. Warning label 3 (the blocking label) returned to conflicting trends, with one of the metrics having a limited positive correlation, two having limited negative correlations and two not exhibiting a trend.

Finally, the supplemental information label showed consistency. All five metrics had trends that aligned.

Looking at the uncertainty levels, most of the labels (except for informational label 1, warning label 3 and the supplemental information label) showed conflicting trends of growing or reducing uncertainty with increased online usage. Note that, for uncertainty, positive for annoyingness was not seen to be at odds with other positive associations, as the uncertainty growth (or decline) would have a similar meaning for all five metrics. Focus now moves on to comparing the different levels of respondents' and respondents' perceptions of others' willingness to use the different labels. Tables 4–6 present these data in terms of income level, political affiliation and online usage levels.

Table 4. Comparison of self and others' willingness to use labels by income level.

	USD 24,999 or Less	USD 25,000–49,999	USD 50,000–74,999	USD 75,000–99,999	USD 100,000–124,999	USD 125,000 or Higher
Informational Label 1						
Self-Willingness	67.9%	62.8%	61.7%	67.6%	56.7%	64.1%
Others' Willingness	67.9%	73.9%	59.2%	71.4%	66.7%	63.3%
Informational Label 2						
Self-Willingness	70.7%	63.4%	59.1%	69.6%	64.5%	70.0%
Others' Willingness	74.0%	71.2%	63.0%	70.2%	86.4%	66.7%
Informational Label 3						
Self-Willingness	65.1%	67.5%	60.8%	68.2%	71.9%	64.1%
Others' Willingness	63.2%	74.0%	52.8%	72.4%	79.2%	61.3%
Warning Label 1						
Self-Willingness	75.3%	74.4%	72.9%	75.0%	71.9%	72.5%
Others' Willingness	73.4%	74.7%	67.9%	80.3%	77.8%	75.7%
Warning Label 2						
Self-Willingness	69.5%	70.6%	65.6%	73.6%	87.1%	70.0%
Others' Willingness	64.4%	78.6%	61.8%	73.2%	84.6%	69.7%
Warning Label 3 (Blocking)						
Self-Willingness	67.1%	65.5%	61.6%	67.6%	54.5%	70.0%
Others' Willingness	63.2%	63.5%	59.4%	72.9%	69.2%	63.9%
Supplemental Information Label						
Self-Willingness	65.9%	65.0%	50.0%	54.5%	65.6%	66.7%
Others' Willingness	61.3%	72.0%	53.9%	56.6%	70.8%	69.7%

Table 4 presents respondents' and respondents' perceptions of others' willingness to use the labels based on respondents' income level. Based on the data presented, warning label 1 was a clear favorite across income levels, with four of the five income levels indicating the highest respondents' wiliness to use this label and three of the five levels having the highest level of others' willingness for this label as well. Notably, the three income levels with respondents indicating that others would prefer an alternate label and the one with respondents themselves indicating that they would prefer an alternate label, use only two other labels: informational label 2 and warning label 2.

While these labels perform the best for given groups, there is also a notable difference, in most cases, between the better performing labels and the underperforming ones. Informational label 1, for example, underperforms warning label 1 by at least 7%, in all cases, and over 10% in several. For the USD 100,000–124,999 income level (where informational label 2 performed the best for others' willingness), it underperformed the best performing label by 20%. Warning label 3 and the supplemental information label also appeared to underperform the best performing label significantly, in most cases (though warning label 3 only slightly underperforms for respondents' willingness for the USD 125,000 or higher group). Notably, while the worst performing labels for each group were less consistent than the best, only four of the labels had worst performing statuses, and all were worst performing for at least two groups. In addition, no label was both a best performer for one group and simultaneously a worst performer for another group.

Given the foregoing, it appears that, in terms of respondents' willingness to use a label, there are clearly preferred labels to select. Despite this, it may still be desirable to support multiple labels to maximize the number of individuals who are willing to use a label (as some may not be willing to use the generally preferred labels).

Table 5. Comparison of self- and others' willingness to use labels by party affiliation.

	Republican Party	Democratic Party	Independent/Other Party
Informational Label 1			
Self-Willingness	51.8%	76.2%	62.8%
Others' Willingness	59.4%	75.2%	64.3%
Informational Label 2			
Self-Willingness	58.8%	75.2%	62.6%
Others' Willingness	64.0%	79.5%	66.7%
Informational Label 3			
Self-Willingness	60.7%	72.2%	63.1%
Others' Willingness	64.4%	71.2%	59.7%
Warning Label 1			
Self-Willingness	70.2%	76.3%	74.5%
Others' Willingness	73.5%	71.8%	75.3%
Warning Label 2			
Self-Willingness	70.2%	74.8%	67.9%
Others' Willingness	66.3%	73.0%	69.3%
Warning Label 3 (Blocking)			
Self-Willingness	64.1%	68.5%	62.2%
Others' Willingness	60.6%	64.7%	66.2%
Supplemental Information Label			
Self-Willingness	63.2%	67.7%	51.1%
Others' Willingness	61.8%	68.4%	57.4%

Table 5 presents respondents' and respondents' perceptions of others' willingness to use the labels based on respondents' political party affiliation. The results for the different political parties are very similar to the income level groups. Warning label 1 is a clear preference, with it being the preferred self-use label for all three groups (tied with warning label 2 for Republicans) and the preferred others' use label for two of the three groups. As with the income level groups, the other two labels that performed best for a group were informational label 2 and warning label 2.

The largest difference between the income level and political affiliation date was the performance of informational label 1 for Democrats. The label was only 0.1% less popular than the best performing label for self-willingness for use. Notably, this label performed well for Democrats and was the worst performing for both self- and others' willingness for use by Republicans. This label clearly had a demonstrable difference in political party affiliation-based perception.

Table 6 presents respondents' willingness and their perceptions of others' willingness, to use the labels based on respondents' online usage level. The results by online usage level have some key similarities to those by income level and party affiliation. Warning label 1, again, performed the best. However, it was principally preferred by those with lower levels of online usage time. The supplemental information label performed, consistently, the worst for users with less than three hours of daily internet usage. For higher levels of use respondents, though, the results were quite different. Informational label 1 was the preferred label for those with more than five hours of daily usage and warning label 2 was the preferred label for those with three to five hours of usage. Warning label 3 was the least preferred for the higher usage level respondents. Notably, the supplemental information label, which was consistently the worst for the lower-usage level respondents, was the best performing for others for one group and just slightly (0.9% lower) less than the best performing for another group.

The data show that there was a demonstrable difference in preference between low-usage and higher-usage level respondents. The higher usage level respondents clearly did not prefer the blocking label. More research will be needed to ascertain whether commonalities between informational label 1, warning labels 1 and 2 and the supplemental information label were responsible for their superior performance for higher-usage level users or if the differences in preference were indicative of true differences in preference between the higher-usage level groups.

Table 6. Comparison of self- and others' willingness to use labels by online usage level.

	1 h or Less	Between 1 and 3 h	Between 3 and 5 h	More than 5 h
Informational Label 1				
Self-Willingness	58.1%	64.5%	69.1%	80.0%
Others' Willingness	64.6%	69.0%	62.0%	72.0%
Informational Label 2				
Self-Willingness	60.8%	67.6%	66.7%	71.0%
Others' Willingness	68.9%	71.1%	69.1%	70.4%
Informational Label 3				
Self-Willingness	62.7%	66.3%	63.8%	73.3%
Others' Willingness	59.8%	69.6%	57.7%	71.4%
Warning Label 1				
Self-Willingness	73.1%	75.3%	70.5%	75.9%
Others' Willingness	71.9%	77.4%	66.7%	75.9%
Warning Label 2				
Self-Willingness	65.6%	71.7%	78.0%	75.0%
Others' Willingness	64.8%	71.8%	72.7%	74.1%
Warning Label 3 (Blocking)				
Self-Willingness	68.2%	63.8%	58.1%	64.5%
Others' Willingness	65.7%	64.7%	61.4%	60.0%
Supplemental Information Label				
Self-Willingness	52.7%	62.8%	59.6%	71.0%
Others' Willingness	54.0%	62.1%	74.1%	75.0%

Finally, focus turns to respondents' comparative perceptions of each label and whether they saw it as most useful for themselves or others. This data are presented in Tables 7–9.

Table 7 presents the data in terms of respondents' income level. There are few patterns in this data, and perhaps the most notable pattern was that the respondents' can be effectively grouped into two groups: those with incomes above and below USD 75,000. Those with incomes below USD 75,000 found informational label 2 most useful for others, consistently, and warning label 3 most useful for themselves. One of the two was a higher-performing label and one was a lower-performing one based on the data in Table 4. However, neither was the highest or lowest performing. The higher income respondents had two labels that were consistently identified as better for others than respondents themselves: warning label 1 and the supplemental informational label, and warning label 2 was identified, consistently, as best for respondents. Warning label 1 was the best performing label overall, and warning label 2 was towards the better performing end of the spectrum. The supplemental information label, conversely, was the poorest performing label.

Given the juxtaposition of the data between Tables 4 and 7, the status of a label as being preferred for respondents own use or others' use is of limited utility. However, the pattern of change at USD 75,000 is an interesting outcome.

Table 7. Do respondents see labels as more valuable to self or others, by income level.

	USD 24,999 or Less	USD 25,000–49,999	USD 50,000–74,999	USD 75,000–99,999	USD 100,000–124,999	USD 125,000 or More
Informational Label 1	Others	Others	Self	Others	Others	Self
Informational Label 2	Others	Others	Others	Others	Others	Self
Informational Label 3	Self	Others	Self	Others	Others	Self
Warning Label 1	Self	Others	Self	Others	Others	Others
Warning Label 2	Self	Others	Self	Self	Self	Self
Warning Label 3 (Blocking)	Self	Self	Self	Others	Others	Self
Supplemental Information Label	Tie	Others	Others	Others	Others	Others

Table 8. Whether respondents saw labels as more valuable to self or others by party affiliation.

	Republican Party	Democratic Party	Independent/Other Party
Informational Label 1	Others	Self	Others
Informational Label 2	Others	Others	Others
Informational Label 3	Others	Self	Self
Warning Label 1	Others	Self	Others
Warning Label 2	Self	Self	Others
Warning Label 3 (Blocking)	Self	Self	Others
Supplemental Informational Label	Self	Others	Others

Table 9. Do respondents see labels as more valuable to self or others, by online usage level.

	1 h or Less	Between 1 and 3 h	Between 3 and 5 h	More than 5 h
Informational Label 1	Others	Others	Self	Self
Informational Label 2	Others	Others	Others	Self
Informational Label 3	Self	Others	Self	Self
Warning Label 1	Self	Others	Self	Others
Warning Label 2	Self	Others	Self	Self
Warning Label 3 (Blocking)	Self	Others	Others	Self
Supplemental Information Label	Others	Self	Others	Others

Table 8 presents the self-versus-others' preference data in terms of respondents' party affiliation. A few interesting patterns are present in this data. Republicans tended to see informational labels as more useful for others, while seeing the warning labels (two of the three) as most useful for themselves. Additionally, they were the only group that found the supplemental information label more useful for their own use. Democrats, on the other hand, seemed to find most labels more useful for their own use. They only identified one informational label and the supplemental information label as being more useful for others. Independent/other party affiliates, on the other hand, had nearly the opposite perspective. They identified six of the seven label types (all except informational label 3) as being more useful for others. This difference in perception may be important when considering how to introduce labels and be indicative of differences in willingness to learn about labels and participate by party affiliation.

Finally, Table 9 presents the self-versus-others' preference data in terms of respondents' online usage level. The patterns in this data are less pronounced than the party affiliation date. Those with the lowest online usage time find the informational labels (excepting number 3) most useful to others and the warning labels most useful to themselves. This may be indicative of the group feeling that they need more explicit guidance due to their lower familiarity with and exposure to the Internet. Those with one to three hours of online usage per day found all labels, except the supplemental information label, to be more useful to others. This group was the only group to find the supplemental information label more useful to themselves than others. An explanation for this could be the group believing that they have enough exposure and experience with internet usage to make their own decisions but requiring the additional support of the extended information to do so.

The higher usage level respondents' responses are more inconsistent. There are three labels that both groups find to be more useful for their own use and one that they find to be more useful to others. Notably, there is a strong transition back to finding labels more useful for self-use between the one to three and 3–5 groups which persists with the more than 5 h group. One interpretation of this is that the lower usage level respondents found the labels useful, as they need the support of them for decision making (and, thus, focus on the warning labels), while the higher usage level respondents see the value in some of the labels for their own use, though there is not a clear label type of preference notable in this data.

8. Conclusions and Future Work

Online content labels are an approach to protecting individuals against the harmful impacts of intentionally deceptive online content without censorship of content creators. They may help prevent the spread of online misinformation and may even increase users' awareness of problematic content through their ongoing use.

To advance the potential future use of online content labeling, this paper presented and analyzed the results and implications of a national survey of consumer perceptions regarding online content labels to ascertain their efficacy. Data were collected from over 500 respondents and analyzed in terms of their key demographics including income level, political party affiliation and online usage level.

The analysis of this data demonstrated a great deal of support for labels, both in general and across various demographic groups. It also demonstrated that some groups had clear preferences for and against certain types of labels. Individuals were also shown to be more or less likely to utilize labels based on key demographic characteristics.

Labels were generally shown to be less well received with increasing income levels. Respondents also indicated greater certainty about their usage decision with higher income levels. The labels that were the best received for those with higher income levels were the ones that made more information available.

Democrats were shown to have a stronger willingness to use labels, in general, and to believe that others would use labels more than Republicans and Independents/other party members. This was true overall and across virtually all label types. However, the first and third warning labels were better received by Independents/other party members than Democrats.

The trends were less clear with regards to online usage levels. The principal trend that was detected, though, for two warning labels was a decline in use with increased online usage.

When looking at preferences, warning label 1 was a strong preference across all income levels for both individuals' own use and use by others. Informational label 2 and warning label 2, though not performing as well as warning label 1, were also well received across income levels. Warning label 1 was also the most popular for use across political affiliations for individuals and others.

Unlike the consistency shown across income levels and political affiliations, differences in a label preference were clear by online usage level. The first warning label was preferred by lower usage groups. However, the label of choice varied among the higher usage groups. The higher usage level groups demonstrated a trend towards being more receptive of labels with extended information on them.

Finally, while individuals' indication of greater usage preference for each level, for both themselves and others, varied by income level and online usage level, notable differences are present between political affiliation groups. Democrats indicated greater preference for all but two of the labels for self-use, while Republicans and Independents/other party members indicated greater preference for the use of labels by others, in most cases.

Knowledge about the demographic groups' preferences and trends can be useful in a number of ways. At the most basic level, computer system operators, users themselves and others can pick the labeling that is most preferred based on the demographics of typical system users. This could also be customized on a per-user basis, informed by the user's demographic characteristics.

Demographic preferences also provide a potential starting point for additional user-specific (or group-specific) customization. They may also provide a starting point for further research into the more specific preferences of particular groups and the development of new and modified types of labels.

The data can also inform decisions regarding the training of groups of user and individual users, allowing focus to be placed on areas that demographic preferences indicate are important. For example, some groups have shown a preference for warning style labels while others have shown a preference for labels with more information (presumably to facilitate the individual making their own informed decision. This type of a preference not only suggests what labels should be presented and suggested to a group of users, but it also has implications regarding what features and capabilities of a labeling system particular demographic groups find most valuable and, thus, how labeling should be presented overall and how training should be presented and focused.

This same knowledge is, thus, inherently useful for product development and feature decision making. Labels that perform well across several groups can be prioritized for implementation over those that are not as well received or as broadly supported.

Author Contributions: Conceptualization, J.S. and M.S.; methodology, J.S. and M.S.; resources, J.S.; writing—original draft preparation, J.S. and M.S.; writing—review and editing, J.S., M.S. and B.F.; project administration, J.S.; funding acquisition, J.S.; visualization, B.F. All authors have read and agreed to the published version of the manuscript.

Funding: Partial support for this work was provided by the NDSU Challey Institute for Global Innovation and Growth.

Institutional Review Board Statement: The study was conducted according to the guidelines of the Declaration of Helsinki and approved by the Institutional Review Board of North Dakota State University (protocol: IRB0003884, approved 23 September 2021).

Informed Consent Statement: Informed consent was obtained from all subjects involved in the study.

Data Availability Statement: A data release, via a data journal publication, is planned once initial analysis of all data is complete.

Acknowledgments: The author are grateful to Jade Kanemitsu, from Qualtrics International Inc., for the management of the data collection process, as well as to Ryan Suttle, Scott Hogan and Rachel Aumaugher, who developed many of the questions that were used in this study during their earlier work (presented in [76]).

Conflicts of Interest: The authors declare no conflict of interest. The funders had no role in the design of the study; in the collection, analyses, or interpretation of data; in the writing of the manuscript, or in the decision to publish the results.

Appendix A

This section presents supporting figures for Section 4. Each figure includes error bars showing the standard error range for the threshold values. Figures A1–A15 present data for the article summary information label (shown in Figure 3). Figures A16–A30 present data for the informational label without article summary (shown in Figure 4). Finally, Figures A31–A45 present data for the informational label with article summary and component score descriptions (shown in Figure 5).

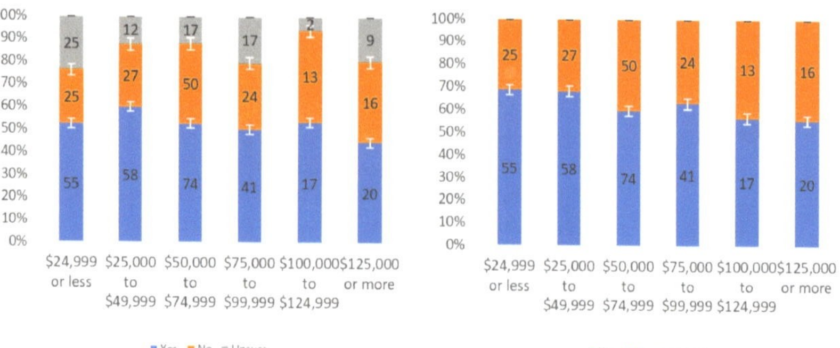

Figure A1. Responses regarding label helpfulness by income level including (**left**) and excluding (**right**) unsure responses.

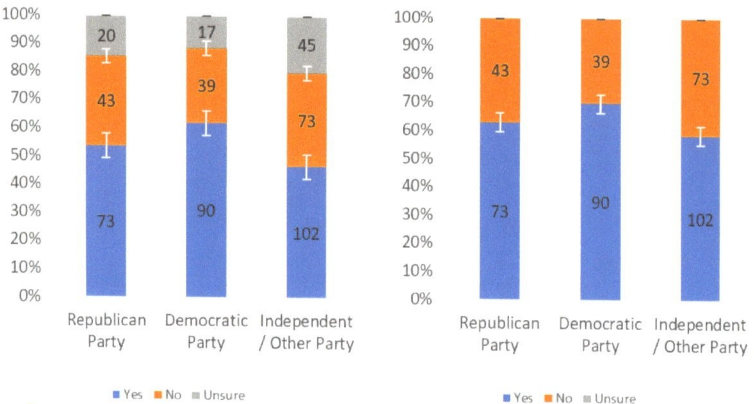

Figure A2. Responses regarding label helpfulness by party affiliation including (**left**) and excluding (**right**) unsure responses.

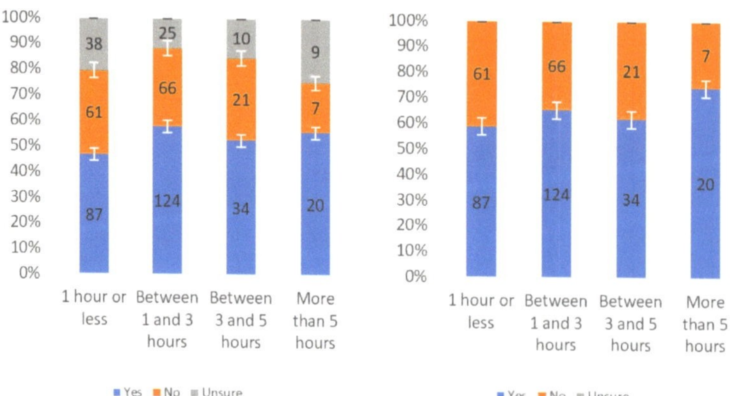

Figure A3. Responses regarding label helpfulness by internet usage level including (**left**) and excluding (**right**) unsure responses.

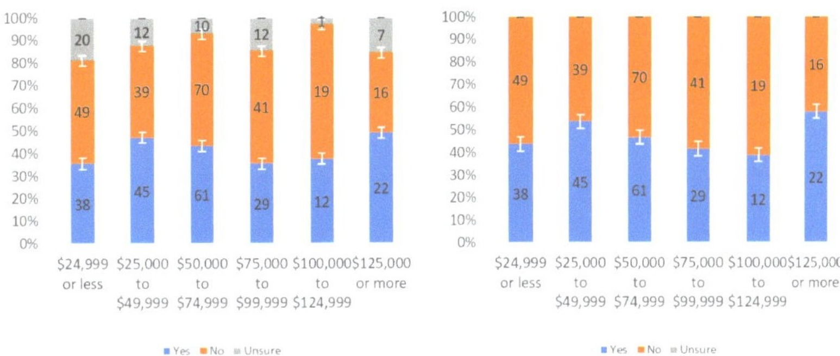

Figure A4. Responses regarding label annoyingness by income level including (**left**) and excluding (**right**) unsure responses.

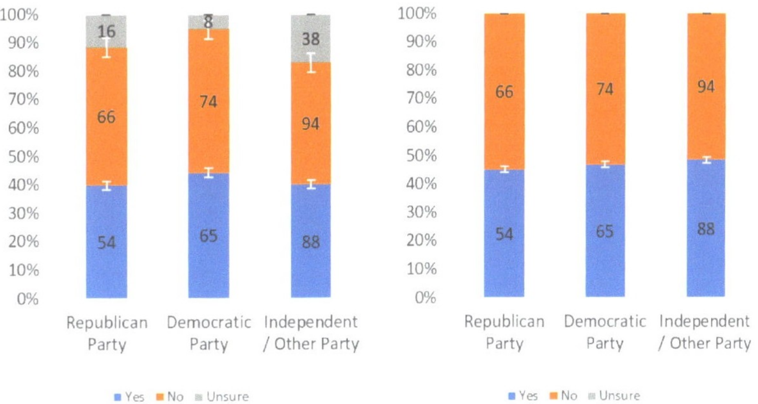

Figure A5. Responses regarding label annoyingness by party affiliation including (**left**) and excluding (**right**) unsure responses.

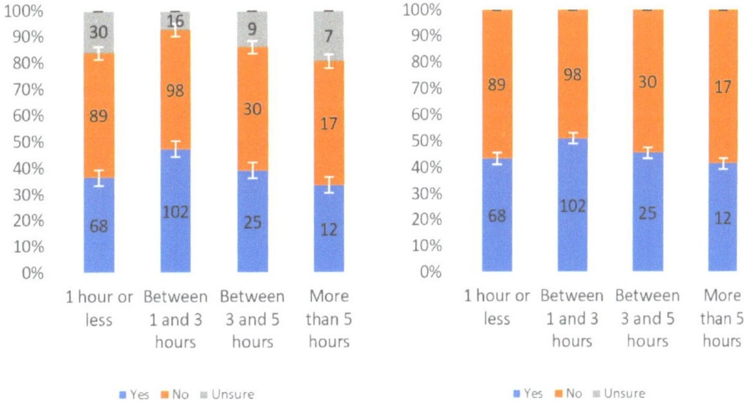

Figure A6. Responses regarding label annoyingness by internet usage level including (**left**) and excluding (**right**) unsure responses.

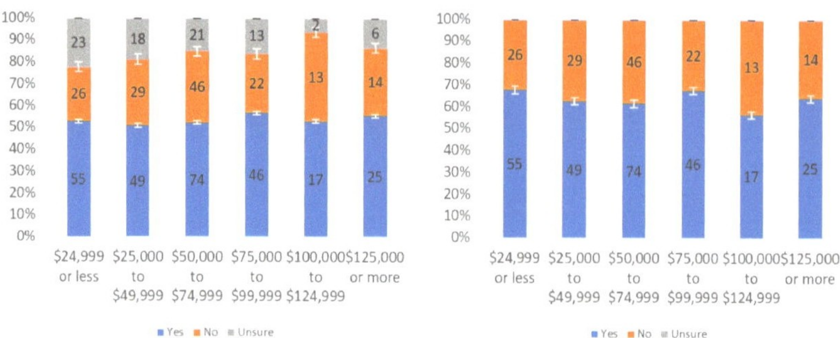

Figure A7. Responses regarding respondents' willingness to review by income level including (**left**) and excluding (**right**) unsure responses.

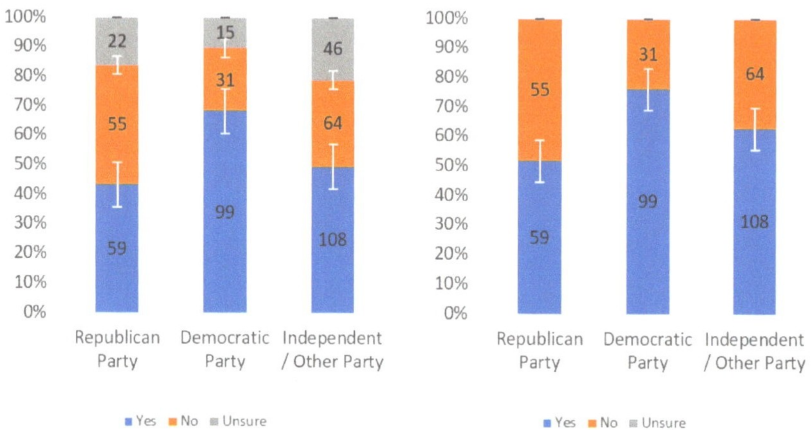

Figure A8. Responses regarding respondents' willingness to review by party affiliation including (**left**) and excluding (**right**) unsure responses.

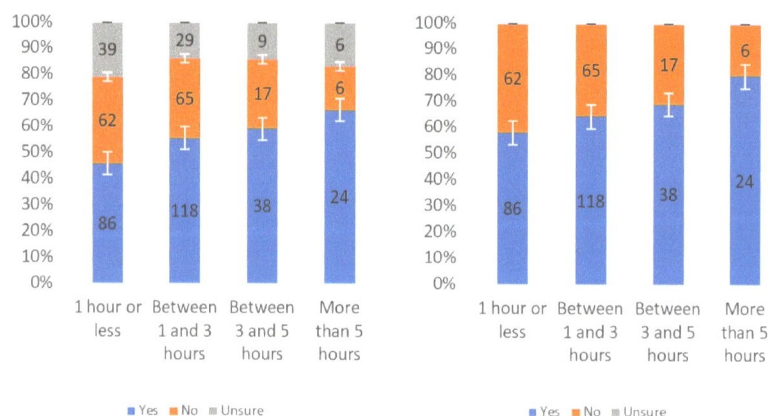

Figure A9. Responses regarding respondents' willingness to review by internet usage level including (**left**) and excluding (**right**) unsure responses.

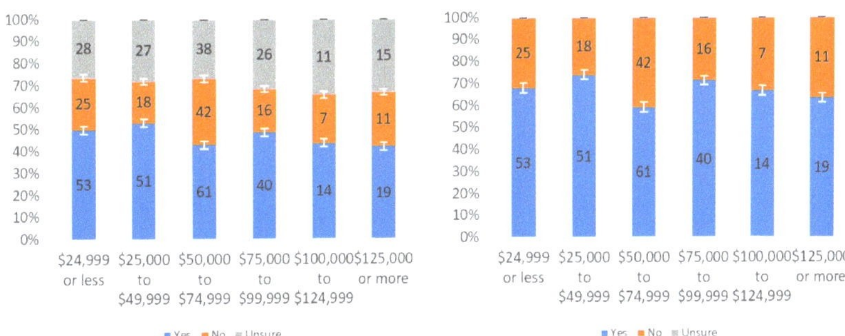

Figure A10. Responses regarding others' willingness to review by income level including (**left**) and excluding (**right**) unsure responses.

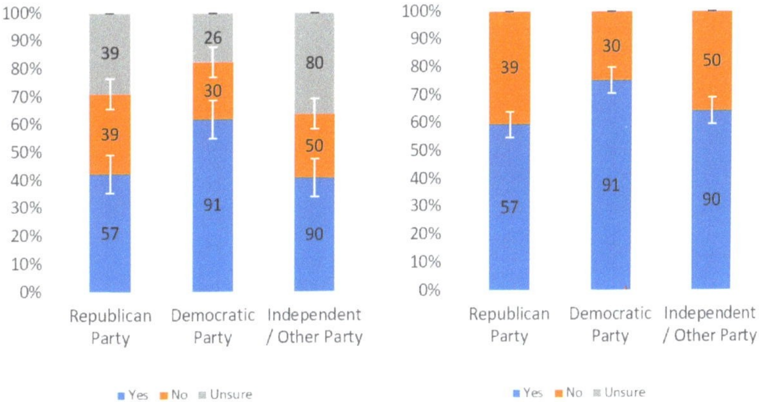

Figure A11. Responses regarding others' willingness to review by party affiliation including (**left**) and excluding (**right**) unsure responses.

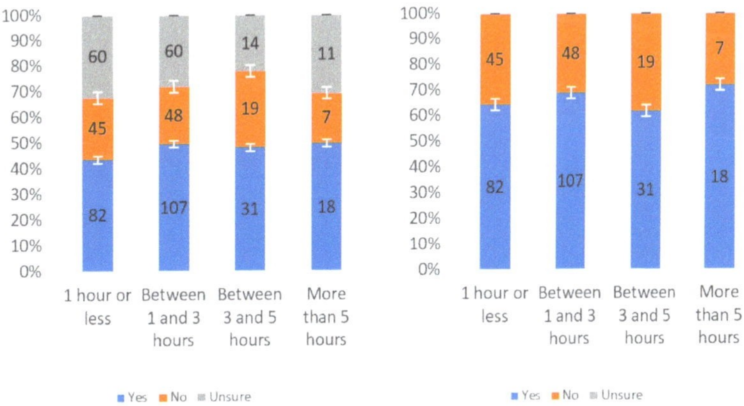

Figure A12. Responses regarding others' willingness to review by internet usage level including (**left**) and excluding (**right**) unsure responses.

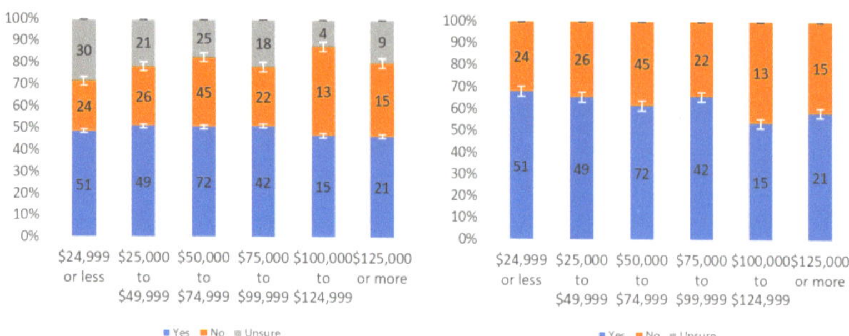

Figure A13. Responses regarding usefulness in judging trustworthiness by income level including (**left**) and excluding (**right**) unsure responses.

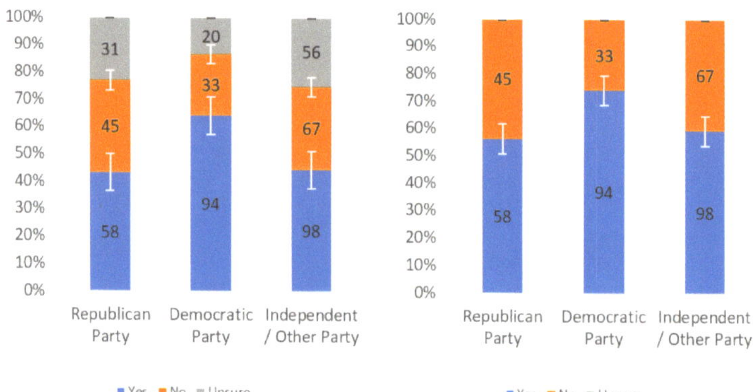

Figure A14. Responses regarding usefulness in judging trustworthiness by party affiliation including (**left**) and excluding (**right**) unsure responses.

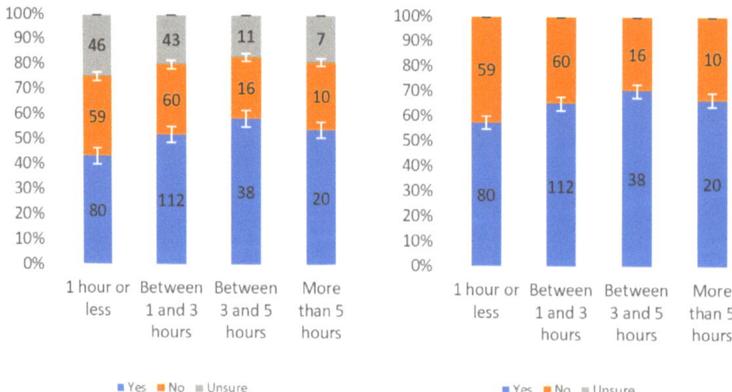

Figure A15. Responses regarding usefulness in judging trustworthiness by internet usage level including (**left**) and excluding (**right**) unsure responses.

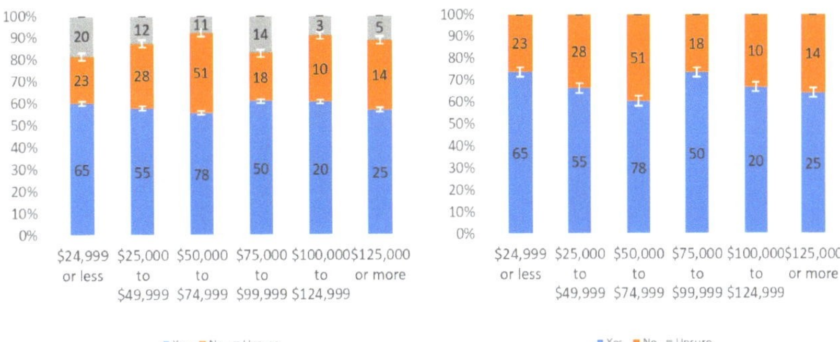

Figure A16. Responses regarding label helpfulness by income level including (**left**) and excluding (**right**) unsure responses.

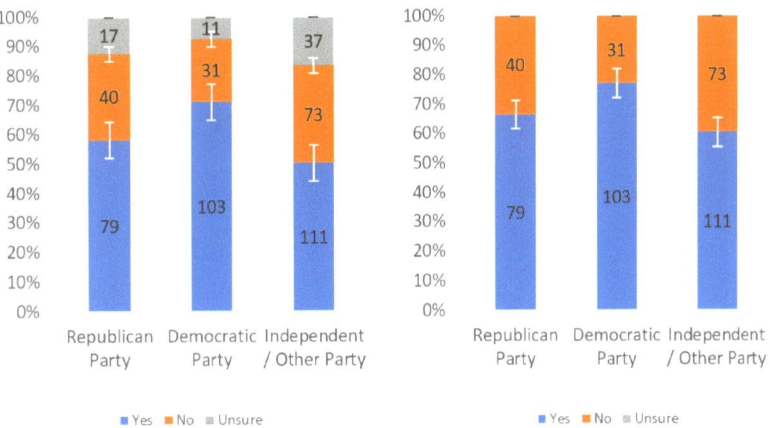

Figure A17. Responses regarding label helpfulness by party affiliation including (**left**) and excluding (**right**) unsure responses.

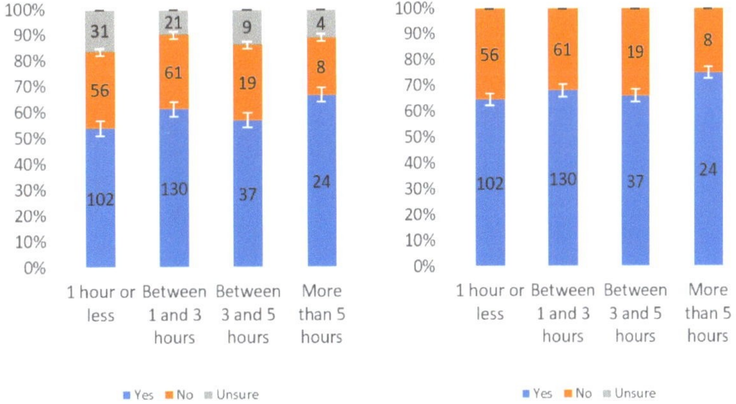

Figure A18. Responses regarding label helpfulness by internet usage level including (**left**) and excluding (**right**) unsure responses.

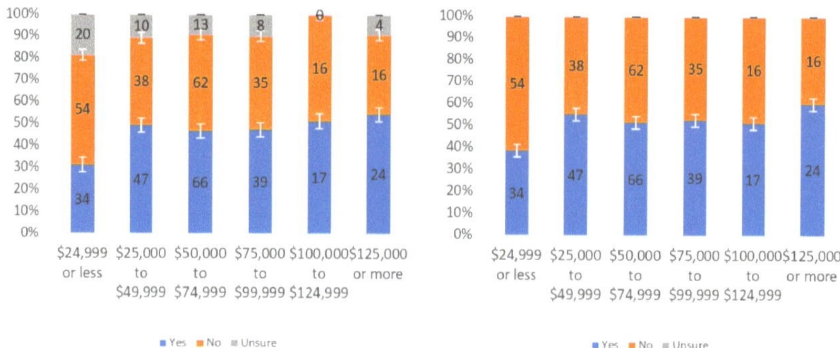

Figure A19. Responses regarding label annoyingness by income level including (**left**) and excluding (**right**) unsure responses.

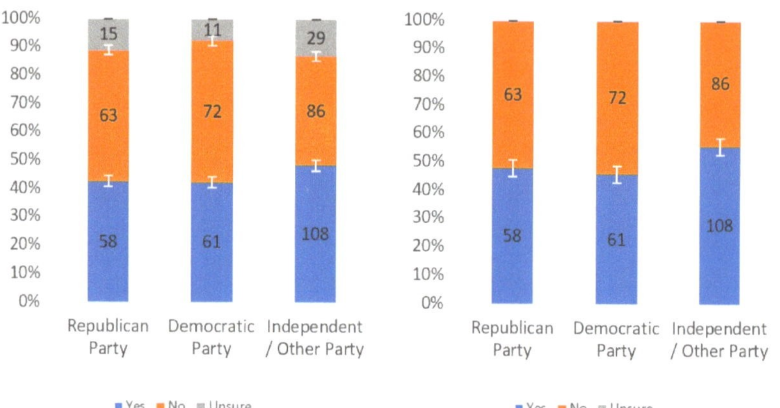

Figure A20. Responses regarding label annoyingness by party affiliation including (**left**) and excluding (**right**) unsure responses.

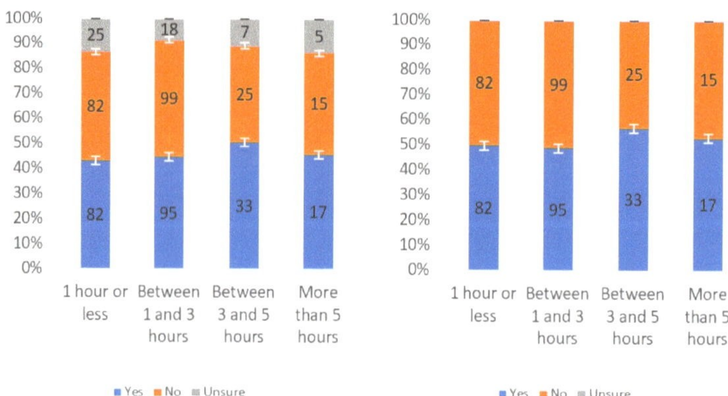

Figure A21. Responses regarding label annoyingness by internet usage level including (**left**) and excluding (**right**) unsure responses.

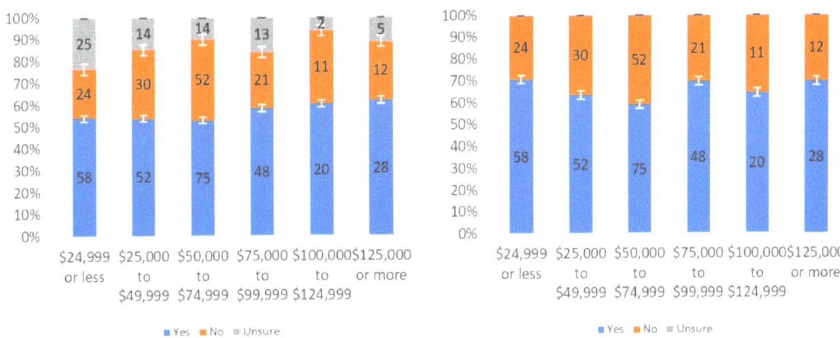

Figure A22. Responses regarding respondents' willingness to review by income level including (**left**) and excluding (**right**) unsure responses.

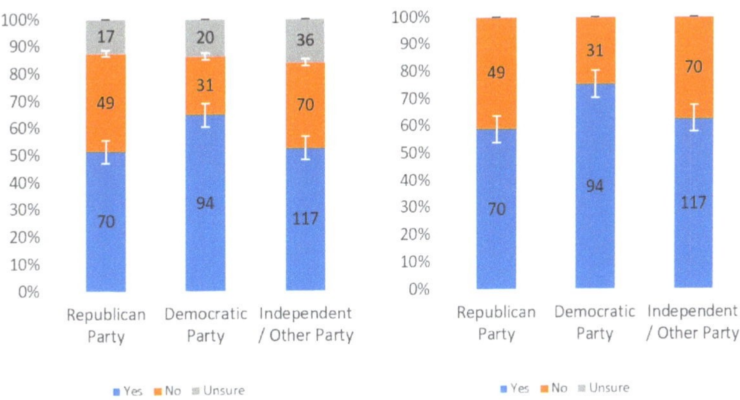

Figure A23. Responses regarding respondents' willingness to review by party affiliation including (**left**) and excluding (**right**) unsure responses.

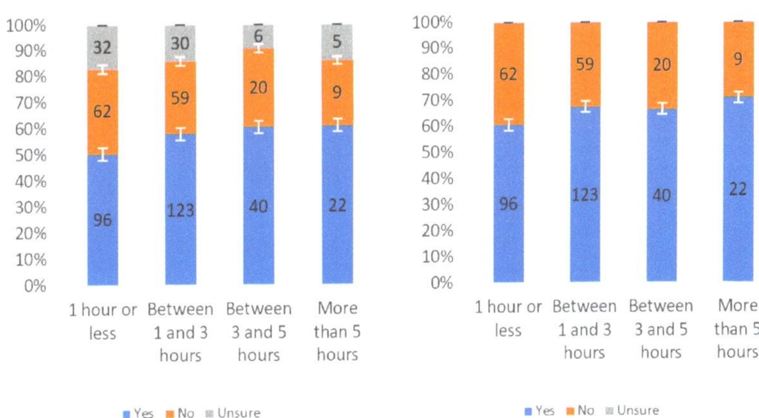

Figure A24. Responses regarding respondents' willingness to review by internet usage level including (**left**) and excluding (**right**) unsure responses.

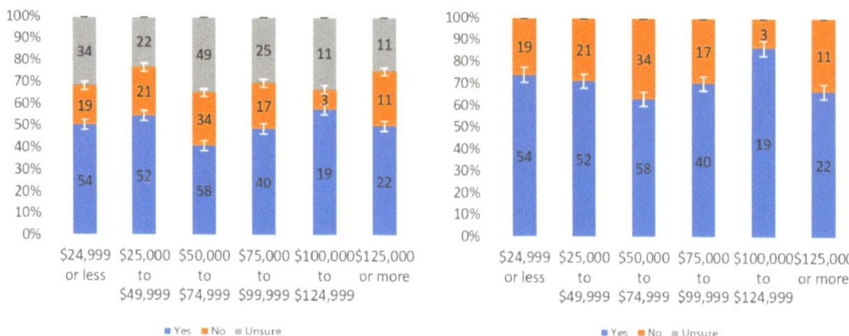

Figure A25. Responses regarding others' willingness to review by income level including (**left**) and excluding (**right**) unsure responses.

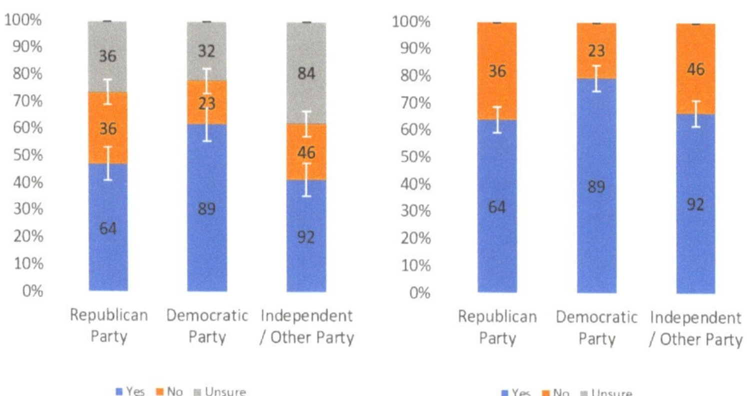

Figure A26. Responses regarding others' willingness to review by party affiliation including (**left**) and excluding (**right**) unsure responses.

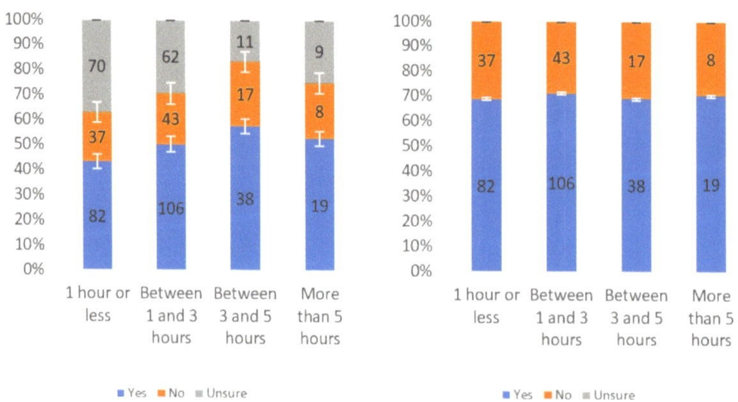

Figure A27. Responses regarding others' willingness to review by internet usage level including (**left**) and excluding (**right**) unsure responses.

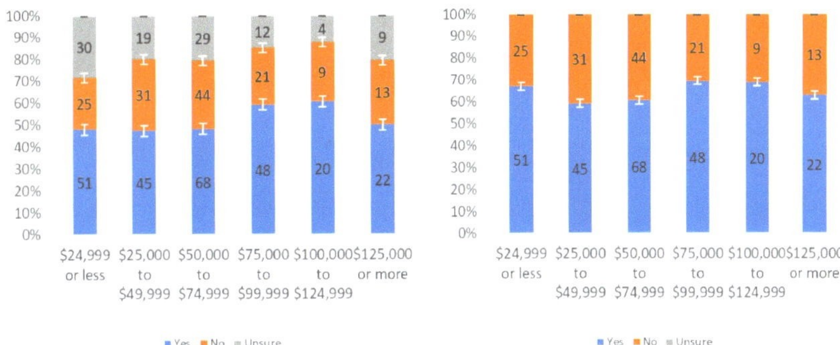

Figure A28. Responses regarding usefulness in judging trustworthiness by income level including (**left**) and excluding (**right**) unsure responses.

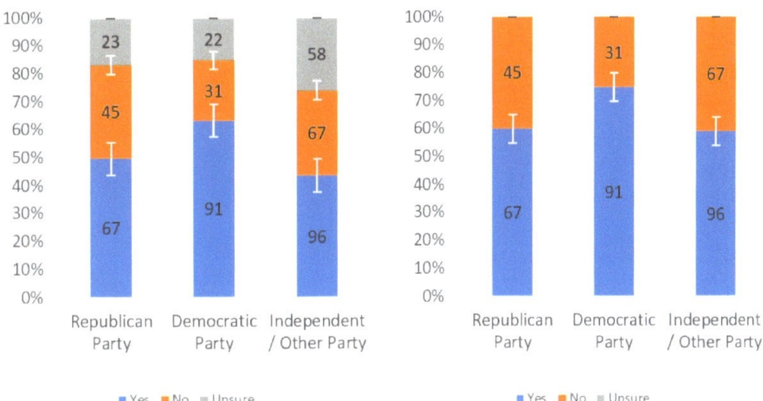

Figure A29. Responses regarding usefulness in judging trustworthiness by party affiliation including (**left**) and excluding (**right**) unsure responses.

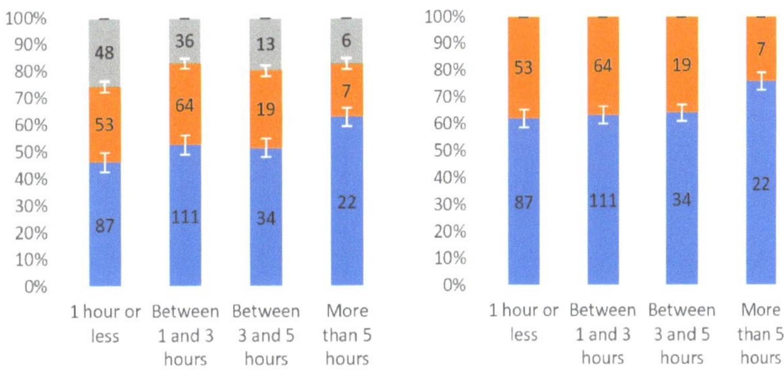

Figure A30. Responses regarding usefulness in judging trustworthiness by internet usage level including (**left**) and excluding (**right**) unsure responses.

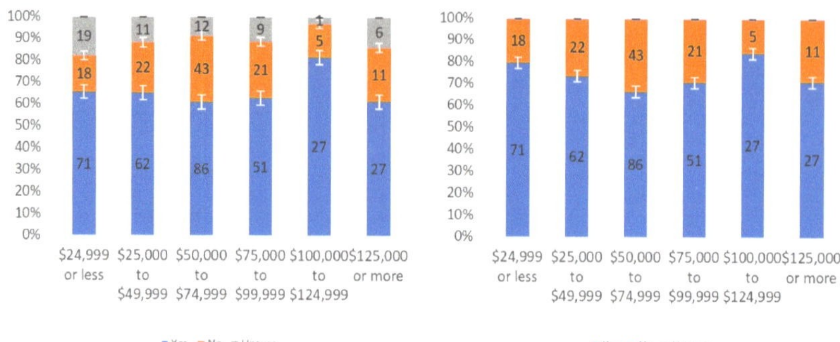

Figure A31. Responses regarding label helpfulness by income level including (**left**) and excluding (**right**) unsure responses.

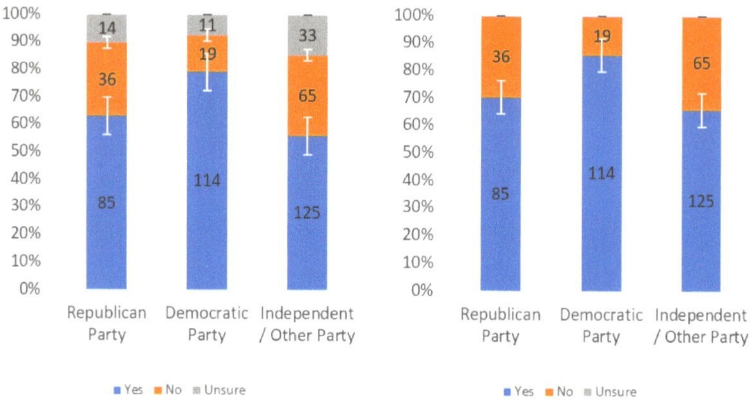

Figure A32. Responses regarding label helpfulness by party affiliation including (**left**) and excluding (**right**) unsure responses.

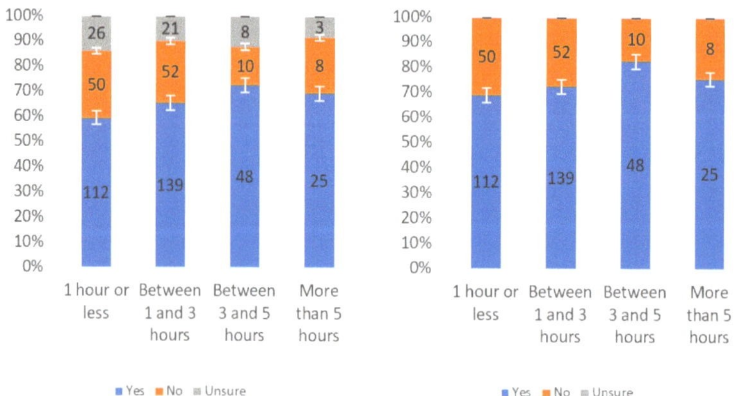

Figure A33. Responses regarding label helpfulness by internet usage level including (**left**) and excluding (**right**) unsure responses.

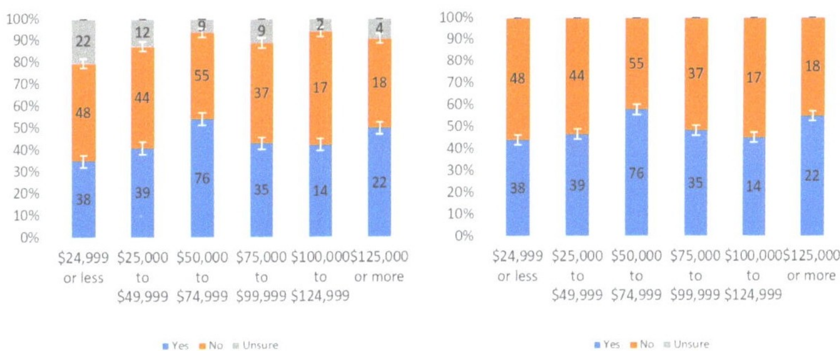

Figure A34. Responses regarding label annoyingness by income level including (**left**) and excluding (**right**) unsure responses.

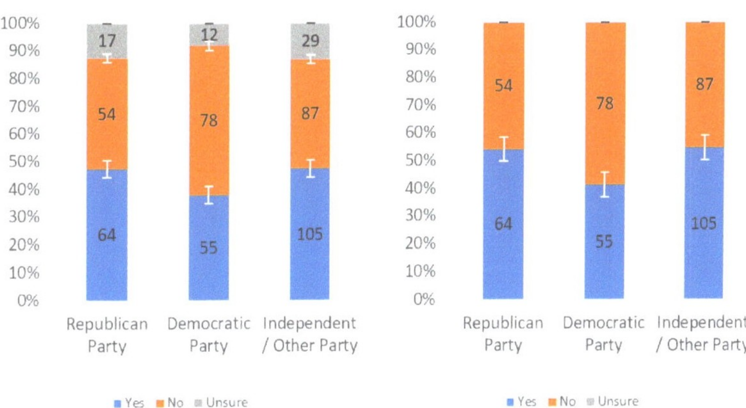

Figure A35. Responses regarding label annoyingness by party affiliation including (**left**) and excluding (**right**) unsure responses.

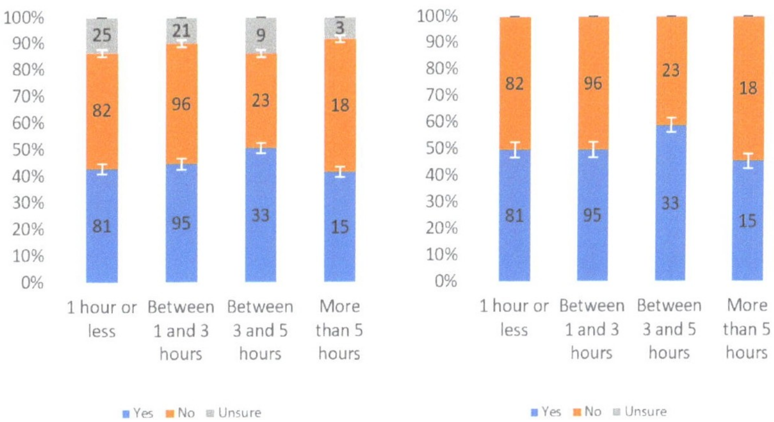

Figure A36. Responses regarding label annoyingness by internet usage level including (**left**) and excluding (**right**) unsure responses.

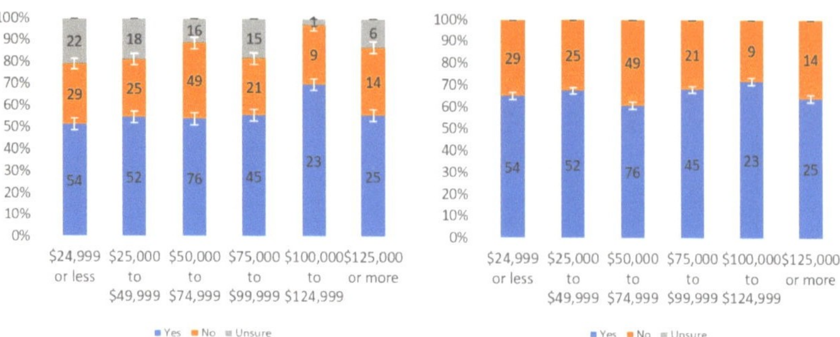

Figure A37. Responses regarding respondents' willingness to review by income level including (**left**) and excluding (**right**) unsure responses.

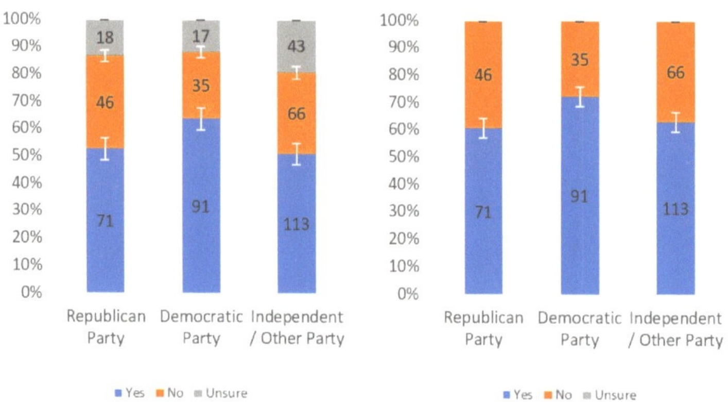

Figure A38. Responses regarding respondents' willingness to review by party affiliation including (**left**) and excluding (**right**) unsure responses.

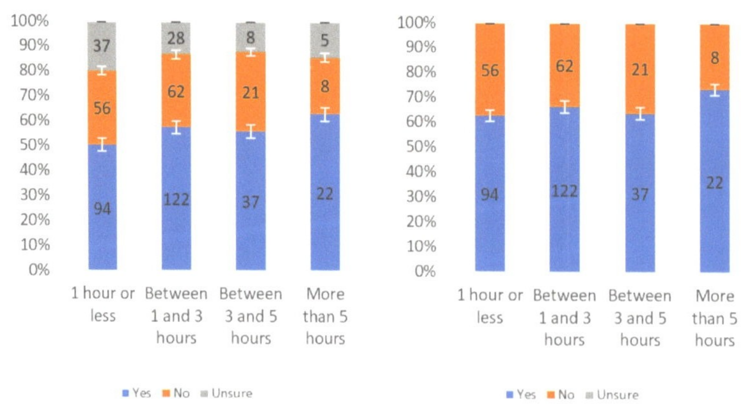

Figure A39. Responses regarding respondents' willingness to review by internet usage level including (**left**) and excluding (**right**) unsure responses.

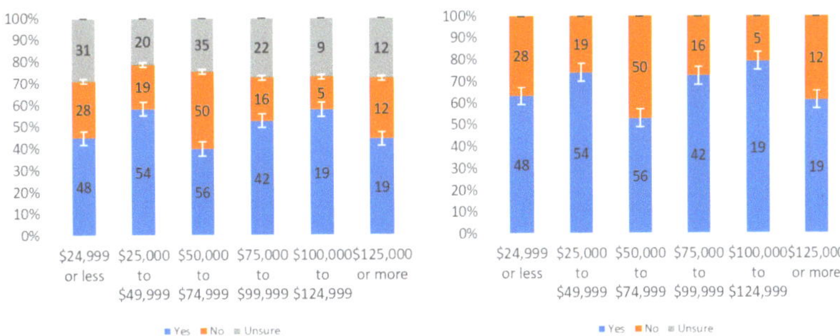

Figure A40. Responses regarding others' willingness to review by income level including (**left**) and excluding (**right**) unsure responses.

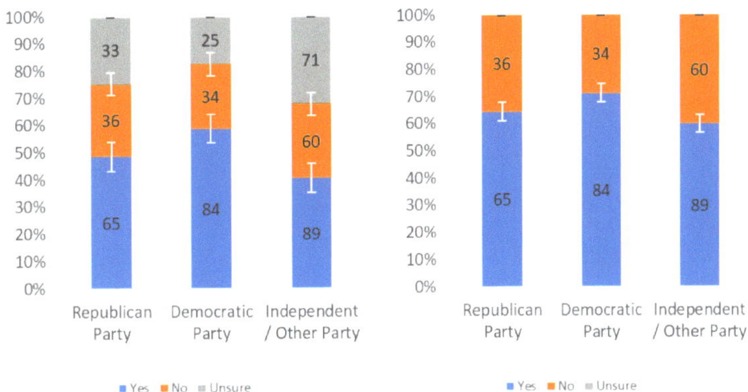

Figure A41. Responses regarding others' willingness to review by political affiliation including (**left**) and excluding (**right**) unsure responses.

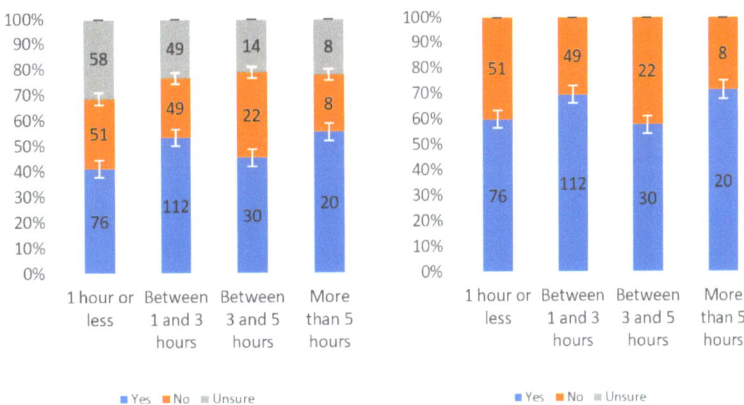

Figure A42. Responses regarding others' willingness to review by internet usage level including (**left**) and excluding (**right**) unsure responses.

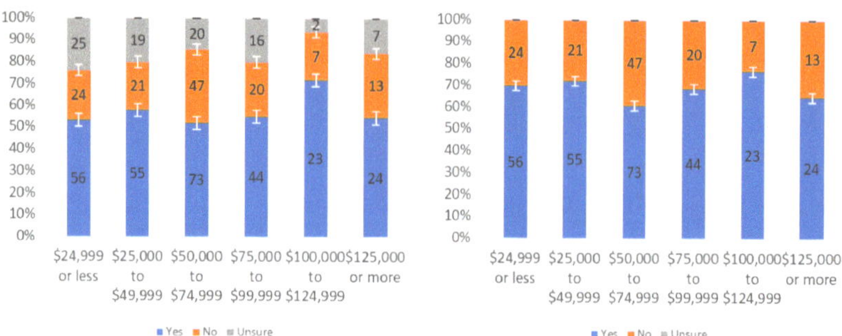

Figure A43. Responses regarding usefulness in judging trustworthiness by income level including (**left**) and excluding (**right**) unsure responses.

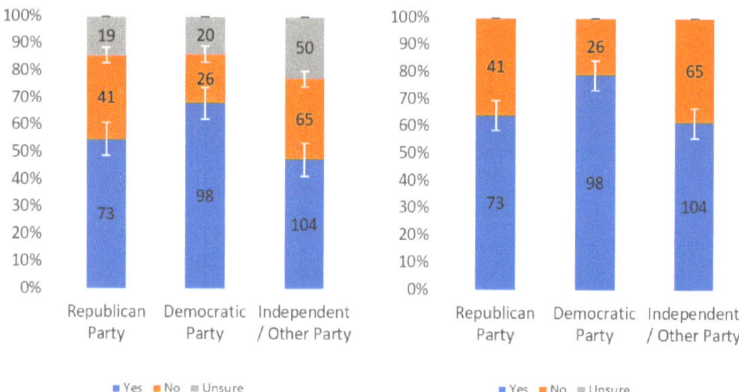

Figure A44. Responses regarding usefulness in judging trustworthiness by party affiliation including (**left**) and excluding (**right**) unsure responses.

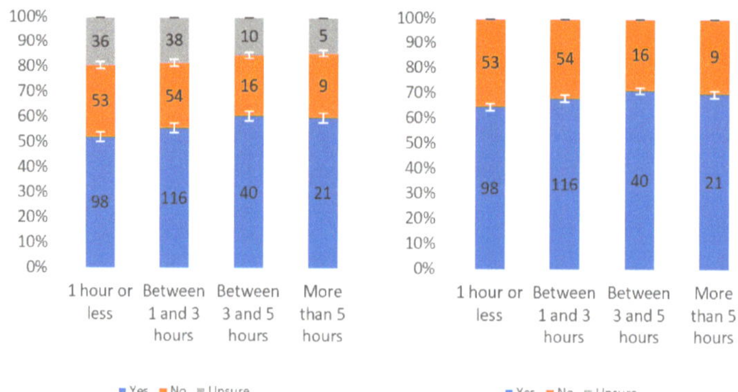

Figure A45. Responses regarding usefulness in judging trustworthiness by internet usage level including (**left**) and excluding (**right**) unsure responses.

References

1. Cunha, E.; Magno, G.; Caetano, J.; Teixeira, D.; Almeida, V. Fake News as We Feel It: Perception and Conceptualization of the Term "Fake News" in the Media. In *Social Informatics*; Lecture Notes in Computer Science; Springer: Cham, Switzerland, 2018; Volume 11185, pp. 151–166. [CrossRef]
2. Tong, C.; Gill, H.; Li, J.; Valenzuela, S.; Rojas, H. "Fake News Is Anything They Say!"—Conceptualization and Weaponization of Fake News among the American Public. *Mass Commun. Soc.* **2020**, *23*, 755–778. [CrossRef]

3. Bastos, M.T.; Mercea, D. The Brexit Botnet and User-Generated Hyperpartisan News. *Soc. Sci. Comput. Rev.* **2017**, *37*, 38–54. [CrossRef]

4. McGaughey, E. Could Brexit be Void? *King's Law J.* **2018**, *29*, 331–343. [CrossRef]

5. Lee, T. The global rise of "fake news" and the threat to democratic elections in the USA. *Public Adm. Policy* **2019**, *22*, 15–24. [CrossRef]

6. Griffiths, J. *The Great Firewall of China: How to Build and Control an Alternative Version of the Internet*, 2nd ed.; Zed Books: London, UK, 2021.

7. Silva, R.M.; Santos, R.L.S.; Almeida, T.A.; Pardo, T.A.S. Towards automatically filtering fake news in Portuguese. *Expert Syst. Appl.* **2020**, *146*, 113199. [CrossRef]

8. Collins, B.; Hoang, D.T.; Nguyen, N.T.; Hwang, D. Trends in combating fake news on social media—A survey. *J. Inf. Telecommun.* **2020**, *5*, 247–266. [CrossRef]

9. Spradling, M.; Straub, J.; Strong, J. Protection from 'Fake News': The Need for Descriptive Factual Labeling for Online Content. *Futur. Internet* **2021**, *13*, 142. [CrossRef]

10. Ott, B. Some Good News about the News: 5 Reasons Why 'Fake' News is Better than Fox 'News'—Flow. *Flow* **2005**, *2*. Available online: https://www.flowjournal.org/2005/06/news-fox-television-reception-the-daily-show-jon-stewart/ (accessed on 8 May 2022).

11. Kim, S. All the Times People Were Fooled by The Onion. Available online: https://abcnews.go.com/International/times-people-fooled-onion/story?id=31444478 (accessed on 4 February 2022).

12. Saez-Trumper, D. Fake Tweet Buster: A Webtool to Identify Users Promoting Fake News on Twitter. In Proceedings of the 25th ACM Conference on Hypertext and Social Media (HT'14), Santiago, Chile, 1–4 September 2014.

13. Grinberg, N.; Joseph, K.; Friedland, L.; Swire-Thompson, B.; Lazer, D. Fake news on Twitter during the 2016 U.S. presidential election. *Science* **2019**, *363*, 374–378. [CrossRef]

14. Lazer, D.M.J.; Baum, M.A.; Benkler, Y.; Berinsky, A.J.; Greenhill, K.M.; Menczer, F.; Metzger, M.J.; Nyhan, B.; Pennycook, G.; Rothschild, D.; et al. The science of fake news. *Science* **2018**, *3*, 1094–1096. [CrossRef]

15. Bovet, A.; Makse, H.A. Influence of fake news in Twitter during the 2016 US presidential election. *Nat. Commun.* **2019**, *10*, 7. [CrossRef]

16. Shearer, E.; Matsa, K.E. News Use Across Social Media Platforms 2018. Available online: https://www.pewresearch.org/journalism/2018/09/10/news-use-across-social-media-platforms-2018/ (accessed on 21 September 2021).

17. Fatilua, J. Who trusts social media? *Comput. Hum. Behav.* **2018**, *81*, 303–315. [CrossRef]

18. Balmas, M. When Fake News Becomes Real: Combined Exposure to Multiple News Sources and Political Attitudes of Inefficacy, Alienation, and Cynicism. *Commun. Res.* **2014**, *41*, 430–454. [CrossRef]

19. Kang, C.; Goldman, A. In Washington Pizzeria Attack, Fake News Brought Real Guns. *New York Times* **2016**, *5*, A1.

20. Haithcox-Dennis, M. Reject, Correct, Redirect: Using Web Annotation to Combat Fake Health Information—A Commentary. *Am. J. Health Educ.* **2018**, *49*, 206–209. [CrossRef]

21. Zhou, X.; Zafarani, R. A Survey of Fake News: Fundamental Theories, Detection Methods, and Opportunities. *ACM Comput. Surv.* **2020**, *53*, 109. [CrossRef]

22. Tandoc, E.C.; Lim, W.; Ling, R. Digital Journalism Defining "Fake News" A typology of scholarly definitions. *Digit. Journal.* **2018**, *6*, 137–153. [CrossRef]

23. Fuhr, N.; Giachanou, A.; Grefenstette, G.; Gurevych, I.; Hanselowski, A.; Jarvelin, K.; Jones, R.; Liu, Y.; Mothe, J.; Nejdl, W.; et al. An Information Nutritional Label for Online Documents. *ACM SIGIR Forum* **2018**, *51*, 46–66. [CrossRef]

24. Hammond, D. Health warning messages on tobacco products: A review. *Tob. Control* **2011**, *20*, 327–337. [CrossRef]

25. Lomeli, N.; Funke, D. Fact check: Cigarette warning labels in US haven't changed since 1984. *USA Today.* 2022. Available online: https://www.usatoday.com/story/news/factcheck/2022/01/27/fact-check-australias-cigarette-package-warning-labels-not-new/6513681001/ (accessed on 8 May 2022).

26. Hiilamo, H.; Crosbie, E.; Glantz, S.A. The evolution of health warning labels on cigarette packs: The role of precedents, and tobacco industry strategies to block diffusion. *Tob. Control* **2014**, *23*, e2. [CrossRef]

27. U.S. Federal Trade Commission Federal Cigarette Labeling and Advertising Act. Available online: https://www.ftc.gov/enforcement/statutes/federal-cigarette-labeling-advertising-act (accessed on 1 March 2022).

28. Hensley, S. FDA Unveils Graphic Cigarette Labels. NPR Website. 2011. Available online: https://www.npr.org/sections/health-shots/2011/06/21/137316580/be-warned-fda-unveils-graphic-cigarette-labels (accessed on 8 May 2022).

29. CBS News Judge Blocks FDA Requirement for Graphic Tobacco Warning Labels. Available online: https://www.cbsnews.com/news/judge-blocks-fda-requirement-for-graphic-tobacco-warning-labels/ (accessed on 1 March 2022).

30. Ingram, D.; Yukhananov, A.U.S. Court Strikes Down Graphic Warnings on Cigarettes. Available online: https://www.reuters.com/article/us-usa-cigarettes-labels/u-s-court-strikes-down-graphic-warnings-on-cigarettes-idUSBRE87N0NL20120824 (accessed on 1 March 2022).

31. U.S. Food & Drug Administration. FDA Proposes New Required Health Warnings with Color Images for Cigarette Packages and Advertisements to Promote Greater Public Understanding of Negative Health Consequences of Smoking. Available online: https://www.fda.gov/news-events/press-announcements/fda-proposes-new-required-health-warnings-color-images-cigarette-packages-and-advertisements-promote (accessed on 1 March 2022).

32. FDA Label Imaegs. Available online: https://web.archive.org/web/20120302084657/http://www.fda.gov/downloads/TobaccoProducts/Labeling/CigaretteWarningLabels/UCM259974.zip (accessed on 1 March 2022).
33. Craver, R. Tobacco Manufacturers Gain Three More Months before Graphic-Warning Labels Required on Cigarette Packs | Local | Journalnow.com. Available online: https://journalnow.com/business/local/tobacco-manufacturers-gain-three-more-months-before-graphic-warning-labels-required-on-cigarette-packs/article_fd8915b6-8f43-11ec-aad6-2f790b9bdb5a.html (accessed on 1 March 2022).
34. U.S. Food & Drug Administration. Cigarette Labeling and Health Warning Requirements | FDA. Available online: https://www.fda.gov/tobacco-products/labeling-and-warning-statements-tobacco-products/cigarette-labeling-and-health-warning-requirements (accessed on 1 March 2022).
35. Baptista, J.P.; Gradim, A. Understanding Fake News Consumption: A Review. *Soc. Sci.* **2020**, *9*, 185. [CrossRef]
36. Braun, J.A.; Eklund, J.L. Fake News, Real Money: Ad Tech Platforms, Profit-Driven Hoaxes, and the Business of Journalism. *Digit. J.* **2019**, *7*, 1–21. [CrossRef]
37. Hoek, J.; Wilson, N.; Allen, M.; Edwards, R.; Thomson, G.; Li, J. Lessons from New Zealand's introduction of pictorial health warnings on tobacco packaging. *Bull. World Health Organ.* **2010**, *88*, 861–866. [CrossRef] [PubMed]
38. Rostron, A. Pragmatism, Paternalism, and the Constitutional Protection of Commercial Speech. *Vt. Law Rev.* **2012**, *37*, 527.
39. Motion Picture Association Inc.; National Association of Theatre Owners Inc. *Classification and Rating Rules*; Sherman Oaks, CA, USA, 2020. Available online: https://www.filmratings.com/Content/Downloads/rating_rules.pdf (accessed on 8 May 2022).
40. WELCOME TO FilmRatings.com. Available online: https://www.filmratings.com/ (accessed on 1 February 2020).
41. The V-Chip: Options to Restrict What Your Children Watch on TV | Federal Communications Commission. Available online: https://www.fcc.gov/consumers/guides/v-chip-putting-restrictions-what-your-children-watch (accessed on 1 February 2020).
42. Harrington, R. Record Industry Unveils Lyrics Warning Label. Available online: https://www.washingtonpost.com/archive/lifestyle/1990/05/10/record-industry-unveils-lyrics-warning-label/6fc30515-ac8a-4e5d-9abd-a06a34cb54f2/ (accessed on 28 February 2022).
43. U.S. Federal Bureau of Investigation FBI Anti-Piracy Warning Seal. Available online: https://www.fbi.gov/investigate/white-collar-crime/piracy-ip-theft/fbi-anti-piracy-warning-seal (accessed on 1 March 2022).
44. United States of America. United States Constitution, First Amendment. In Proceedings of the First Congress of the United States, New York City, NY, USA,, 15 December 1791.
45. U.S. Embassy Beijing New PRC Internet Regulation. Available online: https://irp.fas.org/world/china/netreg.htm (accessed on 28 February 2022).
46. Diagne, A.; Finlay, A.; Gaye, S.; Gichunge, W.; Pretorius, C.; Schiffrin, A.; Cunliffe-Jones, P.; Onumah, C. Misinformation Policy in Sub-Saharan Africa. In *Misinformation Policy in Sub-Saharan Africa*; University of Westminster Press: London, UK, 2021; p. 224. [CrossRef]
47. Haque, M.M.; Yousuf, M.; Alam, A.S.; Saha, P.; Ahmed, S.I.; Hassan, N. Combating Misinformation in Bangladesh. *Proc. ACM Hum.-Comput. Interact.* **2020**, *4*, 130. [CrossRef]
48. Carson, A.; Fallon, L. Fighting Fake News: A Study of Online Misinformation Regulation in the Asia Pacific. *Trobe Rep.* **2021**. Available online: https://opal.latrobe.edu.au/articles/report/Fighting_Fake_News_A_Study_of_Online_Misinformation_Regulation_in_the_Asia_Pacific/14038340/1/files/26480915.pdf (accessed on 8 May 2022). [CrossRef]
49. Yadav, K.; Erdoğdu, U.; Siwakoti, S.; Shapiro, J.N.; Wanless, A. Countries have more than 100 laws on the books to combat misinformation. How well do they work? *Bull. At. Sci.* **2021**, *77*, 124–128. [CrossRef]
50. Kumar, P.J.S.; Devi, P.R.; Sai, N.R.; Kumar, S.S.; Benarji, T. Battling Fake News: A Survey on Mitigation Techniques and Identification. In Proceedings of the 5th International Conference on Trends in Electronics and Informatics (ICOEI), Tirunelveli, India, 3–5 June 2021; pp. 829–835. [CrossRef]
51. Sharma, K.; Qian, F.; Jiang, H.; Ruchansky, N.; Zhang, M.; Liu, Y. Combating fake news: A survey on identification and mitigation techniques. *ACM Trans. Intell. Syst. Technol.* **2019**, *10*, 21. [CrossRef]
52. Wang, W.Y. "Liar, Liar Pants on Fire": A New Benchmark Dataset for Fake News Detection. *arXiv* **2017**, arXiv:1705.00648.
53. Yuan, H.; Zheng, J.; Ye, Q.; Qian, Y.; Zhang, Y. Improving fake news detection with domain-adversarial and graph-attention neural network. *Decis. Support Syst.* **2021**, *151*, 113633. [CrossRef]
54. De Oliveira, N.R.; Pisa, P.S.; Lopez, M.A.; de Medeiros, D.S.V.; Mattos, D.M.F. Identifying Fake News on Social Networks Based on Natural Language Processing: Trends and Challenges. *Information* **2021**, *12*, 38. [CrossRef]
55. Koloski, B.; Stepišnik-Perdih, T.; Pollak, S.; Škrlj, B. Identification of COVID-19 Related Fake News via Neural Stacking. In *Communications in Computer and Information Science*; Springer: Cham, Switzerland, 2021; Volume 1402, pp. 177–188. [CrossRef]
56. Deepak, S.; Chitturi, B. Deep neural approach to Fake-News identification. *Procedia Comput. Sci.* **2020**, *167*, 2236–2243. [CrossRef]
57. Anoop, K.; Deepak, P.; Lajish, L.V. Emotion cognizance improves health fake news identification. In Proceedings of the 24th International Database Engineering & Applications Symposium (IDEAS 2020), Incheon, Korea, 12–14 August 2020; Association for Computing Machinery: New York, NY, USA, 2020.
58. Batailler, C.; Brannon, S.M.; Teas, P.E.; Gawronski, B. A Signal Detection Approach to Understanding the Identification of Fake News. *Perspect. Psychol. Sci.* **2022**, *17*, 78–98. [CrossRef] [PubMed]
59. Pröllochs, N. Community-Based Fact-Checking on Twitter's Birdwatch Platform. *arXiv* **2021**, arXiv:2104.07175. [CrossRef]
60. Bakir, V.; McStay, A. Fake News and The Economy of Emotions. *Digit. Journal.* **2018**, *6*, 154–175. [CrossRef]

61. Chen, W.; Wang, Y.; Yang, S. Efficient influence maximization in social networks. In Proceedings of the 15th ACM SIGKDD International Conference on Knowledge Discovery and Data Mining, Paris, France, 28 June–1 July 2009; pp. 199–207. [CrossRef]
62. Chen, W.; Yuan, Y.; Zhang, L. Scalable influence maximization in social networks under the linear threshold model. In Proceedings of the 2010 IEEE International Conference on Data Mining, Sydney, NSW, Australia, 13–17 December 2010; pp. 88–97. [CrossRef]
63. Budak, C.; Agrawal, D.; Abbadi, A. El Limiting the spread of misinformation in social networks. In Proceedings of the 20th International Conference on World Wide Web, Hyderabad, India, 28 March–1 April 2011; pp. 665–674. [CrossRef]
64. Jain, S.; Sharma, V.; Kaushal, R. Towards automated real-time detection of misinformation on Twitter. In Proceedings of the 2016 International Conference on Advances in Computing, Communications and Informatics (ICACCI), Jaipur, India, 21–24 September 2016; pp. 2015–2020. [CrossRef]
65. World Health Organization Coronavirus Disease 2019 (COVID-19): Situation Report-55. Available online: https://www.who.int/docs/default-source/coronaviruse/situation-reports/20200315-sitrep-55-covid-19.pdf?sfvrsn=33daa5cb_8&download=true (accessed on 5 November 2021).
66. Singh, L.; Bansal, S.; Bode, L.; Budak, C.; Chi, G.; Kawintiranon, K.; Padden, C.; Vanarsdall, R.; Vraga, E.; Wang, Y. A first look at COVID-19 information and misinformation sharing on Twitter. *arXiv* **2020**, *arxiv:2003.13907*. [CrossRef]
67. Scott, M.; Overly, S. Silicon Valley is Losing the Battle against Election Misinformation—POLITICO. Available online: https://www.politico.com/news/2020/08/04/silicon-valley-election-misinformation-383092 (accessed on 4 March 2022).
68. Conger, K.; Isaac, M.; Wakabayashi, D. Twitter and Facebook worked to crack down on election disinformation, but challenges loom. *New York Times*, 2020. Available online: https://www.nytimes.com/2020/11/04/us/politics/twitter-and-facebook-worked-to-crack-down-on-election-disinformation-but-challenges-loom.html (accessed on 8 May 2022).
69. Buntain, C.; Bonneau, R.; Nagler, J.; Tucker, J.A. YouTube Recommendations and Effects on Sharing Across Online Social Platforms. *Proc. ACM Hum.-Comput. Interact.* **2021**, *5*, 11. [CrossRef]
70. Chen, E.; Deb, A.; Ferrara, E. #Election2020: The first public Twitter dataset on the 2020 US Presidential election. *J. Comput. Soc. Sci.* **2021**. [CrossRef]
71. Sanderson, Z.; Brown, M.A.; Bonneau, R.; Nagler, J.; Tucker, J.A. Twitter flagged Donald Trump's tweets with election misinformation: They continued to spread both on and off the platform. *Harv. Kennedy Sch. Misinformation Rev.* **2021**, *2*. [CrossRef]
72. Lespagnol, C.; Mothe, J.; Ullah, M.Z. Information Nutritional Label and Word Embedding to Estimate Information Check-Worthiness. In Proceedings of the 42nd International ACM SIGIR Conference on Research and Development in Information Retrieval, Paris, France, 21–25 July 2019; pp. 941–944.
73. Vincentius, K.; Aggarwal, P.; Sahan, A.; Högden, B.; Madan, N.; Bangaru, A.; Schwenger, C.; Muradov, F.; Aker, A. Information Nutrition Labels: A Plugin for Online News Evaluation. In Proceedings of the First Workshop on Fact Extraction and VERification, Brussels, Belgium, 1 November 2018; pp. 28–33.
74. Gawronski, B. Partisan bias in the identification of fake news. *Trends Cogn. Sci.* **2021**, *25*, 723–724. [CrossRef]
75. Fairbanks, J.; Fitch, N.; Knauf, N.; Briscoe, E. Credibility Assessment in the News: Do we need to read? In Proceedings of the MIS2 Workshop Held in Conjuction with 11th Int'l Conference on Web Search and Data Mining, Los Angeles, CA, USA, 9 February 2018.
76. Suttle, R.; Hogan, S.; Aumaugher, R.; Spradling, M.; Merrigan, Z.; Straub, J. University Community Members' Perceptions of Labels for Online Media. *Futur. Internet* **2021**, *13*, 281. [CrossRef]
77. Straub, J.; Spradling, M. Americans' Perspectives on Online Media Warning Labels. *Behav. Sci.* **2022**, *12*, 59. [CrossRef] [PubMed]

MDPI AG
Grosspeteranlage 5
4052 Basel
Switzerland
Tel.: +41 61 683 77 34

Information Editorial Office
E-mail: information@mdpi.com
www.mdpi.com/journal/information